THE PILLARS OF ISLAM

THE PILLARS OF ISLAM

DA'Ā'IM AL-ISLĀM
of
AL-QĀḌĪ AL-NU'MĀN

Translated by
ASAF A. A. FYZEE

Completely Revised
and Annotated by
ISMAIL KURBAN HUSEIN POONAWALA

Volume II
MU'ĀMALĀT: LAWS PERTAINING TO HUMAN INTERCOURSE

OXFORD
UNIVERSITY PRESS

YMCA Library Building, Jai Singh Road, New Delhi 110 001

Oxford University Press is a department of the University of Oxford.
It furthers the University's objective of excellence in research, scholarship,
and education by publishing worldwide in

Oxford New York
Auckland Cape Town Dar es Salaam Hong Kong Karachi
Kuala Lumpur Madrid Melbourne Mexico City Nairobi
New Delhi Shanghai Taipei Toronto

With offices in
Argentina Austria Brazil Chile Czech Republic France Greece
Guatemala Hungary Italy Japan Poland Portugal Singapore
South Korea Switzerland Thailand Turkey Ukraine Vietnam

Published in India
by Oxford University Press, New Delhi

First published 2004

ISBN-13: 978-0-19-566784-4
ISBN-10: 0-19-566784-0

Typeset in Goudy
by Eleven Arts, Keshav Puram, Delhi 110 035
Printed in India by Pauls Press, New Delhi 110 020
Published by Manzar Khan, Oxford University Press
YMCA Library Building, Jai Singh Road, New Delhi 110 001

Preface

The second volume of the *Da'ā'im*, critically edited by Asaf Ali Asghar Fyzee from six manuscripts, the oldest of which is dated 13th of Dhu 'l-Ḥijja 865/19 September 1461,[1] was published in Cairo, Egypt, in 1961. It was reprinted in 1967. Punctuations in both the editions are not always correct and some typographical errors have escaped the notice of the editor and the proof-reader. A pirated copy, without the critical apparatus, but with all the errors of Fyzee's edition, was published by 'Ārif Tāmir in 1995.[2]

A complete Urdu translation of this volume by Mullā Yūnus Shakīb Mubārakpūrī was published in 1970 in Surat, India. Two years later, Mullā Yūnus followed it up by a Gujarati translation. Both of these translations were meant primarily for the internal use of the Bohra community. Leaving aside a number of errors, both the translations, on the whole, are quite good. The main shortcoming of these renderings, however, stems from a total lack of explanatory notes. This makes it extremely difficult for the layman to follow what Nu'mān is saying. Moreover, the translator has retained the same Arabic technical vocabulary and legal terms, such as *ḥadd, ta'zīr, shuf'a, ṭalāq bā'ina*, etc., without giving any explanation. Hence, the uninitiated reader, not familiar with these terms and not having any background in Islamic law, is simply perplexed and the text remains unintelligible to him/her. At other places, the translation is either vague, or ambiguous and many of the antecedents in long sentences of the Arabic original are never clarified. For example, the following passage:[3]

[1]For its description, see Fyzee, 'An ancient copy'.

[2]*Da'ā'im al-islām*, ed. 'Ārif Tāmir. Beirut: Dār al-aḍwā', 1414/1995.

[3]*The Pillars of Islam*, II, Chap. 11.

[Imam] Ḥasan b. ʿAlī used to marry many women. If he was attracted to a woman while he had four wives, he would divorce one of them and marry the woman. In this manner he married many women and caused them to abstain from that which is unlawful (*fa-aḥṣana kathīr^{an} min al-nisāʾ*).

Here the Urdu translator has rendered the Arabic: *fa-aḥṣana kathīr^{an} min al-nisāʾ*, as 'He made many women *muḥṣana*',[4] with wonderful ingenuity—rendering the Arabic transitive verb *aḥṣana* with its object into a passive participle *muḥṣana*—but without enlightening the reader as he did not bother to explain what *muḥṣana* means in Islamic law. In brief, these translations, without annotation, make Nuʿmān's *Daʿāʾim* incomprehensible to the common reader.

In 1991, Shaykh Aḥmad ʿAlī Rāj and Mullā Qurbān Ḥusayn Rājnagarwālā published in Urdu a summary of the three chapters on Marriage, Divorce, and Inheritance for the benefit of the Urdu-speaking Bohra community.

As stated in the Preface to the first volume, I have treated Fyzee's translation as a first working draft. This volume needed much more meticulous revision and rewriting and has, hence, taken more time than the first volume. Moreover, it covers a wide range of subject matter, from food, drinks, medicine, dress, and perfume to commercial law, family law, penal code, to the question of apostasy and the etiquette of judges. Technical vocabulary and legal terms used in Islamic law recur regularly. Unfortunately, Fyzee's draft was replete with inaccuracies and faulty renderings. One of the reasons for this was that he relied too heavily on the Urdu translation without checking the exact meaning of Arabic terms. Many of the technical expressions and law terms were loosely translated. At times, even Arabic idioms, such as *yad^{an} bi-yad^{in}*,[5] were poorly understood and were incorrectly translated literally 'hand to hand' as opposed to 'on the spot' or 'then and there.'

For some major changes in the format chosen by Fyzee and the method of translation, the reader is advised to refer to the Preface of the first volume. At times, because of the difficulty and ambiguity of the text, faithfulness to the original Arabic has been sacrificed for the sake of fluidity in English. All such places are indicated in the notes. Unfortunately, the punctuations in the edited text are not always correct. The question of where a direct

[4]*Daʿāʾim al-islām*, II, 264 (Urdu trans.). In Urdu it states: *Āpne bekathrat ʿawratūn̐ ko muḥṣana banā diyā thā.*

[5]It should be noted that the translator of Ibn Rushd's *Bidāya* has made the same error, for example, see Ibn Rushd, *Bidāya*, II, 190; trans. II, 233.

quote from a tradition ends is left to the reader to decide. Thus, the difficulty of separating what is reported on the authority of the Imams from what might be an explanation or comment of Nu'mān is not always clearly marked. In all such cases I have followed my own instinct.

In revising and rewriting this translation, I have carefully considered variant readings noted by Fyzee in the footnotes to the Arabic text. Fortunately, I happened to have a very good copy of the second volume of the *Da'ā'im* in the collection of my late father. The manuscript was not only copied with the utmost care but was also collated and corrected. I have consulted this manuscript constantly and have corrected several errors in Fyzee's edition and have amended numerous readings based on it and other parallel sources. I have indicated all those corrections in the footnotes.

The aforementioned manuscript, indicated as MS Q, was transcribed on the 18th of Rabī' II, 1127/23 March 1715, by Raḥīm b. Ṣāliḥ 'Alībhā'ī in Bharampūr[6] in the *dars* (group of students studying under a Shaykh) of Mullā Qāsimkhān b. Mullā Ḥamza. It is written in very elegant *naskhī* handwriting on thick brownish paper. The text is in black ink, while the chapter headings, sectional headings, and key words in the *isnād* of each and every *ḥadīth*, such as *wa-'an*, *wa-'anhu*, *wa-ruwīnā* (or *rawaynā*), are in red ink. In addition to numerous glosses,[7] it contains many marginal and interlinear corrections, all of which suggest that the copy was collated with another manuscript. The manuscript size is $14_{1/2}$ x 25 cm, and the written text is about 10 x$19_{1/2}$ cm; with 18 lines per page. The colophon is followed by eight verses of poetry, as is typically found in such manuscripts. It states that a written book endures for a long time after its scribe has departed from this world and calls upon the reader to pray for his soul. It is followed by a self-testimony written by the scribe that his teacher has given his minor daughter in marriage to him with the dower of forty Indian rupees. A previous seal of ownership on folio 10 recto reads: '*Abd-i dā'ī*

[6]Bharampur is the capital of the Murshidabad district in Bengal. In the 18th century, Murshidabad became the centre of government for the Nawāb of Bengal. Hardy, *Muslims of British India*, 5. The sources at my disposal do not allow me to ascertain Bohra presence in this town during the 17th or the 18th centuries. No such town is to be found in Gujarat. A study of colophons collected from the manuscripts could shed more light on various towns where the religious scholars actively pursued scholarly activities. A detailed and critical history of the Bohras in India is yet to be written.

[7]Besides linguistic explanations, which are at times in Gujarati written in Arabic script, most of the glosses are from *Sharḥ* and *Ḥawāshī* (both by Amīnjī b. Jalāl, see Poonawala, *Biobibliography*, 185, 186), *Yanbū'* (ascribed to Nu'mān, see Poonawala, *Biobibliography*, 54), and *Mukhtaṣar al-muṣannaf* (by Ibn Killis, see Poonawala, *Biobibliography*, 79).

Allāh al-mubīn Amīn b. Mullā Muḥammad Amīn, 1250 [*/1834–5*]. The manuscript is bound with cardboard covers; three dark brown papers added at the beginning and five at the end contain some glosses from the works of Amīnjī b. Jalāl and from an anonymous work, *Majmū' al-fiqh*.

Fyzee's draft of this volume hardly contained any notes, hence, a major part of my endeavour, in addition to revising and rewriting the translation, was spent in annotation. The annotation aims at indicating earlier or parallel sources, explaining technical terms, clarifying difficulties, and identifying individuals and place names. In order to indicate the similarities and differences between Nu'mān's view and that of the Imāmī and the Sunnī schools of law, I have consistently referred to al-Kulaynī's (d. 329/940–1) *Kitāb al-kāfī* and al-Khaṭīb al-Tabrīzī's *Mishkāt al-maṣābīḥ* just as I did in the first volume. In addition to these two sources, I have consulted numerous other sources, especially al-Ṭūsī's (d. 460/1067) *Tahdhīb al-aḥkām* and *al-Nihāya*, and Ibn Rushd's (d. 595/1198) *Bidāyat al-mujtahid*. This has helped me in giving clarity and precision to the meaning of numerous words and phrases used by Nu'mān and in eliminating ambiguities and difficulties in the text of the *Da'ā'im*.

For clarification of certain issues, I have also consulted the following works: *Kitāb al-iqtiṣār*, *al-Urjūza al-muntakhaba*, and *Mukhtaṣar al-āthār* by Nu'mān; *Kitāb al-yanbū'* and *Taqwīm al-aḥkām*, both ascribed to Nu'mān; and *Kitāb al-su'āl wa 'l-jawāb li-mashā'ikh al-hind ma' al-ḥawāshī* by Amīnjī b. Jalāl and *al-Masā'il li-Amīnjī b. Jalāl*. With the exception of *Kitāb al-iqtiṣār*, all these works are in manuscripts in the collection of my late father.

In addition to the sources listed in the Preface to the first volume and its bibliography, more sources have been added that deal with the subject matter of this volume, especially with regard to Islamic law, its various branches, and the Prophet's medicine. As this volume deals more precisely with the law, I have relied on the secondary sources in English, both by Muslim as well as Western scholars, for unravelling the meanings of technical terms and expressions used in legal discourse, besides the Arabic works listed above. Various entries in the *Encyclopaedia of Islam* were also very useful and handy. On issues where there is disagreement among various schools, every effort has been made to give the differing opinions. With regard to family law, I have tried to indicate the recent changes introduced in various Muslim countries.

Since the publication of Joseph Schacht's *The Origins of Muhammadan Jurisprudence* in 1950 and its companion volume, *An Introduction to Islamic Law* in 1964, the field of Islamic law has been completely transformed, hence, a brief note is in order about the origins of Islamic law and the present state of research.

Schacht, following the methodological and historical presuppositions of earlier scholars of Islam, especially Ignaz Goldziher, formulated a thesis on the origins of Islamic law. Accordingly, he demonstrated that the classical theory of *sharīʿa* was the result of a complex historical process spanning a period of about three centuries. He, therefore, completely shattered the historical link between *ḥadīth* and *fiqh* that according to Muslim tradition existed from the very beginning. Moreover, he argued against the traditional Muslim view that the structures of *fiqh* were, at the beginning, independent of the main corpus of traditions (*aḥādīth*). The actual origins of Islamic law, for Schacht, lay in the 'living tradition' of local geographical schools, such as that of Medina and Kūfa, and in juristic adaptation of social norms and legal practices that prevailed in those locations. Gradually, the modus operandi and formal praxis were transformed into the structures of the classical theory of Islamic law.

Furthermore, Schacht claims that his inquiry into the origins of Islamic law confirms what his predecessors, particularly Goldziher and Margoliouth, had concluded about the concepts of *ḥadīth* and *sunna*.[8] He even goes a step further and states that when the *ḥadīth* began to find currency for the first time, it referred not to the Prophet, but to the 'Successors (*tābiʿūn*)', and in the next stage, to the 'Companions (*ṣaḥāba*)', and finally to the Prophet himself. It was Shāfiʿī, according to Schacht, who was able to achieve supreme authority for the traditions of the Prophet.[9]

Put differently, Islamic law, for Schacht, did not exist during the lifetime of the Prophet and for the greater part of the first century of Islamic era. Although the Qur'ān had promulgated new ordinances with regard to family law, marriage, divorce, inheritance, etc., the early Muslims, according to Schacht, did not pay much attention to those ordinances. The *ḥadīth* reports about the purported acts and sayings of the Prophet, he argues, did not come into existence before the end of the first century of Islamic era.

Immediate reaction to Schacht's thesis, in general, was unqualified praise and wholehearted endorsement. Only a few scholars expressed

[8]In his *Muslim Studies*, II, 18–19, Goldziher states:

In the absence of authentic evidence it would indeed be rash to attempt to express the most tentative opinion as to which parts of the *ḥadīth* [*isnād*, the chain of authorities, and *matn*, the content] are the oldest original material, or even as to which of them date back to the generations immediately following the Prophet's death. Closer acquaintance with the vast stock of *ḥadīth*s induces skeptical caution ..., but will probably [lead to the conclusion that] by far the greater part of it [was] the result of the religious, historical and social development of Islam during the first two centuries.

[9]Schacht, *Origins*, 138.

their reservations and criticisms.[10] In 1967, the publication of two works seriously raised questions about Schacht's findings on *ḥadīth*. The first was *Studies in Arabic Literary Papyri*, vol. II, by Nabia Abbott, and the second, *Geschichte des arabischen Schrifttums*, vol. I, by Fuat Sezgin. On the basis of extant manuscripts and other material, both Abbott and Sezgin concluded that traditions were transmitted, both orally and in writing, from the very beginning of the Islamic history, i.e. during the lifetime of the Prophet. In 1978, M. M. Azami published his *Studies in Early Hadith Literature*, which corroborated the findings of Abbott and Sezgin. Like N. Coulson and G. Juynboll, Azami not only severely criticized Schacht for his failure to pay attention to the Qur'ānic legislation, but also challenged his identification of the *fitna* as the civil war following the death of the Umayyad caliph Walīd II b. Yazīd II (125–6/743–4).[11] Refuting Schacht's thesis David Powers, a younger scholar, writes, 'I see no reason to assume that the Qur'ānic legislation on marriage, divorce, and inheritance remained in a state of suspended animation for more than a century after the revelation of the Qur'ān.'[12] In short, a number of younger scholars have scrutinized Schacht's thesis and refuted it in its details as well as in its broad essentials.

David Powers, who has examined the literature about the impact of Schacht on contemporary scholarship, states that Schacht's reasoning suffers from two fundamental weaknesses: the first is his cursory treatment of the Qur'ān, and the second is his blurring of the distinction between jurisprudence and positive law. Based on his own research on the Qur'ānic laws of inheritance, he concludes that Islamic law began to develop with the Qur'ānic legislation, but not in the manner suggested by Islamic tradition. The latter holds that Islamic jurisprudence is a continuous development that started in the lifetime of the Prophet leading to the

[10]For details see Powers, *Studies in Qur'an and Ḥadīth*, 1–8. Rahman's *Islamic Methodology* should be added to the list of authors who criticized some of Schacht's conclusions. Motzki, *Origins of Islamic Jurisprudence*, 1–49; it is a comprehensive survey of research about the beginnings of Islamic jurisprudence done by the Orientalists/Western scholars during the nineteenth and twentieth centuries. In her *Roman, provincial and Islamic law*, 1–17, Crone, who is concerned with the contributions of Roman and provincial law to the *sharī'a*, has given a full survey of the state of the field from that perspective.

[11]Schacht, *Origins*, 36–7. In his 'The Date of the Great *Fitna*', Juynboll examined the use the word *fitna* and concluded that it most probably refers to the revolt of Ibn al-Zubayr (64–71/683–90). It is generally known as the second *fitna*, the first being the series of events, which includes the murder of 'Uthmān and the civil wars that followed during the caliphte of 'Alī. See also *EI*[2], s.v. Fitna.

[12]D. Powers, *Studies in Qur'an and Ḥadīth*, 209.

legal schools of the second and the third centuries of the Hijra. The first stage in the development, according to Powers, was establishing the text of the Qur'ān.[13] The reader is further advised to refer to the works of Wael Hallaq who has published important studies in this area and has refuted Schacht's assumptions.[14] The latest work in this respect is *The Origins of Islamic Jurisprudence* by H. Motzki. It was originally published in German in 1991 and English translation was published in 2002. It deals mainly, as the subtitle, *Meccan Fiqh before the Classical Schools*, suggests, with the problem of how the early history of Meccan jurisprudence can be critically reconstructed from the available sources. He states in the Introduction:[15]

> The present study attempts to demonstrate that Schacht's conceptions, in substantive points, are no longer tenable or are greatly in need of modification—above all, that he estimated the beginning of Islamic jurisprudence a good half to three-quarters of a century too late. The reservations about Schacht's conclusions result in part from the nature of his work itself: it contains a number of questionable premises, historical inferences, and methods.

About the beginning of Islamic jurisprudence he states that already in the first century of the Hijra, Muslims consciously resorted to the Qur'ān and to the ruling of the Prophet as sources of law. Against Schacht's conclusion that traditions from the Companions and Successors are earlier than those of the Prophet, Motzki asserts that authentic traditions from the Prophet and the Companions can certainly be detected. Schacht's assumption that for the better part of the first century of the Hijra, Islamic law did not exist, therefore, must be revised. Motzki contends that the beginnings of a law that was Islamic in the true sense of the word and of theoretical occupation with it are placed by Schacht too late by a good half to three quarters of a century.[16]

A brief note is similarly called for concerning the primary and secondary sources used in annotation, especially for chapters 3–5, on Food,[17] Drinks,

[13]Ibid., 6–7, 209.

[14]W. Hallaq, *Law and Legal Theory* (a number of his articles are reprinted); idem, *A History of Islamic Legal Theories*.

[15]Motzki, *Origins of Islamic Jurisprudence*, xi.

[16]Ibid., 295–7.

[17]In his *Of Dishes*, wherein both primary and secondary sources are listed, G. Gelder explores the theme of representation of food in classical Arabic literature. It focuses on the connections between food and literature, not only in the sense that Arabic texts refer to food and drinks, but also in the sense that 'food goes in where words come out'.

and Medicine. The traditions of the Prophet that were collected and compiled into books did not only deal with legal issues, but also treated a variety of other subjects as well. Among those *aḥādīth*, there were those that contained dietary rules about food and drinks, and advice on the treatment of certain common illnesses. These medical traditions aroused the interest of some *ḥadīth* scholars who collected them into separate books entitled *al-Ṭibb al-nabawī* (The Prophet's Medicine). The earliest collections of this genre go back to the third/ninth century and even earlier. Information about it can be gleaned from Sezgin's *Geschichte des arabischen Schrifttums*, vol. III.[18] In his *Health and Medicine*, Fazlur Rahman has given a comprehensive survey of the Prophet's medicine.

For annotation, I have mainly used three primary works: the first and the second, both entitled *al-Ṭibb al-nabawī*, are by Ibn Qayyim al-Jawziyya, and Muḥammad al-Dhahabī; the third entitled *al-Ādāb al-shar'īya*, is by Ibn Mufliḥ. It should be noted that all of them were contemporaries and lived in Damascus in the first half of the eighth/fourteenth century during the Mamlūk rule. Besides being *ḥadīth* scholars, all three were pupils of Ibn Taymiyya, a famous Ḥanbalī theologian, jurisconsult, and a controversial figure. In addition to these works, I have also used *Ṭibb al-a'imma* (The Imams' Medicine) by Ḥusayn and 'Abd Allāh, the two sons of Bisṭām b. Sābūr al-Nīsābūrī, compiled at the beginning of the fifth/eleventh century. In early Shī'ī works, such as Ibn Bābūya's (d. 381/991–2) *'Ilal al-sharā'i'*, many medical traditions are ascribed to Imam Ja'far al-Ṣādiq. Two recent works in this respect are *Ṭibb al-Imām al-Ṣādiq* by Muḥammad al-Khalīlī,[19] and *Ṭibb al-a'imma* by 'Abd Allāh Shabbar (d.1242/1826–7).[20] Muḥammad Bāqir al-Majlisī has used the fifth chapter from the *Da'ā'im* as a source for his monumental *Biḥār al-anwār*, vol. 62, dealing with the Prophet's medicine. He has reproduced a number of traditions from that chapter and I have indicated them in the footnotes.

All the works entitled *Ṭibb al-a'imma* and *al-Ṭibb al-nabawī*, in addition to citing traditions from the Prophet and the Imams discuss medical theory and list remedies for various diseases, charms, and prayers to be recited.

[18]Band III: *Medizin, Pharmazie, Zoologie, Tierheilkunde*.

[19]The author has used a number of traditions from the *Da'ā'im* as a source in addition to Majlisī's *Biḥār al-anwār*.

[20]In addition to the *Da'ā'im* the author has used the following sources: *Kāfī* by Kulaynī, *'Uyūn akhbār al-Riḍā*, *al-Khiṣāl*, and *Man lā yaḥduruhu al-faqīh* by Ibn Bābūya, *al-Maḥāsin* by Abū Ja'far al-Barqī, *al-Amālī* by Ṭūsī, *Fiqh al-Riḍā* ascribed to 'Alī al-Riḍā, *Da'awāt al-Rāwandī* by Quṭb al-Dīn al-Rāwandī, and *Ṭibb al-a'imma* by the two sons of Bisṭām b. Sābūr al-Nīsābūrī.

The treatment is generally by food, potions, and drugs. They also discuss the diseases, their causes, symptoms, and methods of treatment. Some of these texts include an alphabetic list of medicaments that have special curative characteristics. Here, they noted the powers, effects, and benefits of those drugs and medicines. These texts further suggest that their authors did not dismiss the established Greco-Islamic medicine of Ibn Sīnā' and Rāzī, but they wanted to add an Islamic dimension to it.

The oft-cited tradition states, 'God has created illnesses but He has also created the cures.' The Prophet taught the Muslims to use divine medicaments, especially prayers, alms-giving, fasting, incantations, etc. Besides divine medicaments, the Prophet instructed them on the use of natural medicaments—fruits, vegetables, herbs, and animal products. Of course, religion played an important role in the moral guidelines provided by the authors of those texts. In addition to making available the treatment of physical maladies, those authors also responded to the spiritual needs of the Muslim community.

In recent times, more and more people look outside of conventional medicine for their health care. They take various herbs or herbal supplements to lift their mood, and turn to acupuncture or various types of yogas to alleviate pain. These 'complementary' and 'alternative' medicine and therapies have revolutionized clinical practice and have given birth to 'integrative medicine'.[21] Healing traditions of the Islamic world show broad historical and socio-cultural variation.[22] The twin institutions of Hamdard (meaning companion in pain), both in India and Pakistan, have revived the Greco-Arab-Muslim system of treating illness with herbs. The Hamdard Foundation bases its practice on eastern medical philosophies, including Arab, Indian, and Chinese systems. In addition to clinics, colleges, and pharmacies it publishes books and journals.[23]

Readers of this volume will not fail to notice that 'Alī is portrayed as the most knowledgeable person not only giving the correct advice to the caliphs but also resolving the most complex problems of law. This tendency could be explained as serving the Shī'ī legitimist claim for his succession to the Prophet as well as extolling his excellent knowledge of the Qur'ān and the *sunna*. Schacht has pointed out that the name of 'Alī, who had made Kūfa his headquarters, was invoked to put forward opinions

[21]*Newsweek* issue of 7 Dec. 2002 carried a special report entitled 'The Science of Alternative Medicine'.

[22]*Oxford Ency. of MIW*, s.v. Health care.

[23]Ibid., s.v. Hamdard.

in opposition to the traditional doctrine or to the living tradition.[24] Noth and Conrad have identified some topoi as various types of literary devices employed by Muslim historians. Under one such heading which serves to glorify former times they state that significant personalities of early Islamic history, such as 'Alī, were invoked to great effect by presenting them as the ones who gave the best advice on important matters.[25]

Most recent studies on various issues dealt with in this volume are too numerous to be enumerated here, but are indicated in the footnotes and listed in the bibliography.

Finally, there remains the pleasant duty of thanking my two dedicated and talented students, Karim Jamal Ali and Jihad Turk who have contributed to the making of this book. The former read the entire translation with great care and offered numerous suggestions, emendations, and criticism that have improved the accuracy of the translation. He was also responsible for the major and laborious task of producing the final draft for the press with appropriate format and all of the diacritics. The latter meticulously edited the manuscript chapter by chapter and offered many suggestions for improving syntax and style. If the translation reads smoothly, it is due to his efforts. His insightful observations have also benefited me in clarifying several issues and adding a number of explanatory notes. I am grateful to Dr Talib M. Aziz for elucidating some abstruse and unclear passages. I also wish to thank my son Qays for his help in resolving innumerable computer-related problems that arose from time to time during the preparation of the book. For any inadequacies, errors, and oversights, I alone am responsible.

Revision of this translation was funded by the Academic Senate Grant and G. E. von Grunebaum Center for Near Eastern Studies of the University of California at Los Angeles.

10 January 2003
Rancho Palos Verdes, California

Ismail K. H. Poonawala

[24] Schacht, *Introduction*, 33–4.
[25] Noth and Conrad, *Early Arabic Historical Tradition*, 140, 142.

Contents

Transliteration

The system of transliteration used in this translation is that of the *Encyclopaedia of Islam*, New Edition, with the following changes: j for *jīm* instead of dj; q for *qāf* instead of ḳ. Pairs of letters joined by a bar underneath, such as dh, gh, kh, sh, and th, are written without the bar.

Well-known place names, such as Mecca, Medina, Baghdad, Damascus, as well as certain terms like imam, imamate, caliph, caliphate, vizier, dinar and dirham are retained in their accepted English forms as given by the *Webster's Third New International Dictionary of the English Language*. The two most frequently used words in this translation, viz. 'Muḥammad' and 'Qur'ān,' although accepted in English without diacritics, here retained proper diacritics. All other Arabic words are transliterated.

Table of Transliteration of Arabic Characters

ء	ʾ	س	s	م	m
ب	b	ش	sh	ن	n
ت	t	ص	ṣ	و	u
ث	th	ض	ḍ	ي	y
ج	j	ط	ṭ		
ح	ḥ	ظ	ẓ		
خ	kh	ع	ʿ		
د	d	غ	gh		
ذ	dh	ف	f		
ر	r	ق	q		
ز	z	ل	l		

Long Vowels		Short Vowels		Diphthongs	
ا	ā	ـَـ	a	ـَـو	aw
و	ū	ـُـ	u	ـَـي	ay
ي	ī	ـِـ	i	و	final form ū
				ي	final form ī

Abbreviations

Concordance	Wensinck, *Concordance et Indices de la Traditions Musulmane*
Dodge	Ibn al-Nadīm, *al-Fihrist*, trans. B. Dodge
Dozy	Dozy, *Supplément aux Dictionnaires Arabes*
EI	*The Encyclopaedia of Islam*, 1st ed.
EI^2	*The Encyclopaedia of Islam*, 2nd ed.
EIr	*Encyclopaedia Iranica*
ER	*Encyclopedia of Religion*, ed. M. Eliade
EISup	*Supplement to The Encyclopaedia of Islam*, 2nd ed.
Furāt al-Kūfī	Furāt al-Kūfī, *Tafsīr*
Guillaume	*The Life of Muhammad*, trans. A. Guillaume
History of al-Ṭabarī,	*The History of al-Ṭabarī*, Translated and Annotated by various authors
Ibn Khallikān	Ibn Khallikān, *Wafīyāt al-aʻyān*
Ibn al-Nadīm	Ibn al-Nadīm, *al-Fihrist*
Ibn Saʻd	Ibn Saʻd, *al-Ṭabaqāt*
Kāfī	Kulaynī, *al-Kāfī fī uṣūl al-Dīn*
Kazimirski	Kazimirski, *Dictionnaire Arabe-Français*

Lane	Lane, E., *Arabic-English Lexicon*
Lisān al-ʿArab	Ibn Manẓūr, *Lisān al-ʿArab*
Majmaʿ al-baḥrayn	Ṭurayḥī, *Majmaʿ al-baḥrayn*
Mishkāt	Tabrīzī, *Mishkāt al-maṣābīḥ*
MS	Manuscript
MSS	Manuscripts
MS Q	Manuscript of the *Daʿāʾim*, vol. II, in the collection of Mulla Kurban Husayn Fida Husayn Godhrawala
Oxford Ency. of MIW	*Oxford Encyclopedia of the Modern Islamic World*
pl.	plural
Qāmūs	Fīrūzābādī, *al-Qāmūs al-muḥīṭ*
Qummī	Qummī, *Tafsīr al-Qummī*
Robson	*Mishkat al-masabih*, trans. J. Robson
ShEI	*Shorter Encyclopaedia of Islam*
al-Ṣiḥāḥ	Jawharī, *al-Ṣiḥāḥ*
De Slane	Ibn Khallikān, *Wafīyāt al-aʿyān*, trans. De Slane
Ṭabarī, *Tafsīr*	Ṭabarī, *Tafsīr al-Ṭabarī*, ed. M. Shākir, Cairo ed. (vols. 1–16)
Ṭabarī, *Tafsīr* (Beirut)	Ṭabarī, *Tafsīr al-Ṭabarī*, Beirut ed.
Ṭabarī, *Tārīkh*	Ṭabarī, *Tārīkh al-Ṭabarī*, ed. M. Ibrāhīm
Ṭabrisī	Ṭabrisī, *Majmaʿ al-bayān*
Tāj al-ʿarūs	Zabīdī, *Tāj al-ʿarūs*
Yāqūt	Yāqūt, *Muʿjam al-buldān*

Editor's Introduction

It has been very aptly observed that law represents the distilled essence of a given civilization and that it reflects the people's soul and spirit more than any other discipline of learning.[1] This observation is most appropriate to Islamic civilization. Sir H. A. R. Gibb, a prominent scholar of Islam during the twentieth century and an editor of *The Encyclopaedia of Islam*, states that Islamic law permeated almost every side of social life and every branch of Islamic literature, and it is no exaggeration to see in it, in the words of one of the most penetrating of modern students of the subject [referring to Bergsträsser], 'the epitome of the true Islamic spirit, the most decisive expression of Islamic thought, the essential kernel of Islam.'[2] The observation of Bergsträsser is echoed by Joseph Schacht and David de Santillana, both of them eminent law scholars of the twentieth century.[3] It is for this reason that from the very early period of Islamic history knowledge of the sacred law has enjoyed pride of place among the Muslims and its academic study, viz., the science of jurisprudence (*fiqh*), has remained the most important academic discipline in the curriculum of Islamic education. Islamic jurisprudence has ever since retained its position as the undisputed 'queen of sciences'. Put differently, jurisprudence is theology *par excellence* in the Islamic tradition.

[1]Parry, *Haldane Memorial Lecture*, 3. Both of these sources are also cited by Anderson, *Law Reform*, 1; idem, *Islamic Law*, 17.

[2]Gibb, *Mohammedanism*, 106; see also G. Bergsträsser, *Grundzüge des Islamischen Rechts*, 1; de Santillana, 'Law and Society'.

[3]Schacht, *Introduction*, 1, states, 'Islamic law is the epitome of Islamic thought, the most typical manifestation of the Islamic way of life, the core and kernel of Islam itself.'

In his admirable book *Mohammedanism*, Gibb has remarked with perfect justice that law (*sharīʿa*) was the master science of the Muslim world. It embraced all things, human and divine. For its comprehensiveness and for the ardour with which its study was pursued it would be hard to find a parallel elsewhere, except in Judaism. He further adds that apart from its intellectual pre-eminence and scholastic function, Islamic law was the most far-reaching and effective agent in moulding the social order and the community life of the Muslim peoples, and that it has held the social fabric of Islam compact and secure through all the fluctuations of political fortune.[4]

Jurisprudence is regarded as inclusive of the philosophical foundations of the law. It spills over *kalām* (scholastic theology) and *uṣūl al-dīn* (fundamentals of religion) because, in the discussion about God's attributes, prophethood, etc., there is a strong jurisprudential interest. Divine speech, as one of the attributes of God, for example, takes on special importance for Muslim theology, because it constitutes the transcendental essence of Islamic law. 'Orthodoxy' is not the proper term to use for characterizing Islam's sense of right religion. A better term is 'orthopraxy,' meaning 'right practice', which comes closer to the reality of Muslim devotion and submission to the will of God. Here, Islam is closer to Judaism in spirit and practice than to Christianity.

THE NATURE AND SCOPE OF ISLAMIC LAW

Sharīʿa, literally means a path trodden by camels to a watering place, but in its technical sense is commonly translated as 'Islamic law', or 'Sacred/Divine law', as laid down by God.[5] *Sharīʿa*, therefore, within Muslim discourse, designates the rules and regulations governing the lives of Muslims. It is an all-embracing body of religious duties, the totality of Allāh's commands that regulate the life of every Muslim in all its aspects, religious, political, and civil. In this sense, *sharīʿa* is intimately connected with *fiqh*, which literally means understanding, but in its technical use signifies academic discussion of divine law and the process of jurisprudence by which the rules are derived.

Consequently, the most obvious distinction between the conceptions of law, Islamic and Western, is that the latter is basically secular, whereas

[4]Gibb, *Mohammedanism*, 9–10.

[5]*Sharīʿa* in its broader sense also means a prophetic religion in its totality, such as *sharīʿat Mūsā*, the law/religion of Moses. For its meaning in the Qur'ān and *ḥadīth*, etc., see *EI*[2], s.v. *Sharīʿa*.

the former is essentially religious. It further implies that secular law can be changed by the same human authority that enacted it. Besides the legislature, the courts play an important part in the interpretation and implementation of this law. Islamic law, on the other hand, is regarded fundamentally as divine law, and as such, is generally immutable.[6]

It is necessary to digress here a little and elaborate a point that religion, ethics, and law are so intertwined together in Islam that early authors hardly distinguished between these elements. The *sharīʿa* does not differentiate between purely legal matters, such as contracts or the laws of inheritance, and religious duties, such as prayers and fasting. Goitein has argued that, proportionately, the Qur'ān does not contain less legal matters than the Pentateuch, the Torah, generally known as 'The Law'.[7] Even the earliest *sūras* of the Qur'ān contain legal matters, for instance, when the Prophet enjoins the faithful to keep to their pledges and contracts, to stand by their testimony (70:32–3), and to be just in measure and weight (83:1–3). He further argues that according to the Arab and the old Israelite conception, law is not a fixed order imposed by the power of an organized community, by a king, or by a legal assembly. Rather, law is

[6]This theoretical statement needs to be qualified by adding that there is a fine distinction between *sharīʿa* and *fiqh*. *Sharīʿa* relies on human interpretation and execution. This point is well illustrated in some anecdotal reports of debate between ʿAlī and the Khawārij when the latter raised the well-known slogan *lā ḥukma illā li-llāhi* (the sovereignty belongs to God). ʿAlī responded by saying, 'Their dictum is right, but [their] intention is wrong. It is true that all rule (*ḥukm*) belongs to God, but these people claim that the act of governing belongs to God as well (*lā imrata illā li-llāhi*). The truth is that there is no escape from the fact, that [for better or worse], people will have to rely on good or bad rulers …' *Nahj al-balāgha* (ed. ʿAbduh), I, 57. In another report ʿAlī gathered the people and brought a copy of the Qur'ān. He touched it and addressing the Book proclaimed, 'Speak to the people.' When the people exclaimed that he was mocking them as the Book cannot speak, he said, 'The Qur'ān is but ink and paper … it does not speak by itself. It needs interpreters and the interpreters are human beings.' The contention is that God's sovereignty does not provide escape from human agency to interpret the Qur'ān and the *sharīʿa*. In his *Speaking in God's Name*, 23–4, Abou El Fadl has rightly pointed out that many Muslim fundamentalists and Western scholars have misunderstood the statement 'sovereignty belongs to God', and have taken it to mean that God is the sole legislator and that the *sharīʿa* is immutable. Both the meaning and implications of the above statement were subject to intense debate among the Muslims. *Sharīʿa*, it was argued, is the Divine Ideal, standing as if suspended in midair, unaffected and uncorrupted by the vagaries of life. The *fiqh*, on the other hand, is a human attempt to understand and apply that ideal. *Sharīʿa* is, therefore, immutable, immaculate, but *fiqh* is not. For detailed exposition of the conceptions of law: Islamic and Western, and Western theories of jurisprudence, see Anderson, *Islamic Law*, 1–16; Fyzee, *Modern Approach*, 29.

[7]Goitein, 'Birth-Hour of Muslim Law', 24.

a truth that exists forever and to be discovered by a wise man. He contends that an all-inclusive concept of the *sharī'a* as emanating from God was not the result of post-Qur'ānic developments, but is rooted in the Qur'ān itself.[8]

For a Muslim, there is an ethical quality in every human action. However, this ethical quality cannot be perceived independently by human intellect; instead, man has to depend on divine revelation.[9] Thus, it is the *sharī'a* in its wider connotation that contains the sum total of *al-aḥkām al-khamsa* (the five legal qualifications),[10] whereby all human actions are ethically categorized and subsumed under the following five categories: (i) obligatory or commanded (*wājib, farḍ*), duties that are required and whose performance is rewarded and whose omission is punished. They are further subdivided into those actions which are the individual compulsory duty (*farḍ 'ayn*), such as prayer, fasting, and those which are the collective duty on the community (*farḍ kifāya*), i.e. those duties, such as funeral prayer, which are not incumbent on all members of the community as long as a sufficient number of individuals perform them; (ii) recommended (*sunna, mandūb, mustaḥabb*), duties or acts that are recommended but not required, such as *nāfila* (supererogatory) prayers, night prayers, visiting Medina after the pilgrimage. One who acts accordingly may expect to be rewarded, but one who does not will not be punished; (iii) indifferent (*mubāḥ, jā'iz*), whose performance or omission is neither rewarded nor punished, such as eating while reclining, wearing fine clothes; (iv) reprehensible (*makrūh*), actions that are disapproved. It is better to keep away from them and one who avoids such acts may expect to be rewarded, but one who does not avoid them will not be punished. Examples of this category include prayers without concentration and prayers in the resting place of camels near a waterhole; and (v) forbidden (*ḥarām*), actions that are prohibited, hence punishable, such as stealing, drinking wine, and adultery. It is obvious that much of this law, especially the obligations and the middle three categories, could never be enforced by courts. Islamic law, for this reason, in the words of Snouck Hurgronje, a Dutch Islamologist, is 'a doctrine of duties', a code of obligations. Strictly speaking, there are no rights *as against* God. Abū Ḥanīfa defines law as

[8]Ibid., 27–9.

[9]There is a more nuanced discussion of law and theology, but it is beyond the scope of this brief introduction. Suffice it to state that the Mu'tazila carried their rationalism so far as to claim parity between reason and revelation in the discussion of religious truth. Rahman, *Islam*, 90, 104–5.

[10]Schacht, *Introduction*, 121; Ansari, 'Islamic Juristic Terminology', 294–8.

the soul's cognizance of its rights and obligation, which also clearly demonstrates this essential difference.[11] The application of *sharīʿa* is, therefore, not restricted to positive law, but it also includes moral and ethical precepts and the jurisprudential process in itself.

The above consideration leads to the second basic difference between Islamic law and its Western counterpart. The former is much wider in scope than the latter. Islamic law takes into consideration the whole of human conduct. For this reason the classical books of law, such as *The Pillars of Islam*, deal first with the questions of ritual purity, prayer, fasting, alms tax, pilgrimage, etc., followed by commercial law, the law of contract, then family law (marriage, divorce, guardianship, inheritance), of civil wrongs, the penal code—consisting of *diya* (blood money), *ḥudūd* (divinely ordained punishments), *qiṣāṣ* (retaliation for wrongs), and *taʿzīr* (discretionary punishments)—the law of peace and war, the law of evidence and procedure, and a host of other issues. In short, it covers every field of law: public and private, national and international. This explains Nuʿmān's scheme of division and its respective table of contents in each of the two volumes of *The Pillars of Islam*.

The two major components of *fiqh* (jurisprudence) are: *uṣūl al-fiqh* and *furūʿ al-fiqh*. *Uṣūl* means the roots, or the principles upon which Islamic jurisprudence is based. Accordingly, it varies from one school of law to another. For the Sunnī schools of law (*madhāhib*),[12] the *uṣūl* always includes the Qur'ān, the *sunna* of the Prophet,[13] and *ijmāʿ* (consensus).[14] It is the *ijmāʿ* that, in the final analysis, is the most important source, because the text of the Qur'ān, its right interpretation, as well as the contents of the *sunna* are authenticated through *ijmāʿ*.[15] During the early days of Islam,

[11] Fyzee, *Modern Approach*, 29–30.

[12] The four major Sunnī schools of law are: the Ḥanafī, the Mālikī, the Shāfiʿī, and the Ḥanbalī. The three Shīʿī schools of law are: the Imāmī/the Twelver, the Ismāʿīlī, and the Zaydī.

[13] Ansari, 'Islamic Juristic Terminology', 256–9.

[14] Ibid., 282–7. For Nuʿmān's sources, see Poonawala, 'Al-Qāḍī al-Nuʿmān and Ismaʿili jurisprudence', 127–8.

[15] It is to be noted that the concept of *ijmāʿ* before Shāfiʿī was largely undefined. Practically, *ijmāʿ* is determined after the fact, when a later generation of jurists looks to the past and finds that earlier *mujtahids* have agreed on a particular issue. In Sunnī Islam, *ijmāʿ*, based on the notion that the community is infallible, was both a sanctioning instrument and a material source of law. For the Twelver Shīʿa, *ijmāʿ*, in and by itself, is neither an infallible sanctioning instrument nor a source of law. The Ismāʿīlīs reject it. Rahman, *Islamic Methodology*, 23; idem, *Islam*, 68–75; *Oxford Ency. of MIW*, s.v. Consensus. Fyzee, *Modern Approach*, 28, 31; the *uṣūl* or First Principles may be likened to Western jurisprudence.

any qualified jurist was able to exert the faculty of *ijtihād*, i.e. the right to refer back to the original sources, viz., the Qur'ān and the *sunna*, and to interpret them for himself. With the passage of time and the crystallization of different schools of law and the enunciation of their doctrines, the right of *ijtihād* was progressively curtailed. Later jurists generally followed the dominant opinion that prevailed in their particular school rather than exercising their right of jurisprudential interpretation. This resulted in the lack of vitality in the Sunnī schools.[16]

It is worth noting that the Baghdad school, which produced the principles of jurisprudence (*uṣūl al-fiqh*) for Imāmī Shīʿism, assigned human reason (ʿ*aql*) a fundamental role. Its adoption of reasoned argumentation in jurisprudence and theology paved the way for the future development of *fiqh*.[17] After the Baghdad school, it was the Ḥilla school that steered the development of Imāmī law in the direction which was to prevail universally. Ḥasan b. Yūsuf b. ʿAlī b. al-Muṭahhar al-Ḥillī, generally known as ʿ*Allāma* (the most learned) Ḥillī, provided a theoretical basis for the principle of legal ruling based on *ijtihād* that was disputed until then. He states that *ijtihād* belongs exclusively to the ʿ*ulamā*ʾ to formulate decisions on the basis of general precepts in the Qur'ān and the *sunna* and by weighing contradictory arguments. The characteristic of the ʿ*ulamā*'s *ijtihād* is its fallibility as opposed to the infallibility of the Prophet and the Imams. If a *mujtahid* goes astray with his *ijtihād*, ʿ*Allāma* Ḥillī states, he commits no sin and can always revise his decisions. Thus, the two fundamental characteristics—the fallibility and revisability of *ijtihād* and its restriction to a living authority—give this instrument of legal ruling its flexibility and dynamism.[18]

[16]There were various reasons for it. The qualifications for *ijtihād* were made so rigorous that they were humanly impossible to fulfil. *Ijtihād*, in the sense of reinterpretation of law within one's own school of law continued. Rahman, *Islam*, 78–9; Hallaq, 'Was the Gate of *Ijtihād* Closed?' In his most recent work *Authority, Continuity, and Change in Islamic Law*, Hallaq has demonstrated that both the terms *ijtihād* and *taqlīd* carried multi-layered meanings. He further states that the formation of the major schools of law by the middle of the fourth/tenth century was achieved through the construction of a juristic doctrine called absolute *mujtahid* couched in the authority of the founding imam. The foundational authority gave rise to juristic discourse and hermeneutics. This, in turn, produced a set of positive principles that defined the school as an interpretive doctrine to be studied, defended, and applied. Juristic authority was sustained throughout by passing on its legacy to the next generation. However, it became progressively restrictive.

[17]Halm, *Die Schia*, 62; English trans. 51.

[18]Ibid., 84–90; English trans. 67–71. In his *Roots of Islamic Revolution in Iran*, Algar has analysed the Islamic Shīʿī heritage of Iran and the emergence of a strong class of

The second main constituent of jurisprudence after the principles (*uṣūl*) is *furūʿ*. It means the branches of law[19] wherein disagreement is permitted. It is generally classified into two major categories: *ʿibādāt* (acts of worship) and *muʿāmalāt* (human intercourse). The former regulates the relationship between humans and God, hence it is also known as *ḥuqūq Allāh* (the rights of God over humans).[20] *ʿIbādāt*, therefore, deals with the laws regulating the acts of devotion, rituals, and religious observances.[21] *Muʿāmalāt*, on the other hand, deals with laws pertaining to human intercourse and concerns the rights and duties of people towards each other, hence it is also known as *ḥuqūq al-ʿibād* (the rights of people over one another). It includes a wide range of subjects, such as family law, mercantile law, criminal law, and all the legal issues that arise in social life. Moreover, for the Sunnīs, it includes constitutional law regulating the administration of the state and the conduct of war.[22] The object of these laws is to regulate the conduct of Muslims in their communal relations and to ensure that they conform to juridico-moral concepts of Islam as set out in the Qur'ān and the *sunna*. Put differently, *muʿāmalāt* are strictly concerned with legal subject matter.

Islamic law, as it developed without the formal support of the state, is characterized, in theory at least, by all-inclusiveness. However, in practice, it was dominated by the dualism of religion and state. Consequently, it led to discord between the sacred law and the reality of actual practice, where the regulations were framed by the ruling authorities, or the state, and at times these laws differed from place to place. As the legal theory developed, it ignored the existence of other elements, such as local

---

mujtahids as the directive force in society, a tradition of opposition to the ruling autocratic secular authorities. He has rightly pointed out that the Islamic Revolution has certain particular characteristics that do not permit of an extension beyond Iran. For the most recent developments, see the related articles in Walbridge, *The Most Learned of the Shīʿa*.

[19]Fyzee, *Modern Approach*, 28; he compares the *furūʿ* to Western positive law.

[20]In the Islamic conception, God has rights, but no obligations or duties. God lays down the law that man must obey. However, God is not bound to be pleased with man's actions or his worship. Divine Grace, which is necessary for salvation, is a separate act of Divine Will, quite independent of God's pleasure at man's righteous behaviour. Ibid., 30–31.

[21]See the contents of vol. I, *The Pillars of Islam*. Nuʿmān has included *walāya* and the profession of faith in this category, see *The Pillars of Islam*, I, xxx-xxxiii. Other subjects, such as circumcision (*khitān*), spiritual retreat (*iʿtikāf*), and matters related to funerals (*janāʾiz*) are also included in it.

[22]Nuʿmān has included the constitutional law and the conduct of war in the chapter on *Jihād* in the first volume, see *The Pillars of Islam*, I, xxxii, 422–94.

customs and governmental regulations, and reduced the material sources of Islamic law to the Qur'ān and the *sunna* of the Prophet.[23]

The *sharīʿa* is, therefore, both Islam's outstanding achievement as well as its greatest failure. As a system of divine law, it theoretically governs every aspect of a Muslim's life. However, it failed to measure up to the political and religious aspirations of the early generations of Muslims. Politically, the Islamic state was in a continuous state of disarray. *Sharīʿa* failed to provide guidelines, particularly with regard to constitutional and criminal law. Due to the lack of guidelines the question of succession to the Prophet, especially in the case of the first four caliphs, always created tension within the nascent Muslim community at the death of each caliph. The ensuing crisis was resolved each time on an ad hoc basis. Later on, the Sunnīs accepted the historical order of succession and the first four caliphs were ranked accordingly. The Shīʿa, on the other hand, rejected the historical order and regarded ʿAlī as the only worthy and superior candidate and considered the first three caliphs as usurpers. The debate as to who was superior among those four and the circumstances of their succession remained a subject of heated debate for centuries.[24]

The failure of the caliphal state to realize the Islamic vision of an ideal community and a politically unified *umma*[25] had the effect of placing politics outside the purview of religion. Muslim rulers, beginning with Muʿāwiya and his successors, the Umayyad dynasty, needed no formal authority to legitimize their power. With strong military support, all they needed was the consent of the developing class of ʿ*ulamā*', and in Sunnī communities, it was forthcoming without much difficulty. ʿ*Ulamā*' were appointed as judges (*qāḍīs*) by the rulers/caliphs. Although some ʿ*ulamā*' were often reluctant to compromise the purity of the divine law by serving the corrupt ruling establishment, they lacked the authority to serve as a balance to the growing autocratic powers of the rulers.[26] Hence, both political and religious institutions remained quite separate and distinct from each other.

Although the hereditary caliphate was recognized as a de facto power

[23]In his article 'Islam and the Challenge of Democracy', Abou El Fadl has discussed the fluctuating relations between the '*sharīʿa* law' as articulated by jurists and the administrative practice of the state called *al-aḥkām al-siyāsiyya*.

[24]For the latest comprehensive study of the succession see Madelung, *Succession*.

[25]*EI*[2], s.v. Umma.

[26]Rahman, *Islam*, 237–40; he strongly advocates that the political dogma needs to be reformulated. See also Abou El Fadl, 'Islam and the Challenge of Democracy'.

preferable to anarchy, it was not given de jure recognition by the jurists.[27] As a result, caliphs took over and adopted much of the constitutional, criminal, and commercial law from the practices of the conquered people. The *qāḍī* had no power to enforce his legal decision on the rulers. His jurisdiction was very much limited to public worship, religious obligations, and, mainly, to family law. The rulers, although theoretically and formally committed to uphold the *sharīʿa*, rarely submitted to the decisions of the *qāḍīs* appointed by them, especially when those decisions went against their vested interests. The rulers, on the other hand, established their own *maẓālim* (complaint) courts,[28] which at times overturned the *qāḍī*'s judgment.

Much of jurisprudence, except the five pillars (*ʿibādāt*)[29] and family law, therefore, remained theoretical. Criminal law, developed by the jurists, also remained largely confined to the offences specifically mentioned in the Qur'ān, i.e. the *ḥadd* punishments, such as theft, wine drinking, adultery, slanderous accusation, apostasy, etc. This situation has given rise to twofold legal practice throughout Islamic history. For these reasons, Schacht has aptly remarked:[30]

> Islamic law represents an extreme case of a 'jurists' law'; it was created and developed by private specialists; legal science and not the state plays the part of a legislator, and scholarly handbooks have the force of law. This became possible because Islamic law successfully claimed to be based on divine authority, and because Islamic legal science guaranteed its own stability and continuity.

Moreover, it is to be noted that Islamic law is permeated with religious and ethical considerations.[31]

It is hoped that this brief survey of the nature and scope of Islamic law will help the uninitiated reader to appreciate the whole range of legal topics covered by Nuʿmān in this volume. It should also be borne in mind, as explained in the Introduction to the first volume, that the *Daʿā'im* was commissioned by the Imam-Caliph al-Muʿizz li-Dīn Allāh as a handy reference for the *qāḍīs* and was proclaimed the official code

[27] See Gibb, 'Some Considerations on the Sunni Theory of the Caliphate', idem, 'Al-Mawardi's Theory of the Caliphate', Lambton, *State and Government*.

[28] *EI*[2], s.v. Maẓālim.

[29] The five pillars of Islam according to the Sunnīs are: *shahāda* (profession of faith), *ṣalāt* (prayers), *zakāt* (poor tax), *ṣawm* (fasting), and *ḥajj* (pilgrimage).

[30] Schacht, *Introduction*, 5, 209.

[31] Ibid., 201.

of the Fāṭimid Empire. The juridical legal system that Nuʿmān constructed in the two volumes of the *Daʿāʾim* was, therefore, for the use of both the Fāṭimid state and the Ismāʿīlī community.[32] No doubt after the fall of the Fāṭimid dynasty in Egypt[33] the Mustaʿlī-Ṭayyibī Ismāʿīlī communities that survived in Yemen and later spread and flourished in India under different political regimes have held the *Daʿāʾim* to be a source of supreme authority in family law.

Before we turn our attention to the Indian subcontinent where the bulk of the Ismāʿīlī community is to be found, it should be kept in mind that from the nineteenth century onwards there was a large-scale adoption of European law in the Ottoman Empire and other Muslim countries. As a result, from the later part of that century, the *sharīʿa* law was, more or less, confined to family law. In modern times, in most of the Muslim countries, secular law has not only replaced the sacred law but modernist legislation has severely restricted the field in which the sacred law is applied.[34] Although it is the personal and family law that has always been regarded as the very heart of the *sharīʿa*, in modern times, reforms are affected by a series of ingenious devices, even within the sacred sphere of family law.[35] It is precisely in regard to the law of marriage and divorce that the struggle is still being fought between the traditionalists and the modernists. Anderson's numerous articles and books and other recent studies illustrate how an essentially immutable law can be changed in practice. The Islamic law of inheritance represents the heart of *sharīʿa* as well, as it is based directly on the text of the Qurʾān. For this very reason the law of inheritance has remained a distinctive mark of Islamic society

[32]The relation of Ismāʿīlī Islam or the *daʿwa* to politics, i.e. the Fāṭimid dynasty is beyond the scope of this introduction. According to the theory of the imamate, Imam is the sole interpreter of the Qurʾān and the *sharīʿa*. The role of jurists and *ʿulamāʾ*, in theory at least, is, therefore, subservient to that of the Imam-caliph. The status of the *Daʿāʾim* within the Ismāʿīlī *daʿwa* and to what extent it was implemented by the Fāṭimid courts is discussed in my forthcoming book *Al-Qāḍī al-Nuʿmān: The Ismāʿīlīs from Daʿwa to Dawla*.

[33]The Fāṭimid dynasty was established in north Africa in 297/909 and it ruled there until 362/973 when al-Muʿizz li-Dīn Allāh moved to Cairo. In 524/1130, after the assassination of al-Āmir bi-Aḥkām Allāh his infant son Ṭayyib, designated heir to the throne, went into hiding and the Yemeni *daʿwa* broke off its relations with the Ḥāfiẓī *daʿwa* in Cairo and thus began the Mustaʿlī-Ṭayyibī *daʿwa*. It was headed by a *dāʿī muṭlaq* beginning with the first *dāʿī* Dhuʾayb b. Mūsā al-Wādiʿī. Yemen continued to be the headquarters until the death of the twenty-third *dāʿī* Muḥammad b. Ḥusayn (or Ḥasan) b. al-Walīd in 946/1539. From then onwards, with the twenty-fourth *dāʿī*, Yūsuf b. Sulaymān, the headquarters were transferred to Gujarat on the western coast of India. Poonawala, *Biobibliography*, 12.

[34]Anderson's *Law Reform* is a comprehensive treatment of this subject; idem, *Islamic Law*, 17–37.

[35]For a summary see Anderson, *Islamic Law*, 38–58.

throughout the ages and, like the law of marriage and divorce, is a battleground between the traditionalists and the reformers in recent times.[36]

ISLAMIC LAW IN BRITISH INDIA, KNOWN AS 'ANGLO-MUHAMMADAN LAW' OR 'MUHAMMADAN LAW'

According to the traditional account, it was during the second half of the fifth/eleventh century that missionaries of the Musta'lī-Ṭayyibī *da'wa* succeeded in establishing a foothold in Gujarat on the western coast of India. The subsequent conversion of local Hindu rulers and certain segments of the society are shrouded in legends. By the tenth/sixteenth century, this newly converted community, which came to be known as the Bohras,[37] had grown strong enough that the headquarters of the *da'wa* and the residence of the *dā'ī*, the chief religious authority, were transferred there from Yemen. Although on his Indian campaigns, Maḥmūd of Ghazna (998–1030) had marched through Gujarat, a rich province with commercial and maritime ties with other shores of the Indian Ocean, it was ruled by a local Hindu dynasty under whose protection the Bohras prospered. In 1298, Gujarat came under the rule of the Delhi Sultanate (1206–1555) and was ruled by governors appointed from Delhi until 1583, when it was conquered by the Mughals.[38]

The Mughals professed the Ḥanafī *madhhab*; hence, under their rule from 1526 to 1858,[39] Islamic law, in its Ḥanafī version, was the law of the land. However, the Hindus, the majority of the population, and other Muslim minorities were governed by their own schools of law, particularly in family law and other related matters. The chief *qāḍī* (*qāḍī al-quḍāt*) was the principal judicial officer of the empire. He appointed the provincial *qāḍī*s who tried both civil and criminal cases.[40]

[36]Ibid., 59–80.

[37]The etymological explanation of this term is given as derived from the Gujarati *vyavahār* or *vohorvū*, meaning 'to trade'. The term was applied to the Ismā'īlīs because the early converts came mainly from a trading community. Another explanation is that they were converted from the Hindu Vohra caste. Jhaveri, 'Legendary history', 43–4; Hollister, *Shi'a of India*, 267ff.; Lokhandwalla, 'Bohras', 120.

[38]For the Ghaznawids, the Ghūrids and the Delhi Sultanate, see Majumdar et al., *Advanced History*, 267ff.; Misra, *Rise of Muslim Power in Gujarat*; idem, *Muslim Communities in Gujarat*; Bosworth, *New Islamic Dynasties*, 296–305.

[39]With Awrangzīb's death in 1707 began the decline of the Mughals. The last nominal ruler Bahādur Shāh was deposed and exiled in 1858. Bosworth, *New Islamic Dynasties*, 331–4.

[40]Majumdar et al., *Advanced History*, 550–6; Fyzee, *Outlines*, 48–9; Anderson, *Law Reform*, 20.

In 1610, the British East India Company established factories and trading posts in India. The power of this company kept on growing, and in 1689 it created administrative districts called 'presidency towns' in Calcutta, Madras, and Bombay. The victory of Robert Clive, a company officer, over the army of Sirāj ud-Dawla, the Nawāb of Bengal, at Plassey in 1757 made the company a dominant power in India. British rule in India is, therefore, conventionally described as having begun in 1757. Consequently, the British government established a governor-generalship in India, decreased the administrative control of the company, and made Warren Hastings (1772–85) the first Governor General of India.

He reorganized the courts whereby English law was applied by the courts in the 'presidency towns' of Bombay, Madras, and Calcutta. The new regulations issued by him stated that Hindus and Muslims were to be governed by their respective religious laws in regard to marriage, inheritance, and other religious institutions. As the British judges were not familiar with either the Islamic or the Hindu laws, he advised that the *mawlavī*s (a Muslim scholar of law) or the *muftī*s (a specialist in law who gives an authoritative legal opinion) and pundits (a Hindu scholar of law) should attend the courts to expound the respective law to the judges. Another regulation of 1780 clearly stated:[41]

> That in all suits regarding inheritance, marriage and caste, and other religious usages or institutions, the laws of the Koran with respect to Mahomedans, and those of the Shaster with respect to Gentoos [lit. Gentile, i.e., the Hindus], shall be invariably adhered to.

As no specific directions were given regarding what law was applicable to them in other matters, the following year, i.e. in 1781, Sir E. Impey declared that where no other law was expressly applicable, the courts should decide according to justice, equity, and good conscience. Islamic criminal law, therefore, remained in force for a longer period until 1862, when the Indian Penal Code and Code of Criminal Procedure were implemented.[42] The Islamic law of evidence was abolished with the passing of the Indian Evidence Act in 1872 and similar legislative enactments soon followed.[43]

[41]Cited by Fyzee, *Outlines*, 56.

[42]It is worth noting that the position just before the promulgation of the Penal Code, summarized by Sir George Campbell, was: 'The foundation of our criminal law is still the Mahomedan Code; but so altered and added .... Still the hidden sub-structure on which the whole building rests is this Mahomedan law, take away which and we have no definition of or authority for punishing many of the most common crimes.' Cited by Anderson, *Law Reform*, 24–5.

[43]Fyzee, *Outlines*, 49; Anderson, *Law Reform*, 20–5.

By the end of the nineteenth century Islamic law was, thus, confined to family law, which was left largely inviolate.

The so-called 'Anglo-Muhammadan Law', or 'Muhammadan Law', which still prevails in India and Pakistan, particularly in civil cases involving marriage, divorce, dower, legitimacy, guardianship, gifts, endowments (*waqfs*), wills, and inheritance, is, therefore, an appellation given to an expression of Islamic law that developed and prevailed in British India. It is unique not only in form but also in substance, inasmuch as it has absorbed English influences, especially that of equity.[44] Initially, as explained above, Anglo-Muhammadan law comprised both civil and criminal law. However, after the promulgation of the Indian Penal Code Islamic criminal law was abandoned.[45]

The interpretation of Islamic law during British rule was dependent on Muslim specialists, often called *Mawlavīs* or *Muftīs* who advised the courts, and also on some English translations of the original Arabic sources. Moreover, a growing body of case law provided precedents, which dominated the so-called Muhammadan law. A number of digests and commentaries written by Indian Muslims, British lawyers, and judges also became an influential source.[46]

'Muhammadan law', put differently, is the law applied to Muslims in the Indian subcontinent that is found in the following well-known works of legal texts.[47] The two most authoritative works for the Ḥanafī *madhhab* are: the *Hedaya* (*al-hidāya*, i.e. the Guide),[48] and the *Fatāwā 'Ālamgīrī*. The former is a commentary by the author Burḥān al-Dīn Marghīnānī

[44]Fyzee, *Outlines*, 50–1; Coulson, *History of Islamic Law*, 164–6; Anderson, *Law Reform*, 78; *Oxford Ency. of MIW*, s.v. Anglo-Muhammadan Law.

[45]It should be pointed out that the term 'Muhammadan law' itself and its ugly spelling variants, such as Moohummudun, Mahomedan, Mussalman, coined by the Orientalists and used by eminent scholars such as Schacht and Gibb—a colonial legacy of the past—should be abandoned. Fyzee, *Outlines*, 1–2. Unfortunately, Fyzee did not follow his own advice and giving explanation for his usage states that it is a useful expression so far as India is concerned, for not the whole of the *fiqh*, but only a certain part of it, is applied to the Muslims. By Muhammadan law, therefore, is meant that portion of the Islamic Civil Law, which is applied in India to Muslims as a personal law. It is also to be noted that the first chapter of his book entitled 'Introduction to the study of Muhammadan law', is dated as it was written almost half a century ago.

[46]Fyzee, *Outlines*, 50–1. He states that the negative impact of this source was that it acquired a special kind of authority with the result that new rules cannot be deduced by lawyers of eminence. Consequently, the law remained static, except for legislation and the principles of English equity.

[47]Ibid., 83–4.

[48]Charles Hamilton, *The Hedaya or Guide: A Commentary on the Mussulman Laws*. Reprint of 2nd edn. Introduced by S. G. Grady. Lahore: Premier Book House, 1963.

(d. 593/1197) on his smaller work *Bidāya*. It was translated into English by Charles Hamilton and was published in four volumes in 1791. It should be noted that this translation was sponsored by W. Hastings and is dedicated to him. The latter, on the other hand, is a collection of *fatāwā*, i.e. responses of jurist consults to the questions addressed to them. It was compiled by Shaykh Niẓām Burhānpūrī and four other authors under the orders of the Mughal Emperor Awrangzīb ʿĀlamgīr (1658–1707), hence called *Fatāwā ʿĀlamgīrī*. The third book is a Shīʿī-Imāmī work entitled *Sharāʾiʿ al-islām fī masāʾil al-ḥalāl wa ʾl-ḥarām* (Laws of Islam: Issues that are Permitted or Prohibited) by Najm al-Dīn al-Ḥillī (d. 676/1277). The first volume of Neil Baillie's *A Digest of Muhammadan Law*, published in 1865, is based on the *Fatāwā ʿĀlamgīrī*, while the second volume, published in 1869, is based on *Sharāʾiʿ al-islām*. The fourth book for the Shīʿī-Ismāʿīlīs, both the Bohras and the Āghā Khānī Khojas (Nizārī Ismāʿīlīs), is the present translation of Nuʿmān's *Daʿāʾim al-islām* (*The Pillars of Islam*).

Fyzee has rightly observed that the courts in India used to apply the Imāmī law to the Bohras, because their law was not well known. The old attitude of secretiveness about its religious literature and zealously guarding it from the uninitiated, more particularly from the Sunnī outsiders, still practised by the religious establishment, is to be blamed for this lack of information in the past. In his *Principles of Muhammadan Law*, published in 1913, Faiz Badruddin Tyabji was the first Bohra scholar to point out that the Bohras did possess their own system of jurisprudence by which they are governed.[49] Similarly, Fyzee has observed that prior to the Shariat Act of 1937 the Khojas were governed by the Hindu law of inheritance and succession.[50] After preparing a critical edition of the Arabic text of the *Daʿāʾim*, Fyzee's efforts were directed towards making its contents available in English. Towards this goal, besides publishing several articles and monograms, in his *Compendium of Fatimid Law*, he summarized those chapters of the *Daʿāʾim* which are still valid under the Muhammadan law and the rules that would apply in a court of law in India. He submitted to the court that the Fāṭimid/Ismāʿīlī law expounded by Nuʿmān in *The Pillars of Islam* should apply both to the Bohras and the Khojas alike.[51] It is hoped that this translation will help to crown Fyzee's efforts to achieve

[49]Fyzee, *Compendium*, ix.

[50]Fyzee, *Outlines*, 69–73.

[51]*The Pillars of Islam* is the supreme legal authority for the Bohras. The two most important court cases, viz., the *Chandabhoy Gulla Case* of 1921 and the *Burhanpur Durgah Case* of 1925, give insight into their history and tenets. Accordingly, in the absence of the hidden Imam, the *dāʿī muṭlaq*, the high position of the head of the community, is the authoritative interpreter of religion. Fyzee, *Outlines*, 73–4, 80–1.

the rightful status for *The Pillars of Islam*, similar to that accorded the three aforementioned works, in the courts of India and Pakistan.

In 1937, the Shariat Act, which asserted that the *sharīʿa* law was the fundamental law of all Muslims in India with regard to their personal status, was promulgated. It aimed at restoring Islamic law on a wide variety of Muslim communities and doing away with their local customs, considered to be contrary to the *sharīʿa*. It should be noted that the customary laws of such communities as the Ismāʿīlīi Khojas, the Bohras, and the Memons[52] were, thus, severely limited in favour of the dictates of orthodox Islamic doctrine.[53] In application of Muhammadan law, it is the judge who determines in each case which school of law is applicable. Where both parties to a lawsuit are Muslims belonging to the same school, the law of that school will apply. Where the parties to a lawsuit differ in schools of law, the law of the defendant will apply.[54] Muslim wife's right to dissolve her marriage by legal process was granted by the Dissolution of Muslim Marriages Act, 8 of 1939.[55]

It is true that the development of the so-called Anglo-Muhammadan law exerted an influence on Muslims by bringing their Muslim identity to the centre. It also assumed importance in the political definition of the Muslim community in India. For example, in 1937 when the Shariat Act was passed, it drew considerable Muslim support as a statement of their political identity.[56] Fyzee, on the other hand, has made some pertinent observations in this regard. He states that during the two centuries of British rule, Muhammadan law remained static except for two broadening influences: legislation, and the introduction of the principles of English equity. The Muhammadan law in India is, thus, the *sharīʿa* law modified by the principles of the English common law and equity in the varying social and cultural conditions of India. He further adds that legislation is difficult, because the government does not want to interfere with the

[52]They were converted to Islam in Sindh and Kutch, either by a son or a descendant of ʿAbd al-Qādir al-Jīlānī; are devout Sunnīs; and follow the Ḥanafī school of law. *EI*[2], s.v. Memon.

[53]The three exceptions to this law were: agricultural land, testamentary succession in certain communities, and charities other than *waqfs*. Fyzee, *Outlines*, 50, 55 ff.; Anderson, *Law Reform*, 12. Before the introduction of the Shariat Act, 1937, for instance, the original Hindu customs inherited by the Khojas and Memons, even after their conversion to Islam, excluded females from inheritance. Fyzee, *Cases*, xxviii.

[54]In most of the Islamic countries the general rule is that the school of the litigant is not taken into consideration. It is the *qāḍī* who follows his own school. Fyzee, *Outlines*, 55–87, has given more details on this and other related issues.

[55]Ibid., 471–3; idem, *Cases*, xxxiv.

[56]*Oxford Ency. MIW*, s.v. Anglo-Muhammadan Law.

personal law of the various communities for fear of dissatisfaction, hurting the religious susceptibilities and sensibilities of the Muslims. However, it is also true that changing socio-economic conditions and modernization generate the need for reform and change. As introduction of reform becomes difficult, it creates a tension between the orthodoxy and the reformists.[57] This is precisely the situation at present with the Muslims of India in general and the Bohras in particular.

Article 44, known as the 'Uniform Civil Code' for the citizens, entitled the 'Directive Principles of State Policy', in the Constitution of India (part iv), adopted by the Parliament and signed by the president on 26 November 1949, requires that 'the State shall endeavour to secure for its citizens a uniform civil code throughout the territory of India'. This has given rise to the concept of 'Uniform Civil Code' for all the citizens and has generated great pressure on the Muslims to reform 'Muslim Personal Law'. Article 37 of the Constitution of India, on the other hand, makes it clear that those directive principles, even though 'fundamental in the governance of the country', are not enforceable as such. It should be noted that both Hindus and Muslims bitterly opposed the enactment of Article 44, but in their quest to create a secular, democratic state, and in the national interest of India, the founding fathers of the Constitution did not bow to that pressure.

The Hindus themselves have radically reformed their own personal law by the adoption and promulgation of the Hindu Marriage Act of 1955. It prohibits polygamy and provides for judicial divorce on the basis of strict equity between a husband and a wife. Hence, the question is often posed, why a Muslim man should be allowed to enjoy the 'privilege' of being permitted to marry more than one wife and to divorce his wife at will?

According to Islamic law, a Muslim cannot bequeath more than one-third of his estate. However, under the Special Marriage Act of 1954, if a Muslim registers his marriage, he could have all the powers of a testator under the Indian Succession Act of 1925. For all other purposes, except for this privilege, he is governed by the Muhammadan law. Fyzee, therefore, considers it a most potent influence that helps create the atmosphere of social reform among Muslims.[58]

Unlike the rest of the Muslim world, Anderson, a well-known authority on Islamic law, states that, in India, there has been no dichotomy between the courts which deal with family matters under different religious law

[57]Fyzee, *Outlines*, 51–2.
[58]Ibid., 363–5, 477–8.

on one hand and those which administer the common law of the land on the other. In India it is the same court that applies the general law to all subjects and a whole variety of special systems of law to different religious communities. In all cases, the common law principle of *stare decisis* prevails. This has opened the door to the possibility of law reform through judicial decision. Like Fyzee, Anderson's remarks reiterate that a non-Muslim government hesitates even more than most Muslim governments to introduce legislation which may be regarded by Muslims as contrary to their sacred law.[59]

In January 1972, Anderson was invited first by the then Chief Justice Hidayatullah and the president of the Indian Law Institute to give a series of lectures and to participate in a special seminar on 'Islamic Personal Law in Modern India'. In his erudite paper entitled 'Muslim Personal Law in India', he has analysed polygamy, divorce, inheritance, and the custody of children. He concludes his paper with a very perceptive remark. I would like to quote him at length. He states:[60]

> The Muslim community ... resist[s] even the most obvious reforms in their personal law. They are apt to view any change whatever in the *status quo* as the first step down a slippery slope leading to a uniform code. The greatest need of the moment, as it seems to me, is to convince them that their personal law, as this is at present administered in India, stands in urgent need of reform; that reforms in personal law as administered by the courts have in fact been introduced in most of the leading Muslim countries without any sacrifice of what they consider to be essential Islamic principles; and that the enactment of reforms in those aspects of the Muslim personal law (as at present enforced by the courts in India) which give rise to the most serious criticisms would not necessarily represent a step towards any suppression of their law, but might, indeed, prove the exact opposite. A house which is in good condition is, clearly, much more likely to stand the stresses and strains of the elements than one which is in a sad state of disorder and disrepair. ... It would be infinitely preferable, as I see it, for reforms in Muslim personal law to be proposed by the Muslims themselves rather than imposed on them against their will.

This seminar,[61] in spite of its comparatively representative character and the wide differences in approach, agreed unanimously that 'Muslim Personal Law', as currently applied by the courts in India, did indeed stand in urgent need of reform.[62] In all fairness, it is necessary to add here a few

[59]Anderson, *Law Reform*, 25.

[60]Anderson, 'Muslim Personal Law in India', 35–6.

[61]For various papers see Mahmood, *Islamic Law in Modern India.*

[62]Anderson, *Law Reform*, 214. See also Mahmood, *Islamic Law in Modern India*.

words as postscript. Since 1972, the political, social, economic, cultural, and psychological climate has drastically changed. The *Shah Banu* case was probably a turning point. At the age of 56, she was divorced by her husband who refused to pay alimony. Consequently, she took her case all the way to the Supreme Court, which granted her maintenance beyond the usual period of *'idda* (waiting-period of a woman after termination of marriage before contracting another marriage). If the marriage is dissolved by divorce, the general rule according to the *sharī'a* is that the wife is entitled to maintenance only until the period of the *'idda* expires, unless she is pregnant, in which case the husband's liability continues.

It was unfortunate that inept Muslim political and religious leadership not only rejected the Supreme Court judgement but also launched a huge protest movement. For political gain, and to get Muslim votes, Rajiv Gandhi's government (from 1984 to 1989), enjoying a comfortable majority in the Parliament, enacted a law to overrule the court's verdict. It was argued that the Muslims have a right to follow their *sharī'a* rather than the common law of the land. Afterward, in another rash political move, Rajiv Gandhi unlocked the Babri Masjid, in Ayodhya, which had been shut for a long time. This move would unwittingly invite a hardening of opposing positions on the Babri Masjid issue with one faction claiming that it was originally the site of a temple to Rāma (incarnation of Hindu god Vishnu). Soon, the actions and counteractions of the contending parties pulled the courts deeper into what would become a particularly aggressive and wrenching communal dispute.

The decomposition of the secular character of India that had set in with the Shah Banu case accelerated with the passage of time. The hawks in the fundamentalist parties were waiting for the opportunity and the Rajiv Gandhi government unwittingly offered them on a silver platter. Babri Masjid was completely razed to the ground on 6 December 1992, by a mob of Karsevaks allegedly with the support of the Bharatiya Janata Party (BJP) and other right wing Hindu organizations. The BJP is considered anti-Muslim and it keeps on demanding the enactment of common civil code, hence there is a strong Muslim resistance. BJP rode high to power on the wave of anti-secular ethos. BJP and its axis may have, thus, caused irreparable damage to the democratic, secular constitution, which guarantees by law the absolute equality of all faiths. The Constitution, in accord with age-old Indian tradition of tolerance and religious pluralism is badly shaken. There seems to be a tendency for educational and cultural institutions to be headed by political appointees. The present central government does not diverge from this practice and has allotted key posts in these academies to persons allegedly close to the government. Communal riots, particularly

Gujarat riots of 2002 and the horrendous carnage perpetrated in the wake of those riots have shocked India, including most of the Hindu population. The rise of Hindu right-wing nationalist groups, such as Bajrang Dal, who call themselves 'the warriors of the Hindutva revolution', Sangh Parivar, and the Vishwa Hindu Parishad and their continuing aggressive posture have led to the regression of the liberal, secular ethos. Field studies conducted in India indicate that an overwhelming majority of Muslims represented by The All India Muslim Personal Law Board reject any change in the Muslim Personal Law. It is obvious, therefore, that this issue will have to wait for an opportune future date.[63]

Going back to the major issue that the Islamic law does not differentiate between purely legal matters and religious duties, I would like to add the following. Ṣubḥī Mahmasānī, an eminent lawyer and author from Lebanon, advocates the need to reinterpret and adapt Islamic law to the modern world. He distinguishes between the legal and the religious rulings, similar to that made today between civil and natural obligations. He states that if we refer to the essence of Islamic jurisprudence, we find that the teachings of the Prophet do not bind the Muslims except in cases pertaining to religion and ethics. Traditions which refer to secondary matters of daily living, are not mandatory. Therefore, no relation whatever exists between Islam and matters of daily living, unless these are concerned with a principle of religion.[64]

In his short volume, entitled *A Modern Approach to Islam*, Fyzee, perhaps the soundest scholar of Muhammadan [Islamic] law in the subcontinent, who recommends a liberal study of 'legal pluralism', has made a bold attempt at reinterpretation of Islam. First, he gives a penetrating analysis of law and religion in Islam and Islamic law and theology. Next, he scrutinizes some important documents, such as the Prophet's Last Sermon, 'Umar's instructions to the *qāḍī*, and 'Alī's testament. His analysis of those documents reveals the fusion of law and religion. He then advocates that historical criticism be applied to the study of *sharī'a* and that the law

[63]It should be pointed out that in jurisprudence, mala fide intent is often considered sufficient ground for the inadmissibility of a particular legal position. The current demand for a uniform civil code, especially from the political right (BJP), is mala fide in intent as it is less concerned with providing justice to Muslim women than with forcing a specific political ideology on Muslims. Equal rights advocates have justifiably argued that the real issue in the debate on uniform civil code is neither nationalism nor equality before the law, but gender justice. Viewed from this perspective, it is obvious that even the proponents of a uniform law have failed to see the forest for the trees. The focus of debate, therefore, ought to be not uniformity but reform in Muslim family law and how it can be made acceptable to those for whom it is intended.

[64]Subhi Mahmasani, 'Adaptation of Islamic Jurisprudence'.

should be studied in its relation to social conditions. In the last chapter, entitled 'The Reinterpretation of Islam', which is intensely personal, he affirms his own position as a non-conformist Muslim, rejects secularism in its absolute form, re-evaluates the Islamic tradition, and seeks for an exegetical basis for the reform of Islamic law. He argues the need for a modern Muslim to separate law from religion. He states:[65]

A word may not be out of place about the future. It is the writer's conviction that gradually all individual and personal laws, based upon ancient principles governing the social life of the community, will either be abolished or so modified as to bring them within a general scheme of laws applicable to all persons, regardless of religious differences. This movement is already strong in subjects like industrial legislation ... pertaining to civil marriage and divorce. Such gradual modifications, even of the rules of *sharīʿa* do not destroy the essential truth of the faith of Islam. On a truer and deeper examination of the matter, it will be found that certain portions of the *sharīʿa* constitute only an outer crust which encloses a kernel—the central core of Islam—which can be preserved intact only by re-interpretation and restatement in every age and every epoch of civilization. The responsibility to determine afresh what are the durable and what the changeable elements in Islam rests on us at the present time. The conventional theology of the *ulema* does not satisfy the minds and the outlook of the present century. A re-examination, re-interpretation, reformulation and restatement of the essential principles of Islam is a vital necessity of our age.

In his article 'Islam and the Challenge of Democracy: Can individual rights and popular sovereignty take root in faith?' Abou El Fadl, a younger Egyptian scholar of Islamic law, also advocates separation of law and religion. In order to appreciate his arguments one has to read the aforecited article and his book *Speaking in God's Name*. He states that a religious state law is a contradiction in terms. Either the law belongs to the state or it belongs to God. As long as the law relies on the subjective agency of the state for its articulation and enforcement, any law enforced by the state is necessarily not God's law. Otherwise, we must be willing to admit that the failure of the law of the state is in fact the failure of God's law and, ultimately, of God Himself. In Islamic theology, this [latter] possibility cannot be entertained.[66]

Finally, it will probably become clear to the reader that a major part of the *Daʿāʾim*, composed over a thousand years ago, has fallen into disuse. Even the segment dealing with family law, which is still valid and applied by the courts, is in need of review and reform. However, the religious

[65]Fyzee, *Modern Approach*, 82–3; idem, 'The Reinterpretation of Islam'.
[66]Abou El Fadl, 'Islam and the Challenge of Democracy'.

establishment of the Bohras has shown little or no interest at all either in reinterpretation or introduction of any change. The Āghā Khānī Khojas, on the other hand, have shown remarkable vitality and progressive spirit in addressing the problems of modernity.[67] Their religious leadership, especially under Sulṭān Muḥammad Shāh, Āghā Khān III (1885–1957) and his successor the present Imam Shāh Karīm al-Ḥusaynī, Āghā Khān IV, has taken a keen interest in the affairs of the followers. After extensive consultation with the duly elected community councils on various levels, Āghā Khāns have campaigned and successfully carried out a variety of educational and social reforms.[68] 'The Constitution of the Shia Imami Ismailis in Africa', adopted in 1962 with the blessings of the Āghā Khān is noteworthy in this respect. Important matters connected with the personal law of the community and its legal validity by the territorial courts of various countries where the community members live in were squarely addressed. In his article 'The Isma'ili Khojas of East Africa: A new Constitution and Personal Law for the Community', Anderson has highlighted some of those aspects.[69] The details need not concern us here as this topic of the new constitution is beyond the scope of this short introduction, though it is important to note that polygamy is strictly prohibited and provisions for dower and compensation in cases of dissolution of any marriage are clearly delineated. Even the matter of succession is dealt with wherein it is stated that 'Save as otherwise expressly provided, every Ismaili who is of sound mind and not a minor may dispose of this moveable and immovable property by will, provided such a will be in writing'.[70]

8 March 2003
Rancho Palos Verdes, California

Ismail K. H. Poonawala

[67]It was during the late nineteenth and early twentieth centuries under the leadership of Āghā Khān III that the present religious identity of the community as Shīʿī-Ismāʿīlīs was established. For details see Asani, 'The Khojahs of Indo-Pakistan'.

[68]For modern developments see Daftary, *Short History*, 193–209.

[69]Anderson, 'The Isma'ili Khojas of East Africa'. The history of this constitution goes back to 1905 when the first supreme council for Africa was established in Zanzibar and Ismaili constitution was adopted in 1906. The Ismailis of Bombay and Rangoon also adopted their respective constitutions in the same year. In 1986, a single constitution governing all Ismaili Khoja communities living in various parts of the world was introduced by the present Āghā Khān with the expectation that it would standardize their divergent religious practices. See *The Constitution of the Shia Imami Ismaili Muslims*.

[70]Anderson, 'The Isma'ili Khojas of East Africa', 33.

1

Book of Business Transactions and Rules Concerning Them (Kitāb *al-Buyūʿ wa ʾl-Aḥkām fīhā*)[1]

THE INDUCEMENT TO SEEK THE MEANS OF LIVELIHOOD AND WHAT HAS BEEN SAID THEREABOUT BY THE PEOPLE OF THE HOUSE (AL-ḤAḌḌ ʿALĀ *ṬALAB AL-RIZQ WA-MĀ JĀʾA FĪHI ʿAN AHL AL-BAYT*)[2]

God says: O *ye who believe! When the call is heard for the prayer of the day of congregation, hasten unto remembrance of Allah and leave your trading. That is better for you if ye did but know. And when the prayer is ended, then disperse in the land and seek of Allah's bounty, and remember Allah much, that ye may be successful* (62:9–10).

Jaʿfar b. Muḥammad—his father—his ancestors—ʿAlī: The Messenger of God said, 'When a man is in straitened circumstances, let him go forth from his house and seek the bounty of God by travelling over land, and not cause sorrow to himself or his family.'[3]

ʿAlī: He used to say, 'I dislike the man who is lazy in his worldly affairs; for, if he is lazy in his worldly affairs, he will be more careless of [his spiritual duties], the affairs of the hereafter.'[4]

Jaʿfar b. Muḥammad: A man came to the Imam and asked him to pray

[1] *Buyūʿ* pl. of *bayʿ*, signifies various kinds of selling and buying. Lane, s.v. b-y-ʿ. Schacht, *Introduction*, 151–4; *EI*², Bayʿ. Cf. Mahmasani, 'Transactions in the Sharīʿa'; it deals with property and ownership, contracts, and procedure.

[2] Compare this section with *Kāfī*, V, 61–5, 72–3. For the meaning of *Ahl al-bayt* see *The Pillars of Islam*, I, 38–49; *EI*², s.v. Ahl al-Bayt.

[3] 'Trying to earn a lawful livelihood is an obligatory duty in addition to other obligatory duties.' *Mishkāt*, II, 78; Robson, I, 596 (I have modified his translation).

[4] *Kāfī*, V, 80; it is reported from Abū Jaʿfar [Imam al-Bāqir].

for him for prosperity in his livelihood. The Imam said, 'I shall not pray for you. Seek it as you have been commanded [by God].'[5] And he [Ja'far b. Muḥammad] said, 'Every Muslim should seek his livelihood by undergoing hardship (lit. even by exposing himself to the heat of the sun).'[6]

However, they are too numerous to mention here. The Members of the House of the Prophet transmitted to us many types of prayer about obtaining livelihood [from God]. None of them is prescribed for a particular occasion.

The Messenger of God: On the Farewell Pilgrimage[7] he said, 'I swear by God that, in truth, there is no action which will take you towards the Garden, except that I have apprised you of it; and there is no action which will lead you to the Fire, except that I have warned you against it. Verily the Trusted Spirit (*al-rūḥ al-amīn*) [the Angel Gabriel][8] has whispered to me secretly (*nafatha fī rūʿī*) that no one meets his death until his earthly provision has ended.[9] So fear God, and strive to the best of your capacity to gain your livelihood.

'Every servant of God without exception has a livelihood, between which and him there is a veil. Now, if he exercises patience, God gives him his livelihood lawfully; but if he is unable to do so, he rends the veil and eats it (the livelihood) unlawfully. None of you should dare to seek your livelihood unlawfully in the case in which the means of obtaining livelihood (lawfully) appear to be temporarily blocked; for, without obedience to God, no man can obtain His bounties (lit. what is with Him).'[10]

Ja'far b. Muḥammad: He said, 'Verily, sin bars a man from his livelihood.'

The Messenger of God: During the Battle of Tabūk,[11] he passed by a sturdy youth, who was driving camels which were fat. The Prophet's Companions said to him, 'O Messenger of God, how good it would be if this man's strength and sturdiness, and the fat of his camels were to be used for the cause of God (*fī sabīl Allāh*).' So the Messenger of God called him and said, 'These camels yonder, what do you do with them?' The

[5]A similar tradition in *Kāfī*, V, 73, 74.

[6]Abū 'Abd Allāh [Ja'far al-Ṣādiq] said, 'Verily, I work in some of my country estates until I sweat [profusely] ... so that God will know that I seek livelihood lawfully.' *Kāfī*, V, 72.

[7]It is so called because the Messenger of God bade farewell to the people and died shortly thereafter. *The Pillars of Islam*, I, 21, 26, 360, 368.

[8]For Gabriel see *The Pillars of Islam*, I, 63.

[9]*Majmaʿ al-baḥrayn*, s.v. r-w-ʿ; Ṭurayḥī has cited the tradition.

[10]*Kāfī*, V, 75, 77, reported thrice on different authorities.

[11]For the expedition of Tabūk see *The Pillars of Islam*, I, 432, n. 44.

youth said, 'O Messenger of God, I have a wife and children; so I earn my livelihood by the camels to provide for my family and prevent them from asking people [for money] and incurring a debt upon me.[12] The Prophet said, 'Perhaps there is something else.' The man replied, 'Not at all.' When the man had departed, the Messenger of God said, 'If the man has really spoken the truth, verily he is entitled to a recompense [from God] which is equal to that of a *ghāzī*[13] (one who takes part in a military expedition), or a *ḥājj* (one who makes a pilgrimage), or a *mu'tamir* (one who makes a lesser pilgrimage).'

The Messenger of God: He said, 'On the day when there will be no shadow except the shadow under the Throne [i.e., the Day of Judgement], there will be a man who is [protected by that shadow because he] journeyed into the land to seek by the favour of God, that which kept himself from begging and provided for his family.'

'Alī: He said, 'No day (*ghudwa*, lit. morning) spent by anyone of you in the way of God is greater [in worth] than the day spent by a man in seeking what is beneficial to his children and his family.' And he said, 'The traveller in search of lawful provision [for himself and his family] is [of] similar [worth] to the *mujāhid* in the way of God.'[14]

The Messenger of God: A man asked him and said, 'O Messenger of God, whenever I turned to something [as a means of livelihood], I only failed in it (*ḥūriftu fīhi*, lit. I was turned away from it).' The Messenger of God said, 'Think of something in which you succeeded for once.' The man replied, '[In the business of] *qaraẓ*.'[15] The Messenger of God said, 'Then, stick to it.'

Ja'far b. Muḥammad: [One day] he addressed one of his companions as follows, 'I have come to know that you have increased your absence from your family.' The man said, 'Yes, may I be ransomed for you.' [The Imam] asked, 'Where do you go?' The man replied, 'To Fārs[16] and

[12]The Arabic is *wa-aqḍī dayn^{an} 'alayyā*. I have conveyed the sense rather than the literal meaning.

[13]*Ghāẓī*, a title of honour given to those who distinguished themselves in the *ghazwa*. It became the title of certain Muslim princes, such as the *amīr*s of Anatolia and the first Ottoman sultans. *EI*², s.v. Ghāzī, Ghazw.

[14]*Kāfī*, V, 67, 68–9, 82; three versions of this tradition are reported. *Mujāhid*, active participle of the verbal form III *jāhada*, means 'the one who strives,' and acquired the religious meaning of 'fighter for the faith,' like that of a *ghāẓī*. *EI*², s.v. Mudjāhid.

[15]A plant used for tanning leather. *Lisān al-'Arab*, s.v. q-r-ẓ.

[16]Fārs, the Arabicized form of Pārs, was itself derived from Parsa, the Persis of the Greeks. The province of Fārs was the 'cradle of Persian greatness'. It was conquered by the Muslim Arabs during the caliphate of 'Uthmān. *EI*², s.v. Fārs.

Ahwāz.'[17] [The Imam] asked, 'For what purpose?' The man replied, 'In search of trade and worldly affairs.' The Imam said, 'Look! When you seek the things of the world and fail to obtain them, remember that with which God has distinguished you in regard to religion; and [remember] our *walāya* (devotion)[18] with which He has blessed you; and [remember] the calamities that He has averted from you, because therewith it is more appropriate for you to relinquish those worldly affairs which have escaped you!'

'Alī: Once it came to pass that a man addressed him thus, 'O Commander of the Faithful, I desire to undertake commerce.' 'Alī said, 'Do you have legal knowledge of the religion of God (*a-faqihta fī dīn Allāh*)?' The man said, 'I have [understood] a part of it.' 'Alī said, 'Woe unto you! First [comes] legal knowledge and then business. For, verily, he who buys and sells, and does not ask about what is forbidden and what is lawful, will surely fall increasingly into usury (*ribā*).'[19]

The Messenger of God: He preferred trade in cloth to trade in wheat because that hoarding (*ḥukra*, monopoly) [is involved] in the latter, which is harmful to the believers.[20] But if hoarding were not practised, trading in wheat would not be unlawful.

Ja'far b. Muḥammad: He asked one of his companions as to the profession in which he was engaged. He replied, 'May I be ransomed for you, I have stopped engaging in trade.' [The Imam] asked, 'Why [have you done] this?' The man said, 'I had to wait long [for a profit].' [The Imam] said, 'This action is very surprising; it will deplete your wealth. So do not stop trading, but ask God for His bounty. Open the door [of your shop], spread your carpet, and ask your Lord to provide for you.'[21]

[17]Ahwāz, a town in the Khūzistān plain, was the centre for sugar production and continued to prosper under the Umayyads and 'Abbāsids. *The Pillars of Islam*, I, 281, n. 49.

[18]For *walāya* see *The Pillars of Islam*, I, 2, 18.

[19]*Kāfī*, V, 146, 151; Ṭūsī, *al-Nihāya*, 371; idem, *Tahdhīb al-aḥkām*, VII, 6. *Ribā*, lit. increase, is a technical term for usurious interest, and any unjustified increase of capital for which no compensation is paid. The Qur'ān regards *ribā* as a practice of unbelievers and demands that it should be abandoned. The Prophet also referred to this prohibition in his sermon at the Farewell Pilgrimage. The importance of the prohibition affecting everyday life and the requirements of commerce have given rise to a number of methods of evasion or legal devices called *ḥiyal*. For details see *EI*^{2}, s.v. Ribā, and n. 124 below in this chapter.

[20]*Kāfī*, V, 162; hoarding is condemned. *Mishkāt*, II, 106–7; Robson, I, 619–20; withholding goods until their price rises is condemned. See also Ṭūsī, *al-Nihāya*, 374–5.

[21]*Kāfī*, V, 78, 143–6; Kulaynī reports a slightly different tradition urging people not to stop trading.

The Messenger of God: Once he passed by some tradesmen who in those days were called *samāsira* (sing. *simsār*, broker, middleman), and he told them, 'Harken to me! I do not call you "brokers", but I name you "traders" (*tujjār* pl. of *tājir*). The trader commits foul deeds (*fājir*),[22] and the one who commits foul deeds shall be in the Fire.'[23] So, they locked their doors and stopped their trade.

The next day when the Messenger of God went there, he said, 'Where are the people [brokers]?' He was told, 'O Messenger of God, they heard what you said yesterday and have stopped trading.' The Messenger of God said, 'I say [to you] today the same [explaining what I said yesterday: All will enter the Fire] except those who give and take honestly.'[24]

The Messenger of God: He said, 'My Lord has sent me as a mercy [to mankind], and did not make me a merchant or a tiller of land. Verily the worst ones of this community are [its] tradesmen and [its] agriculturalists, except those who jealously guard the [dictates of] religion.'

The Messenger of God: It is reported that a country Arab (*aʿrābī*)[25] came to him with some camels and said, 'O Messenger of God, I wish to sell these camels of mine, so sell them for me.' The Messenger of God said, 'I am not a merchant plying in the markets.' The country Arab said, 'Then advise me.' The Messenger of God said, 'Sell this for so much and this for so much.'

Jaʿfar b. Muḥammad: He exhorted some of his followers and said, 'Do not roam about the markets, and do not go about making small purchases for yourself. It is not desirable for you, nor for a Muslim of noble

[22]Given the context I have translated *fājir* as the one who commits foul deeds, such as swearing a false oath, or lying, or doing unlawful acts. Lane, s.v. f-j-r.

[23]*Kāfī*, V, 146. 'The trader is a *fājir*, and the *fājir* shall be in Fire.' It is ascribed to ʿAlī. See also Ṭūsī, *al-Nihāya*, 371–2. It should be noted that the *simsār*'s wages are recounted as lawful. *Kāfī*, V, 194–5, 290–1; Ṭūsī, *al-Nihāya*, 406.

[24]Qays b. Abū Ghazara said, 'In the time of God's Messenger we used to be called *samāsira* (brokers), but God's Messenger came upon us one day and called us by a better name than that, saying, "Company of merchants (*tujjār*), unprofitable speech and swearing have a place in business dealing, so mix it with *ṣadaqa*".' Another tradition reports the Prophet as saying, 'The merchants will be raised up on the day of resurrection as evildoers (*fujjār* pl. of *fājir*), except those who fear God, are honest and speak the truth.' *Mishkāt*, II, 82; Robson, I, 599.

[25]*Aʿrābī* is applied to a single person, while *aʿrāb* is the appelation given to those Arabs who live in the desert. *Aʿrāb* occurs in the Qur'ān mostly with a negative connotation, such as *The wandering Arabs are more hard in disbelief and hypocrisy* (9:97); *The wandering Arabs say: We believe. Say (unto them, O Muhammad): Ye believe not, but rather say 'We submit,' for the faith hath not yet entered into your hearts* (49:14). See also *The Pillars of Islam*, I, 15, 90, 120, 190, 232, 245, 287, 426, 457, 484.

descent and religious standing to buy small wares by himself, except such commodities as sheep, camels and slaves.'[26]

Once [the Imam] saw one of his companions carrying some vegetables and he said that he disliked [the action of] a man with dignity (*al-rajul al-sarīy*, high-ranking, noble) to carry such low things, lest some persons be insolent to him.

The Messenger of God: He said, 'Verily, God loves the man who is prompt (*sahl* lit. easy) in buying goods, the man who is prompt in selling them, the man who pays his debts promptly (*sahl al-qaḍā'*),[27] and the man who promptly obtains payment of debts due to him.'[28]

The Messenger of God: He said, 'God will not look [with favour] on three [sorts of] persons on the Day of Judgement, nor will He purify them rather they will have a painful chastisement: (1) The one who swears allegiance to an Imam, and who honours his word only if the Imam gives him something of worldly goods; but if the Imam does not do so, he does not keep his word. (2) The one who has a water well on the road, but refuses it to travellers. (3) The one who swears after the prayer of *'aṣr* that he had been given certain goods [by someone else], and in consequence a third person takes possession of the goods, relying on the man's word; [but, in reality] the man had made a false statement.'[29]

'Alī: He said, 'The market of the Muslims is like their mosque. A man is entitled to sit [and do business] in any place [he stakes out] until he rises, or the sun sets.' By the expression 'the sun sets', 'Alī meant, at a place which does not belong to any particular person.[30]

SALES WHICH ARE FORBIDDEN
(*MĀ NUHIYA 'AN BAY'IHI*)

God says: *O ye who believe! Squander not your wealth among yourselves in vanity, except it be trade by mutual consent* (4:29). He says: *Allah permitteth*

[26] *Kāfī*, V, 85; the commodities specified are: landed property, slaves, and camels.

[27] Jābir reported God's Messenger as saying, 'God shows mercy to a man who is kindly (*rajul^{an} samḥ^{an}*) when he sells, when he buys, and when he makes a claim.' *Mishkāt*, II, 81; Robson, I, 598; transmitted by Bukhārī. About debts see *Kāfī*, V, 87, 89.

[28] *Kāfī*, V, 95.

[29] Abū Dharr reported the Messenger of God as saying, 'There are three [types of persons] to whom God will not speak on the Day of Resurrection, at whom He will not look, ... and they will have a painful punishment.' Abū Dharr said, 'They are losers ... . Who are they, O Messenger of God?' He replied, 'The one who wears a trailing robe, the one who takes account of what he gives, and the one who produces a ready sale of a commodity by false swearing.' *Mishkāt*, II, 81–2; Robson, I, 598; transmitted by Muslim.

[30] *Kāfī*, V, 151; also reported from 'Alī; Ṭūsī, *Tahdhīb al-aḥkām*, VII, 9.

trading (bay') and forbiddeth usury (ribā)[31] (2:275). By 'trading' God means lawful trade with the exclusion of that which He has forbidden in His Book and on the tongue of His Messenger. We shall mention this at the proper place, if God wills.

Ja'far b. Muḥammad—his father—his ancestors—'Alī: The Messenger of God forbade the sale of freeborn men, carrion, blood, pigs, and idols. [He forbade] the hiring of stallions to cover [mares],[32] taking the profit from [the sale of] intoxicating drinks (*al-khamr*), and the sale of dung, [the last of which] he said was like carrion.[33]

Ja'far b. Muḥammad: He said, 'Trade is lawful in things which can be lawfully eaten and drunk, and in other commodities that sustain people if consumed, and if used are beneficial. Forbidden is the sale and purchase of those things which are, in principle, declared to be unlawful.'

This is a comprehensive dictum of Ja'far b. Muḥammad on this topic.

The Messenger of God: He said, 'May God curse wine—its extractor, the one for whom it was extracted, its vendor, its purchaser, the one who drinks it, the one who gives drink [to another], the one who benefits from the price paid for it, its carrier, and the one for whom it is carried.'[34]

The Prophet said, 'He who declared the drinking of intoxicants as unlawful [that is, God] has also declared its sale and taking any profits from it as forbidden.'

Abū Ja'far Muḥammad b. 'Alī: He was asked about a man who owed a certain number of dirhams to another, and so he sold wine or pigs and paid off his debt from the proceeds. [The Imam] said, 'That is all right! It is lawful for the creditor,[35] but unlawful for the seller.'[36]

[31]See a long section on usury in *Mishkāt*, II, 86–91; Robson, I, 602–6; *Kāfī*, V, 139–42.

[32]'Taking hire for a stallion to cover a mare is forbidden.' *Mishkāt*, II, 96, 98; Robson, I, 610, 611; transmitted by Bukhārī.

[33]*Mishkāt*, II, 74; Robson I, 593. The traditions states, 'God and His Messenger have declared forbidden the sale of wine, animals which have died a natural death, swine and idols.' See also Ṭūsī, *al-Nihāya*, 363–5; more forbidden categories are indicated.

[34]'Anas said that God's Messenger cursed ten people in connection with wine: the wine-presser, the one who has it pressed, the one who drinks it, the one who conveys it, the one to whom it is conveyed, the one who serves it, the one who sells it, the one who benefits from the price paid for it, the one who buys it, and the one for whom it is bought.' *Mishkāt*, II, 77; Robson I, 595. See also Ṭūsī, *al-Nihāya*, 363–4.

[35]*Muqtaḍī*: MS Q. *Muqtaḍā* in the edited text is incorrect.

[36]*Kāfī*, V, 231–2; also reported on the authority of al-Bāqir. Two additional traditions are reported on the authority of al-Ṣādiq. Another tradition states: 'Alī al-Riḍā was asked about a Christian who had embraced Islam and had wine and pigs with him, and had debt. 'Can he sell his wine and pigs to pay off his debt?' [The Imam] said, 'No.' See also Ṭūsī, *al-Nihāya*, 403.

Ja'far b. Muḥammad: He was asked about the sale of grapes and dried dates (*tamr*), dry raisins (*zabīb*), and the pressed juice of fruit (*'aṣīr*) to a man who manufactures wine. [The Imam] said, 'There is no harm in it if the sale was lawful, inasmuch as the vendor is not responsible for its unlawful use by the purchaser.'[37]

The Messenger of God forbade profiting from [the sale of] wild and ferocious dog.[38]

'Alī: He said, 'The sale of a dog trained for hunting game is lawful.'

'Alī: He said, 'There is no harm in the sale and purchase of copies of the Qur'ān (*al-maṣāḥif*).'[39]

Ja'far b. Muḥammad said, 'There is no harm if the Book of God is copied for wages.' The expression 'sale' is not applied to the Book of God itself; but to skin (*julūd*, leather for writing) and the two covers (*daffatayn*, or boards) between which the pages of the book are bound.[40] [For instance] you say, 'I sell this [that is, skin and two covers] for so much.'[41]

'Alī: He saw a man carrying a cat and asked him, 'What are you doing with it?' The man said, 'I am selling it.' 'Alī forbade him to do so.[42] The man said, 'But I do not need it.' 'Alī said, 'Well, then, give its price in charity.'

Ja'far b. Muḥammad: He was asked about the purchase of a thing from a person who was known for cheating, stealing, or unfair dealing. [The Imam] said, 'There is no harm in buying the thing so long as it is not known for certain that the thing was obtained fraudulently, by wrongdoing, or by theft. However, if this is known, then its purchase and sale are both forbidden.[43] He who buys anything which is unlawfully

[37]*Kāfī*, V, 231; also reported on the authority of al-Ṣādiq.

[38]'The price paid for a dog is impure, the hire paid to a prostitute is impure ...' transmitted by Bukhārī and Muslim with slight variations. *Mishkāt*, II, 74; Robson, I, 593. Schacht is of the opinion that the sale of dogs was valid. The idea of the ritual uncleanliness of dogs was taken over from Judaism and was expressed in a tradition from the Prophet. Schacht, *Origins*, 216.

[39]*Muṣḥaf* (pl. *maṣāḥif*) is the name given to a complete text of the Qur'ān considered as a physical object. *EI*², s.v. Muṣḥaf.

[40]See Petersen, *The Arabic Book*, 54 ff., 101 ff.

[41]Ibn 'Abbās was asked about payment for writing a copy of the Qur'ān and replied, 'There is no harm. They are just people who draw figures and get a living simply by their handiwork.' *Mishkāt*, II, 78; Robson I, 596. See also *Kāfī*, V, 116–17; all the traditions are reported on the authority of al-Ṣādiq; Ṭūsī, *al-Nihāya*, 368.

[42]'Payments for dogs and cats are forbidden.' *Mishkāt*, II, 75; Robson, I, 593.

[43]*Kāfī*, V, 227–8; has a separate section on selling and buying of stolen goods and on cheating. Ṭūsī, *al-Nihāya*, 401.

obtained (*al-suḥt*, ill-gotten property),[44] will not be excused by God, as he has purchased a thing which was not permissible to him.'

The Messenger of God prohibited the sale of the share of war booty before its distribution.[45]

The Messenger of God: He forbade the sale of water, pasturage, and fire.[46] This is a prohibition expressed in general terms relating to property which [in certain circumstances] can lawfully be sold among Muslims. [The prohibition applies specifically to three cases]: (1) Pasturage on open country;[47] (2) a blazing fire from which people light lamps or take fire [for domestic purposes]; (3) things which do not diminish with use, like flowing water in streamlets (*ghuyūl*), springs (*'uyūn*), overflowing water (*suyūl*), and wells which are in public use and not in private ownership.[48]

Now, [these] things over which private ownership can be established may be sold lawfully. It is not proper to take embers from someone's live fire without his permission because it is a kind of private property.

FORBIDDEN TRANSACTIONS INVOLVING ALEATORY SALES (*MĀ NUHIYA 'ANHU MIN BAY' AL-GHARAR*)[49]

Ja'far b. Muḥammad—his father—his ancestors: The Messenger of God prohibited [the making of] aleatory sales;[50] i.e., a sale in which the thing sold is not known to either one or both of the parties.

[44] *Suḥt* occurs in the Qur'ān 5:42, 62, 63, and it signifies a thing that is forbidden or unlawful, such as the price of a dog, of wine, and of pig. Lane, s.v. s-ḥ-t. *Kāfī*, V, 121–3; has a separate section on *al-suḥt*.

[45] *The Pillars of Islam*, I, 471–3.

[46] 'Excess water must not be sold for the purpose of having the herbage that grows from it sold.' Transmitted by Bukhārī and Muslim. *Mishkāt*, II, 96; Robson, I, 610; Ṭūsī, *Tahdhīb al-aḥkām*, VII, 139 f.

[47] *Kāfī*, V, 281–2.

[48] Ibid., V, 282–3.

[49] *Gharar* lit. means hazard, risk. The Prophet forbade the sale of hazard (*bay' al-gharar*), that which is unknown whether the thing will be delivered or not, such as the sale of fish in the water. It is forbidden because it deceives the buyer and its intrinsic reality is uncertain. Islamic law insists that there must be no doubt concerning the obligations undertaken by the parties to a contract; and the object of the contract must be determined. Lane, s.v. gh-r-r; Schacht, *Introduction*, 146–7.

[50] *Mishkāt*, II, 96; Robson, I, 610; transmitted by Muslim. Robson states that *bay' al-gharar* applies not only to 'the aleatory contracts of sale', but also to the type of transaction in which there is no guarantee that the seller can deliver the goods for which he receives payment, for example, fish which one has not yet caught.

[The Messenger of God]: He forbade the sale of the offspring of the offspring in the belly of the she-camel (*ḥabal al-ḥabala*).[51] [However], there is a disagreement about the meaning of this expression. Some say that it is a sale that was prevalent in pre-Islamic times, in which a she-camel for slaughter (*al-jazūr*) was sold on the condition that the price was to be paid at a later date; and this date specified in the terms of the sale was the time when the pregnant she-camel gave birth to its offspring. Others said that it was a sale where the offspring was sold before it was born. Both these sales are defective (*fāsid*) and neither is permitted.[52]

The Messenger of God: He forbade the sale of *maḍāmīn* (sing. *maḍmūna*),[53] and *malāqīḥ* (sing. *malqūḥa*).[54] As for *maḍāmīn*, it signifies what are in the loins of a stallion. [Pre-Islamic Arabs] used to sell [the offspring] that a stallion would produce during a year or some years, or during one or two services, and the like. *Malāqīḥ* were the fetuses in the wombs of their mothers; [formerly] the progeny was sold even before its birth.

The Messenger of God prohibited the following sales: (1) *mulāmasa*;[55] (2) *munābadha*;[56] and (3) *ṭarḥ al-ḥaṣā*.[57]

As for *mulāmasa*, there is a difference of opinion concerning its significance. Some people say it is the sale of folded (*madrūja*) cloth, which can be felt by hand; but it is not opened nor seen from the inside. Others say, 'It is cloth sold when the vendor says, "The only inspection permissible to you is touching by hand, and you have no option to [open it out and] see it."' Others say, 'The seller says, "As soon as you feel my cloth [by your hand], the sale between you and me is effective."' Others

[51]For the variant shades of its meaning see Lane, s.v. ḥ-b-l; the tradition forbidding such sale is also cited.

[52]*Mishkāt*, II, 96; Robson, I, 610; transmitted by Bukhārī and Muslim.

[53]It signifies what are in the loins of the stallions. Lane, s.v. ḍ-m-n.

[54]It signifies what are in the bellies of the females. Lane, s.v. l-q-ḥ. Some authorities state that the reverse is generally held to be the case, that is *al-malāqīḥ* signifies what are in the loins of the he-camels, and *al-maḍāmīn* signifies what are in the bellies of the females. The sale of both is forbidden.

[55]*Al-Mulāmasa fi 'l-bay'*, or *bay' al-mulāmasa*, is defined in the text. See also Lane, s.v. l-m-s; Schacht, *Introduction*, 147.

[56]*Al-Munābadha* or *bay' al-munābadha* is defined in the text. *Bay' al-ḥaṣāt*, *bay' ilqā' al-ḥajar* or *bay' al-ilqā'*, meaning sale by throwing a pebble signify the same as *al-munābadha*. Lane, s.v. n-b-dh; Schacht, *Introduction*, 147. All three categories belong to *bay' al-gharar*.

[57]According to a tradition of the Prophet transmitted by both Bukhārī and Muslim, all the three types of transactions are forbidden. *Mishkāt*, II, 95–6; Robson, I, 609–10.

say, 'It is to touch certain wares under a cover.' And all these meanings are closely connected with one another. Whenever such a sale takes place, it is defective (*fāsid*).

Similarly, people have differed regarding the *munābadha*. Some say it is this: 'One person throws a piece of cloth to another, and the other throws back another piece and says, "This is for this much," without turning it over or examining [the commodity] closely.' Others say, 'It takes place when a man sees a folded piece of cloth in another's hand, and says, "I buy this from you. So when you throw it towards me, the sale is completed between us," and there is no option to either of them [to withdraw from the contract of sale].'

Others say that *munābadha* (throwing) is the same as *ṭarḥ al-ḥaṣā* (flinging of pebbles). This was a form of sale prevalent in pre-Islamic times; the parties made the contract of sale by throwing pebbles, without uttering words, and [by such action] the contract of sale was completed.

All these forms are *fāsid* (defective, or voidable).

The Messenger of God: He forbade the sale or gift of *walā'* (the relationship of client and patron),[58] and he said, '*Walā'* is a kind of kinship (*nasab*) which cannot be sold or given away.'[59]

The Messenger of God: He prohibited the sale of a runaway slave, or an escaped camel.

'Alī: He said [explaining the above tradition], 'A runaway slave or an escaped camel should not be sold before obtaining possession.'[60]

Ja'far b. Muḥammad said [further explaining the above tradition], 'When a thing is present before you [that is, you have possession thereof], then its sale is permissible, since a sale takes place only when a thing exists before you.'

[Ja'far b. Muḥammad]: He said, 'There is no harm in selling earth laden with minerals for dinars, [provided the transaction] is for ready money then and there;[61] but there is no good[62] in such a sale stipulating future payments (*nasī'a*) [for goods delivered immediately].'

[58]The manumitted slave remains to his former master in a personal relation of clientship (*walā'*). Both the former master/patron and the client are called *mawlā*. This relationship (*walā'*) has certain effects in the law of marriage and inheritance.

[59]*Mishkāt*, II, 102; Robson, I, 615; transmitted by Bukhārī and Muslim.

[60]*Kāfī*, V, 193; Ṭūsī, *Tahdhīb al-aḥkām*, VII, 124; idem, *al-Nihāya*, 409.

[61]The Arabic expression *bi'tuhu yad*[an] *bi-yad*[in] means I contracted a sale with him for ready money, or that payment be made on the spot, or that transaction be carried out then and there. Fayyūmī, *al-Miṣbāḥ al-munīr*, s.v. y-d; Lane, Supp. s.v. y-d.

[62]The Arabic is *lā khayra fīhi*. It implies that it is not approved.

'Alī: He was asked about the sale of fish in the waters of a fen, and milk in the udders [of females],[63] and wool on the backs of sheep.[64] He said, 'The sale of all such things is unlawful, for [the thing sold] is unascertained and unknown; it may increase or decrease, and thus it is an aleatory sale (*gharar*).'

Ja'far b. Muḥammad: He said, 'If fish are collected together in a fen or an enclosed area, and need not be hunted,[65] or there is other fresh milk together with milk in the udders, then such sales are valid.[66] But if the fish cannot be taken without [the uncertainty of] regular fishing operations (lit. hunting), then the sale is void.'

Ja'far b. Muḥammad: He disapproved the practice of sale by *ṣakk*,[67] an order on a certain man to pay a certain amount.

THE SALE OF FRUIT
(*BAY' AL-THIMĀR*)

Ja'far b. Muḥammad—his father—his ancestors: The Messenger of God forbade the selling of fruit[68] until it was clearly ripe (*qabla an yabduwa ṣalāḥuhā*).

Ja'far b. Muḥammad: He explained 'the commencement of maturity' (*bad'u ṣalāḥihā*) as, its shining (*tazhū*) [on the trees]. He was asked, 'What is shining?' He explained, 'It should exhibit the red or the yellow or the black colour.'[69]

Ja'far b. Muḥammad, Muḥammad b. 'Alī, and 'Alī b. Abī Ṭālib: They permitted the sale of fruit when it 'shines brightly' (*idhā zahat*), or when some of it had the colour of maturity, or had become like those which are

[63] *Kāfī*, V, 192; Ṭūsī, *al-Nihāya*, 400.

[64] Ṭūsī, *Tahdhīb al-aḥkām*, VII, 123–5; idem, *al-Nihāya*, 400.

[65] *Kāfī*, V, 193.

[66] Ibid., V, 192.

[67] An Arabicized Persian word, *jak* or *chak*, meaning a written acknowledgement of a monetary debt, or a written statement of a transaction, purchase or sale. Lane, s.v. ṣ-k-k; Schacht, *Introduction*, 78, 193. Gloss in MS Q: *Ṣakk* means '*hundī*' [in Gujarati it means a bill of exchange]. *Bay' al-ṣakk* is where a person sales a thing to another saying that after three months he will pay him a hundred dirhams. Then he says to a third person, 'Give me ninety-five dirhams now and at the end of three months you will take a hundred from that buyer.'

[68] I have preferred the reading *al-thamara* in MS Q. The edited text has *al-tamra*. *Mishkāt*, II, 93 (it is *al-thimār*); Robson, I, 608; transmitted by Bukhārī and Muslim. See also *Kāfī*, V, 172.

[69] Ṭūsī, *Tahdhīb al-aḥkām*, VII, 85–6. "Abd Allāh b. 'Umar said that God's Messenger forbade the sale of fruits till they were clearly ripe, forbidding it both to the seller and to the buyer.' *Mishkāt*, II, 93; Robson, I, 608. See also *Kāfī*, V, 172, 173.

permissible for sale, even if some of it did not attain maturity for a year or two thereafter. This is so because sale can be effected of some of the fruit which had presently attained maturity or of the fruit that was ready for sale. It may happen that some of it does not ripen at all, or that it does not ripen subsequently. This is because many fruits appear to ripen gradually, and so the sale is effective.

The first among [fruit, etc.] to display maturity are the cucumbers and the melons and other fruits as well.

Ja'far b. Muḥammad: He said, 'The prohibition to sell fruit before maturity is not [absolute],[70] as the vendor and purchaser are concerned; in the time of the Messenger of God, people made such transactions, but when some [unforseen] accident occurred whereby fruit was destroyed, they litigated before the Messenger of God. When such disputes increased, he prohibited the sales until the fruit had ripened. The Messenger of God however did not declare such sales totally illegal, but there were restrictions on account of the disputes [that occurred].'[71]

From this it follows that such sales are not illegal so far as the parties involved are concerned, provided that they wish to keep their agreement and neither party comes forward to rescind the sale.

Ja'far b. Muḥammad: He was asked about a man who sells fruit which is still on the trees with the condition that a certain weight thereof would not be sold. He said, 'There is no harm in [such a condition].'

Abū Ja'far: He said, 'There is no objection if a purchaser sells his fruit even before he obtains possession thereof. Such fruits are not like food [grains] which can be measured, and such a sale does not belong to the class of sales which are forbidden.'

The Messenger of God: He prohibited the sale known as *muzābana* which is to sell fresh dates which are still on the trees in return for dried dates by measure.[72] But he permitted such sales in the case of palm trees known as *'arāyā* (sing. *'arīya*).[73]

Abū Ja'far said, 'The term *'arāyā* is employed for a palm tree or two, one-third or one-tenth whereof has already been given away and

[70]The Arabic reads: *laysa … nahya taḥrīm^{in} yaḥrumu shirā'u dhālika wa-bay'uhu 'alā …*

[71]*Kāfī*, V, 172; Ṭūsī, *Tahdhīb al-aḥkām*, VII, 85, 87–8.

[72]Schacht, *Introduction*, 40, 146, 154.

[73]*'Arāya* is defined in what follows in the text. The prohibition of *muzābana* does not apply to the *'arāya*, because a needy man, during the season of fresh ripe dates, having no money with which to buy them for his family, nor any palm trees to feed them therefrom, but only having some dried dates remaining, would come to the owner of palm trees, and say to him, 'Sell to me the fruit of a palm-tree,' or 'of two palm trees,'

harvested by the owner of the trees while they were fresh.' Now the term *'arāyā* is applied to 'gifts' (*'aṭāyā*); and the people have differed as to the meaning of the term *'arāyā*.

Some say that *'arāyā* are the palms, which the owner has excluded from his orchard when he sells the fruit. Thus they do not form part of the fruit sold, because he has reserved them for himself. The quantity of the excluded palms' fruit has not been appraised, since whatever they eat from it is excepted [from sale]. These trees were named *'arāyā* because they were exempted from sale or appraisal for the purposes of charity. So the Prophet permitted the poor and the needy who possessed neither silver nor gold, but had dried dates, to barter them for such fresh dates by conjectural computation of quantity (*kharṣ*). This was done as an act of kindness for poor persons who could not buy fresh dates. But it is not permitted for them [the poor] to buy those fresh dates intended for trading or storing.

Others say that these are trees the fruit of which has already been given away to poor persons and reserved for them. Later the *mu'rā* (the donee), who is the recipient of the gift, comes to the tree to harvest the fruit and this displeases the donor (*mu'rī*, i.e. *wāhib*) because his own family has a share in those trees. Thus the vendor of dates is permitted, as a special case, to buy the dates on the trees from the donee by appraisal [by offering dry dates in exchange for them (as barter)].

Others say: Some people complained to the Messenger of God that they were in need of fresh dates which were available, but they had not

---

and would give him those remaining dried dates for that fruit. The licence was conceded in respect of that fruit when less than five *awsuq* (pl. of *wasq*, a camel's load) in quantity. Lane, s.v. '-r-w.

'Ibn 'Umar said that God's Messenger forbade *muzābana*, which means that a man sells the fruits of his garden, if it consists of palm trees [meaning fresh dates], for dried dates by measure, or if it consists of grapes, for raisins by measure; or if it is corn, he sells it for a measure of corn. He forbade all that.' Transmitted by Bukhārī and Muslim. Another tradition states that the Prophet forbade the sale of *muzābana*, but gave licence for *'arāyā* on the basis of a calculation of what the dates would be when dry, provided they were less than five *awsuq* in quantity. *Mishkāt*, II, 92–3; Robson, I, 607–8.

Schacht states that this is a good example of the element of personal discretion and individual opinion in Islamic law being prior to the growth of traditions from the Prophet. Because of the later success of the Traditionists, most of what had originally been discretionary decisions and the result of individual reasoning by the jurists was put into the mouth of the Prophet. As the pre-Islamic contract of *muzābana* contravened the prohibition of *ribā*, it was rejected. However, to enable poor people, who did not possess palm trees, to acquire fresh dates, certain scholars allowed the exchange of a limited quantity of dried dates for estimated equal quantity of fresh dates on the tree. It was originally a discretionary decision (*istiḥsān*). Schacht, *Introduction*, 40, 154.

the means to buy them and eat with other folk; but they had dried dates. So the Messenger of God allowed the fruit of the *'arāyā* to be bartered by conjectural computation for dry dates which the people possessed.

Others hold similar views regarding *'arāyā*, and all of these are very similar to one another.

Ja'far b. Muḥammad: He said, 'It is not permissible to sell standing corn in exchange for wheat. But there is no harm in selling green corn (unripe), if the ears have appeared, in exchange for wheat, because the sale is effected on a standing crop and not on standing corn. The same is the rule for fresh dates.'

[Ja'far b. Muḥammad]: He was asked about the sale of wheat which had been harvested and fresh dates which had been picked, and he permitted it.

'Alī: He said, 'When a man sells palm trees after they have been pollinated, the fruit belongs to the purchaser unless the vendor has attached a proviso to that sale.[74]

THE PROHIBITION OF FRAUD AND DECEIT IN SALES (*MĀ NUHIYA 'ANHU MIN AL-GHASHSH WA 'L-KHIDĀ' FI 'L-BUYŪ'*)

Ja'far b. Muḥammad—his father—his ancestors: The Messenger of God prohibited people from deceit or adulteration (ghashsh)[75] and from using words to deceive (*khilāba*)[76] or cheat (*khadī'a*),[77] and said, 'He who deceives [others] is not one of us (*laysa minnā*).'[78] He forbade fraud and

[74]*Mishkāt*, II, 101; Robson, I, 614; transmitted by Bukhārī and Muslim. See also *Kāfī*, V, 174, 175.

[75]*Ghashshahu* means he acted towards him, or advised him, dishonestly or insincerely. It also means he dressed up to him an affair [in false colours], or counterfeited it, adulterated it. Lane, s.v. gh-sh-sh.

[76]*Khilāba* means endeavouring to deceive with blandishing speech, deceiving with the tongue. Lane, s.v. kh-l-b.

[77]*Khadī'a* (originally signified concealment) means deceit, and a desire to do to another a foul, or an evil action, without the latter's knowing whence it proceeds. Lane, s.v. kh-d-'.

[78]Abū Hurayra said that God's Messenger once came upon a heap of grain, and when he put his hand into it his fingers felt some dampness, so he asked the owner of the grain how that came about. On being told that rain had fallen on it he said, 'Why did you not put the damp part on the top of the grain so that people might see it? He who deceives has nothing to do with me (*laysa minnī*).' Transmitted by Muslim. *Mishkāt*, II, 96; Robson, I, 611. See also *Kāfī*, V, 157; two slightly different traditions are reported on the same authority; one states *laysa minnā*, and the other *laysa min al-muslimīn*; Ṭūsī, *Tahdhīb al-aḥkām*, VII, 12; identical with that of Kulaynī.

cheating in sale and breaking of contracts (*nakth*). And he said, 'Fulfil your promises in sales and purchases, marriages and oaths, and pacts and charities.'

People have differed in the interpretation of the Prophet's words, 'He who deceives [others] is not one of us.' Some say that it means, 'He is not of "our religion".' Others say, 'He is not "the like of one of us".' Others say, 'He is not one whose morals and actions are like those of the prophets and the righteous.' Others say, 'They are not following us in our conduct,' and they argued, conforming to the saying of Abraham: *But whoso followeth me, he verily is of me* (14:36).

Now whichever of these interpretations the Messenger of God intended, deceit is forbidden.

Ja'far b. Muḥammad: He was asked about [cases in which] food was adulterated so that some parts of it were better than other parts. He said, 'This is deceit (*ghashsh*),' and disapproved of it.[79]

[In adulterated food] when only the better quality is visible [and the inferior quality is not visible], God knows best [whether it is deceit or not]. But [in the opposite case where] the better quality remains hidden and the inferior quality, which forms the greater part, is apparent, it is not deceit, nor it is prohibited.[80]

'Alī: He prohibited the sale [of goods or grain] when the vendor caused the superior quality to appear manifestly and the inferior quality to be hidden. This confirms what we [al-Nu'mān] have said.

'Alī: He prohibited pumping air into meat, i.e. after the animal has been skinned. But to pump air between the skin and the meat is another matter, as this facilitates skinning. The only reason why pumping air into the flesh was forbidden was to prevent it from mixing with the meat, and enlarging the [appearance of] meat, and make it appear as fat, even though it is not.

The Messenger of God: He prohibited the mixing of water with milk when intended for sale, for, this would be adulteration. But there is nothing against a man who mixes water with milk for the purpose of drinking.[81]

[The Messenger of God]: He said, 'When my community begins to give short measure and false weight, and to cheat and break promises,

[79]The tradition states, 'If anyone sells a defective article without drawing attention to it, he will remain under God's anger, or, the angels will continue to curse him.' *Mishkāt*, II, 100; Robson I, 613.

[80]*Kāfī*, V, 180; it states that the better quality should not conceal the inferior quality.

[81]*Kāfī*, V, 157; Ṭūsī, *Tahdhīb al-aḥkām*, VII, 13.

and make a show of piety, they will possess nothing with which to purify their souls.'

Ja'far b. Muḥammad: He was asked about making payments with alloyed dirhams (*al-darāhim al-maḥmūl 'alayhā*) [in which other metals were mixed].[82] He said, 'There is no objection to making payments with them as long as silver is the dominant metal.'[83]

[He was asked about] *sattūq*, i.e. coins made of copper or brass and coated with silver.[84] He said, 'They should be cut [and discarded], and it is not lawful to make payments with them.' The same applies to coins alloyed with quicksilver (*muzaybaqa*)[85] or with antimony (*mukaḥḥala*).[86]

'Alī: He commanded the cashiers of the Public Treasury only to accept good coins.

The Messenger of God: He prohibited the practice of *taṣriya*,[87] and said, 'He who sells a sheep that has not been milked commits a fraud, and the purchaser is entitled to return it when he comes to know of it. He should return a *ṣā'* (small measure)[88] of dry dates while returning the sheep.'[89]

Taṣriya is the practice of leaving the udders of a milch animal unmilked for some days to allow milk to accumulate in them so that it may appear fat.

[The Messenger of God]: He prohibited the practice of *najash*, which

[82]*Al-Darāhim al-maḥmūl 'alayhā*, lit. the [debased] dirhams that are made to accord with the real dirhams.

[83]*Kāfī*, V, 256. If the alloyed dirhams are circulating in the market and are accepted by the merchants, there is no harm.

[84]*Sattūq* or *suttūq* is applied to a worthless dirham and it is unlawful to take it as being a coin. Balādhurī, *Futūḥ al-buldān*, 454; Lane, s.v. s-t-q.

[85]*Dirham muza'baq*, or *dirham muzaybaq* is a dirham done over with quicksilver (*zi'baq*). Lane, s.v. z-'-b-q. See also *Kāfī*, V, 157.

[86]*Al-darāhim al-mukaḥḥala* are alloyed with antimony (*kuḥl*) to inflate its value. Dozy, s.v. k-ḥ-l. The weight of the dirham, the silver unit of the Arab/Muslim monetary system, and its relationship to other metrological units varied widely in different parts of the Islamic world at different times. Dirhams of base silver and copper were also struck by various dynasties. *EI*^{2}, s.v. Dirham.

[87]*Taṣriya* is defined in what follows. See also *Majma' al-baḥrayn*, s.v. ṣ-r-y; the tradition is cited. Lane, s.v. ṣ-r-y.

[88]*Ṣā'*, see *The Pillars of Islam*, I, 331, n. 149.

[89]The buyer has two courses open to him after milking these sheep: he may keep them if he is pleased with them, or he may return them along with a *ṣā'* of dates if he is displeased with them. Another tradition states that the buyer has three days to decide whether to keep them or not. *Mishkāt*, II, 94; Robson, I, 609. Some *Da'ā'im* MSS have the same gloss from Nu'mān's *Mukhtaṣar al-āthār*.

is to offer an increased bid for goods, not with a view to purchase them, but merely that others may hear and offer a higher price.[90]

[The Messenger of God]: He prohibited the townsman (*al-ḥāḍir*) from selling goods for the countryman (*al-bādī*).[91] God knows best, but the obvious meaning of this prohibition is as follows: The townsman should not sell goods for the countryman by going against his wishes and by overpowering his will, making it appear to the countryman that the matter is solely for the townsman's choice; or that the countryman has entrusted the townsman to display the goods for sale and [the townsman] has the authority to sell on his own behalf, or something similar.

On the other hand, if the countryman sends goods to the townsman and asks him to sell them on his behalf, and [the townsman] then displays them [in the market] and tries to get the best price, and informs [the countryman], and the latter takes over the sale by himself, or gives his power of attorney (*wikāla, wakāla*) to the townsmen, such a course is permissible and nothing in such a transaction is against the general prohibition.

The manifest meaning of the rule is against the townsman selling on behalf of the countryman; but, if the countryman, in effect, sells for himself, then such a transaction is not prohibited, as some people with little understanding imagine.[92]

[90]In Islamic law *najash* means he demanded the sale of an article of merchandise for more than its price, not meaning to purchase it, but that another might see him and fall into the snare thus laid for him. Lane, s.v. n-j-sh; *Majmaʿ al-baḥrayn*, s.v. n-j-sh; the tradition is cited. In English such a practice is known as 'puffing'. See also Ibn Rushd, *Bidāya*, II, 162–3; trans. II, 200.

[91]Jābir reported the Prophet as saying, 'A townsman must not sell for a man from the desert; if you leave people alone, God will give them provision from one another.' *Mishkāt*, II, 95; Robson, I, 609; transmitted by Muslim. Ibn 'Abbās, on whose authority this tradition was reported, was asked about its meaning, and he said, 'The townsman should not become a *simsār* (broker, middleman) for the countryman.' Muslim, *Ṣaḥīḥ*, V, 5. See also *Kāfī*, V, 165.

[92]The jurists disagree about the meaning of the Prophet's injunction. Some understood it in absolute terms, but Abū Ḥanīfa and his disciples maintained that there was no harm if the countryman was informed of the price. Mālik disapproved it, but Awzāʿī permitted it. Those who prohibit this sale state that things in countryside are cheaper than they are in urban areas. Therefore, a townsman selling on behalf of the countryman or advising him about [higher] price contradicts the saying of the Prophet, 'The religion consists in sincere advice (*al-dīn al-naṣīḥa*).' Another tradition states, 'The townsman is not to sell on behalf of the countryman; leave the people alone so that Allāh may provide for some of them through others.' For details see Ibn Rushd, *Bidāya*, II, 162; trans. II, 199–200.

[The Messenger of God]: He prohibited the people from going out of the town and meeting riders [to make purchases or sales with them].[93]

Ja'far b. Muḥammad explained, 'The prohibition is to meet riders outside the town and make purchases from them. This causes the suspicion of fraud on the part of the vendors, and prevents the townspeople from obtaining the opportunity to buy goods, because those who go out of the town obtain their goods before the town merchants have an opportunity.'

Ja'far b. Muḥammad: He was asked about the following case. A man goes out to purchase foodstuff [that is sold] either by measure or by weight. He finds that the goods are more in quantity or weight than the measure he had purchased. [The Imam] said, 'If the excess is of such an extent that it is customary for the people to take it,[94] there is no harm. But if the quantity is greatly in excess, it is not good and he should return the excess, in as much as this might have been due to error or oversight on the part of the vendor.'[95]

'Alī: He permitted the purchaser to ask the vendor for some [free] amount [of the goods purchased by him] after they had been measured out. But it is at the discretion of the vendor as to whether or not he will comply with [the request].

[THE CONDITIONS] WHICH ARE FORBIDDEN IN SALES (*MĀ NUHIYA 'ANHU FI 'L-BUYŪ'*)

Ja'far b. Muḥammad—his father—his ancestors: The Messenger of God prohibited [the inclusion of] two conditions in one single sale.[96] People have differed in the interpretation of this rule. Some hold [it to mean] that the vendor says, 'I sell [this] for such and such amount of cash, and for such and such amount of credit [later payment],' and the contract of the sale is concluded in this form.[97]

[93]*Mishkāt*, II, 94; Robson, I, 608; transmitted by Bukhārī and Muslim. *Kāfī*, V, 165–6; the tradition even specifies the limit that constitute going out of town. It should be lesser of a distance than one travels during an early part of the morning (*ghadwa*) or evening (*rawḥa*). Several MSS of the *Da'ā'im* have this gloss from Nu'mān's *Mukhtaṣar al-āthār*. *Ghadwa* and *rawḥa* are about four *farsakhs*, i.e. twelve miles.

[94]The Arabic reads: *mimmā yataghābanu al-nāsu bi-mithlihi*. The word *taghābun* signifies mutual cheating in selling and buying. See Lane, s.v. gh-b-n; *Majma' al-baḥrayn*, s.v. gh-b-n.

[95]*Kāfī*, V, 179.

[96]'Two conditions relating to one transaction are not allowed and neither are two transactions combined in one.' *Mishkāt*, II, 98; Robson, I, 612.

[97]*Kāfī*, V, 204. The vendor cannot put different prices, one for cash and other for credit. He has to sell it for the lower price, even if it is for credit.

Others hold that the vendor says, 'I sell these goods for [so many] dinars on the condition that [after a certain period] when the payment in dinars becomes due, I shall obtain a specified number of dirhams.'

Others say that the vendor sells goods to the buyer on the condition that the buyer will sell those goods to someone else. Others say different things which resemble such conditions, but all such contracts are defective (*fāsid*), unless the parties to the sale disperse while making only one condition. If they include two conditions in one contract, the sale is forbidden; it is like 'two sales' in one, and this is not lawful.

The Messenger of God: He prohibited that a man should take profit from a thing which has not yet come into his possession. People have differed in the interpretation of this rule as well. Some say that this rule only applies to foodstuffs purchased before the purchaser takes possession. Others say that it applies to everything that can be weighed or measured. Others say that it applies to bare necessities (*rizq*) purchased from a large store (or a granary, *hury*) before taking actual possession.[98] Others say that it is when the hirer of a beast or a slave, hires it again [to a third person], at a higher price [than what he hired for]. In respect of such matters, rules have been handed down from the Members of the Prophet's Household, and we shall mention them [in their proper context], if God, the Exalted, wills.

The Messenger of God: He prohibited a sale in which [the vendor] makes an advance.[99] People have differed in the interpretation of this rule. Some say that it means that a man says to another, 'I shall buy your goods for such and such amount, if you advance me a certain sum.' Others say that it means that the vendor advances a loan to a person and then sells him the merchandise for that sum. In both ways the transaction is defective, because the profit of the loan is not known, and therefore the price is not known.

[The Messenger of God]: He prohibited [exchanging] a debt to be paid at a future time for a similar debt [*al-kāli'* or *al-kālī*].[100] That is, to sell one loan (*al-dayn*) for another loan.[101] For instance, a man sells food grains [in advance] to be completed by delivery [and possession] by a certain date, and when that date comes he has no grains to offer. So the vendor

[98]'If anyone buys grain he must not sell it until he received it in full.' *Mishkāt*, II, 94; Robson, I, 608; transmitted by Bukhārī and Muslim.

[99]'The proviso of a loan combined with a sale is not allowable.' *Mishkāt*, 98; Robson, I, 612.

[100]This practice enables a man who cannot pay a debt when it is due to have the period extended but for an additional sum. Lane, s.v. k-l-'.

[101]*Mishkāt*, II, 97; Robson, I, 611; *Kāfī*, V, 94.

would buy such [undelivered] grain from the purchaser for a future date. This in reality is the exchange of one debt for another, and occurs in the advance sale of food grains.[102] The vendor does not pay any money and the debt remains on him, and there are many such examples.

For instance, a man advances a loan to a certain person who manufactures certain goods, and the craftsman pays off his debt later [by making the goods]. Or that some person hires a beast of burden, and then gives it to hire to someone else in lieu of the debt owed by him. There are many such examples.

Ja'far b. Muḥammad: He permitted the selling of a beast in exchange for another, [provided the transaction] is done on the spot (*yad^an bi-yad^in*).

'Alī: He sold his camel at Rabadha[103] for four [specified] (*maḍmūna*) camels, [that is, they were ensured by an acknowledgment of responsibility for their delivery];[104] and sold a she-camel called 'Uṣayfīra[105] for twenty camels to be delivered at a future date. Such a sale is valid when [all the goods] are fully specified.

Ja'far b. Muḥammad: He prohibited the sale of meat in exchange for a living animal.[106]

The Messenger of God: He forbade a person to bargain [and offer a price above] that offered by his brother [a fellow Muslim].[107] The meaning of this prohibition is this: It occurs only when [bargaining takes place], and the vendor [is about to agree and] remains silent just before the transaction is complete. But when a transaction is not almost complete and [the price has not been settled], there is no harm in the purchaser offering a higher price, or the vendor, more goods.

The Messenger of God: He directed a vendor to sell his goods to the person who offers the higher price.[108]

[102]Fayyūmī, *al-Miṣbāḥ al-munīr*, s.v. k-l-'; he cites a similar example.

[103]Rabadha is a village about three miles from Medina on the way to Mecca and the Ḥijāz. Abū Dharr al-Ghifārī is buried there. Yāqūt, s.v. r-b-dh.

[104]Lane, s.v. ḍ-m-n.

[105]With *'uṣfur* (safflower) colour, or inclining to yellowness or ash colour. Lane, s.v. '-ṣ-f-r.

[106]*Mishkāt*, II, 89; Robson, I, 604. The prohibition was connected with pre-Islamic gambling *'maysir'*.

[107]'One must not offer more than the amount agreed by his brother, or ask a woman in marriage when his brother has done so, unless he permits him.' *Mishkāt*, II, 95; Robson, I, 609; transmitted by Muslim.

[108]Anas said that God's Messenger offered for sale a saddle cloth and a drinking vessel, saying, 'Who will buy them?' A man offered to buy them for a dirham, and the Prophet asked, 'Who would offer more?' A man offered him two dirhams and he sold them to him. *Mishkāt*, II, 99; Robson, I, 612.

Ja'far b. Muḥammad: He said, 'A person should not buy foodstuffs that are capable of being weighed or measured and then wish to sell them without weighing or measuring them.[109] But if he has appointed someone as its guardian, such a person may be appointed before the weighing or measuring takes place. There is no harm in selling the whole of the stuff before delivery of the items or recovery of their price. If a person buys foodstuffs, and the vendor assures him that he has measured it, and the purchaser is satisfied that the vendor is truthful, there is no harm in such a sale.[110]

The Messenger of God: He forbade the practice of hoarding commodities (*ḥukra*) and said, 'No one but an erring person hoards foodstuffs.'[111]

'Alī said, 'The hoarder (*muḥtakir*) is a sinful wrongdoer.'[112] He said, 'A calamity smote a group of Israelites; and when they got up in the morning, they had lost the following four kinds of persons: those that measured grain, the singers, the hoarders of foodstuffs, and those that took usurious interest (*ribā*).'

Ja'far b. Muḥammad: He said, 'Hoarding (*ḥukra*) takes place only when one buys foodstuffs not available in town and then hoards it up. If however, the town has foodstuffs, or goods other than the hoarded ones, or such commodities are freely available to the public, there is no harm in hoarding. But if goods are not available, then hoarding is disapproved.'[113]

The prohibition of the Messenger of God against hoarding came when a man from the Quraysh[114] called Ḥakīm b. Ḥizām[115] began to buy all the food that entered the city. So the Prophet passed by and said, 'I

[109] *Mishkāt*, II, 94; Robson, I, 608; transmitted by Bukhārī and Muslim; *Kāfī*, V, 176.

[110] *Kāfī*, V, 176.

[111] 'If anyone withholds goods until the price rises he is a sinner.' *Mishkāt*, II, 106; Robson, I, 619; transmitted by Muslim. For more traditions against hoarding and monopoly see *Concordance*, s.v. ḥ-k-r.

[112] 'He who brings goods for sale is blessed with good fortune, but he who keeps them (*al-muḥtakir*) till the price rises is accursed.' *Mishkāt*, II, 106; Robson, I, 619.

[113] *Kāfī*, V, 161; reported from the same authority.

[114] Quraysh, see *The Pillars of Islam*, I, 37, n. 81.

[115] He is Ḥakīm b. Hizām b. Khuwaylid b. Asad b. 'Abd al-'Uzzā b. Quṣayy, a rich merchant and a notable of Mecca who had bought the *nadwa* (the place of assembly) in pre-Islamic times from the Banū 'Abd al-Dār. Khadīja, the Prophet's wife, was Ḥakīm's aunt. He participated at Badr against the Muslims, but later accepted Islam. Ibn Isḥāq, *al-Sīra*, I, 131, n. 6; 264, 379; II, 125, 269, 274, 320; Guillaume, 160. The Prophet stipulated that Ḥakīm had to fulfil certain requirements before he was permitted to do business. *Kāfī*, V, 147.

warn you not to hoard, O Ḥakīm.'[116] [The Prophet] said, 'Every [act of] hoarding that causes harm to the people and increases the price of goods is no good. [The Prophet] said, 'Hoarding only takes place in the following commodities, and not in others: wheat, barley, oil, dried grapes and [dried] dates.'[117] [The Prophet] used to buy a year's provisions for himself and his family.

'Alī: He said, 'In times of abundance, hoarding takes place if [goods are not released] for forty days; and in times of scarcity, the period is three days. He who exceeds these periods in hoarding, is accursed.'[118]

['Alī]: He wrote to Rifā'a[119] to prohibit hoarding, and punish him who disregards the prohibition, and also to make public what he has hoarded.

Ja'far b. Muḥammad: He was asked about the fixation of prices (*tas'īr*).[120] He said, 'The Commander of the Faithful 'Alī never fixed the price of goods for any person; but if a person sold his goods for a higher price than the market rate,[121] he was told, 'Sell, as the others do; or else arise from the market, unless your grain is superior to that of others.'

'Alī: He was asked about a person whose goods were wrongfully confiscated by the ruler (*sulṭān*), and he had no means wherewith to [pay off the ruler to] release them, except to sell off part of his property. A certain person bought this property, and the question was whether such a sale was considered *bay' al-muḍṭarr* (one who is forced to sell). [The Imam] said, 'The sale is lawful, for this is not the sale of one who is forced to sell. [In fact], such a sale is beneficial to the vendor as he will be able to obtain release of his goods [confiscated by the ruler]. The forced sale, on the other hand, is one not approved by the vendor, but is forced upon him by the purchaser.'[122]

[116]*Kāfī*, V, 162.

[117]Ibid., V, 161.

[118]'If anyone withholds grain for forty days thereby desiring a high price, he has renounced God and God has renounced him.' *Mishkāt*, II, 107; Robson, I, 619. See also *Kāfī*, V, 162; reported on the authority of al-Ṣādiq.

[119]Rifā'a b. Shaddād al-Bajalī, one of the oldest and most trusted associates of 'Alī, was his *qāḍī* at Ahwāz. He was also one of the five leaders of the *tawwābūn* movement and was the only leader to survive that catastrophe. For sources see *The Pillars of Islam*, I, 281.

[120]When prices were high in the Prophet's time the people asked him to fix prices for them, but he replied, 'God is the One who fixes prices, ...' *Mishkāt*, II, 106; Robson, I, 619.

[121]The Arabic reads: *man naqaṣa 'an bay' al-nās*.

[122]'A forced contract is forbidden.' *Mishkāt*, II, 98; Robson, I, 611.

EXCHANGE [OF MONEY AND PRECIOUS METALS] (*AL-ṢARF*)

Ja'far b. Muḥammad—his father—his ancestors: The Messenger of God said, '[To exchange] silver for silver, or gold for gold, in equal amounts, on the spot (*yad^{an} bi-yad^{in}*) [is lawful]; [123] and he who increases or asks for more engages in usury. God has cursed usury (*ribā*); its taker or giver; its seller or purchaser; the one who writes the contract and its two witnesses.'[124]

Ja'far b. Muḥammad: He said, '[Exchanges should be made as follows:] gold for gold, or silver for silver, and in equal amounts. There can be no increase in it and no deferment; and he who increases it or he who asks for an increase, will be in the Fire.'[125]

[123]*Mishkāt*, II, 86–7; Robson I, 602; See also *Kāfī*, V, 247; Ṭūsī, *Tahdhīb al-aḥkām*, VII, 98. In cases of an exchange of monetary assets immediate transfer of ownership (*tamlīk fi 'l-ḥāl*) is required, hence any stipulation of a term (*ajal*) is inadmissible.

[124]'Jābir said that God's Messenger cursed the one who accepted usury, the one who paid it, the one who recorded it, and the two witnesses to it, saying they were all alike.' Transmitted by Muslim. *Mishkāt*, II, 86; Robosn, I, 602.

Ribā is a technical term in Islamic law for usury, or any unjustified increase of capital for which no compensation is given. The Qur'ān expresses it as 'consuming (i.e. appropriating for one's own use) the property of others for no good reason' (4:161). A close scrutiny of the traditions dealing with *ribā* indicates that its rigid prohibition was a gradual development. The *ribā* consisted only in the increase of substance in a business agreement with a fixed period and that there was no *ribā* if the transfer of ownership took place immediately. During the earliest period of Islam the *ribā*, forbidden by the Qur'ān, was understood to have been interest on loans, chiefly of money and foodstuffs.

It should be noted that the Qur'ānic commands, such as the prohibition of *ribā*, though concerned with certain types of legal transactions, are not meant to lay down legal rules regulating those business dealings, but to establish moral norms under which certain transactions are permitted or prohibited. The concept that such transactions, if concluded despite prohibition, are invalid and does not create obligations, does not manifest in the Qur'ān. It was left to Islamic law to establish their legality.

Fazlur Rahman, a prominent liberal reformer, also distinguishes between bank interest and *ribā* (usury) and states that the ban on bank interest (*ribā*) along with the ban on family planning, the veiling of women, etc., are pet issues with the neofundamentalists. *EI*[2], s.v. Ribā; Schacht, *Introduction*, 12, 40, 145–7; Rahman, *Islamic Methodology*, 67, 68, 79; idem, *Islam and Modernity*, 18, 30, 136. See also n. 19 above in this chapter.

[125]Abū Sa'īd al-Khudrī reported God's Messenger saying, 'Gold is to be paid for gold, silver for silver, wheat for wheat ... like for like, with payment being made on the spot. If anyone gives more or asks for more, he has dealt in usury. The receiver and the giver are equally guilty.' Transmitted by Muslim. *Mishkāt*, II, 86; Robson, I, 602.

ʿAlī: He was asked about a man who takes several dirhams for two dirhams, on the spot. He said, 'This is instant usury.'[126]

The Messenger of God: When he used to accept *jizya* (poll tax)[127] from the *dhimmīs* (covenanted people who live under Muslim rule),[128] he accepted it only after making certain conditions one of which was that they should not take usury. Now if someone [from amongst the *dhimmīs*] does that, he forfeits the responsibility (*dhimma*) of God and His Messenger. Those who made a treaty with the Muslims did not stipulate with the Muslims that they were freed from their own religious obligation not to take usury, because taking usury is forbidden according to their law.

God says: *Because of the wrongdoing of the Jews We forbade them good things which were (before) lawful unto them, and because of their much hindering from Allah's way. And of their taking usury when they were forbidden it* (4:160–1). Thus God informed them that He had indeed forbidden usury. He who permitted himself to take it, did so by disobeying God and what their rabbis and their monks distorted [the laws] for them. Hence they declared it to be lawful for them. ʿAlī, therefore, wrote to Rifāʿa[129] commanding him to exclude the *dhimmīs* from transactions of exchange.

Jaʿfar b. Muḥammad: He said, 'Whenever there is disparity (*al-tafāḍul*) [between the price and the commodity sold], this amounts to taking usury.'[130]

[Jaʿfar b. Muḥammad]: He said, 'My father sent me to a money-changer (*ṣarrāf*) from Iraq with a purse containing one thousand dirhams to exchange them for something better [that is dinars]. He told me, "Tell him to sell the dirhams in exchange for dinars, and when he has obtained the dinars and handed over the dirhams let him buy with the dinars which he has obtained in exchange for dirhams the provisions necessary for us."'

[Jaʿfar b. Muḥammad]: He was asked about a person who desired to exchange Syrian dinars for those of Kūfa weight for weight.[131] But the

[126]Cf. *Mishkāt*, II, 87; Robson, I, 603.

[127]For poll tax see *The Pillars of Islam*, I, 457, 468–70.

[128]For *dhimmīs* see *The Pillars of Islam*, I, 143, n. 79.

[129]See n. 119 in this chapter.

[130]Ṭūsī, *Tahdhīb al-aḥkām*, VII, 94.

[131]Ḥajjāj b. Yūsuf, the governor of Iraq, issued dirhams and *al-danānīr al-Dimashqīya* (Damascene dinars) by the order of the Umayyad caliph ʿAbd al-Malik b. Marwān. Balādhurī, *Futūḥ al-buldān*, 452–3. The Syrian dinars are those of the Umayyads and the Kūfan dinars are those of the early ʿAbbāsids.

money-changer (*ṣayrafī*) said, 'I shall not do this transaction unless you give me Yūsufī dirhams for *ghalla*[132] weight for weight.' [The Imam] said, 'There is no harm in it.'[133]

[132]Yūsufī dirhams refer to those issued by the Umayyad governor of Iraq, Yūsuf b. 'Umar. These dirhams were known for their excellence and high purity. Balādhurī states that the 'Abbāsid caliph al-Manṣūr would accept only the dirhams issued by Yūsuf b. 'Umar and his two predecessors (Khālid b. 'Abd Allāh al-Qasrī and Ibn Hubayra, both governors of Iraq) in payment of taxes. Balādhurī, *Futūḥ al-buldān*, 454–5; Ṭabarī, *History of al-Ṭabarī*, XXVI, 4–5, n. 17. *Ghalla* means dirhams that are clipped, or dirhams that are rejected by the state treasury, but taken by the merchants. Lane, s.v. gh-l-l.

I am indebted to Professor Michael Bates for drawing my atttention to Balādhurī. In a communication to me he writes, 'In the late middle [2nd]/8th century, these *ghalla* dirhams would have been older Umayyad Wāsit dirhams struck before the time of [the Umayyad caliph] Hishām [b. 'Abd al-Malik, 105–25/724–43] and dirhams struck at other mints besides Wāsit, as well as Arab-Sasanian and Sasanian dirhams.'

[133]In another communication, Professor Michael Bates writes, 'I find the point of the story unclear, since I would have thought—and all the evidence that we have indicates—that the Umayyad and early 'Abbāsid dinars were of the same purity, in which case there would be no superiority of either one over the other in a weight for weight transaction.

'Possibly, however, the Umayyad dinars were not accepted by the 'Abbāsid government, in which case the 'Abbāsid dinars would exchange at a premium regardless of their identical gold content. The response of the money-changer would then be ironic: "I will accept devalued dinars for good dinars on the basis of equality only if you will give me good [*Yūsufī*] dirhams for [*ghalla*] bad ones on similar terms." Obviously the potential customer would not do so.

'Or possibly the two dinars [*al-Shāmiyya* and *al-Kūfiyya*] were regarded as equivalent, in which case the transaction would have yielded no profit to the money-changer, so he demanded an accompanying transaction that would yield him some profit. This, however, seems indirect and roundabout. Why would he not simply say, "Yes, I will exchange the dinars, but I will keep one dinar (or some sum of money) as my fee."

'Obviously this text is about *ribā*, I don't see the *ribā* involved in these exchanges ... . This text tells us something about early Islamic money, but to me it is not yet clear what it says to us.'

I think Professor Bates misses the very point. If the money-changer had asked to keep one dinar as his fees, it would have been considered *ribā*, which is obvious from the first tradition in this section. The response of the money-changer asking for an accompanying transaction was, therefore, not ironic, but a way to avoid his profit being labelled as *ribā*. It is quite obvious from what follows and the Imam's reply. Schacht (*EI*[2], s.v. Ribā; idem, *Introduction*, 146) states that the exchange of even the same quantities of the same thing, especially of precious metals, was strictly considered *ribā*. Moreover, gold and silver are regarded as *māl ribawī*.

Both Kulaynī (*Kāfī*, V, 250) and Ṭūsī (*Tahdhīb al-aḥkām*, VII, 104–5) report this tradition without the suffix 'dinars' and 'dirhams', implying thereby that in both the transactions 'dirhams' were involved. Kulaynī's text reads: '... a person who desired to exchange *al-Kūfīya* (the Kūfan dirhams) with that of *al-Shāmīya* (the Syrian dirhams)'. This makes more sense as the Umayyad dirhams were known for their excellence as stated by Balādhurī. The money-changer, in exchange for this favour, demanded an accompanying transaction to avoid the

It was said to [the Imam], 'Verily the money-changer wants [to profit by] the excellence of the Yūsufī dirhams over the *ghalla* ones.' [The Imam] said, 'So long as the transaction is weight for weight, and on the spot (*yad*[an] *bi-yad*[in]), there is no harm.'

Then [the Imam] was asked his opinion of a man who wishes to buy one thousand dirhams and one dinar for two thousand dirhams. He said, 'There is no harm in this. My father was bolder than I to the people of Medina and used to say this, and when they used to say, "O Abū Ja'far, this is only a means to escape usury; because if a man came with only one dinar he would not be given a thousand dirhams for it." [Imam al-Bāqir used to say], "The best of ways is to go over from the forbidden to the lawful!"'

A man said to [the Imam al-Bāqir], 'May God have mercy on you, you know that the exchange value of one dinar is nineteen dirhams; now if you went all over the city you would not find a man to give you twenty dirhams for a dinar. Hence, this transaction is nothing but an evasion (*firār*) of usury.' [The Imam] said, 'You have spoken the truth; it is a coming over (*firār*)[134] from falsehood to the truth.'[135]

This objection against [the Imam] (*walīy Allāh*, lit. Friend of God), is the objection of an ignorant person; because there is unanimity among the Muslims that only a transaction in the same commodity be considered usury. It occurs when there is disparity [in the price and amount of] commodities which can be weighed or measured, regardless of whether this disparity is great or small. Now gold and silver are two different commodities, and God has distinguished between them with a *wāw* (and), [that is gold and silver], just as He has distinguished between the sky and the earth. So, disparity [in one of] them does not mean the taking of usury. Now if the same rule were to be applied, [to gold and silver] they would have to be equal in weight. This is not asserted by anyone whom we know. If [when there are two commodities] disparity is permitted in respect of a small quantity, it is also allowed in respect of a large quantity. Neither the Book nor the *sunna*[136] forbid such a course. But such exchanges must

---

ribā. Ṭūsī's text, on the other hand, reads: '... a person who desired to exchange *al-Shāmīya* with that of *al-Kūfīya*'. Unfortunately, both the latter texts are not critical editions, hence the above explanation should remain tentative.

[134]It should be noted that there is an ironic twist in the meaning of the word *firār*, meaning to run away, escape. Hence, Nu'mān's comment follows.

[135]*Kāfī*, V, 249–50; identical report. See also Ṭūsī, *Tahdhīb al-aḥkām*, VII, 104.

[136]*Sunna*, as a technical term, means the exemplary practice of the Prophet embodied in *ḥadīth*. For Islamic law it is the second source after the Qur'ān. For the development of its concept see Schacht, *Introduction*, 8, 17–18, 30–6, 43, 47, 67; Rahman, *Islam*, 43–71; *EI*[2], s.v. Sunna. For Nu'mān's understanding of the *sunna* see Poonawala, 'Al-Qāḍī al-Nu'mān and Isma'ili jurisprudence', 129–30. See also The *Pillars of Islam*, I, 1, n. 2.

take place then and there (*yad^an bi-yad^in*), as the *sunna* lays down, and God willing, we shall mention this later.

As regards the exchange [of gold and silver] there are no fixed rules. This is a matter for agreement between the people and is similar to other sales, cheap or expensive. There is no substance in the objection of the ignorant man who says, 'If the exchange were [conducted] thus, nobody would offer more!' Now there is a consensus between him [the one who objected] and the Muslims, that there is no harm in increasing or decreasing the exchange in such a transaction, for this is essentially a matter for the two parties to the sale.

Jaʿfar b. Muḥammad: He was questioned about swords with ornamental inlaid work and similar goods in which silver was mixed with other metals and whether they could be sold for gold which was to be paid at a specified time. He said, 'Verily, people did not differ about credit sales (*nasīʾa*); they only differed when the sale is made on the spot (*al-yad bi 'l-yad*).' He was asked, 'Could such swords be purchased with dirhams in cash?' He said, 'My father used to say, "It would be preferable if some other commodity (*ʿarḍ*)[137] could be added to the price".'[138]

He was asked, 'What if the silver coins contain more silver than the swords?' [The Imam] asked, 'How would you have knowledge of this?' They said, '[Suppose] they knew it?' [The Imam] replied, 'If they knew this, there is no harm. Otherwise, I would prefer them to add some other goods (*ʿarḍ*) to the price.'

[The Imam] meant that other goods (*ʿarḍ*) should be added to the silver paid. If it was known that the dirhams were greater in weight, silver would have been paid ounce by ounce[139] and the excess would be paid for by the other metal. If however the dirhams were less than the silver, and some other metal was added, the excess of silver would be paid by the other metal.

Jaʿfar b. Muḥammad: He permitted a person to pay his debt of dinars in dirhams, and vice versa.[140]

[137]*ʿArḍ* means commodity, goods other than the dirhams and dinars. *Majmaʿ al-baḥrayn*, s.v. ʿ-r-ḍ.

[138]*Kāfī*, V, 254.

[139]The Arabic is *wazn^an bi-wazn^in*, lit. weight by weight.

[140]Ibn ʿUmar said that he used to sell camels at al-Naqīʿ [a place near Medina] for dinars and take dirhams for them, and vice versa. He went to the Prophet and told him about it and he said, 'There is no harm in taking them at the current rate so long as you do not separate leaving something still to be settled.' *Mishkāt*, II, 99; Robson, I, 612. See also *Kāfī*, V, 248, 251. The tradition states that the exchange rate should not be the current rate, but that prevalent when the original loan was obtained.

Abū Ja'far—his ancestors: 'Alī was asked about loans.[141] He disapproved that the one who loans money should receive any commodity other than what he had advanced. But, if for cordiality of relations, the two agree on a different course of action, there is no objection if the exchange rate is specified.

'Alī: He said, 'It is not permissible to sell silver for gold or gold for silver, except on the spot (*yad*^{an} *bi-yad*^{in}).'

Ja'far b. Muḥammad: He said, 'If you have purchased gold for silver from a man, or vice versa, do not part with him until both of you have obtained possession, even if he has to jump a wall to do so.[142] If a man says, "Send your servant with me so that I shall deliver it to him," do not do so, even if the place is nearby. If however you do send someone else with him, order him to commence the exchange of money immediately, as soon as the cash is presented, and he should conclude the contract with him on that [amount].[143] But if some portion of it remains unpaid, there is no good in it. The payment and the receipt should be exchanged in their entirety then and there.

'If a person buys gold for silver, and then busies himself with something else, and later wishes to complete the transaction, let him renew the contract of sale and say, "I [buy] this with this."'

[Ja'far b. Muḥammad]: He said, 'There is no harm if a man lends [certain kinds of *ghalla*] dirhams [silver coins of base quality] and takes in return better ones [of superior quality], provided there is no specific stipulation in the matter between the two parties. This is [permissible] because [the rule in this type of transaction is] silver for silver, ounce per ounce. It does not matter if the one quantity of silver [that is returned] is better than the other [if it is done willingly]. But this is not lawful if the weight of one lot [either the one lent or returned] is greater. If the weight of both the lots is the same, it is permissible to pay one lot for the other, even though this is not stipulated [in the contract] because different lots of silver are rarely of the same quality in respect to their fineness, and when examined closely one lot may necessarily be slightly better than the other; for, lots of silver come from different places of origin.'[144]

[141] It refers to the previous question of whether a person is allowed to pay his debt of dinars in dirhams, and vice versa.

[142] Jumping a wall is a hyperbolic usage to indicate that the transaction must be completed in one meeting. For a similar expression see Ṭūsī, *Tahdhīb al-aḥkām*, VII, 99. See also *Kāfī*, V, 254.

[143] *Kāfī*, V, 255.

[144] Ibid., V, 256–7.

THE BARTER OF DIFFERENT KINDS OF COMESTIBLES (*BAY' AL-ṬA'ĀM BA'ḌIHI BI-BA'Ḍ*)

We have mentioned earlier that it is not permissible to exchange, in unequal amounts, any one commodity capable of being weighed and measured.[145] But where two different comestibles are bartered, one of them may be given or taken in a greater quantity.[146]

Ja'far b. Muḥammad: He said, 'It is permissible to barter unequal amounts of comestibles, or other commodities that differ from each other, provided the transaction is carried out on the spot (*yad*[an] *bi-yad*[in]), but deferment (*naẓira*) in it is not desirable.'[147]

[Ja'far b. Muḥammad]: He said, 'Wheat and barley are considered one commodity, and no disparity is permitted in a transaction involving them.'[148]

[Ja'far b. Muḥammad]: He said, 'Flour should be equal [in weight] with wheat;[149] and parched barley (*al-sawīq*)[150] should be equal with flour.'

Abū Ja'far Muḥammad b. 'Alī: He was asked about wheat (*burr*) and parched barley. He said, 'They should be [bartered for] equal [amounts].' He was asked, 'But surely, [wheat] is superior to [parched barley].' [The Imam] replied, 'Is there no labour involved in [parched barley]?' They agreed [that there was]. So [the Imam] said, 'This should be bartered for that, [pound for pound].'[151]

'Alī: He said, 'The Messenger of God forbade the sale of dried dates (*tamr*) in exchange for fresh dates (*ruṭab*), because the fresh ones decrease in weight, as they dry. This rule is quite different from the permission granted in the '*arāyā*[152] because in that case the barter is done by a conjectural computation of quantity (*kharṣ*) [in accordance with which fresh dates are exchanged for dry dates, the latter of] which are duly weighed.'[153]

[145]The Arabic term used is *al-tafāḍul*, meaning quantitative disparity between two commodities exchanged.

[146]*Kāfī*, V, 189, 190.

[147]'Gold is to be paid for with gold, silver with silver, wheat with wheat, barley with barley, dates with dates, salt with salt, like for like and equal for equal, payment being made on the spot. If these classes differ, sell as you wish if payment is made on the spot.' *Mishkāt*, II, 86–7: Robson, I, 602; transmitted by Muslim.

[148]*Kāfī*, V, 184; reported from the same authority.

[149]Ibid., V, 185.

[150]*Al-sawīq* is generally a meal of parched barley, or of wheat, cooked with water, or clarified butter, or the fat of a sheep's tail. Lane, s.v. s-w-q.

[151]*Kāfī*, V, 186.

[152]See the section 'The Sale of Fruit' earlier in this chapter.

[153]'The Prophet forbade buying dry dates for fresh, because the fresh dates were diminished when they became dry.' *Mishkāt*, II, 89, 93; Robson, I, 604, 607; *Kāfī*, V, 186.

Ja'far b. Muḥammad: He said, 'There is no harm in selling two pieces of cloth for one, either on the spot, or on credit (*nasī'at^{an}*) where the goods are ascertained.'[154]

The Messenger of God: He forbade the barter of foodstuffs by conjecture (i.e. undetermined quantity, *juzāf*).[155]

Ja'far b. Muḥammad: He was asked about the bartering of whole large cattle or fish (*ḥītān* pl. of *ḥūt*) for butchered ones, without weighing or measuring, and he permitted the practice. He was asked whether selling wheat for future provision of water was lawful, and he allowed it. He was asked, 'Can this be allowed in the case of other consumable liquids such as honey?' He replied, '[No], it would not be correct.' He allowed the barter of flour (*daqīq*) for dried bread (*ka'k*) of equal weight, on the spot; and also vinegar (*khall*) for vinegar, even though the latter differs in kind and variety. The same is the rule for honey (*'asal al-naḥl*) when exchanged for sugar cane juice (*'asal al-sukkar*).[156]

CONDITIONAL BARGAIN (*KHIYĀR AL-MUTABĀYI'AYN*)[157]

Ja'far b. Muḥammad—his father—his ancestors: The Messenger of God said, 'The two parties to a contract of sale have the option [to agree or to annul] until they separate as consenting parties.'[158]

[154]*Kāfī*, V, 188; the exchange of yarn for spread out cloth is permitted.

[155]*Juzāf* or *mujāzafa* means selling and buying by conjecture, without measuring and without weighing. Lane, s.v. j-z-f. *Kāfī*, V, 164, 191; Schacht, *Introduction*, 147.

[156]*Sukkar* is also a kind of sweet fresh ripe date, likened to sugar in sweetness. Lane, s.v. s-k-r.

[157]*Khiyār* is a substantive (*ism*) from *ikhtiyār*, meaning choice or option. As a technical term in Islamic law it means the option for the right of withdrawal for the parties involved in a contract to terminate it unilaterally. *Khiyār* implies a choice on the part of the holder of the right of option, who may either confirm the deal or cancel it. *Khiyār* may be conventional or legal. *Khiyār al-sharṭ* (conditional option) is included among the former type. It is done by inserting a clause in a contract whereby one of the parties, or both of them, reserves the right to confirm or to annul the deal within a specified time. All the four Sunnī schools of law have adopted it. *Khiyār al-ta'yīn* (designation option) is the other conventional option. It is inserted into alternative obligations and allows the one making the stipulation to make his final choice between the different objects of the same obligation. Legal options, on he other hand, are those that the law automatically confers without stipulating them in a contract. According to some jurists they are seventeen, such as fraud, injury, hidden defects, etc. Lane, s.v. kh-y-r; Schacht, *Introduction*, 152–3, 169; *EI*², s.v. K͟hiyār. Although Robson states that 'option' would have been a good translation of *khi'yār*, he renders it 'conditional bargains'. *Mishkāt*, II, 84; Robson, I, 600.

[158]'Both parties in a business transaction have a right to annul it so long as they have

Ja'far b. Muḥammad: He [explained] that this meant a physical separation from the place where the agreement of sale had taken place. [The Imam said], 'My father [Imam al-Bāqir] had verily sold a piece of land called *'urayḍ.*[159] When there was agreement with the purchaser, and the sale was completed, my father got up and walked away. I followed him and asked, "Why did you rise so hastily?" He replied, "I wanted the sale to be binding."'

The Messenger of God said, 'The Muslims are bound by the conditions [to which they have agreed], except those that contravene the Book of God.'[160]

Ja'far b. Muḥammad: He was asked about a man who had sold his house on the condition that if he were to produce its sale price within a year, he would repurchase it for himself. [The Imam] said, 'There is no harm in this, and he is entitled to enforce the condition.' [The Imam] was asked, 'To whom does the usufruct belong?' He said, 'To the purchaser, for, if the house were to be burnt down during the period, the loss would fall on him.'[161]

Ja'far b. Muḥammad: He was asked, 'If a vendor and a purchaser are trading in a commodity and either one of them makes the sale optional but the goods get destroyed prior to the option-holder exercising his option, on whom does the loss fall?' [The Imam] said, 'This will be deemed to be the property of the vendor, so long as the sale has not been completed or the purchaser obtains possession [by notice] only to examine the goods before concluding the deal.'[162] [The Imam] was asked, 'If the sale was completed by the purchaser, although one of the parties had the option [to withdraw from it], but then the property got destroyed?' [The Imam] said, 'The property belongs to the purchaser so long as the option was not exercised by the option-holder. It is well known that in such circumstances, the property belongs to the purchaser, and if it perishes, the loss falls on him.'

---

not separated ....' *Mishkāt*, II, 84–5; Robson, I, 600–1; transmitted by Bukhārī and Muslim; Kāfī, V, 167; Ṭūsī, *Tahdhīb al-aḥkām*, VII, 20; Jazīrī, *al-Fiqh*, II, 169.

[159]*'Urayḍ* is a valley near Medina. Hamdānī, *Ṣifat*, 264, 395. See also *Kāfī*, V, 167. *Al-'Arīḍ* in the printed text of the *Da'ā'im* is incorrect.

[160]'Any condition which is not in God's Book is worthless. Even if there are a hundred conditions, God's decision is more valid and God's condition is more binding.' *Mishkāt*, II, 102; Robson, I, 614; transmitted by Bukhārī and Muslim; Ṭūsī, *Tahdhīb al-aḥkām*, VII, 22. See also *Kāfī*, V, 166.

[161]*Kāfī*, V, 168; reported from the same authority.

[162]Ibid., V, 169; a slightly different version is reported where the goods were stolen before the buyer took possession.

[Ja'far b. Muḥammad]: He said, 'Every purchaser of an animal has the option [to withdraw from the deal] for three days, whether or not this is stipulated [in the contract].'[163]

[Ja'far b. Muḥammad]: He said, 'If a man were to purchase a female slave (*ama*) and have sexual intercourse with her, or kiss her or caress her, or see a portion [of her body] forbidden to strangers, he loses his option [to annul the deal] and the sale shall be deemed binding on him. Similarly, if he causes harm to an animal before exercising the option, the sale is binding upon him, as is the case if he offers the goods purchased for sale [in the open market].'[164]

[Ja'far b. Muḥammad]: He was asked, '[What is the ruling in the case of] a man who purchases goods with an option, then offers them for sale [but, failing to sell], wishes to exercise his option to return them within the period stipulated?' [The Imam] said, 'If he swears by God that he had not exhibited them for sale, and has even hidden his intention to buy, he may return the goods.'

[Ja'far b. Muḥammad]: He was asked about a man who buys cloth or goods with an option and is then offered a profit [to resell it]. [The Imam] said, 'If he wishes to have the profit then he should first buy it for himself [completing the first transaction]. When he does so, he is entitled to the profit [from the second transaction]. In case he does not resell it [for a profit], he is not entitled to return it [to the original vendor] if that sale was final. If the original vendor demands the profit [in case the buyer has resold the goods], then the buyer shall swear that the [first] sale was completed by him before he sold it. If he fails to do that, then the profit goes to the original vendor.'[165]

[Ja'far b. Muḥammad]: He said, 'Two men complete a transaction of sale with a handshake (*ṣafqa*),[166] and then one of them goes to fetch the price. Three days pass by and he does not produce it. After this period, there is no sale even if he claims it, unless the vendor agrees. But if the purchaser returns before three days, he is entitled to the delivery of the goods upon payment of the price.'[167]

[163]Ibid., V, 166; reported from the same authority; Ṭūsī, *Tahdhīb al-aḥkām*, VII, 21–2, 24.

[164]Ṭūsī, *Tahdhīb al-aḥkām*, VII, 24–5. It seems to me to that this means that the buyer can annul the sale if he has not yet placed the items on the market for resale, but if he puts the items on the market, he cannot annul the sale and ask for his money back. Perhaps the reason is to prevent him from putting the items on the market, then simply returning them if he finds they do not yield the profit he hoped for.

[165]*Kāfī*, V, 170; a slightly different case is reported; Ṭūsī, *Tahdhīb al-aḥkām*, VII, 23, 26.

[166]It is a symbolic act. Schacht, *Introduction*, 145.

[167]*Kāfī*, V, 167, 168.

[Ja'far b. Muḥammad]: He was asked about a person who purchases goods for an identified third party stipulating for him an option. The third party remains absent for a long time, then returns, [repudiates the sale], and returns the goods. [The Imam] said, 'In such a case, the [de facto] purchaser should be sworn as to the profits he had received from the goods, if it was capable of producing any, or as to any expenses he had incurred. If he refuses to take oath, the person demanding the oath [the third party] should be told, "Please swear as to what the de facto purchaser has received on your behalf, and take it from him, and pay him his dues." If the [third party] refuses to swear, the goods shall be left as they are, for a great deal of time has elapsed and the goods may have disintegrated. If the goods have improved [in price] or deteriorated, the profit or loss falls on the original [de facto] purchaser as he is liable for the price when he took possession; but even if the time lag is short, it matters not, and the purchaser is bound by his stipulations.'

RULES REGARDING DEFECTS [IN MERCHANDISE] (*AḤKĀM AL-'ŪYŪB*)

We have mentioned earlier that the Messenger of God said, 'He who cheats is not one of us.'[168] The hiding by the vendor of a defect of what he sells is a fraud.

The Household of the Messenger of God—the Prophet: He said, 'Religion [consists in] sincere conduct (*naṣīḥa*).'[169] He also said, 'It is not lawful for a Muslim who, knowing of a defect in merchandise, sells it to his brother without informing him of it. It is not lawful for anyone, if he knows of a defect, to hide it from an intending purchaser whom he sees is ignorant of it.'[170]

Ja'far b. Muḥammad: He said, 'He who concludes a sale (by handshake), and finds a defect after parting from the vendor, has the right to withdraw from the sale because the vendor is responsible [for informing him of the defect].[171]

[Ja'far b. Muḥammad]: He said, 'He who sells a beast or commodity, saying, "I am free from any obligation in respect to any defect," is not free

[168]See n. 78 above in this chapter.

[169]Tamīm al-Dārī told that the Prophet said three times, 'Religion consists in sincere conduct' (*al-dīn^u al-naṣīḥat^u*). He was asked to whom it should be directed. He replied, 'To God, His Book, His Messenger, the leaders (*al-a'imma*) of the Muslims, and to all the Muslims.' *Mishkāt*, II, 608; Robson, II, 1034; transmitted by Muslim.

[170]See n. 79 above in this chapter.

[171]For similar traditions see *Kāfī*, V, 205.

from such an obligation until the vendor informs the purchaser of any defects.'

'Alī: He said, 'If a group of people buy goods and then divide it after assessment (*qawwamūhu*), and thereafter some of them discover a defect in their own portion, such persons are entitled to the price of the defect.[172] If a man buys a certain commodity and finds a defect in it, which has happened either before or after the sale, he may return the defective commodity and take its price, or the value of the defect.'

'Alī: He was asked about a man who purchases a female slave (*jāriya*) and has sexual intercourse with her. Thereafter he finds a defect in her. [The Imam] said, 'The price of such defect shall be paid to him, but the sale shall be deemed binding on him.'[173]

Ja'far b. Muḥammad: He said, 'The above [rule applies] where the slave girl is not pregnant; but if she is, he may return her, and the vendor shall pay to the purchaser one-twentieth of the price.'[174]

Ja'far b. Muḥammad:[175] He said, 'Where a man purchases a slave girl and finds a defect in her, and then he causes her to conceive (a child)[176] after full knowledge of the first defect, the contract is binding upon him, and he has no right to return her or claim damages for the defect [from the vendor].'

'Alī: He said, 'In the case of a slave (*raqīq*), the vendor is responsible for a serious illness contracted during the first year [after the sale]; and for death, if it occurs in the first three days.'

Ja'far b. Muḥammad: He said, 'A slave (*mamlūk*) can be returned if he suffers from a serious illness such as madness (*junūn*), leprosy (*judhām*), leucoderma (*waḍaḥ*),[177] or a *qarn* (fleshy protuberance in the vulva preventing sexual intercourse),[178] contracted during the period of one year [after the sale], except where the vendor has expressly stipulated that there is no such obligation on him.[179] No such obligation exists where the vendor had declared that he was free from any obligation, or in respect

[172]Ṭūsī, *Tahdhīb al-aḥkām*, VII, 60.

[173]*Kāfī*, V, 208, 212, 213; reported from the same authority; Ṭūsī, *Tahdhīb al-aḥkām*, VII, 60–1.

[174]*Kāfī*, V, 212, 214; Ṭūsī, *Tahdhīb al-aḥkām*, VII, 61–2.

[175]As in MS Q. In the printed edition *wa-'an*, is an error.

[176]It is a free rendering of the Arabic *aḥdatha fīhā ḥadath*^an^.

[177]Leprosy, *baraṣ*. Lane, s.v. w-ḍ-ḥ.

[178]A tradition from 'Alī states, 'When a man marries a woman who has *qarn*, [he has the option], he can retain her if he desires or he can divorce her if he likes.' See *Tāj al-'arūs*, s.v. q-r-n.

[179]*Kāfī*, V, 215, 216.

of the sale of inherited property. In such cases, neither the rule of the year, nor the option of three days applies.'[180]

RESALES FOR A FIXED PROFIT (*BAY' AL-MURĀBAḤA*)[181]

Ja'far b. Muḥammad: He said, 'Some goods arrived for my father [Imam al-Bāqir] from Egypt, so he invited some merchants and gave them a feast and they said, "We shall give you [for your every] ten [dinars] twelve (*be-dah davāzdah*)."[182] So he said to them, "I sell these goods to you for twelve thousand."[183] Whereas his purchase was for ten thousand.'

Now *[be] dah davāzdah* is a Persian expression which means 'twelve for ten.' Similarly '*[be] dah yāzdah*' means 'eleven for ten,' an expression used commonly by merchants in the East whereby they give a fixed profit of one dinar or two for every ten. So Abū Ja'far [the Imam] disapproved that the profit be calculated on the capital (*al-māl*), but made it applicable to the commodity (*al-matā'*).[184] For instance, if a man sold cloth for a profit of one or two dirhams; this should not be calculated such that on the capital of every ten dirhams, he should get a determined amount of profit.

Ja'far b. Muḥammad: He allowed that the wages of a fuller (*qaṣṣār*) or a wage-earner (*karī*), or a craftsman who obtains compensation for his labour when the goods are made, should be calculated [on his work as an increase] in the price of the commodity. His resale of the commodity for fixed profit is permitted when he indicates his labour.

[Ja'far b. Muḥammad]: He was asked about a man who buys a large quantity of goods. Later he [sorts them out and] assesses the value of each piece of cloth of the goods with the amount he paid for the whole lot. Is it possible for him to sell [these goods separately] at a profit over and above the price he has paid? [The Imam] said, 'No, unless he makes it clear to the purchaser that he has assessed the price of each piece.'[185]

[Ja'far b. Muḥammad]: He said, 'A man who buys goods on deferred

[180]Ṭūsī, *Tahdhīb al-aḥkām*, VII, 63–4.

[181]A'*ṭāhu mālan murābaḥatan*, means he gave him property on the condition that the gain, or profit, should be [divided] between the two of them. Lane, s.v. r-b-ḥ; Schacht, *Introduction*, 154.

[182]*Davāzdah* or Pehlevi *dōvazdah*. Mu'īn, *Farhang-e Fārisī*, s.v. *Davāzdah*.

[183]*Kāfī*, V, 196. The phrase added at the end is *fa-bā'ahum musāwamatan*, meaning he sold them after bargaining.

[184]The logic of the argument is obvious to avoid any implication of *ribā*.

[185]*Kāfī*, V, 196.

terms (*naẓira*)[186] is not entitled to sell them at a profit unless he makes [the details of his] transaction clear [to the purchaser]. But if he conceals this, the sale is void, unless the purchaser agrees or also buys on deferred terms in the same manner.'[187]

[Ja'far b. Muḥammad]: He said, 'A man buys a cloth [marked] for one dinar but pays the price in dirhams [at the prevailing exchange]. It is thus permissible for him to sell it with a profit [in dirhams], although his purchase was [originally marked] in dinars. The same rule applies in the case of a purchaser [where the price of a thing is fixed] in dirhams but was paid for in dinars. It is therefore possible for him to sell the goods for a greater number of dirhams than what he paid.'

[Ja'far b. Muḥammad]: He was asked about a man who purchases a slave girl and has sexual intercourse with her. Is it permissible for him to sell her at a profitable price? He said, 'There is no harm in it.'

A CONTRACT FOR FUTURE DELIVERY [WITH PREPAYMENT] (AL-SALAM)[188]

God says: O *ye who believe! When ye contract a debt for a fixed term, record it in writing* (2:282). The Word of God clearly shows that the words 'for a fixed period' implies that a *salam* for an indeterminate time in the future is not lawful.

Ja'far b. Muḥammad—his father—his forefathers: The Messenger of God said, 'A transaction of a sale for an undetermined period, or for unspecified goods, is void.'[189]

[186] *Naẓira* lit. means postponement, delay. *Bā'a minhu 'l-shay'a bi-naẓiratin*, means he sold to him the thing with postponement of the payment (or upon credit). Lane, s.v. n-ẓ-r.

[187] *Kāfī*, V, 197; Kulaynī's version is slightly different.

[188] *Salam* and its synonym *salaf* (used by the Iraqi jurists), in Islamic law, means a transaction of sale and purchase where the money is paid by the buyer in advance as the price of a commodity for which the seller has become responsible to deliver at a specified time and place. Since by its very nature a *salam* transaction does not permit the purchaser an 'option after inspection' of the object of sale, an appropriate description of the latter is not only essential but the only possible way of safeguarding it against risk and uncertainty. The object of sale should be fungible, weighable, and measurable. According to Ḥanafī law, animals cannot be the objects of *salam* sale, while in Mālikī law they are allowed. Ḥillī, *Sharā'i' al-islām*, I, 188–91; Lane, s.v. s-l-m; Schacht, *Introduction*, 106, 119, 147, 153, 155; *EI*², s.v. Salam. For the function of documents in Islamic law (with reference to the Qur'ān 2:282), see the English Introduction by Wakin in her book *Function*.

[189] Ibn 'Abbās said that when the Messenger of God came to Medina they were paying one, two, and three years in advance for fruits, so he said, 'Those who pay in advance for anything must do so for a specified measure and weight with specified time fixed.' *Mishkāt*, II, 104; Robson I, 617; transmitted by Bukhārī and Muslim.

ʿAlī: He said, 'Do not pay in advance for the harvest (*ḥaṣād*), or for the cutting off of the fruit of palm trees (*ṣarām*),[190] or for the trampling (or threshing) of corn (*diyās*).[191] Only make advanced payments for a fixed measure, at a determined time.'[192]

The correct form of making a sale with future delivery with advanced payments (*salam*) is for a man to pay dirhams or dinars for certain foodstuffs, specified according to weight or measure, and also to state the place where it will be delivered. The money should be paid in cash before the parting of the two parties at the place where such a contract (i.e. *salam*) has been contracted. Thereafter both the parties should part with mutual consent.

Jaʿfar b. Muḥammad: He was asked about a man who advances a certain number of dirhams for some foodstuffs of a well-known village, at a time when the harvest has not yet commenced to ripen. [The Imam] said, 'Such a sale is invalid, because the purchaser does not know whether the harvest will ripen or not. But what is lawful for the purchaser is to advance cash without condition. There is no harm if the vendor does not have foodstuffs with him [at that time], but when the time [of delivery] comes, he should buy it and pay off his debt.'[193]

[Jaʿfar b. Muḥammad]: He said, 'There is no harm in paying in advance for an animal to be delivered at a specified time when a definite number of teeth would appear.[194] It is lawful for the purchaser to pay a larger sum than the one stipulated, or for the vendor to take a smaller sum by agreement between them and there is no objection in this.'[195]

[Jaʿfar b. Muḥammad]: He said, 'There is no harm in making a transaction of a mortgage (*rahn*) or of a guarantee (*kafīl*) with regard to goods delivered immediately for a deferred payment (*bayʿ al-nasīʾa*).'[196]

Jaʿfar b. Muḥammad: He said, 'There is no harm in immediate delivery of goods where the length, width, and quality are specified or are well known for a deferred payment.'[197]

[Jaʿfar b. Muḥammad]: He said, 'In respect of advanced payments for foodstuffs or other such sales that are legal, if the purchaser fails to obtain from the vendor the goods according to his rights at the specified time,

[190]Lane, s.v. ṣ-r-m.

[191]Lane, s.v. d-w-s.

[192]*Kāfī*, V, 181.

[193]Ṭūsī, *Tahdhīb al-aḥkām*, VII, 39.

[194]*Kāfī*, V, 219, 220; reported from the same authority.

[195]Ibid., V, 220.

[196]"Āʾisha said that God's Messenger bought some grain from a Jew to be paid at a specified time, and gave him his coat of mail as a pledge (*rahn*).' *Mishkāt*, II, 104; Robson, I, 617; transmitted by Bukhārī and Muslim.

[197]*Kāfī*, V, 198; Ṭūsī, *Tahdhīb al-aḥkām*, VII, 27.

there is no harm if the purchaser takes possession of a part of the goods, and for the rest, proportionately goes against the vendor's capital, taking from it a half, or a quarter, or whatever the case may be.'[198]

'Alī: He said, 'When a man purchases foodstuffs to be delivered in the future in a fixed time, and fails to obtain delivery thereof; and the vendor says, "Take the price in cash [for the goods] according to current prices," [in such a case] he should not take an amount in cash which will purchase more than the vendor's obligation. Or he may take the foodstuffs as stipulated. This rule applies to all transactions with prepayment.'[199]

Ja'far b. Muḥammad: He was asked about a buyer who contracts for delivery of foodstuffs with prepayment in dirhams. When the time for delivery arrives, the vendor returns the [prepaid] dirhams and says, 'Purchase the foodstuffs for yourself and satisfy your demand [according to the contract].' [The Imam] said, 'The person [who made prepayment] should not undertake the purchase by himself, but should delegate someone else to do it on his behalf.'[200]

[Ja'far b. Muḥammad]: He was asked about a man who makes prepayment for goods worth twenty dinars, provided that the other party lends him ten dinars, or something similar to this. He said, 'This is not lawful, because a debt induces profit.'[201]

[Ja'far b. Muḥammad]: He said, 'When the specified period of a prepaid purchase ends, and the purchaser does not obtain the goods purchased, but finds [that the vendor has] animals or slaves or [some other] commodity that can satisfy his claims, and the value is the same as that which was contracted for, it is lawful for the purchaser to take such property, [provided its value does not exceed the original contracted price.]'[202]

Similarly, when there is a sale of foodstuffs in exchange for dirhams [to be paid later], and when the term of the sale arrives the purchaser says, 'I have no dirhams to pay, but take foodstuff in exchange.' [The Imam]

[198]*Kāfī*, V, 182; Ṭūsī, *Tahdhīb al-aḥkām*, VII, 28.

[199]*Kāfī*, V, 182.

[200]Ibid., V, 182, 183; Ṭūsī, *Tahdhīb al-aḥkām*, VII 29–30.

[201]Ja'far al-Ṣādiq was asked as to whether a debt that induces profit was lawful, and he said, 'The best of all the debts is the one that induces profit.' *Kāfī*, V, 258. It is not easy to reconcile these contradictory views ascribed to Imam al-Ṣādiq. The editor of *Kāfī* also notes that the consensus of the Imāmī jurists is that any profit connected to a loan is forbidden. In his *Sharā'i' al-islām*, I, 191, Ḥillī writes, 'In loan [giving] there is reward for voluntarily helping the needy and for confining its return to [the loan's] equivalent [the original amount of loan]. If the loan is made on the condition of inducing profit, it is unlawful ... however, if the borrower volunteers to give more than the amount he borrowed, it is permissible.' The editor of *Kāfī*, therefore, states that Kulaynī's tradition should be interpreted in the light of Ḥillī's explanation.

[202]*Kāfī*, V, 183.

said, 'There is no harm in this. He is entitled to dirhams, hence he can take whatever he likes.'

[The Imams] disapproved of prepayment in respect to commodities which do not last long, such as fruit and meat and the like.

[Ja'far b. Muḥammad]: He said of a man who makes a contract for delivery of ten *qafīzes*[203] of foodstuffs with prepayment of ten dinars and pays five dinars immediately, on the understanding that the remaining five would be paid later, [The Imam] said, 'Considering what he has already paid the purchaser's liability in this case is for only five dinars.'

CONDITIONS IN SALES (*AL-SHURŪṬ FI 'L-BUYŪ'*)[204]

Ja'far b. Muḥammad—his ancestors: 'Alī said, 'The believers are bound by the stipulations [made] by them, except those which involve disobedience to God.'[205]

Ja'far b. Muḥammad—his father—his ancestors: 'Alī said, 'If a man were to make a condition which is disapproved, the sale is valid, but the condition is void. Every stipulation which does not declare a legal thing to be illegal, or an illegal thing to be legal, is permissible.'[206]

[Ja'far b. Muḥammad]: '[For instance], a man sells a slave girl on the condition that she should not be sold or given away, and that she should not inherit [any property]. The first two conditions are valid, but not the third regarding the inheritance. Every condition which contravenes the Book of God, should be rejected (lit. returned to the Book of God).[207] If

[203]*Qafīz* pl. *aqfiza* is a dry measure of varying weight used for small quantities of grain in Iraq and Persia. Hinz, *Islamische Masse*, 48–50; *EI*², s.v. Makāyil.

[204]*Sharṭ* pl. *shurūṭ*, broadly means the prerequisites for the validity of a legal act, as opposed to its essential element (*rukn*). For example, in an act of worship the prerequisites are ritual purity, facing the *qibla*, etc. Another set of *shurūṭ* is the 'conditions implied in the nature of the transaction' (*shurūṭ yaqtaḍīha al-'aqd*) and the 'conditions intimately connected with the transaction' (*shurūṭ mulāyima*). Schacht, *Introduction*, 82, 118. For an excellent study of *shurūṭ* literature and a detailed analysis of the Arabic formulary, especially used in the contract of sale, see Wakin, *The Function of Documents*, 1–70.

[205]*Kāfī*, V, 166. 'Muslims are bound by the stipulations made by them, ...' Tirmidhī, *Sunan*, III, 635; also transmitted by Bukhārī, see *Concordance*, s.v. sh-r-ṭ.

[206]The Prophet is reported as saying, 'Muslims must keep to the conditions they have made, except for a condition which makes unlawful something which is lawful, or makes lawful something which is unlawful.' *Mishkāt*, II, 113; Robson, I, 625.

[207]'Any condition which is not in God's Book is worthless. Even if there are a hundred conditions, God's decision is more valid and God's condition is more binding.' *Mishkāt*, II, 102; Robson, I, 614; transmitted by Bukhārī and Muslim.

a man were to purchase a slave girl on the condition that she would be set free, or given the rights of an *umm walad*,[208] such conditions would be valid and he would be bound by them.'

[Ja'far b. Muḥammad]: He was asked about a man who sold a slave and the purchaser discovered that the slave had property (*māl*) [of his own]. [The Imam] said, 'The property [of the slave] reverts to the vendor, unless he had agreed to sell the property with the slave. He had sold the slave, not the property. If the vendor had sold the slave with the slave's property, and the property consisted of movable goods (*'urūḍ*),[209] and he had sold them for cash (*'ayn*),[210] the sale would be valid, whatever be the nature of the movable goods. The same rule applies if the [slave's] property was cash and the vendor had sold them for movable goods. Now if the slave's property consisted of [a certain amount of] cash, and the vendor had sold him for the same amount of cash, [such a sale] would not be permissible, unless the selling price [of the slave] was greater than that of the slave's property. The differential would, therefore, make up for the price of the slave.

'The rule is not applicable where the (slave's) property consists of coined or uncoined silver (*wariq*) and the purchaser buys it with gold nuggets (*tibr*); or the property consists of gold nuggets and the purchaser buys it for coined or uncoined silver. There is no harm in the differential in this transaction because it involves of two different kinds [of valuables].'

JUDICIAL DECISIONS CONCERNING SALES (*AL-AQḌIYA FI 'L-BUYŪ'*)[211]

God says: O *ye who believe! Squander not your wealth among yourselves in vanity, except it be trade by mutual consent* (4:29). Thus God has declared the property of another Muslim unlawful without his consent. [To the best of my knowledge], and I know of no differing opinion, consent is

[208] A slave woman who has borne a child to her master was called *umm walad*. See *The Pillars of Islam*, I, 283, n. 62; also Chap. 12, section on *umm al-walad* in this volume.

[209] *'Urūḍ* means worldly goods, anything except gold, silver (or dinars and dirhams), and immovable property. Contrarily, *'ayn* means gold and silver (or dinars and dirhams). Lane, s.v. '-r-ḍ. See also n. 137 in this chapter.

[210] *'Ayn* means a tangible thing that can be ascertained by weight or measure in a contract of sale in contrast to a counter-value of a claim or debt (*dayn*) that has not been ascertained or whose possession has not been taken. *Dayn* is not tangible as it is associated with the *dhimma* (liability). Schacht, *Introduction*, 134, 144–6, 205; *EI*², s.v. 'Ayn; *EI*², Supp. s.v. Dayn.

[211] *Aqḍiya* pl. of *qaḍā'*, means the judgment given by the *qāḍī*. Schacht, *Introduction*, 123.

when the purchaser says to the vendor, while both of them are in agreement and not under duress, 'Sell this [goods, or property] to me for this [price].' And the vendor says, 'Verily, I have sold it to thee for this price.' And the purchaser says, 'Verily, I have purchased it,' while both of them know what is being sold, and then they separate after mutual satisfaction.

Ja'far b. Muḥammad: He was asked about a man who purchased foodstuffs or cloth or similar things from another man but there were no written contracts.[212] Possession was with the purchaser who affirmed that he paid the price, but the vendor denied having received it. [The Imam] said, 'In such a case, the word rests with the purchaser making a statement on oath, possession being with him. But if the goods have never left the possession of the vendor, then the word is his, and the vendor should give an oath that he had not received the price [which is still unpaid by the purchaser]. Such an assertion [by the vendor] can be disproved by the purchaser if he produces proof that he had paid the price.

'But if the property is such that people ordinarily embody it in a document duly attested by witnesses, such as the sale of animals, large tenement houses (*ribā*ʿ) and the like, then if the parties differ regarding the price, the purchaser says, "I have paid you," but the vendor denies this. In such a case, it is immaterial whether the possession is with the purchaser or not; the proof will lie on the purchaser as to whether he has paid the price or not. The vendor shall state on oath that he has not received the money as he claims.'

[The Imam] was asked, 'What happens where the property is in the joint possession of the vendor and the purchaser, neither has departed with the property?' [The Imam] said, 'The first word [in such a case] is the sworn evidence of the vendor and it is for the purchaser to prove that he had indeed paid the price.'

'Alī: He said, 'It is not permissible for a Muslim to make a mistake [or misrepresentation] in a sale.'[213]

Ja'far b. Muḥammad: He said, 'When a man sells goods to another and then claims that there is an error in the price and says, "I looked into my [account] book (*barnāma*)[214] and found a loss in price and a patent fraud." It is necessary to look into the condition of the goods. If similar

[212]'People are encouraged to have written contracts.' *Kāfī*, V, 151. The Qur'ān states: *O ye who believe! When ye contract a debt for a fixed term record it in writing* ... (2:282).

[213]Cf. *Kāfī*, V, 146–51.

[214]*Barmānjī* in the text seems to be a corruption of *barnāmajī*. Fīrūzābādī (*Qāmūs*, s.v. b-r-j) explains *barnāmaj* as a notebook for keeping account and that it is Arabized from *barnāma*. *Bar*, a preposition, meaning on, upon, and *nāma* meaning letter, book in Persian.

goods are sold for a similar price, or if the shortfall is according to the common usage of the market, the sale is valid; but if the transaction is grossly fraudulent, then the vendor shall take an oath by the one and only God stating that the price quoted by him was an error if he did not have a clear proof. Then the purchaser should be told, "Take the goods at the proper price, or leave them."'

Abū Ja'far Muḥammad b. 'Alī: He said, 'When a man appoints an agent (*wakīl*) to sell his goods and the agent sells them at a low price (*bi-waks^{in} min al-thaman*),[215] the sale is valid except where it is proved that he has committed fraud (*khiyāna*) or shown partiality to the purchaser. Similarly, when someone has authorized an agent to buy and the agent has bought at a high price, but it is not established that he did so deliberately, or fraudulently, or has shown partiality, the sale is also valid. But if it be known that the agent intended to do harm, even to a slight extent, the sale or purchase is to be rejected. If an agent sells only part of a thing, and the sale was proper in other respects, then the sale is valid.

'If a man authorizes two persons to sell a slave (*'abd*) and only one of them sells the slave, the sale is not valid except where both the agents agree individually to the sale. It is their duty to meet together for the transaction.'

'Alī: Two people came to him with their claims. One of them said, 'I sold these baskets of dates (*qawāṣir*)[216] and excepted five among them which were unspecified at the time of sale.' Now some of these baskets were better than others. 'Alī said, 'The sale is invalid as the reservation applies to something which was unspecified.'

Ja'far b. Muḥammad: He was asked about a man who purchases a slave girl [and determines the price] according to his own arbitral decision and sends the amount to the vendor, but the vendor refuses to accept it. So the purchaser says, 'You had made me the arbiter about the price and this is [the appropriate price] in my view.' [The Imam] said, 'If the vendor had appointed the purchaser as the arbiter [of the price], then that is the proper price and the vendor must accept it. But if it be less than that price, then it is for the purchaser to make up the balance.'

Ja'far b. Muḥammad: He said, 'When the ruler (*sulṭān*) or the judge (*qāḍī*) sells a man's goods to pay off his debts, and when the date of maturity

[215]Lane, s.v. w-k-s.

[216]*Al-Qawṣara* or *al-qawṣarra* pl. *al-qawāṣir*, is a receptacle made of reeds or mats in which dates are stored. In conventional language it is so called as long as it contains dates, otherwise it is called *zabīl*. Lane, s.v. q-ṣ-r.

for the payment of the goods [sold] comes and the debtor (*al-gharīm*) is absent or becomes bankrupt, no responsibility attaches to the ruler or judge; but the demand lies against the [original] debtor, or on the owner of the goods if he possesses any.'[217]

[Ja'far b. Muḥammad]: He said, 'The executor, or the legal guardian (*waṣī*) has no right to trade with the property of an orphan, and if he does so, he is responsible for the loss, while the profit belongs to the orphan.'[218]

[Ja'far b. Muḥammad]: He said of a slave (*mamlūk*) who makes a gift of property to a man on the condition that he would buy and emancipate him, 'This is not lawful. If the man buys the slave with that property and emancipates him, and the master comes to know that the property belongs to the slave, the property as well the slave himself, reverts to the ownership of the master as before. Emancipation of a slave by a person is not valid except when a person himself has the means to pay for the price of a slave'.

[Ja'far b. Muḥammad]: He was asked about two people each of whom sold his share of a house, for the share of his friend in another house. He said, 'This is lawful when each party knows what he is buying and what he is selling. But if both of them do not know, or even one of them does not know [the particulars of the transaction], the transaction is not valid.'

'Alī: He was asked about two people who bought goods from a man, and later went to fetch the price. Only one of them returned with the price, and he was told that he would be given possession of the goods only when he paid the price fully. [The Imam said], 'Now [having paid the price fully and having obtained possession], if his companion came later asking for the goods, he cannot obtain them, unless he pays one half of the price to the partner, who paid the full price.'

['Alī]: He was asked about a man who was in the service of the ruler and had died [while in debt to him]. The responsibility of paying off his debts was assumed by one of the deceased's sons. So the son went and sold off a house belonging to his father and paid off the debt due to the ruler [from the price of the house]. Now all the other heirs were present at the sale, but did not consent to the sale. Have they any right in the matter?

'Alī replied, 'If that house was acquired during the course of his public service, and the deceased was indebted during such service, then the debt is payable by all of them. But if it is not so, those of the heirs who did not consent to the sale, are entitled to their rights, and it is not lawful to take possession of the property of a Muslim without his valid consent.'

[217]Cf. *Mishkāt*, II, 111, 112; Robson, I, 623, 624.

[218]*Kāfī*, V, 126, 127; a number of traditions are reported on the authority of Imam Ja'far al-Ṣādiq.

The Messenger of God: At the Farewell Pilgrimage, he said, 'Sanctity attaches to your blood, and property in the same manner as sanctity attaches to this day, in this month of yours, in this land of yours.'[219]

'Alī: The son of the owner of a slave girl sold her but the owner objected. 'Alī held in this case that the sale was void; the slave girl should be returned to her master, and the son should return the sale price to the purchaser.

The Messenger of God: Some of the prisoners from Baḥrayn[220] were brought before him and were drawn up in ranks. He saw a woman weeping and asked her the reason. She said, 'I had a son who was sold among the Banū 'Abs.'[221] The Messenger of God asked, 'Who sold him?' She said, 'Abū Usayd al-Anṣārī.'[222] So the Messenger of God was angered and said [to al-Anṣārī], 'You shall ride and fetch him just as you have sold him.' So Abū Usayd rode off to them and brought him back.[223]

The Messenger of God: He sent Zayd b. Ḥāritha[224] [on a certain mission] and he captured some prisoners among whom was the Ḍamīra (or Ḍumayra) of 'Alī's freedman. The Messenger of God ordered that they be sold, and then he went out and saw them weeping, and said, 'What is it that makes you weep?' They said, 'They have separated us from our brothers.' He said, 'Do not separate them, but sell them together.'[225]

RULES REGARDING DEBTS (*AḤKĀM AL-DUYŪN*)

Ja'far b. Muḥammad—his father—his ancestors: The Messenger of God said, 'Verily, God is with the debtor until he pays off his debt (*dayn* pl. *duyūn*), so long as no action of his displeases God.'[226]

[219] Ṭabarī, *Tārīkh*, III, 151; *History of al-Ṭabarī*, IX, 114.

[220] In early Islamic times the name Baḥrayn was applied to the mainland of eastern Arabia, comprising the oasis of al-Qaṭīf and Hajar (now al-Ḥasā); later it was restricted to the archipelago offshore. Yāqūt, s.v. b-ḥ-r; *EI*², s.v. al-Baḥrayn.

[221] 'Abs was one of the major tribes of northern Arabian tribes Ghaṭafān. *EI*², s. v. Ghaṭafān.

[222] He is Abū Usayd al-Sā'idī al-Anṣārī who was delegated by the Prophet to ask for a woman's hand in marriage for him. Ibn Sa'd, VIII, 102, 103.

[223] For similar traditions see *Kāfī*, V, 218.

[224] Zayd b. Ḥāritha was the Prophet's adopted, freed slave who was killed in the raid on Mu'ta. *EI*, s. v. Zayd b. Ḥāritha. See also *The Pillars of Islam*, I, 54, n. 135.

[225] Cf. *Kāfī*, V, 218.

[226] Abū Hurayra reported the Prophet as saying, 'If anyone borrows other people's money (*amwāl*) intending to return it, God will pay it back for him; but if anyone borrows it intending to squander it, God will destroy his property.' Transmitted by Bukhārī. Robson's translation is unclear. Another tradition states, 'The hand which takes is responsible till

[The Messenger of God]: He said, 'He who lends money to another is credited with the same [reward] as one who gives [a similar amount in] charity.' On the next day he said, 'When a man gives a loan, for each day of the loan he is credited with [recompense] of him who gives [a similar amount to] charity.'

'Alī said, 'O Messenger of God! But yesterday you said, "He who lends money to another is credited with the same [reward] as one who gives [a similar amount] in charity," and today you say, "When a man gives a loan, for each day of the loan he is credited with [recompense] of him who gives [a similar amount to] charity."' The Messenger of God said, 'Yes. When a man lends money to another, he is credited with the same [reward] as one who gives [a similar amount in] charity; but if he defers [receiving the loan amount] after its due terms, then for each day he is credited with [the reward] of him who gives [a similar amount to] charity.'[227]

'Alī: He said, 'No creditor should accept an animal to ride, or the loan of a non-fungible object (*'āriyata matā'in*)[228] [for him to use] on account of the debt loaned by him.[229]

'Alī used to disapprove of the conduct of a creditor (*gharīm*) who would stay with his debtor [as a guest], or eat his food, or consume his drink or fodder.

Abū Ja'far Muḥammad b. 'Alī: He was asked about a man who lent money for profit, and he said, 'Every debt which brings a profit is usury (*ribā*).'[230]

Ja'far b. Muḥammad: He was asked about a man who lent old dirhams

---

he pays.' *Mishkāt*, II, 110–14, 121; Robson, I, 622–6, 631. Many scholars, on the other hand, are of the opinion that debts dissolve when the debtor dies. Ibn Rushd, *Bidāya*, II, 281; trans. II, 343.

[227]Cf. *Mishkāt*, II, 108, 109, 114; Robson, I, 621, 625. It states, 'When anyone has something due him from another, he will be credited with *ṣadaqa* for every day he allows the other to postpone payment.' Another tradition states, 'He who grants respite to one who is in straitened circumstances or remits his debt will be taken by God under His protection.' Transmitted by Muslim.

It should be noted that both in the *Mishkāt* and *Kāfī* there are more traditions emphasizing that debt is a great responsibility until it is paid back.

[228]*'Āriya* or *'ārīya* is a loan of non-fungible objects and is distinguished as a separate contract from the *qarḍ* (loan of money or other fungible objects). It is further defined as putting a person temporarily and gratuitously in possession of the use of a thing and that the use must be lawful. EI^2, s.v. 'Āriyya.

[229]'When one of you makes a loan and the borrower sends him a present or provides an animal for him to ride, he must not accept the former or ride the latter unless it is a practice they followed previously.' *Mishkāt*, II, 91; Robson, I, 606. See also *Kāfī*, V, 97.

[230]*Kāfī*, V, 258. Kulaynī transmitted three traditions on the authority of al-Bāqir and al-Ṣādiq that state, 'The best loan is the one that brings profit.' See n. 201 in this chapter.

(*ghalla*)[231]to another, but the debtor returned new dirhams (*al-darāhim al-ṭāzaja*)[232] out of his own good will. He said, 'There is no harm in it.'

'Alī: He said, 'If a man lends coined or uncoined silver (*wariq*) to a debtor, and did not make any condition except for the return of the same [quantity of silver] but the debtor returns a better kind of silver, [there is no harm in it] and he should accept it.'

Abū Ja'far Muḥammad b. 'Alī: He was asked whether a debtor of money (*darāhim*) or goods (*māl*) may give a present to the creditor. [The Imam] said, 'There is no harm in it.'[233]

All that has come down to us about such transactions, leads to the conclusion that making a condition of obtaining or extracting profit from the debtor, is disapproved (*makrūh*),[234] but if the debtor gives something of his own good will, like a present or some such thing, there is no harm in it.

'Alī: He gave a certain sum of money in a particular town (*min madīnat*[in]) and received it back in another place (*bi-arḍ*[in] *ukhrā*).

Ja'far b. Muḥammad: He permitted the use of bills of credit (*safātij*),[235] and this means that a man obtains a loan at one place, and receives it at another place.[236]

[Ja'far b. Muḥammad]: He was asked about people who engaged in

[231]See n. 132 in this chapter.

[232]*Al-Darāhim al-ṭāzajīya* means fine white dirhams [of high purity]. *Ṭāzaja* is Arabicized of Persian *tāze*. *Majma' al-baḥrayn*, s.v. ṭ-z-j.

[233]'When a man makes a loan to another he must not accept a present.' *Mishkāt*, II, 91; Robson, I, 606; transmitted by Bukhārī. Abū 'Abd Allāh said, 'A man came to 'Alī and said, "I have made a loan to a person and he gave me a present." 'Alī replied, "Consider it as a part of your credit to him."' *Kāfī*, V, 97.

[234]*Al-Aḥkām al-khamsa* (the five religious qualifications) by which every act of man is qualified in Islamic law are arranged on the following scale: (1) *wājib*, *farḍ* (obligatory duty) is of two kinds: *farḍ 'ayn* (the individual duty), such as ritual prayer, fasting, etc., and *farḍ kifāya* (the collective duty), the fulfilment of which by a sufficient number of individuals excuses the others from fulfilling it, such as funeral prayers, *jihād*, etc.; (2) *sunna*, *mandūb*, *mustaḥabb* (recommended); (3) *mubāḥ* (indifferent), should be distinguished from *jā'iz* (allowed, permissible, non-objectionable); (4) *makrūh* (reprehensible, disapproved); (5) *ḥaram* (forbidden), the opposite of *ḥalāl* (that is not forbidden). Schacht, *Introduction*, 121; *EI*[2], s.v. Aḥkām; see also the Editor's Introduction at the beginning of this volume.

[235]*Saftaja* or *suftaja* pl. *safātij* is an Arabicized form of Persian *sufta* meaning promissory note, letter of credit, or a bill of exchange. *Majma' al-baḥrayn*, s.v. s-f-t-j; Mu'īn, *Farhang-e Fārisī*, s.v. s-f-t; Steingass, *Persian English Dictionary*, s.v. s-f-t-j.

[236]*Suftaja* is seen by Islamic law as a form of loan. However, its formation and objectives differ from those involved in loans. The objective of a loan is the acquisition of money, while the objective of *suftaja* is the avoidance of risk in transport. The Ḥanafī and Shāfi'ī schools do not approve of this practice, but the Mālikī school only allows it on the grounds of necessity. The Ḥanbalī school permits it as long as it is done without any material gain. Schacht, *Introduction*, 78, 149; *EI*[2], s.v. Suftadja.

bay' al-'īna (a double sale in one contract to evade *ribā*),[237] [i.e.][238] when there was agreement [for the firtst sale], the parties inserted another sale into the transaction. [The Imam] asked, 'Why?' They said, 'Because the parties disliked what is forbidden.' [The Imam] said, 'When a man desires a lawful thing, there is no harm in it. For instance, if a man were to have sexual intercourse with a woman illegally, both parties consenting to it, and later they considered the situation and married lawfully, such a marriage is permissible.'

[Ja'far b. Muḥammad]: He was asked about a man who says to another, 'Sell me these goods so that I shall make payment later (*nasī'a*) and the vendor sold the goods accordingly.' [The Imam] said, 'There was no harm in it. For, he bought [that is, paid for] the goods after acquiring possession.' [The Imam] was asked, 'If the purchaser wanted [to buy] food, or [some other commodity] with payment delayed, is it correct for the vendor to agree on the price and then purchase the goods [which he did not have] from another place?' He said, 'There is no harm in it.'[239]

[Ja'far b. Muḥammad]: He was asked about a creditor who owes a debt from a debtor that falls due after a certain period. He comes to the

[237]According to the author of *al-Miṣbāḥ al-munīr*, *'īna* is lawful by common consent. It is the case of one man coming to another man to ask for a loan, which the latter does not desire to grant. Coveting profit, which is not to be obtained by a loan, he says, 'I will sell this garment to you for twelve dirhams upon credit, for payment at a certain time, and its value is ten [which you can really obtain by selling it for cash now]. Fayyūmī, *al-Miṣbāḥ al-munīr*, s.v. '-y-n; Lane, s.v. '-y-n; *Majma' al-baḥrayn*, s.v. '-y-n.

Schacht states that *bay' al-'īna* (sale on credit), a popular device (*ḥiyal*), which consisted of a double sale (*bay'atān fī bay'a*) with many variants, was an evasion of the prohibition of *ribā*. The Qur'ān prohibits *ribā*, but there was a demand for the giving and taking of interest in commercial life. Therefore, to satisfy this need, and at the same time to observe the letter of the Qur'ānic prohibition, a number of 'legal devices' (*ḥiyal*), such as *'īna* were developed by the jurists. An example of *'īna* or a double sale is if the prospective debtor sells a slave for a certain amount of cash to the prospective creditor. After obtaining the cash he immediately buys the slave back from him for a greater amount payable at a future date. The cash he took from the first sale amounts to a loan with the slave as security, and the difference between the two prices (the first and the second sale) represents the interest for the creditor. Schacht, *Introduction*, 79, 153.

[238]Addition in MS Q: 'An example of *al-'īna* is that [a moneylender] desires to obtain a greater amount [at a future date] than the sum he loaned. As this is not lawful he inserts [an offer] of some goods or cash [i.e. a second sale] in order to make the first sale [of loan] lawful between the two parties.' This textual addition is reported as glosses in four other MSS of Fyzee's edition.

[239]The marginal note on one manuscript explains it in the following way. The purchaser tells the vendor, 'Sell me ten *ṣā'* of corn for ten dinars on credit.' The vendor agrees on the price and makes the deal. But as he did not have the corn with him, he buys it from another place for eight or nine dinars in cash and delivers it to the purchaser.

debtor and says, 'Pay me so much now and I shall release you from the obligation to pay the balance or I shall give you more time to pay [the balance].' [The Imam] said, 'There is no harm if some kind of payment is made [by the debtor] so long as the capital amount recovered is not increased and there is no harm if a part of the debt is given up, or the time for payment extended.'

ON TRANSFER OF LIABILITY AND SURETYSHIP (*AL-ḤAWĀLA*[240] *WA 'L-KAFĀLA*)[241]

God says in the story of Yūsuf: *They said, approaching them, 'What is it that you are missing? They said, 'We are misisng the king's goblet. Whoever brings it shall have a camel-load, and I [said Joseph] for it am guarantor (zā'īm)* (12:71–2).[242] Now the word *za'īm* is the same as *kafīl*, and *ḥamīl*, and synonymous with it are *qabīl*, *ṣabīr* and *ḍamīn*.

Ja'far b. Muḥammad—his father—his ancestors: The Messenger of God spoke to a member of the Banū Hilāl[243] who asked him for help saying, 'O Messenger of God, verily I am the man who has assumed a guarantee [for the payment of a person] (*taḥammaltu bi-ḥamālat*[in]).'[244] The Messenger of God said, 'It is not permissible to ask for help except for three persons: (i)

[240] *Ḥawāla* means transfer of a claim, or of a debt, by shifting the responsibility from one person to another. *Majma' al-baḥrayn*, s.v. ḥ-w-l; Lane, s.v. ḥ-w-l. *ShEI*, s.v. Ḥawāla; Schacht, *Introduction*, 78, 106, 148–9, 158. *Ḥawāla* is also used as a financial term, in Islamic finance, see *EI*², s.v. Ḥawāla.

[241] *Kafāla* (*ḍamān* in all except the Ḥanafī *madhhab*) corresponds to some extent to the surety bond or bail in Western judicial systems. It means responsibility, guaranty or pledge. In Islamic law it means conjoining of one responsibility to another, i.e. conjoining one's own responsibility to that of another person, with respect to the right of suit. The jurists distinguish between two types of *kafāla*: *kafāla bi 'l-nafs*, that for which the surety (*kafīl*) is binding to secure the appearance of the debtor (*makfūl* or *aṣīl*) in court; and *kafāla bi 'l-māl*, by means of which the *kafīl* stands as a pledge to the creditor (*makfūl lahu*) that the obligation of the principal debtor (*makfūl*) will be fulfilled. Schacht, *Introduction*, 158; *EI*², s.v. Kafāla. See also Ibn Rushd, *Bidāya*, II, 290–5; trans. II, 355–62; Jazīrī, *al-Fiqh*, III, 210–19. It should be noted that Kulaynī transmitted one tradition from Imam al-Ṣādiq that discourages *kafāla*. This section on transfer of liability and suretyship is not to be found in the *Mishkāt*.

[242] Bell, *The Qurān*, I, 224; Arberry, *The Koran*, I, 262.

[243] An Arab tribe in the Najd. It did not accept Islam until after the Prophet's victory over the Hawāzin at the battle of Ḥunayn in 8/630. For details see *EI*², s.v. Hilāl, eponymous ancestor of the tribe of the Banū Hilāl.

[244] Gloss in MS Y: It is not permissible to ask for monetary help except for a person who has provided a guarantee for [another person for] a hundred dinars. The original debtor ran away, so [the creditor] took hold of the guarantor and the latter did not have any money. In such a case it is permissible for him to seek people's help until the debt of the *ḥamāla* is paid off.

the man who had given the guarantee [of money] until it is paid off; (ii) a person afflicted by a calamity; or (iii) a man who faces starvation.

Abū Jaʿfar Muḥammad b. ʿAlī: He said, 'A debtor owes a certain amount to a creditor. The debtor transfers his liability to another person. If, at the time of transfer, the creditor releases the debtor of liability, the debtor is free and the creditor cannot go against him; if not, then the creditor may pursue either of them, since the person to whom the liability was transferred had assumed the pledge.'[245]

[Abū Jaʿfar Muḥammad b. ʿAlī]: He said, 'Where the debtor owes a debt to another, and the debt is guaranteed (*kafala lahu bihi*) by two persons, the creditor is entitled to go against any of them he wishes. But if one of the sureties has transferred his liability, the creditor is not entitled to go against him provided that he has agreed to the transfer of liability.

'Where two persons stand surety (*takaffala*) for a person who owes a hundred dinars, each of them being responsible for the whole of the amount, and one of them is compelled to pay off the debt, the surety [who paid] is entitled to go against the co-surety for half the amount, or if he wishes he can go against the person for whom he guaranteed.

'Where a man obtains a surety, [known as the] *kafāla bi 'l-nafs* (that is, a surety to secure the appearance in court of the debtor, for whom judicial proceedings have been instituted), and later, the debtor obtains another surety [*kafāla bi 'l-nafs*], the liability [to secure the appearance of the debtor in court] extends to both of them.'

[Abū Jaʿfar Muḥammad b. ʿAlī]: He said, 'Where a man becomes a surety [*kafāla bi 'l-wajh = kafāla bi 'l-nafs*] for another for [a specified] period of time, and he fails [in his obligation] to secure the appearance of the debtor [in court] at the end of that period, the surety (*ḥammāla*) should be imprisoned,[246] unless he pays off [the debt of the debtor] as he had assumed the responsibility [for the appearance of the debtor in court].[247] Now if the debtor's whereabouts are known, the surety can go against him. But if the debtor's whereabouts are not known, it is necessary for the surety to secure his appearance [in court] except where the debtor is dead in which case his liability terminates.'

[245]It is called *kafāla bi 'l-māl. Kafi*, V, 98. An interesting gloss in MSS H and Y from Ibn Killis's *Mukhtaṣar al-muṣannaf* states: If the debtor transfers the liability to a bankrupt person and the creditor releases him from liability not knowing that the other person was insolvent he can go against the debtor because he was duped. Contrarily, if the creditor agrees to the transfer of liability knowing full well that the third party was insolvent, he cannot go against the debtor ...

[246]*Kāfī*, V, 99.

[247]Ibid., V, 99; conditions of validity of the surety are specified.

[Abū Ja'far Muḥammad b. 'Alī]: He said, 'Where a slave who is authorized (*al-'abd al-ma'dhūn*)[248] to trade for his master, becomes a surety for another, the slave does not become a surety unless his master agrees.'

'Alī: He said, 'No one can become a surety for a man who has committed a criminal offence (*ḥadd*).'[249]

REVOCATION OF LEGAL COMPETENCE AND BANKRUPTCY (*AL-ḤAJR WA 'L-TAFLĪS*)[250]

God says: *Prove [or test well the] orphans till they reach the marriageable age; then, if ye find them of sound judgement, deliver unto them their fortune* (4:6). Thus God has ordered that the orphans should be tested [to verify that they are of sound mind] till they attain puberty (*balaghū al-nikāḥ*, lit. until they attain marriagable age), and if the necessary understanding is found in them, their property should be delivered over to them. This proves that he who has not acquired proper understanding should not be given his property even if he has attained majority. This is because God has not allowed delivery of property without the presence of two conditions, namely puberty and understanding (*rushd*).[251]

Ja'far b. Muḥammad: He said with regard to the legal guardian (*walīy*) of an orphan, 'When the orphan reads the Qur'ān, attains puberty, and understanding is found in him, the guardian should give him his property. Now even if he attains puberty but does not possess that sound sense which makes him trustworthy (*'aql^un yūthaqu bihi*), the guardian should not hand over his property to him, but provide maintenance for him in all fairness (*bi 'l-ma'rūf*).'

[248] *Ma'dhūn* (as against *maḥjūr*) is applied to a slave who has received from his master permission, in general, for trade. *Ḥajr* implies the revocation of such permission. Schacht, *Introduction*, 126, 129; see also n. 250 below.

[249] For *ḥadd*, meaning punishment of certain acts that are forbidden by the Qur'ān, see *The Pillars of Islam*, I, 50, n. 122, and Chap. 17 in this volume.

[250] *Ḥajara 'alayhi*, infinitive *ḥajr*, means he (i.e. a *qāḍī*) prohibited him (a young or lightwitted person) from disposing of his property according to his own free will. Lane, s.v. ḥ-j-r. *Ḥajr* is, therefore, a technical term in Islamic law for the interdiction, or restriction of the capacity to dispose. A person on whom restriction is put is called *maḥjūr 'alayhi*. The following are subject to *ḥajr*: the minor, the insane, the irresponsible, especially the spendthrift, the bankrupt, the slave, and a person during his mortal illness. The question as to whether *ḥajr* is self-regulating or needs to be imposed by a *qāḍī*, is a subject of debate among the jurists. Schacht, *Introduction*, 125, 126, 129; *EI*[2], s.v. Ḥadjr. *Taflīs* means bankruptcy, insolvency, to be in the state of *iflās*, or to have become *muflis*. Lane, s.v. f-l-s. For more details see Ibn Rushd, *Bidāya*, II, 274–87; trans. II, 334–52; Jazīrī, *al-Fiqh*, II, 339–67.

[251] *Rushd* means maturity of intellect, and rectitude of actions, and good management of affairs. *Balagha rushdahu* means he attained to years of discretion. Lane, s.v. r-sh-d.

The Messenger of God: He said, 'May God have mercy on a faithful one who, when he speaks, gains [admiration] and when he is silent, remains in safety. I dislike palaver (*qīl wa-qāl*), and squandering money, and excess of questioning. So may God have mercy on a faithful one who earns [his livelihood] honestly, and spends it rightfully and turns towards good acts.' That which the Messenger of God has disapproved not only should be avoided, but should be prohibited. Accordingly, the man who acts thus, [should be prevented].

There is agreement among the Muslims that he who is bereft of reason (*al-maghlūbu ʿalā ʿaqlihi*) should be prevented from using his wealth, and [his property] should be protected on account of his ignorance. Even the rational person, when he acts wrongfully, should be prevented from doing that which is forbidden. God indeed has prohibited wastefulness and said: ... *and squander not (thy wealth) in wantonness. Lo! the squanderers were ever brothers of the devils* (17:26–7).

ʿAlī: He came to know of a wasteful act on the part of ʿAbd Allāh b. Jaʿfar.[252] So he took him by the hand and proceeded to [the Caliph] ʿUthmān[253] and said, 'Deprive him of his power to act [in money matters].' ʿUthmān said, 'How can I restrain a man whose partner is al-Zubayr b. al-ʿAwwām [from financial transactions]?'[254] [Nuʿmān said:][255] I do not know how ʿUthmān can escape from the truth by such a statement.[256]

ʿUthmān [b. ʿAffān]: Once he passed by a piece of swampy land which

[252]ʿAbd Allāh b. Jaʿfar b. Abī Ṭālib, the nephew of the caliph ʿAlī, was believed to have been born in Abyssinia where his parents, after their conversion to Islam, had migrated with other Muslims. He is known for his great generosity, and often called *baḥr al-jūd* (the ocean of generosity). After the death of his father Jaʿfar, his mother Asmāʾ b. ʿUmays was married to Abū Bakr, hence Muḥammad b. Abī Bakr was ʿAbd Allāh's half brother. Later on ʿAlī married Asmāʾ. Balādhurī, *Ansāb al-ashrāf* (ed. al-Azem), II, 43–62 and passim; the scattered reports about ʿAbd Allāh b. Jaʿfar are not only interesting but show a stark difference of character between him and his cousins, the Imams of the Ḥusaynī line. *EI*[2], s.v. ʿAbd Allāh b. D̲jaʿfar.

[253]This incident probably happened during the caliphate of ʿUthmān, hence ʿAlī had to take him to the caliph. For ʿUthmān, see *The Pillars of Islam*, I, 23, n. 19. The report suggests that ʿAbd Allāh b. Jaʿfar had some joint business venture with Zubayr.

[254]For Zubayr see *The Pillars of Islam*, I, 23, n. 18.

[255]As in MS Q. In the edited text the following sentence is a continuation of ʿUthmān's reply, but as such it makes no sense. Fyzee's translation of *wa-mā adrī li-hādhā 'l-qawli makhraj*[an] *min al-ḥaqq* (Furthermore, I have no proof of his having done wrong) is incorrect.

[256]Gloss in MSS H and Y states: *And let not thy hand be chained to thy neck [i.e. be niggardly] nor spread it wide open, lest thou sit down rebuked, impoverished* [Qurʾān 17:29]. This Qurʾānic rule should be literally applied both to a spendthrift and a niggard; the former should be restricted in his power to act in financial matters, and the latter should be obliged to spend on himself and his family a certain amount that is commonly held as equitable.

was purchased by 'Abd Allāh b. Ja'far for sixty thousand [dirhams] and he said, '[This land] does not even please me as much as my sandal!' Then he met 'Alī and said, 'Why do you not prevent your nephew and deny him access [to his wealth] by declaring him legally incompetent? He has purchased this swamp for sixty thousand, and it does not even please me as much as my sandal.'

Now here 'Uthmān asks 'Alī to stop 'Abd Allāh, and declare him legally incompetent, but when the *waṣī* ['Alī] had come to ask him for that action, he refused and adduced the reason that Zubayr was 'Abd Allāh's partner [in business]. Now the partnership of Zubayr with 'Abd Allāh does not entitle him [the caliph 'Uthmān] to neglect his legal obligations, and this is clear to every one who ponders over the question.

'Alī: He said, 'When a man becomes bankrupt, and possesses the property of another, the owner of the property is entitled to it.'[257]

Ja'far b. Muḥammad: He was asked about a group of people who were creditors of a man. One of the creditors obtained possession of some goods of the debtor, what is his right? He said, 'The creditors may choose to give him his portion of the goods from the goods in his possession, and take the rest; or give him the whole of the goods he had obtained.' It was said to him, 'Supposing that they accept the goods as belonging to the holder thereof, and there is profit or loss, what then?' [The Imam] said, 'The profit (*ribḥ*) or loss (*waḍī'a*) goes to the debtor and he is responsible for the balance of the debt.'[258]

[Ja'far b. Muḥammad]: He was asked about a man who became indebted and was made bankrupt by his creditors (*ghuramā'* pl. of *gharīm*). After the bankruptcy, a man lent him money as *qirāḍ* (an advance, with the agreement to share profits, the loss if any falling on the capital),[259]

[257]Abū Hurayra reported the Prophet saying, 'If anyone becomes insolvent and a creditor finds his very property with him, he is more entitled to it than anyone else.' *Mishkāt*, II, 108, 111; Robson, I, 621, 623; transmitted by Bukhārī, Muslim, and al-Shāfi'ī.

[258]Cf. *Mishkāt*, II, 112; Robson, I, 624.

[259]*Qirāḍ* and *muqāraḍa*, according to the Mālikī and Shāfi'ī schools, are synonymous with *muḍāraba* (sleeping partnership). It is like a business partnership—treated by Nu'mān under *sharika* (see n. 320 below in this chapter)—wherein an investor (*rabb* or *ṣāḥib al-māl*) entrusts his capital to an agent (*muḍārib*, *'āmil*) who trades with it and shares with the investor a predetermined proportion of the profits. Losses incurred in such a venture are borne by the investor. Lane, s.v. q-r-ḍ; Ibn Rushd, *Bidāya*, II, 232–9; trans. II, 284–92; *EI*², s.v. Muḍāraba; Schacht, *Introduction*, 119, 156–7. Alwi, 'Al-Muḍārabah'; he states that *muḍāraba*, *al-qirāḍ*, *al-muzāra'a*, and *al-musāqāt* were developed in Arabia before the advent of Islam. The main function of Islamic law was to reinstate their applicability in accordance with the jurisprudential principles. These institutions, he concludes, were modified by the succeeding generations, after the Prophet, to keep pace with changing social needs and economic necessity.

and either there is profit or loss. What is the position? [The Imam] said, 'Those who advanced money to the bankrupt after the bankruptcy have priority over the *muqāriḍ* (the man who lent money for profit) and the earlier creditors; and the *muqāriḍ* has precedence over creditors who lent moneys before the bankruptcy. But if the merchant has not become bankrupt, and still trades on his own but [in the meanwhile] he has become indigent, and says, "These goods are intact and belong to so-and-so, and those to so-and-so;" such statements should be verified; but at any rate the man who lent property as *qirāḍ* has priority of claim.'

[Ja'far b. Muḥammad]: He said, 'When the creditors stand up against a bankrupt, he should begin to pay from his own money, first the claims of those who had served him, or workmen who had been employed by him; or dues for the beasts of burden, according to their services, then the creditors are entitled equally after them.'

[Ja'far b. Muḥammad]: He said, 'A man buys property (*matā'*) or a slave or slave girl, and gives the property to charity or emancipates the slave or the slave girl. When the vendor makes his claim, and finds that the debtor has no means [to pay for his purchase], both the emancipation and the gifts to charity are void, and the vendor is entitled to the price of the slave or goods sold by him and if there is an excess in the price after payment of the debt the slave may be emancipated accordingly, or, the property given to charity from the excess.'

[Ja'far b. Muḥammad]: He was told that a patron (*mawlā*) of 'Īsā b. Mūsā died, and left many debts unpaid and many slaves (*ghilmān*) which were security for his debts. Now before his death, he emancipated the slaves; so 'Īsā b. Mūsā asked Ibn Shubruma[260] and Ibn Abī Laylā[261] regarding this question. Ibn Shubruma said, 'You should require of the slaves that they should labour to earn the means of releasing themselves, and then pay that money to the creditors, because the deceased had emancipated the slaves at his death.' Ibn Abī Laylā [on the other hand] said, 'I am of the opinion that you should sell the slaves and give the proceeds to the creditors, for he had no right to emancipate them while he was indebted.' 'Īsā b. Mūsā said, 'By whose [legal] opinion should I issue the order?'[262] They said, 'According to the opinion of Ibn Abī Laylā, as he was on the right way in this case.' Consequently 'Īsā b. Mūsā sold the slaves and paid

[260]Ibn Shubruma was associated with the 'Abbāsid caliph al-Manṣūr. Yāqūt, *Mu'jam al-udabā'*, IV, 1542; Maqrīzī, *Kitāb al-muqaffā*, IV, 201; *Tāj al-'arūs*, s.v. sh-b-r-m.

[261]Ibn Abī Laylā; see Mufīd, *al-Ikhtiṣāṣ*, 202–3; *The Pillars of Islam*, I, 113, n. 323.

[262]Fyzee's edited text is both corrupt and incorrect. I have followed MS Q which reads: *'an ra'yi ayyihimā uṣdiru? Qīla: 'an ra'yi Abī Laylā, wa-kāna lahu fī dhālika huda*^{n}.

the debt. [The Imam] said, 'By God, the truth is as stated by Ibn Abī Laylā.' He then gave a long explanation [of the case].

[Ja'far b. Muḥammad]: He was asked about a man who was in debt but was able to sustain himself and was doing business, buying and selling. He made a charitable gift to his sons and to others. Is it legal for him to do so? [The Imam] said, 'The charity is legal; all his other acts like emancipation, buying, and selling are valid. Now, if the donee claims and states that the donor was buying and selling and was able to sustain himself on the day he made the charitable gift; then he will be asked to prove such an allegation. But if he makes no such claim, he will not be asked and the creditors will be asked for proof that on the particular day [he made the gifts], he was a bankrupt and was not buying or selling. If they prove such a state of affairs, well and good; otherwise they will have no claim.'

[Ja'far b. Muḥammad]: He said, 'Unless the creditors agree, a man who is heavily indebted cannot emancipate a slave, nor can he make a charitable or other gift, regardless of whether or not his debts are due in short or long period. If the man says, "This is my slave girl and my natural daughter," intending thereby that she shall not be sold, his statement shall not be deemed credible unless the fact is well known. Nevertheless his buying and selling is lawful.'

[Ja'far b. Muḥammad]: He said, 'A man is indebted but possesses goods as well as houses. He sells them secretly without informing his creditors, and then he disappears or dies. Now the purchaser either knows that the seller was indebted, or does not know it. When the vendor disappears, the creditors go against the purchaser. The purchaser says, "The debtor sold the property to pay off your debt."'

[The Imam] said, 'If, on the day of sale, the merchant was able to sustain himself and was not a declared bankrupt, and was not stopped from doing business and the sale was regular, there being no suspicion of duress in it, and the sale was proved by honest witnesses, the sale is valid. Similarly, so long as he is not bankrupt, such an admission from the debtor [that he intended to pay off the debt] shall be accepted. But if he is declared bankrupt, and is challenged by the creditors, such a statement will not be accepted without clear proof.'

[The Imam] was asked about the meaning of the word *taflīs* (proclaiming a man bankrupt). He said, 'This occurs when a man is prohibited from using and disposing of his property according to his own free will and is prevented from trading. This can only be done by the state (*sulṭān*).'

[Ja'far b. Muḥammad]: He said, 'A bankrupt person cannot be prevented from marrying. His wife is not entitled to stop him from marrying another woman by reason of her [unpaid] *mahr* (dower).[263] She is merely one of his creditors. None of his other acts, like the payment of debts, can be repudiated while he is able to sustain himself.'

'Alī: He said, 'A destitute person cannot be imprisoned. God says: *And if the debtor be in straitened circumstances, then [let there be] postponement to (the time of) ease* (2:280).[264] So the man who proves his straitened circumstances should be free from imprisonment.[265] If the debtor has received some payment for debts due to him, then at the suit of his opponents, he will have to prove his poverty. But if some part of moneys due to him are not recovered, like money [to be paid for] crime, or as surety, or on transfer of liability, or dower (*ṣadāq*)[266] of his wife, then the debtor will be allowed to prove this by a statement on oath, provided no property is found with him, and another claim is not proved against him.'

TILLING LAND AND TENDING PALM TREES IN RETURN FOR SOME OF THE PRODUCE (*AL-MUZĀRA'A*[267] *WA 'L-MUSĀQĀT*)[268]

Ja'far b. Muḥammad: He was asked about *muzāra'a* and he said, 'The cost belongs to you and the land to the owner. Whatever harvest God

[263] See Chap. 10, section on dower.

[264] Abū Hurayra said that the Prophet told of a man who used to make loans and say to his servant, 'When you come to one who is in straitened circumstances forgive him, for perhaps God may forgive us.' *Mishkāt*, II, 108; Robson, I, 621; transmitted by Bukhārī and Muslim. Several other traditions are reported.

[265] All the jurists agree that when a debtor claims insolvency, the truth of which is not known, he is to be imprisoned until his claim is verified or the creditors acknowledge his insolvency. Ibn Rushd, *Bidāya*, II, 287; trans. II, 357.

[266] See Chap. 10, section on dower.

[267] *Muzāra'a* means making a contract with another, for labour upon land (to till and saw and cultivate) for a share of its produce, the seed being from the owner of the land. Lane, s.v. z-r-'; Jazīrī, *al-Fiqh*, III, 5–25; Schacht, *Introduction*, 119, 155, 156; *EI*², s.v. Muzāra'a. It should be noted that Mālik validated *musāqāt*, basing his validation on the customary practices of Medina and the Prophet's *sunna*, but rejected *muzāra'a*, considering it an aleatory transaction (*bay' al-gharar*), which involves uncertainty and sale of future values. Abū Ḥanīfa also rejected it, however the majority of the jurists regard it permissible and legal. For a recent study see Haque, *Landlord*. See also n. 259 above in this chapter.

[268] *Musāqāt*, lit. giving to drink, refers to a lease of fruit trees, or an orchard, or the employment of a man to manage the cultivating and watering of palm trees or grapevines or fruit trees on the condition of his having a certain share of their produce. Lane, s.v. s-q-y; Ibn Rushd, *Bidāya*, II, 240–6; trans. II, 293–300; Jazīrī, *al-Fiqh*, III, 27–39; Schacht, *Introduction*, 119, 155, 156. The definition of *musāqāt* in *EI*², (s.v. Musāḳāt) as 'a lease of a plantation for one crop period' is incorrect. It seems that the author of the article did not consult the older classical sources. See also n. 259 above in this chapter.

bestows is divided into two halves,[269] and that is how the Messenger of God accepted [the produce of] of Khaybar[270] when the people of Khaybar came to him. He had given them the land to cultivate on the condition that they would take half the produce.'[271]

[Ja'far b. Muḥammad]: He said, 'In such contracts (*muzāra'a*) there is no harm if the proportion fixed is for one-third, one-fourth, one-fifth, or a greater or lesser proportion of the harvest than that, provided the owner of the land does not take from the tiller anything other than what grows on the land.[272] It is not proper [for the landowner] to share [the expenses for] the seed [that is sown][273] or the cattle [with the tiller], but the latter should say to the owner, "I shall cultivate your land and give you so much from the produce."'

[Ja'far b. Muḥammad]: He said, 'There is no harm in letting out one's land for dirhams or dinars for a fixed period, for agricultural purposes.[274] But no good comes where wheat is taken as rent for land where wheat is sown.'[275]

[Ja'far b. Muḥammad]: He said, 'There is no harm if a man gives another his land to till on condition that the tiller pays the land tax (*kharāj*)[276] on it and gives a specific amount to him.[277] If the land contains trees and palms, making a contract is not lawful until the fruit begins to ripen, unless the land contains some vegetables, fresh ripe dates and fruit or some other [harvest] which can be sold.'

[Ja'far b. Muḥammad]: He was asked about *musāqāt* (tending palm trees in return for some of the produce). He said, 'It means that the owner

[269]Any agreement that disregards the actual harvest is invalid because such an agreement cannot guarantee beforehand what a particular piece of land will produce. See *Mishkāt*, II, 127–8; Robson, I, 635–6.

[270]Khaybar, see *The Pillars of Islam*, I, 471, n. 180. The proponents of the pro-*muzāra'a* jurists cite this *ḥadīth* to justify their claim that sharecropping (*muzāra'a*) is legal. Haque, *Landlord*, 51–106.

[271]"Abd Allāh b. 'Umar said that the Prophet handed over to the Jews of Khaybar the palm trees and the land on condition that they should employ whatever equipments belonged to them in working on them and that he should have half the produce.' *Mishkāt*, II, 127–9; Robson I, 635–6; transmitted by Bukhārī and Muslim; *Kāfī*, V, 270; Ṭūsī, *Tahdhīb al-aḥkām*, VII, 193–4, 198.

[272]It is reported that all of the Emigrant families used to cultivate the land either for a third or a quarter of the produce. *Mishkāt*, II, 129; Robson I, 636; *Kāfī*, V, 271; Ṭūsī, *Tahdhīb al-aḥkām*, VII, 194.

[273]In *muzāra'a* contracts, the seed is generally provided by the landowner.

[274]*Mishkāt*, II, 127; Robson, I, 635; *Kāfī*, V, 268.

[275]This is prohibited according to Ja'far al-Ṣādiq because there is no guarantee beforehand of the produce. *Kāfī*, V, 268. Ṭūsī, *Tahdhīb al-aḥkām*, VII, 194–5.

[276]*Kharāj*, see *The Pillars of Islam*, I, 443, n. 75.

[277]*Kāfī*, V, 269.

of a piece of land containing trees or palms says to another, "Give water to this land, and cause it to thrive and cultivate it, and out of the harvest you shall have such an amount." Whatever they agree to is permissible.'

[Ja'far b. Muḥammad]: He was asked about a man who gave his barren land to be cultivated on the condition that the cultivator would take the harvest for a specified number of years.[278] [The Imam] said, 'This is permissible. There is no harm if the owner allows his serf tenants (*'ulūj*)[279] and beasts to remain on the land in accordance with their mutual agreement. This [also] is permissible.'

[Ja'far b. Muḥammad]: He was asked about a man who cultivated the land of another and said, 'He allowed me to cultivate the land on such and such conditions,' but the owner of the land denied his consent. [The Imam] said, 'The statement made by the owner of the land on oath shall prevail. But if at the time of cultivation, the owner knew of it and this [fact] is clearly established, then the declaration of the cultivator on oath that he had the *muzāra'a* contract shall hold sway. [Failing this], the benefit of doubt is given [to the landowner] and the cultivator shall pay a proper rent for the land and the harvest shall not be uprooted.'[280]

[Ja'far b. Muḥammad]: He was asked about a man who ploughs a piece of land, and another tells him, 'Take from me one-half the seed [to sow] and one-half of your cost, and make me a partner [on condition that we shall share the produce equally].' [The Imam] said, 'If they agree on such terms, then it is permissible.'[281]

CONTRACTS OF SERVICE
(*AL-IJĀRĀT*)[282]

In the story of Moses, God says: *Then he turned aside into a shade, till His saying: that thou hirest thyself to me for [the term of] eight pilgrimages* (28:24–7).[283]

[278]Ibid., V, 272; Ṭūsī, *Tahdhīb al-aḥkām*, VII, 201–2.

[279]*'Ilj* pl. *'ulūj* means a strong, sturdy, coarse man. It also means a strong, bulky non-Muslim man of non-Arab origin, or simply an unbeliever. Lane, s.v. '-l-j. *Kāfī*, V, 271, 272, 273; also used for a *dhimmī* (non-Muslim), or serf tenant.

[280]*Mishkāt*, II, 128; Robson, I, 636. See also *Kāfī*, V, 302, for a different version but with the same intent.

[281]*Kāfī*, V, 272–3.

[282]*Ijāra* pl. *ijārāt* means recompense, hire, lease, or wages from one man to another for work, and is synonymous with *kirā'* (rent for a house and the like). Lane, s.v. a-j-r. Ṭūsī, *Tahdhīb al-aḥkām*, VII, 209 ff.; Ibn Rushd, *Bidāya*, II, 214–29; trans. II, 264–81; Jazīrī, *al-Fiqh*, III, 94 ff.; Schacht, *Introduction*, 21, 22, 126, 134, 154f., 191; *EI*[2], s.v. Īdjār, Idjāra.

[283]*Mishkāt*, II, 132; Robson, I, 638.

Ja'far b. Muḥammad—his father—his ancestors: The Messenger of God said, 'Accursed is the man who wrongs a hired worker (*ajīr*) in regard to his wages!'[284] Thus it is lawful for a man to hire a man or a woman or a beast or a slave or a slave girl for a specific job.

The Messenger of God: He contracted the marriage of a woman to one of his Companions on the understanding that he would teach her a chapter of the Qur'ān. We shall discuss the meaning of this in the chapter (*kitāb*) on marriage,[285] if God wills.

[The Messenger of God]: He was asked about a man who used incantations on a person who was bitten by a serpent by chanting (*raqā bi*) a *sūra* of the Qur'ān. The man recovered and gave a compensation for the *ruqya*[286] [performance of the exorcism] and [the Messenger of God] permitted it.[287]

Ja'far b. Muḥammad: He permitted the taking of compensation for giving instruction in a craft which is lawful.

[Ja'far b. Muḥammad]: He said that there is no harm if the muezzin takes remuneration for the *adhān* (call to prayer) from the Public Treasury (*bayt al-māl*), but he cannot do so from his [own] congregation.[288]

[Ja'far b. Muḥammad]: A man comes to another and asks him whether he may purchase for him a piece of land or a house or a slave or a beast or the like for a certain remuneration (*ju'l*).[289] [The Imam] said, 'There is no harm in it.'

[Ja'far b. Muḥammad]: He was asked about a man who is entrusted

[284]The Messenger of God said, 'There are three whose adversary I shall be on the Day of Resurrection: A man who gave a promise in my name then acted faithlessly; a man who sold a free man and enjoyed the price he received; and a man who hired a servant and after receiving full service from him did not pay his wages.' *Mishkāt*, II, 130; Robson, I, 637; transmitted by Bukhārī.

[285]See Chap. 10 on Marriage.

[286]*Ruqya* means a charm, or spell, either uttered or written, by which a person having an evil affliction, such as a fever, epilepsy, etc., is cured. When the charm is in any language other than Arabic, and one does not know what is in it, it is disapproved, lest it involves infidelity. The Qur'ānic verses and other forms of prayer are permitted. For more details see *EI*², s.v. Ruḳya, where recent works in Western languages are cited; Chap. 5, section dealing with amulets and charms.

[287]For similar traditions see *Mishkāt*, II, 131; Robson, I, 637; one of the two traditions is transmitted by Bukhārī.

[288]See *The Pillars of Islam*, I, 184, n. 85. Ibn Rushd, *Bidāya*, II, 217; trans. II, 268; those who forbid remuneration justify their case by citing a tradition that forbids compensation, while those who allow it support their case by stating that giving a call to prayer is not an obligatory act.

[289]It also means a certain reward for a person who brings back a fugitive slave from a distance of more than three days' journey. Schacht, *Introduction*, 159.

with certain goods for sale and is told, 'Sell it, and if you obtain anything over such and such a price the excess is yours.' [The Imam] said, 'There was no objection to it.'

[Ja'far b. Muḥammad]: He said, 'If a man who is hired to do a certain thing, spoils or destroys it, he will be held responsible for it.' [The Imam] added, 'A man hired a porter (*ḥammāl*) to carry a large long-necked bottle filled with oil, and the porter broke the bottle. That man brought the porter to 'Alī, the Commander of the Faithful, and 'Alī held him responsible. It was 'Alī's practice to hold the labourer (or the hireling *ajīr*) responsible [for the loss or damage].'[290]

[Ja'far b. Muḥammad]: He was asked about a porter who is hired to carry oil but spills or loses it. [The Imam] replied, 'If the hirer so wishes, the porter can be punished or arrested. If the porter says that he had been robbed or waylaid, his statement cannot be accepted without proof.'[291]

[Ja'far b. Muḥammad]: He was asked about a tenant who rents a house for a certain amount, and later lets it out for a higher amount. [The Imam] replied, 'No [this is not possible], unless he has added to the premises,[292] or lets out a part of the house for the same [amount of] rent and stays in the remaining part.'[293]

[Ja'far b. Muḥammad]: He was asked about a man who rents a house with trees in it and stipulates that he will take the fruit thereof. [The Imam] said, 'There is no objection to it.'

[Ja'far b. Muḥammad]: He said, 'It is lawful to rent a house by offering goods in return [and not money], or to offer residence in one house in exchange for another.'

[Ja'far b. Muḥammad]: He was asked about the following case: A man agreed to rent a house on a monthly basis on the condition that he would pay a month's rent even if he stayed one day in it. [The Imam] said, 'This is lawful, and the lessee may rent the house for the rest of the month. If a dispute arises about the rent, let the rent be calculated for each day.'

[Ja'far b. Muḥammad]: He said, 'When a man rents a house and finds it in a dilapidated condition or if it gets destroyed, the owner cannot be compelled to repair it. The tenant has a choice. He may stay if he wishes or he may go, and he shall be responsible for the number of days he has stayed.'

[Ja'far b. Muḥammad]: He said, 'The lessee has no right to introduce into the premises things harmful to the house or the neighbours. If he has

[290]For similar traditions cf. *Kāfī*, V, 244–6.

[291]Cf. Ibid., V, 246.

[292]The Arabic is *illā an yuḥditha fīhā shay'an*. It could also mean 'unless he has made improvements in it.'

[293]Cf. *Kāfī*, V, 275, 276. This rule does not apply to land.

rented a house and not stated what he is going to do, the owner has no right to stop the lessee from any occupation in it so long as it is not harmful to the property. The same rule applies to shops (*ḥawānīt* pl. of *ḥānūt*).'

[Ja'far b. Muḥammad]: He was asked about two lessors disagreeing as to rent, either before or after [staying in the house]. He said, 'The final word is with the owner, and both the lessors may either commit to one another by oath [to pay the rent], or both of them may agree together to annul [the contract].'

[Ja'far b. Muḥammad]: He was asked about a dweller in a certain house. The owner of the house says that he rented the house to the dweller,[294] but the dweller in the house says, 'You gave me permission to stay without paying rent.' Neither of them has proof for their statements. [The Imam] said, 'The word of the owner of the house, on oath will prevail; and he is also entitled to the rent. If either party has proof, such proof is preferable.'

[Ja'far b. Muḥammad]: He said, 'Undivided property (*mushā'*)[295] can be rented.'

[Ja'far b. Muḥammad]: He was asked: A man rented a house from another. He alleges that the owner of the house had directed him to repair the house, and the lessee had spent some money on it. This the owner of the house denies. [The Imam] said, 'The claimant shall offer proof [for his statement], and the owner will also make a statement on oath. The lessee is then entitled to undo whatever [he added to the house] and take it away [with him].'

[Ja'far b. Muḥammad]: He was asked: A man hired a house which contained a lot of goods belonging to the owner, on condition that the owner would transfer them; but the owner was too lazy to move them. [The Imam] said, 'The owner is entitled to rent only for that part of the house which was actually occupied by the tenant.'

[Ja'far b. Muḥammad]: He said, 'When a tenant does something in the house without the owner's permission, and such action causes loss, the tenant is responsible for it. But if he acts only as other residents do, he is not responsible.'

[Ja'far b. Muḥammad]: He said, 'When a man hires an animal or a ship to carry a specific thing to a specified destination, and the animal dies

[294]The edited text is incorrect, and both the sentences should be corrected to read (as MS Q): *Akraytuhā iyyāhu. Wa-yaqūlu 'l-sākinu, 'Askantanī bi-lā kirā'in.'*

[295]*Mushā'* means a house or land that is shared in common with joint ownership. It is so called because it is not separated or divided. *Qāmūs*, s.v. sh-y-'; *Tāj al-'arūs*, s.v. sh-y-'; Lane, s.v. sh-y-'; Schacht, *Introduction*, 138; *EI*[2], s.v. Mushā'. Unfortunately, the article is based on modern sources. The author's assertion that the word *mushā'* does not appear in classical Arabic dictionaries is incorrect.

or the ship is destroyed, the contract of hiring becomes void. If such an eventuality takes place after part of the way has been traversed, the payment is to be made proportionately to the distance covered. But if the contract is merely to carry the goods, without specific mention of an animal or a ship, full charges are to be paid up on completion of the task.'

[Ja'far b. Muḥammad]: He said, 'If a man hires an animal for a month to use it for a mill, or perform some other task, or for travelling, and nothing has been specified regarding the service of the animal at a mill, or the load he will bear, or the distance he will travel, the contract of hiring is valid. It is the hirer's duty to use it in accordance with common usage; and if he commits excesses against it [and causes harm to it], he is responsible. The same rule applies to a ship.'

[Ja'far b. Muḥammad]: He said, 'If a man hires a beast of burden or a ship, and the hirer carries wine or pigs or something which God has declared to be unlawful, no responsibility attaches to the owner of the beast [or ship]. But if there was an agreement between the owner and the hirer to carry such goods, the contract is void and the hire for it is unlawful.'

[Ja'far b. Muḥammad]: He was asked about the following case: A man hires a beast or a ship on the condition that it would take him to a particular place on a particular day; and if he was unable to do so on that particular day, the hire would be less than the stipulated one. [The Imam] said, 'A fixed hire is not lawful in such cases; the hirer will be responsible for a proportionate amount only.'[296]

'Alī: A man brought the following case to him: A man had hired an animal to take him to a specified destination; the hirer went beyond the place and the animal perished. 'Alī held the hirer responsible for the price of the animal, and did not award any hire for the extra labour.[297]

Ja'far b. Muḥammad said, 'If the animal does not perish, but the hirer has exceeded the limits [of time] stipulated [in the contract], then the owner of the animal has an option. He may hold the hirer responsible for any loss [of revenue] for the extra period, or he may take the hire of the extra period. The same rule applies when the load on the animal is exceeded beyond the contractual limits.'

[Ja'far b. Muḥammad]: He said, 'A man hires a beast of burden for one day, but detains it for several days more. The owner of the beast has an option. He may either obtain damages for the loss suffered by him or claim hire proportionately.'[298]

[296]For a similar case see *Kāfī*, V, 295–6.

[297]Ibid., V, 294, 295.

[298]Kulaynī narrates a long and interesting tradition where a man in Kūfa hired a mule for going to Qaṣr Ibn Hubayra [a location on the river, Yāqūt, s.v. Qaṣr Ibn Hubayra] and

[Ja'far b. Muḥammad]: He said, 'The parties to a hiring contract differ. The hirer says that the contract was for [carriage to] a certain place, and the owner of the beast claims that it was for another place. Now if one of those two places is farther than the other and involves greater hardship, the burden of proof is on the hirer for what he claims. But if the two places are equidistant—and yet each party sticks to the place he affirms—and the dispute arises before the riding has commenced or when only a small part of the distance has been covered, or before the owner has been paid his hire, then the word of the owner of the beast will be believed and the hirer will be obliged to pay the proper rent paid by people in such cases. Now if no one has ridden, and no payment has been made, let the two take oaths and annul [the contract]. The person who avoids the oath will be bound by the statement of the other party. This occurs when there is no positive proof; but in cases where such proof exists, it is final.'

[Ja'far b. Muḥammad]: He was asked about a hirer who [makes a contract] for going to Iraq, Khurāsān,[299] Africa, Spain, or the like, and names the country but not the exact place where he wishes to go. [The Imam] said, 'The carrier should take him to the best known of the places in that country, such as Baghdad in Iraq or al-Qayrawān[300] in Africa.'

RULES CONCERNING CRAFTSMEN (*AḤKĀM AL-ṢUNNĀ'*)

Ja'far b. Muḥammad—his father—his ancestors: They said, 'Craftsmen (*ṣunnā'*) are responsible for the loss brought about by them, whether

---

return in search of his debtor. When he reached there he was told that he went to … . He followed him to Baghdad and returned after 15 days … he returned the mule to its owner and gave him 15 dirhams to please him, but the owner refused and they agreed to litigate their case before Abū Ḥanīfa … Abū Ḥanīfa asked the man who had hired the mule, 'What did you do with the mule?' The man replied, 'I returned it to the owner in good condition.' The owner said, 'Yes, but after 15 days.' Abū Ḥanīfa said to him, 'What do you want from the man?' He replied, 'The hire of my mule as he retained it for 15 days.' Abū Ḥanīfa said, 'I do not think that you have the right to demand it, because he hired it for going to Qaṣr Ibn Hubayra. He then violated the agreement and rode to Baghdad. He, therefore, is responsible for the price of the mule and the hire is cancelled.' … . The same year the man who had hired the mule went on a pilgrimage and informed Imam al-Ṣādiq about Abū Ḥanīfa's decision and the Imam exclaimed, 'Because of such [an unjust] decision the heavens might withhold its water [blessing] and the earth might keep back its bounty. You should pay the hire from Kūfa to Baghdad and back …' *Kāfī*, V, 296–7.

[299] Khurāsān, see *The Pillars of Islam*, I, 89, n. 240.

[300] It was founded by the Arab Muslim conquerors and is located in central Tunisia. *EI*[2], s.v. al-Ḳayrawān.

intentionally or by mistake, when they work for wages. If however they assert that they did not work for wages and the owners of the goods [deny this] and say, "No, they worked for wages," the owners of the goods will be believed upon their making a statement on oath, and it is the right of the craftsmen to disprove their liability by clear proof.'[301]

[Ja'far b. Muḥammad]: He was asked about a craftsman who accepts a certain work [for a certain price] and thereafter agrees to a reduction in the price. [The Imam] said, 'If the craftsman has laboured at it to some extent, or made plans concerning it, or cut the cloth [being a tailor], or done some work on it, then he is entitled to the higher price; otherwise claiming the higher rate is not good.'

[Ja'far b. Muḥammad]: He was asked about a miller (*ṭaḥḥān*) to whom wheat is sent [for being ground] on the condition that he would deliver a certain amount of flour more than the actual weight of the wheat. He said, 'This is not a good practice; it is the miller's right to receive wages and to deliver the exact weight.'

[Abū Ja'far Muḥammad b. 'Alī][302]—his ancestors: The Messenger of God scarified himself and gave the cupper (*ḥajjām*)[303] his wages. The cupper was a slave who asked his master if he could retain the money [for himself] and the master allowed him.[304]

Abū Ja'far Muḥammad b. 'Alī was asked about the earnings of a cupper. He said, 'I wish that the progeny of Muḥammad had [a share of it],'[305] and he named a large number of people [from Muḥammad's progeny who scarified themselves].

[301]Cf. *Kāfī*, V, 243–5.

[302]According to MS Q, which states: *Wa-ruwīnā 'an abīhi*. The edited text has: *wa-'anhu*.

[303]*Ḥajjām*, also called *maṣṣāṣ* (lit. one who is in the habit of sucking), performs the operation called *ḥajm*, cupping. It is a technique for bloodletting used in traditional Chinese medicine for certain health conditions. Glass or bamboo cups are placed on the skin with suction, which is believed to influence the flow of energy and blood in the body. It is used to treat colds, lung infections, problems in the internal organs, and muscle and joint pain. To create vacuum, a burning cotton ball is placed in an upside down cup. When the oxygen in the cup is burned off, the cup is placed directly on the skin, where it is held in place by a strong suction. Often, the skin inside the cup rises. *Ḥijāma* is the craft of the cupper as well as the operation itself. Lane, s.v. ḥ-j-m; Fleishman, *Acupuncture*, s.v. Cupping; Williams, *Complete Illustrated Guide to Chinese Medicine*, s.v. Cupping; *Gale Encycopedia*, s.v. Cupping.

[304]Ibn 'Abbās reported that the Prophet had himself cupped and gave the cupper his wages. *Mishkāt*, II, 130; Robson, I, 637; transmitted by Bukhārī and Muslim. Contrarily, a tradition transmitted by Muslim states that the earnings of a cupper are impure. *Mishkāt*, II, 74; Robson, I, 593. Ibn Qayyim, *al-Ṭibb al-nabawī*, 65–74; the cupper's name was Abū Ṭayba and his masters had relaxed their imposition on him so that he could retain his wages. Ibn Qayyim has listed the benefits of cupping.

[305]The Imam implies that the profession is honourable as he wishes that they had a share of it.

Ja'far b. Muḥammad: On one occasion, fresh dates were brought to him while a group of his companions were with him, and among them Farqad, the Cupper. So, [the Imam] invited the party [to eat the dates], and all came near except Farqad. So [the Imam] said, 'O my little son! What prevents you from joining [us]?' He said, 'May I be thy ransom! I am a cupper.' So [the Imam] summoned a slave girl who came with water and he directed Farqad to wash his hands. Then he asked Farqad to come near and seated him next to himself, and said, 'Eat.' When Farqad finished eating, he said, 'May I be thy ransom! I am a cupper, and sometimes people speak derisively of my profession, and say that my earnings are unlawful.' Abū 'Abd Allāh [the Imam] replied, 'What they say is not correct. Eat from what you earn, and give in charity, and go to the pilgrimage, and marry!'[306]

Abū Ja'far: He said, 'If a man goes to another and says, "Look at these dinars and dirhams, are they of good quality?" or he says, "Look at this cloth. Will it be sufficient for me?" Such a person may be a tailor or money changer, and he says, "These coins are good, or the cloth is sufficient." Now the man finds that the statements [of the money changer and the tailor] are not correct. If the man was misled and fraud was intended and proved against the referee, the latter should be disciplined and fined. But if it was an opinion expressed [by the referee] to the best of his judgement, he is not culpable.'

[Abū Ja'far]: He said, 'A man gave cloth to a tailor and he sewed a gown (*qabā'*). The owner of the cloth says, "I only asked you to make a shirt (*qamīṣ*)." The tailor says, "No, you asked me to sew a gown." Neither of them has any proof for their statements. In such circumstances, the word of the tailor on oath shall prevail.'

PLEDGES [AND MORTGAGES] (*AL-RAHN*)[307]

God says: O *ye who believe*! *When ye contract a debt for a fixed term, record it in writing*, till His saying: *and cannot find a scribe, then a pledge in hand*

[306]*Kāfī*, V, 110. In this tradition Farqad is asking the Imam whether he should change his profession and the Imam said, 'Eat ... marry! Indeed, the Prophet scarified himself and gave [the cupper] his wages ...'

[307]The Qur'ānic verses 2:282–3 confirm pre-Islamic legal use of *rahn* for the giving of pledges in business as a guarantee and material proof when a written document is unavailable to fulfil one's contract. The traditions are mainly concerned with two issues: (i) What happens to the security in case of non-fulfilment of the contract? Does it pass into the ownership of the creditor or not? (ii) Who is entitled to its use and maintenance? Answers to these questions vary according to various schools of law. Schacht, *Introduction*, 12, 39, 138–40; *EI*[2], s.v. Rahn. See also Ṭūsī, *al-Nihāya*, 431–5; idem, *Tahdhīb al-aḥkām*, VII, 168 ff.; Jazīrī, *al-Fiqh*, II, 319–32.

(shall suffice) (2:282–3). Thus God has mentioned the pledge with possession (*rihān^{un} maqbūḍa*).[308] If therefore possession does not accompany the pledge, as pledges are normally made, the pledge is not valid.[309]

Ja'far b. Muḥammad: He said, 'There cannot be a pledge without possession [of a deposit].'

[Ja'far b. Muḥammad]: He said, 'There is no harm in the mortgaging of houses and lands, divided or undivided (*mushā'*);[310] or [in mortgaging] of ornaments, foodstuffs, or goods of all kinds, when possession is delivered [to the pledgee (*murtahin*), the taker of the pledge]. If possession [of a deposit] is not given, there is no pledge. If possession is delivered, and thereafter the property is returned to the owner (*rāhin*, the giver of the pledge), the pledge becomes void, because returning the property to the owner, invalidates the pledge.'

[Ja'far b. Muḥammad]: He said, 'No profit can be obtained from a pledge. Whatever profit is obtained on a pledge shall be accounted for and compensation paid for it.'[311]

[Ja'far b. Muḥammad]: He said, 'When the property pledged is destroyed, it is deemed to be the property of the pledgor (*rāhin*), and the debt remains intact on him. If the pledgee who has possession claims that the pledged property is lost, and there is no clear proof and the pledgor says that the statement is false, then the pledgee's statement shall not be accepted without proof.'[312]

Abū Ja'far Muḥammad b. 'Alī and Abū 'Abd Allāh Ja'far b. Muḥammad: They said, 'The pledgee claims that the pledge is for a thousand [dirhams]; and the pledgor says it is for a hundred. The word of the pledgor on oath is to be accepted. It is the duty of the man who has possession of the property [pledgee] to prove [by evidence] the extra

[308]It means a deposit may be withheld as a lien.

[309]"Ā'isha said that the Messenger of God bought some grain from a Jew to be paid at a specified time, and gave him his coat of mail as a pledge.' Transmitted by Bukhārī and Muslim. *Mishkāt*, II, 104; Robson, I, 617. See also Ṭūsī, *al-Tibyān*, II, 380.

[310]See n. 295 in this chapter.

[311]Abū Hurayra reported God's Messenger saying, 'An animal may be ridden for payment when it is in pledge and the milk of milch-camels may be drunk for payment when in pledge, payment being made by the one who rides and the one who drinks.' Transmitted by Bukhārī. *Mishkāt*, II, 104; Robson I, 617. Schacht is of the opinion that the taker of the pledge was entitled to use it and maintain it. This practice was found in earlier authorities, but later fell out into disuse. Its use by the taker of the pledge is forbidden except by the Ḥanbalīs. *EI*^{2}, s.v. Rahn.

[312]Cf. *Kāfī*, V, 234, 237; the case cited is where the value of the pledge is more than the debt and the pledge is lost.

amount claimed. The pledgee says that the property is lost, and the pledgor denies this. If there is no proof and there are differences among them as to the price of the pledged article, the sworn testimony of the man in possession is to be believed; and it is for the owner of the pledged property to prove any excess in price.'[313]

Ja'far b. Muḥammad: He said, 'If the pledge is for a certain period, and the pledgor is absent at the end of the term, the pledge shall not be sold unless the pledgor or his agent is present, or he has appointed someone to act in his absence, or has authorized the pledgee.'[314]

[Ja'far b. Muḥammad]: He said, 'If a slave girl or beast of burden or sheep is kept as a pledge, and [any of them] gives birth to a young one, the young will be deemed to be a part of the pledge with their mothers.'

[Ja'far b. Muḥammad]: He said, regarding the hire of beasts of burden or houses which are mortgaged, and the produce of trees and mortgaged estates, that their rents or hire belong to the pledgor [as owner], unless the condition has been made by the pledgee that they will he recovered by him in part payment of the loan.[315]

[Ja'far b. Muḥammad]: He [was asked about] a man who pledges a slave or slave girl, and later decides to emancipate him or her. He has other property to [pay the debt]. [The Imam said], 'The debt shall be paid from his [other] property, and the slave shall be emancipated. It is not necessary to wait for the time of payment, and there is no need for another pledge instead. Similarly, if he has made a written contract with the slave (*kātaba, mukātaba*)[316] that the latter should pay a certain sum as the price of [freeing] himself, and upon the payment thereof he will be free, or if he made the emancipation of his slave to depend upon his own death (*dabbara 'abdahu*),[317] then such arrangements shall be upheld.'

[Ja'far b. Muḥammad]: He said, 'If a man pledges his slave girl (*jāriya*) and wishes to have sexual intercourse with her without the pledgee's permission, he has no right to do so. But if he is able to reach her and have sexual intercourse, he is not guilty of any offence. If the girl becomes pregnant, she should be returned to him, and the debt should be paid from his other property. As soon as a child is born to her she becomes a *umm*

[313]*Kāfī*, V, 238; the figures of a thousand and a hundred are specified as dirhams. Ṭūsī, *Tahdhīb al-aḥkām*,VII, 174.

[314]A tradition states, 'A pledge does not become lost to its owner when he does not redeem it in time. Any increase in its value goes to him and any loss must be borne by him.' *Mishkāt*, II, 105; Robson, I, 617. See also *Kāfī*, V, 233–4.

[315]*Kāfī*, V, 235, 237.

[316]See the section 'Emancipation by Contract' in Chap. 12.

[317]See the section '*Mudabbar* Slaves' in Chap. 12.

walad[318] (a female slave who has borne her master a child) [and cannot be sold].'[319]

MERCANTILE PARTNERSHIP (*AL-SHARIKA/AL-SHIRKA*)[320]

Ja'far b. Muḥammad—his father—his ancestors: The Messenger of God allowed partnerships in estates (*ribā'* pl. of *rab'*)[321] and lands; and he had 'Alī as a partner in his ritual offerings [of camels at the Farewell Pilgrimage].[322]

When two persons contemplate a partnership, each of them should appropriate an equal amount of money, dinars or dirhams, and merge (*khalṭ*) them until they become one fund which is indistinguishable [as to its parts], so that they may sell and buy a variety of merchandise. If there is profit (*faḍl*, surplus) or loss (*waḍī'a*), they share it equally. This then is partnership in its correct form, and there is no divergence of opinion on it, so far as we know. Unless authorized to do so, neither of the partners can buy or sell without the concurrence of the other.[323]

'Alī: He described two persons engaged in *muḍāraba*[324] as follows: There are two persons and one of them gives to the other his money to

[318]*Umm walad*, see *The Pillars of Islam*, I, 283, n. 62.

[319]*Kāfī*, V, 236; Ṭūsī, *Tahdhīb al-aḥkām*, VII, 170.

[320]*Sharika* (partnership or mercantile partnership) is a technical term in Islamic law and takes different forms according to the contents and conditions. It is mainly divided into *sharikat al-milk* (partnership by propety), and *sharikat al-'aqd* (partnership by contract). The Ḥanafī school permits various kinds of partnership. According to liability partnership could be (i) *sharikat mufāwaḍa*, or (ii) *sharikat 'inān*. The former, unlimited, equal mercantile partnership with full power and liability of each partner, is contracted between two persons of equal property and of same religious persuasion. The latter is contracted when each party contributes certain capital. Each partner, accordingly, would become an agent of the other, but not his bail because responsibility and profit are determined by the contract. Schacht, *Introduction*, 119, 155–6; *EI*², s.v. Sharika. See also *Mishkāt*, II, 115–17; Robson, I, 627–8; Ṭūsī, *Tahdhīb al-aḥkām*, VII, 185; Ibn Rushd, *Bidāya*, II, 247–51; trans. II, 301–6; Jazīrī, *al-Fiqh*, III, 63–90.

[321]*Rab'un* a place where people dwell, a place of constant residence. Lane, s.v. r-b-'.

[322]Ṭabarī, *History of al-Ṭabarī*, IX, 111; Balādhurī, *Ansāb*, I, 370, states that the Prophet had brought with him a hundred camels, sixty of which he sacrificed himself and 'Alī the remainder.

[323]It is *sharikat mufāwaḍa*.

[324]*Ḍārabahu fī mālihi* means he traded for his business partner with the latter's property because he who does so generally jouneys in the land seeking gain (from *al-ḍarb fī 'l-arḍ*, journeying in the land for seeking sustenance). This is done by an agent on the condition that the gain should be divided between him and the investor (or the sleeping partner) as agreed upon. Lane, s.v. ḍ-r-b. *Al-Muḍāraba* is also called *al-Muqāraḍa*, see note 259 above in this chapter.

trade with [hence, he becomes a sleeping partner] on the understanding that the profit would be shared according to the agreement between them, but the loss falls on the capital.[325]

Jaʿfar b. Muḥammad: He said, '[If the two had merged their capital] and one of them had advanced a larger sum, the profit is shared according to agreement, while the loss is shared in proportion to their capital.'

ʿAlī: He said, 'When a man takes money by way of *muḍāraba*, he does not become a surety thereby. If he is suspected [of misappropriation], he should be put on oath; but he is not responsible personally for the money deposited with him.'

[ʿAlī]: He said, 'When a man acting in *muḍāraba*, does not act according to the instructions given to him [by his sleeping partner] and transgresses them, he is responsible for the loss or shortfall; and the profit is shared between the two as agreed upon.'

Jaʿfar b. Muḥammad: He said of a man who gives to a certain person money [or goods] to trade with on the condition of allowing him a fixed profit, 'This is *ribā*[326] (unlawful gain) pure and simple. Such a condition is lawful only between a master and slave, because the property belongs solely to the master.'

[Jaʿfar b. Muḥammad]: He said, 'It is not right and proper for a Muslim to act in partnership with a *dhimmī* (a free non-Muslim subject living in Muslim lands),[327] or agree to give his capital, or entrust a thing to him, or [even] give him his sincere affection.'[328]

[Jaʿfar b. Muḥammad]: He [was asked], 'If a man dies indebted and a trust property (*wadīʿa*) is found with him; and he was under a contract of *muḍāraba* but no one could distinguish between such property, [what should be done in such circumstances?].' [The Imam] said, 'The deceased is bound to pay his debt as it was guaranteed by him, although he was not a trustee (*mu'tamin*) for it. As for the rest he is not responsible, except for the debt. As for the things entrusted to him and the *muḍāraba*, he is regarded as trustworthy (*rajul ma'mūn*) [and does not incur any responsibility].'

[Jaʿfar b. Muḥammad]: He said, 'A certain person has goods belonging to another for trade (*qirāḍ*),[329] and he is also indebted. When he dies, if

[325]Ṭūsī, *Tahdhīb al-aḥkām*, VII, 187–8.

[326]*Ribā*, see *The Pillars of Islam*, I, 305, n. 19.

[327]*Dhimmī*, see *The Pillars of Islam*, I, 143, n. 79.

[328]Cf. *Kāfī*, V, 271–2, 291; *musāqāt* and *muzāraʿa* are permitted with the *dhimmīs*. According to a tradition transmitted by Kulaynī this partnership is permitted when there is *tijāra ḥāḍira* provided that the Muslim partner is always present at the time of transaction. See also Ṭūsī, *Tahdhīb al-aḥkām*, VII, 185.

[329]*Qirāḍ*, see n. 259 above in this chapter.

he has clearly indicated that certain goods belonged to a specified person, those should be given over to him. But if the goods as specified by him are not to be found, the remaining part of the estate is for the satisfaction of his creditors.'

[Ja'far b. Muḥammad]: [The following case was brought before him]: Two partners dissolve their partnership and distribute the assets in their hands. A debt due from an absent debtor remains unpaid to them and they agree that each of them will have a share in it. Now [when it is repaid], part of it is destroyed before it reaches [them]. [The Imam] said, 'What is destroyed is a loss which falls on them jointly, as the debt itself cannot be divided.'[330]

[RIGHT OF] PRE-EMPTION (AL-SHUF'A)[331]

Ja'far b. Muḥammad—his father—his ancestors—'Alī: They said, 'There is no right to pre-emption in property which had been divided by metes and bounds (*waqa'at 'alayhi al-ḥudūdu*).[332] The neighbour has no right to pre-empt, although he has his rights and is entitled to consideration.'[333]

The Prophet said, 'The Angel Gabriel[334] gave me good advice

[330]Ṭūsī, *al-Nihāya*, 427. He gives a slightly different case where two partners dissolve their partnership ... . They divide the cash (*naqd*) and the sale on credit (*nasī'a*, whose payment is deferred to a future date). One partner received the credit money, but the other did not receive it. Now, the one who did receive should divide it with his partner and what is destroyed [i.e. the amount the other partner did not receive] is a loss which they both share.

[331]*Shuf'a*, a technical term in Islamic law, means pre-emption, the right of the co-owner to buy out his partner's share that is for sale. If a property is sold to a third party without the approval of the partner, the latter retains his privilege to purchase the said property, even against the will of the third party. The Ḥanafī school gives this privilege to the owners of adjacent properties. Details vary according to different schools of law. It should be noted that Muḥammad al-Aṣamm (d. 347/957) rejected *shuf'a* because it deprives a person of his freedom to sell. *EI*[2], s.v. Shuf'a. For a linguistic explanation see Lane, s.v. sh-f-'; *Majma' al-baḥrayn*, s.v. sh-f-'. See also Ibn Rushd, *Bidāya*, II, 252–9; trans. II, 307–16.

The law of pre-emption was introduced into India by Muslim judges under the Mughal rule. Since then it remained the common law of the country. Modern courts in India, as courts of equity, would not approve of any device which interferes with the right of pre-emption. Fyzee, *Outlines*, 333–54; Anderson, *Law Reform*, 94, 170.

[332]'Jābir said that the Prophet decreed the right to buy neighbouring property applicable to everything which is not divided, but when boundaries were fixed and separate roads made there was no option.' *Mishkāt*, II, 124; Robson I, 633; transmitted by Bukhārī. *Kāfī*, V, 286.

[333]'The neighbour has the best claim by reason of his being near.' *Mishkāt*, II, 124; Robson, I, 633; transmitted by Bukhārī.

[334]Gabriel, see *The Pillars of Islam*, I, 63, n. 164.

concerning the neighbour to such an extent that I thought he would make him an heir.'

[Ja'far b. Muḥammad]: He said, 'The co-sharer (*sharīk*) is legally entitled to pre-empt if he is a Muslim. The *dhimmī* is not entitled to pre-empt. The right of the faithful is valid, whether he is a pre-emptor (*shafī'*) or otherwise. There is no right to pre-emption in respect of distributed property.'[335]

Ja'far b. Muḥammad: He said, 'Pre-emption is lawful in property which has not been distributed. When property is distributed and its boundaries fixed, then there is no pre-emption. The neighbour has no right to pre-empt. Pre-emption takes place according to the proportionate shares of the parties.'[336]

[Ja'far b. Muḥammad]: He said, 'Pre-emption takes place only in undivided property (*mushā'*, shared in common),[337] or where there is a joint right of way (*ṭarīq mushtarak*), or a common wall, wooden or of stone, or a similar structure. People who use a byway (*rā'igha*, a road deviating from the main road)[338] in common, from which there is no outlet (*nāfidha*), have the right to pre-empt, by reason of their common right of passage. Once however division takes place, there is no right for the owner of the higher or lower ground to pre-empt, unless something is in common use between them.'[339]

[Ja'far b. Muḥammad]: He said, 'The right of pre-emption applies to all kinds of immovable property (*'aqār*). *'Aqār* means date palms and lands and houses. There is no right of pre-emption in a ship, stream, or animal.'[340]

[335]'Everything which is shared when undivided, could be pre-empted whether it is a dwelling or an orchard. It is not lawful to sell before informing one's partner who may take it or let it go as he wishes; but if he sells without informing him, he has the greatest right to it.' Transmitted by Muslim. Another tradition states, 'The partner has first right to pre-empt and this option applies to everything.' *Mishkāt*, II, 124, 125: Robson I, 633, 634; *Kāfī*, V, 285, 286; Ṭūsī, *Tahdhīb al-aḥkām*, VII, 164.

[336]Ṭūsī, *Tahdhīb al-aḥkām*, VII, 183.

[337]*Mushā'*, see n. 295 in this chapter.

[338]Lane, s.v. r-w-gh.

[339]'The neighbour is most entitled to the right of pre-emption and its exercise should be waited for even if he is absent, when the two properties have one road.' *Mishkāt*, 125; Robson, I, 633. See also *Kāfī*, V, 285.

[340]According to a tradition transmitted by Mālik the right to pre-emption does not apply to male palm trees. *Mishkāt*, II, 126; Robson, I, 634. According to one tradition, *shuf'a* is permitted with regard to animals, see *Kāfī*, V, 287; Ṭūsī, *Tahdhīb al-aḥkām*, VII, 164–6. The Ḥanafīs make the right of *shuf'a* valid not only to non-fungible properties but also to appendages of the property, such as access and water rights. The Ẓāhirīs extend this right to animals on the basis of a *ḥadīth*.

Abū Jaʿfar Muḥammad b. ʿAlī: He said, 'Where a man gives to his wife a share [of his property] as a dower (*ṣadāq*),[341] no right of pre-emption arises.'

[Abū Jaʿfar Muḥammad b. ʿAlī]: He said, 'Where a slave is the joint property of two persons, and one of them sells his share, the joint owner is the one who is most entitled to buy it. There is no right to pre-empt in respect of an animal.'

ʿAlī: He said, 'A man does not lose his right of pre-emption by reason of absence. The right of pre-emption is possessed both by the absentee and the minor (*ṣaghīr*), and [can be exercised] when the absentee returns or the minor attains majority.'[342]

Jaʿfar b. Muḥammad: He said about a man who is entitled to pre-empt (*shafīʿ*) is absent at the time of sale, 'His right to pre-empt continues till he [returns and] is present; and this is whether he has knowledge of the sale or not.'

[Jaʿfar b. Muḥammad]: He was asked about a pre-emptor who is present at the time of sale but later is absent. Thereafter he returns and claims his right to pre-empt. [The Imam] said, 'He has the right to pre-empt until the time expires; and the period for exercising the right in the case of someone who has attained puberty and is present [at the time of the sale] is one year. If one year elapses after the sale, and he has not claimed the right, the right to pre-empt lapses.'

[Jaʿfar b. Muḥammad]: He said, 'The right to pre-empt arises as soon as the sale is completed, whether possession is delivered or not.'

[Jaʿfar b. Muḥammad]: He said, 'Where the pre-emptor hires the land or the house that is sold, or makes some arrangement about the trees or some other matter, then his right to pre-empt terminates.'

[Jaʿfar b. Muḥammad]: He was asked, 'A certain person claims that he has purchased a piece of land (*shiqṣ*)[343] from an absent owner, and the pre-emptor claims his right.' [The Imam] said, 'No right to pre-empt arises unless the sale is clearly proven.'

[Jaʿfar b. Muḥammad]: He said, 'When the vendor and the pre-emptor differ as to the price of the house, and the pre-emptor cannot furnish any proof, the word of the vendor on oath shall be believed if he brings [evidence of the price paid for] a similar house.'

[Jaʿfar b. Muḥammad]: He said,'There is no right of pre-emption in a

[341] *Ṣadāq*, see Chap. 10, section 'The Account of Dower'.

[342] Ṭūsī, *Tahdhīb al-aḥkām*, VII, 166.

[343] Lane, s.v. sh-q-ṣ.

well, stream, or ship except when it is attached to a piece of land which remains undivided.'[344]

[Ja'far b. Muḥammad]: He was asked, 'Certain lands are endowed as *waqf*[345] to some persons, and one of them builds [a house] and dies. One of the heirs sells his share in the house. Have the co-owners the right to pre-empt?' [The Imam] replied, 'Yes, they have a right because the remaining co-owners may suffer loss if [the purchaser] demolishes a half of the house and, in this manner, some mischief may arise.'

[Ja'far b. Muḥammad]: He was asked, 'If a pre-emptor surrenders his right to pre-empt before sale, can he claim the right to pre-empt after the sale?' [The Imam] said, 'He can do so, so long as he has not surrendered his right after the sale.'

[Ja'far b. Muḥammad]: He was asked, 'A sale takes place in one transaction and [the property sold] consists both of undivided (*mushā'*) and divided property (*maqsūm*). Has the pre-emptor the right to exercise his right over the undivided, and not the divided, part of the property?' [The Imam] said, 'No, he has the right to pre-empt the whole of the property, divided as well as undivided. So, if he desires to pre-empt, he either takes the whole of the property [sold], or relinquishes the whole of it.'

[Ja'far b. Muḥammad]: He said, 'No right of pre-emption exists when a man buys a portion of a slave [held jointly with another], or cloth or jewels or the like.'

[Ja'far b. Muḥammad]: [Someone brought a case to him] saying, 'A pre-emptor claims against a purchaser who says, "I purchased the property for such and such an amount." The pre-emptor agrees to the purchaser's claim. Then the pre-emptor comes to know that the purchaser had bought it for less than the one mentioned. [The Imam] said, 'The pre-emptor, if he wishes to exercise his right, may resile from the original offer [and claim it according to the real price].'

[Ja'far b. Muḥammad]: He said, 'When the vendor deducts some amount from the price to be paid by the purchaser, as is usually done in such cases, a proportionate deduction should be made [in the amount to

[344]The right to pre-empt does not apply to land when boundaries are set up in it, nor does it apply to a well or to male palm trees. *Mishkāt*, II, 126; Robson, I, 634; *Kāfī*, V, 287; it states, 'There is no right of pre-emption in a ship, stream, or road.'

[345]The Arabic word used in the text is *ḥabs* from *ḥabbasa shay'an* meaning he made a thing to remain in itself unalienable, not to be inherited nor sold nor given away, assigning the profits arising from it to be employed in the cause of God. Lane, s.v. ḥ-b-s; *ShEI*, s.v. Waḳf.

be paid by] the pre-emptor. If the amount deducted is so large that it is unusual, then it should be considered a gift (*hiba*) to the purchaser, and no such deduction should be made in favour of the pre-emptor.'

[Ja'far b. Muḥammad]: He said, 'A father should uphold his minor son's right to pre-empt; and so should the executor, or the legal guardian (*waṣī*) for an orphan,[346] or the judge (*qāḍī*) for him who has no executor, if in his opinion, it is for the child's benefit.'

[Ja'far b. Muḥammad]: He said, 'Where a pre-emptor claims against a purchaser, and enforces his right of possession over a part of the property (*shiqṣ*), and afterwards desires to change his mind, he shall not be entitled to do so.'

[Ja'far b. Muḥammad]: He said, 'Where the portion (*shiqṣ*) [to which the pre-emptor is entitled] is sold a number of times during the period of pre-emption, the pre-emptor is entitled to proceed against any of the purchasers he desires.'

'Alī: He said, 'The right of pre-emption due to a Jew or a Christian is lawful between them; but neither of them can claim pre-emption against a Muslim.'

[346]*Kāfī*, V, 286.

2

The Book of Oaths and Vows (*Kitāb al-Aymān wa 'l-Nudhūr*)[1]

THE COMMAND TO FULFIL OATHS AND KEEP PROMISES (*AL-AMR BI-ḤIFẒ AL-AYMĀN WA 'L-'UHŪD*)

God says: *Lo! those who purchase a small gain at the cost of Allah's covenant ('ahd) and their oaths (aymān), they have no portion in the Hereafter. Allah will neither speak to them nor look upon them on the Day of Resurrection, nor will He purify them. Theirs will be a painful doom* (3:77); and He says: *and keep your oaths* (5:89); and He says: *And keep the covenant. Lo! Of the covenant it will be asked* (17:34); and He says: *O ye who believe! Fulfil your undertakings ('uqūd)* (5:1). He says: *Fulfil the covenant of Allah when ye have covenanted, and break not your oaths after the asseveration of them, and after ye have made Allah [a] surety over you* (16:91); and He says: *And make not Allah, by your oaths, a hindrance to your being righteous* (2:224).[2] God praises him who fulfils his covenant and says: *Such as keep the pact of Allah, and*

[1] *Aymān* pl. of *yamīn*. *Ḥalaftu yamīn*[an], I swore an oath. Every statement or undertaking emphasized by the words '*wa 'llāhi* (by God!)', or by a similar formula, is regarded in Islamic law as an oath (*yamīn*). In case of non-fulfilment of such an undertaking an expiation (*kaffāra*) is called for. Schacht, *Introduction*, 117, 159. *Nudhūr* pl. of *nadhr*. *Nadhara 'alā nafsihi an* ..., he made a vow that ... The pre-Islamic concept of *nadhr*, i.e. dedication was modified in Islam. 'Abd al-Muṭṭalib is said to have dedicated (*nadhara*) a son to be slain beside the Ka'ba if he should have ten sons and they grew up, but for his *nadhr* 100 camels were substituted. In Islamic law the vow and the oath are treated together. The Qur'ān 2:225 and 5:89 states that unconsidered expressions (*laghw*) in an oath, especially related to food and women, may be broken and expiated. *EI*², s.v. Nadhr. For more details see Ibn Rushd, *Bidāya*, I, 405–24; trans. I, 488–515; Jazīrī, *al-Fiqh*, II, 56 ff.

[2] *Kāfī*, VII, 475. Swearing by God truthfully or falsely is disapproved of according to al-Ṣādiq.

break not the covenant (mīthāq) (13:20); and He says: *And those who keep their treaty when they make one* (2:177); and He says: *So whosoever breaks his oath, breaks it only to his soul's hurt; while whosoever keeps his covenant with Allah, on him will He bestow immense reward* (48:10).

Ja'far b. Muḥammad—his father—ancestors: The Messenger of God said, 'Evil are those who take oaths without being obedient to God.'

[Ja'far b. Muḥammad]: He said, 'On the Day of Resurrection God will not look at, nor purify three [classes of] persons, and they will suffer a painful torment: (i) A man who swears allegiance to the Imam, but does not honour his pledge unless the Imam gives him some worldly benefit; and if the Imam does not [reward him with worldly goods], he breaks his solemn pledge. (ii) A man who possesses a water [well] by the roadside and yet denies [access to] it to travellers. (iii) A man who swears after the afternoon (*'aṣr*) prayer and falsely says that he had been presented with certain goods, and believing in such false representations, a third person has taken possession of the goods.'

'Alī: He stopped at Kunāsa[3] and said, 'O Merchants, your markets contain a large number of oaths. So mix your oaths with charity, and avoid taking oaths, for God never sanctifies a man who swears by Him falsely.'

['Alī]: He said, 'Fear God when you take a false oath, for verily it causes loss to merchandise and erases God's favour. He who swears falsely, has acted boldly against God; let him then await God's punishment.'[4]

The Messenger of God: He said, 'When God the Mighty and Glorious created Paradise,[5] He made its milk of shining gold, [mixed] with powdered musk, it [Paradise] quivered and exclaimed, "Thou art God. *There is no God save Him the Alive, the Eternal* (2:255). Blessed are those whom thou hast empowered to enter my precincts." And God said, "I swear by My honour and Majesty, nobody shall enter you [Paradise] who does not fulfil My covenant."' The Prophet related the story in detail.

'Alī: He said, 'He who breaks the oath of allegiance will meet God on the Day of Resurrection with his hands severed. He will possess no hand.'

The Messenger of God: He said, 'The oath of one under compulsion (*mukrah*) is void. God says: *save him who is forced thereto and whose heart is still content with the faith* (16:106).

[3]Kunāsa is a name of a quarter in Kūfa. Yāqūt, s.v. k-n-s.

[4]*Kāfī*, VII, 476.

[5]*Jannātu 'adn*^{in}, meaning garden of perpetual abode, occurs several times in the Qur'ān. Rāzī, *al-Zīna*, fol. 104a–104b; he explains the linguistic meanings of *janna*, *firdaws*, *jannat*^{u} *'adn*^{in}, and *jannnat al-khuld*; Lane, '-d-n.

Ja'far b. Muḥammad:[6] He said, 'If a man is under duress (*mukrah*), neither his divorce nor his emancipation [of a slave] are valid.'

Abū Ja'far Muḥammad b. 'Alī: He was asked about a man who takes an oath under duress (*taqīyat*[an]).[7] He replied, 'If you fear about your brother or religion or your property, then swear, if the oath affords relief. But if you find no relief by it, then do not swear. In all matters in which a faithful one fears harm to himself, it is his right to have recourse to *taqīya*.'

Ja'far b. Muḥammad: He said, 'In this community [of the faithful], God has absolved from responsibility persons in the following four cases: where they have no power; where the people are compelled; where they are forgetful; where they are ignorant, until they have knowledge.'

Ja'far b. Muḥammad: Concerning the Word of God: *Allah will not take you to task for vain words (laghw) in your oaths* (2:225),[8] he said, '[This refers to] the saying of a man, "No, by God" and "Yes, by God", but in reality he makes no resolution about any particular action.'[9]

The Messenger of God: He prohibited the use of ambiguous language in oaths and said, 'If a man is wronged (*maẓlūm*), the intention of one who swears will be taken into consideration; but if a man has committed wrong (*ẓālim*), then the intention of the man who calls upon someone to take the oath will be taken into consideration.'[10]

Ja'far b. Muḥammad said, 'The oath [is to be interpreted] according to the intention of one who calls upon another to take the oath.[11] That is, upon the petitioner's intention and purpose; and not the intention of one who takes the oath when he is ambiguous in his oath, or has made a reservation for himself, contrary to the intention of the person who put him on oath, regarding his own claim.'

[6]As in MS Q. In the edited text: *qāla*, instead of *'an*.

[7]*Taqīya*, see *The Pillars of Islam*, I, 77, n. 213.

[8]Bell, *The Qur'ān*, I, 31.

[9]'Ā'isha said that the verse, *Allah will not take you to task for vain words in your oaths*, was sent down about such phrases as 'No, by God', and 'Yes, by God'. *Mishkāt* II, 251; Robson, I, 728; transmitted by Bukhārī. See also *Kāfī*, VII, 484.

[10]In the former case a person swears falsely, while in the latter he hides his intention and calls upon his opponent to swear in order to cover up wrongdoing. In cases of litigation, the jurists agree that oaths are to be construed in conformity with the intention of the person seeking the oath from his opponent. Ibn Rushd, *Bidāya*, I, 413; trans. I, 499. See also *Kāfī*, VII, 485; Ṭūsī, *Tahdhīb al-aḥkām*, VIII, 280.

[11]*Mishkāt*, II, 251; Robson, I, 728. Robson's translation is incorrect and should be corrected to read, 'An oath is to be interpreted according to the intentions of one who calls upon another to take the oath (*al-yamīn 'alā niyyat al-mustaḥlif*).' Transmitted by Muslim.

The Messenger of God prohibited oaths to be taken in the name of any one except God.[12]

Ja'far b. Muḥammad: He said, 'Oaths cannot be taken except in the name of God. The believers are not obligated to oaths taken in the names of anyone else except in the name of God. There is no violation of an oath (*ḥinth*)[13] and no expiation (*kaffāra*)[14] for oaths taken in the names of [persons, etc.] other than God. I am of the opinion that no one has the right to give the oath to any one except in the name of God. The man who swears by God is truthful and does honour to God.'

The Messenger of God: He said, 'A son should not testify on oath against his father, nor should a wife against her husband, nor a slave against his master. If such an oath is taken, it is not an oath, in reality.'[15]

EFFECTIVE AND INEFFECTIVE OATHS
(*MĀ YALZAM MIN AL-AYMĀN WA-MĀ LĀ YALZAM MINHĀ*)[16]

When an oath is taken with a reservation [that is, adding the words, *in shā' Allāh*, if God wills], the man who takes it is free from committing a sin for having violated his oath if it remains unfulfilled. God says: *And say not of anything: Lo! I shall do that tomorrow, except [adding] if Allah will [s]. And remember thy Lord when thou forgettest* (18:23–4).[17]

Ja'far b. Muḥammad: Concerning the Word of God: *And remember thy Lord when thou forgettest* (18:23–4), he said, 'It refers to the oath in which you say, "By God, I shall certainly do such and such," and when you recollect that you have not made a reservation then say, "*in shā' Allāh* (if God wills)."'

[The Imam] said, 'A group of Jews asked the Prophet about something,

[12]A tradition states, 'He who swears by anyone but God is a polytheist. If anyone swears he must swear by God, or keep silent.' *Mishkāt*, II, 249–51; Ṭūsī, *Tahdhīb al-aḥkām*, VIII, 277–9.

[13]Lane, s.v. ḥ-n-th.

[14]*Kaffāra* means an expiatory act which grants remission for grave faults, sins, or violation of oaths. As a technical term it appears in the Qur'ān, for example see 5:49, 89, 95. Etymologically *kaffāra* means 'that which covers' sin, however, it should be noted that the root *kafara* and its derivatives are used in the Qur'ān in the sense of to repudiate, to redeem, and to pardon. Schacht, *Introduction*, 129, 159, 165, 181–3, 185, 207; *EI*^{2}, s.v. Kaffāra; Mir, *Dictionary*, 52–3.

[15]*Kāfī*, VII, 480, 481.

[16]Lit. it means 'what is required of [the person] taking an oath…'

[17]In Pickthall it is 18:24–5. Ibn 'Umar reported the Prophet as stating that if anyone says when swearing an oath, 'If God wills', he is not held accountable if he breaks it. *Mishkāt*, II, 252; Robson, I, 729.

and he said, "Meet me tomorrow and I shall tell you," and he made no reservation. So Gabriel[18] refrained from visiting the Prophet for forty days. Then he came and said to the Prophet: *And say not of anything: Lo! I shall do that tomorrow, except [adding] if Allah will[s]. And remember thy Lord when thou forgettest* (18:23–4).

The Messenger of God: He directed that a reservation should be made in oaths and said, 'Give priority to the will of God (*mashī'a*).'

'Alī: He said, 'If a man takes an oath and then says, "If God wills", there is no sin on him [when he breaks it].'

Abū Ja'far: He said, 'If a man were to move his tongue, even if he does not pronounce the reservation loudly, this is sufficient. But where he has taken the oath loudly, it is better to pronounce the words of reservation loudly.'

'Alī: He said, 'He who takes an oath publicly, should make the reservation publicly; and he who takes the oath secretly should make the reservation secretly.'[19]

The reservation is effective if it is joined to the oath, and in such a case, there is no sin [if he breaks it], and there is a consensus (*ijmā'*)[20] [among various schools of law] on this point as far as we know. But if the reservation is not pronounced immediately after the oath, there is a difference of opinion [as to whether there is sin if it is broken].

Ja'far b. Muḥammad: He said, 'The reservation is valid even after forty days or a year [after the oath].'[21]

The Messenger of God: He said, 'There can be no divorce before marriage, and no emancipation [of a slave] before ownership.'

Ja'far b. Muḥammad: He said, 'There can be no charity by one who does not possess [property].'

Abū Ja'far: Concerning the Word of God: *O Prophet! Why bannest*

[18]See *The Pillars of Islam*, I, 63, n. 164 for Gabriel.

[19]*Kāfī*, VII, 490.

[20]According to the classical theory Islamic law is based on four principles (*uṣūl al-fiqh*): the Qur'ān, the *sunna* of the Prophet, the consensus (*ijmā'*), and the method of reasoning by analogy (*qiyās*). Although *ijmā'* is the third source, in practice, it is the most potent and important factor in the shaping of belief and practice of the Muslims. It is also the most elusive one in terms of its formation and is described as an organic process. Theoretically, it is the unanimous agreement of the *umma* on a regulation (*ḥukm*), but technically it is the unanimous doctrine or opinion of the recognized religious authorities at a given time. For details see Schacht, *Intorduction*, 60–8, 114; Rahman, *Islam*, 68–84; *EI*[2], s.v. Idjmā'. It should be noted that both *ijmā'* and *qiyās* are rejected by Nu'mān as sources of law. Poonawala, 'Al-Qāḍī al-Nu'mān and Isma'ili jurisprudence', 126.

[21]*Kāfī*, VII, 488–90; the reservation could be pronounced even after forty days; Ṭūsī, *Tahdhīb al-aḥkām*, VIII, 281.

thou that which Allah hath made lawful for thee, seeking to please thy wives? (66:1), till His word *and maids* (66:5), he said 'The Messenger of God used to meet Māriya the Copt in privacy before she gave birth to Ibrāhīm. 'Ā'isha came to know of this and the Messenger of God asked her to keep it a secret, while he himself kept away from Māriya. And so 'Ā'isha mentioned it to Ḥafṣa, hence God revealed the above [verse] (66:1–5).[22]

Ja'far b. Muḥammad: He said, 'Where a man denies himself permissible things, and later allows them to himself, he commits no wrong. But if he had sworn not to do that which he was permitted, he may go against his oath, but has to offer expiation. On the other hand, if he were to swear that he would do an unlawful act, and then refrain from it, he has not committed the sin of breaking an oath (*ḥinth*).'

[Ja'far b. Muḥammad]: [He said]: 'Expiation is to be made for oaths only when it is not compulsory for you to do a thing, and you swear not to do it, and later you do it. Here expiation is due. [On the other hand], if a thing is compulsory for you, and you swear that you will not do it, but later you do it, then you are not culpable for breaking an oath and need not expiate it. He who swears that he will disobey God should seek His forgiveness.'[23]

[The Imam] said, 'A man swears that he will perform [a supererogatory] act of obedience, but he does not perform it. He must expiate for it. For example, he swears that he will perform a supererogatory prayer, or fast, or make a charitable gift. [Here expiation is necessary, if the act is not done]. But if he swears that he will not pray [the obligatory prayer] or that he will do wrong, be fraudulent, or commit a sin, and then does not perform [such wrongful action], there is no breaking of an oath and no expiation is necessary for it.'[24]

Ja'far b. Muḥammad: Concerning the Qur'ānic verse: *And make not Allah, by your oaths, a hindrance* (2:224), he said, '[This refers to] a man who swears that he will not speak to his brother or father or some similar act of breaking with blood relations or some other wrong action or sin. It is always his duty to act in consonance with God's command, and thus

[22]Māriya the Copt was the Prophet's concubine and gave birth to Ibrāhīm. See *The Pillars of Islam* I, 278, n. 38; for 'Ā'isha see ibid., 54, n. 137. Ḥafṣa, daughter of 'Umar b. al-Khaṭṭāb, was the Prophet's wife. Her first husband, a Badrī, died at Medina on the return from Badr. *EI*^{2}, s.v. Ḥafṣa.

[23]'If anyone vows to obey God let him obey Him, but if anyone vows to disobey Him let him not disobey Him.' Transmitted by Bukhārī. Another tradition states, 'No vow must be taken to do an act of disobedience, and the atonement for it is the same as for an oath.' *Mishkāt*, II, 253–7; Robson, I, 730–3.

[24]Cf. *Kāfī*, VII, 487; other examples are given.

there is no harm if he had sworn not to do a thing and then breaks his oath.'[25]

Ja'far b. Muḥammad: He said, 'A man swears to divorce [a wife] or emancipate [a slave], and then breaks his oath. He is not culpable either in divorcing his wife, or in emancipating his slave. The same rule applies to one who swears to perform a pilgrimage or offer sacrifices. This is because the Messenger of God forbade oaths except in the name of God, or a divorce except according to the Prophet's *sunna* (practice), or emancipating a slave except for the sake of God, or a pilgrimage except for the sake of God.

[PERFORMING OF] VOWS (*AL-NUDHŪR*)

God says: *Lo! the righteous shall drink of a cup whereof the mixture is of water of Kāfūr,*[26] *a spring wherefrom the slaves of Allah drink, making it gush forth abundantly, [because] they perform the vow and fear a day whereof the evil is wide-spreading* (76:5–7).

Ja'far b. Muḥammad—his father—his ancestors: The Messenger of God forbade the taking of vows except in the name of God. He also forbade vows of disobedience [to God] or breaking ties of blood relationship.[27]

Ja'far b. Muḥammad: He said, 'He who vows [wrongfully] as above, is not deemed to have vowed at all; for, his vow was to disobey God, and thus he is under no obligation. He is like a person who swears by God that he will commit a sinful act if he is able to do it. Although he is able to do the act, he does not do so, and he is not obliged by his oath to do it. Now if this vow consists of some good work in obedience to God, and he has already named the particular act, then it is his duty to fulfil the vow. For instance, he says, "By God I swear to perform so many prayers, or fast for so many days, or perform a pilgrimage, or emancipate [a slave], or do any other pious deeds if God will save me from this [evil], or give me the following means of livelihood, or bestow upon me a spiritual favour or worldly good of a lawful character."'

Ja'far b. Muḥammad: He said, 'If a man vows to do something for God and fails to specify it, then he is under no obligation.'[28]

[25] Ṭūsī, *Tahdhīb al-aḥkām*, VIII, 288.

[26] *Kāfūr*, camphor, a kind of perfume, a certain spring in paradise. Lane, s.v. k-f-r.

[27] Cf. *Mishkāt*, II, 253–7; Robson, I, 730–3. Ṭūsī, *Tahdhīb al-aḥkām*, VII, 303 ff.; Jazīrī, *al-Fiqh*, II, 139–47.

[28] Ibn 'Abbās reported God's Messenger as saying, 'If anyone takes a vow but does not specify it, its atonement is the same as that for an oath.' *Mishkāt*, II, 255; Robson, I,

EXPIATORY OFFERINGS (*AL-KAFFĀRĀT*)[29]

God says: *Allah will not take you to task for vain words in your oaths, but He will take you to task for the oaths which ye swear in earnest. The expiation thereof is the feeding of ten of the needy with the average of that wherewith ye feed your own folk, or the clothing of them, or the liberation of a slave, and for him who findeth not (the wherewithal to do so) then a three days' fast. This is the expiation of your oaths when ye have sworn* (5:89).

Ja'far b. Muḥammad—his father—his ancestors—the Messenger of God: He said, 'Where a man vows to do a certain thing, and later finds that he can do more good by acting in another manner, then let him do that which is better and expiate for [breaking] his oath.'[30]

Ja'far b. Muḥammad: He was asked about the expiation of oaths and he said, 'Wherever the Qur'ān uses the words "or" ... "or," the man has a choice; he may adopt one of the options open to him. But whenever the Qur'ān mentions *if he does not find [the means]*, or *if he is unable to do so*, he must do what is mentioned first, and the second alternative arises only if he is unable to do so. It follows that the man who breaks a vow has a choice; he may feed people, or clothe them, or liberate [a slave]. But if he has not the means to do so, [only] then he has to fast for three [consecutive] days.'[31]

[Ja'far b. Muḥammad]: Concerning the verse of the Qur'ān: *The average of that wherewith ye feed your own folk* (5:89), [Imam al-Ṣādiq] explained, 'It means what your family eats as a rule, i.e. vinegar, oil, and bread. The best [meal] is bread and meat; and the least [acceptable meal] is bread and salt.'[32]

[Ja'far b. Muḥammad]: [He said], 'For expiating a vow, every poor person should be given a *mudd* (a certain measure)[33] of foodstuffs.[34]

---

731. 'If a man vows (*'alayya nadhr^{un}*), he is under no obligation until he specifies it and says that it is for the sake of God (*lillāh*).' Another tradition states, 'If you say, "[I vow] for the sake of God" (*lillāhi 'alayya*), then its atonement is the same as that for an oath.' *Kāfī*, 496, 497; all these traditions are on the authority of al-Ṣādiq.

[29]*Kaffāra* pl. *kaffārāt* see note 14 above in this chapter.

[30]'The atonement for a vow is the same as for an oath.' Transmitted by Muslim. *Mishkāt*, II, 253, 254, 255; Robson, I, 730, 731. *Kāfī*, VII, 498; Ṭūsī, *Tahdhīb al-aḥkām*, VIII, 319 ff.; Jazīrī, *al-Fiqh* II, 76 ff.

[31]*Kāfī*, VII, 493.

[32]Ibid., VII, 494.

[33]*Mudd* is a term used to describe a measure of corn. It is the quantity of corn that fills two hands of a man of moderate size when he extends his arms and hands. Lane, s.v. m-d-d; see also *The Pillars of Islam*, I, 331, n. 149, 340.

[34]*Kāfī*, VII, 493.

[Ja'far b. Muḥammad]: He was asked, 'Can a man feed one beggar for ten days [in expiation]?' He said, 'No, he must feed ten persons as directed by God.'[35] [He was asked], 'Can a man feed poor persons (*ḍu'afā'*) other than followers of the rightful Imams (*ahl al-walāya*)?'[36] [The Imam] said, 'No, feeding the faithful ones (*ahl al-walāya*) if they can be found is more preferable to me; if not, oppressed Muslims (*mustaḍ'afūn*),[37] and if no one is found except a *nāṣibī* (hater of the Imams),[38] he should not be given food. A dirham given to a faithful one (*mu'min*)[39] is better than one thousand given to the non-faithful! God says: *Thou wilt not find folk who believe in Allah and the Last Day loving those who oppose Allah and His Messenger* (58:22).'[40]

'Alī:[41] As to the Qur'ānic dictum: *or the clothing of them* (5:89), he said, '[This means that] two pieces of clothing should be given to each man.'[42]

Abū Ja'far Muḥammad b. 'Alī:[43] He said, 'It is permissible to liberate a newborn baby slave as expiation for breaking a vow. In the case of killing a man, this is not lawful, unless the slave [is old enough] and has professed the unity of God.'

Ja'far b. Muḥammad: He said, 'It is not lawful to free a *mudabbar* (a slave who is already declared to be free after the death of the master)[44] either for expiation for breaking a vow or for *ẓihār* (pre-Islamic form of divorce).[45] It is always best to free a man of sufficient age who can look after himself, but in case of broken vows, a slave child would fulfil the obligation, for God says: *the liberation of a slave* (5:89), without specifying whether he should be a minor or an adult.'

'Alī, and Muḥammad b. 'Alī, and Ja'far b. Muḥammad: They said, 'The expiatory fast [for a broken] vow consists of three consecutive days without a break.'

[35]Ibid., VII, 495; it states, 'If one cannot find more than one or two beggars, he has to feed them again until ten rounds are completed.' Another tradition states, 'If the beggar is a minor then two minors should be fed for one beggar.'

[36]For *walāya* (devotion and obedience to the Imam) see *The Pillars of Islam*, I, 2, 18.

[37]*Mustaḍ'afūn*, see *The Pillars of Islam*, I, 278, n. 39; 323.

[38]*Nāṣib*, see *The Pillars of Islam*, I, 190, n. 128; 191, 294, 361.

[39]For the definition of a *mu'min* see *The Pillars of Islam*, I, 15–17.

[40]MS Q adds: *even though they be their fathers of their sons [or their brethren of their clan]*.

[41]MS Q: '*Anhu* [i.e. Ja'far b. Muḥammad].

[42]Gloss in MS Q: Two medium [-size] pieces of clothing means a loincloth (*izār*) and a loose outer garment (*ridā'*). *Kāfī*, VII, 496; ... 'only one piece of clothing'.

[43]*Abū Ja'far bin Muḥammad*: In the edited text is an error.

[44]See Chap. 12, the section '*Mudabbar* Slaves'.

[45]*Ẓihār*, see Chap. 11, section on *Ẓihār* below.

3

The Book of Food (*Kitāb al-Aṭʿima*)[1]

THE GIVING OF FOOD (*IṬʿĀM AL-ṬAʿĀM*)[2]

God Says: *Lo! the righteous shall drink of a cup whereof the mixture is of water of Kāfūr, a spring wherefrom the slaves of Allah drink, making it gush forth abundantly, (because) they perform the vow and fear a day whereof the evil is wide-spreading, and feed with food the needy wretch, the orphan and the prisoner for love of Him, (saying): We feed you, for the sake of Allah only. We wish for no reward nor thanks from you* (76:5–9), till His saying: *Lo! this is a reward for you. Your endeavour (upon earth) has found acceptance* (76:22).

The Messenger of God: He said, 'When the meals (*mawā'id*)[3] of the progeny of Muḥammad are laid out, angels surround them proclaiming the holiness of God and asking for His forgiveness for the descendants of the Prophet and for those who partook of their meal.' And some of the Prophet's descendants, on whom be salutations, used to say to the guests, 'Eat, O slave of God, and be blessed by the food.'

[1]For this chapter's summary, see Fyzee, *Compendium*, 129–39.

[2]'He who believes in God and the Last Day should honour his guest ...' *Mishkāt*, II, 455; Robson, II, 898; transmitted by Bukhārī and Muslim. See also *Kāfī*, VI, 299. It should be noted that the Bedouin ideal of hospitality is personified in Ḥātim al-Ṭā'ī, a poet who lived in the second half of the sixth century AD. The famous anthology of Arabic poetry entitled 'The *Ḥamāsa* of Abū Tammām' also contains a chapter on hospitality (*ḍiyāfa*). Nicholson, *Literary History*, 85–7; *EI*[2], s.v. Ḥātim al-Ṭā'ī; Ḥamāsa; Gelder, *Of Dishes*, 7–10, 22–4.

[3]*Mā'ida* pl. *mawā'id* means a table with food upon it. *Mā'ida* is an active participle from *māda* (it was in a state of motion), as though the table, which was generally a round piece of leather, was spread upon the ground and was moved about with what was upon it. Lane, s.v. m-y-d.

The Messenger of God: He said, 'Ibn Jud'ān[4] will be among those who suffer least in the lowest rungs of Hell.' It was said to him, 'O Messenger of God, why is that?' He said, 'He used to give food to people.'

[The Messenger of God]:[5] He said, 'That I should gather together a few of my brothers over a measure (*ṣā'*)[6] or two of food is more pleasing to me than going to your market and liberating a slave.'

Ja'far b. Muḥammad: He said, 'Whenever a faithful one gives a sufficiency of food to another believer, God feeds him with the fruits of Paradise; and whenever he gives him a drink [of water] to quench his thirst, God gives him the choicest sealed wine (*al-raḥīq al-makhtūm*).'[7]

The Messenger of God: An Arab from the country [came and] asked him, 'O Messenger of God, tell me of an action which will lead me to heaven.' The Messenger of God said, 'Feed people, greet people often, and pray while the people are asleep.' He said, 'This I cannot do!' The Messenger of God said, 'Have you any camels?' The country man replied, 'Yes.' The Messenger of God said, 'Carry water on it to those people who cannot drink water daily and drink at intervals only. Possibly your camel will not die and your water skin will not be worn out until Paradise is vouchsafed to you.'

'Alī: Seven prisoners were brought to the Messenger of God, so he told me, 'O 'Alī, arise and behead them.' And in the twinkling an eye, Gabriel[8] descended upon him and said, 'O Muḥammad, behead these six, but release this one. The Messenger of God said, 'And what is his special case?' The angel replied, 'He is open-handed (*madakhīyul al-kaff*) and generous with food.' The Messenger of God said, 'Is this [advice] from you or from my Lord?' The angel said, 'From, thy Lord, O Muḥammad.'

Muḥammad b. 'Alī: He said, 'The feeding of a faithful one is equivalent to the liberation of a slave. God is most pleased with the giving of joy to a faithful one when he is fed to his satisfaction, or his debt is paid off.'

Ja'far b. Muḥammad: He said, 'He who feeds a brother in the way of God will obtain the same rewards as feeding [an entire] group of people (*fi'ām*). Livelihood runs towards him who gives food even faster than a knife goes through the hump of a camel. Choose him whom you love for

[4]He is probably 'Abd Allāh b. Jud'ān who was well known for his hospitality. Many times the Prophet was his guest. *Qāmūs*, s.v. j-d-'. Ibn Judh'ān: in the edited text and MS Q is an error.

[5]MS Q: 'Alī.

[6]*Ṣā'*, see *The Pillars of Islam*, I, 45, 331, n. 149.

[7]Alludes to the Qur'ān: *They are given to drink of a pure wine, sealed* (83:25).

[8]Gabriel, see *The Pillars of Islam*, I, 63, n. 164.

the sake of God, for your hospitality (*ṭaʿām*) and your generosity (*māl*).'[9]

[Jaʿfar b. Muḥammad]: He said to one of his companions, 'What prevents you from emancipating a slave every day?' He said, 'My means do not warrant such a course, May I be thy ransom.' [The Imam] said, 'Then feed every day a faithful one (*mu'min*).' The man replied, 'Do you mean a man of means or a needy one?' [The Imam] said, '[Even] a man of means is desirous of food. My father [Imam al-Bāqir] used to say, "It is more desirable for me to give food to ten faithful ones than to liberate ten slaves, that is, other than the faithful. It is more desirable for me to feed one faithful person than to feed a large number (*ufuq min al-nās*)[10] of others." They asked him, "How many persons does the term *ufuq* comprise?" [The Imam] replied, "Ten thousand."'

The Messenger of God: He said, 'No guest arrives among a people without bringing with him his livelihood. Thus, when he alights, he alights with his daily bread; and when he departs, he takes away their sins.'[11] It means that their sins are forgiven, and [even though the guest takes away their sins], he bears no responsibility for them.

[The Messenger of God]: He said, 'Every faithful one extends hospitality to the guest.[12] Hospitality to guests is one of the virtues of character. The limit of hospitality is three days, and any excess [over that period] is charity.'[13]

[The Messenger of God]: He said, 'The noblest virtue in prophets, the truthful [witness] (*ṣiddīqīn*), the martyrs (*shuhadā'*), and the righteous (*ṣāliḥīn*)[14] is visiting [acquaintances] for the sake of God. It is the duty of the visited to proffer to his brother whatever is available to him; even a cup of water, if nothing else.[15] One who refrains from making such an offering to his brother, earns the hatred of God, night and day; and he

[9]Ibn ʿAbbās reported God's Messenger as saying, 'Good comes more quickly to the house in which food is provided than the knife comes to the camel's hump.' *Mishkāt*, II, 459; Robson, II, 902.

[10]*Majmaʿ al-baḥrayn*, s.v. a-f-q.

[11]For similar traditions see *Kāfī*, VI, 298–9.

[12]'One who believes in God and the Last Day should honour his guest.' Ibid., VI, 299.

[13]'He who believes in God and the Last Day should honour his guest. Provisions for the road are what will serve for a day and a night; hospitality extends for three days: what goes beyond is *ṣadaqa*; and it is not allowable that a guest should stay till he makes himself an encumbrance.' *Mishkāt*, II, 455; Robson, II, 898; transmitted by Bukhārī and Muslim. See also *Kāfī*, VI, 297.

[14]Cf. the Qur'ān 4:69. The words *ṣiddīqīn* and *shuhadā'* are translated differently by the Qur'ān translators.

[15]'When your brother visits you offer him food, if he does not eat, offer him water, if he does not drink, offer him [water] to perform the ablution [for the next prayer].' *Kāfī*, VI, 290.

who despises the offering of his brother also earns the hatred of God, night and day.'[16]

'Alī: He said, 'When a faithful brother visits you, give him the best food you have in the house; and if he is fasting, treat him gently [with soothing words].'[17]

Ja'far b. Muḥammad: He said, 'When your brother visits you, give him whatever is to be found in your house; but if you invite him, give him the best that you can afford.'[18]

[Ja'far b. Muḥammad]: He said to some of his companions with whom he was eating, 'The love a man bears to his brother is displayed by the decency with which he eats at his table. I admire the man who eats at my table with decency, and am greatly pleased with him.'[19]

The Messenger of God: He said, 'If I am invited to partake of the shoulder of a sheep, I accept the invitation;[20] and similarly if I am offered the foot [of a sheep or calf], I accept it.' This was because presents [always] gave him great happiness. Giving food to people is one of the ways of nearness to God; so the Messenger of God was not niggardly with Muslims, nor did he deny them the merit of such action.

'Alī: He used to attend feasts and say, 'This is a duty cast on the invitee.[21] But if a man were to attend an invitation as an uninvited guest, he had done something improper.'[22]

Al-Ḥusayn b. 'Alī: He saw a man who was invited to a meal saying to the host, 'Forgive me.' [The Imam] said, 'Arise! There is no question of forgiveness in an invitation. If you are not fasting eat; and if you are fasting, give blessings.'

Ja'far b. Muḥammad: He said, 'If a fasting man visits his brother, and

[16]Cf. *Kāfī*, VI, 291.

[17]The Arabic expression is *fa'dhunhu*, lit. means oint him with oil (namely his hair). Metaphorically, it denotes softness, treating with gentleness. Lane, s.v. d-h-n.

[18]*Kāfī*, VI, 291.

[19]For similar traditions see *Kāfī*, VI, 293–4.

[20]Ibid., VI, 289; the traditions adds, 'because it pertains to religion. But if an infidel or hypocrite invites me to partake of a slaughtered camel, I would not accept it, as it pertains to religion.'

[21]Cf. ibid., VI, 289; all the traditions stress that the invitation of a faithful should not be rejected.

[22]It is to be noted that in classical Arabic literature an uninvited guest or a social parasite, called *ṭufaylī*, was a popular character type in the Arabic *adab* genre. In the anecdotal literature the *ṭufaylī* is characterized as someone who abuses a situation of hospitality. His actions could range from coming uninvited to social functions to consuming more than his share of food and drink, or even to overstaying his welcome. *EI*^{2}, s.v. Ṭufaylī; Gelder, *Of Dishes*, 11.

he invites the visitor to eat, he should do so, unless his fast is in lieu of a compulsory fast, or a specified vow, or else it was past midday.' He also said, 'When your brother says, "Eat", you should eat and not compel him to entreat you (lit. to make an oath); for verily he only desires to show honour to you.'

The Messenger of God: He said, 'When an uninvited guest eats, it is as though a flame of fire is swallowed by him in his belly.'[23] He forbade an invited guest to feed someone else from food offered to him, unless he had been allowed to do so.

[The Messenger of God]: He said, 'When food is before you and a man passes by, if he sends salutations to you, invite him; but if he does not give greetings, then no one should invite him.'

[The Messenger of God]: When a traveller (*ibn al-sabīl*) or hungry man passes by [trees full of] fruit, the Messenger of God allowed him to eat of it. He prohibited that such trees should be surrounded by barriers and denied [to others]. The Messenger of God forbade the man who ate the fruit to damage the tree, or eat more than what was needed by him, or carry away any of it. However, God's Messenger considered this permissible in case of dire necessity.

THE DIFFERENT KINDS OF VIANDS, [THEIR USE AS] TREATMENT, AND THEIR NEED (*ṢUNŪF AL-AṬ'IMA WA-'ILĀJIHĀ WA 'L-ḤĀJA ILAYHĀ*)[24]

Abū Ja'far Muḥammad b. 'Alī: Al-Abrash al-Kalbī asked [the Imam] about the Word of God: *On the day when the earth will be changed to other than the earth* (14:48). [The Imam] said, 'The earth will be changed to another earth and will become like a soft lump of dough (a cake of bread, *khubzat al-niqy*), and the people will eat of it, until the account [taken by God] will be finished.' Abrash said, 'But on that day people will hardly be concerned with eating!' Abū Ja'far replied, 'Those in the Fire will be greatly concerned with it. For God says: *And the dwellers of the Fire cry out unto the dwellers of the Garden: Pour on us some water or some of that wherewith Allah has provided you. They say: Lo! Allah has forbidden both to disbelievers* (7:50). Those in the Fire will eat bitter thorn fruit (*ḍarī'*)[25] and will drink

[23]*Kāfī*, VI, 285.

[24]In the books entitled *Ṭibb al-a'imma* and *al-Ṭibb al-nabawī* the following verse of the Qur'ān is emphasized as a basic principle of good health. O *Children of Adam! … eat and drink, but be not prodigal. Lo! He loveth not the prodigals* (7:31).

[25]*Ḍarī'*, in the Qur'ān 88:6, is said to be the plant which beasts will not approach

boiling water (*ḥamīm*);[26] what then will their condition be during the reckoning? Indeed man has been created by God with a stomach, and he cannot do without food and drink.'[27]

Ja'far b. Muḥammad: Concerning the Word of God, relating the story of Moses: *My Lord! I am needy of whatever good Thou sendest down for me* (28:24), he said, '[Moses] was asking for food, so greatly needed by him.'[28]

The Messenger of God said, 'The chief of the viands of this world and the hereafter is meat (*laḥm*);[29] and the chief of the drinks of this world and the hereafter is water (*mā'*).[30] I enjoin upon you to eat meat, for it increases the growth of flesh, and he who ceases to eat meat for forty days will suffer in his disposition (*khuluq*).'[31]

Abū Ja'far Muḥammad b. 'Alī: He said, 'The eating of meat increases the sense of hearing and sight, and augments strength in the human body.'[32]

Ja'far b. Muḥammad b. 'Alī: He said, 'One of the prophets [of Banū Isrā'īl] complained of weakness to God. And God revealed to him, 'Cook meat in milk (*laban*) and eat them both, for, verily, I have blessed them both.' The prophet did so and God returned his strength to him.'[33]

The Messenger of God: He used to love meat and say, 'Verily we Quraysh[34] are meat eaters (*laḥmīyūn*) [strictly, people of the meat],'[35] and he used to be fond of meat from the shoulder.[36] Once a sheep was

---

because of its bad quality. It is the food of the inmates of Hell and is described as more bitter than aloe, more stinking than a carcass, and hotter than fire. Lane, s.v. ḍ-r-'.

[26]*Ḥamīm*, occurs several times in the Qur'ān, for example: *And those who disbelieve—for them awaits a draught of boiling water, and a painful chastisement, for their disbelieving* (10:4).

[27]*Kāfī*, VI, 300, 301; also reported on the authority of Imam al-Bāqir wherein al-Abrash al-Kalbī asks the Imam.

[28]Ibid., VI, 301; reported on the authority of Imam al-Ṣādiq.

[29]Ibid., VI, 322; Ibn Qayyim, *al-Ṭibb al-nabawī*, 211, 340; Suyūṭī, *al-Manhaj al-sawīy*, 156.

[30]Ibn Qayyim, *al-Ṭibb al-nabawī*, 355; Suyūṭī, *al-Manhaj al-sawīy*, 182.

[31]*Kāfī*, VI, 323; Nīsābūrī, *Ṭibb al-a'imma*, 645. Ibn Qayyim, *al-Ṭibb al-nabawī*, 340; Shabbar, *Ṭibb al-a'imma*, 163.

[32]See Ibn Qayyim, *al-Ṭibb al-nabawī*, 340; in the following pages, i.e. 341–51, he has described various kinds of meat and poultry.

[33]*Kāfī*, VI, 330; Nīsābūrī, *Ṭibb al-a'imma*, 287; the prophet in question was Nūḥ, and the tradition is transmitted on the authority of Imam al-Bāqir; Suyūṭī, *al-Manhaj al-sawīy*, 163.

[34]For Quraysh see *The Pillars of Islam*, I, 37, n. 81.

[35]*Kāfī*, VI, 323.

[36]Ibid., VI, 330.

presented to him, and he desired the shoulder.[37] The sheep cried out, 'I am poisoned!'[38] The Messenger of God said, 'None but the faithful eats a slaughtered camel.'

Ja'far b. Muḥammad: He was asked about the following tradition that people related from the Messenger of God: 'God dislikes those people of the house who are meat eaters.' Ja'far b. Muḥammad said, 'This did not refer to the eating of lawful meat which the Messenger of God liked and ate. This only refers to the "meat" in the Qur'ānic verse: *Would one of you love to eat the flesh of his dead brother* (49:12)? which means backbiting (*ghība*) and concerning oneself with it.'[39]

The Messenger of God said, '*Tharīd*[40] is the fare of the Arabs. The Prophet Abraham[41] was the first to crumble bread in broth and make it into *tharīd*, and the first among the Arabs to crush bread was Hāshim.'[42]

Ja'far b. Muḥammad: He said, '*Tharīd* is a blessing. The food prepared for one suffices for two persons.' [The Imam] meant that it was so nourishing, not that it satisfied or filled [two persons].

[Ja'far b. Muḥammad]: He said, 'The Messenger of God loved honey (*'asal*) and raisins (*zabīb*).'[43]

[37]Ibn Qayyim, *al-Ṭibb al-nabawī*, 210.

[38]After the conquest of Khaybar Zaynab bt. al-Ḥārith, the wife of Sallām b. Mishkam (who was the chief of Banū al-Naḍīr) prepared for the Prophet a roast lamb, having first inquired what cut he preferred. When she learned that it was the shoulder she put a lot of poison in it and poisoned the whole lamb .... The Prophet took hold of the shoulder and chewed a morsel of it, but he did not swallow it ... and spat it out, saying, 'This bone tells me that it is poisoned.' See Ibn Isḥāq, *al-Sīra*, III, 352; Guillaume, 516.

[39]Ṭūsī, *al-Tibyān*, IX, 350; the same interpretation.

[40]*Tharīd* means bread broken into small pieces, with the fingers, then moistened with broth and then piled up in the middle of a bowl and generally has some meat with it. Lane, s.v. th-r-d. 'The food God's Messenger liked best was *tharīd* made from bread and *tharīd* made from *ḥays* (a mixture of dates and clarified butter).' *Mishkāt*, II, 450; Robson, II, 894; *Qāmūs*, ḥ-y-s. See also *Kāfī*, VI, 331–2. "Ā'isha's pre-eminence over the rest of the women was like the pre-eminence of *tharīd* over the rest of the food.' Transmitted by both Bukhārī and Muslim. *Concordance*, s.v. th-r-d; Ibn Qayyim, *al-Ṭibb al-nabawī*, 273.

[41]For Abraham see *The Pillars of Islam*, I, 56, n. 147.

[42]Hāshim b. 'Abd Manāf was the great grandfather of the Prophet. One year when food was scarce in Mecca, he brought baked loaves from Syria, and crumbed (*hashama*) these to make broth (*tharīd*) for the pilgrims; after this he was known as Hāshim, meaning the one who crumbed bread to make broth, but his proper name was 'Amr. He died on a trade journey at Ghazza (Gaza) and left behind in Medina a son 'Abd al-Muṭṭalib by Salmā bint 'Amr of the Najjār clan. Ibn Isḥāq, *al-sīra*, I, 111, 112; Guillaume, 58; *EI*^{2} , s.v. Hāshim b. 'Abd Manāf.

[43]'God's Messenger liked sweetmeats (*ḥalwā'*) and honey.' Transmitted by Bukhārī and Muslim. *Mishkāt*, II, 444; Robson, II, 889. See also Suyūṭī, *al-Manhaj al-sawīy*, 170. For the benefits of raisins see Ibn Qayyim, *al-Ṭibb al-nabawī*, 294–5.

[Ja'far b. Muḥammad]: He said, 'The Messenger of God was fond of *fālūdhaj*.[44] Whenever he wanted to have it he would say, "Make it for us, but sparingly."[45] I believe that was because he wished to avoid taking a large quantity, lest it harm him. The Messenger of God used to give away sugar (*sukkar*) by way of charity. When asked about it he said, "There is no kind of food that I like more, and I wanted to give in charity that which I like most."'

[Ja'far b. Muḥammad]: He used to relish *zīrbāja* (a kind of sweet)[46] and raisins.[47] He used to say, 'We have been granted food of various kinds which were not available to the Messenger of God himself.'

The Messenger of God: He used to love dates (*tamr*) and would say, 'The *'ajwa* (a superior variety of date)[48] comes from Paradise.' He used to put a date above a morsel of food and say, 'This is the seasoning (*idām*) for it!'[49]

'Alī b. al-Ḥusayn used to say, 'I love a man who likes dates because the Messenger of God loved dates. When food was brought to the Messenger of God, and it contained dates, he began with dates.[50] He used to break his fast with dry (*tamr*) or fresh dates (*raṭb*), according to the season.'[51]

Ja'far b. Muḥammad: One of his companions had a meal with him.

[44]Arabicized from the Persian *fālūda* or *pālūda*. It is a kind of sweet prepared from the purest substance of wheat or of starch with water or milk and honey. Lane, s.v. f-l-dh.

[45]*Kafi*, VI, 335.

[46]*Zīrbāja*, arabicized from the Persian *zīrbā*, is a dish made of sugar, almond and vinegar. Dozy, s.v. *zīrbāj*; Mu'īn, *Farhang*, s.v. *zīrbā*; a kind of broth.

[47]*Kāfī*, VI, 365; Ibn Qayyim, *al-Ṭibb al-nabawī*, 294–5; it is good for memory. Zuhrī, a celebrated traditionist and a historian, said that whoever wants to memorize traditions should eat raisins.

[48]It is described as the best kind of dates in Medina; it is large and almost black in colour. Lane, s.v. 'a-j-w. 'He who has a morning meal of seven *'ajwa* dates will not suffer harm that day through poison or magic.' Transmitted by Bukhārī and Muslim. Another tradition states, 'The *'ajwa* dates come from Paradise and contain a cure for poison.' *Mishkāt*, II, 445, 453; Robson, II, 890, 896. See also, *Kāfī*, VI, 361, 363; Ibn Qayyim, *al-Ṭibb al-nabawī*, 313; Suyūṭī, *al-Manhaj al-sawīy*, 381.

[49]'The Prophet took a piece of barley bread and put a date on it, saying, "This is the condiment of this."' *Mishkāt*, II, 450; Robson, II, 894.

[50]According to MS Q, it is a continuation of Imam 'Alī b. al-Ḥusayn's report. Instead of '*wa-'anhu*,' in the edited text, MS Q has '*wa-kāna ṣallā Allāhu 'alayhi wa-sallam* [abbreviated] *idhā* ...' See also *Kāfī*, VI, 359.

[51]"Abdallāh b. Ja'far reported that he saw God's Messenger eating fresh dates with cucumber.' There are several traditions in praise of dates, such as, "Ā'isha said Muḥammad's family did not have a full meal of wheated bread on two successive days, but would have dates on one of them.' Both the traditions are transmitted by Bukhārī and Muslim. *Mishkāt*, II, 444, 445; Robson, II, 889, 890.

When the tray was taken away, Ja'far b. Muḥammad said, 'O slave girl, bring whatever you have.' So she brought dates, and the man said, 'May I be thy ransom, this is the season of fruits (*fākiha*), and grapes (*'inab*),' for it was summer. [The Imam] said, 'Eat, this was the habit of the Messenger of God.' The Messenger of God said, 'There is no disease and no mischief in *'ajwa*.'

The Messenger of God: He said, 'When a man eats a morsel of food with much flesh and fat in it (*luqma samīna*), an equal amount of disease goes out from his body.[52] The meat of cow is a disease, and its clarified butter (*samn*) is a cure and its milk a medicine.[53] Nothing enters the stomach which is as good as clarified butter.'[54]

The Messenger of God: He said, 'Vinegar (*khall*) and [olive] oil are the best of seasonings (*idām*). They are the perfume and seasonings of the prophets of God. It is blessed. The household which has vinegar is never wanting in seasoning.'[55]

Ja'far b. Muḥammad: He said, 'Vinegar quiets disruption of the bile (*mirār*)[56] and gives life to hearts (*yuḥyī al-qulūb*).'

[Ja'far b. Muḥammad]: Once he offered one of his guests vinegar, oil (*zayt*), and a piece of cold meat, and the man ate with him. [The Imam] would break off a piece of meat, dip it in oil and in vinegar, and eat it. The man said, 'May I be thy ransom, is the meat not cooked with the vinegar and the oil?' [The Imam] replied, 'This is our food and the food of the prophets of God.'[57]

[Ja'far b. Muḥammad]: He was asked about the eating of garlic

[52]*Kāfī*, VI, 325.

[53]Ibid., VI, 325; Ibn Qayyim, *al-Ṭibb al-nabawī*, 300; according to 'Alī clarified butter is the best course of treatment.

[54]*Kāfī*, VI, 349–50. MS Q reads: Nothing that enters the stomach is more limpid than clarified butter.

[55]'Vinegar is a good condiment.' Transmitted by Muslim. Another tradition states, 'A house in which there is vinegar is not devoid of condiments.' *Mishkāt*, II, 444, 450; Robson, II, 889, 894. See also *Kāfī*, VI, 343; Ibn Qayyim, *al-Ṭibb al-nabawī*, 211, 283; Suyūṭī, *al-Manhaj al-sawīy*, 169.

[56]*Mirār* pl. of *mirra*, the bile. The four humours of the body are: yellow bile (*ṣafrā'*), black bile (*sawdā'*), blood (*dam*), and phlegm (*balgham*). Lane, s.v. m-r-r. Ibn Qayyim, *al-Ṭibb al-nabawī*, 283; similar benefits are described.

[57]'Ajlān said, 'Once I had my dinner with Abī 'Abd Allāh after dark. He used to eat dinner after dark. Vinegar, oil, and a piece of cold meat was brought. [The Imam] began breaking off a piece of meat to serve me while he ate [bread with] vinegar and oil and did not touch the meat. [As I was surprised, the Imam] said, "This is our food and the food of the prophets."' *Kāfī*, VI, 342. Several traditions stress that the food of the prophets consists of vinegar and oil.

(*thūm*),[58] onion (*baṣal*)[59] and leek (*kurrāth*),[60] fresh as well as cooked, and he said, 'There is no harm in it, but no one eating them raw should enter a mosque lest it disturb others by its odour.'[61]

The Messenger of God: He said, 'You should eat lentils (*'adas*) because they soften the heart, help one to cry tears [of piety][62] and have been sanctified by seventy prophets.[63]

'Alī: He used to eat pomegranates (*rummān*) including the yellow pulp (*bi-shahmihi*) that is amid the seeds of the pomegranate and he would direct others to do the same. He would say that it tans the stomach.[64] Every pomegranate contains a grain of Paradise;[65] if anything drops out from it, find it and eat it. He never used to share his pomegranates with anyone, and he used to pick up what fell from it and say, 'Whoever puts a pomegranate into his stomach, removes thereby the machinations of the devil.'[66]

The Messenger of God: He once cut a quince (*safarjal*) and ate it and

[58]For the benefits of garlic see Ibn Qayyim, *al-Ṭibb al-nabawī*, 272–3; 'one who wants to eat it should cook it.' Besides flavouring in cooking and pickling, it is used in medicine as a digestive stimulant, diuretic, and antispasmodic. It also reduces infection and inflammation of wound. www.folkmed.ucla.edu.

[59]For its benefits see Ibn Qayyim, *al-Ṭibb al-nabawī*, 269–70; the tradition states that it should be cooked and eaten.

[60]It belongs to lily and onion family and is of two kinds: Nabatean and Syrian. For its benefits see ibid., 339–40.

[61]'He who eats [raw] garlic or [raw] onion must keep away from us, or from our mosque.' *Mishkāt*, II, 446; Robson, II, 890; transmitted by Bukhārī and Muslim. See also *Kāfī*, VI, 378–9, 387–8; three separate sections, one on each.

[62]The Arabic reads: *yukthiru al-dam'ata*, lit. means increases tears [in the eye]. It is said that Job's tears (*dam'u Ayyūb*) strengthen one's patience and are diuretic. Lane, s.v. d-m-'.

[63]*Kāfī*, VI, 321, 357–8. One tradition states that lentils are not sanctified by the prophets. Ibn Qayyim, *al-Ṭibb al-nabawī*, 316–17; he rejects this tradition and states that it was a carnal appetite for the Jews and they preferred it over 'the manna and the quails'. He further states that it produces the black bile, one of the four humours of ancient medicine, and causes melancholy and harms the eyesight. Dhahabī, *al-Ṭibb al-nabawī*, 68; 'It softens the heart, increases tears in the eyes, and drives away arrogance.' Shabbar, *Ṭibb al-a'imma*, 201–2.

[64]Tanning is used metaphorically to mean to soften, or to make pliable. It is said in a tradition, 'The tanning thereof [skin] is its purification.' Lane, s.v. d-b-gh. The *ḥadīth* about the pomegranate is transmitted by Ibn Ḥanbal. *Concordance*, s.v. d-b-gh. See also Ibn Qayyim, *al-Ṭibb al-nabawī*, 292; the tradition is narrated from 'Alī. Ibn Qayyim also states its benefits. Suyūṭī, *al-Manhaj al-sawīy*, 289. Its astringent rind is used in medicine and tanning.

[65]*Kāfī*, VI, 363. It states, 'Five kinds of fruits are from Paradise: pomegranates, apples, quinces, grapes, and dates.'

[66]Ibid., VI, 366–9; it has a separate section on pomegranates. See also Nīsābūrī, *Ṭibb al-a'imma*, 622; Shabbar, *Ṭibb al-a'imma*, 217–20.

gave Ja'far b. Abī Ṭālib[67] a portion and said, 'Eat it, O Ja'far, for the quince purifies the heart and fills a coward with courage.'[68]

'Alī: He said, 'You should eat apples (*tuffāḥ*), for they are beneficial to the stomach.'[69]

The Messenger of God: He liked gourd (*dubbā'*)[70] and would lift it from the platter and say, 'It is good for the brain.'[71]

[The Messenger of God]: He said, 'Endive (*hindibā'* or *hindabā'*)[72] is for us, and watercress (*jirjīr*) for the Banū Umayya.[73] [It is as if I see the roots of (*jirjīr*) in Hell][74] while I see the roots of sweet basil (*bādharūj*)[75] in Paradise.'

[The Messenger of God]: He said, 'Parsley (*karafs*)[76] is the vegetable of the prophets (*baqlat al-anbiyā'*), and every leaf of endive (*hindibā'*) contains a drop of the water of Paradise.[77] You should eat gourd (*dubbā'*)

[67]Ja'far b. Abī Ṭālib, see *The Pillars of Islam*, I, 298, n. 156.

[68]*Kāfī*, VI, 370–1; a separate section on quinces. Nīsābūrī, *Ṭibb al-a'imma*, 629; Ibn Qayyim, *al-Ṭibb al-nabawī*, 296–8; all the benefits are enumerated; Suyūṭī, *al-Manhaj al-sawīy*, 291–4; Shabbar, *Ṭibb al-a'imma*, 227–9.

[69]*Kāfī*, VI, 369–70; a separate section on apples; Nīsābūrī, *Ṭibb al-a'imma*, 623; Shabbar, *Ṭibb al-a'imma*, 221–5.

[70]Ibn Ḥajar states that it is a variety of squash (*yaqṭīn*). Lane, s.v. d-b-b.

[71]Anas said, 'A tailor invited the Prophet to a meal which he had prepared and I went along with the Prophet. He presented barley bread and soup containing pumpkin (*dubbā'*) and dried sliced meat, and I saw the Prophet going after the pumpkin in the dish, so I have liked pumpkin since that day.' *Mishkāt*, II, 444; Robson II, 888; transmitted by Bukhārī and Muslim. Suyūṭī, *al-Manhaj al-sawīy*, 163; it strengthens the heart of a grieved person. See also *Kāfī*, VI, 383–4; a separate section on *al-qar'*, which is *al-dubbā'* meaning pumpkin (yellow gourd). Shabbar, *Ṭibb al-a'imma*, 267–8; he cites this tradition from the *Da'ā'im*.

[72]It is of a slender and soft nature; a plant of middling temperament, beneficial for the stomach, the liver and the spleen when eaten; and for the sting of a scorpion when its roots are applied externally. Lane, s.v. h-d-b. See also *Kāfī*, VI, 376–7; all the benefits are enumerated; Nīsābūrī, *Ṭibb al-a'imma*, 640; it enumerates the benefits; Ibn Qayyim, *al-Ṭibb al-nabawī*, 366–7; all the benefits are listed; Ibn al-Bayṭār, *Ṭuḥfa*, 105, 239; Shabbar, *Ṭibb al-a'imma*, 243–7. See also *Majma' al-baḥrayn*, s.v. j-r-r; the *ḥadīth* is cited.

[73]Banū Umayya, see *The Pillars of Islam*, I, 94, 155, 227, 263, 305, 476; *Kāfī*, VI, 381; *jirjīr* is for the Banū Umayya. *Majma' al-baḥrayn*, s.v. j-r-r; the tradition is cited. Ibn al-Bayṭār, *Ṭuḥfa*, 200; Shabbar, *Ṭibb al-a'imma*, 260–1; bad effects of *jirjīr* are enumerated.

[74]Addition from MS Q; it is missing from the edited text. Both the Messenger of God and 'Alī liked *bādharūj*. *Kāfī*, VI, 377–8.

[75]Nīsābūrī, *Ṭibb al-a'imma*, 651–2; '*Bādharūj* is for us, and *jirjīr* for the Banū Umayya.'

[76]As in MS Q and other two MSS of Fyzee. In the edited text: *Karfash* is incorrect. *Karafs*, the herb smallage; apium graveolens of Linnaeus. It is a well-known herb of the leguminous plants that are eaten without being cooked. It is used as a diuretic and to flush the kidneys, liver, and bladder, and to clear obstructions in them. Lane, s.v. k-r-f-s. See also *Kāfī*, VI, 379–80; Ibn Qayyim, *al-Ṭibb al-nabawī*, 339.

[77]Nīsābūrī, *Ṭibb al-a'imma*, 640.

for it sharpens the intelligence and increases brain power.'[78] The Messenger of God also liked purslane (*rijla*)[79] and blessed it.

[The Messenger of God]: He said, 'He who begins his meal and ends it with salt (*milḥ*), is safe from seventy-two diseases, among them leprosy (*judhām*) and leucoderma (*baraṣ*).'[80]

'Alī: He said, 'He who picks up a piece of bread off of the street, and takes it, and rubs it [for cleaning it] and keeps it in a niche, God will write for him a good deed [equal to] ten common good deeds. If he eats it, God will write for him two double good deeds.'[81]

Ja'far b. Muḥammad: He said, 'When my father [Imam al-Bāqir] found any food thrown away in the house, he reduced the food of family to the same extent. Concerning the Word of God: *Allah coineth a similitude: a township that dwelt secure and well content, its provision coming to it in abundance from every side, but it disbelieved in Allah's favours, so Allah made it experience the garb of dearth and fear because of what they used to do* (16:112), [Imam al-Bāqir] said, "This referred to the people of a certain village, to whom God had given ample provision. They found it hard to clean themselves with stones, so they began to use bread shaped like a pestle for toilet purposes. Then God sent them insects smaller than locusts which did not leave for them from God's creation a single tree or vegetable uneaten. The people were so overtaken by [this] great hardship that they began to eat the same pieces of bread which they formerly used for toilet needs."'

'Alī b. al-Ḥusayn: Once he entered the washroom and found a date[82] in it; so he gave it to his slave and said, 'Hold it until I return to you.' The slave, however, took it and ate it. When [the Imam] finished his ablutions and returned, he asked the slave, 'Where is the date?' The slave replied, 'May I be thy ransom, I have eaten it.' [The Imam] said, 'Go, you are free for the sake of God!' [The Imam] was asked about this and what merit there was in the eating of that date which warranted his emancipation. He said, 'As soon as he ate the date Paradise was reserved for him. And

[78]Ibid., 642–3.

[79]It is also called *farfakh* or *al-baqlat al-ḥamqā'*. Lane, s.v. r-j-l. *Kāfī*, VI, 380; *farfakh* was a favourite vegetable of Fāṭima. *Majma' al-baḥrayn*, s.v. r-j-l; it is called *al-ḥamqā'* (dumb) because it grows in river beds.

[80]'Salt is the king of all condiments.' *Mishkāt*, II, 454; Robson, II, 897; Ibn Qayyim, *al-Ṭibb al-nabawī*, 362. *Kāfī*, VI, 340–1; it has a section on the benefits of salt. See also Shabbar, *Ṭibb al-a'imma*, 148–51.

[81]Shabbar, *Ṭibb al-a'imma*, 146–7; the tradition states, 'He who eats what falls from a dining table drives away poverty and increases his means of livelihood.'

[82]'A family which has dates will not be hungry.' *Mishkāt*, II, 445; Robson, II, 889; Ibn Qayyim, *al-Ṭibb al-nabawī*, 270–1.

I disliked that I should be the owner of one of the residents of Paradise!'

Ja'far b. Muḥammad: [One day the Imam] saw some fruit thrown away from his house which had not been fully eaten. He was angered and said, 'What is this? If you are filled, there are many men who are not able to eat to satisfaction; so, serve him who needs food.'[83]

[Ja'far b. Muḥammad]: He said, '[A place in] Paradise is reserved for one who picks up a date or broken piece [of bread] that had been discarded on the ground, wipes it off, and eats it. [His place in Paradise is awarded him] before the food even settles in his stomach.'[84]

Abū Ja'far Muḥammad b. 'Alī: He said, 'Whenever my father 'Alī b. al-Ḥusayn used to see a piece of bread thrown away [on the ground] in his house—even if it were as small as to be [a morsel] pulled by an ant—he used to reduce the quantity of food in the household to the same extent.'

Once [the Imam] al-Mahdī bi 'llāh[85] ordered that thin bread be removed from the daily rations of the household. So some of the people tried to uncover the reason for this, and they were informed that sometimes the Mahdī would enter one of the apartments of the harem unannounced and see that dried pieces of bread were strewn on the ground. So he prohibited this [practice] and when they disobeyed him, he ordered it cut from their rations.

'Alī: Once a dish of *fālūdhaj* was brought and placed before him. He looked at it and saw its beauty, purity, and clarity, and he poked his finger into it and withdrew it without taking any of the sweet and licked his finger. Then he said, 'This is a very lovely sweet, but I do not like that we get used to something with which we are not accustomed. Take it away!' So, they took it away.

The Messenger of God: Once on a Thursday he went to Qubā' (near Medina)[86] while he was fasting. When it was evening, he said, 'Is there any drink?' One of the Anṣār[87] arose and brought him a cup of milk mixed with honey.[88] When the Messenger of God tasted it he threw it away from his mouth and said, 'These are two sauces; one of them is sufficient without the other. I neither drink it nor forbid it. But I show courtesy to my Lord; for, verily God raises him who shows courtesy to Him. He who

[83]*Kāfī*, VI, 312.

[84]Ibid., VI, 314–15; this section is entitled 'Eating of what drops from the plate'.

[85]Al-Mahdī, see *The Pillars of Islam*, I, 71, n. 193.

[86]Qubā', see *The Pillars of Islam*, I, 371, n. 75.

[87]For Anṣār see *The Pillars of Islam*, I, 13, n. 18.

[88]The Messenger of God liked honey. *Kāfī*, VI, 346–7. "Ā'isha said God's Messenger liked sweetmeats and honey.' *Mishkāt*, II, 444; Robson, II, 889; transmitted by Bukhārī. Ibn Qayyim, *al-Ṭibb al-nabawī*, 352–4; he has enumerated the benefits of various types of milk.

shows vanity towards God, God will abase him. He who pursues a moderate path in his mode of life, God will give him his livelihood. He who is extravagant, God will deny him [his needs]. And he who remembers God greatly, will be provided livelihood by God.'[89]

This, and God knows best, is what has come from the Messenger of God showing his humility to God, not that God had declared any good viands to be unlawful.[90] God says: *Say: Who hath forbidden the adornment of Allah which He hath brought forth for His bondmen, and the good things of His providing? Say: Such, on the Day of Resurrection, will be only for those who believed during the life of the world* (7:32).

Ja'far b. Muḥammad: He said, 'There is no extravagance in serving food.'[91] And concerning the Qur'ānic verse: *Then, on that day, ye will be asked concerning pleasure (al-na'īm)* (102:8),[92] he said, 'Now God is too noble to ask you concerning the food that He has bestowed upon you; but you will be questioned about the favours of God through us [the Imams], whether you appreciated them and used them appropriately.[93]

'Alī: He said, 'The more hands that partake of food, the greater the blessing. The Messenger of God has said, "Food for one is sufficient for two; and food for two is sufficient for four."'[94] By sufficiency the Messenger of God meant that which satisfies and removes hunger, not that which satiates and reaches the utmost limit of sufficiency.

The Messenger of God: He forbade the eating of hot food and said, 'It is without blessing.' Once when food which was very hot was brought before him he said, 'God does not wish that fire should be our food. Let it rest for a while, so that it is possible to eat. For, verily, hot food is devoid of blessing, and the devil is a partner in it.[95] When food is [moderately hot and] capable

[89]'God is pleased when a man eats something and praises Him for it, or drinks something and praises Him for it.' *Mishkāt*, II, 446; Robson, II, 891. See also *Kāfī*, VI, 306–11.

[90]It refers to milk and honey in the above report.

[91]*Kāfī*, VI, 295; also reported from al-Ṣādiq.

[92]For a quite different and a mundane explanation of this verse, see *Mishkāt*, II, 458; Robson, II. 901. Ṭabarī, *Tafsīr* (Beirut), XXX, 184–7. According to him, *al-na'īm* means *amn* (safety) and *ṣiḥḥa* (health). He also cites the tradition cited in *Mishkāt* and concludes that *al-na'īm* is used as a general term and does not refer to one particular thing.

[93]The word *al-na'īm* in this verse refers to the *walāya* of 'Alī and the Imams of his progeny. Qummī, II, 477; Furāt al-Kūfī, II, 606; Ṭūsī, *al-Tibyān*, X, 403. For similar traditions on the authority of Imam al-Bāqir and al-Ṣādiq, see *Kāfī*, VI, 295.

[94]'Two people's food is enough for three, and three people's food is enough for four.' Transmitted by Bukhārī and Muslim. Muslim transmitted another tradition, which states, 'One person's food is enough for two, two person's food is enough for four, and four person's food is enough for eight.' *Mishkāt*, II, 443; Robson, II, 888; *Kāfī*, VI, 289.

[95]*Kāfī*, VI, 336.

[of being eaten] it possesses some qualities; it increases the blessing in it and fills to satiety the one who eats it; and it saves man from death.'

The Messenger of God: He forbade that people sniff bread as wild animals.[96] He also forbade that bread be cut by a knife.[97]

Ja'far b. Muḥammad: He was asked about musk (*misk*),[98] amber (*'anbar*)[99] and other odoriferous substances mixed with food. He replied, 'There is no harm in them.'

TABLE MANNERS (*ĀDĀB AL-AKL*)[100]

Ja'far b. Muḥammad—his father—his ancestors: The Messenger of God said, 'God forgives [the sins] of everyone who gathers together with his family and when food is placed before them they mention the name of God before eating and they praise the Lord when finishing it and the tray is taken away.'[101]

'Alī: He said, 'When God is named at the commencement of a meal, and praised at the end of it, and hands are washed at the beginning and end, and many hands join in the meal that is lawfully earned, then verily the blessing of God is perfected.'[102]

[96]Ibid., VI, 317.

[97]Ibid., VI, 318. For different types of bread see Ibn Qayyim, *al-Ṭibb al-nabawī*, 281–2; he rejects the tradition that the Prophet forbade cutting bread with a knife.

[98]Musk is the king of all fragrances. Ibn Qayyim, *al-Ṭibb al-nabawī*, 360–1; Suyūṭī, *al-Manhaj al-sawīy*, 378.

[99]Amber is the best after musk. For its benefits see Ibn Qayyim, *al-Ṭibb al-nabawī*, 314–15.

[100]The term *adab* pl. *ādāb* has a variety of meanings, see n. 1, Chap. 26. There are neither separate sections by this title in *Mishkāt* nor *Kāfī*, however certain aspects are dealt with in the chapter on food. Despite the earthly aspect of eating there is a strong link between eating and etiquette on the one hand, and eating and ethics on the other, in Arabic literature. Table manners are described in works on religious ethics and behaviour, such as Ghazālī's *Iḥyā' 'ulūm al-dīn*, II, 1–21. The Arabic word *adab* used in the classical period for 'belles-lettres' not only meant 'erudition' but also 'good manners, etiquette'. Some scholars have suggested the connection between eating, ethics, and literature by pointing out the apparent etymological link between *adab* (literature, good behaviour) and *ma'duba* (banquet for guests). They further add that as eating is both sustaining and pleasant, so is *adab* instructive and entertaining. Gelder, *Of Dishes*, 3; idem, 'Arabic Banquets'.

[101]'Mention God's name [before eating], eat with your right hand, and eat what is closest to you.' Another tradition states that when God's Messenger finished his food he said, 'Praise be to God who has given us food and drink and made us Muslims.' *Mishkāt*, II, 441, 447; Robson, II, 886, 892; transmitted by Bukhārī and Muslim. *Kāfī*, VI, 310–11.

[102]*Kāfī*, VI, 288–9, 306–11. Suyūṭī, *al-Manhaj al-sawīy*, 180; 'Blessing of food consists in washing [of hands] before and after the meal.'

['Alī]: He said, 'I guarantee that the one who mentions God before his meal will never complain of the food.' Ibn al-Kawwā'[103] said, 'Yesterday I mentioned the name of God before a meal and yet it gave me pain.' The Commander of the Faithful 'Alī said, 'Perhaps you partook of various kinds of food, and mentioned God's name on some of them, but not on others, O base fellow (*luka'*)!'[104] He said, 'So it was, By God, O Commander of the Faithful.'[105]

Ja'far b. Muḥammad: He said, 'When food is placed [before you], mention the name of God, for verily, Satan says to his companions, "Go away, because you have no share in it." Satan has his share of food with him who does not mention the name of God over it.'[106]

[The Imam] said, 'When a man says in the morning, "I begin in the name of God in spite of haste and forgetfulness," such a pronouncement is sufficient [to excuse him] for what he forgets regarding food or drink.'

[Ja'far b. Muḥammad]: He permitted the blowing of breath over food and drink. This is disapproved only when there is some one else with him who may dislike it.

The Messenger of God: He forbade eating food with a back rest.[107] When he ate himself, he sat on one of his legs in an upright posture, not at his ease,[108] and kept the other one free, and he used to say, 'I sit as the slave (*'abd*) does, and I eat as the slave eats.'[109]

'Alī: He said, 'Do not eat lying flat on your back as the tyrants (*jabbārūn*) do, and do not sit cross-legged.'[110]

Abū 'Abd Allāh: He said, 'The Messenger of God never ate with a back rest from the time he received his call till the day of his death.'[111]

[103]He is 'Abd Allāh b. al-Kawwā' al-Yashkurī who evolved in his political orientation from opposition to 'Uthmān, to support for 'Alī, to support for the Khawārij, to support for Mu'āwiya. Ṭabarī, *History of al-Ṭabarī*, XVII, 99, 102, 138.

[104]*Majma' al-baḥrayn*, s.v. l-k-'.

[105]*Kāfī*, VI, 309; it is without the last sentence, i.e. the confession of Ibn al-Kawwā'. See also Nīsābūrī, *Ṭibb al-a'imma*, 256.

[106]'Satan considers food lawful for him when God's name is not mentioned before eating.' *Mishkāt*, II, 441; Robson II, 886; transmitted by Muslim. See also *Kāfī*, VI, 307.

[107]'I do not eat reclining.' *Mishkāt*, 442; Robson, II, 887; transmitted by Bukhārī. *Kāfī*, VI, 286, 287; Ibn Qayyim, *al-Ṭibb al-nabawī*, 212; Suyūṭī, *al-Manhaj al-sawīy*, 179.

[108]*Istawfaza fī qi'datihi* also means that he put down his knees [upon the ground] and raised his buttocks, or he sat in a posture as though he desired to rise and stand up. Lane, s.v. w-f-z.

[109]*Kāfī*, VI, 286, 287; several traditions are reported. See also Ibn Qayyim, *al-Ṭibb al-nabawī*, 212.

[110]*Kāfī*, VI, 287. Ibn Qayyim, *al-Ṭibb al-nabawī*, 213.

[111]*Mishkāt*, II, 442, 448; Robson, II, 887, 893. *Kāfī*, 286; also reported from Imam Ṣādiq.

The Messenger of God: He prohibited people from eating or drinking with the left hand,[112] or walking only with one sandal on. He used to prefer the right hand in everything and used to forbid three things while eating: not to eat with the left hand; not to lie flat on the back; not to lie on the stomach.[113]

Ja'far b. Muḥammad: He said, 'A man should not eat or drink with the left hand; nor should he offer anything to anyone with the left hand without a good cause.'

The Messenger of God: He forbade people to eat with three fingers.[114]

'Alī: He also forbade people to eat with three fingers.

Ja'far b. Muḥammad: He used to eat with five fingers and say, 'This is how the Messenger of God ate his food, not as the tyrants do.'

The Messenger of God: He forbade people to eat from the top [of a bowl or dish of] *tharīd*. He directed that every man should eat what is in front of him;[115] and he permitted that a dish of dried or fresh dates may be eaten from the side of the platter.

[The Messenger of God]: He said, 'When bread and meat are offered to you, begin with bread and satisfy your hunger, and later, eat the meat.'

[The Messenger of God]: He used to lick the bowl [containing food] and say that the last portion contained the greatest blessing. The angels bless those who lick the bowls and pray for a larger share of livelihood for them. He who licks a bowl receives a double reward for a good deed. After a meal, the Messenger of God used to lick his fingers audibly.[116]

Ja'far b. Muḥammad: He related the aforementioned tradition and said, 'My father disliked wiping his hand of food particles with a kerchief

[112]'None of you must ever eat or drink with his left hand, for the devil eats and drinks with his left hand.' *Mishkāt*, II, 441; Robson, II, 886; transmitted by Muslim. *Kāfī*, VI, 288.

[113]*Kāfī*, VI, 286.

[114]Ka'b b. Mālik said that the Prophet used to eat with three fingers and lick his hand before wiping it. *Mishkāt* II, 441; Robson, II, 886; transmitted by Muslim. *Kāfī*, VI, 312; the tradition states, 'The Messenger of God used to eat with three fingers, but not as the tyrants, one of them used to eat with two fingers.'

[115]Ibn 'Abbās told that the Prophet was brought a dish containing *tharīd* (crumbed bread with soup and pieces of meat) and said, 'Eat from its sides and not from the middle, for the blessing descends in the middle of it.' Abū Dāwūd's version reads, 'When one of you eats he must not eat from the top of the dish, but from the bottom, for the blessing descends from the top of it.' *Mishkāt* II, 448, 452; Robson II, 892–3, 895–6. See also *Kāfī*, VI, 311.

[116]Jābir said that the Prophet ordered people to lick their fingers and the dish, saying, 'You do not know in what portion the blessing lies.' Another tradition states, 'When one of you eats he must not wipe his hand until he licks it, or gives it to someone to lick.' Transmitted by Bukhārī and Muslim. *Mishkāt* II, 442, 454; Robson II, 886, 897.

until he had licked his fingers, or given them to be licked by a child sitting next to him to show respect for food. This conduct of the Friends of God (*awliyā' Allāh*) was to show humility to God and give honour to the provisions given by Him, and was contrary to the actions of tyrants among God's creatures.'

The Messenger of God: He forbade to cram two dates or two fruits of any kind in the mouth at the same time.[117] Ja'far b. Muḥammad also confirmed the rule, and said that the [above] rule was for a man eating in company; but he could eat as he wished when alone.

[Ja'far b. Muḥammad]: He disapproved that a man should get up from a meal [while eating]. Sometimes he would summon one of his slaves, and when told that they were eating, he said, 'Leave them until they have done.'

Many forms of prayers, to be said after eating a meal, are reported from the Members of the Prophet's Household, but their mention would lead to prolixity; and none of them are established [practice]. It is sufficient for a man to praise God, to thank Him, and pray to Him to the best of his ability.[118]

The Messenger of God: He said, 'Use a toothpick (*khilāl*) for removing the remains of food. This will be a source of strength for the front and the back teeth; and it will induce livelihood for a man. Bravo to those who use a toothpick while performaing ablution or after a meal![119] Nothing is more painful to the two [recording] angels of a faithful one than the sight of food sticking out from the mouth of a man who is standing and praying.[120] The Messenger of God directed that a reed, or shoot of pomegranate, or sweet basil (*rayḥān*)[121] should not be used for a tooth pick, for they loosen the roots of the teeth.[122]

[The Messenger of God]: He directed the washing of hands after a meal to remove any foul smell of meat and its grease (*ghamar* or *ghamr*) adhering to the hand and said, 'Verily, Satan smells it.'[123]

[117]Ibn 'Umar said that the Messenger of God prohibited anyone from taking two dates together before asking permission from his companions. *Mishkāt*, II, 445; Robson, II, 889; transmitted by Bukhārī and Muslim.

[118]See some references to prayers in *Mishkāt*, II, 446–8; Robson, II, 891–3; *Kāfī*, VI, 306–10.

[119]See *The Pillars of Islam*, I, 132, 146–7.

[120]For the two recording angels and picking the teeth after a meal, see *The Pillars of Islam*, I, 153, n. 131.

[121]*Rayḥān* is mentioned in the Qur'ān 55:12, 56:89. Ibn Qayyim, *al-Ṭibb al-nabawī*, 289–91.

[122]See *The Pillars of Islam*, I, 147, n. 101.

[123]*Mishkāt*, II, 450; Robson, II, 894. See also *The Pillars of Islam*, I, 153, n. 128 and 129.

'Alī: He said, 'The blessings of food lies in ablutions performed before and after it.[124] The devil is fond of the foul smell of meat and its grease adhering to the fingers. When a man reclines on his bed, let him wash both his hands to remove the odour of food.'

['Alī]: He disapproved of the cleaning of hands with something which could be eaten. He used to say, 'Verily, such a course is distasteful to the [food which is] God's benefaction.'

The Messenger of God: He directed that a washbowl (*ṭasht*) should not be raised from the hands of the people until it becomes full.[125]

Ja'far b. Muḥammad: He said, 'When a group of his people are present at a meal, the master of the house should wash his hands last of all, except for his family.'[126]

LAWFUL AND UNLAWFUL FOOD (*MĀ YAḤILL AKLUHU WA-MĀ YAḤRUM AN YU'KAL MIN AL-ṬA'ĀM*)[127]

God says: *Say: I find not in that which is revealed unto me aught prohibited to an eater that he eat thereof, except it be carrion (mayta) or blood (dam) poured forth, or swineflesh (laḥm khinzīr) for that verily is foul—or the abomination which was immolated to the name of other than Allah*. (6:145).[128] Now, if there were nothing in the Qur'ān or the Prophet's *sunna*, laying down rules for declaring eatables as unlawful after this dictum (*āya*), all things would have been lawful to eat except those specified above. But God directed his Messenger to instruct those to whom he was sent that till the time of this revelation only the specified things were unlawful.

But later, God revealed the following verse: *Forbidden unto you [for food] are carrion and blood and swineflesh, and that which hath been dedicated unto any other than Allah, and the strangled, and the dead through beating, and the dead through falling from a height, and that which hath been killed by (the goring of) horns, and the devoured of wild beasts, saving that which ye make lawful (by the death stroke), and that which hath been immolated unto idols. And (forbidden is it) that ye swear by the divining arrows* ... (5:3). God, by His Prophet's tongue, has declared certain other things as unlawful

[124]'The blessing of food consists in ablution before it and after it.' *Mishkāt*, II, 448; Robson, II, 892; *Kāfī*, VI, 304. 'Ablution before eating drives away poverty, and ablution after it repels mental derangement.' Dhahabī, *al-Ṭibb al-nabawī*, 13.

[125]See *The Pillars of Islam*, I, 153, for a similar tradition.

[126]See *The Pillars of Islam*, I, 153; for a similar tradition.

[127]Jazīrī, *al-Fiqh*, II, 1–6.

[128]Pickthall 6:146. See also *Mishkāt*, II, 437; Robson, II, 882.

which have reached us, and we shall mention them if God wills. The first verse (6:145) with which we began [this section] is in the *Sūrat al-An'ām* (Cattle, *sūra* 6) while the second verse (5:3) is from *Sūrat al-Mā'ida* (The Table Spread, *sūra* 5).[129]

'Alī: He said, '*Sūrat al-Mā'ida* (*sūra* 5) was among the last of the revelations of the Qur'ān.'[130]

Ja'far b. Muḥammad: He laid down a comprehensive rule about lawful and unlawful food, and said, 'Lawful foodstuffs growing in the earth are of three kinds: first, grains (*ḥabb*) like wheat (*ḥinṭa*), rice (*aruzz*), legumes (*quṭnīya*), etc.; second, fruits (*thimār* pl. of *thamar*) in their entirety; and third, vegetables (*buqūl*) and plants (*nabāt*). Of these, all those that are healthy and nourishing for man are lawful; and all those that are deleterious are unlawful, except for medical treatment.

It is lawful to eat the following types of animal meat: the flesh of cattle (*baqar*), camels (*ibil*), and sheep (*ghanam*). As for wild game (*luḥūm al-waḥsh*), every animal which does not possess canine teeth or claws [is lawful].[131] All birds (*luḥūm al-ṭayr*) which have gizzards (*qāniṣa*),[132] and all deep-sea fish (*ṣayd al-baḥr*), which have scales (*qishr*) on their bodies are also lawful [to eat].[133]

Apart from these, the flesh of all other animals is forbidden. As for eggs (*bayḍ*), if they are oval, they are lawful,[134] but if the eggs are round, they are unlawful.[135]

The Messenger of God: He said, 'Every animal with [carnivorous] canine teeth (*dhū nāb min al-sibā'*), and every bird with claws (*dhū mikhlab min al-ṭayr*) [to rend meat, etc.], is unlawful.'[136]

[129]*Kāfī*, VI, 257–8.

[130]*Al-Mā'ida* was the last of the revelations. Zarkashī, *al-Burhān*, I, 164. Both Tirmidhī and Ḥākim Nīsābūrī transmitted on the authority of 'Ā'isha that *al-Mā'ida* was the last *sūra* to be revealed. Some traditions state *al-Barā'a* or *al-Tawba* to be the last, yet some other traditions state that both *al-Mā'ida* and *al-Fatḥ* were the last. Suyūṭī, *al-Itqān*, I, 79. Modern Western scholars, such as Weil, Nöldeke and Blachère, after having proposed a variety of dating systems to determine the chronology of the Qur'ānic text, have placed *al-Mā'ida* as the last *sūra* to be revealed. For details see *EI*[2], s.v. Ḳur'ān, 'Chronology of the Text'. See also Darwaza, *al-Tafsīr*, IX, 7–10.

[131]*Kāfī*, VI, 259.

[132]Ibid., VI, 262, 263.

[133]Ibid., VI, 259, 337–8; Ḥillī, *Sharā'i' al-islām*, II, 143.

[134]Most eggs produced by domestic fowl are for human consumption, and come from chickens, ducks, geese, and turkeys.

[135]*Kāfī*, VI, 264; Ṭūsī, *Tahdhīb al-aḥkam* IX, 2–4, 17, 38. These are reptile eggs and they are round.

[136]*Mishkāt*, II, 426, 430; Robson, II, 874, 877; transmitted by Muslim and Tirmidhī.

The Commander of the Faithful 'Alī said, 'Wolf (*dhi'b*), leopard (*nimr*); lynx (*fahd*); lion (*asad*); jackal (*ibn āwā*); bear (*dubb*); hyena (*ḍab*'), or any other animal with claws cannot be eaten.'

The Messenger of God: He permitted the eating of the hare (*arnab*).[137]

[The Messenger of God]: A lizard (*ḍabb*) was brought to him. He did not eat it, and expressed his disgust for it (lit. he shunned it).[138]

'Alī: He prohibited the lizard (*ḍabb*), the porcupine (*qunfudh*) and other creeping things and insects (*ḥasharāt*).

['Alī]: He said, 'The whale (*nūn* means big fish) and the locust (*jarād*) are fit to be slaughtered [and eaten]. Their capture while living is tantamount to ritual slaughter.'[139]

['Alī]: He said, 'Once the Messenger of God passed by a man from Anṣār who was standing by while his horse (*faras*)[140] was in the throes of death.[141] The Messenger of God said, "Slaughter it; you will have two rewards, one for slaughtering the horse ritually; and secondly for consideration towards it." The man said, "O Messenger of God, do I get anything out of it?" The Messenger of God replied, "Yes, eat and feed us." So he sent one leg to the Messenger of God, and he ate some of it and offered the rest of it to us.'

Ja'far b. Muḥammad: He prohibited the slaughter of horses (*khayl*).[142]

Hence, a doubt arises that his prohibition covers all cases of killing horses. His direction however applies to those horses which are healthy and sound, because God had ordered that they should be prepared and caparisoned [for service] in the way of God.[143] The report from the Prophet

[137]*Mishkāt*, II, 430; Robson, II, 877; transmitted by Bukhārī and Muslim. According to some traditions rabbit is forbidden, see Ṭūsī, *Tahdhīb al-aḥkām*, IX, 38–9, 43.

[138]Both Bukhārī and Muslim transmit the tradition that the Prophet neither ate nor prohibited the eating of lizards. Abū Dāwūd, on the other hand, states that the Prophet forbade the eating of lizards. *Mishkāt*, II, 430–1, 434; Robson, II, 877, 880. See also *Kāfī*, VI, 259; it is prohibited.

[139]The eating of locusts and whale is permitted. Ibn Abī Awfā stated, 'We went on seven expeditions along with God's Messenger and ate locusts along with him.' Transmitted by Bukhārī and Muslim. Another tradition states that the Prophet was asked about locusts and replied, 'I neither eat them nor declare them unlawful.' *Mishkāt* II, 431, 435; Robson, II, 878, 881. See also *Kāfī*, VI, 234.

[140]*Faras* is a horse or a mare, but mostly applied to the latter. The name *faras* is given to it because it crushes and breaks the ground with its hoofs. Lane, s.v. f-r-s.

[141]Jurists disagree about the effectiveness of *dhakāt* on an animal that is in the throes of death because of the severity of the disease. The majority of them, however, agree about the effectiveness of *dhakāt* on an animal that is about to die, but not from disease. See Ibn Rushd, *Bidāya*, I, 438–9; trans. I, 533.

[142]*Khayl* is applied collectively to Arabian horses, both males and females. Lane, s.v. kh-y-l.

[143]Cf. *The Pillars of Islam*, I, 429.

concerns a case where the horse was about to die and the rider himself was in great danger [riding such a horse]; but God knows best.[144]

The Messenger of God said, '[The flesh of] domesticated asses (*al-ḥumur al-insīya*) is unlawful. He declared this rule on the day of the Battle of Khaybar.'[145]

Ja'far b. Muḥammad: He said, 'Mules (*bighāl*, pl. of *baghal*) cannot be eaten.'[146]

The Messenger of God: He forbade the meat, milk, and eggs of all living creatures that eat dung (*jallāla*),[147] until they are purified [according to the rules laid down below]. The term *jallāla* is applied to all those creatures who lift up ordure from the dung heaps (*mazābil*) and eat it.

'Alī: He said, 'A she-camel eating ordure should be confined on fodder for forty days; cattle, for twenty days; sheep, for seven days; ducks, for five days; and fowls, for three days. Thereafter their flesh can be eaten; their milk may be drunk, and their eggs can be eaten.'[148]

Abū Ja'far Muḥammad b. 'Alī: He disapproved of vinegar made from wine (*khall al-khamr*) which becomes putrid since it was originally made for the brewing of wine.[149]

Abū 'Abd Allāh: He disapproved the eating of glands (*ghudud* pl. of *ghudda*), marrow of the lumbar region (*mukhkh al-ṣulb*), the spleen (*ṭiḥāl*), the penis of male animals (*madhākir* pl. of *dhakar*, and *qaḍīb*) and the vulvae of females (*ḥayā'*) and the inner part of the kidney (*dākhil al-kulā*).[150]

The Commander of the Faithful ['Alī]: He prohibited [the eating

[144]*Kāfī*, VI, 261; slaughtering horses is not permitted unless circumstances necessitate it. Nu'mān, *Kitāb al-majālis*, 460–1; he asserts his position without the last phrase 'God knows best'.

[145]For Khaybar, see *The Pillars of Islam*, I, 471, n. 180. 'The Prophet forbade [eating] the flesh of domestic asses, but permitted [eating] the flesh of wild asses.' *Mishkāt*, II, 430; Robson, II, 877; transmitted by Bukhārī and Muslim. *Kāfī*, VI, 259, 260, 261; Ṭūsī, *Tahdhīb al-aḥkām* IX, 40.

[146]*Mishkāt*, II, 434; Robson, II, 880.

[147]*Jallāla* is a cow that repeatedly seeks out and eats filth. Its milk is forbidden. *Jallāla* also refers to a beast that eats *jalla*, meaning human ordure. Its flesh is forbidden. Lane, s.v. j-l-l. See also *Mishkāt*, II, 434; Robson, II, 880; *Kāfī*, VI, 266.

[148]*Kāfī*, VI, 266–8; Ṭūsī, *Tahdhīb al-aḥkām*, IX, 45–6.

[149]*Kāfī*, VI, 441; wine could be used to make vinegar provided that the quantity of wine remains small.

[150]Liver and spleen are permitted according to one tradition. *Mishkāt*, II, 434; Robson, II, 881; Dhahabī, *al-Ṭibb al-nabawī*, 66. *Kāfī*, VI, 269; blood (*dam*), testicles (*khuṣyatān*), the penis (*qaḍīb*), the bladder (*mathāna*), glands (*ghudad*), the spleen (*ṭiḥāl*), and the gall bladder (*mirāra*) are prohibited. Several other items are also listed.

of] floating fish (*ṭāfī*), i.e. fish which were dead in the sea before being caught.[151]

Jaʿfar b. Muḥammad: He said, 'No creature living in the sea can be eaten unless they have scales. Eating tortoises (*sulaḥfāt*), crabs (*saraṭān*) and eels (*jirrī*)[152] is disapproved; as are all shellfish (*mā kāna fi 'l-aṣdāf*) and their likes.'

The Commander of the Faithful ʿAlī: He said, 'One who is compelled [by necessity or force] may eat carrion or any forbidden thing.'

Jaʿfar b. Muḥammad: He said, 'One who is compelled [by necessity or force] to eat carrion, may do so until his need is satisfied; and he may drink wine to his satisfaction in similar circumstances; but he cannot return lawfully to such practices unless he again is in dire necessity.'[153]

Jaʿfar b. Muḥammad: He permitted the eating of food [cooked] by the People of the Book and other religious groups, provided it did not contain slaughtered [meat] (*dhabīḥa*).[154]

Abū Jaʿfar Muḥammad b. ʿAlī: He was informed about cheese (*jubn*) made by polytheists and how they manufactured it from the rennet of dead animals and that which is slaughtered without the name of God being pronounced. He said, 'If this is known for certain, it cannot be eaten. But if it was not known by whom the cheese was manufactured and if it was sold in the market of the Muslims: Eat it!'[155]

[Jaʿfar b. Muḥammad]: He was asked about a vessel containing wine. He said that its use is permissible after it is washed.[156]

[151]One tradition states, 'What the sea throws up and is left by the tide you may eat, but what dies in the sea and floats you must not eat.' Another tradition states that fish which have died a natural death are permitted. Both Bukhārī and Muslim transmitted a tradition which stated that on one expedition led by Abū ʿUbayda they suffered severe hunger, and then the sea cast up a huge dead whale and so they ate of it for half a month. When they returned to Medina, they sent some of it to God's Messenger and he ate it. *Mishkāt*, II, 431, 434–5; Robson, 878, 880–1. *Kāfī*, VI, 227–31; floating fish are prohibited.

[152]*Kāfī*, VI, 259; *jirrī* is prohibited.

[153]Under certain circumstances, such as hunger, the eating of animals which have died a natural death is allowable. *Mishkāt*, II, 460; Robson, II, 903.

[154]This is because of the Qur'ānic injunction: *And eat not of that whereon Allah's name hath not been mentioned, for lo! it is abomination* (6:121). *Kāfī*, VI, 277–9; beans and vegetables are permitted provided that their utensils were clean from the traces of wine and pork.

[155]*Kāfī*, VI, 272–3. The traditions transmitted by Kulaynī permit such cheese. The editor notes that the traditions are weak. Ṭūsī, *al-Nihāya*, 588, on the other hand, states that anything which contains even a small amount from dead [animals] is impure and cannot be consumed.

[156]Cf. *The Pillars of Islam*, I, 151; *Kāfī*, VI, 440.

'Alī: He permitted the eating of food and sauce containing dead insects (*khishāsh*), flies (*dhubāb*), and creatures without [warm] blood, and said, 'These insects do not create pollution or unlawfulness. If those which do have [warm] blood die in a liquidy food then it is impure. However, if the food is solid, then the impurity is confined to their surroundings, and the remainder can be [lawfully] eaten.'[157]

[157]See *The Pillars of Islam*, I, 151; *Kāfī*, VI, 276–7. Abū Hurayra reported God's Messenger saying, 'When a mouse falls into clarified butter which is solid throw the mouse and what is around it away; but if it is in a liquid state do not go near it.' Another tradition states, 'When a fly alights in any of your vessels, plunge it in, for in one of its wings there is disease and in the other a cure; it puts forward the one containing the disease, so dip it all in.' *Mishkāt*, II, 433, 436; Robson, II, 880, 882.

*In his *Khiṭaṭ*, II, 341, 342, Maqrīzī states that in the year 395/1004–5 al-Ḥākim issued a decree, which prohibited (i) consumption of Jew's mallow (*mulūkhīya*), ascribed to Mu'āwiya, and watercress (*jirjīr*), ascribed to 'Ā'isha; (ii) selling of fish without scales in the market; (iii) manufacture and consumption of barley wine (*fuqqā'*; see n. 53, Chap. 4).

4

Book of Drinks
(*Kitāb al-Ashriba*)

LAWFUL AND UNLAWFUL DRINKS (*MĀ YAḤILL SHURBUHU WA-MĀ LĀ YAḤILL*)[1]

God says: *We send down purifying water from the sky, that We may give life thereby to a dead land, and We give many beasts and men that We have created to drink thereof* (25:48–9). And He says: *And caused the earth to gush forth springs* (54:12). And He says: *Have ye observed the water which ye drink? Is it ye who shed it from the rain cloud, or are We the shedder?* (56:68–9).

Ja'far b. Muḥammad—his father—his ancestors: The Messenger of God said, 'Water (*mā'*) is the chief of drinks in this world and the next.'[2] The drinking of water created by God, without any act on the part of man, is lawful unless it is mixed with impurity, or something which leads to its being forbidden. There is consensus on this point, according to our knowledge.[3]

Similarly it is lawful to drink the milk (*laban*) of animals, game, and cattle if their flesh is lawful to eat. It is not lawful to drink the milk of animals whose flesh is forbidden, unless compelled [by necessity or duress]. When water is mixed with milk or honey (*'asal*), or with things that are permitted for eating and drinking, such as dates and raisins or other solvent things, the mixture is lawful until its character changes by fermentation or boiling. The extract of grapes, raisins, and dates which is cooked almost to

[1]See Jazīrī, *al-Fiqh*, II, 6–9.

[2]*Kāfī*, VI, 393; it is ascribed to 'Alī, while the Messenger of God is reported to have said, 'Water is the chief of drinks in Paradise.'

[3]*We made every living thing of water* (21:30). Ibn Qayyim, *al-Ṭibb al-nabawī*, 216; 355–60.

the point of boiling and made into a syrup of a consistency like that of honey is lawful to drink, either pure or mixed with water as long as it is not fermented. It is lawful to eat, drink, buy, sell, and make use of it.[4]

'Alī: He used to purify thick pressed grape juice (*ṭilā'*),[5] i.e. grape juice, purified and boiled to make it into a thicker consistency, just as we have described [above].

Abū Ja'far: He was asked about the drinking of [grape] juice. He said, 'There is no harm in drinking it from a clean vessel, one that is not contaminated with wine (*al-ḍārī*).[6] Drink it [any time] during the day or night as long as a large quantity of it does not intoxicate. If its [consumption] in large quantities intoxicates, then even a smaller quantity of it is forbidden.[7] Do not drink it [lest it bring] protracted disgrace; for after an hour or a night, the taste of wine disappears but its sins remain. So fear God and look after your souls. For verily the partisans (*shī'a*) of 'Alī are known for their piety, constant endeavour, safeguarding, avoiding malicious actions, and love for the Friends of God (*awliyā' Allāh*).'

Ja'far b. Muḥammad: He said, 'There is no harm in drinking juice, the portion that flows before its being expressed (*sulāfat^an*)[8] and before it ferments, so long as it does not intoxicate.'

'Alī: He said, 'We used to soak[9] raisins or dates in a vessel (*maṭhara*)[10] in water to sweeten it for the Messenger of God. After a day or two he used to drink it, and when the taste changed he would order it to be thrown away.'[11]

Ja'far b. Muḥammad: He said, 'The lawful way of drinking *nabīdh*[12] is

[4]*Mishkāt*, II, 466; Robson, II, 908; *Kāfī*, VI, 431.

[5]*Ṭilā'* means pressed grape juice cooked until the two thirds of it is evaporated, and is so called by the Arabs because it resembles tar. Lane, s.v. ṭ-l-w. See also *Kāfī*, VI, 432–4; it is permitted.

[6]Gloss in MS Q and Lane, s.v. ḍ-r-w or ḍ-r-y; *ḍariya 'l-inā'^u bi 'l-khamr* means the vessel became seasoned with wine, hence *al-inā' al-ḍārī*. The tradition is also cited.

[7]'I have forbidden you receptacles, for while a receptacle does not make anything lawful or unlawful, every intoxicant is unlawful.' Transmitted by Muslim. Bukhārī and Muslim transmitted another tradition that states, 'Every liquor which intoxicates is forbidden.' *Mishkāt*, II, 311, 467; Robson, II, 776, 908.

[8]Lane, s.v. s-l-f.

[9]The verb is *naqa'a*, and *naqī'* is an infusion, meaning a beverage made by steeping raisins or dates in water. *Lisān al-'Arab*, s.v. n-q-'.

[10]*Maṭhara* means a vessel for purification, i.e. with which one washes himself and performs the ablution. Lane, s.v. ṭ-h-r.

[11]*Mishkāt*, II, 466; Robson, II, 908; *Kāfī*, VI, 437–9; it gives all the details of preparing lawful beverages.

[12]*Nabīdh* is a kind of beverage, made of dates, raisins, honey, wheat, barley, etc. It is so called because one throws those things into a vessel or skin of water, and leaves until it

to steep [dates or raisins] in water and drink it on the same day or the next; but when it changes [that is, begins to ferment] then do not drink it. We [the Imams] drink it sweet before it ferments.'[13]

[Ja'far b. Muḥammad]:[14] He said, 'The water of the well of Zamzam[15] had a salty taste, and [the Arabs] used to throw dates into it so that its water would be sweet.'

DRINKING ETIQUETTE
(*ĀDĀB AL-SHĀRIBĪN*)

Ja'far b. Muḥammad—his father—his ancestors: The Messenger of God forbade eating or drinking with the left hand. He enjoined that the man who drinks should take the name of God when he begins to drink, and should praise Him when he is done. He should also do this when he pauses for breath in drinking.[16]

The Messenger of God: He forbade folding the skin of a water or milk sack (*ikhtināth al-asqiya*),[17] that is, doubling the mouth of the skin and drinking from it. It is said that the prohibition is due to two reasons. First, because of the fear that there may be an insect or serpent which may flow into the mouth of the man who drinks; and second, it may infect (lit. cause an offensive smell to) [the outlet of] the water skin.[18]

The Messenger of God: He used to drink both sitting and standing.[19]

---

ferments, or acquires strength, or conversely not so long as to become intoxicating. It is a lawful beverage before it becomes intoxicating. Lane, s.v. n-b-dh.

[13]'Ā'isha said, 'We used to steep dates for God's Messenger in a skin which was tied at the top and had a mouth. What we steeped in the morning he would drink in the evening, and what we steeped in the evening he would drink in the morning.' Anas said, 'I have given God's Messenger in this cup of mine all kinds of drinks: honey, *nabīdh*, water and milk.' *Mishkāt*, II, 466; Robson, II, 908; both the traditions are transmitted by Muslim. *Kāfī*, VI, 427.

[14]According to MS Q. *'Anhu* is missing from the edited text.

[15]Zamzam, the sacred well of Mecca, is located in the *ḥaram* south-east of the Ka'ba opposite the corner of the Black Stone. The pilgrims drink its water as health-giving and take it home with them to give it to the sick. *ShEI*, s.v. Zamzam. See also *The Pillars of* Islam, I, 26, 394; *Kāfī*, VI, 399–400.

[16]See 'Table Manners' in Chap. 3; Dhahabī, *al-Ṭibb al-nabawī*, 13.

[17]Lane, s.v. kh-n-th. *Mishkāt*, II, 461; Robson, II, 904; transmitted by Bukhārī and Muslim.

[18]Drinking from the mouth of a water skin or having its head inverted and then being drunk from it is forbidden. *Mishkāt*, II, 461; Robson, II, 904. Ibn Qayyim, *al-Ṭibb al-nabawī*, 222.

[19]'Anas said that the Prophet forbade that a man should drink standing.' Transmitted by Muslim. A tradition transmitted by Bukhārī and Muslim states that the Prophet drank

Ja'far b. Muḥammad: He prohibited drinking [water] from the side of the handle of a vessel (*'urwat al-inā'*).[20]

The Messenger of God: He passed by a man who was sipping water by putting his mouth into it.[21] That is he was drinking from the middle of a vessel or the like, and the Messenger of God said, 'Are you drinking like a beast? If you have no vessel for drinking, use your hands, for they are the best of vessels.'[22]

[The Messenger of God]: He said, 'Drink water, sipping it slowly not gulping it down fast, for this may lead to a liver ailment (*kubād*).'[23]

'Alī: He said, 'Many a time I watched the Messenger of God closely while he was drinking water and found that he paused for breath three times,[24] and every time he invoked the name of God when he began drinking, and praised Him when he ended.'

Abū Ja'far and Abū 'Abd Allāh: They said, 'To drink [water] in three breaths is better than to gulp it down at one stretch.'[25] They disapproved that a man should drink like a thirsty camel (*shurb al-hīm*)[26] who does not raise his head from the water till his thirst is quenched.[27]

Ḥusayn b. 'Alī: He used to dislike sipping milk slowly, but would gulp it down quickly. He said, 'Only the residents of Hell drink sip after sip.'

The Messenger of God: When he drank milk, he said, 'O God, bless us with it, and give us more of it.' When he drank water, he said, 'All

---

Zamzam water while standing. A tradition transmitted by Tirmidhī states that God's Messenger drank both standing and sitting. *Mishkāt*, II, 461, 463; Robson, II, 904, 906. *Kāfī*, VI, 396; 'Alī and the Imams al-Bāqir and al-Ṣādiq used to drink water standing.

[20]*Kāfī*, VI, 398; the reason is that Satan sits on the handle and the broken place of the vessel.

[21]*Kara'a fī 'l-mā'* or *kara'a fī 'l-inā'*, he put his mouth into the water, or into the vessel, and so drank. *Lisān al-'Arab*, s.v. k-r-'.

[22]*Kāfī*, VI, 399; Kulaynī states that some people were doing this during the raid on Tabūk.

[23]*Majma' al-baḥrayn*, s.v. k-b-d; the tradition is cited.

[24]'The Messenger of God used to breathe three times in the course of a drink.' *Mishkāt*, II, 461; Robson, II, 904; transmitted by Bukhārī and Muslim. In a version Muslim added that the Messenger of God used to say, 'It is more thirst-quenching, healthier and more wholesome.'

[25]*Kāfī*, VI, 396.

[26]*Hīm* is explained as *al-ibal al-ṣādīya*, camel thirsting vehemently. *Qāmūs*, s.v. h-y-m; Lane, s.v. ṣ-d-y. This expression, i.e. *shurb al-hīm*, occurs in the Qur'ān 56:55 where the Companions of the Left are described as follows: *And you shall fill there with [zakkūm] your bellies and drink on top of that boiling water lapping it down like thirsty camels.* See also Ibn Qayyim, *al-Ṭibb al-nabawī*, 221.

[27]*Mishkāt*, II, 463–4; Robson, II, 906; *Kāfī*, VI, 397.

praise to God Who, by His mercy, has given us sweet and clear water to drink, not salty and brackish water, due to our sins!'[28]

FORBIDDEN DRINKS
(MĀ YAḤRUM SHURBUHU)

God says: O *ye who believe! Wine (khamr) and games of chance and idols and divining arrows are only an infamy of Satan's handiwork. Leave it aside in order that ye may succeed* (5:90).

[The Messenger of God] prohibited wine as he has prohibited all other unlawful things.[29]

Ja'far b. Muḥammad—his father—his ancestors: The Messenger of God said, 'Wine is forbidden.' He cursed wine itself, the extractor of wine, the one who has it pressed, its buyer, its seller, the one who drinks it, the one who serves it, its carrier, the one to whom it is carried, and the one who profits from its price.[30]

Ja'far b. Muḥammad: He said, 'The habitual drinker of wine will meet God, when he does meet Him, as an idol worshipper.[31] When a man drinks a single draught of wine, God will not accept his prayer for forty [days and][32] nights.'[33]

Ja'far b. Muḥammad: He said, 'Paradise is forbidden to three [classes of] persons: the habitual drunkard, the idol worshipper, and the enemy of the family of the Prophet (*'adūw āl-i Muḥammad*).[34] If a man drinks wine and dies within forty days, will meet God as an idol worshipper.'[35]

The Commander of the Faithful 'Alī: He heard the Messenger of God say, 'I do not declare any intoxicant (*muskir*) as lawful; it is forbidden, whether in a large or a small quantity.'[36]

Abū Ja'far Muḥammad b. 'Alī: He said, 'Every intoxicant is forbidden.' He was asked, 'Is this rule laid down by you?' [The Imam] replied, 'No, it is from the Messenger of God.' Then it was said to him, '[Is the intoxicant unlawful] totally?' [The Imam] said, 'Yes, even a mouthful is forbidden.'[37]

[28]*Mishkāt*, II, 464–5; Robson, II, 907; *Kāfī*, VI, 397.
[29]*Kāfī*, VI, 418–19.
[30]*Mishkāt*, II, 77; Robson, I, 595; *Kāfī*, VI, 411, 442.
[31]*Kāfī*, VI, 416; reported from the same Imam.
[32]As in MS Q and the other two MSS of Fyzee.
[33]*Kāfī*, VI, 413–14; most of the traditions have: *yawm^{an}*.
[34]*Āl-i Muḥammad*, see *The Pillars of Islam*, I, 38.
[35]*Kāfī*, VI, 408–14; it gives a detailed list of chastisements.
[36]Ibid., VI, 420–1.
[37]'Every intoxicant is unlawful.' *Mishkāt*, II, 467; Robson, II, 908; *Kāfī*, VI, 421.

Ja'far b. Muḥammad: He said, 'It was the Messenger of God who declared all intoxicating drinks to be forbidden; and what God's Messenger has declared as forbidden, is forbidden [also] by God. Even a small portion of a drink which intoxicates in large quantities, is forbidden.' A man from Kūfa[38] said [to the Imam], 'May God show you the correct path (*aṣlaḥak Allāh*)! The jurists of our country say, "Only that [drink] which [in fact] intoxicates is forbidden."'[39] [The Imam] said, 'Good sir! I do not know what the jurists of your country say. It is related to me by my father [Imam al-Bāqir], from his father [Imam 'Alī b. Ḥusayn], who related from his grandfather ['Alī] that the Messenger of God said, "Even a small portion of what intoxicates in large quantities, is forbidden."'

[Ja'far b. Muḥammad]: He said, 'Precautionary dissimulation (*taqīya*)[40] is my religion and the religion of my forefathers in all matters, except [the following three things:] to declare an intoxicant lawful, not to remove shoes while performing ablutions,[41] and not to utter the *basmala* loudly.' [What the Imam] meant is [at the beginning of every *sūra*] in [the obligatory] prayers where it is to be uttered loudly.[42]

The Messenger of God said, 'The man who treats prayer lightly does not belong to me; and the man who drinks intoxicants does not belong to me. He will not come to me at the Pond [*ḥawḍ* of Kawthar on the Day of Judgement],[43] No, By God [He will not]!'[44]

[38]During the early history of Shī'ism, Kūfa was the main centre of Shī'ī activity. See also *The Pillars of Islam*, I, 296, n. 143.

[39]*Kāfī*, VI, 422. Reported on the authority of the same Imam, but with a variant. The man from Kūfa first asked about *nabīdh*, and the Imam said that it was lawful. Then the man said, 'May God set you right! I asked you about *nabīdh* that had become turbid and [starts] fermenting until it intoxicates.' Abū 'Abd Allāh said, 'The Messenger of God said, "Every intoxicant is forbidden."' The man retorted, 'May God set you right! [The jurists] we have in Iraq say, "What the Messenger of God meant by it is the drinking-cup, which causes intoxication."' Abū 'Abd Allāh replied, 'Even a small portion of what intoxicates in large quantities is forbidden.' The man said '[What about if] I abate its intoxicating influence by mixing water [with it]?' Abū 'Abd Allāh replied, 'No. Water cannot make something lawful that is [already] unlawful. Fear God, and do not drink.' Several similar traditions are narrated.

[40]For *taqīya* see *The Pillars of Islam*, I, 77, n. 213.

[41]For the practice of wiping over shoes during ablution, see *The Pillars of Islam*, I, 136, n. 48.

[42]See *The Pillars of Islam*, 136, n. 47; 201. *Kāfī*, VI, 427; instead of 'uttering the *basmala* loudly', it has '*mut'at al-ḥajj*'.

[43]See *The Pillars of Islam*, I, 37. It refers to the *ḥawḍ* at which on the Day of the Resurrection the Prophet will meet his *umma* (community). The idea of *ḥawḍ* is not found in the Qur'ān, but traditions give a variety of details about it. EI^2, s.v. Ḥawḍ.

[44]*Kāfī*, VI, 412. The tradition states, 'One who treats his prayers lightly will not obtain

'Alī: He said, 'Do not bear affection to him who considers an intoxicant to be lawful. For verily, the man who drinks wine, [despite its being] forbidden will die an easier death than one who either considers it to be lawful, or declares it to be lawful, even if he does not drink it himself. His declaration of the lawfulness [of intoxicants] is sufficient for [his] disavowal [of Islam] and rejection of that which the Prophet brought [i.e. the *sharī'a*] and is pleasing to the devils (*ṭawāghīt* pl. of *ṭāghūt*).'[45]

Ja'far b. Muḥammad: He said, 'The spirit of faith departs from the man who drinks wine and loses his sense.'

Ḥusayn b. 'Alī: He wrote a letter to Mu'āwiya[46] upbraiding and rebuking him for some of his actions. The letter contained the following:

> You have appointed as ruler your son, a young man who drinks wine (*sharāb*) and sports with dogs;[47] thus you have dishonoured your trust and ruined your subjects, and not discharged the obligation of your Lord. How can you appoint over the community of Muḥammad a man who drinks wine? The man who drinks intoxicants is a profligate and a man of vile character. When a man who drinks cannot be trusted with a dirham [penny],[48] how can he be appointed to rule over the [Muslim] community? After a short while you will face your own actions while the pages of [the book of] forgiveness will be folded up.

[The Imam] related the rest of the report in detail.

'Alī b. al-Ḥusayn [Zayn al-'Ābidīn]: He said, 'Wine is of five kinds:[49] [made] from dried dates, raisins, wheat, barley, and honey, apart from grape [wine]. Every intoxicant is known as *khamr*. Now *khamr* is derived from *takhmīr* (covering a thing),[50] and that is to cover it up so that it becomes warm and begins to ferment.'

A lengthy disputation concerning the unlawfulness of intoxicants has been related to us from the People of the House, on whom be salutations, and their partisans, but we have curtailed it in the interests

---

my intercession and will not come to me at the Pond. No, by God, one who drinks intoxicants will not procure my intercession and will not come to me at the Pond. No, by God.'

[45]For *ṭāghūt* see *The Pillars of Islam*, I, 27, n. 47.

[46]Mu'āwiya, see *The Pillars of Islam*, I, 107, n. 300; 480, 483, 486.

[47]Refers to Yazīd b. Mu'āwiya who was addicted to wine and used to amuse himself with dogs, predatory animals, and monkeys. Mas'ūdī, *Murūj al-dhahab*, III, 264–70; *EI*², s.v. Yazīd b. Mu'āwiya.

[48]Dirham, see *The Pillars of Islam*, I, 310, n. 44.

[49]*Kāfī*, VI, 405; reported from the same authority.

[50]Lane, s.v. kh-m-r.

of brevity; and what we have stated [above] from their reports is sufficient and beyond dispute.

The Messenger of God: He forbade the use of wine and intoxicants for medical treatment,[51] or for administration to children and animals.[52] And he said, 'The sin is on him who gives wine to drink.'

Jaʿfar b. Muḥammad: He was asked about the drinking of *fuqqāʿ* (barley wine).[53] [The Imam] asked the questioner, 'Of what is it made up (*kayfa huwa*)?' The questioner told him (*fa-akhbarahu*) [what it constitutes]. Hence, [The Imam] said, 'It is forbidden (*ḥarām*); do not drink it.'

[Jaʿfar b. Muḥammad]: He said, 'Wine and intoxicants cannot be used for medical treatment or by women, for beautifying hair.[54] My father informed me from his father, from his grandfather, that ʿAlī said, "God has not bestowed the quality of healing on impure things which He has declared to be forbidden [whether in large or in small quantities]."'[55]

[Jaʿfar b. Muḥammad]: He was asked about the vessels that have become contaminated with traces of wine (*al-awānī al-ḍārīya*). He said, '*Nabīdh* is not forbidden because of the vessels,[56] but what is forbidden is the intoxicant whether in large or in small quantities.'[57]

[51]*Kāfī*, VI, 425; Ibn Qayyim, *al-Ṭibb al-nabawī*, 154–7; 'One who treats a disease with wine, God will not cure it.' See also Suyūṭī, *al-Manhaj al-sawīy*, 287–8. The Ḥanafī school permits the use of wine as a medicine in cases of emergency and dire need. They justify it on the basis of the Qur'ānic verse 6:119 that states: ... . *He has distinguished for you that He has forbidden you, unless you are constrained to it.* The Shāfiʿīs, on the other hand, allow its external use, i.e. on the body, at the time of necessity. See Nasīmī, *fi 'l-ṭibb al-islāmī*, 45–9.

[52]*Kāfī*, VI, 443.

[53]*Fuqqāʿ*, a kind of wine, is so called because of the froth that rises upon its head. *Tāj al-ʿarūs*, s.v. f-q-ʿ; Lane, s.v. f-q-ʿ. *Kāfī*, VI, 434–7; it contains a section on *fuqqāʿ*. Imam al-Ṣādiq was asked about *fuqqāʿ*, and he said that it was wine. Another tradition reported on the authority of the same Imam states, 'If I had control over the markets of the Muslims I would have removed this wine (i.e. *fuqqāʿ*) from them.' See also Ṭūsī, *al-Nihāya*, 591.

[54]*Imtashaṭa* means 'he combed and dressed his hair', and for a woman *imtashaṭat*. Lane, s.v. m-sh-ṭ.

[55]*Kāfī*, VI, 426; Shabbar, *Ṭibb al-aʾimma*, 85, the author quotes from the *Daʿāʾim*.

[56]It is reported that when a vessel has become seasoned with wine, when *nabīdh* is put into it, it becomes intoxicating. *Lisān al-ʿArab*, s.v. ḍ-r-w; Lane, s.v. ḍ-r-w.

[57]'I have forbidden you receptacles, for while a receptacle does not make anything lawful or unlawful, every intoxicant is unlawful.' Transmitted by Muslim. *Mishkāt*, II, 467; Robson, II, 908.

5

Book of Medicine (Kitāb al-Ṭibb)[1]

THERAPEUTIC TREATMENT (*AL-TADĀWĀ*)[2]

A number of reports concerning what is lawful and what is unlawful in regards to treatments and cures have been reported to us from the Messenger of God and the Imams descended from him. What has come down from

[1]Health concerns and medicine in Islam were viewed through a religio-ethical perspective and visiting the sick and healing the unhealthy were highly regarded virtues. It was this religious motivation that set into motion theoretical and practical processes that were the spiritual and cultural mainstay of the Islamic medical institutions. Traditions ascribed to the Prophet on medicine and spiritual healing provided the theoretical development, while proliferation of the pious foundations known as *awqāf* and Ṣūfī hospices provided the practical side. For a comprehensive survey in English see Rahman, *Health and Medicine*.

In his *Muqaddimah*, Ibn Khaldūn writes:

> The medicine mentioned in religious tradition (*al-nabawīyāt/al-shar'īyāt*) is of the (Bedouin) type. It is in no way part of the divine revelation. (Such medical matters) were merely (part of) Arab custom and happened to be mentioned in connection with the circumstances of the Prophet .... They were not mentioned in order to imply that the particular way of practicing (medicine) is stipulated by the religious law. The Prophet was sent to teach us the religious law (*sharā'i'*) and not medicine ... . None of the statements concerning medicine that occurs in sound traditions (*al-aḥādīth al-ṣaḥīḥa*) should be considered to (have the force of) law .... The only thing is that if that type of medicine is used for the sake of a divine blessing and in true religious faith, it may be very useful. However, that would have nothing to do with humoral medicine (*al-ṭibb al-mizājī*) but be the result of true faith ...

Ibn Khaldūn, *Muqaddima*, III, 117–19; Rosenthal; *Muqaddima*, III, 150–1; with minor changes.

[2]According to MS Q. The edited text has *dhikr al-ṭibb*, which seems to be incorrect.

them will prove to be a blessing and cure for him who [wholeheartedly] accepts it and takes it believing it to be true,[3] God willing; but it will not [benefit] him who does not believe in it and [only] takes it in the form of an experiment.

Ja'far b. Muḥammad:[4] One day he was present at the house of Muḥammad b. Khālid,[5] the governor of Medina, and Muḥammad complained to the Imam about pain in the stomach. [The Imam] said, 'It was related to me by my father, who heard it from his father and grandfather that 'Alī said, "A man complained to the Messenger of God regarding a stomach ache, and the Messenger of God said, 'Take a little honey[6] syrup and put in it three or five or seven [pods of] black caraway (nigella sativa, *shūnīz*,[7]) and drink it. It is possible that by the grace of God you will be cured.' That man did as instructed and he was restored to health." So do accordingly.'

A man of Medina who was present objected and said, 'O Abū 'Abd Allāh, we had heard of this and acted on it, but it did not give us any relief.' So Abū 'Abd Allāh was angered and exclaimed, 'It will benefit only those that have faith in it, and who believe in the truthfulness of His messengers. It does not help hypocrites and those who take it [the medicine] without believing in the Messenger.' So the man [was abashed and he] cast down his eyes.[8]

This whole section is reproduced by Majlisī in his *Biḥār al-anwār*, LXII, 72–3, from the *Da'ā'im*.

[3]*Kāfī*, II, 473; a person should be earnest in his prayer and should have faith before it is fulfilled.

[4]Nu'mān, *Kitāb al-majālis*, 292. The tradition is transmitted by Ja'far b. Muḥammad who stated that he was with his father Muḥammad [Imam al-Bāqir] when they visited the governor. The latter complained to his father [Imam al-Bāqir] … . He, therefore, recalled the Messenger of God's tradition …

[5]Muḥammad b. Khālid b. 'Abd Allāh al-Qasrī was appointed the governor of Medina in 141/758 and was deposed by the 'Abbāsid Caliph al-Manṣūr in 144/761. Ṭabarī, *Ta'rīkh*, VII, 517; *History of al-Ṭabarī*, XXVIII, 74–5, 85.

[6]In his *al-Ṭibb al-nabawī*, 45–9, Ibn Qayyim enumerated all the benefits of honey; Suyūṭī, *al-Manhaj al-sawīy*, 303–7.

[7]*Shūnīz* and *shawnīz*, a Persian word, a kind of black aromatic seed of a species of nigella. In Arabic it is also called *ḥabbat al-sawda*. Lane, s.v. sh-n-z; Mu'īn, *Farhang*, s.v. shūnīz, shīnīz. 'Nigella seed is a remedy for every disease but death.' *Mishkāt*, II, 509–10; Robson, II, 945; transmitted by Bukhārī and Muslim. *Shunūz* is black caraway (*al-kammūn al-aswad*, black cumin) also called *al-kammūn al-hindī*. Some say that it is a mustard seed (*khardal*). Ibn Qayyim, *al-Ṭibb al-nabawī*, 275–8; Suyūṭī, *al-Manhaj al-sawīy*, 280–4, 348. Bīrūnī, *Pharmacy*, 120, 133, 363–4; all the uses and benefits are listed. There is a monograph on *ḥabbat al-sawda* by 'Alī Ibrāhīm.

[8]This part of the *ḥadīth* is slightly different in Nu'mān, *Kitāb al-majālis*, 292.

CURE BY PIOUS ACTIONS
(*AL-TASHAFFĪ BI-A'MĀL AL-BIRR*)[9]

Ja'far b. Muḥammad—his father—his ancestors: He was asked about the Prophet's statement regarding *al-ḥabba al-sawdā'* (black caraway) and he said, 'He verily did say it.' [The Imam] was asked, 'What did he say?' [The Imam] replied, 'It contains a remedy for all disease except *sām*.' *Sām* means death.[10] Then [the Imam] asked the questioner, 'Shall I tell you about [a remedy] concerning which the Messenger of God made no exception?' The questioner replied, 'Oh yes.' [The Imam] said, 'Prayer (*du'ā'*); for verily it wards off a destiny that had been sealed.'[11] Then [the Imam] closed the fingers of both his palms, and put one against the other, the little finger of one hand against the little finger of the other hand, as if he wanted to show you something.[12]

[Ja'far b. Muḥammad]: He said, 'Desire ardently to do works of charity, and perform them early in the morning. Every faithful one who, for the sake of what is with God, does charity early in the morning will be saved by God from the calamities that descend from heaven on that day.' Then he said, 'Do not think lightly of the prayers that the needy make for those of you that are ill; for, verily their prayers for you will be heard, but not their prayers which they make for themselves.'[13]

[Ja'far b. Muḥammad]: One of the members of his household mentioned

[9]Kulaynī has a section on 'Prayers for illnesses and diseases', *Kāfī*, II, 564–8. See also Shabbar, *Ṭibb al-a'imma*, 120–4. Prayers and acts of charity are advocated for healing. Ibn Qayyim states that Prophetic Medicine deals with the overall principles while scientific medicine fills in the details. Man is not merely a body alone but also a mental-spiritual entity. Hence a malady could be treated in three ways: by natural medicine, by divine medicine, and by combination of both. For example, spiritual therapies and the strength of the heart comes from faith in God and trust in him, charity and prayer, repentance and seeking God's forgiveness, doing good to mankind, helping the helpless, and relief of the afflicted. Nīsābūrī, *Ṭibb al-a'imma*, 27, 29; Ibn Qayyim, *al-Ṭibb al-nabawī*, 36; Dhahabī, *al-Ṭibb al-nabawī*, 139–43; Rahman, *Health and Medicine*, 41–9; it summarizes the views expressed in the books on 'The Prophetic Medicine'. Pecho, *Prophet's Medicine*, 65–75. 'Alī Ibrāhīm, *al-Du'ā' al-shāfī*.

[10]*Mishkāt*, II, 509–10; Robson, II, 945; transmitted by Bukhārī and Muslim. See also Nīsābūrī, *Ṭibb al-a'imma*, 309; transmitted from al-Bāqir and al-Ṣādiq.

[11]*Kāfī*, II, 469–70; several traditions are reported under the heading 'Prayer repels calamity and destiny'. Another tradition states, 'Prayer contains a cure for every disease.'

[12]The Imam was probably giving them a tangible image of repelling fate through prayer. This tradition is reported by Majlisī, *Biḥār al-anwār*, LXII, 231, from the *Da'ā'im*.

[13]See *The Pillars of Islam*, I, 299–305.

to him the illness of a certain person [living] with him. So he said to him, 'Send for a large basket; put wheat into it and put it in front of the ill person. Then tell your slaves that if a beggar comes along, he should be brought near the sick man who should hand him [wheat] himself, and ask the beggar to pray for him'. He was asked, 'Should not I distribute dirhams and dinars?' [The Imam] said, 'Do as I have directed you, for that is how it has been related to us.' The man did [as directed] and was cured.[14]

[Ja'far b. Muḥammad]: One of his companions complained about leucoderma (*waḍaḥ*, also leprosy) between his eyes, and said, 'O son of the Messenger of God, this matter has become quite serious with me.' [The Imam] said, 'You should pray while you are prostrating.' He did so, and was cured.[15]

[Ja'far b. Muḥammad]: He said, 'Three things remove forgetfulness and lead to remembrance—recitation of the Qur'ān; [the use of] the toothstick (*siwāk*);[16] and fasting.'

[Ja'far b. Muḥammad]: He said, 'When an anxiety overpowers you, wipe your hand over the place where you prostrate and then wipe it over your face starting with your left cheek, and then move it over your forehead and then your right cheek, and say three times:

In the name of God, the Merciful, the Compassionate; In the name of God, there is no deity other than Him. He possesses knowledge of that which is before us and that which is absent from our sight. He is the Merciful and the Compassionate One. O God remove all anxiety, sorrow and temptations from me; those that are manifest and those that are hidden.'[17]

[Ja'far b. Muḥammad]: He said, 'He who utters thirty times each day [the following prayer], God will remove from him ninety-nine kinds of calamity, the least of them being madness:

In the name of God, the Merciful, the Compassionate. All praise be to the Lord of the worlds. Blessed is God the best of creators. There is no power and no strength save in God, the Sublime, the Great.'

'Alī: He said, 'I complained to the Messenger of God, saying, "My mind often wanders in the recitation of the Qur'ān (*tafallut al-Qur'ān*)." The Messenger of God replied, "O 'Alī, let me teach you certain expressions which will fix the Qur'ān in your heart. Say:

[14]See *Kāfī*, II, 564, for a similar tradition.
[15]See *Kāfī*, II, 564, for a similar *ḥadīth*.
[16]*The Pillars of Islam*, I, 146–7.
[17]Compare *Kāfī*, II, 556–64, 567.

O God, be merciful to me so that I may always avoid disobedience to You as long as You give me life [in this world]. Be merciful to me by keeping away that which does not concern me. Give me true insight into that which pleases you. Obligate my heart to commit Your Book to memory as You have taught me, and to recite it in that manner that will please You. God, give light to my eyes through Your Book; give facility to my tongue to recite it; open my heart to it; and accustom my body to it, and help me with this for there is no one to help me do that except You."'[18]

'I ('Alī) used these words in my prayers, and God fixed the Qur'ān in my heart.'

Ja'far b. Muḥammad: He spoke about a woman who suffered continuously from bleeding even after her days of menstruation and said, 'Let her have a bath before each prayer, seeking reward from God; for, verily any woman who acts in this way will be cured of her disease.'

[Ja'far b. Muḥammad]: He said, 'I guarantee that he who mentions the name of God before a meal will not complain of it [the meal].' Ibn al-Kawwā'[19] said, 'Verily I ate a meal yesterday and took the name of God before it. In the morning [the food] troubled me.' [The Imam] said, 'Possibly you ate a variety of dishes and took the name of God on some but not on others.' The man said, 'And so it was!' [The Imam] said, 'It is for this reason that you have been troubled, O base fellow!'[20]

AMULETS AND CHARMS (*AL-TA'WĪDH*[21] *WA 'L-RUQĀ*[22])

Ja'far b. Muḥammad—his father—his forefathers—'Alī: He said, 'Labīd

[18]*Kāfī*, II, 577; reported on the authority of 'Alī, but without complaining to the Messenger of God. There are some minor variants in the text.

[19]Ibn al-Kawwā' see Chap. 3, n. 103.

[20]The same tradition is narrated before on the authority of 'Alī, see Chap. 3, section 'Table Manners.'

[21]*Ta'wīdh* signifies a kind of amulet, or charm, which bears an inscription and is hung upon a man, woman or child, to protect the wearer against the evil eye, fright, and diabolical possession. It is forbidden to be hung upon the person unless it is inscribed with something from the Qur'ān, or with the names of God. Lane, s.v. '-w-dh; *ER*, s.v. Amulets and Talismans. *Mishkāt*, I, 754–9; Robson, I, 524–8; the chapter is entitled *al-isti'ādha*, meaning 'Seeking refuge in God', and it is quite different from this section. Donaldson, *Wild Rue*, 203–8.

[22]*Ruqya* pl. *ruqa*^{n} means a charm or spell, either written or uttered, by which a person having an evil affection, such as fever, epilepsy, etc., is cured. The term *rāq*^{in} in the Qur'ān 57:27 means 'enchanter', 'one who cures', or 'magician'. *Ruqya* consists in the pronouncing of magical formulae to induce an enchantment. When it is in any other

b. al-A'ṣam, the Jew, and Umm 'Abd Allāh, the Jewess,[23] cast a spell on the Messenger of God by means of knots of red and yellow strings. They wove eleven knots and put them on the spathe of a palm. Then they put them on the stairs of a well in Medina.[24] So the Messenger of God [was afflicted] and lost the power of hearing, sight, understanding, speech, eating, and drinking.

'Consequently Gabriel[25] came to him with two [*suras* of the Qur'ān (113, 114) called the] *mu'awwidhatayn* and said, "O Muḥammad, what is

---

language than Arabic, it is disapproved. Generally something from the Qur'ān or some forms of prayer are approved. It is permitted on the condition that it brings benefit to people and does not harm anyone. A tradition transmitted by Bukhārī and Muslim states, 'The Messenger of God commanded that we use a spell (*ruqya*) against the evil eye.' It is also used against poison, bites, and fever. Another tradition transmitted by Muslim states: 'Awf b. Mālik al-Ashja'ī said, 'In the pre-Islamic days we used to cast spells, and we asked the Messenger of God how he looked upon it.' He replied, 'Submit your spells to me. There is no harm in spells as long as they do not involve polytheism.' In the subsequent centuries *ruqya* proliferated everywhere. Most of the jurists were unanimous in formally forbidding the practice of magic. *Mishkāt*, II, 511, 516, 517; Robson, II, 946–7, 950; Lane, s.v. r-q-y; *EI*[2], s.v. Ruḳya. The last epistle in *Rasā'il Ikhwān al-Ṣafā'*, IV, 283–463, deals with sorcery (*siḥr*), charms (*'azā'im*) and the evil eye (*'ayn*). They affirm that those sciences derive their effectiveness from influences of the human soul. In his *Muqaddima*, Ibn Khaldūn also devotes a long section on sorcery and talismans (*siḥr wa-ṭilasmāt*). He states:

> The religious law makes no distinction between sorcery, talismans, and prestidigitation (*sha'badha*). It puts them all into the same class of forbidden things. The Lawgiver (Muḥammad) permitted us only those actions that are of relevance to us in our religion, which concerns the well-being of our life in the other world, and in our livelihood, which concerns the well-being of our life in this world. Things that are of no relevance in these two respects and that may cause harm ... are forbidden ... Among such (irrelevant and harmful) things are sorcery .... Talismans belong together with it, because the effect of sorcery and talismans is the same.

Ibn Khaldūn, *Muqaddima*, III, 124–37; Rosenthal, *Muqaddimah*, III, 169. Ṣā'im, *Bism Allāh arqīk*.

[23]Labīd b. al-A'ṣam, from the Jews of Banū Zurayq, cast a spell on the Prophet after he had returned from Ḥudaybiya (*The Pillars of Islam*, I, 24, n. 29). The Qur'ān commentators give this incident as the occasion for the revelation of chapters 113 and 114 of the Qur'ān. Chapter 113 refers to '*the evil of women who blow on knots*', a form of witchcraft in which women tie knots in a cord and blow upon them with an imprecation. Ibn Isḥāq, *al-Sīra*, II, 162; Guillaume, 240; Bukhārī, *al-Ṣaḥīḥ*, IV, 20–1; Wāḥidī, *Asbāb al-nuzūl*, 347–8; Ibn Sa'd, II/ii, 4–6; Ṭabarī, *Tafsīr* (Beirut), XXX, 228; Ṭabrisī, V, 568 (*Sūrat al-Falaq*); Ṭūsī, *al-Tibyān*, X, 434; Ṭabāṭabā'ī, *al-Mīzān*, XX, 393. See also Ibn Khaldūn, *Muqaddima*, III, 128; Rosenthal, *Muqaddimah*, III, 160.

[24]Nīsābūrī, *Ṭibb al-a'imma*, 558; name of the well belonging to Banū Zurayq was *dharwān*; see also Yāqūt, s.v. *dharwān*. For Medina see *The Pillars of Islam*, I, 22, n. 13. About the treatment of *siḥr* (sorcery, charm) see Ibn Qayyim, *al-Ṭibb al-nabawī*, 130–3.

[25]For Gabriel see *The Pillars of Islam*, I, 63, n. 164.

your condition?" He replied, "I know not. I am as you see me." Gabriel said, "Verily, Labīd b. al-Aʿṣam and Umm ʿAbd Allāh, the Jew and Jewess, have cast a magic spell on you." Gabriel informed the Messenger of God of the place where the charms were kept, and then recited to him: *In the Name of Allah, the Beneficent, the Merciful. Say: I seek refuge in the Lord of Daybreak* (113, the whole chapter). The Messenger of God repeated it and one of the knots was loosened. Then he recited the other *sūra* and the other knot opened until he recited [alternatively both the *sūras*] eleven times and the eleven knots became loose.[26] Then the Prophet sat up and Gabriel informed him [what had happened].

'The Prophet told me (ʿAlī), "Go and bring the charm to me." So I brought it to him. Then the Prophet called Labīd and Umm ʿAbd Allāh and said, "What prompted you to do what you did?" Then he said to Labīd, "God will not remove you from this world in a good condition." Labīd was a prosperous and rich man. [One day] a boy was passing by with a ring in his ear; Labīd pulled it and the ear of the boy was torn. Labīd was arrested and his hand was cut off. It was cauterized but he died [thereafter].'

[Jaʿfar b. Muḥammad]: He said, 'The Messenger of God used to seat [Imam] Ḥasan on his right thigh and [Imam] Ḥusayn on his left, and used to pray, "I seek protection for you two with God in the name of His perfect words (*al-kalimāt al-tāmma*), from all the devils and poisonous insects (and reptiles *hāmma*) and from all evil eyes (*ʿayn^{in} lāmmat^{in}*)."[27] Then he used to say, "This is how my father [the Prophet] Abraham used to pray for the protection of his sons Ishmael and Isaac."'[28]

Jaʿfar b. Muḥammad: A man complained of a pain from which he suffered. [The Imam] said, 'Say, "In the name of Allah" and massage it [where it pains]. Then say, "I seek protection by the power of God and

[26] *Al-Muʿawwidhatān* are widely used for casting off spells. *Mishkāt*, II, 518; Robson, II, 952.

[27] Belief in the 'evil eye' (*ʿayn*), a universal phenomenon, is well established in Islam. In the Qur'ān (113:5) it is the evil action of an envious glance which is envisaged. A tradition transmitted by Bukhārī states, 'The evil eye is a reality.' Orthodoxy, on the other hand, makes the Prophet condemn it as superstition. Ibn Khaldūn states that the evil eye is a psychic influence exercised by the soul of a person who has the evil eye and that it does not depend on the free choice of its possessor. When a thing or situation appears pleasing to the eye of such a person he likes it outrageously. This creates envy in him and the desire to take it away from its owner. Hence, he prefers to destroy him. The application of the evil eye was involuntary on his part and therefore he should not be punished by death, unlike the sorcerer. Ibn Khaldūn, *Muqaddimah*, III, 170–1; Nīsābūrī, *Ṭibb al-a'imma*, 578; Ibn Qayyim, *al-Ṭibb al-nabawī*, 163–73; it deals with the treatment; Donaldson, *Wild Rue*, 13–23; *EI*[2], s.v. 'Ayn, 'evil eye;'.

[28] *Kāfī*, II, 569; *Lisān al-ʿArab*, s.v. h-m-m; Ibn Manẓūr narrates this tradition.

by His majesty; and by His greatness; and by all the ranks of the *da'wa*,[29] and by His [noble] names,[30] and by the names of the Messenger of God,[31] from the evil which I find in you [i.e. the pain]." You should repeat this seven times.' The man uttered the prayer accordingly and [the traces of] what he had suffered disappeared.

'Alī: He said, '[Once] I fell ill and the Messenger of God visited me. I was restless on my bed. He said, "O 'Alī, the people who are afflicted most with any kind of affliction, by which one's patience (or any other virtue) is tested, are the prophets (*nabīyūn*), then their vicegerents (*awṣiyā'*)[32] and then those that follow them. Rejoice [at good tidings to you!] This is your share of the torment from God, together with the reward that is due to you." Then the Messenger of God added, "Do you wish that God may relieve you from the condition you are in?" I said, "Yes, O Messenger of God." So he said, "Say: O Allāh! Have mercy on this my poor skin and my weak bones. I seek refuge in You from the burning fire. O fever (*umm mildam*),[33] if you believe in God, do not eat [my] flesh, do not drink [my] blood and do not make [my] mouth burn. Go to someone else who associates partners with God. But I bear witness that there is no deity other than God, He is unique and without any associate. I bear witness that Muḥammad is His slave and messenger."' 'Alī said, 'I uttered this and was cured instantly.'

Ja'far b. Muḥammad: He said, 'Whenever I resorted to [the *mu'awwidhatayn*] out of fear, I found them to be beneficial, and we used to teach them to our wives and children.'

Ja'far b. Muḥammad: [34] He said, 'Whenever you wish to seek refuge

[29]The Arabic term is *ḥudūd Allāh*. Its exact meaning of 'legal punishments laid down by God' does not fit in the context. It is, therefore, used as an Ismā'īlī technical term meaning 'various ranks of the *da'wa* hierarchy'. Whether or not the term was so used by Ja'far al-Ṣādiq is questionable. For details on *ḥudūd*, see Zāhid 'Alī, *Hamārē Ismā'īlī*, 299–306; Sijistānī, *Kitāb al-Iftikhār*, 287. For other meanings of *ḥadd* (pl. *ḥudūd*) see *EI*[2], s.v. Ḥadd. The article mentions how the term is used by the Druzes, but fails to mention the Ismā'īlī use.

[30]*To God belongs the Names Most Beautiful; so call Him by them* (7:180; 17:110; 20:8). Muslim piety has picked out from the Qur'ān and supplemented by *ḥadīth*, the ninety-nine most beautiful Names of God. *EI*[2], s.v. Allāh. For handy reference to those names in beautiful calligraphy see Friedlander, *Ninety-Nine Names of Allah*; Sakīna, *Sajda-e Qalam*.

[31]For the names of the Messenger of God, see Ṭabarī, *History of al-Ṭabarī*, IX, 155–6.

[32]For *waṣī* see *The Pillars of Islam*, I, 30, n. 63.

[33]It is an unremitting fever that 'eats flesh and drinks blood'. Pre-Islamic Arabs believed that diseases were spirits in and of themselves capable of independent action. It is also spelled as *umm mildham*. *Qāmūs*, s.v. l-d-m; *Lisān al-'Arab*, s.v. l-d-m; l-dh-m; Ṭabarī, *History of al-Ṭabarī*, IX, 106.

[34]According to MS Q. Printed text has *qāla Ja'far b. Muḥammad*.

[by invoking God], close up your palms, recite the *Fātiḥat al-Kitāb* (The Opening of the Qur'ān, *sūra* 1)[35] and *qul huwa llāh* (*sūra* 112), three times. Then place the two hands on the place where there is pain. Then again close your palms and recite the *Fātiḥat al-Kitāb* and *qul a'ūdhu bi-rabb al-falaq* (*sūra* 113) three times. Then place the hands at the spot where there is pain a second time. Then again close up your palms and recite the *Fātiḥat al-Kitāb* and *qul a'ūdhu bi-rabb al-nās* (*sūra* 114), three times, and place the hands over the pain.'

'Alī: He said, 'Recite the call to prayer (*adhān*) in the ear of a person whose limbs are ill-formed.'

The Messenger of God: He forbade the use of charms (or amulets) except those from the Qur'ān or those which mention the name of God.[36] He said, 'These are the charms which [the Prophet] Solomon son of David[37] used against men, jinns, and vermin (*al-hawāmm*).'[38]

[The Messenger of God]: He said, 'Charms should not be used except in three cases—venomous bites (*ḥuma*), the evil eye (*'ayn*), and blood which does not cease flowing.' The word *ḥuma* means the venom [of an insect or reptile].[39]

[The Messenger of God]: He said, 'There is no such thing as contagion (*'adwā*),[40] a bad omen (*ṭiyara*),[41] or the [bad omen of] an owl (*hām* or

[35]Recitation of the *Fātiḥat al-Kitāb* is a complete cure, an effective medicine, a perfect incantation, a key to success and prosperity, a repellant of anxiety, etc. See Ibn Qayyim, *al-Ṭibb al-nabawī*, 318–19.

[36]'There is no objection to the use of charm as long as polytheism is not involved.' Dhahabī, *al-Ṭibb al-nabawī*, 136. Like the sacred books of many religions, the Qur'ān is believed to possess supernatural power, and it is used in various occult practices. For details see Donaldson, *Wild Rue*, 130–40.

[37] The Biblical king is an outstanding figure in Islamic legends, and is mentioned several times in the Qur'ān. For details see EI^2, s.v. Sulaymān b. Dāwūd.

[38]*Al-Hāmma*, pl. *al-hawāmm*, see *Majma' al-baḥrayn*, s.v. h-m-m; a different *ḥadīth* is cited. 'There is no harm in charms so long as they involve no polytheism.' *Mishkāt* II, 511; Robson, II, 947; transmitted by Muslim.

[39]*Mishkāt*, II, 511, 516; Robson, II, 946, 950–1; the text has *'ayn*, *ḥuma*, and *dam*, meaning bleeding, and it is said that nose bleeding is meant here. 'Spells against evil eye are permitted.' Transmitted by Bukhārī and Muslim. Other traditions mention scorpion stings, small pustules, and skin eruptions, etc. See also Ibn Qayyim, *al-Ṭibb al-nabawī*, 163–85; they should be charmed by reciting the Qur'ānic chapter 1, 112–14; Dhahabī, *al-Ṭibb al-nabawī*, 136; Nasīmī, *Fi 'l-ṭibb al-islāmī*, 105–14.

[40]*'Adwā* means a contagious disease that passes from one person to another, such as mange or scab. *Lā 'adwā* in the tradition means a disease that does not pass by its own agency to a thing. Lane, s.v. '-d-w.

[41]*Ṭiyara* and *ṭīra* means a thing from which one augurs evil, contrary of *fa'l*, fortune. Lane, s.v. ṭ-y-r.

hāma).[42] But the evil eye and divination (*al-fa'l*) are in fact true.[43] When one of you looks at a man or a beast or a beautiful thing and admires it, he should say, "I believe in God and may God bless Muḥammad and his progeny," and his eye will not do harm.'

Abū Ja'far Muḥammad b. 'Alī: He said, 'When one of you wishes to cast a spell (*an tarqiya*) for a wound, i.e. for pain, blood, or that which causes anxiety, then put your hand on the wound and say, "In the name of God I put a spell on you, in the name of God the Greatest, against the sharp [weapons], and the stone cleaving to the ground; and the poisonous tooth.[44] O vein, do not gush forth [blood]; O eye do not abstain from sleep [by night]." He should repeat this three times.'

The Messenger of God: He prohibited the use of *tamā'im*[45] and *tiwala* (or *tuwala*).[46] Now *tamā'im* (amulets) are all writings or beads [strung together and] hung upon a human being. *Tiwala* (charms) are all those things which make women more pleasing to their husbands, such as divination (*kihāna*) and the like. He forbade the use of *siḥr* (sorcery).

Ja'far b. Muḥammad: He said, 'There is no harm in wearing [an amulet inscribed with] a verse from the Qur'ān.'

'Alī: He said, 'One night we were with the Messenger of God when a meteor came down with a flash. The Messenger of God asked the people, "What did you use to say in pre-Islamic times (*al-jāhilīya*)[47] when you beheld such an occurrence?" The people replied, "We used to say that someone great is dead; or someone great is born." The Messenger of God said, "Such a star is not cast down at the death or the birth of any person.

[42]*Lisān al-'Arab*, s.v. h-w-m; the tradition is cited. 'There should be no taking of omens, but the best type is the good omen.' *Mishkāt*, II, 520–1; Robson, II, 955–6; transmitted by Bukhārī and Muslim. Other traditions with some variations are reported both by Bukhārī and Muslim.

[43] 'The evil eye is a reality.' Transmitted by Bukhārī and Muslim. Ibn Qayyim, *al-Ṭibb al-nabawī*, 163.

[44]The Arabic reads: *al-ḥadd wa 'l-ḥadīd, wa 'l-ḥajar al-malbūd, wa 'l-nāb al-asmar*. Meaning of these phrases is not clear and I was unable to find them in the sources that I consulted.

[45]*Tamīma* pl. *tamā'im* is a kind of amulet hung around a person's neck inscribed with a Qur'ānic verse, or the names of God. It also refers to certain beads which the Arabs of the desert used to hang around their children's necks to repel the evil eye. Lane, s.v. t-m-m.

[46]As in *Lisān al-'Arab*, s.v. t-w-l; *Tāj al-'arūs*, s.v. t-w-l. In the edited text and MS Q: *tiwal*, seems to be an error. It is defined as *siḥr*, charm, witchcraft, or refers to some kinds of beads worn around the neck to ward off spells. A tradition transmitted by 'Abd Allāh b. Mas'ūd states, '*Al-Tiwala*, *al-tamā'im* and *al-ruqā* pertain to polytheism.' Ibn Manẓūr cites Abū 'Ubayd and Ibn al-Athīr and states that *al-tiwala* means *siḥr* (and the like) that makes women more pleasing to their husbands and it is prohibited.

[47]For *jāhilīya* see *The Pillars of Islam*, I, 281, n. 46.

But when our Lord decided upon something, the bearers of the Throne proclaimed His glory and said, 'Our Lord has decided upon such [and such].' The residents of the sky who are next to them hear this, and they say the same until its [echo] reaches the inhabitants of the heaven of this world. Now the devils (*shayāṭīn* pl. of *shayṭān*) eavesdropped on [that conversation], and something was recollected by them, and they brought it to the soothsayers (*kahana* pl. of *kāhin*). The devils sometimes embellished or deleted parts [from the stories], and consequently the diviners sometimes spoke the truth and sometimes made mistakes. Then God has guarded the sky [from eavesdropping of the devils] by [shooting] these stars [at them], hence divination ceased, and now it does not exist." The Messenger of God recited the word of the Almighty: *Save him who steals the hearing, and them does a clear flame pursue* (15:18), and He says: *And we used to sit on places (high) therein to listen. But he who listens now finds a flame in wait for him* (72:9).'[48]

TREATMENT AND MEDICINE
(*AL-ʿILĀJ WA 'L-DAWĀ'*)

Jaʿfar b. Muḥammad—his father—his ancestors: The Messenger of God said, 'Treat yourselves medically, for, God never sent down any disease without providing a medicine for it, except *sām*,' which means death. 'There is no remedy for that.'[49]

[Jaʿfar b. Muḥammad]: A group of people from the Anṣār[50] [came to the Messenger of God and] said, 'We have a neighbour who complains of a disorder of the stomach. Will you permit us to treat him?' The Messenger of God asked, 'With what will you treat him?' They replied, 'There is a Jew amongst us who cures this disease.' The Messenger of God asked, 'With what?' They said, 'He opens up the stomach and removes something from it.' The Messenger of God did not like this; so they came back to him two or three times [until finally] he said, 'Do as you wish.' So they called the Jew who cut open the man's stomach and removed from it a large quantity of foul liquid (*rijrij*).[51] Then he washed the stomach,

[48] *Mishkāt*, II, 524, 526–7; Robson, II, 958, 960. Transmitted by Muslim on the authority of Ibn ʿAbbās. A shorter version is transmitted by Bukhārī.

[49] 'God has not sent down a disease without sending down a remedy for it.' Transmitted by Bukhārī. 'There is a medicine for every disease ...' Transmitted by Muslim. *Mishkāt*, II, 509, 512, 513; Robson, II, 945, 947, 948. See also Ibn Qayyim, *al-Ṭibb al-nabawī*, 26–30; Khalīlī, *Ṭibb al-Imām al-Ṣādiq*, 17; the author has used the *Daʿā'im* as a source for his book.

[50] Anṣār, see *The Pillars of Islam*, I, 13, n. 18.

[51] Lane, s.v. r-j-j; Majlisī, *Biḥār al-anwār*, LXII, 73.

stitched it up and treated it with medicine, and the man recovered. The Prophet was informed [about it] and he said, 'Verily, He who has created diseases, has also created medicines for them. The best of medicines is scarification (*al-ḥijāma*), bloodletting (*al-fiṣād*), and black caraway (*ḥabbat al-sawdā'*, i.e. *shūnīz*).'[52]

Ja'far b. Muḥammad: He was asked about a man who was treated by a Jew or a Christian. He said, 'There is no harm in it, for, cure is in the hand of God.'

Ja'far b. Muḥammad: He was asked about a woman who suffers from a physical disorder, and whether it was proper for a man to treat her. He said, 'There is no harm in it if she is under the compulsion [of necessity].'

'Alī: He said, 'He who is a physician should fear God, be sincere, and strive conscientiously.'[53]

The Messenger of God: He forbade that a sick person be restrained from food, except dates in the case of ophthalmia (*ramad*). He saw Salmān (al-Fārisī)[54] eating dates whilst his eyes were affected. He said, 'O Salmān, do you eat dates when you have ophthalmia? If it is inevitable that you have to eat them, eat with the right molars if your left eye is affected, and with your left, if your right eye is affected.'[55]

[The Messenger of God]: He said, 'Avoiding the night meal leads to decrepitude.'[56]

[The Messenger of God]: He said, 'Do not force diseased persons to eat. Verily it is God Who gives them food and drink.'[57]

'Alī: He used to say, 'Although there is no permanence in life, he

[52]For cupping see *Mishkāt*, II, 513, 514, 515; Robson, II, 948, 949. See also *The Pillars of Islam*, I, 126. *Shūnīz* see. n. 7 above in this chapter. This passage is cited by Khalīlī, *Ṭibb al-Imām al-Ṣādiq*, 17.

[53]In his *Biḥār al-anwār*, LXII, 73–4, Majlisī has reproduced this section until here. For the liability of one who practices medicine, see Chap. 16, n. 113.

[54]Salmān al-Fārisī, a Persian by origin, was a Companion of the Prophet. The Prophet ransomed him from slavery and adopted him as his protégé (*mawlā*) and member of his family (*Ahl al-Bayt*). He is one of the most popular figures of Muslim legend and an ardent supporter of 'Alī. *EI*[2], s. v. Salmān al-Fārisī; Jafri, *Origins*, 52, 102, 109.

[55]Majlisī, *Biḥār al-anwār*, LXII, 151; this tradition is cited from the *Da'ā'im*. Nīsābūrī, *Ṭibb al-a'imma*, 419; Suyūṭī, *al-Manhaj al-sawīy*, 332; slightly different version and instead of Salmān it is Ṣuhayb.

[56]Tirmidhī and Ibn Māja transmitted it. Concordance, s.v. t-r-k, '-sh-w; Ibn Qayyim, *al-Ṭibb al*-nabawī, 214. *Kāfi*, VI, 302–4; the night meal should not be avoided.

[57]*Mishkāt* II, 512; Robson, II, 947. The tradition is transmitted by Tirmidhī and Ibn Māja and is discussed in detail by Ibn Qayyim, *al-Ṭibb al-nabawī*, 100–3; Suyūṭī, *al-Manhaj al-sawīy*, 235.

who desires longevity should avoid taking loans (*ridā'*),[58] and should use sandals regularly, eat his morning meal early, and decrease sexual activity.' Ja'far b. Muḥammad said, 'by *ridā'* ['Alī] meant a loan.'

Ja'far b. Muḥammad: He said, 'If people were to be moderate in food their bodies would gain in strength [and stand tall].'

[Ja'far b. Muḥammad]: He said, 'Abandoning dinner leads to the deterioration of the constitution.[59] When a man grows old, it is not proper for him to pass the night without a full stomach.'[60]

The Messenger of God: He said, 'There is no harm in taking a clyster provided it does not increase the size of the abdomen.'

[The Messenger of God]: He said, 'Meat and milk promote the growth of flesh [in the human body] and strengthen the bones.[61] Meat increases hearing and sight; and meat with eggs increases virility.'[62]

The Messenger of God: He said, 'The man who scarifies himself on a Wednesday or a Saturday, and contracts leucoderma (*waḍaḥ*), should blame no one but himself.[63] Scarification of the head is the cure for every disease.[64] Cure[65] can be accomplished in four ways: scarification (*ḥijāma*), taking a clyster (*ḥuqna*), branding (*nūra*), and using an emetic (*qay'*).[66] When the blood becomes restless (or agitated *tabayyagha*), let the man scarify, whatever be the day, and recite the Throne Verse (2:255) and ask God for His forgiveness and seek blessing for the Prophet.' The Prophet said, 'Do not be inimical to certain days, for then they will be inimical to you. When the blood becomes restless (or agitated), let there be a

[58]*Ridā'* also means debt, because it is regarded as a thing that cleaves to the neck of the debtor like the *ridā'* (outer wrapping garment) that cleaves to the shoulders of the wearer. One says, *huwa khafīf al-ridā'*, meaning he is a little burdened in respect of debt. Lane, s.v. r-d-y.

[59]*Kāfī*, VI, 302; reported on the authority of Ṣādiq and ascribed to 'Alī.

[60]Ibid., VI, 302. See also Shabbar, *Ṭibb al-a'imma*, 135–8; additional sources are listed.

[61]*Kāfī*, VI, 351; the tradition mentions milk only, without meat.

[62]Ibid., VI, 339.

[63]*Mishkāt*, II, 514–15; Robson, II, 949. Zuhrī reported it in *mursal* form, i.e. a tradition in which a Successor (*tābi'*, not a Companion) quotes the Prophet directly. Transmitted by Ibn Ḥanbal and Abū Dāwūd, but the latter said that the tradition is not sound. Suyūṭī, *al-Manhaj al-sawīy*, 248–9.

[64]*Mishkāt*, II, 513; Robson, II, 948; several traditions are transmitted about getting cupped.

[65]Reading *al-dawā'* as in MS Q. *Al-dā'* in the edited text seems to be incorrect.

[66]'There is a remedy in three things: The incision of a cupping-glass, a drink of honey, or cauterization by fire.' Transmitted by Bukhārī. *Mishkāt*, II, 509, 510; Robson, II, 945, 946. See also Ibn Qayyim, *al-Ṭibb al-nabawī*, 63, 75; Suyūṭī, *al-Manhaj al-sawīy*, 243–56; it deals with scarification, bloodletting by opening a vein (*faṣd*), diarrhoea (*ishāl*), and use of an emetic. Shabbar, *Ṭibb al-a'imma*, 132–4.

bloodletting, even by a broad (or iron head) of an arrow (*mishqaṣ*) [if nothing else is available].'

And his saying *tabayyagha*, meaning *tabghī* (to exceed just bounds) is from *baghy*.[67]

[The Messenger of God]: He said, 'Fever is from the vehemence (*fayḥ*) of the heat of Hell,[68] so extinguish[69] it with water.' And when he was enervated [by fever], he used to call for water and put his hand in it.

'Alī: He said, 'Ḥusayn became ill and his pain was great. So Fāṭima carried him to the Prophet, and seeking his help and protection, she said, "O Messenger of God, call upon God to cure your child," and placed Ḥusayn in front of him. So the Prophet rose and sat near the head of Ḥusayn. Then the Prophet said, "O Fāṭima, my little one! Verily, it is God Who has given him to you, and it is He Who is able to cure him." Then Gabriel came to him and said, "O Muḥammad, God never revealed any chapter of the Qur'ān to you except that it contained the letter *fā'*, and every occurrence of *fā'* is derived from *āfa* (calamity) except the *Fātiḥa* (*al-ḥamdu lillāh*) which does not contain the letter *fā'*. So call for a bowl of water and recite over it the *Fātiḥa* forty times, then pour it on Ḥusayn and God will certainly cure him." The Prophet did so, and it was as though Ḥusayn was loosened from a shackle.'

The Messenger of God: He prohibited cauterization (*kayy*).[70]

Ja'far b. Muḥammad: He allowed cauterization if there was no fear of death or disfigurement (mutilation).[71]

The Messenger of God: He disapproved that collyrium (*kuḥl*) should be applied except in odd numbers (*witr*[an]).[72] He directed that it be used

[67] *Tabayyagha* is from b-y-gh and not from b-gh-y. It probably is a scribal error. *Lisān al-'Arab*, s.v. b-y-gh; the *ḥadīth* is also cited.

[68] Lane, s.v. f-y-ḥ; the *ḥadīth* is cited.

[69] 'Fever is ... so cool it with water.' *Mishkāt*, II, 510; Robson, II, 946; transmitted by Bukhārī and Muslim. See also Ibn Qayyim, *al-Ṭibb al-nabawī*, 38–45; Suyūṭī, *al-Manhaj al-sawīy*, 358; Khalīlī, *Ṭibb al-Imām al-Ṣādiq*, 17; he cites the *Da'ā'im*.

[70] Some traditions state that cauterization is permitted while the others state that it is forbidden. The apparent contradiction seems to have been a result of misunderstanding the Prophet's intent in prohibiting it. As its misuse could result in serious injury or death the Prophet advised that it should be used as the last resort. *Mishkāt*, II, 509; Robson, II, 945. See n. 66 in this chapter. For a more recent discussion see Nasīmī, *Fi 'l-ṭibb al-islāmī*, 19–40.

[71] Majlisī, *Biḥār al-anwār*, LXII, 74; he has reproduced it from the *Da'ā'im*.

[72] *Al-Iktiḥālu witr*[an]. Explaining this tradition, Ṭurayḥī states that it means that kohl should be applied either three, five, or seven times [in odd numbers], such as four times in the right eye and three times in the left at the bedtime. *Majma' al-baḥrayn*, s.v. w-t-r. See also *Kāfī*, VI, 509; the Prophet used to apply collyrium four times in the right eye and three tims in the left before going to bed. Ibn Qayyim, *al-Ṭibb al-nabawī*, 260.

at the time of sleeping, and that antimony (*ithmad*)[73] should be used as an eye salve. He said, 'I enjoin its use for it removes motes [from the eyes] and clears the sight.'[74]

The Messenger of God: He said, 'The date of the *'ajwa* variety is from heaven, and is a cure for poison.'[75]

Zayd b. 'Alī b. al-Ḥusayn[76] said, 'The way to use it is this. Dried *'ajwa* dates should be taken, their pits should be removed, then they should be ground to a fine texture, and made into a paste mixed with butter made from the milk of an old cow, and then taken out [and preserved]. When the need arises, the paste should be eaten [as a medicine] for poison.'

Ja'far b. Muḥammad: He said, 'Once the Messenger of God was stung by a scorpion, and he shook it off and said, "May God curse you. Neither a believer nor an unbeliever is safe from you." Then he called for salt and put it at the spot where he had been bitten. Then he rubbed it with his thumb until it melted and said, "If the people knew [the properties] of salt, they would not desire *theriaca* (*tiryāq*) in addition to it."'[77]

'Alī: He said, 'The mushroom (*kam'a*) is a part of manna (*mann*), and its juice is medicine for the eyes.'[78] Zayd b. 'Alī b. al-Ḥusayn said, 'The way to use it is this. Take a mushroom and wash it clean; then put it in a cloth and squeeze the juice. The juice should then be heated on the fire

[73]*Ithmad*, an arabicized word, means an ore of antimony, or antimony itself. It is a certain stone from which collyrium is prepared. It is said that the best kind comes from the mines of Iṣfahān. In Persian it is called *surma* and in Hindi *ānjan*. Bīrūnī, *Pharmacy*, 16; Ibn Qayyim, *al-Ṭibb al-nabawī*, 263; Lane, s.v. th-m-d.

[74]Majlisī, *Biḥār al-anwār*, LXII, 151; he has cited it from the *Da'ā'im*. 'Apply antimony, for it clears the sight and makes the hair grow.' Ibn 'Abbās, who narrated the tradition, asserted that the Prophet applied collyrium every night in each eye three times. *Mishkāt*, II, 499, 500; Robson, II, 936; Ibn Qayyim, *al-Ṭibb al-nabawī*, 259, 260. See also *Kāfī*, VI, 508–9; odd numbers are stressed: *yaktaḥilu witr^an witr^an*; *man iktaḥala fa 'l-yūtir*.

[75]*Mishkāt*, II, 518; Robson, II, 953; see also Chap. 3, n. 48; *Kāfī*, VI, 360–3. Ibn Qayyim, *al-Ṭibb al-nabawī*, 106–10, 313.

[76]For Zayd, see *The Pillars of Islam*, I, 428, n. 28; *EI*², s.v. Zayd b. 'Alī.

[77]'Alī said, 'When the Messenger of God was praying one night he placed his hand on the ground and was stung by a scorpion, so he struck it with his sandal and killed it. Then when he departed he said, "God curse the scorpion! It does not leave alone one who is praying, a prophet or anyone else." He then called for salt and water, and putting it in a vessel he began to pour it over his finger where it had stung him. He wiped it seeking refuge in God by reciting the *Mu'awwidhatān*.' *Mishkāt*, II, 518; Robson, II, 952. See also Suyūṭī, *al-Manhaj al-sawīy*, 383.

[78]'Truffles are a kind of manna, and their juice is a medicine for the eyes.' *Mishkāt*, II, 444, 453, 518; Robson II, 889, 953; transmitted by Bukhārī and Muslim. *Kāfī*, VI, 383; it is ascribed to the Messenger of God. See also Nīsābūrī, *Ṭibb al-a'imma*, 400; Suyūṭī, *al-Manhaj al-sawīy*, 335. Its decoction is a curative for the eyes. Bīrūnī, *Pharmacy*, 281; Shabbar, *Ṭibb al-a'imma*, 264–5.

until it becomes thick. Then add to it a kerat (*qīrāṭ*, about 4 gr.)[79] of musk and put it in a bottle to use it as collyrium for all infections of the eye. If it dries up, it should be mixed with rain or other water and then used.'[80]

['Alī]: He said, 'Nothing heals a woman who is confined (due to childbirth (*nafsā'*) better than fresh dates, for, God fed Mary during her confinement (*nifās*) with [fresh and] ripe [dates].'[81]

Ja'far b. Muḥammad: A man complained to the Imam about pain in his side (*khāṣira*).[82] [The Imam] said, 'I enjoin you to eat whatever falls from the plate [of food].' He did so and was relieved.[83]

The Messenger of God: He said, 'The man who eats twenty-one raisins, mixing them with his saliva and removing their seeds, will not suffer from any disease until the illness which causes his death.[84] He who eats seven dried dates before sleeping will be cured of colic (*qūlanj* or *qūlinj*) and the worms in his stomach will be killed.'[85]

[The Messenger of God]: He said, 'The man who eats a pomegranate (*rummān*) with its thin yellow pulp that is amid the seeds, his stomach will be tanned.[86] The quince (*safarjal*) strengthens the weak heart and gives courage to a coward.'[87]

Ja'far b. Muḥammad: A man wrote to [the Imam] from a plague-ridden country and informed him of an epidemic there; so [the Imam] wrote to him, 'I enjoin you to eat apples (*tuffāḥ*).' He did so and was cured. [The Imam] said, 'The apple extinguishes heat and cools the stomach and cures fever.'[88]

The Messenger of God: He said, 'Honey is a cure.'

'Alī: [He said], 'Nothing cures a man [so well] as the use of honey.'[89]

[79]Hinz, *Islamische Masse*, 27. Qīrāṭ, a weight about one half *dāniq* (i.e. one-twelfth of a dirham), it is also a part of dinar, generally one-twentieth. *Lisān al-'Arab*, s.v. q-r-ṭ.

[80]It is reported by Majlisī, *Biḥār al-anwār*, LXII, 151, from the *Da'ā'im*.

[81]It alludes to the story of Mary in the Qur'ān (*Sūrat Maryam*), especially the verses 25–6. See also Ibn Qayyim, *al-Ṭibb al-nabawī*, 110–11, 288.

[82]*Khāṣira* more properly means what is between the crest of the hip and the lowest rib. Lane, s.v. kh-ṣ-r.

[83]*Kāfī*, VI, 314–15.

[84]Ibid., VI, 365; ascribed to 'Alī.

[85]'He who eats seven dates of '*ajwa* variety before going to bed will kill the worms in his stomach.' Ibid., VI, 363.

[86]Ibid., VI, 368. See also n. 64, Chap. 3.

[87]Ibid., VI, 371. See also n. 68, Chap. 3.

[88]Ibid., VI, 369–70. See also n. 69, Chap. 3. Its leaves and extract are beneficial for hot inflammations and are also used as fillers for wounds. The apple is very useful medicinally. Bīrūnī, *Pharmacy*, 91.

[89]*Kāfī*, VI, 346.

Ja'far b. Muḥammad: [He said], 'God has said: *In it [i.e. honey] is healing for mankind*' (16:69).[90]

'Alī: He said, 'Is it not possible for a man, when he is ill, to ask his wife to give him a *dirham* from her *mahr* (dower) and buy honey and drink it with rain water? For verily God says in respect of *mahr*: *But if they are pleased to offer you any of it, consume it with wholesome appetite* (4:4).[91] And He says in respect of honey: *In it is healing for mankind* (16:69). In respect of rain water He says: *And We send down from the sky blessed water* (50:9).'

The Messenger of God: He said, 'I enjoin you to drink the milk of cows, because it is mixed [with the juice of] all trees.'[92]

[The Messenger of God]: He said, 'Butter (*samn*) is a medicine.' And Ja'far b. Muḥammad said, 'It is better [to use it] in the summer rather than in the winter; and nothing entering the stomach [is better] than butter.'[93]

Ja'far b. Muḥammad: He said, 'Vinegar (*khall*) gives relief to the gall bladder (*marāra*), strengthens the heart,[94] kills the worms in the stomach, and is good for the mouth.'[95]

The Messenger of God: Once he walked over a hot sandy tract and his feet were burnt, so he stood on some purslane (*rijla, al-baqla al-ḥamqā'*).[96] He was relieved, so he blessed it. He greatly relished purslane and gourd (*dubbā'*)[97] and used to say that they increase intelligence and brain [power]. He also loved endive (*hindabā'* or *hindibā'*)[98] and said, 'Every leaf of endive contains the water of Paradise.'[99]

Abū Ja'far Muḥammad b. 'Alī: He said, 'I enjoin you the use of black caraway (*al-ḥabba al-sawdā'*), for, it is the cure for all disease except *sām*,' meaning death.[100]

[90]Honey is highly recommended as a remedy. One tradition states, 'If anyone eats honey three mornings every month, he will not be afflicted with any serious trouble.' Another tradition states, 'Make use of two remedies: honey and the Qur'ān.' *Mishkāt*, II, 519; Robson, II, 953; *Kāfī*, VI, 346; Ibn Qayyim, *al-Ṭibb al-nabawī*, 45–9; all the benefits are enumerated.

[91]Arberry, *The Koran Interpreted*, I, 100.

[92]*Kāfī*, VI, 352. Suyūṭī, *al-Manhaj al-sawīy*, 299; 'I enjoin you to drink the milk of cows, because it contains healing power; its butter is a medicine, but its meat is unhealthy.'

[93]*Kāfī*, VI, 349; Imam al-Ṣādiq transmitted it from Imam 'Alī.

[94]The text reads: *yuḥyī al-qalb*. *Kāfī*, VI, 344.

[95]Arabic reads: *yashudd al-fam*. *Kāfī*, VI, 343–4; several traditions are cited with two different readings: *yashudd al-fam*, and *yashudd al-'aql*. See also n. 56, Chap. 3.

[96]Lane, s.v. r-j-l; see also n. 79 in Chap. 3.

[97]Lane, s.v. d-b-b; see also n. 71 and 78 in Chap. 3.

[98]See n. 72 in Chap. 3.

[99]*Kāfī*, VI, 376–7; a separate section on it.

[100]See n. 7 and 10 above in this chapter.

[Abū Ja'far Muḥammad]: He said, 'When you enter a plague-stricken place, eat its onions, for this will protect you from the epidemic.'[101]

The Messenger of God: He said, 'Beware of spurge (*shubrum*),[102] for it is burning hot (*ḥārr*^{un} *yārr*^{un}).[103] Use senna pods (*sanā*)[104] for treatment, if anything were to turn death away, it would be senna.[105] Use fenugreek (*ḥulba*)[106] for medicine; and if my community (*umma*) knew what it contains for them, they would use it as medicine even though it might cost its weight in gold.'

'Alī: He said, 'Every rue plant (*ḥarmal*)[107] is guarded by angels until it reaches those [who need it].'[108] And he said, 'In the root of the rue plant, there is a charm, and in its branch is a cure for seventy-two diseases.'[109]

Ja'far b. Muḥammad: One of his companions complained of a stomach disorder (*ikhtilāf al-baṭn*). [The Imam] directed him to take rice (*aruzz*)[110]

[101]The Messenger of God said, 'When you enter a country (*bilād*), eat its onions, it will drive away the infectious disease (*wabā'*).' *Kāfī*, VI, 388; it contains a separate section on onions. See also Suyūṭī, *al-Manhaj al-sawīy*, 269.

[102]*Shubrum* is a plant of the family Euphorbia. *Lisān al-'Arab*, s.v. sh-b-r-m; the tradition that it is *ḥārr*^{un} *jārr*^{un} is cited. Bīrūnī, *Pharmacy*, 349–50; its fruit is cathartic. Ibn Qayyim, *al-Ṭibb al-nabawī*, 84–6, describes both *shubrum* and *sanā*.

[103]When a loaf of bread is taken out of the oven it is said: *innahu la-ḥārr*^{un} *yārr*^{un}. *Lisān al-'Arab*, s.v. y-r-r; the tradition is cited. *Jārr* and *yārr* are variants in the traditions. Ibn Qayyim, *al-Ṭibb al-nabawī*, 86.

[104]*Sanā* is a plant of the genus Cassia. It has a medical use. Its dried leaflets are used as a purgative. *Lisān al-'Arab*, s.v. s-b-y; the tradition is cited.

[105]Asmā' bt. 'Umays related that the Prophet asked her what laxative she used, and she replied, 'spurge', whereupon he said, 'It is very hot.' She then used senna as a purgative, and the Prophet said, 'If anything contained a remedy for death it would be senna.' *Mishkāt*, II, 512; Robson, II, 948. Suyūṭī, *al-Manhaj al-sawīy*, 297. 'Take senna pods and *sannūt* (cumin seed, dill, etc.), because they contain remedy for every disease except *sām*.' The Prophet was asked, 'What is *sām*,' and he said, 'death'. See also Dhahabī, *al-Ṭibb al-nabawī*, 16, 61–2, 63. It is reported by Majlisī, *Biḥār al-anwār*, LXII, 219, from the *Da'ā'im*.

[106]*Ḥulba*, a leguminous Asiatic herb (Trigonella foenumgraecum) with aromatic seeds is used medicinally. It is made to germinate in a vessel of water and eaten. It is useful as a remedy for diseases of the chest, for cough, asthma, phlegm, haemorrhoids, and for giving strength to the back, the liver, and the bladder. Lane, s.v. ḥ-l-b. Bīrūnī, *Pharmacy*, 127–8; it has many uses.

[107]*Ḥarmal*, is a medicinal plant. It has yellow flowers, sesame-like seeds, and leaves with a bitter taste. Its roots are boiled and given as a drink to a person having a fever. *Lisān al-'Arab*, s.v. ḥ-r-m-l; Bīrūnī, *Pharmacy*, 125; Ibn al-Bayṭār, *Tuḥfa*, 204. The wild rue plant is also used for magical purposes. Its seeds are burned over hot coals and the smoke is allowed to circle about the person concerned. It is believed that it has the power to ward off evil. Donaldson, *Wild Rue*, 146.

[108]Lit. until it reaches those whom it reaches.

[109]Nīsābūrī, *Ṭibb al-a'imma*, 307–8.

[110]Ibn Qayyim, *al-Ṭibb al-nabawī*, 265; all the benefits are listed.

and make some gruel and eat it. He did so and his stomach gained strength. And [the Imam] said, 'I was ill for two or more years, so God gave me the inspiration [to use] rice. So I asked for it, and it was washed, dried, warmed over the fire, and ground into flour. Some of it was made into a kind of dried gruel (*sawīq*) and some into a soup (*ḥasā'*). I ate it and recovered.'[111]

[Ja'far b. Muḥammad]: He said, '*Sawīq* [112] induces the growth of muscle and strengthens the bones.[113] The men suffering from fever should be given *sawīq* washed thrice. It cures the fever (*ḥummā*), dries up the gall (*marāra*) and phlegm (*balgham*), and strengthens the legs.'

The Messenger of God: He prohibited the eating of potter's clay (*ṭafl*)[114] or mud (*ṭīn*) or charcoal (*faḥm*), saying, 'Verily God created Adam from mud, so He declared the eating of mud unlawful for his descendants. Any one who eats mud has verily helped to kill himself. I never said funeral prayers over him who died after eating mud.'[115]

Ja'far b. Muḥammad said,[116] 'The eating of mud causes disloyalty (*nifāq*).'[117]

The Messenger of God: He said, 'The continuous eating of fresh fish melts the body[118] [i.e. reduces its fat].' Whenever he used to eat fish he used to say, 'O God, bless us through it; and in exchange give us something better than it.'[119]

Ja'far b. Muḥammad said, 'Eating dates after [fish] removes its evil effects.'

[Ja'far b. Muḥammad]: He was asked about using the milk of she-asses for medical purposes, and he permitted its use.

The Messenger of God: He forbade the drinking of hot water, that is water heated excessively.[120]

[111]*Kāfī*, VI, 319–21; several traditions are reported.

[112]*Sawīq* is a meal of parched barley or of a similar grain. It is generally made into a kind of gruel with water or clarified butter, and is therefore said to be supped or sipped, not eaten. It is likewise thus called when dry. It is also made of other grains and of several mealy fruits and of carob. Lane, s.v. s-w-q.

[113]*Kāfī*, VI, 319; reported from the same Imam.

[114]*Ṭafl* is applied to anything soft and tender, hence fuller's earth. Lane, s.v. ṭ-f-l.

[115]*Kāfī*, VI, 280.

[116]According to MS Q. The edited text has *wa-'an Ja'far b. Muḥammad.*

[117]*Kāfī*, VI, 280.

[118]Reading *al-jasad* as in MS Q, other MSS and *Kāfī*, VI, 338. The edited text reads: *al-laḥm*. It seems that fish is looked at as a somewhat negative thing. Hence, *yudhību 'l-jasad* (melts the body) means 'reduces fat' in a positive sense. It probably means that it makes one thin and weak. That is why the supplication asks for something better than fish.

[119]*Kāfī*, VI, 337; reported here as a separate tradition.

[120]Ibid., VI, 402; 'Water from hot springs is forbidden because it contains the smell of sulphur.'

6

Book of Dress and Perfume (*Kitāb al-Libās wa 'l-Ṭīb*)[1]

THE ETIQUETTE OF DRESS (*ĀDĀB AL-LIBĀS*)

Jaʿfar b. Muḥammad—his father—his ancestors: ʿAlī used to say, 'When God bestows on man His favour, it behoves him that the results of God's favour should manifestly appear in his dress, so long as it is not showy.'[2]

Jaʿfar b. Muḥammad: Once he saw a companion of his[3] wearing a gown (*jubba*)[4] made of a kind of cloth woven of wool and silk (*khazz*),[5] and a shawl-like garment (*ṭaylasān*)[6] made of the same kind of cloth and looked at him attentively. The man said, 'May I be thy ransom! It is only

[1]For this chapter's summary, see Fyzee, *Compendium*, 146–54.

[2]'God likes the mark of His favour to be seen on his servant.' Another tradition states, 'He who wears grand clothes [to show off] in this world will be made by God to wear humble clothes on the Day of Resurrection.' *Mishkāt*, II, 477, 483; Robson, II, 917, 922; see also *Kāfī*, VI, 453–5, 459–60. People whom God has made prosper should wear clothes suitable for their stations, for the poor may recognize them as people able to give charity. The learned should not conceal their learning, so that others may benefit from it.

[3]He is Yūsuf b. Ibrāhīm who said, 'Once I came to see Abū ʿAbd Allāh wearing ...' *Kāfī*, VI, 457; the whole tradition as reported by Nuʿmān is cited.

[4]See Lane, s.v. j-b-b.

[5]It should be noted that garments of *khazz* are permitted, and they were worn by Companions of the Prophet and the subsequent generation. Contrarily, *ḥarīr*, that is, garments wholly made of silk, are forbidden, but there is no harm in the ornamented border and the warp. *Kāfī*, VI, 465–9; *Mishkāt*, II, 472, 473, 483; Robson, II, 913, 922. Lane, s.v., ḥ-r-r; kh-z-z.

[6]*Ṭaylasān*, arabicized from Persian *tālashān*, is a certain article of apparel worn by the Persians. It is round and its woof and warp are both made of wool. It is [usually] worn by persons of distinction. *Majmaʿ al-baḥrayn*, s.v. ṭ-y-l-s; Lane, s.v. ṭ-l-s.

khazz and its warp is of silk (*ibrīsam*).'[7] So Abū 'Abd Allāh [the Imam] said, 'There is no harm in *khazz*. The day on which [Imam] al-Ḥusayn fell, he had on a gown made from *khazz*.'

Then [the Imam] said, 'When 'Alī, may God bless him, sent Ibn 'Abbās[8] to the Khawārij,[9] Ibn 'Abbās had on him the best of clothes, the best of perfume, and was riding the best of mounts. Then he went to them and overtook them and they said, "You, O Ibn 'Abbās, are the best of men, and yet you come to us in the garb of tyrants (*jabbārīn*) and on their mounts!" So he recited to them: *Say: Who has forbidden the adornment of Allah which He has brought forth for His bondmen, and the good things of His providing? Say: Such, on the Day of Resurrection, will only be for those who believed during the life of the world* (7:32).'[10] Then Abū 'Abd Allāh said, 'Dress and beautify yourselves for God loves beauty so long as it is lawful.'[11]

[Ja'far b. Muḥammad]: One day [the Imam] went out to his companions wearing a gown of yellow *khazz*, a turban of yellow *khazz*, and a square mantle (*miṭraf*)[12] of yellow *khazz*.[13] He spoke of his dress and said, '[The prophet] Joseph son of Jacob[14] used to wear silken gowns (*aqbiyat al-dībāj*)[15] embroidered with gold. He sat on the throne and dispensed justice among the people; and his justice and equity were all that the people needed.'

'Alī b. al-Ḥusayn: During the summer [Imam Zayn al-'Ābidīn] used to wear two Tustarī garments[16] [each] costing five hundred dirhams, and during the winter, he used to wear *khazz*.

['Alī b. al-Ḥusayn]: On the day when al-Ḥusayn b. 'Alī fell [to his

[7]*Al-Ṣiḥāḥ*, s.v. b-r-s-m; an arabicized word.

[8]'Alī sent Ibn 'Abbās to the Khawārij. Ṭabarī, *History of al-Ṭabarī*, XVII, 100; Ibn al-Athīr, *al-Kāmil*, III, 327. For Ibn 'Abbās see *The Pillars of Islam*, I, 86, n. 233.

[9]Khawārij, see *The Pillars of Islam*, I, 50, 94, 190–1, 480.

[10]*Kāfī*, VI, 456–7.

[11]'Alī said, 'God is beautiful and He loves beauty and He loves to see the mark of His favour on His servant.' *Kāfī*, VI, 453, 454.

[12]*Miṭraf* or *muṭraf* is a square or four-sided garment of silk fabric and has ornamental borders. Lane, s.v. ṭ-r-f.

[13]*Kāfī*, VI, 465; it is stated that the Imam prayed in that dress.

[14]Joseph is a favourite subject of Muslim legend. *Sūrat Yūsuf*, chapter 12 of the Qur'ān, deals with his story. In the words of the Qur'ān itself, it is 'the most beautiful of stories'. *EI*[2], s.v. Yūsuf b. Ya'ḳūb. The historicity of the Joseph story as narrated in Genesis is problematic, see *ER*, s.v. Joseph.

[15]*Qabā'* pl. *aqbiya* means an outer garment with full-length sleeves. *Dībāj* is a silk brocade, a kind of cloth, of which the warp and woof are both of silk, and is usually variegated or diversified with colours. Lane, s.v. d-b-j.

[16]Tustar, Arabic form of Shūshtar, a town of south-western Persia in the province of Ahwāz (modern Khūzistān). In medieval times it was famous for its fine clothes and turbans. Yāqūt, s.v. Tustar.

death], he was wearing a gown of *khazz* on which we counted forty cuts and punctures [from swords, lances, and arrows].[17]

Ja'far b. Muḥammad: A man said to him, 'May I be thy ransom! What I like most among men is one who eats coarse food (*jashib*),[18] and wears rough clothes (*khashin*) and abases himself, and the marks of lowliness are apparent on him.' [The Imam] said, 'Woe to thee! Humility (*khushū'*) is a matter of the heart. Have you not heard of a prophet, the son of a prophet, the grandson of a prophet, the great grandson of a prophet, who used to wear gowns of silk brocade embroidered in gold, and used to sit on the throne of the Pharaohs and administer justice.[19] The people had no concern with his dress; they were only concerned with his justice and equity. Similarly, the people are only anxious that the Imam deals out justice to them; when he speaks, he should be truthful; when he promises, he should fulfil his promises; and when he decides, he should be just.

'Verily, God did not forbid any dress, food, or drink which He had already declared to be lawful, but He forbade, in both large and small quantities, only what was declared to be unlawful. God says: *Say: Who has forbidden the adornment of Allah which He has brought forth for His bondmen, and the good things of His providing?*' (7:32)[20]

[Ja'far b. Muḥammad]: A man asked [the Imam], 'O son of the Messenger of God, will it be considered undue expenditure if a man were to bedeck himself with a large number of clothes and preserve some of them?' [The Imam] replied, 'No, this is not undue expenditure. Verily God says: *Let him who has abundance spend of his abundance* (65:7).[21]

[Ja'far b. Muḥammad]: One day Sufyān al-Thawrī[22] came to him and saw that [the Imam] was wearing fine clothes, so he said, 'O son of the

[17] *Kāfī*, VI, 466; there were 63 cuts made by swords, lances, and arrows.

[18] It is applied to wheat or food that is badly or coarsely ground and is without seasoning to render it savoury. It signifies anything disagreeable in taste and dry or tough. Lane, s.v. j-sh-b.

[19] It alludes to Joseph, the firstborn son of Jacob's favourite wife, Rachel. It should be noted that in Jewish tradition Joseph was not a prophet. Sawyer, *Prophecy*; see n. 14 above in this chapter. The Qur'ān (*Sūrat Yūsuf*) calls the account of Joseph's life 'the most beautiful of stories.' In post-Qur'ānic literature the tale of Joseph and Zulaykha (Potiphar's wife) is considerably enlarged and developed into an independent subject of romantic adaptation in Arabic, Persian, and other Islamic languages. *EI*², s.v. Yūsuf and Zulaykhā.

[20] *Kāfī*, VI, 468.

[21] Ibid., VI, 458; three traditions are cited.

[22] Sufyān al-Thawrī al-Kūfī (d. 161/778) was a prominent practitioner of early Islamic law, tradition, and Qur'ān commentary. Occasional suspicion of his alleged sympathising with Shī'ī, including Zaydī, circles, possibly arose as a result of his antagonism towards the 'Abbāsid-inclined Murji'a. It points to an early Kūfan *tashayyu'*, however, without lasting effect on his own tenets. *EI*², s.v. Sufyān al-Thawrī.

Messenger of God, you had spoken to us about ʿAlī and how he used to wear rough and coarse garments (*karābīs*),[23] and you wear *qūhī*[24] and *marwī*[25] [expensive cloth]!' So [the Imam] said, 'Woe to you, O Sufyān, ʿAlī lived in straitened circumstances, and now God has provided us with plenty; and it is desirable that the marks of God's favours be seen manifestly on him who receives them.'[26]

[Jaʿfar b. Muḥammad]: He saw some people wearing cloth made of wool and hair, and said, 'Wear cotton clothes, for, that was the dress of the Messenger of God, and that was the best he could find, and that is (also) our dress.[27] The Messenger of God never wore cloth made of wool or hair, so do not wear it without good cause; for, verily, God is full of beauty and loves it, and [He desires] that the signs of His favour on His bondmen should be seen manifestly.'

ʿAlī b. al-Ḥusayn: During winter he used to feel cold and so he used to wear *khazz*. He used to buy his garment for either five hundred or a thousand dirhams and would give it away in charity after the winter.[28]

Abū Jaʿfar Muḥammad b. ʿAlī: He used to wear a *khazz* garment worth either five hundred or a thousand dirhams, and would give it away in charity after a year. He was asked, 'If you wish, you could sell the clothes and give away the proceeds in charity. Would that not be better?' He said, 'I do not consider it proper that I should sell a garment in which I prayed.'[29]

Jaʿfar b. Muḥammad: He performed a pilgrimage, and during the circumambulation (*ṭawāf*) [of the Kaʿba], while he was wearing two expensive garments, someone suddenly plucked at his gown. So [the Imam] turned towards him, and lo! it was ʿAbbād al-Baṣrī[30] who said, 'O Abū ʿAbd Allāh, do you wear such clothes on such an occasion although you derive your station from ʿAlī, and you certainly know how he dressed!' So Abū ʿAbd Allāh [the Imam] said, 'Woe to thee, O ʿAbbād! ʿAlī used to

[23]*Karābīs* pl. of *kirbās*, arabicized from Persian, means a coarse garment or piece of cloth, or just a piece of cloth made from white cotton. Lane, s.v. k-r-b-s; Muʿīn, *Farhang-e Fārisī*, s.v. *Karbās*.

[24]*Qūhī*, cette étoffe est de peu de valeur. Dozy, s.v. *qūh*.

[25]Marw, a city on the north-eastern fringes of Persia, was known for its silk factories. *EI*[2], s.v. Marw al-Shāhidjān; Dozy, s.v. Marw.

[26]See n. 2 above in this chapter. *Kāfī*, VI, 457; slightly different version.

[27]Ibid., VI, 461, 464.

[28]Ibid., VI, 465; slightly different version is reported on the authority of ʿAlī al-Riḍā.

[29]Ibid., VI, 465; ʿAlī b. al-Ḥusayn used to sell his *miṭraf* in the summer and give away the proceeds in charity.

[30]He was a companion of Jaʿfar al-Ṣādiq. Mufīd, *al-Ikhtiṣāṣ*, 325; the conversation takes place during the pilgrimage, but on a different subject.

dress as befitted his times. If I were to dress as he did, the people would surely say, "The man is verily like 'Abbād!'" Whereupon 'Abbād was rendered speechless, and people around him began to make signs among themselves, for 'Abbād was known for his hypocrisy (*riyā'*).[31]

[Ja'far b. Muḥammad]—his father—his ancestors: The Messenger of God said, 'Whenever a man buys a garment for one dinar, or half a dinar, or [even] one-third of a dinar and wears it praising God, He forgives him as soon as the garment reaches his knee.'[32]

'Alī: Once he came out of the mosque and went to Dār Furāt,[33] where rough clothes (*karābīs*)[34] were sold at the time. He saw an old man selling and said, 'Old man, sell me a shirt for three dirhams.' The man stood up and said, 'Yes, O Commander of the Faithful.' When 'Alī saw that the man had recognised him, he said, 'Sit down,' and then went to another [vendor]. When the same thing happened, 'Alī said, 'Sit down,' and then went to a boy who turned away and did not pay any attention to him. He bought from him a [long] shirt for three dirhams and wore it. It reached down between his shanks and above his ankles. Then he noticed that the sleeves [were long] and came over his hand. He cut off the portion which went beyond his fingers and said, 'All praise to God who has provided me with feathers for beautifying myself among men, for concealing my shame (*saw'atī*) and for covering up my private parts (*'awratī*). All praise to the Lord of the worlds.' A man said to him, 'O Commander of the Faithful, is this a prayer you have uttered, or is it something you have heard from the Messenger of God?' [The Imam] said, 'When the Messenger of God put on a garment, he used to say something similar to this.'[35]

Muḥammad b. 'Alī: He was asked about God's word: *And thy raiment purify* (74:4), and he said, 'It means, "hemming it up".[36] Your garment

[31]*Kāfī*, VI, 457–8; two traditions are cited: in the first, the Imam is confronted with Sufyān al-Thawrī, and in the other with 'Abbād.

[32]'If anyone puts on a garment and says, "Praise be to God who has clothed me with this ...," he will be forgiven his former and latter sins.' *Mishkāt*, II, 476; Robson, II, 916.

[33]It was probably a market place of Kūfa.

[34]See n. 23 above in this chapter.

[35]"Alī bought a garment for three dirhams, and when he put it on he said, "Praise ...". *Mishkāt*, II, 482; Robson, II, 921. *Kāfī*, VI, 472; all the traditions are about extolling Allāh when putting on a new garment.

[36]*Taṭhīr* (cleaning, purification) means *taqṣīr* (making a thing shorter). Qummī, II, 416; *Kāfī*, VI, 469, 470, 471; Ṭabrisī, V, 385; the tradition is reported from Imam al-Ṣādiq and is ascribed to 'Alī. But, this is not the generally accepted meaning of *taṭhīr* by the Sunnīs, see Ṭabarī, *Tafsīr* (Beirut), XXIX, 91–2.

should not exceed your ankle,[37] for trailing clothes is one of the habits of Banū Umayya.[38] 'Alī used to hem up both his trousers and his [long] shirt.'

Ja'far b. Muḥammad: One day he brought out for his companions the shirt in which the Commander of the Faithful, 'Alī b. Abī Ṭālib, was assassinated and there were [stains of] blood on it. He spread it out and they measured it. They found that its length from top to bottom was twelve *shibrs* (span of an open hand), the breadth of the body was three spans, and the length of both his sleeves was three spans.[39]

Abū Ja'far Muḥammad b. 'Alī: He said, 'Whatever goes beyond the ankle [in length] will be in the Fire. Verily, your master, that is, 'Alī, used to buy two shirts, and let his slave choose the one that he likes better between the two, and 'Alī used to wear the other. If the sleeves extended beyond the fingers, he cut them off; and if the length extended beyond the ankles, he cut it off.'[40]

The Messenger of God: [He said], 'If a man keeps hair, he should groom it well;[41] if he takes a wife, he should honour her; if he uses sandals, he should repair them;[42] and if he takes a beast, he should select a lively one; and if he uses a garment he should keep it clean.'[43]

Ja'far b. Muḥammad: He said, 'Cleanliness of clothes humiliates the enemy;[44] washing of clothes removes anxiety and distress;[45] hemming clothes keeps them clean, and this is included in the saying of God: *And thy raiment purify* (74:4);' here it means 'hem them.'[46]

The Messenger of God: He said, 'The felicity of a garment is in its being hemmed;[47] and the felicity of a house is in its being well swept.'

Muḥammad b. 'Alī: He said, 'My father ['Alī b. al-Ḥusayn] used occasionally to buy a square mantle (*miṭraf*) of *khazz* for fifty dinars. He

[37]'The part of the lower garment which goes below the ankles is in Hell.' Bukhārī transmitted it. Another tradition states, 'If anyone trails his garment arrogantly, God will not look at him on the Day of Resurrection.' Transmitted by Bukhārī and Muslim. *Mishkāt* II, 472, 474, 481; Robson, II, 913, 915, 920. Several traditions are reported. See also *Kāfī*, VI, 470.

[38]For Banū Umayya see *The Pillars of Islam*, I, 305, n. 21.

[39]*Kāfī*, VI, 471.

[40]Ibid., VI, 470–1.

[41]'He who has hair should honour it.' *Mishkāt*, II, 496, 502; Robson, II, 933, 938.

[42]*Kāfī*, VI, 476; a separate section on the sandals.

[43]Ibid., VI, 456.

[44]Ibid., VI, 456.

[45]Ibid., VI, 459.

[46]See n. 36 above in this chapter.

[47]*Kāfī*, VI, 493; it adds, 'And it is conducive to longer wear.'

would both pass the winter and enter the mosque wearing it. When summer arrived, he ordered that it be given in charity, or that it be sold and the proceeds be given in charity. Sometimes he would order two *Ushmūnī*[48] (Egyptian) garments be bought and dyed for his use and he would wear them. He used to wear clothes of moderate value and say: *Say: Who has forbidden the adornment of Allah which He has brought forth for His bondmen, and the good things of His providing?*' (7:32)

'Alī: He used to wear patched up clothes, and when asked about it, he said, 'Lowly dress produces humility in the heart.'

Ja'far b. Muḥammad: He said, 'When the body wears soft clothes, it becomes rebellious.' Some of his companions found him wearing worn out and patched up garments, and they spoke to him about it and he said, 'There are no new [clothes] for him who has not [yet] worn out [his old garments].'[49] He possessed two rough garments in which he used to pray in his house. When he wanted to ask something from God, he would wear them.

The Messenger of God: He said, 'Honour your turbans (*'amā'im* pl. of *'imāma*), for they are the crowns of the Arabs.'[50]

[The Messenger of God]: During a war, he wore a tall hat (*qalansuwa*) which was pointed (lit. with two ears).[51]

[The Messenger of God]: His bedding consisted of a piece of leather stuffed with palm fibre. Sometimes they made his bed by doubling over a rug made from [animal] hair. He used to sleep on it till the night was almost over and he wished to rise for prayer. One night they made it fourfold and he slept on it till it was morning. So he said, 'Woe be to you! what was the bedding you laid for me last night?' They said, 'It was [the same] rug, O Messenger of God, but we folded it up four times so that it may be smoother [and more comfortable].' So he said, 'Do not do so! Return to

[48]As in MS Q and H; in the edited text: *Asmūniyān*. *Ushmūn*, a capital town in the districts of Upper Egypt. Yāqūt, s.v. Ushmūn.

[49]It is reported differently and states, '... There is no faith for the one who has no modesty, and there is no wealth for the one who does not appreciate it, and there are no new [clothes] for him who has no worn out [clothes].' *Kāfī*, VI, 474.

[50]'The difference between us and the polytheists is that we wear turbans over caps.' Another tradition states, 'Keep to turbans, for they are the mark of the angels.' *Mishkāt*, II, 475, 481; Robson, II, 916, 920. See also *Kāfī*, VI, 475.

[51]The Arabic term is *al-muḍarraba*, meaning quilted with cotton. The second form refers to a courageous man who rouses his people to ardour in battle. Lane, s.v. ḍ-r-b. See also *Majma' al-baḥrayn*, s.v. ḍ-r-b; this tall cap of the Prophet was called 'the possessor of two ears.' *Kāfī*, VI, 475.

the usual practice, for its smoothness prevented me from [performing] the night prayer.'[52]

One of the companions of Abū Ja'far Muḥammad b. 'Alī: He said, 'I went to the house of [the Imam] and found it well furnished with pillows, carpets, and bedspreads all piled up. Then I went to [the Imam] in another house that was furnished with palm leaf mats, and said [to the Imam], 'What is this house, May I be thy ransom?' [The Imam] said, 'This is my house, and the house you saw earlier was the house of my wife, and I shall tell you a story related to me by my father ['Alī b. al-Ḥusayn].' He said, 'A group of people came to the house of al-Ḥusayn b. 'Alī and found it to be full of carpets and bolsters and they said, "O son of the Messenger of God! We see in your house things we never saw in the house of the Messenger of God."' [The Imam] replied, 'We marry women and give them their dowries (*muhūr*), and they buy with them whatever they wish, and we have nothing to do with it.'[53]

LAWFUL AND FORBIDDEN DRESS (*MĀ YAḤILL MIN AL-LIBĀS WA-MĀ YAḤRUM MINHU*)[54]

Ja'far b. Muḥammad: He made a comprehensive statement regarding lawful dress saying, 'There is no harm in wearing anything made from something which grows in the earth, and in praying in or on it. The same is true for the skins, hair, wool, or fur of all animals whose flesh can be eaten after being slaughtered (*dhukkiya* in the manner prescribed by the law). But if the animal is not slaughtered (in the prescribed manner), there is nothing good in it or in anything that is derived from it.'

[Ja'far b. Muḥammad]—[his father][55]—his ancestors—the Messenger of God: He disapproved of the red-coloured clothes. 'Alī said, 'Saffron (*za'farān*) is for us and red (*'uṣfur*) for the Banū Umayya.'[56]

[52]'The bedding on which God's Messenger slept consisted of leather stuffed with palm fibre.' *Mishkāt*, II, 471; Robson, II, 912; transmitted by Bukhārī and Muslim.

[53]*Kāfī*, VI, 463; it was al-Ḥasan al-Zayyāt al-Baṣrī who visited Imam al-Bāqir with his friend. Kulaynī cites five other traditions, see *Kāfī*, VI, 491.

[54]Jazīrī, *al-Fiqh*, II, 16–20; *The Pillars of Islam*, I, 219–23.

[55]Addition according to MS Q, it is missing from the edited text.

[56]Saffron (*za'farān*) is a deep orange colour while safflower (*'uṣfur, mu'aṣfar*, carthamus tinctorius) is light red. *Mishkāt*, II, 473, 478, 480; Robson, II, 914, 918, 919; four traditions prohibit wearing red garments and one tradition states that the Messenger of God was seen in Minā addressing people and he was wearing a red cloak. *Kāfī*, VI, 461–3; wearing red-coloured garments (*mu'aṣfar*) is permitted. A tradition on the authority of Imam al-Bāqir states, 'Our colour is red (*bahramān*, i.e. ruby or safflower) and the colour of the Umayyads is saffron (*za'farān*).' The Mālikīs do not approve of either colour. See Jazīrī, *al-Fiqh*, II, 16–20.

Ja'far b. Muḥammad: He disliked cloth dyed red [with dyestuff prepared from safflower] and used to say, 'Do not wear red, for it was the dress of both Croesus (*Qārūn*)[57] and the Umayyads;' but he permitted sleeping in red clothing and a red covering.

The Messenger of God: He said, 'There is nothing better than white for your garment; use it for dress and for shrouding your dead.'[58]

'Alī: Once he went out to Ruḥba[59] and was wearing yellow trousers, a black shirt, sandals on his feet, and he had a small spear in his hand.

Ja'far b. Muḥammad: Once he wore a green garment for the *iḥrām*.[60]

'Alī b. al-Ḥusayn: He was once seen in a black woollen coat (*durrā'a*)[61] and an ash-colour (*azraq*)[62] shawl-like garment (*ṭaylasān*).[63]

'Alī: He disapproved of the wearing of pure silk (*ḥarīr*) for men, but permitted [its use] if it was woven with something which grew from the earth. There is no harm [in wearing silk] to show off before the enemy (or to vie with them for superiority in dress).[64] It may also be worn like other garments in which it is not permissible to pray, such as polluted clothes and the skins of dead animals, etc. These kinds of clothes could be used to cover [the body], but not for prayer.

'Alī b. Abī Ṭālib and Muḥammad b. 'Alī b. al-Ḥusayn and Ja'far b. Muḥammad: They said, 'A dead animal and all its parts are impure. The skin of a dead animal cannot be purified even if it is tanned seventy times.'[65] They said the same thing about animals whose flesh was unlawful; 'They fit into the same category as dead animals. There is, however, no harm if their skins are used to cover [the body], but prayers cannot be offered in them.'

Ja'far b. Muḥammad: He was once seen seated on a carpet (*bisāṭ*),

[57]He is the Biblical Korah mentioned three times in the Qur'ān 28:76–82, 29:39, 40:24. In Islam, the legend of Qārūn alludes to his proverbial riches and his special 'knowledge'. *EI*[2], s.v. Ḳārūn.

[58]'Wear white clothes, for they are purer and better; and shroud your dead in them.' *Mishkāt*, II, 475; Robson, II, 915; for related traditions see *Concordance*, s.v. b-y-ḍ. See also *The Pillars of Islam*, I, 286–8.

[59]Ruḥba is a village facing al-Qādisiyya to the south-west of Kūfa, about a day's journey from the latter. Yāqūt, s.v. r-ḥ-b; *Majma' al-baḥrayn*, s.v. r-ḥ-b.

[60]For *iḥrām* see *The Pillars of Islam*, I, 141, n. 65; 372–80.

[61]*Durrā'a*, is a garment of wool, slit in the fore part, with buttons and loops, and is narrow in the sleeve. It is worn in Egypt and North Africa. Lane, s.v. d-r-'.

[62]*Zurqā* is the blueness, grayness, or greenish hue in the eye. Lane, s.v. z-r-q.

[63]*Ṭaylasān*, see n. 6 above in this chapter.

[64]*Kāfī*, VI, 467–9; wearing of silk garments is permitted during a battle. Kulaynī gives more details about silk and silk brocade (*dībāj*). *Mishkāt*, II, 472, 473; Robson, II, 913, 914; The Prophet permitted Zubayr and 'Abd al-Raḥmān b. 'Awf to wear silk because of an itch they had. For more details see Ibn Qayyim, *al-Ṭibb al-nabawī*, 87–91.

[65]See *The Pillars of Islam*, I, 157.

which contained figures (*tamāthīl*) on similar carpets, it cost either one or two thousand [dirhams]. He was asked about it and said, 'The Prophet's practice (*sunna*) was to [only] walk upon it!'[66]

THE WEARING OF ORNAMENTS (*LIBĀS AL-ḤULĪY*)[67]

Ja'far b. Muḥammad—his father—his ancestors—the Messenger of God: He said, 'A woman should never pray without wearing at least an earring (*khurṣ*) as an ornament unless she does not have one.' He commanded women never to be without jewellery and not to resemble men [in the way they dress]. He cursed those who did so.[68]

Abū Ja'far Muḥammad b. 'Alī: He said, 'It does not behove a woman to divest herself of all ornaments; she should at least wear something as minimal as a necklace (*qilāda*) around her neck.'

The Messenger of God prohibited women from stomping their feet on the ground to make their anklets (*khalkhāl*) jingle thereby, disclosing their hidden charm. He meant, [that the rule applies] when she goes out of the house and is in the presence of someone who is not precluded from marrying her (*ghayr dhī maḥram*). This is on account of the Word of God: *And tell the believing women to lower their gaze and be modest* till His saying: ... *and let them not stamp their feet so as to reveal what they hide of their adornment* (24:31).[69]

Abū Ja'far Muḥammad b. 'Alī: He was asked about [the lawfulness] of golden ornaments for women, and he said, 'There is no harm in it, they are only disapproved for men.'[70]

Ja'far b. Muḥammad: He was asked about golden ornaments for children and he said, 'My father used to allow his women and children to use ornaments of gold and silver.[71] There is no harm in adorning swords and Qur'āns (*al-maṣāḥif* pl. of *al-muṣḥaf*) with gold or silver.'[72]

[66]Pictures (i.e. representation of living creatures) are forbidden. *Mishkāt*, II, 504–8; Robson, II, 940–4. 'The angels do not enter a house which contains a dog or pictures.' Transmitted by Bukhārī and Muslim.

[67]Jazīrī, *al-Fiqh*, II, 21–4.

[68]See *The Pillars of Islam*, I, 221; *Kāfī*, VI, 490.

[69]Wearing little bells on the ankles is forbidden. *Mishkāt*, II, 487; Robson, II, 925.

[70]*Kāfī*, VI, 489, 490; *Mishkāt*, II, 487–8; Robson, II, 925, 926; some traditions state that any woman who adorns herself with gold which she displays will be punished for it.

[71]*Kāfī*, VI, 489; *Mishkāt*, II, 489; Robson, II, 926; Mālik said, 'I dislike youths being dressed with any gold, for I have heard that God's Messenger forbade wearing a gold signet ring ...'

[72]*Kāfī*, VI, 489, 490.

The Messenger of God: He saw a man wearing an iron ring on his finger and he said, 'This is an ornament of the people of the Fire. Throw it away; lo! I find the odour and signs of Zoroastrianism (*al-Majūsīya*)[73] in you.' He threw it away and wore a golden ring. The Messenger of God said, 'Indeed, your finger will be in the Fire as long as this ring is in it.' The man said, 'O Messenger of God, then, shall I not wear a ring?' The Messenger of God said, 'Yes, but have a silver one and one not exceeding a *mithqāl*[74] in weight.'[75]

'Alī: He said, 'Do not put iron rings on your children.'

'Alī: He said, 'The Messenger of God's signet ring was of silver,[76] and so was the tip of the scabbard (*na'l*) of his sword.'[77]

The Messenger of God: He forbade men from wearing gold and said, 'It is forbidden in this world.'[78]

[The Messenger of God]: He used to wear a ring in the right hand, and prohibited people from wearing it on the left.[79]

[The Messenger of God]: He said, 'He who wears a cornelian (*'aqīq*) on his ring, God will credit him with good deeds.[80] Crystal (*billawr* or *ballūr*) is the best stone for a ring.'[81]

Al-Ḥusayn b. 'Alī: He said, 'The Messenger of God said to me, "O my little son! Sleep on your back and your stomach will stay lean. Drink water slowly and your food will be wholesome. Apply collyrium [to your

[73]*Majūsīya*, see *The Pillars of Islam*, I, 221, n. 257.

[74]*Mithqāl*, see *The Pillars of Islam*, I, 310, n. 40.

[75]Burayda reported the Prophet as saying to a man who was wearing a ring of yellow copper, 'How is it that I notice the odour of idols in you?' So he threw it away and came wearing an iron ring, and when the Prophet said, 'How is it that I see you wearing the adornment of the inhabitants of Hell?' He threw it away and said, 'O Messenger of God, what material should I use?' The Prophet replied, 'Silver, but do not let it weigh as much as a *mithqāl*.' *Mishkāt*, II, 486; Robson, II, 924. See also Ibn Kathīr, *al-Sīra*, IV, 703–6; *Kāfī*, VI, 482–3; for men silver rings are allowed.

[76]Ibn 'Umar said that the Prophet took a signet ring of gold. A version says that he put it on his right hand, then threw it away and took one of silver on which he engraved, 'Muḥammad God's Messenger.' Transmitted by Bukhārī and Muslim. *Mishkāt*, II, 484–5; Robson, II, 923.

[77]For his swords see Ṭabarī, *History of al-Ṭabarī*, IX, 153–4. The pommel of his sword was of silver. Ibn Kathīr, *al-Sīra*, IV, 707.

[78]'Alī said that God's Messenger forbade wearing Qassī material and anything dyed with saffron, using a gold ring. Transmitted by Muslim. Both silk and gold are forbidden to men. *Mishkāt*, II, 484, 485; Robson, II, 923, 924.

[79]There is no specific tradition which forbids wearing a ring in the left hand. *Mishkāt*, II, 485; Robson, II, 924; *Kāfī*, VI, 483–4; wearing a ring in either of the two hands is permitted.

[80]*Kāfī*, VI, 484–5; several traditions are cited stating that wearing of *'aqīq* brings good fortune.

[81]Ibid., VI, 487.

eyes] an odd number of times and it will give light to your eyes.[82] Anoint [your hair] on alternate days (or frequently) and you will conform to the practice of your Prophet. Keep your sandals in good shape, for verily, they serve as anklets for men. [Keep] your turbans [clean], for they are the crowns of the Arabs. When you cook food, provide a good deal of broth; for if your neighbours do not obtain meat, they will at least get some broth which is a kind of meat. On your ring, put a ruby (*yāqūt*)[83] or a cornelian (*ʿaqīq*),[84] for verily, they are blessed and auspicious. Thus, whenever a man looks at his face in them, the light increases [on his face]; and when one [offers] prayer wearing them, it is like [he is offering] seventy prayers. Put on a ring on your right hand, for that is my practice (*sunna*) and the practice of the apostles. He who does not follow my practice, does not belong to me. Do not put on a ring on the left hand, and do not [wear it] without a ruby or a cornelian on it."'

The Messenger of God: The inscription on the Prophet's signet ring was 'Muḥammad is the Messenger of God.'[85]

ʿAlī: The inscription on ʿAlī's signet ring was, "Alī has faith in God.'[86]

Jaʿfar b. Muḥammad: The inscription on his signet ring was, 'O Lord, make it easy for me. You are the Reliable One, so protect me from the evil of mankind.'[87]

[Jaʿfar b. Muḥammad]: He said, 'Prayer with a ring on which pictures are engraved, is not valid.'[88]

THE VIRTUES AND EXCELLENCE OF PERFUME (*AL-ṬĪB WA 'STIḤBĀBUHU WA-FAḌLUHU*)

Jaʿfar b. Muḥammad—his father—his ancestors—the Messenger of God: He said, 'As soon as the scent of a bondman become pleasant, his intelligence increases.'

[82]See Chap. 5, n. 73.

[83]*Kāfī*, VI, 485–6; ruby drives away poverty.

[84]Ibid., VI, 484–5; cornelian repels hypocrisy; it is blessed; one who wears it attains his wishes; it provides safety during travel and protects from all evils.

[85]*Kāfī*, VI, 487, 488; *Mishkāt*, II, 484–5; Robson, II, 923.

[86]*Kāfī*, VI, 487, 488; the inscription on ʿAlī's signet ring was '*Allāh al-malik*' (God is the sovereign). Kulaynī gives the inscriptions on signet rings of other Imams.

[87]Ibid., VI, 487–8; different inscriptions are cited; 'Oh God, You are the Reliable One, so protect me from the evil of mankind;' 'You are the Reliable One so protect me from mankind;' 'God is my guardian and He is my protector from mankind.'

[88]Pictures of living things and human representations are forbidden. See n. 66 in this chapter, and *The Pillars of Islam*, I, 189.

When the Messenger of God travelled he took with him six things: a long-necked bottle (*qārūra*) [of perfume]; a pair of scissors; a container for collyrium (*mukḥula*); a mirror; a comb; and a tooth-stick (cut from a plant, *siwāk*).[89] He said, 'Three things were gifted by God to the prophets: perfume (*'iṭr*); the tooth-stick; and wives.'[90]

Ja'far b. Muḥammad: He said, 'A pleasant perfume strengthens the intelligence and increases virility.'[91]

Ja'far b. Muḥammad: He said, 'The perfume of men is that whose odour is apparent but whose colour is hidden; and the perfume of women is that whose colour is apparent but whose odour is hidden.'[92]

The Messenger of God: He used to apply perfume plentifully, so much so that his beard and his head would become yellowish. He said, 'When a man goes to the Friday prayer, let him use perfume, even if it be from the bottle of his wife.'[93]

'Alī: He occasionally used the perfume of his wives; and when he offered perfume to anyone who refused it, he said, 'Nobody but an ass refuses the favour (of God).'[94]

The Messenger of God: He said, 'Verily, the excellence that we, the People of the House, possess is superior to that of others just as the ointment of the violet (*banafsaj* lavender) is superior to all others.'[95]

['Alī]: He said, 'Women who apply perfume should not go out and pray in a mosque.' He meant, lest the man proximate to them smell the perfume, and this may be an invitation to the guiles of the devil.

['Alī]: He said, 'It is not proper for a woman to pray without dyeing herself with henna (*ḥinnā'*);[96] and if she has not been able to do so, she

[89]See *The Pillars of Islam*, I, 146.

[90]Anas reported God's Messenger as saying, 'Perfume and women have been made dear to me, but my comfort has been provided in prayer.' *Mishkāt*, II, 669; Robson, II, 1091. See also *Kāfī*, VI, 525; *The Pillars of Islam*, I, 146; Dhahabī, *al-Ṭibb al-nabawī*, 67.

[91]Abū 'Abd Allāh: The Messenger of God said, 'A pleasant perfume strengthens the heart and ...' *Kāfī*, VI, 524.

[92]*Mishkāt*, II, 495; Robson, II, 932; *Kāfī*, VI, 526; reported by Imam al-Ṣādiq from God's Messenger.

[93]'Ā'isha said that she used to perfume the Prophet with the sweetest perfume she could find till she saw the perfume shining on his beard. Another tradition states that the Prophet used to dye his beard yellow with *wars* and saffron. *Mishkāt*, II, 494–6; Robson, II, 931; *Kāfī*, VI, 525, 526. See also *The Pillars of Islam*, I, 225.

[94]*Kāfī*, VI, 526, 527.

[95]Ibid., VI, 534, 535; separate section on the ointment of violet and its benefits.

[96]For its use and benefits see Ibn Qayyim, *al-Ṭibb al-nabawī*, 95, 97–9; Dhahabī, *al-Ṭibb al-nabawī*, 48–50.

should at least apply an aromatic paste (*khalūq*)[97] to the place to be dyed with henna.'

Abū Ja'far Muḥammad b. 'Alī: He said, 'It does not behove a woman to leave her hands undyed with henna. She should at least massage her hands with henna; and this [rule applies], even if she is aged.'[98]

The Messenger of God: He said, 'It is not appropriate for a woman who is menstruating to have locks of hair in front, or [to display] the luxuriance of her hair.'

'Alī: He prohibited women from having locks of hair hanging in front or on the sides, and from using henna to make ornamental designs [on their hands].

[97]*Khalūq* is a certain species of perfume of thick consistence composed of saffron and other things in which redness and yellowness are predominant. It is forbidden to men, because it is the perfume of women. *Mishkāt*, II, 495; Robson, II, 932; forbidden to men. See *The Pillars of Islam*, I, 217, n. 237; *Kāfī*, VI, 531; it has a section on it, but not this tradition.

[98]*Mishkāt*, II, 498; Robson, II, 935; the tradition states that a woman's hands without henna on them are ugly.

7

Book of Hunting[1] (*Kitāb al-Ṣayd*)

LAWFUL AND UNLAWFUL HUNTING (*MĀ YAḤILL MIN AL-ṢAYD WA-MĀ YAḤRUM MINHU*)

God says: *To hunt and to eat the fish of the sea is made lawful to you, a provision for you and for seafarers; but to hunt on land is forbidden as long as ye are on the pilgrimage* (5:96). He says: *But when ye have left the sacred territory, then go hunting (if ye will)* (5:2).

Ja'far b. Muḥammad: The Messenger of God said, 'The bird in the nest is safe in the protection of God; but when it flies away you may hunt it if you wish.'[2] Ja'far b. Muḥammad said, 'Birds cannot be hunted except when they neglect the glorification of God.'[3]

'Alī: He said, 'When a bird is captured [by hawks or falcons] but escapes, and it is later captured [by a person], it is lawful for the person who captures it.'

Ja'far b. Muḥammad: He said, 'This refers [to the capture] by hawks (or falcons, *bāz* pl. *buzāt*) and their kind, because [game captured by them] is lawful.'[4]

['Alī]: He forbade the hunting of pigeons in towns, but allowed hunting them in villages (or in the country).

'Alī: He said, 'Game belongs to the one who seizes it first.'

[1] Jazīrī, *al-Fiqh*, II, 24–36; Ṭūsī, *al-Nihāya*, 574–87; Ibn Rushd, *Bidāya*, I, 450–8; trans. I, 548–59.

[2] *Kāfī*, VI, 226–7, 235. Birds should not be hunted in their nests during the night, and their chicks should not be snatched away. Hunting of birds is permitted only when they are able to fly and during the day.

[3] It implies that when birds are chirping/singing in a tree, i.e. glorifying God, they cannot be hunted. Hunting is, therefore, allowed only when they are flying.

[4] *Kāfī*, VI, 217–19; it cannot be eaten unless it is slaughtered before it is dead.

THE GAME HUNTED BY PREDATORY ANIMALS AND BIRDS (*MĀ AṢĀBAT AL-JAWĀRIḤU MIN AL-ṢAYD*)

God says: *And those beasts and birds of prey (al-jawāriḥ) which ye have trained as hounds* (5:4).[5]

Ja'far b. Muḥammad—his father—his ancestors—'Alī: He was asked about the above verse and he said that it referred to dogs.[6] *Al-Jawāriḥ* (pl. of *al-jāriḥ*) are *al-kawāsib* (pl. of *al-kāsib*),[7] as God says: *And He knows what you have earned (mā jaraḥtum) in the day* (6:60).[8]

[Ja'far b. Muḥammad]: He said, 'Whatever [animal or bird] is hunted by trained hounds may be eaten, even if it has been killed. But what is killed by untrained dogs cannot be eaten.'[9] This means that [game] can be eaten if God's name is mentioned when the hound is sent in pursuit [of the game]. There is no harm in eating game if the mention of God's name has been forgotten.[10]

Abū Ja'far and Abū 'Abd Allāh: They permitted the eating of game which had been hunted by a trained hound even if it had killed and eaten part of it;[11] but [the Imams] did not permit [the eating of game] when a bird had [captured and] eaten part of it.[12]

[5]There is disagreement among the jurists about the different kinds of predatory animals and birds of prey. Ibn Rushd, *Bidāya*, I, 452–4; trans. I, 551–4, discusses the reasons for this disagreement.

[6]*Kāfī*, VI, 213.

[7]*Al-Kawāsib* refers to the limbs (either of a man or of a bird) by means of which sustenance is gained. Lane, s.v. k-s-b.

[8]Here the meaning of *jaraḥtum* is *kasabtum* (i.e. what you earned as sustenance) as explained by the Imam. All the translations of the Qur'ān have conveyed this sense in different ways.

[9]*Kāfī*, VI, 214; it may be eaten, even if the hound had eaten a part of it.

[10]'Adī b. Ḥātim reported the Messenger of God as saying, 'When you set off your dog mention God's name, and if it catches anything for you and you come up to it while it is still alive cut its throat; if you come to it when the dog has killed it but not eaten any of it, eat it; but if it has eaten any of it do not eat it, for it has caught it only for itself. If you find another dog with yours and a kill has been made, do not eat, for you do not know which of them killed the animal. When you shoot your arrow mention God's name, and if the game goes out of your sight for a day and if you find it later with only the wound from your arrow, eat if you wish, but if you find it drowned in water do not eat.' Another tradition states that a catch by an untrained dog is permitted when the hunter is present at the kill. *Mishkāt*, II, 422; Robson II, 870; transmitted by Bukhārī and Muslim. See also Ṭūsī, *Tahdhīb al-aḥkām*, IX, 22–4; Ibn Rushd, *Bidāya*, I 451.

[11]*Kāfī*, VI, 214, 215.

[12]Game captured by falcons cannot be eaten unless it is slaughtered before it is dead. *Kāfī*, VI, 216, 217–19.

[Imam] al-Mahdī bi 'llāh[13] held that when a bird had captured game it could be eaten, and he used to say, 'A dog sometimes [is seized with madness and] eats ravenously (*al-kalbu rubbamā kaliba*).'[14] This does not contradict what his ancestors have said, because they did not allow what was captured by a ravenous dog [to be eaten], they only allowed what was captured by a duly trained hound. As for [Imam] al-Mahdī's saying about what was captured by birds, they are also a kind of predatory animal (*al-jawāriḥ*), and God Himself has permitted the eating of what was captured by them.[15]

Ja'far b. Muḥammad—'Alī: He said, 'Falcons (*ṣaqr* pl. *ṣuqūr*) and hawks (*bāz* pl. *buzāt*) are of predatory birds (*jawāriḥ*).'[16]

Ja'far b. Muḥammad: He said, 'The lynx (*fahd*)[17] which is trained to hunt is similar to a hound. Whatever he captures can be eaten.'[18] This rule follows from what we have said about predatory animals (*al-jawāriḥ*).[19]

The Messenger of God: He prohibited the use of a black dog for hunting, and directed that a black dog should be killed, especially if he was completely black (*bahīm*).[20]

Ja'far b. Muḥammad: He said, 'All dogs, once they are trained [for hunting], are similar, whether they are of the greyhound (*salūqī*)[21] or the Kurdish (*kurdī*) [Kangal/Gammal][22] breed.'

[13]Al-Mahdī, see *The Pillars of Islam*, I, 71, n. 193.

[14]Lane, s.v. k-l-b.

[15]'Adī b. Ḥātim reported the Prophet as saying, 'Eat whatever is caught for you by a dog or a hawk which you have trained and set off when you have mentioned God's name.' He asked whether that applied if it killed the animal and he replied, 'When it kills it without eating any of it, it caught it only for you.' *Mishkāt*, II, 425; Robson, II, 873.

[16]*Kāfī*, VI, 215, 217–19; their kill needs to be slaughtered for lawful eating. Ṭūsī, *Tahdhīb al-aḥkām*, IX, 29, 32.

[17]A well-known beast of prey with which one hunts. Lane, s.v. f-h-d.

[18]*Kāfī*, VI, 214, 216; the lynx's kill needs to be slaughtered, because the lynx is not considered a hound. *Fahd* is a beast of prey (*jawāriḥ*), but not trained as hounds (*mukallibīn*).

[19]Ṭūsī, *Tahdhīb al-aḥkām*, IX, 28–9.

[20]*Kāfī*, VI, 217. Jābir said, 'The Messenger of God ordered us to kill dogs, [so we did] and we even killed a dog brought by a woman from the desert. Afterwards God's Messenger forbade us to kill dogs, saying, "Confine yourselves to the type which is pure black and has two spots, for it is a devil."' *Mishkāt* II, 428, 429; Robson II, 876. Lane, s.v. b-h-m. A group of jurists did not permit black dogs for hunting, however the majority of them permitted the game hunted by it to be eaten, if it was trained. Ibn Rushd, *Bidāya*, I, 452; trans. I, 551.

[21]*Salūqī* is applied to a greyhound and any hunting dog. Lane, s.v. s-l-q.

[22]Kangal/Gammal is the Kurdish national dog. See *www.kurdish.com*. 'The Kurdish dogs when trained [to hunt] are like the greyhound.' *Kāfī*, VI, 215; reported from the same authority.

Jaʿfar b. Muḥammad: He said with regard to hunting, 'One who sends a hound [in pursuit of game] and does not mention the name of God should not eat the game.'[23] This rule applies where the omission of God's name is deliberate; but if he has unwittingly forgotten it, or is ignorant [of the rule], the game is lawful.

We shall mention in the account of slaughter rules which support this view, God willing.

Jaʿfar b. Muḥammad: He was asked about a hound that captures game that is still alive when the hunter reaches it, but then dies there because of the wound.[23A] [Is the game lawful to eat?] [The Imam] said, 'Eat [it], by reason of the Word of God: So *eat of that which they catch for you* (5:4). But if the game is alive when the hunter captures it, and he is dilatory in slaughtering it, or he takes it home, and it dies [on the way] and the dog has not killed it, the game cannot be eaten.'

ʿAlī: Regarding a hound belonging to a Zoroastrian (*al-Majūsī*),[24] he said, 'Game hunted by it cannot be eaten unless the hound was on a leash, and was trained and taken out for hunting by a Muslim. If a Muslim hunts with it, it is lawful to eat what the hound captures, even if it has not been trained by him.'[25]

AN ACCOUNT OF THE GAME HUNTED BY HUNTERS (*MĀ YAQTULUHU AL-ṢAYYĀDŪN MIN AL-ṢAYD*)

God says: O *ye who believe*! *Allah will surely try you somewhat (in the matter) of the game which ye take with your hands and your spears* (5:94).

Jaʿfar b. Muḥammad: He said, 'When a man strikes an animal with a sword, or pierces it with a spear, or shoots it with an arrow and thereby kills it, there is no harm in eating it if he has mentioned the name of God at the time of the act.'[26]

He was asked about a man who shoots at an animal, but fails to

[23] *Kāfī*, VI, 216.

[23A] The Arabic reads: *min fiʿl al-kalb*. I have taken it to mean the wound inflicted by the hound.

[24] See *The Pillars of Islam*, I, 221, n. 257.

[25] *Kāfī*, VI, 219–20; two traditions stress that the hound must be trained by a Muslim, but another tradition states that if the hound was taken out by a Muslim and he mentioned the name of God before sending the hound, then the kill could be eaten. See also *Mishkāt*, II, 425.

[26] *Kāfī*, VI, 221. The jurists agree that *dhakāt* specific to game is to shoot and kill (*ʿaqr*) it, but they disagree over the conditions stipulated for the hunter and the instrument used. For details see Ibn Rushd, *Bidāya*, I, 454–8; trans. I, 554–8.

capture it; and a band of men rush to it and cut it down among themselves; that is they strike it with their swords before the hunter takes the animal, [the Imam] said, 'It is lawful to eat the animal.'[27]

[The Imam] was asked about a wild ass at which a group of people rushed, and cut it down [and divided] the animal amongst themselves. They had taken the name of God [before the kill]. He said, 'This is instantaneous slaughter and the flesh is lawful.'[28]

[Ja'far b. Muḥammad]: He said, concerning a man who shoots at an animal, and [it escapes] with the arrow or the spear in his body; or the animal [escapes] despite the injury (lit. severity of striking) and is lost to sight. The next day the hunter finds the animal dead with his arrow in it, or because of the wound caused by the hunter's arrow/spear, and not by someone else. [The Imam] said, 'It is lawful to eat such game.'[29]

The Messenger of God: He said, 'Eat what you have pursued, or shot, if it has died on the spot in your sight (*aṣmayta*), but do not eat what you have pursued, or shot, when it dies out of your sight (*anmayta*).'[30] Now *iṣmā'* is when the animal is shot and dies on the spot; and *inmā'* means that the hunter hits an animal, then it goes out of his sight, and dies later.

This comprehensive statement and an injunction by the Messenger of God [not to eat game when it dies out of the hunter's sight] or when there is doubt whether the animal had died of the hunter's shot or not is possibly a precautionary prohibition (*nahy ta'dīb*). But the rule we have mentioned from Ja'far b. Muḥammad is a clear explanation, free from any ambiguity; for when it is known [for certain] how the animal died, it is lawful to eat it.

'Alī and Abū 'Abd Allāh: They said about a hunter who wounds an animal [which escapes] and falls into water or fire or a well or from a precipice, and dies. The two [Imams] said, 'Unless [you were able] to slaughter it before it died [from the fall or the fire], it cannot be eaten.'[31]

[27] *Kāfī*, VI, 220, 222.

[28] Wild ass is permitted, see n. 145 in Chap. 3. *Kāfī*, VI, 221; Ṭūsī, *Tahdhīb al-aḥkām*, IX, 38.

[29] *Kāfī*, VI, 221, 222; reported from the same authority. 'When you shoot your arrow and the animal goes out of your sight, eat it when you come upon it, provided it has not a stench.' Transmitted by Bukhārī and Muslim. Muslim transmitted another tradition which permits eating it even if the hunter comes upon the game three days later, provided it has not a stench. *Mishkāt*, II, 423, 425; Robson, II, 871, 873.

[30] Lane, s.v. ṣ-m-y.

[31] *Kāfī*, VI, 222, 225–6; what falls in water and dies should not be eaten.

Abū Jaʿfar Muḥammad b. ʿAlī: He said, 'When an animal has been killed by a stone [from a catapult] or by a pellet [of hardened earth] (*bunduq*)[32] from a crossbow, or the like, it cannot be eaten unless it is slaughtered before it is dead.'[33]

Abū Jaʿfar Muḥammad b. ʿAlī: He disapproved of the eating of game killed by a featherless arrow (*miʿrāḍ*). [Eating of] such an animal is not approved unless it is shot by another arrow [apart from the featherless one].

Miʿrāḍ is an arrow without feathers which strikes the body of an animal with its [thick] middle part [thereby causing death by the shock of a blow, rather than by a wound that bleeds].[34]

The Messenger of God: He forbade the eating of game hunted by Zoroastrians (*al-Majūs*), or animals slaughtered by them. [By this] he meant that game which was killed by them before it could be ritually slaughtered, or which was killed by their hounds which were sent by them.[35]

Jaʿfar b. Muḥammad: He forbade the eating of fish (*ḥūt*) or locusts

[32]Lane, s.v. b-n-d-q.

[33]*Kāfī*, VI, 224; such a kill cannot be eaten. Ṭūsī, *Tahdhīb al-aḥkām*, IX, 36. Jurists disagree about hunting with blunt weapons. Some of them did not permit it, except for those animals that were caught alive and slaughtered, but the others permit it without such qualification. Ibn Rushd, *Bidāya*, I, 452; trans. I, 550.

[34]*Miʿrāḍ* is an arrow without feathers and without a head. It is slender at the two ends and thick in the middle. It goes sideways striking with its middle part and not with its extremities. Sometimes it strikes with its thick middle part in such a manner that it breaks and crushes what it strikes beating the animal to death. Lane, s.v. ʿ-r-ḍ. *Kāfī*, VI, 222–3; some traditions permit the eating of game killed by *miʿrāḍ* on certain conditions, e.g. that the hunter had made such an arrow for that purpose, that he did not have another arrow, and that he had mentioned the name of God before shooting. Ṭūsī, *Tahdhīb al-aḥkām*, IX, 35–6. See also *Mishkāt*, II, 422; Robson, II, 870; it states, 'Eat what the featherless arrows pierce, but what they strike with the middle part and kill is beaten to death, do not eat it.' Transmitted by Bukhārī and Muslim. Some jurists permitted eating an animal killed by the blunt part of *miʿrāḍ* or stone if the body of the animal was torn. This opinion was held by Shāfiʿī, Mālik, Abū Ḥanīfa and others on the basis of the principle that there is no *dhakāt* without a sharpened tool. See Ibn Rushd, *Bidāya*, I, 452; trans. I, 550–1.

[35]Ṭūsī, *Tahdhīb al-aḥkām*, IX, 30. Game caught by a dog belonging to a *Majūsī* is forbidden. *Mishkāt*, II, 425; Robson, II, 873. The jurists disagree about hunting with a dog belonging to a *Majūsī*. Mālik, Abū Ḥanīfa, Shāfiʿī, and others permitted to hunt with it, as the consideration is to be given to the hunter and not to the instrument he employs. Jābir b. ʿAbd Allāh, al-Ḥasan al-Baṣrī, Mujāhid, and al-Thawrī, on the other hand, disapproved of it, because they argue that the Qurʾānic verse 5:4 is addressed to the faithful. Ibn Rushd, *Bidāya*, I, 458; trans. I, 559.

hunted by the Zoroastrians, because they can only be eaten if they are captured alive.[36]

'Alī: He said, 'When [an animal or a bird] is captured in a snare (or a net, *ḥibāla*), and dies in it, it is deemed dead [and cannot be eaten]; but if it is taken alive and duly slaughtered, it may be eaten.'[37]

[36]*Kāfī*, VI, 227–34; contradictory traditions are reported. Ṭūsī, *Tahdhīb al-aḥkām*, IX, 5–10. According to Mālik locusts cannot be eaten without *dhakāt*, and that they are to be killed by cutting off their head or some other part. The jurists generally agree that they may be eaten dead. For details see Ibn Rushd, *Bidāya*, I, 440; trans. I, 534–5.

[37]*Kāfī*, VI, 225; Kulaynī reports several traditions. Ṭūsī, *Tahdhīb al-aḥkām*, IX, 37.

8

Book of Ritual Slaughter (*Kitāb al-Dhabā'iḥ*)[1]

THE ACTS TO BE PERFORMED BY THOSE WHO SLAUGHTER ANIMALS (*AF'ĀL AL-DHĀBIḤĪN*)

God says: *Eat of that over which the name of Allah hath been mentioned, if ye are believers in His revelations* (6:118).[2]

Ja'far b. Muḥammad—his father—his ancestors: The Messenger of God said, 'He who slaughters an animal should sharpen his knife and inflict as little pain as possible on the animal.'[3]

Ja'far b. Muḥammad: He said, 'When you wish to slaughter an animal, do not torture it. Sharpen the knife, turn the head of the animal towards the *qibla*,[4] and do not cut the bone of the neck until it is dead.' By his words *lā tankha'hā* is meant the cutting of the *nukhā'*, which is a bone in the neck.[5]

[1]*Al-Dhabā'iḥ* pl. of *al-dhabīḥa*. The term is applied to a sheep or goat to be slaughtered or sacrificed, but not yet slaughtered. When the act has been executed upon it, it is said to be *dhabīḥ*. Lane, s.v. dh-b-ḥ; *EI*[2], s.v. Dhabīḥa.

[2]Pickthall 6:119.

[3]*Mishkāt* II, 424; Robson, II, 872; transmitted by Muslim. Slaughter has to be performed in a single uninterrupted act. Ibn Rushd, *Bidāya*, I, 443; trans. I, 538–9.

[4]Opinions vary. Some jurists consider it desirable to turn the animal to be slaughtered in the direction of the *qibla*, others consider it obligatory. Ibn Rushd, *Bidāya*, I, 445; trans. I, 541–2.

[5]*Nukhā'* means the spinal cord, or spinal marrow, i.e. what extends from the head through the vertebrae to the end of the tail, like a cord of marrow. Lane, sup. s.v. n-kh-'. *Kāfī*, VI, 242, 245–6; Ṭūsī, *Tahdhīb al-aḥkām* IX, 53, 55.

Abū Ja'far Muḥammad b. 'Alī and Abū 'Abd Allāh: Concerning the man who slaughters without turning the head of the victim towards the *qibla*, [the Imams] said, 'If this was due to a mistake, forgetfulness, or ignorance, there is no harm and the animal slaughtered can be eaten. But if the man did this deliberately, then he has done wrong, and the animal cannot be eaten since the intention was contrary to the *sunna*.'[6]

'Alī: He said, 'When one of you slaughters an animal, let him say, "In the name of God and God is Great (*bismillāh wa 'llāhu akbar*)."' Abū Ja'far said, 'It is enough if he mentions God and whatever glorification (*tasbīḥ*) and declaration of the unity of God (*tahlīl*) that he can. But if he omits the mention of God's name (*tasmiya*) deliberately, the animal cannot be eaten. If however he is ignorant of this [practice] or has forgotten [to mention God's name], he may utter it whenever he recollects it and then eat the animal.'[7]

The Messenger of God: He forbade the mutilation of animals (*al-muthla* or *al-mathula bi 'l-ḥayawān*)[8] and the binding of beasts. *Ṣabr* [in this context] means holding or binding, and he who holds (*ṣabara*) an animal, means that he 'binds' it. For this reason it is said, '*Qutila fulān*^{un} *ṣabr*^{an} (so-and-so was confined to die) when he was bound, or being held until he was put to death.' The words *maṣbūra* and *maḥbūsa* (confined, held) are used for fowls and other living creatures which are bound and left at a place, then they are shot to death.[9]

Abū Ja'far Muḥammad b. 'Alī: He said, 'He who kills a sparrow playfully will be brought on the Day of Resurrection in the presence of the bird who will shriek and say, "My Lord, ask him why he killed me without slaughtering me lawfully." So everyone should be warned not to mutilate or torture animals, but to sharpen the knife [before slaughtering].'[10]

[6]Ṭūsī, *Tahdhīb al-aḥkām*, IX, 54–5. For *sunna* see *The Pillars of Islam*, I, 1, n. 2.

[7]The *ḥukm* of *tasmiya* over the slaughtered animal to be lawful for consumption is a necessary condition described as *sunna mu'akkada* (emphatic practice of the Prophet, an act that was persistently performed). Ibn Rushd, *Bidāya*, I, 444–5; trans. I, 541.

[8]*Lisān al-'Arab*, s.v. m-th-l; tradition of the Prophet is cited.

[9]It is prohibited to keep animals without food and water waiting to be killed or to confine them and use them as targets. *Mishkāt*, II, 424; Robson, II, 872; transmitted by Bukhārī and Muslim.

[10]The Prophet cursed those who would use a living creature as a target. Another tradition states, 'If anyone wrongfully kills a sparrow or anything bigger, God will question him about killing it.' On being asked what the right way was, he replied, 'To cut its throat and eat it, not to cut off its head and [just] throw it away.' *Mishkāt*, II, 424, 427; Robson, II, 872, 874.

The Messenger of God: He prohibited people from skinning an animal or cutting off its head before it has died and lays still.[11]

Ja'far b. Muḥammad: He said, '[Perform the act of] slaughter at the proper place, i.e. the throat near the base of the tongue.[12] The bone of the neck (*nukhā'*) should not be cut, nor should the neck be broken until it dies.'[13]

Abū 'Abd Allāh Ja'far b. Muḥammad: He was asked about the man who cuts the neckbone of the animal before it dies. He meant that he breaks its neck. [The Imam said], 'The man had done wrong but there was no harm in eating the animal.'[14]

The Messenger of God: He forbade cutting off the head of the animal at the time of slaughtering it.

'Alī: He wrote to Rifā'a b. Shaddād, his *qāḍī* at al-Ahwāz,[15] [and commanded him] to direct the butchers (*qaṣṣābīn*) to perform the act of slaughter in an efficient manner, and [he ordered that] those who would strike so hard that [the knife] would penetrate to the neckbone (*ṣammama*) and sever the animal's head should have the animals thus slaughtered thrown away to the dogs.

Abū Ja'far Muḥammad b. 'Alī: He said, 'The man who slaughters should not intentionally cut off the head of the animal, but if this happens due to his ignorance, it does not matter.'[16]

Abū 'Abd Allāh: He said, 'In the case of a man who does not intend to cut off the head of an animal when he slaughters it, but [accidentally] pushes the knife too far and severs the head, then the animal may be eaten if he had no intention [to cut off its head].'

The Messenger of God: He directed that no part of the animal should be cut other than its throat; that is, if this is possible.

Abū Ja'far: He said, 'A slaughtered animal cannot be eaten if its neck is not cut at the proper place.'

Abū 'Abd Allāh Ja'far b. Muḥammad: He said, 'If a bull or camel

[11]*Kāfī*, VI, 242; if it was skinned before it had died, it cannot be eaten.

[12]The Arabic term is *ghalṣama* meaning larynx, or upper part of the windpipe, that is between the head and the neck. Lane, s.v. gh-l-ṣ-m. The rule for *dhabḥ* is the severance of the jugular vein and the pharynx. For details see Ibn Rushd, *Bidāya*, I, 441; trans. I, 536.

[13]Ṭūsī, *Tahdhīb al-aḥkām*, IX, 52–3.

[14]Mālik considered it abominable. If a person did it intentionally and without a lack of knowledge, the slaughtered animal should not be eaten. Ibn Rushd, *Bidāya*, 443; trans. I, 538.

[15]See *The Pillars of Islam*, I, 281.

[16]*Kāfī*, VI, 242, 243.

falls in a well or in the hollow of the earth, or is excited and cannot be slaughtered by slitting the throat (*'alā manḥarihi*[17] *aw madhbaḥihi*),[18] then the name of God should be pronounced and the animal stabbed [with a spear] wherever possible and [then] it may be eaten.'

The Messenger of God: He prohibited people from slaughtering animals except with a steel knife (*al-ḥadīd*).[19]

'Alī, Abū Ja'far and Abū 'Abd Allāh: They said, 'There can be no *dhakāt* (lawful slaughter) without a steel knife (*ḥadīda*).'

The Messenger of God: He disapproved of the slaughter of a pregnant or milk-bearing female animal without a valid reason.

PERSONS WHOSE SLAUGHTERED ANIMAL MAY BE EATEN AND THOSE WHOSE SLAUGHTERED ANIMAL MAY NOT (*MAN TU'KAL DHABĪḤATUHU WA-MAN LĀ TU'KAL DHABĪḤATUHU*)

Abū Ja'far Muḥammad b. 'Alī: He was asked about the slaughter of an animal by a Jew or a Christian or a Zoroastrian,[20] or by one who was opposed to the Imams (*ahl al-khilāf*), and he recited the Word of God: *Eat of that over which the name of Allah has been mentioned* (6:118). He said, 'When you hear the name of God being invoked over the animal, then eat it; but if the name of God has not been mentioned, do not eat it. If a man amongst them is suspected of omitting the mention of God, considering such an omission to be lawful, the animal slaughtered by him cannot be eaten, unless [the Muslim] has seen it [being] slaughtered,

[17]*Manḥar* means the breast or chest. It also signifies the part in which a camel is stabbed, i.e. the uppermost part of the breast, to be sacrificed. Lane, s.v. n-ḥ-r.

[18]See n. 32 below in this chapter.

[19]Bukhārī and Muslim transmitted a tradition which allowed animals to be killed with canes because the people had no knives. The Messenger of God said, 'When God's name is mentioned you may eat what is killed by anything which causes the blood to flow, except a tooth or a claw.' Bukhārī transmitted another tradition where a stone was used as a knife and the Messenger of God allowed [the slaughtered animal] to be eaten. The Messenger of God was asked, 'When one of us catches game and has no knife, may he cut its throat with a flint stone or a splinter of stick?' He replied, 'Cause the blood to flow with whatever you like and mention God's name.' *Mishkāt*, II, 423, 424; Robson, II, 871, 872, 873; *Kāfī*, VI, 239–40; a steel knife is essential; however, in its absence other sharp objects are permitted. The jurists agree that any device that causes the blood to flow from the jugular veins, whether made of iron, rock, or wood, is valid. Ibn Rushd, *Bidāya*, I, 443; trans. I, 539.

[20]The majority of the jurists maintain that the slaughtered animals of the Zoroastrians are not permitted, because they are polytheists. Ibn Rushd, *Bidāya*, I, 448; trans. I, 546.

according to the *sunna*, and that the name of God was mentioned over it. But if the animal was slaughtered in his absence, it cannot be eaten.'[21]

Ja'far b. Muḥammad: He was asked about the meat sold in the markets when it is not known how the animals had been slaughtered by butchers. He did not consider it to be unlawful if it is not known whether the animal had been slaughtered contrary to the *sunna* and [the consumer] had not seen the act of slaughter.[22]

Ja'far b. Muḥammad: He disapproved of the animals slaughtered by Christian Arabs.[23]

Abū Ja'far Muḥammad b. 'Alī and Abū 'Abd Allāh: They permitted a boy to slaughter an animal provided he had the strength and was able to perform the act properly; and similarly, a blind man if he is duly guided or a woman who performs the act efficiently [may also slaughter an animal].[24]

'Alī: He was asked about the slaughter by a man who is not ritually pure, and he permitted it.[25]

Ja'far b. Muḥammad:[26] He allowed a dumb man to slaughter an animal provided he understood the mention of God's name and made a gesture to indicate it.[27]

[21]Ṭūsī, *Tahdhīb al-aḥkām*, IX, 63–70. The general rule is that the animals slaughtered by the People of the Book are not to be consumed unless their slaughter conforms to the conditions laid down by Islam. For details see Ibn Rushd, *Bidāya*, I, 446–7; trans. I, 542–4.

[22]*Kāfī*, VI, 249; meat sold in the markets of the Muslims is allowed for consumption.

[23]I have preferred the reading: Christian Arabs (*Naṣārā al-'Arab*) in MS Q, three MSS of Fyzee's text, and in *Kāfī*, VI, 252. Fyzee's reading *Naṣārā al-A'rāb* (country Arabs who were Christians) is incorrect. Kulaynī has a separate section entitled 'Slaughter of *Ahl al-Kitāb*.' Their slaughter is not permitted unless it is ascertained that God's name was mentioned. The Qur'ānic verse: *The food of those who have received the Scripture is lawful for you, and your food is lawful for them* (5:5) refers to grain, cereals, corn, etc. The majority of the jurists maintain that the *ḥukm* of the slaughtered animals by Christian Arabs (Banū Taghlab) is the same as that for the People of the Book. Some jurists did not permit their slaughtered animals on the grounds that the Qur'ānic injunction '*those who have been given the Book*' (5:5) primarily includes those nations that are distinguished with the possession of the Book, and these are the Banū Isrā'īl and the Byzantines (*rūm*). Ibn Rushd, *Bidāya*, I, 446; trans. I, 544.

[24]*Kāfī*, VI, 249–51; several different traditions are cited. Ṭūsī, *Tahdhīb al-aḥkām*, IX, 73. Slaughter by a person having the following qualifications is unanimously approved: He is a Muslim, a male, major, sane, and regularly observes prayer. The majority of the jurists maintain that animals slaughtered by a Muslim woman and a Muslim minor are permitted. Ibn Rushd, *Bidāya*, I, 445–6, 448; trans. I, 542, 546.

[25]*Kāfī*, VI, 246; reported from Imam al-Ṣādiq.

[26]As in MS Q, the printed text is without 'b. Muḥammad'.

[27]Mālik did not permit the animal slaughtered by an insane or an intoxicated person, but Shāfi'ī did. Ibn Rushd, *Bidāya*, I, 448; trans. I, 546.

THE KNOWLEDGE OF RITUAL SLAUGHTER (MAʿRIFAT AL-DHAKĀT)[28]

God says: *The beast of cattle is made lawful unto you [for food]* (5:1).

Abū ʿAbd Allāh Jaʿfar b. Muḥammad: He was asked about the above verse and he said, 'The foetus (*janīn*) is in the womb of its dam, therefore the slaughter (*dhakāt*) of the dam is its slaughter, provided that its hair and wool have appeared.' He meant that the slaughter of the dam was the slaughter of the foetus. But if no wool or hair has appeared, the foetus cannot be eaten.[29]

He who cuts the throat (*ḥalq*) below its base (*ghalṣama*, the epiglottis, larynx), as is proper to do by the *sunna*, and cuts the throat (*ḥulqūm*), and the gullet (*marīʾ*), and the two jugular veins, and allows the blood to flow until the animal dies, has duly slaughtered the animal. This is by consensus according to our knowledge.

ʿAlī and Abū Jaʿfar: They said, 'The portion of the animal which is cut and severed from its body, before it is duly slaughtered, is carrion (*mayta*) and cannot be eaten. The animal may [thereafter] be slaughtered, and the remaining portion eaten if there was time for the ritual of slaughter to be duly performed.'

[28]*Dhakāt* signifies *dhabḥ*, i.e. the slaughter of an animal for food in the manner prescribed by the law, like *dhabḥ*. Lane, s.v. dh-k-w. Jazīrī, *al-Fiqh*, I, 734–40. Animals with regard to the stipulation of ritual slaughter for the lawful consumption of their meat are divided into two kinds: animals that are not lawful without ritual slaughter, and animals that are lawful without ritual slaughter. The former category includes warm-blooded land animals, while the latter comprises of sea animals. The Qurʾānic verse 5:3 prohibits five kinds of animals. They are: (i) carrion (carcass), blood, swine flesh (also 2:173); (ii) that over which any name other than Allah has been invoked (also 2:173); (iii) that which has been strangled, felled, has tumbled, been gored, or which wild beasts have mangled—unless you come upon them before they die and you have slaughtered them; (iv) that which has been sacrificed on the stone (altar), i.e. immolated to idols; (v) that which you divide by drawing lots by means of arrows as was done in pre-Islamic times (also 2:219, 5:90). For details and disagreements among various jurists see Ibn Rushd, *Bidāya*, I, 436 ff.; trans. I, 529 ff.

[29]'The slaughter of the embryo is included when its mother is slaughtered. Eat it if you wish.' Wool or hair is not mentioned. *Mishkāt*, II, 426, 427; Robson, II, 874. *Kāfī*, VI, 247; Kulaynī's position is identical with that of Nuʿmān. Lane, s.v. dh-k-w; 'The legal slaughter of the foetus, or young in the belly, is the legal slaughter of its mother.' Jurists diagree as to whether the *dhakāt* of the mother is effective for the *janīn* also, because the latter is dead when it comes out. The majority of the jurists, including Mālik and Shāfiʿī, maintained that the *dhakāt* of the mother is the *dhakāt* of the *janīn*. Abū Ḥanīfa, on the other hand, said that if the foetus emerges dead it is carrion and cannot be eaten. Those who maintained the former position stipulated that the foetus must be full grown with the appearance of hair. This was Mālik's opinion, but Shāfiʿī did not stipulate it. Ibn Rushd, *Bidāya*, I, 439; trans. I, 533.

'Alī: He said, 'The sign of a proper and completed slaughter is that the animal twitches its eye, or kicks, or moves its tail or ear.[30] But if none of these things take place and blood has flowed after the slaughter, and yet the animal remains motionless, it cannot be eaten.'

Abū Ja'far Muḥammad b. 'Alī: He said, 'The animal to be slaughtered should be treated kindly and not harshly, both before and after the act.' He did not approve that the achilles tendon (*'urqūb*) of a sheep be stricken with a knife [before the time of slaughter].

[Abū Ja'far Muḥammad b. 'Alī]: He was asked about an animal which falls from a high ledge, into water, or into fire, after being slaughtered. He said, 'If you had slaughtered it properly, and performed all the obligatory [rites], then eat it.'

[Abū Ja'far Muḥammad b. 'Alī]: He prohibited the eating of an animal slaughtered by an apostate (*al-murtadd*).[31]

Ja'far b. Muḥammad: He was asked about slaughtering a sheep while it is standing. He said, 'It was not proper to do this; the *sunna* is to lay it down on the ground, with its head being placed towards the *qibla*.'

[Ja'far b. Muḥammad]: He was asked whether a camel was to be slaughtered [in the manner prescribed by the law, i.e. by cutting the throat] (*dhabḥ*) or in the *naḥr* form.[32] He said, 'The *sunna* is to perform the *naḥr*.' They asked, 'How should the *naḥr* be performed?' He said, 'It should be made to stand facing the *qibla*,[33] and one of its front feet should be tethered. The man performing *naḥr* should also stand towards the *qibla*, and strike the upper part of the chest with a knife until it is cut open and splits.'

[Ja'far b. Muḥammad]: He was asked about whether cattle should be slaughtered by *dhabḥ* or *naḥr*. He said, 'The *sunna* is to perform *dhabḥ* after laying the animal on the ground;[34] but there is no harm if *naḥr* was performed.'

[30] *Kāfī*, VI, 244, 245; several traditions are cited.

[31] See *The Pillars of Islam*, I, 494; *EI*[2], s.v. Murtadd. The majority of the jurists maintain that animals slaughtered by an apostate should not be eaten. Ibn Rushd, *Bidāya*, I, 447; trans. I, 544.

[32] *Dhabḥ* is in the throat, while *naḥr* is in the pit above the breast, between the collar-bones, where camels are stabbed. The jurists agree that the *sunna* for lawful slaughter of sheep and birds is *dhabḥ*, the *sunna* for camels is *naḥr*, and that both *dhabḥ* and *naḥr* are permitted for cows. Lane, s.v. dh-b-ḥ. See also *Kafī*, VI, 240–1; Ibn Rushd, *Bidāya*, I, 440–3; trans. I, 535–9; he discusses in detail.

[33] See n. 4 above in this chapter.

[34] *Dhabḥ* is to be performed on cows and sheep because of the words of the Qur'ān: *God commands you to slaughter/sacrifice (an tadhbaḥū) a cow* (2:67), and *Then We ransomed him with a big slaughtered sacrifice (bi-dhibḥ*[in] *'aẓīm*[in]*)* (37:107). Ibn Rushd, *Bidāya*, I, 440–1; trans. I, 535–6.

[Ja'far b. Muḥammad]: He was asked about the slaughtering of an animal by the nape of the neck (*qafā'*), and he said, 'If this is not intentional, there is no harm. But if the man knows the practice of the Prophet and does this intentionally, the animal should not be eaten and the man should be taught the correct manner.'

'Alī: He was asked about two sheep, one of which was duly slaughtered and the other was not; and it is not known which was and which was not. He said, 'Both of them should be thrown away.'

9

Book of Sacrificial Animals and the Offerings Made for Newborn Children (*Kitāb al-Ḍaḥāyā wa 'l-'Aqā'iq*)

ANIMALS SACRIFICED ON THE *'ĪD* FESTIVAL (AL-ḌAḤĀYĀ)[1]

Ja'far b. Muḥammad—his father—his ancestors: The Messenger of God delivered a sermon on the Day of Sacrifice (*yawm al-naḥr*, i.e. *'īd al-aḍḥā*) and said, 'O People, he who is in easy circumstances should respect the rites (*sha'ā'ir*) of God; and he who is not, [*Verily*] *Allah does not charge a soul beyond its capacity* (2:286).

Ja'far b. Muḥammad: He was asked about sacrificing animals on the Feast of Sacrifice (*uḍḥīya*, pl. *aḍāḥī*), and he said, 'It is incumbent upon all believers except those who possessed none.' It was said to him, 'Is it incumbent upon all the members of the family?' He said, '[No], only upon those who wish to offer it.'[2]

The Prophet: He delivered a sermon on the Day of Sacrifice and said, 'O people! This is a day of spilling blood (*thajj*)[3] and of crying out (*'ajj*).'[4] Now *thajj* means the spilling of blood, 'and he whose intention is

[1]*Ḍaḥāya* pl. of *ḍaḥīya* and *uḍḥīya* pl. *aḍāḥī* means a sheep, goat, camel, bull, or cow that is slaughtered or sacrificed at the time called *al-ḍuḥā* (the early part of the forenoon, after sunrise) on the day called *yawm al-aḍḥā* (the Day of the Sacrifice), i.e. the tenth of Dhu 'l-Ḥijja). Lane, s.v. ḍ-ḥ-w. See *The Pillars of Islam*, I, 405–10.

[2]*Kāfī*, IV, 488–9. The jurists disagree about whether sacrificing animals on the Feast of Sacrifice is obligatory or a *sunna*. For details see Ibn Rushd, *Bidāya*, I, 466; trans. I, 516–17.

[3]*Thajj* signifies the flowing of the blood of an animal brought for sacrifice to Mecca. Lane, s.v. th-j-j.

[4]'Ajj and '*ajīj* means crying out supplicating and begging for aid or succour. It also means raising one's voice with the *talbiya*/saying *labbayk*. It is said in the tradition, 'The

sincere, for him the first drop of blood is the expiation of all his sins.' And *'ajj* is prayer, 'so cry out loudly to God! I swear to you by Him who has in His hand the life of Muḥammad that no one will go from this place but will be forgiven, except he who has committed a major sin (*kabīra*)[5] and persists in it, and does not bring himself to abandon it.'

[The Messenger of God]: He went to Fāṭima[6] on the Day of Sacrifice (*yawm al-aḍḥā*) and said, 'O Fāṭima, arise and witness your sacrifices.[7] Behold, the first drop of blood which falls will be the expiation of your sins. [Listen], the flesh of the animal sacrificed, its faeces and bones and hair and everything will be placed in your balance, and God will increase their weight seventy times [in your favour].' Al-Miqdād b. al-Aswad[8] heard of this and asked the Messenger of God, 'May my father and mother be sacrificed for you! Is this [act of God] restricted to the progeny of Muḥammad, or is it of general application?' God's Messenger replied, 'Indeed, it applies to all Muslims.'

[The Messenger of God]: He delivered a sermon on the Day of Sacrifice; and when he came down, he met a man from Anṣār[9] who said, 'O Messenger of God, I sacrificed my animal before I came out [to go to the place of prayer], and directed my family to prepare it for you, hoping that you would honour me by your presence on this day.' The Prophet said, 'Your sheep was the sheep of meat [not that of sacrifice]; if you possess another, sacrifice it.' The Anṣārī said, 'I have nothing but a small she-kid (*'anāq jadha'a*).'[10] God's Messenger said, 'Sacrifice it; but, verily, after you, the kid will not

---

most excellent [of the actions] of the pilgrimage are the raising of the voice with the *talbiya* and the shedding of the blood of the animals brought for sacrifice to the sacred territory.' Lane, '-j-j.

[5]See *The Pillars of Islam*, I, 54, n. 138.

[6]Fāṭima, see *The Pillars of Islam*, I, 54, n. 138; 288, n. 101.

[7]The Arabic term used is *nusuk*, meaning sacrificial offering.

[8]Al-Miqdād b. 'Amr, from the clan of Bahrā' of Quḍā'a tribe, escaped from Kinda to Mecca in pre-Islamic times and was adopted by a certain Aswad b. 'Abd Yagūth al-Zuhrī of the Makhzūm tribe. Hence he used to be called al-Miqdād b. al-Aswad until the Qur'ānic revelation of 33:5 declaring adoption illegal, whereupon he once again became known as the son of 'Amr. He was one of the seven early converts to Islam. With Salmān al-Fārisī, Abū Dharr al-Ghifārī, and 'Ammār b. Yāsir, these four companions of the Prophet are regarded by the Shī'a as 'the four pillars' (*al-arkān al-arba'a*) who formed the backbone of the first Shī'a. Rāzī, *al-Zīna* in *al-Ghuluww*, 259; Jafri, *Origins*, 52, 75, 76, 86; *EI*[2], s.v. Miḳdād b. 'Amr.

[9]Anṣār, see *The Pillars of Islam*, I, 13, n. 18.

[10]*Jadha'* is a name applied to different kinds of beasts when they are young. Applied to a sheep or goat, it means one year old, in its second year. Sometimes *jadha'*, applied to a sheep, could mean less than a year. Lane, s.v. j-dh-'.

be [sufficient as] a lawful sacrifice for anyone else.' And [the Imam] related the incident in all its details.[11]

Abū Ja'far Muḥammad b. 'Alī and Abū 'Abd Allāh: They said, 'In the towns (*amṣār* pl. of *miṣr*) sacrifices should be made on the Feast of Sacrifice (*yawm al-naḥr*) and the two days following;[12] and at Minā,[13] till the last Day of *Tashrīq*.[14]

The Messenger of God: He let 'Alī participate in his sacrifices. He slaughtered sixty-three large animals (*badana*)[15] with his own hand, and requested 'Alī to slaughter the rest. There were one hundred of them [in all] and all of them were slain on the Day of Sacrifice.[16]

Ja'far b. Muḥammad: He said, 'It is desirable that a man should slaughter his offerings by his own hand. If he is unable to do so, he should keep his hand with the hand of the slaughterer; and if he is unable to do so, he should stand by and recite the name of God until the animal is slain.'

[Ja'far b. Muḥammad]: He said, 'No one but a Muslim can slaughter an animal offered by a Muslim, and at the time of sacrifice, he should say, "In the name of God, God is Great. *Lo!*[17] *I have turned my face toward Him Who created the heavens and the earth, as one by nature upright [and a Muslim], and I am not one of the idolaters* (6:79);[18] *Lo, my worship and my sacrifice and my living and my dying are for Allah, Lord of the Worlds. He has no partner. This am I commanded, and I am first of the Muslims* (6:162–3).

Ja'far b. Muḥammad: He was asked about which animals were the

[11]The Prophet ordered Abū Burda to make the sacrifice again saying, 'A *jadha'* is valid in your case, but for no one other than you.' The majority of the jurists approve of *jadha'* as a satisfactory animal for sacrifice, but a group of jurists insist that a sheep has to be in the second year (*thaniyy*), the least age at which he may be sacrificed. Ibn Rushd, *Bidāya*, I, 430; trans. I, 521–2.

[12]*Kāfī*, IV, 487, 488; in the towns sacrifies should be made on the tenth of Dhu 'l-Ḥijja only.

[13]Minā, see *The Pillars of Islam*, I, 230, n. 298; 405.

[14]The Days of *Tashrīq*, see *The Pillars of Islam*, I, 225, n. 277; 233, 356. Ibn Rushd, *Bidāya*, I, 432–4; trans. I, 524–7; he has a lengthy discussion about the *aḥkām* of slaughter. With respect to the time of its commencement the jurists agree that *dhabḥ* before the ['*īd*] prayer is not permitted. With respect to the end of the period determined for valid sacrificial slaughtering, Mālik maintained that the latest time is by sunset on the third day of the Days of Sacrifice. This was also the opinion of Abū Ḥanīfa, Aḥmad, and other jurists.

[15]*Badana*, a she-camel and a male camel that is slaughtered or brought for sacrifice, so called because they used to fatten them, or because of their bulkiness. Lane, s.v. b-d-n.

[16]*The Pillars of Islam*, I, 405.

[17]As in the Qur'ān and MS Q; it is missing from the edited text.

[18]In Pickthall 6:80.

best for sacrifice and he said, '[The following, in order of priority]: female camels; male camels (*al-ināth min al-ibil, thumma al-dhukūr minhā*); cows; bulls (*al-ināth min al-baqar thumma al-dhukūr minhā*); male sheep (*al-fuḥūl min al-ḍa'n*); gelded sheep (*muwajja'*, sheep whose testicles had been bound until they have deteriorated); ewes (*al-ni'āj*); gelded sheep (whose testicles had been extracted); he-goats; she-goats (*al-faḥl min al-ma'az, thumma al-ināth minhā*). The best of thc rams (*kibāsh* pl. of *kabsh*) are fat, and with big horns, and virile (*faḥl*); eating, drinking, walking, observing and excreting with the flock.[19]

'The Messenger of God used to sacrifice a ram of the same qualities possessed by the ram which came down to Abraham.'[20] He was asked, 'From which place did it descend?' God's Messenger said, 'It came down from the sky to the hill which is to the right of the mosque of Minā.' He was asked, '[What if] such a ram is not available?' The Messenger of God said, 'Then sacrifice whatever you can obtain.'[21]

[Ja'far b. Muḥammad]: He permitted partnerships in sacrificing animals for those who do not have the means to possess their own.[22]

[Ja'far b. Muḥammad]: He said, 'Among cattle and camels, only those that are fully grown (*musinna*) satisfy the obligation, i.e. an animal which has shed its tooth,[23] or is of a greater age. The same condition applies to the eight kinds (four pairs) of cattle[24] with the exception of a *jadha'* (one-

[19]*Kāfī*, IV, 490. *Kabsh* is a ram, or male sheep, whatever be its age. According to some philologists it is a male sheep in its third year. It is also applied to the wild sheep. The female is called *na'ja* pl. *ni'āj*. Lane, s.v. k-b-sh. Ram, as a general term, includes ewes and sheep, etc. In order of priority for sacrifice, therefore, rams come after camels, cows, and bulls.

The jurists disagree about which animals were the best for sacrifice. Mālik maintained that there is greater merit in sacrificing rams (*kibāsh*), followed by cows (*baqar*), followed by camels (*ibil*). This view of his is quite contrary to what he held in the case of offerings during the pilgrimage. Shāfi'ī held the opposite of what Mālik held, that is, camels are the best, then cows, then rams. Ibn Rushd, *Bidāya*, I, 427; trans. I, 517–18.

[20]Alludes to the Qur'ān 37:107. See also Ibn Rushd, *Bidāya*, I, 427; trans. I, 518–19.

[21]*Kāfī*, IV, 488; the least sacrifice is a sheep or ewe.

[22]Ibid., IV, 497–8. Mālik permitted a man to slaughter a ram, a cow, or a camel as sacrifice on his own behalf and on behalf of his family whose maintenance is binding on him. Shāfi'ī, Abū Ḥanīfa, and other jurists permitted a man to sacrifice a camel or a cow on behalf of seven persons. For details see Ibn Rushd, *Bidāya*, I, 430–1; trans. I, 522–3.

[23]The Arabic term is *thanīy*, a camel in its sixth year, the least age at which he may be sacrificed. The term applies to other animals of different ages. Lane, s.v. th-n-y. See also *Kāfī*, IV, 490.

[24]For the four pairs of cattle, see the paragraph above wherein the best of animals for sacrifice are described. They are: female and male camels, cows and bulls, male sheep and ewes, he-goat and she-goat. Eight kinds of cattle are also mentioned in the Qur'ān 39:6.

year-old sheep).[25] It suffices because it is able to mate and to conceive unlike other cattle of a similar age.'

'Alī: He forbade people from sacrificing an animal with a broken horn; or one whose lameness is apparent; or one who is emaciated and his emaciation is apparent;[26] or one whose ears are cut off or damaged. A mere cleft, however, if it is a mark or sign, is not a disqualification.[27] An aged animal, if there is no defect in him and is not emaciated will suffice, but a fat one is desirable.

['Alī]: He said, 'If a man buys a healthy animal, but then it gets sick and dies before the Day of Sacrifice, his obligation is satisfied. But if he obtains another animal in its place for sacrifice, it is better and he should do so.'[28]

Ja'far b. Muḥammad: He was asked about the Word of God: *Eat thereof and feed the beggar (al-qāni') and the suppliant (al-mu'tarr)* (22:36) and *the poor unfortunate (al-bā'is al-faqīr)* (22:28). He said, 'The word *qāni'* implies a beggar who is content with what is given to him and does not turn away his face or contract it contemptuously, belittling what was given; the *mu'tarr* is one who insists on his demand; the *faqīr* is one who does not ask; the *miskīn* is even more needy and the *bā'is* is one whose condition is worse than all the others. Sometimes my father [Imam al-Bāqir] questioned the suppliant to find out who was the contented one, and when such a person stood by, he would give him the head [of the animal], and if he accepted it, he would say, "Put it down," and would give him the meat [instead]. But if he did not accept the head, he would leave him alone and give him nothing.'

'Alī: He said, '[The following] four are instructions from God, but they are not incumbent: (i) His saying: [*And such of your slaves as seek a writing (of emancipation)*], *write it for them if ye are aware of any good in them* (24:33);[29] so he who wishes may make such a contract, and he who does not, does not have to do so. (ii) His saying: *But when ye have left the sacred territory, then go hunting (if ye will)* (5:2); so he who wishes may go hunting, but he who does not, does not have to do so. (iii) His saying:

[25] *Kāfī*, IV, 490, 491.

[26] Ibid., IV, 491, 492, 493. With regard to the condition of sacrificial animals, the jurists agree that a lame, diseased, and emaciated animal should be avoided. For minute details see Ibn Rushd, *Bidāya*, I, 428–30; trans. I, 519–21.

[27] *Kāfī*, IV, 492.

[28] Ibid., IV, 494–7.

[29] The Arabic term is *mukātaba* and signifies that a slave made a written (or other) contract with his master that he should pay a certain sum as the price for his own freedom. Lane, s.v. k-t-b. See also *The Pillars of Islam*, I, 313; Chap. 12 below.

Eat thereof[30] *and feed the beggar and the suppliant* (22:36); so he who wishes to eat [from his sacrifice][31] may do so, and he who does not, does not have to [eat from it]. (iv) His saying: *And when the prayer is ended, then disperse in the land* (62:10);[32] so he who wishes to go about may do so, but he who does not, may sit down [that is, remain in the town or city where he is attending the Friday congregational prayers].'

Ja'far b. Muḥammad—his father—his ancestors: The Messenger of God let 'Alī participate in his sacrificial offerings of one hundred animals. God's Messenger directed that a piece from each animal was to be cooked, and accordingly all of them were cooked. He called 'Alī and both of them ate of the meat and sipped the broth. Thus, following the practice of the Messenger of God, it is desirable to eat some of the sacrificial animals and other offerings.

Abū 'Abd Allāh Ja'far b. Muḥammad: He was asked about the meat of sacrificial animals, and he said, "Alī b. al-Ḥusayn and my father Abū Ja'far used to give one-third to the neighbours, one-third to the beggars, and kept one-third for the family. There are no fixed rules about this, but whatever is given in charity thereof is better.[33] The Messenger of God said, "God has provided you with sacrificial animals so that you may nourish the needy with meat, so give them to eat.""

Ja'far b. Muḥammad: He said, 'The Messenger of God prohibited feeding the polytheists the meat of sacrificial animals because it is [a means of] obtaining communion with God. He also prohibited people from keeping the meat for more than three days, when people were in need of it; but there is no harm in keeping it [longer] today.'

Ja'far b. Muḥammad: He forbade the sale of any parts of the sacrificial animals; but he permitted the use of their skins and wool for defraying the expenses of skinning the animals.[34]

[30]The beginning of the verse reads: *And the beasts of sacrifice—we have appointed them for you as among God's waymarks; therein is good for you. So mention God's name over them, standing in ranks; then when their flanks collapse, eat of them and feed ...* (22:36; Arberry, *The Koran*, II, 31).

[31]Addition from MS Q.

[32]It refers to the Friday congregational prayers in a mosque in a town or city. See *The Pillars of Islam*, I, 223–9.

[33]*Kāfī*, IV, 489. The person who sacrifices an animal is commanded to eat some of his sacrifice and give away the rest as charity. The Qur'ān states: *Then eat thereof and feed therewith the poor unfortunate* (22:28); *eat thereof and feed the beggar and the suppliant* (22:36). Ibn Rushd, *Bidāya*, I, 434–5; trans. I, 527–8.

[34]*Kāfī*, IV, 494, 502, the sacrificial animal could be ridden and milked. The jurists agree that the sale of sacrificial meat is not permitted. However, they disagree about the sale of the slaughtered animal's skin and wool. The majority held that their sale is not

SACRIFICE FOR THE NEWLY BORN CHILDREN (AL-'AQĀ'IQ)[35]

The real meaning of the word *'aqīqa* is the hair with which a baby is born; thence, the sheep which is sacrificed for him at the time of shaving the hair is called *'aqīqa*. This is because [occasionally] a thing is named after another which approximates it or is its cause.[36]

Ja'far b. Muḥammad—his father—his ancestors: The Messenger of God commanded the shaving of a newly born child's hair on the seventh day;[37] and he said, 'Every child that is born is held in pledge for his *'aqīqa* (i.e. for the animal that is to be sacrificed for him when his head is shaven the first time);[38] and his parents may either release him from the obligation or allow him to remain under it [that is, perform or not perform the *'aqīqa*].'

[Ja'far b. Muḥammad]: The Messenger of God sacrificed a ewe (or sheep, *shāt*) on behalf of [Imam] Ḥasan and another on behalf of [Imam] Ḥusayn. He had the head of each one of them shaved on that day, namely the seventh, and he said, 'O Fāṭima, give in charity gold or silver equal to the weight of the hair of the baby.' She weighed [Imam] Husayn's hair and it weighed a dirham and a half.[39]

---

permitted, but Abū Ḥanīfa permitted their barter for things other than dirhams and dinars. Ibn Rushd, *Bidāya*, I, 435; trans. I, 528.

[35]*Kāfī*, VI, 5–56; it is a detailed chapter. Ṭūsī, *Tahdhīb al-aḥkām*, VII, 440–1. *'Aqīqa* pl. *'aqā'iq* signifies that the hair on a newly born infant be shaven off on the seventh day and its weight in silver be given to the poor. The term is also applied to the sheep or goat, generally the latter, that is slaughtered as a sacrifice for the recently born infant on the occasion of the shaving of the infant's hair on the seventh day after his birth. The goat's limbs are cooked with water and salt and given as food to the poor. The majority of the jurists are of the opinion that *'aqīqa* is a *sunna*. Abū Ḥanīfa regarded it neither as an obligation nor a *sunna*, but a voluntary act. If the offering of the *'aqīqa* was neglected on the seventh day after birth, the preferred day by the majority of the jurists, it is permitted on the fourteenth and the twenty-first day. It can be done afterwards, even by the child himself when he attains puberty. It is also recommended that on the day of the *'aqīqa* a name be given to he child. The custom is derived from pre-Islamic practice and a belief that it removes injury from the child. All the jurists maintain that the pre-Islamic custom of smearing the head of the child with the blood of the sacrificial animal stands abrogated in Islam. Ibn Rushd, *Bidāya*, I, 459–61; trans. I, 560–2; Lane, s.v. '-q-q; *EI*[2], s.v. 'Aḳīḳa.

[36]*Kāfī*, VI, 28–31.

[37]Shaving the hair of the infant is explained as removing the impurities with which a child is born, circumcision is also a part of purification. See *The Pillars of Islam*, I, 154.

[38]*Kāfī*, VI, 26–7, 28, 39; it is an obligation, however the poor and impoverished are excused. Some traditions state that the *'aqīqa* cannot be performed after seven days. *Mishkāt*, II, 439; Robson, II, 885.

[39]*Mishkāt*, II, 439; Robson, II, 885; *Kāfī*, VI, 27, 34–5; Ṭūsī, *Tahdhīb al-aḥkām*, VII, 442; Ibn Rushd, *Bidāya*, I, 461; trans. I, 562. Dirham is a weight ca. 3.12 g. Hinz, *Islamische Masse*, 1–8.

The Messenger of God: He said, 'Whoever sacrifices an animal by way of *'aqīqa* for his child should give the midwife (*qābila*) the hind leg [of the animal, i.e. quarter from the back].'[40]

[The Messenger of God]: He spoke of the *'aqīqa* and the baby as follows, 'When it is the seventh day, sacrifice a ram (*kabsh*),[41] cut it limb by limb, and cook it. Then make gifts thereof, and give to charity, and eat of it. Shave the head of the baby [and weigh the hair], and give its weight in gold or silver as charity.'

[The Messenger of God]: He said, 'The animal to be sacrificed is the same, a ewe, both for a male or a female child.'[42]

Ja'far b. Muḥammad: He said, 'The newly born child should be named on the seventh day. The Messenger of God said, "The favour of God will never cease on a family, one of whose members is named after a prophet."'[43]

The Messenger of God: He forbade people from assuming four *kunyas*[44] when they have the name of Muḥammad: Abū 'Īsā, Abū al-Ḥakam, Abū Mālik and Abū al-Qāsim. This prohibition applied to all people except to 'Alī and he said, 'The *Mahdī* will be of my offspring, his name and *kunya* will resemble mine.'[45]

[40]*Kāfī*, VI, 31, 33; the midwife should be given the hind leg with haunch. Another tradition states that she should be given one-third, however, if she is a close relative of the husband she is not entitled to any share.

[41]The ages and the description of the sacrificial animals for this rite are the same as that for the *ḍaḥāya*. The *ḥukm* for the meat, skin, etc., of this rite is the same as that of the sacrificial animals. Ibn Rushd, *Bidāya*, I, 460; trans. I, 562.

[42]'Two sheep are to be sacrificed for a boy and one for a girl, but it does you no harm whether they are male or female.' *Mishkāt*, II, 438–9; Robson, II, 884. *Kāfī*, VI, 27–8; the animal to be sacrificed for a boy or girl is the same. The jurists disagree about the number of animals to be sacrificed. According to Mālik one sheep each is to be sacrificed for the male as well as the female child. Shāfi'ī, Aḥmad b. Ḥanbal and others said that one sheep for a girl and two for a boy. Ibn Rushd, *Bidāya*, I, 459–60; trans. I, 561.

[43]*Kāfī*, VI, 19; Ṭūsī, *Tahdhīb al-aḥkām*, VII, 438, 442–3.

[44]*Kunya* pl. *kunan* means an agnomen consisting of *abū* (father) or *umm* (mother) followed by the name of the son.

[45]According to a widely held Muslim belief, *al-Mahdī* (the rightly guided one) is the appellation of the restorer of religion and justice who will appear and rule before the end of the world. Belief in the coming of the *Mahdī* from the Family of the Prophet became an important part of the faith, especially in radical Shī'ism, the Imāmīs and the Ismā'īlīs, in contrast to Sunnism. Among the Zaydī Shī'a it is a marginal belief. For its origin and early development see *EI*², s.v. al-Mahdī. Nu'mān, *Sharḥ al-akhbār*, III, 353–99; he has cited several traditions. In his *Ismaili Tradition Concerning the Rise of the Fatimids* (97–122), Ivanow has translated these traditions. It should be noted that the first Fāṭimid caliph took *al-Mahdī* as his honorific title.

10

Book of Marriage (*Kitāb al-Nikāḥ*)

THE INDUCEMENTS TO MARRIAGE[1] (*AL-RAGHĀ'IB FI 'L-NIKĀḤ*)

God says: *And of His signs is that He created for you, of yourselves, spouses, that you might repose in them, and He has set between you love and mercy. Surely in that are signs for a people who consider* (30:21);[2] The Mighty and Glorious says: *Marry the spouseless among you, and your slaves and handmaidens that are righteous; if they are poor, God will enrich them of His bounty; God is All-embracing, All-knowing. And let those who find not the means to marry be abstinent till God enriches them of His bounty* (24:32–3);[3]

[1]*Nikāḥ* is the term used in the Qur'ān for the marriage contract. Marriage, in Islamic law, is not a sacrament but a civil contract regulated under religious jurisdiction in order to give its effects a character of sanctity. Its essential constituents (*arkān*) are declaration and acceptance. No religious ceremony, however customary, is legally necessary. The jurists further discuss conditions for a valid marriage under different headings, such as guardians, witnesses, and dower. For marriage customs and *nikāḥ* as a legal institution see *EI*[2], s.v. Nikāḥ. For the Sunnī schools of law, see Ibn Rushd, *Bidāya*, II, 5 ff,; trans. II, 1 ff.; Jazīrī, *al-Fiqh*, IV, 1 ff. For a digest of Muslim law of marriage and recent legislative changes in the Arab countries, see Anderson, *Islamic Law*, 38–58; Nasir, *Status of Women*, 3–68. In her article 'The defective marriage', M. Siddiqui discusses some issues regarding the form of marriage contracts and demonstrates that the marital relationship is viewed primarily as a contract between two parties. In the classical *fiqh* tradition, marriage is thus defined for the most part by using contract terminology.

For a summary of this chapter from a lawyer's perspective, see Najafali, *Law of Marriage Governing Dawoodi Bohra.* A copy of the official marriage form used by the Bohra priests is also given in the Appendix B. In his *Comependium*, 1–41, Fyzee has abridged this chapter.

[2]Arberry, *The Koran*, II, 106–7.

[3]Ibid., II, 50.

and God says: *And He it is who has created man from water, and hath appointed for him kindred by blood and kindred by marriage; for thy Lord is ever Powerful* (25:54).

Ja'far b. Muḥammad—his father—his ancestors: The Messenger of God said, 'He who desires to meet his Lord in a state of purity, ought to live virtuously with his wife.'[4]

[Ja'far b. Muḥammad]: [The Messenger of God] said, 'He who wishes to emulate my character, let him follow my practice (*sunna*),[5] and marriage is [one] of my practices.'[6]

[Ja'far b. Muḥammad]: [The Messenger of God] said, 'Whenever any man marries in his early manhood, the Devil cries out, "O woe to me! This man has protected two-thirds of his religion from me." So, let the man fear God in the remaining third.'[7]

'Alī: He said, 'Whenever any of the Companions of the Messenger of God married, God's Messenger said, "His faith has been perfected."'[8]

'Alī: He said, 'Once 'Uthmān b. Maẓ'ūn[9] came to the Messenger of God and said, "O Messenger of God, I am overwhelmed by pleasurable imaginings (*ḥadīth al-nafs*), but I will not take any action without seeking direction from you first." God's Messenger said, "And what is it that your soul urges you, O 'Uthmān?" He said, "I am anxious to travel in the land." The Messenger of God said, "Do not travel in the land, for verily, the mosques are the visiting places of my community." He said, "I am anxious to give up the eating of meat altogether." The Messenger of God said, "Do not do so. Verily, I desire meat and eat it, and were I to ask God to provide it for me every day, He would do it." 'Uthmān said, "I am anxious to emasculate myself."[10] God's Messenger said, "O 'Uthmān, any one who does this to himself or to anyone else is not one of us. Verily, the

[4]Anas reported God's Messenger as saying, 'Those who wish to be pure and purified when they meet God should marry free women.' Another tradition states, 'There are three [types of man] whom it is right for God to help: ... the man who marries desiring to live a chaste life.' *Mishkāt*, II, 160, 161; Robson, I, 659, 660.

[5]For *sunna* see *The Pillars of Islam*, I, 1.

[6]*Kāfī*, V, 333; transmitted from al-Ṣādiq.

[7]'Oh you young men! Those of you who can support a wife should marry, for it keeps you from looking [at strange women] and preserves you from immorality; but those who cannot should devote themselves to fasting, for it is a means of suppressing sexual desire (*wijā'*).' Transmitted by Bukhārī and Muslim; *Mishkāt*, II, 158; Robson, I, 658.

[8]Anas reported God's Messenger as saying, 'When a man marries he has perfected half of the religion; so let him fear God regarding the remaining half.' *Mishkāt*, II, 161; Robson, I, 660; *Kāfī*, V, 333.

[9]'Uthmān b. Maẓ'ūn, see *The Pillars of Islam*, I, 295, 297.

[10]*Ajubbu nafsī*. The verb *jabba* means he extirpated his testicles. Lane, s.v. j-b-b.

suppression of sexual desire (*waj'*)[11] of my community comes from fasting." 'Uthmān said, "I am thinking of giving up marital relations with my wife Khawla." God's Messenger said, "Do not do so, O 'Uthmān. When a faithful one takes his wife by his hand, God records ten good works to his credit and deletes ten misdeeds; and if he kisses her, God gives him credit for one hundred good works and erases one hundred misdeeds of his; and if he unites with her, God gives him credit for a thousand good works and erases a thousand misdeeds and the angels visit the couple. And when the two take the ritual bath, for every hair that the water touches, God will record for them one good work and delete from the record one misdeed. If this happens to be on a cold night, God tells His angels, 'Observe these two bondmen of mine; they are taking a ritual bath on a cold night, having knowledge that I am their Lord. I bear witness that I have pardoned them;' and if by their association a son is conceived, he will be for them a servitor in Paradise."

'Then the Messenger of God tapped 'Uthmān on the breast and said, "O 'Uthmān, do not turn away from my practice (*sunna*); for, verily he who will turn his face away from my *sunna* will be met by angels on the Day of Resurrection who will turn his face away from my Pond (*ḥawḍ*).'"[12]

The Messenger of God: He said, 'O people, marry, for, on the Day of Resurrection, we together will outnumber the other communities. And the best of women is the affectionate one (*wadūd*) who bears many children (*walūd*).[13] Do not marry the foolish ones, for indeed, association with them is a calamity and their children [who cannot manage their own affairs] will be a [terrible] waste.'[14]

[The Messenger of God]: He said, 'When a faithful one approaches his faithful wife, two angels will surround him, and then he becomes like

[11]It is a free translation. *Waj'un* and *wijā'un* means castration. *Lisān al-'Arab*, s.v. w-j-'; Lane, s.v. w-j-'.

[12]Sa'd b. Abī Waqqās said, 'The Messenger of God objected to 'Uthmān b. Maẓ'ūn living in celibacy. If he had given him permission we would have had ourselves castrated.' *Mishkāt*, II, 158; Robson, I, 658; transmitted by Bukhārī and Muslim. *Ḥawḍ* or *ḥawḍ al-rasūl*, alludes to the pond at which the Prophet will meet his community on the Day of Resurrection and will be given to drink from it. Its waters, according to a tradition, are whiter than the snow and sweeter than honey. The idea of *ḥawḍ* is not found in the Qur'ān, however, in tradition a great variety of details are given. For the related traditions see *Concordance*, s.v. ḥ-w-ḍ; *EI*^{2}, s.v. Ḥawḍ, Kaw<u>th</u>ar.

[13]*Mishkāt*, II, 160; Robson, I, 659; *Kāfī*, V, 328–9, 338; Ibn Qayyim, *al-Ṭibb al-nabawī*, 236, 237.

[14]*Kāfī*, V, 358. One tradition states that a foolish man begets, but a foolish woman does not bear a child.

one who draws his sword in the way of God. And when he is free from her, his sins are shed, just as the leaves fall from a tree in autumn; and when he takes a ritual bath, [behold], he becomes altogether separated from all sins.'

A woman said, 'My father and mother be thy ransom, O Messenger of God, this is for men, but what about the woman?' God's Messenger said, 'When she conceives, God records a compensation for her equal to that of a man who prays and fasts. And when she has the pains of childbirth (*ṭalq*), no one knows the reward she will get except God. And when she is delivered of a child, with every mouthful of milk that the child draws, God rewards her with a good work and erases a misdeed. And when a woman dies in childbirth, she stands before God without any sins[15] because she died in travail.'

[The Messenger of God]: He said, 'He who abandons married life for fear of want, has indeed lost faith in his Lord,[16] for God says: *If they are poor, God will enrich them of His bounty; God is All-embracing, All-knowing*' (24: 32).

Ja'far b. Muḥammad: He said, 'Whenever a faithful couple unite in marriage, it is proclaimed from heaven, "Behold so-and-so has married so-and-so;" and when they separate, it is proclaimed, "Behold, God has permitted so-and-so to separate from so-and-so."'

The Messenger of God said, 'Whenever the faith of a man increases, his love for women increases likewise.'[17]

The [Messenger of God]: He said, 'God has bestowed three [special favours] on the apostles—perfume, wives, and the tooth-stick.'[18]

Ja'far b. Muḥammad: He said, 'There are four qualities which the prophets possess: good organization; the use of perfume; shaving the body,' that is, with a depilatory paste (*nūra*); 'and great virility (*kathrat al-ṭarūqa*)' with women.[19] Then he mentioned [the Prophet] Solomon son of David[20]

[15]It is a free rendering. The Arabic is *bi-ghayr ḥisāb* lit. without reckoning, i.e. without rendering account of one's deeds.

[16]The Arabic expression is *asā'a 'l-ẓanna bi-*, lit. to have a poor opinion of someone, or to think badly of someone. *Kāfī*, V, 334, 335.

[17]*Kāfī*, V, 325; slightly different version reported from al-Ṣādiq.

[18]Ibid., V, 325, 326. See also *The Pillars of Islam*, I, 146, n. 96.

[19]Abū Ayyūb reported God's Messenger saying, 'Four characteristics pertain to the practices of the messengers: modesty (or circumcision), the use of perfume, the use of the tooth-stick, and marriage.' Transmitted by Tirmidhī. *Mishkāt*, I, 122; Robson, I, 80. See also *The Pillars of Islam*, I, 146.

[20]The Biblical king Solomon is an outstanding figure in Islamic legends. The Biblical

and said, 'He had one thousand women in his palace, seven hundred concubines (*surrīya*),[21] and three hundred wives (*mahīra*)'.[22] [The Imam] was asked, 'May I be a ransom for you! How could he satisfy them all?' He said, 'Solomon had the virility of forty men and more, and God gave the same power to the Prophet.' Then they asked about 'Alī and [the Imam] was shy of speaking about him as 'Alī was his ancestor, and because of the status of Fāṭima; so he remained silent and said nothing.

[Ja'far b. Muḥammad]: He said, "Alī left four wives and nineteen concubines.'[23]

Abū Ja'far Muḥammad b. 'Alī: One day he met with his [half-] brother Zayd[24] and both of them counted the women [Imam] Ḥasan b. 'Alī married. They counted fifty-six, but were unable to complete the list.[25]

[Abū Ja'far Muḥammad b. 'Alī]: He said, 'Verily God has removed sexual desire (*shabaq*) from our women and bestowed it on our men; and the same is true of our partisans. And God has taken away sexual power from the men of the Banū Umayya and given it to their women; and He did the same with their partisans.[26]

'It is befitting a man to take more than one wife only when he is able to support them, satisfy them sexually, and deal with them impartially. He should not neglect some of them as it is forbidden by God. If he is unable to comply with those prerequisites, then he is well advised to limit himself to what he can afford.'

Ja'far b. Muḥammad—his father—his ancestors—the Messenger of God: He prohibited a man from eating to his full satisfaction, and not

---

tradition celebrates his wisdom, while the Deuteronomist regards the decline and division of his kingdom as the result of the marriages to many foreign wives. *EI*², s.v. Sulaymān b. Dāwūd; *ER*, s.v. Solomon.

[21]*Surrīya*, a female slave whom one takes as a possession and for concubinage. The term is derived from *sirr* signifying 'concubinage', or 'concealment', because a man often conceals and protects her from his wife. Lane, s.v. s-r-r.

[22]*Mahīra* means a woman to whom a dower has been given, as opposed to *surrīya*. Lane, m-h-r.

[23]'Alī had fourteen sons and nineteen daughters by nine wives and several concubines. *EI*², s.v. 'Alī b. Abī Ṭālib. See also Mufīd, *al-Irshād*, 186–7; he lists twenty-seven children, both male and female, and their respective mothers.

[24]For Zayd b. 'Alī b. al-Ḥusayn see *The Pillars of Islam*, I, 428.

[25]He went from one marriage to another, hence earned for himself the title of *al-Miṭlāq* (the Divorcer). He had sixty, seventy, or ninety wives and three or four hundred concubines. *EI*², s.v. al-Ḥasan b. 'Alī b. Abī Ṭālib. See also Mufīd, *al-Irshād*, 194; he enumerates fifteen children, both male and female, and their mothers respectively.

[26]Compare it to *Kāfī*, V, 343, wherein it is stated that women generally have more sexual desire than men. Banū Umayya, see *The Pillars of Islam*, I, 305, n. 21.

providing for his family; and he said, 'The man who does not provide for those who depend on him for their sustenance deserves destruction.'

[Ja'far b. Muḥammad]: He said, 'If a man collects together several wives without satisfying them sexually, and they commit adultery, the sin lies on his head, for, God says: *And if ye fear that ye cannot do justice (to so many), then one (only) or (the captives) that your right hands possess*' (4:3).

The Messenger of God: He prohibited monasticism(*tarahhub*) and said, 'There is no monasticism (*rahbānīya*) in Islam. Marry, so that I may have the largest number of followers among the various communities.' He prohibited celibacy (*tabattul*) and forbade women from remaining celibate and cutting themselves off from their husbands.

Ja'far b. Muḥammad: He was asked about a man who was so greatly affected by the fear of God that he abandoned women, gave up good food, and he could not lift up his head towards the sky [for fear of God and] in doing honour to Him. [The Imam] said, 'As to what you hold about abandoning women, you know how many of them were with the Messenger of God;[27] and as to your opinion of good food, the Messenger of God used to eat meat and honey;[28] and as to the fear of God which does not enable you to lift up your head to the sky, humility (*khushū'*) is a matter of the heart. Now who was there more humble and more fearful of God than the Messenger of God, but he did not act thus. God says: *Verily in the Messenger of Allah ye have a good example (uswa ḥasana) for him who looketh unto Allah and the Last Day*' (33:21).

THOSE WITH WHOM MARRIAGE IS APPROVED AND THOSE WITH WHOM IT IS NOT APPROVED (*MAN YUSTAḤABB AN YUNKAḤ WA-MAN YURGHAB 'AN NIKĀḤIHI*)

Ja'far b. Muḥammad—his father—his ancestors: The Messenger of God said, 'Choose [a proper resting place] for your seed; for verily the maternal uncle [of your son] has the same character as your wife.'[29]

The Messenger of God: He said, 'Marry among your equals, and give

[27]The Messenger of God married fifteen women and consummated his marriage with thirteen. He combined eleven at one time. Ṭabarī, *The History of al-Ṭabarī*, IX, 126–7.

[28]*Kāfī*, V, 325; slightly different version, but on the same authority and the person concerned was Sukayn al-Nakha'ī.

[29]Ibid., V, 336; reported from the same authority. This is a free translation. The Arabic is *al-khāl aḥad al-ḍajī'ayn*. *Ḍajī'* means a bedfellow. The tradition implies that the son resembles his maternal uncle in character.

[your children] to them in marriage; seek a proper place for your seed. I warn you not to marry Negroes (*zanj*),[30] because they are ugly in appearance (*khalq mushawwah*).'[31] And God's Messenger saying 'Seek a proper place for your seed' is a comprehensive statement to indicate that a man should not marry any other than a chaste woman, or one born in lawful wedlock, and avoid dissolute and suspicious women.

[Ja'far b. Muḥammad]: [The Messenger of God][32] said, 'God says, "When I wish to bestow a favour on a bondsman in this world and the hereafter,[33] I give him a tongue which remembers (Me), and a heart that fears (Me), and a body that is patient in adversity, and a wife who is faithful. She gives the husband happiness to look at her and when he is absent she protects both her person and his property."'[34]

[Ja'far b. Muḥammad]: He said, 'Five things are auspicious: a virtuous wife;[35] good children; righteous friends; livelihood in one's homeland; and love for the progeny of Muḥammad.'

[Ja'far b. Muḥammad]: He said, 'A virtuous wife is [as uncommon] as the crow known as *al-a'ṣam*, which is found but rarely.' A'*ṣam* is a crow with one white foot.[36]

[Ja'far b. Muḥammad]: He said, 'There is no measure (*khaṭar*)[37] for the

[30]*Kāfī*, V, 336; the edict against marrying Negroes is not included in the tradition. The editor also remarks that it is a weak tradition. A separate tradition against marrying Negroes is transmitted by Imam al-Ṣādiq from 'Alī. Ibid., V, 356.

[31]Ibid., V, 356; another tradition adds the Kurds and Khazars (people from the Caspian Sea who were considered unattractive because of their small eyes) to the list. It is reported from al-Ṣādiq.

[32]This addition is from *Kāfī*, V, 331.

[33]When I wish to combine for a Muslim the best of this world and the next ...: in Kāfī. I am unable to find this tradition in *al-aḥādīth al-qudsīya*, however a tradition in *Mishkāt*, II, 207; Robson, I, 694, reads: 'There are four [characteristics which are of such a nature] that one who has been given them has been endowed with what is best in this world and the next: a thankful heart, a tongue which makes mention of God, a body which shows endurance in trial, and a wife who does not seek to be unfaithful to [her husband] in her person and his property.'

[34]I am unable to find this tradition in *al-aḥādīth al-qudsīya*. 'There are four [characteristics which are of such a nature] that one who has been given them has been endowed with what is best in this world and the next: a thankful heart, a tongue which makes mention of God, a body which shows endurance in trial, and a wife who does not seek to be unfaithful to [her husband] in her person and his property.' *Mishkāt*, II, 207; Robson, I, 694.

[35]The Messenger of God said, 'A virtuous wife [brings] happiness to man.' *Kāfī*, V, 332.

[36]*Al-Ghurāb al-a'ṣam* is an epithet applied to anything that is rarely found; and a righteous woman is likened thereto. Lane, s.v. '-ṣ-m. See also *Kāfī*, V, 521; Ṭūsī, *Tahdhīb al-aḥkām*, VII, 401.

[37]For the various meanings of *khaṭar* see Lane, s.v. kh-ṭ-r.

worth of a woman; neither for the righteous, nor for the wicked. As for the righteous, she cannot be measured against gold or silver [for she is superior to both]; and as for the wicked, she cannot be measured against the dust, because the dust is superior to her.'

[Ja'far b. Muḥammad]: He said, 'The world consists of worldly goods, and the best of worldly possessions is a virtuous wife.'

[Ja'far b. Muḥammad]: He said, 'Auspicious for a Muslim are the following: a virtuous wife; a spacious home; a good mount; and a well-behaved child.'[38]

[Ja'far b. Muḥammad]: He prohibited people from marrying a woman for money or beauty and said, 'Her wealth may make her rebellious, and her beauty may destroy her; so I enjoin you to select a religious woman.'[39]

[Ja'far b. Muḥammad]: He said, 'There is no steed better than a black one (*duhm*), and no wife better than a paternal uncle's daughter.'

[Ja'far b. Muḥammad]: He said, 'The best of your women are the women of the Quraysh;[40] they are more considerate to the husband and more affectionate to the children.'[41]

[Ja'far b. Muḥammad]: He said, 'Marry virgins for their mouths are the sweetest, their wombs the most prolific, their affection the most firm, and they are quicker in learning. Marry the spouseless (*ayāmā*) amongst you, for verily God will improve their character and increase their livelihood.'[42]

[38]'The virtuous wife is the best worldly possession.' *Mishkāt*, II, 158; Robson, I, 658; transmitted by Muslim.

[39]'A woman may be married for four reasons; for her wealth, her noble descent, her beauty, and her religion; so get the one who is religious and prosper.' *Mishkāt*, II, 158; Robson, I, 658; transmitted by Bukhārī and Muslim. *Kāfī*, V, 336; a beautiful woman of bad family background should be avoided.

[40]Quraysh, see *The Pillars of Islam*, I, 37, n. 81.

[41]'The best of the women who ride on camels are the good women of Quraysh, for they are the most affectionate to children and the most careful of what belongs to their husbands.' *Mishkāt*, II, 159; Robson, I, 658; transmitted by Bukhārī and Muslim. See also *Kāfī*, V, 330–1; Ṭūsī, *Tahdhīb al-aḥkām*, VII, 404.

[42]I have preferred the translation 'spouseless' of '*ayāmā*' as it occurs in the Qur'ān 24:32. Lexicographers differ as to whether the pl. form *ayāmā* is derived from *ayma*, i.e. a woman whose husband has died, or from *ayyim*, i.e. a woman having no husband. The latter is distinguished from the virgin (*bikr*). Translators have rendered it as follows: 'unmarried' by Bell, 'solitary' by Pickthall, 'single' by Yusuf Ali, 'spouseless' by Arberry, 'die (noch) ledig sind' by Paret, 'les célibataires' by Blachère, and 'single' by Sale with a note stating that it means those who are unmarried, whether they have been married before or not. Lane, s.v. a-y-m; *Mu'jam alfāẓ al-Qur'ān*, s.v. a-y-m. 'Marry virgins, for they have the sweetest mouths, the most prolific wombs, and are the most satisfied with little.' *Mishkāt*, II, 160; Robson, I, 659–60; Suyūṭī, *al-Manhaj al-sawīy*, 222. 'Would you not marry a virgin? She can flirt with you and you can dally with her.' Another tradition states that the

[Ja'far b. Muḥammad]: [The Imam] prohibited a Muslim from rejecting a brother Muslim who asks for the hand of a woman, provided that he approves of his religion. He said: *If ye do not do so, there will be confusion in the land, and great corruption* (8:73).[43]

[Ja'far b. Muḥammad]: He forbade a marriage other than one in the way of God and in the way of chastity. He also forbade marriage for [purposes of] ostentation (*riyā'*) and [bolstering] one's reputation (*sum'a*).

Ja'far b. Muḥammad: He said, 'When a man marries a woman for her beauty or wealth, he has entrusted his affairs to [her beauty and wealth];[44] but if he marries her for her religion and excellence, God will bestow livelihood and beauty.[45] God says: *Marry the spouseless among you, and your slaves and handmaidens that are righteous; if they are poor, God will enrich them of His bounty. God is All-embracing, All-knowing*' (24:32–3).

[Ja'far b. Muḥammad]: He said, 'There is no greater misfortune for a man than his brother's son should come to him and say, "Marry [your daughter] to me," and he says, "I will not do so, for I am richer than you!"'

The Messenger of God: He said, 'Marry women with blue eyes, for they bring good luck.'[46]

[The Messenger of God]:[47] He said, 'Whenever anyone desires to marry a woman, he should inquire about her hair, as he does about her countenance, for verily, hair is one of the two signs of beauty.'

[The Messenger of God]: He said, 'Choose for yourselves servants of short stature, for they will serve your purpose better.'

Messenger of God forbade to have intercourse before loveplay. Dhahabī, *al-Ṭibb al-nabawī*, 18. See also *Kāfī*, V, 338.

[43]'When someone with whose religion and character you are satisfied asks for your daughter in marriage, accede to his request. If you do not do so there will be temptation in the earth and extensive corruption.' Transmitted by Tirmidhī; *Mishkāt*, II, 160; Robson, I, 659; *Kāfī*, V, 350; reported from al-Bāqir and its version is identical with that of Tirmidhī.

[44]The Arabic is *wukila ilā dhālika*; the same in *Kāfī*, V, 337. Gloss in MS Y explains it as: he has left his affairs in the hands of someone else.

[45]*Kāfī*, V, 337; three traditions are cited on the authority of Imam al-Bāqir and al-Ṣādiq.

[46]The Arabic is *zurq* pl. of *zarqā'*, meaning a person whose eye colour is *zurqa*, i.e. blue (light or dark or of a middling tint), blueness of the eye, or grayness of the eye, or a greenish hue in the eye (greenness meaning dust colour intermixed with blackness or deep ash colour in the iris of the eye). Lane, s.v. z-r-q. *Kāfī*, V, 340. I have preferred 'blue eyes' rather than 'deep ash-coloured eyes'. Of course, there are not many blue-eyed Arabs, but they are considered in this tradition very desirable and are thought to bring good luck.

[47]In the text it is *'anhu* meaning that this tradition as well as the following traditions are reported on the same authority as cited in the previous tradition. The Urdu translator has incorrectly taken *'anhu* to mean Ja'far al-Ṣādiq and Fyzee followed it.

[The Messenger of God]: He said, 'It is the good fortune of a woman to have been a virgin [before her marriage].'

[The Messenger of God]: He said, 'Marry a dark woman who is prolific (*walūd*), and not a beautiful woman who is barren (*'āqir*), for verily, I shall pride myself [on your numbers] over other communities on the Day of Resurrection.'[48]

[The Messenger of God]: He said, 'The best of women is the virtuous and the passionate (*ghalima*)'—chaste as regards herself and protective of her treasures, and passionate with her husband.[49]

[The Messenger of God]: He said, 'I warn you not to marry foolish women; for verily, association with them is a calamity and their offspring [who cannot manage their own affairs] will be a [terrible] waste.'[50]

[The Messenger of God]: He said, 'The best women in my community are those that have fair faces and modest dower.'[51]

[The Messenger of God]: He said, 'Women are of four kinds: Uniting, unifying [relatives and friends];[52] spring-like, prolific [bearing children annually];[53] divisive and oppressive;[54] a lice-infected halter round the neck!'[55]

[The Messenger of God]: He said, 'A woman is like a necklace; so let a man consider what he is wearing round his neck.'[56]

[The Messenger of God]: He said, 'If there is any ill luck in anything; it is to be found in a woman (wife), a house, or an animal.'[57]

[48]*Kāfī*, V, 338; variant readings are: Marry an ugly woman (*saw'ā'*) who is prolific; marry a virgin (*bikr^{an}*) who is prolific.

[49]Ibid., V, 329; a tradition of the Prophet transmitted on the authority of Imam al-Ṣādiq.

[50]Ibid., V, 358; Ṭūsī, *Tahdhīb al-aḥkām*, VII, 406. See also n. 14 above in this chapter.

[51]*Kāfī*, V, 329; Ṭūsī, *Tahdhīb al-aḥkām*, VII, 404.

[52]Gloss in MS Y, taken from Ibrāhīm al-Sayfī's *Kitāb al-najāḥ*, explains the Arabic phrase *jāmi'^{un} mujmi'^{un}* as follows: A virtuous wife who advances her husband's affairs as well as hers and unites the family with love and kindness. It could also mean that she possesses good qualities and excellent character.

[53]The Arabic is *rabī'^{un} murba'^{un}*. Gloss from *Kitāb al-najāḥ*.

[54]The Arabic is *ḥarib^{un} muqmi'^{un}*. Gloss from *Kitāb al-najāḥ*. In *Kāfī*, V, 327, 328; two variants: *karib^{un} muqmi'^{un}* (troublemaker), *kharqā' muqmi'^{un}* (stupid).

[55]The Arabic is *ghull^{un} qamil^{un}* lit. a lousy shackle for the neck. It is metonymically applied to a wife/woman of evil disposition; originating from the fact that the *ghull* (shackle) used to be of thongs with hair that became infested with lice. Lane, gh-l-l; gloss from *Kitāb al-najāḥ*.

[56]*Kāfī*, V, 336.

[57]'Ill luck arises concerning a woman, a house and a horse.' *Mishkāt*, II, 159; Robson, I, 659; transmitted by Bukhārī and Muslim. *Kāfī*, V, 569; it adds, 'Ill luck in a woman consists of [her asking] for a lot of bridal money or her having a sterile womb.'

Abū Ja'far Muḥammad b. 'Alī: He said, 'My father ['Alī b. al-Ḥusayn] saw a woman at one of the stations of *ḥajj* (*mashā'ir*) in Mecca. He found her to be pleasing in her manners, and so he asked [people] about her and whether she had a husband. They said, "No." Thereupon he proposed to her and she agreed to marry him. [The Imam] went into his wife but never inquired about her station in life (*ḥasab*).

'A man from the Anṣār[58] who was friendly with [the Imam], upon hearing of this marriage, was troubled and disturbed that she was of a lowly station in life, and [feared that] people would gossip about her. He, therefore, continued to inquire about her until he discovered that she belonged to a house of the Dhu 'l-Jaddayn branch of the Shaybānī tribe.[59] Then he came to [Imam] 'Alī b. al-Ḥusayn and spoke to him about it. The [Imam] said, "Today I shall teach you an opinion sounder than yours. Do you not know that when God sent Islam [to the world], He thereby elevated the low, perfected the imperfect, and honoured those that were censured? No blameworthiness (*lu'm*) attaches to a Muslim, blameworthiness is restricted to the days of the *jāhilīya*.[60] The Messenger of God emancipated a slave girl of his and married her, even though he had wives belonging to the tribe of Quraysh with him,[61] and in the Messenger of God we have a good example (*uswa ḥasana*) for anyone who has hopes in God and the Last Day."'

Abū Ja'far Muḥammad b. 'Alī: He said, 'The Messenger of God delivered a sermon on the day of the conquest of Mecca.[62] He praised God and said, "O people, God has abolished the pretensions (*nakhwa*) of the days of *jāhilīya*, and the boastfulness regarding lineage. Surely, you are all the sons of Adam and Adam [was created out] of earth. The best of the slaves of God are those that are the most pious among them. Arabness does not come from a father or progenitor; but it is [derived from] the spoken

[58]*The Pillars of Islam*, I, 13, n. 18.

[59]Banū Shaybān, an Arab tribe, and an important *baṭn* of Bakr b. Wā'il. *EI*², s.v. Shaybān.

[60]Jāhilīya, see *The Pillars of Islam*, I, 281, n. 46. See also *Kāfī*, V, 348–9. Kulaynī cites three traditions with slight variations.

[61]Six of the Prophet's wives were from the Quraysh. The Prophet had selected Juwayrīya, Ṣafīya, and Rayḥāna from the captives of different campaigns, freed them and married them. Ṭabarī, *History of al-Ṭabarī*, IX, 133–7.

[62]The conquest of Mecca was in the month of Ramaḍān in the year A.H. 8. The Messenger of God stood at the door of the Ka'ba and delivered a sermon. See Ibn Isḥāq, *al-Sīra*, IV, 54–5; Guillaume, 552–3; Ṭabarī, *The History of al-Ṭabarī*, VIII, 181–2. The sentence 'Arabness ... pedigree' as reported by Nu'mān is not in the aforementioned sources.

eloquent tongue. He whose learning is small will not attain that quality by his pedigree. Listen! All the blood-feuds of the pre-Islamic days, and their rancour, are below my feet (or abolished) till the Day of Resurrection.'"

Ja'far b. Muḥammad: He said, 'The Messenger of God contracted the marriage of Miqdād b. al-Aswad[63] with Ḍubā'a bint al-Zubayr b. 'Abd al-Muṭṭalib.'[64] The [the Imam] added, 'Verily the Messenger of God married her to Miqdād to show humility in marriage so that the people would follow the example of the Messenger of God and would learn that *the noblest of you in the sight of God is the most god-fearing of you* (49:13).[65] Now Zubayr was the full brother of 'Abd Allāh, the Prophet's father.'[66]

[Ja'far b. Muḥammad]: [He said], 'The Messenger of God had married several *mawālī*[67] to Qurayshī women to show humility in respect of marriage and [to show] that people follow the example of God's Messenger. The Prophet [for that reason] had married Miqdād b. al-Aswad to Ḍubā'a bint al-Zubayr b. 'Abd al-Muṭṭalib, and had also married Tamīm b. Ḥabīb al-Dārī[68] to a woman of the Hāshimites of [the sub-tribe of] 'Abd Manāf.'[69]

Abū Ja'far Muḥammad [b. 'Alī]:[70] He was asked about a woman who is *mu'mina* (a believer) [of Shī'ī persuasion] and possesses [a lot] of knowledge, but [she lives] in a place where there is no one belonging to her religion. Should she marry among them [outside her circle of religion]? [The Imam] said, 'She should not marry other than one of her own faith.[71]

[63]He is Miqdād b. 'Amr, see n. 8, Chap. 9. The Prophet married him to Ḍubā'a bt. al-Zubayr b. 'Abd al-Muṭṭalib. Ibn Sa'd, III/1, 114–16.

[64]Zubayr b. 'Abd al-Muṭṭalib died while the Prophet was thirty and some years old. Balādhurī, *Ansāb al-ashrāf* (ed. al-Azem), II, 31.

[65]Arberry, *The Koran*, II, 232.

[66]Zubayr was 'Abd Allāh's full brother. Balādhurī, *Ansāb al-ashrāf* (ed. al-Azem), II, 23. *Kāfī*, V, 347; reported on the same authority; Ṭūsī, *Tahdhīb al-aḥkām*, VII, 395.

[67]*Mawālī* pl. of *mawlā* is a term of theological, historical, and legal usage with varying meanings in different contexts. *Mawlā* generally means a person linked by *walā'* to another person. More commonly it designates a person/party to an unequal relationship of assistance, i.e., a master manumitter, benefactor, or patron on the one hand, and a freedman, protégé, or client on the other. For details see *EI*[2], s.v. Mawlā.

[68]Tamīm al-Dārī, a Christian from Palestine, embraced Islam and became a Companion of the Prophet. His *nisba*, Dārī, indicates that he belonged to Dār, a subdivision of the Lakhm tribe (i.e. Arab origin). *EI*[2], s.v. Tamīm al-Dārī.

[69]Hāshim b. 'Abd Manāf was a great grandfather of the Prophet. *EI*[2], s.v. Hāshim b. 'Abd Manāf.

[70]Addition from MS Q.

[71]As in MS Q. The printed text is corrupted. The correct reading is: *Hal tatazawwaj minhum? Qāla, lā tatazawwaj illā man ...*

As for you [men], there is no harm if a man among you marries a simple-minded (*balhā'*)[72] woman belonging to the weaker segment of the society (*mustaḍ'afa*).[73] But as for a woman who bears enmity towards the Imams (*nāṣiba*), and who is the daughter of a Nāṣibī,[74] certainly not. There is no honour in it. The woman takes on the manners of her husband who turns her towards his own opinions. Hence, marry [women] from amongst the skeptics (*shukkāk* pl. of *shākk*, those who entertain doubts about the Imams) if you like,[75] but do not marry your daughters to them. But as for those who oppose the People of the House of Muḥammad and show open hatred to them, and are well known for their feelings, do not mix with them, do not be affectionate to them, and do not enter into marital relations with them.'

[Abū Ja'far Muḥammad b. 'Alī]: He was asked whether a man could marry a wicked and dissolute woman. He said, 'It does not behove him to do so; a woman of chastity and modesty is better. If he has a slave girl, he may, if he wishes, cohabit with her; but he should not make her an *umm walad*[76] by reason of the saying of the Prophet, "Choose [a proper place] for your seed".'

Ja'far b. Muḥammad: He spoke about the Word of God: *The adulterer shall not marry save an adulteress or an idolatress, and the adulteress none shall marry save an adulterer or an idolater. All that is forbidden unto believers* (24:3), and said, 'This verse was revealed in respect of certain polytheistic women who were notorious for adultery; during pre-Islamic times they carried on their trade as prostitutes for hire.[77] Among them was Ḥabība and al-Rabāb and Sārah.[78] On the conquest of Mecca the Messenger of

[72]*Kāfī*, V, 354; *al-bulh* pl. of *al-balhā'*, and they are described as 'those who have no knowledge and bear no enmity [towards the Imams].'

[73]For the explanation of the term see *The Pillars of Islam*, I, 278, n. 39.

[74]*Nāṣib*, see *The Pillars of Islam*, I, 190–1, n. 128; *Kāfī*, V, 352–5; the prohibition applies both to men and women who bear enmity towards the Imams (*nāṣib* and *nāṣiba*).

[75]The vocalization in the edited text *al-shikāk* is incorrect. The Urdu translation is also incorrect, Fyzee was misled by the latter. *Kāfī*, V, 352, 353. Could *shukkāk* refer to *ahl al-shakk* (people of doubt)? The 'doubters' were one of the three *firaq* (groups) that appeared following the third caliph 'Uthmān's murder. The first said that 'Uthmān was killed justly; the second said that he was killed unjustly; and the third professed not to know whether he was killed justly or unjustly. For details see Crone and Zimmermann, *Epistle of Sālim*, 331–2.

[76]*Umm walad*, see *The Pillars of Islam*, I, 283, n. 62. *Kāfī*, V, 357; identical position.

[77]*Kāfī*, V, 358–9.

[78]The Prophet had instructed his commanders when they entered Mecca only to fight those who resisted them, except a small number who were to be killed even if they were found beneath the curtains of the Ka'ba. Among them was ... 'Abd Allāh b. Khaṭal ... . He had two singing girls, Fartanā and her friend, who used to sing satirical songs about the

God had declared their blood to be lawful because they used to urge the polytheists to fight God's Messenger. If, however, a man marries a woman well known for her dissolute behaviour, then he should make her chaste.[79] A man asked the Messenger of God, "O Messenger of God, what is your opinion about my wife who does not repel the advances of any man?" The Messenger of God said, "Divorce her." He said, "But I love her." The Messenger of God said, "If you wish, you may keep her [as your wife]."'

PROPOSING MARRIAGE TO WOMEN (*IKHTIṬĀB AL-NISĀ'*)

The Messenger of God: He forbade a man to propose to a woman after his brother [Muslim] had done so; he meant that [this should not be done] after the two sides had agreed and the woman had consented. But if others had sent in their proposals [before final agreement], there was no harm in it, for the woman can marry the person she desires. This is like more than one offer for merchandise,[80] and we have mentioned this in the Book of Sales.[81]

The Messenger of God: He said, 'When a man desires to marry a certain woman, there is no harm in his having a brief look at her because he is only like a purchaser.'[82] The Messenger of God meant that he should glance furtively at her if the opportunity occurs, without having some secret and evil thoughts, and without deriving any undue pleasure. In His Book, God has commanded the faithful to lower their eyes, and said: *Tell the believing men to lower their gaze and be modest* (24:30).

Ja'far b. Muḥammad: He was asked about a man who, when a woman

Prophet, so he ordered that they should be killed with him ... and Sārah, a freed slave of one of the Banī 'Abd al-Muṭṭalib ... Sārah had insulted the Prophet in Mecca ... . As for Ibn Khaṭal's two singing girls, one was killed and the other ran away until the Prophet, when asked for immunity, gave it to her. Similarly, Sārah [was granted immunity]. Ibn Isḥāq, *al-Sīra*, IV, 51–3; Guillaume, 550–1; Asad, *al-Qiyān*, 86–7, 88.

[79]The Arabic is *fa 'l-yuḥṣin bābahu* lit. fortify his own gate. *Kāfī*, V, 359–60; if someone commits adultery, then repents and marries, the marriage is lawful.

[80]It is a free rendition. The Arabic is [*lā yasūm al-rajul*] or *sawm al-rajul 'alā sawm akhīhi* (anyone of you shall not purchase in opposition to his brother). The prohibition applies both to the seller and the buyer. Lane, s.v. s-w-m. 'A man must not ask a woman in marriage when his brother has done so already, until he marries or gives her up.' *Mishkāt*, II, 171; Robson, I, 668; transmitted by Bukhārī and Muslim.

[81]See n. 107, Chap. 1.

[82]'When one of you asks a woman in marriage, if he is able to look at what will induce him to marry her, he should do so.' *Mishkāt*, II, 163, 164; Robson, I, 661, 662. *Kāfī*, V, 370–1; Ṭūsī, *Tahdhīb al-aḥkām*, VII, 435.

passed by, looked at her from behind. He said, 'Would any of you be happy if a man were to do so at his wife (*ahl*)?[83] Choose for the people what you would for yourselves.'

[Ja'far b. Muḥammad]: He was asked about the Word of God in the story of Moses regarding the saying of the woman: O *my father! Hire him! For the best (man) that you can hire is the strong, the trustworthy* (28:26).[84] As for strength, that was what she saw at the watering of the sheep; and as for her calling him 'trustworthy', when she came to call Moses to her father, she walked ahead of him; so he came forward and walked in front and said, '[Please] remain behind and show me the way, for we are a people who do not look at women from behind.'

'Alī: He was asked about a man who looks at a woman while she passes by. He said, 'You are entitled to look at her for the first time; for the second look, you have no right;[85] and the third look is a poisoned arrow from the arrows of Satan. He who avoids it for none other than God, will be rewarded by God with a faith the taste of which he will enjoy to the full.'[86]

Ja'far b. Muḥammad: He said, 'Those who cast their glances at women from behind, will not be saved from the same trouble in respect of their own women.'

Every one should lower his gaze from women, save those permitted by the Messenger of God, namely the man who looks at a woman for the purpose of marriage. A similar rule applies to casting a glance at those who are forbidden in marriage, and this [principle] is established by the Messenger of God.

Ja'far b. Muḥammad—his father—his ancestors—'Alī: He said, 'A man came to the Messenger of God and said, "Shall I ask permission from my mother to go into her presence?" The Messenger of God said, "Yes. Would it please you if you saw her naked?" The man said, "No." The Messenger of God said, "Then seek her permission." The man said, "What about my sister, O Messenger of God? She displays her hair before me."

[83]*Ahl* also means nearest relative. The last sentence could also be translated as: Permit something to the people what you would permit to yourself.

[84]The woman referred to is the daughter of the prophet Shu'ayb, identified with Jethro, the father-in-law of Moses, mentioned in the Bible. Ṭabarī, *Tafsīr* (Beirut), xx, 39–41; the same explanation as that given by Nu'mān. *EI*[2], s.v. Shu'ayb; Exodus, 2:16–21, 3:1, 18:12.

[85]'Do not give a second look, for while you are not to be blamed for the first, you have no right to the second.' *Mishkāt*, II, 164; Robson I, 662.

[86]'If a Muslim happens to look at a woman's beauties and then lowers his eyes, God will produce for him an act of worship whose sweetness he will experience.' *Mishkāt*, II, 167; Robson, I, 664.

The Messenger of God said, "No [this should not be done]." The man said, "Why?" The Messenger of God said, "I have fears for you if some of her charms are displayed before you, the devil may provoke you!"'[87]

The Messenger of God: He said, 'When one of you happen to kiss a female relation who is not permitted to marry you (*dhāt maḥram*) and who is a menstruating woman, you should kiss her between the eyes or on the head, and avoid the cheeks and the mouth.'

Many prayers (*du'ā'* pl. *ad'iya*) are reported from the People of the House for recitation at marriages and at marriage sermons (*khuṭab* pl. of *khuṭba*) and their mention would involve needless prolixity. None of them is fixed or incumbent; he who prays to God according to his ability and asks for His blessing, will do well, indeed.

When the man who pronounces the contract of marriage praises God, blesses the Prophet, mentions some of his sayings, and then makes the contract as it should be done, he has verily fulfilled his obligation.[88] It is related from the Messenger of God that he said, 'A *nikāḥ* without a sermon is like a mutilated hand.'[89]

Ja'far b. Muḥammad: Concerning the Qur'ānic verse: *There is no sin for you in that which ye proclaim or hide in your minds concerning your troth (betrothal) with women* until the words *except by uttering a recognized form of words* (2:235), he said, 'It is not proper for a man to make a regular [marriage] proposal to a woman during her *'idda* [legally prescribed period of waiting during which a woman may not remarry after being widowed or divorced]. However, God has permitted speaking obliquely (*ta'rīḍ*),[90] i.e. for a man to speak fair words and let the woman understand their true import. But no proposal should be made until the *'idda* is completed.'[91]

[For example] Abū Ja'far Muḥammad b. 'Alī [Imām al-Bāqir] visited Sukayna bint Ḥanẓala when her husband who was her cousin had just died. He saluted her and said, 'How are you, O daughter of Ḥanẓala?' She said, 'Very well, May I be thy ransom, O son of the Messenger of God.'

[87]Cf. *Kāfī*, V, 532–5; women's permission should be sought before entering into her presence.

[88]*Kāfī*, V, 373–9; Kulaynī has reported several sermons.

[89]'Every sermon which does not contain a *tashahhud* is like a hand cut off.' *Mishkāt*, II, 173; Robson, I, 670.

[90]*Ta'rīḍ* signifies speaking obliquely, equivocally, or indirectly; contrary to *taṣrīḥ* (to declare explicitly, openly). Lane, s.v. '-r-ḍ.

[91]*Kāfī*, V, 439–40; the Qur'ānic verse cited is: *But plight not your troth with women except by uttering a recognized form of words. And do not comsummate the marriage until (the term) prescribed is run* (2:235).

The Imam said, 'You know my kinship with the Messenger of God and with 'Alī, and [you know] my right [as Imam] and the [status of] my house among the Arabs.' She said, 'O Abū Ja'far, may God forgive you, are you proposing to me in my *'idda*?' The Imam said, 'I have not done so. I have only informed you of my status and position.'

[Similarly] the Messenger of God visited Umm Salama[92] bint Abī Umayya b. al-Mughīra al-Makhzūmī when she had just lost her husband, Abū Salama, her uncle's son. He continued to mention his own status and position in the eyes of God until the marks of the matting [on which he was sitting] were imprinted on the palms of his hands bearing his weight. But this [too] was not a proposal of marriage.

The Messenger of God: He proposed to Umm Salama, while 'Uthmān b. 'Affān[93] and Ṭalḥa b. 'Ubayd Allāh[94] had also sought her hand. So she sent word to the Messenger of God saying, 'O Messenger of God, I am an aged woman; I have many children; and I am excessively shy.' The Messenger of God said, 'As to your saying that you are aged, I am older than you; as to your saying you have children, your children will be among the children of the Messenger of God; and as to your shyness, I shall pray to God that he may remove it from you.' Now when the Messenger of God married her and she came to him, she said, 'O Messenger of God, it was not that I said a great deal [unnecessarily] to you; but I did not like that I should not inform you about matters concerning me.'

GOING INTO WOMEN AND BECOMING INTIMATE WITH THEM (*AL-DUKHŪL BI 'L-NISĀ' WA-MU'ĀSHARATUHUNNA*)

God says: *Consort with them in kindness* (4:19).

Ja'far b. Muḥammad—his father—his ancestors: When the Messenger of God married Maymūna bint Ḥārith, he gave a feast for her and served *ḥays*.[95]

[Ja'far b. Muḥammad]: He directed that feasts (*walīma*) be given on

[92]Umm Salama, see Ibn Isḥāq, *al-Sīra*, IV, 294; Guillaume, 793; see also *The Pillars of Islam*, I, 277.

[93]See *The Pillars of Islam*, I, 23, n. 19; *EI*², s.v. 'Uthmān b. 'Affān.

[94]In the edited text and MS Q: 'Abd Allāh, seems to be an error. See *The Pillars of Islam*, I, 23, n. 17.

[95]*Ḥays* is a dish made of dates mixed with clarified butter, crumbled bread, etc. Lane, s.v. ḥ-y-s. 'The Messenger of God held a wedding feast with *ḥays* when he married Ṣafiya.' Transmitted by Bukhārī and Muslim. *Mishkāt*, II, 191; Robson, I, 683. For Maymūna's marriage see *Kāfī*, V, 372; Ibn Isḥāq, *al-Sīra*, IV, 296; Guillaume, 794; Ṭabarī, *History of al-Ṭabarī*, IX, 135; Lings, *Muḥammad*, 281; Watt, *Muḥammad at Medina*, 60, 380, 394, 397.

the following occasions: (i) *'urs*, i.e. when a man has his wife conducted to him at the marriage;[96] (ii) *khurs*, i.e. the *'aqīqa* of which we have spoken;[97] (iii) *i'dhār*, i.e. the circumcision of a child;[98] (iv) *wakīra*, i.e. when a man returns from a journey.[99]

[The Messenger of God]: He said, 'As to the marriage feast (*walīma*), it is fit and proper (*ḥaqq*) [to have it on] the first day; the second day is a matter of custom (*ma'rūf*), but thereafter it is hypocrisy (*riyā'*) and show (*sum'a*).'[100]

[The Messenger of God]: Once he passed by [the habitations] of the Banū Zurayq[101] and heard the sound of music and said, 'What is this?' They said, 'O Messenger of God, so-and-so has married.' The Messenger of God said, 'His faith has been perfected; this is a marriage and not immorality (*sifāḥ*). A marriage should never be contracted in secrecy. Smoke [from the fire for cooking food] should be visible, the beat of drum heard. The beat of drum is the distinction between marriage (*nikāḥ*) and debauchery (*sifāḥ*).'[102]

[The Messenger of God]: He passed by a camp of Negroes, and they were beating their drums and singing.[103] When they saw him, they

[96]*'Urs* also means a marriage feast. Lane, s.v. '-r-s. 'The worst kind of food is that at a wedding feast to which the rich are invited and from which the poor are left out ... .' Transmitted by Bukhārī and Muslim. *Mishkāt*, II, 192; Robson, I, 684.

[97]*Khurs* also means a feast prepared on the occasion of the birth of a child. Lane, s.v. kh-r-s. For *'aqīqa* see Chap. 9.

[98]For circumcision see *The Pillars of Islam*, I, 154. *I'dhār* also means food/feast prepared on some joyful occasion or on the acquisition of something new. Lane, s.v. '-dh-r.

[99]*Wakīra* also means food that is prepared on the occasion of building or buying a house. Lane, s.v. w-k-r.

[100]Celebrating a wedding feast is highly recommended. A tradition states, 'God bless you! Hold a wedding feast, even if only with a sheep.' Transmitted by Bukhārī and Muslim. Another tradition states, 'Ibn Mas'ūd reported the Messenger of God saying about the wedding feast, "The food on the first day is a duty, that on the second is a *sunna*, but that on the third day is *sum'a* (to make men to see it and hear of it); and if anyone makes men hear of what he does, God will publish his hypocrisy on the Day of Resurrection."' *Mishkāt*, II, 191, 193; Robson, I, 683, 685. See also *Kāfī*, V, 373; reported from the same authority; Ṭūsī, *Tahdhīb al-aḥkām*, VII, 409.

[101]A clan of Khazraj, see Ibn Isḥāq, *al-Sīra*, III, 295, 358; Ibn Ḥazm, *Jamhara*, 357; Watt, *Muḥammad at Medina*, 154, 180.

[102]Marriage should be made publicly known, hence music, singing, and amusement are permitted. A tradition states, 'The distinction between what is lawful and what is unlawful is the song and tambourine at a wedding.' *Mishkāt*, II, 174; Robson, I, 670.

[103]Singing at weddings is permitted. 'Ā'isha said, 'I had a girl of the Anṣār whom I gave in marriage, and the Messenger of God said, "Why don't you sing, O 'Ā'isha, for this clan of the Anṣār likes singing?"' Transmitted by Ibn Ḥibbān. Another tradition states that the Anṣār liked to sing love songs. *Mishkāt*, II, 174; Robson, I, 670.

remained silent. He said, 'O Banū Arfada (a Negro tribe),[104] continue to do what you were doing, so that the Jews may know that there is latitude (*fusḥa*) in our religion.'

Abū Ja'far Muḥammad b. 'Alī: A man of his partisans came and said, 'O son of the Messenger of God, I came to Medina and stayed with a friend I knew; but I had no knowledge as to how he provided something for his amusement (*lahw*). And, behold, he had all instruments of diversion and pleasure (*malāhī*), and I had an experience the like of which I never had earlier.' The Imam said, 'You should perform the duties of a [good] neighbour until you leave him.' The man asked, 'But what, O son of the Messenger of God, is your opinion of such things?' [The Imam] said, 'The singing girls (*qayna*)[105] are [unlawful and] forbidden, but [the music and festivities] such as those at marriages are permissible.'[106]

Ja'far b. Muḥammad: He said, 'On the night when 'Alī married Fāṭima, the Messenger of God heard the beating of the tambourine (*daff*)[107] and asked, "What is this?" Umm Salama[108] said, "O Messenger of God, this is Asmā' bint 'Umays[109] beating the tambourine in order to give pleasure to Fāṭima so that she may not feel the absence of her mother who is dead." The Messenger of God raised his hands to the skies and prayed, "O God, give as much pleasure to Asmā' bint 'Umays as she has given to my daughter." Then he called Asmā' and asked her, "O Asmā', what is it that you say when you beat the tambourine?" Asmā' said, "We do not know

[104]Banū Arfada (or Arfida), mentioned in a tradition, is a class of the Abyssinians who danced. *Lisān al-'Arab*, s.v. r-f-d; Lane, s.v. r-f-d; see also Ibn Ḥazm, *Jamhara*, 4; Abyssinians are traced back to Arfida. The tradition that there is latitude (*fusḥa*) in our religion is transmitted by Ibn Ḥanbal. *Concordance*, s.v. f-s-ḥ.

[105]*Qayna* pl. *qaynāt* or *qiyān* means female singing slave. Following the Arab-Muslim conquests, music and singing developed in the holy cities of the Ḥijāz. However, due to later judicial disputations about the admissibility of the two pursuits, attempts were made to stem their spread. *EI*², s.v. Ḳayna; contains a bibliography of older sources and recent studies.

[106]'Āmir b. Sa'd said, 'I called on Qaraẓa b. Ka'b and Abū Mas'ūd al-Anṣārī at a wedding where slave girls were singing and said, "Is this being done in the presence of you two who are Companions of the Messenger of God and were present at Badr?" They replied, "Sit down if you wish and listen along with us, or go away if you like, for we have been given licence of amusement (*lahw*) at a wedding."' Transmitted by Nasā'ī. *Mishkāt*, II, 175; Robson, I, 671.

[107]Al-Rabayyi', daughter of Mu'awwidh b. 'Afrā', said, 'The Prophet came and entered when I had been conducted to [the home of] my husband, and sat on my bedding ... . Some little girls of ours began to play the tambourine ...' Transmitted by Bukhārī. *Mishkāt*, II, 171; Robson, I, 668. See also *EI*², s.v. Duff.

[108]Umm Salama, see n. 92 above in this chapter.

[109]She was married to Ja'far b. Abū Ṭālib, see *The Pillars of Islam*, I, 283, n. 59; 289.

what we speak, O Messenger of God. I only desired to give her pleasure." The Messenger of God said, "Do not use foul language (*hujr*)."'

In this report and similar ones, there is permission (*rukhṣa*) to use [music and entertainment] to induce people to attend a marriage and to distinguish it from debauchery.

Ja'far b. Muḥammad: He was asked about entertainment and music (*lahw*)[110] on occasions other than marriage and he forbade them, and recited the Word of God: *We created not the heaven and the earth and all that is between them in play. If We had wished to find a pastime (lahw^an), We could have found it in Our presence—if We ever did. Nay but We hurl the true against the false, and it doth break its head and lo! it vanisheth. And yours will be woe for that which ye ascribe (unto Him)* (21:16–18).

The Messenger of God: He said, 'I prohibit my community from dancing (*zafn*),[111] playing the flute (*mizmār*),[112] beating drums (*kūba*)[113] and playing a string instrument (*kinnāra*).'[114]

'Alī: A man was accused before him of having broken a Persian lute (*barbaṭ*),[115] and 'Alī dismissed the suit and did not make any order against the accused person.

Ja'far b. Muḥammad: He said, 'God never looks at those who participate in a gathering devoted to music and song (*majlis al-ghinā'*).[116] Singing is

[110]'Ā'isha said that when a bride was transferred to [the house of] one of the Anṣār, the Messenger of God said, 'Have you no amusement (*lahw*)? The Anṣār are delighted by amusement.' Transmitted by Bukhārī. *Mishkāt*, II, 171; Robson, I, 668. *Lahw* means game, pastime, amusement, while *malāhī* (pl. of *malhā*) refers to musical instruments, among other things.

[111]*Qāmūs*, s.v. z-f-n; Lane, s.v. z-f-n.

[112]*Mizmār*, a musical reed, or pipe, and what is called in Persian *nāy* (a flute). Lane, s.v. z-m-r; *EI*², s.v. Mizmār.

[113]*Kūba* pl. *kūbāt* means small drums, slender in the middle, and according to some the musical instrument called *barbaṭ*. Lane, s.v. k-w-b. Traditions about its prohibition are transmitted by Ibn Ḥanbal and Abū Dāwūd. *Concordance*, s.v. k-w-b; see also *Lisān al-'Arab*, s.v. k-w-b.

[114]*Kinnāra* pl. *kinnārāt*, for its different meanings see *Lisān al-'Arab*, s.v. k-n-r; a tradition prohibiting various instruments is cited.

[115]Lane, s.v. b-r-b-ṭ.

[116]The specific meaning of *ghinā'* is song or singing, however, it refers to music in general. *Ikhwān al-ṣafā'* (I, 183–241), whose Ismā'īlī authorship is accepted by the scholars, endorse this interpretation. At the beginning of Islam there was no opposition to singing, yet the four Rightly Guided Caliphs are reported to have been in opposition to any indulgence in listening (*al-samā'*) to singing or any music. As a result the rigid schools of jurisprudence prohibited it altogether and a whole library of literature—both for and against—came into existence. For details see *EI*², s.v. Ghinā'; Samā'.

the vilest of God's creations; it produces mischief (*nifāq*) and leads to poverty.'

[Ja'far b. Muḥammad]: He was asked about the Word of God: *And of mankind is he who payeth for mere pastime of discourse (lahw al-ḥadīth), that he may mislead from Allah's way* (31:6). [The Imam] said, 'Abū Ja'far [Imam al-Bāqir] said, "This refers to singing (*ghinā'*) and God has promised retribution by the Fire."'

[Ja'far b. Muḥammad]: He was asked about singing and he replied, 'Woe to you! When God will distinguish between the true and the false, where, in your opinion, will singing be?' The man said, 'By God, among the false, May I be your ransom.' The Imam said, 'This is sufficient for you [as an answer].'

[Ja'far b. Muḥammad]: He asked about the affairs of one of his acquaintances who visited him, and who said, 'May I be a ransom for you! Yesterday a certain person came to me, took me by the hand and led me to his house. He had a girl who sang and played [an instrument], and I was with him till evening.' [The Imam] said, 'Woe be to you! Did you not fear [what would have happened to you] if the command of God had come to you [that is, you had died] while you were there? It was a gathering at whose members God does not look. Singing is the vilest of God's creations, and the most evil; it leads to poverty and dissension (*nifāq*).'

[Ja'far b. Muḥammad]: He said, 'When a man plays the Persian lute in the morning, God will depute an evil spirit for forty days who will overpower all his limbs; and when this happens, God will remove modesty from him, and he will not care what he speaks or what is said to him.'

Abū Ja'far Muḥammad b. 'Alī: He said, 'Singing breeds dissension (*nifāq*) in the heart in the same manner as a palm tree grows a spadix.'

Ja'far b. Muḥammad: He said, 'A house of a song is a place not spared by calamity, it is a place where prayers are not accepted and where the angels do not enter.'

[Ja'far b. Muḥammad]: He was asked about the Word of God: *And those who will not witness vanity, but when they pass near senseless play (laghw), pass by with dignity* (25:72). He said, 'Among these are singing and chess (*shaṭranj*).'

[Ja'far b. Muḥammad]: He said to one of his companions, 'Where were you yesterday [evening]?' The man said, 'I thought he knew where I had been, so I said, "I passed by so-and-so, and he took hold of me and took me home. Then he sent for a girl of his and she sang."' [The Imam] said, 'Did you seek the protection of God for your property and family? Verily God does not look at the people of such a gathering.'

[Ja'far b. Muḥammad]: He said, 'While I was a young boy I stood listening at a place where there were flute players (*zammārīn*), drummers (*ṭabbālīn*), and other entertainers (*la''ābīn*), and my father [Imam Bāqir] passed by. So he took me by the hand and said, "Possibly, you have come across those who took malicious pleasure in Adam's [discomfiture]." I said, "And what may that be, O my dear father?" He said, "All that you see here of pastime, entertainment, and singing was created by the devil for his own malicious satisfaction when Adam was evicted from Paradise."'

[Ja'far b. Muḥammad]: He heard of the arrival of a group of people from Kūfa[117] who camped at the house of a singer, so he asked them, 'Why did you act in this way?' They said, 'We found no room anywhere else, O son of the Messenger of God, and did not know [his profession] till after we had camped.' [The Imam] said, 'If that is so, behave with dignity, for verily God says: *When they pass near senseless play, pass by with dignity*' (25:72).

[Ja'far b. Muḥammad]: He said, 'The buying and selling of song (*ghinā'*) is unlawful; listening to it is hypocrisy and teaching it produces disbelief.'[118]

[Ja'far b. Muḥammad]: On singing being mentioned, he said, 'My ears have never heard it, I swear by God.'

[Ja'far b. Muḥammad]: He was asked about the Qur'ānic verse: *So shun the filth of idols, and shun lying speech* (22:30), and he explained that 'the filth of idols' was chess, and 'lying speech' was song.

[Ja'far b. Muḥammad]: He was asked about listening to music and he forbade it, and recited the verse of the Qur'ān: *Lo! the hearing and the sight and the heart—of each of these it will be asked* (17:36). The hearing will be asked as to what it had heard, and the heart will be asked as to what it had believed, and the sight will be asked as to what it had seen.

All these reports have been related only to show that the lawfulness of the beating of drums at marriage feasts should not make a man believe that listening to singing is permissible. He should know that this was only for publicity at marriages which was duly approved.

The Messenger of God: He said, 'Lead your brides to their new homes [that of the bridegrooms] at night, and give a feast during the forenoon.'[119]

[117]During those days, Kūfa was the centre of Shī'ī activities even though the Imams lived in Medina. Generally the Kūfan partisans of the Imams would visit Medina when they came to perform their pilgrimage.

[118]Lengthy gloss in MS Y taken from Nu'mān's *Mukhtaṣar al-āthār* states that this prohibition does not apply to military parades and other celebrations attended by the Imams/caliphs and army commanders. The reason is that music and singing on such occasions are not meant for revelry and [sensual] delight.

[119]*Kāfī*, V, 372.

[The Messenger of God]: He said, 'There is no remaining awake at night except for three purposes: Reading the Qur'ān steadfastly (*tahajjud bi 'l-qur'ān*); seeking knowledge; leading the bride to her [new] home.'

[The Messenger of God]: He said, 'Let a man prepare himself to go to his wife as he desires her to prepare herself for him.' Abū Ja'far [Imam al-Bāqir] said that by this, the Messenger of God refers to cleanliness.

The Messenger of God: He said, 'When a wife is brought to her husband [after the marriage], let him pray two *rak'as* of prayer and put his hand on her forehead and say:

O God, make my wife auspicious for me, and make me auspicious for her. As You have united us, unite us in goodness, success, and blessing, and when you separate us, separate us in fairness. Then he should say: O God, all praise to God Who has guided me rightly when I was on the wrong path; Who has brought me from poverty to riches; has raised me from my lowly position, given honour to me in my debased condition, given protection to my family, coupled my celibacy with marital life, given a servant for my service, has made my loneliness amusing, and removed my baseness. O Lord, [I thank] you profusely, kindly invoking [your] blessing for what You have given me, and for what You have deemed to be my portion to honour me!'

Abū Ja'far Muḥammad b. 'Alī: A man said to the [Imam], 'O son of the Messenger of God, as you see, I am a man of great age. I have married a young virgin, and have not consummated the marriage, fearing that if she comes to me and sees me, she will take a disliking to me on account of my old age.' Abū Ja'far [the Imam] said, 'When she comes to you, tell [her relatives] that she should be ritually pure, and you too should be in the same condition. Then do not go to her until you have prayed two *rak'as* of prayer, and direct them to call upon her to do the same. Then praise God and bless the Prophet, and supplicate, and ask them to say "amen", while you are supplicating. Then say:

O God, provide me with her love, companionship, and consent, and similarly provide her with my love; and unite us with the best bonds and companionship; for You love what is lawful and hate what is forbidden and disharmonious [between us].'[120]

Ja'far b. Muḥammad: He said, 'When a man wishes to have sexual intercourse with his wife, let him take the name of God, and pray to Him to the best of his ability. He should say:

[120]Ibid., V, 507; reported from the same authority.

O God! If You have decreed that a successor should follow me, then let him be sincere to You [in faith] and do not give Satan any share, or interest, or portion in him; and make my child intelligent, and do not create in him any deficiency or superfluity [in limbs] and make his end happy.'[121]

The Messenger of God: He said, 'When a man has sexual intercourse with his wife, he should not bring about her orgasm quickly and when he has intercourse with her [he should satisfy her fully], and should give her *ṣadāq* (dower).'[122]

'Alī: He disapproved that a man should have sexual intercourse while facing the *qibla*.

['Alī]: He said, 'When a man has sexual intercourse with a woman and finds that he is about to ejaculate, and [therefore] separates from her and allows the semen to fall outside (*'azl* i.e. coitus interruptus), it is a kind of secret burying of a child at its birth (*al-wa'd al-khafīy*);[123] so do not do so.

'The Messenger of God prohibited people from practising *'azl* with a free woman without her consent, and with a slave girl (*ama*) without her master's consent.'

This arises when a slave girl has a husband for her [newly conceived] child would be the slave of her master, and so *'azl* is not permitted without her master's consent. Similarly, a free woman has the right to have a child, and therefore *'azl* is only permissible with her consent. As to the slave girl (*mamlūka*) there is no harm in practising *'azl*, as her consent need not be obtained.[124]

'Alī: He used to practise *'azl* with a slave girl (*jāriya*) named Jumāna [or Umm Jumāna].[125]

[121]Ibid., V, 508–10; similar traditions; Ṭūsī, *Tahdhīb al-aḥkām*, VII, 411.

[122]My translation of this passage is guided by glosses in MSS Q and Y taken from Nu'mān's *Kitāb al-īḍāḥ*. The scribe of MS Y could not understand the last word of this tradition, hence he writes: *wa-qawluhu fal-yaṣduqhā, wa-llāhu a'lam*. For the dower see 'The Account of Dower' below in this chapter and *Kāfī*, V, 417–18.

[123]Gloss in MS Q: This was a pre-Islamic practice due to their aversion to female babies. The Qur'ān states: *When the buried infant shall be asked for what sin she was slain* (81:8–9). When the Prophet was asked about *'azl* he said that it was *al-wa'd al-khafīy*.

[124]According to both Bukhārī and Muslim coitus interruptus (withdrawal of the penis before emission of semen to avoid conception) was permitted by the Prophet. Ibn Māja transmits that the Prophet forbade *'azl* from a free woman unless she gives permission. However, another tradition transmitted by Muslim states that practising *'azl* amounts to 'secret burying alive' (*al-wa'd al-khafīy*), and it refers to the Qur'ān: *And when the girl child that was buried alive* ... (81:8). *Mishkāt*, II, 182–5; Robson I, 677–9. *Kāfī*, V, 510; *'azl* is left to man's discretion.

[125]Addition in MS Q and some other MSS of Fyzee.

Ḥusayn b. ʿAlī: He used to practice *ʿazl* with a concubine (*surrīya*) of his.

Abū Jaʿfar Muḥammad b. ʿAlī: He was asked about *ʿazl* and he said, 'As for the slave girl (*ama*), there is no harm in it; but with a free woman, I disapprove of it, unless this was agreed to at the time of marriage.'[126]

Jaʿfar b. Muḥammad: He said, 'There is no harm in practising *ʿazl* with a free woman with her consent, or with a slave girl with her master's permission. There is no objection that it be stipulated at marriage. There is no harm in practising it with a feeding mother, fearing that conception might hurt the [breastfed] child.' This [the Imam] related from the Messenger of God.

[Jaʿfar b. Muḥammad]: He forbade sexual intercourse with a free woman when there was another [free woman] in the house, or when a child was looking on from its cradle.[127]

Abū Jaʿfar Muḥammad b. ʿAlī: He said, 'There is no harm if a man sleeps between two wives or concubines; but he should not have intercourse with one of them while the other is looking on.'

ʿAlī: He said, 'Looking at people having sexual intercourse leads to blindness.'[128]

Abū Jaʿfar: He used to forbid people from conversing during sexual intercourse and said, 'Verily, this is the cause of dumbness.'[129] He disapproved of sexual intercourse [with one's wife] while there was another [male] person in the house. But in the case of a slave girl, he permitted it.[130]

Abū Jaʿfar Muḥammad b. ʿAlī: He was asked whether he disapproved of any particular time [during the day or night] for having sexual intercourse. He replied, 'Yes. From the early dawn to the rising of the sun; from the setting of the sun to the end of twilight; during the night, when there is the eclipse of the moon, and during the day when there is the eclipse of the sun; during the day or the night when an earthquake takes place; and during the times of yellow, black, or red wind.[131]

[126]Ṭūsī, *Tahdhīb al-aḥkām*, VII, 417.

[127]*Kāfī*, V, 507; Nīsābūrī, *Ṭibb al-aʾimma*, 619–20.

[128]Nīsābūrī, *Ṭibb al-aʾimma*, 615–16, n. 1; the editor reports a slightly different tradition from Ṭabrisī.

[129]Ibid., 615; the editor reports from Ṭabrisī.

[130]Ṭūsī, *Tahdhīb al-aḥkām*, VII, 413.

[131]Ibid., VII, 411; Nīsābūrī, *Ṭibb al-aʾimma*, 615; reported from the same Imam. Yellow, red, and black winds refer to sandstorms when the horizon changes colours from yellow to red to black depending on the intensity of the storm.

'The Messenger of God once spent a night with one of his wives during which there was an eclipse of the moon, and nothing happened [that is, the Prophet did not have intercourse with his wife]. When it was dawn, he went to his prayer mat and the wife said, "O Messenger of God, why this hardship (*jafā'*) from you this night?" The Messenger of God said, "There was no hardship, but there was a solemn sign and I did not like to enjoy during this time; I did not wish to be among those pointed out by God in His Book: *And if they were to see a fragment of the heaven falling [down upon them], they would say: [It is only] a heap of clouds* (52:44)."'[132]

Then Muḥammad b. 'Alī [Imam al-Bāqir] said, 'I swear by Him Who sent Muḥammad with the apostleship and chose him for the prophethood and selected him for singular honour that when a man refrains from intercourse during these periods, he will be blessed with children who will make him happy.'[133]

Ja'far b. Muḥammad: He said, 'When a man marries a wife of tender age, he should not have sexual intercourse with her till she completes the age of nine years from the date of her birth.'[134]

'Alī: He disapproved of sodomy with a wife.[135]

The Messenger of God: He prohibited people from conversing with those women with whom marriage was lawful. He said, 'Men should never meet women in private; for, when a man meets a woman in privacy, Satan is the third among them.'[136]

Ja'far b. Muḥammad: He said, 'Conversing with women is one of the snares of Satan.'

The Messenger of God: He said, 'Fear God when you deal with women[137] for they are weak (*'ayy*), open, and exposed (*'awra*); they have been declared lawful to you by the trust [reposed in you] by God. They

[132]It refers to the pagan Meccans and their defiance to the Prophet. It means that if the Meccans should see a part of the heaven falling on them, they would not believe it until they were crushed to death by it. Bayḍāwī, *Tafsīr*, 696; Sale, *Koran*, 507. Nīsābūrī, *Ṭibb al-a'imma*, 615.

[133]*Kāfī*, V, 505–6; reported from the same authority with some variations in the wording; Nīsābūrī, *Ṭibb al-a'imma*, 617.

[134]*Kāfī*, V, 402; she should be either nine or ten.

[135]Intercourse with women through the anus is prohibited. *Mishkāt*, II, 184; Robson I, 678–9. See also *Kāfī*, V, 543, 547–54; Ṭūṣī, *Tahdhīb al-aḥkām*, VII, 415; Ibn Qayyim, *al-Ṭibb al-nabawī*, 241–7; a detailed discussion on the subject.

[136]'Whenever a man is alone with a woman the devil makes a third.' *Mishkāt*, II, 166; Robson, I, 663.

[137]*Mishkāt*, II, 16, 202; Robson, I, 546, 690; it is in the Prophet's sermon at the Farewell Pilgrimage. See Ṭabarī, *History of al-Ṭabarī*, IX, 113.

have been with you since you married them (*'awān*),[138] so treat their weakness with silence and conceal their bodies (*'awrāt*) in your homes.'[139]

[The Messenger of God]: He said, 'The best occupation for a faithful woman is spinning [thread or yarn].'[140]

[The Messenger of God]: When he administered the oath of allegiance to women, he took their promise that they would speak only with those men who were forbidden to marry them by law (*dhū maḥram*).

Ja'far b. Muḥammad: He said, 'Once a blind man sought the permission to be in the presence of Fāṭima whereupon she veiled herself. The Prophet said to her, "Why do you veil yourself from him when he cannot see you?" Fāṭima said, "O Messenger of God, even if he does not see me, I can see him and he smells the scent!" The Messenger of God said, "I bear witness that you are a portion of myself."'[141]

'Alī: He said, 'The Messenger of God asked us what was the best thing for a woman to do. None of us could answer; so I asked Fāṭima and she said, "The best thing for a woman is that she should not see any man, and that no man should see her." So I mentioned this to the Messenger of God and he said, "She spoke the truth. Verily, she is a part of me."'

The Messenger of God: He forbade women from looking at men, or going out of the house without the permission of their husbands, or entering the [public] baths without proper cause. And he said, 'Whichever woman discards her veil (*khimār*) in a house other than her husband's has indeed, disgraced her veil (*ḥijāb*).'[142]

[138]'*Awān* means a woman of middle age, neither young nor old, or a woman who has had a husband. Lane, s.v. '-w-n.

[139]'Act kindly towards women, for they were created from a rib and the most crooked part of a rib is its top. If you attempt to straighten it you will break it, and if you leave it alone it will remain crooked; so act kindly towards women.' Transmitted by Bukārī and Muslim. *Mishkāt*, II, 198; Robson, I, 688. See also *Kāfī*, V, 518–19, 539.

[140]Cf. *Kāfī*, V, 521.

[141]'Fāṭima is a piece of me, so he who angers her angers me.' Transmitted by Bukhārī and Muslim. *Mishkāt*, III, 255; Robson, II, 1350. 'Once Ibn Umm Maktūm, who was blind, came to see the Prophet while he was with 'Ā'isha and Ḥafṣa, so he said to his wives, "Stand up and go inside the house." They said, "But, he is blind." The Prophet said, "Even if he does not see you, you can see him."' *Kāfī*, V, 538.

[142]Gloss in MS Y states that both *khimār* and *ḥijāb* are used metonymically, the former alludes to body exposure and the latter to disgrace. The word *ḥijāb*, commonly translated as 'veil' and used to refer to Muslim women's traditional head, face, or body coverings, occurs seven times in the Qur'ān. The Qur'ānic usage provides valuable information about its basic and metaphorical meanings. *Ḥijāb*, according to Muslim scholars, was imposed at first on the Prophet's wives. The Qur'ānic verse 33:53 is interpreted as having such an injunction, see for example Ṭabarī, *Tafsīr* (Beirut), XXII, 25–9; Wāḥidī, *Asbāb al-nuzūl*, 254–5. It is worth noting that the said verse reads: .... *And when you ask his (the Prophet's)*

[The Messenger of God]: He said, 'A woman should not walk naked in front of her husband; nor should a man be naked with his wife.'

[The Messenger of God]: He forbade women from walking in the middle of a road and said, 'They have no right to the centre of the road.'[143] He forbade women from wearing conspicuous clothes and clanging ornaments when they go out of the house. He cursed women who resembled men (*al-mudhakkarāt min al-nisā'*), and men who resembled women (*al-mu'annathūn min al-rijāl*) [in clothes or deportment]. He forbade women from raising their voices except for necessity, and from staying the night at places other than their homes. And he forbade men from saluting women.[144]

[The Messenger of God]: A woman sent word to him and said, 'O

---

wives for any object, ask them from behind a curtain, (or a barrier, or a partition, min warā'i ḥijāb[in]); that is cleaner for your hearts and theirs. It does not mean veiling of women from head to toe. *Ḥijāb* in its Qur'ānic use does not refer to woman's clothing/veil, rather to a barrier, curtain. See for example 7:46, 17:45, 38:32, 41:5, 42:51, for its use in non-gender contexts.

The separation was later extended to all free Muslim women according to 33:59. It states: *O Prophet! Tell thy wives and thy daughters and the believeing women to draw their cloaks (jalābīb) round them (when they go out). That will be better, so that they may be recognized and not annoyed.* Both Qummī, II, 196, and Wāḥidī, *Asbāb al-nuzūl*, 257, consider that *ḥijāb* was imposed by this verse. Ṭabarī, *Tafsīr* (Beirut), XXII, 33–4, states that before the revelation of this verse free women as well as slave girls used to dress alike, and when they would go out in the evenings (they) would be annoyed by some wicked people. God, therefore, commanded the believing women not to resemble the slave girls in their clothing. Ṭabarī then discusses the differing opinions as to whether it implies veiling of the head and the face as well.

Another verse 24:31 states: *And tell the believing women to lower their gaze and be modest (or guard their private parts), ... and to draw their veils over their bosoms (wa 'l-yaḍribna bi-khumurihinna 'alā juyūbihinna).* Here the word *khimār* means 'a veil covering head and face'.

The Qur'ān stressing the desirability of modesty by further referring to the contrasting concept of *tabarruj* (immodesty). The verse 33:33 states: *Do not dress up fancily the way they used to dress during the Time of Ignorance (al-jāhiliyya).* Islam did not introduce veiling or seclusion, but it existed long before Islam in Byzantine and Sasanid Persia. In the Middle East the veil was historically worn to distinguish women of high status in society. With the expansion of Islam, wearing of the veil spread, especially in towns where intellectual movements developed. This spread contributed, to a large extent, to the keeping of Muslim women in seclusion. Most of the Muslim reformists have denounced this practice. In contemporary times *ḥijāb* is identified as part of an emergent Islamic consciousness and movement that has spread all over the Islamic countries. Most recently this movement has shifted from establishing Islamic identity and morality to asserting Islamic nationalism, resisting authoritarian regimes (that prevail throughout the Arab Muslim countries), and Western dominance. Resistance through *ḥijāb* or against it, has generated a heated discourse on gender, Islamic ideals, and women's status and liberation. *EI*[2], s.v. Ḥidjāb; *Oxford Ency of MIW*, s.v. Ḥijāb.

[143]*Kāfī*, V, 524.

[144]Ibid., V, 538; men should not salute women first.

Messenger of God, verily my husband went on a journey and ordered me not to go out of my house. Now my father is at the point of death. Can I go out to him?' The Messenger of God told the messenger, 'Tell her to remain at home and obey her husband.' She did so and her father died. So the Messenger of God sent word to her and said, 'Verily, God has pardoned your father for the obedience you showed to your husband.'[145]

[The Messenger of God]: A woman asked him, 'O Messenger of God, what is the right of the husband over the wife?' The Messenger of God said, 'She should not give in charity anything from his house without his permission; she should not refuse herself to him even if she is on the packsaddle;[146] she should not perform the supererogatory fast without his permission; she should not go out of the house without his permission. If she acts otherwise, she will be cursed by the angels of the sky and the earth, and the angels of God's anger and pleasure.' The woman asked, 'Among all the people, who are the persons who have the greatest rights over men?' The Messenger of God said, 'His parents.' The woman asked, 'Who are the persons who have the greatest rights over women?' The Messenger of God replied, 'Her husband.' The woman asked, 'O Messenger of God, have I no right [over him] as he has over me?' The Messenger of God said, 'No, not even one in a hundred.[147] If I had the

[145]Ibid., V, 519; despite several requests by the woman the Prophet advised her not to disobey her husband's command.

[146]'When a woman who has been called to come to her husband's bed refuses and he spends the night angry, the angels curse her till the morning.' Transmitted by Bukhārī and Muslim. Another tradition states, 'When a man calls his wife to satisfy his desire she must go to him even if she is occupied at the oven.' *Mishkāt*, II, 199, 203; Robson, I, 689, 691. See also *Kāfī*, V, 515.

This tradition, and many others transmitted by Nu'mān and other transmitters of Prophetic traditions, have grave theological, moral, and social consequences. They not only support the concept of mandating obedience to husbands, but also contribute to the denigration of the moral status of women. Regardless of the apologists' jargon as to how Islam liberated and honoured women, these traditions subjugate their honour to the will of men. It is highly unlikely that the Prophet or the early Shī'ī Imams would have uttered those words. A modern Syrian scholar of *ḥadīth*, Nāṣir al-Dīn al-Albānī (d. 1999), was revolted by the ugliness of these traditions, and did not accept them. He states that the *sharī'a* cannot endorse this genre of traditions as they violate the ethical principles of the Islamic message. Abou El Fadl, *Speaking in God's Name*, chap. 7, is a comprehensive treatment of the subject and is appropriately entitled, 'Faith-based assumptions and determinations demeaning to women.'

[147]The Messenger of God was asked, 'What right can any wife demand of her husband?' He replied, 'That you should give her food when you eat, clothe her when you clothe yourself, not beat her on the face, and do not revile her (or separate from her) except in the house.' *Mishkāt*, II, 203; Robson, I, 691. *Kāfī*, V, 513; reported on the authority

right to do so, I would have ordered a wife to prostrate herself before her husband.'[148]

[The Messenger of God]: He said, 'When a woman has knowledge of her Lord, believes in Him and His Prophet, and knows the excellence of the Prophet's family,[149] and prays five times, and fasts during Ramaḍān, and remains faithful to her husband and obeys him, she will enter Paradise by any of its gates as she wishes.'[150]

[The Messenger of God]: In speaking of women, he said, 'How will it be [on the Day of Judgement] with those women who [bedeck themselves] with gold [ornaments], put on silk [clothes], and take a great deal of trouble for the rich, but tire the poor?'

'Alī:[151] He said, 'He who complies with the wishes of his wife in four things, God will hurl him headlong in the Fire.' He was asked, 'What is this compliance, O Commander of the Faithful? 'Alī said, 'The demand to attend [marriage] feasts (*'urusāt*), to join mourning sessions (*niyāḥāt*), to go visiting the sick (*'iyādāt*)[152] and to visit [public] baths (*ḥammāmāt*).'

The Messenger of God: He prohibited people from beating women without good reason.[153]

'Alī: A man from the Anṣār came to the Messenger of God with his

---

of al-Bāqir. Instead of 'If I had the right ... her husband,' this tradition ends with the woman inquirer saying, '[I swear] by the One who sent you with truth as a prophet that no man will ever exercise authority over myself.' In another tradition a woman asks, 'O Messenger of God, [has the wife to be obedient to her husband] even if he is tyrannical?' The Messenger of God replied, 'Yes.' She exclaimed, '[I swear] by the One who sent you with truth that I will never marry a man.' *Kāfī*, V, 514.

[148]'If I were to order anyone to prostrate himself before another, I would order a woman to prostrate herself before her husband.' *Mikhkāt*, II, 203, 205–6; Robson, I, 691, 693. See also *Kāfī*, V, 514. According to *ḥadīth* scholars, the authenticity of these traditions ranges from weak (*ḍa'īf*) to good (*ḥasan gharīb*). Again, all of them are *āḥādī* (reports of singular transmission) and not *mutawātir*, i.e. transmitted throughout the first three generations of Muslims by a large number of transmitters that it is highly unlikely that they are fabricated. Abou El Fadl, *Speaking in God's Name*, 212ff.

[149]*Kāfī*, V, 557; 'And knows the rights of 'Alī.'

[150]A tradition reported by Anas states, 'When a woman observes the five prayers, fasts during Ramaḍān, preserves her chastity, and obeys her husband, she may enter Paradise by any of its gates she wishes.' *Mishkāt*, II, 202–3; Robson, I, 691.

[151]According to MS Q; in the edited text it is: *wa-'anhu*, i.e. the Messenger of God, which is incorrect.

[152]*Kāfī*, V, 522; instead of *'iyādāt*, it has *'īdāt*. It also adds, 'her demand for fine clothes'.

[153]'None of you must whip his wife as a slave is whipped and then have intercourse with her at the end of the day.' Transmitted by Bukhārī and Muslim. Another tradition states, 'A man will not be asked about why he beat his wife.' *Mishkat*, II, 199, 206; Robson, I, 688.

daughter and said, 'O Messenger of God, verily her husband has beaten her, leaving marks on her face, so award her compensation [retaliation].' The Messenger of God said, 'That is your right.'[154]

Thereupon God revealed the following: *Men are the qawwāmūn over women,*[155] *because Allah hath made the one of them to excel the other, and because they spend of their property (for the support of women). So good women are the obedient, guarding in secret that which Allah has guarded. As for those from whom ye fear rebellion, admonish them and banish them to beds apart, and scourge them. Then if they obey you, seek not a way against them* (4:34).[156]

The word '*qawwāmūn*'[157] means that men are *qawwāmūna bi 'l-adab*.[158] So, the Messenger of God said, 'I desired a certain thing, but God desired something else.'[159]

[154]This was the occasion of revelation for 4:34. See Ṭabarī, *Tafsīr*, VIII, 290–2; Wāḥidī, *Asbāb al-nuzūl*, 105–6.

[155]The word *qawwāmūn* in the above Qur'ānic verse is often used by the exegetes to argue the superiority of men over women by virtue of their physical strength. The word is generally translated as 'Men are in charge of women' (Pickthall), or 'Men are protectors and maintainers of women' (Yusuf Ali), 'The men are overseers over the women' (Bell), 'Men are the managers of the affairs of women' (Arberry), 'Men shall have the pre-eminence above women' (Sale), 'Les hommes ont autorité sur les femmes' (Blachère), 'Die Männer stehen über den Frauen' (Paret). Al-Hibri ('Muslim women's rights,' 51; idem, 'Islam, Law and Custom') has argued that the meaning of *qawwāmūn* as 'those of guiding and advising' in ancient Arabic dictionaries is more consistent with the general Qur'ānic view of gender relations than the one preferred by male jurists and traditional patriarchal exegetes. Furthermore, she adds, by restricting the woman to the home, society insured that women will almost always need to be supported and advised by some male. This point of view has encouraged oppressive males to move away from the Islamic ideal of marital relationships. See also *Majma' al-baḥrayn*, s.v. q-w-m.

[156]Muslim jurists of the past have generally understood this reference to beating in this verse of the Qur'ān restrictively. They have held that beating cannot be to the face and cannot cause pain. Abou El Fadl, *Conference*, 167–76, 177–88; idem, *Speaking in God's Name*, 210.

[157]This same word is used in the Qur'ān at two other places (4:135, 5:8), where Muslims are commanded to be the *qawwāmūn* of justice. Of course, it is translated differently by the translators. Abou El Fadl, referring to the verse 4:34, states that the word *qawwāmūn* is ambiguous. He further adds that the verse seems to hinge on the status of being a maintainer, guardian, or protector. Abou El Fadl, *Speaking in God's Name*, 210.

[158]As stated in the previous note the word *qawwāmūn* is ambiguous. The word *adab* also carries several meanings, hence it is not clear what Nu'mān meant by this expression. Given the tenor of Nu'mān's thought, he probably meant that men are overseers of good discipline of the mind and manners. In a report, Ṭabarī (*Tafsīr*, VIII, 291) explains the meaning as *al-rijāl ya'khudhūna 'alā aydīhinna wa-yu'addibūnahunna*, very similar to that of Nu'mān.

[159]It is obvious from the above report that the Messenger of God wanted to discipline the husband for beating his wife, but then he received the revelation 4:34, whereby God annulled retaliation (*qiṣāṣ*). Ṭabarī, *Tafsīr*, VIII, 291; Wāḥidī, *Asbāb al-nuzūl*, 106.

The Messenger of God: He said, 'Self-respect (*ghayra*) is a part of faith.[160] Any person who has discovered immorality even to the slightest extent in his wife (*fī ahlihi*), and has not felt it keenly, will be visited by a bird sent by God for forty mornings, consecutively. Each morning when he enters his house or goes out the bird will say to him, "Have self-respect." If the man still does not have any feeling [of remorse], the bird will rub his eyes with its wings, and [as a consequence,] if there is something good, the man will not see it; and if there is something vile, he will not object to it.'[161]

'Alī: He said, 'There is no bashfulness (*ghayra*) in doing a lawful thing.'[162]

The Messenger of God: He said, '*Jihād*[163] is prescribed for the men of my community, and bashfulness (*ghayra*) for the women; now the woman who exercises patience hoping for reward, will be given the same compensation as a martyr.'[164]

MARRIAGE CONTRACTED BY GUARDIANS AND THE EVIDENCE OF MARRIAGES (*NIKĀḤ AL-AWLIYĀ' WA 'L-ISHHĀD FI 'L-NIKĀḤ*)

God says: *So wed them [women] by permission of their folk* (4:25).

Ja'far b. Muḥammad—his father—his ancestors: The Messenger of God said, 'There is no marriage without a guardian (*walīy*) and two reliable witness (*shāhiday 'adl*).'[165]

[160]*Ghayra* also signifies jealousy, or a man's dislike of another's participating in that which is his right over his wife, or care of what is sacred, or inviolable. Lane, s.v. gh-y-r. See also *Kāfī*, V, 511; the section is entitled 'Jealousy of Women'.

[161]It implies that the man will be divested of 'the spirit of *īmān*', and will be called 'cuckold' (*dayyūth*, without jealousy and regardless of shame) by the angels. See *Kāfī*, V, 539–40; has a separate section on *al-ghayra*.

[162]Ibid., V, 541; reported from al-Ṣādiq.

[163]See *The Pillars of Islam*, I, 3, 422.

[164]*Kāfī*, V, 514; 'A woman's *jihād* consists of being obedient to her husband (or that she adorned herself for her husband).'

[165]The fundamental principle for a valid marriage in Ismā'īlī law is to have a guardian representing the bride and two witnesses. Even if the woman is a major she should have a guardian. In certain circumstances she can appoint her own guardian. 'There is no marriage without a guardian.' Transmitted by Bukhārī, Abū Dāwūd, Tirmidhī, Ibn Māja, Dārimī, and Ibn Ḥanbal. 'Marriage without two witnesses is not permissible.' Transmitted by Bukhārī. *Concordance*, s.v. n-k-ḥ; *Mishkāt*, II, 169; Robson, I, 665–6. According to the Twelvers, a woman who has reached maturity and is in control of her affairs can be married without *walīy*, or, if she likes, can appoint a guardian. *Kāfī*, V, 395–6; Ṭūsī, *Tahdhīb al-aḥkām*, VII, 377; idem, *al-Nihāya*, 467. The Mālikīs, Shāfi'īs, and Ḥanbalīs insist that even an adult

Ja'far b. Muḥammad: He said, 'The guardian should himself take responsibility for the contract of marriage; now the marriage of a man who marries a woman without a guardian, is void.'[166]

The Messenger of God: He forbade that a woman be married without being consulted.[167]

'Alī: He said, 'No man should give his daughter in marriage until he consults her respectfully; for, she knows best what is good for her. If she remains silent [when asked], or cries, or laughs, then she has consented; but if she refuses, the guardian should not contract her in marriage.'

'Alī: He said, 'Marriages contracted by the fathers of children below the age of puberty, are lawful; but when they grow up [and attain majority] the fathers have no such right.'[168]

'Alī: He said, 'When a marriage is contracted by an agent (*wakīl*), it is valid.'

['Alī]: He said, 'Where a Muslim woman appoints her Christian father or brother as her agent for the marriage, such a marriage is valid. But if a Christian agent arranges her marriage while she is a child this is not permissible, for, a non-Muslim cannot possess guardianship over a Muslim.'

['Alī]: He said, 'Where a woman appoints two agents and deputes to them the right to contract her marriage; and each of them marries her to a [different] man, the marriage which takes place first is valid.'[169]

---

woman must be contracted in marriage by her guardian. The Ḥanafīs, on the other hand, allow an adult woman to contract herself in marriage provided that she chooses a husband who is her 'equal' in respect of family, social standing, etc. Anderson, *Islamic Law*, 43–4.

The essential features of Islamic law of marriage go back to the pre-Islamic customary law. The Prophet reformed those old laws in a far-reaching way by improving the woman's position. The most important provisions are: the marriage contract must be concluded between the bridegroom and the bride's *walīy* (guardian), who must be a free Muslim of age and of good character; the guardian is bound to carry out the contract in accordance with the wishes of the woman; the marriage must be concluded in the presence of at least two witnesses who possess the legal qualifications for a witness, however according to both Kulaynī and Nu'mān a marriage without any witness is valid. *EI*², s.v. Nikāḥ.

[166]'If any woman marries without the consent of her guardian, her marriage is void.' *Mishkāt*, II, 168–9; Robson, I, 666.

[167]'A woman without a husband (whether previously married or not) must not be married till she is consulted, and a virgin must not be married till her permission is asked.' *Mishkāt*, II, 168; Robson I, 665; transmitted by Bukhārī and Muslim. *Kāfī*, V, 396–8.

[168]*Kāfī*, V, 403–4. All schools of law allow a guardian to contract a marriage of his minor ward. According to the Ḥanafīs the minors have an option to repudiate such a marriage when they attain majority in cases in which the guardian who acted for them was other than their father or grandfather. The Imāmī position is very similar to that of the Ḥanafīs. Anderson, *Islamic Law*, 44.

[169]Cf. *Kāfī*, V, 400, 401; Kulaynī cites quite different cases.

Abū Ja'far and Abū 'Abd Allāh: They said, 'The paternal grandfather represents his son [the father of the girl] in the marriage of his infant daughter; for the paternal grandfather has the prior right [of guardianship] unless the father of the girl has already given her in marriage. If both the father and the grandfather have contracted the child in marriage [to different persons], the marriage which takes place first is valid.'[170]

Ja'far b. Muḥammad: He said, 'If the father is absent and the brother contracts the marriage after being deputed by the woman, the marriage is valid.'

Abū Ja'far Muḥammad b. 'Alī: He was asked about a marriage contracted without witnesses. He said, 'God has mentioned witnesses only in divorce; and if a man did not have witnesses in a marriage, no blame attaches to him because it is a matter between him and God. But he who has witnesses, has made the question of inheritance certain, and is safe from the fear of the punishment of the ruling authority. The evidence of witnesses in a marriage is the more trustworthy and just course, and this is the rule of action.'[171]

Abū Ja'far Muḥammad b. 'Alī: He said, 'In a marriage, witnesses that can testify in matters of property are permissible, as is the testimony of women and slaves.'

Ja'far b. Muḥammad: He said, 'Where in a marriage one witness testifies that the bride's father gave her in marriage while the bride disapproved of it, and the other witness says that the marriage was with her consent, the marriage is valid.

'If in a marriage, one witness says that the *mahr* was one thousand [dirhams] and the other says the amount was two thousand and the wife claims the higher amount, the wife should be sworn and so too her witness.

'Where in a marriage one witness says that the wife was a virgin and of age,[172] and the other says that she was not a virgin (*thayyib*)[173] and she was married without her consent, the evidence is void [and the marriage is valid].'

[170]Ṭūsī, *al-Nihāya*, 465.

[171]*Kāfī*, V, 392. A marriage without witnesses is valid. In Sunnī law the presence of two eligible witnesses is a requirement of a valid marriage, but not in Shī'ī law. The Mālikīs dispense with the need for such witnesses provided that adequate publicity is given to the occasion when the wife is transferred to her new home. Anderson, *Law Reform*, 105.

[172]A variant reading: *bāligh*, gloss in MS Q. In the edited text and MS Q: *ṭifl* (an infant).

[173]*Thayyib* means a woman who has become separated from her husband because he has died, or who has been divorced, and has then become eligible for marriage. Lane, s.v. th-w-b.

DOWER
(*AL-MAHR*)[174]

God says: *And give unto the women [whom ye marry] free gift of their marriage portions* (*ṣaduqāt* pl. of *ṣaduqa*)[175] (4:4).

Ja'far b. Muḥammad—his father—his ancestors: 'Alī said in respect of the above verse, that God says, 'Give to them their *ṣaduqāt* whereby you made sexual intercourse lawful with them. Thus he who wrongs a woman in respect of her dower (*ṣadāq*) has indeed committed fornication by making her lawful to himself [without the payment of *mahr*].'[176]

[Ja'far b. Muḥammad]: The Messenger of God said, 'Verily, God forgives every man his sins except the man who wrongfully takes away the *mahr* of a woman, wrongfully denies payment to a labourer, or sells a free man as a slave.'[177]

'Alī: He said, 'The Messenger of God married each of his wives with a *mahr* of twelve and one half *ūqīya*[178] of silver. He married Fāṭima to me with a similar [amount of *mahr*].'[179] Each *ūqīya* is forty dirhams.

Ja'far b. Muḥammad [Imam al-Ṣādiq] said that each dirham at that time was of the weight of six *qīrāṭ*.[180] This amount is not fixed for *mahr*;

[174]*Mahr* (pl. *muhūr*) or *ṣadāq* in Islamic law is a gift given by the bridegroom to the bride at the time of the marriage contract and which becomes the wife's property. In pre-Islamic days, *mahr* was an essential condition for a legal marriage. Likewise, all the Prophetic traditions stress that the *mahr* is an essential part of the marriage contract. According to a tradition, transmitted by Bukhārī, the *mahr* is not only an essential condition for the legality of the marriage, but 'every marriage without *mahr* is null and void.' The jurists differ as to whether the *mahr* is a foundation of the marriage contract or its consequence. The Ḥanafīs, Shāfi'īs, and Ḥanbalīs consider it a result of the contract based on the Qur'ānic verse 2:236. The Mālikīs, on the other hand, basing their view on the verse 4:24 maintain that the *mahr* is an element in the conclusion of the contract and not its consequence. For details see *EI*^{2}, s.v. Mahr; El-Alami, *Marriage Contract*, 107–13. For dower cases in the Indian subcontinent, see Pearl, *Muslim Family Law*, 190–201.

[175]Both the words *ṣadāq* and *ṣaduqa* appear in the traditions. *EI*^{2}, s.v. Ṣadāḳ.

[176]'One who fixes the dower, but does not intend to fulfil his words is like a thief.' Another tradition states, 'One who marries a woman without intending to pay the dower is indeed committing fornication.' *Kāfī*, V, 388–9.

[177]Ibid., V, 387; reported from the same authority.

[178]*Ūqīya* is a weight of varying magnitude. Hinz, *Islamische Masse*, 34–5. See *Mishkāt*, II, 186; Robson, I, 681; the total of twelve and a half *ūqīya* was five hundred dirhams. Transmitted by Muslim. *Kāfī*, V, 380.

[179]Fāṭima's dower was insignificant. According to one tradition it consisted of an old and worn out garment, a coat of mail and a mattress of sheep's skin. Another tradition states that the *mahr* consisted of a coat of mail worth thirty dirhams. *Kāfī*, V, 381–2.

[180]*Qīrāṭ* (kerat, carat) is a measure of weight. Hinz, *Islamische Masse*, 27. See also *Kāfī*, V, 381.

but it is the *mahr* which the Messenger of God fixed for his wives because he liked equality between them, and God says: *And give unto the women (whom ye marry) free gift of their marriage portions* (4:4), and God did not fix either more or less in this regard. God says: [*And if ye wish to exchange one wife for another*] *and ye have given unto one of them a sum of money (however great), take nothing from it. Would ye take it by the way of calumny and open wrong?* (4:20).

Ja'far b. Muḥammad: He was asked about *mahr* and he said, 'It consists of what people agree to,[181] but it must necessarily be a known *mahr*, regardless of whether it be great or small, and there is no harm if it is commodities.'[182]

'Alī: He said, 'A man came to the Messenger of God and said, "O Messenger of God, I desire to marry this woman." The Messenger of God asked, "How much *mahr* will you give her?" The man said, "I have nothing." The Messenger of God observed that he was wearing a ring, so he said, "Is this ring yours?" The man replied, "Yes." The Messenger of God said, "Then marry her for the ring [as dower]."'

'Alī: He said, 'It is good fortune for a woman to have ease in marriage,[183] and to be prolific.'[184]

'Alī: He said, 'Do not be excessive in respect of the dower of women for this may lead to enmity.'[185]

Abū Ja'far Muḥamamd b. 'Alī: He said, '[Once Imam] al-Ḥasan[186] b. 'Alī married a woman and sent her one hundred slave girls, and with each of them a thousand dirhams.'

Ja'far b. Muḥammad: He said, 'It is a man's right to marry a woman on the condition that he would teach her a chapter of the Qur'ān [as *mahr*], or give her something or other.'[187]

[181]*Kāfī*, V, 382–3; reported from al-Ṣādiq.

[182]As the *mahr* is a token for the validity of the marriage, goods given as *mahr* need not be expensive. A tradition states, 'If anyone gives as a dower to his wife two handfuls of flour or dates, he makes her lawful for him.' Another tradition states that a woman of the Banū Fazāra was married for a dower of two sandals. *Mishkāt*, II, 189; Robson, I, 682.

[183]To have ease in marriage (*taysīru nikāḥihā*) means a woman who does not ask for excessive *mahr*.

[184]This is a free rendering of *taysīru raḥimihā*, in the light of what Nu'mān has discussed earlier in this chapter. Fyzee's translation, 'easy [good] relations with her kindred', probably influenced by Mubārkpūrī's literal Urdu translation of the Arabic, does not convey the intended meaning of the tradition.

[185]'Do not go to extremes in giving women their dower ...,' is ascribed to 'Umar b. al-Khaṭṭāb. *Mishkāt*, II, 189; Robson, I, 681.

[186]According to MS Q, in the edited text: al-Ḥusayn. In MS Q also it was al-Ḥusayn, but then it was corrected.

[187]The Messenger of God arranged for the marriage of a woman and asked the man

'Alī: He said, 'Marriage does not take place without a *mahr*.'

Ja'far b. Muḥammad: He was asked about the Word of God: *O Prophet! Lo! We have made lawful unto thee thy wives* (33:50), and he said, 'God made it lawful for him to marry [any number of] wives he desired, and He allowed him to marry believing women without *mahr*. This is [the meaning of] the verse [as it further states]: *... and a believing woman if she give herself unto the Prophet, and the Prophet desire to ask her in marriage* (33:50). Then God made it explicit that this was a command restricted to the Prophet as God says: *A privilege for thee only, not for the (rest of) the believers—We are aware of that which We enjoined upon them concerning their wives and those whom their right hands possess—that thou mayst be free from blame*' (33:50).

Then Ja'far b. Muḥammad [Imam al-Ṣādiq] said, 'It is not lawful [for a woman] to give herself to any one except the Messenger of God. As for the others, it is not lawful for them to marry without the payment of *mahr* which should be determined before the consummation of marriage, [regardless of] whether it be clothes, money, something else, great or small [in value].'[188]

'Alī: A man married a woman [on the condition that the *mahr* would be] according to her desire (*'alā ḥukmihā*). Later she demanded an excessive [amount of *mahr*] from him. [The case was brought before 'Alī], so he decided that she was entitled to a *ṣadāq* equal to that of a woman of her like [i.e. her station in life], without any decrease or increase (*lā waks wa-lā shaṭaṭ*).[189]

Ja'far b. Muḥammad: He was asked about a man who was deputed to fix the *ṣadāq* of his wife, and fixed it for a small amount. [The Imam] said, 'She is entitled to a *mahr* equal to that of a woman of her like [the same station in life].'

Abū Ja'far Muḥammad b. 'Alī: He was asked about a man who married a woman leaving the amount of *mahr* to her decision (*'alā ḥukmihā*). He said, 'If she is excessive in her demand, she will not be entitled to any more than the *mahr* of the Prophet's wives, namely five hundred dirhams.'[190]

Abū Ja'far Muḥammad b. 'Alī: He said, 'If a man marries a woman and she agrees to his decision (*'alā ḥukmihi*) as to dower, whatever has

---

to teach her some of the Qur'ān. Transmitted by Bukhārī and Muslim. Another tradition states that Abū Ṭalḥa married Umm Sulaym and the dower between them was his acceptance of Islam, because Umm Sulaym had embraced Islam before Abū Ṭalḥa. *Mishkāt*, II, 188, 190; Robson, I, 681, 682. See also *Kāfī*, V, 384, 385.

[188] *Kāfī*, V, 389–90; 392–3.

[189] Lane, s.v. sh-ṭ-ṭ; the tradition is cited.

[190] Ṭūsī, *Tahdhīb al-aḥkām*, VII, 356.

been fixed by him is valid.' He was asked, 'How is it that the husband's decision against her is lawful, whereas, if she has fixed the amount higher than that of the wives of the Prophet, her decision against him is not valid?' He said, 'When she had agreed to the husband's decision [as to dower], she has no right to deny herself to him whatever be the amount he has fixed. But when the husband leaves the decision to the wife, she has no right to go beyond [the amount of] the *sunna*.[191] But if he divorces her or dies before consummation and the dower has not been fixed, then she is entitled to a *mut'a* (present),[192] or inheritance, but not dower.'[193]

The Messenger of God: He prohibited *shighār* in marriage. The meaning of *shighār* is that A gives his daughter in marriage to B, on the condition that B gives his daughter in marriage to A, and no *ṣadāq* is paid by either party. He said, 'There is no *shighār* in Islam.'[194]

'Alī[195] said, 'This [*shighār*] was a form of marriage prevalent in pre-Islamic times. There is no harm in contracting a marriage without naming [a *mahr*], but the husband should not consummate the marriage until he gives the wife something. God says: *It is no sin for you if ye divorce women while yet ye have not touched them, nor appointed unto them a portion (farīḍa)*[196] *[i.e. dower or bridal gift]*' (2:236).

Ja'far b. Muḥammad: About the case of a man who marries a woman but does not fix her *ṣadāq*, and he dies or divorces her before consummation, he said, 'If he divorces her, she is not entitled to *ṣadāq*; but she is entitled to a present (*mut'a*) and she need not observe the *'idda*.[197] If he dies before consummation, she is not entitled to *ṣadāq*,[198] but she inherits from him, and he inherits from her, and she has to observe the *'idda*. [On the other hand] if he has fixed the amount of the *ṣadāq* and then divorces her before

[191] *Kāfī*, V, 383–4; reported from the same Imam.

[192] It is called *mut'at al-ṭalāq*, see Chap. 11, section 'Gifts to a Divorced Wife.'

[193] *Kāfī*, V, 384; a separate tradition transmitted from the same Imam.

[194] It is prohibited. *Concordance*, s.v. sh-gh-r; transmitted by Bukhārī, Muslim, and others. *Kāfī*, V, 365–6; Ṭūsī, *Tahdhīb al-aḥkām*, VII, 355.

[195] 'Alī: is dropped in MS Q, hence it is a continuation of the quote from the Messenger of God.

[196] The Arabic term used in the Qur'ān is *farīḍa*. Ṭabarī, *Tafsīr*, V, 120, states that it means 'the obligatory dower (*ṣadāq*).' See also Ṭūsī, *al-Tibyān*, II, 269.

[197] *'Idda* is the waiting period imposed on a widow or a divorced woman before she may remarry, see Chap. 11.

[198] Ibn Mas'ūd was asked about a man who had married a woman without fixing any *mahr* and died without consummating. He said that she should receive the type of dower given to women of her class, nothing less and nothing more, observe the *'idda*, and have her share of the inheritance. *Mishkāt*, II, 189; Robson, I, 682.

consummation, she is entitled to one-half of her *ṣadāq*; but if the husband or the wife dies, the *ṣadāq* is to be paid wholly.'

'Alī: Where a man marries a woman on the condition that he would give her a servant (*waṣīf*), he said, 'There can be no decrease or increase in this.'

Ja'far b. Muḥammad: He said, 'If a man marries a woman on the condition that he would give her a house and a servant (*khādim*), the woman is entitled to a house and a servant, and it should not be exceeded nor decreased.'[199]

[Ja'far b. Muḥammad]: He said, 'Where a man marries a woman and the *mahr* is not known, the marriage is not invalid. The woman is entitled to a *mahr* equal to that of a woman of her station in life, so long as it does not exceed the *mahr* of the *sunna*, i.e. five hundred dirhams.'[200]

[Ja'far b. Muḥammad]: He said, 'If a man marries a woman on the condition that he would give to his wife a slave girl (*jāriya*) to be emancipated upon his own death (*mudabbara*),[201] and he divorces her before consummation, the wife is entitled to one-half the service of the slave girl, and the slave girl serves the [divorced] wife and her master on alternate days. If the girl's master dies, she is emancipated. If, however, he divorces her after consummation, she is entitled to the service of the slave girl; and when the master dies, the slave girl is emancipated.'[202]

'Alī:[203] With regard to the story of Moses [in the Qur'ān]: *He said: Lo! I fain would marry thee to one of these two daughters of mine on condition that thou hirest thyself to me for [the term of] eight pilgrimages. Then if thou completest ten it will be of thine own accord, for I would not make it hard for thee* (28:27),[204] he said, 'He made the marriage contract for a fixed [period of] service. But in Islam, marriage is not lawful for service to the guardian [of the bride], because the woman is more entitled to her own dower.'[205]

Ja'far b. Muḥammad: He said, 'If a man marries a woman for one

[199]*Kāfī*, V, 385; both the servant and the house should be of average quality.

[200]Ibid., V, 386; without the last phrase that it should not exceed the amount of the *sunna*.

[201]Lane, s.v. d-b-r; see also Chap. 12.

[202]*Kāfī*, V, 384. Instead of 'the master dies', it states, 'If the slave girl to be emancipated dies before her master and the woman, who would inherit [her property]?' [The Imam] said, 'The woman will have half of what she left behind and the other half for her master.'

[203]As in MS Q; in the printed edition: *'anhu*, is incorrect. Following the Qur'ānic verse it should read: *fa-qāla 'alayh al-salām* as in MS Q; in the printed text: *fa-qāla 'Alī*.

[204]See n. 84 above in this chapter.

[205]*Kāfī*, V, 389. 'If a man marries a woman and fixes her dower at twenty thousand [dirhams] and assigns ten thousand for her father, the dower is valid but the portion assigned to her father is invalid.'

thousand dirhams, but instead gives her a runaway slave (*'abd ābiq*)—i.e. a slave who, to her knowledge, had run away—and a garment of Yamanī fabric (*thawba ḥibarat*ⁱⁿ),[206] and she consented to it, there is no harm if she took the garment and agreed to the slave. If the husband divorces her before consummation, she should return five hundred dirhams to him, and the slave shall be her property, she may have him when she obtains possession of him.'[207]

[Ja'far b. Muḥammad]: He said, 'Where a man marries a woman for a certain sum as *ṣadāq* to be paid after a certain time, the *nikāḥ* is valid. But he must necessarily give her something before consummation, however little it may be,[208] to legalize the marriage. If, however, he possesses nothing, there is no harm and he has the right to consummate the marriage and the *ṣadāq* will remain a debt on him.'

'Alī: [The following case was brought before him]: A man marries a woman on the condition that he would pay her *ṣadāq* within a certain period; and that if he did not do so, he would have no right over her. 'Alī decided that the sexual intercourse (*buḍ'*)[209] of the wife is in the hand of the husband, the *ṣadāq* is an obligation on him, and the marriage is not dissolved by the [breaking of a] condition.[210]

Ja'far b. Muḥammad: He said, 'Where a man marries a woman for a certain dower, a part of which is prompt and the other deferred,[211] and both the parties vied in hastening to consummation, the wife shall not be compelled to agree to intercourse until the prompt portion has been paid. She has no right to the payment of the deferred portion, except after consummation. If the period is specified [for the deferred portion], the husband is bound to pay it within that period, but if the period is not fixed, then he has the right to consummation [after the prompt portion has been paid].

'If the woman denies that the husband has paid the prompt portion,

[206]See *The Pillars of Islam*, I, 287, n. 89.

[207]*Kāfī*, V, 385; also reported from al-Ṣādiq.

[208]Lit. give her a garment or a small thing.

[209]Lane, s.v. b-ḍ-'.

[210]*Kāfī*, V, 405; reported on the authority of Imam al-Bāqir and states that the sexual intercourse of the wife is in the hand of the husband and such a condition is of no avail.

[211]The practice of dividing *mahr* into two parts, *muqaddam* or *'ājil* (prompt) and *mu'akhkhar* or *ājil* (deferred), is quite common in the Ḥanafī school. Prompt *mahr* is payable at the time of the marriage contract or upon its conclusion while the deferred *mahr* must be paid at the specified time or only on termination of the marriage. The woman may refuse to allow consummation of the marriage if the prompt part is not paid. The wife's claim for the unpaid (deferred) portion of her *mahr* is legally considered an unsecured debt ranking equally with other unsecured debts due after her husband's death from his estate. *EI*², s.v. Mahr; Esposito, *Women in Muslim Family Law*, 25.

and the marriage has been consummated, and the husband claims that he has paid the prompt portion, the husband's word shall be accepted after administering the oath to him. If the husband claims that he has paid the deferred portion and the wife denies it, her word is to be accepted after oath; and the husband has to prove by clear evidence that he has paid the deferred portion.'

'Alī: He said, 'Where a man marries a woman for a certain *ṣadāq*, and there are witnesses for a secret deal, and there are witnesses for a public announcement for a greater amount, the first agreement is valid and the amount of dower will be paid accordingly.'[212]

['Alī]: He said, 'When a man goes in to a woman, closes the door, or lets the curtain down, the whole of the dower is due, whether he had sexual intercourse with her or not.'

Abū Ja'far said, 'I married a woman in the time of my father 'Alī b. Ḥusayn, and I desired to go in to her at midday. So my father said, "O my little son, do not go in to her at this time." But I did so, and when I went in to her, I disliked her and rose to go out. So a slave girl of hers got up, closed the door and let the curtain down. And I said, "Gently! Leave it; for you have become entitled to what you wish."'[213]

'Alī, and Abū Ja'far and Abū 'Abd Allāh: Concerning a man who frees his slave girl (*ama*) with the intention of marrying her and declares her emancipation as her dower; and the slave girl consents to this arrangement, they said, 'This is lawful.'

Abū Ja'far [Imam al-Bāqir] said, 'I would prefer him to give her something.'[214]

And Abū 'Abd Allāh [Imam al-Ṣādiq] said, 'If he divorces her before consummation, she is entitled to half her price [as dower].'

'Alī: He said, 'He who steals property and gives it as *ṣadāq* to his wife, or buys a slave girl, is entitled to sexual intercourse [with either of them]; but he is responsible for the property, and the sin will lie on his head.'

CONDITIONS IN MARRIAGE
(*AL-SHURŪṬ FI 'L-NIKĀḤ*)

We have mentioned earlier the established principle which has come down from the People of the House regarding conditions [in marriage],

[212] *Kāfī*, V, 386; reported from al-Ṣādiq.

[213] It means that she became entitled to the whole dower, irrespective of whether the marriage was consummated or not as the previous tradition states.

[214] *Kāfī*, V, 483–4.

namely that no condition is valid unless it conforms with the Qur'ān and the *sunna*; and what contravenes them is void.[215]

Ja'far b. Muḥammad—his father—his ancestors—'Alī: Where a man marries a woman and stipulates to her people that if he marries another wife or takes to himself a concubine (*surrīya*), the woman he marries would be *ipso facto* divorced, or that the slave girl (*surrīya*) be emancipated, 'Alī decided that the condition imposed by God takes precedence over the conditions laid down by men. If the husband wishes he may keep his promise; but if he so wishes, he may marry another wife or take a concubine [and if he does so], the wife he marries need not be divorced, and the slave girl need not be emancipated.[216]

Abū Ja'far Muḥammad b. 'Alī: He said, 'Where a man makes a condition with his [first] wife that if he marries another, or harms her, or removes her [from his home], or takes to himself a concubine, the first wife will be divorced, the conditions laid down by God have precedence over the conditions agreed to by men. It does not behove him to harm her or to ill-treat her, but he may marry another wife or keep a concubine [without being divorced from his first wife].'[217]

'Alī: He said to a man who married a woman on the condition that sexual intercourse would be at her choice, and she would have the right to divorce him, 'You have gone against the *sunna* and deputed the right to someone other than the one who is entitled to it.' He decided that dower is incumbent upon the husband and sexual intercourse and divorce are in his hand, and he declared the condition to be void.[218]

[215]Most jurists divided the conditions inserted in marriage contracts into three categories: those that reinforce legal effect of marriage, e.g. stipulations concerning the *mahr*; those that are contrary to the nature of marriage, e.g. stipulation of a fixed duration of the marriage; and those that might be considered as attempts to change the normal legal effects of marriage, e.g. stipulation that the husband will not take any additional wives. The last category caused controversy among various schools. All the Sunnī schools, except the Ḥanbalīs, hold that such conditions are null and void, while the marriage itself is valid. The Ḥanbalīs further argue that although the *sharī'a* permits polygamy it does not enjoin it. Hence, a husband who agrees not to exercise his right for additional marriages must be held to his undertaking. Should he, nevertheless, marry another wife; the first wife would be entitled to a judicial annulment of her marriage. It should be noted that this Ḥanbalī doctrine was included in the Ottoman Law of Family Rights, as well as in the legislations of Jordan, Syria, and Morocco. Anderson, *Islamic Law*, 50–1.

[216]Cf. *Kāfī*, V, 406–7; such a case was brought before Imam al-Ṣādiq.

[217]'A man divorced his wife and she was separated from him. Later he decided to remarry her. The woman said, "Nay, by God I will never marry you until you solemnly agree that you will neither divorce me nor take another wife." The man agreed. When the Imam [Mūsā al-Kāẓim] was informed of this he said, "He should fulfil the condition."' *Kāfī*, V, 407.

[218]Ibid., V, 407; reported from the same authority. Instead of 'he declared the

Ja'far b. Muḥammad: He said, 'It is a valid condition if a man marries a woman and stipulates [with her family] that she may stay with them,[219] or at a known place. A condition between Muslims which does not render lawful that which is unlawful, or renders unlawful that which is lawful, is valid.'

Ja'far b. Muḥammad: He said, 'If a man marries a woman and the parties agree to the condition that the husband would visit her every month or every Friday, and that he would not spend more than a certain sum on her, the marriage is valid but the condition is void. She does, however, have the right to her subsistence allowance and an equal division [of time with other wives], according to what wives are entitled. If he desires to keep her, let him take her according to what is incumbent on him, or let him divorce her. If the wife agrees to this and dislikes *ṭalāq*, then it is up to her to reach a compromise. God says: *If a woman fears ill-treatment from her husband, or desertion, it is no sin for them twain if they make terms of peace between themselves. Peace is better* (4:128). Such a case arises where a man dislikes his wife and wishes to divorce her, and she dislikes divorce, so she makes peace with him, giving up a part of her interest in equal division [of time with other wives], or from her allowance, or something similar, and both agree to the terms of the pact. Now such a settlement is lawful.'[220]

The Messenger of God: He forbade a woman from asking [her husband] to divorce her sister [co-wife] for the purpose of denying livelihood to her.[221] Surely God will provide for her.

Ja'far b. Muḥammad: He said, 'No man shall marry a woman on the condition that he should divorce one of his wives.'

The Messenger of God: He declared temporary marriage (*mut'a*)[222] to be forbidden.

---

condition to be void,' it states, 'and that is the *sunna*.' See also Chap. 11, section entitled 'Divorce by mutual consent.'

[219]*Kāfī*, V, 405–6; reported from the same Imam.

[220]Ibid., V, 406. Two traditions are reported, one each from al-Bāqir and al-Ṣādiq. According to al-Ṣādiq such a condition is valid. The second tradition transmitted by al-Bāqir is similar to that of Nu'mān.

[221]The Arabic is *li-taktafi'a ṣaḥfatahā* lit. to turn her bowl upside down. *Lisān al-'Arab*, s.v. k-f-'; the tradition is cited.

[222]The word *mut'a* literally means 'enjoyment', hence in its legal context it is rendered as a 'marriage for pleasure', or 'temporary marriage', which is contracted for a fixed period on rewarding the woman with a specified amount of money. It is regarded as the survival into Islam of an old Arabian custom. It seems that it was tolerated by the Prophet for some time, but all Islamic schools of law, except the Imāmī (Ithnā 'Asharī) school are agreed that

'Alī: He said, 'A valid marriage [takes place] with a guardian and two witnesses, but not for one or two dirhams, or for one or two days. This [type of marriage, i.e. for a short duration and for a few dirhams] is debauchery (*sifāḥ*),[223] and [specification of a definite time period] is not a valid condition in marriage.'

Ja'far b. Muḥammad: A man asked him about a *mut'a* marriage. [The Imam] said, 'Describe it to me.' The man said, 'A man meets a woman and says, "I shall marry you for this dirham or for two dirhams, for one communion or for one or two days."' [The Imam] said, 'This is unlawful intercourse (*zinā'*), and no one but an immoral person acts thus.

'The refutation of the *mut'a* marriage is contained in the Qur'ān, for God says: *And who guard their modesty—save from their wives or the (slaves) that their right hands possess, for then they are not blameworthy. But whosoever craveth beyond that, such are transgressors* (23:5–7). Thus God did not

---

he finally declared it unlawful. This sharply distinguishes the Ismā'īlī law from that of the Imāmīs.

According to some traditions it was 'Umar who first prohibited *mut'a*. In spite of their refusal to recognize *mut'a*, the Sunnī jurists made concessions by which *mut'a* gained a footing in different form. The practice was not to insert a definite time period in the contract, hence any agreement made outside the contract was not affected by the law. In his *Kitāb al-umm*, al-Shāfi'ī declared a marriage valid when it is concluded without uttering the resolution (*niyya*) to observe it for only the period of a stay at a place or for only a few days, as long as it is not expressly stipulated in the contract.

A good example of how the two opposite points of view are expressed in interpreting the Qur'ān is the case of verse 4:24. It states: *Since you have thereby [such wives] sought enjoyment with them (fa-mā 'stamta'tum bihi minhunna), give them their wages (marriage portions) as a duty (as stipulated) (fa-ātūhunna ujūrahunna)*. The Sunnīs refer to it as a regular marriage (*nikāḥ*) and state that *ujūr* (pl. of *ajr*) is the *mahr*. The Imāmīs justify *mut'a* on the basis of this verse and consider the traditions of 'Umar prohibiting it not authoritative. Ṭabarī (*Tafsīr*, VIII, 175–9; see also *Qummī*, I, 164) states that Ibn 'Abbās and others read the above verse as follows: ...*sought enjoyment with them for a fixed term (ilā ajal^{in} musammā)*. *EI*^{2}, s. v. Mut'a. For the twelver position see *Kāfī*, V, 455–62; Ṭūsī, *Tahdhīb al-aḥkām*, VII, 240–1, 248–52.

Haeri's *Law of Desire* is a study of the institution of temporary marriage, popularly known as *sighe*, in contemporary Iran. It demonstrates the tension that exists between the religious acceptance of *mut'a* and its cultural disapproval because of its association with prostitution. Consequently, those who practise it tend to keep it secret. A *Mut'a* contract is private and does not require witnesses. There seems to be a widespread moral ambivalence toward *sighe* and especially towards women who practise it. According to Haeri, most of the contemporary *'ulamā'* defend this institution by stressing its contractual aspect, and instead of referring to it as *mut'a*/*sighe* they call it *izdiwāj-i muwaqqat* (temporary marriage). Some *'ulamā'* have even shifted their tactics from the defensive to the offensive. They criticize the Western-style 'free' male-female relationship as decadent and propose temporary marriage instead, the latter being legitimate and morally superior.

[223] MS Q and five MSS of Fyzee: like debauchery (*shibh al-sifāḥ*).

apply the term *nikāḥ* except to the relationship with the wife or the slave, and He mentions the divorce which separates the spouses; and makes the spouses heirs to each other; and necessitates the observance of the *'idda* on women who are divorced.

'Now the *mut'a* marriage is different from this. For those who consider it to be lawful, it means that a man and a woman may agree on a certain period [for marital life], and when the period ends, there is separation between them without *ṭalāq*. The woman has no obligation to observe *'idda*; the children of the marriage have no relationship with the father; the husband need not make a promise for the wife's sustenance; and the two do not inherit from each other. Now this is without doubt what is known as *zinā'* (unlawful intercourse).'

'Alī: [The following case was brought before him]: A man makes a proposal for a woman to her father and he gives her in marriage to him. She has a sister, and when the time for consummation comes, the father sends the sister. Now 'Alī decided that *ṣadāq* is to be paid to the sister with whom consummation took place, or the husband returns the obligation [to pay *mahr*] to the father [because of his deception]. She who was originally contracted in marriage is his wife, but the husband should not consummate the marriage with her until the *'idda* of her sister terminates.[224]

['Alī]: He decided that if a slave fraudulently marries a free woman, representing himself to be a free man and she believes him, she may stay with him if she wished, or separate from him.[225]

Abū Ja'far Muḥammad [Imam al-Bāqir] said, 'If he has consummated the marriage, *ṣadāq* is due to her; but if he has not, she has no right over him if she chooses to separate from him. But if the husband has consummated the marriage after she knew that he was a slave, then he is her husband.'[226]

'Alī: A man married a woman and she gave birth to a child. Then a [different] man proved conclusively that she was his slave (*ama*). 'Alī decided in favour of the latter [and declared her to be his slave]. He also decided that the man who deceived the husband to marry her, should pay [a sum of money by way of] reparation for the child and for causing distress and disgrace [to the husband], and he cancelled the *ṣadāq* of the husband for [legalizing] the intercourse.

Ja'far b. Muḥammad [Imam al-Ṣādiq] said, 'If no one had deceived him, or if the deceiver possesses nothing, the child should not be declared

[224]*Kāfī*, V, 409; similar in content but slightly different in wording.
[225]Ibid., V, 413–14.
[226]Ibid., V, 414.

a slave if the husband had no knowledge that she was a slave, but a price should be fixed [for the child to be paid by the husband]. If however the husband knew that his wife was a slave, then the child of the marriage is a slave (*raqīq*).'[227]

['Alī]: He said, 'A man purchases a slave girl (*jāriya*) and makes her bear a child. Later another person proves that he is her owner; the latter takes her and [pays] the price of her child.'

['Alī]: He was asked about a *mujabbab* (a man with his genitals cut off)[228] who had deceived a woman and she had agreed to marry him. When he consummated the marriage, she came to know of it, and made a legal claim against him. 'Alī decided that he should be punished with stripes, and the two should be separated.[229] If he has had intimacy with her, the whole of the *mahr* is to be paid to her, otherwise he has to pay her half the *mahr*. They asked him, 'And what do you say about an impotent man (*'innīn*)?'[230] He said, 'He is in the same position.'[231]

'Alī: He said, 'A woman can be rejected [after marriage] if she suffers from a defect in the vulva preventing intercourse (*qarn*),[232] leprosy (*judhām*), madness, or leucoderma (*baraṣ*). If there has been intimacy between the couple, the husband has to pay *mahr*, and he may take her or leave her. The obligation to pay *mahr* shall be upon the man who deceived him to marry her; whereas, if the wife has deceived the husband, the husband has the claim against her [she has to repay the *mahr*], and he may leave for her a small amount for legalizing the intercourse. If the husband has had no intercourse, he may leave her if he so desires and there is no claim on the husband [for dower].'[233]

[227]Ibid., V, 407–8; all the three traditions are slightly different.

[228]*Majbūb* means having the genitals, or the testicles and the penis, cut off entirely, or extirpated, or having the penis cut off. Lane, s.v. j-b-b.

[229]*Kāfī*, V, 414, 415; instead of *mujabbab* it has *khaṣīy* (castrated).

[230]*'Innīn*, on the measure of *fi''īl* in the sense of the measure *maf'ūl*, means a man incapable of going into women, or who does not go into women by reason of impotence. Lane, s.v. '-n-n.

[231]*Kāfī*, V, 414; '... they should be separated, however if he has intercourse with her once, they should not be separated. A man should not be rejected because of a flaw.' In another tradition the decision to separate or to remain together is left to the wife.

[232]*Qarn* or *'afal* means a certain excrescence of flesh in the vulva of a woman, or a swelling between the vagina and rectum of a woman, hence her vulva is contracted and prevents penetration. Lane, s.v. '-f-l; Fayyūmī, *al-Miṣbāḥ*, s.v. '-f-l; *Majma' al-baḥrayn*, s.v. q-r-n; the tradition, cited on the authority of al-Ṣādiq, states that a woman can be rejected on account of four things, *qarn* being one of them.

[233]Cf. *Kāfī*, V, 410–13. Traditions reported from al-Ṣādiq are brief and apparently inconsistent.

[ʿAlī]: Concerning a man who marries a woman and finds her to be blind, or lame, or suffering from leucoderma, he said, 'She can be returned to her guardian. If she suffers from chronic illness (*zamāna*), such as cannot be seen by men, the testimony of [other] women is permissible against her.'

[ʿAlī]: He said, 'The woman suffering from leucoderma or leprosy is to be rejected.' He was asked, 'What about a woman blind in one eye?' He said, 'She cannot be rejected. A woman can be rejected only for leprosy, leucoderma, madness, or a genital disease preventing sexual intercourse.'[234]

ʿAlī: A man said to him, 'O Commander of the Faithful, I married a virgin; but when I went into her, I found her not to be a virgin.' He said, 'Woe to thee! Virginity is lost by jumping, leaping, menstruation, ablution and prolonged celibacy (*taʿnīs*)!'[235]

[ʿAlī]: A woman sued her husband [bringing the case] before ʿAlī. She said that she had been married to him for several years but he had not been able to consummate the marriage with her. ʿAlī asked the husband and he confirmed her statement. So he appointed the term of one year [to consummate the marriage], and after a year said to the wife, 'If you agree to merely food and raiment, [it is your choice,] otherwise you are your own mistress [i.e. free to marry someone else].'[236]

Jaʿfar b. Muḥammad: He said, 'So long as the wife of an impotent person does not complain, the man is entitled to remain as her husband. But if she sues him, a year's term is to be fixed. If, during that period, the husband is unable to consummate the marriage, they shall be separated. If the husband had been intimate with her, she is entitled to the whole of the *mahr*, and she has to observe *ʿidda* and later she can marry any one whom she wishes.'[237]

[234]Ibid., V, 410.

[235]Ibid., V, 417. *Taʿnīs* means a woman became of middle age, remaining a virgin, not having married, or she stayed long with her family after attaining puberty without marrying until she ceased to be reckoned among virgins. Lane, s.v. ʿ-n-s.

[236]'A man marries a deflowered woman who [then] marries another man. She alleges that [the first husband] did not consummate the marriage. In such a case, the word of the man [i.e. the first husband] on oath that indeed he had intercourse with her should be believed, because she is the claimant. However, if a man marries a virgin and she alleges that he did not have intimacy with her, it could be verified by women. Hence, if some trusted women look into it and testify that she is a virgin, the Imam should give the man one year [to consummate the marriage]. If he consummates the marriage [well and good], otherwise they should be separated. She should be given half the *mahr*, but there is no *ʿidda* for her [to be observed].' *Kāfī*, V, 415; reported from al-Bāqir.

[237]Ibid., V, 415–16; Kulaynī gives four different and interesting cases. Where the wife alleges that her husband is impotent, the man is put to test in an ingenious way to

LAWFUL AND UNLAWFUL MARRIAGE (*AL-NIKĀḤ AL-MANHĪY 'ANHU WA 'L-NIKĀḤ AL-MUBĀḤ*)

God says: *And marry not those women whom your fathers married* (4:22),[238] and he says: *Forbidden unto you are your mothers, and your daughters* (4:23).

Ja'far b. Muḥammad—his father—his ancestors—'Alī: He used to say, 'When a man has married a woman, and whether he has gone into her or not, her mother is forbidden to him. This follows from the Qur'ān: [*Forbidden unto you are*] ... *and your mothers-in-law* (4:23). Thus, mothers-in-law are absolutely (*mubhama*) forbidden in the Book of God.'[239]

[Ja'far b. Muḥammad]: Concerning the Qur'ānic verse: *And your step-daughters who are under your protection (fī ḥujūrikum) (born) of your women unto whom ye have gone in* (4:23), [the Imam] said, 'These are the daughters of your wives with whom you have consummated your marriage and they are forbidden. But if you have not gone in to them [your wives], then marriage to the step daughters is lawful.' And concerning the words *fī ḥujūrikum* (4:23), [the Imam] said, 'The word *ḥujr* means protection, therefore [it means] "under your protection". This expression is similar to the Word of God: *cattle and crops are forbidden*' (6:137). The word *ḥijr* means *muḥarram*, i.e. forbidden.[240]

[Ja'far b. Muḥammad]: He said, 'If a man has a slave girl (*ama*) and has sexual relations with her, her daughter is forbidden to him; free women and slaves are equal in this respect. Similarly, the mother is forbidden where sexual relations have taken place with the daughter, whether she is free or bonded.'[241]

Abū Ja'far Muḥammad b. 'Alī: He was asked if a man can marry the daughter of a woman he had married and had seen her head or some other parts of her body. [The Imam] said, 'When a man looks at such parts of a

---

verify her allegation. In the second case if the husband had intercourse at least once, the wife has no choice. Another case is given where a man is able to perform [the act] with other women, but not with his wife. In such a case he can retain her.

[238]Cf. *Mishkāt*, II, 178; Robson, I, 674.

[239]The word *mubham*, when applied to prohibited things, means 'not allowable in any manner, nor for any cause'. It is prohibited unconditionally, as the prohibition of the marriage with the mother, or the sister, and the like. Such a woman is said to be *mubhama 'alā al-rajul*, absolutely prohibited as though she were closed against him. Lane, s.v. b-h-m. *Mishkāt* II, 181; Robson, I, 676; Ṭūṣī, *Tahdhīb al-aḥkām*, VII, 272. These sources are without the word *mubhama*.

[240]Ṭūṣī, *Tahdhīb al-aḥkām*, VII, 273.

[241]*Mishkāt* II, 181; Robson, I, 676.

woman's body which are forbidden to others, it is not lawful for him to marry her daughter.'

'Alī: In respect of the Qur'ānic verse: *And marry not those women whom your fathers married* (4:22), he said, 'Where a man marries a woman and divorces her, or dies, she cannot be married to any of his sons whether he has gone into her or not. No man can marry the wife of his grandfather, for she is forbidden to all of his sons [and grandsons], regardless of generational distance.'[242]

'Alī: He once bared the leg of one of his slave girls, and then gave her as a gift to Ḥasan, and told him, 'Do not go near her for she is not lawful to you.' This happens only when the father looks with passion at a portion of the body which is forbidden to others. If however he looks at her without passion; like a man turning a woman round at the time of buying her [as a slave], or looks at her while she was the slave of another, she would not become unlawful for his son.

Abū Ja'far [Imam al-Bāqir] said, 'Where a father looks at a girl for purchasing her [as a slave], there is no harm in his son having sexual intercourse with her after she has been gifted to him, unless the father has seen her private parts.'[243]

Abū Ja'far: He said, 'Where a man strips a slave girl [of her clothes] and places his hand on her, she becomes unlawful both to his father and to his son.'

'Alī: Concerning the Qur'ānic verse: *And (It is forbidden unto you) that ye should have two sisters together, except what has already happened (of that nature) in the past* (4:23), he said, 'This refers to marriage [of two sisters together].' [The Imam] added, 'If a man married a woman and went to another country and there married her sister, without knowing [her relationship with his wife], it is his duty to withdraw from her as soon as he comes to know of it.'[244]

'Alī: He said that a man should not have sexual relations with two sisters who are his slaves.[245] There is another tradition wherein he was

[242] *Kāfī*, V, 422; Ṭūṣī, *Tahdhīb al-aḥkām*, VII, 281.

[243] *Kāfī*, V, 423.

[244] Ibid., V, 435–9; Kulaynī reports several traditions. One tradition reported on the authority of Imam al-Bāqir states that in such a situation, the man has to decide which of the two sisters he will retain as his wife. Mishkāt, II, 179; Robson, I, 675; Ṭūṣī, *Tahdhīb al-aḥkām*, VII, 284–6.

[245] He cannot have sexual relations with both of the sisters. If he has sexual relations with one, he cannot go into the other unless the first is sold for some pressing need or gifted. See the details in Ṭūsī, *al-Nihāya*, 455; *Kāfī*, V, 437, 438.

asked about this and said, 'One Qur'ānic verse legalizes such sexual relations, and another forbids them. But, for myself, I abstain from such a course and forbid my children from following it.'[246]

Ja'far b. Muḥammad said, 'When 'Alī abstained from a course himself and prohibited his children from it, it is clear that the faithful should also abstain from the practice followed neither by 'Alī nor by his descendants.'

Ja'far b. Muḥammad: He said, 'If a man has two sisters as slaves, and has sexual relations with one of them and later desires to have sexual intercourse with her sister, it is not proper for him to do so until the first is removed from his ownership either by gift or sale.[247] The legal obligation will not be satisfied if he gives away one sister to his son; for if he has sexual relations with the second sister, the first is forbidden to him until her sister dies. [If he disregards the rules, then] he has verily sinned and transgressed against the limits laid down by God.'

'Alī: He said, 'When a man divorces his wife, he cannot marry her sister till the *'idda* terminates.'

The Messenger of God: He forbade a man from marrying a woman and her paternal aunt, or a woman and her maternal aunt, as co-wives.[248]

Ja'far b. Muḥammad: He said, 'There is no harm if a man marries a woman who was the wife of another and her step-daughter; that is the daughter must be the daughter of another woman. [Similarly, he can marry] an *umm walad*[249] who is not the mother of the wife and may have them as co-wives if he wishes.'

[Ja'far b. Muḥammad]: He was asked whether it is lawful for a son to marry or take as a concubine his father's wife's or concubine's daughter

[246]The jurists agree that two sisters are not to be combined in marriage because of the Qur'ānic verse 4:23. However, they disagree about combining them through 'the ownership of the right hand (*milk al-yamīn*).' In general the jurists prohibit it except a group that holds that it is permissible. The reason for this disagreement stems from a different way of reading the verses 4:23–4. The latter group argues that *save those (captives) whom your right hand possess* (i.e. *milk al-yamīn*, 4:24) is exempted from the general rule stated in the previous verse, i.e. 4:23. Those who uphold the prohibition in *milk al-yamīn* further disagree in a case where one of the two sisters was associated through marriage while the other through ownership. Mālik and Abū Ḥanīfa prohibit it, but Shāfi'ī permit it. Ibn Rushd, *Bidāya*, II, 42; trans. II, 47–8.

[247]As indicated in the previos note both Kulaynī and Ṭūṣī empahsize that the sale must be for a pressing need. If he sells her merely to enjoy the other sister he has not fulfilled the legal obligation.

[248]*Mishkāt*, II, 176: Robson I, 672; transmitted by Bukhārī and Muslim. See also *Kāfī*, V, 428–9; here such a marriage is permitted if approved by both of the women.

[249]*Umm walad*, see *The Pillars of Islam*, I, 283, n. 62.

by another father. [The Imam] said, 'If the girl was born before the marriage of the father with the woman, it is lawful for the son to marry or have sexual relations with her. But if the girl was born after the marriage (or concubinage), I disapprove of it.'

It is related from another source that [Imam al-Ṣādiq] said, 'A man marries a divorced woman and children are born to her. There is no harm if this woman's son marries the daughter of another woman by her former husband.'[250] The reason which would bring doubt in this case, and was disapproved by [the Imam], is if the son was born near the time of divorce. But if there is no doubt about the birth, or if the son was born much earlier than the divorce or death, then it is not disapproved. And God knows better.

'Alī: He said, 'If a man has four wives and divorces one of them, he has no right to marry a fifth, until the *'idda* of the divorced woman ends.'[251]

'Alī and Abū Ja'far and Abū 'Abd Allāh: They said concerning a man who has illicit relations with the mother, or sister, or daughter of his wife, 'Such an action does not render the wife unlawful to him. He deserves the punishment for illicit intercourse; but a forbidden act does not render unlawful, what [in its nature] is lawful.'

Abū Ja'far [Imam al-Bāqir] said, 'If a man has illicit relations (*fajara*) with a woman, he cannot marry her daughter, real mother, or foster-mother.'[252]

'Alī: He said, 'If a man has illicit relations (*yaznī*) with a woman and then wishes to marry her, there is no harm if both of them repent.'[253]

['Alī]: He said, 'Where a man marries a woman, but she commits fornication before consummation, they should be separated, and she is not entitled to *ṣadāq* because she is responsible for her sin (*ḥadath*, misdeed).' This rule applies when the husband wishes divorce; but if he desires to maintain the marriage, then we have mentioned earlier the rules regarding the marriage of immoral persons (*fawājir* pl. of *fājir*), as laid down by the Members of the House of the Prophet.

Abū Ja'far Muḥammad b. 'Alī: He was asked about a man at the point of death who desires to marry a woman in order that she may inherit from him. He said, 'There is no harm in this, and the marriage is valid if contracted lawfully.'

[250] *Kāfī*, V, 402–3.

[251] Ibid., V, 434–5.

[252] 'What is unlawful by reason of consanguinity (*al-wilāda*) is unlawful by reason of fosterage (*al-raḍā'a*).' Transmitted by Bukhārī and Muslim, Muslim's version is slightly different. *Mishkāt*, II, 176; Robson, I, 672. See also *Kāfī*, V, 419–21.

[253] *Kāfī*, V, 360–1.

Ja'far b. Muḥammad: He was asked about a man who marries two sisters[254] or five women by one contract of marriage.[255] He said, 'Of the two sisters, the one whose name was mentioned first, is duly proved to be married. The four women whose names were mentioned first are also duly married, and the marriage of the rest is void. If it is not known as to which of the women were mentioned first, the whole of the contract of marriage is void.'

'Alī: He decided a case in which a woman's husband had died while she was pregnant. She married before the expiry of the four months and ten days [of the '*idda*]. He held that the couple be separated, and that he should not propose to her until both the terms [i.e. the period of the '*idda* and the period of pregnancy] are over.[256]

Ja'far b. Muḥammad [Imam al-Ṣādiq] said, 'This rule applies if there was no consummation; but if a man marries a woman during her '*idda* and consummation takes place, then they should be separated and she can never be lawful to him, but she is entitled to *ṣadāq* for legalizing her union with him. If there has been no consummation, they should be separated, and after the expiry of the '*idda*, he may marry her if the two so wish it.'

This rule applies where both parties knew that this course was unlawful;[257] but if the two were ignorant and consummation has taken place, they shall be separated until the '*idda* expires, and they may then marry if they so desire.

[The Imam] was asked, 'If one of them deliberately acted thus, and the other was ignorant, what then?' He said, 'The man who intended to act thus is not entitled to return to his companion, but people excuse ever greater errors on the score of ignorance.'

[254]Ibid., V, 435–9; it is forbidden.

[255]Ibid., V, 434–5; one cannot have five women by one contract of marriage, he has to let go one or if he has four, he has to divorce one and cannot marry the fifth before the '*idda* of the divorced one expires. For a case where a man is married to more than four wives and then embraces Islam, see Schacht, *Introduction*, 41.

[256]A pregnant woman's husband had died. After she had delivered a baby, but before the expiry of four months and ten days [of the '*idda*], she married. Imam al-Ṣādiq said, 'If consummation took place, the couple should be separated and she can never be lawful to him. She has to complete the remaining period of the first '*idda* and has to resume the second '*idda* of three menstrual cycles for the second [illegal marriage]. On the other hand, if there was no consummation, the couple should be separated, and she has to complete the remaining period of the first '*idda*. After that, he can propose.' Another version of this tradition is reported on the authority of Imam al-Bāqir. *Kāfī*, V, 431–2. If the woman is pregnant, the '*idda* continues until her delivery.

[257]Ibid., V, 431, 433; these traditions are presented separately and are not connected with the aforementioned case as depicted by Nu'mān.

[Ja'far b. Muḥammad]: He said, 'A man from Anṣār married a woman while he was still observing *iḥrām*,[258] and the Messenger of God declared the marriage to be void.'

'Alī: He said, 'The man observing *iḥrām* cannot marry or be married, and if he marries, the marriage is void.'

Ja'far b. Muḥammad said, 'Where a man observing *iḥrām* marries, the parties should be separated. If he has consummated the marriage, he shall pay *mahr* to legalize the intercourse, and he shall also expiate for [breaking] his *iḥrām*.[259] The *muḥrim* should not [explicitly] utter the proposal of marriage. If he knew that it is illegal, marriage will never be lawful with the same woman; but if he was ignorant [of this fact], and wishes to marry the woman after completing the *iḥrām*, he has the right to do so. If either of the two parties to the marriage knew [that an explicit proposal of marriage] was illegal [when they were observing *iḥrām*], it is not lawful for that person to [marry] the other.'

The Messenger of God: He directed that a man should not marry his midwife (*al-qābila*)[260] or her daughter.

MISSING HUSBANDS (*AL-MAFQŪD*)

Ja'far b. Muḥammad—his father—his ancestors—'Alī: He said, 'When the address of a missing person is known, his wife cannot be [re]married.'

This is [a deduction from the rule] relating to missing persons; the reason is that when the address of a man is known, he is not a missing person (*mafqūd*). The term *mafqūd* can only be applied to a person who goes out of his home and it is not known where he has gone, what he has done, or what his news and affairs are.[261] A man who goes out travelling is not a missing person, whether his address is known or not. In the case

[258] *Iḥrām* means the consecrated state in which one performs the *ḥajj* and *'umra*. Marriage is forbidden in such a state, see *The Pillars of Islam*, I, 381.

[259] He will have to make a sacrifice in expiation and to make a fresh pilgrimage the following year because his *ḥajj* is void. See *The Pillars of Islam*, I, 380.

[260] *Lisān al-'Arab*, s.v. q-b-l. See also *Kāfī*, V, 454–5.

[261] The jurists differ about the missing person in 'the land of Islam' (the territory in which the law of Islam prevails). According to Mālik, if the wife takes her case to the ruling authority (*ḥākim*), he should set a limit of four years. When that period expires, she should begin the period of waiting (*'idda*, four months and ten days). As to whether his property could be inherited, the requisites are more stringent. Rules about persons missing in war are different. Ibn Rushd, *Bidāya*, II, 52–3; trans. II, 61–2. The missing person is declared dead only after 90 or 120 lunar years have elapsed since his birth. Schacht, *Introduction*, 124.

of such a person, his wife cannot [re]marry until there is news of his death, or a divorce [pronounced by him]. [If this occurs,] she should observe the waiting period (*'idda*).

Ja'far b. Muḥammad: He said, 'So long as the wife of a missing person remains silent, she should be left alone. If, however, she takes her case to the ruling authority (*wālī*), he should fix a term of four years, and should write to the place where the man was last known and seek information regarding him. If no news is available, then after four years, the *wālī* should call the *walīy* (the nearest relative) of the missing husband and ask him, "Has the missing person any property?" If there is, the *wālī* should say [to him], "Give her maintenance." If the missing person has no property, and the *walīy* was supporting her from his own resources, then she has no right to [re]marry so long as he maintains her. But when the *walīy* refuses to maintain her, the *wālī* should compel the guardian to divorce her by a single [pronouncement of the] *ṭalāq*, pronounced during a period of [her] purity,[262] and she should commence the *'idda*. Thus, the *ṭalāq* of the *walīy* becomes the *ṭalāq* of the [missing] husband.

'If the husband returns before the expiry of the *'idda*, counting it from the day of the *walīy*'s divorce, and desires to return to her, she is legally his wife. She continues to be his wife on account of the two remaining pronouncements of the *ṭalāq*.[263] But if the period of *'idda* expires before the [missing] husband returns or withdraws [the *ṭalāq*], she can be [re]married lawfully [to another man], and no man has any right over her. But if the *walīy* says, "I shall maintain her," he cannot be compelled to pronounce divorce. If the missing man has no *walīy*, the ruling authority (*sulṭān*) should divorce her.'

People asked [the Imam], 'O son of the Messenger of God, what happens if the woman says, "I desire what all women desire [namely married life], and I can no longer exercise patience." [The Imam] said, 'She has no such right, nor is there any honour [in acting thus] so long as the missing man's *walīy* maintains her.'

Abū Ja'far Muḥammad b. 'Alī: He said, 'When the news of the death

[262]It is the *ṭalāq al-sunna*, see Chap. 11, n. 8.

[263]For a *ṭalāq* to be valid, it should be pronounced thrice in accordance with the rules, and not in immediate succession. The threefold pronouncement as well as the period of waiting in between them allow the man an opportunity to atone for a hurried pronouncement of *ṭalāq* by withdrawing it. If the missing husband returns before the expiry of the waiting period, the *ṭalāq* pronounced by the *walīy* is counted as the first pronouncement. It is for this reason that if the husband desires to return to her he can withdraw the *ṭalāq*. For details see *EI*[2], s.v. Ṭalāḳ.

of a [missing] man comes to his family, or that man's family informs his wife that he has divorced her, she should observe the waiting period and thereafter she can marry. But if her husband returns [thereafter], he has the greater right to her than the man whom she has married, whether the latter has consummated the marriage or not. If he has consummated the marriage, she is entitled to *mahr* in order to legalize the union.'

FOSTERAGE
(*AL-RAḌĀʿ*)[264]

After mentioning those blood relations who cannot be lawfully married, God says: *And your foster-mothers, and your foster-sisters* (4:23).

Jaʿfar b. Muḥammad—his father—his ancestors: The Messenger of God said, 'Whatsoever is prohibited [for marriage] by reason of consanguinity (*al-nasab*), is also prohibited by reason of fosterage.'[265]

The explanation of what is laid down in the above revelation [and tradition] is as follows. When a man's wife gives suck to a baby girl, the girl is forbidden in marriage to that man, his father, and his grandfathers, both paternal and maternal, regardless of generational distance. [The girl is also forbidden] to her foster mother's sons, and grandsons, i.e. her son's sons, and her daughter's sons, and all subsequent generations.

If the breastfed baby is a boy, his foster mother and her descendants, and the descendants of his foster father are forbidden to him. No man should marry his foster-daughter, or her descendants, regardless of generational distance. A man should not marry his foster sister, her descendants, his foster brother's children, or his paternal or maternal aunt by fosterage. He should not have as co-wives two foster sisters; a woman and her foster paternal aunt, or a woman and her foster maternal aunt.

Thus all those who are forbidden on grounds of blood relationship (*al-nasab*) are forbidden by reason of fosterage. [This is] on account of the tradition of the Messenger of God, 'Whatever is prohibited by consanguinity is prohibited by fosterage.'

[264]*Raḍāʿ* or *riḍāʿ* or *raḍāʿa*, suckling, as a technical term, the suckling produces the legal restriction in marriage of foster-kinship. In pre-Islamic Arabia, the Meccans used to give their infants to Bedouin wet nurses. Suckling thus creates fraternal bonds which have a widespread social and moral effect. Milk produces an effect comparable to that of blood. Shīmā, daughter of the wet nurse Ḥalīma, was the foster-sister of the Prophet. Legal aspects of *raḍāʿa* are addressed by the Qurʾān and *aḥādīth*. For details see *EI*[2], s.v. Raḍāʿ.

[265]*Mishkāt*, II, 176; Robson, I, 672; transmitted by Bukhārī. See also *Kāfī*, V, 442–3; Ṭūsī, *Tahdhīb al-aḥkām*, VII, 312.

There is no harm if a man marries the wet nurse of his son; and likewise, she can marry that man's sons, except the son whom she has suckled. She is not forbidden to them as she is not their mother. She is only the foster-mother of their brother, but not the wife of their father. God has forbidden only the wives of the fathers, and she is by no means in that category. Similarly, they can marry the foster sister of their brother, her children, and her descendants.

Similarly, a man can marry the daughters or grand daughters of the foster-mother of his son, because they are not foster relations, nor are they related to him in such a way as to cause illegality. The daughters of the foster-mother are forbidden only to the one who was suckled.

A man may marry a foster paternal uncle's daughter, a foster paternal aunt's daughter, a foster maternal uncle's daughter, and a foster maternal aunt's daughter, because cousins are [also] lawful [for marriage] if they are related by blood (*al-nasab*).

Thus, we see that those foster relations are lawful for marriage which are lawful if they were related by consanguinity. Do you not see that a man may marry a woman and his son can marry her step daughter? Similarly, a man may marry a woman and his father can marry her step daughter. A father and son can each marry one of two sisters.

'Alī: He said, 'I said to the Messenger of God, "O Messenger of God, why is it that you marry women of the Quraysh, but leave us [our family] alone?"' The Messenger of God replied, 'Have you any one [in mind]?' 'Alī said, 'Yes, the daughter of Ḥamza.' The Messenger of God said, 'She is not lawful to me for she is the daughter of my foster-brother; and whatever is forbidden by consanguinity (*al-nasab*) is also forbidden by fosterage.'[266]

'Alī: He said, 'The prohibition by fosterage arises [regardless of] whether the quantity (of milk) is small or great; even a single mouthful renders marriage unlawful.' This is a dictum the soundness whereof is clear to him who ponders over it and is endowed with understanding, for God says: *And your mothers who have given you suck* (4:23). Therefore the rule of fosterage applies whether the quantity is great or small. Accordingly, to him who asserts that [a small quantity of milk] which does not cause the growth of flesh or blood, nor strengthen the bone, cannot cause the

[266]*Mishkāt*, II, 176; Robson, I, 672; transmitted by Muslim; *Kāfī*, 443; Ṭūsī, *Tahdhīb al-aḥkām*, VII, 326. Thuwayba, a slave girl of Abū Lahab, was the first wet nurse to suckle the Prophet. Before that she had suckled Ḥamza, who was younger than 'Abd Allāh, the Prophet's father. Hence, Ḥamza, the Prophet's uncle was also his foster-brother. Ibn Isḥāq, *al-Sīra*, I, 170, n. 6. For Ḥamza see *The Pillars of Islam*, I, 23, n. 22.

unlawfulness [of marriage to such a person, we say] that even a small quantity that enters [the body] increases the growth of flesh, blood, and bone, in proportion to its quantity, when it mixes with its counterpart.[267]

The Messenger of God: He prohibited suckling (a child) after weaning it (*fiṭām*).[268]

'Alī: He said, 'Fosterage occurs during the period of [the child's first] two years, and there is no fosterage after weaning. God says: *Mothers shall suckle their children for two whole years [that is] for those who wish to complete the suckling*' (2:233).

['Alī]: A man asked him, 'Verily, my wife suckled a grown-up slave girl (*jāriya*) in order to render her unlawful to me.' 'Alī said, 'Punish your wife, and you can go into your slave girl. There is no fosterage after weaning.'[269]

Ja'far b. Muḥammad: He was asked about [a man's] wife who had suckled a slave girl. Would the slave girl be lawful to his son by another woman? He said, 'No. She will be deemed to be a foster-sister by relationship with his father, because she had shared in the milk of the father.'[270]

[Ja'far b. Muḥammad]: He said, 'The milk of the male renders (a person) unlawful [in marriage].' The meaning of 'the milk of the male' is this: that many children [not of the same family] may share the milk produced by one man's [marriage or intercourse], and all those who have shared the milk become unlawful to one another [in marriage]. In the case where the man has wives or mothers of [his] children (*ummahātu awlād*^{in}) [i.e. female slaves], each child, male or female, which is breastfed by some woman or other, may in a sense, be said to share the milk of the male, and they are all unlawful to one another [in marriage]. [This rule applies] even if the children have not shared in common one woman's milk. The male is the connecting link between all these women [wives and slaves] and, therefore, the children are all inter se his foster children.[271]

[267] 'Being suckled once or twice does not make marriage unlawful.' Transmitted by Muslim. Another tradition transmitted by Muslim states: 'Ā'isha said that in what was revealed in the Qur'ān, ten known sucklings make marriage unlawful, but they were abrogated by five known sucklings. When the Messenger of God died, these words were among what was recited in the Qur'ān. *Mishkāt*, II, 177; Robson, I, 672. See also *Kāfī*, V, 443–6; traditions reported on the authority of Imam al-Ṣādiq are similar to those transmitted by Muslim and diametrically opposed to what Nu'mān states.

[268] *Kāfī*, V, 449.

[269] Ibid., V, 451; reported on 'Alī's authority.

[270] Ibid., V, 445, 450, 451.

[271] Ibid., V, 446–9; Ṭūsī, *Tahdhīb al-aḥkām*, VII, 322–3.

'Alī: He said, 'Fosterage in relation to the father, renders a person unlawful in the same manner as consanguinity.'

Ja'far b. Muḥammad: A man asked him regarding a slave girl born in his household and with whom he intended to have sexual intercourse. However, his female slave who has borne a child to him (*umm walad*) told him that she had suckled her. [The Imam] said, '[Because] she makes a statement which suits her, she is to be suspected and not believed.'

[Ja'far b. Muḥammad]: He was asked about a woman who says that she suckled a boy and a girl then resiles from her statement. [The Imam] said, 'When she denies the statement, it may be [investigated and] confirmed.' It was said to him, 'But [what] if she returns to her previous statement and says that she has suckled them both?' [The Imam said], 'This statement need not be confirmed.'[272]

The evidence of a single woman is permissible in fosterage, as long as it is made by a reliable and competent witness who is not suspected; but if she is suspected and not reliable, her evidence is not acceptable.

'Alī: He said, 'If a boy is given milk as medicine through the mouth or the nose, during [his first] two years [of fosterage], it will be deemed to be fosterage.'[273]

The Messenger of God: He prohibited that an illegitimate child (*walad al-zinā'*) be suckled (*muẓā'ara*).[274]

Ja'far b. Muḥammad: He said, 'If a slave girl is guilty of fornication and gives birth to a child, the slave mother should not be employed as a foster-mother (*ẓi'r*, i.e. *murḍi'a*).'

[Ja'far b. Muḥammad]: He was asked, 'If a boy slave has intercourse with a girl slave, and a child is born, and the master requires the milk of the slave girl, [is this lawful?].' He said, 'If the master allows the two slaves to [lawfully] have intercourse,[275] then there is no harm in it.'

'Alī and Abū Ja'far [Imam al-Bāqir]: They permitted a Jewish, Christian, or Zoroastrian (*Majūs*)[276] woman to be employed as a foster-mother. And

[272]*Kāfī*, V, 452.

[273]*Awjarahu dawā'an* means he poured medicine into his (a child's) mouth. *As'aṭahu dawā'an* means he poured medicine into his (a man's, child's) nose. Lane, s.v. s-'-ṭ, w-j-r; *Majma' al-baḥrayn*, s.v. w-j-r; he cites a similar tradition. 'The only suckling which makes marriage unlawful is that which is taken from the breast and enters the bowels, and is taken before the time of weaning.' Transmitted by Tirmidhī. *Mishkāt*, II, 178–9; Robson, I, 674.

[274]From *ẓā'arat* meaning she took to herself a child to suckle. Lane, s.v. ẓ-'-r.

[275]The Arabic reads: *in aḥalla lahumā mā ṣana'ā*. I understand the term *aḥalla* here to mean to allow, permit, and not in the sense of declaring something lawful.

[276]*Majūs*, see *The Pillars of Islam*, I, 221, 469.

Abū 'Abd Allāh[277] [Imām al-Ṣādiq] said, 'When those women are employed as foster mothers they should be forbidden to drink wine, or eat unlawful things.'[278]

[Ja'far b. Muḥammad]: He said, 'To employ a Jewish or Christian woman to suckle a child is preferable to employing a *nāṣibīya* (one who bears enmity toward the Imams). Beware of asking them to suckle your children, marrying them, or befriending them!'[279]

[Ja'far b. Muḥammad]: He was asked if it is lawful for a man to sell his servant girl (*khādima*) who had suckled him? He said, 'The servant girl has the right against him [not to agree to this course].'

[Ja'far b. Muḥammad]: He said, 'Forbidden milk (*laban al-ḥaram*)[280] does not render unlawful that which is lawful. An illustration of this rule is [the following]: A woman suckles a male child with the milk [produced by having a child with] her husband. Thereafter [she fornicates] and suckles [a girl] by the milk [produced as a result of this] debauchery.' He said, 'A person who suckles a girl by the milk of debauchery, does not render her marriage unlawful [by fosterage] because forbidden milk does not render unlawful that which is lawful.'

Abū Ja'far: He was asked about a woman who suckled her slave. He said, 'As soon as she suckled him, he became emancipated.'[281]

'Alī: A man married a woman and gave *ṣadāq* (dower) to her, but did not consummate the marriage; later it was discovered that there was [a prohibition by] fosterage between them. 'Alī decided that the woman should return what she had taken from him [as *mahr*].

The Messenger of God: He prohibited women from suckling a lot of children (lit. 'right and left'), and he said, '[This is] because they forget [their foster-children].'[282]

[277]MS Q: Ja'far b. Muḥammad.

[278]Ṭūsī, *al-Nihāya*, 504.

[279]Marriage with a *nāṣibīya* is prohibited. *Kāfī*, V, 352–6. For *nāṣib* see *The Pillars of Islam*, I, 190, 191, 294, 361.

[280]Towards the end of her pregnancy, a woman's breasts enlarge and get ready to produce milk. 'Forbidden milk', therefore, refers to a woman's pregnancy and milk produced by illicit sex. In the illustration, a woman first suckles a baby with the milk produced by legal pregnancy as she was impregnated by her husband. In the second case, she had illicit sex with another man that resulted in pregnancy and she suckled a baby girl. When this baby girl attains maturity and gets married, her lawful marriage, in no way, is rendered unlawful because of the fact that she was suckled by a woman with the milk [produced as a result of] debauchery.

[281]'He is her foster-child and it is unlawful for her to sell him and benefit from his price.' *Kāfī*, , V, 453.

[282]Ibid., V, 453; reported on the authority of 'Alī.

MARRIAGE OF SLAVE WOMEN (*NIKĀḤ AL-IMĀ'*)[283]

God says: *And whoso is not able to afford to marry free, believing women, let them marry from the believing maids whom your right hands possess*, till the Word: *This is for him among you who fears to commit sin ('anat)*[284] (4:25). Thus, God has not permitted marriage with bondmaids except on two conditions—that a man cannot afford to marry a free woman, and that he fears the commission of sin.[285]

Ja'far b. Muḥammad—his father—his ancestors—'Alī: He said, 'Marriage with bondmaids (*imā'*) is not permissible except for him who fears the commission of sin,' i.e. unlawful intercourse (*zinā'*). 'In the case of a man who has the means to marry a free woman, [already] has a free woman for a wife, or is not compelled to marry, it is extremely improper for him to marry a bondmaid, and if he does so, they should be separated and reprimanded (*'uzzira*),'[286]

Abū Ja'far and Abū 'Abd Allāh: They said, 'There is no harm if a free man were to marry a bondmaid when he is compelled by necessity to do so.' Abū Ja'far said, 'Unless two conditions coexist, a free man should not marry a slave—[fear of] sin (*'anat*) and lack of means (*'adam al-ṭawl*). Even if unnecessary marriages with slaves, save for the purpose of producing a slave child, were not declared to be disapproved, such marriages should never be performed unless a man is compelled by necessity and no other course is left open to him.'

The Messenger of God: He prohibited people from marrying a female slave (*ama*) in addition to a free woman, and an unbelieving woman (*kāfira*) in addition to a Muslim woman.[287]

'Alī: Concerning the man who, having a free wife, marries a female slave (*ama*), he said, 'Both the man and the female slave should be separated, and he should be compelled to pay *ṣadāq* for legalizing the intercourse if consummation had taken place. But if there had been no consummation, she has no such right against him.'[288]

['Alī]: A man married a slave girl (*ama*); thereafter, he found the means to marry a free woman, but disliked the idea of divorcing the slave girl as

[283]*Imā'* pl. of *ama*.

[284]For various shades of meaning see Lane, s.v. '-n-t.

[285]*Kāfī*, V, 364; 'There is no objection if he is compelled to marry a slave girl.'

[286]For *ta'zīr* punishment see n. 117 in Chap. 17.

[287]Ṭūsī, *Tahdhīb al-aḥkām*, VII, 419.

[288]*Kāfī*, V, 364; 'If a man, having a free wife, marries a slave girl, such a marriage is not valid.'

he was attached to her. 'Alī decided that he could marry the free woman in addition to the slave girl who was [his first wife] chronologically, and he should divide his time between them in the following manner: two nights to the free woman and one to the slave girl.[289] Similarly, he should show preference in maintaining the free woman without causing harm to the maid nor giving her less than what is sufficient.

Ja'far b. Muḥammad: He said, 'If a man, not possessing the means to marry a free woman and fearing that he might commit immorality (*'anat*), marries a slave girl (*ama*) and later finds the means to marry a free woman and marries her without the free woman knowing that her husband has a slave wife, the free woman has an option [to free herself] when she comes to know of it. She may stay with him or she may separate from him if he is deeply attached to the slave wife. If she separates before consummation, she has no right against him, but if he has consummated the marriage, she is entitled to *ṣadāq* to legalize the union with him. If, however, the husband divorces the slave girl, the free woman has no option [to separate from him].'[290]

'Alī: He said, 'If a free man fears that he might commit immorality (*'anat*) and has not the means to marry a free woman, he should not marry more than one slave girl (*ama*). He has no right to marry one slave girl after another, because, [having one wife], he cannot fear sinfulness (*'anat*).'

'Alī: He said, 'Where a man marries a slave girl (*ama*) belonging to another person and makes it a condition with him that all the children of the slave girl will be free, the condition is lawful.'

'Alī: He said, 'When a free man marries a slave girl and does not make any condition regarding her service, her service belongs to her masters during the day, but they should allow the husband and wife to meet freely at night. In such a case, her maintenance will be the obligation of her husband; but if the masters do not free her at night, she has no right of maintenance against the husband. It is not proper for her masters to prevent the husband from intercourse with her, whether by day or by night.'

Ja'far b. Muḥammad: He was asked about a slave girl (*mamlūka*) jointly owned by two persons. One of them married her during the absence of the other. Is such a marriage lawful? [The Imam] said, 'If the absent owner disapproved of it, the marriage is not valid.' That is to say that [it is invalid] when he has not given the joint owner permission, authority, or licence to marry the girl.

'Alī: He said, 'It is not lawful for a Muslim to marry a polytheist slave

[289]Cf. ibid., V, 364, 365.
[290]bid., V, 364; slightly different version.

girl (*al-ama al-mushrika*) because God has permitted him the believing maids as He says: ... *let them marry from the believing maids* ... (4:25).' [And 'Alī related that] the Messenger of God disapproved that Jews and Christians should have the children of Muslims as their slaves.

Ja'far b. Muḥammad: He was asked about a man who had a small child, and the child had a slave girl (*jāriya mamlūka*). Is it lawful for the father to have sexual intercourse with the slave girl? He said, 'This is not lawful for the father unless he fixes an adequate price for the slave girl. He may then take her and the child is entitled to the price of the slave girl.'[291] He also said, 'It is not lawful for the man to take any property belonging to his child without the latter's consent unless he is compelled by necessity; and then he should only take what is necessary for his food, but not for his pleasure.'

Ja'far b. Muḥammad: He was asked about a woman who directed her son to have intercourse with the father's slave girl in order to make her illegal to his father. The son did so, and [the Imam] said, 'The mother and her son have sinned, but I do not approve of the father having intercourse with slave girl even though a forbidden act does not render a lawful act unlawful.'

'Alī: He did not approve of a man having sexual intercourse with a slave girl (*ama*) held in partnership with another.

['Alī]: He was asked about the marriage of a *mukātaba* (a slave girl who has made an agreement with her master to purchase her freedom in instalments).[292] He said, 'Marry her if you wish.' That is, marry her with her consent and the consent of her master, even though she is adjudged as emancipated [by her contract]. We will deal with this issue in its appropriate place.[293] He also said, 'Know that the children of the *mukātaba* born during the period prior to her emancipation would be either free or bonded depending on [the contract] into which she has entered.'

['Alī]: He said, "Ā'isha desired to buy a slave girl called Barīra[294] and the owners asked for the condition that her *walā'*[295] should belong

[291]Ibid., V, 478.

[292]For further details on *mukātab* slaves see Schacht, *Origins*, 279–81; Chap. 12 in this book.

[293]See the section 'Emancipation by Contract' in Chap. 12 of this book.

[294]Barīra, a slave woman who had arranged to buy her freedom in nine, or five annual instalments, appealed to 'Ā'isha who agreed to pay the whole amount. The owners were willing to sell her, but insisted on retaining the right of inheritance from her. For details see *EI*², s.v. Barīra; Schacht, *Origins*, 173.

[295]*Walā'*, a technical term, means the right to the inheritance of the property left by an emancipated slave. The right of *walā'* (inheritance) belongs to the one who sets a slave free. *Kāfī*, VI, 208; Tahānawī, *Kashshāf*, IV, 388–9; Schacht, *Origins*, 161–2. See also Chap. 12, section on '*Walā'*.'

to them. She agreed to the condition. The Messenger of God came to know of this, so he ascended the pulpit and praised God and sent laudations to Him and said, "What do the people think when they make conditions which are not to be found in the Book of God? [For instance,] a man sells a slave and makes it a condition that he retains the *walā'* even though *walā'* belongs to him who emancipates a slave. The conditions laid down by God are more firm [than those laid down by men]. Every condition contrary to the Book of God is void." When Barīra was finally emancipated, the Messenger of God gave her the choice [to either stay] with her husband [Mughīth, who was a black slave] whom she had married while she was a slave [or to free herself from him]. She chose [to be free], and then the Messenger of God said, "Observe the *'idda* [of divorce] for three menstrual periods."'

Ja'far b. Muḥammad said, 'The husband of Barīra, [the slave woman] to whom the Messenger of God gave the choice, was [also] a slave. Choice is only necessary in the case of a slave. If the husband was a free man, she would have become free in accordance with his status.'[296]

'Alī: He said, 'It is not lawful for a person to have sexual intercourse with his slave girl (*mamlūka*) who is held in partnership with another.'

Ja'far b. Muḥammad: He forbade lending (women) for sexual intercourse (*'āriyat al-furūj*); for instance, a man permitting another to have sexual intercourse with his slave girl; or a woman permitting her husband, or someone else, to have intercourse with her slave girl (*ama*) without marriage or proprietary right.

Ja'far b. Muḥammad said, 'The lending of private parts (*'āriyat al-furūj*) is fornication, and I dissociate myself before God from anyone who acts thus, for the Qur'ān speaks of it and God says: *And who guard their private parts (furūj) save from their wives or the [slaves] that their right hands possess, for then they are not blameworthy. But whosoever craveth beyond that, such are transgressors* (23:5–7). Accordingly, God does not permit sexual intercourse, except under two conditions, marriage or proprietary right [in slaves].'

MARRIAGE OF MALE SLAVES (*NIKĀḤ AL-'ABĪD*)

Ja'far b. Muḥammad—his father—his ancestors: The Messenger of God forbade slaves to marry without the permission of their masters.[297] He

[296] *Mishkāt*, II, 186; Robson, I, 680; transmitted by Bukhārī and Muslim. Mughīth loved Barīra, but she hated him.

[297] *Kāfī*, V, 485.

said, 'Whichever free woman marries a slave without the permission of his owner has indeed permitted sexual intercourse and she has no right to *ṣadāq*.'[298]

Ja'far b. Muḥammad:[299] He said, 'The slave is not permitted to marry or to divorce without the master's permission. If a slave marries without his master's permission, he may allow him to remain so or may separate (them).'[300]

'Alī: He said, 'A slave cannot marry more than two women; more than two are not permissible to him.'

Ja'far b. Muḥammad explained that this rule relates to free women. It is, however, his right to marry four slave women where such permission is given to him by his master. He may also buy as many slave girls as he likes and have intercourse with them by his proprietary right with his master's permission and authority.[301]

Ja'far b. Muḥammad: When a man desires that his slave should marry his slave girl (*ama*), he should say, 'Verily, I have married thee to so-and-so;' and the master should give her something on his behalf, even one dry measure (*mudd*)[302] of food.[303]

[Ja'far b. Muḥammad]: He said, 'Where a master marries his slave to his slave girl (*ama*), it is [his right] to take her away from her husband [whenever he chooses] without [pronouncing] divorce.[304] But if he marries her to a free man, or to the slave of another person, he cannot withdraw her from her husband without a divorce.

'If he sells the slave girl, it is [the right of] the purchaser to separate her from her slave husband. The sale of the girl is equivalent to her divorce, but if the purchaser agrees to the marriage, she may retain her status as married with the vendor.'

[298]Ibid., V, 486–7; reported on the authority of Imam al-Ṣādiq.

[299]According to MS Q, and five other MSS of Fyzee. In the edited text Fyzee has retained 'Abū Muḥammad' as in MS S.

[300]*Kāfī*, V, 485, 487; if a slave girl marries without the permission of her master, such a union is unlawful.

[301]Ibid., V, 484; the same rule. The slave is permitted to a maximum of two wives, except in the Mālikī view, which grants him four, just like a free man. This was also the opinion of the Ẓāhirites. The reason for disagreement was whether bondage is effective in discarding this number, just as it is effective in remitting one-half of the *ḥadd* punishment that is obligatory on the freeman for adultery. Ibn Rush, *Bidāya*, II, 41; trans. II, 47; Qurṭubī, *al-Kāfī*, 245.

[302]*Mudd* is a measure of varying magnitudes; see *The Pillars of Islam*, I, 331, n. 149.

[303]*Kāfī*, V, 487; 'the master should give her something on his behalf, or on behalf of his slave ...'

[304]Cf. ibid.,V, 488.

'Alī: He said, 'Where a woman acquires the ownership of her slave husband, either wholly or in part, she is forbidden to him, and he to her, because a male slave cannot marry his mistress.'[305]

THE MARRIAGE OF POLYTHEISTS (*NIKĀḤ AL-MUSHRIKĪN*)

God says: *Wed not idolatresses till they believe* (2:221), and He says: *This day are (all) good things made lawful for you,* till His word, *and the virtuous women of those who received the Scripture* (5:5).

Ja'far b. Muḥammad—his father—his ancestors—'Alī: He said, 'God has made the women of the People of the Book lawful for Muslims in marriage only when there is a shortage of women among Muslims; but when there are a number of Muslim women, He says: *And wed not idolatresses till they believe* (2:221) and He says: *And hold not to the ties of disbelieving women*' (60:10).[306]

The Messenger of God prohibited a Muslim to marry a non-Muslim woman when Muslim women were available; and a polytheist shall not marry a Muslim woman. When a polytheist becomes a Muslim and has a polytheist wife, he may, if he chooses, retain her if he is attached to her, for it is possible that God may guide her rightly. It is also his right to marry three other Muslim wives, as long as they know about her [i.e. the polytheist wife].

Abū Ja'far Muḥammad b. 'Alī [Imam al-Bāqir]: He said concerning a man who has a polytheist wife and marries a Muslim woman, 'If a man marries a free Muslim woman and he has a Jewish or a Christian wife unknown to the Muslim wife, and she comes to know of this when consummation takes place, she has the right to keep what she has taken of her *mahr* and stay with him if she so desires, or to go back to her own people. Thereafter, when she goes through the three periods of menstruation, or three months expire if she is not menstruating, she is entitled to marry without a regular divorce.' He was asked, 'What if her husband divorces the Jewish or Christian woman before the expiration of the *'idda*,[307] can he bring back the Muslim wife to his home?' [The Imam] said, 'Yes.'

'Alī: He was asked the following question: [What is the case of] a polytheist woman who accepts Islam and has a polytheist husband?[308]

[305]Ibid., V, 491–2; several traditions are cited.

[306]Ṭūsī, *Tahdhīb al-aḥkām*, VII, 297–9.

[307]For *'idda* see *The Pillars of Islam*, I, 118, n. 334, and Chap. 11, section on *'idda*.

[308]A Muslim woman cannot marry a polytheist, hence as soon as she embraces Islam her husband is divorced. It is explained in a tradition below.

'Alī said, 'If he becomes a Muslim before the expiry of the *'idda*, the marriage subsists. If, however, the *'idda* expires, she is entitled to marry any Muslim she likes. If her [unbelieving] husband embraces Islam after the *'idda*, he may become one of her suitors, and if she agrees, a fresh marriage can take place.[309]

'If an unbeliever is converted to Islam and has a polytheist wife, the marriage continues if she accepts Islam; but even if she does not become a Muslim, she may continue as his wife, if he so wishes.'

['Alī]: He said, 'If a polytheist [man] becomes a Muslim while [simultaneously] married to two free sisters, or more than four free women, the sister that he married first may be left with him as his wife; similarly the first four women he married [may be retained as his wives]. The second sister and all of the women except the first four should be separated from him.'[310]

Ja'far b. Muḥammad: He said, 'If a *ḥarbī* (foreign national of a non-Muslim state)[311] comes to an Islamic country (*dār al-islām*)[312] and becomes a Muslim, and thereafter his wife joins him, their marriage may continue.'[313]

The Messenger of God: He said, 'When pre-Islamic Arabs (*ahl al-jāhilīya*) are converted to Islam, they retain the status of their marriage, divorce, and inheritance so long as their laws conform with those of Islam; but if an unbeliever accepts Islam and has a spouse who is forbidden [by the laws of Islam], the two should be separated.'

'Alī: If a Zoroastrian woman (*Majūsīya*) becomes Muslim before the

[309]Cf. *Kāfī*, V, 441; Ṭūsī, *Tahdhīb al-aḥkām*, VII, 300–1.

[310]Cf. *Mishkāt*, II, 179; Robson, I, 674; *Kāfī*, V, 442.

[311]*Ḥarbī* lit. means warlike or bellicose. It is an adjective denoting non-Muslim neighbours and is defined as those who have refused to be converted to Islam after being duly invited, and against whom warfare is permissible. *EI*[2], s.v. Dār al-ḥarb.

[312]*Dār al-islām* lit. 'the Land of Islam', is the territory in which the law of Islam prevails. Everything outside of it is *dār al-ḥarb* (the Land of War). In classical Islamic legal writings the world was divided into the *dār al-islām* (abode of Islam) and the *dār al-ḥarb* (abode of war, or abode of non-believers), with the implication that the latter has to be subdued by the former to establish Islamic hegemony over the entire world. Sachedina states that both the terms, *dār al-islām* and *dār al-ḥarb*, were legal constructs of Muslim jurists with the rise of political Islam that gave the normative foundation of Muslim religious convictions about forming a transcultural, transnational *umma* that must subdue and dominate non-believers. He argues that the Qur'ān does not support such constructs, rather, the Qur'ān considers the world as one stage of a struggle between the forces of *īmān* and *kufr*. In modern times it is, therefore, a defunct legal construct, but still used by neo-Orientalists to indicate the Muslim extremists' threat by arguing that they are reviving the notion of *jihād* to destabilize the secular world order. Khadduri, 'International Law'; idem, *War and Peace*; *EI*[2], s.v. Dār al-Ḥarb, Dār al-Islām; Sachedina, *Islamic Roots*, 5, 54, 135,148.

[313]Cf. *Kāfī*, V, 440–1.

consummation of her marriage with [a Zoroastrian] husband who has refused to become Muslim, she is entitled to one-half her *mahr*. ʿAlī said, '[The acceptance of] Islam does nothing but increase her honour.'[314]

ʿAlī: He said, 'When a man becomes an apostate (*irtadda*), he is (ipso facto) divorced from his wife.[315] If he is asked to recant and repents before the expiry of the *ʿidda*, their marriage continues; but, if the period of the *ʿidda* has expired, and he repents afterwards, her husband may become one of her [possible] suitors. If the husband goes to a non-Muslim country (*dār al-ḥarb*),[316] all his ties with her are broken. If both of them become apostates, or both of them go to a non-Muslim country, and afterwards accept Islam and when asked to recant [their apostasy] they repent, their marriage continues.'

[ʿAlī]: He said, 'Where a woman from a non-Muslim country (*ahl al-ḥarb*) comes into an Islamic country (*dār al-islām*) seeking refuge, and leaves her husband in that country, her husband has no right over her and she may marry whom she likes without observing *ʿidda*. If her husband accepts Islam, he may become one of her suitors.'

[ʿAlī]: He said, 'It is not lawful for a Muslim to marry an alien woman (*ḥarbīya*) in a non-Muslim country (*dār al-ḥarb*).'

[314]Ibid., V, 442. For the case of a Christian couple see ibid., V, 441.

[315]In its verdict dated 5 August 1996, the Egyptian Court of Cassation (*maḥkamat al-naqd*), which is the final appeal court against a definitive ruling of the appeal court (*maḥkamat al-istiʾnāf*), declared Naṣr Ḥāmid Abū Zayd, a professor of Arabic language and literature at the University of Cairo and a theorist of hermeneutics and the Qurʾānic exegesis in the contemporary Arab world, to be an apostate. The said court, therefore, even without consulting his wife, ordered his separation from her (who is a Muslim) and invited him to repent and recant his 'un-Islamic' views. The views expressed by Abū Zayd in his book *Naqd al-khiṭāb al-dīnī (Critique of Religious Discourse*, first published as a book in 1990, second edn. Cairo, 1994) were cited as offensive to Islam and the Muslims. In this book Abū Zayd distinguished between the religion as revealed in the Qurʾān and the religious discourse dealing with religion, systematized and institutionalized by various groups over the course of fourteen centuries of Islamic history. He simply advocated that the religious texts must be interpreted in the light of their historical and social contexts. His wife Ibtihāl Yūnis, also a professor, was outraged and protested vehemently against the court verdict stating that it violated the sanctity of her private life. The couple was forced to leave Egypt for their own safety. Now, they live in the Netherlands.

Unfortunately, in 1993 this climate of intimidation and terror against the intellectuals in Egypt led to the assassination of another thinker Faraj Fouda. Again in 1997, yet another leading intellectual Ḥasan Ḥanafī, professor of philosophy at the University of Cairo, was threatened by a small but vocal group of Azharite conservative *ʿulamāʾ*. The same oppressive climate prevails in the rest of the Islamic world including the Ismāʿīlī community of both the Bohras and the Khojas.

[316]See n. 312 above in this chapter.

['Alī]: He said, 'When a polytheist man and his wife are captured in war, their marital status continues. Where, however, one of them is made captive and safely guarded in an Islamic country, but the other is not [because he or she has escaped to his or her country], their ties are broken.'

THE RIGHT TO EQUITY BETWEEN CO-WIVES (*AL-QASMA BAYN AL-ḌARĀ'IR*)[317]

God says: *Ye will not be able to deal equally between [your] wives, however much ye may wish (to do so). But turn not altogether away (from on), leaving her as in suspense* (4:129). Thus God has informed [you] that justice between wives is unattainable. The reason is that it is possible for a man to be just in regard to maintenance, residence at night, gifts, and with other material possession; but justice is unattainable regarding desire, passion, and joy in sexual intercourse. Thus, it is incumbent upon a man to be equitable as far as possible. God has made allowances concerning things which cannot be attained, but commanded justice otherwise where possible. He said: *Allah tasketh not a soul beyond its scope* (2:286).

Ja'far b. Muḥammad—his father—his ancestors—'Alī: He said, 'A man is entitled to marry four wives. If he marries only one wife, he must stay with her one night in every four and during the remaining three nights he may do what God has made lawful for him.'

Ja'far b. Muḥammad said, 'If a man has two wives, he should select

[317] *Ḍarā'ir* pl. of *ḍarra*. *Ḍirr* means taking a second wife (concurrent with a first). Lane, s.v. ḍ-r-r. I have preferred this translation of *qasma* by El-Alami, *Marriage Contract*, 128. Robson rendered it 'Sharing visits to one's wives equally'. Fyzee had rendered it 'The division of time between co-wives'. It is true that most of the traditions transmitted by Nu'mān in this section and Tabrīzī in his *Mishkāt al-maṣābīḥ*, II, 195–7; Robson, I, 686–7, deal with the division of time between the wives. However, as stated by Nu'mān equitable treatment of wives is based on the Qur'ānic verse 4:129. Polygamy is, thus, conditional upon the maintenance of equity. If a man fears that he will not be able to do justice between wives, then he should restrict himself to one. Abū Hurayra related the Prophet as saying, 'When a man has two wives and does not treat them equally he will come on the Day of Resurrection with his scale hanging down.' In another tradition 'Ā'isha related that the Prophet used to divide his time among his wives equally and say, 'O God, this is my division concerning what I possess, so do not blame me concerning what Thou possessest and I do not.'

Modern Muslim reformers addressed the problem of polygamy and as a result of their efforts many Muslim countries have enacted legislation imposing legal restrictions in an attempt to restrict it. Turkey and Tunisia have abolished the capacity of the husband to contract a second polygamous marriage. For details see Anderson, *Law Reform*, passim; Pearl, *Muslim Family Law*, 241–73. For Egyptian and Moroccan laws about polygamy, equity, and divorce on grounds of harm due to polygamy, see El-Alami, *Marriage Contract*, 129–36.

one of them and stay three nights with her and one night with the other. If he has three wives, he should stay one night with each and the fourth night may be spent with any of them. If he has four wives, he should not show preference to one wife above the others.'[318]

'Alī: He was asked about the Qur'ānic verse: *If a woman fears ill-treatment from her husband, or desertion, it is no sin for them twain if they make terms of peace between themselves. Peace is better* (4:128). 'Alī said, 'This concerns [the case of] a man who has two wives and wearies of one of them, or [finds] one of them ugly (*damīma*) and turns against her wishing to divorce her. If she dislikes this course, they may settle the affair by mutual consent [agreeing] that he will come to her [only] once in a while, or that she will give up this right entirely.'

['Alī]: He said, 'If a man has one, [two], or three wives and marries a virgin, he should stay seven nights with her,[319] and if he marries a woman who is not a virgin (divorcee or widow), he should stay three nights with her; and then he should distribute his time equally between them.'[320]

Ja'far b. Muḥammad: He was asked about a man who has several wives and has sexual intercourse with some of them to the exclusion of others. He said, 'His only obligation is to stay with each wife the night appointed for her and spend the afternoon siesta with her. However, he is not obliged to have sexual intercourse[321] with her if he takes no pleasure in it.'

'Alī: He said, 'When a man has several wives and returns after having gone out travelling, he should begin by spending the night with the woman whose turn it is.'

THE OBLIGATION TO PROVIDE MAINTENANCE TO WIVES (*AL-NAFAQĀT 'ALA 'L-AZWĀJ*)[322]

God says: *We are aware of that which We enjoined upon them concerning their wives and those whom their right hands possess* (33:50). He says: *But feed and clothe them from it, and speak kindly unto them* (4:5).

[318]Ṭūsī, *al-Nihāya*, 483.

[319]Ibid., 483; 'if he marries a virgin he could stay with her three to seven nights.'

[320]*Mishkāt*, II, 195; Robson, I, 686; transmitted by both Bukhārī and Muslim; Ṭūsī, *Tahdhīb al-aḥkām*, VII, 420.

[321]Ṭūsī, *al-Nihāya*, 483; 'he has to share time between his wives, but is not obliged to have intercourse.'

[322]Maintenance for the wife consists of providing for her food, clothing, housing, and running a household. The basis for it is the Qur'ān 2:233, 65:6 and the *sunna* of the Prophet. The jurists agree that the obligation of maintenance is a consequence of the marriage contract. The Mālikīs further hold that this obligatory is subject to fulfilment of

Ja'far b. Muḥammad—his father—his ancestors: The Messenger of God delivered a sermon on the Farewell Pilgrimage and mentioning wives, he said, 'They are entitled to receive maintenance and clothing in accordance with custom (or with moderation recognized as reasonable *bi 'l-ma'rūf*).'[323]

[Ja'far b. Muḥammad]: He prohibited people from feeding themselves and keeping their families hungry. He said, 'A man who harms those who are under his care deserves destruction. It is a grave sin for him to harm those who depend on him.'[324]

[Ja'far b. Muḥammad]: He said, 'There are seven good deeds that have priority over all others, and it is incumbent upon you to discharge them.' Among them, he mentioned maintenance of the family.[325]

Abū Ja'far Muḥammad b. 'Alī: He said, 'He who believes in the reward of the hereafter (*khalaf* lit. recompense) is generous in providing for his family.'

Ja'far b. Muḥammad: In regard to the Word of God: *and squander not [thy wealth] in wantonness* (17:26), he said, 'There can be no squandering in obedience to God.'

The Messenger of God: He said, 'Kindness (*rifq*) is one-half of livelihood, and he who is moderate will not deviate from the right course.'

[The Messenger of God]: He said, 'When God the Blessed and Exalted desires the welfare of a family, He instructs them in religion, provides for them in kindness, and teaches them moderation in life.'

[The Messenger of God]: He said, 'He who acts in moderation in his way of living, God will provide for him; and he who squanders his wealth, God will deprive him of his livelihood.'

'Alī: He said, 'He who bought what he does not need, has indeed sold what he needs.'

['Alī]: He said, 'The greatest perfection consists in understanding of religion (*al-tafaqquh fi 'l-dīn*), patience in adversity, and thoughtfulness in living.'

---

certain conditions, such as the consummation of marriage. Maintenance may be suspended on account of wife's disobedience to her husband. It terminates on the death of either of the parties to the marriage. For details about Egyptian and Moroccan laws regarding maintenance see El-Alami, *Marriage Contract*, 113–28. In recent times the question of maintenance has become 'alive'. For details of court cases in India, Pakistan, and Bangladesh, see Pearl, *Muslim Family Law*, 201–26.

[323]Ṭabarī, *Tārīkh*, III, 151; *History of al-Ṭabarī*, IX, 113. See also *Mishkāt*, II, 231; Robson, I, 714; transmitted by both Bukhārī and Muslim.

[324]Cf. *Mishkāt*, II, 232; Robson, I, 714; transmitted by Muslim.

[325]'When God makes any of you prosperous, he should spend first on himself and his family.' *Mishkāt*, II, 231; Robson, I, 714.

The Messenger of God: He said, 'Having numerous children and a paucity of means are [the cause] of the greatest of calamities. A small number of children is one of the two ways of ease [in life].'[326]

'Alī: He said, 'When a man has no means whereby to maintain his wife, a little time may be afforded him, and if he is able to provide her with something, they should not be separated; but if he cannot provide anything, a time limit should be fixed and then they should be divorced.'

'Alī: A woman asked him for help against her husband saying that he refused to give her any maintenance in order to cause her hardship, so 'Alī imprisoned him for it.[327]

['Alī]: He said, 'A woman who goes out of her husband's house without his permission is not entitled to maintenance until she returns.'

['Alī]: Once he gave a decision in favour of a woman against her [divorced] husband while she was suckling his child. He decreed that the husband should pay one-fourth of a *makkūk*[328] of food and one pitcher of water [per day].

On the issue of maintenance, there is no fixed measure; and God has distinguished between people in accordance with their means and said: *The rich according to his means, and the straitened according to his means* (2:236). It is likely that 'Alī decided upon [the above measure] based upon the means of the man.

['Alī]: Concerning the Qur'ānic verse: *A mother should not be made to suffer because of her child, nor should he to whom the child is born (be made to suffer) because of his child. And on the (father's) heir is incumbent the like of that (which was incumbent on the father)* (2:233),[329] he said, 'After the death

[326]It raises the issue of family planning introduced by some Muslim governments in recent times. See Rahman, *Health and Medicine*, 113–18; Halm, *Shi'a Islam*, 150–2.

[327]The Muslim woman is an independent legal entity even after her marriage and retains her financial independence. She can own property in her own right and her husband cannot access her funds or demand any form of financial support from her. The husband is obliged to support his wife. Al-Hibri, 'Muslim Women's Rights', 46–7.

[328]*Makkūk* is a grain measure of varying magnitude. Hinz, *Islamische Masse*, 44–5. The *makkūk* of Aleppo and Tripoli contained 83.5 kg. of wheat. *EI*[2], s.v. Makāyil.

[329]It is worth noting that Khumaynī's *fatwā* regarding birth control and family planning is fairly and squarely based on this verse. The first part of the verse, not quoted by Nu'mān, states: *Mothers shall suckle their children for two whole years; (that is) for those who wish to complete the suckling. The duty of feeding and clothing nursing mothers in a seemly manner is upon the father of the child. No one should be charged beyond his capacity.*

The strict observance of instructions in the above verse is in itself a kind of contraception that will minimize the possibility of early pregnancy. The later half of the verse is another evidence that implies family planning. Based on this verse '*ulamā*' state that the pregnancy of a woman is permissible only if she is physically ready. Secondly, the child should not

of the father, the heir has the same obligation regarding maintenance and suckling as the father had. The harm that the child suffers from the mother is that although she is able to suckle him she refuses to do so. In this there is harm as well to the father [in regard to the child]. It is also an obligation on the father that he should not harm the mother by refusing her to suckle the child and by asking someone else to do so. In the same manner as the parents, the heir should also not harm the child either in respect of suckling and in respect of maintenance.'

['Alī]: Concerning a man who divorces his wife while she is suckling her baby, he said, 'Verily she has prior right to suckle her child if she so desires, and she may take [the wages] which a wet nurse is given.'[330]

Ja'far b. Muḥammad: He was asked about the following case: A man died leaving his widow and his child by her. She gave the child to a servant girl (*khādima*) for suckling. Later she (servant girl) came to the legal guardian and claimed the remuneration for suckling. [The Imam] said, 'The *khādima* should be paid the same amount as one in her position,[331] and the legal guardian has no right to take the child away from her bosom.'

---

deprive the mother of having a decent life. Moreover, the father should have sufficient means to support the family. The *fatwā* concludes by stating, 'so it can be said that Islam's support of more children is not everlasting, it may be subject to the mental, physical, and economic conditions of parents. The application of various methods of contraception has been discussed by Muslim jurists, scientists, and scholars who have generally concluded that methods not harmful to women are permitted.' The *fatwā* was published in the newspaper *Kayhan International*, 22 April 1993; Halm, *Der Schiitische Islam*, 166–8; English trans. *Shi'i Islam*, 150–2. See also Juynboll, 'The *Ḥadīṯ* in the Discussion of Birth-Control'.

[330] All jurists agree that according to the Qur'ān 2:233, it is imperative for the mother to suckle her baby, whether she is married to its father, or divorced. However, the positions of various schools of law differ as to whether the mother should be ordered by the court to suckle the baby. Nasir, *Status of Women*, 119–20.

[331] It should be noted that according to the Imāmīs the mother is entitled to receive payment for nursing her own child during the continuation of marriage, during or after the *'idda* of a revocable or irrevocable divorce. The husband may even hire her for fostering. The Sunnī schools of law and the modern laws of Syria, Morocco, and Jordan rule on the contrary. All schools of law, Sunnī and Shī'ī alike, hold that the mother, whether she is separated or living with her husband, has the first claim to the custody of her child. The Imāmīs rule that the mother's custody for the male child shall continue for the duration of suckling, and for the female child until the age of seven. Some jurists, however, extend the custody to seven years for the boy and to nine years for the girl. The Sunnī schools differ widely in this respect. The Mālikī law enshrined in the Moroccan legislation rule that the mother's custody of the boy shall continue until he attains puberty, and of the girl till she is married. For details and modern legislations, see Nasir, *Status of Women*, 121–36.

11

Book of Divorce (*Kitāb al-Ṭalāq*)[1]

FORBIDDEN AND LAWFUL DIVORCES (*AL-ṬALĀQ AL-MANHĪY 'ANHU WA 'L-ṬALĀQ AL-MUBĀḤ 'ANHU*)

God says: *O Prophet! When ye (men) put away women, put them away for their (legal) period, and reckon the period, and keep your duty to Allah, your Lord* till His saying: *Allah has set a measure for all things* (65:1–3).[2]

Divorce, according to the Book of God and the *sunna* of the Messenger of God, is permitted for a man who wishes it, and the right of divorce belongs to men; so he who dislikes his wife and desires separation from her, has the right [to divorce her] with or without any cause. Separation

[1]The chapter on divorce shows that there are a number of ways in which a marriage may be terminated in Islamic law. Some of these forms, such as *īlā'*, *ẓihār*, and *li'ān*, may appear exotic, but they are not practised today. The two most common forms of divorce, based on mutual consent, are *khul'* and *mubāra'a*. Under the *sharī'a* marriage may be dissolved during the lifetime of the spouses either by the act of the husband, by mutual agreement between the husband and the wife, or by a judicial order of the court. Modern personal status legislation in Muslim countries shows an increasing tendency to curb the unilateral right of the husband. Under some legislation, no divorce is effective outside the court. These are the recognized forms of dissolution of marriage in most of the Muslim countries. For details see Nasir, *Status of Women*, 69–96. For recent changes in the Islamic law of divorce in various Muslim countries, see Anderson, *Islamic Law*, 38–58. In his *Compendium*, 42–71, Fyzee has given the summary of this chapter.

[2]In the Qur'ān 65:1–3, it is also stated: ... *Expel them [your women] not from their houses nor let them go forth unless they commit open immorality ... when they have reached their term, take them back in kindness or part from them in kindness ...* . The husband has to provide maintenance to the wife during *'idda*. The pregnant wife should be provided for until she delivers. Kulaynī elaborates this aspect in his *Kāfī*, VI, 97–101, 107–8.

however is disapproved after affection and association when there is no cause, but the disapproval does not amount to a [legal] prohibition.[3]

Ja'far b. Muḥammad—his father—his ancestors—'Alī: One day while Umm Sa'īd, a slave girl of 'Alī, was pouring water on his hands, he said, 'O Umm Sa'īd.' She said, 'Here I am, O Commander of the Faithful.' 'Alī said, 'I greatly desire to become a bridegroom!' Umm Sa'īd said, 'And what prevents you from this, O Commander of the Faithful?' 'Alī said, 'Woe to thee! [What] After having four wives in the Ruḥba?'[4] Umm Sa'īd said, 'Divorce one of them and bring another in her place.' 'Alī replied, 'Woe to thee! I certainly know of this [option]; but divorce is reprehensible and I disapprove of it.'[5]

[Imam] Ḥasan b. 'Alī used to marry and divorce many women. If he was attracted to a woman while he had four wives, he would divorce one of them and marry the woman. In this manner he married many women and caused them to abstain from that which is unlawful (*fa-aḥṣana kathīr*[an] *min al-nisā'*).

Abū Ja'far Muḥammad b. 'Alī [Imam al-Bāqir] said, 'Once 'Alī said to the people of Kūfa, "Do not marry [your daughters] to Ḥasan, for he is a man who divorces women freely (*miṭlāq*)."'[6]

[3]Divorce without any good reason is disapproved. *Kāfī*, VI, 57–8. According to the teachings of *fiqh* (jurisprudence) on *ṭalāq* the husband has the right to pronounce divorce on his wife even without giving the reasons, however his pronouncing it without good reason is considered reprehensible, and by the Ḥanafīs even as forbidden. It should be noted that the institution of the unilateral *ṭalāq* has been subjected to severe criticism. Both Western as well as Muslim scholars have rightly observed that it is the Islamic law of divorce—not polygamy—which stands out in the whole range of the family law as causing the gravest suffering to Muslim women. The 'triple pronouncement of *ṭalāq*' in one sitting is also the main target of Nu'mān's criticism in the following pages. Since the beginning of the twentieth century, increasing dissatisfaction with traditional divorce laws and rapid socio-economic changes, have led to several changes and the enactment of legislation in all Muslim countries. Relevant legislative particulars are listed in *EI*², s.v. Ṭalāḳ; Anderson, *Law Reform*; Pearl, *Muslim Family Law*, 286–382. Unfortunately, the Bohra religious establishment has not shown any sign of reform concerning divorce practices in the community or enhancing the status of women.

[4]Ruḥba, see Chap. 6, n. 59.

[5]'The lawful thing which God hates most is divorce.' *Mishkāt*, II, 209, 212; Robson, I, 696, 698.

[6]The title *al-Miṭlāq* (the Divorcer) was given to Ḥasan because of his numerous marriages. He had married sixty or seventy or ninety times. *EI*², s.v. Ḥasan b. 'Alī b. Abī Ṭālib. See also *Kāfī*, VI, 59. After 'Alī's statement Kulaynī's tradition adds: Then a man stood up and said, 'Oh yes! We will certainly marry [our daughters] to him. Verily, he is the [grand]son of the Messenger of God and the son of Fāṭima. If he is pleased with her he will keep her and if he dislikes her he will divorce her.' *Majma' al-baḥrayn*, s.v. ṭ-l-q; he cites the tradition of 'Alī. See also Chap. 10, n. 25.

The [type of] divorce which is proper—and no other is permissible—is the one according to the Book of God and the practice (*sunna*) of the Messenger of God; and that which is not in consonance with this rule is not a [proper] *ṭalāq*, as God says: *Such are the limits (imposed) by Allah; and whosoever transgresseth Allah's limits, he verily wrongs his soul* (65:1).

Ja'far b. Muḥammad—his father—his ancestors: Once Ibn 'Umar[7] divorced his wife while she was in her menses. The Messenger of God heard of this and repudiated his action and commanded him to take her back, and divorce her, if he so desired, according to the *sunna* form of divorce (*ṭalāq al-sunna*).[8] This is a well-known tradition, on which there is a consensus, and we shall mention it at its proper place and clarify its meaning, if God wills.[9]

'Alī: Once he wrote to Rifā'a[10] a letter which contained the following: 'Beware of speaking on matters relating to divorce, and wherever there is a way out, keep yourself away from it. Where any such matter is forced upon you, refer it to me and I shall show them the right path. The correct ways of divorce and marriage have been obliterated, and the innovators have altered them.'

Abū Ja'far Muḥammad b. 'Alī: He said, 'People cannot be brought back to the right path in the matter of divorce except by means of the sword; and if I were the ruler over people, I would have brought them back to the Book of God.'[11]

Ja'far b. Muḥammad: He said, 'If I were in charge of the affairs of men, I should certainly have taught them [the correct laws of] divorce,

[7]'Abd Allāh b. 'Umar, see *The Pillars of Islam*, I, 326, n. 113.

[8]*Ṭalāq al-sunna* (in conformity with the dictates of the Prophet) is the approved form of divorce as opposed to *ṭalāq al-bid'a*, which is disapproved. Accordingly, one single pronouncement of *ṭalāq* is made in a period of *ṭuhr* (purity, when the woman is free from her menstrual course). It is further explained in what follows. For details see also Fyzee, *Outlines*, 152–4; *EI*[2], s.v. Ṭalāḳ.

[9]'Abd Allāh b. 'Umar said that he divorced a wife of his while she was menstruating and that when 'Umar mentioned the matter to the Messenger of God, he became angry and said, 'He must take her back and keep her till she is purified, then has another period and is purified. Then if it seems good to him to divorce her, he may do so when she is pure from the menstrual discharge and before having intercourse with her, for that is the period of waiting which God has commanded for the divorce of women.' *Mishkāt*, II, 208; Robson, I, 695; transmitted by both Bukhārī and Muslim. See also Ṭūsī, *Tahdhīb al-aḥkām*, VIII, 55. The case of Ibn 'Umar is referred to by Marwazī, *Ikhtilāf al-fuqahā'*, 236–40, while discussing the definition of *ṭalāq al-sunna*.

[10]Rifā'a b. Shaddād, see *The Pillars of Islam*, I, 281.

[11]*Kāfī*, VI, 59, 60; reported from the same authority.

and no person brought before me who had broken the law would have escaped my punishment of scourging.'[12]

'Alī: He said, 'Divorce with reference to the *'idda* (*al-ṭalāq li 'l-'idda*) [takes effect] when the woman is pure and no sexual intercourse has taken place [during the period of purity in which the divorce was pronounced as well as during the whole of the *'idda*].'

Abū Ja'far and Abū 'Abd Allāh: They said, 'The divorce with reference to the *'idda* (*ṭalāq al-'idda*) is that which is mentioned by God: ... *put them away for their (legal) period* (65:1).[13] When a man wishes to divorce his wife with reference to the *'idda*, let him wait till she menstruates, and is free from her menstrual period, and then he should divorce her. She should be pure, in a period of purity during which he should not have touched her. [He should pronounce] one *ṭalāq* and this should be witnessed by two competent witnesses.[14] It is the husband's right to return to her, and he may do so for some days after [the first pronouncement] but prior to the next menstruation; this return must be witnessed by two witnesses and then he may cohabit with her and remain with her till she menstruates.

'When she menstruates and becomes free from her menses, he may pronounce another divorce as long as no intercourse has taken place; two witnesses should witness this divorce pronouncement. He may also resume his marriage whenever he wishes but before she menstruates [again]. He should have witnesses for the resumption (*raj'a*), and may cohabit with her until the third menstrual period [begins].

'When she is free from her menses and becomes pure, he may divorce her for the third time, as long as he has had no intercourse with her. Two witnesses should witness the divorce pronouncement. When this is accomplished, she is divorced absolutely by three divorce pronouncements, and the woman is not lawful to him until she marries another husband.[15] If the wife is one of those women who do not menstruate, he should divorce her for a period of [three] months.'

If the husband divorces her with one pronouncement as we have described it, and then it occurs to him to have her, she may remain with

[12]Ibid., VI, 60. These traditions suggest that the right of divorce was greatly abused and the proper procedure was not followed.

[13]This verse is unanimously interpreted to mean that it is forbidden to pronounce the *ṭalāq* during the woman's period of menstruation. Qummī, II, 389; Ṭabarī, *Tafsīr* (Beirut), XXVIII, 83–5.

[14]Bukhārī, *Matn al-Bukhārī*, III, 268; *Kāfī*, VI, 62, 65. It is also called revocable divorce.

[15]*Kāfī*, VI, 78–9. The third *ṭalāq* is considered definite.

him for the period of two remaining divorce pronouncements. And if he has divorced her twice, she may remain with him till one more pronouncement. But if he divorces her for the third time, he has no right to return to her, and she is not lawful to him until after another husband.

These rules apply when he returns to her before the expiry of the *'idda.* But if he has divorced her once or twice, and he leaves her till the *'idda* expires, he has no right to return to her. He then becomes just another of her suitors, and if she agrees to a marriage with him, he may marry her by a fresh contract.[16]

This is the divorce according to the Prophet's practice (*ṭalāq al-sunna*). For him who wishes the divorce to be effective, it is laid down that he should pronounce *ṭalāq* once, leave her, and not return to her until the *'idda* expires. Then, the separation is completed and she is more entitled to manage her own affairs thereafter [than anyone else]. If both parties agree, they may return to each other by a fresh marriage, and if they do not desire to do so, she may marry anyone she likes.

So far as I [Nu'mān] know, this is the divorce on which there is a consensus of opinion among the jurisconsults. It is the form of divorce commanded by God and laid down in the practice (*sunna*) of the Messenger of God. When Ibn 'Umar divorced his wife, contravening the law, the Messenger of God ordered him to return to his wife. If the divorce had been pronounced as it ought to have been done, the Messenger of God would not have ordered him to return to her.

Those who express a contrary opinion [to this], thereby deviating from and being ignorant of the Book of God and the practice of the Messenger of God, have, according to [their learned jurists], sinned and transgressed the limits set down by God. For instance, a man pronounces divorce on his wife while she is menstruating, as did Ibn 'Umar with his wife, or while she is in the period of purity in which he had touched her, or he does so without witnesses, or divorces her three times [three consecutive pronouncements] at one sitting. All such pronouncements of divorce are contrary to what God has ordered in His Book and contrary to the *sunna* of His Messenger. Yet, in spite of disapproval [of such a divorce] by [their jurists], [the commonalty] confirm the divorce pronoucned by [Ibn 'Umar]. They [the commonalty], thereby, prohibit the husband from having lawful intercourse with his wife,[17] and make such [unlawful] intercourse with her lawful to another man[18] contrary to the Book and

[16]Ibid., VI, 67–71; *ṭalāq al-sunna wa 'l-'idda* is explained.

[17]This is because they approve of such a divorce and the couple is separated.

[18]Divorce was invalid and without reference to the *'idda*, hence she could marry

the *sunna*. For him who thinks over it, the plain meaning of what we have stated is a sufficient refutation of the view of its proponent.

Abū Ja'far and Abū 'Abd Allāh: They said, 'Every divorce which contravenes [the rules] laid down by God is void.' Thus if a man were to divorce a woman while she is menstruating, or during post-partum bleeding, or after he has had intercourse but before she has menstruated, or if he divorces her in a period of purity, without having had intercourse with her but without two competent witnesses being present as commanded by God, it is not a valid divorce. He must divorce her according to the Book and the *sunna* as we have described above.[19]

Abū Ja'far Muḥammad b. 'Alī: Once he went to the mosque, and behold, he saw a man delivering legal opinions and around him were a number of people. He asked, 'Who is this?' They said, 'It is Nāfi',[20] the emancipated slave of Ibn 'Umar.' So [the Imam] called him and he came, and [the Imam] said, 'O Nāfi', I hear that you say that Ibn 'Umar divorced his wife only once, and the Messenger of God asked him to return to her even though he thought it to be a valid divorce.' Nāfi' replied, 'That is what I heard, O son of the Messenger of God.' Abū Ja'far [the Imam] said, 'You have lied against the Messenger of God, O Nāfi'. Ibn 'Umar divorced her three times, and therefore the Messenger of God did not see him.'[21]

The rule stated by Nāfi' and supported by those of the commonalty who concur with him, that the Messenger of God held the divorce of Ibn 'Umar to be valid, and ordered him to take his wife back, is unsound by their own views. If the divorce pronounced by Ibn 'Umar was a single pronouncement, as they allege, and was made while his wife was menstruating was valid, the Messenger of God would never have asked him to take her back. The command of the Messenger of God [to take her back] is a *farḍ* (mandatory obligation); and it cannot be obligatory for a man who has legally divorced his wife to take her back.[22]

'Alī: He said, 'A man divorces his wife, takes her back, and purports

---

another man immediately. As a result they make the intercourse of another man [i.e. her new husband] with the still wedded wife of the first husband lawful, even though it is sinful. Nu'mān discusses this *ṭalāq al-bid'a* in great detail in the following pages.

[19] *Kāfī*, VI, 62, 64.

[20] *EI*[2], s.v. Nāfi', the *mawlā* (freedman) of 'Abd Allāh b. 'Umar. His fame rests mainly in his alleged position in *isnāds* in the Sunnī *ḥadīth* collections. The Nāfi'—> Ibn 'Umar—> Prophet, strand, according to Juynboll, ('Nāfi', the *mawlā* of Ibn 'Umar'), supports relatively late Ḥijāzī counterparts of *matns* first put into circulation elsewhere, as well as earlier Ḥijāzī *matns*. See also Schacht, *Origins*, 176–7.

[21] *Kāfī*, VI, 64; reported on the same authority.

[22] See the paragraph with n. 25 below for further explanation.

to divorce her again before he has touched her. This is not effective as a second divorce.'

Ja'far b. Muḥammad: He was asked about a man who divorced his wife while she was in her menses. He said, 'A *ṭalāq* which does not conform with the *sunna* is void.'

Abū Ja'far: A man asked [Imam al-Bāqir], 'O Son of the Messenger of God, I have heard that you say that if a man were to divorce [his wife] without following the rules of the *sunna*, his divorce would not be permissible.' [The Imam] replied, 'Not I, but God says this: *Why do not the rabbis and the priests forbid their evil-speaking and their devouring illicit gain? Verily evil is their handiwork* (5:63). If we were to deliver opinions dishonestly, we would be worse than they!'[23]

Abū Ja'far and Abū 'Abd Allāh: They said, 'Every *ṭalāq* pronounced in anger or [as part of] an oath is void.'

Abū Ja'far: He said, 'A man purports to divorce [his wife] with reference to the *'idda*, but pronounces more [divorces] than one. Every pronouncement except the first is void. If a man divorces a woman without two competent witnesses, this is not a *ṭalāq*. The evidence of women is not permissible in divorce.[24] If a man pronounces *ṭalāq* but does not intend it, no *ṭalāq* takes place, i.e. in intention which is between him and God. If a man pronounces a divorce according to the *sunna* and is duly witnessed and then says, "I did not intend *ṭalāq*," the legal decision does not take effect to his statement [of divorce], [25] for his intention is between him and God.'

'Alī: A man came to him and said, 'O Commander of the Faithful, I have verily divorced my wife.' He asked, 'Have you any proof for this?' The man said, 'No.' 'Alī said, 'Go away [from me]!'[26]

Abū Ja'far Muḥammad b. 'Alī: He said, 'If I had been appointed to deal with the affairs of the people, I would have taught them [the rules of] *ṭalāq* and how divorce should be pronounced. Then, if a man had been brought to me who had gone against the rules, I would have scourged his back. And he who had divorced [his wife] in contravention of the *sunna*, I would surely have sent him back to the Book of God even though he

[23]*Kāfī*, VI, 60; reported from the same authority.

[24]Ibid., VI, 70.

[25]His *ṭalāq* is null and void: as in *Kāfī*, VI, 64–5; it is reported on the same authority. The Ḥanbalīs, Ḥanafīs, and Shāfi'īs demand corresponding intention for the *ṭalāq*, but the Mālikīs pay no heed to the intention. *EI*[2], s.v. Ṭalāḳ.

[26]*Kāfī*, VI, 61; it is reported on the same authority. Instead of *ughrub* (go away) *Kāfī* has *u'zub*, with the same meaning.

may have been humbled thereby. If I had been given power over men, I would have put them right by sword and lash until they [had learnt] to divorce with reference to the *'idda* according to the commands of God.'

'Alī: A man asked him, 'I have divorced my wife with reference to the *'idda* without witnesses.' He said, 'This is not a divorce, so return to your wife.'

Ja'far b. Muḥammad: He said, 'Where a man divorces his wife with reference to the *'idda* three times [with three pronouncements] at one sitting and has witnesses for it, the woman is divorced once. This saying of his is clear for one who thinks over it. When the husband says, "She is divorced," she is divorced once, and his repetition of the words three times is equivalent to his saying it a thousand times! The man who opposes us does not see the true effect of pronouncing more than three times. Now whether it is one, a thousand, or even more pronouncements [than that], they are all over and above the first pronouncement. The reason is that whether it is a small number or a large number, if the smaller number is not proved, neither is the larger number. I [the Imam] do not see any difference in it. The Messenger of God declared void the divorce of Ibn 'Umar, in which he pronounced divorce three times during his wife's menstruation. If he had pronounced it according to the *sunna*, it would have been valid as a single pronouncement [of divorce] because when the husband said, "She is divorced," one divorce was effectively pronounced.'[27]

Ja'far b. Muḥammad: He said, 'A divorce repeated three times, if it is pronounced in a period of purity as prescribed, is valid as a single [pronouncement of] divorce; but if it is not pronounced in a period of purity, it does not take effect at all.'[28]

[27]Ibid., VI, 73.

[28]In principle, a *ṭalāq* does not constitute a final separation of the spouses since the husband might retract the repudiation during the wife's *'idda*. He is permitted to do so twice against the same wife. The third *ṭalāq* is, therefore, final and irrevocable. The term irrevocable 'triple *ṭalāq*,' i.e. three repudiations pronounced thrice successively on the same occasion, is derived from the above rule. It was also held to be possible for a husband to affect an immediate and irrevocable divorce by adding to a single repudiation on oath or some form of solemn expression of finality. The traditions are divided on this issue. Some authorities approve of it while the others not only disapprove of it but also hold it to be invalid. Some of those traditions suggest that such a *ṭalāq* was considered to be a single one and that 'Umar was the first to introduce into jurisprudence his view that it was a threefold pronouncement. It is argued that he did this in order to restrain people by fear of the undesirable consequences of its abuse. Although the overwhelming majority of the Sunnī jurists considered both of these types of *ṭalāq* 'blameworthy' morally, but nonetheless valid and effective. Shī'ī law held them to be null and void, or at least to constitute only a single, revocable *ṭalāq*. Cf. *Mishkāt*, II, 211–12; Robson, I, 698; *EI*[2], s.v. Ṭalāḳ; Coulson, *Succession*, 18.

[Ja'far b. Muḥammad]: He was asked about a man who says, 'Every woman whom I marry [hereafter] is divorced.' [The Imam] said, 'This statement is of no effect.' Then he was asked, 'If a man says, "If I marry so-and-so or if I marry at such and such a place, she is divorced."' He said, 'There can be no divorce or emancipation except after possession.'[29]

The Messenger of God: He prohibited [the marriage] of women divorced three times without observing the period (*'idda*), for, he said, 'They still have their husbands.'

Ja'far b. Muḥammad: One of his companions asked him about a man of the commonalty (*'āmma*)[30] who had divorced a woman, without reference to the *'idda* and wanted to remarry her. [The Imam] said, 'Consider [the matter] when you see him. Tell him, "You had divorced so-and-so when you knew that she was pure in a period of purity during which you had not touched her." When he says, "Yes," [then inform him], "That was the first divorce. Leave her until she completes her *'idda*, and then marry her, if you wish to do so, because she has been separated from you absolutely due to your first pronouncement." There should be two witnesses when you ask him, so the divorce will be in the presence of two witnesses.

'The divorce of Ibn 'Umar, which is held by consensus to be valid by our opponents, was either valid or invalid. If it was valid, then what was the import of its repudiation by the Prophet, and his command to return to her when the divorce was permissible? If it was invalid, how could the *'idda* be observed as our opponents allege?'

In addition to the tradition from Abū Ja'far [Imam al-Bāqir] in which we have reported earlier that Ibn 'Umar had divorced his wife thrice during her menses, there is another tradition from the [same Imam] which says that [the Imam] said to Nāfi', 'I heard 'Abd Allāh Ibn 'Umar saying, "I had divorced her thrice when she was in her menses, and the Messenger of God asked 'Umar[31] [my father] to order me to return to her and said, 'Verily the divorce of 'Abd Allāh three times, while his wife was menstruating, was not a divorce.'"'[32]

[29]'Alī reported the Prophet saying, 'There is no divorce before marriage, and no manumission until one has possession ...' *Mishkāt*, II, 209–10; Robson, I, 696; *Kāfī*, VI, 65, 66. 'If I marry thee, thou art divorced,' is recognized as valid by 'Abd Allāh b. Mas'ūd, 'Abd Allāh b. 'Umar, Nakhā'ī and Zuhrī, while others deny it. *Ṭalāq* presupposes a valid marriage. *Ṭalāq* pronounced on condition that the marriage is carried through is invalid according to the Shāfi'īs and Ḥanbalīs. *EI*², s.v. Ṭalāḳ.

[30]It means non-Shī'ī. For Nu'mān's use of this term for the Sunnīs see *The Pillars of Islam*, I, 5.

[31]According to MS Q. 'Ibn 'Umar' in the printed edition is an error.

[32]*Kāfī*, VI, 61, 62. *Ṭalāq al-bid'a* is unlawful according to the Shī'a. For the position of various Sunnī schools see Jazīrī, *al-Fiqh*, IV, 210 ff.

So a man said to [Imam] Ja'far b. Muḥammad and this he related from his father—that the people say that Ibn 'Umar had divorced her once when she was menstruating. [The Imam] said, 'If Ibn 'Umar had the right to return to her, what is it that the Messenger of God asked him to do? They have lied. He divorced her thrice,[33] so the Messenger of God ordered him to go back to her and said, "If you wish to divorce her, do so; and if you wish to take her back, do so." Those who oppose us uphold the *ṭalāq al-bid'a* (divorce of innovation),[34] which they consider to be permissible, to be the divorce of disobedience (*ṭalāq ma'ṣiya*).[35] They, however, say that such a divorce [being valid] separated them [the couple], but [on the other hand] they do not hold that a marriage of disobedience (*nikāḥ al-ma'ṣiya*) is valid. The result is that when they separate the couple on the ground of disobedience, they make the intercourse of another man with the [still wedded] wife lawful, even though it is sinful.'

There is no difference between those two things, for, if he divorced her without observing the *'idda*, she marries another man immediately thereafter. When they forbid her from intercourse [with her husband] by being disobedient, they permit her to have intercourse with another man by this act of disobedience. But a sinful person can only emerge from his sinful condition by repentance, and repentance in such a case, is to go back from a forbidden act to the lawful one. The man who divorces a woman contravening the *sunna*, does not repent from his sin. So their action confirms the action of a sinful man, and they consider sexual intercourse—a major sin—to be lawful, and they permit it even though it is contrary to what God mentions in His Book on the subject of divorce. They did not consider it to be lawful in marriage because He commanded that divorce should be with reference to the *'idda* and prohibited marriage during the *'idda*. They contravened His command and did what He prohibited. Now in the contravention of this command is the permissibility of a prohibition, for, when they declared intercourse [with the still wedded wife] to be forbidden, they declared it to be lawful to another, despite its sinfulness. This is clear to him who thinks and is endowed with intelligence.

According to their opinion, if a man were to pray all the prayers of the day and the following night in the morning, none of his prayers would be valid except the one which was offered at its proper time. This is because God has made prayer compulsory at its proper time, and the man who prays before its time, has not prayed correctly according to

[33]*Kāfī*, VI, 63; reported on the same authority.

[34]*Ṭalāq al-bid'a* is the one wherein the requirements of *ṭalāq al-sunna* are not observed.

[35]*Ṭalāq* pronounced during the woman's period of menstruation is regarded as a sin (*ma'ṣiya*) and error (*khaṭā'*), but its validity is not disputed. *EI*[2], Ṭalāḳ.

them. The same rule applies to *ḥajj*, the fast of Ramaḍān, and all obligatory acts which are enjoined by God at a specified time. Such acts cannot be performed before their appointed time.

Divorce is similar, because God has fixed the limits of its time, made it clear, and prohibited the transgression of its limits. The divorce of one who transgresses its limits is void, just as his fasting, prayer, and pilgrimage would be void, as the mandatory act in all those should be performed within the time limited for it. When a time limit is fixed, it is mandatory; so the act of one who breaks the limits laid down by God is void, for, if an act is permissible on account of a certain reason, it may also become lawful for another reason.

The arguments concerning this are numerous, and if we were to deal exhaustively with them, mentioning and refuting the reasoning of those who uphold the *ṭalāq al-bid'a*, it would exceed the limits of this book. What we have mentioned in this respect is sufficient for him who is rightly guided.

'Alī and Abū Ja'far and Abū 'Abd Allāh: They said, 'Five kinds of women can be divorced in all circumstances: the pregnant woman; the woman whose marriage has not been consummated;[36] the minor who does not menstruate;[37] the old woman who no longer menstruates;[38] and the woman whose husband has been absent for long.'[39]

The divorce of a pregnant woman is [executed by] a single pronouncement and the husband is entitled to return to her so long as she has not delivered the baby. But as soon as she has delivered she is absolutely separated from him and the husband becomes one of her [potential] suitors (*khuṭṭāb* pl. of *khāṭib*).[40] The woman with whom marriage was not consummated is absolutely separated from her husband when there is a single pronouncement of divorce. If he pronounces a divorce after this [first divorce], and before he returns to her, the second divorce does not take effect, as the first pronouncement separated her absolutely from him. He only divorces a divorced woman.

As for him who has been absent from his wife for long, when he divorces her once, she is absolutely separated from him when her *'idda* expires before he reaches her and returns to her. If he does reach her before

[36] *Kāfī*, VI, 87–8.

[37] Ibid., VI, 88–9.

[38] Ibid., VI, 89–90. The Qur'ān states: *And for such of your women as despair of menstruation, if ye doubt, their period (of waiting) shall be three months, along with those who have it not. And for those with child, their period shall be till they bring forth their burden* (65:4).

[39] *Kāfī*, VI, 82; reported on the same authority.

[40] Ibid., VI, 85–7.

the expiry of the *'idda* and returns to her before the end of the *'idda*, he is entitled to do so and she remains with him until two more divorce pronouncements. If he divorces her a second time while he is absent and has not returned to her, the second *ṭalāq* does not apply to her because he has divorced a woman who has been divorced already.[41]

The pronouncement of divorce that is legally effective is for a man to say to his wife, as we have already mentioned earlier in the account of the *sunna* form of *ṭalāq*, 'You are divorced', or he should take her name and say, 'So-and-so is divorced', either expressly or by necessary implication; or she may be mentioned to him [by somebody] and he should say, 'She is divorced.' Any language can be used for the pronouncement of divorce.

Similarly, if the husband says to his wife, 'Choose,' and she chooses herself, this is a valid *ṭalāq*. But if she chooses him, there is no *ṭalāq*. Also, he may say, 'Observe *'idda*,'[42] intending thereby a divorce, and it will be a divorce.

Abū Ja'far and Abū 'Abd Allāh: They said, 'A man says to his wife, "You are released (*khalīya minnī*), or free (*barī'a*), or separated (*bā'in*), or cut off (*batta*), forbidden (*ḥarām*), to me." This is not a divorce until he says to her in a period of purity in which no intercourse has taken place and with two competent witnesses, "You are divorced", or "Observe *'idda*", intending *ṭalāq* thereby.'[43]

It was said to Abū 'Abd Allāh [Imam al-Ṣādiq], '[Some of] the reporters of Kūfa relate from 'Alī that he said, "Every one of the three [pronouncements of] *ṭalāq* separates absolutely, so the woman is not lawful to her husband until she marries another." [The Imam] said, 'They have lied against him, may God curse them. 'Alī did not say that, but they have lied against him.'[44]

Abū Ja'far [Imam al-Bāqir] said, "Alī was asked about a man who said to his wife, "You are released (*khalīya*), or free (*barī'a*), or separated (*bā'in*), or cut off (*batta*), or forbidden (*ḥarām*)," and 'Alī said, 'These are among *the footsteps of the devil*,[45] and are of no effect. The man should be punished as a means of correcting him.'

Abū Ja'far: He was asked about a man who said to his wife, 'You are forbidden (*ḥarām*) to me.' He said, 'If I had the authority, I would have hit

[41] Ibid., VI, 82–4.

[42] The Arabic *i'taddī* means for a woman to observe the *'idda*. The Urdu translator has incorrectly rendered it 'prepare yourself'.

[43] *Kāfī*, VI, 71, 142.

[44] Ibid., VI, 141; instead of 'Kūfa' it has 'Iraq.'

[45] Alludes to the Qur'ān: *Follow not the footsteps of the devil.* 2:168, 208; 6:142; 24:21.

him on his head and said, "God has made her lawful to you and you make her forbidden to yourself!" What he said was no less than a lie for he asserted that what had been made lawful for him was forbidden to him. This is not *ṭalāq* nor does *kaffāra*[46] become due as a result of this statement.'

It was said to him, 'God says: O *Prophet! Why bannest thou that which Allah hath made lawful for thee, seeking to please thy wives?* (66:1). And God imposed expiation upon him.' [The Imam] said, 'The Messenger of God became intimate with Māriya the Copt,[47] before she gave birth to Ibrāhīm.[48] When 'Ā'isha[49] came to know of this, she became displeased [and angry with him]. The Messenger of God swore to 'Ā'isha that he would not go to Māriya and would make her forbidden to him. He asked

[46]A technical term, used in the Qur'ān, means an expiatory and propitiatory act which grants remission for faults of some gravity. *EI*^{2}, s.v. Kaffāra.

[47]Māriya, see *The Pillars of Islam*, I, 172, n. 37; *EI*^{2}, s.v. Māriya; this incident as well as other traditions are reported.

[48]Ibrāhīm, see *The Pillars of Islam*, I, 278, n. 36.

[49]'Ā'isha bt. Abī Bakr, see *The Pillars of Islam*, I, 54–5, 326, 488, 489, 490; *EI*^{2}, s.v. 'Ā'isha bint Abī Bakr. The aforecited verses (66:1–5) allude to an event or events wherein God reproaches the Prophet concerning his wives and reminds him that one of them has divulged a secret that he had entrusted to her. An allusion is made to the alliance of the two wives against the Prophet and the verses end with a threat of repudiation. The *mufassirūn*, the authors of *asbāb al-nuzūl* (occasions of revelation), and the *muḥaddithūn* explain these verses as follows: The Prophet, during a temporary absence of Ḥafṣa, had invited into her room Māriya the Copt and had relations with her there. Ḥafṣa, returning, surprised them and created a scene. The Prophet placated her, swearing that he would have no more relations with Māriya, but he insisted that she should not disclose it to someone else. But Ḥafṣa did not keep her word and told her friend 'Ā'isha and the news leaked out. The Prophet was annoyed and divorced Ḥafṣa, but soon revoked his resolution because of the revelation. The Prophet freed himself from the oath that he had taken concerning Māriya by offering a *kaffāra*. He also avoided his wives for twenty-nine days. See Ṭabarī, *Tafsīr* (Beirut), XXVIII, 100–5; Qummī, II, 392–3; Wāḥidī, *Asbāb al-nuzūl*, 312–14; *EI*^{2}, s.v. Ḥafṣa.

Some *muḥaddithūn* were not happy about this story, hence they asserted that the secret confided to Ḥafṣa, and her disclosure to 'Ā'isha, was about his succession, that Abū Bakr would succeed him and 'Umar would succeed the latter. Balādhurī, *Ansāb al-ashrāf*, I, 423–4.

Both Bukhārī and Muslim have a slightly different version according to which 'Ā'isha said that the Prophet used to spend time with Zaynab bt. Jaḥsh and that he once drank honey at her house, so Ḥafṣa and she agreed that the one whom the Prophet visited first should say, 'I notice that you have an odour of the gum of the mimosa. Have you eaten some?' When the Prophet visited one of them and she said that to him he replied, 'Don't worry; I drank some honey at the house of Zaynab, but I swear that I shall not do it again. Do not tell anyone of that.' He said this to please his wives, and then came down the revelation: *O Prophet! Why bannest thou that which Allah hath made lawful for thee, seeking to please thy wives?* (66:1). *Mishkāt*, II, 209; Robson, I, 696; transmitted by Bukhārī and Muslim. See also Balādhurī, *Ansāb al-ashrāf*, I, 424–7.

'Ā'isha to keep this secret, but she informed Ḥafṣa [thereby betraying the secret],[50] so the above verse was revealed. God then commanded him to break the oath, offer expiation, and return to Māriya; when Ibrāhīm was born, she became his *umm walad*.'[51]

Ja'far b. Muḥammad: He was asked about *khiyār* (choice in divorce).[52] He said, 'Verily Zaynab[53] said to the Messenger of God, "You are the Messenger of God and yet you do not do justice [to us]!" And Ḥafṣa said, "If you were to divorce us, we would find our equal [in marriage] among our people." So God humbled His Messenger and withheld revelation for twenty days. Then God revealed to him: O *Prophet! Say unto thy wives: If ye desire the world's life and its adornment, come! I will content you and will release you with a fair release. But if ye desire Allah and His Messenger and the abode of the Hereafter, then lo! Allah hath prepared for the good among you an immense reward* (33:28–9).[54]

'So the Messenger of God withdrew from them for twenty-nine nights at Mashrabat Umm Ibrāhīm.[55] Thereafter, he called them and gave them the choice [to be free], and they chose him. Had they chosen to be free, it would have amounted to one [pronouncement of] absolute divorce (*bā'in*).'[56]

[Ja'far b. Muḥammad]: He said, 'If a man gives a choice to his wife, she has this choice as long as they remain together in the same meeting. It

[50]Ḥafṣa, daughter of 'Umar b. al-Khaṭṭāb, was one of he wives of the Prophet. Her first husband, a Badrī, died at Medina on return from Badr. The Prophet married her in Sha'bān 3/February 625, after his marriage with 'Ā'isha and before the Battle of Uḥud; she was his fourth wife. Ṭabarī, *History of al-Ṭabarī*, IX, 131–2, 179; *EI*[2], s.v. Ḥafṣa.

[51]For *Umm al-walad* see *The Pillars of Islam*, I, 283, n. 62.

[52]*Kāfī*, VI, 142–3; this *khiyār* was the Prophet's privilege only.

[53]Zaynab bt. Jaḥsh, cousin of the Prophet, was previously married to Zayd b. Ḥāritha. The Prophet married her in Dhu 'l-Qa'da 5/627. Ṭabarī, *History of al-Ṭabarī*, IX, 23, 127, 134, 168; other sources are indicated therein.

[54]Qummī (II, 192) explains the occasion of revelation as follows. After the conquest of Khaybar the Prophet's wives asked for their share in the booty. When the Prophet said that he had distributed it among the Muslims as commanded by God, they became angry and said, 'You think that perhaps if you were to divorce us, we would not find our equal among our people.' So God humbled His Messenger and commanded him to keep away from his wives. The Messenger of God, therefore, withdrew from them to Mashrabat Umm Ibrāhīm for twenty-nine days. Ṭabarī, *Tafsīr* (Beirut), XXI, 97–9, states that 'Ā'isha and other wives asked for more things. See also Ṭūsī, *al-Tibyān*, VIII, 333–4; he states that 'the choice' was not in divorce, but between the world and the hereafter. Ṭabrisī, IV, 353–4; he elaborates on the explanation of the word 'choice (*takhyīr*).'

[55]Mashrabat Umm Ibrahīm, see *The Pillars of Islam*, I, 172.

[56]"Ā'isha said that the Messenger of God gave us the choice [to divorce] and we chose God and His Messenger. This was not reckoned against us [as divorce].' Transmitted by Bukhārī and Muslim. *Mishkāt*, II, 208; Robson, I, 695 (translation is mine). *Kāfī*, 144–5; Kulaynī's version is the same as that of Nu'mān's.

is of no effect unless she is pure in a period of purity during which no intercourse has taken place. If she chooses him, it is not a divorce; but if she chooses herself, it amounts to a single [pronouncement of] irrevocable divorce, and the husband becomes one of her [potential] suitors. She can marry him on the same day, but if she wishes to marry someone other than her husband, then her *'idda* must be completed. If she does not respond on the spot,[57] or if he goes to her and places his hand upon her, or if he kisses her before she speaks, this does not amount to anything [either separation or reunion] unless she responds at that very spot [before she stands up from her place].'

[Ja'far b. Muḥammad]: He said, 'Where a man divorces a woman during his illness, but is [still] of sound mind, the divorce is valid. If he or she dies before the expiry of the *'idda*, the two inherit from each other. But if her *'idda* expires, and the husband dies of the illness he was suffering from, she inherits from him so long as she remains unmarried.'[58]

[Ja'far b. Muḥammad]: He said, 'The divorce of a lunatic, i.e. a man of unsound mind, is not lawful;[59] neither is that of a drunken man who does not understand [what he is doing];[60] nor that of a sleeping man, when he pronounces the divorce while sleeping and does not understand [what he is doing]; nor that of a man who is compelled to pronounce divorce;[61] nor that of an infant before he has reached the age of puberty.'[62]

[Ja'far b. Muḥammad]: He said, 'A divorce cannot be broken up into fractions. Where a man pronounces a divorce as it should be pronounced, and says to his wife, "You are divorced to the extent of one-half, or one third or one-fourth of a divorce," or uses a similar expression, this pronouncement [is valid] as a single [pronouncement of] divorce.'

'Alī: He said, 'Where a man makes a reservation in divorce [i.e. he says, "*in shā' Allāh*" (if God wills)] and makes the reservation aloud, the divorce does not take effect. But if he pronounces the divorce aloud, and

[57] It is a free translation, the lit. translation is 'stands up from her place' (*qāmat min makāniha*).

[58] *Kāfī*, VI, 127–9; traditions in this section are contradictory, some state that a sick man cannot divorce, while others state that the divorced wife inherits from her husband so long as she is unmarried.

[59] *Kāfī*, VI, 131–2; *Mishkāt*, II, 210; Robson, I, 697.

[60] *Kāfī*, VI 132–3. Anderson, *Islamic Law*, 53, states that in the Ḥanafī law pronouncements of *ṭalāq* uttered under the influence of intoxication or intimidation were held valid. It was the miserable lot of Ḥanafī wives that urged the Ottomans to introduce reforms in the family law as early as in 1915.

[61] *Kāfī*, VI, 133–4; *Mishkāt*, II, 210; Robson, I, 697.

[62] *Kāfī*, VI, 130–1; *Mishkāt*, II, 211; Robson, I, 697.

makes the reservation secretly, the divorce pronounced aloud will be held to be valid.'

A NEGOTIATED DIVORCE AT THE REQUEST OF THE WIFE AND A DIVORCE BY MUTUAL CONSENT (*AL-KHUL' WA 'L-MUBĀRA'A*)[63]

Ja'far b. Muḥammad—his father—his ancestors: 'Alī said, '*Khul'*[64] is permissible when the man makes use of it on the proper occasion. This is when his wife tells him, "I fear I shall not be able to keep within the limits fixed by God with respect to you, and so I give to you such and such [property];" and the husband says, "I fear I shall not be able to keep within the limits fixed by God with respect to you." Now, whatever they agree between them concerning this, is permissible for them.'

Ja'far b. Muḥammad said, 'In such circumstances in which a wife tells her husband, "I shall not obey your order, fulfil my oaths to you, or bathe after impurity (*janāba*),[65] rather I shall trample upon your bed and enter your presence without asking permission;" if a wife uses similar expressions, briefly or at length, implying similar insubordination, or she says, "I shall not follow the limits laid down by God (*ḥudūd Allāh*) regarding you," it is permissible for the husband to release the wife on such terms as are agreed upon between them or for the wife to divorce her husband by giving him back some of the property which he had given her or by giving him some other property which he may take from her.

'*Khul'* operates as a single, irrevocable divorce (*taṭlīqa bā'ina*); the

[63]*Khul'* is a technical term that refers to a man divorcing his wife in exchange for some of her property which she gives him as a ransom to be released from him. It is generally at the request of the wife. Lane, s.v. kh-l-'; EI^2, s.v. Ṭalāḳ. *Mubāra'a* is a technical term meaning a mutual separation by the common consent of the husband and wife whereby they free themselves by a reciprocal renunciation of all rights. Lane, s.v. b-r-'; EI^2, s.v. Ṭalāḳ.

When married parties disagree and are apprehensive that they cannot observe the bounds prescribed by the divine law, the woman can release herself from the tie by giving the husband some property in consideration of which the husband consents to the divorce. When the desire to separate emanates from the wife, it is called *khul'*, but when the divorce is affected by mutual aversion and consent, it is known as *mubāra'a* (lit. freeing one another mutually). Fyzee, *Outlines*, 163–4. It should be noted that in 1967 the Supreme Court of Pakistan upheld a case of *khul'* divorce. Recently the governments of Egypt and Jordan have introduced legislation that this form of divorce be allowed by the courts. Anderson, *Law Reform*, 80, 136.

[64]For details and varying views of different schools see Jazīrī, *al-Fiqh*, IV, 371–406.

[65]*Janāba*, major ritual impurity after sexual intercourse, which warrants a ritual bath; see *The Pillars of Islam*, I, 140.

husband has no right to return to her unless they marry again by common consent.[66] The husband retains the right to pronounce the remaining *ṭalāq*s and this follows from the Word of God: *And it is not lawful for you that ye take from women aught of that which ye have given them; except (in the case) when both fear that they may not be able to keep within the limits (imposed by) Allah. And if ye fear that they may not be able to keep the limits of Allah, in that case it is no sin for either of them if the woman ransom herself* (2:229).

Ja'far b. Muḥammad: He said, '*Khul*' takes place when the two spouses desire separation without any harm being done by the husband to the wife, and on the understanding that the wife should give to the husband some of the property he had given to her; or that she may give up some of her right against him, or something else may be done so that she may free herself thereby. This can take place if she does not transgress in speech. It is not lawful for the husband to take more than what he had given to her, but if she is excessive in her words and wishes to ransom herself without any harm coming to her from him, she has the right to give back to him all that he had given to her and even more. This is permissible.'[67]

'Alī: He said, '*Khul*' and *mubāra'a* can only take place in the presence of two witnesses in a period of purity during which no intercourse has taken place just as is the case with *ṭalāq* and *takhyīr* (choice).'[68]

Ja'far b. Muḥammad: He said, 'If hostility (*nushūz*)[69] exists on the part of the wife but not on the part of the husband, then it is lawful for the husband to take from her whatever is agreed upon between them. But if both are hostile to each other, and each of them is on bad terms with the other, then the husband shall take no more than what he had given her.'

'Alī: In regard to the Word of God: ... *appoint an arbiter (ḥakam) from his folk and an arbiter from her folk* (4:35), he said, 'They have no right to

[66]*Kāfī*, VI, 145–50; both *khul*' and *mubāra'a* are treated separately. Kulaynī has another section dealing with the maintenance and residence of women divorced by mutual consent. Ibid., VI, 150–1.

[67]Ibn 'Abbās related that the wife of Thābit b. Qays came to the Prophet and said, 'O, Messenger of God, I do not reproach Thābit in respect of character or religion, but I do not want to be guilty of infidelity regarding Islam?' The Messenger of God asked her if she would give him back his garden, and when she replied that she would, he told him to accept the garden and make one declaration of divorce [*khul*']. *Mishkāt*, II, 208; Robson, I, 695; transmitted by Bukhārī.

[68]*Kāfī*, VI, 149–50.

[69]*Nushūz*, in Islamic law, means violation of marital duties on the part of either the husband or the wife. Lane, s.v. n-sh-z. The term occurs in the Qur'ān 4:34, 128. *Kāfī*, VI, 151–2.

arbitrate unless both spouses agree and authorize them to either bring them together or separate them.'[70]

['Alī]: A man came to him with his wife and with each of them there were a large number of people. So he ordered each spouse to appoint an arbitrator from their folk, and they did so. Then he called the arbiters and said, 'Do you know what your duty is? If you decide that they should come together, you should bring them together; but if you think they should separate, then you should separate them.' Then the woman said, 'I am content with what is laid down in the Book of God regarding my rights and obligations.' And the husband said, 'As to separation—no!' So 'Alī said, 'You lie, By God. Unless you agree as she has done [no arbitration will take place].'[71]

Abū Ja'far Muḥammad b. 'Alī and Abū 'Abd Allāh: In regard to the Word of God: ... *appoint an arbiter from his folk and an arbiter from her folk* (4:35) they said, 'The arbiters have no right to separate them unless both the husband and the wife authorize them [to do so].'[72]

VOW OF CONTINENCE (*AL-ĪLĀ'*)[73]

God says: *Those who forswear (yu'lūna* [from *ālā*]) *their wives must wait four months ...* (2:226).[74]

Ja'far b. Muḥammad—his father—his ancestors: 'Alī said, '*Īlā*' takes place when a man says to his wife, "I swear by God, I shall certainly make you angry; I swear by God, I shall harm you," and then leaves her and does not have sexual intercourse [with her] for four months. After

[70]Ṭabarī, *Tafsīr*, VIII, 320–31; he states that there is a difference of opinion as to who is authorized to appoint both the arbiters and what alternatives are permitted for them to decide.

[71]It is transmitted by Ṭabarī, *Tafsīr*, VIII, 320–1. The editor states that it is transmitted by Shāfi'ī in his book *Kitāb al-Umm*.

[72]*Kāfī*, VI, 152–3.

[73]*Īlā*' is a technical term in Islamic law that refers to a vow of continence not to have sexual intercourse with one's wife for four months or more. It was a pre-Islamic practice which, if kept, produced a divorce automatically at the end of four months. It was regulated by the Qur'ān. For details see Jazīrī, *al-Fiqh*, IV, 450–66; Schacht, *Origins*, 215; Fyzee, *Outlines*, 162; Lane, s.v. a-l-w. See also Ṭabarī, *Tafsīr*, IV, 456–65. This form of divorce is not of much importance today in dissolution of marriage.

[74]Bukhārī, *Matn al-Bukhārī*, III, 275–6. After citing the above verse he quotes a tradition that states, 'The Messenger of God took a vow of continence with respect to his wives ... and stayed in his Mashraba for twenty-nine days ...'

this period, he should be summoned either to go back to her or divorce her.'[75]

'He[76] summoned 'Amr[77] b. al-Ḥārith who had taken a vow of continence with respect to his wife and four months had elapsed, so 'Alī directed him either to go back to her or to divorce her. [The Imam] said, 'If a man takes a vow of continence with respect to his wife, nothing is incumbent upon him until four months elapse. After that period, he should be informed either to return to her or to divorce her at once. But if the woman does not come forward to make a claim nothing happens and no divorce takes place.[78] If four months have passed before being summoned, and the woman claims her right against him, he should be instructed to either return to her or to give her a divorce. He is at liberty [to do what he likes] until he is summoned.'

Ja'far b. Muḥammad said, 'She is his wife and cannot be separated [from him] until he is summoned, even though he has kept [away from] her for a year. The wife has no claim for four months. If four months had passed before he touched her, and she remains silent and contented, then he is within his rights for what is permissible to him. But if she takes her case to the ruling authority (*wālī*), he should be told, "Either return to her or divorce her." If the woman claims her right after four months, he should be summoned, even if some time has passed.'

[The Imam] said, 'The return in such a case is [indicated by] sexual intercourse. If the husband is unable to have intercourse because of disease, a valid excuse, or travels, it will be sufficient if he agrees [to take her back] by his word. But if he is able to have intercourse, his obligation is not fulfilled until he actually cohabits with her, unless something prevents their coming together and there is no way out of it. In such a case, when he says definitely that he returns to her, and this is witnessed, it is lawful.'[79]

'Alī: He said, 'When the maker of such a vow is duly summoned, and he intends to divorce [his wife], he should be separated from her until she menstruates and then becomes pure. When she is in a period of

[75]'One who swears to stay away from his wife must be made to return to her or divorce her at the end of the period.' Bukhārī, *Matn al-Bukhārī*, III, 276; *Mishkāt*, II, 213–4; Robson, I, 699; Ṭūsī, *Tahdhīb al-aḥkām*, VIII, 2. See also Ṭabarī, *Tafsīr*, IV, 462, 463.

[76]According to MS Q: *wa-annahu*. In the edited text: *wa 'anhu* seems to be an error.

[77]'Amr: according to MS Q, in the edited text: 'Umar. He is most probably 'Amr b. Abī 'Amr = 'Amr b. al-Ḥārith, a Badrī. Ibn Sa'd, III/1, 304.

[78]*Kāfī*, VI, 139; Ṭūsī, *Tahdhīb al-aḥkām*, VIII, 3–4.

[79]*Kāfī*, VI, 137–9.

purity, he should divorce her. He is entitled to return to her so long as three menstruations have not been completed.'[80]

There is a similar report from Abū 'Abd Allāh [Imam Ja'far al-Ṣādiq] who said, 'Two just witnesses should testify to a divorce.'

Abū Ja'far and Abū 'Abd Allāh: They said, '*Īlā'* does not take place unless a man has consummated his marriage with his wife; likewise it does not apply to a woman whose marriage has not been consummated.'[81]

'Alī: A man came to him and said, 'O Commander of the Faithful, my wife has given birth to a son and verily I said to her, "By God, I shall not go near you until you wean him," fearing that she may conceive again.' 'Alī said, 'In such an adjustment, *īlā'* does not apply to you.'[82]

Ja'far b. Muḥammad [Imam al-Ṣādiq] said, 'This is not *īlā'* and there is no obligation on him.'

'Alī: He said, 'A man who swears that he will not have sexual intercourse with his wife for two years is not one who has made an *īlā'*.'[83]

Ja'far b. Muḥammad: He said, 'If a man avoids his wife for more or less a year, without [making] an oath with regard to her, this is not *īlā'* and he can go to her.'

'Alī: A man came to him and asked him about someone who had pronounced both *īlā'* and *ẓihār*[84] within an hour of each other. He said, 'Only one expiation (*kaffāra*) [is due from him].'

['Alī]: He said, 'When a man who has taken the vow of *īlā'* is duly summoned, it is not proper for the ruling authority (*imām*) to compel him to withdraw from it.' That is, the proper course for the ruling authority (*ḥākim*) is to give him a choice between returning [to her] or divorcing her, and if he neither returns [to his wife] nor divorces her, the authority should compel him to take a decision one way or the other. The choice should be left to the husband, but after four months, there must be, of necessity, either a return or a divorce.[85]

[80]Ibid., VI, 138, 139.

[81] Ibid., VI, 140–1; Ṭūsī, *Tahdhīb al-aḥkām*, VIII, 7.

[82]*Kāfī*, VI, 138. In his *Tafsīr*, IV, 457–60, Ṭabarī reported several such reports from 'Alī and they are summed up as follows: *Īlā'* takes place only in anger; if you intend something good, *īlā'* does not apply.

[83]Ṭūsī, *Tahdhīb al-aḥkām*, VIII, 7.

[84]For *ẓihār* see the following section.

[85]Kulaynī states that 'Alī used to detain the husband until he divorced his wife. Another tradition on the authority of Imam al-Ṣādiq states that if the husband refuses either of the two choices he should be executed. *Kāfī*, VI, 139–40.

['Alī]: He said, 'When a man retracts his *īlā'* [by sexual intercourse], an expiation is due from him.'

['Alī]: He said, 'Where a slave takes the oath of *īlā'* regarding his wife, the rules of *īlā'* take effect, and the limit for him is fixed at two months, and he should be summoned after two months.'

['Alī]: He said, 'When an oath of *īlā'* is taken, it is not [regarded in law as an] *īlā'* until the time limit [i.e. four months] has elapsed.'

Ja'far b. Muḥammad: He said, 'As to the return of the man [to his wife] who has taken the oath of *īlā'*, when he says, "I have done it [sexual intercourse]" and the woman denies it, the man's word shall be accepted, and there is no *īlā'* [i.e. divorce].'

[Ja'far b. Muḥammad]: He said, 'If a man takes a vow that he will not go near his wife for four months, there is no *īlā'* in this, but if he vows for a period longer than four months, that is an *īlā'*. There is no *īlā'* in a period of four months or less.'[86]

INJURIOUS COMPARISON (*AL-ẒIHĀR*)[87]

God says: *Such of you as put away your wives (by saying they are as their mothers)—They are not their mothers* (58:2–4), to the end of the *ẓihār* account.[88]

Ja'far b. Muḥammad: He said, 'A man came to the Prophet and said, "O Messenger of God, I have pronounced *ẓihār* on my wife." The Messenger of God said, "Go and emancipate a slave." The man said, "I have none." The Messenger of God said, "Then fast for two months consecutively."

[86]Ṭūsī, *Tahdhīb al-aḥkām*, VIII, 6.

[87]'Incestuous comparison' or 'injurious comparison' is a vague translation of *ẓihār*, a form of repudiation not recognized by Islam. It consists of a declaration by the husband that his wife is to him like a relative in a prohibited degree of marriage. The most common formula is that the husband says to his wife, 'Thou art to me (as untouchable) as the back (*ẓahr*) of my mother.' The formula meant that intercourse with the wife was being considered as unlawful or incestuous as intercourse with one's mother. In this formula, one could equate any part of the body of one's wife other than 'the back' with that of a woman one could not marry without committing incest. *Ẓihār* was a pre-Islamic method of repudiation and is condemned in the Qur'ān. The special atonement is specified (33:4; 58: 2–4). For the Ḥanafīs, it has no further legal effect on the marriage. The Mālikīs and Shāfi'īs deal with *ẓihār* as *īlā'*. *EI*[2], s.v. Ṭalāḳ; Schacht, *Introduction*, 165; Jazīrī, *al-Fiqh*, IV, 467–85; Fyzee, *Outlines*, 162. This form of divorce may be dismissed as virtually extinct today.

[88]The rest of the verses are: *As to those among you who divorce their wives by declaring that they will thereafter regard them as their mothers; (let them know that they are) not their mothers*. Sale, *Koran*, 524. Kulaynī explains the occasion of its revelation, *Kāfī*, VI, 158–9.

The man said, "I am unable to do so." The Messenger of God said, "Go and feed sixty poor persons." The man said, "I cannot." The Messenger of God said, "Take this wheat (*burr*) and feed sixty poor persons." The man said, "I swear by Him Who sent you with the truth, I do not know anyone between the two tracts of black stone [of Medina][89] more needy than I and my family." The Messenger of God, therefore, said, "Go and eat, and feed your family." '[90]

'Alī: He said, '*Ẓihār* does not take effect unless it is pronounced in a period of purity [during which] no intercourse [has taken place].'

['Alī]: He decided that a man who has pronounced *ẓihār* three times has to give three expiations.[91] A similar tradition is reported from Abū Ja'far and Abū 'Abd Allāh [the Imams al-Bāqir and al-Ṣādiq].

'Alī: He said, 'This occurs only when the man utters *ẓihār* on several [different] occasions, even though the matter is one and the same. He is then liable for several expiations, but if he utters *ẓihār* repeatedly at one sitting, then there is only one expiation.'[92]

Ja'far b. Muḥammad: He said, 'When a man pronounces *ẓihār* on four wives, he has to offer four expiations;' that is where he singles out every one of the four for *ẓihār*.[93] This is because it is related from 'Alī that when he was asked about a man who uttered *ẓihār* on four wives at one sitting, by one expression, he said that there is only one expiation.

'Alī and the Imams: They said, '*Ẓihār* [is uttered in reference to] every female relation which cannot be married [such as] one's mother, sister, paternal or maternal aunt, or those that are similar to them in being forbidden in marriage. When a man says to his wife, "You are to me

[89]The Arabic term is *Lābatayn* for Medina, see *The Pillars of Islam*, I, 370, n. 69.

[90]Abū Salama related that Salmān (or Sulaymān) b. Ṣakhr, also known as Salama b. Ṣakhr al-Bayāḍī, declared his wife to be like his mother's back to him till the end of Ramaḍān, but when only half the month had gone, he had intercourse with her during the night and went to the Messenger of God and mentioned that to him. He told him to set free a slave, but he replied that he could not get one; so he told him to fast two consecutive months, but he replied that he was unable to do that; he then told him to feed sixty poor people, but he replied that he did not possess the means. The Messenger of God then said to Farwa b. 'Amr, 'Give him that '*araq* (date basket holding fifteen or sixteen *ṣā*'s) so that he may feed sixty poor people.' *Mishkāt*, II, 214; Robson, I, 699–700. See also *Kāfī*, VI, 161; Ṭūsī, *Tahdhīb al-aḥkām*, VIII, 15. For a similar tradition in a different context see *The Pillars of Islam*, I, 339–40. Wāḥidī, *Asbāb al-nuzūl*, 292; Aws b. al-Ṣāmit was the one who had pronounced *ẓihār*. Ṭabarī, *Tafsīr* (Beirut), XXVIII, 2–6; it was Aws b. al-Ṣāmit.

[91]*Kāfī*, VI, 162, 163; for every pronouncement of *ẓihār* one expiation is due.

[92]Ṭūsī, *Tahdhīb al-aḥkām*, VIII, 19, 22.

[93]Ibid., VIII, 21.

like the back of my mother, sister, maternal or paternal aunt," this amounts to a declaration of *ẓihār*.'[94]

Ja'far b. Muḥammad: He was asked about a man who pronounces *ẓihār* on his wife before the consummation of marriage, and he said, 'There can be no *ẓihār* or *īlā'* unless he has consummated the marriage.'[95]

'Alī: He said, 'There can be no *ẓihār* between a free man and his slave girl. I will contend with anyone willing by imprecating the curse of God upon whichever of us is wrong[96] as to the permissibility of *ẓihār* with regard to a slave girl. This is because God says: *Such of you as put away your wives (by saying that they are as [the back of] their mothers)* (58:2). Now a slave girl is not a wife.'

Ja'far b. Muḥammad: He said, '*Ẓihār* on a slave girl is like the *ẓihār* on a free woman;' he meant, when she is his wife. But if a man utters *ẓihār* on his slave girl, it does not take effect as *ẓihār*.[97]

Ja'far b. Muḥammad: He said, '*Ẓihār* cannot take effect by an oath. A *ẓihār* is effective only when a man says to his wife, while she is pure and [in a period of purity] during which he has not had intercourse with her, "You are to me like the back of my mother;" or he says, "Bear witness against me that she is [to me] like the back of my mother." He should not say, "If you do this or that, then you are to me like the back of my mother." '[98]

A man asked [the Imam], 'O Son of the Messenger of God, verily I said to my wife, "You are to me like the back of my mother if you go out from the door of the room," and she did go out.' [The Imam] said, 'There is no obligation on you.' The man said, 'I am able to offer expiation by [emancipating] a slave or two.' [The Imam] said, 'There is no obligation on you whether you are able [to emancipate] or not.[99] When you take an oath in uttering *ẓihār*, it is not a *ẓihār*.[100] *Ẓihār* only takes place when you say to your wife at a time when she is pure in a period of purity in which you have not touched her and in the presence of two witnesses or more, "Bear witness against me that she is [to me] like the back of my mother," and you do not add, "If she does this or that." '

[94]*Kāfī*, VI, 160.

[95]Ibid., VI, 165; Ṭūsī, *Tahdhīb al-aḥkām*, VIII, 21.

[96]The Arabic is: *man shā'a bāhaltuhu*. Urdu translation is incorrect and Fyzee was misled by it. Lane, s.v. b-h-l.

[97]*Kāfī*, VI, 160, 161; different *ḥadīth* but with the same intent.

[98]Ṭūsī, *Tahdhīb al-aḥkām*, VIII, 9.

[99]*Kāfī*, VI, 160.

[100]Ibid., VI, 161, 165.

[Ja'far b. Muḥammad]: He said, 'There can be no *ẓihār* except in a period of purity during which no intercourse has taken place. There must be two witnesses to give evidence, and there must not be any vow,[101] as in *ṭalāq*. But if there is any variation in these conditions, however slight, then there is no *ẓihār*.'

A tradition is reported from Abū Ja'far and Abū 'Abd Allāh in the following way: The reporter of this tradition reported from one of the two [Imams] saying, '*Ẓihār* is of two kinds; in one of them, expiation has to be made before sexual intercourse, and in the other, after intercourse. The one in which there is expiation after the intercourse, the man says, "You are to me like the back of my mother if I come near you." He has to make expiation after the intercourse. The other is when he says, "You are to me like the back of my mother" and does not say, "If you do such and such a thing."' This report might raise doubt in the mind of him who is of lesser understanding, that *ẓihār* contrary to what has been stated, does not take place with an oath. The expiation in [the first case] is only in respect of the vow of continence (*īlā'*).[102]

Ja'far b. Muḥammad—his father—his ancestors: 'Alī was asked about a man who pronounced *ẓihār* and *īlā'* on his wife at the same time, and he said, 'There is only one expiation.'

[Ja'far b. Muḥammad]: In regard to expiation for *ẓihār*, [Imam al-Ṣādiq] said, 'If a man has a slave to manumit he should do so. If he has no slave, he should fast two months consecutively, and if he is unable to do so, he should feed sixty destitutes.' This is according to the text of the Qur'ān and what we have related from the Prophet in the earlier part of this section. Fasting does not fulfil the obligation of him who can emancipate a slave; and feeding poor persons does not fulfil the obligation of him who is able to fast.

Ja'far b. Muḥammad: He said, 'Wherever the expressions *aw* and *aw* (or, or) occur in the Qur'ān, the man has a choice; he may choose what he wishes; but when the expression in the Qur'ān is, "If he has none," or "if he is not able to do so," there is no choice. The first alternative is his duty; it is only "if he is unable" or "if he has none" that the second alternative applies, and then the other alternatives successively.'

'Alī and Abū Ja'far and Abū 'Abd Allāh: They said, 'A man who has pronounced *ẓihār* should not approach his wife to the slightest extent

[101] Ibid., VI, 159; reported on the authority of Imam al-Bāqir. *Ẓihār* cannot be pronounced in a state of anger. Ibid., VI, 166.

[102] Ibid., VI, 167; reported on the authority of Imam al-Ṣādiq.

until he has made expiation. When he intends to return to his wife on whom he has pronounced *ẓihār*, he should make expiation.'

Ja'far b. Muḥammad was asked about a man who utters *ẓihār* and has intercourse with his wife before expiation, and he said, 'This is not how a man who knows the law should act.'[103] It was said to him, '[What about] if he does so?' [The Imam] said, 'He has transgressed one of the divine ordinances of God (*ḥudūd Allāh*), and has committed a great sin.' It was said to him, 'Has he to make any expiation apart from the first?' [The Imam] said, 'Let him seek the pardon of God, and repent, and remain away from his wife, and not go to her until he has made expiation.'[104]

[Ja'far b. Muḥammad]: He was asked about *ẓihār*, 'When does it become incumbent on a man to offer expiation?' He said, 'When he wishes to have intercourse with his wife.' It was said to him, 'But if he divorces her before he has intercourse, is there any obligation to make expiation?' He said, 'No, the expiation abates.'[105]

Abū Ja'far: He was asked about a man who pronounces *ẓihār* on his wife and then divorces her with a single [pronouncement of] divorce. He said, 'The *ẓihār* becomes void when he divorces her.'

Abū 'Abd Allāh [Imam al-Ṣādiq] was asked, 'What is the position of a man who pronounces *ẓihār* and then divorces his wife with a single [pronouncement of] divorce and then returns to her?' He said, 'She is his wife. His obligation is that of a person who has pronounced *ẓihār* before he touches her. So, when he desires to have intercourse, he should first make expiation and then have her.' It was said to him, 'If he leaves her until her *'idda* expires, and she becomes her own mistress and he seeks her in marriage and marries her, is expiation necessary for him before he touches her?' He said, 'No, because she had been separated from him, and she became her own mistress, and this is a new marriage.'

Abū Ja'far Muḥammad b. 'Alī: He was asked about a man who pronounced *ẓihār* on his wife and did not go near her, but forsook her and would see her alone without touching her. Is there anything that is due from him? He said, 'She is his wife. Nothing is forbidden to him except sexual intercourse; i.e. until expiation.' It was said to him, 'If she took him before the sovereign authority (*sulṭān*) and said, "This is my husband. He has pronounced *ẓihār* and has detained me, but does not have marital intercourse fearing that he may have to pay the expiating fine of one

[103]Ibid., VI, 167.

[104]Ibid., VI, 167. For a different tradition see *Mishkāt*, II, 214, 215; Robson, I, 700. Kulaynī transmits the same tradition in *Kāfī*, VI, 166.

[105]*Kāfī*, VI, 162, 163, 165.

who pronounces *ẓihār*.'" [The Imam] said, 'The sovereign cannot compel him to emancipate a slave, or fast, or give food when he has no slave to emancipate, no strength to fast, and no means to feed the needy. But if he has the means, the authority (*imām*) can compel him to emancipate a slave, or if he has no slave to emancipate and says that he is unable to fast, the *imām* can compel him to give in charity. This should be done before he touches her, but if he has not made expiation before touching her, it may be done after intercourse.'[106]

Abū Ja'far and Abū 'Abd Allāh: They said, 'The free and the bonded are equal in regard to *ẓihār*, except that the obligation of the slave is only one-half of that of the free man.'[107]

Abū 'Abd Allāh [Imam al-Ṣādiq] said, 'In fasting, the slave should fast only for one month and is not obliged to emancipate a slave or [do charity] for expiation,[108] because the property of the slave belongs to the master. He has no right to emancipate or do charity from the master's property unless the master permits it and voluntarily allows him to do so. This will fulfil his obligation.'[109]

Ja'far b. Muḥammad: He said, 'In *ẓihār*, the obligation is fulfilled by emancipating a slave who prays and fasts, does not pray or fast, is a child, or is aged.'[110]

'Alī said, '[The emancipation of] a Jew or a Christian slave or an *umm al-walad* (a female slave who has borne her master a child)[111] fulfils the obligation for expiation in *ẓihār*, but not a lunatic, or a slave with a serious [physical] defect.'

Abū 'Abd Allāh [Imam al-Ṣādiq] said, 'Neither a *mudabbar* (slave to be emancipated after a term)[112] nor a *mukātab* (slave who has purchased his freedom)[113] can be offered in expiation for *ẓihār*.'

'Alī: He said, 'The fasting in expiation of *ẓihār* is for two months consecutively, as God says [58:4]. If the man who fasts obtains the means to emancipate a slave before the end of his fast, he may do so and end his fast. But if he has completed his fast, and at that very hour it is possible

[106]Ibid., VI, 168; the beginning of this tradition is different, but the later part is the same as the one in the *Da'ā'im*.

[107]Ibid., VI, 162, 163.

[108]The edited text reads: *wa-laysa 'alayhi 'itq*[un] *wa-lā kaffārat*[un]. In *Kāfī*, VI, 163: *wa-laysa 'alayhi kaffāratu ṣadaqat*[in] *wa-la 'itq*[in].

[109]Ṭūsī, *Tahdhīb al-aḥkām*, VIII, 24.

[110]*Kāfī*, VI, 165.

[111]*Umm walad*, see *The Pillars of Islam*, I, 283, n. 62; also Chap. 12 below.

[112]*Mudabbar*, see Chap. 12 below.

[113]*Mukātab*, see *The Pillars of Islam*, I, 313; Chap. 12 below.

[for him to emancipate a slave], his obligation is fulfilled and no liability remains on him.'

Abū 'Abd Allāh: He said, 'Where a man fasts in expiation of *ẓihār* for a month or less, and then breaks his fast for [either] a good or bad reason, he has indeed destroyed his fast, and it is incumbent on him to fast for two months consecutively on some future occasion. But if he has fasted for a month, and entered upon the second month, and then his fast comes to an end, his only obligation is to fast for the days that remain out of the two months, because he has fasted both months successively.'[114]

'Alī: He said, 'As to feeding poor persons in expiation of *ẓihār*, the man should feed sixty destitute persons giving each of them one half of a *ṣā'*.'[115]

Ja'far b. Muḥammad: He said, 'One *mudd* (handful)[116] for each person fulfils the obligations of feeding the poor in expiation of *ẓihār*.'

It is possible that the half of a *ṣā'* mentioned by 'Alī was of barley (*sha'īr*), and the one *mudd* referred to by Ja'far b. Muḥammad [Imam al-Ṣādiq] was of wheat (*burr*) as both of them are about equal and equivalent in price and sufficiency. The rule which comes from 'Alī was directed to a man who is able [to afford it] and the *mudd* mentioned by Ja'far b. Muḥammad was a rule of concession and permissibility; and the rule which comes from 'Alī is to be preferred.

MUTUAL IMPRECATION (*AL-LI'ĀN*)[117]

God says: *As for those who accuse their wives but have no witnesses except themselves; let the testimony of one of them be four testimonies, (swearing) by*

[114]*Kāfī*, VI, 162.

[115]For *ṣā'* see *The Pillars of Islam*, I, 331, n. 149; 346, it is the same expiation for breaking the fast because of illness. Ṭūsī, *Tahdhīb al-aḥkām*, VIII, 23.

[116]*Mudd*, see *The Pillars of Islam*, I, 331, n. 149; 340.

[117]*Li'ān* is a technical term in Islamic law. If a husband accuses his wife of infidelity, but is unable to prove the allegation, he might adopt the procedure of *li'ān*. It consists of taking an oath by which a husband may allege, without legal proof, adultery on the part of his wife without his becoming liable to the punishment prescribed for this (i.e. *qadhf*, false accusation of adultery), and the possibility of denying the paternity of a child borne by the wife. The evidence thus given by the husband is strengthened by oaths, by which the husband and the wife each invokes the curse and the wrath of God upon themselves if they should lie. This procedure frees the husband from the legal punishment (*ḥadd*) for *qadhf* and the wife from the legal punishment for incontinence. This procedure is in itself not a divorce but it could lead to the dissolution of the marriage. *Li'ān* was taken recourse to in extreme cases, and with the introduction of modern legal codes into many Islamic countries and the

Allah that he is of those who speak the truth till His saying: ... *that Allah is Clement, Wise* (24:6–10).[118]

Ja'far b. Muḥammad—his father—his ancestors: 'Alī said concerning God's Word (see above, 24:6–10), 'He who maligns his wife is not obliged to utter an imprecation unless he claims to have seen a man copulating with her with his own eyes.'[119]

Ja'far b. Muḥammad: He said, '*Li'ān* takes place when a man tells his wife in the presence of the governor (*wālī*), "Verily I have seen a man [behaving] with her as I would do;"[120] or he denies the paternity of her child and says, "This child is not mine." When this happens, they should both imprecate each other before the *wālī* (governor, or some government officer). This is where the man sticks to his word and does not go back on it. But he should not have acknowledged the paternity of the child on an earlier occasion; and should he have acknowledged the paternity of the child and later denied it, his denial will not be permitted and he cannot pronounce a *li'ān*.'

[Ja'far b. Muḥammad]: He said, 'Where a man accuses his wife [of adultery] and then retreats the accusation, he should be scourged with eighty stripes[121] and the wife should be returned to him. If he persists in the affirmation of the charge, he should utter an imprecation against her. Mutual imprecation takes place as follows:

'The husband should swear by God and bear witness four times before the authority (*imām*) that he is a truthful person. He should say, "I bear witness by God that I saw a man behaving with her as I would do," or he

creation of legal mechanisms for resolving the disputes over paternity *li'ān* has fallen into disuse. *EI*², s.v. Li'ān, Ṭalāḳ; Fyzee, *Outlines*, 166–8; Anderson, *Law Reform*, 136, 141.

[118] The complete text of the Qur'ān reads: *And for those who launch a charge against their spouses, and have (in support) no evidence but their own, their solitary evidence (can be received) if they bear witness four times (with an oath) by God that they are solmnly telling the truth. And the fifth (oath should be) that they solemnly invoke the curse of God on themselves if they tell a lie. But it would avert the punishment from the wife, if she bears witness four times (with an oath) by God, that (her husband) is telling a lie. And the fifth (oath) should be that she solemnly invokes the wrath of God on herself if (her accuser) is telling the truth. If it were not for God's grace and mercy on you, and that God is Oft-Returning, full of wisdom (ye would be ruined indeed)*. Yusuf Ali, *The Holy Qur'ān*, 24:6–10; see also Sale, *The Koran*, 343–4.

[119] Several traditions state that mutual imprecation cannot take place until the man says that he had seen her doing such and such, or that he had seen it with his own eyes. People are urged to follow this procedure and not to take the law into their own hands by striking the adulterer with the sword. *Kāfī*, VI, 173, 174; *Mishkāt*, II, 219; Robson, I, 703–4; transmitted by Bukhārī and Muslim. See also Ṭūsī, *Tahdhīb al-aḥkām*, VIII, 184.

[120] It is a free rendering of *ra'aytu rajul*an *makāna majlisī minhā*.

[121] See Chap. 17 below for *qadhf*.

may say, "I bear witness by God that this child is not mine." He should say this four times, and each time he should say, "Verily I am a truthful person in all that I have said." And the fifth time he should say, "The curse of God be upon me if I am one of the lying ones." Then he should say, "If I speak falsely in this my statement, the curse of God be upon me."

'Then the wife should bear witness and say four times, "Verily he is one of the perjurers in slandering me," and the fifth time she should say, "The wrath of God be upon me if he is speaking the truth." The *imām* should corroborate the statement of each party by saying "Amen" at the end.' [Imam al-Ṣādiq] said, 'The *sunna* for the *imām* is to sit for the imprecators and make them stand facing the *qibla* before him.'[122]

'Alī and Ja'far [*Imam* al-Ṣādiq]: They said, 'When two parties imprecate each other before the *imām*, they shall be separated[123] and they can never be united in marriage again.[124] Union is forbidden to them.[125] The lineage of the child imprecated will be established through his mother[126] and her relations, and his affairs and status will be with them. He who slanders the child will be punished criminally, and the relationship between the child and the person who imprecated his mother will be cut off. There will be no inheritance between them. His mother and [other] persons tracing kinship through her will be entitled to inherit from him.'[127]

'Alī: He said, 'Regarding two who imprecate each other, if a man accuses his wife before the *wālī* and then fails to utter the imprecation, he should be punished as a criminal and scourged. If the man utters the imprecation and the woman does not, she should be stoned [as an adulteress].[128] If both utter the imprecation and the man denies the paternity of

[122]*Kāfī*, VI, 170; Kulaynī narrates a case before the Prophet. See also Ṭūsī, *Tahdhīb al-aḥkām*, VIII, 185, 191. The *imām* should sit turning his back to the *qibla* while the imprecators should stand facing the *qibla* before him; the man on his right and the woman of his left, and the mutual imprecation should begin with the man. *Kāfī*, VI, 172.

[123]The Qur'ān does not touch upon the question of whether *li'ān* makes separation between the couple necessary. Schacht is of the opinion that in many traditions, separation is so expressly affirmed that there must have been a school which approved the continuity of the marriage after the *li'ān*. *EI*², s.v. *Li'ān*.

[124]Mālik states that after the *li'ān*, the husband and wife could never marry one another again. *EI*², s.v. Li'ān.

[125]*Kāfī*, VI, 170.

[126]The lineage of the child in such a case is traced to its mother. *Mishkāt*, II, 217–18; Robson, I, 702; transmitted by Bukhārī and Muslim.

[127]*Kāfī*, VI, 170.

[128]This is the general rule. However, Bukhārī transmitted a tradition wherein a woman accused of infidelity hesitated and drew back when she was testifying the fifth time. She said, "I shall not disgrace any people forever," and went on with her fifth declaration. It

the child, whether born or unborn, and later, after the imprecation, the husband claims the child,[129] the child inherits from him, but he does not inherit from the child on account of the imprecation and his denial [of the paternity]. [If he claims the child] before the imprecation, he should be scourged, the child will belong to him and the woman retains her status [as his wife].'

Ja'far b. Muḥammad: The following case of *li'ān* was brought before him. A man slandered his wife, and denied the paternity of the child. He imprecated her and separated from her. After this he said, 'The child is my child.' Then he declares himself a liar. [The Imam] said, 'As for the wife, she can never return to him, but the child will be returned to him and he should not abandon it. He does not inherit from the child. The child inherits from the father, but the father does not inherit from the child. The mother, his maternal uncles and those who claim [lineage] through the mother will inherit from the child.[130]

'If a man declares himself to be a liar before the imprecation, he should be punished as a criminal [for slander]. His wife and child belong to him. If a man slanders his wife during pregnancy, he should not imprecate her before childbirth. If she gives birth to a child and he claims it, the child is his even though he had denied paternity earlier, and the woman also remains his wife, but he should be punished with *ḥadd* punishment as a slanderer.'

Ja'far b. Muḥammad: He said, 'A Muslim shall utter an imprecation against his *dhimmī* (free non-Muslim) wife if he slanders her. This is manifestly according to the Book of God because it says: *Those who accuse their wives* ... (24:6); and this (*dhimmī* woman) is his wife.'[131]

[Ja'far b. Muḥammad]: He said, '*Li'ān* can take place between every

---

was a case of adultery and after she had given birth to a child, the Messenger of God said, 'If it were not for what has already been stated in the Book of God, I would have dealt severely with her.' *Mishkāt*, II, 218–19; Robson, I, 703.

[129]Kulaynī reports a tradition where the imprecation takes place when the wife is pregnant. After she delivers, the man claims that the child is his. In such a case the child will be returned to him, and the man will not be punished as the imprecation had already taken place. *Kāfī*, VI, 172, 173.

[130]*Kāfī*, VI, 171; Ṭūsī, *Tahdhīb al-aḥkām*, VIII, 187, 194–5.

[131]A tradition transmitted by Ibn Māja states, 'There are four types of women with whom there can be no invoking of curses: a Christian woman married to a Muslim, a Jewess married to a Muslim, a freewoman married to a slave, and a slavewoman married to a freeman.' *Mishkāt*, II, 223; Robson, I, 707. *Kāfī*, VI, 172; Kulaynī expresses the same view as that of Nu'mān. On this question, whether *li'ān* is possible if one partner is not a Muslim, or not free, there is a difference of opinion among the jurists.

couple, free or bonded. A free man can utter an imprecation on his slave wife; a slave, on his free wife; and a slave, on his slave wife.'[132]

A similar report comes from 'Alī who said, 'There can be no *li'ān* between two children before they attain puberty. When they do attain puberty, there cannot be any *li'ān* regarding the accusation made by the husband when both of them were children.'

['Alī]: He said, '*Li'ān* cannot be uttered between the spouses until the husband consummates the marriage with his wife.'[133]

['Alī]: He said, 'Where husband and wife are dumb, there can be no *li'ān*, because an imprecation can only be uttered by the tongue.'

Ja'far b. Muḥammad said, 'When a man accuses his dumb wife, they shall be separated.'[134]

Ja'far b. Muḥammad: He said, 'Where a man accuses his wife on suspicion and addresses her, "O adulteress", there shall be no imprecation until he claims to be an eyewitness [of her infidelity], or denies the paternity of her child, born or unborn. If the husband says, "I do not find you a virgin," this is not a valid cause for *li'ān*, and if he accuses her before consummation, he has not imprecated her but he should be punished with *ḥadd* punishment [for this].'

[Ja'far b. Muḥammad]: He said, 'Where a man backs out at the fifth [oath or affirmation],[135] she remains his wife and he should be scourged;[136] and similarly, if the wife backs out at the fifth [oath or affirmation], she should be stoned.'

[Ja'far b. Muḥammad]: He said, 'Concerning a man who accuses his wife of infidelity and later divorces her, if he confesses to having accused her falsely, he should be flogged; but if he still persists in his accusation while she is in her *'idda*, he shall utter the *li'ān*. If she dies and a person among her people represents her, then this man pronounces the imprecation on her husband [on her behalf]. In such a case, the husband will not be entitled to inherit from her; but if none among her close relatives (*awliyā'*) stands up to represent her, he will inherit from her.'

[Ja'far b. Muḥammad]: He said, 'Where a husband accuses his wife

[132]See the previous note. *Kāfī*, VI, 172; Kulaynī expresses the same view as that of Nu'mān.

[133]Ibid., VI, 169; Ṭūsī, *Tahdhīb al-aḥkām*, VIII, 188.

[134]*Kāfī*, VI, 172, 174; another case of a dumb and deaf wife, and a case of a deaf husband whose wife accuses him of infidelity. They should be separated. Ṭūsī, *Tahdhīb al-aḥkām*, VIII, 193.

[135]See the Qur'ānic pronouncement at the beginning of the section.

[136]*Kāfī*, VI, 171.

of infidelity, but no imprecation takes place, and one of them dies, the other has the right to inherit, unless the imprecation has taken place earlier. But when the imprecation has taken place, they are separated and neither inherits from the other.'

[Ja'far b. Muḥammad]: He was asked about the following case: A man divorces his wife before consummation, and she claims that she is pregnant by him. [The Imam] said, 'If she proves that he had intercourse with her and then he denies the paternity of the child, the husband must perform the *li'ān* and she should be separated from him, and he has to pay the *mahr* in full.[137] In the same way, *li'ān* does not render nugatory [the wife's right] to obtain *mahr* from the husband, regardless of whether the *li'ān* is completed and the spouses separate, or whether it is not completed and the spouses do not separate and remain husband and wife.'[138]

WAITING PERIOD (AL-'IDDA)[139]

God says: *Such of you as die and leave behind them wives, they (the wives) shall wait, keeping themselves apart, four months and ten days* (2:234),[140] and God says: *Women who are divorced shall wait, keeping themselves apart, three (monthly) courses (qurū')* (2:228).[141] He says: *If ye wed believing women and*

[137]Ibid., VI, 173. See also Chap. 10, 'The Account of Dower (*Mahr*).'

[138]Nu'mān does not discuss the question as to how the annulment of the marriage as a result of *li'ān* is to be carried out. Is it by a triple pronouncement of *ṭalāq* by the husband, or by the decision of the *qāḍī* before whom the *li'ān* took place, or by the *li'ān* itself? For different views see *EI*[2], s.v. *Li'ān*.

[139]'*Idda*, from '*adda*, to count (days of menstruations), is a technical term in Islamic law for legally prescribed period of waiting during which a woman may not remarry after being divorced or widowed. It was unknown in pre-Islamic Arabia and was instituted by the Qur'ān. The three main objectives of observing the '*idda* are: (i) to ascertain whether the wife if pregnant, and if so, the paternity of the child; (ii) to provide the husband with an opportunity to reconsider and return to the wife (if the divorce is revocable); (iii) to mourn the deceased husband, in the case of the widow. *EI*[2], s.v. 'Idda; Nasir, *Status of Women*, 99–106.

[140]A widow must observe the '*idda* of four months and ten days after her husband's death. A tradition states, 'It is not lawful for a woman who believes in God and the Last Day to observe mourning for one who has died more than three nights, except for the four months and ten days in the case of a husband.' Transmitted by Bukhārī and Muslim. *Mishkāt*, II, 226; Robson, I, 709. See also *Lisān al-'Arab*, s.v. ḥ-d-d.

[141]*Qurū'* (pl. of *qar'* or *qur'*) carries two contradictory meanings, either one monthly (menstrual) period, or conversely a state of purity from the menstrual discharge, i.e. the inter-menstrual period of purity. The Mālikīs, Shāfi'īs, the Ja'farī Shī'a, and the Ismā'īlīs

divorce them before ye have touched them, then there is no period that ye should reckon (33:49).[142] He Who has no partner says: *And for those with child, their period shall be till they bring forth their burden* (65:4),[143] and He says: ... *and reckon the period, and keep your duty to Allah, your Lord. Expel them not from their houses nor let them go forth unless they commit open immorality* (65:1). He means [committing immorality] during the period.[144]

Jaʿfar b. Muḥammad—his father—his ancestors—the Commander of the Faithful [ʿAlī]: One of the wives of the Messenger of God asked him, 'The husband of so and so has died. Can she go out of the house to attend to some urgent business?' The Messenger of God said, 'Out upon thee (*uff*)![145] Before I was sent [as a Messenger to you], you were the same women. When one of you became a widow, she would pick up the droppings of animals and throw it behind her back and say, "I will not use collyrium [for my eyes], nor comb my hair, nor use henna for a whole year."[146] I have ordered you [retreat] only for four months and ten days and yet you cannot have patience. Do not comb your hair, or use henna or collyrium, and do not go out of the house during the day, and do not stay out of the house at night.' The lady said, 'O Messenger of God, what is she to do if an important matter arises?'[147] The Messenger of God said, 'She should go out after the night has vanished[148] and return by evening,

---

assert the latter meaning, while the Ḥanafīs, Ḥanbalīs, and the Zaydīs the former. Because of this difference there are slight variations in the calculation of the period of the *ʿidda*. Lane, s.v. q-r-'; *EI*², s.v. 'Idda.

[142]The law insists that women observe an *ʿidda* only when the marriage has been consummated.

[143]For a pregnant woman following the death of her husband, divorce, or annulment, the *ʿidda* lasts until she delivers a baby.

[144]It is the right and duty of every woman who is observing an *ʿidda* to do so in the house of her former husband. *Kāfī*, VI, 101.

[145]*Uff*, an interjection, expressing displeasure, dislike, or hatred. Lane, s.v. a-f-f.

[146]A woman came to the Prophet and said, 'O Messenger of God, my daughter's husband has died and her eye is troubling her, may we apply collyrium?' He said, 'No,' twice or thrice ... then he said, 'It is only four months and ten days, whereas in the pre-Islamic period none of you threw away the piece of dung until a year had passed.' Transmitted by Bukhārī and Muslim. *Mishkāt*, II, 225–6; Robson, I, 709; Lane, s.v. b-ʿ-r.

[147]The Arabic is: *in ʿaraḍa lahā ḥaqq^un*. The primary significance of *ḥaqq* is suitableness to the requirements of wisdom, justice, right, fact, or to the exigencies of the case. Lane, s.v. ḥ-q-q. Al-Furayʿa bt. Mālik, sister of Abū Saʿīd al-Khudrī, went to God's Messenger and asked to be allowed to return to her folks after her husband was killed, because he had not left her in a house which belonged to him, nor had he left any maintenance. The Prophet granted her request, but when she was in the courtyard or in the mosque he called her and said, 'Stay in your house until the prescribed period is over.' *Mishkāt*, II, 226; Robson, I, 710.

[148]The Arabic expression is *baʿda zawāl al-layl*. It implies that she should go out early

so that she does not pass the night out of the house.' The lady asked, 'Can she go on the pilgrimage?' The Messenger of God replied, 'Yes.'[149]

'Alī: He was asked about the *'idda* of a woman whose husband had died before consummation and whether she was obliged to reckon a period of *'idda*. He said, 'Yes, she has to observe *'idda* and she is fully entitled to inheritance. She reckons the period of four months and ten days, the *'idda* of one whose husband has died after consummating the marriage; and this whether she has attained puberty or not, and whether she menstruates or not.'[150]

'Alī and Abū Ja'far and Abū 'Abd Allāh: They said, 'The widow may observe the *'idda* either at the house of her former husband, or elsewhere as she desires.'[151] She should observe all the rules applicable to her as it is incumbent upon her, and we have mentioned this earlier.

'Alī and Ja'far b. Muḥammad: They said, 'The *'idda* of the divorced

---

in the morning so that she might finish all her work and return to her house by evening. *Kāfī*, VI, 121–3. Kulaynī reports another tradition, which states that she can go out after midnight. Several other traditions stress that she can move her residence from one house to another every few weeks and can go out for important business. The Gujarati and Urdu translator has incorrectly rendered the above Arabic expression to mean 'in the afternoon.' Fyzee was misled by it.

[149]The Bohras confine their widows during the *'idda* to a room in a house, completely screened from the outside world to such an extent that she is not allowed to gaze at the sky. She is permitted to see only close male relatives with whom it is unlawful for her to marry. Hence, even a baby who does not qualify for the above relationship is barred from entering into her presence. I am told that she cannot receive a telephone call from a male relative with whom it is lawful for her to marry. She is, therefore, a virtual prisoner in a room or a house and is not permitted to wear anything other than white clothes. All these practices are not in conformity with the teachings of the Qur'ān and the *sunna* of the Prophet. Unfortunately, the religious authorities have shown no interest in addressing this and other pressing social issues except by harassing the reformists who advocate changes. See two independent investigative reports issued by the commissions appointed by the Human Rights Commision of India and the Citizens for Democracy into the alleged infringment of human rights of reformist Dāwūdī Bohras by their High Priest and his religious establishment. *Nathwani Commission Report, Tewatia and Nayar Commission Report*.

[150]Widows are obliged to observe the *'idda* whether or not the marriage has been consummated and whether or not they have reached the age of puberty. The only condition being that the marriage has been validly concluded. The idea of avoiding uncertainty of birth seems to be the reason behind this strict rule. *Kāfī*, VI, 123–5; the same position in several traditions, but in one tradition Imam al-Ṣādiq abstained from replying about the *'idda*. The editor comments that the *'idda* in such cases are for precaution (*lil-taqīya*).

[151]*Mishkāt*, II, 226; Robson, I, 710. *Kāfī*, VI, 121; she can observe the *'idda* wherever she likes. Kulaynī states that when 'Umar died 'Alī brought his daughter Kulthūm to his home.

woman, whose menstruation appears manifestly, is three *qurū'*.'[152] We have mentioned earlier the account of this from the Book of God.

'Alī and Abū Ja'far and Abū 'Abd Allāh: They said, 'The divorcee should not observe *'idda* anywhere except in her husband's house, and she should not emerge from it except after the *'idda*.'[153]

['Alī and Abū Ja'far and Abū 'Abd Allāh]: They said, 'As regards the widow who is pregnant, she should observe *'idda* for the longer of the two periods. If she gives birth to a child before four months and ten days, she should wait [before remarrying] until the whole period of the *'idda* (i.e. four months and ten days) is over.[154] And if childbirth takes longer than four months and ten days, she should wait till childbirth. The period for the divorced pregnant woman is, on the other hand, as laid down in the Qur'ān, namely until she lays down her burden; and whatever be the nature of the foetus she gives birth to, whether it is a fully formed child or not, the termination of the pregnancy ends the *'idda*.[155]

'If the woman is pregnant, and the husband divorces her by a revocable divorce, and then dies before childbirth, the wife has to commence the *'idda* for her deceased husband, so long as her [previous] *'idda* [of divorce] has not been completed. But if the *ṭalāq* is irrevocable, and he divorces her while he is in health, and then dies, and later she delivers her child, then her *'idda* is [considered] terminated. [This legal result follows] even if the husband has not yet been buried, or if she is delivered of her child immediately after his death.'

'Alī: He said, 'Where a woman bears twins, her *'idda* does not terminate till after the birth of the second child.'

[152] *Kāfī*, VI, 67–70; traditions mention three *qurū'* or three months.

[153] *Mishkāt*, II, 224–5; Robson, I, 708–9. Muslim transmitted a tradition wherein a divorcee was forbidden by a man to go out, hence she went to the Prophet and he said, 'Certainly, [go out and] cut down fruit from your palm trees ...' Kulaynī also transmitted this tradition. *Kāfī*, VI, 94–100; a number of traditions stress that she can go out if there are pressing matters; Ṭūsī, *Tahdhīb al-aḥkām*, VIII, 131–2.

[154] 'Subay'a al-Aslamīya gave birth to a child after some nights of her husband's death. Then she went to the Prophet and asked permission to remarry. He gave her permission and she married.' Transmitted by Bukhārī. *Mishkāt*, II, 225; Robson, I, 709. *Kāfī*, VI, 118–20. Kulaynī's position is the same as that of Nu'mān, i.e. the woman should observe the longer of the two periods.

For a pregnant woman, whether divorced or widowed, the *'idda* lasts until she delivers. All the Shī'a, the Imāmīs, the Ismā'īlīs, and the Zaydīs, prolong the *'idda* beyond the delivery until the period of four months and ten days as stipulated by the Qur'ān only in the case of a widow. This period of deferment, they argue, not only avoids a confusion in establishing birth, but also honours the memory of the deceased. *EI*², s.v. 'Idda.

[155] For details see Jazīrī, *al-Fiqh*, IV, 510–21.

[ʿAlī]: He said, ʿWhere the husband pronounces divorce on his wife once or twice and then he dies, the wife should observe the *ʿidda* of a widow for four months and ten days, and she inherits from him.'[156]

[ʿAlī] and Abū Jaʿfar and Abū ʿAbd Allāh:[157] They said, ʿAs regards the woman whose husband is absent, and she hears of her husband's death, she should observe the *ʿidda* from the date when she is informed of his death.'

Jaʿfar b. Muḥammad: He said, ʿA woman's husband is absent and he divorces her. If she knows the date on which he has divorced her, she should observe the *ʿidda* from that day; but if the date of the divorce is not known, [she should reckon the *ʿidda*] from the day she receives the news.[158]

ʿSince mourning (*iḥdād*) is necessary for a widow, she cannot reckon the *ʿidda* from the date of the death of the husband, but only from the date she receives the news, for, the widow is bound to commence mourning [immediately after the death of the husband].[159]

ʿThe divorcee is not obliged to mourn; she reckons the period of *ʿidda* from the date of the divorce, if it is known; but where this is not known, then from the day she receives the news. And if he has divorced her before consummation, she is separated from him immediately, and may marry during that very hour [immediately], if she so desires, for God says: *... divorce them before ye have touched them, then there is no period that ye should reckon*' (33:49).

Jaʿfar b. Muḥammad: He said, ʿThe *ʿidda* for a woman who does not menstruate any longer [because of age or for some other reason], or who has in fact never menstruated, is the three months after her divorce.'[160]

[Jaʿfar b. Muḥammad]: He said, ʿAs regards the divorced woman who suffers from haemorrhage,[161] she should reckon the *ʿidda* by her monthly periods; and if she is doubtful, then by months.' We have discussed earlier, in the Book of Ritual Purity,[162] the woman who suffers from haemorrhage, and we have distinguished between haemorrhage and menstruation. If the divorced woman knows the duration of her monthly courses, she

[156]This is because the third pronouncement was not made, hence the divorce was not absolute.

[157]In MS Q: Abū Jaʿfar and Abū ʿAbd Allāh.

[158]*Kāfī*, VI, 115–17.

[159]Ibid., VI, 117–18.

[160]Ibid., VI, 94, 101–2, 103.

[161]*Mustaḥāḍa*, a woman continuing to have a flow of blood after her days of menstruation.

[162]See *The Pillars of Islam*, I, 158–60.

should reckon accordingly; but if she is doubtful, she should reckon by months. This is the meaning of the above report.

[Ja'far b. Muḥammad]: He was asked about the Word of God: *And for such of your women as despair of menstruation, if ye doubt, their period (of waiting) shall be three months* ... (65:4). He said, '*Al-rība* (doubt) means the period which exceeds a month. If a month passes and she does not menstruate, and she is in the position of one who despairs of menstruation, let her reckon by months.[163] If she menstruates again before her '*idda* ends, let her begin her '*idda* again and reckon it by menstruations (*aqrā'*). If she menstruates one or two courses and then ceases to menstruate, she should begin the reckoning again by months.[164] Where a man divorces a woman by pronouncing *ṭalāq* once or twice and dies, she should commence the '*idda* from the day of his death and reckon it as the '*idda* of her husband's death. This is because she comes under the force of the second rule [i.e. the '*idda* after death] before she emerges from the force of the first [i.e. the '*idda* after divorce].'

'Alī: He said, 'If a man divorces a woman and then returns to her, and then divorces her without touching her, the second *ṭalāq* does not apply.'

Ja'far b. Muḥammad: He said, 'The divorcee should reckon the '*idda* from the day she was divorced because the divorce has necessarily to precede the '*idda*.'

[Ja'far b. Muḥammad]: He said, 'A *khul'*[165] is equivalent to one irrevocable divorce (*ṭalāq bā'in*) and the woman separated by *khul'* should observe her '*idda* in her own house, as a divorced woman, except that the husband has no right to return to her without her consent. If both parties agree to a return, they should marry by a fresh contract.'

'Alī and Abū 'Abd Allāh: They said, 'When the master of an *umm walad*[166] dies, she should observe the '*idda* of a widow;[167] and if he has freed her, she should observe the '*idda* of a divorcee.'[168]

'Alī and Abū Ja'far and Abū 'Abd Allāh: They said, 'A free woman whose husband is a slave should observe the '*idda* in the case of [her husband's] divorce or death in the same manner as she would if he were a free man. Similarly, the slave [husband] has to pronounce divorce three times to her just as a free man would pronounce.

[163] *Kāfī*, VI, 104; three months is the limit.
[164] Ibid., VI, 105.
[165] *Khul'*, see n. 63 above in this chapter.
[166] *Umm al-walad*, see *The Pillars of Islam*, I, 283, n. 62.
[167] This '*idda* is four months and ten days. *Kāfī*, VI, 179–81.
[168] This '*idda* is three menstrual periods. Ibid., VI, 179–81.

'A slave girl, whether her husband is free or bond, observes the *'idda* of a slave girl both in divorce or death, and this is one half of that of a free woman. In death it is two months and five days,[169] and in divorce, it is two [full] monthly courses if she menstruates.[170] [The latter is not merely one and a half cycles] because a monthly course cannot be divided. If she is one that does not menstruate, her period is a month and a half.'[171]

Ja'far b. Muḥammad said, 'If she is emancipated before her *'idda* expires, her *'idda* is completed.'

MAINTENANCE FOR WOMEN OBSERVING *'IDDA* AND FOR THEIR CHILDREN (*AL-NAFAQĀT LI-DHAWĀT AL-'IDAD*[172] *WA-AWLĀDIHINNA*)

Concerning divorced women, God says: *Lodge them where ye dwell, according to your wealth, and harass them not so as to straiten life for them. And if they are with child, then spend for them till they bring forth their burden* (65:6).[173]

Ja'far b. Muḥammad—his father—his ancestors—'Alī: He said, 'The term [of support] of the pregnant woman is till she brings forth her burden. It is the husband's duty to provide maintenance for her according to what is approved by common usage (*bi 'l-ma'rūf*) until she is delivered of her child. That is the Word of God: *And for those with child, their period shall be till they bring forth their burden*' (65:4).[174]

Ja'far b. Muḥammad: He said, 'Where a man divorces a woman while she is pregnant it is his duty to maintain her [in kindness] until childbirth.' [The Imam] meant [that this applies] when both parties are free, and whether he has the right to return to her or not. This is a point about which there is no difference [of opinion].

'Alī:[175] He said, 'The right of the divorced woman to reasonable maintenance during *'idda* depends upon his means. But when the terms

[169]Ibid., VI, 179, 183; according to Kulaynī the *'idda* of a slave girl after the death of her husband is the same as that of a free woman.

[170]Ibid., VI, 175.

[171]Ibid., VI, 178.

[172]MS Q: *al-'idda*. *'Idad* pl. of *'idda*.

[173]The Qur'ān continues: *Then, if they give suck for you, give them their due payment and consult together in kindness; but if ye make difficulties for one another, then let some other woman give suck for him. Let him who hath abundance spend of his abundance, and he whose provision is measured, let him spend of that which Allah hath given him* ... (65: 6–7). The rights and obligations of a woman observing *'idda* vary according to whether she is a widow or divorced.

[174]*Kāfī*, VI, 107–8.

[175]As in MS Q. In the edited text: *Qāla 'Ali.*

[of *'idda*] ends, then—*a reasonable maintenance (matāʿun bi 'l-maʿrūf), a duty upon those who act piously*' (2:241).[176] The divorced woman is thus entitled to residence and maintenance during the *'idda* whether she is with child or not, so long as the husband has the right to return to her.[177]

Jaʿfar b. Muḥammad: He said, 'The woman divorced irrevocably (*al-bā'in*) does not possess the right of residence or maintenance.'[178]

'Alī: Concerning the Word of God: [179] ... *And on the (father's) heir is incumbent the like of that (which was incumbent on the father)* (2:233), 'Alī said, 'God has prohibited harming the child or his mother during the period of suckling; and it is not proper for the mother to take more than two years to wean the child, but if the two agree by mutual consent on weaning (*fiṣāl*) the child, they may do so. *Fiṣāl* is the same as *fiṭām* (weaning);[180] and it is not proper for the heir to harm the woman, and say, "I shall not allow the child to go to her."'

[176]The verse reads: *Women who are divorced have a right to reputable [or reasonable] maintenance* ... Bell, *The Qur'ān*, I, 34. See also Yusuf Ali, *The Holy Qur'ān*, 2:241. Medinese opinions share the tendency to impose 'the obligatory gift' (*matāʿun bi 'l-maʿrūf*) in a wider range of cases than the Iraqians. Schacht, *Origins*, 101–2. See also *Kāfī*, VI, 109–10; according to some it is obligatory. See the section 'Gift to a divorced wife', below in this chapter.

[177]*Kāfī*, VI, 109; Ṭūsī, *Tahdhīb al-aḥkām*, VIII, 132–3. For the viewpoints of different schools see Jazīrī, *al-Fiqh*, IV, 544–56. According to Mālik, Awzāʿī, and Shāfiʿī she is entitled to residence only in strict conformity with the Qur'ānic verse 65:6; Marwazī, *Ikhtilāf al-fuqahā'*, 276–9.

[178]*Kāfī*, VI, 108–9; Ṭūsī, *Tahdhīb al-aḥkām*, VIII, 133. The rights of the woman divorced irrevocably vary according to different schools. The Ḥanafīs maintain that her former husband is responsible for her maintenance during the *'idda*. The other schools are not that liberal. Some schools grant her only the right to be housed. If she is pregnant, because of the Qur'ānic injunction (65:6), the husband is required to provide her with complete *nafaqa* until she delivers. *EI*[2], s.v. 'Idda.

[179]The verse begins with: *Mothers shall suckle their children for two whole years; (that is) for those who wish to complete the suckling. The duty of feeding and clothing nursing mothers in a seemly manner is upon the father of the child. No one should be charged beyond his capacity. A mother should not be made to suffer because of her child, nor should he to whom the child is born (be made to suffer) because of his child. And on the (father's) heir* ... (2:233). Ṭabarī, *Tafsīr*, V, 54–66, states that exegetes differ on the meaning of *wa-'ala 'l-wārith (and on the heir)*. Generally it is taken to mean that the duty of feeding and clothing an infant orphan and his nursing mother falls on the deceased father's heir, his agnatic relatives.

It should be noted that a widow never has the right to full maintenance (*nafaqa*), even if she is pregnant. The wife's right to *nafaqa* ceases on the death of her husband, for her right of inheritance supervenes. The widow is therfore not entitled to maintenance during the *'idda*. Kulaynī states that a pregnant widow cannot claim *nafaqa*. *Kāfī*, VI, 119–20.

[180]*Majma' al-baḥrayn*, s.v. f-ṣ-l; Ṭurayḥī quotes both the Qur'ān and Imam al-Ṣādiq. *Bukhārī*, *Matn al-Bukhārī*, III, 288; *Kāfī*, VI, 108.

Abū Ja'far [Imam al-Bāqir] said that the above verse (2:233) refers to maintenance.

['Alī]: He said, 'The woman should not be compelled to suckle the child nor should the child be taken away from her without her consent. She has the greater right to suckle the child for such compensation as another woman would accept; but she has no right to suckle it for more than two years.'

'Alī and Abū 'Abd Allāh: They said, 'Where a man divorces a woman who claims to be [pregnant] with child, she should wait for nine months. If she gives birth to a child [well and good], otherwise she should observe *'idda* for three months and then there is an absolute separation between them. This rule applies when her pregnancy is not manifest; but if it is determined that she is with child, he should provide for her until she gives birth to the child as God says: *And if they are with child, then spend for them till they bring forth their burden* (65:6).'[181]

MOURNING
(*AL-IḤDĀD*)[182]

God says: *Such of you as die and leave behind them wives, they (the wives) shall wait, keeping themselves apart, four months and ten days* (2:234). So God, in His Book, made the *'idda* of four months and ten days compulsory for the widow; and he made mourning compulsory for her by the tongue of His Prophet.[183]

Ja'far b. Muḥammad—his father—his ancestors—'Alī: He said, 'The Messenger of God forbade the woman who is mourning from combing her hair, using collyrium, dyeing her hair, or using ornaments until her *'idda* expires.[184] He directed her not to go out of the house during the day and not to stay out of her house at night. If it was necessary for her to go out for an important matter, she should do so after the night had vanished

[181]Ṭūsī, *Tahdhīb al-aḥkām*, VIII, 134.

[182]*Iḥdād* refers to a woman who abstains from the wearing of ornaments and the use of perfumes and dye for the hands and who puts on the garments of mourning after the death of her husband. *Lisān al-'Arab*, s.v. ḥ-d-d; Lane, s.v. ḥ-d-d.

[183]See n. 140 above in this chapter.

[184]'A woman must not observe mourning for one who has died more than three [nights], except for four months and ten days in the case of a husband, and she must not wear a dyed garment except one of the type made of dyed yarn, or apply collyrium, or touch perfume except for a little costus or *aẓfār* (odorous substance) when she has been purified after her courses.' *Mishkāt*, II, 226; Robson I, 709; transmitted by Bukhārī and Muslim.

and return by evening.[185] She should not stay out of her house overnight during her *'idda*.'

'Alī: He said, 'The mourning woman should not use perfume, or dyed (coloured) clothes, and should not stay the night away from her house.'

Ja'far b. Muḥammad: He said, 'The mourning woman should not wear coloured clothes, use collyrium, use perfume, nor adorn herself until her *'idda* expires. There is no harm if she wears clothes dyed black.'

Al-Ḥusayn b. 'Alī: He said, 'Asmā' bint 'Umays said,[186] "When the news of the death of Ja'far b. Abī Ṭālib[187] came, the Messenger of God looked at me and perceived the signs of weeping, feared that I might lose my sight, and saw that my forearms had been split. So he consoled with me on the loss of Ja'far and said, 'I beseech you, O Asmā', put collyrium [in your eyes] and yellow colour on your forearms.'"'

'Alī: He said, 'The widow should not wear coloured clothes and should not touch perfume or make up her hair. If it is very necessary to comb her hair, let her do so but without any perfume. She should not apply collyrium unless she is afflicted with an eye disease, in which case she may use it.' Here, the meaning is that the collyrium is used for the treatment of an ailment, and not for adornment, similarly, she is forbidden to use coloured clothes, but allowed to wear black, which is not an adornment.

Ja'far b. Muḥammad: He said, 'Mourning has to be observed only by a widow and it is not lawful for a woman to mourn for more than three days for anyone except her husband. There is no mourning in divorce. A divorced woman may use collyrium and perfume and dye her hair, and dress as she wishes. She may appear before her husband so long as he can return to her. Mourning is not prescribed for her, and it is incumbent only on a woman whose husband has died.'

GIFTS TO A DIVORCED WIFE (*AL-MUT'A*)[188]

God says: *It is no sin for you if ye divorce women while yet ye have not touched them, nor appointed unto them a portion [i.e. dower or bridal gift]. Provide for*

[185] See n. 148 above in this chapter.

[186] Asmā', see *The Pillars of Islam*, I, 283, n. 59; 289.

[187] For Ja'far see *The Pillars of Islam*, I, 298.

[188] *Mut'a* or *mut'at al-ṭalāq* is a technical term in Islamic law meaning a gift which a husband should always give to his wife on repudiating her, unless she had been seriously at fault. The Mālikīs regard it as a legal rather than moral obligation and permit a wife to go to court to demand it. Only the Ḥanafīs interpret the *mut'a* as referring to a sort of substitute

them (matti'ūhunna), the rich according to his means, and the straitened according to his means, a fair provision. (This is) a bounden duty for those who do good (2:236). He also says: *Women who are divorced have a right to reputable [or reasonable] maintenance (matā'un bi 'l-ma'rūf) an obligation on the godfearing* (2:241).[189]

Ja'far b. Muḥammad—his father—his ancestors—'Alī: He used to rule that the divorced woman be given a gift (*mut'a*) as stated in the Book of God—*the rich according to his means, and the straitened according to his means* (2:236).

Abū Ja'far: He said, 'The gift to [divorced] women is incumbent, whether the marriage has been consummated or not.'[190]

Ja'far b. Muḥammad: He said, 'The gift to [divorced] women is mandatory, and no amount is fixed for it, as God says: *The rich according to his means, and the straitened according to his means*' (2:236).

Ja'far b. Muḥammad: He said, 'The well-to-do may give a slave or slave girl and the man of limited means may give clothes, wheat, raisins, and money (dirhams). The least that a man can give is a veil (covering head and face, *khimār*) or the like.[191] [Imam] 'Alī b. al-Ḥusayn used to give a riding beast.'

Ḥusayn b. 'Alī: He once gave a divorced woman twenty thousand dirhams and some skins full of honey and she exclaimed, '[What] a meagre gift from a departing beloved!'

Abū Ja'far: He said, 'When a man wishes to divorce his wife, he may, if he wishes, give her the [departing gift] before divorce.'

Ja'far b. Muḥammad said, 'He may give her [the departing] gift after the *ṭalāq* or even after the end of the *'idda*. This is a more generous way of giving the present.'

If, according to the report from Abū Ja'far [Imam al-Bāqir], a man gave the present before the divorce, but while intending to give *ṭalāq* and while informing her accordingly, and did this before the *'idda* [commences] and in the presence of the witnesses for the divorce, this will be a sufficient fulfilment of his obligation.

---

for dower (*mahr*), in the case that no *mahr* had been specified, due from a husband who divorces his wife before consummation. *Majma' al-baḥrayn*, s.v. m-t-'; *Tāj al-'arūs*, s.v. m-t-'; Schacht, *Introduction*, 167; Coulson, *History of Islamic Law*, 31–2; Anderson, *Law Reform*, 60, 124–5.

[189]See n. 176 above in this chapter. Also refer to the Qur'ān 33:28 and 65:1–2. *Kāfī*, VI, 109–10; Ṭūsī, *Tahdhīb al-aḥkām*, VIII, 139.

[190]*Kāfī*, VI, 109; it is obligatory; Ṭūsī, *Tahdhīb al-aḥkām*, VIII, 140–2.

[191]*Kāfī*, VI, 110; Ṭūsī, *Tahdhīb al-aḥkām*, VIII, 139–40.

'Alī and Ja'far b. Muḥammad: They said, 'All divorced women shall receive a *mut'a* except the woman divorced by *khul'*; she is not entitled to a *mut'a*.'[192]

RECONCILIATION WITH A DIVORCED WIFE (*AL-RAJ'A*)

God says: *O Prophet, when ye [men] put away women, put them away for their (legal) period, and reckon the period*, till His saying: *Then, when they have reached their term, take them back in kindness or part with them in kindness* (65:1–2). He says: *Women who are divorced shall wait, keeping themselves apart, three (monthly) courses*, till His saying: *And their husbands would do better to take them back in that case if they desire a reconciliation* (2:228).

We have mentioned earlier that the man who divorces his wife according to the *sunna* or with reference to the period of waiting (*'idda*) has the right to return to her so long as the *'idda* has not expired. If the term has ended, and he has divorced her three times, she is absolutely separated from him, and she is not lawful to him until she marries another husband. If he has divorced her only once according to the *sunna*, and then leaves her until her *'idda* expires, then indeed she is separated from him, and he becomes one of her [potential] suitors. They may then marry afresh by common consent and the husband possesses the right to pronounce [two] remaining *ṭalāqs*.

'Alī and Ja'far b. Muḥammad: Concerning the Word of God: *Retain them not to their hurt so that ye transgress (the limits). He who doeth that has wronged his soul* (2:231), they said, 'That is the case of a man who desires to divorce a woman, and divorces her once and then returns to her when he does not need her. Again he divorces her and returns to her when her *'idda* is about to expire and when he has no need for her except to prolong the period of *'idda* and thus do her harm. God prohibited this [course of action].'

Ja'far b. Muḥammad: He said, 'Where a man wishes to return to his wife after divorcing her, it is proper for him to have his return witnessed in the same manner as his divorce. Now if a man overlooks this, or is ignorant of it, and does not have witnesses, there is no sin on him. Witnesses are considered necessary only because there is room for denial before the sovereign and the heirs lest it may be said, "He had divorced her and did not return to her." If a man returns to his wife without there

[192] Ṭūsī, *Tahdhīb al-aḥkām*, VIII, 137. According to Mālik three types of women are not eligible to receiving a *mut'a*: those divorced by *khul'*, those divorced by mutual imprecation, and those divorced before consummation of the marriage. Qurṭubī, *al-Kāfī fī fiqh ahl al-Madīna*, 291. For *khul'* see n. 63 above in this chapter.

being any witnesses, let him have the return witnessed when he recollects it or comes to know [of the rule].[193]

'Where his return has been witnessed before the expiry of the *'idda*, she remains his wife whether she knows it or not. If he has had sexual intercourse with her before the end of the *'idda*, then he has indeed returned to her even though he may not have used the word "return (*raj'a*)" and may not have had witnesses. Therefore, let him have the return witnessed whenever he recollects it or comes to know [that it is obligatory].'

'Alī: He said, 'Where a man divorces his wife and then returns to her, he is more entitled to her [than anyone else],[194] regardless of whether he informs her about the return or not.

'If a husband publicly divorces a woman and keeps his return [to her] a secret and then goes away and upon return, he finds her married to someone else, [in such a case,] he has no right over her because he made the divorce public but kept the return secret.'[195] This means that he had no witnesses for the return and did not inform the wife about it. But if he had the return witnessed or informed the wife of the return, then she is his wife and is not lawful to anyone, except after being divorced and the expiry of the *'idda*, or after the [husband's] death and the completion of the *'idda*.

'Alī: He said, 'When a man has divorced his wife, he should not ask her permission to go into her so long as he has the right to return to her. But where he has divorced her in a way which does not permit the return, he should not go into her either during or after the *'idda*, without her permission.'

Abū Ja'far [Imam al-Bāqir]: He said, 'So long as a husband has the right to return to her, the wife may glance at him and present herself before him.'

'Alī and Abū Ja'far and Abū 'Abd Allāh: They said, 'The *qar'* [or *qur'*] *al-ṭuhr* is the state of purity between two monthly courses.[196] Accordingly,

[193]*Kāfī*, VI, 75. For the Mālikī position see Qurṭubī, *al-Kāfī fī fiqh ahl al-Madīna*, 291–2.

[194]According to al-Bāqir he is more entitled to return to her as long as she has not seen the blood of the third menstrual course. As soon as she sees it her *'idda* terminates and the husband who divorced her cannot return to her. *Kāfī*, VI, 91.

[195]Ibid., VI, 77. Kulaynī cites a different case on Abū Ja'far's authority where a husband's return was witnessed, but the wife was informed neither by the husband nor by the witnesses. Hence, the woman did not know about it until after the *'idda* had expired. The Imam said that in such a case the woman has a choice either to remarry him or someone else. However, if she gets married before she comes to know about it, the former husband has no claim on her.

[196]See n. 141 above in this chapter; *Kāfī*, VI, 93–4.

when the divorced woman sees the blood of the third menstrual course, she is finally separated from him and the husband who divorced her cannot return to her.'[197]

Ja'far b. Muḥammad: He said, 'The smallest period of a monthly course is three days and the smallest period of purity is ten nights. [The responsibility of reckoning] the *'idda* and menstruation is on women; when they say something, they [are presumed to] speak the truth as long as it is plausible,[198] and the above is the least plausible [period].

'If a woman is divorced by her husband, and she claims that she has menstruated after ten nights of purity, she should be believed. Then if she claims that she is pure after three nights, she should be believed also. Then if she claims that she menstruated after ten nights, she should be believed, and this procedure should be followed till her *'idda* has been completed. If she is charged with making false statements, she should be given the oath unless she produces just women witnesses who support her statement.

'If she is married and is later charged with making false statements, she should not be sworn, and her word should be accepted. If she goes back on her oath or declares herself to be a liar after the expiry of the *'idda*, she should not be believed because her second husband is her protector[199] and she cannot get out of his protection by such an allegation.'

LEGALIZATION OF MARRIAGE WITH A WOMAN DIVORCED THREE TIMES (*IḤLĀL AL-MUṬALLAQA THALĀTH*[AN])[200]

God says: *And if he hath divorced her* (the third time), *then she is not lawful unto him thereafter until she hath wedded another husband* (2:230).[201]

[197]Ibid., VI, 91, 92.

[198]Ibid., VI, 105. Abū Ja'far said, '[The obligation of computing] the *'idda* and menstruation is on women. When she makes a claim, she should be believed.'

[199]The Arabic term is *'iṣma*. *'Iṣmat al-nikāḥ* means the bond of marriage, or *'iṣmat al-mar'a* means the woman's matrimonial bond, which is her husband's hand, or power. Lane, s.v. '-ṣ-m.

[200]*Iḥlāl* (or *taḥlīl*, lit. making lawful) is a form of legal device (*ḥiyal* pl. of *ḥīla*) that aims at removing the impediment to legalizing the marriage of a couple irrevocably divorced after a triple repudiation by arranging for the marriage of the woman to another husband with the understanding that this marriage would be immediately dissolved after consummation. It is to be noted that the attitudes of different schools of law differ towards the *ḥiyal*. Ibn Taymiyya declared the *ḥiyal* in general and the *taḥlīl* in particular invalid. Schacht, *Introduction*, 81–2; El-Alami, *Marriage Contract*, 25–6.

[201]'Ā'isha related that Rifā'a al-Quraẓī's wife came to the Messenger of God and said, 'I was married to Rifā'a but he divorced me, making my divorce irrevocable. Afterwards

Ja'far b. Muḥammad—his father—his ancestors—'Alī: He said, 'When a man divorces his wife three times, as it behoves him to do so, she is not lawful to him until she marries another husband.' It was said to him, 'Would a marriage without having sexual intercourse make her lawful to him?' 'Alī took out his hairy arm [from his mantle] and said, 'No, not until he [the second husband] has had actual physical intercourse with her'.[202]

Abū Ja'far and Abū 'Abd Allāh: They said, 'If a man divorces a woman three times with reference to *'idda*, she is not lawful to him until she marries another husband and he consummates the marriage and each of the spouses have enjoyed the delight of intercourse with one another (*yadhūq 'usaylatahā wa-tadhūq 'usaylatahu*).'[203]

'Alī: He decided as follows: A man divorced his wife and both of them repented [after the *'idda* has expired], and so they agreed as directed by 'Alī that she should marry a man to make her lawful to her husband. He said, 'She will not be lawful to him until she marries a husband with pleasure (*nikāḥ^u ghibṭat^in*), and not for convenience (*muwāṭa'a*, lit. means secret understanding, collusion), and he has sexual intercourse with her.[204]

I married 'Abd al-Raḥmān b. al-Zubayr, but all he possesses is like the fringe of a garment.' The Messenger of God understood that she wanted to return to Rifā'a and said, 'No, not until you and 'Abd al-Raḥmān have experienced the sweetness of intercourse with one another.' Ṭabarī, *Tafsīr*, IV, 589–96.

[202]Lit. until he shakes her in copulating with her (*ḥattā yahuzzahā bihi*, the last pronoun refers to *jimā'*). Anderson, *Law Reform*, 72–3; idem, *Islamic Law*, 42–3, without indicating his source, states that a woman came to the Prophet saying that a marriage she contracted in her youth had not been a success and it had ended in divorce. Since then she married another man who had also divorced her. Now being older and wiser, might she not remarry her first husband? The Prophet gave her permission and it is said that it was the occasion of the revelation of the verse 2:230. Thus, according to the Qur'ān remarriage after a triple pronouncement of divorce is permitted only if the woman concerned had experienced an intervening marriage.

It seems that this concession led to the expedient that a husband who had triply divorced his wife, but then regretted his action would procure a *muḥallil*, who would marry her and then divorce her in order to make it lawful for him to remarry her. All jurists agree that this intervening marriage must be consummated. However, some jurists refuse to recognize such a deliberately contrived marriage and insist that the intervening marriage, to be effective, must be contracted in good faith. Mālikīs do not approve of such devices (*ḥiyal*); hence the Tunisian Law of 1956 prohibits a man from remarrying his triply divorced wife.

[203]*Mishkāt*, II, 213; Robson, I, 699; transmitted by Bukhārī and Muslim. *Kāfī*, VI, 79. See also Lane, s.v. '-s-l, for linguistic explanation of *'usayla*.

[204]*Mishkāt*, II, 213; Robson, I, 699. 'The Messenger of God cursed the man who made a woman lawful for her husband and the one for whom she was made lawful.' Robson comments that it refers to an arrangement to marry a divorced woman and to divorce her after having intercourse so that the one who had divorced her might remarry her.

Thereafter if he divorces her or dies, and she completes the *'idda*, the parties may marry again if they both agree.'

Ja'far b. Muḥammad: He was asked about a man who divorced his wife three times, and so she married a slave who then divorced her. Is she lawful to the first husband? He said, 'Yes. God says: ... *until she hath wedded another husband* (2:230); and the slave is a husband.'

[Ja'far b. Muḥammad]: He said, 'If a man divorces his wife three times, and she weds herself to a *majbūb* (man with an amputated penis)[205] or a boy who has not yet attained puberty[206] and the second husband divorces her or dies, she is not lawful to the first husband until she marries some one who makes her lawful to him as it ought to be [that is, by actual sexual intercourse].'

[Ja'far b. Muḥammad]: He said, 'If a man divorces his wife and she marries another husband in the *mut'a* marriage,[207] such a marriage does not make her lawful to the first husband.'[208]

[Ja'far b. Muḥammad]: He said, 'Where a man marries a slave girl (*ama*), and then divorces her [three times], and she returns to her master and he has sexual intercourse with her, and later her husband wishes to return to her, she is not allowed to do so until she marries another husband.'

[Ja'far b. Muḥammad]: He said that in the following four cases the man and the woman can never marry each other again:

A woman against whom her husband has uttered *li'ān* is never lawful to him even if she marries another husband.[209]

If a man marries a woman during the *'idda*, and he knows that it is unlawful, they should be separated and they can never marry again.

A man divorces his wife in a form whereby she can never be lawful to him without marrying another husband. Then he returns to her three times, after she has married three other husbands. After such a procedure [three returns, nine *ṭalāqs*], she can never be lawful to her first husband in future.[210]

A *muḥrim*[211] who knows that it is unlawful to marry during *iḥrām*, and yet he marries a woman during that period should be separated [from her] and she can never be lawful to him in the future.

[205]For *majbūb* see n. 228 in Chap. 10.

[206]*Kāfī*, VI, 79; marriage with a minor does not satisfy the requirement.

[207]*Mut'a* marriage see Chap. 10, n. 222.

[208]Ṭūsī, *al-Nihāya*, 515.

[209]*Kāfī*, VI, 170, 171, 174. For *li'ān* see n. 117 in this chapter.

[210]*Kāfī*, VI, 80; Ṭūṣī, *al-Nihāya*, 514.

[211]*Muḥrim* is one who has entered the state of ritual consecration for performing the *ḥajj*; he is forbidden to marry, or contract anyone in marriage. See *The Pillars of Islam*, I, 381.

'Alī: He was asked about a man who marries a slave girl (*ama*) and then divorces her in a form whereby she can never be lawful to him without marrying another husband. If he then buys her, is it permissible for him to have intercourse with her by right of property? He said, 'One verse of the Qur'ān makes her lawful to him and another unlawful. The verse making her unlawful is ... *then she is not lawful unto him thereafter until she hath wedded another husband* (2:230); and the verse which makes her lawful is ... *or (the captives) that your right hands possess* (4:3). I disapprove of this practice and consider it forbidden for myself and my children.'

Ja'far b. Muḥammad: He was asked about a man who marries a slave girl and then divorces her in a form whereby she can never be lawful to him without marrying another husband. If he then buys her, is it possible for him to have intercourse with her by right of property? He said, 'Has 'Alī not already decided and said, "One verse of the Qur'ān makes her lawful and another makes her unlawful. I have forbidden this for myself and my children."[212] 'Alī has made it clear that when it is forbidden to him and his children, it is [also] not lawful for the buyer to have intercourse with her until she marries another husband. She has to enter into [the second marriage][213] in the same way as she emerged from [the first], but he can engage her services. If he has divorced her [with a revocable] divorce whereby he is able to return to her without an intervening marriage, he has the right to have intercourse with her.'

'Alī and Abū Ja'far and Abū 'Abd Allāh: They said, 'Where a man has divorced his wife with one or two divorce pronouncements, and then left her until her *'idda* has expired, and she marries another husband who dies or divorces her, and she observes the *'idda* and marries her former husband, she remains with him and the remaining pronouncements of *ṭalāq* can be given to her, and this right [of the husband] is not destroyed by his past pronouncements of divorce.'[214]

THE DIVORCE OF SLAVES (ṬALĀQ AL-MAMĀLĪK)

God says: *Allah coineth a similitude: (on the one hand) a (mere) chattel slave ('abd^{an} mamlūk^{an}), who has control of nothing* (16:75).[215]

[212] *Kāfī*, VI, 181; reported on the same authority.

[213] Ibid., VI, 182; slightly different wording.

[214] Ibid., VI, 80; the new marriage has annulled his previous pronouncements of *ṭalāq*, and has renewed the three pronouncement *ṭalāq* option. See also Ḥillī, *Sharā'ī' al-islām*, II, 59.

[215] The remainder of the verse states: *and (on the other hand) one on whom We have*

Ja'far b. Muḥammad—his father—his ancestors: 'Alī said, 'When a man marries his slave to his slave girl, he has the right to separate them whenever he wishes,'[216] and recited the above Qur'ānic verse. He then said, 'There is no marriage and no divorce without the permission of his master.'

Abū Ja'far and[217] Abū 'Abd Allāh: Both of them equally said the same. Abū 'Abd Allāh was asked, 'A man marries his slave (*'abd*) to a slave girl (*jāriya*) of another tribal group or to a free woman. Is it lawful to him to separate them without a divorce?' He replied, 'Yes. A slave (*mamlūk*) has no right to go against his master in any matter, for, as God says, ...' and he recited the Qur'ānic verse cited above (16:75).[218]

[Abū Ja'far and Abū 'Abd Allāh]: They said, 'A slave has no right to divorce or to marry without the permission of his master. If the master marries him, it is permissible. God says: *A (mere) chattel slave, who hath control of nothing* (*lā yaqdir 'alā shay'*) (16:75), and divorce and marriage are each of them a "thing" (*shay'*).'[219]

'Alī and Abū Ja'far and Abū 'Abd Allāḥ: They said, 'Divorce and *'idda* are matters pertaining to women. If a free woman is married to a free man or to a slave, her divorce consists of three pronouncements; and if a slave woman (*ama*) is married to a free man or to a slave, her divorce consists of two pronouncements.[220] She will be separated absolutely after the second pronouncement as the free woman is separated after the third.'

---

bestowed a fair provision from Us, and he spendeth thereof secretly and openly. Are they equal? It should be noted that *ṭalāq* between slaves is not regulated in the Qur'ān. '*Abd*[an] *mamlūk*[an] means a slave who is himself a piece of property.

[216]*Kāfī*, VI, 175–6, 177; this rule applies when both the slave and slave girl belong to one master.

[217]According to MS Q, it is missing from the edited text.

[218]*Kāfī*, VI, 176; in such a situation divorce is permitted.

[219]Ibid., VI, 176. When a master permits his slave to marry a free-woman or a slave girl of [another tribal] group, the right of divorce rests with the slave. However, if the slave has married without his master's permission, the right of divorce rests with the master.

[220]Ibid., VI, 175, 178.

12

Book of the Emancipation of Slaves (*Kitāb al-ʿItq*)

THE INDUCEMENTS FOR EMANCIPATION (*AL-RAGHĀʾIB FI ʾL-ʿITQ*)[1]

God says: *But he hath not attempted the Ascent (al-aqaba)*[2]*—Ah, what will convey unto thee what the Ascent is! (It is) to free a slave, and to feed in the day of hunger an orphan near of kin, or some poor wretch in misery* (90:11–16).

ʿAlī: He said, 'The Messenger of God said, "When a man emancipates a slave, whether *muʾmin* or *muslim*,[3] God will protect each of the limbs of the emancipator from the Fire [in requital for] each of the limbs of the slave."'[4]

ʿAlī, Abū Jaʿfar, and Abū ʿAbd Allāh said the like of this.

ʿAlī b. al-Ḥusayn [Zayn al-ʿĀbidīn]: He said, 'No faithful person emancipates a faithful slave but God will protect from the Fire each of

[1]Slavery was practised in pre-Islamic Arabia as in the ancient and medieval world. The Qurʾān has endeavoured to moderate the institution of slavery and mitigate its legal and moral aspects. Spiritually, the slave has the same value as the free man, and the same eternity is in store for his soul. The most important Qurʾānic legal enactments and reform have been with regard to women and slavery. The Qurʾān, throughout, makes the emancipation of slaves a meritorious act. It bans the prostitution of female slaves. The traditions enjoin real kindness towards them. For more details see Rahman, *Islam*, 38–9; *EI*[2], s.v. ʿAbd.

[2]ʿ*Aqaba* means a mountain road, or most difficult of ascent. *Iqtaḥama ʾl-ʿaqaba* is metaphorically used to mean he entered upon a difficult affair. Lane, s.v. ʿ-q-b; *Muʿjam alfāẓ al-Qurʾān*, s.v. q-ḥ-m.

[3]For the distinction between a *muʾmin* and a *muslim*, see *The Pillars of Islam*, I, 15–17.

[4]'If anyone emancipates a Muslim slave, God will set free from Hell a limb of the body for every limb of his, even his private parts for his.' Transmitted by Bukhārī and Muslim. *Mishkāt*, II, 241; Robson, I, 721. See also *Kāfī*, VI, 188–9; Ṭūṣī, *Tahdhīb al-aḥkām*, VIII, 216.

the limbs of the emancipator—including his private parts—for each of the slave's limbs.'

Ja'far b. Muḥammad: He said, 'If a man were to perform one of the following four acts for [the pleasure of] God, he will be assured of Paradise: gives water to a beast dying of thirst;[5] feeds a hungry man; clothes a naked body; or emancipates a faithful slave.'

[Ja'far b. Muḥammad]: He was asked about a man who emancipates a slave. He said, 'God will free from the Fire a limb of the emancipator for each limb of the slave. It is commendable to free a slave on the eve of the Day of 'Arafa.'[6] I think there is a virtue in it and we have mentioned this is the chapter of pilgrimage.

'Alī: He used to work with his hands, fight in the way of God, and take his share of booty. He was sometimes seen with a caravan of camels laden with date stones, and people would say, 'What is this, O Abu 'l-Ḥasan?' He would say, 'Palm trees, God willing!' He would plant them without losing a single stone.

He continued to wage religious war throughout the life of the Messenger of God and from the time he ruled over the people until God summoned him. During the interlude [i.e. after the death of the Messenger of God and his assumption of the caliphate], he used to work on his estate and had emancipated a thousand slaves, all with his own earnings, peace be on him.

The Messenger of God: Describing emancipation, he said, 'Emancipation is wonderful.'

Abū Dharr al-Ghifārī[7] asked him, 'Which kind of slave is most excellent [to emancipate], O Messenger of God?'

He replied, 'The one which is dearer in price and more valuable to his masters.'

Abū Dharr asked, 'If the man has no wealth [with which to free a slave], O Messenger of God?'

[5]'Forgiveness was granted to an unchaste woman who, coming upon a dog panting and almost dead with thirst at the mouth of a well, took of her shoe, tied it with her head covering and drew some water for it ... a reward is given in connection with every living creature.' Transmitted by Bukhārī and Muslim. Another tradition states, 'If any Muslim clothes a Muslim when he is naked, God will clothe him with some of the green garments of paradise; if any Muslim feeds a Muslim when he is hungry, God will feed him some of the fruits of paradise; and if any Muslim gives a Muslim drink when he is thirsty, God will give him some of the pure wine which is sealed [ref. Qur'ān 83:25] to drink.' *Mishkāt*, I, 597, 599; Robson, I, 404, 406.

[6]For the Day of 'Arafa, see *The Pillars of Islam*, I, 399. *Kāfī*, VI, 188.

[7]Abū Dharr was noted for his piety. *The Pillars of Islam*, I, 37, n. 83.

The Messenger of God said, '[Let him give charity with his] surplus of food (*'afw^u ṭa'āmihi*).'

Abū Dharr said, 'But if the man has no surplus of food?'

The Messenger of God replied, 'Then let him give prudent advice to his companion.'

Abū Dharr said, 'But if he has no prudent advice to offer?'

The Messenger of God said, 'Then let him serve the weak among you with his strength.'

Abū Dharr asked, 'And if he cannot do so?'

The Messenger of God replied, 'Then you[8] should look after your own hereafter and help the wronged ones.'

Abū Dharr said, 'And if I do not do so, O Messenger of God?'

The Messenger of God responded, 'Then remove from the path of people things that hurt them.'

Abū Dharr asked, 'And if I do not do so?'

The Messenger of God replied, 'Then refrain from giving trouble to people; for this is a charity you can do to yourself.'

Ja'far b. Muḥammad: A man asked [Imam al-Ṣādiq], 'Which [among my] slaves shall I emancipate?' He said, 'Emancipate the one who has made himself free from want.'[9]

Abū Ja'far Muḥammad b. 'Alī and Ja'far b. Muḥammad: They were asked about the emancipation of children, and they said, "Alī emancipated a large number of children.'[10] Ja'far b. Muḥammad [Imam al-Ṣādiq] said, 'Their names are written down with us.'[11]

'Alī: He emancipated a Christian slave who embraced Islam as soon as he was freed. Thus the emancipation of a Christian is permissible but the emancipation of a faithful one is more meritorious.

[8]From this point onwards the Arabic text of the dialogue abruptly changes from the third person to the first and second persons. In this respect it is similar to a slightly different and shorter version transmitted by Bukhārī and Muslim on the authority of Abū Dharr who said that he asked the Prophet what action was most excellent and he replied, 'Faith in God and *jihād* in His path.' He then asked which kind of slave is most excellent [to emancipate] and he replied, 'The one whose price is highest and who is held in most esteem by his masters.' He asked [what he should do] if unable to act accordingly and the Prophet replied, 'You should assist a workman, or work for one who is unskilled.' He asked [what he should do] if unable to act accordingly. The Prophet replied, 'Do no harm to others, for that is a charity (*ṣadaqa*) you bestow on yourself.' *Mishkāt*, II, 241; Robson, I, 721; Bukhārī, *Matn al-Bukhārī*, II, 79 (*Kitāb al-'itq*).

[9]*Kāfī*, VI, 190, 207; Ṭūsī, *Tahdhīb al-aḥkām*, VIII, 218.

[10]*Kāfī*, VI, 189.

[11]The Imam implies that his family has preserved the record of those whom 'Alī emancipated.

Ja'far b. Muḥammad: He emancipated a slave and wrote a document testifying to it as follows:

This [document] is to certify that Ja'far b. Muḥammad has emancipated his slave, so and so, for the sake of God,[12] without desiring a requital or his thanks, on the condition that he [the slave] should be devoted to the Friends of God (*awliyā' Allāh*), disclaim association with the enemies of God, perform his ablutions fully and pray regularly, give the alms tax, perform the pilgrimage, fast during the month of Ramaḍān, and fight in the way of God. Three witnesses to this are so-and-so, so-and-so, and so-and-so.[13]

UNCONDITIONAL EMANCIPATIONS AND WHAT IS LAWFUL AND WHAT IS UNLAWFUL AMONG THEM ('*ITQ AL-BATĀT WA-MĀ YAJŪZ MINHU WA-MĀ LĀ YAJŪZ*)[14]

Ja'far b. Muḥammad—his father—his ancestors—'Alī: The Messenger of God prohibited emancipation of slaves except for the sake of God.

Ja'far b. Muḥammad: He said, 'There is no emancipation unless it is performed for the sake of God,[15] and he who says, "All the slaves I possess are free," or swears to it, or is forced to say so, but does not intend to do so for the sake of God, and does not say so, his emancipation is void.'

[Ja'far b. Muḥammad]: He said, 'He who is obligated to emancipate a slave does not fulfil his obligation by emancipating a blind man, a cripple, or a useless person, except when he had already determined to do so [earlier].'

The Messenger of God: He said, 'There is no emancipation except after ownership.' A similar report comes from 'Alī.[16]

Ja'far b. Muḥammad: He said, 'A man says, "If I buy a slave, he is emancipated for the sake of God;" or, "if I buy this cloth, it is charity in the way of God;" or "if I marry so and so, she is divorced."' [The Imam] said, 'All these statements are null and void. A man can only divorce, emancipate, or give in charity what he [already] possesses.'

Ja'far b. Muḥammad: About a man who emancipates a share in a

[12]'There is no manumission except for the sake of God.' *Kāfī*, VI, 187.

[13]Ibid., VI, 190; some variation in the wording.

[14]'*Itq al-batāt* means absolute, irrevocable emancipation for the sake of God. Lane, s.v. b-t-t.

[15]*Kāfī*, VI, 187.

[16]'There is no manumission till one has possession.' *Mishkāt*, II, 210; Robson, I, 696. *Kāfī*, VI, 187; Ṭūsī, *Tahdhīb al-aḥkām*, VIII, 217.

slave who belongs wholly to him, he said, '[Here,] the slave becomes wholly free because God has no partner.'[17]

[Ja'far b. Muḥammad]: He was asked about a man who emancipated one-third of his slave at the time of his death. The deceased had no other property other than the slave. [The Imam] said, 'One-third of the slave is emancipated and two-thirds belong to the heirs.'[18]

'Alī, Abū Ja'far, and Abū 'Abd Allāh: They said, '[If a man shares the ownership of a slave and] emancipates his share thereby emancipating his portion and leaving the residue to enure to the benefit of his partners, it is incumbent on the emancipator, if he is well-to-do, to emancipate the remaining part of the slave and to pay off the part owners their share of the price of the slave on the day of emancipation.[19] If, however, he is in straitened circumstances, the partners are entitled to their shares. When the slave or the emancipator pays for his freedom, the slave will be wholly emancipated, otherwise, the slave will either serve them according to their shares or the owners may permit him to ransom himself if they agree on the terms of his service (*si'āya*).[20]

'If one of the part owners of the slave emancipates him to the extent of his share, and the first emancipator is in straitened circumstances, but the second emancipator is well-to-do, it is the duty of all the remaining co-owners, except the first, jointly to emancipate the slave. Later, if the first co-owner becomes well off, recourse may be had to him and to each of the co-owners, one after the other [according to priority].' This is the

[17]'If anyone emancipates a share in a slave, he is to be completely emancipated if he has money; but if he has none, the slave will be required to work to pay for his freedom, but must not be overburdened.' Transmitted by Bukhārī and Muslim. Another tradition states that a man emancipated a share in a slave, and the matter was mentioned to the Prophet, and he said, 'God has no partner,' and decided that he should be emancipated [fully]. *Mishkāt*, II, 244, 246; Robson, I, 723, 724. Ṭūsī, *Tahdhīb al-aḥkām*, VIII, 221–2.

[18]According to Islamic law, a Muslim cannot dispose of more than one-third of his net estate. The remaining two-thirds must go to his heirs. Fyzee, *Outlines*, 360. See also *Mishkāt*, II, 244–5; Robson, I, 723; see also Chap. 14, n. 2 below.

[19]'If anyone emancipates his share in a slave and has enough money to pay the full price for him, a fair price for the slave should be fixed, his partners given their shares, and the slave be thus manumitted; otherwise he is emancipated only to the extent of the first man's share.' Bukhārī and Muslim transmitted it. *Mishkāt*, II, 244; Robson, I, 723. See also *Kāfī*, VI, 191–2.

[20]The Arabic is *istas'ā 'l-'abda*, meaning he required of the slave that he should labour to earn for releasing himself completely, when he had been emancipated in part. *Si'āya* or *sa'y*, in this context, signifies the work so imposed for acquiring his freedom. Lane, s.v. s-'-y; Schacht, *Introduction*, 129.

purport of what has been related from [the Imams], however, their words may vary in some respects.

Jaʿfar b. Muḥammad: He said, 'If a man emancipates a slave at the time of his death, and owes a debt equal to the price of the slave, the slave, [in this case], should be sold [to pay off the debt] and the emancipation is not permitted. However, if the debt is less [than the price of the slave] and the slave has already been emancipated[21] to the extent of one-sixth [of the slave's value] or more, the emancipation is permitted, as long as [one-sixth of his value], the share which has already been emancipated, can come out of the [bequeathable] third after the payment of the debt.'

[Jaʿfar b. Muḥammad]: He was asked about a man who emancipates a slave at his death while having no property except his slave and while having also a debt to pay. [The Imam] asked, 'How much is the debt?' It was said to him, 'As much as the price of the slave or more.' [The Imam] said, 'If the debt is for the same amount as the price of the slave, the slave should be sold and the debt paid off. If the debt is more than the price of the slave, the creditors will share rateably the price of the slave among themselves.' It was said to him, '[If] the debt is less than the price of the slave?' [The Imam] said, 'Then you may calculate [the figures] as you wish.'

The man asked, 'What do you say about the slave whose price is six hundred [dirhams] and the debt is five hundred [dirhams]?' [The Imam] replied, 'The slave should be sold; five hundred should be paid to the creditors and the heirs shall receive one hundred.' The man said, 'Is it not that the surplus from the slave's price is one hundred [dirhams] and he is entitled to receive one-third of it and will be emancipated proportionately?'

[The Imam] smiled and said, 'This is a bequest and the slave is not entitled to a bequest.' It was said to him, 'What if the price of the slave is six hundred [dirhams] and the debt four hundred?' [The Imam] said, 'The same rule applies. The slave should be sold, the creditors will be paid four hundred, and the residue will go to the heirs.' It was said to him, 'What if the debt is three hundred and the price of the slave six hundred [dirhams]?' [The Imam] replied, 'From this proportion on, things are different even though you have considered them to be the same, and you did not understand the *sunna*. Where the property of the heirs is equal to the debt of the creditors, or the property of the heirs is greater in value, the bequest will be permissible and the testator will not be blamed for his bequest. The slave will be summoned [and dealt with as follows]: three hundred will be for the creditors, two hundred will be for the heirs, and

[21]Read *ʿutiqa*, passive voice; vocalization in the edited text is incorrect.

[one hundred] will be taken by the slave as one-sixth [his value] and he will emerge a free man [proportionately].'

This follows from what I [Nu'mān] have related from him [Imam al-Ṣādiq] in the preceding report. Thus, it is a mandatory obligation to take the rule from [Imam al-Ṣādiq] or from any of the other Imams and follow it, for, obedience to them is obligatory. No objection can be raised to what they say. We have mentioned that the *sunna* is what [the Imam] says, and that the *sunna* is according to his word.

[Ja'far b. Muḥammad]: [Concerning the case of] a man who has no property except slaves, emancipates some of them at the time of his death, but fails to mention, by name, which of them is to be freed first, [the Imam] said, 'Lots should be drawn among them and they should be emancipated one by one according to their [respective turn] until the [bequeathable] third is exhausted.'

Abū Ja'far Muḥammad b. 'Alī [Imam al-Bāqir] said, 'But if he has named them and said, "Emancipate so and so, and so and so for my sake," the total of the prices of the slaves should be calculated and [considered in relation to] the [bequeathable] third. Then, you should begin by emancipating the slaves in the order in which they are mentioned, and if the [bequeathable] third is more than the price of the slaves taken together, all of them will be emancipated. But, if the price of the last slave exceeds the limit of the [bequeathable] third by one-sixth or more, he should be detained for the balance of what remains on him. The remaining slaves form part of the heritable estate. [In any case,] a beginning should be made only with those slaves which the testator had mentioned by name, according to their priorities.' This dictum is that of Abū Ja'far [Imam al-Bāqir] and the fixation of the residue beyond the bequeathable third as mentioned above is according to Abū 'Abd Allāh Ja'far b. Muḥammad b. 'Alī [Imam al-Ṣādiq].[22]

Ja'far b. Muḥammad: He was asked about a man who buys a slave or

[22] 'Imrān b. Ḥusayn said that a man who had no other property, emancipated six of his slaves at the time of his death. God's Messenger called for them, and after dividing them into three groups, casting lots among them, and setting two free and keeping four in slavery [because a Muslim cannot dispose of more than one-third of his estate], he spoke severely of him [the dead man]. Transmitted by Muslim and Nasā'ī. Another tradition states that a man of the Anṣār declared that a slave would be free after his death and he had no other property. Hence, when the Prophet heard of that he said, 'Who will buy him from me?' Nu'aym bought him for eight hundred dirhams .... The Prophet handed them over to the man and said, 'Spend first on yourself giving yourself *ṣadaqa*, if anything is left over give it to your family ... give it to your relatives ... and do thus and thus.' Transmitted by Bukhārī and Muslim. *Mishkāt*, II, 244, 245; Robson, I, 723–4.

slave girl for a price to be paid at a future date, then emancipates the slave, or makes the slave girl bear a child and emancipates her, at which time, the seller demands the price of the slave but the purchaser has no money. [The Imam] said, 'The emancipation is valid if the purchaser had the means to pay the price on the day he emancipated the slave or impregnated the slave girl. However, if he was poor and had no money, the emancipation is void and both the slave girl and her child revert to the seller.'[23]

'Alī : He emancipated [the four slaves] Abū Bīruz,[24] Ḥabtarā,[25] Riyāḥ, and Zurayq on the condition that they should work on his estate for four years and then be free. They laboured accordingly and became free.[26]

Abū Ja'far:[27] He said, 'If a man buys a slave or slave girl and emancipates him/her on the condition that when the emancipated slave earns money to the extent of his/her own price, he/she will return it to the emancipator, it is binding upon him/her when he/she obtains the money. Muslims are bound by their stipulations. If the man emancipates his slave on the condition that he marries the emancipator's slave girl, the emancipated slave is bound by such a condition. If the man makes the condition that the emancipated slave, when he marries some other woman, bond or free, in order to remove his children from the master's ownership, the slave will pay a certain amount of money, such a condition is valid.'

Ja'far b. Muḥammad: He said, 'If a slave mixes up [his own] property with that of another man who purchases and emancipates him, and the owner of the slave has no knowledge of the property and has not given the slave any such permission, [in such cases,] the owner has an option; if he so wishes, the slave will revert to him and his property will be sequestered; or, he may return the property to the slave.'[28]

Abū Ja'far and Abū 'Abd Allāh: They said, 'If a man emancipates his slave knowing that the slave has some wealth, such property belongs to the emancipated slave should he allow the slave to retain it. However,

[23]*Kāfī*, VI, 204.

[24]MS Q: Abū Bīdhar. Six MSS of Fyzee: Abū Bīzar.

[25]In six MSS of Fyzee: Jubayl, probably an error for Jubayr.

[26]Safīna said, 'I was a slave of Umm Salama, and she said, "I shall emancipate you on the condition that you should serve God's Messenger as long as you live." I replied, "Even if you do not make a stipulation with me, I shall not leave the Messenger of God as long as I live." She then emancipated me and made the stipulation with me.' *Mishkāt*, II, 246; Robson, I, 724. Kulaynī gives three names: Abū Nīzar, Rabāḥ and Jubayr, and states that they were to work for five years. *Kāfī*, VI, 188.

[27]MS Q adds: Muḥammad b. 'Alī.

[28]*Kāfī*, VI, 205. Concerning the case of a slave who gives money to a third party in order to be purchased and emancipated by that third party, Abū Ja'far said, 'It is not permitted.'

if the owner did not know of it and he or his heirs came to know about it, in such a case, the property belongs to the emancipator or his heirs, as the case may be.'[29]

'Alī, Abū Ja'far, and Abū 'Abd Allāh: They said, 'A slave can possess nothing except what his owner gives him. A slave is not allowed to emancipate another slave, give in charity, or make a gift of anything in his possession except as empowered by his master. [In addition to such an empowerment, a slave may do charitable works] if the master has granted him a portion of his property (*aqṭa'ahu mālan*), or has approved of what he did, or has allowed him to keep [the balance of his earnings] after paying the [fixed] impost (*ḍarībatahu*)[30] [levied upon him by the master].'[31] This is the purport of what has been related to us from [the Imams], although their words may vary in some respects.

['Alī, Abū Ja'far, and Abū 'Abd Allāh]: They said, 'If anyone gets possession of a relative who is so closely related to him as to be forbidden in marriage, then the slave becomes emancipated and the owner has no right over him.'[32]

['Alī, Abū Ja'far, and Abū 'Abd Allāh]: They said, 'Where a man marries a slave girl and makes a condition with her owners that the children will be free, such a condition is valid. Similarly, if they stipulate that the first child will be free but the rest will be slaves, this condition is valid as well. If twins are born, both of them are free with immediate effect.'[33]

Ja'far b. Muḥammad: He said, 'If some of the heirs testify that the deceased had emancipated a slave of his, the witness need not be guaranteed because the evidence affects only the share of the heir so testifying.'

[Ja'far b. Muḥammad]: He said, 'The emancipation of a slave [is not valid] if a man [only] writes it down, but does not pronounce it [by word of mouth]. It is of no effect until he utters it.'

[29]'Anyone who emancipates a slave that owns property gets the slave's property, unless the master stipulates otherwise.' *Mishkāt*, II, 246; Robson, I, 724. See also *Kāfī*, VI, 201.

[30]The Arabic term is *ḍarība*, and *ḍarībat al-'abd* means that what the slave pays to his master, of the impost that is levied upon him. *Lisān al-'Arab*, s.v. ḍ-r-b; Lane, s.v. ḍ-r-b.

[31]*Kāfī*, VI, 200.

[32]'If anyone gets possession of a relative who is within the prohibited degrees of marriage, that person becomes free.' *Mishkāt* II, 245; Robson I, 724. *Kāfī*, VI, 185–7. According to Kulaynī, a man cannot possess his parents, sister, or maternal or paternal aunts. When a slave becomes the property of a very close relative, emancipation follows automatically: according to the Shāfi'īs, this only applies in the ascending and descending lines; the Mālikīs add brothers and sisters; the Ḥanafīs, on the other hand, extend the rule to all relatives within the prohibited degrees of marriage. *EI*^{2}, s.v. 'Abd.

[33]*Kāfī*, VI, 206.

[Ja'far b. Muḥammad]: He said, 'Where a man emancipates a slave on the condition that the emancipator would receive some property from the slave, this is permissible.'

[Ja'far b. Muḥammad]: He said, 'A woman has the right to emancipate [her slave] and do what she likes with her property without let or hindrance from her husband or anyone else. Her husband has no right in her property except what she gives him by her own free will.'

[Ja'far b. Muḥammad]: He said, 'It is lawful for a man to emancipate the unborn child of his slave, or say to her, "Whoever is born to you, or your first-born is free." If she gives birth to twins, they are both emancipated.'

[Ja'far b. Muḥammad]: He said, 'If a man emancipates his slave girl (*ama*), but makes an exception in the case of what is in her womb, the exception is not lawful. She will be emancipated and the child born to her, will be free.'

[Ja'far b. Muḥammad]: He said, 'The emancipation made by a dumb person is valid provided it is made public or in writing if he knows how to write.'

EMANCIPATION BY CONTRACT THROUGH PERIODIC PAYMENTS (*AL-MUKĀTABŪN*)[34]

God says: *And such of your slaves as seek a writing (of emancipation), write it for them if ye are aware of aught of good in them* (24:33).

Ja'far b. Muḥammad—his father—his ancestors: 'Alī said, 'The first man who made a contract of emancipation was Luqmān, the wise man (*al-ḥakīm*).[35] He was an Abyssinian slave.'

[Ja'far b. Muḥammad]: He said, 'Four [rules from the Qur'ān] are instructions, but are not obligatory: (i) *write it for them if ye are aware of*

[34]The word *mukātab* is derived from the Qur'ānic passage 24:33. Hence, under a *mukātaba* contract, the master allows his slave to purchase his freedom by his own earnings and pay in instalments the sum of money agreed between them. This slave was called *mukātab*. Concerning the decision as to when the *mukātab* becomes free, there is a difference of opinion. Schacht, *Origins*, 173, 279–81; *EI*², s.v. 'Abd. See also Ṭūsī, *Tahdhīb al-aḥkām*, VIII, 265 ff.; *The Pillars of Islam*, I, 313.

[35]Luqmān, a legendary hero and sage of pre-Islamic Arabia, is mentioned in the Qur'ān as a monotheist and a wise father giving admonitions to his son. In Islamic lore, he is credited with many fables. The Qur'ān commentators relate traditions that Luqmān was a 'thick-lipped, flat-footed black slave' of Ethiopian or Nubian origin. Ṭabarī, *Tafsīr* (Beirut), XXI, 43. For details see *EI*², s.v. Luḳmān.

aught of good in them (24:33), he who wishes to make a contract of emancipation with his slave may do so, and he who does not, need not do so. (ii) ... *but when ye have left the sacred territory, then go hunting (if ye will)* (5:2); he who wishes to hunt after leaving the sacred territory may do so, but he who does not, is not obliged to do so.[36] (iii) ... *eat thereof and feed the beggar and the suppliant* (22:36); he who wishes to eat of his sacrificial animals may do so, and he who does not, is not obliged to do so.[37] (iv) *And when the prayer is ended, then disperse in the land* (62:10); he who wishes to disperse may do so, and he who does not, may sit in the mosque.'[38]

[Ja'far b. Muḥammad]: He was asked about a slave who asks for *mukātaba*; is it proper for the master to only make a contract at a high price? [The Imam] said, 'That is a matter for him [the master] to decide and there are no fixed rules applicable to him in such a contract.'

[Ja'far b. Muḥammad]: Concerning the Qur'ānic phrase ... *write it for them if ye are aware of aught of good (khayr) in them* (24:33), [the Imam] said, 'It (*khayr*) refers to his capacity to pay compensation.'[39]

Abū Ja'far and Abū 'Abd Allāh: They said, 'The word *khayr* in the above verse means "property". God says: ... *if he leave wealth (khayr), that he bequeath unto parents and near relatives in kindness* (2:180), i.e. property. He [among the slaves] who is able to earn and pay money is a person who has *khayr* (property).'

'Alī: He said, 'The owners of Barīra[40] (a slave girl) made a contract of emancipation for her even though she used to beg from people. 'Ā'isha[41] mentioned this to the Prophet, but he did not repudiate the contract while she continued to beg.'

'Alī: Once he was sitting and distributing property amongst the Muslims. An old man came and stood by and said, 'O Commander of the Faithful, I am an old man, as you see. I am a *mukātab* (having a contract of emancipation), so [give me] some of this property and assist me.' 'Alī said, 'By God, these goods are not of my earning; nor have I received them as an inheritance from my father, but it is a trust property which I have to look after and distribute among those that are entitled to it. Nevertheless, do take your seat.' He sat down while the people

[36]See *The Pillars of Islam*, I, 380–9.

[37]See Ibid., I, 406, 410.

[38]See ibid., I, 226.

[39]*Kāfī*, VI, 197; *khayr* is explained as having property (*māl*), or property and faith (*dīn*).

[40]Barīra, see n. 294 in Chap. 10.

[41]'Ā'isha bt. Abī Bakr was the wife of the Prophet, see *The Pillars of Islam*, I, 54, n. 137.

were around the Commander of the Faithful. ʿAlī looked at them and said, 'May God have mercy on him who helps this old man who is bearing a heavy burden.' Thereupon, people began making gifts to him.

Jaʿfar b. Muḥammad: He was asked about a slave who asks his master to emancipate him by a contract (*kitāba*) even though he has no property whatsoever. He said, 'Let him emancipate him by contract, even though the slave has to beg for it, for verily, God provides for some of his bondmen through others.'[42]

ʿAlī: He said, 'Concerning the Word of God: ... *And bestow upon them of the wealth of Allah which He has bestowed upon you* (24:33), the Messenger of God said, "This refers to one-fourth of the price of *kitāba*."' And ʿAlī said, 'A quarter of the *kitāba* may be bequeathed to the slave [under a contract of emancipation].'

Abū Jaʿfar said, 'Do not say, "I give you a contract of emancipation for five thousand, and bequeath you one thousand." Rather, look at the amount you have determined [in your mind] for him and give him a portion of it.'[43]

Jaʿfar b. Muḥammad said, 'Do not increase the amount and then deduct the excess, but reduce the amount already fixed for his [your slave's] emancipation.'

Abū Jaʿfar: He said, 'Where a man emancipates a slave either [outright] or by a contract, and knows that the slave has some property which the master has not excluded [from the contract], the property belongs to the slave.'[44]

[Abū Jaʿfar]: He said, '[It is valid] to stipulate in a contract of emancipation that if the slave fails to perform his part of the contract, he returns to the status of slavery, for Muslims are bound by the conditions they make.'

Jaʿfar b. Muḥammad said, 'If such is the stipulation and the slave fails to perform his part of the contract, he returns to slavery. Formerly, people did not make such conditions, but now they do so, and Muslims are bound by the stipulations they make.'[45]

[Abū Jaʿfar]: He was asked concerning a *mukātab* who was bound by a condition not to marry without the master's permission until he had paid the whole of the amount [that was stipulated]. [The Imam] said, 'The slave is bound by the condition, and if he does marry, the marriage

[42] *Kāfī*, VI, 197–8.
[43] Ibid., VI, 197.
[44] *Mishkāt*, II, 246; Robson, I, 724.
[45] *Kāfī*, VI, 195.

is invalid (*fāsid*) and susceptible to being rescinded (*mardūd*). He may, however, marry again after the emancipation.'

'Alī: A *mukātab* was referred to him against whom his masters had made the condition that, on his emancipation, they would be entitled to his inheritance. 'Alī declared the condition void and said, 'The condition imposed by God takes precedence over the condition made by men.'[46]

Abū Ja'far and Abū 'Abd Allāh: They said, 'The position of a *mukā*tab with whom a stipulation is made that if he fails to perform his part of the contract, he returns to slavery, is that of an ordinary slave in all matters save in respect of the property given to him [by his master]. For verily, it is his duty to pay his instalments (*nujūm*);[47] and when he is emancipated, the balance that remains with him becomes his property. He is entitled to buy and sell and if he contracts a debt in his trade during the contractual period of emancipation and cannot pay it, it is for his master to pay his dues, for, the *mukātab* is his slave and the master has to pay his unpaid debts for him. Such a slave neither inherits, nor is inherited, and he possesses the same rights and obligations as all other slaves. It is not lawful for him to emancipate a slave, make a gift, marry, or undertake a pilgrimage, except with the consent of his masters, until he has paid off all his dues.[48]

'Where, however, the amount for his instalments has been fixed and no stipulation has been made that, on breach of contract, he returns to slavery, he becomes free upon the payment of his first instalment to the extent of his payment, and he confirms slavery in proportion to the unpaid balance. The same is his position in respect to all matters and all things which can be divided into parts such as: inheritance,[49] criminal punishments (*ḥudūd*), emancipation, gifts, and crimes. He is entitled to them in proportion to his emancipation and the rest will be declared void.

'The return to slavery is according to the conditions stipulated; if it is stipulated that he returns after failure of the first or the second or the third instalment, or according to some other stipulation, he will return to slavery pursuant to the agreed conditions.'

[46]Refers to Qur'ān 24:33.

[47]*Najm* pl. *nujūm* means the time when a payment falls due, hence an instalment. *Lisān al-'Arab*, s.v. n-j-m.

[48]*Kāfī*, VI, 195–6.

[49]'When a slave who has made an agreement to purchase his freedom gets blood money or an inheritance, he can inherit in proportion to the extent to which he has been emancipated.' *Mishkāt*, II, 247; Robson, I, 725.

'Alī: He said, 'A *mukātab* should not be returned to slavery until he fails to pay two consecutive instalments.' That is to say, time should be given to him after his failure to pay the first instalment till the time of the second instalment; and when the time for the second instalment has expired and he fails to pay, he returns to slavery.[50]

'Alī and Ja'far b. Muḥammad:[51] They said, 'If a *mukātab* wishes to pay his instalments in advance and if it is stipulated that the *mukātab* returns to slavery if he fails to pay an instalment, the owner cannot be forced to accept such payment, and the emancipator may refuse to accept payment except at the times stipulated for each instalment, for it is possible that the slave fails to pay and returns to slavery. However, where there is no such condition, and the time for an instalment has come, and the slave pays that instalment together with the balance, the master cannot refuse, because emancipation has already begun and the slave can never return to slavery. In fact, it is the slave's duty to hasten payment of the balance due.

'Those children of the *mukātab* which do not form part of the contract [and are born during the period of the contract], are all slaves; and those born after his emancipation, whether to his slave (*ama*) or to his free wife, are all free. The children born to his free wife during his contract are also free; but the children of a slave girl belonging to some other master, belong to the master of the girl provided that no conditions for their freedom have been made.' We have mentioned this in the Book of Marriage.[52] If he has bought a slave girl (*jāriya*) and she gave birth to a child, the child is his.

Ja'far b. Muḥammad: He said, 'If a *mukātab* dies after paying some of his instalments, and has a son by a slave girl (*jāriya*) and if the slave has agreed to the stipulation that his failure to pay would return him to slavery, his son and his slave girl go back to his owner as slaves. If there had been no such condition, his son would become free upon paying the remaining instalments and would inherit the rest of the property.[53] In

[50]'A slave who has entered into an agreement to purchase his freedom is a slave as long as a dirham of the agreed price remains to be paid.' *Mishkāt*, II, 246, 247; Robson, I, 725. Early opinions vary as to when the *mukātab* slave becomes free. See Schacht, *Introduction*, 42–3.

[51]As in MS Q. Ibn Muḥammad: missing from the edited text.

[52]See Chap. 10 on marriage in this book.

[53]A slave made a contract with his master to purchase his freedom for one thousand dirhams. There was no stipulation that if he failed to pay he would return to slavery. The *mukātab* had paid five hundred dirhams and died. He left behind a son who had attained the age of puberty and some property. The Imam said that the property should be divided equally between the master and the *mukātab*'s son because when he died, he was half

the case of a *mukātab* slave girl who gives birth to a son, her son has the same status as herself; he will be free with her emancipation and will return to slavery, if she has to.

'The owner of a *mukātab* cannot, in an attempt to rescind the contract of emancipation, sell him so long as he pays his instalments. If such a *mukātab* is sold, he remains with the purchaser on the same terms as Barīra was sold.[54] This is permissible. The *mukātab*'s position with the purchaser is the same as with the previous owner and he becomes emancipated as soon as he has paid off his last instalment [as stipulated in the contract].'

'Alī: He said, 'If a man makes a contract of emancipation with a slave girl, he should not have sexual intercourse with her.'[55] He also said, 'There is no harm in writing a contract of emancipation with a minor slave,[56] and there is no harm if someone else guarantees the terms of the contract.'

['Alī]: He said, 'When a *mukātab* pays some of his instalments and delays the rest, even though he has the means to pay, he should be confined to prison. If his insolvency is manifest, he should be released in order that he may try to labour to earn the means to pay his debt.' By this, 'Alī meant the case of a man who has not contracted to go back to slavery if he is unable to pay. However, if he has so contracted, he goes back to slavery. When he says that he is unable to pay, he goes back to his master to return to slavery. His master, however, has an option. If he knows that the slave has property, he may ask the slave to return to slavery or he may demand the property. If the goods are clearly in his possession, they may be seized from him and sent to the master, and he (the slave) becomes free.

MUDABBAR SLAVES (AL-MUDABBARŪN)[57]

The word *tadbīr* means that the master of a slave, who is legally competent to do so, whether in health or otherwise, tells his slave, 'You are free

emancipated. The *mukātab*'s son has the same status as his father: he is half free and half slave and when he pays the remaining amount he will be free. *Kāfī*, VI, 196.

[54]See n. 294 in Chap. 10.

[55]*Kāfī*, VI, 196.

[56]*Raqīq*[in] *mawṣūf*[in] as in MS Q. *Mawṣūfīn* in the edited text as well as the pirated text of A. Tāmir is incorrect. *Waṣīf* means a young slave who has not attained puberty. *Lisān al-'Arab*, s.v. w-ṣ-f; *Majma' al-baḥrayn*, s.v. w-ṣ-f; Bustānī, *Qaṭr al-muḥīṭ*, s.v. w-ṣ-f.

[57]*Mudabbar* is a slave to whom the master has promised freedom, to take effect on his death. It is derived from *dabbara 'abdahu*, i.e. he declared that his slave would be free after his own death, saying to him, 'Thou art free after my death.' Lane, s.v. d-b-r. Schacht, *Origins*, 265, *EI*[2], s.v. 'Abd.

after my death, for the sake of God,' or 'When I die you will be a *mudabbar*,' or some similar expressions. When the master says this, the slave becomes a *mudabbar* in his master's lifetime, and after his death the slave becomes free, his price being deducted from the bequeathable third. As far as we know, there is a consensus about this rule.

'Alī, Abū Ja'far, and Abū 'Abd Allāh: They said, '[The price of] the *mudabbar* is to be deducted from the bequeathable third.'[58]

The Messenger of God: He permitted the master of a *mudabbar* to sell him if he so wishes.[59]

Abū Ja'far and Abū 'Abd Allāh: They said, 'The *mudabbar* is a slave [in all respects] till his master dies, without having revoked the *tadbīr*. He is a slave, and his master can sell him, make a gift of him, emancipate him, continue with the *tadbīr*, or revoke it.[60] The master is like a testator who makes a will; he may change it if he so wishes before his death, and the will may be revoked to the extent that it is nullified. If, however, he allows it to stand, the will takes effect from the bequeathable third.'[61]

[Abū Ja'far and Abū 'Abd Allāh]: They said, 'There is no harm in selling the service of a *mudabbar* slave provided the master does not revoke the *tadbīr*. In such a case, the purchaser obtains his service, and when the master dies, the slave will be emancipated from the bequeathable third.'

[Abū Ja'far and Abū 'Abd Allāh]: They said, 'There is no harm if the master has sexual intercourse with his *mudabbar* slave girl (*jāriya*).'[62]

[Abū Ja'far and Abū 'Abd Allāh]: They said, 'The children of a *mudabbar* slave girl have the same status as she has; they become emancipated with her emancipation, and they remain slaves so long as she remains a slave.' [The Imams] meant [that this rule applies] when the master continues the *tadbīr*; but if the master revokes the *tadbīr* in respect of some or all of them then they remain in their former status.[63] If the master dies while he is indebted, the status of the *mudabbar* is the

[58]*Kāfī*, VI, 193.

[59]See n. 22 above in this chapter.

[60]*Kāfī*, VI, 193.

[61]Ibid., VI, 194; Ṭūsī, *Tahdhīb al-aḥkām*, VIII, 258–9. Kulaynī gives another example of a *mudabbar* slave who was a well-to-do merchant. He bought a slave girl with his master's permission and she gave birth to several children. The *mudabbar* died before his master. Abū Ja'far said, 'Whatever *mudabbar* left behind belongs to his master ... his children are *mudabbarūn* like their father and when the master dies they become free.'

[62]*Kāfī*, VI, 195; Ṭūsī, *Tahdhīb al-aḥkām*, VIII, 263.

[63]*Kāfī*, VI, 193, 194.

same as that of a slave who has been bequeathed his freedom, and we have discussed his case earlier.[64]

Ja'far b. Muḥammad: He said, 'The emancipation of a slave by *tadbīr* does not fulfil the obligation of a compulsory emancipation [that is done in expiation for a sin or for some act which makes expiation obligatory].'

SLAVE WOMEN WHO HAVE BORNE CHILDREN TO THEIR MASTERS (*UMMAHĀT AL-AWLĀD*)[65]

We have mentioned earlier that when a man has sexual intercourse with his slave girl (*ama*), and she is delivered of what is known to be a child, she is granted the status of an *umm al-walad* (mother of the child).

'Alī, Abū Ja'far, and Abū 'Abd Allāh: They said, 'When a man dies and he has an *umm al-walad*, she becomes free by his death. She is not to be sold unless it be for a debt incurred by the deceased to purchase her, and there is no other property beside her.'[66]

This [rule] is proved to have been laid down by 'Alī. We have mentioned earlier how an emancipated slave can be sold for his unpaid debt. Before her master's death, the *umm al-walad* is, in most cases, governed by rules applicable to slaves, and we have mentioned some of these principles earlier.[67]

Ja'far b. Muḥammad: He said, 'Where a man gives his *umm al-walad* in marriage [to someone] and she gives birth to a child, the child will have the same status as its mother. The child will serve its mother's master, and when he dies, and the mother is emancipated, the child will become free.

'If the father of the child is a free man and he dies, the child should

[64] Ṭūsī, *Tahdhīb al-aḥkām*, VIII, 260–1.

[65] When a concubine (*surrīya*) has a child by her master, she enjoys the title of *umm al-walad*, and an improved status in that she cannot be sold. She becomes free on her master's death. The child and any other children she may subsequently have are all free. See *The Pillars of Islam*, I, 283, n. 62; *EI*², s.v. Umm al-Walad.

[66] Jābir said, 'In the time of God's Messenger and of Abū Bakr['s caliphate], we sold slave women who had borne children, but when 'Umar [assumed power], he forbade us to do so and we so stopped.' *Mishkāt*, II, 246; Robson, I, 724. The view that the *umm al-walad* cannot be sold is held by Abū Ḥanīfa, Ibn Ḥanbal, and Shāfi'ī. For details see *EI*², s.v. Umm al-Walad. *Kāfī*, VI, 202–3; her sale is permitted with certain qualifications.

[67] See the last paragraphs of the previous section. Ṭūsī, *Tahdhīb al-aḥkām*, VIII, 238.

be purchased [and emancipated with the proceeds] from the estate he inherits from his father, and the child will be the heir to the remainder of the estate.

'If a master of an *umm al-walad* gives her in marriage [to someone] and the husband dies or divorces her, she returns to her master. She observes the *'idda* of death for two months and five days, or the *'idda* of divorce for two menstrual courses if she menstruates. If she is one of those that do not menstruate, then she observes [*the 'idda*] for a month and a half. Thereafter, her master may have intercourse with her by right of property without a marriage.'

PATRONSHIP (AL-WALĀ')[68]

Ja'far b. Muḥammad—his father—his ancestors: The Messenger of God said, '*Walā'* belongs to him who emancipates a slave.'[69]

[Ja'far b. Muḥammad]: He said, 'He who is born in Islam is an Arabian (*'arabī*); he who was first a slave and then freed is a *mawlā* (client); and he who freely entered Islam is a *muhājir* (emigrant).'[70]

[Ja'far b. Muḥammad]: He said, 'The client of the tribe belongs to them; the son of the sister of the tribe is one of them; the ally (*ḥalīf*) of the tribe is one of them.'

'Alī: He said, '*Walā'* is inherited by the nearest relations according to priority.[71] When the relations are equal in degree,[72] then the full (*banu 'l-*

[68]In Islamic law *walā'* is a contractual clientage (syn. *muwālāt*), the relationship of patron and client created between the manumitter and his manumitted slave. In early Islam, *walā'* provided a solution to the problem of affiliating non-tribesmen to a tribal society. The persons linked to one another by *walā'* were known as *mawlā* (pl. *mawālīn*). It should be noted that, in pre-Islamic poetry, *walā'* generally indicated an egalitarian relationship between the two parties, but in later literature, it denotes an unequal relationship, *mawlā* being a master, manumitter, benefactor, or patron, and a freedman being a client or protégé. *Walā'* is important for purposes of inheritance, blood money, and giving of women in marriage. Tahānawī, *Kashshāf*, s.v. *walā'* (IV, 388–9); Schacht, *Origins*, 161–2, 173; *EI*², s.v. 'Abd, Ḥilf, Mawlā.

[69]*Kāfī*, VI, 208; reported from the same authority.

[70]Ṭūsī, *Tahdhīb al-aḥkām*, VIII, 250.

[71]The Arabic reads: *yarithu al-walā' al-aq'adu fa 'l-aq'adu*. The saying *wirthuhu bi 'l-iq'ād* means his inheritance is by reason of nearness of relationships. Lane, s.v. q-'-d.

[72]The Arabic reads: *idhā 'stawa 'l-qu'dud*. *Qu'dud* or *qu'dad* means nearness of relationship, a man closely related to the father of the tribe, a man near in lineage to the chief, or the oldest ancestor of his family. Lane, s.v. q-'-d.

umm wa 'l-ab) [i.e. from the same parents] are preferred to the consanguine kindred (*banu 'l-ab*).'

['Alī]: He said, 'When a man emancipates a slave, the slave's *walā'* belongs to the emancipator and the emancipator has to pay for the wrongs done by the slave.'

Ja'far b. Muḥammad: He was asked about a man who emancipates a slave in expiation (*kaffāra*) of an oath, for *ẓihār*,[73] or some act which makes expiation obligatory. Who possesses the *walā'*? [The Imam] said, 'The emancipator.'

[Ja'far b. Muḥammad]: He said, 'Where a slave is owned by two persons jointly, and they both emancipate him, they are the joint owners of the *walā'*.'

The Messenger of God: He said, 'May God curse him who assumes the *walā'* for someone other than his master or one who claims his lineage through someone who is not his father.'[74]

[The Messenger of God]: He forbade the sale or gift of *walā'*.[75]

Ja'far b. Muḥammad: He said, 'Where a man emancipates a slave without retaining his *walā'* (*sā'iba*),[76] it is for the slave [to choose] the *walā'* of whom he desires.[77] If a certain man agrees to accept his *walā'*, it is he who inherits from the slave and it is he who pays for the wrongs done by the slave.'

'Alī: He said, 'Where a woman emancipates a slave, his *walā'* belongs to her.'[78]

['Alī]: He also said, 'He who inherits the inheritance, inherits the *walā'*.'[79]

'Alī and Abū Ja'far: They said, 'When the father is emancipated, he becomes responsible for the *walā'* of his children. The son, when he is emancipated, similarly becomes responsible for the *walā'* of his children. For example: Where a slave marries a free woman, his children become free and their lineage share the same fate as that of their mother. When

[73] *Ẓihār*, see Chap. 11, section on *ẓihār*.

[74] This tradition is transmitted by Ibn Ḥanbal. *Concordance*, s.v. l-'-n.

[75] Schacht, *Origins*, 173.

[76] *Sā'iba* generally means a beast that is left to pasture where it will, without a pastor. Hence, it is applied to a slave emancipated so that the emancipator has no claim to inherit from him, for such an emancipated slave may bestow his property on whom he pleases. Lane, s.v. s-y-b.

[77] *Kāfī*, VI, 208.

[78] Ibid., VI, 208.

[79] Ṭūsī, *Tahdhīb al-aḥkām*, VIII, 254–5.

the master emancipates their father, the *walā'* goes to the master, and he becomes the owner of their *walā'*.'

'Alī: He used to say, 'The foundling (*manbūdh*)[80] is a free man.'

['Alī]: He said, 'The *walā'* belongs to the foremost [i.e. nearest of kin].'[81] The meaning of this is as follows: A man emancipates his slave and then dies, leaving [behind] his two sons. When the emancipator dies, the *walā'* belongs jointly to the two sons. If, however, one of the sons dies before the emancipator leaving a son of his own, and, thereafter, the emancipator dies, the *walā'* belongs to the emancipator's son and not to his grandson [whose father has predeceased the emancipator].

[80]*Manbūdh* is a child, be it a bastard or lawfully begotten, cast out by its mother in the road and picked up and maintained by a Muslim. Lane, s.v. n-b-dh. See also n. 19 in Chap. 22.

[81]The tradition states, '*Al-Walā' li 'l-kubr.*' Lane explains it as the right to inherit of the property left by an emancipated slave. It belongs to the nearest of kin [to the emancipator]. The right to the inheritance would thus belong to the emancipator's son, not his grandson. Lane, s.v. k-b-r; *Concordance*, s.v. k-b-r (*kubr*); Schacht, *Introduction*, 40.

13

Book of Benefactions (*Kitāb al-ʿAṭāyā*)[1]

THE ACTS OF KINDNESS TOWARDS MANKIND (*IṢṬINĀʿ AL-MAʿRŪF ILA ʾL-NĀS*)

Jaʿfar b. Muḥammad—his father—his ancestors: The Messenger of God said, 'Every kind act (*maʿrūf*) is charity.'[2]

[Jaʿfar b. Muḥammad]: He said, 'Mankind is the family of God. The man whom God loves most is the one who benefits his children and brings joy to the members of his house; and for a man to walk with a brother Muslim in his hour of need is more pleasing to God than for him to sit in retreat (*iʿtikāf*)[3] for two months in the Sacred Mosque [at Mecca].'[4]

ʿAlī: He said, 'The people who do acts of kindness are in greater need of performing them than those who desire them for themselves. This is because they obtain praise, recompense, and remembrance [from God]. He who does an act of kindness brings good to himself [when it is done] without demanding gratitude for help given to himself from someone else. Nonetheless it is incumbent on the person favoured to thank his benefactor for his kindness, for, if he fails to do so, he [is considered as] having denied them.'[5]

[1]ʿ*Aṭāyā* pl. of ʿ*aṭīya*, means a gift or present. For the summary of this chapter, see Fyzee, *Compendium*, 72–82.

[2]'Every act of kindness is *ṣadaqa*.' Transmitted by Bukhārī and Muslim. 'Do not consider any act of kindness insignificant, even meeting your brother with a cheerful face.' Transmitted by Muslim. *Mishkāt*, I, 595; Robson, I, 403.

[3]*Iʿtikāf*, see *The Pillars of Islam*, I, 160, 333, 356–8.

[4]Ibid.,I, 25, 68, 390, 397.

[5]*Kafara ʾl-niʿmata*, he covered or denied the favour or benefit conferred upon him. Lane, s.v. k-f-r. 'If anyone is given a gift and has the means, he should make a return for

Abū Ja'far Muḥammad b. 'Alī: He said, 'When God resurrects a faithful from the grave, there emerges with him a beautiful apparition (*mithāl^{un} ḥasan^{un}*). When he comes across tribulations, the apparition will say, "Fear not; no harm will come to you." The apparition will not cease to console him and to give him good tidings until he takes him to God. Then God will take his reckoning lightly, and command him to be taken to Paradise. The believer will exclaim,"Who are you? May God have mercy on you! For you have promised me [good things], and declared me to be faithful and protected me from fear." And the apparition will say, "I am a creation of my Lord who created me from that joy which you used to give to the faithful, and so today, I give you joy."'

Ja'far b. Muḥammad: He said, 'The *ma'rūf* (kindness) is like its name; nothing is superior to it than the reward for it. The *ma'rūf* is a gift from God to His faithful slave. Not every one who wishes to do a kind act to the people can do it; not every one who wishes to do it, has the power to do so; and not everyone who has the power is given the permission to do it. So when God favours a man, He combines the desire to do good with the capacity and His permission. Thus is completed the felicity and the honour on the man who wishes to do the desired act.'

Abū Ja'far: Hẹ said, 'The doing of good actions repels the evil effects of bad acts; every kindness is a charity. Those who do good acts in this world [are recepients of] kind acts in the hereafter. The first of those who enter Paradise are those who do acts of kindness.'

Ja'far b. Muḥammad: He said, 'I have seen that a benefaction is not completed without three qualities: to do it humbly (*taṣghīruhu*); to do it willingly (*taysīruhu*), and to do it quickly (*ta'jīluhu*). So, when you consider it a small matter, you have made it great for the man for whom you have done it. When you have done it willingly, you have verily completed it; and when you have done it quickly, you have given joy with it. If you do it in any other way, you have verily erased it and made it paltry.'

[Ja'far b. Muḥammad]: He said, The best of Muslims is he who unites [people by his affection][6] and who helps and benefits [others].'[7]

'Alī: He said that the Messenger of God said, 'He who has benefitted

it, but if he has not the means, he should express commendation, for he who expresses commendation has given thanks. He who conceals a matter has been ungrateful (*man katama fa-qad kafara*), and he who decks himself with what he has not been given is like him who puts on the two garments of falsehood.' *Mishkāt*, II, 141–2; Robson, I, 646.

[6]For similar traditions see *Mishkāt*, II, 597–9; Robson, II, 1024–6.

[7]*Mishkāt*, I, 595; Robson, I, 403.

by a kind act should return the favour. If he cannot, let him give praise. If he does not do so, he has verily denied the favour.'[8]

LAWFUL GIFTS
(*AL-HIBĀT WA-MĀ YAJŪZ MINHĀ*)[9]

Ja'far b. Muḥammad: He was asked concerning a man who makes more gifts and presents to some of his children than to others. He said, 'There is no harm in it. The donor can do with his wealth whatever he wants to do if he is in health; but if he is ill and dies of his disease, then it is not permissible.'[10] He [further] said, 'When a man gives to his son what he wishes, and gives to some of his sons more than to others, and takes something out of his own possession and transfers it to one of his children while in health and competent to do legal acts, there is no harm in it.[11] A man's property belongs to him; he may do what he likes with it. 'Alī did similarly with his son Ḥasan; and Ḥusayn did this with his son 'Alī, and my father did so, and so did I.'

[Ja'far b. Muḥammad]: He said, 'A gift is effective when accepted, whether possession is handed over or not, and whether it is divided by metes and bounds or not.'[12]

[8]'If one is done a kindness and expresses to his benefactor a desire that God may give him a good reward, he has fully expressed his commendations.' *Mishkāt*, II, 142; Robson, I, 646.

[9]*Hiba* pl. *hibāt* means a gift, one that is freely and disinterestedly given, not for any compensation. As a technical legal term, *hiba* means a gift *inter vivos*, that transfers the ownership of a thing during the lifetime of the donor to the donee. A gift is a contract formed by an offer and an acceptance (*ījāb wa-qabūl*). Although this mutual agreement is indispensable, it does not have the same juridical value in all the law schools. Gifts are of two kinds: of the corpus (*'ayn*) or of the usufruct (*manfa'a*). The former is subdivided into those whose aim is to obtain reward, either from God or from the creatures, and those whose aim is not for reward. There is no disagreement among the jurists about the permissibility of gifts not intended for seeking reward. However, they disagree about their rules (*aḥkām*). Similarly, they disagree about the gifts intended for seeking reward. For details see Lane, s.v. w-h-b; *EI*[2], s.v. Hiba; Fyzee, *Outlines*, 217–73; Ibn Rushd, *Bidāya*, II, 324–30; trans. II, 397–404; Jazīrī, *al-Fiqh*, III, 283–308.

[10]Ṭūsī, *Tahdhīb al-aḥkām*, IX, 156.

[11]'Fear God and act equally with your children.' Transmitted by Bukhārī and Muslim. *Mishkāt*, II, 140–1, 144; Robson, I, 645, 647. Abū 'Abd Allāh was asked about a person who singles out some of his children [to the exclusion of others] for gifts. He said, 'It is permitted if he is well-to-do, but not if the is poor.' Ṭūsī, *Tahdhīb al-aḥkām*, IX, 156.

[12]Ṭūsī, *Tahdhīb al-aḥkām*, IX, 156. According to all the jurists offer and acceptance are must in a gift. Among the conditions for the donee is that he must be one whose acceptance

[Ja'far b. Muḥammad]: He said, 'When a man makes a gift desiring merit in the eyes of God, or for obtaining a reward in the next life, or for gaining the affection of his kindred, then it cannot be revoked; but he who makes a gift wishing thereby to obtain a return [gift], has the right to revoke it when no return [gift] has been made.'[13]

Ja'far b. Muḥammad: He said, 'The donor can revoke a gift, whether possession has been handed over to the donee or not, except when it is made to a relative or to some person from whom he will receive a recompense for it.[14] In all cases except the above, the donor can revoke the gift if the subject of the gift exists; but if the gift itself is non-existent, then the donor cannot obtain it.'[15] [The Imam] said that if a man owes a certain number of dirhams to another, and the creditor makes a gift of them to the debtor, such a gift cannot be revoked by him.[16]

[Ja'far b. Muḥammad]: He said, 'A poet came to the Prophet, gave him fulsome praise and asked for a reward. The Prophet told one of his Companions, "Arise and cut off his tongue!" The man went out, returned, and asked, "O Messenger of God, shall I indeed cut off his tongue?" The Prophet said, "I only asked you to cut off his tongue [i.e. silence him] by a gift ('*aṭā*')!"'

Abū Ja'far: The poet Kumayt[17] came to him and recited verses which he had composed concerning [the Imam]. Abū Ja'far [the Imam] said, 'May God have mercy on you, O Kumayt. If we had possessed wealth, we would have given you to your full satisfaction.' Kumayt said, 'May I be made thy ransom! By God, I did not praise you for a worldly reward, but for merit in the eyes of God and His Messenger.' [The Imam] responded,

---

and possession is valid. However, the jurists disagree whether possession is a condition for the validity of the contract or not. Al-Thawrī, Abū Ḥanīfa, and Shāfi'ī agree that possession is among the conditions of *hiba*'s validity. Therefore, as long as the donee has not taken possession, it does not become binding on the donor. Mālik, on the other hand, states that the contract is concluded with acceptance and that the donee is to be compelled to take possession as in sale. In other words, possession, according to Mālik, is a condition of completion of *hiba* and not a condition of its validity. See Ibn Rushd, *Bidāya*, II, 326; trans. II, 399.

[13]*Kāfī*, VII, 39, 42; Ṭūsī, *Tahdhīb al-aḥkām*, IX, 152, 153, 158. About revocation of gifts, there is a difference of opinion among the scholars of law. *EI*[2], s.v. Hiba.

[14]*Kāfī*, VII, 40; Ṭūsī, *Tahdhīb al-aḥkām*, IX, 154, 158.

[15]*Kāfī*, VII, 41; Ṭūsī, *Tahdhīb al-aḥkām*, IX, 153.

[16]*Kāfī*, VII, 41; Ṭūṣī, *Tahdhīb al-aḥkām*, IX, 154.

[17]Al-Kumayt b. Zayd al-Asadī, an Arab poet of Kūfa, was known for his hostility towards the Umayyads. He acquired distinction with the composition of poems in praise of the *Ahl al-bayt*. His renown, in Shī'ī circles, rests mainly on the *Hāshimīyāt*, praises aimed mainly at the Prophet, 'Alī, and his descendants. He died in 126/743. *EI*[2], s. v. Kumayt.

'By your praising us, you deserve what the Messenger of God said to 'Abd Allāh b. Rawāḥa[18] and Ḥassān b. Thābit,[19] "You will always receive help from the Holy Spirit (*rūḥ al-qudus*)[20] for the defence you have put up for us by your tongue."'

Ja'far b. Muḥammad: He permitted the gift of a *mushā'* (undistributed share in property)[21] when it is accepted, and possession handed over, as is necessary in the case of a *mushā'*.

'Alī: A lady made a gift of a slave girl (*walīda*)[22] to her daughter, later the daughter died, leaving her mother as her sole heir. 'Alī decided that the slave girl should be returned to the mother by way of inheritance.

Abū Ja'far: He was asked about allowances (*jawā'iz*) received from aggressors,[23] and he said, '[Imams] Ḥasan and Ḥusayn used to accept allowances from such aggressors as Mu'āwiya,[24] because they were truly entitled to what they received. What is in the hands of aggressors is unlawful for them, but it is permissible (*wāsi'un*) for the people [to take of it] when the property is given to them in charity (*fī khayr*) and they should take it rightfully.'

Ja'far b. Muḥammad: He said, 'But allowances which are paid to those that serve them in disobeying God are unlawful to them, and constitute wrongful gain (*suḥt*).'[25]

'Alī: He said, 'The *'umrā*[26] and the *ruqbā*[27] are equal [in the eyes of the law].'

[18]'Abd Allāh b. Rawāḥa, a Khazrajī of the most esteemed clan of the Banu 'l-Ḥārith, was one of the twelve *naqībs* of the Anṣār who gave their pledge to the Prophet at the second pledge of al-'Aqaba. Besides his military talents, he was a poet and acted as a scribe for the Prophet. *EI*², s.v. 'Abd Allāh b. Rawāḥa.

[19]Ḥassān b. Thābit al-Khazrajī, generally known as the 'poet laureate' of the Prophet, was the most prominent poet to be associated with the rise of Islam. He had already established his reputation in pre-Islamic times. *EI*², s.v. Ḥassān b. Thābit.

[20]*Rūḥ al-qudus*, mentioned in the Qur'ān 2:87, 253; 5:110 and 16:102, is identified with the Angel Gabriel. *The Pillars of Islam*, I, 14, 63.

[21]*Mushā'*, see Chap. 1, n. 295.

[22]*Walīda*, a female slave, is so called because she was born in servitude. Lane, s.v. w-l-d.

[23]The Arabic term is *mutaghallibīn* meaning those who gain power by force.

[24]Mu'āwiya, see *The Pillars of Islam*, I, 107, n. 300.

[25]*Suḥt*, see Chap. 1, n. 44.

[26]*'Umrā*, derived from *a'marahu dāran*, refers to one man assigning to another a house for the life of either the latter or the former. It was a pre-Islamic practice. Lane, s.v. '-m-r.

[27]*Ruqbā* refers to one's giving to another person a possession, such as a house, on the condition that it should be the property of the survivor of the two of them. The term is derived from *murāqaba* because each of the two persons looks for the death of the other in

Abū 'Abd Allāh [Imam al-Ṣādiq] said, 'In *'umrā* and *suknā*[28] a man gives to another the right to reside in his house for his lifetime. Similarly, he may give him the house for his life and to his survivors till they all die. They have no right to sell the house and when they all die, the house returns to the original owner.'[29]

Abū Ja'far Muḥammad b. 'Alī: He was asked about *'umrā* and *suknā*. He said, 'In these transactions, the parties are bound by their stipulations. *Suknā*, *'umrā*, and *ruqbā* all stand on the same footing, except that the conditions of holding property are distinguishable. In *suknā*, a man gives to another the right to stay in his house for a known period. The owner allows him to stay without any recompense. In *'umrā*, the man is allowed to stay in the house for his lifetime, and if his survivors are also allowed to stay, this is permissible,' as we have said before. 'In *ruqbā*, a man is allowed to stay until one of them dies; and when one of them dies, by his death, the injunction of *ruqbā* comes to an end and the house returns to the original owner.'[30]

---

order that the property may be his. Put differenctly, *ruqbā* signifies donation with the proviso that it shall either revert to the donor after the donee's death or become the donee's property upon the donor's death. Lane, s.v. r-q-b. See also *Mishkāt*, 139; Robson, I, 644.

[28]*Suknā*, derived from *askanahu al-dār*, means giving a man a place to inhabit without rent. It is similar to *'umrā*. Lane, s.v. s-k-n.

[29]'*'Umrā* (life tenancy) of a house is a gift.' Transmitted by Bukhārī and Muslim. 'What is given in life tenancy is part of the inheritance of those who receive it.' Transmitted by Muslim. 'If anyone has property given him as life tenancy for him and his descendants, it belongs to the one to whom it is given and does not return to the one who gave it because he gave a gift which may be inherited.' Transmitted by Bukhārī and Muslim. Another tradition states, 'The life tenancy, which the Messenger of God permitted, was only that one should say, "It is for you and your descendants." When he says, "It is yours as long as you live," it returns to its owner.' Transmitted by Bukhārī and Muslim. *Mishkāt*, II, 138–9; Robson, I, 643. Contradictory traditions, cited above concerning *'umrā* where the stipulation is for the duration of the lifetime of the donee, have resulted in wide disagreement among the jurists. According to Thawrī, Abū Ḥanīfa, Shāfi'ī, and Ibn Ḥanbal it is an absolute gift, i.e. the gift of the corpus (*hibat li 'l-riqba*). Mālik, on the other hand, states that the only thing in it that is for life is the utility (*manfa'a*). Hence, if the donee dies the corpus reverts to the donor or to his heirs. Mālik further adds that if the donee's successors are stipulated in such a *hiba*, then the gift reverts to the donor or his heirs when the donee's successors die. Dāwūd and Abū Thawr assert that when the donor states to the donee that this is for you and your successors, the corpus passes to the donee's ownership. However, if it is not stipulated then the corpus reverts to the donor or his heirs on the death of the donee. Ibn Rushd, *Bidāya*, II, 328; trans. II, 401–2. See also Ṭūsī, *al-Nihāya*, 600–1.

[30]*Kāfī*, VII, 42, 43, 48; Kulaynī reports some complex cases.

MUTUAL GIFTS AND CREATING GOODWILL (*AL-TABĀDHUL WA 'L-TAWĀṢUL*)

Ja'far b. Muḥammad—his father—his ancestors—'Alī b. al-Ḥusayn: They[31] said, 'The Messenger of God said, "On the Day of Resurrection, when God will resurrect the people, He will proclaim that the generous (*ahl al-faḍl*) should arise. Then a large number of people will arise and angels will greet them and give them good tidings of Paradise and ask [them], 'What are your acts of generosity which entitle you to Paradise before the reckoning?' They will say, 'We used to forgive those that wronged us, be friendly with those that dissociated with us, and be considerate with those who behaved badly with us.' Then they will be told, 'Enter Paradise. What an excellent recompense for those who do good works!'

'"Then, a proclamation will be made that the patient ones (*ahl al-ṣabr*) should arise. A large number of people will arise and be greeted by angels and given good tidings of Paradise and will be asked, 'What is the patience which entitles you to Paradise before the reckoning?' They will say, 'We used to be patient in obedience to God, and we used to be patient regarding sins against God.' They will be told, 'Enter Paradise. What wonderful recompense for those that do good works!'

'"Then, a proclamation will be made that the neighbours of God in the abode of peace should arise. A large number of people will arise, and the angels will greet them and give them good tidings of Paradise, and they will ask, 'What is the merit (*mā faḍlukum*) by which you became neighbours of God in the abode of peace?' They will say, 'We used to have mutual affection for one another; we used to visit one another, have friendly relations with one another (*natawāṣal*), and make mutual gifts (*natabādhal*), for the sake of God.' And it will be said to them, 'Enter Paradise, for you are the neighbours of God in the abode of peace.'"'

'Alī: The Messenger of God said, 'If I were invited to [partake of] a shoulder of mutton, I would accept the invitation; and if I were presented with a trotter, I would accept it.'[32]

['Alī]: He said, 'For a man to show honour to his brother is to accept his gift, and make a gift of what he possesses without constraining himself.

[31] As in MS Q, in the edited text: *annahu qāla* is an error.

[32] Abū Hurayra reported God's Messenger as saying, 'If I were invited [to eat] a trotter, I would accept the invitation, and if I were presented with a front leg, I would accept it.' *Mishkāt*, I, 575; Robson, I, 387; transmitted by Bukhārī. Another tradition states, '... and a woman should not despise even the gift of half a sheep's trotter from her neighbour.' *Mishkāt*, II, 143; Robson, I, 647.

I have heard the Messenger of God say, "God does not love those who use forced manners [in their speech or behaviour] (*mutakallif*)."'[33]

The Messenger of God: He said, 'When God provides a man with livelihood for which he has not moved his foot, tightened his stirrups, or made an effort, he is one of those whom God mentions in the Qur'ān[34] and recited: *And whosoever keeps his duty to Allah, Allah will appoint a way out for him, and will provide for him from (a quarter) whence he hath no expectation*' (65:2–3).

'Alī: He said, 'When a man honours his brother with a generous gift (*al-karāma*), he should accept it. If he is a needy person, let him use it for his need. If he is not needy, let him keep it in a place of need so that the donor receives its recompense. If a man can return the favour, let him do so; and if he has not the means, let him give fair praise and prayers.'

['Alī]: He was given *fālūdhaj*[35] (a sweetmeat) one day, and he asked, 'What is this?' and they said, 'It is the New Year (*nayrūz*)[36] today.' So he said, 'Celebrate *nayrūz* each day, if you are able to,' i.e. make gifts to one another and show mutual affection for the sake of God.

The Messenger of God: He said, 'Shake hands with one another and give presents, for, verily, a handshake increases affection, and a present removes bad blood.'[37]

[The Messenger of God]: He said, 'O you who are related to one another, visit one another, do not argue among yourselves, and give mutual gifts, for, verily, visits increase affection, contentions produce discord, and gifts remove hatred.'

'Alī: He said, 'Show special favour to your intimate friends and brothers.'

['Alī]: He said, 'It is wrongful gain (*suḥt*) to make a gift in expectation of a larger return. This follows from the Word of God: *And show not favour, seeking worldly gain*' (74:6).

[33]*Takallafa amr^{an}* refers to a person who imposes upon himself a thing, or an affair in spite of difficulty. *Takalluf* signifies straining. Lane, s.v. k-l-f. 'He who does not thank people does not thank God.' Another tradition states, 'If one is done a kindness and expresses to his benefactor a desire that God may give him a good reward, he has fully expressed his commendation.' *Mishkāt*, II, 142–3; Robson, I, 646.

[34]As in MS D. Edited text as well as MS Q: *al-samā'*, which is incorrect.

[35]It is a kind of sweet dish, see Chap. 3, n. 44.

[36] It is *nawrūz*, the first day of the Persian solar year, the day of the vernal equinox. It is marked with popular festivities. *EI*^{2}, s.v. Nawrūz. The Coptic *nawrūz*, the first day of the Coptic calendar, was celebrated by the Copts and the Muslims alike in Fusṭāṭ and Cairo. Maqrīzī, *Itti'āẓ*, I, 214, 224; Sanders, *Ritual*, 44, 81, 83, 118.

[37]'Give presents to one another for a present removes grudges.' *Mishkāt*, II, 142–3; Robson, I, 647.

Ja'far b. Muḥammad: Concerning the Word of God: *That which ye give in usury in order that it may increase on [other] people's property hath no increase with Allah* (30:39), he said, 'This refers to giving a present to a man expecting a return greater than the gift; and that is usury (*ribā*).'[38]

Whatever is to be found in this chapter, regarding the merit of gifts and the command to accept them, refers to those gifts which are made only for the sake of God and for mutual goodwill through them. Gifts made for any reason other than a present or gift or for giving food are all unlawful gain (*suḥt*), for instance, what is given for fear of a man, in dissimulation [to avoid] evil from him, to make his heart turn towards you, to satisfy the need of the donor, to ward off evil from him, to avoid oppression, to ask for some need, etc. It is forbidden to take such gifts, to accept them, or to eat them. They are included in the prohibition laid down by the Imams, the blessings of God on them.

Ja'far b. Muḥammad: Concerning a man who asks for some favours from another, or requests him to ask the sovereign (*sulṭān*) or some other authority for his need, and for this purpose makes a gift to him, [Imam al-Ṣādiq] was asked, 'What do you think of accepting a gift for this purpose?' He said, 'The acceptance of such a gift is not lawful and this is unlawful gain. It is proper, for a man who is capable, to assist a faithful one for such a purpose. He who is capable of helping his brother should do so; but if he takes remuneration, a gift, or a meal for it, then all of these are unlawful gain, and taking them is forbidden.'

THE EXCELLENCE OF CHARITABLE GIFTS (*FAḌL AL-ṢADAQA*)

Ja'far b. Muḥammad—his father—his ancestors: 'Alī said, 'I gave one dinar in charity on a certain day and the Messenger of God said to me, "O 'Alī, do you not know that as soon as [the money for] charity leaves the hand of the faithful, the jaws of seventy devils are disjointed!"'[39]

[Ja'far b. Muḥammad]: He said, 'A man came to the Messenger of God and said, "O Messenger of God, I do not know what the matter is with me; I do not love death." The Messenger of God said, "Have you any wealth?" The man replied, "Yes." The Messenger of God asked, "Have you arranged for someone to inherit it [after your death]?" The man replied, "No." The Messenger of God said, "That is the reason why you do not like death, because the heart of a man is in his wealth."'

[38]For *ribā* see Chap. 1, n. 124.
[39]*The Pillars of Islam*, I, 301.

[Ja'far b. Muḥammad]: The Messenger of God was asked, 'Which charity is the most meritorious?' He said, '[That which is the result of] labour by a poor man.'[40]

[Ja'far b. Muḥammad]: He said, 'Three persons came to the Messenger of God and one of them said, "O Messenger of God, I had one hundred *ūqīya*[41] of gold and I gave ten of them in charity;" the second said, "O Messenger of God, I had one hundred dinars and I gave ten of them in charity;" the third said, "I had ten dinars and I gave one in charity," and the Messenger of God said, "All of you are equal in respect of reward."'[42]

Ja'far b. Muḥammad: He said, 'Any man who does even one of the following things will gain paradise: Providing [for dependents] during hard times (*al-munfiq min iqṭār*); meeting all people with a cheerful face (*al-bishr bi-jamī' al-nās*); doing justice to oneself (*al-munṣif bi-nafsihi*).'

[Ja'far b. Muḥammad]: Concerning the Word of God: ... *and seek not the bad (with intent) to spend thereof (in charity)* (2:267), he said, 'When the people embraced Islam, they had earnings of usury (*ribā*) and abominable wealth (*amwāl khabītha*), and would deliberately give to charity out of these funds, so God forbade them to do so.'

Al-Ḥusayn b. 'Alī: He was told, 'Verily 'Abd Allāh b. 'Āmir[43] gave to charity such and such property, and emancipated so many slaves,' and he said, 'The case of 'Abd Allāh b. 'Āmir is like that of a man who robs a pilgrim and gives it to charity. Verily, true charity is that which is made by the sweat of the brow and the dust of the face.' It was said to Abū 'Abd Allāh, 'To whom did [Imam Ḥusayn] refer [in that remark]?' He said, 'He meant 'Alī.'

'Alī: He said that the Messenger of God said, 'When a man gives a loan to another, he obtains the same reward as [one who gives a similar amount] in charity.' Later he said, 'When a man gives a loan to another, he obtains for each day [of the loan] the same reward as for a charity.' So 'Alī said, 'O Messenger of God, formerly you said, "He obtains the same reward as for a charity," and today you say, "He obtains for each day the same reward as for a charity." The Messenger of God replied, "Yes, when

[40]'The most excellent *ṣadaqa* is what a man with little property can afford to give; you should begin with those for whom you are responsible.' *Mishkāt*, I, 606; Robson, I, 411.

[41]*Ūqīya* is a weight of varying magnitude. Hinz, *Islamische Masse*, 34–5.

[42]*The Pillars of Islam*, I, 304–5.

[43]'Abd Allāh b. 'Āmir, a member of the 'Abd Shams clan and a maternal cousin of the caliph 'Uthmān, was appointed by the latter as governor of Baṣra to succeed Abū Mūsā al-Ash'arī. He was celebrated for his military abilities and also for his generosity. He fought against 'Alī at the Battle of the Camel and later joined Mu'āwiya. *EI*², s.v. 'Abd Allāh b. 'Āmir.

a man gives a loan to another, it is as though he gave it to him in charity; but if he allows him time for repayment, then, for each day he receives the reward for a charity." '[44]

Ja'far b. Muḥammad: Concerning the Word of God: *If ye publish your almsgiving, it is well, but if ye hide it and give it to the poor, it will be better for you* (2:271), [Imam al-Ṣādiq] said, 'This is not *zakāt* but it is alms which a man gives on his own. *Zakāt* is always given publicly, and not secretly.'[45]

[Ja'far b. Muḥammad]: The Messenger of God said, 'Verily secret charity extinguishes the fire of God's anger;[46] when a man gives charity with his right hand, let not the left hand know of it.'[47]

Abū Ja'far Muḥammad b. 'Alī: When he began to bathe his father, [Imam] 'Alī b. al-Ḥusayn, [after his death], some of his followers among the People of the House were present. They observed the places of prostration such as his knees, the outer part of his feet, the inner part of his palms, and his forehead, and found that they had hardened as the result of his prostrations and had become like pads on the knees of a camel. [Imam] 'Alī b. al-Ḥusayn used to pray during each day and night one thousand units (*rak'a*) of prayer. They then looked at the vein of his shoulder and found that it had marks which had hardened. So they asked Abū Ja'far [Imam al-Bāqir], 'We have understood that the marks we have seen are the result of [prolonged] prostration, but what is this that is on his shoulder?' [The Imam] said, 'By God, no one knew it, and he did not know that I have come to know of it. But for his being dead, I would not have informed you. When the earlier part of the night had passed and the people were sleeping in the house, he would perform his ablutions and pray two units of prayer very lightly [quickly]; then he would look at the surplus food left over in the house, and put it in a sack, and putting the sack on his shoulder, he would silently slink out of the house, so that no one would come to know it. He would then go to the houses of poor persons and distribute it while they did not know who he was, except that they knew he was coming and expected him. When he would arrive, they would say, "Here is the man with the sack;" and would open the doors to him so that he could distribute to them what was in the sack and depart after emptying it. By this, he wished to obtain the merit of secret alms, and of charity during the night, and of giving charity by his own hand. Then he would return and standing in his archway (*miḥrāb*) say

[44]See n. 227 in Chap. 1.
[45]For the distinction between *zakāt* and *ṣadaqa*, see *The Pillars of Islam*, I, 299, n. 1.
[46]*Kāfī*, IV, 10, 11.
[47]*The Pillars of Islam*, I, 301.

the remaining prayers of the night. What you see is the mark made by the sack on his shoulder.'[48]

The Messenger of God: He said, 'Secret charity extinguishes the anger of the Lord. Verily, almsgiving extinguishes sin as water extinguishes fire and it saves [a man] from an evil death. The doer of good acts parries an evil death. The affection for [one's] kindred increases livelihood and age, and wards off poverty; and saying "there is no power and no strength save in God" is one of the treasures of Paradise and is a cure for ninety-nine diseases, the first of which is anxiety.'

Ja'far b. Muḥammad: He said, 'Even if a man is full of sin from the crown of his head to his feet, there are four things whereby God will forgive him and substitute for them good actions and these are: charity, modesty, courteous behaviour, and gratitude.'

The Messenger of God: He said, '[A man receives for good actions the following rewards from God]: for charity, ten times; for a loan, eighteen times; for affection to brothers [in faith], twenty times; and for affection to relatives,[49] twenty-four times. Affection for [one's] kindred increases the age of a man and removes poverty.'

[The Messenger of God]: He said, 'Charity wards off diseases (*dā'*), tumours (*dubayla*),[50] burning, drowning, destruction [by accident], and madness, [etc.]' and mentioned seventy calamities (*balā'*).[51]

Ja'far b. Muḥammad: He said, 'Have a keen desire for charity, and do it early in the day; for when a man does an act of charity in the morning for the sake of God, He will save him from all the calamities which descend on him from the sky on that day.' And he said, 'Do not belittle the prayers of the destitute for [recovery] of your sick ones, for their prayers for you will be accepted while their prayers for themselves will not be accepted.'

[Ja'far b. Muḥammad]: He had a slave whom he had emancipated (*mawlā*), and the slave and another man owned a house jointly. The slave died and [the Imam] inherited the share in the house with the man. [The Imam] sent someone to the man to divide the house with him. The man was an astrologer and delayed the distribution awaiting

[48] See *The Pillars of Islam*, I, 300–1.

[49] '*Ṣadaqa* given to a poor man is just charity, but when given to a relative, it serves a double purpose, being both charity and a connecting link (*ṣila*).' *Mishkāt*, I, 606; Robson, I, 411.

[50] *Dubayla* is a certain malady in the belly. It is either a collection of corrupt matter therein or an ulcer that discharges internally and the sufferer from it seldom recovers. It might also be a large tumour. Lane, s.v. d-b-l.

[51] *The Pillars of Islam*, I, 301; *Kāfī*, IV, 8.

an auspicious moment. When the auspicious constellation appeared in the heavens he came to Abū 'Abd Allāh [Imam al-Ṣādiq] and [the Imam] sent a man with him to divide the house. The man preferred the distribution of the house by lots, and the lot turned in favour of Abū 'Abd Allāh.

When the man [sent by the Imam] saw what had transpired, he informed [the Imam] of all the facts. [The Imam] said, 'Shall I show you a way better than what you have said?' The man said, 'Yes, may I be your ransom!' [The Imam] said, 'Give in charity in the morning and it will keep bad luck away from you for the day. Give in charity in the evening and it will keep bad luck away from you for the night. If it were not for your belief in the auspiciousness of stars, we would have left our share in the house as an inheritance for you.'[52]

The Messenger of God: He said, 'The beggar is a messenger from the Lord of the Worlds; he who gives him charity, gives to God; and he who refuses him, refuses God.'[53] The Messenger of God meant that begging has been sent [to the world] by God as an examination for His creatures and as a reason for giving a recompense to those whom He wishes to honour by His reward.

[The Messenger of God]: He said, 'Give to the beggar, even if only a charred, cloven hoof [of a sheep].'[54]

[The Messenger of God]: He said, 'But for the fact that beggars tell lies, those who refuse alms to beggars would never be saved; so do not refuse a beggar.'

[The Messenger of God]: He said, 'When a beggar begs for necessity, he receives the same reward as one who gives charity to him.'

'Alī: He said, 'Give to the beggar even if only a piece of a date; bestow on the beggar even though he comes on horseback.'[55]

['Alī]: He said, 'Often, the People of the House were put to the test by a beggar who was neither a jinn[56] nor a man. Verily God has angels in

[52]*Kāfī*, IV, 9; slightly different version and ends as follows: Abū 'Abd Allāh said, 'Before I left the house I began [my day] with charity. This is better for you than astrology.'

[53]*The Pillars of Islam*, I, 303.

[54]'Put something in his [the beggar's] hand, even if only a burnt hoof.' See *The Pillars of Islam*, I, 303, n. 17.

[55]*The Pillars of Islam*, I, 303.

[56]According to the Qur'ān, jinn were created of smokeless flame while mankind and the angels were created of clay and light. Jinn, according to the Muslim conception, are intelligent, imperceptible to our senses, and capable of appearing under different forms and of carrying out heavy labours. The Prophet was sent to them as well as to mankind. They are capable of salvation and some will go to Paradise while others will be cast into

the shape of men who come to beg from human beings, and when they give them something, the angels give it to the destitute.'

Abū Ja'far Muḥammad b. 'Alī: One day [Imam al-Bāqir] said to his companions, 'Do not refuse a beggar.' One of those that were present exclaimed, 'O son of the Messenger of God, sometimes a man who does not deserve charity may ask for alms. [What do we do then?] [The Imam] said 'We fear that if they refuse a man whom they think to be undeserving, the beggar may well be among the deserving ones. I fear that what befell [the Prophet] Jacob—and I seek God's refuge—may befall them.' The man said, 'O son of the Messenger of God, and what befell Jacob?'[57]

[The Imam] said, 'Jacob used to slaughter a sheep each day for his family, and together with that, he used to distribute food which was sufficient for them [his family] to eat their fill. There was, in Jacob's day, a prophet among God's prophets who was held in high estimation by God, but [had no family] to return to at night. So the prophet made himself nameless, took to travel, forsook the world, and did not engage in any occupation. When he became exhausted, he would stand at the doors of prophets, sons of prophets, and righteous persons. He would stand and beg without being recognised. When he obtained his barest necessities,[58] he would move away from the house.

'One night, he stood silently pleading at the gate of Jacob. They had finished their meal and yet had a large amount of food left with them. He pleaded, but they turned away and did not give him anything, nor did they ask him to go. He stood there for a long while in expectation, until, by prolonged waiting, exhaustion overtook him and he fell down and fainted. He did not regain consciousness until a part of the night had passed. He then rose and went on his way.

'That night, Jacob dreamt that an angel came to him and said, "O Jacob—so says the Lord of the worlds—I have enlarged your resources and have increased My favour on you. A prophet, who is held in high estimation by Me, came to your door and begged humbly. He bore his

---

the Fire. Their relation to Iblīs, the *shayṭān* is obscure. In the Qur'ān, Iblīs is said to be a jinn, but in other places he is said to be an angel. Hence, many legends and hypotheses grew on the subject. In folklore they are associated with magic. The binding of jinn to talismanic service is an important aspect of popular novels, such as the *Thousand and One Nights*. *EI*², s.v. D̲j̲inn; Adams, 'Islamic Faith,' 41–2 .

[57]Ya'qūb, the Arabic name for the Old Testament Patriarch Jacob, son of Isḥāq (Isaac), a son of Ibrahīm (Abraham), is numbered in the Qur'ān among the prophets. *EI*², s.v. Ya'ḳūb; *The Pillars of Islam*, I, 9, 85, 304.

[58]The Arabic expression is *yumsik al-ramaq* meaning sustenance that arrests the remains of life, or that which will maintain the strength. Lane, s.v. r-m-q.

misfortune till the limit of his exhaustion was reached, but you and your family turned away from him even though you had plenty to share from the bounties I had bestowed on you. A little of that would have revived him, but you neither gave him nor asked him to go. He, therefore, begged from other persons until he fainted and collapsed on the ground. He lay there for most of the night while you were sleeping in your beds, belly downwards, enjoying My favours. Both of you were within My sight, and I swear by My honour and majesty that I shall visit you with a tribulation (*balīya*) which will make of you a tale [to be remembered] from among the bygone people."

'Jacob was terrified but wary. He ran to his archway (*miḥrāb*) and began to weep out of fear and sorrow until morning. That is when his sons came to ask him for permission to take Joseph away to the fields. Joseph was the one he loved most among his sons, and Jacob began to ponder about what he had seen in his dream and God had warned that what was going to happen might be related to Joseph. He did not anticipate that the calamity would be caused by his own sons. He was rather afraid that some beast of prey may destroy him [Joseph].'[59]

Abū Ja'far [Imam al-Bāqir] then related the story of Joseph fully till the end. All that we have mentioned about giving to suppliants in charity is a recommendation and is not obligatory. Only the alms tax is obligatory, and everything else is good works, a means which leads to communion with God (*taqarrub ila 'llāh*). These are acts of *sunna* which should not be avoided. They are supererogatory and approved acts of charity.

Ja'far b. Muḥammad: He mentioned obligatory and supererogatory acts of charity. It is recommended that charitable acts be directed towards suppliants (*sā'il*), deprived persons (*maḥrūm*), [the poor but] contented (*al-qāni'*), and the one who pleads silently (*mu'tarr*).[60] [He also mentioned] gifts (*hibāt*),[61] favours (*ṣilāt*),[62] emancipation (*'itq*),[63] commodate loans (*'āriya*),[64] loans (*qarḍ*)[65] and different acts of beneficence (*wujūh al-ma'rūf*)

[59]See *The Pillars of Islam*, I, 304; the same story with slight variation in words.

[60]*And feed such as (beg not, but) live in contentment (al-qāni'), and such as beg with due humility (al-mu'tarr)* 22:36. Yusuf Ali. *And give to eat thereof both unto him who is content (with what is given him, without asking), and unto him who asketh.* (*Or, unto him who asketh in a modest and humble manner, and unto him who wanteth but dare not ask*). 22:36. Sale, *Koran*, 331. For the linguistic explanation of *mu'tarr* see Lane, s.v. '-r-r.

[61]See n. 9 above in this chapter.

[62]See section on 'Mutual Gifts and Creating Goodwill' in this chapter.

[63]See Chap. 12.

[64]See Chap. 21.

[65]See Chap. 1, section on 'Rules Regarding Debts'.

all of which are supererogatory. These are the means employed by human beings to do good deeds, but they are not mandatory obligations that cannot be omitted, nor are they established *sunna*, omission whereof is forbidden.

We shall relate some of the reports handed down from [the Members of] the House of the Prophet, which, when read with those which we have already related, show that giving in charity is not a mandatory obligation except in the case of the obligatory alms tax (*zakāt*).

Ja'far b. Muḥammad—his father—his ancestors: The Messenger of God said, 'Observe the suppliant; if your hearts are satisfied with his sincerity, give him charity, for verily, he is truthful.'

Abū Ja'far Muḥamamd b. 'Alī: A beggar shouted at his door and said, 'May God make you and me free from want.' He persisted in repeating the same thing, so [the Imam] said, 'If you so wish, come tomorrow, God willing.' It was Thursday, so [the Imam turned to] his companions and said, 'Verily an act of charity done on a Friday [earns] a double [reward].' [The Imam] used to give a dinar in charity every Friday.

Ja'far b. Muḥammad: He was once [sitting] with a group of his companions when a suppliant came, and [the Imam] gave him some charity; then came another and [the Imam] gave him; them came a third one and [the Imam] gave him. Then came a fourth, and [the Imam] said, 'May God provide for us and for you.'

Then he said to his companions, 'If a man had a hundred thousand [dirhams],[66] and wanted to put them to their proper use, he would surely find the place for them.' In this report there is a clear indication that *ṣadaqa* and *zakāt* are distinguishable. Charity is an approved and desirable act, but it is not mandatory as is the alms tax; nor is refusing to give to a beggar unlawful or forbidden. But the merit of charitable acts, some of which we have mentioned, is great. They ward off calamities[67] as we have noted earlier.

That which we have not mentioned is what is related from [Imam] 'Alī b. al-Ḥusayn: Once upon a time he cast his eyes on the pigeons of Mecca and said, 'Do you know how it is that pigeons exist in this sanctuary (*ḥaram*)?'[68] They said, 'You know better, O son of the Messenger of God, so inform us.' He said, 'During times past, there was a man in whose house a pigeon had taken refuge. Near his house there was a palm tree, and the pigeon built its nest in the cleft of its trunk. The man used to keep an eye on the chicks, and when they were about to fly away, he would ascend

[66]As in MSS Y and A.

[67]*Kāfī*, IV, 7–10.

[68]The sacred territory of Mecca is called *ḥaram*. *The Pillars of Islam*, I, 141, 303, n. 14.

the tree, catch the young ones and kill them, and the pigeon would look on with great sorrow. A long time passed in this way, and not a single one of the progeny of the pigeon could fly away, so it complained to God, the Mighty and Glorious, and God said, "If the man attempts to do the same again with these birds, I shall hasten his death before he reaches them." The next time the pigeon laid eggs and the chicks began to gather strength, the man climbed the tree according to his habit. But when he was [halfway] up the tree, a beggar came to his door and [began to beg], so he came down and gave him something. Then he ascended the tree and slaughtered the young ones while the pigeon looked on. So the pigeon [called upon God and] said, "What is this, O my Lord?" God said, "Verily, My slave gave to charity before My calamity reached him; for, charity wards off calamities. But I shall give a good recompense to the pigeon, and its descendants will survive as long as the world lasts." The pigeon said, "O my Lord! You have promised me and I trust in Your promise and You indeed do not break [Your] promise."[69] Then God inspired it to travel to this sanctuary, and forbade the hunting [of game] and so its tribe increased as you see. That pigeon was the first to stay in the sanctuary.'[70]

Abū Ja'far Muḥammad b. 'Alī: He mentioned charity and its merit, and what calamities it wards off, and said, 'There was a man in times past who had much wealth, but was not blessed with a son. During the last part of his life, he at last had a son who was the dearest of the children to him. When the boy reached the age of maturity, he engaged him to one of the most beautiful and well-born of girls, and had them married. On the night the marriage [contract was concluded], an apparition visited the man in his sleep and said, "O man, verily, your son who has married and will spend the night with his wife, will die tonight." So the man awoke from his sleep in fright and began to postpone the coming together of the couple, without disclosing the real object. Then the mother of the son insisted. Nonetheless, a considerable delay occurred. So the man said to himself, "Possibly what I saw [in the dream] was from Satan, or perhaps these are [nothing more than] nightmares,"[71] and although fearful and apprehensive, he allowed the young couple to come together.

'On the night of consummation, the man was greatly perturbed, he would sit and rise and pray and entreat until it was morning; then he asked for his son and found him to be in the best condition. When he slept that

[69]*Lo! Thou breakest not the promise.* (3:194).

[70]See *The Pillars of Islam*, I, 303; the story is repeated there with some variations in the wording.

[71]The Arabic is *aḍghāthu aḥlām*^{in}, meaning jumbled dreams, as in the Qur'ān 12:44.

night, the apparition came to him again and said, "What I had said was true, O man, but God warded off the calamity from your son, increased his life, and delayed his death on account of what he did for a suppliant."

'So when it was morning, he sent for his son and asked him, "O my little son! What good act did you do for the beggar?" The son did not know what to say, and the father said, "It is absolutely necessary for you to tell me about it, as it is a serious matter." The son said, "Verily, I do not know who the suppliant was. When the people departed and I was left alone with my wife, I looked at her and was full of joy and admiration. When I intended to go to her, a beggar stood at the door and cried, 'Feed the hungry beggar from what God has given you.' So I said to myself, possibly what he says is true, and I am not going to lose my wife; so, I left her and went to him, and let him into the house and offered him the food of the wedding feast and said, 'Here you are. Eat!' He ate his fill while I stood by him with guests holding water. When he had finished, I said, 'Please eat more,' and he said, 'It is sufficient for me. May God ward off disagreeable things from you as you have removed from me a great hunger.' I said, 'Have you any children?' The beggar said, 'Yes, by God, they are even more needy than I. I could hardly swallow the food that I ate without them.' I said, 'Here you are! Take it and carry for them what you wish.' He began to take food but was shy, so I increased it and he carried away as much as he could carry and was averse to taking more. He prayed to God [for us] and went away. Then I went in to my wife and spent the night happily."

'The father then related to him all that had happened, told him the story, and greatly praised God and thanked him.'[72]

LAWFUL AND UNLAWFUL CHARITIES (*MĀ YAJŪZ MIN AL-ṢADAQA WA-MĀ LĀ YAJŪZ*)

Ja'far b. Muḥammad: He was asked about a man who gave [property] in charity in partnership with another, and [the Imam] said that this was lawful. He was also asked whether *mushā'* (undivided property) could be given in charity, and he said, 'It is lawful, possession can be taken as that of the *mushā'*.'[73]

[Ja'far b. Muḥammad]: He was asked whether a man can give in

[72]Nu'mān reports this story with some variations in the first volume, see *The Pillars of Islam*, I, 301–2.

[73]Ṭūsī, *Tahdhīb al-aḥkām*, IX, 139; idem, *al-nihāya*, 596. For *mushā'* see n. 295 in Chap. 1.

charity [property of which] he had not obtained possession. He said, 'If the donee had accepted the gift, or, if someone else had accepted it on behalf of a minor donee, the gift to charity would be lawful, regardless of whether possession had been handed over or not. But if [the donee] had not accepted it, the gift would be ineffective until it is accepted.'[74]

Al-Ḥusayn b. 'Alī: He inherited certain lands and property and gave them in charity before obtaining possession of them.

Ja'far b. Muḥammad: He was asked whether it is proper for a man to later revoke and take back the property that he made as a charitable gift to his son or some other person. He said, 'The Messenger of God said, "He who makes a charitable gift and then revokes it is like a person who returns to his vomit."'[75]

Ja'far b. Muḥammad: A man asked him, 'O son of the Messenger of God, my father made a charitable gift of a house to me. Later it occurred to him to revoke it. The judges of our province have decided that the house belongs to me and that he had no right to revoke the gift after having given it to me as a charitable gift. I do not know whether the decision of the judges is correct or not.' [The Imam] said, 'What your judges have decided is wonderful and what your father has done is bad. A charitable gift is given only for the sake of God, and that which is given for the sake of God cannot be revoked. If you are litigating against your father, do not raise your voice against him. If he raises his voice against you then lower your voice.' The man said, 'Verily my father has just died.' [The Imam] said, 'Then enjoy the house happily.'

[Ja'far b. Muḥammad]: He was asked, 'A man makes an irrevocable (*mabtūla*)[76] gift to charity for the sake of God. Has he the right to revoke such a gift?' [The Imam] said, 'When a man makes a gift to charity for the sake of God, it is intended for the poor and the wayfarers and he has no right to revoke it.'

'Alī: He said, 'When a man makes a charitable gift [of a certain property] and later inherits it [from somebody], it is his by right of inheritance and there is no harm in taking it.'

Ja'far b. Muḥammad:[77] When a man makes a charitable gift [of a certain

[74]Ṭūsī, *Tahdhīb al-aḥkām*, IX, 139.

[75]'One who seeks to take back a gift is like a dog which returns to its vomit.' Another tradition states, 'None of you may take back his gift, except in the case of a father taking it from his child.' *Mishkāt*, II, 140–1; Robson I, 645.

[76]*Ṣadaqat^{un} batlat^{un}* signifies a gift for the sake of God irrevocably cut off from its giver and to be dovoted to he casue of God. Lane, s.v. b-t-l.

[77]As in MS Q, in the edited text: *qāla*.

property], it is not lawful for him to purchase it, to request it to be given him as a gift, or take possession of it after the dedication to charity. The only exception to the rule is inheritance; when property reverts to him by inheritance, it is lawful for him.

'Alī b. al-Ḥusayn: If he gave something to a beggar, and the beggar considered it to be paltry,[78] [the Imam] would snatch it away from him and give it to someone else. This is in accordance with the rule we have stated earlier, that a charitable gift is revokable so long as it has not been accepted; and being discontented (*tasakhkhuṭ*) with a gift is tantamount to rejecting it.

Abū Ja'far Muḥammad b. 'Alī: He was asked about a man who had a slave girl and whose wife caused him unhappiness as a result. So the man said to his wife,[79] 'I present her to you as a charitable gift.' [The Imam] said, 'If the man had said "for the sake of God", then the gift is effective; but if he did not say so, he is entitled to revoke it.'

'Alī: He said, 'Nothing remains with a man after his death except a continuing charity, right knowledge, and the prayers of [his] children.'

Ja'far b. Muḥammad: He said, 'Nothing brings in a reward to a man after his death except three things: A charity established in his lifetime which continues to give benefit after he dies; righteous children who pray for him; or a righteous practice established by him which continues to be followed after his [death].'[80]

'Alī: He said, 'A charitable gift (*ṣadaqa*) and a *waqf* (*ḥubs*)[81] are two treasures, so leave them [after you] till their day [Day of Resurrection].'

Ja'far b. Muḥammad: He mentioned 'Alī, Commander of the Faithful, and said, 'He was one of God's slaves for whom He had reserved Paradise. He made an irrevocable charity which continued to benefit the poor after him, and dedicating it, he said, "O God, I have done this only that You may turn away the Fire from my face, and turn my face away from the Fire."'

Ja'far b. Muḥammad: He said, 'The Messenger of God dedicated certain properties as *waqf*, and used to spend the income from them for guests.

[78]The Arabic, *tasakhkhaṭahu*, means that he became displeased, angry with him, or deemed it little. Lane, s.v. s-kh-ṭ.

[79]Gloss in MS Q: i.e. he said in jest without intending it for the sake of God.

[80]*Kāfī*, VII, 66.

[81]*Ḥubs*, *ḥabs*, or *ḥubus* means what is bequeathed or given unalienably, not to be sold nor inherited, and the profit arising therefrom to be used in the cause of God or religion. Lane, s.v. ḥ-b-s. *Waqf*, in legal terminology, means a pious foundation or endowment. For details see *EI*[2], s.v. Waḳf; Fyzee, *Outlines*, 274–332.

Later, he dedicated them to Fāṭima.[82] The [estates] were: al-'Awāf;[83] Burqa; al-Ṣāfiya; Mashrabat Umm Ibrāhīm;[84] al-Ḥusnā, or al-Ḥasnā; al-Dalāl; and al-Mīthab.'[85]

[Ja'far b. Muḥammad]: He said that the Messenger of God distributed *fay*'[86] lands and 'Alī received a parcel. He dug a well in it and the water spurted from it in the shape of a camel's neck. When a man came to give him the good news, 'Alī told him, 'Inform the heirs (*al-wārith*).[87] This is a charitable gift, for travellers and pilgrims to the House of God. It is irrevocable, [untransferable,] and shall not be sold, nor given away [as gift], nor inherited. The curse of God, His angels, and all men shall be on him who sells it or makes a gift of it. God will not accept anything else from the man as [equitable] exchange for it.'[88] 'Alī named the spring Yanbu'.[89]

'Alī: He dedicated certain *waqf*s from his property. He mentioned them in his written testament wherein it is stated:

[82]Fāṭima was the youngest daughter of the Prophet, see *The Pillars of Islam*, I, 288, n. 101.

[83]In Yāqūt: A'waf. MSS Q, Y, D, and Ṭ: al-'Awālī; an estate near Medina, according to Yāqūt, s.v. 'Awālī.

[84]Mashrabat Umm Ibrāhīm, see *The Pillars of Islam*, I, 172, 372. *Kāfī*, VII, 58; it is spelled as *Mā li-Umm Ibrāhīm*.

[85]Al-Mīthab: According to Yāqūt. Al-Maythab: According to *Kāfī*. Al-Manbat: MSS Q, Z, Y, A, and D. Al-Mant: In the edited text.

Yāqūt (s.v. Mīthab) states that before he died, Mukhayrīq, the Jew, who had embraced Islam, gave these seven fenced gardens near Medina as a gift to the Prophet. Kulaynī (*Kāfī*, VII, 58–9) also lists these gardens and states that, after the Prophet's death, 'Abbās, the Prophet's uncle, unsuccessfully contested Fāṭima's right to those estates. Later, Fāṭima bequeathed them to 'Alī. Kulaynī further states that Salmān al-Fārisī had made the *mukātaba* contract (to win his freedom) to work on the orchard al-Maythab. See also *Majma' al-baḥrayn*, s.v. b-r-q, ḥ-s-n, d-l-l, ṣ-f-y, '-w-f.

[86]*Fay*' lands, in theory, arise from unconditional surrender, see *The Pillars of Islam*, I, 327, n. 118.

[87]Gloss in MS Y: *al-wārith* refers to those for whom the estate was bequeathed as a charitable endowment.

[88]The Arabic idiom *lā yuqbalu minhu ṣarf^{un} wa-lā 'adl^{un}*, means that neither *ṣarf* nor *'adl* shall be accepted from him. By *ṣarf* is meant repentance and by *'adl*, ransom, i.e. he did not accept from him repentance nor ransom, but he required from him more than that. For detailed explanation see Lane, s.v. ṣ-r-f.

[89]*Kāfī*, VII, 64; Ṭūsī, *Tahdhīb al-aḥkām*, IX, 148–9; Yāqūt, s.v. Yanbu'; he states that there are two places with this name: (1) in the direction of the ocean, about seven way stations (*marāḥil*) from Medina, a night's journey from Raḍwā, and belongs to the descendants of Ḥasan b. 'Alī; (2) a fortified place with palm trees, a plantation, and water wells. This is where 'Alī's religious endowments are located.

This is what ʿAlī b. Abī Ṭālib dedicated as *waqf* from his property, seeking merit from God, in order that He may lead me to Paradise and turn me away from the Fire and turn the Fire away from me, on the day when [some] faces will be white and [some] black. Whatever property belongs to me at Yanbuʿ,[90] and what is known to be mine around it, is a charitable gift. All my slaves [working on that estate] except Riyāḥ,[91] Abū Bīruz,[92] and Ḥabtarā[93] are emancipated, and no one has a right over them. They are my clients (*mawālī*); they shall work on my estate for five years, and from it, they shall have their allowances, livelihood, and provision for their families.

One-third of my property[94] at Wādī al-Qurā[95] belongs to the children of Fāṭima; and the slaves [on that estate] are *ṣadaqa* (dedicated to charity). Whatever property and slaves that I own at Burqa[96] are *ṣadaqa*, and Zurayq[97] has the same rights that I have written for his companions. Whatever property and slaves that I own at Udhayna[98] are *ṣadaqa*. What I have written about my aforesaid property as an irrevocable charitable gift (*ṣadaqa*) is binding and irrevocable. Whether I am alive or dead, the income of all those charitable gifts should be spent for the sake of God, in the way of God, for His pleasure, and for any relations of Banū Hāshim[99] and Banū ʿAbd al-Muṭṭalib.[100]

Ḥasan b. ʿAlī should manage these [trusts] and eat out of the income according to custom; he should spend in lawful ways as God shows him, and nothing should stand in his way. If he wishes to spend the charity money in place of some other funds, he may do so, and he should not be prevented. If he wishes, he may sell part of the property to pay debts, for he is at liberty to do so. All the children of ʿAlī and his property are in the hands of Ḥasan b. ʿAlī. Apart from the houses dedicated to charity, Ḥasan may sell any of his houses he so desires, and nothing should stand in his way. If he sells a house, it shall be

[90]See the previous paragraph.

[91]Rabāḥ: *Kāfī*, VII, 59 (not vocalized). For the names of ʿAlī's emancipated slaves see Chap. 12, n. 24–6.

[92]Abū Nīzar: *Kāfī*, VII, 59 (not vocalized).

[93]Jubayr: Ibid.

[94]All of it: Ibid.,VII, 60.

[95]Wādī al-Qurā (the Valley of Villages) was once a prosperous region in northern Ḥijāz. It is four or five days' journey to the north of Medina and stretches along the road to Syria. It was conquered by the Prophet in the year 7 AH. Several prominent Companions, including ʿAlī, are known to have owned estates there. Guillaume, 516; *History of al-Ṭabarī*, VIII, 95–6, 124–5; al-Hamadānī, *Ṣifat*, 273, 274, 332; Yāqūt, s.v. Wādī al-Qurā; *EI*², s.v. Wādī 'l-Ḳurā.

[96]Burqa, see n. 85 above. Dīma: *Kāfī*, VII, 60.

[97]Zurayq, see Chap. 12, the paragraph with n. 26.

[98]Udhayna, is the name of a valley. Yāqūt, s.v. Udhayna.

[99]Banū Hāshim, see *The Pillars of Islam*, I, 43; *EI*², s.v. Hāshim b. ʿAbd Manāf, great grandfather of the Prophet.

[100]Banū ʿAbd al-Muṭṭalib, see *The Pillars of Islam*, I, 20.

distributed in three parts—one-third in the way of God; one-third for Banū Hāshim,[101] and one-third for the family of Abū Ṭālib.[102] He should spend it as God shows him.

If a calamity befalls Ḥasan, and Ḥusayn is alive, verily, [this trusteeship] will pass to Ḥusayn b. ʿAlī, and he should act as I have instructed Ḥasan; and Ḥusayn has the same rights and obligations as Ḥasan. The rights enjoyed by the children of Fāṭima in the charities of ʿAlī are similar to those enjoyed by the children of ʿAlī. Verily, what I have provided for the children of Fāṭima, I have provided for the sake of God, for honouring[103] the sanctity of Muḥammad, for declaring the greatness of God and His Messenger and their nobility, and for [acquiring] their pleasure.

If a calamity befalls Ḥasan and Ḥusayn, the child of the survivor of them should look into the affair. If, in his opinion, someone else among the descendants of ʿAlī who is satisfactory in respect of religion, belief, and honesty should be appointed [as manager], he may appoint him, if he so wishes. But if he finds none suitable among them, then he should select one from the descendants of Abū Ṭālib, according to his discretion. If he finds that among the descendants of Abū Ṭālib, none is suitable in respect of dignity, judgement, and age, then he may, if he so wishes, appoint one of the Banū Hāshim. He should make it a condition with the man so appointed that he should allow the property to remain in the original condition, and should use the profits as I have instructed in the way of God, for His sake, and for any kindred of Banū Hāshim and ʿAbd al-Muṭṭalib. [Charitable property] shall not be sold, gifted, or inherited. Verily, the property of Muḥammad where it is located belongs to the children of Fāṭima, and similarly the property of Fāṭima, to her children.

He went on relating the rest of the testament.[104]

Abū ʿAbd Allāh Jaʿfar b. Muḥammad: He said, "ʿAlī, the Commander of the Faithful, dedicated to charity a house belonging to him in Medina which was situated in the quarter of the Banī Zurayq.[105] He wrote as follows:

In the name of God the Compassionate, the Merciful. ʿAlī b. Abī Ṭālib, who is alive and in good health, has dedicated to charity his house in the quarter of the Banū Zurayq [in Medina], which cannot be sold, gifted, or inherited until God,

[101] And Banū ʿAbd al-Muṭṭalib: addition in some MSS and *Kāfī*, VII, 60.

[102] Abū Ṭālib, the father of ʿAlī, was the son of ʿAbd al-Muṭṭalib. *EI*^{2}, s.v. Abū Ṭālib.

[103] Reading *li-takrīm* as in MS Q; *li-karīm* in the edited text seems to be an error.

[104] Kulaynī reports the rest of the testament which deals with ʿAlī's seventeen female slaves. There were four witnesses to it, and it was written by ʿAlī himself on 10 Jumādā I, 37 AH. *Kāfī*, VII, 59–61.

[105] Banū Zurayq was a clan of the Khazraj tribe in Medina. Ibn Ḥazm, *Jamharat ansāb*, 356–8, 472.

the inheritor of the heavens and the earth, gives it as inheritance. 'Alī has given his maternal aunts the right to reside in the house for their lifetime. Thereafter, their descendants may reside there so long as any of them survive and upon the death of such descendants, the poor among the Muslims may stay there. May God be a witness [to this dedication].

Abū Ja'far Muḥammad b. 'Alī: He said to Abū Baṣīr:[106] 'O Abū Baṣīr, may I read to you the testament of Fāṭima?' Abū Baṣīr replied, 'Yes, please do so as a favour to me. May I be your ransom.' [The Imam] had a basket or a small box and he took out a document from it and began to read:

In the name of God, the Beneficent, the Merciful. This is what Fāṭima, the daughter of Muḥammad, has bequeathed. She has seven estates (*ḥawā'iṭ*):[107] al-'Awāf, al-Dalāl, al-Burqa, al-Manbat, al-Ḥusnā, al-Ṣāfiya, and Mashrabat Umm Ibrāhīm.[108] They are all for 'Alī b. Abī Ṭālib; and if he be dead, then to al-Ḥasan; and if he be dead, to al-Ḥusayn, and then to the eldest of his descendants. May God, [in addition to] Miqdād b. al-Aswad,[109] and Zubayr b. al-'Awwām, be a witness to this.[110] Written by 'Alī b. Abī Ṭālib.[111]

Ja'far b. Muḥammad: He said, 'There is no harm if a man makes a *waqf* (*ḥubs*) for his daughters on the condition that the one among them who marries, loses her interest in the *waqf*; and if [later] she is widowed, she regains her interest in the *waqf*.'

[Ja'far b. Muḥammad]: He said, 'If a man makes a *waqf* and says, "If I need it, I am the most entitled to it." When he dies, the properties will be distributed [according to the rules of] inheritance.'[112]

Abū Ja'far Muḥammad b. 'Alī: He said, [Imam] al-Ḥusayn b. 'Alī gave a house in charity; so [Imam] al-Ḥasan b. 'Alī told him to turn away from the house [i.e. to have no personal interest in it].'

[Abū Ja'far Muḥammad b. 'Alī]: One of his companions[113] wrote to him that a certain person had purchased an estate (*ḍay'a*), dedicated it to charity, and given [the Imam] one-fifth of the income. He also said

[106] Abū Baṣīr, see *The Pillars of Islam*, I, 95, n. 267.

[107] *Ḥawā'iṭ* pl. of *ḥā'iṭ* could either be a garden or a date palm orchard surrounded by a wall or fence. Lane, s.v. ḥ-w-ṭ.

[108] For these seven estates, see n. 83–5 above in this chapter.

[109] Miqdād, see Chap. 9, n. 8.

[110] Zubayr, see *The Pillars of Islam*, I, 23, n. 18.

[111] *Kāfī*, VII, 59; reported from the same authority through Abū Baṣīr.

[112] Such a condition is valid and he has the right of disposal. However, if he dies without expunging such a stipulation, the property will revert to his estate as inheritance. Ṭūsī, *al-Nihāya*, 595–6.

[113] He was 'Alī b. Mihryār (Mihzyār: in the text). *Kāfī*, VII, 45.

that grave differences had arisen among those to whom the *waqf* was granted, and there was no certainty that the situation among them would not become serious. He asked for [the Imam's] opinion. [The Imam] wrote to him, 'If the final dedication to God has not been made and if you think it fit, please sell my share in the estate and send the proceeds to me. If grave differences arise among the people, they should sell the estate, for, sometimes, differences lead to loss of life and property.'

14

Book of Wills (*Kitāb al-Waṣāyā*)[1]

THE INJUNCTION TO MAKE WILLS AND WHAT MAY BE BEQUEATHED (*AL-AMR BI 'L-WAṢĪYA WA-MĀ YŪṢĀ BIHI*)[2]

God says: *It is prescribed for you, when one of you approacheth death, if* he *leave wealth* (*khayr*[an]), *that he bequeath unto parents and near relatives in kindness*. (*This is*) *a duty for all those who ward off* (*evil*) (2:180). And God says: O *ye who believe! Let there be witnesses between you when death draweth*

[1]This chapter was edited and translated by Fyzee in his *The Ismaili Law of Wills*, and summarized in *Compendium*, 90–6.

[2]Reading *mā yūṣā bihi* as in MS Q. *Mā yurḍā bihi* in the edited text as well as the pirated text of A. Tāmir is an error. *Waṣīya* pl. *waṣāya*, as a technical term in Islamic law, means the last will, testament, or legacy. The bequest verses (2:180, 240) revealed during the early period of the Prophet's mission, encourage the faithful anticipating death to make his testament in favour of parents, relatives, and wives. Howver, later revelation of 4:11–12 apparently seems to curtail the testamentary freedom by assigning specific fractional shares of the estate to parents and wives. The jurists came to consider the latter verses as obligatory commands and thereby abrogating the former verses. In his *Studies in Qur'an*, 21–52, D. Powers has discussed this issue and argued against this position taken by the overwhelming majority of Muslims.

The Shī'a claim that their system of inheritance is more Islamic and more Qur'ānic than that of the Sunnīs. The historians of Islam uphold the Shī'ī claim but add that it was influenced by their political claim for the leadership of the Muslim community. Powers has argued cogently that the Sunnī law of inheritance too is conditioned by considerations related to the issue of political succession. The following two points need to be stressed in his discussion. First, the division of the Prophet's estate, which created a bitter controversy between Fāṭima and Abū Bakr, may have contributed to the transformation of Islamic law of inheritance. Second, after careful scrutiny of the

nigh unto one of you, at the time of bequest—two witnesses, just men from among you, or two others from another tribe (5:106).[3]

Ja'far b. Muḥammad—his father—his ancestors: The Messenger of God said, 'It does not befit a Muslim to pass two nights without having a written testament under his head.'[4]

Abū Ja'far Muḥammad b. 'Alī: He said, 'The making of a will is incumbent on every Muslim.'[5]

Ja'far b. Muḥammad: He was told, 'When your emancipated slave (*mawlā*) A'yan[6] was about to die, the pangs of death were very painful to him. Then his [health] improved such that we thought he had recovered, but he later died.' [The Imam] said, 'This is the restfulness which precedes] death (*rāḥat al-mawt*). Lo, behold, not a single person dies without God returning to him his reasoning, hearing, and sight. A'yan enumerated his property for bequests, some of which he bequeathed and some he left to be inherited.'[7]

The Messenger of God: He said, 'He who does not make his will in the proper manner at the time of his death is faulty with respect to his consideration (*murū'a*) and his intellect.' They said, 'O Messenger of God, how should a dying man make his will?' The Messenger of God said, 'When death approaches him and people foregather, he should say:

meaning of the word *kalāla* and older exegetical sources Powers proposes an alternative reading of the consonantal text of the second half of 4:12 as follows: *Wa-in kāna rajul^un yūrithu kalālat^an aw imra'at^an ... yūṣī bihā ...* (*If a man designates a daughter-in-law or wife as heir, ... after any legacy he bequeathes ...*). The established reading of the 'Uthmānic text, therefore, eliminates the embarassing reference to the possibility of the testator designating an heir. For details see the first chapter in the aforecited work; *EI*[2], s.v. Waṣīya; Schacht, *Origins*, 201–2; idem, *Introduction*, 173–4; Fyzee, *Outlines*, 355–74; Anderson, *Islamic Law*, 66; Nu'mān, *Urjūza*, 38–9; Ibn Rushd, *Bidāya*, II, 331–5; trans. II, 405–10; Jazīrī, *al-Fiqh*, III, 307–43.

[3]*Kāfī*, VII, 10–13. Explaining the Qur'ānic injunction ... *or two others*, Kulaynī states that they should be Muslims. If that is not possible, then they may be either Jews or Christians. Women witnessses are allowed, but for only one-fourth of the testament.

[4]'It is the duty of a Muslim who has something to be given as a bequest not to have it for two nights without having his will written down.' *Mishkāt*, II, 155; Robson, I, 656; transmitted by Bukhārī and Muslim.

[5]*Kāfī*, VII, 10; reported on the authority of al-Bāqir as well as al-Ṣādiq.

[6]A'yan was a Greek slave. He was bought by a man from Banū Shaybān who educated, freed, and later adopted him. He was a *ḥāfiẓ* and a learned man. His sons, Zurāra and Ḥumrān, were companions of Imam al-Bāqir and al-Ṣādiq. See Poonawala, 'The Imām's Authority.' 112, n. 45; older sources are listed therein.

[7]*Kāfī*, VII, 10; it is without the last sentence: *Wa-'addada ashyā'a li 'l-waṣīya* (i.e. A'yan spelled out his property for bequests).

O God, Creator of the Heavens and the Earth, Knower of what is manifest and what is concealed, the Compassionate, the Merciful, verily I have sworn allegiance to Thee in this world. Verily, I bear witness that there is no deity other than Thee, Unique art Thou and without any associate, and [I bear witness] that Muḥammad is Thy slave and Thy messenger. And [I bear witness] that the Garden, the Fire, the Resurrection, the Reckoning, the Divine Decree (*al-qadar*), and the Balance (*al-mīzān*) are all true. And [I bear witness] that religion is as Thou hast described; and Islam as Thou hast prescribed (*shara'ta*), and the Word (*al-qawl*) as Thou hast uttered, and the Qur'ān as Thou hast revealed, and that Thou art Allāh, the manifest Truth.

May God requite Muḥammad with the best of requitals on our behalf, and may He greet him with greetings of peace. O God, my support in times of anxiety, my companion in times of adversity, and my guardian in times of ease. O God of mine and my ancestors, do not leave me to myself for the twinkling of an eye, for if Thou doest so, I shall draw nigh to evil and recede from the good. Console me in the loneliness of the grave, and consider me within Thy covenant on the day I shall meet Thee.[8]

Then he may bequeath according to his need. This is the covenant of the dying. The making of a will is incumbent on every Muslim.

'Alī said, 'The Messenger of God taught me this testament, and he said to me, "Gabriel, on whom be peace, taught it to me."'[9]

'Alī: He said, 'When a man feels that he is about to die, it is proper for him to affirm his covenant and to renew his testament.' He was asked, 'How should he make a will, O Commander of the Faithful?' 'Alī said, 'The man should say:

In the name of God, the Merciful, the Compassionate. This is a testimony from God, to which so-and-so, the son of so-and-so, bears witness. *Allah (Himself) is witness that there is no God save Him. And the angels and the men of learning (too are witness). Maintaining His creation in justice, there is no God save Him, the Mighty, the Wise* (3:18). O God, [all beings] come from Thee and they return to Thee, and they are within Thy possession and power. Thy hands are far-reaching, Thou providest as Thou wishest, and Thou art the All-subtle, the All-aware.[10]

In the name of God, the Merciful, the Compassionate. This is the will of so-and-so, the son of so-and-so. He makes his will and bears witness that there is no deity other than Him, unique and without associate, and that Muḥammad is His slave and messenger. He sent him [Muḥammad] with Guidance [the Qur'ān]

[8]Ibid., VII, 9; reported on the authority of Imam Ja'far.
[9]Ibid., VII, 9.
[10]Alludes to Qur'ān 6:103, 22:63, 31:16, 67:14.

and the true faith, *to warn whosoever liveth, and that the word may be fulfilled against the disbelievers* (36:70).[11] O God, I call You to bear witness—and You are sufficient as a witness—and those who carry Your Throne, and those who reside in Your heavens and Your earth, and those whom You have created and brought into being and originated and caused to grow and caused to flow, that You are verily God, there is no deity other than You, unique and without any associate, and that Muḥammad is Your slave and Your messenger; that the Hour is doubtless to come; and that God will resurrect those in the grave; and that the Garden and the Fire are realities. I utter these words of mine along with him who utters them, and I defend them from him who denies [them]. There is neither power nor strength save in God, The Exalted and Mighty. O God, write my testimony with the testimony of him who bears witness to what I bear witness; and as for him who refuses, write my testimony in place of his; and allow me to enter Your covenant with it—a covenant which You will fulfil with me on the day I meet You alone. *Lo! Thou breakest not the promise* (3:194).

'Then his bed should be laid in the direction of the *qibla* and he should say, "I am a follower of the religion of the Messenger of God, *as one by nature upright, and I am not of the idolaters* (6:79),[12] and then he should make a will as directed by the Messenger of God.'

Ja'far b. Muḥammad: He said, 'The Messenger of God's testament to 'Alī contained the following, "O 'Alī, I command to you certain virtues for your own sake, which you must always remember." Then he said, "O God, help him [adhere to these virtues]; first, [tell] the truth (*ṣidq*), never utter a falsehood from your mouth; secondly, [have] piety (*wara'*), never venture upon dishonesty; thirdly, fear of God, [fear Him] as if He is ever within your sight; fourthly, weep excessively [in the fear of] God, for every tear, a thousand mansions will be built for you in Paradise; fifthly, shed your blood and spend your money for your religion; sixthly, adhere to my practice in fasting, prayer, and charity. As for the prayer, it is fifty-one *rak'as*[13] and as for fasting it is three days in every month; a Thursday in the first part [the first Thursday]; a Wednesday in the middle, and a Thursday in the last part [the last Thursday].[14] As for charity, strive in it till it is said that you are extravagant, but [in reality] you have not been extravagant. I enjoin you [to offer] the night prayers. Offer the night prayers! Offer the

[11]It is 36:69 in Pickthall.

[12]In Pickthall 6:80.

[13]During the course of a day and night the mandatory prayers consist of seventeen *raka'āt* and that of the *sunna* thirty-four *raka'āt* totalling fifty-one *raka'āt*. *The Pillars of Islam*, I, 258–9.

[14]For supererogatory fasts see *The Pillars of Islam*, I, 352.

night prayers![15] I enjoin you [to pray] the prayers of the declination of the sun, *ṣalāt al-zawāl, ṣalāt al-zawāl;*[16] I enjoin you to recite the Qur'ān under all circumstances; raise your hands in prayer;[17] and use a tooth-stick during every ablution.[18] As for good manners, hold fast to them, and as for bad manners, avoid them. If, [in the end,] you do not act in accordance with this advice, do not blame anyone except yourself." '

'Alī b. al-Ḥusayn and Muḥammad b. 'Alī [Imam al-Bāqir]: They mentioned the testament of 'Alī and said, "Alī made a testament in favour of Ḥasan, while [his sons] Ḥusayn and Muḥammad [ibn al-Ḥanafīya], all of 'Alī's children, the leaders of his supporters (*shī'atihi*), and the people of his house all bore witness. He handed over to Ḥasan the books and weapons,[19] and then said to him, "The Messenger of God ordered me to give you my testamentary directions and to give you my books and weapons, even as the Messenger of God gave me [his dying] injunctions and handed over to me his books and weapons. He charged me to command you to deliver them over to your brother Ḥusayn when you are face-to-face with death." Then, he turned to Ḥusayn and said, "The Messenger of God has ordered you to deliver them [likewise] to this son of yours." Then he caught hold of Ḥusayn's son, 'Alī b. Ḥusayn[20] by the arm and embraced him, and said to him, "The Messenger of God has commanded you, O my little son, to deliver them to your son Muḥammad [al-Bāqir], so convey to him my salutations and those of the Messenger of God."[21]

'Then he turned to his son Ḥasan and said, "O my son, you are the man in charge (*walīy al-amr*)[22] and the avenger (or guardian) of blood (*walīy al-dam*). If you forgive, it is with you that the decision rests, but if you wish to kill (avenge), then return blow for blow, and do not transgress (*lā ta'tham*)."[23] Before this, he had singled out Ḥasan and Ḥusayn for injunctions whereby he confided in them writing the names of the [future]

[15]The night prayers should be said after the *'ishā'*. *The Pillars of Islam*, I, 259.

[16]*Ṣalāt al-zawāl*, see *The Pillars of Islam*, I, 259.

[17]See *The Pillars of Islam*, I, 197, 203.

[18]Ibid., I, 132, 146–7.

[19]For the books and weapons see *The Pillars of Islam*, I, 28, n. 50.

[20]According to Nu'mān, *Sharḥ al-akhbār*, III, 275, 'Alī Zayn al-'Ābidīn died at the beginning of 94/712 at the age of 58. He was thus born in one of the following years 36/656–7, 37/657–8, or 38/658–9. They are all mentioned in different sources.

[21]See Mufīd, *al-Irshād*, 254; it is known as *ḥadīth al-lawḥ* transmitted by Jābir from the Prophet.

[22]It could also mean 'the man in charge of the imamate'.

[23]As in MS Q and other MSS of Fyzee. The edited text reads: *lā ta'tam*. These instructions refer to the punishment of Ibn Muljam, 'Abd al-Raḥmān al-Murādī, the murderer of 'Alī. For details see *EI*², s.v. Ibn Mul<u>dj</u>am.

kings, the period of existence of this world, and the names [of all] of the *dāʿīs*[24] [that will come] till the Day of Resurrection. He handed over to them the text of the Qurʾān and the Book of Knowledge; then, when the people gathered around, ʿAlī said to them what he said. Then ʿAlī wrote [dictated] a testament as follows:[25]

In the name of God, the Merciful, the Compassionate. This is the testament of the servant of God, ʿAlī b. Abī Ṭālib, made in his last moments in this world, while he is about to travel towards 'the halfway house of the dead' (*barzakh*),[26] and away from his people and friends. He bears witness that there is no deity other than God, who is unique and without associate, and that Muḥammad is His slave, messenger, and Trusted one, [may] the blessings of God [be] on him, his progeny, and his fellow apostles and worthy descendants.

May God, on our behalf, requite Muḥammad with the most excellent of requitals as may be made to a prophet by his community. I enjoin you, O Ḥasan,[27] those who are present from amongst the People of My House, my children, and my partisans, to all fear God, *and die not save as those who have surrendered (unto Him, i.e. become Muslims), and hold fast, all of you together, to the cable of Allah, and do not separate* (3:102–3). For, verily, I have heard the Messenger of God saying, 'The composing of differences between the people of discord is better than all fasts and prayers.' I enjoin you to act before you are overtaken by suppressed anger [for not acting fast enough]. I enjoin you to take advantage of health before disease overtakes you and before *a soul should say: Alas, my grief that I was unmindful of Allah, and I was indeed among the scoffers! Or should say: If Allah had but guided me I should have been among the dutiful!* (39:56–7) But how and whence can this be now? For you were ruled by your passions; then will his sight be uncovered and his veils rent asunder in accordance with God's word: *Now We have removed from thee thy covering, and piercing is thy sight this day* (50:22). Whence can he have sight now? Lo, did he not see the harm before this time and before the curtain was dropped on penitence by the descent of calamity? And the soul desires that if it could return, it would act in fear of God, but these wishes are of no avail.

I enjoin you to avoid passion, for verily, passion leads to blindness, and it is straying from the right path both in this world and in the next. I enjoin you to

[24]*Dāʿī*, a technical term, means a missionary; a rank in the Ismāʿīlī *daʿwa* hierarchy. It is possible that *duʿāt* is a later interpolation for *aʾimma* (Imams).

[25]In his *Kāfī*, VII, 61–2, Kulaynī transmits, in a much shorter version, the following testament of ʿAlī.

[26]The word *barzakh* occurs thrice in the Qurʾān, 23:100, 25:53, 55:20. One of the explanations is that it is a barrier between Hell and Paradise. Another is that it refers to the grave which lies between this life and the next. In eschatology, it is used to describe the boundary of the world of human beings, which consists of the heavens, the earth, and the nether regions, and its separations from the world of pure spirits and God. *EI*^{2}, s.v. Barzakh.

[27]Some parts of this testament are reported by Kulaynī with slight variations. *Kāfī*, VII, 61–2.

be sincere [in your devotion] to God; and why should you not be sincerely devoted to God Who has brought you forth from the loins of the polytheists and rescued you from the persistent denial of the agnostics (*ahl al-shakk*)? So worship Him out of hope and out of fear. This will not go unrewarded by Him. I enjoin you to be sincerely devoted to Muḥammad, the righteous Guide and Messenger, and one of the ways in which you can show devotion to him is that you should pay him his dues. God says: *Say (O Muhammad, unto mankind): I ask of you no fee [reward] therefor [i.e. for the revelation], save loving kindness towards kinsfolk* (42:23).[28] A man who repays to Muḥammad his dues by showing affection towards his relations, has verily returned what was entrusted to him. He who has not returned it, has become his adversary; and he who becomes the Prophet's adversary, contends with the Prophet, and he who contends with the Prophet, verily brings upon himself the wrath of God and *his habitation is the Fire, a hapless journey's end* (3:162).

O People, behold, Muḥammad is not loved but for the sake of God,[29] and the progeny of Muḥammad are not loved but for the sake of Muḥammad; so he who wishes may increase or decrease [his love]. I enjoin you to be affectionate to us and to be kind to our partisans (*shīʿatinā*), for he who does not do so, is not one of us.[30] I enjoin you [to love] the Companions of Muḥammad who were not innovators (*lam yuḥdithū ḥadath*^{an}),[31] did not shelter a criminal,[32] and did not deny the rights of [*ahl al-bayt*].[33] For, surely, the Messenger of God left them to our care, and cursed the innovator amongst them and amongst others.

I enjoin you to be clean ritually, without which prayer is not complete; and to pray, which is the prop of faith, and the mainstay of Islam; so neglect it not.[34] [I enjoin you to give] *zakāt* which completes prayer;[35] and to observe the fast of Ramaḍān, *and pilgrimage to the (sacred) House (is a duty unto Allah), for mankind, for him who can find a way thither* (3:97), and to fight in the way of God, for it is the best (lit. apex) of actions and the glory of the faith and Islam. [I enjoin] fasting for you, for it is a shield from the Fire. I warn you to observe strictly the hours of prayer, for verily he who misses prayer is not one of my people. I enjoin you to offer the prayer of the declination of the sun (*ṣalāt al-zawāl*), for verily it is the

[28]See *The Pillars of Islam*, I, 85–8.

[29]*Illā lillāh*: as in MS Q. *Illa 'llāh* in the edited text is an error.

[30]See *The Pillars of Islam*, I, 85–98.

[31]*Ḥadath* is an innovation, particularly in matters of religious doctrine or practice. It is a practice that is not known in the *sunna*. It is therefore disapproved. Lane, s.v. ḥ-d-th; *Majmaʿ al-baḥrayn*, s.v. ḥ-d-th.

[32]*Āwā muḥdith*^{an} means that he harboured a criminal or an offender in his dwelling and protected him from retaliation. Lane, s.v. ḥ-d-th.

[33]According to the Shīʿa, the Prophet vested ʿAlī with the authority for the leadership of the Muslim community, but as ʿAlī was set aside, most of the Companions had reneged on what they had professed. See *The Pillars of Islam*, I, 18ff.

[34]See *The Pillars of Islam*, I, 167.

[35]*Perform the prayer, and pay the alms tax*, is repeated numerous times in the Qur'ān.

prayer of the penitent ones (*ṣalāt al-awwābīn*).[36] I enjoin you to pray the four *raka'āt* [*taṭawwu'*] after the *maghrib* prayer,[37] so do not forsake them even if you fear an enemy. I enjoin you to remain awake at night [praying], from the beginning to the end; but if sleep overcomes you, [keep awake praying] in the last part of the night.[38] He who is prevented by disease, verily, God will excuse him. He who omits the *witr* prayer or delays the two *raka'āt* of the morning prayer[39] does not belong to me or my partisans.

He who devours property unlawfully will be unable to present himself to the Messenger of God, by God, never; by God, never; by God, never. He will not be able to drink from his Pool (*ḥawḍ*),[40] or obtain the Messenger of God's intercession (*shafā'a*),[41] never, by God. Nor shall he who habitually drinks any of the intoxicating drinks, nor he who commits adultery with a married woman (*muḥṣana*),[42] by God, never. Nor he who does not recognize my right or the right of the People of My House, and these [rights] are most obligatory for them, by God, never. No one who follows his passion, or whose stomach is full while his neighbour is hungry, or who does not rigorously follow justice for the sake of God, will be able to enter the presence of the Messenger of God.

Verily, the Messenger of God enjoined me and said, 'O 'Alī, *Enjoin that which is just, and forbid that which is reprehensible* (31:17)[43] by your hands; and if you cannot do so, then by your tongue; and if you cannot do so, then by your heart. Otherwise, do not blame any one except yourself. I warn you to avoid backbiting, for verily, it nullifies [good] works. Show affection to your kith and kin; scatter greetings, and pray while the people are asleep. I enjoin you, O descendants of 'Abd al-Muṭṭalib[44] in particular, to show your generosity to those who are good to you, and to fulfil the hopes of those who have hopes in you, for verily, this

[36]See *The Pillars of Islam*, I, 259.

[37]Ibid., I, 259.

[38]Ibid., I, 260–4.

[39]Ibid., I, 259–60.

[40]*Kawthar* (Qur'ān 108:1) is regarded as the proper name of a river or pond in Paradise designated for the Prophet. *Ḥawḍ* has become synonymous with *Kawthar*, 'the Prophet's Pool', at which the faithful will quench their thirst when entering Paradise. *EI*², s.v. Kawthar. See also *The Pillars of Islam*, I, 37.

[41]The Prophet's *shafā'a* is recognized by the *ijmā'* (consensus of the *umma*) and is based on the Qur'ān 17:79 and 93:5. In popular piety, it is believed that martyrs, saints (*awliyā'*), etc., could intercede on behalf of their followers. For details see *EI*², s.v. Shafā'a; Poonawala, 'Pilgrimage to the Shrines'.

[42]See Chap. 17, n. 43 for *muḥṣana*.

[43]'Commanding right and forbidding wrong' is a central moral tenet mentioned several times in the Qur'ān. In his *Commanding Right and Forbidding Wrong in Islamic Thought*, M. Cook has mapped the history of Islamic reflection on this obligation covering all the major Islamic sects and schools of thought, and its significance in both Sunnī and Shī'ī thought today. The book therefore contributes to the understanding of contemporary Islamic politics and ideology and raises important questions for the comparative study of ethics.

[44]'Abd al-Muṭṭalib was the Prophet's grandfather, see *The Pillars of Islam*, I, 20, 464.

befits your [noble] ancestry. Avoid hatred towards your kindred who are faithful, for it produces discord in religion (*al-ḥāliqa li 'l-dīn*).[45] I enjoin you to be civil to people, for verily, this is charity. Repeat very often the saying, 'There is neither power nor strength save in God, the High, the Great;' and teach it to your children. Be expeditious in the circumcision (*khitān*)[46] of your children, for verily, it is cleaner for them. Never utter a falsehood from your mouth so long as you live; do not use obscene language, for it befits neither us nor our partisans (*bi-shīʿatinā*). A man with a foul tongue cannot be truthful. The conceited man (*mutakabbir*) is accursed and the courteous man (*mutawāḍiʿ*) is held high in the estimation of God. Beware of conceit for it is the Cloak of God, the Mighty and Glorious, and God will shatter him who contends with God for His Cloak.

Fear ye God, fear ye God, with respect to orphans. Never allow them to remain hungry in your presence. Fear ye God, fear ye God, concerning the traveller (*ibn al-sabīl*). Let him not feel loneliness and yearn for his kinsfolk when he is your guest. Fear ye God, fear ye God, regarding a guest. Never let him depart without being grateful to you. Fear ye God, fear ye God, concerning the fight with your [carnal] souls, for verily, they are the most inimical of your enemies and, verily, God says: *Lo! the (human) soul enjoineth unto evil, save that whereon my Lord hath mercy* (12:53). Verily, the first of sins is to give support to the baser spirit and to rely upon passion. Fear ye God, fear ye God, do not desire the world, for the world is the source of all errors, and is bound to vanish in course of time. Beware of envy, for it was the first sin to be found in jinns[47] before human beings. Beware of trusting women, for it was they who caused your father [Adam] to depart from paradise and who rendered him to the affliction of this world.[48] Beware of thinking ill of others, for such conduct renders [good] actions nugatory, *Guard your duty to Allah, and speak words straight to the point; He will adjust your works for you and forgive you your sins* (33:70–1).

I enjoin you to obey him [the Prophet] whose disobedience will not be

[45]*Ḥāliqa*, is either a year of drought or that which destroys and utterly cuts off religion like a razor. Lane, s.v. ḥ-l-q.

[46] For *khitān* see *The Pillars of Islam*, I, 154.

[47]Jinn, see Chap. 13, n. 56.

[48]It should be noted that the Qur'ānic account about Adam and Iblīs does not ascribe blame to Eve rather than Adam, or vice versa. The Qur'ān states categorically that both of them slipped, and both of them acknowledged their error and asked God for forgiveness. *The Satan caused them to slip* (2:36); *the Satan whispered to them* (7:19–23); and *then Satan whispered to him* (20:120–3). Nuʿmān's projecting of his own attitude towards women onto ʿAlī reflects the values of highly patriarchal Arab society and culture, which are in conflict with the basic teaching of Islam. It should be noted that the famous Sunnī traditionist Bukhārī's attitude towards women is not different from that of Nuʿmān. Bukhārī transmitted a tradition which states that when the Messenger of God heard that the people of Persia had made Kisrā's daughter their queen he said, 'People who make a woman their ruler will never prosper.' *Mishkāt*, II, 322; Robson, I, 785. See also Murata and Chittick, *Vision of Islam*, 142; Hibri, 'Muslim Women's Rights'.

excused in you; [I enjoin you] to obey us, the People of the House, for God has coupled obedience to us with obedience to God Himself and His Messenger, and He has said this in a verse of His Book as a favour on you and on us. God has made obedience obligatory to Him and His Messenger and to those from among the People of the House who are possessed of authority (*wulāt al-amr*).[49] God has commanded you to ask [questions] to the People of the Reminder (*ahl al-dhikr*), and by God, we are the People of the Reminder.[50] Anyone who makes this claim but is not of us, is a liar. The Word of God confirms this: *Now Allah hath sent down unto you a Reminder, a messenger reciting unto you the revelations of Allah made plain, that He may bring forth those who believe and do good works from darkness unto light* (65:10–11), and then He says: *Ask the People of the Reminder (ahl al-dhikr) if you know not* (16:43). We are the People of the Reminder; so accept our authority and abstain from what we have forbidden. We are the doors concerning which you are commanded to *go to houses by the gates thereof* (2:189);[51] and we, by God, are the gates of these houses; no one else has this status and no one except us can make this claim.

O people, if there is any one amongst you who can complain of an unjust decision or wrong done to his person or his property, let him rise and I shall give him justice regarding it. A man among the people rose and praised him and eulogized him and mentioned his attainments in a long discourse. Then 'Alī said, 'O you (slave) who speaks! This is not the time for praise, and I do not desire to be face-to-face in this place of gathering with any one who is not sincere towards me. God is the witness against him who, having seen something of which he disapproves, does not inform me about it. For verily, I desire to be well pleased with my soul before I die.

O God, Thou art witness, and Thou art sufficient as a witness, verily, I and three members of my family (*ahl baytī*) covenanted with Thy Messenger and Thy Proof (*ḥujja*)[52] in Thy earth, Muḥammad, that, for the sake of God, we shall not leave any commandment but obey it, and we shall not leave any prohibition but abstain from it. None of his [the Prophet's] friends will remain unbefriended by

[49] It refers to the Qur'ān 4:59; *wulāt al-amr* are the *ulu 'l-amr* mentioned in the verse, see *The Pillars of Islam*, I, 27; *Kāfī*, I, 192.

[50] It refers to the Qur'ān 16:43, see *The Pillars of Islam*, I, 36, 98; Nu'mān, *Sharḥ al-akhbār*, II, 344.

[51] The verse reads: *They ask thee, (O Muhammad), of new moons. Say: They are fixed seasons for mankind and for the pilgrimage. It is not righteous that ye go to houses by the backs thereof (as do the idolaters at certain seasons), but the righteous man is he who wardeth off (evil). So go to houses by the gates thereof, ...* . The well-known Shī'ī tradition states God's Messenger as saying, 'I am the city of knowledge (or wisdom) and 'Alī is its gate; he who wishes [to acquire] knowledge should enter through its gate.' Furāt al-Kūfī, I, 13–14; Nu'mān, *Sharḥ al-akhbār*, I, 89–90; the editor has indicated more Sunnī sources. Ṭabrisī, I, 282–4, II, 343, 417–18. They relate the tradition as an explanation of the above verse. See also *Mishkāt*, III, 244; Robson, II, 1341.

[52] For *ḥujja* see *The Pillars of Islam*, I, 17, n. 29.

us, and none of his enemies will but be treated as an enemy by us. We shall not turn our backs to the enemy; we shall not grow weary of obligatory acts; we shall not augment towards God and His Messenger aught but sincerity. My companions were killed, may the mercy and approval of God be on them, and all of them were People of My House. 'Ubayda b. al-Ḥārith died a martyr at the Battle of Badr;[53] my uncle Ḥamza died a martyr at the Battle of Uḥud,[54] and my brother Ja'far died a martyr at the Battle of Mu'ta,[55] may God's mercy be upon [them all]. Then God revealed for me and my companions: *Of the believers are men who are true to that which they covenanted with Allah. Some of them have paid their vow by death (in battle), and some of them still are waiting; and they have not altered in the least* (33:23).[56] I am, by God, the expectant one and have not changed in the least. Out of His kindness, He promised us a good reward and said: *Say: In the bounty (faḍl) of Allah and in His mercy (raḥma): therein let them rejoice. It is better than what they hoard* (10:58).[57] The time has come, in what has befallen me, to rejoice in the favour of God.

The people then praised him greatly and wept. Then said 'Alī:

I want you to bear witness that no one among you rose, saying, 'I desired to speak but was afraid.' As between you and me, I absolve you from all blame, unless indeed there is someone desirous of doing me wrong, or wants to make a complaint against me regarding an offence I have not committed; then, take heed, I have

[53]He is 'Ubayda b. al-Ḥārith b. 'Abd al-Muṭṭalib. He fell in the Battle of Badr. Ibn Isḥāq, *al-Sīra*, II, 364; Guillaume, 328, 336; Wāqidī, *Kitāb al-maghāzī*, I, passim; Ibn Sa'd, III/1, 34–5. For the Battle of Badr see *The Pillars of Islam*, I, 284, n. 67.

[54]Ḥamza b. 'Abd al-Muṭṭalib, see *The Pillars of Islam*, I, 23, n. 22; 284, 288, 297. For the Battle of Uḥud see *The Pillars of Islam*, I, 296, n. 145.

[55]Ja'far b. Abī Ṭālib, see *The Pillars of Islam*, 298, n. 156. Mu'ta, a town near the Dead Sea in what is now Jordan, was the place where the Muslim expedition was defeated in the year 8/629. *EI*^{2}, s.v. Mu'ta.

[56]*... have paid their vow by death (in battle)*, are Ḥamza and Ja'far, and ... *still are waiting*, is 'Alī. Qummī, II, 188–9; Ṭūsī, *al-Tibyān*, VIII, 327–31; Ṭabrisī, IV, 349–50. Ṭabarī, *Tafsīr*, (Beirut), XXI, 92–4, on the other hand, states that ... *have paid their vow by death*, are those who fell at Badr and Uḥud, and *still are waiting*, are those who await their martyrdom in the future. After this general import, Ṭabarī states that, according to some authorities, the above verse was revealed concerning Anas b. al-Naḍr and his companions. Wāḥidī, *Asbāb al-nuzūl*, 250–1, states that ... *have paid their vow* refers to Ṭalḥa b. 'Ubayd Allāh, while ... *true to ... they covenanted* refers to Anas b. Muḍar. It should be noted that Ṭabrisī also reports different explanations.

[57]It is 10:59 in Pickthall. Bounty (*faḍl*) refers to the Messenger of God and 'mercy' (*raḥma*) refers to 'Alī. *Let them rejoice* means let our partisans (*shī'atunā*) rejoice at what 'bounty' and 'mercy' they possess rather than the worldy goods that our enemies possess. Furāt al-Kūfī, I, 179–81; Qummī, I, 341–2; Ṭūsī, *al-Tibyān*, V, 397. Ṭabarī, *Tafsīr*, XV, 105–8, states that *faḍl* and *raḥma* refer to Islam and the Qur'ān, and the verse is addressed to the Prophet.

never taken either the life or the property of a person unless it was lawful for me to do so. I waged war in the company of the Messenger of God by the command of God and His Messenger. When God summoned His Messenger, I waged [religious] war against those of the rebels whom the Messenger of God ordered me to fight and he named each one of them to me and urged me to fight against them and said, 'O 'Alī, you will fight the breakers of promises (*nākithīn*)'[58] and he named them to me; 'and the wrongdoers (*qāsiṭīn*)' and he named them to me; 'and those that deviate (*māriqīn*),' and he named them to me. Therefore, let there not be variance in your opinions; for, verily, man is most truthful in this condition.

And the people praised him greatly and spoke good words and wept. Then he turned to Ḥasan and said:

O Ḥasan, you are the avenger of my blood (*walīyu damī*), and he [Ibn Muljam,[59] the curse of God be on him] is with you, and I have handed him over to you. No one else has authority in this matter. If you wish to kill him, do so; if you wish to forgive him, do so. You are the Imam after me, the heir to my knowledge, the most excellent of those that I leave behind after me, and the best of my successors amongst the People of My House. The Messenger of God has given good tidings to you and to your brother, the son of your mother [Ḥusayn],[60] so you two should be glad at the good tidings given to you and act in obedience to God. You two should be grateful to Him for (His) bounty.

Then he continued to say:

O God, save us from thy accursed enemy [Satan]. O God, I make Thee a witness that Thou art God, and that there is no deity other than Thee, and that Thou art One, everlasting. Thou dost not beget nor art Thou begotten, and there is none to equal Thee. To Thee, all praise for Thy numerous bounties and Thy kindness to me. So pardon me and be kind to me, for Thou art the kindest of the merciful ones.

He continued to say:

There is no deity other than God. Thou art one and there is no associate with Thee, and Muḥammad is Thy slave and messenger. [This confession is] a provision

[58]For those three groups see *The Pillars of Islam*, I, 61, n. 160; 62, n. 162; 480.

[59]Ibn Muljam, 'Abd al-Raḥmān al-Murādī, was the murderer of 'Alī. The sources describe 'Alī as always scrupulous in the application of the *sharī'a*. In the case of his murderer, they are almost unanimous in insisting on the fact that he ordered Ḥasan that the *lex talionis* (law of retaliation) be strictly observed. Some of the sources even stress 'Alī's magnanimity. For details see *EI*^{2}, s.v. Ibn Muld̲j̲am.

[60]It refers to the Prophet's saying concerning Ḥasan and Ḥusayn, 'They are the lords of the youth of Paradise, ...' *The Pillars of Islam*, I, 48.

for this halting place [in this world], and for each of the halting places after it. O God, give to Muḥammad from us the best of rewards and the best of requitals, and convey to him from us the best of salutations. O God, unite me with him [the Prophet] and do not separate me from him. Verily Thou art the Hearer of prayer, the Clement, the Merciful One.

Then he turned his eyes to the People of his House and said, 'May God protect you, and may God protect your Prophet among you.[61] I leave you in the hands of God and I send you my greetings.' He continued to repeat, 'There is no deity other than God, and Muḥammad is the Messenger of God,' until he died on the twenty-first night of Ramaḍān in the fortieth year of the Hijra.[62] May the blessings, mercy, and approval of God be upon him.

LAWFUL AND UNLAWFUL BEQUESTS (*MĀ YAJŪZ MIN AL-WAṢĀYĀ WA-MĀ LĀ YAJŪZ MINHĀ*)[63]

Ja'far b. Muḥammad—his father—his ancestors—'Alī: He came across an impecunious man who said to him, 'May I not make a will, O Commander of the Faithful?' 'Alī said, 'Admonish [your heirs] to fear God. As for your property, leave it to your heirs, because it is small and trivial, and God says: ... *if he leave wealth, that he bequeath* ... (2:180), while you do not leave wealth which you can bequeath.'

[Ja'far b. Muḥammad]—the Messenger of God: He said, 'A man has the greatest right to his third; he may deal with it as he likes.'[64] 'Alī told

[61]The edited text is identical with that in *Kāfī*, VII, 62. MS Q reads: *Ḥafiẓakum Allāhu wa-rasūluhu, min ahli baytihi, wa-ḥafiẓa fī-kum nabīyakum*.

[62]*Kāfī*, VII, 62: He died on Friday night, the twenty-third of Ramaḍān, in the fortieth year of the Hijra. He was struck on the twenty-first night.

[63]The four constituent elements of a bequest are: testator (*mūṣī*), legatee (*mūṣā lahu*), bequeathed property (*mūṣā bihi*), and testament (*waṣīya*). The jursists agree that the testator could be any owner with a legally valid ownership. In the case of the legatee, they further agree that a bequest is not valid for an heir. They disagree about a bequest for deceased person. For details see Ibn Rushd, *Bidāya*, II, 331–35; trans. II, 405–10.

[64]The Islamic law permits a Muslim to give away the whole of his property by gift *inter vivos*, but restricts him to one-third in his testamentary capacity. This was established when the Prophet told Sa'd b. Abī Waqqāṣ that he might bequeath no more than one-third of his estate to legatees. The jurists interpret the Prophetic dictum to strike a balance between the compulsory heirs (to the extent of two-thirds) and the legatees (to the maximum of one-third). Schacht's assertion that the restriction of legacies to one-third of the estate was of Umayyad origin connected to their fiscal interests is refuted by Coulson and Powers. Powers further argues that the one-third restriction was originally introduced to strike a balance between the entitlement of the testamentary heir (minimum of two-

a man to bequeath a third of his property, and a third is a considerable portion. Ja'far b. Muḥammad said that a woman has the same rights.[65]

'Alī: He said, 'I prefer that bequests should be restricted to one-fifth [of the estate]. Verily, God is well pleased with one-fifth from his slaves.[66] One-fifth is the course of moderation and one-third is a hardship for the heirs; a bequest of one-fourth is more pleasing to me than that of one-third.'[67]

Ja'far b. Muḥammad:[68] He said, 'He who bequeaths one-third has, [in reality], not left anything for the heirs and caused them harm; a bequest of one-fourth or one-fifth is more excellent than that of one-third.'[69]

This, then, is the preference concerning which we related a report from ['Alī]; but bequest to the extent of one-third is lawful. If the heritable estate is considerable and the heirs are rich, there is no harm in dealing with the whole of the third; but if they are poor, then to restrict it to less than one-third is better. To bequest a greater amount than one-third is not permissible unless the heirs agree to it. All the heirs should have the capacity to act and a single heir may permit it from his own share.

'Alī: He said, 'It is not permissible for a man to bequeath more than one-third or the whole of his property. He should be dissuaded from his plan and directed to one that is reasonable rather than reprehensible. If a man wrongs himself concerning the bequest and acts unjustly (*ḥāfa*[70] *fīhā*),[71] the bequest will return to that which is proper and the heirs will receive their proper shares.'[72]

---

thirds) and legatees (maximum of one-third). *EI*², s.v. Waṣīya; Schacht, *Origins*, 201–2; idem *Introduction*, 173–4; Coulson, *History of Islamic Law*, 65–9; Powers, *Studies in Qur'ān*, 50–1; idem, 'The Will of Sa'd b. Abī Waqqāṣ.'

[65] Ṭūsī, *Tahdhīb al-aḥkām*, IX, 191–8.

[66] It should be noted that *khums*, a religious tax, was originally paid to the Prophet according to the Qur'ān 8:41, *And know that whatever ye take as spoils of war, lo! a fifth thereof is for Allah, ...*

[67] *Kāfī*, VII, 18–19.

[68] According to MS Q. In the printed edition it is a continuation.

[69] A tradition transmitted by Bukhārī and Muslim states that the Prophet permitted Sa'd b. Abī Waqqāṣ to will away a third of his estate and said, 'You may will away a third, but that is a lot. To leave your heirs rich is better than to leave them poor and begging from people ...' *Mishkāt*, II, 155; Robson, I, 656.

[70] According to MS Q. *Khāfa* in the edited text as well as the pirated edition of Tāmir is an error. See also *Kāfī*, VII, 19, 29.

[71] Refers to the Qur'ān 2:182, it states: *But he who feareth from a testator some unjust or sinful clause, and maketh peace between the parties, (it shall be) no sin for him.*

[72] 'If anyone deprives an heir of his inheritance, God will deprive him of his inheritance in Paradise on the Day of Resurrection.' *Mishkāt*, II, 157; Robson, I, 657.

Abū Ja'far and Abū 'Abd Allāh: They said, 'Where a man makes certain bequests in which the emancipation of a slave is mentioned, the price of the slave should first be taken out of his third and the slave be manumitted, and then the residue should be allowed to [be used for] the remaining bequests.'[73]

Ja'far b. Muḥammad: He said, 'Similarly, if a man makes a bequest for a pilgrimage to be performed on his behalf, the testator never having performed it himself, such a bequest should be given preference over all others [out of the third].'[74]

Ja'far b. Muḥammad: A man amongst his companions told him, 'A woman among us disposed of her third by will and said, "A *juz'* (part) from it may be given to a certain man, and a *juz'* to a certain woman." The case was referred to Ibn Abī Laylā,[75] and he disallowed the bequest saying, "She only mentioned a thing (*shay'*) and she did not specify [the word *juz'* being a general term and uncertain in meaning]."' Abū 'Abd Allāh [Imam al-Ṣādiq] said, 'Ibn Abī Laylā did not know the correct rule. The word *juz'* is applied to one-tenth of a thing.' By this [the Imam] meant that *ajzā'* consist only of ten parts. What is less than that is said to be one-half or one-third or one-fourth, and so on till we come to one-tenth. A fractional part less than one-tenth is not known as a *juz'*.[76]

[Ja'far b. Muḥammad]: Concerning a man who bequeaths a *sahm* (general word for 'part') from his third to a certain man, [the Imam] said, 'Let one-sixth be given to him, as a *sahm* is one-sixth of a thing.'[77]

'Alī, Abū Ja'far, and Abū 'Abd Allāh: They said, 'There shall be no bequest to an heir.'[78]

[73]*Kāfī*, VII, 25–6.

[74]Cf. *Kāfī*, VII, 23; Ṭūsī, *Tahdhīb al-aḥkām*, IX, 219.

[75]Ibn Abī Laylā, see *The Pillars of Islam*, I, 113, n. 323. See also *EI*[2], s.v. Ibn Abī Layla.

[76]*Juz'* meaning one-tenth of a thing is derived from the Qur'ān 2:260 (... *then place a part of them on each hill*, ...). There were ten hills, according to a tradition, hence *juz'* is one-tenth. *Kāfī*, VII, 49, 50. The words *juz'* and *sahm*, although general terms, have come to possess a definite technical meaning. It illustrates how jurists, in the past, construed words when their connotation was left unspecified by the testator, or where the exact fractional share was not indicated. These rules, therefore, serve as modern counterparts of interpretation.

[77]*Sahm* signifies the measure of six cubits, as used in sales and purchases in measurings of land. Lane, s.v. s-h-m. *Sahm* means one-eighth of a thing. This interpretation is derived from the Qur'ān 9:60 wherein eight categories are indicated as recepients of the obligatory alms. *Kafī*, VII, 50–1.

[78]'... and no legacy must be made to an heir.' Another version of this tradition states, 'No legacy is to be left to an heir unless the other heirs are agreeable.' *Mishkāt*, II, 156; Robson, I, 656–7.

So far as we know, there is a consensus of opinion on this point. If a bequest were permissible to an heir, verily, a greater portion than that which has been fixed by God would be bequeathable to him. He who bequeaths to the heir, belittles the right given to the heir by God and contravenes His Book, and he who contravenes the Book of God, acts unlawfully.

A tradition attributed to Ja'far b. Muḥammad [Imam al-Ṣādiq] has created doubt in the minds of some of those who adopt his view [stated above]. He was asked about a man who made a bequest to his relatives and said that it is permissible according to the Word of God: *If he leave wealth, that he bequeath unto parents and near relatives* (2:180). That which we have related from him and from his saintly ancestors earlier, is more authentic and there is a consensus about it among the Muslims.[79]

The Messenger of God: He said, 'There shall be no bequest to the heir. God has assigned to the persons entitled to inherit their specific shares (*farā'iḍ*).'[80]

If the opinion handed down from Ja'far b. Muḥammad [Imam al-Ṣādiq] and reported by us latterly is correct, then by 'parents and near relatives', [the Imam] meant persons other than heirs, such as those relations

[79]Bequests to heirs, according to the Twelvers, are permissible, see *Kāfī*, VII, 16–17; Ṭūsī, *Tahdhīb al-aḥkām*, IX, 199–200. The Ismā'īlīs, in this respect, agree with the Sunnīs and the Zaydīs.

[80] *Farā'iḍ* pl. of *farīḍa*, a technical term in law, means a primarily apportioned inheritance assigned by the Qur'ān. *'Ilm al-farā'iḍ* or *al-farā'iḍ* means the science of the division of inheritance. *Dhawu 'l-farā'iḍ*, the quota heirs whose shares are fixed by the Qur'ān are: (i) the children, (ii) the father, (iii) the mother, (iv) the relations of the father, (v) the relations of the mother, and (vi) spouses. Their shares are assigned usually as follows, but such cases occur rarely and the actual distribution is quie complicated. 1. The daughter is entitled to half the estate, two or more daughters get two-thirds, but if they inherit along with sons, they become the normal heirs. 2. The daughter of a son is in the same position as a daughter; inheriting along with the son of a son, she becomes the normal heir. 3. The father's quota is always one-sixth of the estate. 4. The parental grandfather (in default of the father) receives one-sixth, but is excluded by the father. 5. The mother gets one-sixth of the estate if there are children; otherwise one-third (the father in this case gets two-thirds). 6. The grandmother always gets a sixth; the mother's mother is excluded by the mother, and the father's mother by the father and mother. 7. A full sister receives half, two or more such sisters get together two-thirds, but along with a full brother or the grandfather, she becomes the normal heir. 8. The half-sister on the father's side is similar to that of the full sister; along with a half-brother on the father's side, she becomes a normal heir. 9. The widower receives half of the estate, but only a quarter if there is a child. 10. The widow receives half of what a widower would receive under that same circumstances; if the deceased leaves more than one widow, they share equally the quota alloted to the widow. For details and exceptions from the general rules see *EI*^{2}, s.v. Farā'iḍ; Lane, s.v. f-r-ḍ.

who do not inherit, because he who is near [in degree of relation] excludes the more remote, like parents who are slaves or polytheists. We have mentioned in an earlier portion that a slave can be purchased from the inheritance of his master and freed, and [as a free man] he inherits the rest. We shall discuss this fully hereinafter, God willing.

It is probable that the meaning of the Qur'ānic expression 'bequests to parents and near relatives in kindness', is as God has laid down in the Qur'ān, namely the portion of property to which they are entitled as inheritance. This is well known. For example, a man, who, faced with death, may bequeath his properties to the heirs according to what God has fixed for them or hand over to them their specific shares according to what God has fixed for them during his life, lest they quarrel after his death or lest some of them deny others their relationship with the deceased.

Ja'far b. Muḥammad: He said that any present (*'aṭīya*) or a gift (*hiba*) made to an heir during the course of a disease from which the giver of the present or gift dies, is void. This confirms what we have said before.

Ja'far b. Muḥammad was asked concerning a man who, in his terminal illness, had acknowledged a debt to one of his heirs. [The Imam] said, 'It is necessary to consider the position of the man who acknowledges the debt. If he is a just man free from an inclination [to do a wrong],[81] his admission is lawful; if, however, he is not such a person, his admission is not lawful unless the heirs agree to it.'[82]

'Alī: He said, 'The Messenger of God decreed the debt before the legacy, even though you read the reverse order [in the Qur'ān]: *after any legacy he may have bequeathed, or debt (has been paid)*' (4:11).[83]

Al-Ḥakam b. 'Utayba:[84] He said, 'I[85] was sitting at the door of Abū Ja'far [Imam al-Bāqir] when a woman came and said, "Ask permission of

[81]The Arabic expression is *ma'mūn min al-janaf*. The word *janaf* occurs in the Qur'ān 2:182 which states: *And he who fears from the testator an inclining [to a wrong course], or a declining [from the right course]*. Lane, s.v. j-n-f.

[82]*Kāfī*, VII, 51–2; the dying man's admission is generally accepted when the debt is less than one-third of his legacy.

[83]Abū 'Abd Allāh [Imam al-Ṣādiq] said, 'Funeral expenses should be paid first, then the debt, then the legacy, then the inheritance.' *Kāfī*, VII, 32.

[84]'Utayba: according to *Kāfī*, VII, 33; see also Mufīd, *al-Ikhtiṣāṣ*, 254, 287. 'Uyayna: in the edited text as well as the pirated edition of Tāmir. In MS Q it was 'Utayba, then it was corrected to 'Uyayna. Al-Ḥakam b. 'Utayba al-Kindī, an eminent jurist of Kūfa, was a Zaydī and a Mu'tazilī leader. Jafri, *Origins*, 253, 306; older sources are listed therein. As pointed out in *The Pillars of Islam*, I, 103, n. 286, Nu'mān does quote the views of the Zaydīs, but here it is cited to show that it is erroneous.

[85]We (I myself and a group of people) were waiting at the door for the [Imam] to come out: in *Kāfī*, VII, 33.

Abū Jaʿfar for me [to see him]." She was told, "What do you want from him?" She said, "I wish to ask him concerning a matter." She was told, "Here is al-Ḥakam, an expert in *fiqh* from the people of Iraq, so ask him." She said, "Verily, my husband died and left one thousand dirhams, and he owed me five hundred dirhams for my dower (*ṣadāq*). So I took my dower, and took my share of inheritance. Then a man came and said,[86] 'He [the deceased] owed me one thousand dirhams.' As I knew of this, I testified to the truthfulness [of the claim].'"

Al-Ḥakam said, 'Wait until I think over your problem and calculate.' He began to calculate and Abū Jaʿfar [the Imam] came out of the house while he was still calculating. So [the Imam] said, 'What is this, O Ḥakam, which is causing your fingers to move?' Ḥakam informed him, and before he could finish what he had to say, Abū Jaʿfar said, 'She has acknowledged his right to two-thirds of what is in her hands and there is no inheritance for her until she pays him off.'[87]

ʿAlī and Abū Jaʿfar: [Concerning the case] in which a testator makes a bequest to a man who was absent [at the time of the bequest], and then dies without altering his will and when the matter is investigated, it is found that the legatee (*al-mūṣā lahu*) had died before the testator (*al-mūṣī*), they said, 'The legacy is void.[88] If the legatee were absent at the time of the bequest, but died later than the testator, the matter may be considered. If the legatee had accepted the legacy, then it goes to his own heirs; whereas, if he had not accepted it, then it goes to the testator's heirs.'

Abū Jaʿfar and Abū ʿAbd Allāh: They said, 'A man is entitled to revoke his will both in health and in disease, and he can alter it as he wishes; for, in this matter, he has a choice.[89] [A bequest which is not altered or revoked] till the testator's death, is to be paid from the bequeathable third.'

ʿAlī, Abū Jaʿfar, and Abū ʿAbd Allāh: They said, 'When a man makes a bequest, it shall be paid out of his third. This is the case even though it

[86]And alleged: in *Kāfī*.

[87]*Kāfī*, VII, 33; Abū Jaʿfar said, 'She has acknowledged the third that is in her hands, and there is no inheritance for her.' Al-Ḥakam said, 'By God, I do not think that I have ever understood Abū Jaʿfar.'

Ibn Abī ʿUmayr gave the following explanation of Abū Jaʿfar's [legal decision]: There is no inheritance for her until she pays off the debt. He [her husband] left one thousand dirhams, but he owed a debt of one thousand and five hundred jointly to his wife and the man. Hence, she will have one-third of a thousand and the man will have two-thirds.

[88]*Kāfī*, VII, 21; Ṭūsī, *Tahdhīb al-aḥkām*, IX, 230–1. If the testator dies without altering or revoking his will, then the legacy goes to the legatee's heir. Hence, the Twelver view is different than that of the Ismāʿīlīs.

[89]*Kāfī*, VII, 14–16, 20; a man is entitled to do whatever he wishes with his wealth as long as he is alive. See also Ṭūsī, *Tahdhīb al-aḥkām*, IX, 186–8.

may be in favour of a Jew, a Christian, or for some other purpose. This should surely be done on account of the Word of God: *And whoso changeth (the will) after he hath heard it—the sin thereof is only upon those who change it* (2:181).'[90] The three [Imams] mean that the testator makes the will to do acts which are permissible for the living Muslim to do. However, if the testator makes a bequest for an unlawful purpose, the bequest is not lawful.

Abū 'Abd Allāh Ja'far b. Muḥammad: He was asked about a man who had made a bequest for a pilgrimage [to be made on his behalf], and the executor used it for [emancipating] a slave (*nasama*).[91] [The Imam] said, 'The executor should be penalized to the extent to which he has acted against the testator's wish. The legacy is to be spent in accordance with the testator's direction.'[92]

[Abū 'Abd Allāh Ja'far b. Muḥammad]:[93] He said, 'Fāṭima bint Asad b. Hāshim,[94] the mother of 'Alī b. Abī Ṭālib, made a will and said, "O Messenger of God, set free my female servant so-and-so." The Messenger of God said, "Lo! Whatever property you have given away [in charity], you will find it [in the next world]." When she died, the Messenger of God stood at her grave before she was laid in it and said, "Wait." Then he descended and reclined in her grave, and emerged and said, "Lower her; I did what I did desiring that God may increase [His mercy] on her. For behold, no one profited me as much as she and Abū Ṭālib[95] did." The Messenger of God upheld her will and executed it according to her instructions.'

Ja'far b. Muḥammad: He said, 'When a man bequeaths a legacy to another, the legatee has the option to accept or refuse the legacy if he [the legatee] is present. If the legatee refuses the legacy in the presence of the testator, he is not obligated to it. But if the legatee was absent when

[90]*Kāfī*, VII, 22.

[91]*Nasama* means living creature. It can be used to refer to a person or a slave, male or female. *Majma' al-baḥrayn*, n-s-m.

[92]*Kāfī*, VII, 30; it adds the Qur'ānic verse 2:181.

[93]'Alī: in MS Q.

[94]Fāṭima bint Asad b. Hāshim b. 'Abd Manāf was an early convert and had migrated to Medina. She bore all the children of Abū Ṭālib: Ṭālib, Umm Hāni', 'Aqīl, Ja'far, and 'Alī. Ibn Ḥazm, *Jamhara*, 14. See also Balādhurī, *Ansāb al-ashrāf* (ed. al-Azem), II, 38, 39, 40, 41.

[95]Abū Ṭālib son of 'Abd al-Muṭṭalib b. Hāshim was the Prophet's uncle. After the death of 'Abd al-Muṭṭalib, he looked after Muḥammad and continued to protect him unflinchingly after he received the revelation. He died shortly after the end of the Quraysh boycott of Banū Hāshim. Soon, thereafter, the Prophet's wife, Khadīja, died. Hence, the tenth year of the mission is known as *'ām al-ḥuzn* (the year of sorrow). *EI*[2], s.v. Abū Ṭālib.

the bequest was made to him, and then the testator dies, it is not proper for the legatee to refuse the legacy. For, on the death of the testator [the legacy lapses] and it becomes a right among the rights of God [that is, it must be executed).'[96]

[Ja'far b. Muḥammad]: He said, 'When a man bequeaths one-third of his property to his slave, then let the slave be valued. If the third thus bequeathed is less in value than the price of the slave but not less than one-fourth of the slave's price, [the slave shall be emancipated to the extent of the legacy] and he will be allowed to emancipate himself by paying off the difference.[97] If the legacy is in excess of the price of the slave, the slave shall be emancipated and the excess shall be given to him. If he is not emancipated except to the extent of less than one-sixth [of his value], there shall be no legacy to him.'[98]

'Alī: He was asked about bequests made by, and bequests made to, *mukātabs* (slaves to be emancipated by contract and by paying instalments). He said, 'The legacy is permissible to the extent to which he is emancipated.'[99] This is a brief statement, and we have explained it fully in the Chapter of *Mukātabs*.[100]

The meaning is that this statement applies only to him [the *mukātab*] who does not have the condition [in his agreement] that if he fails [to make an instalment], he returns to slavery. But as for him who has stipulated this condition, his status is the same as that of a slave, until he pays off the last instalment [of his contract]. We have mentioned the question of legacies to slaves in the preceding chapter.

[96]*Kāfī*, VIII, 13–14; Ṭūsī, *Tahdhīb al-aḥkām*, IX, 205–6. If the legatee was absent when the bequest was made to him, he could refuse it provided that the testator is still alive and is informed that the legatee has declined. But, if the testator dies before receiving that news, the legatee is obliged to accept the legacy and fulfil it.

[97]For example, the price of the slave is 300 dirhams. The bequeathable third is 200 dirhams, as the testator left the property worth 600 dirhams. In this case the slave is manumitted to the proportionate extent and he has to earn to pay off the difference.

[98]For example, the price of the slave is 700 dirhams, and the bequeathable third is 100 dirhams. This being the case, the legacy is less than one-sixth of the price. Hence, there is no legacy at all and no proportionate emancipation can take place. *Kāfī*, VII, 36. A man on his deathbed manumitted his slave whose price is 600 dirhams, and left a debt of 300 dirhams and did not have any other property. The Imam said that the slave be emancipated to the extent of one-sixth of his value, because after paying the debt, he has the legacy of one-third from 300 dirhams, which is one-sixth of his price.

[99]I have read *'utiqa* (passive voice) as in MS Q and a variant reading in one of Fyzee's MSS. See also *Kāfī*, VII, 36. In the edited text: *'ataqa*.

[100]See 'Emancipation by Contract', in Chap. 12.

'Alī, Abū Ja'far, and Abū 'Abd Allāh: They said, 'There shall be no bequest to a slave.'[101]

Ja'far b. Muḥammad: He said, 'When a testator bequeaths legacies in excess of the bequeathable third, and the heirs agree to this in his lifetime; but later, after his death, if it occurs to them to go back upon their consent to such legacies, they have no right to do so.'[102]

[Ja'far b. Muḥammad]: He said, 'Umāma bint Abi 'l-'Āṣ[103] b. al-Rabī', the daughter of the Messenger of God's daughter Zaynab, whom 'Alī married after Fāṭima and whom al-Mughīra b. Nawfal[104] married after 'Alī, became ill and lost the power of speech. Ḥasan and Ḥusayn came to her, and despite Mughīra's disinclination, began to speak to her, "You have emancipated so and so," and she nodded her head signifying her assent, and they said, "You have given in charity for such and such a cause," and she nodded her assent, and then she died. They [Ḥasan and Ḥusayn] held her bequests to be lawful.'

Ja'far b. Muḥammad said, 'A sign, when understood to be signifying a bequest, is valid in the case of one who is unable to speak.'

[Ja'far b. Muḥammad]: Concerning a man who bequeaths a sum of one hundred dinars for emancipating a slave girl who is found to be of less value, [the Imam al-Ṣādiq] said, '[She should be emancipated and] the excess is to be returned to the slave girl if she had been specifically named by the testator. But if he had used general words with respect to the slave girl, it is the duty of the executor to buy a slave girl worth one hundred dinars [and emancipate her] if he finds her in accord with the terms of the bequest.'

[Ja'far b. Muḥammad]: If a man who is himself indebted bequeaths to another, and the executor removes property of the value of the debt

[101]This seems to be inconsistent with the previous tradition from Imam al-Ṣādiq.

[102]*Kāfī*, VII, 19–20.

[103]Al-'Āṣī: in Ibn Ḥazm, *Jamhara*, 16, 70, 77, and MS Q before correction. Abu 'l-'Āṣ al-Rabī' b. 'Abd al-'Uzzā b. 'Abd Shams was an important person in Mecca. He had wealth and respect. He was married to his cousin Zaynab, the Prophet's eldest daughter. Khadīja was his aunt and she used to regard him as her son. When the Prophet was honoured with revelation, Khadīja and her daughters embraced Islam, but Abu 'l-'Āṣ persisted in his polytheism. He joined the Quraysh in their expedition against the Muslims at Badr and was taken prisoner. Zaynab sent a necklace, which her mother had given her on her wedding, as ransom money for her husband. Soon, she migrated to Medina and died there in 8 AH. Abu 'l-'Āṣ accepted Islam a few years later, migrated to Medina, and died in 12 AH. Ibn Isḥāq, *al-Sīra*, I, 202; II, 306–14; Guillaume, 83, 313–17; Balādhurī, *Ansāb al-ashrāf* (ed. al-Azem), I, 138, 355, 480–5.

[104]He is al-Mughīra b. Nawfal b. al-Ḥārith b. 'Abd al-Muṭṭalib. Balādhuī, *Ansāb al-ashrāf* (ed. al-Azem), II, 138, 352, 381, 514; Ibn Ḥazm, *Jamhara*, 16, 70.

from the bulk of the testator's property, takes possession of it, and sends it to his own house, then divides the residue among the heirs and gives effect to the legacies, but thereafter, the property [of the value of the debt] is stolen from the executor's house, [the Imam] said, 'The executor will be liable for the property, as he had no right to take possession of the creditor's property without their authority.'[105]

[Ja'far b. Muḥammad]: He was asked about the testament of a person who commits suicide. He said, 'If the will is made after he committed the act which led to his death, the will is not valid.'[106]

[Ja'far b. Muḥammad]: He said, 'If a man bequeaths certain legacies and dies but prior to that he had already sent maintenance [money] for a certain period to his family, then whatever remains over after deducting the maintenance [of his family] till the day of his death, is inheritance, and legacies will be paid out of that remainder.'

'Alī: He said, 'Nothing deprives an executor of his executorship except loss of reason, apostasy, prodigality, fraud, or abandoning the *sunna*.[107] The sovereign (*sulṭān*) is the executor of him who has no executor, and he is the overseer (*nāẓir*) of him who has no overseer.'

Abū Ja'far Muḥammad b. 'Alī: He said, 'If the testator permits the executor to carry on trade with the property of his infant children, he is entitled to do so, and is not responsible for the loss. However, if the testator has permitted the executor to trade [the property] with profits, the condition is valid and binding.'[108]

Ja'far b. Muḥammad: He said, 'When an executor trades with the property of an orphan and no such right was given to him by will, he stands surety for any loss which may occur and any profit goes to the orphan.'

Abū Ja'far Muḥammad b. 'Alī: He said, 'If a man makes a will and leaves heirs who are absent and the executor refers the matter to the *qāḍī*, the *qāḍī* should appoint an agent to take charge of the property of the absent heirs.'

[105] *Kāfī*, VII, 32; slightly different version.

[106] The addition in *Kāfī*, VII, 55, states, 'If the will was made before he committed such an act, it is valid to the extent of one-third of his property. One who commits suicide is in Hell forever.' See also Ṭūsī, *Tahdhīb al-aḥkām*, IX, 207.

[107] It is the customary practice established by the Prophet which constitutes legally binding precedents. *The Pillars of Islam*, I, 1, n. 2.

[108] *Kāfī*, VII, 72; slightly different version.

15

Book of Inheritance
(*Kitāb al-Farā'iḍ*)[1]

THE SHARES OF CHILDREN
(MĪRĀTH AL-AWLĀD)

God says: *Allah chargeth you concerning (the provision for) your children: to the male the equivalent of the portion of two*

[1]For *al-farā'iḍ* see Chap. 14, n. 80. Fyzee, *Outlines*, 387–467; for the Ismā'īlī law of inheritance, see Fyzee, *Compendium*, 97–118. In pre-Islamic Arabia the estate of the deceased went to the nearest male relative in accordance with the patriarchal tribal system of society. In his *Studies in Qur'an*, D. Powers asserts that the Qur'ānic legislation introduced a complete new system of inheritance containing provisions for both testate and intestate succession thereby supplanting the pre-Islamic customary tribal law. Therefore, the Islamic law of inheritance, like the Islamic law of marriage and divorce, represents the heart of the *sharī'a* because it is based directly on the Qur'ānic text and expanded on the traditions of the Prophet. Thus, the Islamic family law, comprising the laws of marriage, divorce, and inheritance, has been characteristic of Islamic society throughout the ages. It is still applied in almost all the Muslim countries.

The Islamic law of inheritance displays the following peculiarities: (i) in addition to obligations entered into by the deceased, the debts of the estate include the funeral expenses and religious obligations omitted by the deceased, e.g. neglected fasts of Ramaḍān, the pilgrimage not undertaken without good reason; (ii) the Qur'ān gives specific shares to certain individuals; (iii) bequests are limited to one-third of the estate.

In the afore-cited book D. Powers maintains that the Islamic law of inheritance elaborated by the jurists is not identical to that which was revealed to the Prophet. He argues at great length that the operation of the law of inheritance is predicated upon a series of secondary assumptions about the reading of the Qur'ānic verses and the traditions. Basing his analysis on linguistic, lexicographic, and historical evidence, Powers reconstructs what he calls 'the proto-Islamic law of inheritance'. Unlike Islamic law, which imposes compulsory rules for the division of the estate, proto-Islamic law permits a Muslim to decide who his heirs will be and how much they will inherit. He further suggests that the transformation

females[2] till His saying: *then to his mother appertaineth the sixth, after any legacy he may have bequeathed, or debt (hath been paid)* (4:11).[3]

'Alī, Abū Ja'far, and Abū 'Abd Allāh: According to their fundamental teaching (*'alā aṣli qawlihim*), they said, 'When a man dies leaving behind surviving male and female offspring, and there are no other heirs, then the share of the male is twice that of the female. If he leaves only one son, the whole of the inheritance goes to him. If he leaves only one daughter, she obtains one half by inheritance and the other half returns to her (*yuraddu 'alayhā*)[4] by consanguinity (*bi 'l-raḥim*), i.e. if there is no one else more closely related to the deceased.'[5]

It is not as our opponents say to those who are in similar circumstances as Fāṭima, but do not have the ties of kinship. They wish to deny the right of Fāṭima[6] in the inheritance of the Messenger of God. God has clearly repudiated their opinions, for they said, 'The daughter is not entitled to more than half as mentioned in the Book of God. The second half goes to the agnatic heirs (*'aṣaba*).'[7] But they turned away from the Word of God: *And those who are related by consanguinity (ūlu 'l-arḥām) shall be deemed the nearest of kin to each other according to the Book of God* (8:75).[8] This dictum includes agnatic relations (*'aṣabāt*) as well as others. But they say that if

---

from proto-Islamic to Islamic law of inheritance was triggered by political, social, and religious crises the Muslim society passed through during the first century of the Islamic era.

It should be noted that the Shī'ī law of inheritance differs in certain ways from that of the Sunnīs. This was due mainly to their theological-political doctrine that 'Alī and Fāṭima were the only heirs to the Prophet to he exclusion of 'Abbās, the Prophet's uncle. See *EI*², s.v. Mīrāth; Schacht, *Introduction*, 169–74; Anderson, *Islamic Law*, 59–80; Pearl, *Muslim Family Law*, 439–85; idem, *Textbook*, 114–57; Coulson, *Succession*; a comprehensive study on the subject with a discussion on important changes that were introduced into the law of inheritance in modern times.

[2]The male gets double the share of a female because he supports the family, wages *jihād*, and pays blood money. *Kāfī*, VII, 93–4.

[3]Ibid., VII, 82–3.

[4]*Radd*, a technical term, means the law of reversion. First, the estate is divided among the quota heirs (*farā'iḍ*), and if there is any remainder, it is further apportioned by the law of reversion (*radd*) among the latter. *EI*², s.v. Farā'iḍ. See also n. 67 below in this chapter.

[5]Ṭūsī, *al-Nihāya*, 632–3.

[6]For the question of Fāṭima's inheritance see *EI*², s.v. Fadak.

[7]'*Aṣaba* are the relations on the side of the male. In Islamic law, it means the heirs of a man who has left neither parent nor offspring, and with respect to the inheritance, they do not have a *farīḍa* named, but who receive a portion if there remains anything after the distribution of the *farā'iḍ*. Thus, the '*aṣaba* are the normal heirs. Lane, s.v. '-ṣ-b; *EI*², s.v. Mīrāth.

[8]Sale, *Koran*, 177. Yusuf Ali translates: *But kindred by blood have prior rights against each other in the Book of God.* See also the Qur'ān translations by Bell, Blachère, and Paret.

her father is a slave and she purchases and emancipates him, then she obtains her half share of inheritance mentioned [in the Qur'ān] for her, and the second half by *walā'* belongs to the emancipator because the Messenger of God said, '*Walā'* belongs to him who emancipates.'[9] They gave inheritance on the ground of *walā'*, but abandoned the principle of consanguinity (*al-raḥim*) which is obligatory and has priority.

Ja'far b. Muḥammad—his father—his ancestors: They said, 'Fāṭima had kept to herself what she inherited from the Messenger of God even though those who wanted to take away her inheritance [attempted] to do so.'

Ja'far b. Muḥammad: He said, 'If a man dies leaving behind a daughter and a sister or a son's daughter, the whole property belongs to the daughter. The same would be the result if with her there was a sister or a son's son. The whole of the estate would go to the daughter, one half by inheritance and one half by consanguinity (*bi 'l-raḥim*).'

Similarly, 'Alī, Abū Ja'far [Imam al-Bāqir], and Abū 'Abd Allāh [Imam al-Ṣādiq] said, 'If the deceased leaves behind two daughters [and no one else], they will get one-third each, as God said, and the residue will return to them on account of the blood (uterine) relationship.'[10] Thus, as we have said, the estate will be divided into two halves between them.

If, in addition to the son, there is someone who is entitled to a Qur'ānic share (*farīḍa*), a beginning will be made with such a share and given to him, and the residue will be given to the son, as we have mentioned.

The sons' sons represent the sons when there is no son surviving,[11] and male and female descendants have the same rights as male and female children. The son of a son represents the son and the son of a daughter represents the daughter. Those who oppose us deny that the sons of daughters come under the general term son (*walad*). They say that they are descendants of another people, i.e. they refer to their fathers [not to their mothers]. God has declared their falsity in His Book, by the tongue of His Messenger, and even through their own arguments. They manifested the ugliness of their undue assumption clarifying what they really intended, namely, invalidating the inheritance of Fāṭima. This was due to their hatred for those to whom loving kindness was made obligatory by God's word, as spoken by the Prophet: *Say [O Muhammad, unto mankind]:*

[9]*Kāfī*, VII, 181; see also Chap. 12, n. 68.
[10]Ṭūsī, *al-Nihāya*, 633.
[11]Ibid., 634.

I ask of you no fee [reward] therefor [i.e. for the revelation], save loving kindness towards kinsfolk (42:23).[12]

These people relate from Ibn 'Abbās,[13] and they arrogate to themselves that the descendants of Ibn 'Abbās are the true claimants of the Imamate, while [in reality] they are the usurpers of the heritage of the rightly guiding Imams. They claim what their ancestors never claimed and invoke their parentage [in justification of their claim], but it is [just] their own [invented] idea.

It was said to 'Abd Allāh Ibn 'Abbās, 'Who are the relations which God means in the Qur'ānic verse: *Say, (O Muhammad unto mankind) I ask of you no fee [reward] therefor, save loving kindness towards kinsfolk* (42:23)?' He said, "Alī, Fāṭima, Ḥasan, Ḥusayn, and their descendants.' Threrefore, Ibn 'Abbās never claimed anything for himself, for his father, or for any of his sons, and they relate this tradition from him and declare it to be authentic.

As for the Qur'ān, God says: *That is Our argument. We gave it unto Abraham against his folk. We raise unto degrees (of wisdom) whom We will. Lo! thy Lord is Wise, Aware. And We bestowed upon him Isaac and Jacob; each of them We guided; and Noah did We guide aforetime; and of his seed, (We guided) David and Solomon and Job and Joseph and Moses and Aaron. Thus do We reward the good. And Zachariah and John and Jesus and Elias. Each one (of them) was of the righteous* (6:83–5).[14]

Who does God mean as between Noah and Abraham? Jesus was among his progeny through his daughter Mary, and not through a male descendant. They have contradicted the word of the Messenger of God [as transmitted through] their own reports that they have reported from various sources and which they consider to be authentic. These reports are great in number and their mention would lead to prolixity. Verily, the Messenger of God used to call Ḥasan and Ḥusayn his 'sons', and when he saw each one of them for the first time, he said, 'Show me my son!' He continued to call them his sons till his death. The Messenger of God did not call them by this name frivolously (*'abath^{an}*) or insincerely (*takalluf^{an}*), for, as God says: *Nor doth he speak of (his own) desire* (53:3). Those who oppose us base their opposition on the reports of the Prophet in accordance with the letter and the meaning and the story [of this verse]. They, therefore, fling the Book of God behind their backs and contradict the practice

[12]For the explanation see *The Pillars of Islam*, I, 85–9.

[13]'Abd Allāh b. al-'Abbās, see *The Pillars of Islam*, I, 86, n. 233.

[14]Pickthall 6:84–6.

of the Prophet in enmity to those for whom God has prescribed loving kindness and in opposition to those to whom God has prescribed obedience. We seek God's refuge from going astray and from following those ignorant in matters of religion.

God Himself declares them to be untruthful about the following point: Regarding God's Word: *If a man die childless and he have a sister, hers is half the heritage* (4:176),[15] they say that if a man dies leaving a son, then the sister obtains nothing, as God gives to her one-half if there is no son, but if there is a son, he has more right than her, and the whole goes to him. But if there is a daughter, she obtains one-half and the sister gets one-half.

We say, 'How is this? Is not the daughter [considered] a child (*walad*)? For according to you, without any difference of opinion, as respects God's Word: *And unto you belongeth a half of that which your wives leave, if they have no child (walad); but if they have a child then unto you the fourth of that which they leave, after any legacy they may have bequeathed, or debt (they may have contracted, hath been paid). And unto them belongeth the fourth of that which ye leave if ye have no child (walad), but if ye have a child then the eighth of that which ye leave* ... (4:12),[16] you deprive the husband of the half if the woman leaves a daughter surviving her, and the wife of the one-fourth if the man leaves a daughter surviving him. This is because she is [considered] a child (*walad*), as God says, and so in this context, according to you she is a child (*walad*). But with the sister she is not [considered] a child (*walad*). Such ignorance cannot be hidden and such contradiction does not escape a man of perception.

'Furthermore, they say in regard to the daughter's son, that it is not lawful for him to marry his mother's father's wife, for, verily, God says: *And marry not those women whom your fathers married* (4:22). It is not lawful for the grandfather to marry his daughter's son's wife on account of God's word: *And the wives of your sons who [spring] from your own loins* (4:23). Those who say that the evidence of a father concerning a son, and that of a son concerning the father is not permissible, also say that the evidence of a man regarding his mother's father is not legal, because he is a son. Similarly, they say that the evidence of a maternal grandfather, because he is a father, is not valid. So the son of a daughter is, according to you, in these cases, considered a child (*walad*), but he is not a child (*walad*) in inheritance. By this, you only intend to invalidate the claims of Ḥasan and Ḥusayn to be related to the Messenger of God by direct descent, and

[15]In Pickthall it is 4:177.

[16]In this verse, *walad* means either a male or female child or offspring. Ṭabarī, *Tafsīr*, VIII, 51–2; Ṭabrisī, II, 17. See also Ṭūsī, *al-Nihāya*, 640.

to repudiate the claims of the pure and rightly guided Imams descended from him, and you do this in a bold rejection of the Book of God and what comes from His Messenger.'

These are some of the things that God has shown to be falsehoods according to the utterances of their own tongues. [He has shown] their arguments to be against their own selves just as He has shown their opposition to the Book of God and to the practice of the Prophet, may God bless him and his progeny. There are many other things which, if we had described at length, would have increased the size of the book and would have gone beyond the limits set for it.

Jaʿfar b. Muḥammad: He said, 'The son's daughters, when there are no sons or daughters, stand in the same position as would the daughters.'[17]

[Jaʿfar b. Muḥammad]: Concerning a man who dies leaving a daughter, a son's son, and a son's daughter [the Imam] said, 'The whole estate belongs to the daughter, as she is nearest of kin.'[18]

[Jaʿfar b. Muḥammad]: Concerning a man who dies leaving a father and a son's son [the Imam] said, 'The father will get one-sixth and the residue will go to the son's son who represents his deceased father. Similarly, the son of a son or any male descendant thereafter, when there is no son nearer than him to the deceased, shall represent the son.

'He who is nearer excludes the more remote. Similarly, the descendants of the daughter are like the son (*walad*). When [the children of the daughter] coexist with the children of the son, the latter will get the share of their father, and the former will get the share of their mother, regardless of whether they are great or small in number and of whether they are male or female, because they are entitled to claim through the person they represent. Accordingly, if a man were to leave surviving him the daughter of a son and the son of a daughter, the son of a daughter will obtain one-third and the daughter of the son will obtain two-thirds.'

THE SHARES OF PARENTS WITH CHILDREN AND BROTHERS (*MĪRĀTH AL-WĀLIDAYN MAʿ AL-WALAD WA 'L-IKHWA*)

God says: *And if he have no son and his parents are his heirs, then to his mother appertaineth the third* (4:11).

[17]*Kāfī*, VII, 97.

[18]According to Abū Mūsā, in a case involving a daughter, a son's daughter, and a sister, the daughter gets half and the sister gets half. According to Ibn Masʿūd, the daughter gets half, the son's daughter a sixth, and what remains goes to the sister. *Mishkāt*, II, 152; Robson, I, 653.

Ja'far b. Muḥammad—his father—his ancestors—the Prophet: He said, 'If a man dies leaving his parents, his mother obtains a third and his father two-thirds.'[19]

God says: *And the parents (of the deceased) shall have each of them a sixth part of what he shall leave if he have a child* (4:11).[20] According to the principles stated above, God has named the parents in this place, given them their shares, and given the residue to the sons.

Ja'far b. Muḥammad: He said, 'If a man leaves behind his parents and a son, each of his parents obtains one-sixth and the residue goes to the son, i.e. two-thirds. If he leaves behind his parents and male and female children, then one-sixth goes to each of his parents and the remainder to his children with each male taking the share of two females.'[21]

[Ja'far b. Muḥammad]—his father—his ancestors—'Alī: The Messenger of God said, 'If a man leaves behind his parents and one daughter, the daughter gets three-fifths (three portions)[22] and the parents one-fifth each (a total of two portions),' i.e. the property should be divided into five parts, three of them go to the daughter and two to the parents.[23]

'If a man leaves behind a daughter and mother, the daughter receives three-fourths (three portions) and the mother one-fourth (one portion),' i.e. the property is to be divided into four portions, three to the daughter, and one to the mother. In the same manner, if the survivors are a daughter and a father, three potions should go to the daughter and one to the father.[24]

This is taken from the Scroll of Inheritance (*ṣaḥīfat al-farā'iḍ*). It was dictated by the Messenger of God and was in the handwriting of 'Alī.[25] As laid down by the Messenger of God, the *radd* (return or increase of shares) is [to be calculated] according to the fractional shares and not according to the original [share of] inheritance. The Messenger of God explained that the *radd* returns to the parents and children by reason of blood relationship. However, if the deceased leaves behind brothers, God has said: *If he have no son and his parents are his heirs, then to his mother appertaineth*

[19]*Kāfī*, VII, 100; Ṭūsī, *Tahdhīb al-aḥkām*, IX, 269, 270; idem, *al-Nihāya*, 624.

[20]Sale, *Koran*, 73. Ṭūsī, *al-Nihāya*, 624.

[21]Ṭūsī, *al-Nihāya*, 624.

[22]The Arabic expression is *thalāthat^{u} ashum^{in}*. *Sahm* pl. *ashum* is applied to a share or portion, whatever it may be. Testamentary disposition is generally divided into six or eight shares. The reason for it is that the least share decreed by the Qur'ān is one-eighth, the share of a widow with a child. *Majma' al-baḥrayn*, s.v. s-h-m.

[23]*Kāfī*, VII, 103; Ṭūṣī, *Tahdhīb al-aḥkām*, IX, 270, 272; idem, *al-Nihāya*, 624.

[24]Ṭūsī, *al-Nihāya*, 625.

[25]*Kāfī*, VII, 103; Ṭūṣī, *Tahdhīb al-aḥkām*, IX, 270. For the scroll, see *The Pillars of Islam*, I, 28, n. 50.

the third; and if he have brethren, then to his mother appertains the sixth (4:11). Therefore, the brothers deprive the mother of her third,[26] and as no part of the inheritance is named for the brothers, the residue goes to the father. This is proved by the Word of God: *If his parents are his heirs* (4:11).

Ja'far b. Muḥammad—his father—his ancestors—'Alī: The Messenger of God said, 'If a man leaves behind his parents, the mother gets one-third and the father two-thirds, as mentioned by God in His Book.[27]

'If the deceased has brothers, full or half (paternal), five-sixths goes to the father, and one-sixth to the mother. The share of the father has been increased to provide for his children when both the parents are heirs. However, the uterine brothers are not related to the father, hence, they do not inherit or deprive the mother of her third [i.e. decrease the share of the mother].[28]

'If a man dies leaving a mother, full brothers and sisters, paternal brothers and sisters, and uterine brothers and sisters, and the father is not alive, they do not inherit, nor do they deprive the mother of her share, because *kalāla*[29] cannot inherit[30] when a mother, father, son, or daughter survives. If any one of these four survives, *kalāla* do not inherit according to the Word of God: *Say: Allah hath pronounced for you concerning al-kalāla* (4:176).[31] Where there is a father, mother, son, or daughter, [*kalāla*], do not inherit; but a husband or wife always inherits.'

This is also from the Scroll of Inheritance mentioned before, and we

[26]Ṭūsī, *al-Nihāya*, 628–9.

[27]Ibid., 624.

[28]*Kāfī*, VII, 101.

[29]The word *kalāla* occurs twice in the Qur'ān in *Sūrat al-Nisā'* 4:12 and 4:176. There was an extensive debate about its precise meaning among the early exegetes of the Qur'ān. In his *Studies in Qur'an*, 23–8, 30–43, D. Powers has given a lengthy analysis of Ṭabarī's explanation and its elucidation in other sources. He contends that the generally accepted meaning of *kalāla* as distant kindred, or as other than one's parents or children is not correct and that it was projected back onto the Qur'ānic text because of the issue of political succession following the death of the Prophet. He asserts that *kalāla* is a loan word from another Semitic language and it signifies 'a daughter-in-law', i.e. a man's own wife or his son's wife. His proposed alternative reading of the consonantal Qur'ānic text of the second half of 4:12 would read as follows in translation: *If a man designates a daughter-in-law or wife as heir, and he has a brother or sister, each one of them [brother and sister] is entitled to one-sixth. If they [brother and sister] are more than that, they are partners with respect to one-third, after any legacy he bequeaths or debt, without injury.*

Strangely enough Ṭabrisī, II, 17, 149, states on the authority of the Imams, without citing the name of the Imam, that *kalāla* means brothers and sisters.

[30]*Kāfī*, VII, 101.

[31]In Pickthall 4:177.

have mentioned earlier the argument for the inheritance of the daughter rather than the sister or others in a similar position.

Ja'far b. Muḥammad: He said, 'If a man leaves behind two or more brothers, full or half (through the same father), or one full and one half (through the same father), they deprive the mother of her third. However, two or three sisters do not deprive the mother of her share. Not until there are four or more sisters, full or half (same father), or at least one brother and two sisters [does the mother become deprived of her share].'[32]

THE INHERITANCE OF SINGLE OR MULTIPLE SPOUSES (*MĪRĀTH AL-ZAWJAYN WAḤDIHIMĀ WA-MA' GHAYRIHIMĀ*)

God says: *And unto you belongeth a half of that which your wives leave, if they have no child; but if they have a child then unto you the fourth of that which they leave, after any legacy they may have bequeathed, or debt (they may have contracted, hath been paid). And unto them belongeth the fourth of that which ye leave if ye have no child, but if ye have a child then the eighth of that which ye leave, after any legacy ye have bequeathed, or debt (ye may have contracted, hath been paid)* (4:12). This is what God has Himself laid down in His Book as explanation and exposition.

Ja'far b. Muḥammad—his father: They said, 'Verily God has included the husband and the wife in [the compulsory] shares, and thus there can be no increase or decrease in their shares. The husband takes one-half or one-fourth always; and the wife, one-fourth or one-eighth.[33] There can be no decrease from the fourth of the husband or from the eighth of the wife, whoever may be the other heirs with them; or from his half or her fourth, if there be none.'

Abū Ja'far and Abū 'Abd Allāh: Concerning a man who dies leaving behind his wife and parents, [the Imams] said, 'The wife will get one-fourth, the mother one-third, and the father, the residue.'[34]

[Abū Ja'far and Abū 'Abd Allāh]: [The two Imams] mentioned a decision from the Scroll of Inheritance dictated by the Messenger of God and written down by 'Alī. If a woman dies leaving behind her husband and her parents, the husband will get one-half (three shares), the mother one-third (two shares), and the father one-sixth (one share).[35]

[32]*Kāfī*, VII, 101, 102; Ṭūsī, *al-Nihāya*, 630.

[33]*Kāfī*, VII, 92.

[34]The estate should be divided as follows: 3/12 to the wife, 4/12 to the mother, and 5/12 to the father. Ṭūsī, *al-Nihāya*, 625.

[35]*Kāfī*, VII, 107, 108; Ṭūṣī, *al-Nihāya*, 627.

It was said to Abū 'Abd Allāh [Imam al-Ṣādiq], 'How does the mother get a greater share than the father?' He said, 'Do you not see that in one case, the father gets five-sixths and the mother one-sixth? This is laid down by God's manifest command, because He prescribed one-half for the husband, one-fourth for the wife, and one-third for the mother, but did not lay down anything for the father. Consequently, he gets the residue.'

THE INHERITANCE OF BROTHERS, GRANDFATHER, AND GRANDMOTHER (*MĪRĀTH AL-IKHWA WA 'L-JADD WA 'L-JADDA*)

God says: *They ask thee for a pronouncement. Say: Allah hath pronounced for you concerning al-kalāla* (4:176).[36]

Ja'far b. Muḥammad—his father—his ancestors: They said, 'Concerning the last verse of *Sūrat al-Nisā'* (Women)—*They ask thee for a pronouncement. Say: Allah hath pronounced for you concerning al-kalāla. If a man dies childless and he have a sister, hers is half the heritage and he (the deceased) would have inherited from her had she died childless. And if there be two sisters, then theirs are two-thirds of the heritage, and if they be brethren, men and women, unto the male is the equivalent of the shares of two females* (4:176),[37] their shares increase or decrease between them. The same is the rule with sons and daughters who get a greater or lesser portion [according to circumstances].'

Ja'far b. Muḥammad: Concerning God's Word: *And if a man designates a daughter-in-law (kalāla) or wife as heir, and he has a brother or sister, then each one of them is entitled to one-sixth. If they are more than that, they are partners with respect to one-third* (4:12),[38] [Imam al-Ṣādiq] said that this verse relates to a uterine brother or sister. This is mentioned as an explanation of God's decision in His Book.

I have mentioned in the earlier part of [this chapter] that brothers or sisters of any sort, do not inherit with the father, the son, [the son's son],[39] the mother, or the daughter, and that they inherit only when they [the latter] do not coexist. If full, half (paternal), and uterine brothers and sisters coexist, the half (paternal) brothers and sisters are excluded. If there

[36]In Pickthall 4:177. Ṭūsī, *Tahdhīb al-aḥkām*, IX, 319.

[37]In Pickthall 4:177.

[38]I have adopted an alternative reading as suggested by Powers. See n. 2, Chap. 14, and n. 1 and 29 in this chapter.

[39]Additions in MS Q, and gloss in MS S from Nu'mān's *Mukhtaṣar al-āthār*.

are no full brothers or sisters, the half (paternal) brothers and sisters inherit in their place.[40]

'Alī: He said, 'The Messenger of God decided that relations by full blood (*awlād al-a'yān*)[41] have precedence over relations by half blood (*banu ' l-'allāt*);[42] thus full brothers and sisters are nearer than half (paternal) brothers and sisters, and they exclude the latter brothers and sisters [from inheritance]. Similarly, full brothers exclude half (paternal) brothers.'

Ja'far b. Muḥammad: He said, 'If a man dies leaving behind full, half (paternal), and uterine brothers, the uterine brothers get the one-third mentioned by God, and the residue [two-thirds] goes to the full brothers, half (paternal) brothers being excluded. Among uterine brothers and sisters, males and females share the one-third equally; and the full brothers and sisters share their inheritance with the male getting twice the shares of the female.[43]

'If [a man dies] leaving a uterine brother, a uterine sister, a half (paternal) brother, and a full sister, the uterine brother and sister get one-third and share it equally, the full sister gets one-half as well as the residue, and the half (paternal) brother and sister are excluded.'

'Alī, Abū Ja'far, and Abū 'Abd Allāh: They related from the Scroll of Inheritance dictated by the Messenger of God and written by the hand of 'Alī: The grandfather stands in the same position as the full brother;[44] he has the same position as one of the males. This is what is well known as reported from 'Alī among the (select) *khāṣṣa* and the (commonalty) *'āmma*. That the grandfather is of the same degree as the brother may be shown in respect of his nearness of kinship with a common ancestor (*qu'dad*)[45] [i.e. the father] of the deceased. (The brother) is related to the deceased's father as the son, while (the grandfather), as the father. Both of them are equal in nearness to the father, and the relationship

[40]For the inheritance of brothers and sisters, see Ṭūsī, *al-Nihāya*, 635–40; various hypothetical cases are cited.

[41]*Awlād al-a'yān* means the sons of the same father and mother. Lane, s.v. '-l-l.

[42]*Banu 'l-'allāt* means the sons of one father by different mothers. Lane, s.v. '-l-l. '... the sons of the same mother (*a'yān bani 'l-umm*) inherit from one another, but not the sons of one father by different mothers (*banu 'l-'allāt*). A man inherits from his brother who has the same father and mother, but not from his brother who has the same father but a different mother.' *Mishkāt*, II, 151; Robson, I, 652.

[43]Cf. *Kāfī*, VII, 119–20.

[44]Ibid., VII, 117–19; Ṭūsī, *al-Nihāya*, 650.

[45]*Qu'dad* or *qu'dud* signifies nearness of relationship, a man near in lineage to the chief, or oldest ancestor of a family or tribe. *Al-Mīrāth al-qu'dud*, the inheritance of him who is nearest of kin to the deceased. Lane, s.v. q-'-d.

is the same [i.e. one generation], one being the son, and the other the father.

Those who oppose us rely on the doctrine of Abū Bakr[46] when he gave the grandfather the same position as the father. They argued about the expressions in the Qur'ān: 'O *Children of Adam*,'[47] or 'O *Children of Israel*,'[48] or '*the creed of your father Abraham*,'[49] and said, 'When all mankind is descended from Adam, he is their father.' He who is endowed with intelligence will perceive that people do not inherit in this manner; God has given them inheritance by descent and relationship and not by names [which are metaphorical].

God says: *The believers indeed are brothers* (49:10),[50] but they do not inherit one another by such a nomenclature unless they are descended from a single man or woman. Our opponents cannot escape this [reasoning]. If people inherit from one another by such a nomenclature, on the condition that Adam is their father, then not a single mother will ever inherit her full share of one-third, because the deceased has left behind many so-called brothers.

Similarly, God says: *The Prophet has a greater right (awlā-bi) over the believers than their selves, and his wives are their mothers* (33:6).[51] From this nomenclature, none of the wives of the Prophet inherit from any one of the faithful. Similarly, God says: ... *and your foster-mothers, and your foster-sisters* (4:23). None of them inherits by this name. Thus, it is clear that inheritance can only be taken by blood relationship[52] and nearness,[53] and not merely by names which have a metaphorical significance and interpretation.

Ja'far b. Muḥammad: Once he opened the Scroll of Inheritance dictated by the Messenger of God and written by the hand of 'Alī, and the first thing he saw was: The son of a brother and the grandfather share the inheritance equally.[54]

Abū Ja'far and Abū 'Abd Allāh: They said, 'The son of a brother

[46]Abū Bakr, see *The Pillars of Islam*, I, 22, n. 15; 49, 50, 51, 52, 475.

[47]Qur'ān 7:26, 27, 31, 35.

[48]Qur'ān 2:40, 47, 122; 61:6.

[49]Qur'ān 22:78.

[50]Arberry, *Koran*, II, 231.

[51]All the translators have rendered the word *awlā* in this verse as 'closer' or 'nearer'. *Awlā-bi* means worthier, more deserving, or more suitable.

[52]The Arabic term is *ansāb* pl. of *nasab* meaning lineage, kinship.

[53]The Arabic term is *qarāba* meaning kinship, relation.

[54]*Kāfī*, VII, 121; Ṭūsī, *al-Nihāya*, 651–2.

and the grandfather are in the same position and both of them share the property equally. If someone says, "This contradicts what we have given as an illustration, cannot be deducted from the verses which are revealed in regard to the inheritance of the grandfather, and goes beyond the limits." He should be told, "Both of the rules have come down from the Messenger of God and God has said: *And whatsoever the Messenger [of God] giveth you, take it. And whatsoever he forbiddeth, abstain (from it)* (59:7). Therefore, there can be no objection to the Book or the *sunna*, and what is demanded of them is acceptance and submission. God says: *But nay, by thy Lord, they will not believe (in truth) until they make thee judge of what is in dispute between them and find within themselves no dislike of that which thou decidest, and submit with full submission* (4:65).'"

Ja'far b. Muḥammad: He said, 'The paternal grandfather and the paternal grandmother take the inheritance when there is no other heir; and similarly, so do the maternal grandfather and the maternal grandmother. If they all coexist, the maternal grandfather and grandmother get the mother's one-third share and the paternal grandfather and grandmother take the father's two-thirds share. Males take the share of two females.[55] If there is only one claimant on the maternal side, and two on the paternal side, or two claimants on the maternal side, each one of them receives the share of the person through whom the heir claims, one-third to the maternal side, whether there be one or two heirs, and two-thirds to the paternal side, in the same manner. The nearer grandparents exclude the more remote. The inheritance returns to one of them as it returns to all remote kindred when there are no others [nearer than them].'

The Messenger of God: Once he gave one-sixth to the [paternal] grandmother even though the son was living.[56] He saw the children dividing the estate and felt compassion for her, and gave her one-sixth which then became a compulsory share for her. God says: *And whatsoever the Messenger [of God] giveth you, take it. And whatsoever he forbiddeth, abstain (from it)* (59:7). This is what we have said before and there can be no objection to the Book and the *sunna*.

[55]Ṭūsī, *al-Nihāya*, 648.

[56]*Kāfī*, VII, 122–3. Ibn Mas'ūd said about a case where there was a grandmother and her son, that she was the first grandmother to whom God's Messenger gave a sixth which was not due to her having a son who was still alive. *Mishkāt*, II, 153; Robson I, 654. Another tradition, cited before the latter, states that when a grandmother came to Abū Bakr asking him for her share of an estate, he told her that nothing was prescribed for her in God's Book or in the *sunna* of God's Messenger, but asked her to go home till he had questioned the people.

THE INHERITANCE OF AGNATES, COGNATES, AND OTHER KINDRED (*MAWĀRĪTH DHAWI 'L-ARḤĀM*[57] *WA 'L-'AṢABĀT*[58] *WA 'L-QARĀBĀT*)[59]

Ja'far b. Muḥammad: Concerning God's Word: *And unto each We have appointed heirs (mawālī) of that which parents and near kindred (al-aqrabūna) leave* (4:33), he said, 'By these, He meant blood relations (*ūlu 'l-arḥām*) in the inheritances and did not mean the benefactors (or possessors of *walā'*, *awliyā' al-ni'ma*).[60] The first of them are those who are more closely related to the deceased by kinship (*aqrabuhum bi 'l-raḥim*). This is what causes the inheritance to go to them.'[61]

[Ja'far b. Muḥammad]—his father—his ancestors—the Messenger of God: He forbade that the property of a deceased person who had a paternal or maternal aunt surviving him should escheat to the Public Treasury.

Abū Ja'far: He said, 'Your son is nearer to you than your son's son; your son's son is nearer to you than your brother's son; your full brother's son is nearer to you than your half (paternal) brother's son; your half (paternal) brother's son is nearer to you than your paternal uncle; your full paternal uncle is nearer to you than your half paternal uncle; the son of your full paternal uncle is nearer to you than the son of your half paternal uncle.'[62]

[57]*Dhawu 'l-arḥām* or *ūlu 'l-arḥām* (Qur'ān 8:75; 33:6) means the relations by the women's side (or on the maternal side). In Islamic law, it means any relations that have no portion of the inheritances termed *farā'iḍ* and are not such heirs as are designated by *'aṣaba* with respect to the *farā'iḍ*. Lane, s.v. r-ḥ-m.

[58]See n. 7 above in this chapter.

[59]*Qarāba* generally signifies relationship on the female side. Lane, s.v. q-r-b. *Qarāba*, kinship, has the meaning of closeness, proximity. As a technical term, it seems to be of post-Hijra usage. The Qur'ān uses *dhu 'l-qurbā*, *dhawu 'l-qurbā*, and *ūlu 'l-qurbā*. Kinship itself is not clearly defined. Uterine siblings, in a patriarchal society, are not part of the family and hence have no inheritance rights. In the absence of direct heirs, however, they inherit. *EI*², s.v. Ḳarāba.

[60]Abū 'Abd Allāh [Imam al-Ṣādiq] said, "Alī did not claim the inheritance of any of his emancipated slaves (*mawālīhi*) if they left behind any relative.' *Kāfī*, VII, 143; Ṭūṣī, *Tahdhīb al-aḥkām*, IX, 328–9.

[61]*Kāfī*, VII, 86. See also Ṭūṣī, *al-Nihāya*, 652–62; various situations are considered.

[62]'Your son is nearer to you than your son's son; your son's son is nearer to you than your brother; your full brother is nearer to you than your half (paternal) brother; your half (paternal) brother is nearer to you than your uterine brother; your full brother's son is nearer to you than your half (paternal) brother's son; your half (paternal) brother's son is nearer to you than your paternal uncle; your full paternal uncle is nearer to you than your half paternal uncle; your half paternal uncle is nearer to you than your uterine paternal uncle; your cousin from your full paternal uncle is nearer to you than your cousin from your

'Alī: He decided about paternal and maternal aunts thus: To the paternal aunt he gave two-thirds; and to the maternal aunt, one-third.[63] He gave inheritance to blood relations (*dhawu 'l-arḥām*) in preference to the possessors of *walā'* (*mawālī*).

Ja'far b. Muḥammad: He gave inheritance to the maternal and paternal uncles and aunts as follows: the maternal uncle and aunt, one-third, to be shared equally by the male and the female; the paternal uncle and aunt, two-thirds, with two shares going to the male and one share to the female. The descendants of such uncles and aunts will represent their parents.

If the surviving relations are a maternal uncle's son, a paternal uncle, and a paternal aunt, the uncle and aunt will inherit as they have a greater right to the inheritance.

If the surviving relations are paternal uncle's sons and daughters and maternal uncles and aunts, then the maternal uncles and aunts or any one of these will inherit, and the paternal uncle's sons will be excluded.

If a man dies leaving behind a paternal uncle's son and a paternal uncle's daughter; or a brother's son and a brother's daughter, all of these by the same father (thus, full or half paternal), they all inherit, and each male shall take the share of two females. If the heirs are descendants of different brothers, each of the heirs will represent their father, the nearest excluding the more remote; and agnates and cognates, whether male or female, will inherit equally according to their nearness in degree.[64]

[Ja'far b. Muḥammad]: He said, 'Inheritance is transferred first [to those specified in] the Book, then to those that are nearer in degree (*al-aqrab*), [and then to others] according to the general statement in the Book: *And those who are related by consanguinity (ūlu 'l-arḥām) shall be deemed the nearest of kin to each other according to the Book of* God (8:75).[65] Everyone who is entitled to inherit is distinguished by nearness in degree of relationship from him who is not. They obtain their rights by representation through intervening relations. According to the law of reversion, [the remainder of the property] returns to the heir just as it returns to the person through whom he is making his claim.'

Abū Ja'far: He said, 'He for whom a prescribed share of inheritance

---

half paternal uncle; your cousin from your half paternal uncle is nearer to you than your cousin from your uterine paternal uncle.' *Kāfī*, VII, 86.

[63] *Kāfī*, VII, 128; Ṭūṣī, *Tahdhīb al-aḥkām*, IX, 324–5; the same rule.

[64] See *Kāfī*, VII, 129–32; various hypothetical survivors and their shares are enumerated.

[65] Sale, *Koran*, 177. See n. 7 in this chapter.

(*farīḍa*) is mentioned [in the Qur'ān], has a greater right to it than he who is not mentioned,[66] and the agnates (*'aṣabāt*) have no special rights when coexisting with cognates (*dhawu 'l-arḥām*).'

'Alī: He said, 'The Messenger of God forbade that any agnatic heir should inherit when there is a child or grandchild of either gender.'

THE QUANTUM OF SHARES AND THEIR UNJUST CHANGE BY *'AWL* (*MABLAGH AL-SIHĀM WA-TAJWĪRUHĀ MIN AL-'AWL*)[67]

Ja'far b. Muḥammad—his father—his ancestors—the Messenger of God: In the Scroll which he dictated to 'Alī and is written by the hand of 'Alī,

[66] *Kāfī*, VII, 86–7.

[67] *'Awl* lit. means 'deviation by excess' from the prescribed limits of the primary portions of the *farīḍa*, which are all fractional shares allotted to the Qur'ānic heirs. Given this situation, the fractions taken together may be (i) equal to the whole, or (ii) more than the whole, or (iii) less than the whole. Cases of the first category occur rarely and no difficulty arises.

In cases that equal more than the whole anomaly arises as the fractions allotted to the Qur'ānic heirs should not amount to more than the whole. In order to resolve this anomaly, *'awl* is practised, i.e. artificial inflation of the denominator to make it equal to the sum of the numerators. Its real effect is the proportionate reduction of each share. For instance, if a woman dies leaving a widower and two full sisters, the share of the widower would be 1/2, that of the two full sisters 2/3. The total of these fractions, reducing them to a common denominator is 3/6 + 4/6 = 7/6. The anomaly is resolved by increasing the denominator to make it equal to the sum of the numerators—individual numerators remaining the same—thus, proportionately decreasing the share of each heir. The artificial inflation of the denominator is called *'awl*. The share of the husband will, therefore, reduce to 3/7 and that of the two full sisters to 4/7 respectively. Another example is where a woman is survived by her husband, father, mother, and two daughters. The appropriate quota shares are: 1/4 for the husband, 1/6 each to both father and mother, and 2/3 for the two sisters. But these shares add up (1/4 + 1/6 + 1/6 + 2/3 = 3/12 + 2/12 + 2/12 + 8/12) to an aggregate of 15/12, i.e. three to the husband, two each to the parents, and eight to the daughters. Hence, the shares are reduced to unity by the expedient of making the total numerator 15 into the new denominator. Thus, the husband gets 3/15, the parents 2/15 each, and the daughters 8/15 between them.

This particular problem is called *al-mas'ala al-minbariyya*. It is ascribed to 'Alī who is reported to have solved it off-hand when it was submitted to him while he was on the *minbar* (pulpit). The *'awl* is accepted by all the Sunnī schools of law. The Ibāḍīs (Khawārij) recognize it, but they (like Nu'mān) ascribe its introduction to 'Umar b. al-Khaṭṭāb. The Shī'a, both the Ismā'īlīs and the Twelvers, reject it. They assert that the Qur'ānic quota shares should not be regarded as piecemeal reforms to be superimposed on the pre-Islamic agnatic system but as the foundation for the new Islamic system. The agnates, therefore, have no priority over cognates. In his *Studies in Qur'an*, D. Powers has cogently argued that the Qur'ānic inheritance legislation was a complete system of inheritance, both for testate and intestate succession, replacing the pre-Islamic tribal customary law. He also

he said, 'The [Qur'ānic] shares do not deviate [by excess] from the limit of the designated portions (*anna 'l-sihām lā ta'ūl*).'[68]

Abū Ja'far and Abū 'Abd Allāh: They said, 'The man who knows the numbers of [sand dunes collected together at] Raml 'Ālij,[69] knows that the shares of the Qur'ānic heirs (*al-farā'iḍ*) do not change (*lam ta'ul*).' They also said, 'The shares (*sihām* pl. of *sahm*) do not vary (*lā ta'ūl*), and are not more than six.'[70] The meaning of what the two [Imams] said is that the shares—as mentioned by God in His Book—do not exceed six.

The greatest size of a share is two-thirds, and it is God's saying: ... *and if there be women [daughters] more than two, then theirs is two-thirds of the inheritance* (4:11). Also, like the share of the father [when he inherits along] with the mother as indicated in the Word of God ... (*and if he have no son*) *and his parents are his heirs, then to his mother appertaineth the third* (4:11), thus proving that two-thirds belong to the father.

The next largest share is one-half. It is [specified in] the Word of God: *And if there be one [daughter only], then the half* (4:11); and His saying: *And unto you belongeth a half of that which your wives leave* (4:12).

The next largest share is one-third. That is [specified in] the Word of God: *(and if he have no son and his parents are his heirs), then to his mother appertaineth the third* (4:11), and ... *if they be more than two [brother and sister], then they shall be sharers in the third* (4:12).

The next size share is one-fourth. That is [specified in] God's saying: ... *but if they [your wives] have a child, then unto you the fourth* .... *And unto them [your wives] belongeth the fourth of that which ye leave if ye have no child* (4:12).

---

refuted 'the superimposition theory' advanced by Marçais and subsequently accepted by most legal historians. The Shī'a further claim that their system of inheritance is more Islamic and more in line with the Qur'ānic instructions than that of the Sunnīs.

Radd, the contrary of *'awl*, is applied to cases where the sum total of the fractions of the Qur'ānic heirs is less than the whole and there are no agnatic heirs to take the residue. The residue thus returns to the Qur'ānic heirs in proportion to their shares and is called *radd*, return. Ḥanafīs, most Shāfi'īs, and Ḥanbalīs agree in this regard. The Mālikīs, on the other hand, make no provision for the return to quota shares, rather they give the remainder to *bayt al-māl*. See also n. 4 above in this chapter. Lane, s.v. '-w-l; *EI*[2], s.v. 'Awl; Fyzee, *Outlines*, 416–18; Anderson, *Islamic Law*, 65–6.

[68]*Kāfī*, VII, 90; Ṭūsī, *Tahdhīb al-aḥkām*, IX, 247–8; Ḥillī, *Sharā'i' al-islām*, II, 184–5; the principle of *'awl* is rejected.

[69]*Raml 'Ālij* is a mountain range stretching from Wādī al-Qurā and Taymā' in the Ḥijāz to al-Dahnā', between Yamāma and Basra. *Raml 'Ālij* is metaphorically used for most of Arabia which is surrounded by desert. Bakrī, *Mu'jam*, III, 178–9 (s.v. 'Ālij); *Lisān al-'Arab*, s.v. '-l-j; *Majma' al-baḥrayn*, s.v. '-l-j.

[70]*Kāfī*, VII, 90–1.

The next size share is one-sixth. That is [specified in] God's saying: ... *And to each of his parents a sixth of the inheritance* (4:11), and His saying ... *and if he have brethren, then to his mother appertaineth the sixth* (4:11), and His saying: ... *and he have a brother or a sister (only on the mother's side, then) to each of them twain (the brother and the sister) the sixth* (4:12).

The smallest size share is one-eighth. It is [mentioned in] the Word of God: *But if ye have a child, then [to the widow] the eighth (of that which ye leave* (4:12).

These are the [fractions of] shares mentioned by God in His Book, not one-ninth, one-seventh, or one-fifth. The possessors of the Qur'ānic shares (*sahm*) are six: first, the children; second, the father; third, the mother; fourth, the relations of the father; fifth the relations of the mother; sixth, the spouses. This is how the Qur'ānic shares (*farā'iḍ*) are determined and God knows better. If there were a share for one in preference to the others, He would have mentioned him/her and so also his/her share.

Apart from this, it is mentioned that the first who unjustly altered the Qur'ānic shares (*man a'āl al-farā'iḍ*) was 'Umar b. al-Khaṭṭāb.[71] When the people qualified in the law of descent and distribution of the shares (*ahl al-farā'iḍ*) came to him and with differing opinions, 'Umar said, 'By God, I do not know which of you is given precedence by God and which of you is deferred. I find nothing better (*awsa' min*) than to distribute the property by [changing the denominator] according to the portions of the sum (*bi 'l-ḥiṣaṣ*).' Hence, everyone's designated share was unjustly altered by *'awl*.

It is said that the first who did this was Zayd b. Thābit,[72] but whichever of the two did it should not be followed, as he was ignorant of the Book of God and the practice (*sunna*) of the Prophet.

'Alī, Abū Ja'far, and Abū 'Abd Allāh: They distributed the Qur'ānic

[71]See *The Pillars of Islam*, I, 22, n. 16; for his lack of legal knowledge and references to it, see ibid., index.

[72]Zayd b. Thābit al-Anṣārī al-Khazrajī plays the central role in all the traditions about the collection of the Qur'ān. He is also described by Ibn Sa'd as the most knowledgeable about *al-farā'iḍ* (inheritance). He acquired the art of writing from a prisoner of Badr. 'Abd Allāh b. Mas'ūd, one of the famous collectors of the Qur'ān, bragging about his own *qirā'a* (reading of the Qur'ān) is reported to have said, 'I received seventy some *sūras* directly from the mouth of the Messenger of God while Zayd was a young boy playing with his mates.' He died in 45/665–6. Ibn Sa'd, II/1, 14; II/II, 105, 109–10, 112–13, 115–17; Ibn Ḥajar, *al-Iṣāba*, I, 561–2; *EI*², s.v. Zayd b.Thābit. Although the first chronologically arranged version of the Qur'ān is attributed to 'Alī, and his knowledge of the Book and the *sunna* aided the caliphs in resolving various legal problems, he was not included in the committee charged with the task of collecting the Qur'ān.

shares according to the Book of God without unjustly altering them as did those who held *'awl* to be permissible. That is because they began with the heir mentioned first by God and gave him priority, and placed the heir later whom God had placed later; and they did not drop any heir to a lower rank than that to which God Himself dropped him.

An example of that is as follows: A woman died leaving behind her husband, uterine brothers, and a half (paternal) sister. Abū Ja'far [Imam al-Bāqir] said, 'The husband gets one-half, i.e. three shares, the uterine brothers [one-third],[73] i.e. two shares, and the half (paternal) sister gets the residue, one share, (i.e. one-sixth).' It was said to him, 'Those who held the principle of *'awl* gave three shares to the half (paternal) sister and changed three-sixths to three-eighths.' Abū Ja'far said, 'Why did they do so?' They said, 'God says: *[If a man die childless] and he have a sister, hers is half the heritage.*' (4:176).[74] Abū Ja'far replied, 'If the sister were a brother?' They said, 'He would get one-sixth only.' [The Imam] said, 'Why do they decrease the share of the brother and not that of the sister when he has been given more? For the sister, God says: *hers is half the heritage* (4:176), whereas for the brother, God says: ... *and he would have inherited from her [had she died childless* (4:176), i.e. all of the property. Thus, they give to the residuary, whom God gave all the property, no more than one-sixth, and give the full one-half to the one entitled to only one-half.'

There are many examples of this principle, and if we were to discuss them [fully], the book would become lengthy. Accordingly, we have mentioned only that part of the argument which pertains to the diminution of the share by *'awl* and the principle of unjust change in shares resulting from its application. This is sufficient, God willing.

PERSONS WHO CAN LAWFULLY INHERIT AND THOSE WHO CANNOT DO SO (*MAN YAJŪZ AN YARITH WA-MAN LĀ MĪRĀTH LAHU*)

We have mentioned in the Book [Chapter] of Divorce, the inheritance of children who were not acknowledged as legitimate (*ibn al-mulā'ana*).[75]

Ja'far b. Muḥammad—his father—his ancestors[76]—'Alī: The

[73]According to MS Q. *Al-thulth* is missing in the edited text, as well as the pirated text of A. Tāmir.

[74]It is 4:177 in Pickthall.

[75]See Chap. 11, section '*Li'ān*,' in this book. *Kāfī*, VII, 170–3; Ṭūsī, *Tahdhīb al-aḥkām*, IX, 338–43.

[76]According to MS Q, and a variant in Fyzee's MS Y. In the edited text: his grandfather.

Messenger of God laid the responsibility of paying the blood money of the illegitimate child (*walad al-zinā'*) on the people of the mother's group. Therefore, it is the mother and the relations claiming through her that inherit from him.[77]

Ja'far b. Muḥammad: He said, 'The foundling (*al-laqīṭ*) cannot be inherited, nor can he inherit from his parents. However, if he happens to have a child, the child inherits from him. A foundling inherits and can be inherited on the ground of affinity through marriage.'[78]

[Ja'far b. Muḥammad]: He said, 'If, during one period of purity, both the owner and another man have sexual intercourse with one slave girl and a child is born, it is not lawful for the owner [of the slave girl] to sell the child. The child is a portion of his inheritance.[79]

'If a woman is divorced by a man and marries before the *'idda* has expired, and a child is born to her within six months [of the marriage], the child belongs to the first husband, but if it is born after six months then it belongs to the second husband.'

[Ja'far b. Muḥammad]: He used to give inheritance to the acknowledged kinsman (*ḥamīl*).[80] A *ḥamīl* is a person born in a non-Islamic country (*balad al-shirk*), but his kinship is recognized and acknowledged by some persons in the country of Islam (*dār al-islām*),[81] until they die, then they inherit from one another on this basis.

The same principle applies to persons coming from distant lands whose pedigrees are unknown, but are acknowledged as kinsmen by some persons among them. One of them says, 'This is my brother, son, uncle, cousin, etc.' On the basis of mutual acknowledgement, their kinship is established and proved even though the people [of *dār al-islām*] have not witnessed the marriage of the spouses, known of the acknowledgement of their parents, or witnessed their living together or the birth of children.

[77] *Kāfī*, VII, 174–5; Ṭūsī, *Tahdhīb al-aḥkām*, IX, 344–5. The traditions are contradictory. The consensus seems to be that the illegitimate child neither inherits nor is inherited by his parents. His legacy goes either to one who stands guarantee for his offence or to the Imam of the Muslims.

[78] 'A woman gets inheritance from the following three: one she has set free (*'atīqahā*), a foundling (*laqīṭahā*), and her child whose paternity is the subject of mutual imprecation (*mulā'ana*).' *Mishkāt*, II, 150; Robson, I, 651.

[79] Cf. *Kāfī*, VII, 176, for a slightly different version.

[80] *Ḥamīl*, one who is carried as a child from the country of the unbelievers to that of Islam, and who is therefore not allowed to inherit without evidence. The woman who carried the child should say that it is her son, relation, or kinsman, in the territory of the unbelievers. Lane, s.v. ḥ-m-l. See also *Kāfī*, VII, 177–8; they inherit by their own testimony.

[81] For the concept of *dār al-islām*, see n. 312, Chap. 10.

[Their kinship is established even though] their kinship is not known beyond general repute.

'Alī, Abū Ja'far, and Abū 'Abd Allāh: They said, 'A newborn child, if born alive, can inherit and be inherited, whether he cries at birth (*istahalla*)[82] or not. [He is considered alive if] life can be seen through his movement, breathing and similar indications.[83] It is possible that the child cries only when it suffers pain, and occasionally, the child never suffers pain before death.' Abū 'Abd Allāh [Imam al-Ṣādiq] said, 'He may also be dumb.'[84]

Ja'far b. Muḥammad:[85] He said, 'The Muslim inherits from the unbeliever (*al-kāfir*), but the unbeliever does not inherit from the Muslim.[86] The unbelievers are entitled only to inherit from one another.' He was told, 'The people relate from the Prophet that he said, "The people of two different communities (*ahlu millatayn*) do not inherit from one another."'[87] Abū 'Abd Allāh [Imam al-Ṣādiq] said, 'We inherit from them, but they do not inherit from us; for Islam primarily increased the Muslim's right.'[88]

The reply of Abū 'Abd Allāh[89] [Imam al-Ṣādiq] confirms the saying of the Messenger of God because the latter's saying, 'People of two communities do not inherit from each other' is not contrary to what [the Imam] Abū 'Abd Allāh said, 'We inherit from them but they do not inherit

[82] *Istahalla 'l-ṣabīyu bi 'l-bukā'* means that the child raised its voice and cried at birth. *Lisān al-'Arab*, s.v. h-l-l.

[83] 'When an infant has raised its voice [and then dies], prayer is offered over it and it is treated as an heir.' The position in such a case is that when the heir of someone who has died is expecting a child, the division of the property must not be made till the child is born. If the child lives long enough to cry or to raise its voice, it is entitled to a share in the inheritance. *Mishkāt*, II, 149; Robson, I, 651. 'If a man dies leaving behind his pregnant wife who delivers a son, but he dies soon thereafter and the midwife testifies that the child cried when he was born and died later, her testimony is approved for one-fourth inheritance of the child.' *Kāfī*, VII, 166. See also Ṭūsī, *Tahdhīb al-aḥkām*, IX, 391.

[84] *Kāfī*, VII, 166; Ṭūsī, *Tahdhīb al-aḥkām*, IX, 391–2.

[85] In the edited text: *wa 'anhu 'an Ja'far b. Muḥammad.* It seems to me that originally it was: *wa 'anhu*, referring to Abū 'Abd Allāh, however, it could also refer to 'Alī. In order to remove the ambiguity of the referent, the scribe might have added *'an Ja'far b. Muḥammad* in the margin or above *wa 'anhu* and later on the scribes might have added it to the text. In MS Q: *qāla Abū Ja'far Muḥammad.*

[86] 'A Muslim may not inherit from an infidel or an infidel from a Muslim.' Transmitted by Bukhārī and Muslim. *Mishkāt*, II, 148; Robson, I, 650. *Kāfī*, VII, 152; Ṭūsī, *Tahdhīb al-aḥkām*, IX, 366; the same position as that of Nu'mān.

[87] 'People of two different religions may not inherit from one another.' *Mishkāt*, II, 149; Robson, I, 651.

[88] *Kāfī*, VII, 152; Ṭūsī, *Tahdhīb al-aḥkām*, IX, 366–7.

[89] Addition in MS Q: Ja'far b. Muḥammad.

from us.' This is because the words of the Messenger of God, 'These people do not inherit *mutually*' do not differ from what Abū 'Abd Allāh [Imam al-Ṣādiq] said, 'The Muslim inherits from the unbeliever, but the unbeliever does not inherit from the Muslim.'

The meaning of *yatawārathu* and its import is determined by the grammatical form *yatafā'alu* [form VI].[90] The form *yatafā'alu* cannot be used unless it has at least two subjects, nor can it be used when one person does a thing but not the other. If a man beats another, you say *ḍaraba fulānun fulānan* (so-and-so beat so-and-so), but you do not say *taḍārabā* until each one of them beats the other. This is the grammatical rule regarding the form *mufā'ala* in the Arabic language as affirmed by the philologists. This will be clear to anyone who thinks and is endowed with intelligence.

'Alī, Abū Ja'far, and Abū 'Abd Allāh: Concerning a freed slave or an unbeliever who becomes a Muslim before the distribution of the inheritance, they said, 'They have their rights in the inheritance, even if the emancipation or acceptance of Islam happens after the death of the deceased, but before the distribution of the estate. However, if the estate already has been distributed, then they have no right.'[91]

'Alī: He used to give inheritance to the Zoroastrian (*al-Majūsī*)[92] in two ways. The meaning of this is that if a Zoroastrian were to marry his own daughter[93] and a son was born to her, and then they became Muslims, the woman would be the mother as well as the sister of the son; and both wife and daughter of the man.[94]

[90]The sixth form *tafā'ala* is the reflexive (*muṭāwi'*) of the third form and implies reciprocity. Wright, *Grammar*, I, 38–40.

[91]Ṭūsī, *Tahdhīb al-aḥkām*, IX, 369; they inherit if they embraced Islam before the distribution of the estate. Cf. *Mishkāt*, II, 153; Robson, I, 654.

[92]See *The Pillars of Islam*, I, 221, n. 257; 469, n. 168. The Urdu translator did not render this passage. In his *Kitāb al-majālis*, 477, Nu'mān reports that an Ismā'īlī *dā'ī* had won a large number of Zoroastrians for the *da'wa* in an Eastern part of the 'Abbāsid empire, while they were still keeping their religion. He allowed them to follow their earlier customs which contravene Islamic laws, such as marriage with close female relatives of a man.

[93]Xvétōdāt, a next-of-kin marriage, namely with a sister, daughter, or mother, which existed from remote antiquity, was still a living practice within the Mazdean community during the fourth/tenth century as attested by Nu'mān's report in the preceding note. For more details see *Dénkart*, book III, 85–90; de Menasce, 'Zoroastrian Literature'; Frye, 'Zoroastrian Incest'. I am thankful to my colleague Professor M. Morony for guiding me to these references. See also Abū Tammām, *Bāb al-Shayṭān*, 118–19.

[94]''Alī used to give inheritance to a Zoroastrian married to his mother or daughter in two ways: first, on the ground that she is his mother [or daughter]; second, on the ground that she is his wife.' Ṭūsī, *Tahdhīb al-aḥkām*, IX, 364; idem, *al-Nihāya*, 683–4; here he notes that there is a difference of opinion among the Imāmī jurists concerning this matter.

['Alī]: He said, 'When an apostate (*al-murtadd*)[95] dies or is killed, his property is distributed among his heirs according to the Book of God.'[96]

Abū Ja'far and Abū 'Abd Allāh: They said, 'A free man and a slave cannot inherit from each other.'[97]

'Alī: He said, 'If a man dies without any heir except one who is a slave, the slave should be purchased from the estate of the deceased and set free, and then the rest of the estate should be given to him as inheritance.'[98]

'Alī, Abū Ja'far, and Abū 'Abd Allāh: They said, 'A man who kills another cannot inherit from him.'[99]

'Alī said, 'A man who kills his brother (*ḥamīm*),[100] whether intentionally or accidently, cannot inherit from him.'[101]

Kulaynī, on the other hand, without quoting any Imam's authority, states that the Zoroastrians inherit according to their kinship (*min wajh al-qarāba*) in consistence with the Islamic principles of inheritance. Inheritance on any other ground is not permitted because some of them contract marriage with their close female relatives (*dhāt al-maḥārim*), namely a mother, sister, or daughter. After citing the above tradition, Ṭūsī also states that the Imāmī jurists differ as to whether a Zoroastrian could inherit on the grounds of marriage relation (*min wajh al-sabab*) when he is married to a close female relative. Ṭūsī upholds the tradition and states that such a practice of marriage is permissible in accordance with their religion, and it has nothing to do with whether it is lawful or not under Islamic law.

The above discussion raises another issue: that at times, non-Muslim subjects appealed to Muslim authorities in their disputes knowing that they would get better treatment than from their own religious authorities. Nu'mān's report suggests that the couple was converted to Islam and for that reason, their case was brought before 'Alī. What is surprising is that 'Alī would have allowed double inheritance to a female after the couple had embraced Islam.

[95]*Murtadd* means 'one who turns back', especially from Islam, see Chap. 19 below in this book.

[96]*Kāfī*, VII, 162–3; Kulaynī cites two traditions from Abū 'Abd Allāh; Ṭūsī, *Tahdhīb al-aḥkām*, 373–4; his estate is distributed among his Muslim heirs.

[97]*Kāfī*, VII, 159.

[98]Ibn 'Abbās said that a man died leaving behind no heir but a youth whom he had emancipated. When the Prophet asked whether he had any heir and was told that he had none but a youth of his whom he had emancipated, he assigned his estate to him. *Mishkāt*, II, 153; Robson I, 654. See also *Kāfī*, VII, 144.

[99]*Mishkāt*, II, 149; Robson, I, 651; *Kāfī*, VII, 149; Ṭūsī, *Tahdhīb al-aḥkām*, IX, 377.

[100]*Akh*[an] (brother): MS Q. *Ḥamīm* has a variety of meanings; it occurs in the Qur'ān 70:10. Sale, Bell, and Yusuf Ali: friend; Pickthall: familiar friend; Arberry: loyal friend; Paret: Freund; Blachère: ami fervent. I have preferred 'brother', and the context also corroborates this meaning. See *Tāj al-'arūs*, s.v. ḥ-m-m; *Majma' al-baḥrayn*, s.v. ḥ-m-m (one who is close in kinship); Lane, s.v. ḥ-m-m (a man's brother).

[101]*Kāfī*, VII, 149–51; Ṭūsī, *Tahdhīb al-aḥkām*, IX, 378–81; if one kills his kinsman who belongs to the rebellious group (*ahl al-baghy*) this rule does not apply. 'On fighting with rebels', see *The Pillars of Islam*, I, 479–89.

['Alī, Abū Ja'far, Abū 'Abd Allāh]:[102] They said, 'The heirs inherit the blood money (*diya*).'[103]

Abū Ja'far and Abū 'Abd Allāh said, 'The uterine brothers [and sisters] are an exception; they do not inherit any portion of the *diya*.'[104]

['Alī, Abū Ja'far, and Abū 'Abd Allāh]:[105] They said, 'The hermaphrodite (*al-khunthā*)[106] inherits and is inherited according to his organ of urination, that is how the principle is established.'[107] If he urinates from his penis (*dhakar*), he is a male and has his rights and obligations. If the urine comes out of the vulva (*farj*), the hermaphrodite is deemed to be a woman and has her rights and obligations. If he urinates from both organs together, it must be seen from which organ the urine comes out first and the law is to be applied accordingly.

However, if the urine comes out together, then it has been related from 'Alī as follows: Verily a woman came to Shurayḥ[108] and said, 'O *qāḍī*,

[102] As in MS Q (*wa-'anhum*). *Wa-'anhu*: in the edited text is an error.

[103] The heirs, including the wife, inherit the blood money paid for her husband. Cf. *Mishkāt*, II, 153; Robson, I, 654. About *diya* see Chap. 16 below in this book.

[104] *Kāfī*, VII, 148; the same rule is reported on the authority of 'Alī, al-Bāqir, and al-Ṣādiq.

[105] As in MS Q (*wa-'anhum*). *Wa-'anhu* in the edited text is an error.

[106] *Dorland's Medical Dictionary* defines hermaphrodite as follows: An individual having hermaphroditism, i.e. the presence of both male and female gonadal (primary sex gland) tissue in the same individual. They have existed throughout world history. Hermaphroditos, in Greek mythology, was the son of Hermes and Aphrodite who became joined in body with the nymph Salmacis. Lloyd-Jones, *The Greek World*, 235.

Although the words *mukhannath* and *khunthā* are derived from the same root *kh-n-th*, the lexicographers make a subtle distinction between the two. The former means an effeminate man who resembles a woman in gentleness, in softness of speech, and in an affectation of languor of the limbs. The latter, on the other hand, means one who has what is proper to the male and what is proper to the female. In the language of the jurists, it means one who has what are proper to both sexes, and they are subject to special laws. Lane, s.v. kh-n-th. It is to be noted that in pre-Islamic and early Islamic times there existed a form of publicly recognized and institutionalized effeminacy/transvestism. The *mukhannathūn* were allowed free association with women on the assumption that they had no sexual interest in them. For an interesting article on the effeminates, see Rowson, 'The Effeminates of Early Medina'.

[107] *Kāfī*, VII, 167–9; Ṭūsī, *Tahdhīb al-aḥkām*, IX, 353–4.

[108] Shurayḥ b. al-Ḥārith (or b. Shuraḥbīl) b. Qays, al-Kindī was an early *qāḍī* of Kūfa. According to some accounts, 'Umar appointed him as the judge of Kūfa and 'Uthmān, 'Alī and Mu'āwiya confirmed him in his position. 'Alī called him 'the best *qāḍī* among the Arabs'. However, their relationship appears to have been uneasy. 'Alī upbraided him for giving a wrong decision and even dismissed him, but later reinstated him. The contradictory pronouncements ascribed to him as well as the inconsistencies in his biography have led some scholars, especially Schacht, to regard elements of his biography

I am a claimant [in a lawsuit].' He said, 'Where is your opponent?' She said, 'You are my opponent! Let there be privacy for me.' He gave her privacy and said, 'Speak.' She said, 'Verily I am a woman; I have a penis as well as a vulva.' Shurayḥ said, 'There was a similar case with the Commander of the Faithful ['Alī], and he gave inheritance according to the emergence of the urine.' She said, 'The urine comes out simultaneously from both the penis and the vulva.' Shurayḥ replied, "Alī decided according to the priority of the emergence of the urine from the organs.' She said, 'There is no priority. The urine comes out together and ceases together from both organs.' Shurayḥ said, 'You inform me of something very strange.' She said, 'I shall inform you of something stranger than this. My uncle's son married me and gave me a female slave, so I had intercourse with her and she bore a child. I have come to you to look into my affair, and if I am a man you should separate me from my husband.'

Shurayḥ rose from the place where he used to sit to administer justice (*majlis al-qaḍā'*) and went to ['Alī] the Commander of the Faithful and related the story to him. 'Alī ordered the woman to come to his presence. When she came, he asked her and she related the same story. 'Alī summoned the husband and said, 'Is this your wife and your uncle's daughter?' The man said, 'Yes.' 'Alī asked, 'Did you give a servant girl to her?' The man replied, 'Yes.' 'Alī said, 'Did your wife have intercourse with her and produce a baby?' The man said, 'Yes.' 'Alī asked, 'Did you have intercourse with your wife after that?' The man replied, 'Yes.' 'Alī said, 'You are more daring than the one who would castrate a lion! Bring me a cupper (*ḥajjām*) for a dinar and two women.' They were brought to him. 'Alī said, 'Take this woman into a house and count her ribs on both sides.' They did so and then came out and said, 'We counted them.' 'Alī asked, 'What did you find?' They said, 'On the right side we found twelve ribs and on the left, eleven ribs.' The Commander of the Faithful ['Alī] said, 'God is great. Bring the cupper.' They brought him, and 'Alī said, 'Cut the hair of this man.' Then he took away the outer wrapping garment (*ridā'*) from her, and clothed her with the mantle of a man (*ilḥāf al-rajul*) and said, 'Go. This man [the husband] has no power over you. Marry women who are lawful to you.' The husband said, 'O Commander of the Faithful, she is my wife and my uncle's daughter and you have considered her to be a man. From where did you adopt this rule?' 'Alī said, 'From my father, Adam. Verily

---

as legendary and he maintained that Shurayḥ was only a *ḥakam* (arbiter). This view has since been challenged by Sezgin and Motzki. *EI*[2], s.v. Shurayḥ.

Eve was created from Adam's rib[109] and men have fewer ribs than women.'[110]

Ja'far b. Muḥammad—his father—his ancestors—'Alī: He said, 'If a hermaphrodite urinates from both organs together, it should be observed from which organ the urine emerges first. If the urine comes out simultaneously the hermaphrodite obtains one-half of the inheritance of a man and one-half of [the inheritance] a woman.'[111]

It is possible that, in the report which we [Nu'mān] have just mentioned in which the number of ribs was taken into consideration, [the Imam Ja'far al-Ṣādiq] said that [the fewer number of ribs on the left side] was due to the son he had procreated. This [additional consideration] was because the urine came out simultaneously; and when the man spoke of his son, a different rule was to be applied. The first person to decide about a hermaphrodite in Islam was 'Alī.

'Alī:[112] He was sitting in the Ruḥba[113] when a group of five persons came and saluted him. He returned the greeting but he did not know them. He asked, 'Are you from Syria or the Jazīra?'[114] They said, 'From Syria, O Commander of the Faithful.' 'Alī asked, 'What is it that brought you here?' They said, 'There is a difference of opinion among us about a matter.' 'Alī asked, 'What is that?' They said, 'We are all brothers; our father died leaving a large estate. One of our brothers has[115] a vulva like a woman, and a penis like a man. We thus gave him the inheritance of a woman, but he refused it and insists on a man's portion.' 'Alī asked, 'Where were you that you did not go to Mu'āwiya?'[116] They said, 'We want your decision, O Commander of the Faithful.' 'Alī said, 'I shall not decide between you until you give me full information.' They said, 'We went to

[109]The name of Ḥawwā' (Eve) does not occur in the Qur'ān. The legendary story of her creation is adapted in Islamic tradition from Biblical sources. She was created in Paradise from a left rib of Adam while he slept. *Genesis*, 2:21–5; Kisā'ī, *Tales*, 31–3; she was called Ḥawwā' because she was made from a living being (*ḥayy*), as God said: O *mankind! Fear your Lord, who created you of a single soul, and from it created its mate*, ... (4:1). See also Ibn Kathīr, *Qiṣaṣ al-anbiyā'*, 20: EI^2, s.v. Ḥawwā'.

[110]Ṭūsī, *Tahdhīb al-aḥkām*, IX, 354–5; the whole story is reported with minor variations.

[111]*Kāfī*, VII, 167–8; Ṭūsī, *Tahdhīb al-aḥkām*, IX, 354.

[112]As in MS Q. In the edited text: *wa-'anhu*.

[113]Ruḥba, see Chap. 6, n. 59.

[114]The land between Tigris and Euphrates. *The Pillars of Islam*, I, 322, n. 95.

[115]*Wa-hādhā minnā lahu*: As in MS Q and variant in three of Fyzee's MSS. In the edited text: *Wa-hādhā mabāluhu farj*[un] *ka-farj al-mar'a*. This text already implies that he urinates from the vulva, but it was established later by 'Alī as the tradition reports.

[116]Mu'āwiya was the governor of Syria and fought against 'Alī, see *The Pillars of Islam*, I, 107, n. 300; 480, 483, 488.

him, but he did not know how to decide between us. He [Muʿāwiya] said, "This is a great deal of property and I do not know how to decide. Go to ʿAlī, for, verily, he will find a way out for you. He might ask you whether you came to me, but please say that you did not."' ʿAlī said, 'May God curse a people who are satisfied with our decisions, but [criticize and] attack us in our religion. Depart with your companion and give him [water] to drink, then observe the place from which the urine emerges. If it comes out of the penis, then he is entitled to a man's share; but if it comes out of the vulva, then he is entitled to a woman's share.' He urinated from his penis and they gave him a man's share.

[ʿAlī]: He said, 'Where a hermaphrodite urinates both from the vulva and the penis, his case should be observed, and his share of inheritance should be determined by the organ whereby he urinates first.'

Jaʿfar b. Muḥammad: He was asked about a newborn child whose organs were neither like those of a man nor of a woman, and he said, '... *So blessed be Allah, the Best of Creators!* (23:14); *Thy Lord bringeth to pass what He willeth and chooseth. They have never any choice* (28:68). In this case the Imam should draw lots; he should write *ʿAbd Allāh* (slave of God) on one of the arrows and *Amat Allāh* (handmaiden of God) on another, and then the drawer Imam should say, "O God, Thou art God; there is no deity other than Thee. Thou art the knower of the seen and the unseen, and Thou decidest between thy slaves in matters wherein they differ. Thou hast created this creature as Thou wishest and shaped him as Thou willeth. O God, we do not know what he is and no one knows it but Thee. So make his affair clear to us and tell us what Thou hast made obligatory for him." Then the Imam should throw the two arrows among others (*mubhama*) and mix them up; and then draw lots and give inheritance accordingly.'[117]

ʿAlī, Abū Jaʿfar, and Abū ʿAbd Allāh: They said, 'Where several persons die by fire, drowning, or destruction [of property, etc.],[118] and it is not known who died before his companion, they all inherit from one another.'[119]

Abū ʿAbd Allāh [Imam al-Ṣādiq] said, '[The following is an example of] this: If two brothers board a ship and both of them are drowned, and

[117]About the practice of casting lots with arrows, see the well-known story of ʿAbd al-Muṭṭalib's vow to sacrifice his son in Ibn Isḥaq, *al-Sīra*, I, 160–4; Guillaume, 66–8. *Kāfī*, VII, 168–9; Ṭūsī, *Tahdhīb al-aḥkām*, IX, 356; reported from the same authority. Both Kulaynī and Ṭūsī transmitted a few more strange traditions.

[118]About destruction of property, see Ṭūsī, *Tahdhīb al-aḥkām*, IX, 359.

[119]*Kāfī*, VII, 144–5; 'this is how it is in the Book of ʿAlī.'

it is not known who died first, and each of them has his own heirs and one of them has a hundred thousand [dirhams][120] and the other has nothing, then the man who has nothing will inherit a hundred thousand, and his heirs will inherit the said amount and the heirs of the other man [the owner of the hundred thousand dirhams] will inherit nothing.'[121]

It is according to this illustration that the inheritance will be given, namely, that when it is not known who died first by drowning, each of them will inherit from the other. If one of them has little wealth, and the other has much wealth, they will stand in the place of those who inherit from each of them. It will be deemed that the wealthy man died before the poorer one, and if the poorer man is the sole heir, he will inherit the whole of the property; and if he has sharers in the inheritance, he will inherit his share, and each one of the other heirs will get his share.

Thereafter, it will be deemed as if the wealthy brother is alive and the man with little wealth died before him. Thus, each one will inherit from his companion, and the heirs of each of them will receive their share according to his portion.

We have mentioned the inheritance of the *mukātab* (a slave who has made a contract with his master stipulating that he should pay a certain sum for his freedom) in the chapter on *mukātabs*,[122] and the inheritance of divorced persons in the Book of Divorce[123] according to similar principles, and we shall mention them here as well.

Abū Ja'far and Abū 'Abd Allāh: They said, 'Where a man divorces his wife with reference to the *'idda* or the *sunna*, they inherit from each other so long as the husband has the right to return to her; but when the marriage is terminated, there is no inheritance between them.'

This is the rule if the man is in good health. However, if he divorces her when he is ill, [the Imams] said that when the *'idda* expires, he does not inherit from her, but if he dies of his illness the wife inherits from him. She does so unless he recovers from his illness or the wife marries another husband.[124]

[120] Addition of 'dirhams' from *Kāfī*, VII, 145; Ṭūsī, *Tahdhīb al-aḥkām*, IX, 360.

[121] According to Kulaynī, this story in its two versions was inserted by Abū Ḥanīfa, the founder of the Ḥanafī school, into the previous report from 'Alī, and Imam al-Ṣādiq had heard about it. The editor of *Kāfī* comments that this happens only when there is none more closely related to either of them and that both of them do not have any heir except themselves. *Kāfī*, VII, 145–6. Ṭūsī, *al-Nihāya*, 674, states that, under those circumstances, the man with little wealth should be given precedence over the man with much wealth.

[122] See Chap. 12.

[123] See Chap. 11.

[124] *Kāfī*, VII, 141–2. The normal rule is that a final form of divorce terminates the mutual

We have mentioned that [inheritance by] *walā'* belongs to him who emancipates; for, he who emancipates [a slave], inherits from the freedman. Thus, he who inherits the estate, inherits *walā'* as well.[125]

'Alī, Abū Ja'far, and Abū 'Abd Allāh: They said, 'If a freedman (*mawlā*)[125A] dies and leaves as his heir his blood relation (*dhū raḥim*) to whom a share [of the inheritance] is allotted, whether mentioned in the Qur'ān or not, then the inheritance goes to the relations rather than to the emancipators (*mawālī*).' The emancipator does not inherit in the company of relatives (*dhawi 'l-arḥām*). They recited the verse of the Qur'ān: *And those who are related by consanguinity (ūlu 'l-arḥām) shall be deemed the nearest of kin to each other according to the Book of God* (8:75).[126]

Ja'far b. Muḥammad: He said, 'The emancipator (*mawlā*) inherits from the freedman if the latter dies without leaving an heir [through kinship].'

'Alī: He said, 'The Messenger of God never descended from the pulpit without saying, "When a man dies leaving property, the property is for his heirs; but if he leaves a debt or loss, the responsibility is on me."'

Abū Ja'far [Imam al-Bāqir] confirmed that the said responsibility is also on the Imam.

Abū 'Abd Allāh said, 'The property of one who dies without leaving an heir forms part of the spoils (*al-anfāl*)[127] and escheats to the Public

---

rights of inheritance between spouses. If this rule was to apply to divorces during terminal illness, the divorced spouse could no longer claim any share of the inheritance, but might take up to one-third of the net estate by way of gift (*mut'at al-ṭalāq*) or bequest. The ultra vires doctrine, stated here, is directed only to this issue. Thus, the divorce during the terminal illness will be valid and effective for all other purposes, including that of extinguishing the sick husband's right of inheritance from his divorced wife in the event she dies before her husband. Accordingly, the wife's right to inheritance is not extinguished. In Shāfi'ī law only a *ṭalāq* pronounced in a final form during the husband's terminal illness has the effect of immediate extinction of the wife's right to inherit. All other schools of law presume that such a *ṭalāq* had the improper motive of depriving the wife of her right of inheritance. Therefore, her right of inheritance will not be extinguished. Coulson, *Succession*, 276–7.

[125]See Chap. 12, n. 68; *Kāfī*, VII, 181–2.

[125A]*Mawlā* belonged to the category of *aḍdād* (pl. of *ḍidd*) words, which according to the definition of Arab philologists, have two contrary meanings. Thus, *mawlā*, depending on the context, could mean a patron, master or a client, freedman. *EI*², s.v. Aḍdād; see also n. 68 in Chap. 12.

[126]*Kāfī*, VII, 143; Ṭūsī, *al-Nihāya*, 669.

[127]Ṭabarī states that the commentators of the Qur'ān (*ahl al-ta'wīl*) differ among themselves about the meaning of *anfāl* (pl. of *nafal*). In addition to its meaning of *ghanīma* (the spoils of war), he cites various other interpretations. In expressing his own opinion, he states that *anfāl* refers to what the commander (*imām*) gives to his warriors in addition to their share of the spoils. Ṭabarī, *Tafsīr*, XIII, 361–82. Lane, s.v. gh-n-m, states that

Treasury. This is because the damages to be paid for his crimes are also to be paid by Treasury. Unbelievers who are the heirs of a deceased (Muslim) do not inherit from him. The deceased [in this case] will be treated as one who has left no heirs.'

Abū Ja'far [Imam al-Bāqir] was asked about the Qur'ānic verse: *They ask thee (O Muhammad) of the spoils of war (al-anfāl). Say: The spoils of war belongs to Allah and the Messengers* (8:1). He said, 'If a man dies without leaving behind heirs or possessors of *walā'*, the property is treated as spoils of war.'[128]

'Alī: He said, 'When certain heirs agree to recognize an unknown person as an heir, he will be deemed to be an heir and his share will be allotted to him; but his descent will not be established [by this] and he will not get his share of inheritance by his own testimony. He will be deemed to be an heir, and it will be calculated as to which of the heirs has suffered in his share by such recognition, and such heir will be paid the balance from the share of the recognized heir.'[129]

The Messenger of God: He said, 'The first thing to be paid from the property of the deceased is [the expense] of his shroud [burial]; then the debt; then the legacy; then the inheritance.'[130]

'Alī and Abū 'Abd Allāh said, '[The expenses of] the burial (*al-kafan*) should be taken out of the assets of the deceased; no other expense should be incurred before this.'[131]

EXPLANATION OF SOME OF THE QUESTIONS WHICH ARISE IN THE LAW OF INHERITANCE (*TAFSĪR MASĀ'IL JĀ'AT MIN AL-FARĀ'IḌ MUJMALA*)

We have related from the People of the House, the blessings of God on them, several questions regarding inheritance which have been reported briefly, but which have not been explained by anyone and, consequently, doubts have arisen among many people concerning them. We have, therefore, deemed it advisable to explain their meaning in order to show their real significance, and we rely on God for direction. We have not planned this book for the solution of that which is impossible,[132] as an

---

ghanīma is more general in signification than *nafal*, and *fay'* is more so than *ghanīma*. See also *Lisān al-'Arab*, s.v. n-f-l.

[128] *Kāfī*, VII, 180; Ṭūsī, *Tahdhīb al-aḥkām*, IX, 386–7.

[129] *Kāfī*, VII, 178; Ṭūsī, *Tahdhīb al-aḥkām*, IX, 373–4; idem, *al-Nihāya*, 685, 687.

[130] Ṭūsī, *Tahdhīb al-aḥkām*, IX, 171.

[131] Ibid., IX, 171.

[132] The Arabic expression is *fatḥ al-muqfal*.

explanation of difficulties, or as an exposition of divergencies. We have restricted ourselves to brevity and confined ourselves to well-established questions and reports rather than mentioning those that are not authentic and rejecting those that are weak or those that have been interpolated. However, when we saw that the apparent meaning of some of the questions was at variance with the Book, the *sunna*, or the consensus (*ijmā'*) among the Imams and the community, and doubts were arising among our followers, and the commonalty were reproaching us for them, we decided to clarify them, asking God for help. Among them are questions which we have already mentioned and those which we are about to mention, and provide their exposition, God willing. For instance, we mentioned earlier bequests to heirs, and the arguments against our positions. We have also mentioned the arguments that God provided for us and we mentioned what we were able to do by the direction of God, the Exalted. We have avoided those whose explanation would be lengthy. There are many of them, and some of these we shall explain in the present section.

Among the decisions of 'Alī, there is one in which he said that when a man dies leaving no heirs other than his widow, he gave her the whole of the inheritance; similarly, when a woman dies leaving no heir but her husband, 'Alī gave him the whole of the inheritance.

We have already mentioned the largest shares to which the spouses are entitled, and, in this, there is no difference of opinion. This has been clarified by God in His Book, namely, that the largest share of the husband from his wife's estate is one-half of the inheritance, and the largest share of the wife from the husband's estate is one-quarter, with the residue going to blood relations only.

What has been reported from 'Alī appears to be contrary to this and also to other reports from 'Alī himself. This seeming contradiction exists if only the apparent meaning of the Qur'ān, *sunna*, and what has been handed down authentically from him and other Imams is taken into consideration.

This is not an abstruse doctrine, difficult to comprehend, nor is it a doubtful matter requiring proof; rather it is manifest and patent, clear and well known. What is doubtful because of its brevity requires an explanation in comparison with its contrary opinion [and evidence]. It is not impossible that the spouses in this particular case were related to one another, or that there was a freedman but no other heir [by relationship], and so 'Alī made the husband heir by marriage and kinship. This explanation of the problem was omitted because the hearer's knowledge was assumed, as there was no alternative explanation; alternatively, it is possible that 'Alī considered the husband or the wife deserving of the residue to the estate as if it consisted of the spoils of war (*anfāl*). God has said: *They ask thee (O Muhammad) about the spoils of war. Say: The spoils of war belong to Allah and the Messenger* (8:1). We have mentioned at another place that [the powers] which the Messenger of God possessed, belong as well to the Imam of the time who is one of the People of his House. This property was entrusted to ʿAlī [as Imam] and he gave it as God prompted him.

It is related from ʿAlī that a man sent him some trove property buried by earlier owners, and he said, 'We are entitled to one-fifth (*khums*)[133] of it, but we will return it to you.' This is because ʿAlī felt that the man deserved it.

[ʿAlī]: He judged in the case of a man newly converted to Islam who was killed by mistake and who had no heir. ʿAlī said, 'Distribute the blood money (*diya*)[134] among a number of those who have been converted to Islam.'

This and similar reports coming from ʿAlī establish the permissibility of a man who dies with no heirs to bequeath the whole of his estate to the poor.[135] He rendered the bequest permissible. This was because ʿAlī [as Imam] was entitled to two-thirds of the estate, and decided to allocate the bequest to the poor.[136]

The Messenger of God: The case of a man from the tribe of Khuzāʿa[137] was referred to him. The man died without leaving any heirs, so the Messenger of God ordered that his property be given to a man from the tribe of Khuzāʿa. This is just one of many such reports. Similar precedents are great in number but would increase the size of the book.[138]

Among these is a report from Abū Jaʿfar [Imam al-Bāqir] and Abū ʿAbd Allāh [Imam al-Ṣādiq]. They said, 'Where a man dies leaving sons, the eldest of them is entitled to the sword (*sayf*), the coat of mail (*dir*ʿ), the ring (*khātam*), and the [copy of the] Qur'ān (*muṣḥaf*). If something happens to the eldest son, then the next son is entitled to them.'

This dictum taken at its face value seems to be contrary to the Book, the *sunna*, and the sayings of the Imams and the community (*al-umma*).

[133]*Khums* is the share of the Imam, see *The Pillars of Islam*, I, 321.

[134]*Diya*, see Chap. 16.

[135]*Kāfī*, VII, 181; Ṭūsī, *Tahdhīb al-aḥkām*, IX, 387.

[136]ʿĀ'isha said that a freedman of God's Messenger died leaving some property, but no relative or child, and God's Messenger said, 'Give his property to a man from his village.' *Mishkāt*, II, 150–1; Robson, I, 652.

[137]Khuzāʿa, see *The Pillars of Islam*, I, 457, n. 108.

[138]Burayda said that a man of Khuzāʿa died and his estate was brought to the Prophet who gave instructions to look for his heir or some relative, but they found neither. So God's Messenger said, 'Give it to the leading man (the nearest in kin to the man's closest ancestor) of Khuzāʿa.' *Mishkāt*, II, 151; Robson I, 652.

The survivors of the deceased may be, apart from the eldest son, other sons and daughters, and parents and wives. God says: *Unto the men (of a family) belongeth a share of that which parents and near kindred leave, and unto the women a share of that which parents and near kindred leave, whether it be little or much—a compulsory (legal, mafrūḍ) share* (4:7). How, after such a rule, can one of the heirs be preferred over the others? Is this not contrary to the Book of God? All the common people are in unanimity against this. We have mentioned what each one of the heirs is entitled to inherit according to the Imams; how, then, is it proper to give a lot to one of the heirs and nothing to the others?

I have seen some of our judges pointing to this rule as well as to other similar ones as being invalid, and this is the least that a helpless person can do. There are others who, when the books of the People of the House are read to them and they are asked about similar rules, say that its explanation will come later. Then, when the reader reads, the explanation never comes. Yet others say that they have understood its meaning and found the answer, namely, that it is due the status of the eldest son. This is due to ignorance on the part of the exponent. How can it be possible for one of the heirs [to have more] because of his status when all the others are partners in the heritage? The rule of distribution for a partner is that the estate should be divided, if it is possible to do so, or that it may be sold and its price distributed so that the partners are satisfied by their portions. We have never known a partner to allow his co-partner to take more than his right because of his position, as this man says. It is not lawful for one partner to take a thing without allowing his partner to have a similar thing [in return] unless there is an agreement between them.

The true meaning of this report—and God knows best—is that this rule is meant especially for the vicegerents (*awṣiyā'*)[139] and the Imams rather than other people. These are things which are transmitted from one Imam to another such as the signet ring of the Imamate (*khātam al-imāma*),[140] the authentic text of the Qur'ān (*muṣḥaf al-Qur'ān al-thābit*),[141] the books of knowledge (*kutub al-ʿilm*), and the weapons (*al-silāḥ*).[142]

[139]*Awṣiyā'* pl. of *waṣī*, see *The Pillars of Islam*, I, 21, 27, 30, 34, 62, 69.

[140]Before the Messenger of God died, he gave his signet ring to ʿAlī which the latter wore round his finger. *Kāfī*, I, 236.

[141]Only the Imams possess the whole of the Qur'ān as it was revealed and collected by ʿAlī. *Kāfī*, I, 228.

[142]About the books and the weapons, see *The Pillars of Islam*, I, 28, n. 50.

These are not the private property of any single person to whom the rules of inheritance are applicable, rather, they are passed on from one to another, from him who precedes to him who succeeds.

We have mentioned in the Book of Wills[143] that the Messenger of God transmitted his books and weapons to his *waṣī* (vicegerent) ʿAlī, the Commander of the Faithful. He commanded ʿAlī to transfer them to his son Ḥasan; Ḥasan to Ḥusayn, Ḥusayn to his son ʿAlī, he commanded ʿAlī b. Ḥusayn to transfer them to his son Muḥammad b. ʿAlī and to give him the Prophet's salutation.[144] This is the true reason for the rule contained in the report, and it bears no other interpretation. Thus, either he [the Imam] explained the rule and the reporters omitted the explanation, or he stated the rule briefly being satisfied with the knowledge of those to whom it was transmitted. It is also possible that it contains an allusion (*ramz*) from the Friend of God (*walīy Allāh*) from whom it has come.

Another such report is the one related from Abū Jaʿfar [Imam al-Bāqir] and Abū ʿAbd Allāh [Imam al-Ṣādiq]. They said, 'Women do not inherit any landed property, but a woman should be given her share [of money] liquidated.'[145] The apparent meaning of this report contradicts the Book of God, the *sunna*, and the consensus of the opinions of the Imams and the community. It demands the same explanation as in the previous report and the same defect is to be found in it.

In my opinion, the real reason—and God knows best—is, as in the previous report, that it is a brief statement containing an allusion or that the explanation of it is omitted. The reason why such land cannot be inherited by women is that it is land endowed as *waqf* on men and not on women, like territory conquered by force and endowed as *waqf* for assisting Muslim men for religious war or helping them against unbelievers. Additionally, it may be, as we have mentioned, that the lands may be endowed as *waqf*s for one group of persons and not for others, and that the women have no share in it. The women are only entitled to their share when liquidated and, thus, the men are entitled to its benefit and not the women. They are entitled only when liquidation takes place.

[143]See Chap. 14.

[144]Nuʿmān alludes to a well-known Shīʿī tradition where Muḥammad al-Bāqir meets the Prophet's Companion, Jābir b. ʿAbd Allāh al-Anṣārī, who conveyed the Prophet's greetings to him. Nuʿmān, *Sharḥ al-akhbār*, III, 276–7.

[145]*Kāfī*, VII, 135–7; 'A woman does not inherit any landed property (*ʿaqār*), but gets her share liquidated.' She also cannot inherit hamlets (*qurā*), large homes (*dūr*), weapons (*silāḥ*), or riding animals (*dawābb*).

As for land that is the private property of the deceased, women have a share in it just as God has said. This is the only lawful course.

A SUMMARY OF THE CALCULATION OF THE DIVISION OF INHERITANCE (*IKHTIṢĀR ḤISĀB AL-FARĀ'IḌ*)

We have already mentioned that there are six various proportions of the Qur'ānic heirs as mentioned by the People of the House and in the Book of God. He who wishes to obtain the shares without any defect should multiply the fractions [and reduce them to a common denominator].

The compulsory shares mentioned by the People of the House are based upon two principles. The first is when there is a fixed portion [for particular heirs] and the residue goes to the others. The second is when there is a fixed portion [for certain heirs] and the residue is further apportioned by the law of reversion (*radd*)[146] to those who are named in the fixed portion [and not to others].

As for the case where there is a compulsory share to particular persons and the residue goes to others, the shares will be taken from the least number of portions which satisfy the case. For instance, if one-half is allotted, it will be taken from two portions; and if one-third, then from three portions; and if one-fourth, then from four portions, and so on. If, however, there are two or three compulsory sharers and the residue is for those that remain, the fractions should be reduced to the least common denominator. For instance, if the shares are one-half and one-third and the residue to the residuary, the shares will be calculated from six shares because the least common denominator is six. Similarly, if the shares be one-half and one-sixth, then again they will be taken from six portions. Where the shares are one-half and one-eighth, they shall be calculated from eight portions. This is how shares are to be allotted where there is a fixed portion [for certain heirs] and the residue for a single residuary.

If the residue is to be distributed to two or more persons equally, the residue is to be divided according to the portion of each person. If the residue is not easily divisible, then consider the fractional residue left after the compulsory shares are allotted. Thereafter, multiply the fractional shares to reduce them to the least common denominator. Then, the fractions will be correctly calculated. For this purpose, if the shares are multiples of two, three, or four, as the case may be, multiply them by the said number and divide accordingly.

[146]See n. 4 above in this chapter.

For instance, if you are told that a woman leaves behind her husband and six sons, then you know that this problem contains one-fourth [for the husband] and the residue [for the sons]. So when you give one-fourth to the husband, there remain three-fourths as residue [1/4 + 3/4 (6 shares)]. This fraction, three-fourths, cannot be divided among the six sons without reducing them to a common denominator. When you look at three, you find it to be one-half of six, so you take two and multiply it by four to obtain eight [1/4 + 3/4 = 2/8 + 6/8]. The calculation will be correct, two shares [one-fourth] to the husband, and there remain six shares [one-eighth] each for the sons. So, calculate accordingly in any case that arises.

However, when the residual fraction does not accord with the portions of those who are entitled to them, then multiply the figure with the fractional share of the claimants and you will have the correct solution, God willing. For instance, if you are told that a woman dies leaving a husband and five sons, the distribution is from four shares, one-fourth to the husband, and three-fourths to the sons. Three-fourths cannot readily be divided into five portions, so take the number of claimants, i.e. five, and multiply it by four, which is the basic principle in this division. You will obtain twenty portions [1/4 + 3/4 (5 shares) = 5/20 + 15/20]. Thus, five portions are for the husband, and fifteen portions [should be divided amongst] the sons, each of them taking three portions.

Similarly, if you are told that a woman dies leaving a husband, five full sisters, and one consanguine grandfather, the distribution is from two shares, one-half to the husband and the residue to the others. There are seven shares in the residue, i.e. one-half. Each sister gets one share, and the grandfather gets two shares. Multiply seven by two, which is the basic principle in this division, and you obtain fourteen—the husband gets seven shares; the five sisters get one share each; and the grandfather gets two shares [1/2 + 1/2 (7 shares) = 7/14 + 5/14 + 2/14].

The second principle deals with the question of *radd* (the law of reversion) as it may arise before you. Here, you have to consider the original shares allotted to each heir before giving them the residue. Say the property, consisting of such and such things, is distributed in a certain number of shares. If there remains a residue, it goes back to the heirs in proportion to their shares. For instance, you are told that a man dies leaving behind a daughter, a father, or a mother, then the daughter gets one-half (three shares) and the parent one-sixth (one share) and the residue returns to them in proportion to their shares (*sihām*) and not according to the original portion of the inheritance. Therefore, the estate will be divided into four portions, three-fourths to the daughter and one-fourth to the father or mother (with a proportion of three to one).

If there be both father and mother, then the property will be divided into five portions, three of them to the daughter and one each to the parents [3/5, 1/5, 1/5 come to 5/5; therefore, the denominator is reduced]. Thus, whenever a problem arises, calculate accordingly and you will find the correct solution.

If, with the heirs entitled to the *radd*, there is a spouse, then multiply the residue after deducting the share of the husband by the number of their shares and divide the residue proportionately. For instance, if you are told that a woman leaves behind a husband, a daughter, and her father. The husband is entitled to one-fourth, i.e. one out of four shares, and the remaining three shares are to be divided between the daughter and the father in the proportion of one-half and one-sixth [i.e. three to one out of four shares]. Multiply the original fraction of three-fourths by four and you will obtain sixteen shares. Four go to the husband and the remaining twelve shares are divided between the daughter and father with nine-sixteenths going to the daughter and three-sixteenths going to the father [thereby preserving the proportion of three to one].

If, instead of the father, there is a mother, then you should calculate accordingly. Every problem in which there is a spouse and the heirs entitled to the *radd* are many, then take out first the share of the spouse and then distribute the rest according to their shares. If they cannot be readily distributed, then multiply the denominator by the number of sharers.

If you are told that a man dies leaving behind a wife, twenty daughters, and a father, then it is from eight shares with one-eighth going to the wife and seven-eighths being divided between the daughters and the father. This is between five shares. This cannot be readily distributed, so multiply five by eight and it becomes forty. So give one-eighth to the wife, i.e. five shares, and divide the remaining thirty-five shares between the father (1/5) and the daughters (4/5), i.e. seven and twenty-eight shares respectively. There are twenty daughters and division [of twenty-eight shares between them] is not possible. So multiply the twenty [daughters' shares] by forty and you have eight hundred shares: one hundred shares go to the wife; one hundred and forty go to the father, and five hundred and sixty shares go to the twenty daughters, i.e. twenty-eight shares each.

Calculate accordingly in cases that come to you and the calculation will be correct.

16

Book of Blood Money (*Kitāb al-Diyāt*)[1]

THE UNLAWFUL AND REPREHENSIBLE NATURE OF SHEDDING BLOOD UNJUSTLY (*TAḤRĪM SAFK AL-DIMĀ' BI-GHAYR AL-ḤAQQ WA 'L-TAGHLĪẒ FĪ DHĀLIKA*)

God says: *And slay not the life which Allah hath forbidden save with right. Whoso is slain wrongfully, We have given power unto his heir* ... (17:33); And He says: *And those who cry not unto any other god along with Allah, nor take the life which Allah hath forbidden save in (course of) justice* ... (25:68); and

[1]*Diyāt* pl. of *diya*, is a technical term for a fine, a specified amount of money or goods, for homicide or other injuries unjustly inflicted upon another person. It is paid to the nearest of kin in cases of murder and intentional injury if the victim or his family forgo their rights of retribution. It is a substitute for the law of private vengeance used as a measure to safeguard public order and as a means of compensation for the loss and injury. Hence, it corresponds to *wergeld* of the ancient Roman and Germanic laws. In pre-Islamic Arabia it rested upon a tribal basis in the absence of any political authority. In cases of homicide, the principle of *tha'r* (vengeance) was supreme. The possibility of voluntary renunciation of the right of vengeance was made possible by the payment of *diya*. Its amount was fixed at one hundred camels. The Qur'ān confirmed this practice, but with certain modifications. The most important change was the rule which made *diya* obligatory in cases of accidental homicide.

It is optional in the case of offences committed deliberately (*'amd^{an}*), but obligatory in all other cases. The integration of this pre-Islamic custom in the Qur'ānic legislation had the effect of fixing it in a definite form in the Islamic law. As the Islamic society developed into a unified community and organized as a state, the principle of *diya* was found out of tune with the new developments. The system of *diya* is, therefore, partially in force in several countries, such as Saudi Arabia, Yemen, Oman, Sudan, and Persia. It also survives at present among the Bedouin tribes of Jordan, Syria, and Egypt. The Bedouin

He says: *For that cause We decreed for the Children of Israel that whosoever killeth a human being for other than manslaughter or corruption in the earth, it shall be as if he had killed all mankind, and whoso saves the life of one, it shall be as if he had saved the life of all mankind* ... (5:32); and He says: *O ye who believe! Squander not your wealth among yourselves in vanity, except it be trade by mutual consent, and kill not one another. Lo! Allah is ever Merciful unto you. Whoso does that through aggression and injustice, We shall cast him into Fire, and that is ever easy for Allah* (4:29–30). And He says: *Whoso slayeth a believer of set purpose, his reward is Hell forever. Allah is wroth with him, and He has cursed him and prepared for him an awful doom* (4:93).

Ja'far b. Muḥammad—his father—his ancestors: The Messenger of God said, 'Verily, there is a valley in Hell called *sa'īr*[2] (blazing fire), and when it is opened, there will be in it a blazing fire which God has prepared for murderers.'[3]

[Ja'far b. Muḥammad]—[The Messenger of God]:[4] He said, 'The most criminal of God's creatures is one who kills a man who is not his murderer,[4A]

---

tribes of Sinai, Sudan, and Somalia, on the other hand, apply *diya* laws derived from customary practices rather than those derived from the *sharī'a*. *EI*², s.v. Diya; *EIr*, s.v. Dīa; Alfi, 'Punishment in Islamic Criminal Law'.

[2]*Sa'īr* is so called because it burns fiercely. *Nār*[un] *sa'īr*[un] signifies fire made to burn with other fire. According to Rāzī, *Kitāb al-zīna*, II, 206–8, the seven names of Hell are: *laẓ*[an] (blazing fire, occurs once in the Qur'ān); *sa'īr* (occurs several times in the Qur'ān); *ḥuṭama* (a vehement fire that breaks in pieces that which is cast into it, occurs twice in the Qur'ān); *jaḥīm* (flaming vehemently, occurs several times in the Qurān); *jahannam* (Hell-fire, occurs most frequently in the Qur'ān); *hāwiya* (abyss, infernal depth, bottomless pit, occurs once in the Qur'ān); *saqar* (Hell, occurs four times in the Qur'ān). *Nār* is the other most frequent word that occurs in the Qur'ān denoting the eternal fire of Hell. *EI*², s.v. Djahannam; Nār; it gives the full range of knowledge about fires and their varieties, esp. fire in the Qur'ān and in Arabic writings.

[3]'The blood of a Muslim who testifies that there is no god but God and that I am God's Messenger may not lawfully be shed but for one of three reasons: a life for a life; a married man who commits adultery; and one who turns aside from his religion and abandons the community.' Transmitted by Bukhārī and Muslim. *Mishkāt*, II, 258; Robson, I, 734.

[4]Addition from *Kāfī*, VII, 300; reported by Imam al-Ṣādiq.

[4A]'The most criminal of God's creatures' is a free rendering of the Arabic: *a'tā al-khalqi 'ala 'l-nās man* .... A literal translation would be: The most hardened of mankind in disdain of God .... *A'tā* is the noun of pre-eminence (*ism al-tafḍīl*) from *'atīy* meaning insolent, presumptuous. In the Qur'ān 19:69, it reads ... *ashaddu 'ala 'l-raḥmāni 'itīy*[an] (*the most hardened in disdain of the All-Merciful* ...; in 25:21, it reads ... *wa-'ataw 'utūw*[an] *kabīr*[an] (*and became greatly disdainful*). The next question in this tradition is: How can a man who has already been killed kill a person? I think that this phrase in Arabic *man qatala ghayra qātilihi* (which also occurs in a tradition transmitted by Ibn Ḥanbal, *Musnad*, IV, 614 and Kulaynī, *Kāfī*, VII, 300) is a clever rhetorical way of saying that the only justifiable reason for killing a person is if he killed you. In that case, of course, it would be impossible for a person to kill the one who killed him, since he is already dead. Thus, there really is no justifiable reason for killing someone.

or one who strikes a man who has not assaulted him, or [a freedman] who claims someone as a master (*mawlā*) who is not his master, or who claims descent from one who is not his father.'[5]

[Ja'far b. Muḥammad]—the Messenger of God: A murdered man found between the houses of the Anṣārs,[6] was brought to him and he said, 'Is he a known person?' They said, 'Yes, O Messenger of God.' He said, 'If the whole community had united in killing a faithful one, God would hurl all of them headlong into the Fire.'[7]

'Alī: He said, 'Among the most heinous offences (*al-kabā'ir*)[8] is the deliberate murder of a believer;[9] fleeing from encountering the enemy in war;[10] practising usury (*ribā*)[11] after clear proof [of its prohibition]; eating the property of an orphan wrongfully; becoming an Arab of the desert after emigration [for the sake of Islam];[12] and slandering virtuous women behind their backs.'[13]

The Messenger of God: He delivered a sermon at Minā[14] on the Day of Sacrifice[15] and said, 'O people, do not return to disbelief after me,[16]

[5]Ibn Isḥāq, *al-Sīra*, IV, 253; Guillaume, 652; part of the Prophet's sermon during the Farewell Pilgrimage; Ya'qūbī, *Tārīkh*, II, 101. See also Ṭabarī, *The History of al-Ṭabarī*, IX, 114, n. 778.

[6]For Anṣār see *The Pillars of Islam*, I, 13, n. 18.

[7]'If the inhabitants of heaven and earth were to share in [shedding] the blood of a believer (*mu'min*), God would throw them into Hell.' *Mishkāt*, II, 262; Robson, I, 737.

[8]*Al-Kabā'ir* is a technical term for major sins, see *The Pillars of Islam*, I, 169, n. 21.

[9]'God may forgive every sin except the one who dies a polytheist or one who purposely kills a believer (*mu'min*).' *Mishkāt*, II, 263; Robson, I, 738. See also *Kāfī*, VII, 298, 301, 302.

[10]See *The Pillars of Islam*, I, Chap. 9.

[11]*Ribā*, see Chap. 1, n. 124.

[12]The Arabic expression is *al-ta'arrub ba'd al-hijra*. The fifth form *ta'arraba* means he became an Arab of the desert, he returned to the desert after he had been dwelling in a region of towns and of cultivated land. The exclusive word for the nomads and the bedouins of the desert used in the Qur'ān is *a'rāb*, in pl. only. The Qur'ān is critical of the nomads. It states: *Bedouins are more stubborn in unbelief* (9:97); *the Bedouins say, 'We believe.' Say (unto them, O Muhammad): Ye believe not, but rather say, 'We submit,' for the faith hath not yet entered into your hearts* (49:14). The above expression, therefore, means that a person having embraced Islam has reverted back to infidelity (*kufr*). Another expression clearly states, 'It is infidelity to become a country Arab after emigration.' *Lisān al-'Arab*, s.v. '-r-b; *Majma' al-baḥrayn*, s.v. '-r-b; Lane, s.v. '-r-b. The issue of *hijra* addressed by the Qur'ān (see 'Abd al-Bāqī, *al-Mu'jam al-mufahras*, s.v. h-j-r) is resistance to oppression whether it is pursued actively or passively. A tradition states, 'There is no *hijra* after the conquest [of Mecca].'

[13]See Chap. 17, n. 105.

[14]Minā, see *The Pillars of Islam*, I, 230, n. 298.

[15]The Day of Sacrifice is the day of *'īd al-aḍḥā*, see *The Pillars of Islam*, I, 229; another part of the sermon is reported.

[16]*Kāfī*, VII, 299, 301.

killing one another; for, verily, I have been commanded to only fight people until they say, "There is no deity other than God;" and when they say that, then their lives and their property are under my protection until they meet their Lord on the day when He will take their reckoning. [Harken to me!] Have I conveyed [the message to you]?' They said, 'Yes.' The Messenger of God said, 'O God, bear witness.'[17]

This is a concise statement and the polytheists will be fought against until they agree to proclaim the unity of God and that Muḥammad is His slave and messenger and until they truly repent. Their repentance consists in giving up polytheism, in believing with their hearts; establishing prayer; rendering the alms tax; and accepting all the compulsory obligations of Islam. These are its conditions and limitations; insistence on all of them is to be found in the Book of God. If they agree to the conditions, they should be accepted. If they do not, the conditions should be presented to them and their protection vouchsafed[18] *[if] they agree to pay the poll tax (jizya) readily, being brought low* (9:29).[19] If they do so, well and good, otherwise they will be fought against and killed.

[The Messenger of God]: He said, 'He who commits a wrongful act (*man aḥdatha ḥadath*[an])[20] in Medina, or gives protection to a wrongdoer (*āwā muḥdith*[an]) is cursed by God.' It was said to Abū 'Abd Allāh [Imam al-Ṣādiq], 'What is a *ḥadath*?' He said, 'A murder.'[21]

[The Messenger of God]: He said, 'Your blood and your property are as sacred as the sanctity of this day, in this month, in this town of yours.'[22]

'Alī: Concerning the Words of God which mention the people of Hell: *Our Lord! Show us those who beguiled us of the jinn and humankind. We will place them underneath our feet that they may be among the nethermost* (41:29), he said, '[The reference is to] Satan [Iblīs][23] and the son of Adam who killed his own brother, because the former [Iblīs] was the first

[17]This part of the sermon is reported by Ya'qūbī, *Tārīkh*, II, 102. It is neither reported by Ibn Isḥāq nor by Ṭabarī, see Ṭabarī, *The History of al-Ṭabarī*, IX, 112–14.

[18]'If anyone kills a man who has made a covenant (*mu'āhid*) [used for a member of protected communities], he will not experience the fragrance of Paradise ...' Transmitted by Bukhārī. *Mishkāt*, II, 259; Robson, I, 735.

[19]*Jizya*, see *The Pillars of Islam*, I, 457, n. 105; 468–71.

[20]*Aḥdatha ḥadath*[an] denotes that he originated an innovation. *Āwā muḥdith*[an] signifies that he harboured a criminal, or an offender, in his dwelling and protected him from retaliation. Lane, s.v. ḥ-d-th; see also *The Pillars of Islam*, I, 125, n. 13 and 16.

[21]*Kāfī*, VII, 300, 301.

[22]It is from the Prophet's sermon during the Farewell Pilgrimage. Ya'qūbī, *Tārīkh*, II, 100; Ṭabarī, *The History of al-Ṭabarī*, IX, 112–14; *Kāfī*, VII, 299.

[23]For details see *EI*[2], s.v. Iblīs.

jinn to disobey and the latter [Adam's son] was the first man to disobey.'[24]

Abū Ja'far Muḥammad b. 'Alī: Concerning the Qur'ānic verse: *Whosoever killeth a human being for other than manslaughter or corruption in the earth, it shall be as if he had killed all mankind, and whoso saveth the life of one, it shall be as if he had saved the life of all mankind* (5:32), [the Imam] said, 'He will have a place in Hell [so painful] that if he had killed all mankind, the torment could not be greater.'[25]

[Abū Ja'far Muḥammad b. 'Alī]: He said, 'Verily a man will come on the Day of Resurrection and there will be with him as much blood as is to be found in a cupping glass, and he will say, "By God, I have not killed, nor have I been an accomplice in the killing of, any man." Then he will be told, "Oh yes! You spoke [ill] of [my slave][26] so-and-so and the matter escalated [to the point] that he was slain, and it is his blood that is on your hands."'[27]

ON RETALIATION FOR WRONGS (*AL-QIṢĀṢ*)[28]

Says God: *And there is life for you in retaliation, O men of understanding ...* (2:179).[29]

[24]Although the Qur'ān does not give the names, it tells the story of the two sons of Adam, Hābīl and Qābīl, the latter of whom killed the former because his own sacrifice was refused while his brother's was accepted, see Qur'ān 5:27–32. *EI*[2], s.v. Hābīl wa Ḳābīl.

[25]*Kāfī*, VII, 297, 298; reported from the same Imam.

[26]Addition from *Kāfī*, VII, 299; reported from the same Imam.

[27]This is a more idiomatic rendering of the Arabic, which is unclear: *fa-taraqqā dhālika ḥattā qutila, fa-aṣābaka, hādhā min damihi.* It probably means that he betrayed him to the unjust rulers who executed him.

[28]*Qiṣāṣ*, in Islamic law, is applied in cases of killing and in cases of wounding that do not prove fatal. The former is called *qiṣāṣ fi 'l-nafs* while the latter *qiṣāṣ fī-mā dūn al-nafs*. The term *qiṣāṣ* is generally used for the former and the term *qawad* for the latter. However, at times they are used interchangeably. Blood vengeance was common in pre-Islamic Arabia. Schacht states that the evidence of the Qur'ān and the *sīra* (biography of the Prophet) suggest that the Prophet did not recognize the blood feud, but allowed *qiṣāṣ* as personal vengeance. Moreover, he subjected its application to certain limitations, endeavoured to free it from tribal customs, and brought it closer in character to a punishment. For details see *EI*[2], s.v. Ḳiṣāṣ. Ibn Rushd, *Bidāya*, II, 391–404; trans. II, 479–90.

[29]The Qur'ān mentions both deliberate and accidental homicide. The punishment for the former is prescribed in 2:178–9 while the latter is addressed in 4:92. Based on these verses the jurists laid down the principle that no *qiṣaṣ* is called for an accidental homicide but only the blood money and *kaffāra*. The punishment for deliberate homicide is *qiṣaṣ*, i.e. the taking of the culprit's life. In modern times, it means death penalty for murder. The Imāmī as well as Ḥanafī and Mālikī schools hold that in case of intentional or deliberate homicide or injury the remedy is *qiṣāṣ*, i.e. punishment or talion and *diya* is not an option.

Ja'far b. Muḥammad—his father—his ancestors: One day, 'Alī held his beard and said, 'By God, this will be dyed by this,' [30] and he pointed to his head and to his beard. A group of persons who were with him said, 'O Commander of the Faithful, if someone were to do this to you, we would destroy his family.' And he said, 'Alas and alack! This would be an aggression, as God says only a life can be taken for a life.'

The Messenger of God: He said, 'The blood of all the faithful is of equal value with respect to [retaliation].[31] The lowest of the Muslims can assume the responsibility [on behalf of the victim] in demanding retaliation. All Muslims are in league against all others.'[32] This makes it obligatory to give compensation for life (*qiṣāṣ fi 'l-nafs*, blood vengeance) and for wounds that do not prove fatal (*qiṣāṣ fī-mā dūn al-nafs*).[33] The compensation is the same for the strong and the weak, the high and the low, the defective and the sound, the handsome and the ugly,[34] and the one with a disfigured face (*mushawwah*)[35] and the one with a beautiful face (*wasīm*). In this respect, there is no difference between the faithful.

'Alī: He wrote to his governors ('*ummāl* pl. of '*āmil*), 'Blood should not flow in Islam without compensation.'[36] He wrote to Rifā'a,[37] 'Blood should not flow in Islam without compensation and the implementation of the *ḥadd* punishments[38] should not be neglected [lit. annulled].'

[30]The Prophet said to 'Alī while pointing to his beard and head, 'By God, you will be dyed from here to here.' Ṭabarī, *Kitāb al-dīn wa 'l-dawla*, 45; 169; Nu'mān, *Sharḥ al-akhbār*, II, 445; Mufīd, *Irshād*, 169.

[31]This tradition is transmitted by Ibn Ḥanbal, Abū Dāwūd, Nasā'ī and Ibn Māja. *Concordance*, s.v. k-f-'.

[32]When a Muslim kills another Muslim intentionally his penance will not be accepted until he pays blood money to the guardians, emancipates a slave, and fasts for two consecutive months.' Ṭūsī, *Tahdhīb al-aḥkām*, X, 164.

[33]*Qiṣāṣ fi 'l-nafs* can only be applied after definite proof of guilt is established and certain conditions are fulfilled. *Qiṣāṣ fī-mā dūn al-nafs* is applicable only when the wounds are inflicted deliberately and illegally. It excludes the wounding of someone in self defence, i.e. who tries to murder, injure, or rob a fellow man. Injuring someone in this case is permissible if it is not possible to repel him. For example, it is permitted to strike a man in the eyes or throw something in his eyes if he forces his way into another's house without permission. *EI*[2], s.v. Ḳiṣāṣ.

[34]I have preferred the reading: *damīm* in the MSS of Fyzee, while in the edited text it is *dhamīm*.

[35]It means one whose face is rendered unseemly or ugly by God. Lane, s.v. sh-w-h.

[36]The Arabic expression is *ṭulla damuhu*, which means that his blood was made to go for naught, unretaliated, and uncompensated by a fine imposed for the offence. Lane, s.v. ṭ-l-l.

[37]Rifā'a was 'Alī's *qāḍī* at Ahwāz. *The Pillars of Islam*, I, 281.

[38]For *ḥadd* punishments, see *The Pillars of Islam*, I, 50, n. 122; 187, n. 104; 327, 446; Chap. 17 below in this book.

['Alī]: He said, 'If you do three things, no calamity will ever befall you: [first] to wage war against your enemy; [second] refer criminal matters (*ḥudūd*) to your Imams so that they can decide justly, and [third] give sincere advice to your Imams.'

['Alī]: One day, he entered the mosque of Kūfa by the front door.[39] He met a certain number of people among whom was a young man who was weeping. The people were asking him to be quiet[40] so the Commander of the Faithful stood among them and asked the young man why he was crying. The young man replied, 'O Commander of the Faithful, these people went on a journey for trade with my father; they returned but my father did not. I asked them about it and they said that he died. Then, I asked them about his property and they said he had left none. I brought them to Shurayḥ,[41] but he did not decide anything. He only asked them to take an oath.[42] I knew, O Commander of the Faithful, that my father had a lot of property with him.' The Commander of the Faithful ['Alī] said, 'Return with the young man to Shurayḥ.'

Then,[43] 'Alī went to Shurayḥ and said, 'What does this young man say, O Shurayḥ?' Shurayḥ replied, 'O Commander of the Faithful, this young man made a claim against these people so I asked for proof and none was given. Therefore, I asked them to take an oath.' The Commander of the Faithful said, 'Alas, O Shurayḥ, this is not the way to decide such a case.' Shurayḥ asked, 'Then how shall I decide the case, O Commander of the Faithful?' 'Alī said, 'I shall deal with the case; I shall decide this as no one else has done since the Prophet David.'[44]

Then, 'Alī sat in the place where he used to sit to administer justice (*majlis al-qaḍā'*) and called[45] 'Ubayd Allāh b. Abī Rāfi'[46] who was his scribe

[39]*Al-bāb al-qiblī* lit. southern gate facing the direction of Mecca/*qibla*.

[40]This report is related by Kulaynī, *Kāfī*, VII, 406–8, and by Mufīd, *al-Irshād*, 115–17. I have noted below the major variants only.

[41]Shurayḥ, see Chap. 15, n. 108.

[42]He asked me to drop the case against them: *Irshād*.

[43]This paragraph is not in the *Irshād*; instead, it states: The young man accused them of killing his father for his property.

[44]Dāwūd (David) is mentioned in several places in the Qur'ān. Islamic traditions stress his wisdom and the ability to do justice in difficult issues. *EI*[2], s.v. Dāwūd. See also Nu'mān, *Kitāb al-majālis*, 63.

[45]*Kāfī*: ['Alī said], 'O Qanbar, call for me *shurṭat al-khamīs*.' So he called them and ['Alī] put one officer (*shurṭī*) in charge of each man.' *Irshād*: 'Alī said to Qanbar, 'Gather those people and call for *shurṭat al-khamīs*'. For *shurṭat al-khamīsī*, see *The Pillars of Islam*, I, 461, n. 125.

[46]According to MS Q; Mas'ūdī, *al-Tanbīh*, 297, 301; Mufīd, *al-Ikhtiṣāṣ*, 4; idem, *al-Irshād*, 115. He was a freedman (*mawlā*) of the Messenger of God. 'Abd Allāh, instead of 'Ubayd Allāh, in the edited text seems to be an error.

(*kātib*). He ordered him to bring a scroll and an ink-pot. Then, he asked the people to go in the different directions of the mosque and for each of them to sit near a pillar (*sāriya*). He had one man accompanying each of them. He ordered that their heads be covered [with cloth] and said to those around him, 'When you hear me saying the *takbīr* (*Allāhu akbar*), say it also.'

Then,[47] he sent for one of the men, uncovered his face, looked at him and paused.[48] Then he said, 'Do you think that I do not know what you have done with the father of this young man? If that is the case, I am an ignorant man.' When he[49] addressed him and asked him, the man said, 'O Commander of the Faithful, the man had died.' 'Alī then asked him about his illness, how many days he was ill, where he fell ill, the full details of his illness, the circumstances of his death, who had closed his eyes, his ritual bath, his shroud, who had carried him, who had offered prayers, and who had buried him. When he had completed his interrogation, he raised his voice and exclaimed, 'Arrest him, arrest him.'[50] Then, 'Alī and his companions uttered the *takbīr*, and the group doubtlessly suspected that their companion had confessed. Then, 'Alī called another of them and questioned him as he did the first. He replied, 'O Commander of the Faithful, I was the only one of the group who was unwilling to murder the man.' He thereby confessed the murder. Then, 'Alī called each one of the group and all of them, except the first, confessed their guilt. They also admitted [to stealing] the property then returned it [to the boy] and paid the compensation for the murder.[51]

Shurayḥ said, 'O Commander of the Faithful, what was the decision of the Prophet David in the case like this one from which you claim to have derived inspiration?'[52] 'Alī said, 'David passed by a group of boys who were playing. One of them called out to his companion, "*Yā māta 'l-dayn* (O you whose debt is dead),"[53] and he responded to them. So David

[47]Then ['Alī] called for 'Ubayd Allāh b. Abī Rāfi', his scribe ...: *Kāfī*, *Irshād*.

[48]*Irshād*: Their faces were not covered, and 'Alī would question each of them in a very low voice so that the others would not be able to hear what each of them will confess to 'Alī.

[49]*Kāfī*: Then, 'Alī said to 'Ubayd Allāh b. Abī Rāfi', 'Write his confession and whatever he says.' In *Irshād*, it is slightly different.

[50]*Kāfī*: 'Alī ordered that his head be covered and that he be led to prison.

[51]*Irshād*: They returned the property, which they had buried near Kūfa. The young man forgave them their crime, hence 'Alī did not impose the death penalty on them but gave them severe punishment.

[52]*Irshād*: How did you decide [to proceed as you did] in a case like this?

[53]There is an irony in this name as well as in its substitute. Those who murdered the man probably owed him a large debt or thought that they would get away with the crime and sarcastically might have suggested that name.

came to them and said, "O boy, what is your name?" He said, "*Māta 'l-dayn*." David asked, "Who gave you this name?" The boy replied, "My mother." David asked, "Where is your mother?" The boy answered, "At home." David said, "Come with me to her." The boy went and the mother came out of the house. David asked her, "Is this your son?" She replied, "Yes." David asked, "What is his name?" The woman said, "*Māta 'l-dayn*." David asked, "Who gave this name to him?" The woman replied, "His father." David asked, "Where is his father?" The woman replied, "He went out to trade with a group of persons[54] and they returned but he did not. I asked them about him and they said that he died. I asked them about his property and they said that it was lost. Then, I asked them whether he had left any instructions to me about any matter. They said, 'Yes. He told us that you were pregnant and that when you give birth to the child,[55] you should name him *māta 'l-dayn*.'" David asked, "Where are these people?" The woman said, "They are here." David said, "Come with me to them." David assembled them and did with them as I did, and decided as I decided.[56] David told the woman, "Name your son *'āsha 'l-dayn* (the debt is alive).'"'

Ja'far b. Muḥammad: He performed the *ḥajj* and met Abū Ja'far al-Manṣūr[57] who was also performing the pilgrimage.[58] When he was performing the circumambulation, a man cried out, 'O Commander of the Faithful, one night, these two men came to my brother and led him out of the house and he did not return. I do not know what the two did

[54]Addition in *Irshād*: And I was pregnant.

[55]*Irshād*: Whether a boy or a girl.

[56]*Irshād*: David convicted them of murder and extracted from them the property.

[57]The second 'Abbāsid Caliph reigned from 136/754 to 158/775. *EI*[2], al-Manṣūr, Abū Dja'far 'Abd Allāh. Manṣūr, having faced the threat of an 'Alid uprising, had taken repressive measures against the Shī'a and had Ja'far al-Ṣādiq closely watched. Given those circumstances, one might question this Shī'ī report transmitted by Kulaynī and Nu'mān. 'Spring of Abū Zayd,' an estate of Ja'far al-Ṣādiq, was seized by the caliph and when al-Ṣādiq asked for its return the caliph retorted, 'Your Mahdī [alluding to the rebellion of al-Nafs al-Zakīya in 145/762] has already seized it.' However, in his letter to al-Nafs al-Zakīya, the caliph referring to al-Ṣādiq writes, 'After 'Alī, there was no one among you to equal his son, Muḥammad b. 'Alī [al-Bāqir] … . Further, there is no one equal to his son, Ja'far [al-Ṣādiq] … . He is certainly better than you …' Thus, if these reports are authentic, the caliph picked al-Ṣādiq out as the noblest of the 'Alids then living in order to settle his claims against those of al-Nafs al-Zakīya. Ṭabarī, *History of al-Ṭabarī*, XXVIII, 172, 188, 222. See also Nu'mān, *Sharḥ al-akhbār*, III, 302–7; Mufīd, *al-Irshād*, 272–3.

[58]In 136/753, when the first 'Abbāsid caliph al-Saffāḥ died, Abū Ja'far was, at the time, in Mecca and the oath of allegiance had been rendered to him. He also made the pilgrimage in 140/757 and 147/765. Ṭabarī, *The History of al-Ṭabarī*, XXVIII, 1–2, 60; XXIX, 39.

with him.' Abū Ja'far [al-Manṣūr] said, 'Bring them to me at the time of the afternoon prayer.' He did. Then, al-Manṣūr took Abū 'Abd Allāh Ja'far b. Muḥammad [Imam al-Ṣādiq] by the hand and said, 'O Abū 'Abd Allāh, decide between them.' [The Imam] said, 'Nay, but you can decide between them.' Al-Manṣūr said, 'By the right I have, I swear that you should decide.'

Abū 'Abd Allāh [the Imam] left [the immediate vicinity of the Ka'ba] and a prayer carpet[59] was spread for him and [the Imam] sat on it. The contending parties came to him and they stood before him.[60] Then, he asked the complainant, 'What do you say?' The complainant said, 'O son of the Messenger of God, these two came to my brother one night and led him away. They took him from his house. I swear by God, he did not come back to his house and I do not know what they did with him.' [The Imam] said to the two, 'What do you two have to say?' They said, 'O son of the Messenger of God, we spoke with him and then he returned to his house.' Then, Abū 'Abd Allāh [the Imam] said to his attendant (*ghulām*), 'O attendant, write, "In the name of God the Merciful and Compassionate. The Messenger of God said, 'The man who comes knocking at the door by night and takes away a man out of his house, is responsible [for his safety] unless he proves clearly that he had returned to his house.'"' Then, [the Imam] said to the complainant, 'O young man, choose either of these two [men] and behead him.' One of the two said, 'By God, O son of the Messenger of God, I did not kill him but only held him until this man came and struck him.' Ja'far b. Muḥammad [the Imam] said, 'I am the son of the Messenger of God, O young man [the complainant], take the other man and strike off his head.'[61] The man said, 'O son of the Messenger of God, I did not torture him but killed him with one stroke.' [The Imam] ordered the brother of the murdered man [the complainant] to behead him. The complainant did so and [the Imam] commanded that the accomplice should be beaten on both his sides; then, he was committed to prison and [the following] verdict was recorded against him:[62] He should be imprisoned for life and struck fifty lashes each year.[63]

[59]Made of reed: addition in *Kāfī*, VII, 315. It is reported with minor variations in wording.

[60]Sat before him: *Kāfī*, VII, 315.

[61]This man gave you the choice, so strike off the head of the other man: in MS Q. The Arabic is *takhayyarahu hādhā*, instead of *khudh hādhā* in the edited text.

[62]Fyzee, misled by the Urdu translation, rendered this idiomatic expression incorrectly: He was bound and fell headlong into prison.

[63]It should be noted that, according to Islamic law, the ruler cannot pardon crimes incurring *qiṣāṣ* penalties. However, if the nearest of kin (of the victim) grants a pardon, the ruler may, in his discretion, impose discretionary punishment.

'Alī: He allowed the person accused of murder to confess, and to be treated with kindness while obtaining it. He also said, 'Retaliation (*qawad*)[64] and criminal punishment (*ḥadd*) cannot be implemented against an accused when his confession is procured through frightening, binding, striking, or restraining him.'

['Alī]: He said, 'The evidence of women is not lawful in criminal punishments (*ḥudūd*)[65] and retaliation.' He used to say, 'The evidence of children is permissible against other children in cases involving injury, so long as they have not dispersed, met their relatives, or met someone who tutors them.' This is the rule only when the evidence of children is contrary to (*laṭkh*^{an}) the fifty statements of men on oath (*al-qasāma*).[66]

'Alī: A man who had been heard to have threatened to murder 'Alī was brought to him. 'Alī said, 'Release him; if he murders me, the decision [to punish him] will rest with the avenger of my blood (*walīy al-dam*).'

'Alī: With respect to a man who had murdered a woman intentionally, he said, 'The inheritors (*awliyā'*) of the woman have a choice; they may kill the murderer and pay one-half of the blood money to the inheritors of the man or they may take one-half of the blood money from the murderer himself if he gives it to them.'[67]

Abū 'Abd Allāh: He said, 'If a woman intentionally kills a man, she should be put to death for it. There is no more responsibility than this either on her or on any one else on her behalf.'

Abū 'Abd Allāh also said, 'For wounds, the woman is on a par with the man, i.e. for one-third of her blood money, but when that portion exceeds one-third [of her blood money], her portion of the blood money for the wounds is half of that of the man.[68] For instance, if a man cuts off

[64]See n. 28 above in this chpater.

[65]For *ḥudūd* see n. 38 above in this chapter.

[66]*Al-Qasāma*, a technical term in law, although derived from *qasam*, differs from it in its mode of being taken and its strict area of application. It is repeated fifty times in penal procedure, either by the inheritors (*awliyā'*) of the victim of a murder, or by the inhabitants of the place where the crime was committed in order to assert the guilt or innocence of the accused. In Mālikī law, the *qasāma* is a procedure of accusation, while in Ḥanafī law, it is a procedure for the defence of the one presumed guilty. For details see *EI*^{2}, s.v. Ḳasam; *Kāfī*, VII, 394–7; Ḥillī, *Sharā'i' al-islām*, II, 278–88; *Majma' al-baḥrayn*, s.v. q-s-m. See also the section on *al-qasāma* below in this chapter.

The Arabic reads: *fa-hādhā innamā yakūn shahādat al-ṣibyān laṭkh*^{an} *ma' al-qasāma*. The Urdu translation is incorrect because the translator failed to grasp the meaning of the last two words in that sentence. Gloss in MS Q states: The evidence of children is permissible in cases of murder if it is corroborated by the *qasāma*. However, if the evidence of children is dubious in cases of murder the *qasāma* procedure is to be performed.

[67]*Kāfī*, VII, 327, 329, 330.

[68]The blood money for a man's murder is 100 camels; for the cattle owner, 200 cattle;

the finger of a woman, [the compensation] is one hundred dinars; if he cuts two fingers, then [the compensation] is two hundred dinars; for three fingers, three hundred dinars; and for four fingers, two hundred dinars, because when her [compensation] exceeds one-third of [her] blood money, it comes down to fifty dinars for each finger. This is because the blood money of a woman is five hundred dinars, and for wounds not exceeding one-third of her blood money, her compensation is the same as that of a man.'[69]

'Alī, Abū Ja'far, and Abū 'Abd Allāh: They said, 'When a group of people kill a man intentionally and it is not known by whose blow he died, the avenger of the murdered man's blood (*walīy al-dam*) should choose one man and kill him. As to the rest, the guardians have the right to receive blood money from them. If there were three of them, one of them is to be killed by way of retaliation (*qawad*) and the remaining two should pay two-thirds of the blood money.[70] They should also be beaten and, in this manner of accounting, a proportionate amount should be paid [depending on the number of murderers].' They also said that the Messenger of God said, 'Two persons cannot be killed for the murder of one man.'

'Alī: He judged in the case of a man who killed another while his accomplice held him [during the act] and a third man kept a watch to see that no man came to them. 'Alī decided that the murderer should be killed and the man who held him should be imprisoned. He should also be beaten with stripes and imprisoned for life. He should also be beaten fifty stripes each year as a deterrent punishment (*nakāl*). Both the eyes of the man who kept a watch should be put out.[71]

Abū 'Abd Allāh: He said, 'If a slave murders a free man intentionally,

---

for the sheep owner, 1,000 sheep (with middle incisor); for the people possessing gold, 1,000 dinars; for the people possessing silver, 10,000 dirhams, etc. *Kāfī*, VII, 306–9. For the wounds ibid., VII, 327–30.

[69]For one of her fingers, ten camels are due to her, just as in the case of the man's finger; for two of her fingers, twenty camels; and for three of her fingers thirty; but for four of her fingers, only twenty, because they exceed one-third of her blood money, therefore, the portion is reduced to one-half of what is due to the man. The amount varies according to the schools of jurisprudence. Lane, s.v. '-q-l. There is disagreement over the *diya* of a woman. The majority view is that her *diya* is half that of a man. The Imāmī, Mālikī, and Ḥanbalī schools maintain that a woman's *diya* is equal to that of a man until it reaches two-thirds of the value. This is the reason that it leads to peculiar results as cited in the above case.

[70]*Kāfī*, VII, 309–11.

[71]'If one man seizes another and a second man kills him, the one who killed him is to be killed and the one who seized him is to be imprisoned.' *Mishkāt*, II, 266; Robson I, 740. *Kāfī*, VII, 315. Kulaynī reports another tradition which states, 'If a man hires someone to kill another man, the assailant should be killed and the one who ordered assassination should be imprisoned for life.' Ibid., VII, 312.

he should be killed for the offence.[72] However, if he kills him by mistake, then the owner of the slave may surrender him for the crime or, if he wishes to ransom him, he should do so by paying the blood money.[73]

'If a slave kills another slave intentionally, then, if his master so chooses, he may surrender him to the owner of the murdered slave, but, if he wishes to ransom him, the owner may pay the price of the slave as blood money, and the slave should be beaten rigorously for what he did.[74]

'If a free man kills a slave intentionally, he has to pay a fine to the extent of the price of the slave and be severely beaten.[75] However, the compensation [of a slave] should not exceed the blood money of a free man.[76] Evidence regarding the compensation of a slave being greater than the blood money of a free man is void.

'When a free man kills his own slave, the sovereign (*al-sulṭān*) should reprimand him severely; but it is obligatory on him, between himself and God, to either emancipate a slave or fast for two months consecutively and to repent before God.[77] No *qiṣāṣ* (retaliation) for killing the slave should be implemented against the free man. If the free man had mutilated the slave, he should be punished and the slave made free.'[78]

[Abū 'Abd Allāh]: He said, 'If a Muslim kills a Jew or a Christian, he should be severely reprimanded and be fined the blood money, which is eight hundred dirhams. If the killer is a habitual murderer, and the inheritors (*awliyā'*) of the murdered man are willing to pay the difference between his blood money and that of a *dhimmī*,[79] he may be killed. The *dhimmīs*, when they kill one another [intentionally],[80] should be put to death.'[81]

[72]The slave should be surrendered to the guardians of the murdered. They may kill him, imprison him, or enslave him. *Kāfī*, VII, 335.

[73]Ibid., VII, 337; Kulaynī gives the example of a *mudabbar* slave who kills a man by mistake. His master may ransom him or surrender him to the guardians of the murdered person to serve them. When his master dies he becomes free.

[74]Ibid., VII, 338. If a man has two slaves and one kills the other, the master may kill the murderer or forgive him.

[75]Ibid., VII, 334.

[76]Ibid., VII, 335, 336.

[77]Ibid., VII, 332–3. If the free man is a habitual killer, he should be killed. If he tortured his slave until he died, then the free man should be struck a hundred stripes, imprisoned for a year, and be fined the price of the slave.

[78]Ibid., VII, 334.

[79]Ibid., VII, 340, 342. If a non-Muslim kills a Muslim and then embraces Islam when he is caught, he should be killed. However, if he does not embrace Islam, he should be surrendered to the guardians of the murdered person. They may kill him, pardon, or enslave him. For *dhimmī* see *The Pillars of Islam*, I, 143, n. 79.

[80]Addition from *Kāfī*, VII, 341.

[81]Ibid., VII, 341.

[Abū 'Abd Allāh]: He said, 'If a man kills his blood or near relation, he should be killed for the offence. He who kills his mother should be disgraced and killed and neither he nor his heirs can inherit property from her.[82] Near relations who kill one another shall be killed,[83] except a father when he kills his son.'[84]

[Abū 'Abd Allāh]: He said, 'When a man strikes another intentionally and, as a result, the man dies, retaliation is obligatory because such a killing is deliberate. It is only considered an unintentional murder when a man intends to strike something other than the person killed, but the blow falls on him; or when he does something without the intention to kill and the blow falls on a man and he is killed.'[85]

[Abū 'Abd Allāh]: He said, 'If a man is killed and his inheritors (*awliyā'*) are infants or absent, then any one of them present may claim retaliation.'[86] He added, '[Imam] Ḥasan took vengeance [for his father's death] upon Ibn Muljam [the murderer],[87] may God curse him, even though, at that time, 'Alī had little children. [Imam] Ḥasan did not wait until they attained full maturity [before deciding to take vengeance].'

'Alī: He said, 'In an intentional murder, the avenger of the blood has a choice. If he so desires, he may kill the murderer, accept blood money,[88] or forgive him.' He also said, 'Every heir [of the deceased], except the husband or the wife, has the power to forgive in the case of blood.[89] They [the husband or the wife] have no right to forgive. He who forgives has no right to blood money unless he has made this a condition.'

Ja'far b. Muḥammad: He said, 'If some of the inheritors (*awliyā'*) of a

[82]Ibid., VII, 326.

[83]Fyzee, misled by the Urdu translation, rendered *aqāda* as 'paying compensation'.

[84]'A father is not to be killed for his son.' *Mishkāt*, II, 263; Robson, I, 738; *Kāfī*, VII, 326.

[85]'If anyone kills a man deliberately, he is to be handed over to the relatives of the one who has been killed. If they wish, they may kill him, but if they wish, they may accept blood money.' *Mishkāt*, II, 264; Robson, I, 739. *Kāfī*, VII, 304, 305–6; gives more examples. Ṭūsī, *Tahdhīb al-aḥkām*, X, 155–6.

[86]*Kāfī*, VII, 391. The guardians are both infants and adults. If the adults forgive the murderer, he should not be killed, but when the infants attain adulthood they have the right to demand their share of blood money.

[87]Ibn Muljam, see Chap. 14, n. 59.

[88]'If anyone kills a man hereafter, his people will have a choice to either kill him, if they wish, or to accept blood money, if they wish.' *Mishkāt*, II, 260; Robson, I, 736.

[89]Abū 'Abd Allāh said, 'Women have no right either to forgive or to retaliate.' *Kāfī*, VII, 391. The old Arab idea that the husband and wife have no share in matters of retaliation was a primitive feature in the doctrine of Ibn Abī Laylā and was dropped from Abū Ḥanīfa onwards. Schacht, *Origins*, 292.

murdered man forgive a murderer, the offence is mitigated.[90] If some of the guardians accept the blood money, and the others pardon it, the blood money will be decreased proportionately to the extent of their shares. If all of them accept the blood money and none of them has given it up, they will share it [proportionately].'

[Ja'far b. Muhammad]: He said, 'Where a man[91] kills another intentionally and the deceased has no inheritor (*walīy*) except[92] for a *dhimmī*, then the Imam should offer Islam to the relatives who are *dhimmīs*. He who accepts Islam is his guardian. The murderer should be surrendered to him. He may, if he so wishes, kill the murderer, pardon him, or take from him the blood money. However, if none of the relations accepts Islam, then the Imam is the murdered man's guardian and may either kill him or take the blood money and put it in the Public Treasury.'[93]

[Ja'far b. Muḥammad]: He was asked about a man who murders or steals and then takes refuge in the *ḥaram* (sanctuary at Mecca).[94] He said, 'He should not be given help, food, or drink, nor should a compact be made with him. When he comes out of the *ḥaram*, he should be given the *ḥadd* punishment.'

The Messenger of God: He said, 'It is a great calamity for a man to be brought forward and killed while bound (*yuqtalu ṣabr*^{an});[95] for a prisoner to be held and bound; and for a man to see another man on the stomach of his wife [committing adultery].'

He said, 'There is no retaliation [for murder] except with the sword.'[96]

[90]*Kāfī*, VII, 390–2; the offence is mitigated in the case of a murderer of a man who has two guardians and one forgives. In another case, if a man with two guardians is murdered and one forgives while the other refuses to forgive, the latter may kill the murderer and pay half the blood money to the guardians of the man slain in retaliation.

[91]A Muslim kills another Muslim: *Kāfī*, VII, 393.

[92]As in MS Q: *illā min*. The edited text and the pirated edition of Tāmir are without *illā*. *Kāfī*, VII, 393: the deceased has no Muslim guardians except *dhimmīs* among his relations.

[93]The tradition in *Kāfī*, VII, 393, stresses the point that the Imam does not have the right to forgive, because that right belongs to all the Muslims. He, therefore, may kill him or accept the blood money.

[94]For *ḥaram* see *The Pillars of Islam*, I, 303, n. 14; 374, 377.

[95]*Qatalahu ṣabr*^{an} means that he confined him to die, was confined alive until he was put to death, or he was bound hand and foot until he was beheaded. Lane, s.v. ṣ-b-r.

[96]The jurists disagree concerning the means by which the death penalty should be carried out in cases of *qiṣāṣ*. The Ḥanfīs and the Ḥanbalis maintain that the culprit should be killed by the sword, whether or not he has killed his victim in this manner. The Mālikīs and the Shāfi'īs hold that the murderer should be put to death in he same manner in which he killed his victim. The former view asserts that the punishment should be carried out in the easist and most efficient way that causes the least possible pain to he culprit. El-Awa, *Punishment*, 72.

'Alī said, 'No blood revenge (*qawad*) shall be taken from anyone except with the sword in cases of murder, even though the man may have killed with something other than a sword. The manner of retaliation for the eye is that cotton should be bound on one eye. Then, a mirror should be heated and brought before the eye on which revenge is to be taken. It should be cut open until [the liquid] flows [from it],[97] even though the man on whom revenge is taken may have done the criminal act by putting out the eye in another manner.'

The Messenger of God: He prohibited mutilation (*muthla*). 'Alī said, 'He who mutilates another should be mutilated for the offence.'

BLOOD MONEY
(*AL-DIYĀT*)

God says: *He who hath killed a believer by mistake must set free a believing slave, and pay the fixed blood money to the family of the slain, unless they remit it as a charity* (4:92).[98]

Ja'far b. Muḥammad—his father—his ancestors: They said, 'Blood money should be recovered from the property which the owners possess; from the owners of camels, camels should be recovered; from the owners of cattle, cattle; from the owners of sheep, sheep; from the owners of clothing, clothing;[99] from the owners of gold, gold; from the owners of silver (*al-wariq*), silver. No one should be burdened to pay what one does not possess.'

[97]The Arabic is *ḥattā tasīl*. The cells of the conjunctiva, a thin transparent membrane surrounding the white of the eye, produce a fluid that lubricates the lids and the cornea. Between the cornea and the iris, there is a small compartment containing a clear fluid called *acqueous humour*, which protects the lens and nourishes the cornea. Hence, when this liquid is drained out, it goes blind. *Kāfī*, VII, 352: ... thus the fat (soft part and the lubricant) melts. The eye [physically] remains but the sight is gone.

[98]The Qur'ān fully states: *It is not for a believer to kill a believer unless (it be) by mistake. He who hath killed a believer by mistake must set free a believing slave, and pay the blood money to the family of the slain, unless they remit it as a charity. If he (the victim) be of a people hostile unto you, and he is a believer, then (the penance is) to set free a believing slave. And if he cometh of a folk between whom and you there is a covenant, then the blood money must be paid unto his folk and (also) a believing slave must be set free. And whoso hath not the wherewithal must fast two consecutive months* ... (4:92). *Kāfī*, VII, 303–4. One who assaults and, as a result, is assaulted, no retaliation is permitted. Ibid., VII, 320.

[99]The Arabic term is *ḥulal* pl. of *ḥulla*, meaning a dress or garment. Lane, s.v. ḥ-l-l. According to the Imāmī school of law the full fixed *diya* could be paid in the following six types: 100 camels, 200 cows, 1,000 sheep, 100 two-piece garments, 1,000 dinars (gold coins), or 10,000 dirhams (silver coins). The offender or the party that bears the financial liability selects the type of *diya*. In cases of intentional crimes, however, both parties will reach a settlement about the type of *diya*. *EIr*, s.v. Dīa.

Ja'far b. Muḥammad said, 'Blood money [is to be recovered from the owners as follows]: (i) owners of gold, one thousand dinars; (ii) of silver, ten thousand dirhams; (iii) of camels, one hundred camels worth ten dinars each; (iv) of cattle, two hundred heads, each worth five dinars; (v) of sheep, two thousand sheep, each worth half a dinar; (vi) of cloth (*bazz*), one hundred pieces of clothing (*ḥulla*), each worth ten dinars.'[100]

This is the blood money for a Muslim who is a free man. The blood money of a woman is one-half for her life; and for her wounds, one-third.[101]

[Ja'far b. Muḥammad]: Concerning the Qur'ānic verse: *And for him who is forgiven somewhat by his (injured) brother, prosecution according to usage and payment unto him in kindness* (2:178), [Imam al-Ṣādiq] said, 'This rule is for him who accepts blood money. God orders him to enforce his right with kindness and not to be hard on him who pays. For him who has to pay, [God orders] that he should not do any wrong and should pay with kindness.'[102]

'Alī: He said, 'He who has killed a man by mistake, even though his people have denied the charge, will meet God, the Blessed and Exalted, on the Day of Resurrection, with the blood.'

Ja'far b. Muḥammad: Concerning the Word of God: *But whoso forgoeth it (in the way of charity) it shall be expiation for him* (5:45), [Imam al-Ṣādiq] said, 'His sins will be expiated to the extent that he has pardoned the [retaliation].'

[Ja'far b. Muḥammad]: He was asked about the Word of God: *He who transgresseth after this will have a painful doom* (2:178). He said, 'This refers to a man who accepts blood money and then kills [in retaliation]. For him, there will be a painful doom and he will be killed and not forgiven.'

[Ja'far b. Muḥammad]: He said, 'The expiation of murder is the emancipation of a slave. If he has no slave to emancipate, he should fast for two consecutive months. If he is incapable of observing the fast, he should feed sixty poor persons.'[103]

[Ja'far b. Muḥammad]: He said, 'The repentance for murder is to confess [the crime] to the guardians of the man slain, and, if the guardians have pardoned him or accept blood money, then he should have contrition, which is between him and God.'

[100]*Kāfī*, VII, 306–9; more specifications about camels, cattle, and sheep are given. Ṭūsī, *Tahdhīb al-aḥkām*, X, 158–61.

[101]The exact amount of blood money differs slightly in the traditions. *Mishkāt*, II, 268–72; Robson, I, 741–6.

[102]No punishment should be inflicted on the assailant for which *qiṣāṣ* is prescribed if the victim forgives the accused, especially after being compensated.

[103]Ṭūsī, *Tahdhīb al-aḥkām*, X, 164; it is the expiation of murder by mistake.

THE BLOOD MONEY PAYABLE BY THE AGNATIC RELATIONS (*AL-DIYA ʿALA ʾL-ʿĀQILA*)[104]

God says: *It is not for a believer to kill a believer unless (it be) by mistake. He who has killed a believer by mistake must set free a believing slave, and pay the blood money to the family of the slain* (4:92).

Jaʿfar b. Muḥammad—his father—his ancestors: In the case of a killing by mistake, ʿAlī decided that blood money should be paid by the agnatic relations [of the slayer]. He said, 'The blood money should be paid over three years, one-third being paid each year.'

[ʿAlī]: A man who had killed another man by mistake was brought to him.[105] ʿAlī asked him, 'What is your tribe (*ʿashīra*)[106] and who are your relations?' The man replied, 'I have no tribe or relations in this place [Kūfa].' ʿAlī asked, 'From which place do you come?' The man answered, 'I am from Mosul[107] where I was born. I have my relations and family there.' ʿAlī inquired in Kūfa about his family and relations and found that he had none. Then, ʿAlī wrote the following to his governor (*ʿāmil*) at Mosul:

So-and-so, the son of so-and-so, whose appearance is such and such, has killed a Muslim by mistake. He has declared that he is a man from Mosul and his relations and family reside therein. I have sent him with my messenger, the son of so-and-so, and his appearance is such and such. When he comes to you, God willing, and you have read my letter, make inquiries about his affairs and ask about his Muslim relations. Assemble them together and look at them. If there is someone among them who can inherit from a Qurʾānic share of inheritance and is not excluded by some other relation, then fix the responsibility of the blood money upon him and take one instalment (*najam* pl. *nujūm*) from him for each of the three years.

However, if there is no one who inherits as a Qurʾānic heir but there are other relations who are related to him through his father and his mother, then fix the responsibility for paying the blood money on male relations on the father's

[104]ʿ*Āqila* is a technical term in Islamic penal law that signifies the group of persons upon whom devolves a joint liability, along with the person who has committed homicide or inflicted bodily harm, to pay compensation in cash or in kind. It has its roots in the pre-Islamic Arab tribal principle of joint responsibility. All of the schools of law are unanimous in the view that the *ʿāqila* comprises the *ʿaṣāba* (paternal or agnate relations) of the guilty party. *ʿAql* is also used as a verb, for example *ʿaqaltu al-qatīl* or *al-maqtūl* means I gave the blood money to the heir or next of kin of the slain person. For details see Lane, s.v. ʿ-q-l; ʿ-ṣ-b; *EI*², s.v. ʿĀḳila. Now, this practice has fallen out of use.

[105]It is reported by Kulaynī, *Kāfī*, VII, 398–9; with minor variations.

[106]*EI*², s.v. ʿAshīra.

[107]Mawṣil, in Arabic, is a city in northern Iraq on the west bank of the Tigris and opposite to the ancient Nineveh. It was the capital of Diyār Rabīʿa in early Islamic times. At present, it is the third largest city of the Republic of Iraq. *EI*², s.v. Mawṣil.

and the mother's side. Fix two-thirds of the *diya* on the relations of the father's side, and one-third on those of the mother's side. If there are no male relations on the father's side, then fix the responsibility on the male members of the mother's side. Fix the *diya* and take it within three years.

If there are no relations either on the father's or on the mother's side, then fix the responsibility on the people of Mosul who were born there. Do not procrastinate. Do not fix the responsibility for such payment on people who were not born there. Recover the *diya* from them in three years in instalments of one-third each year until they render the whole of the amount, God willing.

If there are no relations of so-and-so the son of so-and-so, and if he is not from Mosul, then send him back with my messenger so-and-so. Since I am his guardian, I shall pay on his behalf, for the blood of a Muslim cannot remain without compensation.

Abū Ja'far Muḥammad b. 'Alī: As regards manslaughter and wounds for which retaliation is due, [Imam al-Bāqir] said, 'For intentional crimes, retaliation (*qawad*) [is lawful] and for unintentional wrongs, the responsibility for paying blood money is on the agnatic relations (*'āqila*).'

'Alī: He said, 'For an intentional assault, there is no responsibility to pay blood money on the agnatic relations; they are only responsible for unintentional assaults. For wounds, they are only responsible where the compensation amounts to one-third of the blood money or more. What is less than one-third should be recovered from the offender's property and not from his inheritors (*awliyā'ihi*).'

['Alī]: He said, 'The agnatic relations shall not pay compensation for an intentional act of slaying (*'amd*an), for [the slaying] by a slave (*'abd*an),[108] for a compromise [reached by the assailant] (*ṣulḥ*an),[109] or for admission of guilt (*i'tirāf*an).'[110]

['Alī]: He said, 'Compensation is not payable by agnatic relations amongst the *dhimmīs*. Whenever they commit the crimes of murder or wounding, whether intentional or by mistake, then the criminals are personally responsible to pay compensation from their own property.'

['Alī]: He said, 'If a man has admitted killing or wounding a man by

108 According to Abū Ḥanīfa, it does apply to the case of a slave who commits a crime against a free man. Lane, s.v. '-q-l.

109 All jurists agree that it is permissible for the nearest relative of the victim and the assailant/culprit to settle the matter peacefully on the supposition that the culprit may pay more money that the amount fixed for *diya*. El-Awa, *Punishment*, 76.

110 Abū Ja'far said, 'The agnatic relations do not pay compensation for intentional assault, admission of guilt, or for a compromise [reached by the assailant].' *Kāfī*, VII, 400. See also Ṭūsī, *al-Nihāya*, 737; *EIr*, s.v. Dīa. Both Fyzee and the Urdu translator failed to grasp the meanings of *'abd*an and *ṣulḥ*an.

mistake, the blood money must be paid from his property over three years. However, if witnesses testify that he has killed a person by mistake and they spoke the truth, the responsibility for paying the blood money is on the agnatic relatives. No responsibility (*khaṭa'*) attaches to the relatives unless by the evidence of just witnesses. Compensation shall not be paid by them on the admission of the slayer or by his settlement [with the inheritors of the victim] (*bi-ṣulḥihi*).'

THE OFFENCES FOR WHICH COMPENSATION IS TO BE PAID (BY AGNATIC RELATIVES) AND FOR WHICH RETALIATION IS NOT LAWFUL (*AL-JINĀYĀT ALLATĪ TŪJIB AL-'AQL WA-LĀ TŪJIB AL-QAWAD*)

Ja'far b. Muḥammad—his father—his ancestors—'Alī: Where two riders collide and both of them die, or one of them dies, or they both sustain fractures or wounds, he said, 'If both or one of them acted intentionally, then, with respect to acts deserving retaliation, retaliation is due and, with respect to acts deserving blood money, blood money is due. If the act was unintentional, the family (*'āqila*) of each shall pay blood money. If both acted intentionally, they shall pay each other one-half of the blood money, because the injury was mutual. Where the collision is unintentional, the responsibility is borne by their families. If one of them acted intentionally, the striker shall himself pay the blood money. If the act is unintentional, the family of the striker shall pay the man struck down. The injuries received by the striker are without compensation as they are from his own doing, just as are injuries sustained by a rider falling from his mount or a man struck down by a falling wall or any other similar accident.'

[Ja'far b. Muḥammad]: He said, 'No retaliation (*qiṣāṣ*) is due from children. Their intentional acts are deemed to be unintended and compensation (*'aql*) is payable by their families.'

[Ja'far b. Muḥammad]: He said, 'Where a child or lunatic whose reason is impaired, kills someone, the act will be deemed to be unintentional and compensation is payable by their families.'

Abū Ja'far Muḥammad b. 'Alī: He said, 'If a man kills another intentionally and then becomes insane after the murder, but was sane at the time of murder, the avenger of the blood of the slain (*walīy al-dam*) may kill him.[111] The responsibility for the criminal acts of infants or insane persons is on their respective families.'

[111]*Kāfī*, VII, 323; blood money could be paid from his property, if he has any, otherwise blood money could be paid from the Public Treasury.

'Alī: He said, 'He who practises medicine or veterinary science should obtain his freedom from responsibility from the person who follows him [i.e. is treated by him],[112] otherwise, the unskilled person [who does harm to his patient] will be responsible.'[113]

['Alī]: He held a professional circumciser (*khattān*) responsible for cutting off the head of the penis[114] of a boy. A woman who circumcised girls (*khattāna*) performed circumcision on a girl who bled and died. 'Alī held her responsible for it and said, 'Woe be to you! Why did you not spare some part of [the clitoris] of the girl?' He decreed blood money for the deceased and the relations (*'āqila*) of the female circumciser had to pay it. A similar responsibility lies on the person who unintentionally causes injury or death during circumcision. However, if he intended the act, the relations are not responsible for paying the compensation.

'Alī, Abū Ja'far, and Abū 'Abd Allāh: They said, 'If one man falls on another and one of them or both die or are injured, the injuries of the man who falls are not compensated if the act was intentional, but he is responsible to the man on whom he falls for compensation (or retaliation, *qawad*). If the act was unintentional, the relations (*'āqila*) are responsible for the blood money. If some other man had intentionally pushed the man who fell, he is responsible for the injuries sustained by both of them; but, if he unintentionally pushed him, the relatives of the man who pushed are liable to pay compensation to both the persons injured.'

Abū Ja'far and Abū 'Abd Allāh: They said, 'The man who digs a well or commits an act on a road used by Muslims to which he is not entitled is responsible for any damage caused to one who is injured or perishes thereby.'[115]

[112]From his guardian (*walīyihi*): *Kāfī*, VII, 398.

[113]'Anyone who practices medicine when he is not known as a practitioner will be held responsible.' *Mishkāt*, II, 272; Robson, I, 745. See also Ibn Qayyim, *al-Ṭibb al-nabawī*, 139–44; Dhahabī, *al-Ṭibb al-nabawī*, 109; Suyūṭī, *al-Manhaj al-sawīy*, 384. Ibn Rushd states, 'The rule in Mālik's opinion is that the artisans compensate all that is caused at their hands ..., except where the risk is inherent in the work, for example, ... the death of the patient through the doctor's treatment ... . If the doctor is qualified, but makes a mistake, there is no liability on him for the loss of life, and the *diya* beyond one-third is to be paid by the *'āqila*, while less than one-third is to be paid by the doctor. If he is unqualified, he is to be punished with stripes, imprisoned, and made to pay the *diya* from his property. Ibn Rushd, *Bidāya*, II, 227; trans. II, 279.

[114]*Ḥashafa* is the head of the penis. If this is cut off, the whole price of blood is due. Lane, s.v. ḥ-sh-f. For circumcision (*khitān*), see *The Pillars of Islam*, I, 154.

[115]*Kāfī*, VII, 382–3, 412. '[Anyone who has dug a mine or a well in a place where he is entitled to do so is not responsible if someone falls in].' *Mishkāt*, I, 567; II, 274; Robson, I, 380, 747; transmitted by Bukhārī and Muslim.

'Alī: A certain number of persons from Yemen who were inheritors (*awliyā'*) of a deceased man came to him to litigate about a case. Some people came to a pitfall (*zubya*) wherein a lion had fallen and they were looking at it. One of them fell into the ditch. As he was falling, he seized the second man who, in turn, seized the third, and third seized the fourth. All four fell into the pit and the lion tore them up. The inheritors claimed their rights and 'Alī decided that the first was the prey of the lion and he was responsible for one-third of the blood money of the second; the second was responsible for two-thirds of the blood money of the third; the third was wholly responsible for the blood money of the fourth; and that the fourth was not responsible for the blood money at all. They had differences regarding the decision of 'Alī, so they came to the Messenger of God, and mentioned the decision of 'Alī to him. The Messenger of God said, 'The decision is as 'Alī has decided between you.'

[The above incident] has been related to us in a different manner from 'Alī. Some people crowded round the pitfall of a lion and four fell into it; the first grabbed the second, the second the third, and the third the fourth. 'Alī decided that for the first, one-fourth of the blood money was due because he died on account of the three who fell over him; for the second, one-third of the blood money was due, because he died on account of the two who fell over him; for the third, one-half of the blood money was due, because he died on account of the one who fell over him; and for the fourth, the whole of the money was due. He made all the people who were present at the ditch responsible for the blood money.[115A]

This report is similar to the one about the collision of two riders, which we mentioned previously, and where both of them died by mutual acts. This report, however, varies from the last report, and each of them is correct according to their [true] meaning.

In the previous report, the first man slipped by his own act without being pushed by any one. He seized the second, the second seized the third, and the third the fourth. Therefore, the first became the prey of the lion, and his blood is without compensation because no one acted against him. As for the fourth, the whole of the blood money is due because he acted against no one. The other two come under the rule of responsibility, so the inheritors of the fourth are entitled to the whole of the blood money against all the other three, and each of them is responsible to the extent of the one-third because the three of them pulled him. The inheritors of the first pay the inheritors of the second one-third of the blood money;

[115A]Both the versions are presented by Ḥillī, *Sharā'i' al-islām*, II, 297; the first on the authority of Imam al-Bāqir and the second on the authority of Imam al-Ṣādiq.

the inheritors of the second take the one-third and pay the inheritors of the third two-thirds of the blood money, adding one-third to what they had received; and the inheritors of the third add one-third to what they had received and pay the full amount to the [inheritors of the] fourth, as he did not do any wrong to any one, but the three previous ones did wrong to him.

This is the meaning of the first report. The meaning of the second report varies from this because the people crowded round the ditch and, consequentially, four fell into it. Therefore, ʿAlī made blood money payable by all those who were present, for, when they crowded round and pressed, they joined in pushing those that fell into the ditch.

ʿAlī: He said, 'The owner of an animal is responsible for the damage it causes, and a similar responsibility is on the leader (*qāʾid*), driver (*sāʾiq*), and rider (*rākib*).'[116] This is a brief statement which was fully explained by Jaʿfar b. Muḥammad [Imam al-Ṣādiq].

He said, 'If a man were to stop an animal on the road or in a market [in an improper manner], or where he is not supposed to, he is responsible for the damage caused by the animal and in whatever manner the deed is done. The rider is responsible for the damage caused by the forefeet or what it knocks down or bites. Such responsibility is on him because, by God's permission, he owns it. There is no responsibility if the animal flings a small stone behind by its forefeet when it is going at a quick pace and which could not be prevented. Similarly, there is no responsibility if some damage is caused by the rear part, such as the saddle or tail, except when it tramples upon something as a result of the rider spurring it. He [is also responsible if he] hits the animal and its tail strikes something, or if the animal kicks it; or if he pulls back on its rein and it goes backward and destroys something or something similar occurs. The driver is responsible, in all such cases, for what falls from it as well, such as a saddle, a pack-saddle, what is carried on its back (*ḥiml*),[117] or whatever else it carries. In such cases, the rider and the driver are responsible for the damage.'[118]

ʿAlī: Where one person rides behind another on the back of the same beast and it causes damage, he used to make both of them responsible equally.

ʿAlī and Abū Jaʿfar: Where there is a wall which leans and [a call for] security was given to the owner,[119] or it leans so visibly that it is not

[116]*Kāfī*, VII, 386, 387; Ḥillī, *Sharāʾiʿ al-islām*, II, 296.

[117]*Ḥiml* could also mean a litter/howdah (*hawdaj*). Lane, s.v. ḥ-m-l.

[118]*Kāfī*, VII, 384.

[119]According to MS Q, which reads: *idhā tuquddima ilā ṣāḥibihi fīhi ḍamān^{un}*. The edited text is without *ḍamān*, and it does not make any sense.

safe from falling and the owner has knowledge of it and yet allows it to remain standing and does not destroy it or prop it up and the wall falls and causes injury, the owner is responsible for the damage.[120]

'Alī: He said, 'Where a man hires a labourer who is not a minor and competent to deal with his own affairs (and with whom a contract is lawful) and he seeks his help or employs him to do a job and the labourer helps him and dies during the course of the work without any wrong done by the hirer, the hirer is not responsible. His death is [accidental] and no compensation is due for it. However, if the hirer seeks the help of a boy who is a minor without the permission of his guardian who looks after him and whose directions are lawful for him, or if he employs a slave without the permission of his master, and the employee dies, the hirer is responsible. However, if the hiring had taken place with the permission of the owner of the slave or the guardian who is competent to act, the hirer is not responsible.'

'Alī: He decided that where a man entered the house of certain persons without their permission and their dog bit him, the people were not responsible for the harm. He was asked, 'But if he had entered with their permission?' 'Alī said, 'Then they are responsible.'[121]

['Alī]: He said, 'There is no retaliation for [a blow] which cleaves the skin and touches the outer layer of a bone (*munaqqila*),[122] a grazing wound in the head (*simḥāq*),[123] or what is less [severe] than that.' He meant a wound to the brain or head which is less [severe] than those. He said, 'In such wounds, blood money is due. Retaliation (*qawad*) is not due for a fracture of the head (*ma'mūma*),[124] a stomach wound (*jā'ifa*),[125] or the fracture of a bone, and, in these cases, blood money (*'aql*) is due.'

[120]Cf. *Kāfī*, VII, 386.

[121]'If anyone were to look into your house without receiving your permission and you were to throw a pebble at him and put out his eye, you would be guilty of no offence.' Transmitted by Bukhārī and Muslim. *Mishkāt*, II, 275; Robson, I, 747. See also *Kāfī*, VII, 385, 387.

[122]*Munaqqila* is a wound in the head or the face that cleaves its skin or its flesh. Lane, s.v. sh-j-j; n-q-l. Compensation for the *muaqqila* is fifteen camels. *Kāfī*, VII, 360, 361.

[123]*Simḥāq* is the pericranium, i.e. the thin skin above the skull. Lane, s.v. s-m-ḥ-q. The indemnity for it is four camels. *Kāfī*, VII, 360, 361.

[124]*Ma'mūma* is a wound by which the head is broken reaching to the part called *umm al-dimāgh* or *umm al-ra's*, hence there remains between it and the brain only a thin skin. The blood money for it is one-third of the whole price of blood. Lane, s.v. a-m-m. For this injury, one-third of the blood money or thirty-three camels are due. *Kāfī*, VII, 360, 361.

[125]*Jā'ifa* is a spear wound or the like, that reaches the interior (*jawf*) of the body or head. Lane, s.v. j-w-f. The indemnity for this injury is one-third of the blood money. *Kāfī*, VII, 361.

The principle upon which retaliation for wounds and crimes on the human body is envisaged is that nothing more or nothing less should be awarded, that excess should be guarded against, and that there should be no fear of death for the offender. In such cases, retaliation is permissible, but for every other wrong, blood money is due from the property of the offender if he is a free adult capable of acting in his own affairs and has intentionally committed the act. Blood money is due from the family (*'āqila*) of the offender where it is permissible, if the act is unintentional. We have already mentioned earlier the unintentionally caused wounds for which the family pays the blood money.

'Alī: He said, 'If a woman cuts off the penis of a man, or a man causes injury to the private parts of a woman, there is no retaliation between them, but each of them is responsible for the blood money to the other from his or her own property.[126] They should be punished rigorously and, if the [injured] woman is the wife of the man, the man should be forced to retain her [as his wife].'

Ja'far b. Muḥammad: He said, 'If a man has intercourse with his wife and splits the vaginal passage during the act, and the woman is unable to stop urinating, and if the woman is a person of such age that intercourse with her like cannot be had or the husband has treated her with unusual roughness, he is liable for blood money.'[127]

'Alī: He said, 'A woman who splits the vagina of a virgin (*jāriya*) should pay her dower (*mahr*) and should be punished painfully.'

'Alī: He decided that the [blood money] of the unborn child (*janīn*) of a slave girl was one-tenth of her price.

'Alī, Abū Ja'far, and Abū 'Abd Allāh: They said, 'The human foetus is to be considered in its five stages, for each of which a part of the blood money is prescribed. If a woman is beaten and aborts a fecundated ovum (*nuṭfa*) before the foetus has begun to change, the blood money is twenty

[126] *Kāfī*, VII, 347. A man who causes injury to the private parts of a woman is responsible for blood money; if he refuses to pay, the woman may cut off his penis.

[127] A gloss in one MS (taken) from Nu'mān's *Mukhtaṣar al-īḍāḥ* states: The woman of such an age that intercourse with her cannot be had refers to a girl less than nine years of age. If this is the case, then the man is responsible for the injury because intercourse with a girl (of her age) cannot be had. However, if the woman is older than that and intercourse with her can be had and is legal and the injury is unintentional, there is nothing against him if he retains her. If the woman was not his wife and he committed adultery with her, either with her consent or without, and thereby caused the injury, then he has to pay the blood money and the *ḥadd* punishment must be imposed on him. The Commander of the Faithful ['Alī] said, 'When a man consummates the marriage with his wife and she dies due to injuries sustained in such an act, he is not responsible for the blood money.' Kulaynī transmits a tradition with the same content, see *Kāfī*, VII, 347–8, on the authority of al-Ṣādiq.

dinars; for a soft clot of blood (*'alaqa*), forty dinars; for a little lump (*muḍgha*), sixty dinars; where bone (*'iẓām*) appears, eighty dinars; when flesh (*laḥm*) grows and its shaping is completed, one hundred dinars, which is one-tenth[128] [of the blood money]. If life appears in the foetus, then the whole of the blood money, one thousand dinars, is due.[129] This is in accordance with God's Word: *We formerly created man of a finer sort of clay (ṭīn); afterwards we placed him in the form of seed (nuṭfa) in a sure receptacle; afterwards we made the seed coagulated blood ('alaqa); and we formed the coagulated blood into a piece of flesh (muḍgha); then we formed the piece of flesh into bones ('iẓām); and we clothed those bones with flesh (laḥm); then we produced the same by another creation [i.e. producing a perfect man, composed of soul and body]. Wherefore blessed by God, the most excellent Creator!*' (23:12–14).[130]

'Alī: He decided that the [blood money] of the unborn child (*janīn*) of a slave girl was one-tenth of her price.

Ja'far b. Muḥammad: He said, 'Verily, the Messenger of God declared that all acts which are unlawful against a living person are unlawful against a dead person. If a man deals with a dead person in such a manner that if he were alive, it would lead to his death, the person so acting is responsible for blood money and is also liable proportionately for a lesser injury.

'The blood money [for an injury to] a dead person is the same as that for a foetus before it is quick with life and that for injuries to limbs is according to the same proportion. The blood money is not inherited, because what is done to the man is after his death. If the dead body is mutilated, the blood money due on it belongs to the deceased person and not to his heirs. Debts can be paid from it, a pilgrimage made on his behalf if necessary, slaves can be emancipated, and acts of charity and piety may be done for his benefit.'[131]

'Alī: He said, 'If a man loses his life by being crushed to death by a group of persons crowding one another, the blood money is payable by

[128]*Al-'Ushr*: as in MS Q and Fyzee's MSS. In the edited text: *al-ghurra*. It means a slave boy or girl. 'The Messenger of God decided that the blood money for the foetus (*janīn*) is *ghurra*.' The jurists interpret the term *ghurra* to mean a slave whose price is one-tenth of the blood money. *Majma' al-baḥrayn*, s.v. gh-r-r; *Kāfī*, VII, 376, 377. 'The Messenger of God decided that a male or female slave of the best quality (*bi-ghurrati 'abd^in aw walīdat^in*) be paid for a child (*janīn*) killed in its mother's womb.' *Mishkāt*, II, 273; Robson, I, 746.

[129]*Kāfī*, VII, 375, 376; addition in it states: The whole of the blood money is due if it is male, and 500 dinars if it is female.

[130]Sale, *Koran*, 335–6.

[131]*Kāfī*, VII, 380–1. The Imāmī and the Ismā'īlī schools are the only schools of law that set specified *diyas* for the mutilation of a corpse.

that group, if they can be identified; but, if they cannot be identified, the blood money is to be paid from the Public Treasury.'[132]

['Alī]: A man asked for drinking water from a group of persons, but they did not give it to him. They let him die of thirst, even though they had water to spare. 'Alī decreed blood money against them.

['Alī]: Six boys entered a body of water and one of them perished. Three of them gave evidence that the remaining two drowned the boy, and two gave evidence that the three drowned him. 'Alī decreed the blood money and divided it into five portions; three portions to be paid by the two boys, and two by the three boys.

['Alī]: Four persons drank wine and knifed one another. They were brought to 'Alī who imprisoned them; later two of them died and two survived. The families of the two deceased said to 'Alī, 'Order compensation to be paid to us by the survivors.' But none of them confessed to the crime and there was no clear proof against them. So 'Alī said, 'It is possible that each of the two killed the other!' They said, 'We do not know.' So 'Alī decreed the blood money against all four of them, and deducted the blood money for the wounds suffered by the two survivors.

['Alī]: He decided that a man who kills an animal without cause, cuts a tree, destroys standing crops or a house, or damages a well or a canal, should be fined to the extent of the damage or destruction and should be punished with a certain number of stripes as a deterrent. If he had done this unintentionally, without intending any harm, he is liable for the fine but not for imprisonment or punishment. He is liable for the harm done to the animal as much as it has decreased its price.

The Messenger of God: A man implored his assistance against a person and said, 'O Messenger of God, verily, a bull belonging to this person has killed my donkey.' So the Messenger of God said, 'The two of you should go to Abū Bakr,[133] ask him [for a decision] and come back to

[132]'Alī said, 'Whoever loses his life by being crushed to death by a crowd on Friday, on the Day of 'Arafa, or on a bridge, and the killer cannot be identified, the blood money is to be paid from the Public Treasury.' *Kāfī*, VII, 388, 389.

[133]Abū Bakr, see *The Pillars of Islam*, I, 22. Kulaynī transmitted two versions of this tradition on the authority of Imam al-Bāqir. The second version is similar to that of Nu'mān while the first is slightly different but in a more plausible setting. It states, 'They brought the matter before the Messenger of God while he was with his Companions including Abū Bakr and 'Umar. So the Messenger of God said to Abū Bakr, "Decide the matter between the litigants." He replied, "O Messenger of God, a beast killed a beast, it does not matter." Then the Messenger of God asked 'Umar ... and he said the same as Abū Bakr. Next, the Messenger of God asked 'Alī ... .The Messenger of God raised his hands towards the heaven and said, "All praise ..." *Kāfī*, VII, 385.

me and tell me what he says.' So they asked him and he said, 'There is no compensation (*qawad*) against beasts.' They returned to the Messenger of God and informed him. He said, 'Go to 'Umar,[134] ask him, and come back to me and tell me what he says.' So they asked him and he said the same as Abū Bakr did. They informed the Prophet and he said, 'Go to 'Alī and tell me on your return what he says.' So they went to him and he said, 'If the bull entered the place of the donkey and killed it, then the owner of the bull is responsible. But if it was the donkey that entered the place of the bull and the bull killed it, the owner of the bull is not responsible.'

They returned to the Prophet and informed him what 'Alī had said, and the Prophet said, 'All praise to God who created someone amongst the People of My House who adjudicates according to the rule of the prophets.'

'Alī: In a case from Yemen, where a horse had escaped and kicked a man who then died, 'Alī declared his death to be without compensation and said, 'If the horse had escaped, there is no liability against the owner; but if he had released it or tied it in an improper manner, the owner is responsible.'[135] The Yemenis were not pleased with his decision and went to the Messenger of God and said, 'O Messenger of God, 'Alī has done wrong. He gave no compensation for our companion,' and they informed him of the events. So the Messenger of God said, 'Verily, 'Alī is not a wrongdoer and was not created for doing wrong. The decision of 'Alī is like my decision and his word is my word and he is your guardian (*walīy*) after me.[136] None but an unbeliever rejects his word or decision and none but a believer is well pleased with his word or decision.' When the Yemenis heard what the Messenger of God said, they said, 'O Messenger of God, we are satisfied with the decision of 'Alī.' The Messenger of God said, 'This is your repentance!'

Ja'far b. Muḥammad: He said, 'So long as the beasts of cattle are untied and free (*mursala*), the owners shall not be fined for their acts.'[137] That is to say, where the beasts belong to them but have run away from them [there is no fine].

[134]'Umar, see *The Pillars of Islam*, I, 22.

[135]'Alī decided this case while he was in Yemen on a mission sent by the Messenger of God. *Kāfī*, VII, 386.

[136]Indeed, the *walāya* belongs to 'Alī after me: *Kāfī*, VII, 386. For the *walāya* of 'Alī see *The Pillars of Islam*, I, 18.

[137]*Kāfī*, VII, 384, 412; reported from the same authority. 'No retaliation is payable for a wound caused by a dumb animal.' The reference is to an animal which is not, at the time, under anyone's charge. *Mishkāt*, I, 567; II, 274; Robson, I, 380, 747; transmitted by Bukhārī and Muslim.

[Ja'far b. Muḥammad]: A Bactrian camel[138] became wild (*ightalama*),[139] escaped from the house (stable or pen), and killed a man. The deceased's brother came and killed the Bactrian camel. [The Imam] said, 'The owner of the camel is responsible for the blood money of the deceased and may recover the price of the camel;'[140] this happens if he had let the camel loose, as we had said before.

WHERE NEITHER BLOOD MONEY NOR RETALIATION IS DUE (*MĀ LĀ DIYA FĪHI WA-LĀ QAWAD*)

Ja'far b. Muḥammad—his father—his ancestors—'Alī: A man entered a woman's house and had sexual intercourse with her against her will and killed her son. When he went out, she took a pickaxe and killed him. 'Alī decided that there was no compensation for his blood, and that the woman's compensatory dower (*'uqr*)[141] and the son's blood money was to be paid from the man's property.[142]

Ja'far b. Muḥammad: He said, 'If a man tried to seduce a woman, and she repelled and killed him, no blood money was to be paid for him.'[143] He also said, 'The blood of a thief is without compensation, and no liability arises from a man's action in self-defence.'

'Alī: One man bit another who then took his hand away by force. The injured person thereby broke the assailant's two front teeth. 'Alī decided that no compensation was to be paid for the teeth.

Ja'far b. Muḥammad: He said, 'Where a man intends to strike another,

[138]*Bukhtī* is the large, two-humped Bactrian, camel. Lane, s.v. b-kh-t. The Bactrian is the camel most commonly found in Central Asia, whereas in the Middle East the dominant camel is the one-humped dromedary.

[139]*Ightalama* describes a camel when it is excited by vehement lust to cover. Lane, s.v. gh-l-m.

[140]*Kāfī*, VII, 384; reported from the same authority.

[141]*'Uqr* is a kind of dower or compensation given to a woman when connection has been had with her in consequence of dubiousness or as a fine for ravishing her. It is a similar amount to a dower in the case of a free woman. Lane, s.v. '-q-r.

[142]Kulaynī has a slightly different version. It states, 'A thief entered a woman's house to steal her property. When he had gathered the clothes, she followed him and he overpowered her and raped her. Her son moved [to help her], but the thief killed him with a pickaxe which he carried. Then the thief picked up the clothes he had gathered and went out. She [followed him] carrying a pickaxe and killed him. His family members came demanding blood money.' Abū 'Abd Allāh said, '... The Messenger of God said, "One who has sexual intercourse with a woman against her will and she then kills him, there is neither blood money nor retaliation."' *Kāfī*, VII, 321. See also Ḥillī, *Sharā'i' al-islām*, II, 293, for a similar version.

[143]*Kāfī*, VII, 319.

and the person protects himself using something and the thing causes injury, such injury is without compensation.'[144]

Where a rider intends to trample a man down and the man strikes the animal, and the rider falls down, the [Imam] said, 'The striker is not liable for anything.' [The Imam] meant that the man did this in self-defence, as others do, and he did not intend to cause the fall of the rider. But, if he had done this intentionally to bring him down, for instance, by hindering the animal, or in any other manner, the man is liable.

The Messenger of God: He said, 'If a man peeps through gaps in a house to look at the private parts of some people and they put his eye out, there is no compensation for such an injury.'[145]

'Alī: He said, 'When a dead man's body is found in a tribal habitation (*qabīla*), and there are no marks [of foul play] on it, there is no liability on them, for he may have died a natural death.'[146]

'Alī: He said, 'A man who dies while being punished for a *ḥadd* crime, or by the law of retaliation (*qiṣāṣ*), is a person slain by [the command of] the Qur'ān, and there is no blood money for him.'[147]

AN OATH PRONOUNCED FIFTY TIMES IN A PENAL PROCEDURE (*AL-QASĀMA*)[148]

Ja'far b. Muḥammad—his father—his ancestors—'Alī:[149] The Messenger of God decided by *qasāma* and oath taking (*yamīn*) with the evidence of a single witness, especially in regard to property. 'Alī decided similarly at Kūfa, and so did Ḥasan.

[144]bid., VII, 318, 319.

[145]Abū Dharr reported that the Messenger of God said, 'If anyone removes a curtain and looks into a house before receiving permission and sees anything therein which he should not have seen, he has committed an offence which it is not lawful for him to commit. If a man confronted him when he looked in and put out his eye, I would not blame him; but if a man passes a door that has no curtain and is not shut and looks in, he has committed no sin, for the sin pertains only to the people inside.' *Mishkāt*, II, 277; Robson, I, 749. See also *Kāfī*, VII, 318, 319.

[146]A man was killed in or near a village, but there was no clear evidence against the people of that village that he was killed while he was with them. Hence, there is no liability on them. *Kāfī*, VII, 389.

[147]Ibid., VII, 318, 319.

[148]*Qasāma*, see note 66 in this chapter. In the case of a murder, the claimant of blood money or the plaintiff has to take the oath first and produce fifty men to swear that so-and-so killed so-and-so ... if this is not possible, then the defending party has to produce fifty men to swear that they did not kill and have no knowledge as to who committed that act. Now, the practice of *qasāma* has fallen out of use.

[149]MS Q: Ja'far b. Muḥammad—'Alī.

Ja'far b. Muḥammad said, 'Our enemies will not be well pleased with *qasāma* and our friends will never dislike it. *Qasāma* is a true principle, and we believe that it is definitely prescribed [by the *sharī'a*]. If it were not so, people would kill one another and nothing would happen. Verily, *qasāma* is a way of absolution for the people at large.[150] The burden of proof in all matters is on the plaintiff. An oath is to be taken by the defendant except in the case of blood.'

The Messenger of God was once sitting at Khaybar[151] when the Anṣār[152] lost a man and found him murdered. They said, 'O Messenger of God, a certain Jew, so and so, has killed our companion.' So the Messenger of God said, 'Bring the evidence of two just witnesses who do not belong to your group and I shall give you full compensation,' that is to say, if the Jew denies the guilt. 'But if you do not find two witnesses, then find fifty persons who will take the oath (*qasāmat khamsīna rajul*[an]) and I shall give you full compensation.' They said, 'O Messenger of God, we have no witnesses, and we dislike swearing to something which we have not actually seen.' He said, 'Let the Jews swear (*taḥlif*) [fifty oaths][153] that they have not killed him and do not know the slayer.'[154] They said, 'O Messenger of God, they are Jews and will swear [accordingly].'[155] So the Messenger of God gave the blood money from his own [property][156] and said, 'God has protected the blood of Muslims by *qasāma*, because, if a vicious evil-doer finds the opportunity, only the fear of *qasāma* will restrain him from the act.'[157]

When a murdered man is found among a certain group of people, it is their obligation to produce fifty persons to swear that they have not killed him and do not know who the murderer was. They will be fined the blood money if the murdered man was found among them, that is to say, when there is no suspicion entitling the avengers of the blood of the dead man (*awliyā' al-dam*) to swear and ask for retaliation (*qawad*), as

[150]*Kāfī*, VII, 394.

[151]Khaybar, see *The Pillars of Islam*, I, 471, n. 180.

[152]Anṣār, see *The Pillars of Islam*, I, 13, n. 18.

[153]Addition from Ibn Isḥāq, *al-Sīra*, III, 370; Guillaume, 524.

[154]And they will be free from the guilt of his blood: Addition in Ibn Isḥāq.

[155]In Ibn Isḥāq: They answered, 'We cannot accept the oaths of Jews. Their infidelity is so great that they would swear falsely.'

[156]Another version states: The Messenger of God wrote to the Jews of Khaybar when the Anṣār spoke to him: 'A dead man has been found among your dwellings. Pay his blood money.' The Jews wrote back swearing by Allāh that they had not killed him and did not know who had, so the Messenger of God paid the blood money from his own property. Ibn Isḥāq.

[157]*Kāfī*, VII, 395.

the Messenger of God said to the Anṣār. The Messenger of God said this only because a murdered man from Anṣār was found in an ancient well[158] among the wells of the Jews in Khaybar.

It is said that it was ʿAbd Allāh b. Sahl[159] and his uncle's son, Muḥayyiṣa b. Masʿūd,[160] who went out for some need at Khaybar.[161] It is [also] said that as they felt exhausted [after a long journey from Medina] both of them separated at the gardens of Khaybar in order to collect [and carry away] the dates (*li-yuṣībā min al-thimār*).[162] Their separation took place after *ʿaṣr* (late afternoon) and ʿAbd Allāh was found murdered in the evening before nightfall. Khaybar was populated entirely by Jews and there were none others among them and there was manifest bad blood between them and the Anṣār. Such circumstances are suspicious and require *qasāma*. When, however, there is no suspicion and no proof, it is necessary for the people among whom the slain was found to take an oath. Fifty of them should take an oath that they did not kill him and that they did not know the murderer. Then, all of them will be fined the blood money in accordance with the report of the Messenger of God. If, however, the slain man has said [just before his death], 'So-and-so has killed me,' it is an accusation (*laṭkh*) and *qasāma* will be necessary [on behalf of the accused].

Abū Jaʿfar Muḥammad b. ʿAlī: He said, 'If a dead man was brought to ʿAlī, the Commander of the Faithful, he would place the responsibility of the blood money on the vicinity (*ṣaqab*).'[163] Abū Jaʿfar [the Imam] said, 'The *ṣaqab* is the village which is nearest to the slain person. If ʿAlī found the dead man at the gate of a village, he made the people of the village responsible; if he found the body between two villages, he would measure the distance between the two villages and place the responsibility on

[158]The Arabic term is *qalīb* which means an ancient well situated in a desert. It might or might not be cased within [a wall] and it might or might not contain water. Lane, s.v. q-l-b.

[159]Sahl: according to Ibn Isḥāq, *al-Sīra*, III, 369; Guillaume, 524; *Mishkāt*, II, 279; Robson, I, 751; transmitted by Bukhārī and Muslim. Another version is transmitted by Abū Dāwūd. In the edited text and MS Q: Suhayl.

[160]Masʿūd: according to MS Q, Ibn Isḥāq and *Mishkāt*. In the edited text: Saʿūd.

[161]He had gone there with his friends to take away the dates: Ibn Isḥāq.

[162]The Jews of Khaybar had capitulated to the Prophet and the under the terms of the agreement, they were to remain there and cultivate the land, but were to hand over one-half of the produce to the Muslims. For the historical context of this passage see Ibn Isḥāq. In the *ḥadīth* version transmitted by Bukhārī and Muslim it reads: *atayā khaybar, fa-tafarraqā fi 'l-nakhli, fa-qutila ʿAbd Allah b. Sahl* (both of them came to Khaybar and when they had separated among the palm trees ʿAbd Allāh b. Sahl was killed).

[163]*Ṣaqab* signifies vicinity or nearness. A tradition states, 'The neighbour has the best claim to pre-emption by reason of his being near (*al-jāru aḥaqqu bi-ṣaqabihi*). Lane, s.v. ṣ-q-b.

those nearest the dead man; and if he found the body in an open country (or waterless desert, *falāt*) and not in a village, he ('Alī) paid the blood money from the Public Treasury. He used to say, "Blood shed in Islam cannot remain without compensation."'[164]

Ja'far b. Muḥammad: He said, 'For intentional murder, the oath taking of fifty persons is obligatory; for unintentional killing, twenty-five persons,[165] and for wounds, a proportionate number.'

CRIMES RELATING TO LIMBS (*AL-JINĀYĀT 'ALA 'L-JAWĀRIḤ*)[166]

Ja'far b. Muḥammad—his father—his ancestors—'Alī: The Messenger of God decided that if the hair of the head is plucked and does not grow, the whole of the blood money was payable;[167] but if some grows but not all, then the blood money is awarded proportionately.

Ja'far b. Muḥammad [Imam al-Ṣādiq] said, 'If [all] the hair grows, then twenty dinars [are due]. If a man shaves the head of a woman, he should be imprisoned in a jail until the hair grows. [During this period], he should be brought out and flagellated and then returned to prison. When her hair has grown, an amount [of money] should be taken from him which is equal to the *mahr*[168] of a woman of similar status, unless it is greater than the *mahr* of *sunna*,[169] in which case, only the *mahr* of *sunna* should be taken.'

The Messenger of God: He decided that if the skin of the head is totally removed, the whole of the blood money is due; and for a wound in the forehead, if it heals without a blemish, one hundred dinars.

'Alī: He decided that if the temple (*ṣudgh*) of a man is wounded so badly that he cannot face anyone without turning his body, one half of the blood money (i.e. five hundred dinars) is payable; and for a lesser injury, a proportionate amount.[170]

[164] *Kāfī*, VII, 396–7.

[165] Ibid., VII, 397.

[166] Retaliation for injuries is not clearly prescribed either in the Qur'ān or the *sunna*, hence opinions vary.

[167] Abū 'Abd Allāh [Imam al-Ṣādiq] was asked, 'What is the case of a man who goes to a bathhouse and the keeper of the bathhouse pours hot water over his head and, as a result, the hairs are plucked out and do not grow.' [The Imam] replied, 'The whole of the blood money is due.' *Kāfī*, VII, 349.

[168] *Mahr*, see Chap. 10, n. 174.

[169] *Mahr al-sunna*, see Chap. 10, n. 174. The *sharī'a* lays down no maximum amount to the *mahr*, and the traditions endeavour to show that the *mahr* must be neither too high nor too low. The Prophet used to give a *mahr* of hundred dirhams to his wives.

[170] *Kāfī*, VII, 343.

['Alī]: He decided that where both the eyebrows (*ḥājib*) are plucked and hair does not grow, the whole of the blood money is payable; one-half, for each eyebrow;[171] if hair grows, then blood money for each eyebrow is ten dinars; and if an eyebrow is partially injured, a proportionate amount is payable.

['Alī]: He said, 'If an upper eyelid (*shufr*)[172] is injured and inverted, one-third of the blood money for the eye is due, and for the lower eyelid, one-half.[173] For injuries to the eye, a proportionate amount is due. If the eyelashes (*ashfār*) of both the eyes are plucked and do not grow, the whole of the blood money [for the eye] is due, and for each of the eyelashes, one-quarter is due. This is the case whether it is the upper or lower eyelid.'

['Alī]: He said, 'For [blinding] both eyes, the whole of the blood money is due; for one eye, one-half [five hundred dinars].'[174]

'Alī: He said, 'For the good eye of a one-eyed person (*a'war*), the whole of the blood money is due,'[175] i.e. when no blood money had been paid for the blind eye.

Ja'far b. Muḥammad [Imam al-Ṣādiq] said, 'When the good eye of a one-eyed person is intentionally put out and he becomes totally blind, he may, if he so wishes, put out one of the eyes of the assailant and take one-half of the blood money; or, if he so wishes, he may take the whole of the blood money and not put out the eye of the assailant.'[176]

'Alī: He said, 'If a one-eyed person blinds the eye of another, the good eye of the one-eyed person may be put out.' It was said to Abū 'Abd Allāh [Imam al-Ṣādiq], 'But then he would become [totally] blind.' He said, 'It is but right that the injured person should blind him [the assailant].'[177]

'Alī: He decided that, for the putting out of a good eye whose pupil (*ḥadaqa*) is normal but whose vision is defective, the blood money is one hundred dinars.[178]

[171] For the eyebrow, half the blood money of the eye is due. Ibid., VII, 365.

[172] *Shufr* pl. *ashfār* is the place where eyelashes grow, i.e. the edge of the eyelid; it can also signify an eyelash. Lane, s.v. sh-f-r.

[173] *Kāfī*, VII, 365.

[174] *Mishkāt*, II, 269; Robson, I, 742; *Kāfī*, VII, 343.

[175] *Kāfī*, VII, 351.

[176] Two other traditions on the authority of Imam al-Ṣādiq state that, for the good eye of a one-eyed person, the whole of the blood money is due. Ibid., VII, 351.

[177] A free rendition of *al-ḥaqqu a'māhu*, lit. 'It is [the dispensation of] justice that made him lose his eyesight.' See also *Kāfī*, VII, 353, 354. This is listed by Kulaynī in a separate section about wounds for which the victim may demand retaliation.

[178] For the putting out of an eye whose vision is defective, the blood money is half of that for the good eye. Another tradition states that the blood money for such an eye is one-fourth of that for the good eye. *Kāfī*, VII, 351, 352. *Mishkāt*, II, 271; Robson, I, 745; one-third of the blood money should be paid for loss of eyesight when the eye is not removed.

['Alī]: He said, 'When a man is injured and loses part of his sight, the blood money should be given to him in proportion to his loss of sight. [It should be determined as follows:] An egg should be cleaned of its contents and suspended by a hair and held by the hand of a person. The injured eye should be bound up, [the good eye left open], and the person should show him the egg and move away from him [the injured man]. So long as he says that he can see it, the man should keep moving away until he says, "I cannot see anything." The spot should be marked, and the person should return to the injured man. Then, the person should walk away in a different direction until the injured man says he cannot see the egg. This spot should also be marked. This process should be followed in four directions and each of these distances should be measured. If the distances are equal, then this is confirmed; but if some of these distances are more than others, he should be told that he has lied. The whole process should be repeated in all four directions until the distances are equal.

'It would be proper to cover the man walking with the egg so that the injured man cannot count his steps. When the distances are found to be equal in all directions, then the correct limit of his vision will be known.

'Next, the injured man's good eye should be bound up, the injured eye left open, and the whole process repeated. When the measurements are completed accurately, then the two distances should be compared, and the blood money awarded proportionate to the loss of vision.'[179]

[The Imam] said that the same should be done in the case of the ear, and the sound should be made by jingling dirhams.

Abū Ja'far: He was asked about a blind man who blinded a good eye of another. He said, 'The man should be fined the blood money and punished rigorously if he did it intentionally. However, if the act was done unintentionally, the blood money should be paid by the family (*'āqila*).'[180]

'Alī: He said, 'When a man is injured and completely loses his hearing (*sam'*), the whole of the blood money has to be paid.[181] But if it is suspected that he has [partially] lost his hearing, a sound should be made near him by beating something which he cannot see and of which he is not aware. He should be watched for his reaction to such a sound and to conversation, until the loss of hearing is established.'[182]

The Messenger of God: He decided that if both the ears (*udhun*) are uprooted, the whole of the blood money is due. For each ear

[179]*Kāfī*, VII, 356–7; 358. Several traditions are reported.
[180]For *'āqila*, see n. 104 above in this chapter.
[181]*Kāfī*, VII, 343.
[182]Ibid., VII, 355, 356.

unintentionally uprooted, half of the blood money is due.[183] If done intentionally, retaliation should be awarded.

If a nose is cut (*judiʿ*) unintentionally, the whole of the blood money was decreed;[184] if done intentionally, retaliation should be awarded; the same applies to the eyes. If the nose is flattened (*fuṭis*), fifty dinars should be awarded.

Jaʿfar b. Muḥammad: He said, 'If the two lips (*shafa*) are uprooted, the whole of the blood money is due.[185] For the upper lip, one-half is due; and for the lower lip, two-thirds, because it can hold food and saliva.'[186]

Abū Jaʿfar Muḥammad b. ʿAlī: He said, 'In regard to unintentional injury to the front teeth (*asnān* pl. of *sinn*),—which are twelve in number,—fifty dinars are awarded per tooth. The front teeth are called *thanāyā*,[187] *rabāʿiya*[188] and *anyāb*;[189] and the back teeth are called *aḍrās* [molars].[190] For each molar, twenty-five dinars are awarded; and there are sixteen of them, four on each side. This is the complete blood money for the teeth; and, [for some of them], a proportionate amount is due.[191]

'Some people have twenty molars, five on each side [of the jaw]. Only sixteen of the molars count for compensation. A man who has twenty molars shall receive for each molar twenty-five dinars;[192] and if all twenty are broken, then only four hundred dinars are due, the same amount is due for someone with sixteen [molars]. For a lesser number, a proportionate amount is awarded for each tooth and molar. If a tooth is injured and becomes black [dead], the whole of its blood money is due.'

[183]Ibid., VII, 343, 367–8; for the earlobe, one-third of the blood money for the nose.

[184]Ibid., VII, 345, 366. When the cartilage (*mārin*) of the nose is broken, the whole of the blood money is due. If the tip of the nose (*rawtha*) is cut off, 500 dinars; if it is pierced (*kharm*) one-third of the blood money of the nose. See also *Mishkāt*, II, 268; Robson, I, 742.

[185]*Kāfī*, VII, 343, 366; *Mishkāt*, II, 268; Robson, I, 742.

[186]*Kāfī*, VII, 344, 366; for the upper lip, 4,000 dirhams; for the lower, 6,000 dirhams. The amounts vary among the Imāmī jurists.

[187]*Thanīya* pl. *thanāya* are the foremost teeth in the mouth, the central incisors. They are four in number, two above and two below. Lane, s.v. th-n-y.

[188]*Rabāʿiya* pl. *rabāʿiyāt* is the tooth between the central incisor and the canine tooth. They are four in number, two above and two below. Lane, s.v. r-b-ʿ.

[189]*Nāb* pl. *anyāb* is the canine tooth that is behind the *rabāʿiya*. They are four in number. Lane, s.v. n-y-b.

[190]*Ḍirs* pl. *aḍrās* are the molar teeth, or grinders. They are next behind the canine teeth. Lane, s.v. ḍ-r-s.

[191]*Kāfī*, VII, 345; for all of the teeth, the whole blood money is due. See also *Mishkāt*, II, 268, 269; Robson, I, 742.

[192]For each of the broken front teeth, five hundred dirhams [12 x 500=6,000], and for each back tooth two hundred and fifty dirhams [16 x 250=4,000]. *Kāfī*, VII, 364, 368–9.

'Alī: He said, 'For the milk tooth of a child, when the permanent tooth does not grow, the blood money for a grown man's tooth is due; but if it grows, ten dinars are due.'

The Messenger of God: He said, 'When the tongue (*lisān*) is wholly uprooted, the whole of the blood money is due;[193] and proportionately, if it is partly cut. Similarly, a proportionate amount is due depending on the defect in speech.'

'Alī: He said, 'A man whose tongue is cut or injured and is therefore unable to pronounce some words should be examined. It should be ascertained which letters of the alphabet he is unable to pronounce and a proportionate amount is due to him. The [Arabic] alphabet consists of twenty-eight letters, and for each letter, thirty-five and four-fifths dinars should be awarded.'[194]

['Alī]: He said, 'For the tongue of a dumb man (*akhras*), one-third of the blood money is due.'[195]

['Alī]: He said, 'If the beard (*liḥya*) is plucked or shaved or the hair removed by hot water and the hairs do not grow back, the whole of the blood money is payable;[196] and proportionately if the injury is lesser. For the moustache (*shārib*), when it does not grow, one-third of the money for the upper lip is due; and for a lesser injury, a proportionate amount. If the moustache grows, then twenty dinars are payable. These amounts are for unintentional acts; if the act is intentional, retaliation is to be awarded.'

'Alī: He said, 'When the two jaws (*laḥy*, *laḥyān*) are broken and healed without any defect, the blood money is one hundred and forty dinars; for each jaw, seventy dinars. But if the jaws are crushed, then one-fourth of the blood money, i.e. two hundred and fifty dinars. If the chin is crushed, then one-third of the blood money is due; but if it is broken and healed without defect, one hundred dinars. If some defect remains, then one hundred and thirty dinars are due; and if the chin is split, three-fifths of the total money for the chin.'

['Alī]: He decided that, for a collarbone (*tarquwa*) which is broken and healed without defect, the blood money is forty dinars; and if it is merely split, four-fifths of this amount, i.e. thirty-two dinars.'[197]

['Alī]: He said, 'For a broken shoulder (*mankib*), one-fifth of the blood

[193]Ibid., VII, 345.

[194]Ibid., VII, 355.

[195]Ibid., VII, 351.

[196]If the beard is shaved and the hairs do not grow back, the whole blood money is due; if the hairs grow, then one-third is due. Ibid., VII, 349.

[197]Ibid., VII, 369.

money for a hand, i.e. one hundred dinars should be awarded. If there is merely a split, then eighty dinars.'[198]

['Alī]: He said, 'For a broken upper arm (*'aḍud*) that healed without any defect, one hundred dinars should be awarded.'[199]

Ja'far b. Muḥammad: He said, 'For a broken elbow (*mirfaq*), that healed without any defect, one hundred dinars should be awarded.'[200]

[Ja'far b. Muḥammad]: He said, 'For a broken forearm (*sā'id*) that healed without any defect, one-third of the blood money for a life is due. For one of the bones (*qaṣaba*) [of the forearm],[201] one-fifth of the blood money for the hand must be awarded.'[202]

[Ja'far b. Muḥammad]: He said, 'For a crushed wrist (or ankle *rusgh*) that healed without any defect, one-third of the blood money due for the hand should be awarded.'[203]

[Ja'far b. Muḥammad]: He said, 'For a broken palm of the hand (*kaff*) that healed without defect, the blood money is one-fifth of that of the hand. If it is dislocated, one-third of the blood money of the hand is due.'[204]

Ja'far b. Muḥammad: He said, 'For each finger (*iṣba'* pl. *aṣābi'*), one hundred dinars should be awarded.[205] For each finger joint (*mafṣil*), except that of the thumb (*ibhām*), one-third of the blood money of a finger is due, for each thumb has only two joints [and, accordingly, each one is worth one-half of the blood money for the finger].'

'Alī: He said, 'When a finger is disabled (or withered), its full blood money is due.'

Ja'far b. Muḥammad: He said, 'For a disabled hand or finger, one-third of the respective blood money is due.'

The Messenger of God: He decided that for both the hands, the whole of the blood money is due. For each hand, one-half thereof is due.[206]

'Alī: He decided that when the chest (*ṣadr*) is broken and its two halves bent, one-half the blood money, i.e. five hundred dinars, is due. For each half of the chest, one-quarter is due. If the chest is bent together

[198]Ibid., VII, 369.
[199]Ibid., VII, 369.
[200]Ibid., VII, 369–70.
[201]Addition from *Kāfī*, VII, 370.
[202]In the edited text as well as the pirated edition, the previous paragraph is repeated.
[203]*Kāfī*, VII, 370.
[204]Ibid., VII, 370–1.
[205]For each finger, ten camels or 1,000 dirhams are due, and for the fingernail, five dinars. For a finger wound reaching to the bone, a tenth of the blood money for the finger is due. Ibid., VII, 362, 363, 365, 361; more detailed. *Mishkāt*, II, 269; Robson, I, 742.
[206]*Kāfī*, VII, 343.

with the two shoulders (*katif*), then the whole of the *diya* [one thousand dinars] is due.[207]

['Alī]: He decided that if the spine (*ṣulb*) is broken and does not heal, the whole blood money is due.[208] Similarly, the whole blood money is due when it heals imperfectly and makes the man hunchbacked. If the chest heals and there is no defect, then one hundred dinars are due.

['Alī]: He said, 'When a rib (*ḍil'* pl. *ḍulū'*, *aḍlā'*) that is part of the chest is broken, the blood money is twenty-five dinars; and for ribs that are part of the sides (*'aḍud*), ten dinars per rib.'[209]

['Alī]: He said, 'For a spear wound that penetrates into the interior of the body (*jā'ifa*), one-third of the blood money is due, and if the wound goes right through to the other side, then two-thirds of the blood money.'

Ja'far b. Muḥammad said, 'For a slit in the stomach (*baṭn*), one-third of the blood money is due. If there is a swelling but no slit, and the size is that of a walnut, one hundred and twenty dinars are due; if it is of the size of a date, one hundred dinars; if it is of the size of an egg and makes a sound and moves, then one-third of the *diya*.'

'Alī: He said, 'When the hip bone (*warik*) is broken and heals without any blemish, two hundred dinars are due; and for its cracking, one hundred and sixty dinars.'[210]

The Messenger of God: He decided that for removing a penis (*dhakar*) from its roots, the whole of the blood money was due.[211]

'Alī: He said, 'For [cutting off] the head of the penis (*ḥashafa*),[212] the whole of the blood money is due; for the two testicles, the whole of the blood money;[213] and for one testicle (*bayḍa*), one-half thereof, each of the testicles being equal. If a man is injured and both his testicles (*unthayān*) are crushed and the liquid flows, four hundred dinars are due; and for each testicle [so injured], two hundred dinars.'

['Alī]: He said, 'For the pudendum of a woman (*farj*), the whole of the blood money is due;[214] and for a broken coccyx (tail bone, *'uṣ'uṣ*),

[207]Ibid., VII, 371–2.

[208]If the spine is broken and the person is unable to sit, the whole of the blood money is due. *Kāfī*, VII, 345; *Mishkāt*, II, 269; Robson, I, 742.

[209]*Kāfī*, VII, 372.

[210]Ibid., VII, 372.

[211]*Kāfī*, VII, 343; *Mishkāt*, II, 268; Robson, I, 742.

[212]For *ḥashafa*, see n. 114 above in this chapter. The penis, when its glans and what is above it is cut off, the whole blood money is due. *Kāfī*, VII, 343–4, 345.

[213]Ibid., VII, 343; *Mishkāt*, II, 268; Robson, I, 742.

[214]*Kāfī*, VII, 347.

resulting from a man who has lost control over himself, the whole of the blood money.'[215]

Ja'far b. Muḥammad: He said, 'For a broken thigh (*fakhdh*) that heals without a blemish, two hundred dinars are due; but if it swells, then one-third of the blood money.'[216]

[Ja'far b. Muḥammad]: He said, 'For the fracture of a knee (*rukba*), two hundred dinars are due; and for splitting it, four-fifths of the blood money of a fracture. These amounts are due when the wounds are healed without any defect. The same rule applies for a shank (*sāq*).'[217]

Ja'far b. Muḥammad: He said, 'For a broken ankle (*ka'b*) that heals without any defect, one-third of the blood money is due,' i.e. three hundred thirty-three and one-third dinars.[218]

'Alī: He said, 'For each toe (of the foot, *aṣābi' al-rijl*), one hundred dinars are due; and for each of the fingertips (*unmula* pl. *anāmil*), a proportionate amount.' We have mentioned this earlier.

The Messenger of God: He decided to award one-half of the blood money for each leg (*rijl*).[219]

FACE/HEAD WOUNDS (*AL-SHIJĀJ*)[220]

Ja'far b. Muḥammad—his father—his ancestors: 'Alī decided that the following amounts be paid as blood money: If a man is struck in the face

[215] Ibid., VII, 346, 348. If the perineum (*'ijān*) is broken and one has no control over himself, the whole of the blood money is due.

[216] Ibid., VII, 372.

[217] Ibid., VII, 373.

[218] Ibid., VII, 373.

[219] Ibid., VII, 343, 345.

[220] *Shajja* pl. *shijāj* is a wound to the head or face in which the skin or flesh is split open. *Shijāj* are of ten different kinds and each one is distinguished by a different epithet in Arabic and Islamic jurisprudence. They are as follows: (i) *Ḥāriṣa*, which scrapes off the skin, but does not bleed; (ii) *Dāmiya*, which bleeds; (iii) *Bāḍi'a*, which cleaves the flesh slightly and bleeds; (iv) *Mutalāḥima*, which cleaves the flesh much; (v) *Simḥāq*, which leaves between it and the bone a thin layer of flesh. According to the Sunnī schools of law, for these five wounds, there is no retaliation and no fixed compensation, only adjudication by a judge or an arbitrator (*ḥukūma*, see also n. 232 in this chapter). In such a case, a judge estimates how much the bodily harm in question would reduce the value of a slave, and determines the corresponding percentage of the blood money to be paid. Ibn Rushd states that, although adjudication is generally accepted, opinions vary and a fixed compensation is reported on the authority of 'Umar, 'Uthmān, 'Alī, and Zayd b. Thābit. (vi) *Mūḍiḥa* (vii) *Hāshima*(viii) *Munaqqila* (ix) *Ma'mūna* [vi to ix are explained in the footnotes that follow] (x) *Dāmigha*, which reaches the brain. One-third of the whole blood money is

and his face reddened, two and one-half dinars are due; if it becomes green or black, three dinars; if the blow is on the eye and it reddened greatly, three dinars; if the eye and all round it became green, six dinars; and for a lesser injury, a proportionate amount.[221]

For bleeding wounds (*dāmiʿa*),[222] if the skin is broken and the wound bleeds like tears (*al-dāmiʿa al-ṣughrā*), five dinars are due; and for a larger wound which bleeds profusely (*al-dāmiʿa al-kubrā*), ten dinars. For a *fāqira*,[223] where the skin has broken but not the flesh, twelve and one-half dinars are due. For a *bāḍiʿa*,[224] where both the flesh and skin are cut, twenty dinars. When the flesh is broken (*mutalāḥima*),[225] thirty dinars. For a *simḥāq*,[226] where the skin and flesh are broken and the wound has reached the outer bone of the head, forty dinars. Where the bone is exposed (*mūḍiḥa*),[227] fifty dinars; regardless of whether the wound is on the face or the head, the same blood money is due. For all wounds that expose and fracture the bone of any part of the body, one-quarter of the blood money. For the fracture of every bone, we have already mentioned the amounts.

ʿAlī, Abū Jaʿfar, and Abū ʿAbd Allāh: They said, 'For a *hāshima*,[228] one hundred dinars should be awarded. A *hāshima* is an injury where the

---

due. *Kāfī*, VII, 363–4; Ṭūsī, *al-Nihāya*, 775–6; Ibn Rushd, *Bidāya*, II, 415–16; Ibn al-Farrā', *al-Aḥkām al-sulṭāniyya*, 277–8; Māwardī, *al-Aḥkām al-sulṭāniyya*, 234–5. Lane, s.v. sh-j-j. See also Schacht, *Introduction*, 185–6.

[221]For the reddened face, a dinar and a half; for the green face, three dinars; for the black face six dinars. *Kāfī*, VII, 367; Ṭūsī, *al-Nihāya*, 776.

[222]*Shajja dāmiʿa* is a wound on the head from which blood flows in small quantities, or in drops like tears. It ranks after the one termed *dāmiya*, that which bleeds but does not flow. Lane, s.v. d-m-ʿ.

[223]*Fāqira* is an act that breaks the vertebrae of the back. Hence it is used for a calamity or misfortune. Lane, s.v. f-q-r. In the Qur'ān 75:25, it occurs in the sense of great disaster. *Fāqira*, as it is used in this text, is not found in the classical Arabic dictionaries.

[224]*Bāḍiʿa* is a wound to the head in which the skin or flesh is split open, but does not reach the bone. Lane, s.v. b-ḍ-ʿ. The blood money is two camels. *Kāfī*, VII, 360, 361, 363.

[225]*Mutalāḥima* is a wound that cleaves the flesh much, but does not reach to the bone. *Lisān al-ʿArab*, s.v. l-ḥ-m; Lane, s.v. sh-j-j. The blood money is three camels, *Kāfī*, VII, 360, 363–4.

[226]*Simḥāq* is the pericranium, i.e. the thin skin above the skull, or the skin that is between the bone and the flesh. Hence, *simḥāq* is a wound which leaves between it and the bone only a thin piece of tissue. Lane, s.v. s-m-ḥ-q. The blood money is four camels, *Kāfī*, VII, 360, 361, 364.

[227]*Mūḍiḥa* is a wound to the head or face, that shows the whiteness of the bone, or which reaches the bone and for which the blood money is five camels. Lane, s.v. w-ḍ-ḥ; sh-j-j; *Kāfī*, VII, 360; Ibn Rushd, *Bidāya*, II, 416.

[228]*Hāshima* is a wound in the head which breaks the bone, and for which the blood money is ten camels. Lane, s.v. sh-j-j, Supp. s.v. h-sh-m; *Kāfī*, VII, 364; Ibn Rushd, *Bidāya*, II, 416.

bone of the head is crushed. For a *munaqqila,*[229] one hundred fifty dinars are due. This is where the bones are broken to pieces by the blow and fall off the parts broken, either in small or large quantities.'

'Alī: He decided that when any bone of the body is crushed and has moved from one place to another, but does not fall out in two pieces, the blood money is one-half of the fracture of the bone. We have explained this earlier.[230]

['Alī]: He decided that for a *ma'mūma,*[231] one-third of the blood money for a life is due. This is an injury which reaches the brain after crushing the skull.

He said that those who oppose us in regard to wounds which are lesser than those which expose the bone (*mūḍiḥa*), [assert that the victim is entitled to a compensation known as] *ḥukūmatu 'adl*^{in},[232] for they do not fix any definite sum.[233] They say that if the man struck down is a slave, his price before he was struck and after the assault should be compared and the loss in his price should be awarded as blood money. They said the same with regard to the beard when it is plucked. This opinion is opposed to that of the Messenger of God. God has forbidden any opposition to him and warned those who oppose him of a painful torment and mischief (*fitna*); for the Messenger of God said, 'The blood of all the Muslims is of equal value.'[234]

[229]*Munaqqila* is a wound to the head, by which bone is moved, from one place to another, and for which the blood money is fifteen camels. Lane, s.v. sh-j-j, Supp. s.v. n-q-l; *Kāfī*, VII, 360, 361, 364; *Mishkāt*, II, 269; Robson, I, 742; Ibn Rushd, *Bidāya*, II, 416.

[230]See the previous section 'Crimes Relating to Limbs'.

[231]*Ma'mūna* is a wound to the head reaching to the part called *umm al-dimāgh*, so that there remain between it and the brain only a thin piece of tissue. It is the most severe of wounds (*shijāj*) and for which the blood money is one-third of the whole price of blood or thirty-three camels. Lane, s.v. a-m-m, sh-j-j; *Kāfī*, VII, 360, 361, 364; Ibn Rushd, *Bidāya*, II, 416; *Mishkāt*, II, 269; Robson, I, 742.

[232]If the fixed amount or percentage of the blood money is not prescribed for the penalty of wounds, the victim is entitled to a compensation known as *ḥukūmatu 'adl*^{in}. In such a case the amount is to be determined by the *qāḍī*. He could either follow the instructions laid down by the Prophet in his letter to 'Amr b. Ḥazm when the latter was deputed to Yemen, or follow his own *ijtihād*. The compensation is generally estimated, as Nu'mān himself explains in the following passage, by how much the bodily harm in question would reduce the value of a slave. Hence, the corresponding percentage of the blood money must be paid. Mālik, *al-Muwaṭṭa'*, 523; Shāfi'ī, *al-Risāla*, 422–3; trans. 261–2; Schacht, *Origins*, 186; See also n. 220 above in this chapter. The Urdu translator and Fyzee failed to grasp the meaning of this term.

[233]For these lesser wounds, there is no retaliation nor any fixed amount of blood money. Ibn Rushd, *Bidāya*, II, 403, 415; see also n. 220 above in this chapter.

[234]See n. 31 above in this chapter.

[Let us take the case of] a free man who is short, ugly, and black, who is being hit. If he was a slave before and after he was hit, we find that, when assessed before and after the assault, his price may increase rather than decrease in [the estimation of] a purchaser who desires to use him for aggressive purposes (*li 'l-ḥarb*). His scars may prove his aggressiveness and strength. If his price decreases, it may not be to a large extent. However, if he is well built and handsome, his price may diminish greatly. Thus, they differentiated between the blood money of a Muslim whom the Messenger of God had declared equal. They also assessed the value of free men who have no price and it is not proper to put a price on those who cannot be sold. This is contrary to God and His Messenger. He who follows passion as his god will be led astray and blinded by God. May God protect us from following passions and giving opinions on religion and legal provisions (*aḥkām*) by mere opinion. For their assertion that this is the rule of adjudication [known as] *ḥukūmatu 'adl*^{in} is, in reality, tantamount to the rule of *ḥukūmatu jawr*^{in} (unjust adjudication). The former only resembles the latter. This cannot escape him who is endowed with intelligence and a sense of justice when he examines his conscience.

17

Book of Divinely Ordained Punishments (*Kitāb al-Ḥudūd*)[1]

THE ESTABLISHMENT OF DIVINELY ORDAINED PUNISHMENTS AND THE PROHIBITION OF GIVING THEM UP (*IQĀMAT AL-ḤUDŪD WA 'L-NAHY 'AN TAḌYĪ'IHĀ*)[2]

Ja'far b. Muḥammad—his father—his ancestors: A woman who had a high status and was respected among her people had committed theft

[1]For *ḥudūd* see *The Pillars of Islam*, I, 50, n. 122. Jurists differ on the number of *ḥudūd* offences. According to the most liberal count, they are seven: theft (*sariqa*), highway robbery (*qaṭ' al-ṭarīq*), adultery (*zinā'*), defamation (false accusation of adultery, *qadhf*), wine drinking (*shurb al-khamr*), apostasy (*ridda*), and rebellion (*baghy*). Some jurists omit rebellion while others classify wine drinking and apostasy as crimes of *ta'zīr* (the offences for which the *sharī'a* does not prescribe a penalty and punishment of these offences is left to the discretion of the sovereign). Neither the Qur'ān nor the *sunna* prescribed specific penalties for them. See Aly Mansour, 'Hudud Crimes'; Alfi, 'Punishment in Islamic Criminal Law'; Schacht, *Introduction*, 175–87; these punishments come under penal law.

[2]The Qur'ān states: *These are the limits (imposed by) Allah (ḥudūd Allāh). Transgress them not* (2:229). At another place it states: *Such are the limits (imposed by) Allah; and whoso transgresseth Allah's limits, he verily wrongeth his soul* (65:1). A *ḥadd* offence is considered a breach of obligation towards God. The principle of the legality of punishment has been applied strictly to *ḥudūd* crimes and may never be abrogated, either by an individual or by society through its duly constituted authorities. The *ḥadd* punishment cannot be inflicted if there is any doubt concerning the material elements of the crime or if the circumstances surrounding the crime motivate its commision. A tradition states, 'Avert the infliction of *ḥudūd* punishments on Muslims as much as you can. If there is any way out, let a man go, for it is better for the Imam to make a mistake in forgiving than to make a mistake in punishing.' *Mishkāt*, II, 292; Robson, I, 762. Most Sunnī jurists agree that, in accordance with the principle of equality of all persons before the law, the *ḥadd* punishment can be imposed even

and was brought to the Messenger of God. The Messenger of God ordered her hand to be cut off. People of the Quraysh[3] gathered together and came to the Messenger of God and said, 'O Messenger of God, do you cut off the hand of a noble woman like so-and-so for a small fault?' He said, 'Yes. The people who lived before your time perished for such an error. They used to enforce the divinely ordained punishments on the weak amongst them, and used to set free the strong and the highborn, and so they perished.'

[Ja'far b. Muḥammad]: He forbade people from cancelling the divinely ordained punishments. He said, 'The Israelites perished because they enforced the divinely ordained punishments against the lower classes but not against the higher.'

'Alī: He wrote to Rifā'a[4] as follows: Execute the divinely ordained punishments against those that are near [you] so that those who are distant may fear it [the punishment]. Blood does not go unrecompensed and the divinely ordained punishments are not suspended.

['Alī]: Once he was in the presence of 'Uthmān[5] and they brought Walīd b. 'Uqba[6] as one who deserved the divinely ordained punishment. 'Uthmān said, 'He who holds that Walīd deserves such a punishment should stand up and punish him.' Knowing the opinion of 'Uthmān, the people were reluctant to act. So 'Alī stood up, took up the thong and delivered the strokes by his own hand.

['Alī]: In exhorting some people, he said, 'I enjoin you to enforce the divinely ordained punishments on those who are near and those who are distant,[7] and to judge by the Book of God whether it is agreeable

---

on the Imam/Caliph (Head of the Islamic State). Aly Mansour, 'Hudud Crimes'; Alfi, 'Punishment in Islamic Criminal Law'.

[3]Quraysh, see *The Pillars of Islam*, I, 37, n. 81.

[4]Rifā'a was 'Alī's *qāḍī* at Ahwāz, see *The Pillars of Islam*, I, 281.

[5]'Uthmān b. 'Affān was the third caliph, see *The Pillars of Islam*, I, 23, n. 19.

[6]Walīd b. 'Uqba b. Abī Mu'ayṭ was 'Uthmān's governor in Kūfa from 26/646 to 30/650. He was accused of wine drinking. Sa'īd b. al-'Āṣ flogged al-Walīd, who was wearing a coarse mantle, and 'Alī b. Abī Ṭālib ripped it from him. Ṭabarī, *The History of al-Ṭabarī*, XV, 5, 15–17, 45–54. Walīd was addicted to wine and Mas'ūdī's narrative of his misbehaviour during prayer is provocative. Ṭabarī's report that Sa'īd flogged Walīd is inconsistent with what Mas'ūdī relates. He reports that 'Alī first asked his son Ḥasan to flog Walīd, but he excused himself realizing that those who were present were reluctant to anger the caliph. Finally, when 'Alī stood up, Walīd called him names and 'Aqīl b. Abī Ṭālib, who was present, reprimanded him. Mas'ūdī, *Murūj*, III, 78–80.

[7]'Enforce God's prescribed punishments on those who are near and those who are distant, and let no one's blame come upon you [regarding their enforcement].' *Mishkāt*, II, 296; Robson, I, 765.

to you or not, and to distribute [property] justly between the red [Arabs] and the black [Negroes].'[8]

['Alī]: He used to visit the prisons every Friday. He would inflict the divinely ordained punishments on those who were guilty and discharge those who were innocent.[9]

['Alī]: He said, 'He who deserves the divinely ordained punishment should be punished. There should be no delay in [carrying out] the divinely ordained punishments.'[10]

The Messenger of God: He forbade people from interceding in [the implementation of] the divinely ordained punishments (for criminal offences). He said, 'God will punish those persons on the Day of Judgement who intercede to annul a divninely ordained punishment or who generally try to render nugatory those rules (of divinely ordained punishment).'[11]

'Alī: He had arrested a man from the tribe of the Banū Asad[12] who had been guilty of a *ḥadd* offence and was to be punished for it. The Banū Asad went to al-Ḥusayn b. 'Alī to intercede on their behalf and he refused. They went to 'Alī and asked him. He replied, 'If you ask for something I possess, I will give it to you.' They went away happy. They passed by al-Ḥusayn and informed him of what 'Alī had said and he responded, 'If you have some need on behalf of your companion, go, but it is possible that his affair is finished.'

They went to 'Alī and found that he had inflicted the *ḥadd* punishment on the man. The tribesmen said to 'Alī, 'Did you not promise us, O

[8]The Arabic terms are *al-aḥmar wa 'l-aswad*. A tradition of the Messenger of God says, 'I have been sent to the white (*al-aḥmar*) and the black;' because these two epithets comprise all mankind. *Al-Aḥmar* means the white and the red races, and *al-aswad* means the Negroes. Some authorities hold that by the former foreigners are meant, and by the latter Arabs are meant. Lane, s.v. ḥ-m-r. Gloss in MS Q: *al-aḥmar* means non-Arabs (*'ajam*), *al-aswad* means Arabs. The Byzantines were called Banū Aṣfar (sons of the Yellow/Red One) by the Arabs. See Ṭabarī, *History of al-Ṭabarī*, IX, 48, n. 346.

[9]Cf. Alfi, 'Punishment in Islamic Criminal Law', 235.

[10]*Kāfī*, VII, 227; '... there should not be even a short delay.'

[11]Once Usāma b. Zayd spoke to the Messenger of God concerning a Makhzūmī woman who had committed theft. The Messenger of God said, 'Are you interceding regarding a *ḥadd* punishment ordained by God?' He then got up and addressed [the people saying], 'What destroyed the people who preceded you was nothing more than the following: When a person of high rank among them committed a theft, they left him alone, but when a weak one of their number committed a theft, they inflicted the *ḥadd* punishment on him. I swear by God that if Fāṭima, daughter of Muḥammad, should steal I would have her hand cut off.' *Mishkāt*, II, 302; Robson, I, 769; transmitted by Bukhārī and Muslim. See also *Kāfī*, VII, 278.

[12]Banū Asad, see *The Pillars of Islam*, I, 492, n. 279.

Commander of the Faithful?' 'Alī said, 'I did promise you [something from] what I possessed; but this belongs to God and I have no power over it.'

['Alī]: He said, 'There is no harm in interceding for a *ḥadd* crime appertaining to the rights of men (*ḥuqūq al-nās*)[13] before it has been taken [to the authority concerned]. Once, however, the Imam begins deliberation over the matter, no intercession is possible.'[14]

['Alī]: An embroidered black gown (*khamīṣa*)[15] belonging to Ṣafwan b. Umayya[16] was stolen. He brought the thief to the Prophet who ordered his hand to be amputated. Ṣafwān said, 'O Messenger of God, I did not think that the affair would culminate in this. I make a gift of the gown to him.' The Messenger of God said, 'Why was this not done before you came to me with him? When the accused person upon whom the *ḥadd* punishment is to be carried out is brought before the governing authority, he cannot abandon it.'[17]

Abū Ja'far [Imam al-Bāqir] said, 'No one below the rank of the Imam can forgive a crime against God [i.e. the offences that 'transgress God's limits']; but those offences that are against the rights of men can be forgiven by an officer below the rank of an Imam.'

Ja'far b. Muḥammad [Imam al-Ṣādiq] said, 'No person who forgives an accused person of a *ḥadd* crime has the right to withdraw from such a decision.'

The Messenger of God:[18] He said, 'The back of a believer is protected except against a divinely ordained punishment.' He forbade that the punishments laid down by God be increased and made more excessive. He said, 'God has clearly mentioned all of the punishments ordained [in

[13]Crimes such as murder, false accusation of fornication, theft, brigandage, and battery, are crimes against men.

[14]'Forgive the infliction of *ḥudūd* punishments among yourselves, for any *ḥadd* penalty of which I hear, must be carried out.' *Mishkāt*, II, 292; Robson, I, 762.

[15]A *khamīṣa* is a black, square garment with two ornamental or coloured borders of either wool or silk at each end. Lane, s.v. kh-m-ṣ.

[16]Ṣafwān b. Umayya had fought the Muslim army entering Mecca, but then surrendered. He was among those 'whose hearts were to be reconciled (*al-mu'allafa qulūbuhum*)', and the Prophet gave him one hundred camels from the booty captured at Ḥunayn. Ṭabarī, *The History of al-Ṭabarī*, IX, 7, 10, 32.

[17]Ṣafwān b. Umayya came to Medina and slept in the mosque using his cloak as a pillow. A thief came and took his cloak. Ṣafwān seized him and brought him to the Prophet who then ordered that his hand be be cut off. Ṣafwān said, 'This was not my intention. I give it to him as *ṣadaqa*.' The Messenger of God replied, 'Why did you not do so before bringing him to me?' *Mishkāt*, II, 298–9; Robson, I, 767. See also *Kāfī*, VII, 275–6.

[18]As in MS Q.

the Qur'ān], and has laid down a punishment for everyone who transgresses [God's] limits.'

[The Messenger of God]: He said, 'The most abominable creature in the sight of God is one who bares the back of a believer without having any right [to do so];[19] one who strikes a man who had not struck him and without any justification; or one who kills a man who did not kill him.'

'Alī: He commanded Qanbar[20] to strike a man. Qanbar made a mistake and administered three stripes in excess. 'Alī gave the accused the right of retaliation, who, in turn, gave Qanbar three stripes.[21]

['Alī]: He wrote to Rifā'a,[22] 'Protect the faithful one as far as possible, for, verily, he is in the protection of God, his life is held sacred by God, to him is due a reward from God, and the one who wrongs him is the adversary of God, and you should not become the adversary of God.'

The Messenger of God: He forbade people from inflicting divinely ordained punishments in a mosque.[23] 'Alī used to order out of the mosque the one against whom the *ḥadd* punishment was to be carried out.

'Alī: A group of people had refused to come out of enemy territory and had demanded a pact that they should not be held responsible for any of their obligations [while they were there]. 'Alī said, 'This is not proper, for religious war (*jihād*) is waged only to establish the penalties laid down by God and to repel the wrongs done to the people of those territories. When an army fights in an enemy country, and they find that someone has committed a *ḥadd* (punishable) offence, their case should be delayed until they come out of the enemy territory. Thereafter, the *ḥadd* punishments should be inflicted upon them so that their protective instinct does not lead them to remain in the enemy country.'[24]

The Messenger of God said, 'When a man commits an offence and has been punished for it in this world, God is too just to duplicate the punishment on the creature [in the next world].[25] When a man commits

[19]*Kāfī*, VII, 286.

[20]Qanbar was a slave of 'Alī. See *The Pillars of Islam*, I, 64, n. 168.

[21]*Kāfī*, VII, 285–6; Alfi, 'Punishment in Islamic Criminal Law', 233.

[22]Rifā'a, see *The Pillars of Islam*, 281, n. 48.

[23]*Mishkāt*, II, 263; Robson, I, 738. See *The Pillars of Islam*, I, 187.

[24]It was the Umayyad practice not to apply *ḥadd* punishments on the army in enemy territory for fear of desertion. Abū Ḥanīfa introduced a systematic theory of the applicability of religious punishments and their territorial limits. The Medinese did not recognize the practice, but Mālik made the concession that the commander might postpone the *ḥadd* punishment if he was engaged in enemy country. Schacht, *Origins*, 209. 'Alī said, 'The *ḥadd* punishment should not be carried out in enemy territory.' *Kāfī*, VII, 235.

[25]*Kāfī*, VII, 291.

a sin and God has veiled him from discovering it in this world, God is too noble to return to something [in the next world] which he had already overlooked.'

'Alī: When he stoned Shurāḥa al-Hamdānīya[26] [for adultery], there was a large crowd, so the gates of the Ruḥba[27] were closed. He took her out and she was put in a pit and stoned until she died. Then, the gates of the Ruḥba were opened and people entered and began to curse her. When 'Alī heard this, he had a proclamation made to this effect, 'O people, no divinely ordained punishment [for a crime] is ever inflicted on anyone except as a complete expiation thereof, just as one debt is extinguished by another.'[28]

'Alī: He said, 'I heard the Messenger of God say, "God has provided seventy-two veils to His faithful servant; when he commits a sin, one of these veils is torn asunder. If he repents, God returns the veil and adds seven others. If the sinner refuses [to repent] and goes straight on with his sins, his veils are rent; but if he repents, the veil is restored and seven others added. However, if he persists in wrongdoing and goes on with his sins, his veils will be torn and he will have no veil left and God will ask the angels to veil him with their wings. If he still refuses and goes on with his sins, the angels will complain to God and God will command them to raise [their wings] from him. Then, if he commits a wrong in the darkness of night, or the light of day, in a cave, or in the depths of the sea, God will make it manifest against him and it will run on the tongues of the people." Therefore, ask God not to rend asunder your veils.'

'Alī: He said, 'If I were to see an indecency being committed by a believer, I would cover it up by this robe of mine'[29] or, he is reported to

[26]Shurāḥa al-Hamdānīya confessed to 'Alī that she had committed adultery. *Majma' al-baḥrayn*, s.v. sh-r-ḥ; *Tāj al-'arūs*, s.v. sh-r-ḥ.

[27]Ruḥba, see Chap. 6, n. 59.

[28]To extinguish one debt by another is a metaphorical language. What it means is that she committed an adultery, i.e. incurred a debt, and it was extinguished by bringing upon herself another debt, i.e. the *ḥadd* punishment. Her crime was paid off by undergoing the punishment, hence she should not be cursed. See also 'Abd al-Razzāq, *Muṣannaf*, III, 537. After she died a person criticized her and said that she died an evil death. On hearing it 'Alī beat the man with a staff that was in his hand.

[29]Mā'iz came to he Prophet and confessed that he [committed adultery] ... [The Prophet] ordered him to be stoned to death, but said to Hazzāl, 'If you had covered him with your garment, it would have been better for you.' Hazzāl was one of the two persons who had asked Mā'iz to go to the Prophet and tell him. *Mishkāt*, II, 292; Robson, I, 761. Another version of this tradition is as follows:

When Mā'iz al-Aslamī came to God's Messenger and said that he had committed fornication he turned away from him. He came a second time. The Prophet turned away from

have said, by his robe. He raised his hands [in prayer and said], 'Verily, repentance is between the believer and God.'

['Alī]: He said, 'There are three [known] truths: (i) God does not become the guardian of a servant in this world and then appoint someone else to judge him in the next; (ii) God does not act the same towards a man who has a share in religion as He does towards one who has no share in it; (iii) when a man accompanies a people of Islamic faith in good things and not in bad, he will surely appear with them on the Day of Judgement. The fourth, [if I were to reveal and] if I were to swear to it, I would be doing a good act, is that whenever God covers up [the sins of] a man in this world, He also screens him in the Hereafter.'

THE PUNISHMENTS FOR ADULTERERS AND ADULTERESSES (*ḤADD AL-ZĀNĪ WA 'L-ZĀNIYA*)[30]

God says: *And come not near unto adultery. Lo! it is an abomination and an evil way* (17:32); and God says: *The adulterer and the adulteress, scourge ye each one of them (with) a hundred stripes* (24:2), till His saying:[31] *... all that is forbidden unto believers* (24:3); and God says: *And who guard their modesty, save from their wives or the [slaves] that their right hands possess, for then they are not blameworthy. But whoso craveth beyond that, such are transgressors* (23:5–7). And God says: *And those who cry not unto any other god along with Allah, nor take the life which Allah hath forbidden save in (the course of) justice, nor commit adultery—and whoso doeth this shall pay the penalty; the doom shall be doubled for him on the Day of Resurrection, and he will abide therein disdained forever; save him who repenteth* (25:68–70).

---

him. He came round again, and when he said it a fourth time, God's Messenger gave the command. He was taken out to the *ḥarra* and stoned. When he felt the effect of the stones, he ran away vigorously till he passed a man who had the jawbone of a camel. That man struck him with it and the people struck him till he died. They then mentioned to God's Messenger that he had fled when he felt the effect of the stones and the touch of death. He said, 'Why did you not leave him alone? Perhaps he might have repented and been forgiven by God.'

Mā'iz was turned away three times and was punished after his fourth confession. In order to implement the *ḥadd* punishment for adultery, confession must be made on four separate occasions. The reason for it is that, in this case, four male witnesses are required instead of the normal two, and they must testify as eyewitnesses to the act of intercourse itself. Schacht, *Introduction*, 177; idem, *Origins*, 106.

[30]For a summary in Arabic, see Māwardī, *al-Aḥkām al-sulṭāniyya*, 223–6; Ibn al-Farrā', *al-Aḥkām al-sulṭāniyya*, 263–6.

[31]The rest of the verse is: *And let not pity for the twain withhold you from obedience to Allah, if ye believe in Allah and the Last Day. And let a party of believers witness their punishment. The adulterer shall not marry save an adulteress or an idolatress, and the adulteress none shall marry save an adulterer or an idolater.*

Ja'far b. Muḥammad—his father—his ancestors—'Alī: The Messenger of God said, 'The wrath of God is kindled on a woman who introduces an outsider to [the privacy of] a people, who then sees their women and tramples upon their beds. The man who will suffer the most torment on the Day of Resurrection is he who plants his seed in a womb forbidden to him.'

['Alī]:[32] He said, 'On the Day of Resurrection, the adulterer will be brought above the people in Hell and a drop shall emerge from his private parts. It will cause pain to the people of Hell because of its stench. They will ask the keepers of Hell, "What is this awful stench?" They will reply, "It is the odour of an adulterer." Then, the adulteress will be brought and a drop shall exude from her private parts and it will also cause torment to the people of Hell.'

['Alī]: He said, 'Except polytheism, there is no sin greater in the eyes of God than [for a man] to place his seed in a womb which is not lawful for him.'

['Alī]: He said, 'Adultery and goodness (*khayr*) cannot live together in one house.'

['Alī]: He said, 'The wrath of God descends vehemently upon a woman who introduces an outsider to her people who then enjoys their property[33] and looks at their private parts.'

['Alī]: He said, 'The man who deceives and corrupts[34] another man's wife is not one of us.'

['Alī]: He ascended a pulpit and said, 'There are three persons, *God shall not speak to them on the Day of Resurrection, neither purify [or absolve] them; there awaits them a painful chastisement* (2:174)[35] [and these are:] an aged adulterer (*shaykh*^{un} *zān*^{in}), a tyrannous king (*malik*^{un} *jabbār*^{un}), an impecunious cheat (*muqill*^{un} *mukhtāl*^{un}).'

['Alī]: He said, 'An adulterer, at the time of committing adultery, is not possessed of faith.'[36]

Ja'far b. Muḥammad:[37] He said, 'When an adulterer descends upon

[32]In the edited text and MS Q: *wa-'anhu*. The referent, therefore, is not clear.

[33]The text is: *fa-akala min ḥarā'ibihim*. *Ḥarība* (pl. *ḥarā'ib*) is the wealth or property of which one is despoiled, or the wealth by means of which one lives. Lane, s.v. ḥ-r-b. In MS Q and other MSS of Fyzee: *khazā'inihim*, instead of *ḥarā'ibihim*.

[34]The Arabic is *khabbaba*. It means that he corrupted and rendered her disaffected to her husband. Lane, s.v. kh-b-b; gloss in MS Q.

[35]Arberry, *Koran*, I, 50. It is worth noting that the verse does not refer to these three categories of people, rather it refers to *Those who conceal what the Book of God has sent down on them, and sell it for a little price* [*the Jews*].

[36]Bukhārī, *Matn al-Bukhārī*, IV, 171.

[37]According to MS Q. In the edited text: *qāla*.

the belly of the adulteress, the spirit of faith departs from him. When he stands up, and if he asks God for His forgiveness it returns.'

Ja'far b. Muḥammad:[38] He said, 'There are three persons, *God shall not speak to them on the Day of Resurrection,*[39] *neither purify [or absolve] them; there awaits them a painful chastisement* (2:174)—an aged adulterer, a cuckold[40] who collects people for committing adultery in his house, and a woman who tramples upon the bed of her husband.'

Abū Ja'far Muḥammad b. 'Alī: He said, 'Among things revealed to Moses[41] son of 'Imrān is [the following:] "O Moses, forbid the Israelites from committing adultery, for, verily, adultery will be committed against him who commits adultery. O Moses, become pure and your people will also become pure. O Moses, if you wish good to increase in your house, be warned against adultery. O Moses, son of 'Imrān, as you behave [towards men] so shall they behave towards you."'

[Abū Ja'far Muḥammad b. 'Alī]: He said, 'The verse of stoning was in the Qur'ān [and it read]: *The old man and the old woman, if they commit adultery, stone them both [to death] (outright) without fail, for verily they have satisfied themselves (of their lusts).*'[42]

[38]In MS Q: *'anhu.*

[39]*On the Day of Resurrection*: as in the Qur'ān and MS Q; it is dropped in the edited text.

[40]The Arabic term is *dayyūth*, a man without jealousy nor shame, and acts the part of a pimp to one's own wife. Lane, s.v. d-y-th.

[41]See *The Pillars of Islam*, I, 56.

[42]Mālik reported it in his *Muwaṭṭa'*, 542. 'Umar said, 'God sent Muḥammad with the truth and sent down the Book to him. The verse of stoning was included in what God sent down. The Messenger of God stoned [the adulterer and the adulteress] to death and we have also been doing it since his death. Stoning is a duty laid down in God's Book for married men and women who commit adultery when proof is established, or if there is a pregnancy, or a confession.' Transmitted by Bukhārī and Muslim. *Mishkāt*, II, 287–8; Robson, I, 757. See also *Kāfī*, VII, 189–90, reported on the authority of Imam al-Ṣādiq.

This so-called 'verse of stoning' is said to have been an original part of the Qur'ān and to have been acknowledged as such by the second caliph, 'Umar b. al-Khaṭṭāb. It is improbable that this verse is genuine. Similarly, the reports that the Prophet punished the guilty by stoning are unworthy of credence. The stoning punishment entered Islam quite early and came from Jewish law (Deuteronomy XXII, 21–4), as can be seen in *ḥadīth*. Some jurists refused to recognize stoning to death because it is based on the *sunna* and not mentioned in the Qur'ān. J. Burton has argued that the story about the verse of stoning was put into circulation by Shāfi'ī scholars who did not accept the principle that a *sunna* can abrogate a Qur'ānic verse. Hence, they were forced to find a source with higher authority, i.e. the Qur'ānic revelation, for the lawfulness of stoning. For the question as to whether this is an alleged instance of the *naskh* (abrogation) of the Qur'ān by the *sunna*, or an instance of a third mode of *naskh*: the suppression of the wording without, however, the

'Alī: He decided that a married man (*muḥṣan*) and a married woman (*muḥṣana*)[43] found guilty of adultery should first be given one hundred stripes each and then stoned.[44]

Ja'far b. Muḥammad:[45] He said, 'No man or woman should be stoned until four competent and just witnesses have given evidence against them that they have seen them having intercourse and have witnessed the penetration and the extraction [of the penis] like a style in the collyrium case.[46] Thus, they are not to be punished if they are unmarried and unless such evidence is forthcoming. If they [the man and the woman] are found covered in one sheet, they shall be scourged with ninety-nine strokes. A similar punishment is to be awarded to two men or two women if they are found covered in one sheet without proper cause. This is because they are suspected [of a misdeed] but there is doubt. This decreases their punishment to something below the limit.'[47]

The Messenger of God: A man came to him and said, 'O Messenger of God, I have committed adultery.' The Messenger of God turned away

---

suppression of the ruling (*naskh al-tilāwa dūna 'l-ḥukm*) see Burton, *Collection of the Qur'ān*, 86–104; Ibn Sallām, *Kitāb al-nāsikh*, English introduction, 24–42; *EI*^{2}, s.v. Zinā or Zinā'.

In its report of 29 December 2002, Associated Press reported that Āyatollāh Nāṣir Makārim Shīrāzī and Āyatollāh Ḥusayn Mūsawī Tabrīzī have introduced a bill in the Iranian Majlis (parliament) for the abolition of stoning punishment. They said that their move was in response to the demands of modern age. Any punishment, they argued, including stoning, that defames Islam or depicts a bad picture of the religion in the world is harmful to Islam and it is fully Islamic to stop it.

[43]In Islamic penal law the terms *muḥṣan* and *muḥṣana* are applied only to adult free persons with two different meanings: (i) a *muḥṣan* in the sense of being a free person who has never committed unlawful intercourse, and is protected against *qadhf* (see n. 105 below); (ii) a *muḥṣan* in the sense of a free person who has concluded and consummated a valid marriage, and is subject to a more severe punishment, if he or she should afterwards have illegal intercourse. Schacht, *Introduction*, 125; see also n. 57 below. All schools of jurisprudence agree that *zinā'* is to be punished with stoning if the offender is *muḥṣan*. Ḥanafīs and Ḥanbalīs require that parties in *zinā'* be *muḥṣan* for stoning to be applied.

[44]I have avoided the repetition found in the Arabic text. The married person is first flogged, then stoned. *Mishkāt*, II, 288; Robson, I, 758; transmitted by Muslim.

[45]According to MS Q, the edited text is without *'an*.

[46]As a counterweight to the severe punishment, the law stipulates definite requirements for the proof necessary to establish the crime. The jurists are not satisfied with the mere requirement of four reliable witnesses, but further stipulate that they must testify that they have witnessed the physical act of sexual intercourse. *Kāfī*, VII, 1, 97–8; all the traditions emphasize the above prerequisites. Ṭūsī, *Tahdhīb al-aḥkām*, X, 2–3.

[47]*Kāfī*, VII, 194–6, 215. In all such cases, both men and women shall be punished to the full extent of the law. If a man is found with a boy covered in one sheet, he should be flogged and the boy chastised.

from him three times and said to those who were with him, 'Is your companion devoid of reason?' They said, 'No.' The man then confessed a fourth time[48] and the Messenger of God ordered him to be stoned. A pit was dug for him and he was stoned. When the stones began to hurt him, he began to run away and Zubayr[49] overtook him, struck him with the jawbone of a [dead] camel and killed him. The Prophet was informed of this and said to Zubayr, 'Oh yes, you should have let him escape.' The Prophet also said, 'It would have been better for him to have it hidden [rather than confess] provided he had repented.'[50]

'Alī: He once stoned a woman. A pit was dug for her and she was put into it; then, he himself, peace be upon him, began to stone her and commanded the people to do likewise and they did. 'Alī said, 'The Imam is the one most entitled to begin the stoning in [cases of] adultery.'

Ja'far b. Muḥammad said, 'The adulterer and the adulteress should be buried up to their waists. The Imam should stone first and then the people should follow. Smaller stones should be used because they can be easily thrown and are less hurtful to the criminal.[51] His face should be

[48]This doctrine of confession from a person who has committed adultery before incurring the *ḥadd* punishment, based on the analogy of four witnesses prescribed by the Qur'ān (24:4), has survived in the Ḥanafī school. It was an original Iraqi doctrine that spread into Ḥijāz and was expressed in a group of traditions ascribed to the Prophet, but it did not prevail in the school of Medina. Schacht, *Introduction*, 38; idem, *Origins*, 106–7.

[49]He is probably Zubayr b. al-'Awwām, see *The Pillars of Islam*, I, 23, n. 18.

[50]*Mishkāt*, II, 288–89, 291; Robson, I, 758–9, 761. Two traditions on the authority of Abū Hurayra, with slight variations, are cited. Bukhārī and Muslim transmitted the first. Zubayr's name is not given. *Kāfī*, VII, 198–9. Kulaynī transmits two traditions. In the first, the name of the person stoned is given as Mā'iz b. Mālik (as in *Mishkāt*). In both the traditions, it was Zubayr who delivered the last blow. See also n. 29 above in this chapter.

This tradition, as well as others reported in *Mishkāt*, suggest that the Prophet would have preferred geuine repentance and rehabilitation rather than severe punishment. A tradition states, 'Forgive the infliction of prescribed penalties among yourselves, for any *ḥadd* penalty of which I hear must be carried out.' Another tradition states, 'Avert the infliction of *ḥadd* punishment on Muslims as much as you can. If there is any way out, let the accused go, for, it is better for the Imam to make a mistake in forgiving than to make a mistake in punishing.' *Mishkāt*, II, 292; Robson, I, 762.

Kulaynī cites a long tradition in which a pregnant woman came to 'Alī and confessed to committing adultery. There were no witnesses, but she insisted that he purify her by inflicting the punishment on her. 'Alī sent her back saying that she should return after she had delivered the baby. When she returned, 'Alī sent her back saying that she should nurse the baby for two years. She returned after two years and, again, 'Alī sent her back to make sure that she found someone who will nurture her baby when she is dead. Finally, 'Alī was forced to carry out the punishment because she insisted on it and had confessed to the offence four times. *Kāfī*, VII, 199–201.

[51]*Kāfī*, VII, 198–9.

turned towards the *qibla* and he should not be stoned [from the front] of his face. He should be stoned until he dies.'

'Alī was asked about two unmarried persons (*bikr*) who had committed fornication. He said that they should be punished with a hundred stripes each, and then recited the Word of God: *The adulterer and the adulteress, scourge ye each one of them [with] a hundred stripes. And let not pity for the twain withhold you from obedience to Allah* (24:2).[52]

Ja'far b. Muḥammad:[53] He said: The stripes inflicted on the adulterer should be the most severe. After the unmarried (*bikr*) fornicator has been scourged, he should be banished from the town (city) for one year. If one of the adulterers is married (*thayyib*) and the other unmarried (*bikr*), then each one should be scourged with one hundred stripes; the unmarried one should be banished and the married one should be stoned.'[54] A person, whether male or female, who has no spouse, is called a *bikr*, and a person who has (or had) a spouse is known as a *thayyib*.[55]

'Alī: A man was brought to him who had acknowledged that he had committed adultery. 'Alī asked him, 'Have you married?'[56] He said, 'Yes.' Then 'Alī said, 'In that case, you will be stoned.' 'Alī ordered him to be taken to prison. When it was evening, people gathered to stone him. A man among them said, 'O Commander of the Faithful, he certainly has married a woman, but he has not consummated the marriage with her.' 'Alī was relieved and scourged him with stripes [instead].

Ja'far b. Muḥammad said, 'Only after one legally marries, consummates, and lives with a spouse does he achieve [the state of] *iḥṣān* (unblemished reputation)[57] and thereby, become liable to stoning punishment. If the man and wife deny that they had sexual intercourse (*dukhūl*) after having lived together, they should not be believed.

[52]The last part of the verse according to MS Q, it is missing in the edited text.

[53]According to MS Q. *Qāla*: in the edited text.

[54]'An unmarried man who committed fornication should receive one hundred lashes and be banished for a year.' Transmitted by Bukhārī. *Mishkāt*, II, 287; Robson, I, 757. See also *Kāfī*, VII, 190, 211–12. On banishment, see Schacht, *Origins*, 53, 209.

[55]Lane, s.v. th-w-b.

[56]The Arabic expression is *uḥṣinta*, from the fourth form, *aḥṣana*, and means that he protected himself. *Aḥṣanahu al-tazawwuju* means that marriage caused him to abstain from that which is unlawful, and *iḥṣān* is a verbal noun from it. Lane, s.v. ḥ-ṣ-n; see also n. 106 below in this chapter.

[57]*Iḥṣān* is a technical term in Islamic law denoting a certain personal status (see the previous note). It applies to one who is married (and the marriage has been duly consummated), free, and Muslim. The quality of *iḥṣān* resides in each spouse when both satisfy all the above three criteria. *EI*[2], s.v. Muḥṣan.

'Alī:[58] He said, '[The state of] *iḥṣān* is not achieved through a *mut'a* marriage.[59] The man who is absent from his wife and the woman who is absent from her husband are not considered to be *muḥṣan* [persons possessing the quality of *iḥṣān*].[60] [The state of] *iḥṣān*, which makes stoning obligatory, only occurs when a man is staying with his wife and a woman with her husband.'

['Alī]: He said, 'Neither the evidence of women nor hearsay evidence is lawful in divinely ordained punishments. At least four witnesses must give testimony for the offence of *zinā'* according to the Word of God (4:15; 24:4). If three persons testify to the offence, but a fourth witness is not available, the three witnesses shall be scourged as defamers (*ḥadd al-qādhif*).[61] If three men and two women bear witness to the offence, the punishment [for *zinā'*] becomes obligatory, but if only two men and four women testify, [there is no *ḥadd* punishment] and the witnesses will be scourged as defamers.'[62]

'Alī: With reference to the Word of God: *And let a party (ṭā'ifa) of believers witness their punishment* (24:2), he said, 'The word *ṭā'ifa* is a party comprising anywhere from one to ten persons.'

['Alī]: With reference to the Word of God: *And let not pity for the twain withhold you from obedience to Allah* (24:2), he said, '[Regarding] the infliction of punishment, if the adulterer is found naked, he should be scourged[63] naked; if he is found clothed, he should be scourged with his clothes on. The criminal should be scourged severely. Men should be beaten while standing and women while sitting. All of the bodily limbs should be

[58]According to MS Q. 'An 'Alī: is missing from the edited text. Hence, it is a continuation of Imam al-Ṣādiq's report.

[59]*Kāfī*, VII, 191; *iḥṣān* does not take place because the *mut'a* marriage, in its nature, is not permanent. For *mut'a* marriage, see Chap. 10, n. 222.

[60]Abū 'Abd Allāh [Imam al-Ṣādiq] was asked about a man who committed adultery while he was in the Ḥijāz and his wife was in Iraq. The Imam said, 'He should be scourged with a hundred stripes, the punishment of a fornicator, and should not be stoned.' In another tradition, the Imam was asked to define the word *muḥṣan*. He said, 'A *muḥṣan* is one who has adequate legitimate means through which he can satisfy his sexual needs and may be stoned if he commits adultery.' For more examples, see *Kāfī*, VII, 191–2.

[61]*Kāfī*, VII, 226. If there are three witnesses, but the fourth does not come forward right away, the three should be punished for defamation. If three witnesses testify for *zinā'* and the fourth express reservation, the *ḥadd* punishment cannot be carried out.

[62]Evidence of women alone is not admissible. Testimony of two men and four women is admissible for beating, but not for stoning. If the testimony of all four witnesses varies, the *ḥadd* punishment cannot be carried out. Ḥillī, *Sharā'i' al-islām*, II, 244–5.

[63]I have preferred the reading *julida* as in MS Q and other MSS of Fyzee. In the edited text: *ḍuriba*.

beaten save the face and the private parts and the beating should be as severe as possible.'[64]

The Messenger of God: An ill person was brought to him who had dropsy (*ḥaban*), whose stomach was enlarged, whose veins were very swollen, and who was suffering from a chronic disease. He had committed an offence worthy of a *ḥadd* punishment. The Messenger of God said, 'You should have busied yourself with something other than this illegal act.' The man said, 'O Messenger of God, a sudden impulse came to me and I could not control it.' The Messenger of God asked for a date palm spadix (*'urjūn*)[65] that had on it one hundred twigs (*shimrākh*).[66] With this, he scourged the man once.[67]

Ja'far b. Muḥammad [Imam al-Ṣādiq] cited the Word of God: *Take in thine hand a branch (ḍighth)*[68] *and smite therewith, and break not thine oath* (38:44),[69] saying, 'This should only be done—and God knows better—when a person is ill and has given up all hope of recovery. But if he is one of those for whom recovery is hoped, [the punishment] should be delayed until he recovers. Only at that point should it be inflicted.'

'Alī: He said, 'No *ḥadd* punishment is to be inflicted on a man who has smallpox (*mujaddar*) or measles (*ḥaṣba*) until he recovers. I am afraid to inflict punishment on him lest his boils burst and he dies; but when he is free from disease, we shall punish him.'[70]

['Alī]: He said, 'No *ḥadd* punishment shall be inflicted on a pregnant woman until she gives birth to her child. Similarly, it should not be inflicted either on a woman who is [in the state] following childbirth or on one who is menstruating, until she is free from that condition.'

['Alī]: He saw a woman being led away, so he asked, 'What is this?' They said, "Umar[71] has ordered her to be stoned, as she conceived a child without having a husband.' 'Alī asked, 'Is she [really] pregnant?'

[64]*Kāfī*, VII, 196–7.

[65]*'Urjūn* is a raceme of a palm tree or dates that has become dry and curved and from which the fruit stalks are cut off. It occurs in the Qur'ān 36:39. Lane, s.v. '-r-j-n.

[66]*Shimrākh* or *shumrūkh* are the fruit stalks of the raceme of a palm tree upon which are dates. It is also a slender and soft branch that has grown forth, upon the upper part of a thick branch within a year. Lane, s.v. sh-m-r-kh.

[67]*Mishkāt*, II, 293–4; Robson, I, 763; the man is described as sick and of deficient build. He was found in the act of illicit intercourse with a slave woman. See also *Kāfī*, VII, 266.

[68]*Ḍighth* is a handful of twigs of trees, or fruit stalks of the raceme of a palm tree. Lane, s.v. ḍ-gh-th.

[69]In Pickthall it is 38:45. *Kāfī*, VII, 266.

[70]*Kāfī*, VII, 267.

[71]'Umar b. al-Khattāb the second caliph, see *The Pillars of Islam*, I, 22, n. 16.

They said, 'Yes.' 'Alī, therefore, rescued her from them and went to 'Umar and said, 'Although you have power over her, you have no right on what is in her womb.' 'Umar said, 'If it wasn't for 'Alī, 'Umar would surely have perished!'[72]

['Alī]: He said, 'A servant girl belonging to one of the progeny of the Messenger of God committed an immoral act. The Messenger of God said to me, "O 'Alī, go and punish her."[73] I went to her and found her to be suffering from continuous haemorrhage, and I informed the Messenger of God and he said, "Leave her until her blood stops, then punish her.[74] The *ḥadd* punishments should also be inflicted on (the slaves) that your right hands possess."'

['Alī]: He said, 'If a married man (*muḥṣan*) confesses four times to adultery, he should be stoned.'

Ja'far b. Muḥammad [Imam al-Ṣādiq] said, 'If he goes back upon his statement, [it should not be accepted and he should be punished but not stoned. If he is married and revokes his confession],[75] he should be scourged with stripes and set free.'

'Alī:[76] Concerning a man who had intercourse with a slave girl (*walīda*) belonging to his wife, he said, 'His punishment should be the same as for adultery. I have punished by stoning everyone who has been brought to me for having intercourse with his wife's slave.'

['Alī]: A woman brought her husband to him and said, 'He has committed adultery with my slave girl and the man admitted that he had sexual intercourse with her and said, "She gifted the girl to me."' 'Alī asked for proof of the gift but no proof was forthcoming. Accordingly, he ordered him to be stoned. When the wife saw this, she said, 'He spoke the truth. I did give my slave girl to him.' Thereupon, 'Alī ordered the man to be set free and his wife to be scourged with the punishment of a defamer.[77]

['Alī]: He said regarding a man who has intercourse with a slave girl

[72]See *The Pillars of Islam*, I, 106, 116, 163, 191.

[73]The Arabic is *fa-aqim 'alayhā 'l-ḥadda*.

[74]'Alī said, 'O people, carry out the *ḥadd* punishments on your slaves ... for a slave woman belonging to God's Messenger committed fornication and he ordered me to beat her. However, she had recently given birth to a child and I was afraid that, if I beat her, I might kill her. So I mentioned that to the Prophet and he said, "You have done well."' Transmitted by Muslim. In a version by Abū Dāwūd, he said, 'Leave her until her blood stops flowing and then carry out the punishment on her ...' *Mishkāt*, 290–1; Robson, I, 760–1.

[75]Addition marked by the brackets is according to MS Q. It is missing from the edited text as well as from the pirated edition of Tāmir.

[76]According to MS Q, in the edited text: *wa-'anhu*.

[77]*Kāfī*, VII, 222. The case was brought before 'Alī and the tradition is reported on the authority of Imam al-Bāqir.

that he owns jointly with another man, 'He should be punished with fifty stripes.'[78]

Ja'far b. Muḥammad: He said, 'If an unmarried elderly woman commits an indecency with a boy who has not attained puberty or if an unmarried grown-up man behaves indecently with a female child who has not attained puberty, the person who has attained puberty should be punished with the punishment of *zinā'*. There is no liability on children, but they should be disciplined severely.'[79]

Ja'far b. Muḥammad: He said, 'An unmarried man who marries a woman who still has a husband shall be punished with stripes. The woman shall be stoned after being scourged. If both are married persons, both shall be scourged and stoned.'[80] [The Imam] meant that [this was the rule] when the man knew that the woman was married, but if he had no such knowledge, there is no punishment for him.

Abū Ja'far Muḥammad b. 'Alī: He was asked about a woman who married [another man] during the *'idda* of divorce in a case where the husband had the right to return to her. He said, 'The punishment is stoning. But if she married during an *'idda* in which the husband had no right to return, then she would be punished with one hundred stripes for fornicating as an unmarried woman. The same would be the case if she married during the *'idda* of death.' This occurs where the second husband actually consummates the marriage. It was said to him, 'But, please tell us! What if the act was done by reason of ignorance?' [The Imam] said, 'There is not a single Muslim woman who does not know that she is duty bound to observe the *'idda* of divorce or of death. Even the women of pre-Islamic times knew of this rule.' It was said to him, 'But, if, in fact, she did not know?' He said, 'The rule still applies to her. She should ask until she knows.'[81]

[Abū Ja'far Muḥammad b. 'Alī]: He was asked about a woman who

[78]Ibid., VII, 208–10; it contains more details and variations on the same theme.

[79]If a boy who has not yet attained puberty commits adultery with a woman, he should be flogged less than the prescribed punishment and the woman punished to the full extent. She should not be stoned even if she is *muḥṣana* because the one who had intercourse with her had not attained puberty. Conversely, if a man is found having intercourse with a girl not yet matured, the man should be punished to the full extent of the law, and the girl be flogged less than the prescribed punishment. Ibid., VII, 193. On the authority of Imam al-Bāqir, Kulaynī states that a fifteen-year-old boy and a nine-year-old girl are liable for a full *ḥadd* punishment; see ibid., VII, 212.

[80]The woman should be stoned if her first husband resides in the same town and both of them see each other. However, if the husband is absent or lives in the same town but they do not see each other, she should be scourged. Ibid., VII, 206–7.

[81]Ibid., VII, 207; reported from the same authority. It is like our dictum: Ignorance of law is no excuse.

married even though she had a husband who was absent. He said, 'They should be separated and she should be punished for adultery.'[82]

The Messenger of God: He said, 'When the people of Lot[83] did what they did, the sky and the earth complained to God and God commanded the sky to pelt them [with stones] and the earth to engulf them.'

[The Messenger of God]: He said, 'There are four ages (*qarn* pl. *qurūn*) and I am in the best of them [the first].[84] Then, there will be a second and a third and, when it comes to the fourth age, men will satisfy themselves with men and women with women. When this happens, God will take away His Book from the breasts of men (*banī Ādam*) and send a black wind (i.e. plague, epidemic, *rīḥ sawdā'*), which will not spare any [except] the Friends of God (*walīy Allāh*).[85] Thereafter, there will be [an age of] engulfment and transmutation (*maskh*).'[86]

The Messenger of God: He said, 'The sodomist (*Lūṭī*), if married, shall be stoned; if not married, shall be scourged with one hundred stripes.'[87]

The Messenger of God: He cursed effeminate males (*al-mukhannathīn min al-rijāl*), and said, 'Remove them from your homes.' He also cursed masculine females (*al-mudhakkarāt min al-nisā'*) and effeminate males (*al-mu'annathīn min al-rijāl*).[88]

[82]Ibid., VII, 207–8; reported from the same authority.

[83]Lūṭ is the Biblical Lot (*Genesis*, xiii, 5–13, xvii-xix) and his story is told at several places in the Qur'ān, for example, in *Sūrat Hūd*, *Sūrat al-Ḥijr*, and *Sūrat al-Shu'arā'*. Besides the refusal to believe, the people of Lūṭ persisted in vices, such as inhospitality and homosexuality. At four places in the Qur'ān 7:81, 26–165–6, 27:55, 29:29, they are accused of 'coming with lust unto men instead of women'. Qur'ān commentators and authors of 'the stories of the prophets' have augmented the Qur'ānic story with vivid details. Despite Abraham's intercession, they were punished and their sinful city was destroyed. *EI*², s.v. Liwaṭ, Lūṭ; Kisā'ī, *Tales of the Prophets*, 155–9; see *The Pillars of Islam*, I, 429, n. 31.

[84]The generation of the Prophet, the first generation of Muslims, is said to have been the best. Then, a process of irreversible decline set in. See *The Pillars of Islam*, I, 13, n. 19.

[85]*Walīy Allāh*, see *The Pillars of Islam*, I, 2, 14, 229, 463. The Arabic text seems to be corrupt.

[86]For *maskh* see *The Pillars of Islam*, I, 188, n. 110. The tradition refers to the apocalypse. Although there is no exact equivalent term for it in Arabic, the material found in *ḥadīth* collections under the title *Kitāb al-fitan wa-ashrāṭ al-sā'a* (Book on civil strife and the signs of the Last Hour) deals with the extraordinary events that will precede the Last Judgment and forms the basis of apocalyptic traditions in Islam. For details see *EIr*, s.v. Apocalyptic, in Muslim Iran.

[87]'The thing I fear most for my people is what Lot's people did.' *Mishkāt*, II, 294; Robson, I, 763. See also *Kāfī*, VII, 212–5; some traditions state that they should be killed. Ṭūsī, *Tahdhīb al-aḥkām*, X, 51–7. It should be noted that the Arabic term *Lūṭī* for a homosexual is derived from Lūṭ, meaning one who is addicted to the practice of the people of Lot.

[88]This tradition is transmitted by Bukhārī, Tirmidhī, Dārimī, and Ibn Ḥanbal. The

'Alī: He said, 'The man who is obedient to his baser spirit will fall headlong into passion for women.'

['Alī]: He said, 'When a man speaks and walks like a woman and has an inclination to have sexual intercourse like a woman, then stone him and do not allow him to live.'[89]

['Alī]: He stoned to death a man in Kūfa who used to allow people to commit sodomy with him (*yu'tā fī duburihi*).

Ja'far b. Muḥammad: He said, 'Persons committing sodomy should be stoned, both the one who does it and the one to whom it is done.'[90]

'Alī:[91] He spoke of sodomists and said, 'Sodomy (*liwāṭ*) is a crime not committed by any community except one, and God did with them what is mentioned in His Book, [namely,] He pelted them with stones. So you too stone them as God had done.'[92]

'Alī:[93] He said, 'Lesbianism between females (*al-saḥq fi 'l-nisā'*) is like sodomy between males, but the punishment is one hundred stripes, as there is no penetration (*īlāj*) in it.'[94]

'Alī:[95] A man who had committed fornication with his father's wife was brought to him. He was not a married man (*lam yakun uḥṣina*), but [the Imam] ordered him to be stoned.

Arabic words used are: *al-mukhannathīn min al-rijāl, al-mutarajjalāt min al-nisā', al-mutashabbihīn min al-rijāl bi 'l-nisā'*, and *al-mutashabbihāt min al-nisā' bi 'l-rijāl*. Bukhārī, *Matn al-Bukhārī*, IV, 38; *Mishkāt*, II, 493; Robson, II, 930; Concordance, s.v. kh-n-th.

[89]*Kāfī*, VII, 294.

[90]*Mishkāt*, II, 294; Robson, I, 763.

[91]As in MS Q. In the edited text: *wa-'anhu* [i.e. Ja'far b. Muḥammad], which is incorrect as the following traditions clearly indicate.

[92]Refer to n. 83 above in this chapter. The word 'homosexuality', derived from the Greek *homos*, meaning 'same', refers both to sex between males and sex between females, though 'lesbianism' is used to refer to the latter. In the history of Western culture, the image of homosexuality appears in the social, medical, and religious discourse. The image equates the sexual behaviour, personal identity, and sociosexual orientation of a person, often under a negative rubric. Since about the eleventh century, homosexuality has been seen as antithetical to Western ideas of church, family, and state, and this attitude to homosexuality reflects a traditional Judeo-Christian cosmology. Some scholars have argued that homosexuality is universal and that it is culture-bound to certain societies or historical periods. It has been demonstrated that polytheistic societies are generally more tolerant of homosexuality than are monotheistic ones. However, there are many exceptions. The literature on this subject is immense and varied. See a comprehensive article in *ER*, s.v. Homosexuality. The learned author of the above article observes that Islamic societies held a more tolerant and informal attitude towards homosexuality.

[93]As in MS Q.

[94]*Kāfī*, VII, 216–17; Ṭūsī, *Tahdhīb al-aḥkām*, X, 57–60.

[95]As in MS Q.

ʿAlī:[96] He said, 'If a man were to have intercourse with a woman forbidden to him in marriage (*dhāt maḥram*), he should be killed.'[97]

ʿAlī:[98] He said, 'If a man compels a woman to copulate with him, against her wishes, he should be put to death. If he compels her, she is not guilty at all and is entitled to have, from the man's property, a dower (*mahr*) of a woman of similar status.'[99]

ʿAlī:[100] He heard that ʿUmar had ordered an insane woman (*majnūna*) to be stoned for adultery. ʿAlī went to him and said, 'Have you not heard that God has exempted three persons from legal liability[101]—a sleeping man until he wakes up; a lunatic (or insane person, *majnūn*) until he regains his sanity; and a child until he reaches puberty? This is an insane woman and God has declared her free from responsibility.'[102] So ʿUmar released her.

Jaʿfar b. Muḥammad: He said, 'If a man has intercourse with an animal, he should be beaten with stripes to the full extent of the law (*ḥadd*). The flesh and milk of the animal should be declared unlawful. If the animal is one which is lawful to eat, it should be slaughtered and burnt to prevent anyone from eating it. If the animal does not belong to the accused, its value should be paid from his property.'[103]

ʿAlī: He said, 'Where a male or female slave commits fornication, each of them should be scourged with fifty stripes, whether they are Muslims or non-Muslims. A slave cannot be punished with banishment or stoning.'

We have mentioned in the chapter of emancipation by contract (*mukātab* slaves)[104] that a slave who has been partially emancipated should be punished fully [as a free man] in proportion to the degree of his freedom;

[96]As in MS Q.

[97]*Kāfī*, VII, 204–5; he should be killed.

[98]As in MS Q.

[99]For similar traditions see *Mishkāt*, II, 292, 295; Robson, I, 762, 764. *Kāfī*, VII, 203; the man should be killed.

[100]As in MS Q.

[101]The Arabic expression is *rafaʿa Allāhu 'l-qalama* or *rufiʿa 'l-qalam*^{u}, which means that God withheld the pen [of the recording angel from writing the deeds of] .... See *The Pillars of Islam*, I, 242; *ḥadīth* sources are indicated therein.

[102]*Kāfī*, VII, 205–6. Kulaynī first reports from ʿAlī that an insane woman should not be punished, but then reports another tradition from Imam al-Ṣādiq that if an insane man commits adultery, he should be punished.

[103]For similar traditions, see *Mishkāt*, II, 294, 296; Robson, I, 763, 765. *Kāfī*, VII, 219–20. He should be beaten less than the full extent ... and banished. He should be given the full (*ḥadd*) punishment only in the case of penetration. See also Ṭūsī, *Tahdhīb al-aḥkām*, X, 60–2; the punishment varies.

[104]See the section 'Emancipation by Contract' in Chap. 12.

and should be awarded half the punishment in proportion to the degree of his enslavement.

THE PUNISHMENT FOR SLANDEROUS ACCUSATION OF FORNICATION (*AL-ḤADD FI 'L-QADHF*)[105]

God says: *Lo! as for those who falsely accuse women in wedlock (al-muḥṣanāt)*,[106] *who behave in a negligent manner (al-ghāfilāt)*,[107] *but are true believers, shall be cursed in this world and the Hereafter. Theirs will be an awful doom* (24:23). And He says: *And those who accuse honourable women but bring not four witnesses, scourge them (with) eighty stripes and never (afterward) accept their testimony—They indeed are evil-doers—Save those who afterwards repent and make amends. (For such) lo! Allah is Forgiving, Merciful.* (24:4–5).[108]

Ja'far b. Muḥammad—his father—his ancestors: 'Alī said, 'The major sins (*kabā'ir*)[109] are: Associating any one with God (*al-shirk bi 'llāh*); intentionally killing a faithful one; fleeing from battle, except for turning round to fight back or to take sides in favour of a particular party; taking usury (*ribā*) after [knowing about] clear evidence [against its lawfulness];[110]

[105]The Arabic term is *qadhf*. The verb *qadhafa* means that he charged a chaste or a married woman with adultery. The active participle is *qādhif*. *Lisān al-'Arab*, s.v. q-dh-f. The person guilty of making such an accusation is punished by a fixed penalty (*ḥadd*) of eighty lashes as stipulated in the Qur'ān. *Qadhf* occurs, according to the majority of jurists, only if the expressions used by the slanderer expressly relate to the fornication or illegitimate descent. It should be pointed out that on account of the very restrictive interpretation of *qadhf* by the majority of legal schools, including the Ismā'īlīs, certain slanderous accusations do not warrant the *ḥadd* punishment prescribed by the Qur'ān. The *qāḍī* has discretionary powers, viz., *ta'zīr*, to apply a lesser penalty than the Qur'ānic *ḥadd*. For details see *EI*[2], s.v. Ḳadhf; Aly Mansour, 'Hudud Crimes', 199. For a summary in Arabic, see Māwardī, *al-Aḥkām al-sulṭāniyya*, 229–31; Ibn al-Farrā', *al-Aḥkām al-sulṭāniyya*, 270–2.

[106]The term *muḥṣana* is applied to a woman who is chaste or abstains from what is neither lawful nor decorous. It can also just mean a married woman. According to some lexicographers, it has the latter signification and means 'caused to be chaste or to abstain from that which is unlawful or indecorous by her husband.' *Muḥṣanāt*, therefore, means women who have husbands. Lane, s.v. ḥ-ṣ-n; see also n. 56 and 57 above in this chapter.

[107]i.e. those who may be less careful in their conduct and more free in their behaviour, but conscious of no ill. See Sale, *Koran*, 345. In translating this verse I have deviated from Pickthall.

[108]In the edited text: *ilā qawlihi*, is incorrect.

[109]For the list of *kabā'ir*, see *The Pillars of Islam*, I, 169, n. 21.

[110]*Kāfī*, VII, 263; for the first time, he should be reprimanded. If he does it again, he should be disciplined. If he goes back to the old habit, he should be killed. For *ribā* see Chap. 1, n. 124.

wrongfully defrauding an orphan of his property; becoming a country Arab after emigration [to Medina];[111] defaming heedless yet believing married women (*al-muḥṣanāt*).'[112]

Ja'far b. Muḥammad: He said, 'Those who abuse a faithful man or woman for something of which they are not guilty will be sent by God to a festering water in Hell[113] [and they will stay there] until they find a way out from what they alleged.'

[Ja'far b. Muḥammad]: He said, 'When you see a man who is not ashamed of what he says or of what is said to him, then know that he is damned (*lu'na*) or in the snare of the devil.'

[Ja'far b. Muḥammad]: He said to one of his companions, 'What did your creditor do?' He said, 'That is the son of an immoral woman (*ibn al-fā'ila*)!'[114] Abū 'Abd Allāh [the Imam] stared angrily at him, and the man said, 'May I be thy ransom, he is a Zoroastrian who has married his sister.' [The Imam] said, 'Is it not true that, in their religion, this is a lawful marriage?'[115]

[Ja'far b. Muḥammad]: Concerning a man who slanders a believing married woman, he said, 'He should be given the *ḥadd* punishment, declare himself a liar before the people, and repent before God for what he has done. When he does this, bears witness against himself, and repents, his testimony may be accepted [in future cases].'

[Ja'far b. Muḥammad]: He said, 'The punishment of a slanderer is

[111]The Arabic expression is: *ta'arraba ba'da hijratihi*. It means that he became an Arab of the desert or returned to the desert after emigration (for the sake of Islam). The word *a'rāb* has a negative connotation. The Prophet is reported to have stated that a *Muhājir* (emigrant) is not like an *A'rābī*. A tradition states that becoming a country Arab after emigration is a major sin because it implies apostasy (*irtidād*). *Lisān al-'Arab*, s.v. '-r-b; *Concordance*, s.v. '-r-b.

[112]*Qadhf*, in the technical sense, only occurs if the slandered person is *muḥṣan* (see n. 57 above in this chapter). Thus, slanderous accusations, except in Mālikī law, of fornication can only be applied to a person who has reached puberty. The accused person, being in possession of reason, must be a free Muslim who has no previous convictions for fornication. If he lacks one of the above qualifications, the slanderer may be given the lesser punishment than the Qur'ānic penalty (*ḥadd*) of eighty lashes.

[113]The Arabic is *ṭīnat al-khabāl* and the Prophet is said to have explained it as 'the sweat discharged by the inhabitants of Hell'. *Mishkāt*, II, 312; Robson, I, 776; transmitted by Muslim.

[114]Gloss in MS Q: *ibn al-fā'ila ay walad al-zinā'*. It means that the Imam's companion reviled his creditor who was a Zoroastrian. *Kāfī*, VII, 221, 222. Kulaynī reports three different traditions where the same expression, *ibn al-fā'ila*, is used and, in all cases, it entails *ḥadd* punishment.

[115]See Chap. 15, n. 93. *Kāfī*, VII, 261; reported from the same authority.

eighty stripes, as God says.[116] The fornicator should be scourged more severely than the man who defames; the defamer should be scourged more severely than the man who drinks [intoxicants]; and the man who drinks should be struck more severely than the one who is to be punished by way of correction (*ta'zīr*).'[117]

Abū Ja'far Muḥammad b. 'Alī: He said, 'A man from the tribe of Hudhayl[118] used to abuse the Prophet. When he came to know of this, the Prophet said, "Who [will deal with] this man?" Two men of the Anṣār[119] arose and said, "We, O Messenger of God." They rode their camels and came to 'Arafa.[120] They asked for him and learnt that he had just then left[121] to gather his sheep. They overtook him while he was in the midst of his family and his sheep. The two did not salute him so he said, "Who are you and what are you [seeking]?" They said, "We are seeking [an offender].[122] Are you so-an-so, the son of so-and-so?" He said, "Yes," so they pounced upon him and beheaded him.'

[Abū Ja'far Muḥammad b. 'Alī]: He said, 'He who abuses the Prophet should be killed and should not be given the opportunity to repent.'[123]

[116]The Messenger of God said, 'The fornicator should be flogged more severely than the man who drinks wine, and the latter should be flogged more severely than the defamer, and the latter should be flogged more severely than the one who is given a *ta'zīr* punishment.' *Kāfī*, VII, 220, 230–1.

[117]*Ta'zīr*, a technical term in Islamic law, is a discretionary punishment by the *qāḍī* for the offences for which no *ḥadd* punishment is stipulated. In theory, *ta'zīr* punishments should be lower than the lowest *ḥadd* penalty. *EI*², s.v. Ta'zīr; Benmehla, 'Ta'azir Crimes'.

[118]A tribe of northern Arab descent living in the vicinity of Mecca and Ṭā'if belonged to the branch of Muḍar known as Khindif. It was closely related to Kināna and Quraysh. For details see *EI*², s.v. Hudhayl.

[119]Anṣār, see *The Pillars of Islam*, I, 13, n. 18.

[120]'Arafa, see *The Pillars of Islam*, I, 7, n. 9. 'Araba: in *Kāfī*, VII, 293. The name of a place near Medina. *Qāmūs*, s.v. '-r-b. 'Urana: in Ṭūsī, *Tahdhīb al-aḥkām*. A place in 'Arafāt other than the halting place. *Qāmūs*, s.v. '-r-n. 'Araba seems to be more probable.

[121]He just escaped/fled (*haraba*): MS Q.

[122]The Arabic is: *bāghiyān*, and it could also mean 'tyrants', i.e. we will punish you. Another reading in some MSS is: *yā ghabīn*, which means, 'O, he who is weak in his intellect and in religion.'

[123]*Kāfī*, VII, 292. 'A man reviled the Messenger of God during Ja'far b. Muḥammad's lifetime and was brought before the governor of Medina ... 'Abd Allāh b. al-Ḥasan, al-Ḥasan b. Zayd, and others said, "His tongue should be cut off." ... Rabī'a, the speculator, and his group said, "He should be disciplined." Abū 'Abd Allāh [Imam al-Ṣādiq] exclaimed, "Praise the Lord! So, there is no distinction between the Messenger of God and his Companions!"' Ṭūsī, *Tahdhīb al-aḥkām*, X, 85; idem, *al-Nihāya*, 730; the reviler should be killed if there was no danger in killing him. See also *Kāfī*, VII, 293–4. A person was sentenced to death because he said that the Messenger of God does not have precedence over anyone

Abū ʿAbd Allāh Jaʿfar b. Muḥammad [Imam al-Ṣādiq] said, 'Let the man who participates in abusing the Prophet be killed by the lowest of the low.'[124] It was said to him, "Should he not be brought to the governor (*al-wālī*)?" [The Imam] said, "Yes, the Muslims may do so if they deem themselves safe from the governors of wrongdoers (*wulāt ahl al-jawr*). If they are not safe from them, the Muslims should leave him alone. However, if there is a just Imam, it is not proper for anyone to execute such an act without him."'

ʿAlī: He wrote to Rifāʿa,[125] 'Do not enter into a controversy with one who describes the shortcomings of the prophets.'

Jaʿfar b. Muḥammad: He was asked about a man who abused ʿAlī.[126] [The Imam] said, 'He does not deserve to live, not even for a day. The man who abuses the Imam should be killed in the same manner as he who abuses the Prophet.'[127]

Jaʿfar b. Muḥammad: He said, 'If a man slanders a community, i.e. even by one phrase [or expression] and they bring him as a group to the governor (*sulṭān*), he should punish him for one offence. However, if they bring him individually or in small groups, then the governor should punish him for every time some individual or group brings him before the *sulṭān*.[128] However, if he had abused every single member of the group individually, he should be punished accordingly, whether they come singly or in groups.'[129]

[Jaʿfar b. Muḥammad]: He said, 'It is not proper and not fitting that a Muslim should defame a Jew, a Christian, or a Zoroastrian on matters on which he has no information. The least that should be done in such a case is that he should be declared a liar.'[130]

[Jaʿfar b. Muḥammad]: He said, 'When the People of the Book[131]

---

of Banū Umayya with respect to noble descent. *Kāfī*, VII, 295–6. In his *Muhammad at Medina*, 328, Watt writes: The individuals who were assassinated had forfeited any claim to friendly treatment by Muhammad through their propaganda against him.

[124]*Kāfī*, VII, 284, 296. The Mālikīs of Morocco and Spain had instituted trials for *zandaqa*, especially for insults to the honour of the Prophet. *ShEI*, s.v. Zindīḳ.

[125]Rifāʿa b. Shaddād was ʿAlī's *qāḍī* at Ahwāz, see *The Pillars of Islam*, I, 281.

[126]Gloss in MS Q: *tanāwala ay sabba*, meaning to abuse, revile. Cf. *Majmaʿ al-baḥrayn*, s.v. n-w-l.

[127]*Kāfī*, VII, 296; shedding his blood is lawful. Ṭūsī, *al-Nihāya*, 730; ... he should be killed if there was no danger in doing so.

[128]*Kāfī*, VII, 225, 226; reported from the same authority.

[129]The governor should carry out the punishment for each instance, whether they have come in individually or in small groups.

[130]*Kāfī*, VII, 261; reported from the same Imam.

[131]People of the Book, see *The Pillars of Islam*, I, 290, n. 109.

defame one another, [the authority] should punish them with the punishment fixed for the defamer, whether the defamer belongs to the community of the defamed person or to other polytheists.'[132] He said, 'The People of the Book should be punished, taking into consideration what they consider to be lawful.'

[Ja'far b. Muḥammad]: He said, 'Where a Muslim defames a non-Muslim woman (*mushrika*) whose husband or son is a Muslim; or where a Muslim defames a non-Muslim (*mushrik*) whose son is a Muslim and the Muslim claims the *ḥadd* punishment for slander, such punishment shall be inflicted.'

[Ja'far b. Muḥammad]: He said, 'A non-Muslim who defames a Muslim should be scourged, his head and beard shaved, and he should be taken round among his own non-Muslim people to furnish them with a severe warning.'[133]

[Ja'far b. Muḥammad]: He said, 'It is not proper to defame a slave.' There are strict injunctions and severe punishments in this regard. A man of the Anṣār asked the Messenger of God about his wife who had defamed her slave girl. The Messenger of God said, 'Ask her to request forgiveness,[134] otherwise, the girl will have the right to retaliate on the Day of Resurrection.'

Ja'far b. Muḥammad:[135] He said, 'A man who defames the slave of someone else should be punished severely. If the mother of the slave is a free woman and the defamation relates to her, the defamer should be scourged for defamation. The man who defames his own slave has sinned. It is proper for him to ask the slave to overlook it and forgive him.'

Abū Ja'far and Abū 'Abd Allāh: They said, 'A slave who defames a free man should be fully punished with the *ḥadd* punishment.[136] This is only the punishment of a free man to be inflicted on the slave's back.'

Ja'far b. Muḥammad: He said, 'The defamer shall be punished no matter what language he uses, e.g., Arabic or any other language ('*ajamī*).'[137]

[132]*Kāfī*, VII, 260.

[133]*Kāfī*, VII, 260. 'Where a Christian defmames a Muslim, he should be flogged eighty stripes per the legal claim of the Muslim and an additional seventy-nine stripes as a safeguard for Islam. His head should be shaved and he should be taken round among his own community to teach them a lesson.'

[134]The Arabic according to MS Q reads: *fa-l-taṣbir lahā nafsahā*. Gloss in the same MS explains it as: *ay tas'al 'inda mamlūkat*[in] *al-'afw kamā qadhafathā*. Following the Urdu translation, Fyzee also rendered it literally 'to have patience', which is incorrect.

[135]According to MS Q. In the edited text: *wa-qāla*.

[136]*Kāfī*, VII, 254.

[137]'*Ajam* means foreigners, non-Arabs, like barbarians, especially Persians. '*Ajamī*

[Ja'far b. Muḥammad]: He was asked about two men who had mutually defamed each other. He said, 'Two men who had defamed each other were brought to 'Alī. He exempted them both from the *ḥadd* punishment and administered a warning (*'azzara*)[138] to them.'

[Ja'far b. Muḥammad]: He said, 'If a man accuses his wife of infidelity and she complains about him [to the authority],[139] he should be scourged unless he claims to have seen [the immoral act] with his own eyes[140] or denies the paternity of her child. In that case, he has to utter an imprecation (*li'ān*).[141] If he says to her, "O adulteress, I committed adultery with you,"[142] he should be punished for defamation. He cannot be punished for *zinā'* unless he confesses to it four times or its proof is forthcoming.'[143]

'Alī:[144] He said, 'A man says to his wife, "I do not find you a virgin," he is not liable to punishment, because virginity is lost even without intercourse.'[145]

Ja'far b. Muḥammad:[146] He said, 'The man should be warned (*yu'addabu*) if the matter is different from what he says (*khilāf mā qāla*), if he intends to abuse (*shatm*) her, or if he makes an accusation expressed by an allusion (*ta'rīḍ*);[147] for instance, during an argument between them.'

'Alī and Abū 'Abd Allāh: They said, 'If a person who defames a woman against whom mutual imprecation (*li'ān*) has been pronounced

---

signifies one who is of the race of the *'ajam*. *'Ujma* implies that one has an impediment or a difficulty in his speech, especially in speaking Arabic. Lane, s.v. '-j-m.

[138]*'Azzarahu* means that he disciplined the man so that he would turn away from foul conduct. It could also mean that he inflicted upon the man a beating less than that prescribed by the law (i.e. a *ḥadd* punishment). For the full range of its meaning, see Lane, s.v. '-z-r. See also n. 117 above in this chapter.

[139]Reading with the addition of *ila 'l-wālī*, as in MS Q and another MS of Fyzee.

[140]The Qur'ān states: *As for those who accuse their wives but have not witnesses except themselves; let the testimony of one of them be four testimonies, (swearing) by Allah that he is of those who speak the truth* (24:6).

[141]See Chap. 11, section on 'Mutual Imprecation'.

[142]The Arabic reads: *yā zāniya anā zanaytu biki*. When a man accuses his wife of infidelity he may call her *zāniya*, but why would he say that he committed adultery with her? Could it be a way of expressing, metaphorically, that he disassociates himself with her because she is an adulteress, therefore acts of intercourse with her were adultery?

[143]*Kāfī*, VII, 227–8; several traditions with some variants are reported.

[144]MS Q: 'Alī and Abū 'Abd Allāh: They said ...

[145]*Kāfī*, VII, 229.

[146]As in MS Q, in the edited text: *qāla*.

[147]*Kāfī*, VII, 229. It should be noted that only the Mālikīs consider an accusation expressed by allusion or preterition to be *qadhf*. This considerably expands the scope of the offence. *EI*², s.v. Ḳadhf.

or if he defames the woman's son, that person shall be scourged with the punishment of a defamer.'[148]

'Alī and Abū Ja'far: They said, 'If the person pardons the defamer before the case is taken to the sovereign authority (*sulṭān*), the pardon is effective, and the person defamed has no right to go back upon such a pardon. However, if he has already taken the matter to the ruling authority, his pardon is not effective.'[149]

Abū 'Abd Allāh Ja'far b. Muḥammad: He was asked about a person who slanders an insane person or a male or female child. [The Imam] said, 'No punishment is due to him who defames one who cannot be punished.[150] However, the defamer is a sinful person and the least that should be done is for him to be declared a liar.'

'Alī: He said, 'A son should be punished when he defames his father, but the father should not [be punished] when he defames his son.'[151]

Ja'far b. Muḥammad: He was asked concerning a person who calls another, saying, 'O Lūṭī [belonging to the people of Lot].'[152] [The Imam] replied, 'If, by these words, he did not intend to defame him, there cannot be a punishment for him, for he only said that he was one of the people of Lot. However, if he had said, "Verily, you act like the people of Lot," then he should be punished.'[153]

'Alī: Concerning a man who defames another for being a catamite, and addresses him by such expressions as, 'O *mankūḥ* (passive agent in marriage i.e. coition),' or 'O *ma'fūj* (one who is struck),'[154] [the Imam] said, 'He is liable for punishment.'

['Alī]: Where a man commits a culpable act, but is defamed for another offence, the defamer is liable for a *ḥadd* punishment.

['Alī]: He said, 'If a man slanders a dead man and one of his legal heirs (*awliyā'*) takes action on his behalf, the defamer shall be punished.'[155]

[148] *Kāfī*, VII, 221, 223, 224.

[149] Ibid., VII, 276, 277.

[150] Ibid., VII, 220, 221, 225, 277.

[151] Ibid., VII, 229.

[152] See n. 83 and 87 above in this chapter.

[153] 'Ikrima reported on the authority of Ibn 'Abbās that the Prophet said, 'If you find anyone doing as Lot's people did, kill both the one who does it and the one to whom it is done.' Another tradition states, 'Accursed is he who does what Lot's people did.' *Mishkāt*, II, 294, 296; Robson, I, 763, 765. See also *Kāfī*, VII, 223.

[154] '*Afj* is used for sodomy. *Lisān al-'Arab*, s.v. '-f-j.

[155] The slandered person need not be alive at the time of the action. According to the majority of the jurists, all of the heirs of the deceased, or [at least] certain heirs, may institute a legal action against the slanderer if the slandered person did not do so in his lifetime.

['Alī]: He said, 'If a person denies that someone else is the son of his father, the slanderer shall be scourged. However, if a person denies that someone else has the lineage of his tribe, he shall only be disciplined.'

['Alī]: He said, 'If a man abuses (*yasubb*) another, makes an accusation by allusion (*yu'arriḍu bihi al-qadhf*), saying, for instance, "O swine", "O donkey", "O dissolute one", "O immoral man", "O cuckold", or some similar expression, or, in a quarrelsome manner, says, "You have committed an indecent act with your mother or sister," or uses similar expressions, in all such cases, he should be warned and instructed, but the full *ḥadd* punishment [for slander] shall not be inflicted.'[156]

THE PUNISHMENTS FOR DRINKING INTOXICANTS (*AL-ḤADD FĪ SHURB AL-MUSKIR*)[157]

We have already mentioned in the Book of Drinks[158] the illegality of wine[159] and intoxicants[160] and the severity with which their consumption is forbidden.

Ja'far b. Muḥammad—his father—his ancestors: They said, 'Eighty

[156] *Kāfī*, VII, 262.

[157] *Muskir* pl. *muskirāt* is an alcoholic beverage or intoxicating liquor. Drinking wine was prevalent in pre-Islamic Arabia and the Qur'ān did not prohibit it in one instance, but did it gradually. The earliest revelation states: *They question thee about wine (strong drink) and games of chance. Say: In both is great sin, and (some) utility for men; but the sin of them is greater than their usefulness* (2:219). Later, it was revealed: O *ye who believe! Draw not near unto prayer when ye are drunken, till ye know that which ye utter* ... (4:43). Finally, it was prohibited as the Qur'ān states: O *ye who believe! Strong drink (wine) and games of chance and idols and divining arrows are only an infamy of Satan's handiwork. Leave it aside in order that ye may succeed. Satan seeketh only to cast among you enmity and hatred by means of wine and games of chance, and to turn you from remembrance of Allah and from (His) worship. Will ye then have done?* (5:90–91).

The prophet was asked about wine which had been turned into vinegar and he forbade it. When he was told that someone had made wine only as a medicine, he replied, 'It is not a medicine, but a disease.' Another tradition states, 'We told the Messenger of God, "We live in a cold land and do heavy work and we make a liquor from wheat to get strength from it for our work and to stand the cold of our country." He asked, "Does it intoxicate?" We replied, "Yes." He said, "You must avoid it."' *Mishkāt*, II, 312, 314; Robson, I, 777, 778. For a summary in Arabic see Māwardī, *al-Aḥkām al-sulṭāniyya*, 228–9; Ibn al-Farrā', *al-Aḥkām al-sulṭāniyya*, 268–70.

[158] See Chap. 4.

[159] 'Wine comes from five things: grapes, dates, wheat, barley, and honey. Wine is what veils (or obscures) the intellect.' Transmitted by Bukhārī. *Mishkāt*, II, 311; Robson, I, 776.

[160] 'Every liquor that intoxicates is forbidden.' Transmitted by Bukhārī and Muslim. *Mishkāt*, II, 311; Robson, I, 776.

strokes is the punishment for wine, whether the quantity is large or small, and the same rule applies to all intoxicating drinks.[161] If a man is punished [for drinking intoxicants] and repeats the offence three times, he should be punished each time [and, on the third occasion, he should be] killed.[162] A man who drinks an intoxicant should be severely scourged when he drinks it, even if he is not intoxicated.'

Ja'far b. Muḥammad: He said, 'The test of an intoxicated man is that he cannot read [a page or book] when asked to do so or that he cannot distinguish between his own and someone else's clothes.'

'Alī: The poet Najāshī[163] was brought to him. He had drunk wine during Ramaḍān so 'Alī scourged him with eighty stripes. Thereafter, 'Alī imprisoned him and, on the following day, he brought him out and scourged him with thirty-nine stripes.[164] The poet asked, 'Why this excess, O Commander of the Faithful?' 'Alī replied, 'For your defiance of God and for breaking the fast in the month of Ramaḍān.'

Ja'far b. Muḥammad: He said, 'Where a man drinks wine but does not

[161]'The Prophet gave a beating with palm branches and sandals, while Abū Bakr gave forty lashes.' Transmitted by Bukhārī and Muslim. Another tradition transmitted by Bukhārī states that, 'When a drinker was brought [for punishment] during the time of God's Messenger, during Abū Bakr's caliphate, and in the beginning of 'Umar's caliphate, we beat him with our hands, sandals and cloaks, but at the end of 'Umar's caliphate, he inflicted forty stripes, and when people were immoderate and excessively wicked, he inflicted eighty stripes.' A tradition transmitted by Mālik states that 'Umar sought the counsel of 'Alī about the prescribed punishment for drinking wine and 'Alī said, 'I think you should give one who drinks it eighty lashes, for when he drinks, he becomes intoxicated, and when he is intoxicated, he raves, and when he raves, he makes up lies.' So 'Umar inflicted eighty lashes. *Mishkāt*, II, 304, 306; Robson, I, 771, 772. See also *Kāfī*, VII, 231–2. Schacht (*Origins*, 75, 126) notes that there was an ancient practice to apply the *ḥadd* punishments for drinking wine only if the culprit was taken in a state of drunkenness. This doctrine of Ibn Abī Laylā, followed by Abū Ḥanīfa and Abū Yūsuf, was extended by analogy to all *ḥadd* crimes that lapse after a short period of prescription. Shāfi'ī did not accept this principle, but made allowances for the common tendency to drink by letting all *ḥadd* punishments lapse through repentance.

[162]'Beat anyone who drinks wine, and if he does it a fourth time, kill him.' The same tradition adds, 'A man who had drunk wine four times was brought to he Prophet who then beat him, but did not kill him.' *Mishkāt*, II, 305; Robson, I, 771. See also *Kāfī*, VII, 235–6. There is a difference of opinion as to whether he should be killed on the third or the fourth occasion, however the majority of the traditions state that the offender should be killed on the third occasion. Ṭūṣī, *al-Nihāya*, 712; should be killed if he is caught the third time.

[163]Qays b. 'Amr al-Najāshī al-Ḥārithī was a well-known poet from Yemen. In Kūfa, he was one of 'Alī's poets and composed several lampoons of Mu'āwiya at the Battle of Ṣiffīn. Due to his disorderly life, he lost 'Alī's favour and, after a drinking bout in Ramaḍān, he was punished by lashes of the whip. Later on, he was expelled by 'Alī and went over to Mu'āwiya. *EI*[2], s.v. al-Nadjāshī.

[164]Twenty stripes: *Kāfī*, VII, 234.

know that it is forbidden and this fact is established by proof, he shall not be punished.'

[Ja'far b. Muḥammad]: He said, 'If a man confesses to having drunk wine or an intoxicating drink, he shall be scourged.' [The Imam] said, 'This is according to the Messenger of God's dictum, "Punish the man who confesses to drinking wine and then retracts the statement!"'

'Alī: He said, 'Both the free man and the bondsman shall be scourged with eighty stripes for drinking wine or intoxicating date wine (*nabīdh*). Similarly, the Jew or the Christian will be punished if he drinks openly in a Muslim town. They are only allowed to drink in their own homes. If they do so publicly, they shall be scourged.'[165]

DECISIONS IN CRIMINAL OFFENCES (*AL-QAḌĀYĀ FI 'L-ḤUDŪD*)

Ja'far b. Muḥammad—his father—his ancestors—'Alī: A man who had stolen a coat-of-mail was brought to him and [two] witnesses testified against him. The accused began to adjure 'Alī regarding [the falsity of] the allegations and said, 'By God, if I had been brought before the Messenger of God, he would never have cut off my hand.' 'Alī said, 'And why?' He said, 'His Lord would have informed him that I was innocent. My innocence would have profited me.' When 'Alī saw his earnest pleading, he summoned the two witnesses and appealed to them and said, 'Verily, repentance is nigh; so fear God and do not cut the hand of a man wrongfully.' They did not shrink [from their accusation] so 'Alī said, 'Let one of you hold his hand, and the other cut it off.' When he said this, both of them entered the crowd of people and fled from his presence. Thus, they did not complete their evidence and stand their ground. 'Alī, therefore, said, 'Whoever will point out to me these two untruthful witnesses I will punish them in an exemplary manner.'

The Messenger of God said, 'Annul the *ḥadd* punishments by doubts, and make light[166] of the shortcomings of the noble ones, except where the punishments are laid down by God.'

[The Messenger of God]: He said, 'Where in [the facts of] a criminal offence there are doubts (lit. "it is possible" *la'alla*, or "it is probable" *'asā*), the punishment is annulled.'

'Alī: A woman who was caught red-handed committing an immoral

[165]Ibid., VII, 232, 233.

[166]The Arabic is *wa-aqīlū* ... it means to cancel, dismiss.

act with a man was brought to him. She said, 'O Commander of the Faithful, By God, I had not consented to the act, but he forced me to it.' 'Alī excused her from the punishment.

Ja'far b. Muḥammad said, 'If those people [the opponents of the Imam] had been asked about this case, they would have said that the woman did not speak the truth, but, by God, thus acted the Commander of the Faithful.'

'Alī: He said, 'In criminal offences, there can be no guarantee (*kafāla*);[167] no evidence to rebut evidence; and it is not permissible for one judge to write to [or consult] another about it.'

The Messenger of God: He prohibited people from taking oaths in criminal cases.

'Alī: A man complained to him that someone had defamed him, but did not bring any proof and said, 'O Commander of the Faithful, ask him to take an oath regarding me.' 'Alī said, 'There is no oath in a criminal offence.'[168]

['Alī]: He said, 'If a man confesses to a crime because he is frightened, imprisoned, or beaten up, such a confession does not go against him and he shall not be punished.'[169]

['Alī]: A man confessed to a crime (*i'tarafa bi-ḥadd*[in]) without specifying it. 'Alī ordered him to be scourged until the man begged the striker to desist. When eighty stripes had been delivered, the man said, 'This is enough,' and 'Alī said, 'Release him.'

['Alī]: He said, 'If a man who is punished for a criminal offence dies, neither blood money nor retaliation is due.'

['Alī]: A man was brought to him who had committed an offence for which the punishment was death and 'Alī put him to death. Abū Ja'far [Imam al-Bāqir] said, 'If a man has been found guilty of several offences, one of which was a capital offence, the lower punishments should be inflicted first and then he should be put to death.'

'Alī and Abū 'Abd Allāh [Imam al-Ṣādiq]: They said, 'The [right of] criminal punishment cannot be bequeathed.'[170] What they meant by it is that it is the right of the aggrieved person [to ask for the criminal punishment against his aggressor]. If he does not ask for it until he dies, then his heirs do not inherit this right.

'Alī: He said, 'After the infliction of the *ḥadd* punishment for a crime,

[167]*Kāfī*, VII, 279; Ṭūsī, *Tahdhīb al-aḥkām*, X, 147. For *kafāla* see Chap. 1, n. 241.
[168]*Kāfī*, VII, 279–80.
[169]Ibid., VII, 286.
[170]Ibid., VII, 279; reported from the same Imam.

the criminal cannot be imprisoned unless he is a thief who has committed his third offence and has already had his hand and foot cut off.'[171] We shall mention this case at its proper place, God willing.[172]

['Alī]: The Messenger of God said, 'Do not ask a lewd woman, "Who committed lechery with you?" For, just as it was easy for her to act immorally, so also it would be easy for her to accuse an innocent Muslim.'

'Alī said, 'If she says that so-and-so had unlawful intercourse with her, then she deserves the punishment for slander.'[173]

Ja'far b. Muḥammad: He said, 'No person has the right to disregard the proper authority (*sulṭān*) and inflict criminal punishments on his male or female slaves himself.'

Abū Ja'far and Abū 'Abd Allāh: The narrator of this tradition relates that one of these two [Imams] said, 'If a man sells his wife, his hand should be cut off. If the purchaser is a married man and knows that she is a free woman and has intercourse with her, he should be stoned. If unmarried, he should be scourged. If the woman consented to the intercourse, she too should be stoned.'

Ja'far b. Muḥammad: He said, 'He who commits *zinā'* in Ramaḍān should be punished for the offence and chastised for breaking the fast during the month, as 'Alī did with Najāshī. If the man commits the offence three times, he should be put to death.'

Abū Ja'far Muḥammad b. 'Alī: He said, 'If a man defames another and is scourged and then tells the defamed person, "I did not say anything about you but the truth," [in such a case,] a second punishment is not called for; but if he repeats [the false allegations], he shall be scourged again.'

[171]Ibid., VII, 296.

[172]See Chap. 18.

[173]'She deserves two punishments: first, for her immorality and second for slandering a Muslim.' Ṭūsī, *Tahdhīb al-aḥkām*, X, 67.

18

Book of Thieves and Robbers (*Kitāb al-Surrāq wa 'l-Muḥāribīn*)

THE RULES [OF DECISION] FOR THIEVES (*AL-ḤUKM FI 'L-SURRĀQ*)[1]

God says: *As for the thief, both male and female, cut off their hands* (*fa 'qṭa'ū aydiyahumā*, 5:38).[2]

Ja'far b. Muḥammad—his father—his ancestors: The Messenger of God said, 'I saw a man in the Fire who had taken an *'abā'a* (or *'abāya*, a

[1]For a summary in Arabic see Māwardī, *al-Aḥkām al-sulṭāniyya*, 226–8; Ibn al-Farrā', *al-Aḥkām al-sulṭāniyya*, 266–8. Jurists define theft as 'taking someone else's property by stealth'. They disagree concerning the value of the stolen property for the *ḥadd* punishment to be imposed, how the hand should be cut off, and the question of the places from where property is stolen. Ibn Rushd, *Bidāya*, II, 441–9; trans. II, 536–46; El-Awa, *Punishment in Islamic Law*, 2.

[2]The rest of the verse is: *It is a reward of their own deeds, and exemplary punishment from Allah. Allah is Mighty, Wise.* Classical Arabic dictionaries give innumerable examples for metaphorical usages of the word *qaṭa'a*. (See for example, *Tāj al-'arūs*, s.v. q-ṭ-'). Nu'mān has given a good example that a poet came to the Prophet, recited a eulogy and expected a reward. The Prophet, therefore, told one of his Companions, 'Arise [and] *fa 'qṭa' lisānahu* (lit. cut off his tongue; see Chap. 13 above). The Prophet used it metaphorically, not literally, which meant 'silence him by giving a gift'. In his article 'Islam and the Challenge of Democracy', Abou El Fadl entertains the idea that the verb *qaṭa'a* in this verse could also mean to deal firmly, to bring an end, to restrain, etc. His assertion is that whatever the meaning derived from the Qur'ānic text by human interpretation cannot claim with certainty that it is identical to that intended by God. Even the issue of meaning is resolved, it is impossible for human beings to determine or enforce the law in such a fashion that the possibility of a wrongful result is completely eliminated. No doubt that the legal requirements for the *ḥadd* punishments are very rigorous. The spirit of Islamic law, on the other hand, is well expressed by the Prophet and 'Alī in the following utterances cited earlier by Nu'mān in Chap. 17. After inflicting the *ḥadd* punishment on a person who had confessed to his sin four times,

woolen cloak with stripes) deceitfully; and I saw in the Fire a man with a stick having a bent handle (*miḥjan*) by which he stole the goods of pilgrims; and I saw in the Fire a woman who had a cat, who used to seize it with her nails both from the front and from behind, and who used to keep it bound and did not feed it, nor did she release it, so it ate the insects of the earth.'[3]

Ja'far b. Muḥammad: He said, 'At the time of committing theft, the thief does not possess faith.'

[Ja'far b. Muḥammad]: He said, 'Where a man catches a thief stealing his property and forgives him, there is no harm. But when the thief has been brought to the authority (*sulṭān*), his hand should be cut off. If the complainant forgives him or says, "I have made a gift to him of what he has stolen;" such forgiveness is not possible after the thief has been presented to the authority, and his hand should be cut off.'[4]

'Alī: A man suspected of theft was brought to him. I [the narrator of the tradition][5] felt that 'Alī feared that when questioned, the accused would be frightened and confess to something he did not do. So 'Alī said to him, 'Have you committed the theft? Say, no, if you wish.' The man said, 'No.' There was no proof against him and 'Alī released him.

Abū Ja'far and Abū 'Abd Allāh: They said, 'The least amount for which the hand of a thief is cut is one fifth of a dinar, or a thing worth one fifth of a dinar.'[6]

'Alī and Abū 'Abd Allāh: They said, 'The hand of a thief should be amputated from the base of the four fingers, and the palm of the hand

---

the Prophet said, 'It would have been better for him to have it hidden [rather than confess] provided he had repented.' Similarly, 'Alī said, 'If I were to see an indecency being committed by a believer, I would cover it up by this robe of mine [provided he had repented].'

[3] *Mishkāt*, II, 119; Robson, I, 630.

[4] *Ḥadd* punishments are not remissible after being reported to the authorities. See Chap. 17, n. 17.

[5] Gloss in MS Q: *Aẓunnuhu* (I presume), is a statement of Sayyidnā [al] Qāḍī al-Nu'mān.

[6] The rule for applying the *ḥadd* penalty of amputation is that the value of the property stolen should reach a certain minimum value called *niṣāb*. Jurists, however, disagree as to the exact amount and often use crude analogy for arriving at a fixed value. According to Mālik and Shāfi'ī, it is a quarter of a dinar or three dirhams; the jurists of Iraq say it is ten dirhams. These differences are probably due to the different interpretations of the then existing monetary value. Ibn Rushd, *Bidāya*, II, 442–3. A tradition transmitted by Bukhārī and Muslim states, 'A thief's hand should be cut off only for a quarter of a dinar and upwards.' *Mishkāt*, II, 297; Robson, I, 766. Kulaynī transmitted two traditions from Imam al-Bāqir stating the minimum amount to be a fifth of a dinar, other traditions put the amount at a quarter of a dinar. *Kāfī*, VII, 238–40. See also Schacht, *Origins*, 107, 261; idem, *Introduction*, 38–9; El-Awa, *Punishment in Islamic Law*, 3–5.

and the thumb should be left to him.[7] The foot should be cut from [the part that is in front of the] heel, and the heel should be left for him to walk with.[8] Therefore half the foot should be cut.'

Ja'far b. Muḥammad: He said, 'The right hand of the thief should be cut off. 'Alī recited: *As for the thief, both male and female, cut off their hands* (5:23).' Abū 'Abd Allāḥ [Imam al-Ṣādiq] said, 'If the right or left hand be disabled (*ashall*), the right hand shall be cut no matter the circumstances.'[9]

'Alī: He ordered the right hand of a thief to be cut, but he put forward his left one, and they cut it, thinking it to be the right. Later they came to know and produced the thief before 'Alī, and he said, 'Leave him! I am not going to cut his right hand after his left has been cut off!'[10]

'Alī: A thief was brought to him and he cut off his right hand. The same thief was brought to him a second time, so he cut off his left foot and said, 'I would be ashamed before God not to leave him a hand with which he can eat or clean himself.' 'Alī [further] said, 'The Messenger of God never exceeded beyond cutting off one hand and one foot.' If a thief was produced before 'Alī for the third time, his hand and foot having been cut off on two previous occasions, he would imprison him for life and provide for him from the booty (*fay'*)[11] belonging to the Muslims, and if the thief committed theft in the prison, 'Alī would put him to death.[12]

['Alī]: When he ordered the hand of a thief to be cut, he also ordered that it should be cauterized, lest the thief should bleed to death.[13]

['Alī]: He said, 'If a man committed theft and had his hand or foot cut off and the man died therefrom, no blood money is due for him, for the death was justifiable.'

Abū Ja'far and Abū 'Abd Allāh: They said, 'When a thief is caught, [his hand] should be cut off. If what he has stolen is found in his hands, it should be taken and returned to the owner. If he has wasted the goods, the loss should be calculated, and it should come out of his property.'[14]

[7]Jurists disagree as to how the hand should be amputated. El-Awa, *Punishment in Islamic Law*, 5–6.

[8]*Kāfī*, VII, 240, 243.

[9]Ibid., VII, 243; from the same Imam.

[10]Ibid., VII, 241.

[11]*Fay'*, see *The Pillars of Islam*, I, 327, n. 118.

[12]*Kāfī*, VII, 240–1. A tradition states, 'If a thief steals cut off his hand, if he steals again cut off his foot, if he steals again cut off his hand, and if he steals [yet] again cut off his foot.' Another tradition states that a thief was killed when he was brought a fifth time. *Mishkāt*, II, 299; Robson, I, 767. For differing opinions of jurists see Ibn Rushd, *Bidāya*, II, 447–8.

[13]'Maim him, then cauterize him.' *Mishkāt*, II, 299; Robson, I, 768.

[14]*Kāfī*, VII, 243.

ʿAlī: He ordered the hands of some thieves to be cut off; when that was done, he ordered them to be cauterized,[15] and that was done. Then he said, 'O Qanbar,[16] take them to yourself and treat their wounds and be good to them. Inform me when they recover.' When they were cured, Qanbar came to him and said, 'O Commander of the Faithful, their wounds have healed.' ʿAlī said [to him], 'Go and clothe them with two garments each and bring them to me.' Qanbar acted accordingly, and brought them to ʿAlī as if they were people who had donned the ritual garment for *iḥrām*,[17] each having a sheet and an undergarment. They remained standing before him for a while; he then lowered his gaze on the ground and began to mark it with his finger in a pensive mood for some time. Then ʿAlī raised his hand and said, 'Open your hands,' and they opened them. Then he said, 'Raise them to the sky and say: O God, ʿAlī has amputated us.' They did so and ʿAlī said, 'O God, [I did this] according to Your Book and the practice of Your Prophet.' Then he said, 'O you people, your hands have preceded you in the Fire; if you repent, you will snatch your hands from the Fire, otherwise you will join them in it.'[18]

[ʿAlī]: When he cut off [the hand of] a thief and the thief recovered from his injuries, ʿAlī banished him from Kūfa to some other place.[19]

THOSE WHOSE [HAND] SHOULD BE AMPUTATED AND THOSE WHO SHOULD BE EXCUSED (*MAN YAJIB ʿALAYHI AL-QAṬʿ WA-MAN YUDRAʾ ʿANHU*)

Jaʿfar b. Muḥammad—his father—his ancestors—ʿAlī: He said, 'The [hand of a] man who snatches a thing (*mukhtalis*) should not be cut,[20] nor should [the hand of a] guest who steals while he is the guest of his host.'[21]

[ʿAlī]: He said, 'There is no amputation for your workman[22] or one whom you have allowed entry into your house, when he steals;' i.e. [if the theft is committed] during the time when you allowed him to enter your house.

[15] *Mishkāt*, II, 299; Robson, I, 768.

[16] Qanbar was ʿAlī's slave, see *The Pillars of Islam*, I, 64.

[17] *Iḥrām*, consecrated state for the *ʿumra* and the *ḥajj*, see *The Pillars of Islam*, I, 141, n. 65.

[18] *Kāfī*, VII, 243.

[19] Ibid., VII, 250.

[20] *Mishkāt*, II, 298; Robson, I, 767; *Kāfī*, VII, 249.

[21] *Kāfī*, VII, 247.

[22] Ibid., VII, 245, 246, 247.

Ja'far b. Muḥammad:[23] He said, 'A man whom you allow entry into your house is a trusted man. When he steals, [his] hand should not be amputated; but he is responsible for what he has stolen.'

'Alī: He said, 'When a slave steals from the property of his master, [his hand] shall not be cut off,[24] but when he steals from someone else's property, his hand shall be cut off.'

['Alī]: He said, 'When the slaves of government (*imāra*)[25] steal the property of government (*māl al-imāra*), their hands shall not be cut off; but if they steal from any other property, their hands shall be amputated.'

['Alī]: He gathered together the people of Kūfa to distribute goods which were gathered with him. One of them stood, took a helmet and hid it amid his goods. He was brought before 'Alī and he said, 'His [hand] shall not be amputated because he is a partner in the goods. He is not a thief, but a cheat.'[26]

['Alī]: He said, 'If a man steals from the property of his son; or a son from the property of his father; or a husband from the property of his wife; or a wife from the property of her husband; or a brother from the property of his brother, none of them shall have their hands amputated.'[27]

['Alī]: About one who snatches away goods (*mukhtalis*), he said, 'His hand should not be cut, but he should be scourged and imprisoned.[28] He who is trusted with something should not have his hand amputated for cheating; for there is no amputation with regard to *ghulūl*.'[29]

The Messenger of God: He said, 'Annul *ḥadd* punishments where there are doubts.'[30]

[23]According to MS Q. In the edited text: *qāla*.

[24]*Mishkāt*, II, 300; Robson, I, 768; Ibn Rushd, *Bidāya*, II, 446.

[25]*Imāra* means possession of command, the office of a commander, or governor. It is also used for *ṣāḥib al-imāra*, i.e. the governor, or prince. Lane, s.v. a-m-r.

[26]*Kāfī*, VII, 245, 251; one who steals from booty, his hand shall not be amputated, because he has a share in it.

[27]Ibn Rushd, *Bidāya*, II, 446.

[28]*Kāfī*, VII, 244, 245.

[29]The general meaning of *ghulūl* is that he acted unfaithfully. *Ghalla min al-maghnam* means he acted unfaithfully in taking from the spoil or booty. *Ghulūl*, thus, signifies stealing or unfaithfulness in respect of a hidden thing. Such conduct is termed *ghulūl* because the hands have been erroneously put upon a thing and hidden amid one's own goods. Lane, s.v. gh-l-l. *Kāfī*, VII, 245.

[30]Application of the *ḥadd* penalty involves a great deal of uncertainty and doubt. Jurists have cited several cases in which this penalty was avoided. The general rule holds that this penalty should not be applied in case of doubt. It seems that flogging was the punishment for theft during most of the Umayyad period. Schacht, *Origins*, 191, 208.

ʿAlī: A man who had [a bundle of] cloth on him was brought to him. The people alleged that he had stolen it from a man, but there was no proof against him. The man who was found with [the bundle of] cloth said, 'I took it from him playfully.' ʿAlī asked the owner of the cloth, 'Are you acquainted with this man?' He said, 'Yes.' ʿAlī, therefore, released the man and said, 'His hand should not be cut.'

Jaʿfar b. Muḥammad: A man who had a bundle of clothes belonging to another person was brought to [the Imam]. The man who had the bundle said, 'The owner has given it to me.' He did not confess to the theft and no proof was adduced against him. [The Imam] said, 'His hand should not be cut.'[31]

[Jaʿfar b. Muḥammad]: He said, 'The hand of a cutpurse (*ṭarrār*,[32] who cuts purses by slitting a man's sleeve or the clothe [in which he carries his money]) and the hand of a *mukhtalis* (one who snatches away something [while its owner is unaware]) should not be cut;[33] but both of them should be severely scourged and imprisoned.'[34]

ʿAlī: A thief who had made a hole [through a wall] of a house was brought to him. The people had made haste in arresting him. ʿAlī said, 'You have made haste with him,' and scourged him. He said, 'Neither a man who makes a hole through a wall of a house, nor a man who breaks a lock can be punished with cutting [off the hand]. Similarly, the hand of a man who breaks into a house and takes goods but does not go out of the precincts (*ḥirz*)[35] of the house shall not be cut, but he shall be scourged severely, imprisoned, and made responsible for the goods spoilt.'[36]

[31]*Kāfī*, VII, 242.

[32]Derived from *ṭarr*, the act of slitting/cutting. Lane, s.v. ṭ-r-r. The closest English equivalent would be 'a pickpocket'.

[33]*Kāfī*, VII, 244, 245.

[34]'Cutting off the hand is not to be inflicted on one who is treacherous, one who plunders, or one who snatches something.' *Mishkāt*, II, 298; Robson, I, 767.

[35]*Ḥirz* means a place that is fortified, protected against attack, or one in which a thing is kept and guarded. *Hataka 'l-sāriqu 'l-ḥirza* means the thief broke into the place of custody. Lane, s.v. ḥ-r-z. All the jurist agree upon the stipulation of *ḥirz* for the obligation of amputation. However, they differ about what constitutes *ḥirz*. The commonly accepted definition of *ḥirz* is that it is a place or a condition in which wealth is preserved in a way that its stealing is made difficult. The act committed by the thief, i.e. theft (*sariqa*), is taking away of property from the *ḥirz*. Ibn Rushd, *Bidāya*, II, 444; trans. II, 540; El-Awa, *Punishment in Islamic Law*, 6–7.

[36]*Kāfī*, VII, 242. A requirement for the *ḥadd* punishment is that the thief must commit the theft with clear intent to acquire the stolen property. In addition to that, he must carry the property away from the place where it is usually kept. Ibn Rushd, *Bidāya*, II, 444–5.

Abū 'Abd Allāh [Imam al-Ṣādiq] was asked, 'If the thief is found in the house after having taken the goods and [the owner] brings him out of the house, is he to be punished with amputation?' [The Imam] said, 'No. Not until the thief had removed the goods outside the precincts of the house.'

'Alī: A mad man who had committed theft was brought to him. He released him and said, 'A mad man cannot [have his hand] amputated.'

['Alī]: He said, 'A thief who commits theft in a year of famine (*fī 'āmi sanat^in^*)[37] cannot [have his hand] amputated.'[38]

['Alī]: He said, 'I heard the Messenger of God saying, "A person who steals a stone shall not [have his hand] cut off except in the case of precious stones (*jawhar*)."' Ja'far b. Muḥammad said, '[By stone,] he meant marble and the like.'[39]

'Alī: The Messenger of God said, 'A man who steals sheep from a grazing ground shall not be punished by having his hand amputated. Rather, he shall be given the discretionary penalty of *ta'zīr*[40] and shall make good what he has stolen or spoilt.'

'Alī: The Messenger of God said, 'There is no cutting [of the hand] for [stealing] fruit or the pith of the palm tree (*kathar* or *kathr*, syn. *jummār*).' He also said, 'The man who steals these shall be given the *ta'zīr* penalty and he shall be made to pay their price.'[41]

'Alī: He said, 'There is no amputation for [stealing cooked] food.'

['Alī]: He said, 'There is no amputation where theft occurs at a place where no permission is required for entry [public places], such as mosques, caravanserais (*khānāt*), [public] baths (*ḥammāmāt*), the vicinity of wells (*arjāz*), and similar places.'[42]

['Alī]: A man who had stolen an ostrich whose price was one hundred dirhams was brought to 'Alī. Another man was brought who had stolen a pigeon. He said, 'No cutting [of the hand] is permissible for [the theft] of a bird or anything feathery.'[43]

['Alī]: He said, 'No amputation is permissible for stealing the following:

[37] *Sanat^un^* is used alone to signify drought, or barrenness. Lane, s.v. s-n-w.

[38] *Kāfī*, VII, 251–2; theft in this case refers to food.

[39] Ibid., VII, 250.

[40] For the *ta'zīr* penalty, see Chap. 17, n. 117.

[41] 'For taking fruit or the pith of the palm tree, the hand is not to be cut off.' Another tradition states that if anyone steals fruit which was hung up in a place where it is dried and it amounts to the price of a shield, i.e. three dirhams, his hand must be amputated. *Mishkāt*, II, 297–8; Robson, I, 766. See also *Kāfī*, VII, 250, 251.

[42] *Kāfī*, VII, 251.

[43] Ibid., VII, 250.

seed produce (*zar*ʿ);[44] sheep, until they reach a pinfold; fruits; trees; palm trees; or roaming camels unless they are contained behind a fence.'

[ʿAlī]: A man came to him and said, 'Verily I have committed theft;' so ʿAlī chided him. Then the man said, 'O Commander of the Faithful, verily I have committed theft.' Then ʿAlī said, 'Do you testify twice against yourself?' ʿAlī then amputated [his hand].[45]

Jaʿfar b. Muḥammad: He said, 'Where a man confesses to a theft and then retracts, his hand should be cut off and no attention should be paid to his denial.'

[Jaʿfar b. Muḥammad]: He said, 'If a man steals and runs away, and it was not possible to arrest him, and he then steals for a second time and is caught, his hand shall be cut off and he will be responsible for the loss [of goods].'

ʿAlī: He said, 'If a man is recognized as having stolen goods in his hands, but he says, "I have purchased them," and does not admit the theft and no proof is forthcoming, his hand should not be cut off. But, if proof is established by the plaintiff against him, the goods will be taken from him [and given to the owner].'

ʿAlī: A boy who had committed theft was brought to him. He scraped off the flesh below the thumb and the index finger until they bled. ʿAlī then said, 'If you repeat it, I shall cut them off.' He [further] said, 'Listen, verily, no one has acted thus since the Messenger of God except myself,' and he said, 'A boy cannot be punished until he attains puberty and his armpits begin to smell.'

It is reported that in this case ʿAlī [probably] scratched off (*qaṭaʿa*) the fingers. [It appears that] the term *qaṭ*ʿ is applied to bruising or rubbing (*ḥakk*). This is not a *ḥadd* punishment but only a chastisement. It is necessary to discipline a boy to indicate that were he a grown-up man, he would have been given a *ḥadd* punishment. There is a severity in ʿAlī's bruising the fingers together with the warning he administered, and there is an indication that if he repeated the offence, his hand would be cut off. It is possible that this was the real implication of his words: 'If you repeat it, I shall cut off [your hand],' i.e. if you repeat it after attaining maturity. ʿAlī therefore made good on this threat to him. He said it vaguely but severely

[44]*Zar*ʿ signifies seed produce, while in growth i.e. standing corn and the like, or the seed produce after it has been reaped. Its prominent application is to wheat and barley. Lane, s.v. z-r-ʿ.

[45]The *ḥadd* punishment for theft could be applied only after a twofold confession by the culprit. Schacht thinks that this rule was derived by analogy with the two witnesses required in such cases and this doctrine is expressed in a tradition from ʿAlī, but not all Iraqis hold it. Schacht, *Origins*, 107, 297.

so that the boy will not repeat the offence. In such cases, there are no fixed limits as to correction.[46]

['Alī]: He amputated the hand of a grave-robber (*nabbāsh*) who had dug up the grave and had taken off the shroud from the body [of the dead man].[47]

['Alī]: He said, 'The hand of the grave-robber should be cut when he is a chronic offender.'

Ja'far b. Muḥammad [Imam al-Ṣādiq] said, 'The hand of a grave-robber should not be cut unless he is caught in the act repeatedly. Each time he should be chastised, punished severely, and imprisoned.'

'Alī: A man stole a she-camel who later foaled. 'Alī ordered the man to return the she-camel with the young one [to the owner].

['Alī]: He said, 'When several persons conspire to commit theft, the hand of each of them shall be cut off.'

THE RULES REGARDING ROBBERS OR BANDITS (*AḤKĀM AL-MUḤĀRIBĪN*)[48]

God says: *The only reward of those who make war upon Allah and His Messenger and strive after corruption in the land will be that they will be killed or crucified, or have their hands and feet on alternate sides cut off,*[49] *or will be expelled out of the land* (5:33).[50] We have mentioned earlier in the book

[46] *Kāfī*, VII, 252–4; if boys commit theft they should be given a stern warning, if they repeat, a *ta'zīr* punishment should be given, if they return again, then their fingers should be bruised.

[47] *Mishkāt*, II, 300–1; Robson, I, 768; *Kāfī*, VII, 247–8.

[48] The word *muḥārib* pl. *muḥāribūn* is an active participle from the verb *ḥārabahu* meaning he waged war with him. *Muḥāraba* or *ḥirāba*, therefore, means banditry, brigandage. All the jurists agree that *ḥirāba* is a show of armed force and obstruction of the highways outside the city. They disagree about the brigands within the city. For Mālik they are the same. Shāfi'ī stipulated power (*shawka*), not the number. He further asserted that if the [legitimate] political authority weakens and domination by another is found in the city, it amounts to *muḥāraba*. The Arabic term *qaṭ' al-ṭarīq* for highway robbery is a post-Qur'ānic development, as robbery was not considered a crime by the pre-Islamic Arabs. The penalty is defined in the Qur'ān (5:33). Jurists disagree as to whether these punishments are to be applied alternatively or differently according to circumstances. Some jurists have interpreted exile (*expelled out of the land*) to include imprisonment. Lane, s.v. ḥ-r-b; Ibn Rushd, *Bidāya*, II, 450–4; trans. II, 547–52; Aly Mansour, 'Hudud Crimes', 198–9; Schacht, *Introduction*, 9; El-Awa, *Punishment in Islamic Law*, 7–10.

[49] It is understood to mean the right hand and the left foot.

[50] Although this verse is regarded by most jurists as referring to bandits, some state that it was revealed with regard to some people who apostatized during the time of the Prophet and drove off his camels. Ibn Rushd, *Bidāya*, II, 450; see also the following note in this chapter. Māwardī, *al-Aḥkām al-sulṭāniyya*, 62–4; the verse refers to *muḥāribūn wa-*

that where the Qur'ān mentions the words *aw...aw* (or ... or), the man has a choice of alternatives.

Ja'far b. Muḥammad—his father—his ancestors: 'Alī said, 'A group of the tribe of Banū Ḍabba[51] came to the Messenger of God. They were ill and the Messenger of God said to them, "Stay with me [for a while], when you have recovered, I shall send you on an expedition (*sarīya*)."[52] They found Medina to be unhealthy for them, so the Messenger of God sent them out to [a place where] some camels given as payment of *ṣadaqāt* (obligatory alms) [were kept] and he asked them to drink their milk and use their urine as medicine. When they recovered and became strong, they killed three of the men who were shepherding and looking after the camels, and they drove off the camels to their own destination. When the Prophet heard about them he sent me to seek them. I overtook them near the land of Yemen; they had entered a valley from which they could not emerge. So I arrested them and brought them to the Messenger of God, and he recited the verse: *The only reward of those who make war upon Allah and His Messenger* till the end of the verse (5:33). Then he said, "Amputation!" And their hands and feet were cut off on alternate sides.'[53]

Ja'far b. Muḥammad: He said, 'The rule regarding the bandit (*muḥārib*), i.e. a man who intercepts people on the road, robs them on the highway, plunders the goods, or does similar acts, is that the decision [as to what

---

quṭṭā' al-ṭarīq; see also Ibn al-Farrā', *al-Aḥkām al-sulṭāniyya*, 57–60. Both of them distinguish between a bandit and a rebel (*bāgh^in* pl. *bughāt*, also called *ahl al-baghy*).

[51]Ḍabba b. Udd ... b. Muḍar b. Nizār b. Ma'add was a well-known Arab tribe. *EI*², s.v. Ḍabba. Nu'mān's report of this incident does not concur with other historical sources. It is narrated that a group of Banī 'Urayna (or of Qays of Kubba of Bajīla) came to Medina and accepted Islam. They were suffering from fever, so the Prophet allowed them to go to the pasture grounds of his private herd of camels to enjoy the plentiful milk. But when they recovered their health, they killed the Prophet's shepherd Yasār and drove off with his camels. The Prophet sent Kurz b. Jābir in pursuit; he overtook them and brought them to him. He cut off their hands and feet and put them to death. According to Wāqidī, the verse 5:33 was revealed on this occasion. Ibn Isḥāq, *al-Sīra*, IV, 290; Guillaume, 677–8; Wāqidī, *Kitāb al-maghāzī*, II, 568–70; Ṭabarī, *History of al-Ṭabarī*, IX, 146; Watt, *Muhammad at Medina*, 43. The tradition is transmitted both by Bukhārī and Muslim, see *Concordance*, s.v. j-w-y; Ibn Qayyim, *al-Ṭibb al-nabawī*, 59; it was a group of Banū 'Urayna.

[52]*Sarīya* pl. *sarāya*, means a portion of an army marching secretly by night. Afterwards it was used for such a march by day. It consisted of anything from five persons to three hundred. But, it is related that the Prophet sent a single person as a *sarīya*. The term is used in contradistinction to *maghāzī* or *ghazawāt* wherein the Prophet himself participated. *Sariyya* is also translated as a raiding party. Lane, s.v. s-r-y; Ṭabarī, *History of al-Ṭabarī*, IX, 118.

[53]*Kāfī*, VII, 267–8; reported from Imam al-Ṣādiq. Kulaynī's report is identical with that of Nu'mān.

type of punishment be meted out to him] rests with the Imam. If he so wishes, he may put him to death, crucify him, cut off [his hand and foot from opposite ends], or expel him. The Imam may punish the offender according to his offence.'

'Alī: A bandit (*muḥārib*) was brought to him. He ordered him to be crucified alive. A pillar was erected on the ground. The bandit's face was turned towards the *qibla* where the people stood and his back towards the pillar. When the bandit died, 'Alī left him for three days, then ordered him to be brought down. He prayed for him and buried him.[54] We have mentioned earlier the manner of amputation and its limits.

Ja'far b. Muḥammad: He was asked about the expulsion of a bandit and he said, 'He may be expelled from one town (*miṣr*) to another. Verily, 'Alī expelled two persons from Kūfa to another place.'[55]

'Alī: He said, 'Where a bandit kills a person, the matter rests with the Imam.[56] Even if the avenger of the victim's blood (*walīy al-dam*) forgives him, the Imam can arrest him for the offence.'

The Messenger of God: He said, 'The man who is killed [defending] his property, is a martyr.'[57]

Abū Ja'far [Imam al-Bāqir] said, 'If a man forsakes his property for the robber, there is no harm; it is not incumbent on him to fight the bandit. Where he is afraid of losing his life, I prefer that he should protect it [by escaping and abandoning his property]. If the man fights the robber and dies [trying to protect] his property, he is a martyr just as the Messenger of God said.'

[54]Ibid., VII, 269; the man was crucified in Ḥīra. Ḥīra was the capital of the pre-Islamic Lakhmids and was located to the south-east of present-day Najaf.

[55]'Alī expelled ... from Kūfa to Basra: Ibid., VII, 269.

[56]Ibid., VII, 268, 271; the Imam can decide either for amputation, execution, crucifixion, or banishment, depending on the nature of the crime.

[57]*Mishkāt*, II, 274; Robson, I, 747; transmitted by Bukhārī, Muslim, Abū Dāwūd, Tirmidhī, Nasā'ī, Ibn Māja, and Ibn Hanbal. *Concordance*, s.v. sh-h-d.

19

Book of Apostasy and Innovation (*Kitāb al-Ridda wa 'l-Bid'a*)

RULES REGARDING THE APOSTATE (*AḤKĀM AL-MURTADD*)[1]

God says: *And verily it hath been revealed unto thee as unto those before thee (saying): If thou ascribe a partner to Allah, thy work will fail and thou indeed wilt be among the losers* (39:65). And He says: *How shall Allah guide a people who disbelieved after their belief* (3:86). And He says: *And whoso becomes a renegade and dies in his disbelief: such are they whose works have fallen both in the world and the Hereafter. Such are rightful owners of the Fire: they will abide therein]* (2:217).[2]

Ja'far b. Muḥammad—his father—his ancestors: 'Alī did not allow the renegade [to live] for more than three days after he requested him to repent. When it was the fourth day, 'Alī put him to death, without asking

[1]*Murtadd*, lit. one who goes back, or turns back, especially from Islam, is an apostate. *Irtidād* or *ridda* meaning apostasy may be committed verbally by denying a pillar of Islam or by an action, for example, to reject the obligations imposed upon a Muslim by the Qur'ān. Rejecting Islam by omission is to refrain from performing an obligatory act. It should be noted that, in the Qur'ān, the apostate is threatened with punishment in the Hereafter only. In many traditions, however, one finds a new punishment, the death penalty. But from the very beginning, there was no agreement on the nature of the death penalty. 'Ikrima and Anas b. Mālik criticized 'Alī for having burned apostates. Traditions also differ on the question of whether the apostate should be given an opportunity to repent or not. For details see *EI*[2], s.v. Murtadd; Aly Mansour, 'Hudud Crimes', 197; El-Awa, *Punishment in Islamic Law*, 49–56. In most Muslim countries today, conversion is no longer punishable by death.

[2]Shāfi'ī adduced this verse as the main evidence for the death penalty for the apostate. See also the following verses in the Qur'ān: 3:82, 85–90; 4:137; 5:54; 9:66; 16:106.

the apostate to repent.[3] Then, he would recite: *Lo! those who believe, then disbelieve, and then (again) believe, then disbelieve, and then increase in disbelief, Allah will never pardon them, [nor will he guide them unto a way]* (4:137).

The meaning of apostasy is 'return', and the name apostate (*murtadd*) is applied to a person who comes out of something and then returns to it. So it is said: *irtadda*, that is he returned to something from which he had come out. This is like an unbeliever who used to believe in his own religion, accepts Islam, and then returns to the religion in which he believed formerly. It is he who should be asked to repent.

The Messenger of God said, 'Kill him who changes his religion.'[4]

'Alī: He used to ask the apostate to repent when he adopted Islam and then went back to his old faith. He said, 'Only he who enters a religion and then goes back on it should be asked to repent; but he who is born in Islam, we kill him and do not request him to repent.'[5]

['Alī]: A man named Mustawrid al-'Ijlī[6] was brought to 'Alī. It was said that he had adopted Christianity and hung a cross round his neck. Before questioning him and before any testimony was given against him, 'Alī said to him, 'Woe be to you, O Mustawrid, it has been represented to me that you have become a Christian and wish to marry a Christian woman. We shall marry you to her.' The man said, 'Holy! Holy!' 'Alī said, 'Perhaps you have inherited [a fortune] from a Christian and believe that we shall not give the inheritance to you. But, we shall give the inheritance to you because we [Muslims] inherit from them [Christians],

[3]*Kāfī*, VII, 283. Traditions differ on the question whether the apostate should be given an opportunity to repent or not. Some traditions do not accept the repentance of an apostate, while others state that the Prophet forgave apostates. *EI*^{2}, s.v. Murtadd; sources are indicated therein.

[4]*Mishkāt*, II, 281; Robson, I, 752; transmitted by Bukhārī, Abū Dāwūd, Tirmidhī, Nasā'ī, Ibn Māja and Ibn Ḥanbal. *Concordance*, s.v. b-d-l.

[5]*Kāfī*, VII, 280, 282. Leaving aside the Qur'ān and the *aḥādīth*, in the books of jurisprudence there is unanimity that the male apostate, if he is an adult (*bāligh*), sane (*'āqil*), and has not acted under compulsion (*mukhtār*), should be put to death. A woman, on the other hand, is to be imprisoned until she recants and adopts Islam again. This is the rule according to the Ḥanafī and Shī'ī schools, while according to Awzā'ī, Ibn Ḥanbal, the Mālikīs, and the Shāfi'īs, she should also be killed. Some early jurists make a distinction between the apostate born in Islam and one converted to Islam. According to them the former is to be put to death at once, while others insist on three attempts at conversion (relying on the verse 4:137), or have him imprisoned for three days in order to give him a chance for recanting. For older sources see *EI*^{2}, s.v. Murtadd.

[6]'Ijl, an ancient Arabian tribe, is reckoned part of Bakr b. Wā'il. *EI*^{2}, s.v. 'Idjl. Māwardī, *al-Aḥkām al-sulṭāniyya*, 56; he mentions this case.

but they do not inherit from us.' He said, 'Holy! Holy!' 'Alī asked, 'Have you then become a Christian as it is alleged?' He replied, 'Yes, I have become a Christian.' Then 'Alī asked him a second time, 'Have you become a Christian?' He said, 'Yes, I have become a Christian.' 'Alī exclaimed, 'God is Great.' Mustawrid said, 'The Messiah (*al-Masīḥ*)[7] is greatest.' Then, 'Alī held him by the fold of his dress and threw him down on his face, and said, 'O servants of God, trample upon [him],' and the people trampled upon him till he died.[8]

'Alī: He said, 'When a woman becomes an apostate, the rule with regard to her is that she should be imprisoned until she becomes a Muslim or dies;[9] but she should not be killed. If she is a slave girl and her owners desire her service, she should be utilized for service. She should be treated with the utmost harshness and clothed in the coarsest cloth which is just sufficient to cover her modesty and save her from dying from heat or cold. She should be given the meanest food for her survival and the maintenance of her life. The same is the rule with regard to the *umm al-walad*.[10] The male slave is to be treated in the same manner as a free man.' We have mentioned his case earlier.

'Alī: He said, 'The apostate's wife shall be separated from him;[11] and so long as he is an apostate, the animal slaughtered by him shall not be eaten.[12] His apostasy shall be deemed to be a divorce (*furqa*), but if he becomes a Muslim before the end of the '*idda*, he is the person most entitled to her.[13] Where a woman apostatizes and goes over to an enemy country (*arḍ al-ḥarb*), her husband is entitled to marry four wives, even her sister, i.e. when the wife's '*idda* is over.'

['Alī]: He said, 'The young children of an apostate are Muslims.'

[7]*Al-Masīḥ* in Arabic is a loan word from the Aramaic, where it was used for the Redeemer. The word is used in the Qur'ān. However, its exact meaning is not clear. One can assume with reasonable certainty that *al-Masīḥ* is used in the Qur'ān as a title of Jesus, and does not mean a messianic figure. *EI*², s.v. al-Masīḥ.

[8]Cf. *Kāfī*, VII, 280; Ṭūsī, *Tahdhīb al-aḥkām*, X, 137; very brief account and the person who had adopted Christianity his name is not given.

[9]*Kāfī*, VII, 280; Ṭūsī, *Tahdhīb al-aḥkām*, X, 143.

[10]*Umm al-walad* is a female slave who has borne her master a child. See *The Pillars of Islam*, I, 283, 362, and Chap. 12, section entitled '*Umm al-Walad*' in this volume.

[11]The marriage of the *murtadd* becomes void. If he had *umm al-walad*, she becomes free; the *kitāba/mukātaba* continues, but other legal activities are suspended. For details see *EI*², s.v. Murtadd; Ṭūṣī, *Tahdhīb al-aḥkām*, X, 137.

[12]*Kāfī*, VII, 283.

[13]It seems that, in this case, the apostate might have escaped into the *dār al-ḥarb* or hidden himself from the authorities.

RULES REGARDING INNOVATION AND HERETICS (*AL-ḤUKM FĪ AHL AL-BIDʿA*[14] *WA ʾL-ZANĀDIQA*)[15]

Jaʿfar b. Muḥammad—his father—his ancestors: ʿAlī used to ask heretics (*zanādiqa*) to repent, but he did not ask those of Muslim parentage to repent. He used to accept the evidence of two just witnesses that a certain person was a heretic; and [even] if a thousand persons were to testify that he was free from heresy, he would not listen to their evidence.[16]

[ʿAlī]: A number of heretics were brought to him from Basra, so he put forward Islam to them [for their acceptance] and asked them to repent. They refused, so he dug a pit for them and said, 'I shall fill [the pit] with flesh and fat.' Then he ordered that they should be beheaded. He had their bodies thrown in the pit, then he lit a fire and burnt them. That is how he used to act with apostates and those who changed their religion.[17]

ʿAlī ordered the burning of a Christian who had apostatized. His relations offered to pay a hundred thousand dirhams for his body, but ʿAlī refused, and by his order he was burnt by fire. ʿAlī said, 'I am not going to help Satan against them nor be one of those who sell the body of a

[14]The term *bidʿa*, meaning innovation, is used more precisely for any doctrine or practice not attested in the time of the Prophet. The term is, therefore, the opposite of *sunna*. Soon, it became necessary to distinguish between 'good' and 'bad' innovations. In several contexts, *bidʿa* was translated as 'heresy', however, the two terms are not exact equivalents. *EI*², s.v. Bidʿa; Lewis, 'Observations', 52–3; *The Pillars of Islam*, I, 52, 110, 119, 180, 264. Nuʿmān uses it as a synonym for heresy (*zandaqa*).

[15]The word *zindīq* pl. *zanādiqa* is arabicized from Persian *zand* (the book of Zoroaster) or from *Zandīk* (Magian, Manichaeans). It was originally used for the Dualists, one who does not believe in the unity of the Creator, or one who conceals unbelief and makes a show of belief. Later, it was applied to all who held unorthodox and suspect beliefs, especially those who were considered dangerous to the state and society. *EI*², s.v. Zindīḳ; Lewis, 'Observations', 54–6; *The Pillars of Islam*, I, 494. There is no special section by this title in *al-Aḥkām al-sulṭāniyya* of either Ibn al-Farrā' or Māwardī. Their definition of *ahl al-baghy* (rebels) as 'those who oppose the community and stand alone with a religious creed they innovated (*khālafū ra'y al-jamāʿa wa 'nfaradū bi-madhhab*ⁱⁿ *ibtadaʿūhu*)', seems inclusive of this group. Muslim historians recording on heresies had classified the Ismāʿīlīs among the extreme (*ghulāt*) Shīʿīs or as *zanādiqa*. One can understand Nuʿmān's purpose in refuting them. Similarly, he included fighting with rebels (*ahl al-baghy*) in the 'Book of Jihād', as a religious obligation. See *The Pillars of Islam*, I, 479–94; Abou El-Fadl, *Rebellion and Violence*; is a recent comprehensive study on this subject.

[16]*Kāfī*, VII, 283, 442.

[17]There was no agreement on the nature of the death penalty. Anas b. Mālik and ʿIkrima criticized ʿAlī for having burned them. *EI*², s.v. Murtadd; older sources indicated therein.

disbeliever.' When 'Alī burnt the heretics that we have mentioned, he used to ask Qanbar[18] to burn them and say:

'When I saw a nauseous thing this day,
I kindled a fire, and called upon Qanbar.'[19]

['Alī]: The Messenger of God said, 'The magician (*sāḥir*)[20] of the Muslims should be put to death,[21] but not the magician of the unbelievers.' It was said, 'And why so, O Messenger of God?' He said, 'Because attribution of a partner to God (*shirk*) and magic resemble each other closely; and between the two, *shirk* is worse.'[22]

'Alī said, 'It was for this reason that the Messenger of God did not kill the Jew Ibn A'ṣam[23] who had performed magic.' He also said, 'When two just witnesses testify that a person works magic, the magician should be killed, because it is equivalent to disbelief (*kufr*).

[18]Qanbar was 'Alī's slave. *The Pillars of Islam*, I, 64, n. 168.

[19]See *The Pillars of Islam*, I, 64; it is the same verse except the variant *al-yawm* instead of *al-amr*.

[20]*Siḥr*, generally translated as magic, includes several concepts. The following three are worth noting. (i) It is applied to that which entrances the eye and acts on the psyche of a person making him believe that what he sees is real while it is not so. It is called *ruqya* (charm, incantation), also known as 'white' or 'natural magic'. (ii) It refers to things, the apprehension of which is subtle, for example, poetry and eloquence, especially of the Qur'ān. Bukhārī transmitted a tradition which states that when two men coming from the east made a speech and the people were charmed with their eloquence, the Messenger of God said, 'In eloquence there is magic.' In this case *siḥr* consists of a falsification of the reality of things and actions. Hence, it is reprehensible, as it is allied to falsehood and trickery. (iii) It is applied to any action effected through recourse to a demon and with his assistance. It is known as 'black magic'.

Siḥr and its derivations occur more than forty times in the Qur'ān. In some verses it is equated with *kufr* (disbelief) and is said to have been derived from demonical origin, taught to men by two fallen angels. It is seen as an enchantment exerted over spirits as a falsehood, as possession by jinn. What is probited is the 'black magic'. For details and sources see *EI*², Ruḳya, Siḥr; *Mishkāt*, II, 571; Robson, II, 1000. It is worth noting that the last epistle of the *Epistles of Brethren of Purity* (*Rasā'il ikhwān al-ṣafā'*) deals with the quiddity of magic, charms (or spells) and evil eye (*māhīyat al-siḥr wa 'l-'azā'im wa 'l-'ayn*).

[21]'Kill every *sāḥir* (magician) ... and *sāḥira* (female magician).' (Ibn Ḥanbal). 'The *ḥadd* punishment of the *sāḥir* [is decapitation] by the sword.' (Tirmidhī). 'Among the seven sins which merit death are the attribution of a partner to God (*shirk*) and magic (*siḥr*).' (Bukhārī and Muslim). *Concordance*, s.v. s-ḥ-r; *EI*², s.v. Siḥr.

[22]*Kāfī*, VII, 285. Another tradition states that he should be struck on the crown with a sword.

[23]As in MS Q and other sources indicated below. 'Āṣim: in the edited text is an error. He is Labīd b. A'ṣam from the Jews of Banū Zurayq who had cast a spell over the Prophet. See Chap. 5, n. 23.

'Magic is disbelief, and God mentions this in His Book and says: *And follow that which the devils falsely related against the kingdom of Solomon. Solomon disbelieved not, but the devils disbelieved, teaching mankind magic [sorcery]*[24] *and that which was revealed to the two angels in Babel, Hārūt and Mārūt.*[25] *Nor did they (the two angels) teach it to anyone till they said: We are only a temptation, therefore disbelieve not (in the guidance of Allah)* ... till the end of the verse (2:102). Thus, God says that magic is disbelief, so he who performs magic becomes an unbeliever. The magician of the Muslims should be killed because he becomes an unbeliever after [accepting Islam] as is related from the Messenger of God.' 'Alī said, 'This is the evidence from the Qur'ān.'

'Alī: A man who was originally Christian but who had adopted Islam was brought to 'Alī. With him was found the flesh of swine; he had fried it and wrapped it up with some sweet smelling plant (*rayḥān*). 'Alī said, 'Woe to you! What impelled you to do what you have done?' He said, 'O Commander of the Faithful, I became ill and craved it.' 'Alī said, 'Woe be to you! What keeps you from [eating] mutton so that you would be free [from such a desire]? If you had eaten it, I would have punished you fully with the *ḥadd* penalty; but I shall scourge you in such a manner that you will never return to it.' 'Alī scourged him until the man urinated standing on his legs.[26]

'Alī: He said, 'A man who goes to a fortune-teller (*'arrāf*),[27] asks him,

[24]The Biblical king Solomon is an outstanding personality in Islamic lore wherein special emphasis was put on his wonderful powers of magic and divination. This particular verse refers to the occult science practised by the Jews, the origin of which was ascribed to Solomon. The Qur'ān refutes the charge of idolatry against him. *EI*², s.v. Sulaymān b. Dāwūd; Ṭabarī, *Tafsīr*, II, 405–42; Kisā'ī, *Tales*, 300–21.

[25]It refers to a legend concerning the fallen angels who made themselves masters of the arts (magic) forbidden to men. Both the angels had come to Babylon with instructions to avoid grave sins, but were captivated by a wondrously beautiful woman. Being caught unaware at the very moment she was granting them her favours, they killed the man who had witnessed their misconduct. As a punishment, they were imprisoned and hung by the feet in a well in Babylon where they have been tormented ever since. For details and sources see *EI*², s.v. Hārūt wa-Mārūt.

[26]The Arabic *shaghara bi-bawlihi* primarily signifies raising the leg or hind leg. It is used metaphorically to refer to the copulation and urination of animals. Lane, s.v. sh-gh-r. This tradition is cited in *Majma' al-baḥrayn*, s.v. sh-gh-r, without the name of 'Alī. *Kāfī*, VII, 292; reported on the authority of Imam al-Ṣādiq.

[27]*'Arrāf* means a diviner. According to Rāghib al-Iṣfahānī, the *'arrāf* is one who informs of future events and the *kāhin* is one who informs of past events. Lane, s.v. '-r-f. A tradition transmitted by Muslim states, 'Whoso comes to an *'arrāf* and asks him concerning a thing, prayer of forty nights will not be accepted from him.' Muslim, *Ṣaḥīḥ*, VII, 37; also transmitted by Ibn Ḥanbal, *Concordance*, s.v. '-r-f; *EI*², s.v. 'Arrāf.

and believes in what he says, has indeed denied what God revealed to Muḥammad. ʿAlī used to say, 'Many of the charms (*ruqya*)[28] and necklaces of amulets (*tamāʾim*)[29] are parts of idolatry (*ishrāk*).'

Abū Jaʿfar Muḥammad b. ʿAlī: He said, 'If a faithful one who used to do good works falls into sin[30] and becomes an unbeliever and thereafter repents, he is entitled to the reward of all the actions committed by him during the period of belief. His disbelief will not erase them if he has repented after disbelief.'

[28]See Chap. 5, n. 22.

[29]*Tamīma* pl. *tamāʾim* and the synonyms *taʿwīdh*, *ʿūdha*, means amulet or talisman. Originally it meant a stone with white speckles on a black field or vice-versa which was threaded on a thong or cord and worn around the neck to avert danger. Pre-Islamic Arabs believed that it would protect them from the evil eye, ill fate, and sickness, having, thereby, recourse to other than God. As this practice was associated with a power other than God's, the Prophet condemned such belief; but, when these *tamāʾim* contain verses from the Qurʾān, they are lawful.

'Among the ten faults detested by the Prophet ... is wearing *tamāʾim*.' Another tradition states, 'Three practices stem from *shirk*: *ruqā* (charms), *tamāʾim*, and *tiwala* (spells by means of which a woman seeks to gain a man's love).' Lane, s.v. t-m-m; *EI*[2], s.v. Tamīma; *Concordance*, s.v. t-m-m (*tamīma*). See also Chap. 5, n. 21.

[30]The Arabic *aṣābathu fitnat*[un], means he was afflicted with a trial. *Fitna* has a wide range of meanings. The Qurʾān (2:191) states: *And infidelity, or unbelief (al-fitna) is more excessive than slaughter*.

20

Book of Usurpation and Transgression (*Kitāb al-Ghaṣb wa 'l-Ta'addī*)

USURPATION (AL-GHAṢB)[1]

God says: *And eat not up your property among yourselves in vanity, [nor seek by it to gain the hearing of the judges that ye may knowingly devour a portion of the property of others wrongfully]* (2:188). And says God: *Do not begin hostilities. Lo! Allah loves not aggressors* (2:190).

Ja'far b. Muḥammad[2]—his father—his ancestors—'Alī: The Messenger of God delivered a sermon to the people at Minā[3] on the Day of Sacrifice[4] at the Farewell Pilgrimage[5] while riding his she-camel

[1]*Ghaṣb*, according to Arab Lexicographers, means usurpation, wrongful appropriation, or taking something unjustly or by force. There is no agreed upon definition of 'wrongful appropriation' among the various schools of law. It is neither robbery nor larceny, both of which are dealt with in criminal law. *Ghaṣb*, the illegal appropriation of something belonging to another or the unlawful use of the rights of another is restricted to civil law and comes under obligations arising from a tort. It is considered a sin and the usurper (*ghāṣib*) is liable to discretionary punishment (*ta'zīr*). He has to return the unlawfully taken object to the deprived person (*maghṣūb minhu*) or pay him compensation. The usurper is liable for the loss of the usurped object. He is further liable for a dimunition of the value of the usurped object. Schacht observes that Islamic law treats *ghaṣb* in great detail, with the tendency to protect the lawful owner as much as possible. Lane, s.v. gh-ṣ-b; Ibn Rushd, *Bidāya*, II, 312–20; trans. II, 383–93; Ḥillī, *Sharā'i' al-islām*, II, 150–8; both of these sources cover items not dealt with by Nu'mān; Mahmasani, 'Transactions in the Sharī'a', 189; Schacht, *Introduction*, 160, 200; *EI*[2], s.v. Ghaṣb.

[2]As in MS Q. The edited text adds: b. 'Alī.

[3]See *The Pillars of Islam*, I, 230, n. 298.

[4]See *The Pillars of Islam*, I, 410.

[5]See *The Pillars of Islam*, I, 360, n. 5; 368.

Qaṣwā'.[6] He said, 'O People, I fear I shall not meet you in this place after this year. So listen to what I say and profit by it.' Then he said, 'Which day is the most sacred?' They said, 'This day, O Messenger of God.' He said, 'Which month is the most sacred in the eyes of God?' The people said, 'This month, O Messenger of God.' He said, 'Which country is the most sacred?' They said, 'This country, O Messenger of God.' The Prophet said, 'The sanctity of your property and of your lives (lit. blood) is like the sanctity of this day of yours, in this month of yours, in this country of yours. [This will be the case] until you meet your Lord when He will ask you about your actions. Hark! Have I conveyed [to you the message of God]?' They said, 'Yes.' The Prophet said, 'O God, bear witness.'[7] Then [the Imam] related the whole tradition fully.

The Messenger of God:[8] He said, 'Every property owner is most entitled to their own property.'[9]

Ja'far b. Muḥammad: He said, 'Return goods entrusted to you, even if it be to the murderer of [Imam] al-Ḥusayn[10] b. 'Alī.[11] Whoever receives either goods or property from a Muslim should return them [to their rightful owner, thereby] avoiding the crime [of usurpation] and freeing himself from any liability that he might incur. If the owner/donor dies [before the trustee absolved himself of the accountability], then the trustee should hand over the property to the heirs. He should also repent his infraction before God until God manifests the signs of contrition, repentance, and absolution.' He further said, 'I am not going to hold you responsible for the interpretation (*ta'wīl*) of the punishment regarding the goods of the people. However, I am of the opinion that the goods should be given back [to those entitled], if they still exist *in specie* in the hands of those who appropriated them wrongfully. They should clear themselves from the responsibility [by returning the goods] to the rightful owners. If the goods are destroyed, let the usurper (*mughtaṣib*) give their value to those entitled to them. If they are not known, then the goods [or

[6]The name of the Prophet's she-camel is spelled slightly different in the MSS; al-Qaṣwā' (with *alif* and *hamza*, a sign of prolongation, *al-alif al-mamdūda*), and al-Quṣwā (with *al-alif al-maqṣūra*, and the vowel *ḍamma* on the first letter). *Lisān al-'Arab*, s.v. q-ṣ-w; *Majma' al-baḥrayn*, s.v. q-ṣ-w; *The Pillars of Islam*, I, 399, n. 242.

[7]For the full text of the Prophet's sermon see Ibn Isḥāq, *al-Sīra*, IV, 250–2; Guillaume, 650–2; Ṭabarī, *History of al-Ṭabarī*, IX, 112–14; Lings, *Muhammad*, 332–6.

[8]As is MS Q; in the edited text: *wa-'anhu*.

[9]A similar tradition is transmitted by Ibn Ḥanbal and Ibn Māja. *Concordance*, s.v. ḥ-q-q.

[10]As in MS Q, in the edited text: al-Ḥasan, is incorrect.

[11]*Kāfī*, V, 128; '... even if it be to the murderer of 'Alī ...'

their value] should be given in charity to the poor and the indigent on behalf of the rightful owner and the usurper should repent before God of what he has done.'[12]

[Ja'far b. Muḥammad]: He said, 'If a man forcibly takes away a slave girl [belonging to someone else] and begets a child on her, the owner shall take possession of the slave girl and the child will be held in slavery. Where a man buys a slave girl [from one] who has wrongfully taken her and begets a child on her, the true owner shall seize the girl and, if the buyer did not know that the girl was taken away forcibly, obtain the price of the child.'[13]

[Ja'far b. Muḥammad]: He said, 'If a man forcibly takes a beast and she foals and produces young ones, both the dam and her young will be recovered by the true owner.[14] The same is the rule regarding a slave girl who bears children.'

Abū Ja'far Muḥammad b. 'Alī: He said, 'If a man forcibly takes away a slave girl and she dies, he is responsible for her price [to the owner]. If the usurper has intercourse with the slave girl and she becomes pregnant and later, her true owner claims her and gets her back while she is pregnant and she dies in childbirth, the usurper is responsible for her price [to the owner].'

[Abū Ja'far Muḥammad b. 'Alī]: He said, 'If a man forcibly takes away a slave and makes him work for wages, or if the slave himself works for wages, and later, the owner claims his rights, he will obtain both the slave and the wages [from the usurper or the slave].'

[Abū Ja'far Muḥammad b. 'Alī]: He was asked about a man who forcibly takes the property of another and works it or increases its value. 'In such cases,' he said, 'the usurper is entitled to the produce or the increase in value. However, the owner does receive any increase in value [or goods] that takes place without the labour of the usurper. [In either case] the loss is borne by the usurper.'[15]

[12]He who wrongfully appropriates property must restore it to its rightful owner. If it has been consumed, destroyed, or lost, as a result of his transgression or otherwise, he must replace it if it is replaceable. Otherwise, he must pay its value at the prevailing price.

[13]Cf. Ḥillī, *Sharā'i' al-islām*, II, 156.

[14]'No one must milk a man's animal without his permission. Would any of you like his upper chamber to be intruded and his treasury broken into ...' *Mishkāt*, II, 118; Robson, I, 629.

[15]'If anyone takes a span of land unjustly, its extent taken from seven earths will be tied round his neck on the Day of Resurrection.' Transmitted by Bukhārī and Muslim. Another tradition states, 'If anyone makes barren land fertile, it belongs to him, but no right pertains to one who plants wrongfully in land another has brought into cultivation.'

FORCIBLE DISPOSSESSION (*AL-TAʿADDĪ*)[16]

Jaʿfar b. Muḥammad—his father—his ancestors—ʿAlī: He said, 'If a man forcibly dispossesses someone of property, the acquisition whereof is not lawful [in the first place], and destroys it, his act is not culpable.' A man who had destroyed a lute (*barbaṭ*)[17] was brought to ʿAlī and he rejected the (owner's) claim [for compensation].

Abū Jaʿfar Muḥammad b. ʿAlī: He said, 'A man who breaks a *barbaṭ*, a plaything (*luʿba*), a musical instrument (*malāhī* pl. of *malhā*),[18] or pierces a wine skin (*ziqq*) containing an intoxicant or wine, has done well and there is no fine on him.'

Jaʿfar b. Muḥammad: He prohibited [people] from gaming (*qimār*),[19] and looting [on festive occasions] when [fruits, walnuts, almonds, sugar, and silver and gold coins] are scattered.[20] By this, [the Imam] meant

---

Mishkāt, II, 118, 120; Robson, I, 629, 630. Compensation for the loss of use of profit sustained as a result of wrongful appropriation is disputed among jurists. Mahmasani, 'Transactions in the Sharīʿa,' 189. See also Ḥillī, *Sharāʾiʿ al-islām*, II, 156.

[16]Lit. to go beyond what is right, transgression. In Islamic law, it is a tort or negligence. Questions of liability form a very intricate subject matter in the Islamic law of obligations. Liability may arise from the non-performance of a contract, from a tort (*taʿaddī*), or from a combination of both. The depositary and other persons in a position of trust (*amīn*) are not liable for accidental loss, but they lose their privileged position through *taʿaddī*, i.e. illicit acts not compatible with the fiduciary relationship, such as using the deposit and losing it, whether the loss is caused by the unlawful act or not. The concept of *taʿaddī* is not limited to liability. It refers to torts in general. Schacht, *Introduction*, 147–8.

[17]*Barbaṭ*, a certain musical instrument of the Persians, is an arabicized word that means the breast of the duck, because of its resemblance thereto. Lane, s.v. b-r-b-ṭ; Muʿīn, *Farhang-e Fārisī*, s.v. b-r-b-ṭ. Arab authors used the terms *ʿūd* (lute) and *barbaṭ* synonymously, but there seems to have been a fundamental distinction between the two. The *barbaṭ* had its sound chest and neck made in one graduated piece, whereas the sound chest and neck were separate in the *ʿūd*. *EI*², s.v. ʿŪd.

[18]The term *malāhī* is used figuratively for musical instruments and, at times, is replaced by another term *ālāt al-lahw*. It is usually connected to the word *lahw*, which means amusement, pastime, or game. The usage of the term with the sense of musical instrument most probably arose during the third/ninth century. Religious authorities opposed to music seized upon this association with amusement and emphasized this pejorative connotation and attack what they considered as the negative aspect of music and its emotive power. This term disappeared after the fourth/tenth century as the Muslim philosophers and theorists wrote against the identification of music with amusement and playing. *EI*², s.v. Malāhī.

[19]It is a game of hazard, such as that called *maysir* in the Qurʾān (2:219, 5:90–1). Lane, s.v. q-m-r.

[20]I have preferred the reading in MS Q: *nahā ʿan al-qimār wa ʾl-nuhba fi ʾl-nithār*. In the edited text: *nahā ʿan al-qimār wa ʾl-nuhba wa ʾl-nithār* is an error.

[looting] by persons not invited [to a feast] with whom the scatterer was not pleased and who snatched and seized the things strewn in a raiding-like fashion. However, where a man invites people and distributes food or perfume, it is permissible to partake. Each person at the party should take what is put before him and what happens to come in front of him, without snatching or behaving arrogantly over any one else. This is permissible and is like food to which people are invited. It is placed before them and they are permitted to eat it. There is no difference of opinion [concerning this] among the people, so far as we know. There is also no difference of opinion regarding the rule that each man should eat what is in front of him. Snatching or taking food forcibly from another is disapproved. It is also disapproved that someone not invited should eat among them. Scattering [of fruits and money on festive occasions] is a similar case [to being a guest at a meal and the same rules apply]. God knows best.

[Ja'far b. Muḥammad]: He forbade Muslims from extending their walls into the streets of the Muslims. He said, 'He who extends his wall into a street that does not belong to him ought to return it to its [original] place. How can he extend his house to a space which does not belong to him? For whom will he leave it [as an inheritance]? Will he live in it [for ever]? [Nay], he will shortly depart from it [die] and will approach one [God] who will not excuse him for such an act. He will leave the house to one who will neither praise him nor benefit him. How heedless the heir is as to what might happen to the inherited property—enjoying the house and spending the wealth. The pledges of the testator are unredeemable! [If the testator knew this,] he would be filled with anger and would wish that he did not leave behind anything.[21]

'Alī: He wrote to Rifā'a[22] as follows:

> Return the things deposited with you and fulfil your promises.[23] Do not cheat him who cheats you and do good to him who does ill to you. Repay him who does good to you. Forgive him who does wrong to you. Pray for him who helps you. Make a gift to one who deprived you of [your rights]. Be courteous to him who is generous to you. Thank God profusely for what He has conferred upon you (*mā awlāka*) and praise Him for the trials which He has sent you (*mā ablāka*).[24]

[21]The Arabic text is unclear. I have tried to convey the sense from its context.

[22]Rifā'a b. Shaddād was 'Alī's *qāḍī* at Ahwāz, *The Pillars of Islam*, I, 281.

[23]The Arabic is *waffi ṣafqataka* which lit. means fulfil the terms of your agreement.

[24]*Ablāhu* means that He (God) tried, proved, or tested him. For, God tries his servant (*yablūhu*) by, or with, a benefit, to test his thankfulness; and by, or with, a calamity, to test his patience. Lane, s.v. b-l-w.

Ja'far b. Muḥammad: He was asked, 'If a man [called X] has a [just] claim against another man [called Y], but Y denies it and brings some goods to X and leaves them with him for safekeeping, or X obtains possession of some goods from Y, is it lawful for X to take possession of the property of Y to the extent of his claim?' [The Imam] said, 'No; this would be dishonesty. X cannot take anything from Y unless Y gives it to X freely or unless X obtains a decree against Y.'

[Ja'far b. Muḥammad]: He said, 'The people in a Muslim country (*dār al-islām*),[25] including opponents [of the state] and others, all have the benefits of a treaty obligation. So, [for example,] their lost animals should be returned to them;[26] the goods deposited by them should be returned; and the promises made to them should be fulfilled. Verily, goods entrusted to a person must be returned to him, regardless of whether he is virtuous or wicked; a promise made must be respected, irrespective of whether the man is virtuous or wicked.[27] So, return the deposits to the person who trusted you, do not deceive one who deceives you, and do not unlawfully take something from someone who denies your [just] claim.'

[25]See n. 312, Chap. 10.

[26]*Kāfī*, V, 132–6; several traditions are cited for *al-luqṭa wa 'l-ḍālla* (a thing lost and found and a lost animal). See also Ḥillī, *Sharā'i' al-islām*, II, 173–9.

[27]*Kāfī*, V, 128.

21

Book of Commodate Loans and Deposits (*Kitāb al-ʿĀriya wa ʾl-Wadīʿa*)

COMMODATE LOANS (*AL-ʿĀRIYA*)[1]

God says: *And forget not kindness among yourselves* ... (2:237).

Jaʿfar b. Muḥammad: He said, 'Giving [money] loans (*qarḍ*), commodate loans, and [extending] hospitality to guests are among the Prophet's practice (*sunna*).'

[Jaʿfar b. Muḥammad]: He said, 'The thing loaned by way of *ʿāriya* belongs to the lender. The borrower does not possess any ownership rights except those given to him by the lender. None of the rights of the lender over the thing loaned are destroyed by loaning it to the borrower.'

[Jaʿfar b. Muḥammad]: He said, 'The thing loaned as *ʿāriya* must be returned.[2] It is the right of the borrower to use it according to the permission granted to him by the lender.'

[1]*ʿĀriya* or *ʿārīya* is a loan of non-fungible objects and is distinguished as a separate contract from fungible objects, such as *qarḍ* (loan), or a loan of money. It is defined as putting someone temporarily and gratuitously in possession of the use of a thing, the substance of which is not consumed by its use. The intended use of such a thing must be lawful. It is described as a charitable contract because the lender puts the borrower in possession of the use of a thing without asking anything in exchange. The borrower's position is that of a trustee, the returning of the thing is obligatory when the thing itself remains in existence. In principle, he is not responsible for damage or loss arising directly from the authorized use of that thing. The Sunnī schools of jurisprudence differ about the details. The Ḥanafī and the Mālikī schools are more favourable to the borrower than the other schools. Ibn Rushd, *Bidāya*, II, 309–11; trans. II, 379–82; Schacht, *Introduction*, 134, 157, 168; *EI*², ʿĀriyya; Lane, s.v. ʿ-w-r; Mahmasani, 'Transactions in the Sharīʿa,' 186–7, 199–200. For the summary of this chapter, see Fyzee, *Compendium*, 82–6.

[2]*Mishkāt*, II, 122; Robson, I, 632.

[Ja'far b. Muḥammad]: He said, 'If the borrower transgresses (*qad ta'addā*)[3] [the limits set by the lender][4] and uses the thing borrowed wrongfully thereby damaging it or destroying it partly or wholly, he is responsible for the destruction or the loss.'

[Ja'far b. Muḥammad]: Concerning a thing lent that is destroyed without any wrong done by the borrower, [the Imam] said, 'If the lender had asked for a guarantee or if the borrower had guaranteed it at the time of the loan, the borrower is liable for the damage done. However, if the borrower had neither guaranteed it, made any wrongful use of the thing, nor broken any of the conditions, he is not liable.[5]

'The Messenger of God had borrowed eighty[6] coats of mail from Ṣafwān b. Umayya[7] for the Battle of Ḥunayn.[8] Ṣafwān asked, "[Is it] a guaranteed loan?" The Messenger of God replied, "Yes, a guaranteed loan (*'āriya maḍmūna*)" [i.e. a loan with a guarantee for its return]. The words of the Messenger of God (*'āriya maḍmūna*)[9] indicate [grammatically] an indefinite [form]. If the [form] were definite and [the words used were] "[all] the loans are guaranteed" (*al-'awārī maḍmūna*), the Messenger of God would have said, "The loan is [always] guaranteed (*al-'āriya maḍmūna*)." However, his words "a guaranteed loan", mean that there are some loans that are

[3]*Ta'addī* lit. means transgression, but here it has a technical meaning 'from tort;' i.e. illicit acts not compatible with the fiduciary relationship. The concept of *ta'addī* is not limited to the doctrine of liability, but refers to a tort in general. See Schacht, *Introduction*, 148.

[4]In today's legal terminology, we might say, of *qad ta'addā* 'if the person went beyond the bounds of what should be reasonably expected of him while in possession of the property.'

[5]*Kāfī*, V, 239–41.

[6]Ibid., V, 241: Seventy.

[7]Umayya b. Ṣafwān quoted his father as saying that, at the Battle of Ḥunayn the Prophet borrowed his coats of mail and he asked, 'Are you taking them by force, O Muḥammad?' The Prophet replied, 'No, it is a loan with a guarantee of their return.' *Mishkāt*, II, 122; Robson, I, 632; Ṭūsī, *Tahdhīb al-aḥkām*, VII, 182–3. When the Prophet decided to go out against Hawāzin, he was told that Ṣafwān b. Umayya had some armour and weapons, so he sent to him even though he was a polytheist at that time, saying, 'Lend us these weapons of yours so that we may fight our enemy tomorrow.' Ṣafwān asked, 'Are you demanding them by force, Muḥammad?' The Prophet said, 'No, they are a loan and a trust (*'āriya wa-maḍmūna*) until we return them to you.' Ṣafwān said that, in that case, there was no objection and he gave him one hundred coats of mail with sufficient arms to go with them. Ibn Isḥāq, *al-Sīra*, IV, 83; Guillaume, 567.

[8]For the Battle of Ḥunayn, see *The Pillars of Islam*, I, 459, n. 120.

[9]Grammatically, it is not a complete nominal sentence, but a phrase, the second word *maḍmūna* (guaranteed) is an adjective of *'āriya* (loan). *'Āriya* is an indefinite noun without the definite article *al*.

not guranteed. Furthermore, [it was] the Messenger of God who was asked for an explanation. If the loan was guaranteed, even though no [specific] guarantee was given, he would have said to Ṣafwān when he assured him, "It is guaranteed (*hiya maḍmūna*)." You would have [also] said those words. Otherwise, he would have [used another form and] said, "The loan is [always] guaranteed (*al-'āriya maḍmūna*).'"

What is clearly indicated by the guarantee of the Messenger of God to Ṣafwān is that Ṣafwān knew that a loan is not guaranteed unless done so specifically. Therefore, we have mentioned this case. This is the most cogent proof and the clearest interpretation for one who is endowed with its understanding, God willing.

Ja'far b. Muḥammad: He said, 'When the borrower claims the destruction of the thing borrowed, cannot produce any proof for this, and he is not above suspicion, he should not be believed and should be held responsible for the loss.'[10]

[Ja'far b. Muḥammad]: He was asked about a man who borrowed a thing and mortgaged it with some other goods, i.e. without the owner's permission. Then the borrower became a bankrupt, disappeared, or died. [The Imam] said, 'The owner of the thing borrowed should seize his property and the creditor [of the mortgage] should go against the debtor for his loan.'[11]

DEPOSITS
(AL-WADĪ'A)[12]

God says: *Lo! Allah commandeth you that ye restore deposits (al-amānāt) to their owners*[13] ... (4:58).

Ja'far b. Muḥammad: He said, 'The deposit (*al-amāna*) shall be returned

[10]*Kāfī*, V, 240; if the man is known for his honesty, he is not held responsible.

[11]Ibid., V, 240.

[12]*Wadī'a* (pl. *wadā'i'*, deposit, trust) is when an owner places his property in the custody of another person for safekeeping. The property deposited is on trust in the possession of the person receiving it, consequently, the latter is not liable if it is destroyed or lost unless he is guilty of negligence, a fault, or a wrongful act. However, if the deposit has been made for safekeeping in consideration of a fee and the thing deposited is destroyed or lost for some preventable cause, the trustee is liable. This voluntary contract may be terminated at the will of either party. Ibn Rushd, *Bidāya*, II, 306–8; trans. II, 375–8; Lane, s.v. w-d-'; Schacht, *Introduction*, 157; Mahmasani, 'Transactions in the Sharī'a,' 200; *EI*[2], s.v. Wadī'a.

[13]It should be noted that the word *wadī'a* does not occur in the Qur'ān, rather, the word *amāna* is used. In 33:72, the same word is used with a different type of trust. 'The hand which takes is responsible until it pays back.' *Mishkāt*, II, 121; Robson, I, 631.

to [the owner, whether he be] virtuous or wicked.'[14] We have mentioned aspects of this in the [previous] section on commodate loans.

[Ja'far b. Muḥammad]: In giving an extended exhortation to some of his partisans (*min shī'atihi*), he said, 'Fear God, your Lord. Return deposits (*al-amāna*) to the white and the black, whether he be a Khārijī (*Ḥarūrī*),[15] a Syrian, or an enemy.'[16]

[Ja'far b. Muḥammad]: He said, 'Where a man guards deposits (*wadī'a*) carefully, as they should be guarded, and later some are destroyed, displaced before they could be protected, are lost, forgotten by him, or are destroyed without his fault or destructive action, he is not responsible [for the loss].'

[Ja'far b. Muḥammad]—his father—his ancestors—'Alī: The Messenger of God said, 'There is no responsibility on a depositary (*mustawda'*).'[17]

'Alī: He said, 'There is no responsibility on a person entrusted [with some thing] (*mu'taman*).'

Ja'far b. Muḥammad: He said, 'The depositary (*ṣāḥib al-wadī'a*) and the owner (depositor *ṣāḥib al-biḍā'a*) are both to be trusted. [In a dispute,] the word of a depositary is to be believed if he says that the thing deposited is lost; but if he is suspected, an oath should be administered to him.'[18]

Abū Ja'far Muḥammad b. 'Alī: He was asked about a man who had deposited a thing with someone who then says, 'Yes, you had deposited the thing with me, but you had instructed me to give it to so-and-so,' but depositor denies this. [The Imam] said, 'The burden of proof is on the depositary because [he says] that the depositor had commanded him to deliver it [to someone else]. The depositor, [on the other hand,] should

[14]*Kāfī*, V, 128.

[15]For a fuller version of this tradition and explanation of a Ḥarūrī and a Syrian, see *The Pillars of Islam*, I, 93–4.

[16]Cf. *Kāfī*, V, 128.

[17]Liability can only be granted to the depositor if negligence or transgression is proved against the depositary. This occurs (i) when he deposits the *wadī'a* with a third party; or (ii) if he uses it for deriving benefits from it and, thereby, wears it out or damages it. *EI*[2], s.v. Wadī'a.

[18]A man deposited a thousand dirhams with someone and they were lost. The depositary said that it was a deposit, while the depositor claimed that it was a loan. The Imam said, 'The depositary is responsible unless he produces evidence that it was a deposit.' Another tradition states a man deposited a certain thing with someone. The depositary then put that deposit in his neighbour's house and it was lost. Is he responsible for the loss? The Imam said, 'Yes, because he violated the depositor's command and took it out of his possession.' *Kāfī*, V, 241. See also Ibn Rushd, *Bidāya*, II, 406–8, for different cases and differing opinions of the jurists.

take the oath that he had not authorized him to deliver it [to someone else].'

[Abū Jaʿfar Muḥammad b. ʿAlī]: The Imam said, 'A man had deposited a thing with a person. The depositor said to the depositary that if so-and-so came to him, he should deliver the said thing to him. Accordingly, the depositary delivered it to him; but the man who was to receive the thing denied the receipt of the thing.' [The Imam] said, 'The word is with the depositary when he says that he gave it. If he is suspected, he should be sworn because the depositor had agreed that the depositary should deliver the thing to someone else.'

ʿAlī: Two thieves came to a well-to-do Qurayshī[19] lady during the time of ʿUmar[20] and deposited one hundred dinars with her. They said to her, 'Do not give any of the money to either one of us without the other. When we come to you together, return the money to us.' They concealed their deceitfulness with her and went away. Then, one of them returned and said, 'Verily, my companion is faced with a situation which prevents him from returning with me and has instructed me to come to you so that you may give the property to me.' He mentioned to her certain signs between her and the absent person. She was a simple and naïve woman, so she gave him the money and he went away with it. Then [later], the second man came to her and said, 'Give me[21] the money!' She said, 'Your companion had come with [a clear] indication from you, so I paid [the money] to him.' He said, 'I did not send him,' and brought her to ʿUmar; but he did not know how to decide between them and sent the two to the Commander of the Faithful, ʿAlī. ʿAlī said to the man, 'As you two had jointly instructed her that no portion of the money should be given to one without his companion, so you have no right to obtain any portion of it without your companion. Go and bring your companion, and obtain your right.' Thus, he failed in his purpose and went away.

Jaʿfar b. Muḥammad: He said, 'Where a man has received a deposit, it is improper for him to spend from it or to borrow from it with intent to return it [later]. If he is compelled [by circumstances] to do so, and is capable of returning it, he should do so immediately, because he does not know how long he will live. If he is not capable of returning it, then it is not proper for him to borrow it in the first place, nor is it lawful for him to consume any of it without the depositor's consent.[22] The same

[19]See *The Pillars of Islam*, I, 37, n. 81.
[20]He was the second caliph, see *The Pillars of Islam*, I, 22, n. 16.
[21]According to MS Q and other MSS of Fyzee. In the edited text: *al-māl*.
[22]Cf. Ibn Rushd, *Bidāya*, II, 307.

rule applies to the agent (*muḍārib*)[23] [who trades with the capital of an investor and shares with him a pre-determined percentage of the profits].'

[Ja'far b. Muḥammad]: He said, 'If a man entrusts a child under the age of puberty with a deposit and the child loses [or destroys] it, there is no responsibility on the child.[24]

'If a man entrusts a slave to a child under the age of puberty and the child kills the slave, the child's family is responsible [for the blood money]. The evidence on oath of the child's family will determine the price of the slave unless the guardian of the slave can prove a higher value, in which case, the higher value shall be paid.'

[Ja'far b. Muḥammad]: He said, 'If a man entrusts a slave with a deposit, there is no responsibility on the slave if he loses it. If the slave is empowered to do business, the owner of the slave will not be responsible for anything unless the slave was empowered to accept deposits [from others], or unless the deposit is in the way of business. Even in the latter case, it is a loan to the slave and when he (the slave) is enfranchised, the deposit can be demanded; but if the slave admits the deposit, his admission shall not be accepted [against the owner].'

[23]For *muḍāraba* see Chap. 1, n. 324.

[24]The Ḥanafīs do not stipulate the adulthood of both parties and accept that a minor who has permission to trade is able to deposit his property freely. *EI*[2], s.v. Wadī'a.

22

Book of Finds, The Foundling, and The Runaway Slave
(*Kitāb al-Luqṭa wa 'l-Laqīṭ wa 'l-Ābiq*)

FINDS
(*AL-LUQṬA*)[1]

Ja'far b. Muḥammad—his father—his ancestors—'Alī: The Messenger of God once saw a date thrown away on the road and he picked it up. Later he came across a beggar and gave it to him and said, 'If you had not come to it, it would have come to you.'

'Alī: Once he came to Fāṭima[2] and found Ḥasan[3] and Ḥusayn[4] weeping before her. He asked, 'What is the matter with them?' She said, 'They wish to eat, but there is nothing in the house.' 'Alī said, 'Why not send someone to the Messenger of God?' Fāṭima said, 'Yes,' and sent someone to say, 'O Messenger of God, your two children [Ḥasan and Ḥusayn] are crying and there is nothing [to eat] for them. If you have

[1]*Luqṭa* and *Luqaṭa* lit. mean what is picked up or taken from the ground. It signifies an article found. The picking up of articles found is permitted, however, it is sometimes also said to be more meritorious to leave them so that the owner might remember and return to retrieve it. The person who finds it is bound to advertise the article for a year unless it is insignificant in value or perishable. After the period expires, according to Mālik and Shāfi'ī, the finder has a right to dispose of it as he pleases; but according to Abū Ḥanīfa, only if he is poor. If the owner claims it before the period expires, he receives the object back, as he does even after the period expires if it is still with the finder. If the finder has disposed of it in keeping with the law, he is liable for its value. Ibn Rushd, *Bidāya*, II, 300–4; trans. II, 368–74. Schacht, *Introduction*, 137; *EI*[2], s.v. Luḳaṭa. For the summary of this chapter, see Fyzee, *Compendium*, 86–9.

[2]See *The Pillars of Islam*, I, 42, 44, 48, 54, n. 138.

[3]Ḥasan, see *The Pillars of Islam*, I, 23, n. 24.

[4]Ḥusayn, see *The Pillars of Islam*, I, 23, n. 25.

anything, send it to us.' The Messenger of God looked around and found nothing in the house but some dates and he sent them, but that was not enough for them.

'Alī, therefore, went out to obtain a loan or the like, but whenever he intended to speak to anyone about it, he became shy of asking and went away. While he was walking about, he suddenly came across a dinar, so he came with it to Fāṭima and informed her. She said, 'If you pawned it for food today, and if its owner came along, we hope that we could find something with which to redeem it, God willing.' So he went with it to buy flour and tried to pay from the dinar by pawning it, but the man refused to take it and said, 'Whenever it is easy for you to pay the price, come with it,' and swore that he would not take the price [from the dinar]. Then, he passed by a butcher and bought meat worth a dirham and offered the dinar as a pawn, but he too refused it in the same manner and swore that he would not take it.

'Alī then went to Fāṭima with the meat and the flour and said, 'Make haste [in cooking], for I am afraid the Messenger of God would not have sent [mere] dates to his children if he had any [other] food with him.' She [cooked] hurriedly and 'Alī went with the food to the Messenger of God. They had hardly begun eating when they heard a boy asking people whether they had found the dinar, adjuring God and Islam. Then, 'Alī informed the Messenger of God of the whole story and the Messenger of God sent for the boy and asked him; he said, 'My people sent me to buy food for one dinar, and it fell out of my hand.' The Messenger of God returned the dinar to him after the boy had described it.[5]

To pick up found articles (*luqṭa*) with the intent to return it to one who swears it to be his property or to keep it at the place where it is found are both permissible according to what has come down from the Messenger of God. There is no harm in leaving it where it is until its true owner comes along.

Ja'far b. Muḥammad: He said, '[Imam] 'Alī b. al-Ḥusayn[6] and his freed slave passed by some lost articles (*luqṭa*); so the freed slave wanted to pick them up. [The Imam] forbade it, but the freed slave went and picked it up anyway. They walked a little and found its owner and the freed slave returned the thing to him and said to [Imam] 'Alī b. al-Ḥusayn,

[5]Cf. *Mishkāt*, II, 146–7; Robson, I, 649; a very brief tradition, which states that the dinar was lost by a woman.

[6]'Alī b. al-Ḥusayn, see *The Pillars of Islam*, I, 55, n. 140.

'Is this not a good thing [that I have done]?' [The Imam] said, 'If you and everyone else would have left it where it was, the owner would have come to retrieve it.'

'Alī: He was asked about found articles. He said, 'If you have passed by them, do not turn back towards it. However, there is no harm in picking them up if you inform people about them for one year,[7] so that their true owner may come along. If he does not appear, make them part of your property, and let them take the same course as your property, until someone comes along to seek them.'

Ja'far b. Muḥammad: He was asked about a man who had found a dinar in the sanctuary (*ḥaram*) [of Mecca] and picked it up: What should he do with it? [The Imam] said, 'He did a bad thing in picking it up. Finds in the *ḥaram* cannot be picked up.[8] It is in the sacred precinct of God until its true owner comes along and takes it.' It was said, 'The man was afflicted by picking it up. [How can he redeem himself?]' [The Imam] said, 'He should make it known [to the people].' It was said, 'He did it, [but no one came to claim it].' [The Imam] said, 'Then he should dedicate it to charity for the families of Muslims and if its true owner came along, he is responsible for it.'

We have mentioned earlier what has been transmitted of the command concerning giving good counsel to a Muslim. One of the ways of imparting such advice is to [ask him to] guard the property of another for him and to return it to him when he comes to claim it. So long as he does not find the true owner and gives up all hope of finding him, he should treat the property as belonging to an unknown owner. Therefore, the proper way of dealing with the property is to add it to the Public Treasury. We have mentioned the same rule for a man who dies without leaving an heir (escheat).

What is related from Abū 'Abd Allāh Ja'far b. Muḥammad [Imam al-Ṣādiq] as regards dedicating found property (*luqṭa*) to charity is because the Public Treasury, in his time, was in the hands of usurpers and, therefore, he did not deem it proper to put anything into it. His rule on this issue was to have it submitted to him so that he would spend it as he thought fit.

[7]'Making the matter known to people for a year,' seems to be the *sunna*. *Mishkāt*, II, 145; Robson, I, 648. A find less than a dirham in value need not be announced to people. *Kāfī*, V, 133.

[8]'The Messenger of God prohibited picking up what a pilgrim has dropped.' *Mishkāt*, II, 145; Robson, I, 648.

[Ja'far b. Muḥammad]: He said, 'No one eats [the meat] of lost camels (*ḍawāll* pl. of *ḍālla*) except one who goes astray.'[9]

Ja'far b. Muḥammad: He said, 'Found property cannot be sold or gifted.'

Ja'far b. Muḥammad: He said, 'When a man finds lost property, he should make it known for a year and then place it among his own belongings[10] so that what happens to them, happens to it until he finds someone claiming it. If he dies, he should bequeath it. If he has given it as charity, he is responsible for it, and if the true owner comes along, he should give it or its equal value to him.'[11]

'Alī: He said, 'A man came to the Messenger of God and said, "O Messenger of God, I have found a goat." The Messenger of God said, "It is for you, your brother, or the wolf." [12] The man said, "I have found a camel." The Messenger of God said, "Its hoof is its shoe [feet] and its stomach is its water skin [water supply]; so do not disturb it."'[13]

'Alī: He had a penfold for straying animals (*ḍawāll*) and used to give them fodder which neither fattened them nor made them slim. He provided the fodder from the Public Treasury. The animals would raise their heads and he who could furnish something of a proof [that the animals belonged to him] from [the masks on] their necks would take them, otherwise, 'Alī would continue with them in this condition but would not sell them.

The Messenger of God: A man asked him, 'O Messenger of God, I

[9]'He who shelters a stray camel is astray himself as long as he does not make the matter known [to people].' *Mishkāt*, II, 145; Robson, I, 648; transmitted by Muslim. *Ḍālla* is a beast that has strayed or a camel that remains in the place where it was lost.

[10]*Kāfī*, V, 132.

[11]'He who finds something should call one or two trustworthy people as witnesses and should not conceal it or cover it up. Then, if he finds its owner, he should return it to him, otherwise, it is God's property, He gives to whom He will.' *Mishkāt*, II, 147; Robson, I, 649. See also *Kāfī*, V, 135.

[12]The Messenger of God was asked about stray sheep (or goats) and he replied, 'You, your brother, or the wolf may have them.' Transmitted by both Bukhārī and Muslim. *Mishkāt*, II, 145; Robson, I, 648; *Kāfī*, V, 135.

[13]The Messenger of God was asked about stray camels and replied, 'What have you to do with them? [Leave them alone.] They have their water skin [water supply] and their feet. They can go down to water and eat trees until their owner finds them.' Transmitted by Bukhārī and Muslim. *Mishkāt*, II, 145; Robson, I, 648; *Kāfī*, V, 135. Kulaynī transmitted another tradition from Imam al-Ṣādiq which states, 'If, on the other hand, one finds a camel in a desert that is exhausted and abandoned by its owner and he takes it and spends money on its maintenance thereby rescuing it from inevitable destruction, it belongs to him. The original owner cannot and must not claim it.' *Kāfī*, V, 135.

have found a goat in the desert.' The Messenger of God said, 'That is for you, your brother, or the wolf. Seize it and make it known [to people] where you found it. If the animal is recognized, return it to its owner. If the beast is not recognized, then eat it. [If the owner turns up later,] you are responsible for it.'

'Alī: He was asked about the food bag of the traveller (*sufra*)[14] tht is found on the road discarded, full of bread, meat, cheese, and eggs. 'Alī said, 'Its value should be determined and the food eaten since it would spoil and would not last. If its owner came, they should pay its value to him.' The people said, 'O Commander of the Faithful, it was not known whether the *sufra* belonged to a *dhimmī*[15] or a Zoroastrian.'[16] 'Alī said, 'So long as the people did not know about it, they were free to eat from it.'

['Alī]: He was asked about *wariq* (silver, coined or uncoined) found in a house. He said, 'If the house was inhabited, it belongs to its owner; but if the house was in ruins,[17] it is to be treated as would found property.'[18]

THE FOUNDLING AND THE RUNAWAY SLAVE (*AL-LAQĪṬ*[19] *WA 'L-ĀBIQ*)

Ja'far b. Muḥammad—his father—his ancestors: 'Alī said, 'The foundling (*manbūdh*) is a free man [and not a slave].'

[14]*Sufra* is the food of the traveller or the food for a journey. It is the primary signification. Hence, it is used for the receptacle thereof or for the piece of skin in which it is put. This receptacle is generally of a round shape with a running string and can be converted into a bag to hold the food. When the traveller wants to eat, he could spread it flat on the ground and eat upon it. Lane, s.v. s-f-r.

[15]The People of the Book, see *The Pillars of Islam*, I, 143, n. 79.

[16]See *The Pillars of Islam*, I, 139, 221, 469.

[17]*Kāfī*, V, 133: ... if the house was in ruins and its inhabitants have departed, then he [the person who found *wariq*] is more entitled to it.

[18]The Messenger of God was asked about found property and he replied, 'If it is in a frequented road and a large town, make the matter known for a year. If its owner comes, give it to him, but if he does not, it belongs to you. However, what is found in a place which had been laid waste or if it is a hidden treasure (*rikāz*) [belonging to ancient times], it is subject to the one-fifth tax (*khums*).' *Mishkāt*, II, 146; Robson, I, 649.

[19]*Laqīṭ*, the same as or in the sense of *malqūṭ*, is a child that is cast out and found by another person or picked up, and whose parentage and status (free or slave) is unknown. The person who finds the child must swear in the presence of witnesses that he has found him, so that he may not subsequently claim him as his own son or slave. The child's paternity must be established by proper means. The person who has picked up a child must be free, a Muslim, and of good character. The child is presumed to be of free status until proved otherwise. He is also presumed to be a Muslim if found by a Muslim. It is the finder's responsibility to look after the foundling. Some jurists differ in this respect and

Jaʿfar b. Muḥammad: He said, 'The foundling (*manbūdh*) is free; if he wishes it, he may make the person who looks after him his patron (relationship of *walāʾ*) or may give the patronship (*walāʾ*) to someone else. If the man who looks after him requests money for providing for the foundling, the latter may give it to him if he is well-to-do; but if the foundling is not well-to-do, whatever has been spent upon him will be treated as charity (*ṣadaqa*).'[20]

[Imam al-Ṣādiq] further said, 'No good comes from an illegitimate child.[21] It is not proper for a man to take up [and raise] an illegitimate child of a slave girl. A man should not pollute himself by marrying a child of fornication. If the illegitimate child belongs to a slave girl, it is lawful for her owner to own him, sell him, use his services, and, if he so wishes, [sell him and] perform the *ḥajj* by his price.'[22]

ʿAlī:[23] He was asked about remuneration (*juʿl*)[24] for [returning] a runaway slave and he said, 'This is not necessary. A Muslim should return the dues of a [brother] Muslim, even when he has not been employed therefor.'

Jaʿfar b. Muḥammad: He said, 'If a man brings back a runaway slave and demands remuneration [from the slave's owner], he has no right [to claim it] unless a remuneration was fixed for him.'

[Jaʿfar b. Muḥammad]: He said, 'If someone captures a runaway slave in order to return him [to his owner], but the slave escapes from him, he is not responsible.'

---

charge the upbringing to the Public Treasury. Ibn Rushd, *Bidāya*, II, 305; trans. II, 374. Lane, s.v. l-q-ṭ; Schacht, *Introduction*, 159, 166; *EI*[2], Laḳīṭ.

[20]*Kāfī*, V, 223–4; reported from the same Imam. The foundling cannot be sold, bought, or gifted.

[21]Ibid., V, 224.

[22]Opinions vary on this issue, see Ibid., V, 225.

[23]As in MS Q. In the edited text: *wa-ʿanhu*, [i.e., Jaʿfar b. Muḥammad].

[24]Islamic law imposes the obligation of paying a reward called *juʿl* for bringing back a fugitive slave from a distance of more than three days' journey, except between near relatives. It was originally based on a public offer of reward, and was fixed at 40 dirhams. Schacht, *Introduction*, 159–60. For other meanings of *juʿl*, see Lane, s.v. j-ʿ-l.

23

Book of Partition and Construction (*Kitāb al-Qisma wa 'l-Bunyān*)

ON DIVISION (*AL-QISMA*)[1]

Everything which is owned by two or more persons should be divided when some or all of the persons claim it, but [it should be done] so that no harm (*ḍarar*) comes to any partner. We have mentioned earlier the distribution of war booty (*fay'*) and other goods. Where property is such that harm would be caused by its distribution, or where the property cannot be partitioned, then it should be sold and its price distributed,[2] because, in His Book, and on more than one occasion, God has prohibited the causing of harm [without good reason]. He said: ... *and harass them not (lā tuḍārrūhunna) so as to straiten life for them* (65:6), and He says: *Retain them not to their hurt (ḍirār) so that ye transgress (the limits)* (2:231), and He says: A *mother should not be made to suffer (lā tuḍārra) because of her child, nor should he to whom the child is born (be made to suffer) because of his child* (2:233).

As we have mentioned earlier, the Messenger of God prohibited the waste of property.

[1]Ibn Rushd, *Bidāya*, II, 260–6; trans. II, 317–24. According to him, the origin of the term *qisma* goes back to the Qur'ān: .... *And when kinsfolk and orphans and the needy are present at the division (qisma of the heritage)* (4:7–8). Hence, the discussion revolves around the distributor (*qāsim*), the divisor (number of shares by which something is divided, *maqsūm 'alayhi*), and the division (*qisma*) itself. *Qassām*, the title given in Ottoman law to the trustee responsible for the division of an estate between the heirs of a deceased person, is the noun of intensiveness (*ism al-mubālagha*) from *qāsim*. *EI*[2], s.v. Ḳassām.

[2]Ṭūsī, *al-Nihāya*, 429; Ḥillī, *Sharā'i' al-islām*, II, 215.

Ja'far b. Muḥammad[3]—his father—his ancestors—'Alī: The Messenger of God said, 'There shall be no loss (*ḍarar*) nor the causing of loss (*iḍrār*).'[4]

'Alī: He wrote to Rifā'a b. Shaddād:[5] There should not be a partition [of goods] which cannot be divided. He meant by this, property that is not capable of being partitioned according to the shares of the partners.[6]

Ja'far b. Muḥammad: He was asked about the partition of a watercourse (stream, *majrā 'l-mā'*). He said that this was one of the things which cannot be partitioned.[7]

'Alī: He was asked about a group of persons who distributed a house or tract of land in such a fashion that one of them had no right of passage to it. He said, 'This is not a [proper] partition among Muslims. Such a partition should be cancelled and it should be done in a fair and reasonable way.'

'Alī: He said, 'There is no escape from a distributor of property (*qāsim*), and from his proper remuneration.'[8]

Ja'far b. Muḥammad: He was asked about a house belonging to two persons. They partitioned it. One of them got the top and the other got the lower portion. He said, 'This is permissible, except in the case of a clear fraud or wrong. Unless both the parties knew and agreed to it the partition should be revoked.'

[Ja'far b. Muḥammad]: He was asked about a group of persons who partitioned a house that had only one way [into it]. The ownership of the way was given to one of them and the others were given the right of walking through the passage. He said, 'There is no harm in it and there is no harm in a man purchasing nothing more than the right of way through a house or the land belonging to another.'[9]

[Ja'far b. Muḥammad]: He was asked about a group of persons who

[3]As in MS Q. In the edited text: Abū Ja'far Muḥammad.

[4]*Concordance*, s.v. ḍ-r-r; transmitted by Ibn Ḥanbal; see also *Kāfī*, V, 298, 299.

[5]*Rifā'a* b. Shaddād was 'Alī's *qāḍī* at Ahwāz. *The Pillars of Islam*, I, 281.

[6]Ibn Rushd, *Bidāya*, II, 261–3; trans. II, 318–21; dwellings, animals, and certain goods or commodities fall into this category. Ibn Rushd cites several examples.

[7]Cf. *Kāfī*, V, 299.

[8]The tradition stresses the need for a professional distributor of inherited property through lots after equalization of shares and proper evaluation of the property. Property could be of three types: (i) fixed and immovable, such as house and real estate; (ii) movable that cannot be measured or weighed, such as animals; and (iii) movable that can be measured or weighed, such as precious metals. Division is a binding contract and cannot be revoked except in the case of a contingency. Moreover, the *qāsim* should be well versed in *'ilm al-farā'iḍ* (in the calculation and the division of inheritance). This being a professional work the person performing such a task should receive his remuneration. See also n. 1 above in this chapter.

[9]Cf. *Kāfī*, V, 298, 300.

partitioned a house amongst themselves in such a way that one of them got only a fraction of his share and left the remaining portion of his share to be distributed among others. [The Imam] said, 'There is no harm in it if they all agree to it.'

[Ja'far b. Muḥammad]: He was asked about a group of persons who were joint owners of several houses. Some of them said, 'I shall take my share in each house;' and others said, 'Let each of us have his share at one place.' [The Imam] said, 'The matter should be considered. If all the houses are equally well kept, and of even value with respect to salability and are equally desirable by people, the distribution should be such that each man has his share in one place. On the other hand, if the houses differ widely [in their condition and desirability] each house should be divided into portions and each co-owner may have his rights therein.'

[Ja'far b. Muḥammad]: He was asked, 'If there are several walled gardens (of palm trees *ḥawā'iṭ* pl. of *ḥā'iṭ*) at different places at distances which would take a day or so to reach, how is the partition to be made?' He said, 'The share of each person should be distinctly marked within certain limits [in each garden and made known.'

[Ja'far b. Muḥammad]: He said, 'If a group of persons are co-owners of some walled gardens (of palm trees) and plots of land, some of which are closer to each other than others, and all co-owners desire to have a portion from each property, there is no harm in it. If they desire that each one should have his shares together in one parcel of property by a calculation based on a fair price, that also is permissible. If, however, not all the plots of land and walled gardens can be divided according to the several portions or, if so divided, it would cause loss to some partner whose rights cannot be enjoyed proportionately, then the right of each co-owner should be united in one portion of land by a calculation based on a fair price [of each property].'

[Ja'far b. Muḥammad]: He was asked, 'If a group of co-owners own several gardens situated at different places each containing different kinds of fruit, how is the partition to be made?' He said, 'The share of each partner should be determined by a fair price. All of the gardens and all of the shares should be combined together and, if [the lands produce] corn and fruits which cannot be divided, then the produce should not be divided with lands, but the lands may be divided by metes and bounds.'

[Ja'far b. Muḥammad]: He was asked about the distribution of fruits and a harvest by conjectural computation of quantity (*khirṣ*).[10] He said,

[10]Also *khurṣ* and *kharṣ*. Lane, s.v. kh-r-ṣ.

'Conjectural computation of quantity is used amongst us as for the measure (*kayl*) of dry [produce]. It is to be used [as a measure] only for dates, grapes, and cereals (*ḥubūb*) and it is not used for measuring apples, plums, and the like, which can be counted individually. The conjectural computation of quantity may only be used for what can be measured and weighed.'

[Ja'far b. Muḥammad]: He was asked about the distribution of vegetables (*baql*) among co-owners. He said, 'The harvest cannot be divided when standing, but the crops should be sold and the price divided. Conversely, they can be harvested and then distributed as is the custom in such things, except when they all agree on the former course. Additionally, it is possible to divide it justly [in some other way]. The same rule applies to any standing harvest which does not appear to be ripe.'

[Ja'far b. Muḥammad]: He said, 'Where a group of persons jointly inherit land watered by a certain place of watering (or by watering right, *shirb*) and they have made the distribution of land among themselves, each one of them has a right in the watering according to his share.'

[Ja'far b. Muḥammad]: He was asked about co-owners of a piece of land with several kinds of trees. He said, 'Each tree should be distributed with the land, so that one man's tree is not to be found in another man's land.'

[Ja'far b. Muḥammad]: He said, 'If there are several co-owners of a house from which they are absent but which they know well enough, and they divide it according to its description, and each one knows his share in it, it is lawful. Likewise, the sale of a house from which the buyer and the seller are absent, but which is known to both of them [is also lawful]. However, if they do not know the house or if some of them know it, but not others, then the distribution is not valid until they or their agents are present at the division. The same rule applies to land and trees.'

[Ja'far b. Muḥammad]: He was asked about a group of persons who distributed a large house (or mansion, *dār*), but made claims against one another regarding a chamber (*bayt*) in it that was not in the individual possession of any one of them. They differed as regards its boundaries [and their shares]. He said, 'If there is no clear proof, let them take oaths, and the partition should be annulled.'

[Ja'far b. Muḥammad]: He said, 'With regard to the partition of mansions, there is no harm if the rooms are distributed by their prices, and an open space (courtyard) by measurement. A passage may be left in an open space which is common to all owners.'

[Ja'far b. Muḥammad]: He was asked about the distribution of an upper and a lower storey. Who is responsible for disrepair in the lower storey?

He said, 'The owner of the lower storey, because it is like land for the upper-storey owner. Although the upper-storey owner benefits from [the upkeep of] the lower storey, the owner of the lower storey cannot destroy [the foundation or the ceiling] and then ask the owner of the upper-storey to put a [new] roof over [his dwelling]. Rather, it is the duty of the lower-storey owner to repair the lower storey when it needs repair, so long as the owner of th upper-storey has not done any harm to it.'

[Ja'far b. Muḥammad]: He said, 'Whatever is destroyed or sequestered, as of right, from the property of joint owners before distribution is to be calculated [as a loss] from the total assets of all the parties. However, whatever is destroyed after distribution, falls as a loss on the share of the particular person to whom it was allotted. If the share of one of the co-owners is wholly or partly claimed, the distribution shall be made again.'

[Ja'far b. Muḥammad]: He said, 'Whenever the lower portion is in disrepair and it is possible and feasible to repair it to support the upper part, it is the duty of the owner of the lower part to repair it and support, thereby, the upper part. If that is not possible, the owner of the upper part should demolish it. It is the duty of the lower owner to repair the lower part. Then, the owner of the upper part may build on it according to his right. Where the whole building is destroyed, it is the duty of each one to repair his portion as needed. [Regarding] the portion which is common to them both, the needed repairs should be carried out and the cost borne by each co-owner according to his share. This is the case unless there is a lawful and permissible agreement between them, in which case, the agreement shall prevail.'

[Ja'far b. Muḥammad]: He said, 'When one of the shareholders claims that a fraud is committed while the rest deny it, the burden of proof rests with the claimant. If the claimant tells the judge, "Come with me or send someone to see and verify it," the judge has an option either to comply with the request or decline it. If, after verification, he finds that a fraud or a grave error has, in fact, been committed, he should distribute [the property] anew. The same rule applies where the witnesses testify to a fraud.'

[Ja'far b. Muḥammad]: He said, 'Division may be of two kinds. The first is a division by consent. Where the partners agree and consent and all of them are competent to act and each one knows what his share is, the division shall stand among them. The second is again of two kinds: (a) where the thing to be distributed is cereals (or corn) and the distributive shares are equal, [the division shall be in kind]; and (b), where the shares are unequal, some being greater than others, the price of the harvest should be taken into consideration and distribution made accordingly.'

ON CONSTRUCTION [OF BUILDINGS, WALLS, ETC.] (*AL-BUNYĀN*)

Ja'far b. Muḥammad: He was asked about a wall which stood as a barrier of privacy (*sutra*) between the owner of the wall and his neighbour. The wall fell down and the owner refused to rebuild it. [The Imam] said, 'The owner cannot be forced to do so unless the neighbouring owner had a right [to demand it] or unless it was an essential condition of the ownership of the property. However, the owner of the neighbouring house may be told, "You may take such steps that secure your privacy as you are entitled."'

[The Imam] was asked, 'If the wall had not fallen by itself, but had been destroyed or demolished with the intent to cause harm to the neighbour and without any need for demolition?' He said, '[The wall should] not be left [in a demolished state], for the Messenger of God said, "There shall be no loss nor the causing of loss." If the neighbouring owner had demolished it, he should be compelled to rebuild it.'

[Ja'far b. Muḥammad]: He said, 'There was a wall belonging to one of the owners of two contiguous houses; it fell and the owner refused to rebuild it. The owner of the other house asked him to rebuild it and said, "You deprived my family of privacy; cover up that which is between you and me."' [The Imam] said, 'The owner of the wall is responsible for its rebuilding or for somehow covering up between the two houses so that no part of the privacy of his neighbour is invaded.'

[Ja'far b. Muḥammad]: He was asked concerning a wall jointly owned by two owners. It fell and one of the two owners asked his companion to rebuild it and he refused. [The Imam] said, 'If the wall is of a kind that can be divided, it should be divided between them and each of the two should either build his part or leave it, provided it does not harm his companion. If the wall cannot be divided, he should be told, "Build, sell, or hand over your portion to your companion if he is willing to build it. In the latter case, it will become his." However, if the two owners agree that the original claimant should build it and the other co-owner should also benefit from it, then he should pay one-half of the charges [to the builder].'

[Ja'far b. Muḥammad]: He said, 'No one has the right to open a garret window (*kuwwa*) in his own wall to be able to look into his neighbour's house. However, he cannot be prevented from doing so if he opens such a window for light at a place from which nothing can be seen.'

[Ja'far b. Muḥammad]: He was asked about a man who increases the height of his building so that his neighbour is deprived of sunshine. [The Imam] said, 'This is his [the builder's] right and is not an injury that can prevent him from building. He may also increase the height of his wall as he wishes, provided this does not enable him to have a view of the inside of his neighbour's house.'

[Ja'far b. Muḥammad]: He said, 'Anyone who wishes, may alter the position of the gate of his house from a certain place [to another] or open another door on a (frequented) thoroughfare, unless there is a clear loss [to someone]. However, if this is in a by-path (*rā'igha*) and not a thoroughfare that is (widely) used, the door cannot be opened, nor can a door be moved from elsewhere, unless the residents of the by-path agree.'

[Ja'far b. Muḥammad]: He said, 'No one has the right to alter the condition of a well-travelled road (*sābila*) used by the generality of Muslims. However, if the road belongs exclusively to a certain group of eminent persons and they agree to change it to another place and do not injure anyone thereby, or if it is in the possession of someone who allows them to alter it, then it is permissible. The same rule applies when people wish to protect the path or put a lock on it. This is possible only when the road belongs exclusively to certain eminent persons and they agree; but no one is permitted to do this on an open, well-travelled road.'

[Ja'far b. Muḥammad]: Concerning the case of a man who has a right of way through the garden of another person who wishes to put a gate in it, [the Imam] said, 'He has no right to do so without the permission of the one who has the right of way.'

24

Book of Evidence
(*Kitāb al-Shahāda*)[1]

THE COMMAND TO ESTABLISH EVIDENCE AND TO PROHIBIT FALSE EVIDENCE
(*AL-AMR BI-IQĀMAT AL-SHAHĀDA WA 'L-NAHY 'AN SHAHĀDAT AL-ZŪR*)

God says: *And keep your testimony upright for Allah* (65:2);[2] And He says: *And call to witness, from among your men, two witnesses. And if two men be not (at hand) then a man and two women, of such as ye approve as witnesses* (2:282);[3] He says: *And have witnesses when ye sell one to another* (2:282).[4]

We have mentioned in the chapters on business transactions, marriage, divorce, divinely ordained punishments, and at other places, certain aspects of the law of evidence.

Ja'far b. Muḥammad—his father—his ancestors—'Alī:[5] The Messenger of God said, 'The false witness will be raised on the Day of Resurrection

[1]*Shahāda* pl. *shahādāt* it testimony or deposition. The discussions of witnesses and testimony generally revolves around three things: qualification, gender, and number. The most important qualifications for the acceptance of a witness are: *'adāla* (probity, moral uprightness), puberty (*bulūgh*), Islam, freedom (*ḥurrīya*), and the absence of any accusation against him (*nafy al-tuhma*). Some of these qualifications are agreed upon, while others are disputed. For details see *EI*[2], s.v. S̲h̲āhid; Ibn Rushd, *Bidāya*, II, 457–61; trans. II, 556–60.

[2]*Kāfī*, VII, 415; it refers to concealing evidence.

[3]Ibn Rushd, *Bidāya*, II, 460–1; trans. II, 556–60; gives more details about women's testimony.

[4]'The Messenger of God gave a decision on the basis of an oath and a single witness.' Transmitted by Muslim. *Mishkāt*, II, 342; Robson, I, 801; *Kāfī*, VII, 420.

[5]'An 'Alī is missing from MS Q.

with his tongue lolling out in Fire in the same manner as a dog hangs his tongue out in a vessel.'[6]

[The Messenger of God]: He said, 'When the angel of death descends [to the earth] to take possession of the life of the wicked man (*fājir*), he has with him a spit (*saffūd* or *suffūd*) of fire.' 'Alī said, 'O Messenger of God, will it strike a member of your community?' The Messenger of God replied, 'Yes, the unjust ruler; a person who wrongfully devours the property of an orphan; and a false witness.'[7]

[The Messenger of God]: He said, 'The false witness is one who have gone astray and one of the infamous ones.' He said, 'A great calamity will befall those who give evidence without being called upon to do so.'

Abū Ja'far Muḥammad b. 'Alī: He said, 'The witness should render as evidence only what he is asked to witness[8] and should fear God, his Lord. For a man to give evidence of what he does not know or to deny what he does know is an untruth. God has said: *So shun the filth of idols, and shun lying speech, turning unto Allah (only), not ascribing partners unto Him* (22:30–31). Thus, God has equated the giving of false evidence with polytheism (*shirk*).'[9]

Ja'far b. Muḥammad: He said, 'As soon as the false witness steps out of the place where he has testified, he is sentenced to [be punished by] the Fire.'[10]

[Ja'far b. Muḥammad]: He said, 'The false witness is to be scourged, but [the number] of stripes have not been determined. This is for the Imam to decide. He should be taken round the town so that the people may know. If after this, he offers repentance and improves, his evidence will be accepted.'

[Ja'far b. Muḥammad]: He said, 'The repentance of a false witness is that he should restore the loss he has caused by his evidence. The false witness becomes responsible for the loss he has caused as soon as he comes to know of it. He should render the cost of the damages to the owner.'[11]

[6]'If anyone appropriates by his oath what rightly belongs to a Muslim, God has made Hell necessary for him and deprived him of Paradise.' Transmitted by Muslim; *Mishkāt*, II, 342; Robson, I, 800.

[7]'Among the most serious of major sins are attributing a partner to God, unfilial behaviour, and deliberate perjury.' *Mishkāt*, II, 345; Robson, I, 803.

[8]*Kāfī*, VII, 416–17; a man has a choice either to testify or to observe silence, but he is obliged to testify against the oppressor.

[9]*Mishkāt*, II, 346; Robson, I, 803–4.

[10]'If anyone swears a false oath near this pulpit of mine, ... he will certainly go to Hell.' *Mishkāt*, II, 345; Robson, I, 803. See also *Kāfī*, VII, 417.

[11]*Kāfī*, VII, 418–19; one who retracts his testimony has to compensate for the damages.

[Ja'far b. Muḥammad]: He said, 'Do not imprison yourself and lose your property by giving false evidence, for there is no defect (*wakaf*) in a man's religion or sin in the eyes of God that cannot be removed according to his capacity.'

LAWFUL AND UNLAWFUL EVIDENCE (*MAN YAJŪZ SHAHĀDATUHU WA-MAN LĀ YAJŪZ SHAHĀDATUHU*)[12]

The evidence of a man who is faithful (*mu'min*), an adult (*bāligh*), free (*ḥurr*), sane (*'āqil*), capable of speech (*nāṭiq*), and of known parentage, is permissible with regard to things about which he is not prejudiced, provided he is virtuous (*'adl*) and not charged (*muttaham*) nor suspected (*ẓanīn*).

Ja'far b. Muḥammad: He was asked about the evidence of a father in favour of his son, of a son in favour of his father; and of brothers, relations, and spouses, testifying for each other. He said, 'The evidence of those of them who are virtuous (*'udūl* pl. of *'adl*) is permissible for each other.'[13] This is [also] related to us from 'Alī, and there is no difference of opinion in this respect among us.

[Ja'far b. Muḥammad]: He said, 'Where a man testifies to a matter in which he has an interest, his evidence will not be permissible, not in his own favour nor in favour of any other person who has testified in his favour along with him [in the same matter].'[14]

Abū Ja'far and Abū 'Abd Allāh: They said, 'The evidence of a blind man regarding something which is heard is permissible in the same way as the evidence of a man having eyes as to things which can be seen. The same is the rule regarding a man's evidence according to his knowledge.'[15]

Ja'far b. Muḥammad: He said, 'The evidence of a dumb person (*akhras*) is permissible when his gestures (*ishāra*) are known and understood. A non-Arab slave girl was brought to the Messenger of God on a complaint made with regard to her. He said to her, "Who am I?" She pointed to the sky and then to him and then to the people, indicating that he was the Messenger of God to the people, and the Prophet said, "She is a Muslim, so teach her Islam."

[12]Lit. translation is 'Persons whose testimony is permissible and those whose testimony is not permissible.'

[13]*Kāfī*, VII, 429–30.

[14]In today's legal terminology, it amounts to conflict of interest.

[15]*Kāfī*, VII, 437–8.

'The Messenger of God once prayed with the people in a sitting posture on account of illness. They stood behind him and he indicated to them by his hand to sit down and they sat down. Thus, a gesture which is understood, stands in the same position as speech when it is known.'

'Alī, Abū Ja'far, and Abū 'Abd Allāh: They said, 'The testimony of slave in favour of a person other than his patron is lawful if he is a person of good reputation (*'adl*). God says: *And call to witness, from among your men, two witnesses* (2:282); and a slave is to be counted as a man.'

Ja'far b. Muḥammad: He was asked concerning a man who died leaving behind a brother who inherited two slaves and a slave girl. He emancipated the two slaves. After emancipation, the two [former] slaves gave evidence that the deceased used to have sexual relations with the slave girl and that she had given birth to a son who had died after him. [The Imam] said, 'Their evidence in favour of the slave girl is lawful if they are of good character, and the two should return to the status of slavery as before [for they are rightfully the property of the *umm al-walad*].'[16]

[Ja'far b. Muḥammad]: He said, 'The evidence of a boy is not permissible until he attains puberty.'

[Ja'far b. Muḥammad]: He said, 'When the people of the desert (*ahl al-bādiya*) give evidence about a right among themselves, their evidence is lawful if they are upright. However, when they give evidence against townspeople (*ahlu qarya*) from whom they lie at some distance, their evidence would be less [in value] than that of the townspeople whose evidence is more appropriate in such a case. In such cases the evidence of the Bedouin is suspect.'[17]

It is reported that the evidence of an adversary (*khaṣm*)[18] and doubtful persons (*ẓanīn*) is not permissible. As regards the omitting of the evidence of neighbours, townspeople of good reputation, people of equitable composition amongst them, and, in place, the asking for evidence from persons living in the desert at a distance, it is something which leads to doubts and suspicion, rendering the evidence null and void.

'Alī: He said, 'The evidence of an illegitimate child is not permissible.'[19]

[16]The slave girl was the *umm walad*, the female slave who has borne a child to her master which he has recognized. Hence she becomes free by law on her master's death and inherits from him. See Chap. 12, section on *ummahāt al-awlād*.

[17]'The testimony of a nomadic Arab against a townsman is not allowable.' *Mishkāt*, II, 346; Robson, I, 804. Ibn Rushd states that the testimony of a Bedouin is not acceptable against a town-dweller because a Bedouin rarely gets the chance to witness what is happening in a town. *Bidāya*, II, 459; trans. II, 558. See also n. 111 in Chap. 17.

[18]*Kāfī*, VII, 432.

[19]Ibid., VII, 432.

['Alī]: He said, 'The evidence of one partner in favour of a co-partner is not permissible in a matter that is litigated between them;[20] but the evidence of a partner is permissible in all other cases such as inheritance, emancipation, offences involving killing, divorce, marriage, crimes, and the like.'

Ja'far b. Muḥammad: He was asked about the evidence of a hireling (*ajīr*)[21] or follower (*tābi'*).[22] He said, 'He is a suspected person (*ẓanīn*) and his evidence is not permissible.'

[Ja'far b. Muḥammad]—his father—his ancestors—'Alī: The Messenger of God forbade that the evidence of one who is party [to the litigation], a suspected person, or a neighbour, be adduced against any persons.

'Alī; He said, 'The evidence of a person charged with an offence (*muttaham*) is not admissible.'[23]

['Alī]: He said, 'The evidence of sectarians (*ahl al-ahwā'*) is not permissible against the faithful (*mu'minīn*).'

Abū Ja'far [Imam al-Bāqir] said, 'The evidence of a Khārijī (*Ḥarūrī*),[24] a believer in free will (*qadarī*),[25] a Murji',[26] an Umayyad, an enemy of the Imams (*nāṣib*),[27] or a libertine (*fāsiq*)[28] is not permissible.' By this, he meant a person who openly manifests such qualities and whose enmity [towards the Imams] clearly appears. However, he who hides such feelings, does good openly, and is honest in his conduct, his evidence is admissible. This is the rule to be followed.

Abū 'Abd Allāh Ja'far b. Muḥammad:[29] He said, 'The evidence of a slanderer (*qādhif*) who repents and becomes virtuous is permissible.[30] God

[20]Ibid., VII, 430.

[21]Ibid., VII, 431.

[22]It also means a subordinate, adherent, or partisan.

[23]*Kāfī*, VII, 431, 432; testimony of both the *ẓanīn* and the *muttaham* is not admissible. A *fāsiq* (dissolute, adulterer) and a *khā'in* (disloyal, traitor) fall in the same category as a *ẓanīn*.

[24]For Ḥarūrī and Umayyad, see *The Pillars of Islam*, I, 94.

[25]Qadariyya is a name used to denote a group of theologians who represented the principle of 'free will' in the early part of Islam, from about 70/690 to the consolidation of the Mu'tazila at the beginning of the third/ninth century. *EI*², s.v. Ḳadariyya.

[26]*Murji'* = *Murji'a*, see *The Pillars of Islam*, I, 5, n. 2.

[27]See *The Pillars of Islam*, I, 190, 191, 294, 361.

[28]A *fāsiq* is an unjust man who is guilty of *fisq*, i.e. one who has committed one or more of the 'major sins' (*kabā'ir*). In legal terminology, *fāsiq* is the antonym of '*adl*. *EI*², s.v. Fāsiḳ. For *kabā'ir* see *The Pillars of Islam*, I, 169, n. 21.

[29]Abū Ja'far: MS Q.

[30]*Kāfī*, VII, 434–5.

says: *Truly, God loves those who repent, and He loves those who cleanse themselves* (2:222).[31] There is no reason to reject the evidence of those whom God loves when they are equitable. God has made an exception in the case of those who repent after being slanderers in respect of their evidence and He says: *[And those who accuse honourable women ...] And never (afterward) accept their testimony* (24:4) and then God makes an exception and says: *Save those who afterward repent [and make amends]* (24:5).

Abū Ja'far Muḥammad b. 'Alī:[32] He said, 'The evidence of the following persons is not admissible: (i) accused persons (*muttaham*); (ii) illegitimate persons (*walad al-zinā'*); (iii) persons suffering from leucoderma (*abraṣ*); (iv) those who drink intoxicating liquor (*shārib al-muskir*); (v) those who associate with worthless persons (*baṭṭāl*);[33] (vi) and with singers (*mughannin*); (vii) those who do evil acts (*ahl al-munkar*) in association with prostitutes (*'awāhir*); (viii) those who commit suspected acts (*aḥdāth fi 'l-rība*); (ix) those who expose their private parts (*yakshifūna 'awrātahum*) in public baths and elsewhere; (x) those who sleep together as a group (*jamā'atan*) under one sheet; (xi) those who trifle with weights and measures (*yuṭaffifūna 'l-kayla wa 'l-wazna*); (xii) those who frequent fortune-tellers (*kuhhān* pl. of *kāhin*);[34] (xiii) those who dislike the norms sanctioned by the tradition (*sunan* pl. of *sunna*); (xiv) those debtors who put off the payment of debts [time after time] while they are in a position to pay what they owe;[35] (xv) those who fail to pray; (xvi) or to pay the alms tax (*zakāt*); (xvii) those who have committed actions which amount to criminal offences (*ḥadd*)[36] or deserve *ta'zīr*[37] punishments; (xviii) those who cause trouble to their neighbours; and (xix) those who sport with dogs, pigeons, and cocks.[38] The evidence of such persons is not admissible so long as they continue in their [vain] occupations.'[39]

[31]Arberry, *Koran*, I, 59.

[32]MS Q: *wa-'anhu* [Abū Ja'far].

[33]*Baṭṭāl* signifies a man having a vain pursuit, one who is diverted from that which would bring profit in the present life or in the life to come. Lane, s.v. b-ṭ-l.

[34]For details see *EI*², s.v. Kāhin; Kāhina.

[35]The Urdu translator has omitted this category, probably because it was incomprehensible to him. Fyzee's translation was off the mark due to the last phrase *wa-huwa wājidun*.

[36]*Ḥadd*, see Chap. 17. If a person convicted of a *ḥadd* crime repents publicly or before the Imam, his testimony could be accepted. *Kāfī*, VII, 435.

[37]*Ta'zīr*, see Chap. 17, n. 117.

[38]Kulaynī adds to this list persons who play backgammon (*nard*), cards (*al-arba' 'ashar*), and chess (*shāhayn*).

[39]This is a comprehensive list of persons whose evidence is not admissible. *Mishkāt*, II, 346; Robson, I, 804, adds the following: A deceitful man (*khā'in*) or woman, an immoral

The Messenger of God: He said, 'You should think well of him who prays five times a day in a congregation and permit him to give evidence.' He meant that this should be the rule when nothing is known to disqualify him from giving evidence.

'Alī: He said, 'He who resembles a member of the community [in appearance] is to be counted as one of them.'

The Messenger of God: He prohibited that an unbeliever's evidence be accepted against a Muslim.

Abū Ja'far Muḥammad b. 'Alī: Concerning the Qur'ānic verse: ... *or two others from another folk* (5:106),[40] [Imam al-Bāqir] said, 'It meant from amongst the People of the Book.'

Abū Ja'far Muḥammad b. 'Alī said, 'Where a man is travelling and is about to die and does not find any Muslim to bear witness to his will and calls as witnesses two *dhimmīs*[41] who agree, such evidence is permissible in regard to the will, as God has said [5:106].[42]

Ja'far b. Muḥammad [Imam al-Ṣādiq] said, 'Where a man is in a foreign country where there are no Muslims and is about to die and calls two non-Muslims to testify to his will, the two witnesses should be sworn by God that, "We have not borne witness except the truth. So-and-so has made a will for such and such objects." That is according to the Word of God: ... *shall be two men of equity among you; or two others from another folk ... they shall swear by God*' (5:106).

'Alī, Abū Ja'far, and Abū 'Abd Allāh: They said, 'Where an unbeliever is called upon to give testimony while he is an unbeliever; or a small child (is called upon to give testimony) during his minority, and the unbeliever gives his testimony after having embraced Islam, and the minor (does so) after having attained majority,[43] their testimony is lawful provided they are approved persons.'

---

man (*zān*[in]) or woman, one who harbours rancour against his brother, one who has been flogged for criminal punishment (*ḥadd*), one who is suspected regarding the patrons (*walā'*) he claims or relationships, and one who is dependent on a family.

[40] Arberry, *Koran*, I, 144.

[41] *Dhimmī*, see *The Pillars of Islam*, I, 143, n. 79.

[42] The Qur'ān reads: *O believers, the testimony between you when any of you is visited by death, at the bequeathing, shall be two men of equity among you; or two others from another folk, if you are journeying in the land and the affliction of death befalls you.* Arberry, *Koran*, I, 144.

[43] 'The minor can testify after attaining puberty if he has not forgotten the testimony.' Another tradition on the authority of Imam al-Ṣādiq states, 'A child's testimony is admissible only in the case of homicide; his initial statement should be accepted, but not the later [as he might have been coached].' 'When the child is ten years old, his testimony becomes permitted.' *Kāfi*, VII, 424–5.

'Alī b. al-Ḥusayn: [The Umayyad Caliph] 'Abd al-Malik[44] wrote to [Imam Zayn al-'Ābidīn] asking for the rule concerning the testimony of the *dhimmīs* given among themselves and he wrote as follows:

My father [Ḥusayn] related from my grandfather, the Messenger of God, that certain Jews came to him with a man and a woman [and alleged that] they had committed adultery. The Jews then gave evidence that the couple had committed adultery and were married persons, so the Messenger of God stoned them both.

[The Imam] said, 'Therefore, the evidence of *dhimmīs* against one another is permissible if the witnesses are persons of good reputation according to them; but their evidence against Muslims is not admissible except, as God mentions, in the case of wills.'[45]

'Alī, Abū Ja'far, and Abū 'Abd Allāh: They said, 'The same witnesses, being women or slaves,[46] are eligible to give evidence in marriage just as in the case of property. The evidence of women is not admissible in divorce or criminal punishments (*ḥudūd*),[47] but it is admissible in cases of property[48] and in matters in which none but women have knowledge, because it is only they who can actually see [other] women. For example, [she can testify about] the cries of a child at his birth (*istihlāl*),[49] and in cases of his delivery (*nifās*), childbirth (*wilāda*), menstruation (*ḥayḍ*), and the like.[50] The evidence of a midwife (*qābila*) is admissible in such matters if she is approved.[51] There is suspicion in the evidence of women in cases of murder and, in such cases, an oath pronounced fifty times (*qasāma*)[52] is necessary.'

[44]'Abd al-Malik reigned from 65/685–86/705. *The Pillars of Islam*, I, 476, n. 207.

[45]*Kāfī*, VII, 435–7; identical position to that of Nu'man.

[46]'A slave's testimony is accepted if he is of good character.' Ibid., VII, 425–6.

[47]The only exception in which her testimony is accepted is the case of homicide. Kulaynī reports this on the authority of Imam al-Ṣādiq. For the stoning penalty if there are three men witnesses, then two women's testimony is admissible. Ibid., VII, 426.

[48]Ibid., VII, 426; her testimony is admissible is cases of financial claims (*dayn*).

[49]This is important for matters of inheritance and for determining whether prayers should be offered for him of not. Different rules apply depending on whether the child dies after birth or is stillborn. See *The Pillars of Islam*, I, 292.

[50]*Kāfī*, VII, 426, 427, 428; also in the case of establishing the virginity of a girl. Another tradition states that a maiden was accused of fornication, so 'Alī asked the women to inspect her and they testified in her favour. 'Alī, therefore, acquitted her. Ibid., VII, 442. The independent testimony of women, i.e. unaccompanied by male witnesses, is acceptable, according to the majority of the jurists, in matters of personal law that are usually not accessible to men, such as birth, consummation of a marriage, etc. For more details and the positions of various schools, see Ibn Rushd, *Bidāya*, II, 460–1; trans. II, 560.

[51]*Kāfī*, 426, 428.

[52]See Chap. 16, section on *qasāma*.

ʿAlī: He did not allow one witness to contradict another in criminal cases.

ʿAlī: He said, 'Where witnesses give evidence of unlawful sexual intercourse and differ regarding the place where the offence was committed, they should be scourged [for slander].' As regards divergence in testimony, we have mentioned this earlier at another place.[53]

Jaʿfar b. Muḥammad: He was asked about providing testimony based on written [evidence] (*al-shahāda ʿala 'l-khaṭṭ*). He said, 'I heard my father say that the Messenger of God said, "Give not evidence on a matter which you do not remember; for verily, he who wishes can write a letter and impress a seal."'[54] [Imam al-Ṣādiq did not decide cases merely on the basis of written evidence.][55]

Abū ʿAbd Allāh Jaʿfar b. Muḥammad: He was asked by a man as follows, 'O Son of the Messenger of God, some of my neighbours came with a writing and stated that they would make me a witness of what was written in it. The writing contained my name in my own handwriting which I recognized, and have no doubt about it. But I did not recollect the [nature of that] evidence. What do you think?' [The Imam] said, 'Do not testify until you recollect the evidence for which you had been asked to give testimony. God says: ... *saving him who beareth witness unto the Truth knowingly*' (43:86).

ʿAlī: A man was brought to him and he was told that the man had committed theft. Two witnesses gave evidence against him, so ʿAlī, because of their evidence, cut off the thief's hand. Then, the two [witnesses] came with another man and they said, 'We made a mistake regarding the first. Verily, this is the thief.' ʿAlī disbelieved their evidence against the second person, and made the two responsible for the blood money of the hand of the man against whom they had given their evidence, and whose hand was cut off by their testimony.[56] ʿAlī said, 'If I knew that you have done this intentionally, I would cut off your hands.'

ʿAlī: He said, 'Four persons testified to the adultery of a man who was then stoned. Then, one of the witnesses went back on his evidence

[53]See Chap. 17, especially the last section.

[54]*Kāfī*, VII, 417–18; Kulaynī reports four traditions, one is exactly the same as reported by Nuʿmān.

[55]I have added this last sentence from MS Q and other MSS of Fyzee. It reads: *wa-kāna lā yaqṭaʿu bi-shahādat al-khaṭṭ*. The gloss in MSQ reads: *lā yaqṭaʿu ay lā yujawwizu*. The edited text is without it. See also *Kāfī*, VII, 417; the Imam advised against testifying unless one is absolutely sure about it. Wakin, *Function of Documents*.

[56]*Kāfī*, VII, 420; reported from the same authority. "Alī did not permit their testimony against the other [i.e. the second person].' Kulaynī reports other traditions stating that when a person retracts his testimony, he is liable for the damages, see ibid., VII, 419.

and said that it was doubtful to him. This man should be fined one-quarter of the blood money (*diya*). If two witnesses go back on their evidence, they should be fined one-half of the *diya*. If all four of them go back on their word and say that they testified falsely, then retaliation (*qawad*) should be ordered against them.'

Ja'far b. Muḥammad: He said, '[In a case in which] two witnesses give evidence against a man for a certain property and then retract at the time of [formal] evidence the evidence should be regarded as false if the judge has not given his decision; but if the judge has passed the order, the two witnesses are responsible for the decree passed by their evidence.'

Abū Ja'far Muḥammad b. 'Alī: He said, 'Two witnesses gave evidence that a man who was absent had given divorce to his wife. The judge decided according to their evidence [and decreed divorce]. The woman observed '*idda* and then remarried. [Later,] one of the witnesses retracted, and so [the Imam] said, "There should be a separation between the woman and her second husband. She should observe the '*idda* and return to her first husband. She is entitled to a dower (*ṣadāq*) from her second husband if he had consummated the marriage, and the second husband may turn to the witness for his *ṣadāq*."'

'Alī: He said, 'Where a man gives evidence before us and later requests us to annul it, we shall release him [from responsibility];' i.e. so long as no decree has been passed.[57]

Ja'far b. Muḥammad: With respect to the Word of God: ... *and the witnesses must not refuse when they are summoned* (2:282), he said, 'It refers to the place where they are invited as witnesses before any verdict (*al-kitāb*) has been reached [by the judge]. It is not proper for any of them to say, "I shall not testify for you." When you are called upon to testify, you should comply with the request. When you are asked to be a witness and are summoned to give evidence, it is not lawful for you to avoid it.[58] This is because of the Word of God: *Hide not testimony. He who hideth it, verily his heart is sinful* (2:283).'[59]

Abū Ja'far Muḥammad b. 'Alī: He said, 'Where a man is present at the accounting of a certain group of persons and is asked to give evidence according to what he had heard, the matter is at his discretion. He may choose whether or not to give evidence, except when they summon him to give evidence. If he gives evidence, he should testify to the truth; and if he does not give evidence, there is nothing against him because he

[57]Ibid., VII, 417.
[58]Ibid., VII, 414–15; Kulaynī transmitted several traditions.
[59]Ibid., VII, 415–16.

was not summoned.[60] He should not give evidence unless he had retained the [actual] words, corroborated [the statement], and understood well [what was said].'

Ja'far b. Muḥammad: He was asked about a man who had possession of a house in which he stayed for over fifty or sixty years. A certain person proceeded against him and claimed the house [from him] and proved that it originally belonged to him. The man who was in actual possession said, 'I purchased it from persons who are now no more and the proof is also no longer extant.' He brought a group of persons who stated that, according to what they had heard, the man had purchased it as mentioned. [The Imam] said, 'If they give evidence [by hearsay] that the present owner purchased it from the claimant's relations and the claimant claims it [precisely] on account of his kinship to them [that he inherited it], his claim becomes null and void. Otherwise the original owner's right prevails.'[61] This is so because hearsay evidence is admissible in respect of genealogy, death, pious endowments (*aḥbās* pl. or *ḥubs*)[62] and the like.

[60]Ibid., VII, 416–17; this section deals with one who hears the testimony (hearsay) but does not witness it.

[61]Cf. *Kāfī*, VII, 458–9; a slightly different tradition but the same rationale.

[62]*EI*[2], s.v. Waḳf; Lane, s.v. ḥ-b-s.

25

Book of Claims and Clear Proofs (*Kitāb al-Daʿwā*[1] *wa ʾl-Bayyināt*)[2]

God says: *And eat not up your property among yourselves in vanity, nor seek by it to gain the hearing of the [unjust ruling] authorities (al-ḥukkām)*[3] *that ye may knowingly devour a portion of the property of others wrongfully* (2:188).

Jaʿfar b. Muḥammad—his father—his ancestors—ʿAlī: The Messenger of God prohibited people from depriving Muslims of their property by a false oath.

[The Messenger of God]: He said, 'I give judgment between yourselves by relying only on clear proofs and oaths (*aymān* pl. of *yamīn*).[4] Some of you may be smarter and more articulate (*alḥan*) than others in argument. Thus, every person to whom I give a property from the property of his

[1]*Daʿwā*, is a legal action, a lawsuit, or a case. It is defined as 'the action by which a person claims his right against another person in the presence of a judge.' The plaintiff is called *muddaʿī*, the defendant, *muddaʿā ʿalayhi*, and the object of the claim, *muddaʿā*. *EI*², s.v. Daʿwā; Schacht, *Introduction*, 189.

[2]*Bayyina* (pl. *bayyināt*), the feminine adjective is used in the Qurʾān as a noun and means 'manifest or clear proof'. Chapter (*sūra*) 98 itself is entitled '*al-Bayyina*'. In legal terminology, it denotes the proof *par excellence* that is established by oral testimony. Nonetheless, it came to be applied to the giving of testimony and to the witnesses themselves. *EI*², s.v. Bayyina; Schacht, *Introduction*, 192.

[3]Bell, Pickthall, Yusus Ali, Blachère, Paret, and Arberry have rendered *al-ḥukkām* as judges. Irving has rendered it: *... nor try to bribe authorities*. *Kāfī*, VII, 451; *al-ḥukkām* in this context refers to unjust rulers. Ṭabrisī, I, 282; he reports a tradition from Jaʿfar al-Ṣādiq that urges the faithful not to bring their disputes before unjust rulers for legal decision. I have followed Kulaynī and Ṭabrisī in the translation of *al-ḥukkām* in this verse. See also Ṭabarī, *Tafsīr*, III, 548–52; Ṭūsī, *al-Tibyān*, II, 138–40.

[4]Ibn Rushd, *Bidāya*, II, 457–66; trans. II, 560–7; about oaths. Most of the jurists agree that the claim against the defendant is dismissed because of the oath when the plaintiff does not have evidence.

brother and who knows that he is not entitled to it, to him I only give a piece of Hell-fire.'[5]

'Alī: He said, 'I decide between you by means of manifest proofs. Verily, David,[6] the blessings and peace of God be on him, said, "O my Lord, I decide matters between Thy creatures in a manner which is perhaps not in consonance with Thy knowledge." So God sent him the following revelation:

> O David, decide between them by oaths and manifest proofs, and concerning things which are hidden to you, entrust the parties to Me and I shall give judgment between them in the Hereafter.

'David said, "O my Lord, inform me regarding the judgment of the Hereafter." So God sent a revelation to him:

> O David, what you have asked for [is a thing] about which I have informed none of my creatures. It is not proper for any one except Myself to decide between My creatures in that manner.

'This did not prevent David from asking God again. God revealed to him:

> O David, none of the prophets before you had ever asked what you have asked. I shall inform you; but neither you nor any one of my creatures in the world will have the strength to bear it.

'A man came to David claiming a cow from another. The other man denied it and produced the proof. Testimony was given that it belonged to the person who possessed her. So God revealed to David:

> Take the cow from the person in whose possession she is and give it to the claimant. Give the claimant a sword and ask him to behead the possessor of the cow.

'David did as commanded by God and did not know the reason for it. This preyed heavily on the mind of David and the Israelites refused to accept the decision as correct.[7]

'Then, there came an old man and with him was a youth who had a bunch of grapes. The old man said, "O Prophet of God, this young man

[5]Transmitted by Bukhārī, Muslim, and others. *Concordance*, s.v. ḥ-j-j; see also *Kāfī*, VII, 454. This tradition is also cited in *Lisān al-ʿArab*, s.v. l-ḥ-n; *Majmaʿ al-baḥrayn*, s.v. l-ḥ-n; partially cited.

[6]See *The Pillars of Islam*, I, 353.

[7]Kulaynī gives two short versions of this story. *Kāfī*, VII, 454–5, 472–3.

entered my garden, destroyed the vines, ate from them without my consent, and took this bunch of grapes without my permission." David asked the boy, "What have you to say?" The boy admitted the alleged facts. God revealed to David:

> Command the young man to behead the old man, and give the garden to the boy. Then, command the boy to dig at a certain place and, behold, he will find forty thousand dirhams which the old man had buried there. Let the young man take them.[8]

'David acted accordingly and this increased his perplexity. The Israelites talked about this and showed an increased dislike about this affair to David. They had gathered together to speak to David about it. They were with him for this purpose and preparing to talk with him when, suddenly, there came an ox running along. The ox had escaped from custody and was running away and they were looking at him. Then, a man came out of a house, caught the ox, and bound him up. He went in his house, brought out of a knife, and slaughtered and skinned the ox. He began cutting the flesh and hauling it into his house while they looked on.

'When this was going on, a man came running and said to some of the men, "Perhaps you have seen an ox running by." They said, "Yes. There it is, that man has slaughtered it." The man ran up to him, held him, and brought him to David and said, "O Prophet of God, an ox belonging to me escaped and I found that this man had slaughtered and skinned it, cut it to pieces, and took it into the house. Here is the head of my ox and its skin." He took the testimony of the people who were present and they said that it was so. David turned to the man who had slaughtered the bull and asked him, "What have you to say?" He said, "O Prophet of God, I do not know what they say, but I went out of the house this day, for there was nothing [for us to eat] in my house. I found a derelict bull and slaughtered it and took it to my house as he claims. What is necessary for me to do? Pass [whatever] order [you wish against me]." Hence, God revealed to David:

> Ask the man who came to claim the bull to lie down and command the man who slaughtered the bull to slaughter him in the same manner as he slaughtered the bull. Give him all that the slaughtered man possesses and is in his hands.

'David did accordingly. His perplexity doubled and the Israelites came to him and said, "O Prophet of God, what are these decisions? We had

[8]Ibid., VII, 461–2.

heard some reports about you and had come to speak about them, but we have seen something which is even worse than them." David said, "I swear by God, I did not do this, but God has done it and He ordered me." David informed them of what God had asked him to do. Then, David entered his niche [of prayer] and asked God to explain the meaning of what was ordered so that he could go with the explanations to the Israelites. God then revealed to him:

O David, as to the owner of the cow [its possessor], he came across the father of the latter [claimant] and killed him and took the cow from him. The son of the murdered man recognised the cow but found no one to give evidence for him and did not know that the present owner had murdered his father. I knew all this and decided according to My knowledge.

As to the man with the bunch of grapes, the owner of the garden had murdered the father of the boy, taken his wealth, bought the garden from it, and buried the balance of the wealth in his land in the garden. The boy knew nothing about this and, thus, I decided according to My knowledge.

As to the owner of the bull, he had killed the father of the man who slaughtered the bull and had taken a great deal of property from him. That was the basis of his wealth. The man [who slaughtered the ox] did not know of this, so I decided according to My knowledge. These, O David, are the judgments of the Hereafter and I have postponed them to the Day of Judgement. Do not ask Me to hasten things which I have deferred. Give decisions between my people according to what you have been ordered.'

Jaʿfar b. Muḥammad—his father—his ancestors—ʿAlī: The Messenger of God said, 'The burden of proof in claims of property lies on the plaintiff. The defendant has to take the oath.'[9]

ʿAlī said, 'In matters relating to the killing of a man, the proof has to be adduced by the person who denies having committed the offence. The accuser has to take the oath.'[10]

We have mentioned regarding claims and proofs in murder cases in the Book of Blood Money.

The Messenger of God: He forbade that anyone should be given an oath in the name of anyone except God. He said, 'He who is given an oath in the name of God should consent to it. He who does not do so, is not a Muslim.'[11]

Jaʿfar b. Muḥammad said, 'No one should be given an oath in the

[9]Ibid., VII, 455.

[10]Ibid., VII, 455.

[11]'He who swears by other than God has indeed committed polytheism.' *Concordance*, s.v. ḥ-l-f; a number of similar traditions are reported.

name of any object or being other than God. The People of the Book should be asked to swear on their books and on their communities.' What [the Imam] meant is that when they (the People of the Book) do not consider it proper to swear on anything but their books and consider it a sin for a man to swear by God, [they should be asked to swear on their books.]

[Ja'far b. Muḥammad]: A man claims a right, but has no proof. It is decided in the plaintiff's favour that the defendant should take the oath. The defendant returns the oath to the plaintiff and says that his claim would be valid and the defendant would give to the plaintiff what he asks for, if he stated it on oath. [The Imam] said, 'This right belongs to the defendant and if the plaintiff refuses to take the oath, he has no right.'[12]

Where a claim is established by proof against a defendant and he still refuses and asks for an oath by the plaintiff, such a right belongs to the defendant and it never fails him. This right belongs to the defendant. Sometimes rights fail because it is not known who possesses the right. Where a man does not know his own right, it is for the authority (*ḥākim*) to inform him of it. If a man asks for an oath [by the opponent], it is his right to do so.

Where a plaintiff makes a claim and the defendant denies it and asks the plaintiff to swear and the plaintiff swears and the plaintiff then brings his proof, such proof must be taken into consideration.[13]

The Messenger of God: He used to allow the evidence of a single witness along with an oath by the claimant, especially in property cases.[14] This view is held by [Imams] 'Alī, Abū Ja'far [al-Bāqir], and Abū 'Abd Allāh [al-Ṣādiq].

'Alī: When two people claim the same thing and the evidence adduced is of equal value on both the sides and neither of them is in possession of the property, 'Alī would decide the matter by drawing lots. If the property was in the possession of both of them and they both either take or refrain from taking the oath, then the property would be divided equally between them. However, if one of them takes the oath and the other avoids it, the property goes to the man who takes the oath. If the property is in the

[12]*Kāfī*, VII, 456–8.

[13]'The proof lies on the plaintiff and the oath must be taken by him who rejects the claim.' *Mishkāt*, II, 341; Robson, I, 800. See also *Kāfī*, VII, 455. The expression we use in English is: 'The burden of proof is upon the plaintiff.'

[14]'Ibn 'Abbās said that the Prophet gave a decision on the basis of an oath and a single witness.' *Mishkāt*, II, 342; Robson, I, 801.

hands of one of them, then the claimant has to prove his claim. We have mentioned earlier that the burden of proof is on the claimant and the oath should be taken by the defendant.

'Alī, Abū Ja'far, and Abū 'Abd Allāh: When the matter was dubious, they made it incumbent that the decision be given by drawing lots. We have mentioned earlier similar matters. In matters resembling them and related to them, the same rules are applicable.

Abū 'Abd Allāh Ja'far b. Muḥammad said, 'Where the matter is dubious, what decision can be more cogent than the drawing of lots? Is it not a relegation direct to God, Glorious is His mention?'

Abū 'Abd Allāh [Imām al-Ṣādiq] then related the story of Jonah (Yūnus) as mentioned in the Word of God: *And then drew lots and was of those rejected* (37:141);[15] and the story of Zachariah[16] and God's saying: *Thou wast not present with them when they threw their pens (to know) which of them should be the guardian of Mary* (3:44);[17] and the story of 'Abd al-Muṭṭalib[18] when he made votive offering (*nadhr*) to God that he would slaughter the child born to him.[19] 'Abd Allāh, the father of the Messenger of God, was born to him and God put love into the heart of 'Abd al-Muṭṭalib who began to cast lots between 'Abd Allāh and the camels which he would slaughter in place of the son. The lot by arrows always fell to the son until the number of camels came to one hundred. Then, the lot was drawn in favour of the camels. He cast lots repeatedly and they all fell to the camels. Then he said: Now I know that my Lord has consented. He then slaughtered the camels.

Abū 'Abd Allāh [Imam al-Ṣādiq] related these stories fully and the decision of 'Alī concerning the case of a hermaphrodite that was dubious

[15]*Sūra* 10 in the Qur'ān is called *Sūrat Yūnus*, after the prophet Jonah. However, a fuller story of him is given in *sūra* 37. He fled on a ship that was overloaded. He was condemned by drawing lots and was swallowed by a fish. For details of his story in Muslim legends, see *EI*[2], s.v. Yūnus b. Mattai.

[16]Zakariyyā', the father of John the Baptist, is mentioned in the Qur'ān along with John, Jesus, and Elias as being righteous. *EI*[2], s.v. Zakariyyā'.

[17]*Idh yulqūna aqlāmahum* (lit. when they threw their pens), the expression means, when they drew their lots. Ṭabarī, *Tafsīr*, VI, 407–9.

[18]'Abd al-Muṭṭalib was the paternal grandfather of the Prophet. *The Pillars of Islam*, I, 20, n. 7.

[19]When 'Abd al-Muṭṭalib encountered the opposition of Quraysh while he was digging the well of Zamzam, he vowed that if he should have ten sons to grow up and protect him, he would sacrifice the tenth one to God at the Ka'ba. When the man took the arrows to cast lots with them, 'Abd Allāh's arrow came out. For details, see Ibn Isḥāq, *al-Sīra*, I, 160–4; Guillaume, 66–8; Lings, *Muhammad*, 12–14.

to him and which he decided by drawing lots. We have related these [reports] earlier.[20]

It is related from ʿAlī that three persons from the Yemen came to him litigating about a woman. All of them had intercourse with her during one period of purity. She had given birth to a child and each one of them claimed it. He drew lots and gave the child to the person to whom the lot fell. This came to the ears of the Prophet and he laughed so heartily that his molars were visible. He said, 'I know of no decision in this matter save that of ʿAlī.'

ʿAlī: Two men had a dispute about a wall which stood between their two houses; each of them claimed it as his own and neither of them had any proof. He decided that it should go to the person who had a rope or fetter attached to it; if it was of unburnt brick or stone, the matter should be considered further. If it is attached to the foundation of one of the two houses then it belongs to that owner. If it is attached to the foundation on both sides, it is their common property. Similarly, if it is not attached to the property of either of them and they both take the oath, it is their common property. Where the wall is attached to the house of one or both of them, and one of them takes the oath but the other refuses, the wall belongs to the one who takes the oath. If the wall is made of reeds, then consider the rope fastening and where it is attached; this stands in the same position as an attachment.

The Messenger of God: He said, 'A neighbour cannot prevent his neighbour from putting pieces of wood on his wall.' This—and God knows best—is an instruction or recommendation and not an absolute rule. We have already reported the Prophet's saying, 'Every owner is more entitled to his property [than any one else].' [The rule about the wall] is similar.

Jaʿfar b. Muḥammad: He said, 'This saying of the Messenger of God points towards several of his exhortations regarding neighbours. It is a command to persuade people concerning it. The people are commanded to respect the rights of the neighbourhood; but it cannot be the basis of a decision against a man who refuses to do so.'

Jaʿfar b. Muḥammad: He was asked about neighbour X who permits neighbour Y to place a load on his wall. Can X remove the load any time he wishes? [The Imam] said, 'If X wishes to remove the load for a necessity that has arisen and does not wish to harm Y, he is entitled to do so. However,

[20]See Chap. 15, section 'Persons who can lawfully inherit ...' No such case is related earlier.

if X merely wishes to harm his neighbour Y thereby, I do not think he can do so.'

Abū Ja'far Muḥammad b. 'Alī: He was asked about a girl of seven about whom two persons, a man and a woman, had a dispute. The man said that she was his slave; the woman said that she was her daughter. Abū Ja'far [Imam al-Bāqir] said, "Alī had decided such a case.' It was said to him, 'What did he decide?' [The Imam] said, "Alī said, "All people are free except he who, being an adult, acknowledges himself to be a slave or unless someone proves that he is a slave." If the man brings honourable witnesses and proves that she is his slave, even though they do not know whether he has sold her, given her as a gift, or freed her, then he takes possession of her. On the other hand, if the woman is free and proves that the girl is her daughter whom she actually bore, or if she proves that she was a slave of this man or someone else, but was later manumitted, [then the woman is entitled to the girl].'[21]

Ja'far b. Muḥammad: He was asked [about the following case]: A man gave dinars or dirhams to another, and the receiver took possession of them, went away, and then returned and said, 'The coins were bad,' and were accordingly found to be so. The person who had given the coins said, 'I gave [you] nothing except good coins.' [The Imam] said, 'If the receiver has proof that the bad coins he is returning are the same ones that were given to him, he may return them to the giver and the giver should exchange them. If the receiver has no proof, the giver shall swear by God that he did not give him any coins except good ones. He shall also irrevocably swear that he did not give him these bad coins. If the giver refuses to take the oath, then the receiver should swear that these are the very dirhams [he received]. Then, the receiver shall return them to the giver and receive good coins from him.'

The same rule applies if the quantity is less.

Ja'far b. Muḥammad: Concerning a man and a woman both of whom claim the goods to be found in a house, [the Imam] said, 'If one of them has proof for it, he or she is more entitled to it than the one who has no proof. If neither can furnish any proof, they should both take oaths. If one of them swears, but the other fails to take the oath, then the one who swears is more entitled to it. If both take the oath or both refuse it, then the goods which are used by men, go to the man; and the goods usually used by women, go to the woman. The same rights apply to their heirs.'

[21]*Kāfī*, VII, 461; it adds: If both the parties cannot adduce evidence, the girl is free to choose either of the two parties. For a similar case see Ṭūsī, *al-Nihāya*, 344.

[Ja'far b. Muḥammad]: Concerning the case of a man who claims a garment that is in the possession of another man who says, 'You had pawned it to me (*'indī rahn*^{un}),' and the claimant says, 'No, I had deposited it with you (*'indaka wadī'at*^{un}),' [the Imam] said, 'It is the claimant whose word will prevail. It is for the possessor to prove that this was a pawn in his hands.'

[Ja'far b. Muḥammad]: He was asked about the following sale transaction: A man sells some goods and, after the sale, the vendor claims that there was a mistake in the price. [The Imam] said, 'The quality of the goods must be seen. If such goods can be sold for the above price or a similar one, the sale is valid. However, if the difference is great or if there is a clear fraud, the vendor shall swear that he had made a mistake in the price and that the price of the goods should be fixed as mentioned. Then, the buyer should be told, "If you desire to purchase it, take it for the price mentioned; if not, leave it."'

26

Book of the Etiquette of *Qāḍīs* (*Kitāb Ādāb al-Quḍāt*)[1]

God says: *Lo! Allah commandeth you that ye restore deposits to their owners, and, if ye judge between mankind, that ye judge justly* (4:58). And He, blessed are His names, says: *So judge between them by that which Allah hath revealed, and follow not their desires* (5:49). And He says: O *David! Lo! We have set thee as a viceroy in the earth; therefore judge aright between mankind* (38:26).[2]

Ja'far b. Muḥammad—his father—his ancestors—the Messenger of God: He prohibited all persons from seeking the office of the [supreme] commander over the people and from seeking to judge[3] between the people. He said, 'One who seeks an office of a [supreme] commander will be entrusted with it [over the people], but will not be helped [to discharge

[1]The word *adab* pl. *ādāb*, in this context, is not easy to translate, but 'the etiquette' is preferable. *Adab al-qāḍī* lays down 'the unwritten code of honour which discountenances certain practices in this profession'. It is a large subject and the material dealing with it is interspersed in a variety of books. In his article 'The *Adab al-Qāḍī* in Islamic Law', Fyzee has listed the foremost authorities and has covered briefly the following topics: Qualifications, appointment, seat of the court, remuneration, deportment, corruption, and arbitration. See also Ṭūsī, *al-Nihāya*, 337–55.

[2]In Pickthall 36:27.

[3]The Arabic reads: *annahu nahā an yataʿarraḍa aḥad*[un] *li 'l-imāra wa 'l-ḥukm*. *Yataʿarraḍu* refers to one who petitions another for a thing that he wanted. The meaning of *imāra* in this context is the office of the Imamate/Caliphate. In the reports on the meeting of the *Saqīfa banī Sāʿida*, the word *amīr* is used for the head of the Muslim community. During the Medinan Caliphate, the commanders of armies and the governors were also called *amīrs*. See *Mishkāt*, II, 316; the chapter is entitled '*Kitāb al-imāra wa 'l-qaḍā*';' Robson, I, 780; he translates it 'The offices of commander and of qadi'. Lane, s.v. a-m-r. Māwardī, *al-Aḥkām al-sulṭāniyya*, 30–54, reflects the full development of the institution of *imāra* (amirate) and *amīr*. *EI*[2], s.v. Amīr.

it]. He who achieves it without asking for it will be helped [by God to discharge it].'[4]

Ja'far b. Muḥammad:[5] He said, 'It is a compulsory duty (*farḍ*) laid down by God to have *walāya*[6] for the People of Justice [i.e. the Imams] to whom God has ordered devotion (*walāya*). It is also a duty to appoint them to executive positions (*tawliyatuhum*), to acknowledge their positions and to actively support them.[7] Obedience to them [the Imams] is obligatory. It is not lawful for those who are commanded to do certain duties for them [the Imams] to turn away from the orders received from them. As regards the rulers of the wrongdoers (*wulāt ahl al-jawr*), their followers, and their officers, they are in disobedience to God.[8] It is not permissible for those who are summoned by the unjust rulers to serve them, to work for them, to help them, or to accept [their authority].

'Our opponent's excuse that they are merely following the orders of their [false] Imams does not relieve them from their responsibility to avoid blindly following in acts of wrongdoing and transgression. Similarly, it does not allow them to deem lawful such unlawful acts as shedding of innocent Muslim blood, the taking of their property unjustly, and other wanton acts of aggression and injustice. They fall into error because they accept the decisions of those who permit such actions. They do not see that none save those who have absolute power of discernment (*naẓar*) can authorize others to act by their authority. They accept the idea that those whose mistakes, wrongdoing, and bad character are notorious could have absolute power of discernment. [These persons bear such a character] that, if they come forward as witnesses before you [for a case involving an insignificant amount, even as little as] one penny (lit. one dirham), their evidence would not be accepted. Sufficient for them is this shame

[4]'Do not ask to be in the position of the commander over the people (*imāra*), for if you are given it after asking, you will be left to discharge it yourself; but if you are given it without asking, you will be helped [by God] to discharge it.' Transmitted by Bukhārī and Muslim. Another tradition states, 'You will be eager for the office of an *amīr* (*imāra*), but it will become a cause of regret on the Day of Resurrection. It is a good suckler but an evil weaner.' *Mishkāt*, II, 320; Robson, I, 783; transmitted by Bukhārī. Nu'mān presents the Shī'ī point of view of the Imamate. See Chap. 2 in *The Pillars of Islam*, I.

[5]The Arabic text of the following two paragraphs is somewhat obscure and difficult to translate. I have tried to convey the approximate meaning.

[6]For the definition of *walāya*, see *The Pillars of Islam*, I, 2, n. 6, and chapter 2 'The Book of *Walāya*.'

[7]Cf. *Kāfī*, VII, 445.

[8]Shī'ī jurists have consistently viewed any government not headed by the Imam or in the absence of the Imam as illegitimate (*jā'ir*) and oppressive (*ẓālim*).

and warning. It is sufficient to prove the ignorance of those that follow them and to show the degree to which they are astray.'[9]

It has reached us that a letter was read to an officer of a *qāḍī* of Ifrīqiya[10] in order to record and confirm the evidence of certain persons who were present. When the reader read the words, 'This is a letter from the *qāḍī* so-and-so, the son of so-and-so', one of the companions of the *qāḍī* who was present smiled. The *qāḍī* observed this and, later, pulled him aside privately. The *qāḍī* asked, 'Why did you smile when the letter was being read? Did you find in it something which you disliked?' The man said, 'A very great thing!' The *qāḍī* asked, 'What was it?' The man said, 'Your words: From the *qāḍī* ...' The *qāḍī* asked, 'What did you dislike in this?' The man asked, 'Who appointed you to be a *qāḍī*?' The *qāḍī* replied, 'The Amīr Ibrāhīm b. Aḥmad.'[11] The man asked, 'If he came to give evidence before you would you accept his testimony?' The *qāḍī* replied, 'No!' The man asked, 'How then can you be a *qāḍī*?' The *qāḍī* fell silent and was speechless.

The Messenger of God said, 'He who gives judgment for a thing worth ten dirhams and makes an error regarding the command of God will come with his hands manacled on the Day of Judgement. He who gives judgment without knowledge will be cursed by both the angels of the sky and the angels of the earth.'[12]

Ja'far b. Muḥammad: He said, 'Judgments are of two kinds—the judgments of God and the judgments of the *jāhilīya* (Days of Ignorance). Whoever makes a mistake in the judgment of God judges according to the rules of the *jāhilīya*.'[13]

[9]'No obedience is to be given to anyone in an act which entails disobedience to God. Obedience is to be given only regarding what is good (*ma'rūf*).' *Mishkāt*, II, 317; Robson, I, 780; transmitted by both Bukhārī and Muslim.

[10]It refers to the eastern part of the Maghrib. Al-Maghrib, the name used by Arab historians, refers to that part of Africa which Europeans called Barbary or Africa Minor and then North Africa. It includes Tripolitania, Tunisia, Algeria, and Morocco. It should be noted that the boundaries of Ifrīqiya were never stated precisely. *EI*[2], s.v. Ifrīḳiya, al-Maghrib.

[11]He is Abū Isḥāq Ibrāhīm II b. Aḥmad of the Aghlabid dynasty in Ifrīqiya. Their capital was in Qayrawān. He was a sadistic tyrant whose cruelty spared no member of even his own family. It was during his reign that the Fāṭimid *dā'ī*, Abū 'Abd Allāh, was gaining ground politically. In 289/902, on the command of the 'Abbāsid caliph, Ibrāhīm II abdicated in favour of his son. *EI*[2], s.v. Aghlabids; Bosworth, *New Islamic Dynasties*, 31–2.

[12]'The Day of Resurrection will come to the just *qāḍī* and he will wish he had never given judgment between two men about a single date [i.e. the most insignificant matter].' *Mishkāt*, II, 335; Robson, I, 795.

[13]*Jāhilīya* refers to the pre-Islamic days, see *The Pillars of Islam*, I, 281, n. 46. *Kāfī*, VII, 446. Compare the above *ḥadīth* with the following, which contradicts the former and states, 'When a judge (*ḥākim*) gives a decision having tried his best to decide correctly

[Ja'far b. Muḥammad]: He said, 'Whoever decides between two persons and errs by [as little as] two dirhams becomes an unbeliever. God says: *Whoso judgeth not by that which Allah hath revealed: such are disbelievers*' (5:44).[14] One of the companions said, 'O son of the Messenger of God, sometimes there is a dispute between two persons of our partisans concerning a thing and they agree on a man [as an arbitrator] among us. [What happens to him?]' [The Imam] said, 'This case is not on a par with those which I mentioned. The [above] rule is applicable to him who compels obedience to his decisions with the sword and the thong.'

We have mentioned earlier the excellence of knowledge, the virtues of the learned ones, and the inducements of seeking knowledge.[15]

'Alī: He said, 'The Messenger of God sent me [as a judge] to the Yemen and I said, "O Messenger of God, you are sending me but I am a young man who will decide between them without knowing how to judge!" He slapped my chest and said, "O God, guide his heart rightly and make his tongue sound." By Him who splits the seed and creates man, from that day forth, I never had a doubt regarding a decision in a dispute between two persons.'[16]

['Alī]: He said, 'I once entered the mosque and, behold, there were two men from the Anṣār[17] who wanted to have their dispute decided by the Messenger of God. One of them said to his companion, "Come, let us litigate before 'Alī." I was hesitating about his suggestion when the Messenger of God looked at me and said, "Go and decide between the two." I said, "How can I decide in your presence, O Messenger of God?" He said, "It is alright, do it." I went and decided between them. [From that day forward,] the correct decision has been made perfectly clear to me in every case that I have decided.'

['Alī]: He wrote to Rifā'a,[18] 'Do not appoint anyone as an officer who

---

and is right, he will have a double reward; and when he gives a decision having tried his best to decide correctly but is wrong, he will have a single reward.' *Mishkāt*, II, 333; Robson, I, 793; transmitted by Bukhārī and Muslim.

[14]*Kāfī*, VII, 447.

[15]See *The Pillars of Islam*, I, 98–122.

[16]'Alī said, 'God's Messenger sent me to the Yemen as *qāḍī* and I said, "Messenger of God, are you sending me when I am young and have no knowledge of jurisprudence (*qaḍā'*)?" He replied, "God will guide your heart and keep your tongue true. When two men bring a case before you, do not decide in favour of the first till you hear what the other has to say, for it is best that you should have a clear idea of the right decision."' 'Alī said, 'I had no doubts about a decision afterwards.' *Mishkāt*, II, 335; Robson, I, 794.

[17]See *The Pillars of Islam*, I, 13, n. 18.

[18]Rifā'a was 'Alī's *qāḍī* at Ahwāz. *The Pillars of Islam*, I, 281.

does not believe you to be truthful and does not confirm your statements about us; otherwise, God will be your opponent and demand [an explanation]. Do not entrust the affairs of the market[19] to anyone whose actions are at variance with the *sunna* (*dhū bidʿat*[in]), otherwise, you know best [what will happen].'

'Alī: He said, 'Every ruler (*ḥākim*) who pronounces a judgment without considering our legal judgments (*aḥkām*)—being the People of the House (*ahl al-bayt*)—is a false deity (*ṭāghūt*).'[20] 'Alī then recited the Word of God: ... *how they would go for judgment (in their disputes) to false deities when they have been ordered to abjure them? Satan would mislead them far astray* (4:60), and said, 'I swear by God that this is exactly what they [the majority of the Muslims] did. They presented their case before a false deity and Satan lead them far astray. Nobody except us and our partisans have escaped from [the implication of] this verse; the rest have been ruined [and have strayed from the right path]. May the curse of God be upon anyone who does not know the rights [of *ahl al-bayt*] (*ḥaqqahum*).'[21]

Jaʿfar b. Muḥammad: Concerning the Word of God: *And eat not up your property among yourselves in vanity, nor seek by it to gain the hearing of the [unjust ruling] authorities (al-ḥukkām)*[22] (2:188), [Imam al-Ṣādiq] said, 'Verily, God knows that there are in the community officials (*ḥukkām*) who behave corruptly (*yajūrūna*); but, listen, He does not mean the officers of the People of Justice (*ahl al-ʿadl*). Rather, He means the officers of the people of corruption (*ahl al-jawr* lit. people of injustice). Listen, whenever one of you has a case against another and he asks him to go to the People of Justice and he refuses to do so and, instead, refers the case for adjudication to an officer of the people of corruption, he is truly a person who goes for decision to a false god (*ṭāghūt*). That is the Word of God: *Hast thou not seen those who pretend that they believe in that which is revealed unto thee and that which was revealed before thee, how they would go for judgment (in their disputes) to false deities when they have been ordered to abjure them?*' (4:60).[23]

[Jaʿfar b. Muḥammad]: One day, he said to his companions, 'I warn

[19]The *muḥtasib* was the person entrusted in a town with the application of 'promoting good and forbidding evil' in the marketplaces. He had to be a person known for his moral integrity and for his competence in Islamic law. *EI*[2], s.v. Ḥisba. See also Buckley, *The Book of the Islamic Market Inspector*, for a full range of the inspector's responsibility.

[20]*Ṭāghūt*, see *The Pillars of Islam*, I, 27.

[21]*Ḥaqqahum*: as in MS Q. It is missing from the edited text and the pirated one.

[22]See n. 3 in Chap. 25, for the meaning of *al-ḥukkām*.

[23]*Kāfī*, VII, 451.

you not to take your disputes for decision to the people of corruption (*ahl al-jawr* lit. unjust people, oppressors). Rather, identify someone among your own people who knows something of our decisions and leave the matter to him for, verily, I have made him a *qāḍī*. Litigate your disputes before him.'[24]

'Alī: He delivered a sermon at Kūfa and said, 'Verily, the like of Mu'āwiya[25] is not fit to be a protector of public safety, of God's ordinances (*aḥkām*), of sexual chastity, of war booty, and of alms tax (*ṣadaqa*).[26] He is unfit in his own character and in his religion.[27] He is habituated to fraud with respect to things entrusted to him. He is a breaker of the *sunna* and one who blatantly violates everything that is inviolable (*al-musta'ṣil li 'l-dhimma*). He is a forsaker of the Book and a cursed one, the son of the cursed one. In fact, the Messenger of God cursed him on ten occasions as he did his father and his brother.[28] It is not proper to have a greedy person [as a ruler] over Muslims who will satisfy his inordinate desires from their property. The ruler should not be a person ignorant [of the Book and the *sunna*] who leads them to their damnation by his ignorance. He should not be a miserly person who denies them their rights; nor a rude person who, by his wrongs, leads them to coarse actions. He should not be one who is afraid of the vicissitudes of time (*al-khā'if li 'l-duwal*) and who, therefore, leans towards one community rather than another.

[24]Ibid., VII, 451; reported from the same Imam. See also Poonawala, 'Imām's Authority', 119.

[25]For Mu'āwiya, see *The Pillars of Islam*, I, 107, n. 300; the older sources are indicated threrein.

[26]It is a free rendering of: *lā yajūz an yakūn amīn^{an} 'ala 'l-dimā' wa 'l-aḥkām wa 'l-furūj wa 'l-maghānim wa 'l-ṣadaqa.*

[27]The Arabic reads: *al-muttaham fī nafsihi wa-dīnihi* lit. means of doubtful character and faith.

[28]Mu'āwiya's father, Abū Sufyān, was the Meccan leader against the Muslims at the Battle of Uḥud. During the course of that battle, Hind, Mu'āwiya's mother, mutilated the corpse of the Prophet's uncle, Ḥamza, and chewed his liver as an act of vengeance. Hence, Mu'āwiya was called *ibn ākilat al-akbād* (the son of the liver eater). Both Mu'āwiya and his father were considered to be *ṭulaqā'* (set free) and *'utaqā'* (emancipated), i.e. those Meccans who remained heathen until the surrender of Mecca. They were also under the Qur'ānic category 'those whose hearts were to be reconciled' (*al-mu'allifati qulūbuhum*).

Mu'āwiya was known for his *ḥilm*, i.e. 'the patient and tireless cunning in the manipulation of men through knowledge of their interests and passions'. Yazīd b. Abī Sufyān, the elder brother of Mu'āwiya, was a commander in the Arab-Muslim army that conquered Syria. After the death of Abū 'Ubayda and Yazīd in the plague of 'Amwās (in the year 18/639), 'Umar appointed Mu'āwiya over the forces in Damascus and its *kharāj*. *EI*[2], s.v. Mu'āwiya I; Ṭabarī, *History of al-Ṭabarī*, XIII, 100.

He should not be [a corrupt person] who takes bribes for dishonestly adjucating cases thereby destroying the rights of men.[29] Similarly, the ruler should not be a person who annuls the *sunna* and thus leads the community (*umma*)[30] to its perdition.'

The Messenger of God: He said, 'He who does wrong either deliberately or by mistake will be in the Fire.'

'Alī: He said, 'When adultery becomes widespread, deaths will occur suddenly; and when the ruler is unjust, there will be a famine.'

['Alī]: He said, 'Judges are of three kinds, one of them will be in Heaven and two, in Hell. A man who does wrong deliberately will be in the Fire as will the man who errs in his decision. The man who acts rightly will be in Heaven.'[31]

['Alī]: He wrote to Rifā'a,[32] his *qāḍī* at Ahwāz, as follows:

O Rifā'a, know that this position of authority (*imāra*) is a trust; he who acts dishonestly in it, will be cursed by God until the Day of Resurrection; and he who appoints a corrupt officer, [the Prophet] Muḥammad will dissociate himself from him both in this world and in the hereafter.'

Ja'far b. Muḥammad: He said, 'Bribe taking in deciding cases is a type of unlawful gain (*suḥt*).'[33] It was said to him, 'O Son of the Messenger of God, even if he decides rightly?' [The Imam] said, '[Yes,] even if he decides rightly; but if he decides wrongfully, that is unbelief. God says: *Whoso judges not by that which Allah hath revealed: such are disbelievers* (5:44).'[34]

[29]'May God curse the giver of bribes (*rishwa*), [who aids another to do what is wrong], the receiver thereof, and the one who is an agent between the two, regulating the amount of the bribe.' *Mishkāt*, II, 339; Robson, I, 798; Lane, s.v. r-sh-w.

[30]Cf. *Nahj al-balāgha*, I, 144.

[31]'*Qāḍīs* are of three types, one of whom will go to Paradise and two to Hell. The one who will go to Paradise is a man who knows what is right and gives judgment accordingly; but a man who knows what is right and acts tyrannically in his judgment will go to Hell, as will a man who gives judgment for people when he is ignorant.' *Mishkāt*, II, 334; Robson, I, 793. Cf. *Kāfī*, VII, 446. '*Qāḍīs* are of four kinds: three of them will be in Hell, and one in Heaven. A man who deliberately decides unjustly will be in the Fire; a man who unknowingly decides unjustly will be in the Fire; a man who decides rightly but unknowingly will be in the Fire; a man who pronounces judgment rightly knowing [that it is the right decision] will be in Heaven.' Reported on the authority of Imam al-Ṣādiq. Gleave, 'Two classical Shī'ī theories', has cited this tradition from *Kāfī* to show that the office of *qāḍī* is held in low prestige by most Shī'ī authors.

[32]*The Pillars of Islam*, I, 281.

[33]*Kāfī*, VII, 449; transmitted from the same authority. *Suḥt* is a thing that is forbidden, unlawful, or from ill-gotten gain. See n. 44, Chap. 1.

[34]'If anyone intercedes for someone who, in turn, gives him a present for it, and he accepts it, he has been guilty of a serious kind of usury (*ribā*).' *Mishkāt*, II, 340; Robson, I, 799.

'Alī: He chided[35] Ibn Harma[36] for his dishonesty, while he was [an officer] at the market[37] of Ahwāz. He wrote to Rifā'a:

When you read this letter of mine, remove Ibn Harma from [his post] in the market; make him stand before the people, and imprison him. Make a proclamation, and write to your officers informing them of the opinion I have formed with regard to him.

Let not neglect or negligence seize you in this matter, lest you be destroyed by God and dismissed by me with the greatest disgrace. I seek refuge from God for you in this respect. When it is Friday, take him out of prison and scourge him with thirty-five stripes. Then, take him around the markets. If a man has a claim against him, make him and his witness take an oath. Pay the amount proved against him from the wealth of Ibn Harma and order him into prison, despised, disgraced, and reviled like a dog. Bind his legs with a thong and release him at the time of prayer. Do not obstruct anyone from bringing him food, drink, clothes, or bedding. Do not allow anyone to approach him who eggs him on to violence or gives him hope of escape. If you know definitely that someone has prompted him to hurt a Muslim, then scourge him and imprison him till he repents.

Order the inmates of the prison, except Ibn Harma, to be taken out in the courtyard at night in order that they may relax. However, if you fear the death of Ibn Harma, then take him out with the other prisoners to the courtyard. If you find that he has the strength [to bear the punishment], scourge him another thirty-five stripes thirty days after the first thirty-five stripes have been administered. Write [to me] as to what you have done regarding the market, and whom you have chosen to replace that dishonest fellow. [Lastly,] cut off his salary.

The Messenger of God: He forbade the *qāḍī* to favour one party over another in a legal suit by constantly looking at him and paying undue attention to him. He directed that witnesses should neither be led nor treated with hostility.

Abū Ja'far Muḥammad b. 'Alī: He said, 'There was a *qāḍī* among Israelites who used to decide cases rightly. When he was about to die, he said to his wife, "When I am dead and my body is lowered in the grave, please descend [into the grave] and look at my face. I am sure that you will see something which will gladden you, God willing."[38] She did [as

[35]It is a free rendering of *istadraka 'alā*, lit. he rectified what was wrong.

[36]Ibrāhīm b. 'Alī b. Salama b. 'Āmir b. Harma, born in 90/709, known as Ibn Harma, a poet of Medina and an 'Alīd supporter, was probably the grandson or great grandson of Ibn Harma. *EI*[2] s.v. Ibn Harma.

[37]He was probably a *muḥtasib*, see n. 19 above in this chapter.

[38]'When I am dead wash my body, shroud me, lay the body down on my bed, and cover my face. Indeed, you will not see anything unpleasant.' .... She uncovered his face to see and ... *Kāfī*, VII, 449; reported from the same Imam.

directed] and saw a huge worm moving about in his nostrils. She was frightened thereby. When it was night, she saw him in her dream and he said, "Were you frightened at what you saw concerning me?" She said, "Yes, I was frightened." He said, "What you saw was entirely on your account. Your brother came before me claiming a right against some other person. When the two sat before me, I said to myself, 'O God, give him [the wife's brother] the right and turn the case against the opponent.' What you saw happening to me was on account of this." '

'Alī: He used to say, 'It is not proper for a *qāḍī* to pay attention to one of the parties and not the other. He should divide his attention equally between them with justice. He should not allow one party to show hostility to the other.'

The Messenger of God: When he sent 'Alī as a judge to the Yemen, he said to him, 'When you, O 'Alī, decide between two persons, do not pass judgment in favour of the first without listening to what the other has to say.'[39] The Messenger of God also prohibited the judge from speaking until he had heard both parties; by speaking, he meant delivering a judgment.

'Alī: He heard that Shurayḥ[40] used to decide cases in his own house, so he said, 'O Shurayḥ, sit [as a judge] in the mosque. This is more fair to the people. It is a form of weakness in a *qāḍī* that he sits in his own house.'[41]

['Alī]: When he appointed Shurayḥ as a *qāḍī*, he made it a condition that he should not issue judicial decisions without referring them to him ['Alī].[42]

['Alī]: When he appointed Rifā'a as a judge at Ahwāz,[43] he wrote a letter to him which contained the following:

Avoid ambitious designs, fight vain desires, and adorn your knowledge with righteous conduct. The best help to religion is patience. If patience were a man, he would be a righteous person. Avoid weariness [with a case], for it is a form of

[39]See note 16 in this chapter.

[40]Shurayḥ, see n. 108, Chap. 15.

[41]He held court in the mosque and, on rainy days, he would sit in judgment at home. See n. 108 in Chap. 15. The *qāḍī* should sit and exercise his power at a place accessible to the public. It should be in the middle of the town, should be no barrier, nor should people be intimidated. The Caliph-Imam al-Manṣur had ordered Nu'mān to sit within the threshold of the royal palace. The Caliph-Imam al-Mu'izz finding that it was inaccessible for the poor, the sick, and the women, who were scared to come within the precincts of the palace, ordered a new building to be built where Nu'mān could sit. Nu'mān, *Kitāb al-majālis*, 69–70.

[42]*Kāfī*, VII, 445. Another tradition criticizes Shurayḥ for assuming the office of *qāḍī*.

[43]*The Pillars of Islam*, I, 281.

folly and vileness. Do not allow persons who do not resemble you [in character and opinions] to be in your company. Choose [suitable persons] for your private worship. Decide cases on clear and manifest grounds. Leave esoteric [meanings] (*bāṭin*) to the learned. Give up [expressions like], 'I think', 'I consider', and 'I am of the opinion'. In religion, there are no doubtful matters. Do not engage in controversies with fools or jurists; the latter will keep his goodness from you and the former will make you sad by his foolishness. Do not engage in argumentation with the People of the Book except in the best manner and use the Qur'ān or the *sunna*.

Do not accustom yourself to laughter, because it decreases dignity and emboldens parties to take undue liberties. I warn you against accepting presents from litigating parties. Be warned against the secret intentions of a man who trusts a foolish woman; he who seeks her advice will regret it. Beware of the tears of a faithful one, for they break [destroy] him who causes them to flow and extinguish the ocean of fires for the one from whose eyes they flow. Do not treat the parties rudely nor deride the applicant. Do not allow anyone but a jurist to sit in a legal session. Do not consult anyone in the matter of [your] judgment. Consultation is only [proper] in matters relating to war and urgent matters. Religion does not admit of personal opinions (*al-ra'y*); it is only a question of obedience (*ittibā'*) [to rules laid down]. Do not forsake the compulsory religious duties (*farā'iḍ*) and rely on supererogatory performances (*nawāfil*). Be good to him who treats you badly and pardon him who harms you. Pray for him who helps you, give to him who denies [something] to you, be courteous to one who favours you, give thanks to God for what He provides for you, and give Him praise for the trials He sends you.

Religious knowledge consists of three things: a clear [Qur'ānic] verse (*āya muḥkama*); a *sunna* to be followed; and a just religious duty (*farīḍa*). It is our command that establishes those precepts.

Ja'far b. Muḥammad: He was asked about [the authority] on which a *qāḍī* decides a case. He said, 'The Book.' It was said to him, 'If it is not found in the Book?' [The Imam] said, 'By the *sunna*.' It was said to him, 'Where the question is not to be found either in the Qur'ān or in the *sunna*?' [The Imam] said, 'There is nothing in religion which is not to be found in the Qur'ān or the *sunna*. Indeed, God has perfected religion and says: *This day have I perfected your religion for you ...* (5:3).' Then, [the Imam] said, 'For this, God guides and gives strength to whomsoever of His creatures He wishes; and the matter is not as you think.'[44]

[44]The Ismā'īlīs recognize the Qur'ān, the *sunna* of the Prophet as handed down by the *ahl al-bayt*, and the teaching and authority of the Imams as the three sources of law. *Ijmā'* (consensus of the community), *qiyās* (reasoning by deduction) and *ijtihād* (jurisprudential interpretation) are rejected. Fyzee, *Compendium*, introduction; al-Nu'mān, *Kitāb Ikhtilāf*

[Ja'far b. Muḥammad]: He said, 'The Messenger of God prohibited judicial decisions to be based on personal opinion (*al-ra'y*) or deduction (*al-qiyās*).[45] The Messenger of God said, "The first person to rely on deductive reasoning was Satan (*Iblīs*). Anyone who exercises his own opinion in any matter concerning the religion of God goes out of it."'

Abū Ja'far Muḥammad b. 'Alī: It was reported to [Imam al-Bāqir] that 'Ubayda al-Salmānī[46] had reported a tradition in which 'Alī [permitted] the sale of slave girls who had borne children to their masters (*ummahāt al-awlād*).[47] Abū Ja'far [Imam al-Bāqir] said, 'They forged a lie against 'Ubayda; or 'Ubayda fabricated a tradition by 'Alī. The people only intended that they would attribute to 'Alī a decision by the use of deductive reasoning (*al-qiyās*). This can never be proved by them. We are the children of 'Alī whatever we relate to you from 'Alī, is his saying; and whatever we deny is a fabrication. We know that *qiyās* (deductive reasoning) is not a part of 'Alī's religion. Only someone who does not know the Qur'ān and *sunna* uses deduction, so let not their reports mislead you. They never make claims [about 'Alī] except to mislead. It will not gladden you to meet the likes of *Yagūth*, *Ya'ūq*, and *Nasr*[48] whom God mentions in the Qur'ān and who mislead greatly. You should beware of meeting them.'

Ja'far b. Muḥammad: He said, 'It is not lawful for anyone to employ his own personal opinion or make use of deduction when speaking about the religion of God. Woe to the theologians (*aṣḥāb al-kalām*)[49] who claim that some things can be deduced and some things cannot be deduced. Verily, the first to make a deduction was Satan, may God curse him, when

uṣūl al-madhāhib, introduction. See also *The Pillars of Islam*, I, 20, 111–12, for the context of the verse.

[45]Ansari, 'Islamic Juristic Terminology', 288–94; *EI*², s.v. Ahl al-ra'y, Ḳiyās.

[46]'Ubayda al-Salmānī al-Murādī was a member of *shurṭat al-khamīs* (see *The Pillars of Islam*, I, 461) and accompanied 'Alī and Ibn Mas'ūd. Mufīd, *al-Ikhtiṣāṣ*, 3.

[47]See Chap. 12, section *Umm al-Walad*.

[48]It refers to the Qur'ān 71:23. They were heathen deities. *Yaghūth* was venerated by Murād in Yemen, *Ya'ūq* was venerated both by Hamdān and Murād, and *Nasr* was worshipped by Dhu 'l-Kilā' in Yemen. Blachère, *Coran*, 617–18; Bell, *Qur'ān*, II, 608; Yusuf Ali, *Holy Qur'ān*, 1619–23.

[49]Fārābī defines *'ilm al-kalām*, generally translated as 'theology', as 'a science which enables a man to procure the victory of the dogmas and actions laid down by the Legislator of the religion, and to refute all opinions contradicting them'. Ījī states, '*Kalām* is the science which is concerned with firmly establishing religious beliefs by adducing proofs and with banishing doubts.' *Mutakallim* is the one who practicies *'ilm al-kalām*. The Mu'tazila were one of the great schools of *kalām*. *EI*², s.v. 'Ilm al-Kalām.

he said: *I am better than he. Thou createdst me of fire while him Thou didst create of mud* (7:12). He held his own opinion and said out of his disbelief that fire was greater in worth than earth. It became apparent to him through deduction that the higher being should not prostrate before a lower being. He was cursed for this and became a rebellious Satan.[50]

'If deduction were permissible, each person who makes an incorrect deduction would still have an ample scope for such an activity, because [he thinks that] it is *qiyās* (deduction) whereby religion is completed. This is not objectionable to the people of the opposition. The condition of the Israelites (*banū Isrā'īl*) remained moderate [and sound] until there grew amongst them half-breeds (*muwalladūn*) and the children of prisoners, they began to use personal opinion and deduction, and they forsook the practice of the prophets, the blessing of God on them. This is how they went astray and misled others.'

[Ja'far b. Muḥammad]: He said to one of his companions, 'Beware of two destructive traits: that you use your own opinion to decide between people and that you profess as religion something you do not know. Verily, the first to make deductions was Satan. Verily, the first ones to lay down practice on the basis of deduction are well known.'[51]

The Messenger of God: Usāma[52] had asked a favour from the Messenger of God for one of the parties litigating before him. The Messenger of God said, 'O Usāma, you had asked for a favour when I was seated as a judge [to decide judicially between two litigants]. Verily, legal rights are matters on which there can be no intervention (*shafā'a*).'

[The Messenger of God]: He forbade any litigating party from staying with the judge. A man stayed with 'Alī at Kūfa and he entertained the man. Then, he came [before 'Alī] to litigate, and so 'Alī said to him, 'Are you a party to the suit? Go away from me for, verily, the Messenger of God forbade a party to a suit from staying [with the judge] unless his opponent is also with him.'[53]

[The Messenger of God]: He forbade a *qāḍī* to pronounce judgment while he was angry, hungry, sleepy. He said, 'God says, "O son of Adam! Remember me when you are angry, and I shall remember you when I am

[50]Alludes to the Qur'ān 4:117.

[51]The Imam refers to *aṣḥāb al-ra'y*, especially Ibn Abī Layla, Abū Ḥanīfa, and his disciples. *The Pillars of Islam*, I, 108, 110, 112–13, 113–18.

[52]Usāma was the son of Zayd b. Ḥāritha, the Prophet's freed slave. *The Pillars of Islam*, I, 54.

[53]*Kāfī*, VII, 453.

angry, otherwise, I shall erase you along with the others that are erased [destroyed]!"'[54]

[The Messenger of God]: He said, 'Anger corrupts faith as aloes (*ṣibr*)[55] spoil honey.'

'Alī: He said to Rifā'a,[56] 'Do not pronounce judgment when you are angry[57] or are intoxicated by sleep.'

Ja'far b. Muḥammad: He said, 'When it is clear to the judge that he had decided incorrectly, he should cancel the judgment and decide correctly. Similarly, if the judgment of some other judge is brought to him, he should cancel it and decide rightly.'

Ja'far b. Muḥammad: He said, 'Anyone who wishes to obtain a thing or to be free from the responsibility of something, is considered to be a claimant (*mudda'in*) and the burden of proof is on him.'[58]

'Alī: He said, 'There is no escape from the office of *amīr* (*imāra*)[59] and remuneration for him; nor from an administrative officer (*'arīf*)[60] and remuneration for him; nor from a [*muḥtasib*][61] and remuneration for him; nor from a judge (*qāḍī*) and remuneration for him.' He disliked that the remuneration of judges should come from the litigants. [He held that] it should come from the Public Treasury (*bayt al-māl*).[62]

[54]'No judge (*ḥakam*) must give judgment between two people when he is angry.' *Mishkāt*, II, 333; Robson, I, 793; transmitted by Bukhārī and Muslim. See also Ṭūsī, *al-Nihāya*, 338.

[55]Lane, s.v. ṣ-b-r.

[56]Rifā'a b. Shaddād, see *The Pillars of Islam*, I, 281.

[57]Cf. *Kāfī*, VII, 453.

[58]Ibid., VII, 455.

[59]See n. 3 above in this chapter. When Abū Bakr became caliph, he said, 'My people know that my trade was not incapable of supporting my family, but I have become occupied with the affairs of the Muslims. Therefore, Abū Bakr's family will be supported from this property [i.e. *bayt al-māl*] while he works for it on behalf of the Muslims.' *Mishkāt*, II, 337; Robson, I, 797; transmitted by Bukhārī.

[60]'*Arīf*, in the sense of the measure '*ārif*, is a manager of the affairs of a people, i.e. one who knows his companions. During the Medinan Caliphate, he collected taxes from the tribes and handed them over to the *muṣaddiq* who was appointed by the caliph. From the time of 'Umar b. al-Khaṭṭāb, the office of '*arīf* is mentioned frequently with regard to the military organization of the Muslim empire. Lane, s.v. '-r-f; *EI*[2], s.v. 'Arīf. Cf. *Mishkāt*, II, 324, 325; Robson, I, 786, 787.

[61]*Ḥāsib*: in the edited text as well as in the pirated edition and in MS Q. It seems to be an error. For *muḥtasib*, see n. 19 in this chapter.

[62]'When we appoint someone to an administrative post and provide him with an allowance, anything he takes beyond that is unfaithful dealing (*ghulūl*).' *Mishkāt*, II, 337, 338; Robson, I, 797. The conception of *bayt al-māl* as the State or Public Treasury as distinct from private ownership and the idea that these properties and monies were designed to serve the interests of the Muslim *umma* (community) began with the institution of the *dīwān* during the caliphate of 'Umar. *EI*[2], s.v. Bayt al-Māl.

'Alī: He used to walk in the markets, whip (*dirra*) in hand, by which he would strike any dealer who gave short measure (*muṭaffif*)[63] or who practised fraud (*ghashsh*) in trading with Muslims. Aṣbagh[64] said, 'I told him one day, "I shall do this for you, O Commander of the Faithful, and you may sit in your house." 'Alī said, "You did not give me [good] advice, O Aṣbagh."'

'Alī used to ride Shahbā',[65] the mule belonging to the Messenger of God and go round the markets one by one. One day, he came to the butcher's quarters (*ṭāq al-laḥḥāmīn*) and said, 'O group of butchers (*qaṣṣābīn*)! Do not make haste [cutting up the animals] until they are clearly dead. I warn you not to blow [breathe] on the meat.' Then, he went to the date sellers (*tammārīn*) and said, 'Show your poor quality dates in the same manner as you exhibit the good ones.' Then, he went to the fishmongers (*sammākīn*) and said, 'Do not sell any spoiled fish, only the good ones; I warn you not to sell fish which float [i.e. are stale and rotting].' Then, he went to the quarter [of Kūfa] called Kunāsa[66] and, at that place, there were a number of trades, such as cattle dealers, slave traders (*nakhkhās*), dealers in ropes (*qammāṭ*), camel dealers, money changers (*ṣayrafī*), cloth merchants (*bazzār*), and tailors (*khayyāṭ*). He raised his voice and proclaimed loudly, 'O Merchants, in these markets of yours are many oaths [that you swear]. Requite your oaths with charity and stop taking oaths for, verily, God does not sanctify the person who swears falsely in His name.'

Abū Ja'far Muḥammad b. 'Alī: He said, 'Verily, a lawsuit (*khuṣūma*) effaces and erases religion, renders good actions nugatory, and begets enmity.'

Abū 'Abd Allāh Ja'far b. Muḥammad: He exhorted a person and said, 'Whatever kindly act you can do, do it. I warn you not to intervene between two persons when there is a lawsuit. I am a warner for you; I am a warner for you; I am a warner for you.'

'Alī: He said, 'There should be no imprisonment merely on the basis of an accusation, except in cases of murder. It is wrong to imprison someone after the truth has been ascertained [and the accused is found to be innocent].'

['Alī]: He said, 'Anyone imprisoned permanently should be given subsistence from the Public Treasury. No one should be imprisoned

[63]Referred to in he Qur'ān 83:1.

[64]He is Aṣbagh b. Nubāta, see *The Pillars of Islam*, I, 489.

[65]Shahbā', see *The Pillars of Islam*, I, 488.

[66]Yāqūt, s.v. Kunāsa.

permanently except in three cases: one who is awarded a life imprisonment;[67] a woman who has apostatized until she repents;[68] and a thief after his hand and foot are cut off.' In the case of the latter, he meant a thief who has committed theft for a third time.

['Alī]: He said, 'It is not lawful to imprison a person who is in straitened circumstances on account of debt.'

['Alī]: He said, 'When witnesses give evidence against a man for a monetary right and the *qāḍī* does not know about their integrity, but another *qāḍī* in some other place does know [the integrity of those witnesses], the *qāḍī* [hearing the case] should accept a letter from such a *qāḍī*.

'However, if the evidence is given in a divorce case or a criminal offence (*ḥadd*), the letter of one *qāḍī* to another is not to be accepted. In these cases [i.e. criminal offences] a witness who gives evidence against another witness is not to be accepted and a letter from one *qāḍī* to another is not to be accepted.'

'Alī: He said, 'The letter of a *qāḍī* of the people of rebellion (*ahl al-baghy*)[69] shall not be enforced nor should he be written to.'

['Alī]: He said, 'If a man appoints an agent, a decision shall be given against the agent. Agency (*wikāla*) is lawful, even without the presence of the principal.'

Ja'far b. Muḥammad: He was asked about a man against whom a decree has been passed and who asks for time. [The Imam] said, 'If the man wishes thereby merely to delay matters, time should not be given to him. However, if he wishes to sell his property in lots, piece by piece, the matter should be considered for that purpose.'

[Ja'far b. Muḥammad]: He said, 'If a man refuses to pay his opposing party [in a lawsuit] his dues even though he is well-to-do and able to pay, he should be scourged until he does pay his dues. If he is a man who has nothing except goods, he should give a surety (*kafīl*); if he cannot provide a surety, he should be imprisoned till he is able to sell [part of his goods] and pay his dues [with the proceeds].'

[Ja'far b. Muḥammad]: He used to consider it proper to judge an absent man. He would postpone matters for proof if the absent man had any. If a debtor against whom a decree was passed was not to be trusted, a surety should be appointed to pay the dues from the property of the

[67]One who is held until death.

[68]A man born a Muslim who apostatizes and does not recant shall be killed. In case of a woman, she should be imprisoned until she recants or dies. *The Pillars of Islam*, I, 494.

[69]For the people of rebellion, see *The Pillars of Islam*, I, 479–89.

absent person. However, if the absent person has a proper defence, the property may be returned to him.

[Ja'far b. Muḥammad]: He said, 'If a case relating to the People of the Book is brought to the judge, he should decide it according to the revelations of God, as God says: *So judge between them by that which Allah has revealed* (5:49).'

'Alī: He delivered a sermon to the people at Kūfa and said, 'O People, God has granted to me a certain right over you by giving me command over you and by virtue of my status. It is my responsibility to give you friendly admonition and justice.[70] Verily, a right does not go to anyone unless it is conferred on him; and a right is not bestowed on anyone unless he is fit for it.'

['Alī]: He said, 'Anyone who wrongfully strikes another with even one lash, God will strike him with a thong of fire.'

Ja'far b. Muḥammad: He said, 'The prayer of the just Imam is not rejected and the petition of a wronged person is not rejected. When a wicked ruler disobeys God and you obey him, this is one of the greatest calamities (*qawāṣim al-ẓahr*)!'[71]

[70]Cf. *Nahj al-balāgha*, I, 53.

[71]The Sunnī position is 'No obedience is to be given [to the caliph/ruler] in actions that entail disobedience to God.' Transmitted by Bukhārī and Muslim. However, in the case of an unjust or tyrannical ruler, most of the traditions are condescending. For example, a tradition states, 'After my death you will see [rulers] appropriating the best things for themselves and other matters which you will disapprove.' The Messenger of God was asked what he commanded them to do and he replied, 'Give them what is due to them and ask God for what is due to you.' Another tradition states, 'If anyone sees in his *amīr* what he dislikes, he should show patience, for no one separates a span's distance from the community and dies without dying like those of pre-Islamic times.' Transmitted by Bukhārī and Muslim. *Miskhāt*, II, 317, 318; Robson, I, 781, 782. See also Rahman, *Islam*, 237–40; he argues that the inherited political dogma needs to be reformed. Justice ('*adl*) and knowledge ('*ilm*) are the main constituents in the Shī'ī theory of the Imamate, as the Imam upholds and promulgates the rule of justice and equity. See Sachedina, *The Just Ruler*.

Glossary

This glossary contains technical terms, mainly of Arabic origin, used in Islamic law, theology, and other Islamic sciences. Technical terms used by the Shīʿa, especially the Ismāʿīlīs, and their meanings are indicated by an asterisk. These terms appear frequently in the text and are explained in the notes.

al-ʿabd al-maʾdhūn	a slave who has his master's permission to trade
ābiq	runaway slave
adab al-qāḍī	the etiquette of the judge (*qāḍī*)
āda (pl. *ādāt*)	custom, habitual practice
ʿadāla	the quality of religious probity and moral integrity a witness must possess for his testimony to be admissible; a person of such character is called *ʿadl*
ʿadam al-ṭawl	lack of means
adhān	call to prayer
ʿadl (pl. *ʿudūl*)	virtuous, fair, just, a person of good reputation whose profession is mainly that of public notaries, see *ʿadāla*
aḥdatha ḥadath^{an}	to commit a wrongful act
ʿāhir (pl. *ʿawāhir*)	prostitute
aḥkām (pl. of *ḥukm*)	positive commands, rules of law, judgments; the effects of a contract
al-aḥkām al-khamsa	the five legal qualifications: *wājib*, *sunna*, *mubāḥ*, *makrūh*, and *ḥarām*
ahl al-ʿadl	the People of Justice
ahl al-bayt	House of the Prophet, *Messenger of God's family (restricted to the Prophet, ʿAlī, Fāṭima, Ḥasan, Ḥusayn, and their descendants)

ahl al-farā'iḍ	those entitled to prescribed Qur'ānic shares, people qualified for inheritance
ahl al-ḥadīth	traditionists as opposed to the *ahl al-ra'y*; the scholars who favour literal approach in the analysis of texts
ahl al-ḥall wa'l-'aqd	lit. those who are qualified to unbind and bind, the representatives of the community who appoint and depose a caliph/ruler
ahl al-ikhtiyār	(on the caliphate/imamate) the supporters of free election
ahl al-jawr	the people of corruption
ahl al-ra'y	as opposed to *ahl al-ḥadīth* who emphasize the role of reason in legal analysis
ahl al-shawka	people with power, notables
ahl al-walāya	*the rightful Imams
ajal	term, appointed time
ajīr	hired worker, labourer
ama	female slave, concubine
amān	safe conduct
amāna	deposit, trust
amīn	a person in a position of trust
amīr	commander, governor, prince, a person invested with command (*amr*)
'āmma	commonalty, the masses
'anat	sin, immorality
anfāl	spoils
'aqār	immovable property
'aqd (pl. *'uqūd)*	a contract that is concluded through an offer and acceptance during the contract session
aq'ad	nearness of relationship
'āqila	agnatic relations upon whom devolves a joint liability for the blood money in cases of homicide, wounding, and assault
'aql	compensation/blood money payable by the agnatic relatives
'āqir	a woman who is barren
aqḍiya (pl. of *qaḍā'*)	judicial decisions
'aqīqa (pl. *'aqā'iq*)	offering made for a newborn child
'arāya = bay' al-'arāya	
'arḍ	commodity, goods other than cash dinars and dirhams
'arīf	an officer who collects taxes from the tribes for the *muṣaddiq*
'āriya	commodate loan, loan of non-fungible things, gratuitous loan or transfer of the uses of property

'āriya maḍmūna	guaranteed loan
'arīya (pl. *'arāyā*)	a palm tree, which its owner assigns to a needy to consume its fruit during a year
arsh	a penalty for certain wounds, see *ḥukūma*
'aṣaba (pl *'aṣabāt*)	agnates, agnatic relations
aṣḥāb al-ḥadīth = ahl al-ḥadīth	
aṣḥāb al-kalām	theologians
'ashīra	tribe
aṣīl	the principal
'aṭīya (pl. *'aṭāya*)	benefaction, present
āwā muḥdith^{an}	to give protection to a wrongdoer
'awl	an artificial inflation of the denominator to make the various fractional shares equal to the whole that results in proportional reduction of shares of heirs
awlād al-a'yān	relations by full blood, children of the same father and mother
'awra	private parts of the human body to be covered in prayer and in the presence of others
aymān (pl. of *yamīn*)	oaths
'ayn	tangible thing that can be ascertained by weight or measure, gold and silver coins, the substance/ corpus of property; evil eye
ayyām al-tashrīq	three days following the Day of Sacrifice (*'īd al-aḍḥā*)
'àzl	coitus interruptus
bāḍi'a	wound in the head that cleaves the flesh and bleeds
baghy	rebellion
bāligh	of age, adult
banu 'l-ab	children of the same father by different mothers
banu 'l-'allāt	relations by half blood, children of one father by different mothers
banu 'l-umm wa 'l-ab	full children (from the same parents)
barnāma	account book
barzakh	a barrier between Hell and Paradise
bāṭil	null and void, invalid
bay'	sale, exchange
bay' al-'arāya	barter of dried dates for fresh dates on the tree
bay' al-dayn bi 'l-dayn	exchange of one obligation for another
bay' al-ḥaṣāt= ṭarḥ al-ḥaṣā	
bay' al-gharar	aleatory sales, hazardous sales
bay' al-'īna	sale on credit consisting of a 'double sale' to evade *ribā*

bay' al-muḍṭarr	one who is forced to sell
bay' al-mulāmasa	a mode of bargaining by touching a thing without opening or inspecting, an aleatory transaction
bay' al-munābadha	a mode of bargain by throwing a piece of cloth, an aleatory transaction
bay' al-nasī'a	deferred sale, forward buying
bay' al-wafā'	sale of real property with the right of redemption
bay'atān fī bay'a	'double sale' in one sale for evading the prohibition of *ribā*
bayt al-māl	public treasury
bayyina (pl. *bayyināt*)	clear proof, evidence; the term is applied not only to giving testimony but also to the witnesses themselves
bikr	unmarried person
buḍ'	sexual intercourse
bughāt (pl. of *bāghin*)	rebels
buyū' (pl. of *bay'*)	business transactions, selling and buying
ḍaḥīya (pl. *ḍaḥāya*)	sacrificial animal for the Day of Sacrifice
ḍālla (pl. *ḍawāll*)	lost she camel, strayed animal
ḍamān	the civil liability arising from the non-performance of a contract or from a tort or negligence, suretyship, guarantee
dāmi'a	bleeding wound
dāmi'a al-kubrā	a wound that bleeds profusely
dāmi'a al-ṣughrā	a wound that bleeds like tears
dāmigha	a wound in the head that reaches the brain
ḍāmin	liable, see *ḍamān*
dāmiya	wound in the head that bleeds
dār al-ḥarb	abode of war or unbelievers, land of war (defunct medieval legal concept)
dār al-islām	abode of Islam, the country of Islam (defunct medieval legal concept)
al-darāhim al-ghalla	older Umayyad dirhams struck before the time of the Hishām b. 'Abd al-Malik
al-darāhim al-maḥmūl 'alayhā	alloyed dirhams, debased dirhams
al-darāhim al-mukaḥḥala	coins alloyed with antimony
al-darāhim al-muzaybaqa	coins alloyed with quicksilver
al-darāhim al-ṭāzaja	fine white dirhams of high purity
ḍarar	damage, prejudice; cruelty (in the context of divorce)
ḍarībat al-'abd	an impost imposed upon a slave by his master
ḍarra (pl. *ḍarā'ir*)	taking a second wife concurrent with a first
ḍarūra	necessity as a dispensing element

daʿwā	claim, a legal action, a lawsuit
dayn (pl. *duyūn*)	loan, debt; obligation
dhabīḥa (pl. *dhabāʾiḥ*)	ritual slaughter
dhabḥ	proper manner of slaughtering the cattle and birds in the throat
dhakāt=tadhkiya	
dhāt maḥram	female relatives forbidden for marriage
dhawāt al-ʿidad	women observing the *ʿidda*
dhawu ʾl-arḥām	lit. 'the possessors of a uterine relationship (*dhū raḥim*),' relations by the women's/maternal side, related by consanguinity, cognates, uterine heirs
dhawu ʾl-qurbā	kinship
dhimma	obligation, responsibility, undertaking
dhimmī	covenanted people living under Muslim rule, a free non-Muslim subject living in Muslim lands, esp. the Jews and the Christians
dhū maḥram	a person related to another within the forbidden degree of marriage
dhū raḥim	blood relation
dinar Dimashqī=dirham Dimashqī	
dirham Dimashqī	issued by the order of the Umayyad caliph ʿAbd al-Malik
dirham Yūsufī	issued by Yūsuf b. ʿUmar, the Umayyad governor of Iraq
diya (pl. *diyāt*)	blood money, compensation due in cases of homicide, wounding, and assault
dukhūl	consummation of marriage
faḍl	surplus, profit
fājir (pl. *fawājir*)	immoral person
faqīh (pl. *fuqahāʾ*)	jurist, legal scholar, a specialist in Islamic law
farāʾiḍ (pl. of *farīḍa*)	apportioned inheritance assigned by the Qurʾān, the quota heirs whose shares are fixed by the Qurʾān
farḍ (pl. *farāʾiḍ*)	synonym of *wājib*, precept of the divine law, mandatory obligation, obligatory duty; fixed share of an heir (see *farāʾiḍ*)
farḍ ʿayn	the individual duty
farḍ kifāya	the collective duty
farīḍa	obligatory *mahr*; apportioned inheritance assigned by the Qurʾān (see *farāʾiḍ*)
fāriqa	an act or a wound that breaks the vertebrae of the back
fāsid	invalid, defective

fāsiq	libertine, sinner, an impious person
faskh	annulment of a contract, rescission
fatwā (pl. *fataāwā*)	non-binding legal opinion issued in response to a legal problem, the considered opinion of a *muftī*, opinion of a jurist on a legal problem
fay'	in early Islamic times it meant immovable properties acquired by conquest in contrast to the moveable booty called *ghanīma*
fiqh	lit. understanding, the science of jurisprudence, the sacred law (*sharī'a*) of Islam
fiṣāl=fiṭām	
fiṭām	weaning
fitna (pl. *fitan*)	a Qur'ānic term with the meaning of temptation or trial of faith; revolt, civil war
furū' (pl. of *far'*)	the branches, positive law as opposed to *uṣūl*
ghalima	a passionate woman
ghalla=al-darāhim al-ghalla	older Umayyad dirhams struck before the time of the Hishām b. 'Abd al-Malik
ghanīma	booty, esp. moveable as opposed to *fay'*
gharar	uncertainty, risk, hazard, particularly with regard to commercial contracts
gharīm (pl. *ghuramā'*)	creditor, debtor
ghaṣb	in civil law, usurpation, wrongful/illegal appropriation of something belonging to another, unlawful use of the rights of another
ghashsh	adulteration, counterfeit
ghāṣib	usurper (see *ghaṣb*)
ghayba	in law, is the state of being not present at the place where one should be
ghayra	self-respect, bashfulness
ghāzī	a title of honour given to one who distinguished himself in the *ghazwa*
ghirra	blood money payable for the destruction of a foetus
ghurra = ghirra	
ḥabal al-ḥabala	offspring of the offspring in the belly of the she-camel
ḥabs	retention of a thing to secure a claim, lien
hadr or *hadar*	not protected by criminal law
ḥadath	misdeed, sin, innovation, particularly in matters of religion
ḥadd = ḥudūd	
ḥadd al-qādhif	the punishment for defamer

ḥadd al-zānī	the punishment for adulterer
ḥadd al-zāniya	the punishment for adulteress
ḥadīth al-nafs	pleasurable imaginings
ḥā'iṭ (pl. *ḥawā'iṭ*)	walled gardens of palm trees
hajj	pilgrimage to Mecca at least once in one's lifetime, if one is able to do physically and financially
hājj	one who makes a pilgrimage to Mecca
ḥajjām	cupper
ḥajr	interdiction, revocation of legal competence; husband's desertion of the marriage bed to rebuke his wife
ḥakam	arbitrator
ḥākim	ruling authority
ḥākimīya	sovereignty /dominion of God
ḥalāl	permitted, lawful, not forbidden
ḥalīf	an ally
ḥamīl	a person born in a non-Islamic country but acknowledged by some in the country of Islam
ḥaqq	proper, duty
ḥaram	a sanctuary, sanctuary of Mecca
ḥarām	forbidden, unlawful
Ḥarūrī = Khawārij	
ḥarbī	foreign national of a non-Muslim state, enemy alien
ḥārisa	wound in the head that scrapes off the skin
hāshima	wound in the head that breaks the bone
ḥawāla	transfer of debts
ḥawḍ	the pond at which the Prophet will meet his community on the Day of Resurrection
hiba (pl. *hibāt*)	gift, present, grant, the gratuitous transfer of the corpus of property
ḥijr	forbidden
ḥīla (pl. *ḥiyal*)	legal device, stratagem, evasion
ḥinth	violation of an oath
ḥirāba	see *muḥārib*
ḥirz	lit. a fortified place where a thing is kept, the place of safe custody
ḥisba	the function of ensuring that the precepts of the *sharī'a*, esp. of moral and religious nature, are observed, the office of the *muḥtasib*
ḥubs (pl. *ḥubūs*)	what is bequeathed is not be sold nor inherited, and the profit from it to be used in the cause of God, a pious endowment
ḥudūd (pl. of *ḥadd*)	a fixed punishment of certain crimes in the Qur'ān, divinely ordained punishments are:

theft, highway robbery, adultery, defamation, wine drinking, apostasy, and rebellion

ḥudūd Allāh — the divine ordinances of God

ḥujr — protection

ḥukm — Decree of God, a legally binding judgment, ruling of law, see also *aḥkām*

ḥukm qiyāsī — ruling arrived at through the use of analogy (*qiyās*)

ḥukm sharʿī — the rule of the *sharīʿa*

ḥukra — monopoly, hoarding of goods

ḥukūmatu ʿadl[in] — if no percentage of the blood money is prescribed for the penalty or compensation of a wound, the so-called *ḥukūma* becomes due, i.e. the compensation to be decided by a *qāḍī* through special *ijtihād* (an assessment of the actual loss suffered and is determined by reference to the market value of slave before and after a similar injury, then it is decided that the corresponding percentage of the blood money must be paid)

ḥuqūq Allāh — rights of God upon humanity, the infraction of which may or may not be forgiven

ḥuqūq al-ʿibād — rights of individuals upon each other, the infraction of which God will not forgive unless the wronged person forgives

ḥuqūq al-nās — the rights of people

ḥurr — a free person

ibn al-fāʿila = walad al-zināʾ

ibn al-mulāʿana — child not acknowledged as legitimate

ibn al-sabīl — traveller

ʿidda — legally prescribed waiting period during which a woman may not marry after being divorced or widowed (during which the legal rights and obligations of the spouses are not completely extinguished)

idhn — permission, authorization necessary to conclude legal and commercial transactions

iʿdhār — feast for a joyful occasion; celebration at the circumcision of a child

īfāʾ — fulfillment of an obligation

iḥdād — mourning of a widow after the death of her husband

iḥlāl — making lawful the remarriage of a couple irrevocably divorced by arranging for the marriage of the woman to another husband, a marriage

	intended to legalize the remarriage of a couple irrevocably divorced
iḥrām	consecrated state in which one performs the *ḥajj* and *'umra*; the state of consecration during the prayers
iḥṣān	unblemished reputation; one who is married, free, and Muslim
ījāb wa-qabūl	an offer and an acceptance of a contract
ijāra (pl. *ijārāt*)	lease, hire
ijmā'	consensus of opinion
ijtihād	jurisprudential interpretation, the exercise of human reason to ascertain a rule of *sharī'a*
ikhtilāf	divergence of juristic opinions/doctrines, disagreement
ikhtiṭāb	marriage proposal
ikhtiyār	choice
ikrāh	duress
īlā'	vow of continence/abstinence by the husband not to have sexual intercourse with his wife for four months (two months if the wife is a slave) at the end of that period the marriage is automatically broken up in Ḥanafī law
'illa (pl. *'ilal*)	effective/operative cause, the ascertainment of the reason (*'illa*) underlying a legal rule, an essential step in the process of *qiyās*
'ilm al-farāiḍ=farā'iḍ	
imām	ruling authority, authority
imāra	position of authority, the office of the supreme commander, i.e. the caliphate/imamate
'īna	a device consisting of a 'double sale' in one contract to evade *ribā*
'innīn	impotent
iqrār	affirmation, acknowledgement, recognition of rights; admission, confession
iṣmā'	an animal that is shot dies on the spot within the hunter's sight
isnād	chain of authorities/transmitters in a tradition
isqāṭ	relinquishment of a claim
istahalla	a child raised its voice and cried at birth
istihlāl = istahalla	
istīlā'	usurpation
i'tikāf	pious retreat in a mosque for a certain number of days with the observance of certain conditions and occupying oneself in prayer and recitation of the Qur'ān

ʿitq	emancipation of a slave, manumission
ʿitq al-batāt	unconditional emancipation
ʿiwaḍ	compensation, exchange value
ʿiyādāt	to go visiting the sick
jāhilīya	pre-Islamic days, Days of Ignorance
jāʾifa	a (spear) wound that penetrates the interior of the body or head
jāʾiz	allowed, permissible, to specify that the judicial act is legitimate
janāba	a major ritual impurity after sexual intercourse
janaf	an inclination to do a wrong
jāriya	female slave, slave girl
jazūr	a she-camel for slaughter
jihād	an effort directed towards a determined goal; religious war
jināya	tort
jizya	poll tax levied on non-Muslims in Muslim states
juʿl	remuneration, reward for bringing back a fugitive slave
juzāf	selling and buying by conjecture, without measure and weight, undetermined quantity
juzʾ	one-tenth of a thing
kabīra (pl. *kabāʾir*)	a major sin as opposed to *ṣaghāʾir*, an offence
kafāʾa	compatibility of social status of the two parties to a marriage, social equality of the spouses in a marriage
kafāla	suretyship, surety bond, bail, guarantee
kafāla bi ʾl-māl	monetary pledge
kafāla bi ʾl-nafs	pledge to secure the appearance of the debtor in court
kafāla bi ʾl-wajh = kafāla bi ʾl-nafs	
kaffāra	expiation, propitiatory act which grants remission for faults of some gravity
kafīl	guarantor, surety
kāhin (pl *kuhhān*)	fortune-teller, soothsayer, diviner
kalāla	a daughter-in-law, one's own wife
kālī= kālīʾ	
kālīʾ	a practice that enables a man who cannot pay a debt when it is due to have the period extended for an additional sum
kathrat al-ṭarūqa	great virility
kātib	scribe, secretary whose role is to draft official documents
khabar (pl. *akhbār*)	a report, piece of information; tradition

khaḍīʿa	deceit by concealment
khafḍ	female excision as opposed to *khitān*
khalwa	privacy between the spouses, the consummation of marriage
kharāj	land-tax
kharṣ = khirṣ	
khaṣm	party to a lawsuit
khāss	the elite, notables as opposed to *ʿāmma*
khāṣṣa = khāṣṣ	
khattān	professional circumciser
Khawārij	the earliest of the religious sects of Islam, those who seceded from ʿAlī's camp at the Battle of Ṣiffīn
khilāba	to deceive with blandishing speech
khimār	head and face covering
khirṣ	conjectural computation of quantity only for dates, grapes, and cereals
khitān	male circumcision
khiyāna	embezzlement
khiyār	option, conditional bargain, option either to confirm a deal or to withdraw, right of rescission; choice in divorce
khiyār al-majlis	'the option of the session,' the right of a party to repudiate unilaterally a contract just concluded as long as the 'session' lasts
khulʿ	a form of divorce by which the wife redeems herself from the marriage for a consideration, a negotiated divorce at the instance of the wife
khums	one-fifth share of the Prophet and the Imams
khunthā	hermaphrodite
khurṣ = khirṣ	
khurs	feast on the occasion of the birth of a child (*ʿaqīqa*)
khuṣūma	litigation
kihāna	divination, see *kāhin*
kitāba	a contract of emancipation, see *mukātab*
lā waks wa-lā shaṭaṭ	without any increase or decrease
lahw	amusement, music
laqīṭ	the foundling, a child whose parentage and status (free or slave) is unknown
liʿān	mutual imprecation by a couple, a procedure by which a husband accuses his wife of infidelity and may repudiate paternity of a child born to his wife; the oath which gives a husband the

possibility of accusing his wife of adultery without evidence and without becoming liable to the *ḥadd* punishment of *qadhf*

liwāṭ — sodomy, homosexuality

luqṭa — find, article or thing found, what is picked up, lost and found

lūṭī — sodomite, a homosexual playing the active part in the act of sodomy as opposed to *ma'būn*

ma'būn — the passive partner in sodomy as opposed to *lūṭī*

ma'dhūn — a slave who has been given permission by his master to trade

maḍmūn (pl. *maḍāmīn*) — what is in the loins of the stallions

maḍmūn = *maḍmūna*

maḍmūna — a thing ensured by an acknowledgment of responsibility for its delivery

mafqūd — a person who at a given moment is not present at the place where he should be and concerning whose existence there is uncertainty, a missing husband

ma'fūj — one who is struck in sodomy

maḥārim (pl. of *maḥram*) — a person related to another within the forbidden degree of marriage

maḥjūr — a person who is prohibited from disposing of this property

mahr (pl. *muhūr*) — dower, the gift given by the bridegroom to the bride when the contract of marriage is made and which becomes the wife's property

mahr al-mithl — the *mahr* appropriate to the similar status of a woman

mahr mu'ajjal = *mahr mu'akhkhar*

mahr mu'akhkhar — deferred dower

mahr muqaddam — prompt dower

mahr al-sunna — *mahr* of the *sunna*, i.e. neither too high nor too low

mahīra — a woman to whom a dower is given, wife

makīl — things that can be measured

makrūh — reprehensible, disapproved

malāhī (pl. of *malhā*) — instruments of diversion and pleasure, musical instruments

mālik — owner

malqūḥa (pl. *malāqīḥ*) — what is in the belly of the female

mamlūk — slave

ma'mūna — a deep wound in the head almost reaching the brain

manbūdh	a foundling
mandūb = *sunna*	
manfa'a (pl. *manāfi'*)	usufruct
mankūḥ	passive agent in sodomy
mansūkh	the repealed verse, see *naskh*
māriqīn	those who strayed from true path, the Khawārij
ma'rūf	a kind act, kindness
mas'ala minbariyya	a particular problem of inheritance, which 'Alī is reported to have solved off-hand when it was submitted to him while he was on the minbar
mashā'ir al-ḥajj	stations of pilgrimage
maskh	transmutation, metamorphosis of men into animals
matn	text; the content of a tradition as distinct from the *isnād*
mawāt	dead lands, uncultivated lands belonging to nobody
mawlā (pl. *mawālī*)	a patron; a freedman, client
maẓālim	the prerogative jurisdiction exercised by the political authority
mayta	animals not ritually slaughtered
miḥrāb	the prayer niche in the mosque indicating the direction of the prayer
milk	ownership
mi'rāḍ	featherless arrow
mīrāth	inheritance, share
mithqāl	a measure of weight
miṭlāq	a man who divorces women freely
mu'āmala (pl. *mu'āmalāt*)	the bilateral contracts as opposed to *'ibādāt*, transactions
mu'annathīn min al-rijāl	effeminate males
mubāḥ	indifferent (neither obligatory nor reprehensible), permissible, lawful
mubāra'a	a form of divorce by agreement with mutual waiving of financial obligations
mubhama	absolutely
mudabbar (pl.*mudabbarūn)*	a slave who is declared to be free after the death of his master, manumitted by *tadbīr*
muḍāraba	a commercial association whereby the investor entrusts his capital to an agent who trades and shares a predetermined proportion of the profits; losses incurred in the venture is borne by the investor; sleeping partnership
muḍārib	an agent who trades with the capital of an investor and shares a predetermined profits

mudd	handful
muddaʿā	the claim, lawsuit
muddaʿā ʿalayhi	the defendant, the litigant against whom a claim (*daʿwā*) is made
muddaʿī	the plaintiff, the litigant who makes a claim and upon whom rests the burden of proof
mūḍiḥa	a head wound that shows the whiteness of the bone
mudhakkarāt min al-nisāʾ	masculine females
muflis	bankrupt
mughtaṣib	usurper
muḥarram	forbidden
al-muḥarramāt min al-nisāʾ	women with whom marriage is forbidden on grounds of blood relationship, marriage, or suckling
muhājir	an emigrant from Mecca to Medina
muḥārib (pl. *muḥāribūn*)	robber, bandit, a criminal engaged in gross acts of violence
muḥrim	one who is in the state of *iḥrām*, see iḥrām
muḥṣan	in law it denotes a certain personal status: married, free, and Muslim; a free person who has never committed unlawful intercourse is protected against *qadhf*; a free married person who is subject to severe punishment if found guilty of adultery
muḥṣana (f. of *muḥṣan*) = *muḥṣan*	
muḥtasib	the person entrusted in a town with the application of 'promoting good and forbidding evil,' the market inspector, the official exercising the function of *ḥisba*
muḥtakir	the hoarder, speculator on rising food prices
mujabbab	a man with his genitals cut off
muʿāhad	an unbeliever connected with the Islamic state by treaty
mujāhid	a fighter for the faith
mujtahid	one who exercises *ijtihād*, a qualified lawyer who uses *ijtihād*
mukātab	a slave who has purchased his freedom by concluding a contract with his master
mukātaba	manumission by contract, see *mukātab*
mukhannathīn min al-rijāl	effeminate males
mulāmasa = *bayʿ al-mulāmasa*	
munābadha = *bayʿ al-munābadha*	
munaqqila	a wound in the head or the face that cleaves its

	skin and the bone is moved, a fracture with displacement of a bone
muqāriḍ	the man who lends money for profit
mu'rā	a donee, a recipient of the gift
murābaḥa	resale for a fixed profit
murḍi'a	foster-mother, wet nurse
mu'rī	a donor
murji'ī	an adherent of Murji'a, a polito-religious movement that refers to those who identified faith with belief to the exclusion of acts stating that those who committed grave sins do not cease to be Muslims and believed in the suspension of judgment, politically quietists/passive
murtadd	lit. one who turns back, an apostate
murtahin	the pledgee
al-mūṣā bihi	bequeathed property
al-mūṣā lahu	the legatee
musāqāt	lease of fruit trees on the condition to share their produce
mushā'	undivided property with joint ownership, shared in common
muṣḥaf (pl. *maṣāḥif*)	the Qur'ān
mushrik	polytheist
mushrika (f. of *mushrik*)	
al-mūṣī	the testator
muskir (pl. *muskirāt*)	alcoholic beverage, intoxicating liquor
mustaḍ'afa (f. of *mustaḍ'af*)	lit. weak, oppressed; a group of early Muslims who were clanless and without protection
mustaḥabb =*sunna*	
musta'man	an unbeliever who enters an Islamic country after being given a safe conduct
mut'a	temporary marriage; gift to a divorced wife, see *mut'at al-ṭalāq*
muṭaffif	one who gives short measure
mut'at al-ṭalāq	gift to a divorced wife
mutalāḥima	wound in the head that cleaves deeply the flesh but does not reach to the bone
mu'tamin	trustee
mu'tamir	one who makes a lesser pilgrimage (*'umra*) to Mecca
muthla	mutilation
muttaham	the accused
muwālāt	contract of clientship
muwallad (pl. *muwalladūn*)	half-breed, hybrid, of mixed blood

muẓā'ara	suckling
muzābana	sale/exchange of fresh dates on the palm trees for dried dates by measure, a contract of exchange of fruits growing on the tree for their calculated value in harvested fruits of the same species
muzāra'a	sharecropping, lease of agricultural land in return for some of the produce
nabīdh	intoxicating date wine, intoxicating drinks made from barley, honey, and dates
nadhr (pl. *nudhūr*)	vow, votive offering
nafaqa (pl. *nafaqāt*)	maintenance of a divorced woman
nāfila (pl. *nawāfil*)	supererogatory performances
nafy	banishment
naḥr	proper manner of slaughtering camels by stabbing in the pit above the breast, one of the two methods of slaughtering animals
najash	practice to offer an increase bid for a commodity, not to purchase it, but that another buyer may hear and offer a higher price
najm (pl. *nujūm*)	instalment payment of a *mukātab*
nākithīn	those who violated their covenant and fought against 'Alī in the Battle of the Camel
nasī'a	credit sale, sale stipulating future payments, see also *bay' al-nasī'a*
nāṣib	one who bears enmity toward the Imams
nāṣiba (f. of *nāṣib*)	
nāsikh	the repealing verse, the abrogator, see *naskh*
naskh	the doctrine that God abrogated some verses/laws of the Qur'ān after they were revealed, repeal, the act of cancellation
naṣṣ (pl. *nuṣūṣ*)	text; an explicit provision of the Qur'ān or the *ḥadīth* (from which the law is derived
naẓira	a transaction on deferred payment
nifās	delivery
nikāḥ	marriage
nikāḥ al-ma'ṣiya	lit. marriage of disobedience, marriage contracted with a woman divorced by *ṭalāq al-bid'a* or *ṭalāq al-ma'ṣiya*
nisāb	the value of the stolen property should reach a certain minimum value for applying the *ḥadd* penalty
niyāḥa	mourning sessions
nushūz	violation of marital duties on the part of either spouse

qabḍ	taking possession of things
qābila	midwife
qabūl	acceptance (a constitutive element of a contract)
qaḍā'	payment of a debt; both the office and the sentence of the *qāḍī*
qadhf	a slanderous accusation of adultery punishable by *ḥadd* punishment, defamation
qādhif	a slanderer
qadarī	a believer in free will, early theological school (precursors of the Mu'tazila)
qafīz	a dry measure of varying weight
qar' (pl. *qurū'*, *aqrā'*)	menstrual period
qar' al-ṭuhr	a monthly/menstrual period; inter-menstrual period of purity
qarābā (pl. *qarābāt*)	kinship, the closest relatives who have a claim to inherit from a man, relationship on the female side
qarḍ	loan of money or other fungible objects for consumption
qāsim	professional distributor of inherited property, one who distributes property in accordance with the *sharī'a*
qāsiṭīn	those who acted wrongfully and fought against 'Alī at the Battle of Ṣiffīn
qasma	the right to equity between co-wives
qasāma	an oath pronounced fifty times in a penal procedure
qaṣṣāb (pl. *qaṣṣābūn*)	butcher
qatalahu ṣabr^{an}	one who is confined to death, to kill someone while bound
qaṭ' al-ṭarīq	highway robbery
qatl	homicide
qawad	retaliation for wounds, blood revenge
qawāṣir (pl. of *qawṣara*)	a reed basket of dates
qayna	singing girls
qibla	the direction of Mecca in prayers
qirāḍ	an advance in trade with the agreement to share profits
qiṣāṣ	the legal sanction in cases of homicide and wounding, retaliation for wrong
qiṣāṣ fi 'l-nafs	retaliation for homicide
qiṣāṣ fī-mā dūn al-nafs	retaliation for wounds
qisma	partition, division (of property)
qiyās	deductive reasoning, deduction by analogy

qubḥ	ugliness, immorality as opposed to *ḥusn* (that which is good and moral)
qu'dad = qu'dud	
qu'dud	nearness of relationship with a common ancestor
qur'=qar'	
qur' al-ṭuhr=qar' al-ṭuhr	
raḍā'	fosterage
radd	the distribution of the residue of the estate, the law of reversion in the distribution of inheritance
rahbānīya	monkery, celibacy, monasticism
rāhin	the giver of the pledge, pledgor
rahn	mortgage, pledge, security, pawn
rā'igha	a by-path, by-road
ra'y	personal opinion, juristic speculation
raj'a	resumption of married life after the pronouncement of divorce, reconciliation with a divorced wife before the final pronouncement or the expiry of the *'idda*, husband taking back his divorced wife
rak'a (pl. *raka'āt*)	a basic unit of prayer consisting of standing, bowing, prostrating, and sitting
raqīq	slave
raqīq mawṣūf	a minor slave
ribā	usury, interest on a capital loan
ribā' (pl. of *rab'*)	estates
ridda	apostasy
riyā'	show, hypocrisy
rufi'a al-qalam	exempted from legal liability
rūḥ al-qudus	the Holy Spirit; the Angel Gabriel
ruqbā	life tenancy of a house, refers to a donation of a house with the proviso that it shall either revert to the donor after the donee's death or become the donnee's property upon the donor's death
ruqya (pl. *ruqā*)	charm, spell
sābila	a well-travelled road
ṣadaqa	charity, charitable gift, voluntary alms
ṣadaqa batta	irrevocable gift for the sake of God
ṣadāq	dower, see *mahr*
ṣaduqa (pl. *ṣaduqāt*)=*ṣadāq*	
ṣafqa	handshake/handclasp for the completion of a sale transaction
safātij (pl. of *saftaja/suftaja*)	bills of credit
ṣaghā'ir (pl. of *ṣaghīra*)	minor sins as opposed to *kabā'ir*
ṣaghīr	minor

sahm (pl. *sihām*)	one-sixth of a thing; fixed share of an heir
saḥq fi 'l-nisā'	lesbianism
sā'iba	refers to an emancipated slave where the former master did not retain his *walā'*
salam	contract for delivery with prepayment
ṣaqab	vicinity, nearness
sattūq	copper or brass coins coated with silver
ṣarf	exchange of cash/money or precious metals; contract of exchange
sariqa	theft
ṣarrāf	money changer
sa'y = *si'āya*	
ṣayrafī = *ṣarrāf*	
ṣā'	a small measure
shabaq	sexual desire
shafā'a	intercession, intervention
shafī'	pre-emptor
shahāda (pl. *shahādāt*)	evidence of witnesses, testimony; confession of faith
shāhid (pl. *shuhūd*)	witness
shāhid[u] 'adl[in]	reliable witness
shar' = *sharī'a*	
sharī'a	Islamic law; besides positive law it includes moral and ethical values, and the jurisprudential process itself
sharīk	partner
sharika	partnership
sharṭ (pl. *shurūṭ*)	condition, stipulation, prerequisite
sharṭ al-khiyār	the stipulation of the right of rescission
shawka	power
shibr	span of an open hand
shighār	A gives his daughter to B on the condition that B gives his daughter in marriage to A and no dower is paid by either party
shijāj	wounds in the head
shirk	polytheism
shirka = *sharika*	
shuf'a	pre-emption
shukkāk (pl. of *shākk*)	those who entertain doubts about the Imams
si'āya	signifies the work imposed on a slave for acquiring his freedom when he has been emancipated in part
sifāḥ	immorality, debauchery
simḥāq	grazing wound in the head, which leaves between it and the bone a thin layer of flesh
simsār (pl. *samāsira*)	broker, middleman

suftaja	bill of exchange
suḥt	a wrongful gain, unlawful gain
suknā	life-tenancy of a house without rent
ṣulḥ[an]	compromise reached between the assailant/culprit and the nearest relative of the victim
sulṭān	sovereign authority, ruling power
sum'a	show
sunna (pl. *sunan*)	the exemplary practice of the Prophet, recommended practice versus *farḍ*, normative legal custom
surrīya	a concubine
sutra	a barrier of privacy
tabādhul	mutual exchange of gifts
tabattul	celibacy
tadbīr	manumission of a slave that takes effect upon the death of the owner, see *mudabbar*
ta'addī	transgression, illicit act, tort, forcible dispossession
tadhkiya	slaughter in the manner prescribed by the law
tafāḍul	disparity between two commodities exchanged
taflīs	bankruptcy
tafrīq	dissolution of marriage
ṭāghūt	a false deity
taḥlīl= iḥlāl	
takhyīr =khiyār	
taklīf	legal charge, obligation, the duties imposed by God upon human beings
ṭalāq	divorce, unilateral repudiation of his wife by a husband
ṭalāq bā'in	a single pronouncement of absolute, irrevocable divorce
ṭalāq al-batta	irrevocable divorce
ṭalāq al-bid'a	disapproved form of divorce as opposed to *ṭalāq al-sunna*
ṭalāq al-'idda	divorce with reference to *'idda*
ṭalāq al-ma'ṣiya	lit. divorce of disobedience, *ṭalāq* pronounced during the woman's period of menstruation is regarded as a sin
ṭalāq raj'ī	revocable divorce
ṭalāq al-sunna	divorce in conformity with the dictates of the Prophet, an approved form of divorce
ṭalq	the pains of childbirth
tamīma (pl. *tamā'im*)	amulets
taqīya	dissimulation, dispensation from the requirements of religion under compulsion

tarahhub = rahbānīya	
taʿarraba baʿda hijratihi	to become a country Arab after emigration, i.e. apostasy
ṭarḥ al-ḥaṣā	a sale by throwing a pebble, an aleatory transaction
taʿrīḍ	to speak obliquely
al-taʿarrub baʿd al-hijra = taʿarraba baʿda hijratihi	
tasʿīr	price fixing
tasmiya	mentioning the name of God
taṣriya	practice of allowing milk of sheep or goats to remain unmilked in the udders
taṭlīqa bāʾina=ṭalāq bāʾin	
taʿzīr	discretionary punishments as opposed to *ḥadd* punishments, the offences for which neither the Qurʾān nor the *sunna* prescribe specific penalty, hence it is left to the discretion of the *qāḍī*
tawāṣul	to create mutual goodwill
taʿwīdh	amulet, charm
taʾwīl	interpretation
thayyib	married person
tibr	gold nuggets
ṭiwal	charms
uḍḥīya (pl. *aḍāḥī)=ḍaḥīya*	
ʿudūl = ʿadl	
ʿulūj (pl. of *ʿilj*)	serf tenants
ūlu ʾl-arḥām=dawu ʾl-arḥām	
ūlu ʾl-qurbā=dhawu ʾl-qurbā	
umm walad (pl. ummahāt al-awlād)	a slave woman who has borne a child to her master
umma	community, Muslim community
ʿuqr	a compensatory dower to be paid to the owner of a female slave for unlawful intercourse
ʿumrā	life-tenancy of a house without rent
ʿurs (pl. *urusāt*)	marriage feasts, celebration when a bride is transferred to her new home
ʿurūḍ	worldly goods, anything except gold and silver, immovable property
wadīʿa (pl. *wadāʾiʿ*)	trust property, deposit
waḍīʿa	loss
wajʿ	suppression of sexual desire
wājib	obligatory, synonym of *farḍ*
wakāla=wikāla	
wakīl	agent, representative of a party
wakīra	celebration when a man returns from a journey

walā'	a contractual clientage, patronship; the right to inherit from a manumitted slave
walad al-zinā'	illegitimate child
walāya	*walāya* of the Imams, *the first and the most excellent pillar of Islam
wālī	ruling authority, governor
walīda	a female slave, so called because she was born in servitude
walīma	feast, marriage feast
walīy (pl. *awliyā'*)	guardian, nearest relative, inheritor, legal heir
walīy Allāh (pl. *awliyā' Allāh*)	Friend of God, i.e. the Imams,
walīy al-amr	the person with authority; the Imam*
walīy al-dam (pl. *awliyā' al-dam*)	the next of kin with the right to demand retaliation, the avenger or guardian of blood, blood warden
walūd	a woman who bears many children
waqf	religious endowment, see also *ḥubs*
wariq	coined or uncoined silver
waṣī (pl. *awṣiyā'*)	executor or guardian appointed by testament, *vicegerent
waṣīya (pl. *waṣāyā*)	bequest, testament, the last will, legacy
waṣīf	a young slave, a servant
wikāla	power of attorney
wulāt ahl al-jawr	the rulers of the wrongdoers
wulāt al-amr	people with authority
yad[an] bi-yad[in]	on the spot, then and there
yamīn (pl. *aymān*)	oath
yawm al-aḍḥā=yawm al-naḥr	
yawm al-naḥr	the Day of Sacrifice, i.e. *'īd al-aḍḥā*
zakāt	alms tax, poor tax
ẓanīn	doubtful person, suspected person
ẓann	speculative, the legal value attached to the result of juristic reasoning, uncertain as opposed to *qaṭ'* (certain, definitive)
zawāj mu'aqqat	temporary marriage, see also *mut'a*
zawāj al-mut'a=mut'a	
zawāj al-taḥlīl=iḥlāl	
ẓihār	pre-Islamic form of divorce which uses the formula 'you are for me (as untouchable) as the back of my mother'
zinā'	adultery, unlawful intercourse punishable by *ḥadd* punishment
ẓi'r=murḍi'a	

Appendix I

Lawful Food, Drinks, and Herbs

'Ajwa (a superior date of Medina)
All juices before they ferment
Amber (*'anbar*)
Apple (*tuffāḥ*)
Beef (*laḥm al-baqar*)
Birds (*luḥūm al-ṭayr*) that have gizzards
Black caraway (*shūnīz*, *ḥabba sawdā'*)
Clarified Butter (*samn*)
Dry Dates (*tamr*)
Eggs (*bayḍ*) that are oval
Endive (*hindibā'*)
Fālūdhaj (*fālūdā*) a sweet made of flour and honey
Fenugreek (*ḥulba*)
Fish (*samak*, *ṣayd al-baḥr*) that have scales
Flesh of camels (*laḥm al-ibil*)
Fresh Dates (*raṭb*)
Fruits (*fākiha* pl. *fawākih*, *thamar* pl. *thimār*)
Garlic (*thūm*)
Gourd (*dubbā'*)
Grains (*ḥabb*)
Grapes (*'inab*)
Hare (*arnab*)
Honey (*'asal*)
Idām (seasoning)
Leek (*kurrāth*)
Legumes (*quṭniya*)
Lentils (*'adas*)
Locust (*jarād*)

Manna (*mann*)
Meat (*laḥm*)
Milk (*laban*)
Mushroom (*kam'a*)
Musk (*misk*)
Mutton (*laḥm al-ghanam*)
Nabīdh (beverage from dates, raisins, honey, barley, etc. before it ferments)
Oil (*zayt*)
Onion (*baṣal*)
Parsley (*karafs*)
Plants (*nabāt*)
Pomegranate (*rummān*)
Purslane (*rijla, al-baqla al-ḥamqā'*)
Quince (*safarjal*)
Raisins (*zabīb*)
Rice (*aruzz*)
Rue plant (*ḥarmal*)
Salt (*milḥ*)
Sawīq (a gruel of parched barley, or of similar grain)
Senna (*sanā*)
Spurge (*shubrum*)
Sugar (*sukkar*)
Sweet basil (*bādharūj, rayḥān*)
Tharīd (broth with meat and bread)
Vegetable (*baqla, buqūl*)
Vinegar (*khall*)
Water (*mā'*)
Water-cress (*jirjīr*)
Whale, big fish (*nūn*)
Wheat (*ḥinṭa*)
Wild Game (*luḥūm al-waḥsh*)
Zīrbāja (a kind of sweet)

Appendix II

Disapproved Food

Crab (*saraṭān*)
Eels (*jirrī*)
Glands (*ghudud*)
Inner part of the kidney (*dākhil al-kulā*)
Marrow of the lumbar region (*mukhkh al-ṣulb*)
The Milk and meat of animals that eat dung should not be consumed until those animals are prevented from eating it and purified according to the rules
Penis of male animals (*madhākīr*, *qaḍīb*)
Shellfishes (*mā kāna fi 'l-aṣdāf*), such as lobster, clam
Spleen (*ṭiḥāl*)
Tortoises (*sulaḥfāt*)
Vulvae of female animals (*ḥayā'*)

Appendix III

Unlawful Food and Drinks

Bear (*dubb*)
Birds with claws (*dhū mikhlab min al-ṭayr*)
Blood (*dam*)
Carnivorous animals with canine teeth (*dhū nāb min al-sibāʿ*)
Carrion (*mayta*)
Domesticated Asses (*al-ḥumur al-insīya*)
Eggs (*bayḍ*) that are round
Floating (dead) fish (*ṭāfī*)
Fuqqāʿ (barley wine)
Hyena (*ḍabʿ*)
Horse (*faras*); it is allowed in certain circumstances; slaughter of *khayl* is prohibited
Insects & creeping things (*ḥasharāt*)
Intoxicants (*muskir*)
Jackal (*ibn āwā*)
Leopard (*nimr*)
Lion (*asad*)
Lizard (*ḍabb*)
Lynx (*fahd*)
Mules (*bighāl*)
No sea creature can be eaten unless it has scales
Porcupine (*qunfudh*)
Pork (*laḥm khinzīr*)
Vinegar made of wine (*khall al-khamr*)
Wine (*khamr, sharāb*)
Wolf (*dhi'b*)

Appendix IV

Head/Face Wounds and Their Compensation According to Nu'mān, Kulaynī, Ṭūsī, Ibn Rushd, Ibn al-Farrā', and Māwardī

Nu'mān

Dāmi'a ṣughrā: 5 dinars
Dāmi'a kubrā: 10 dinars
Fāqira: 12 1/2 dinars
Bāḍi'a: 20 dinars
Mutalāḥima: 30 dinars
Simḥāq: 40 dinars
Mūḍiḥa: 50 dinars
Hāshima: 100 dinars
Munaqqila: 250 dinars

Ma'mūma: 1/3 blood money

Kulaynī

Ḥāriṣa
Dāmiya: 1 camel
Bāḍi'a: 2 camels
Mutalāḥima: 3 camels
Simḥāq: 4 camels
Mūḍiḥa: 5 camels
Hāshima:
Munaqqila: 15 camels
Ma'mūma: 33 camels or 1/3 blood money
Jā'ifa (body wound): 1/3 blood money

Ṭūsī

Ḥāriṣa/ Dāmiya: 1 camel
Bāḍi'a: 2 camels
Mutalāḥima: 3 camels
Simḥāq: 4 camels
Mūḍiḥa: 5 camels
Hāshima: 10 camels
Munaqqila: 15 camels
Ma'mūma: 33 camels or 1/3 blood money
Jā'ifa (body wound)

Ibn Rushd

Dāmiya
Ḥāriṣa
Bāḍi'a
Mutalāḥima
Simḥāq
Mūḍiḥa: 5 camels
Hāshima: 10 camels
Munaqqila: 15 camels
Ma'mūma: 1/3 blood money
Jā'ifa (body wound): 1/3 blood money

Ibn al-Farrā' and Māwardī

Ḥāriṣa *Dāmiya* *Dāmiʿa* Mutalāḥima	Adjudication (*Ḥukūmatu ʿadl*^{in})

Bāḍiʿa
Simḥāq
Mūḍiḥa: 5 camels
Hāshima: 10 camels
Munaqqila: 15 camels
Ma'mūma/Dāmigha: 33 camels or 1/3 blood money

Bibliography of Cited Works

This bibliography is in addition to that given in the first volume. Book titles are abbreviated by the first word (or words); other abbreviations are indicated in parenthesis. The Arabic letter *'ayn* and the definite article *al-* are disregarded in classifying the following entries.

Abou el-Fadl, Khaled. '*Ahkam al-Bughat*: Irregular Warfare and the Law of Rebellion in Islam', in J. T. Johnson and K. Kelsay (eds). *Cross, Crescent, and Sword: The Justification and Limitation of War in Western and Islamic Traditions*. Westport, CT: Greenwood Press, 1990.

______. 'Legal Debates on Muslim Minorities: Between Rejection and Accommodation', *Journal of Religious Ethics* 22 (1994), 127–62.

______. 'Islamic Law and Muslim Minorities: The Juristic Discourse on Muslim Minorities from the second/eighth to the eleventh/seventeenth centuries', *Islamic Law and Society* 1 (1994), 141–87.

______. *The Conference of the Books*. Lanham, Maryland: University Press of America, 2001.

______. *Speaking in God's Name: Islamic Law, Authority and Women*. Oxford: One World, 2001.

______. *And God Knows the Soldiers: The Authoritative and Authoritarian in Islamic Dicourses*. Lanham, Maryland: University Press of America, 2001.

______. *Rebellion and Violence in Islamic Law*. Cambridge: Cambridge University Press, 2001.

______. 'Islam and the Challenge of Democracy: Can individual rights and popular sovereignty take root in faith?', *Boston Review*, April/May, 2003.

Abū Tammām. *An Ismaili Heresiography: Bāb al-Shayṭān* from *Kitāb al-Shajara of Abū Tammām*. Edited and translated by W. Madelung and P. Walker. Leiden: Brill, 1998.

Abū Ya'lā, Muḥammad b. al-Ḥusayn al-Ḥanbalī. *al-Aḥkām al-Sulṭāniyya*. Edited by Muḥammad Ḥāmid al-Fiqī. 2nd edn. Cairo: Muṣṭafā al-Bābī al-Ḥalabī, 1386/1966.

Abū Zayd, Naṣr Ḥāmid. *Naqd al-khiṭāb al-dīnī*. 2nd edn. Cairo: Sīnā li 'l-nashr, 1994.

Adams, Charles. 'Islamic Faith', in R. M. Savory (ed.). *Introduction to Islamic Civilization*. Cambridge: Cambridge University Press, 1976, 33–44.

al-Aḥādīth al-qudsīya. Beirut: Dār al-Kutub al-'Ilmiyya. n.d.

al-'Ajam, Rafīq. *Mawsū'at muṣṭalaḥāt uṣūl al-fiqh*. Beirut: Maktabat Lubnān, 1998. 2 vols.

el-Alamai, Dawoud. *The Marriage Contract in Islamic Law in the Sharī'ah and Personal Status Laws of Egypt and Morocco*. London: Graham & Trotman, 1992.

al-Alfi, Ahmad Abd al-Aziz. 'Punishment in Islamic Criminal Law', in M. C. Bassiouni (ed.). *The Islamic Criminal Justice System*. London: Oceana Publications, 1982, 227–36.

Algar, Hamid. *Roots of Islamic Revolution in Iran*. Revised and Expanded edn. Oneonta, NY: Islamic Publications International, 2001.

'Alī b. Abī Ṭālib (ascribed to). *Dīwān al-imām 'Alī*. Collected by Na'īm Zarzūr. Beirut: Dār al-kitāb al-'ilmiyya, 1416/1995. (ed. Zarzūr)

______. *Dīwān al-imām 'Alī*. Collected by al-Sayyid Muḥsin al-Amīn. Beirut: Dār al-Murtaḍā lil-ṭibā'a, 1420/2000. (ed. al-Amīn)

'Alī Ibrāhīm, Marzūq. *Min asrār al-ṭibb al-nabawī: Mu'jizat al-shifā' bi 'l-ḥabbat al-sawdā'*. Cairo: Dār al-faḍīla, n.d.

______. *al-Du'ā' al-shāfī*. Cairo: Dār al-faḍīla, n.d.

'Alī Rāj, Shyakh Aḥmad and Mullā Qurbān Ḥusayn Rājnagarwālā. *Nikāḥ, Ṭalāq awr Wirāthat ke ahamm aḥkām*. Udaipur: Tanẓīm-e ishā'at-e islāmī ta'līm, 1412/1991.

Alwi, Abdullah bin Haji Hasan. '*Al-Muḍārabah* (Dormant Partnership) and its Identical Islamic Partnerships in Early Islam', *Hamdard Islamicus* 12 (1989), 11–38.

Aly Mansour, Aly. 'Hudud Crimes', in M. C. Bassiouni (ed.). *The Islamic Criminal Justice System*. London: Oceana Publications, 1982, 195–201.

Amīnjī b. Jalāl. *Kitāb al-su'āl wa 'l-jawāb li-mashā'ikh al-hind ma' al-ḥawāshī*. MS Collection of Mullā Qurbān Ḥusayn Godhrawala (Poonawala).

______. *al-Masā'il li-Amīnjī b. Jalāl*. MS Collection of Mullā Qurbān Ḥusayn Godhrawala (Poonawala).

Anderson, Norman. *Islamic Law in the Modern World*. [New York]: New York University Press, 1959.

______. 'The Isma'ili Khojas of East Africa: A New Constitution and Personal Law for the Community', *Middle Eastern Studies* 1 (1964), 21–39.

______. 'Muslim Personal Law in India', in Tahir Mahmood (ed.). *Islamic Law in Modern India*. Bombay: N. M. Tripathy Private Ltd., 1972, 34–49.

______. *Law Reform in the Muslim World*. London: University of London, 1976.

Ansari, Zafar Ishaq. 'Islamic Juristic Terminology before Shāfi'ī: A Semantic Analysis with Special Reference to Kūfa', *Arabica* 19 (1972), 255–300.

Arnold, Sir Thomas and Alfred Guillaume (eds). *The Legacy of Islam*. Reprint of 1931. London: Oxford University Press, 1965.

al-Asad, Nāṣir al-Dīn. *al-Qiyān wa 'l-ghinā' fi 'l-'aṣr al-jāhilī*. 2nd edn. Cairo, 1968.

Asani, Ali. 'The Khojahs of Indo-Pakistan: The Quest for an Islamic Identity', *Journal Institute of Muslim Minority Affairs* 8 (1987), 31–41.

el-Awa, Mohamed. *Punishment in Islamic Law: A Comparative Study*. Indianapolis: American Trust Publications, 1982.

al-Azami, M. Mustafa. *On Schacht's Origins of Muhammadan Jurisprudence*. Oxford: Oxford Centre for Islamic Studies, 1996.

al-Bakrī, Abū 'Ubayd 'Abd Allāh al-Andalusī. *Mu'jam ma 'stu'jima min asmā' al-bilād wa 'l-mawāḍi'*. Edited by Jamāl Ṭalaba. Beirut: Dār al-kutub al-'arabiyya, 1418/1998. 5 vols.

al-Balādhurī, Aḥmad b. Yaḥyā. *Futūḥ al-buldān*. Reviewed and corrected by Riḍwān Muḥammad Riḍwān. Beirut: Dār al-kutub al-'ilmiyya, 1412/1991.

_______. *Ansāb al-ashrāf*. Edited by Maḥmūd Firdaws al-'Aẓim. Damscus: Dār al-yaqẓa al-'arabiyya, 1997–2001. 15 vols. (ed. al-Azem)

al-Bayḍāwī, 'Abd Allāh b. 'Umar. *Anwār al-tanzīl wa-asrār al-ta'wīl*, generally known as *Tafsīr al-Bayḍāwī*. Beirut: Dār al-jīl, 1329 [1911]. (*Tafsīr*)

Benmehla, Ghaouti. 'Ta'azir Crimes', in in M. C. Bassiouni (ed.). *The Islamic Criminal Justice System*. London: Oceana Publications, 1982, 211–25.

al-Bīrūnī, Abū al-Rayḥān Muḥammad. *Kitāb al-ṣaydana fi 'l-ṭibb* (*Al-Biruni's Book on Pharmacy and Materia Medica*). Edited and translated by al-Hakīm Muḥammad Sa'īd and Rānā Iḥsān Ilāhī. Karachi: Hamdard National Foundation, 1973. 2 vols. (Pharmacy)

Bos, Gerrit. 'Ibn al-Jazzār on medicine for the poor and destitute', *Journal of the American Oriental Society* 118 (1998), 365–75.

Bosworth, Clifford, E. 'An Early Arabic Mirror for Princes: Ṭāhir Dhū l-Yamīnain's Epistle to his son 'Abdallāh (206/821)', *Journal of Near Eastern Studies* 29 (1970), 25–41.

_______. *The New Islamic Dynasties: A Chronological and Genealogical Manual*. New York: Columbia University Press, 1996.

Buckley, R. P. *The Book of the Islamic Market Inspector*. Translation of *Nihāyat al-rutba fī ṭalab al-ḥisba* by 'Abd al-Raḥmān al-Shayzarī. Oxford: Oxford University Press, 1999.

Burhanpur Dargah Case. *Judgment in Civil Suit No. 32 of 1925, Commonly known as Burhanpur Durgah Case*, delivered by G. S. Kher on 2 January 1931. Bombay: Britannic Durbar Printing Works, 1931.

al-Bustānī, Buṭrus. *Qaṭr al-muḥīṭ*. Beirut, 1869. 2 vols.

Calder, N. *Studies in Early Muslim Jurisprudence*. Oxford: Oxford University Press, 1993.

The Constitution of the Shia Imami Ismaili Muslims. Pakistan, [1986].

Cook, Michael. *Commanding Right and Forbidding Wrong in Islamic Thought*. Cambridge: Cambridge University Press, 2000.

Coulson, N. J. A *History of Islamic Law*. Edinburgh: Edinburgh University Press, 1964.

_______. *Conflicts and Tensions in Islamic Jurisprudence*. Chicago: The University of Chicago Press, 1969.

_______. *Succession in the Muslim Family*. Cambridge: Cambridge University Press, 1971.

Crone, P. *Roman, provincial and Islamic law: The origins of the Islamic patronate*. Cambridge: Cambridge University Press, 1987.

Crone, P. and F. Zimmermann. *The Epistle of Sālim Ibn Dhakwān*. Oxford: Oxford University Press, 2001.

Daftary, Farhad. *A Short History of the Ismailis: Traditions of a Muslim Community*. Edinburgh: Edinburgh University Press, 1998.

Dallal, Ahmad. 'Science, Medicine, and Technology: The Making of a Scientific Culture', in J. Esposito (ed.). *The Oxford History of Islam*. New York: Oxford University Press, 1999, 155–213.

Darwaza, Muḥammad 'Izzat. *al-Tafsīr al-ḥadīth: Tartīb al-suwar ḥasab al-nuzūl*. 2nd edn. Beirut: Dār al-gharb al-islāmī, 1421/2000. 10 vols.

Dénkart. *Le Troisième Livre du Dénkart*. Traduit de pehlevi par J. de Menasce. Paris: Librairie C. Klincksieck, 1973, 85–90.

al-Dhahabī, Abū 'Abd Allāh Muḥammad b. Aḥmad. *al-Ṭibb al-nabawī*. Cairo: Muṣṭafā al-Bābī al-Ḥalabī, 1380/1961.

Dodge, Bayard. 'The Fāṭimid Legal Code', *Muslim World* 50 (1960), 30–8.

Donaldson, Bess A. *The Wild Rue: A Study of Muhammadan Magic and Folklore in Iran*. London: Luzac & Co., 1938.

Donohue, John and John Esposito (eds). *Islam in Transition: Muslim Perspectives*. New York: Oxford University Press, 1982.

Dutton, Yasin. *The Origins of Islamic Law: The Qur'ān, the Muwaṭṭa' and Madinian 'Amal*. London: Curzon Press, 1999.

Esposito, John. *Women in Muslim Family Law*. Syracuse: Syracuse University Press, 1982.

_______ (ed.). *Oxford Encyclopaedia of the Modern Islamic World*. New York: Oxford University Press, 1995. 4 vols. (*Oxford Ency. of MIW*).

al-Fayyūmī, Aḥmad b. Muḥammad. *al-Miṣbāḥ al-munīr fī gharīb al-sharḥ al-kabīr lil-Rāfi'ī*. Edited by 'Abd al-'Aẓīm al-Shannāwī. 2nd edn. Cairo: Dār al-ma'ārif, [1994].

Fleischman, Gary. *Acupuncture: Everything You Ever Wanted to Know*. Barrytown, NY., 1998.

Friedlander Shems and al-Hajj Shaikh Muzaffereddin. *Ninety-Nine Names of Allah*. Hattat [Khaṭṭāṭ] Hamid al-Amidi. English trans. T. Topuzoglu. New York: Harper Colophon Books, 1978.

Frye, R. N. 'Zoroastrian Incest', in G. Gnoli and L. Lanciotti (eds). *Orientalia Iosephi Tucci Memoriae Dicta*. Rome: 1985, 445–55.

Fyzee, A. A. A. 'Bequests to Heirs: Ismā'īlī Shī'a Law', *Journal of the Bombay*

Branch of the Royal Asiatic Society, New Series 5 (1929), 141–5. It was also published in *Bombay Law Reporter*, 1929, 84–7.

———. 'The Ismāʿīlī Law of Mutʿa', *Journal of the Bombay Branch of the Royal Asiatic Society*, New Series 8 (1932), 85–92.

———. 'An Ancient Copy of *Daʿāʾim al-Islām*', *Bombay University Journal* 2 (1934), 127–33.

———. 'The Impact of English Law on the *Shariat* in India', *Revue Egyptienne de Droit International*, 18 (1962), 1–27.

———. 'The Relevance of Muhammadan Law in the Twentieth Century', *The Cambridge Law Journal*, 1963, 261–9.

———. 'Muhammadan Law in India', *Comparative Studies in Society and History*, 5 (1963), 401–15.

———. *A Modern Approach to Islam*. Delhi: Oxford University Press, 1981. Second Impression of the 1st edn. 1963.

———. 'The *Adab al-Qāḍī* in Islamic Law', *Malaya Law Review* 6 (1964), 406–16.

———. *Cases in the Muhammedan Law of India and Pakistan*. Oxford: Clarendon Press, 1965.

———. 'Aspects of Fatimid Law', *Studia Islamica* 31 (1970), 81–91.

Gelder, Geert Jan van. *Of Dishes and Discourse: Classical Arabic Literary Representations of Food*. Richmond, Surrey: Curzon, 2000. (Published in the States under the title *God's Banquet: Food in Classical Arabic Literature*, New York: Columbia University Press, 2000.)

———. 'Arabic Banqueters: Literature, Lexicography and Reality', in R. Gyselen (ed.). *Banquets d'Orient* (*Res Orientales*, 4). Bures-sur-Yvette, 1992, 85–93.

Gibb, H. A. R. *Mohammedanism: An Historical Survey*. New York: Oxford University Press, 1962.

———. 'Al-Mawardi's Theory of the Caliphate', in S. Shaw & W. Polk (eds.). *Studies on the Civilization of Islam*. London: Routledge & Kegal Paul Ltd., 1962, 151–65.

Gleave, R. 'Two classical Shīʿī theories of *qaḍāʾ*', in Hawtings et al (eds.). *Studies in Islamic and Middle Eastern Texts and Traditions in Memory of Norman Calder*. Oxford: Oxford University Press on behalf of the University of Manchester, 2000, 105–20.

Goitein, S. D. 'The Birth-hour of Muslim Law?' *Muslim World* 50 (1960), 23–9.

Goldziher, Ignaz. *Muslim Studies* (*Muhammedanische Studien*). Translated from the German by C. Barber and S. M. Stern. London: George Allen & Unwin Ltd., 1967–71. 2 vols.

Haeri, Shahla. *Law of Desire: Temporary Marriage in Shiʿi Iran*. Syracuse: Syracuse University Press, 1989.

Haji Hasan, Abdullah Alwi bin. '*Al-Muḍārabah* (dormant partnership) and its identical Islamic partnership in early Islam', *Hamdard Islamicus* 12 (1989), 11–38.

Halkim, A. S. 'The *Ḥashwiya*', *Journal of the American Oriental Society* 54 (1934), 1–28.

Hallaq, Wael B. *Authority, Continuity, and Change in Islamic Law*. Cambridge: Cambridge University Press, 2001.

______. *A History of Islamic Legal Theories: An Introduction to Sunnī Uṣūl al-Fiqh*. Cambridge: Cambridge University Press, 1997.

______. *Law and Legal Theory in Classical and Medieval Islam*. Aldershot: Variorum, 1995.

______. 'Was the Gate of *Ijtihād* Closed?' *International Journal of Middle Eastern Studies* 16 (1984), 3–41. Reprinted in Hallaq, *Law and Legal Theory in Classical and Medieval Islam*.

______. 'Was al-Shāfi'ī the Master Architect of Islamic Jurisprudence?' *International Journal of Middle Eastern Studies* 25 (1993), 587–605. Reprinted in Hallaq, *Law and Legal Theory in Classical and Medieval Islam*.

Halm, Heinz. *Die Schia*. Darmstadt: Wissenschaftliche Buchgesellschaft, 1988.

______. *Shiism*. Translated by Janet Watson. Edinburgh: Edinburgh University Press, 1991.

______. *Der Schiitische Islam: Von der Religion zur Revolution*. München: Verlag C. H. Beck, 1994.

al-Hamdānī, al-Ḥasan b. Aḥmad. *Ṣifat jazīrat al-'arab*. Edited by Muḥammad b. 'Alī al-Akwa'. Riyad: Manshūrāt dār al-Yamāma, 1397/1977.

Hamilton, Charles, trans. *The Hedaya or Guide: A Commentary on the Mussulman Laws*. [Translation of al-Marghīnānī's Hidāya]. Reprint of the 2nd edn. Lahore: Premier Book House, 1963.

Haque, Ziaul. *Landlord and Peasant in Early Islam: A Study of the Legal Doctrine of Muzāra'a or Sharecropping*. Islamabad: Islamic Research Institute, 1977.

Hardy, P. *The Muslims of British India*. Cambridge: Cambridge University Press, 1972.

al-Hibri, Azizah Yahia. 'Muslim women's rights in the global village: Challenges and opportunities', *Journal of Law and Religion* 15 (2000–2001), 37–66.

al-Ḥillī, Ja'far b. al-Ḥasan al-Muḥaqqiq. *Sharā'i' al-islām fi 'l-fiqh al-islāmī al-Ja'farī*. Beirut: Dār maktabat al-ḥayāt, 1406/1986. 2 vols.

Hollister, John N. *The Shi'a of India*. London: Luzac & Company, 1953.

Ibn al-Athīr. *al-Kāmil fi 'l-ta'rīkh*. Edited by C. J. Tornberg. Photoreprint of 1st edn. Beirut: Dār Ṣādir, 1399/1979. 13 vols.

Ibn Bābūya, Muḥammad b. 'Alī. *'Ilal al-sharā'i'*. Foreward by Muḥammad Ṣādiq Baḥr al-'Ulūm. [Beirut]: Dār al-balāgh, 1386/1966.

Ibn al-Bīṭār, Ḍiyā' al-Dīn 'Abd Allāh. *Tuḥfat ibn al-bīṭār fi 'l-'ilāj bi 'l-a'shāb wa 'l-nabātāt*. Edited by Abū Muṣ'ib al-Badrī. Cairo: Dār al-faḍīla, 1992.

Ibn Buṭlān. *Taqwīm al-ṣiḥḥa*. Édition critique, traduction, commentaire par Hosam Elkhadem. Louvre: Académie Royale de Belgique, 1990.

Ibn Ḥazm, Abū Muḥammad 'Alī al-Andalusī. *Jamharat ansāb al-'Arab*. Edited by 'Abd al-Salām Muḥammad Hārūn. 5th edn. Cairo: Dār al-ma'ārif, 1982.

Ibn Kathīr, Abū al-Fidā' Ismā'īl. *al-Sīra al-nabawīya*. Edited by Muṣṭafā 'Abd al-Wāḥid. Beirut: Dār iḥyā' al-turāth al-'arabī, 1386/1966.

______. *Qiṣaṣ al-anbiyā'*. Edited by Muḥammad Aḥmad 'Abd al-'Azīz. Beirut: Dār al-nadwa al-jadīda, 1401/1981.

Ibn Khaldūn. *Muqaddimat ibn Khaldūn*. Edited M. Quatremère. Photoreprint of the 1st edn. 1858. Beirut: Maktabat Lubnān, 1992. 3 vols.

______. *The Muqaddimah: An Introduction to History*. Translated from the Arabic by Franz Rosenthal. 2nd printing of 2nd edn. Princeton: Princeton University Press, 1980. 3 vols.

Ibn Qayyim al-Jawziya. *al-Ṭibb al-nabawī*. Edited by Muḥammad Fatḥī Abū Bakr. Cairo: al-Dār al-Miṣriyya al-Lubnāniyya, 1409/1989.

Ibn Rushd. *The Distinguished Jurist's Primer: Bidāyat al-Mujtahid wa Nihāyat al-Muqtaṣid* [by] Ibn Rushd. Translated by Imran Ahsan Khan Nyazee, reviewed by Mohammad Abdul Rauf. Reading: Garnet Publishing, 2000. 2 vols.

Ibn Sallām, Abū 'Ubayd al-Qāsim. *Kitāb al-nāsikh wa 'l-mansūkh*. Edited with a commentary by John Burton. Cambridge: E. J. W. Gibb Memorial Trust, 1987.

Ivanow, W. *Ismaili Traditions Concerning the Rise of the Fatimids*. London: Oxford University Press, 1942.

Jhaveri, Dewan Bahadur K. M. 'A Legendary History of the Bohoras', *Journal of the Bombay Branch of the Royal Asiatic Society*, vol. 9 (1933), 37–52.

Juynboll, G. H. A. 'The *Ḥadīth* in the Discussion of Birth-Control', in *Actas IV congresso de estudos arabes e islāmicos*, Coimbra-Lisboa 1 a 8 de Setembro de 1968. Leiden: E. J. Brill, 1971, 373–9. Reprinted in his *Studies*.

______. 'The Date of the Great *Fitna*', *Arabica* 20 (1973), 142–59.

______. *Muslim Tradition: Studies in chronology, provenance and authorship of early ḥadīth*. Cambridge: Cambridge University Press, 1983.

______. 'Nāfi', the *mawlā* of Ibn 'Umar, and his position in Muslim *Ḥadīth* Literature', *Der Islam* 70 (1993), 207–44. Reprinted in his *Studies*.

______. *Studies on the Origins and Uses of Islamic Ḥadīth*. Variorum, 1996.

Kamali, Mohammad. 'Law and Society: The Interplay of Revelation and Reason in the *Shariah*', in J. Esposito (ed.). *The Oxford History of Islam*. New York: Oxford University Press, 1999, 107–53.

Khadduri, Majid and H. Liebesny (eds). *Law in the Middle East, vol. I: Origin and Development of Islamic Law*. Washington, DC: The Middle East Institute, 1955.

Khadduri, Majid. 'International Law', in Khadduri, M. and H. Liebesny (eds). *Law in the Middle East, vol. I: Origin and Development of Islamic Law*. Washington, DC.: The Middle East Institute, 1955, 349–72.

______. *War and Peace in the Law of Islam*. Baltimore: Johns Hopkins University Press, 1955.

al-Khalīlī, Muḥammad. *Ṭibb al-imām al-Ṣādiq 'alayhi al-salām*. 4th edn. Najaf: Manshūrāt al-maktaba al-Ḥaydariyya, 1385/1966.

Kisā'ī. *The Tales of the Prophets of al-Kisā'i*. Translated from the Arabic with notes by W. M. Thackston Jr., Boston: Twayne Publishers, 1978.

Kraemer, Joel. 'Apostates, Rebels and Brigands', in J. Kraemer and I. Alon (eds.),

Religion and Government in the World of Islam. Tel Aviv: Tel Aviv University, 1983, 35–73.

Krapp, Kristine and J. L. Longe (eds.). *The Gale Encyclopedia of Alternative Medicine*. Detroit: Gale Group, 2001. 4 vols.

Lambton, Ann. *State and Government in Medieval Islam: An Introduction to the Study of Islamic Political Theory: The Jurists*. Oxford: Oxford University Press, 1985.

Lent, van. J. and H. Qureshi (compiled by). *Glossary and Index of Technical Terms of Encyclopaedia of Islam, 2nd edn*. Vols. I–VII, and to Supplement, Fascicules 1–6. Leiden: E. J. Brill, 1995.

Lewis, Bernard. 'Some observations on the significance of heresy in the history of Islam', *Studia Islamica* 1 (1953), 43–63. (Observations)

Lloyd-Jones, H. (ed.). *The Greek World*. Penguin Books, 1965.

Lokhandwalla, Shamun T. 'The Bohras: A Muslim Community of Gujarat', *Studia Islamica*, 3 (1955), 117–35.

Mahmasani, Subhi Rajab. 'Transactions in the *Sharī'a*', in Khadduri, M. and H. Liebesny (eds), *Law in the Middle East, vol. I: Origin and Development of Islamic Law*. Washington, DC.: The Middle East Institute, 1955, 179–202.

______. *Falsafat al-Tashrī' fī al-Islām: The Philosophy of Jurisprudence in Islam*. Translated by Farhat Ziadeh. Leiden: E. J. Brill, 1961.

______. 'Adaptation of Islamic jurisprudence to modern social needs', in J. Donohue and J. Esposito (eds.). *Islam in Transition*, 181–7.

Mahmood, Tahir (ed.). *Islamic Law in Modern India*. Bombay: N. M. Tripathy Private Ltd., 1972.

______. *Family Law Reform in the Muslim World*. New Delhi, 1972.

Majumdar, R. C., H. C. Raychaudhuri, and K. Datta. *An Advanced History of India*. 3rd edn. London: Macmillan, 1967.

Mālik b. Anas. *al-Muwaṭṭa'*. Photographic reproduction from an MS dated 1094/ 1682. Kuwait: Markaz al-buḥūth wa 'l-dirāsāt al-Kuwaytiyya, 1421/ 2000.

Mallat, Chibli and Jane Connors (eds.). *Islamic Family Law*. London: Graham and Trotman, 1990.

Mallat, Chibli. *The Renewal of Islamic Law: Muhammad Baqer as-Sadr, Najaf and the Shi'i International*. Cambridge: Cambridge University Press, 1993.

Mandviwalla, J. M. *Mussalman Wakf Act and the Dawoodi Bohra Community*. [Memorandum] submitted to the President and Members of the Parliamentary Joint Select Committee of Indian Reforms, London. Bombay: Satya Mitra Press, 1933.

Maqrīzī, Taqī al-Dīn Aḥmad. *Kitāb al-mawa'iẓ wa 'l-i'tibār bi-dhikr al-khiṭaṭ wa 'l-āthār*, generally known as *al-Khiṭaṭ al-Maqrīziya*. Photo offset copy of Bulaq ed. of 1294 AH. Baghdad: Maktabat al-Muthannā, 1970. 2 vols.

Al-Marwazī, Abū 'Abd Allāh Muḥammad. *Ikhtilāf al-fuqahā'*. Edited by Muḥammad Ṭāhir Ḥakīm. Riyad: Aḍwā' al-salaf, 14120/2000.

al-Mas'ūdī. *Murūj al-dhahab wa-ma'ādin al-jawhar*. Edition de B. de Meynard et P. Courteille, reveue et corrigée par C. Pellat. Beirut: Publications de l'Université Libanaise, 1966–79. 7 vols.

———. *Kitāb al-tanbīh wa 'l-ishrāf*. Edited by M. de Goeje. Reprint of Leiden edn. 1894. Beirut: Dār Ṣādir.

Maydani, Riyad. "*Uqūbāt*: Penal Law', in Khadduri, M. and H. Liebesny (eds.). *Law in the Middle East, vol. I: Origin and Development of Islamic Law*. Washington, DC.: The Middle East Institute, 1955, 223–35.

de Menasce, J. 'Zoroastrian literature after the Muslim Conquest', in R. N. Frye (ed.). *The Cambridge History of Iran, vol. IV: The Period from the Arab Invasion to the Saljuqs*. Cambridge: Cambridge University Press, 1975, 543–65.

Mir, Mustansir. *Dictionary of Qur'ānic Terms and Concepts*. New York: Garland Publishing, Inc., 1987.

Misra, Satish C. *The Rise of Muslim Power in Gujarat: A History of Gujarat from 1298 to 1442*. Bombay: Asia Publishing House, 1962.

———. *Muslim Communities in Gujarat: Preliminary Studies in their History and Social Organization*. Bombay: Asia Publishing House, 1963.

Modarressi, Hossein. An Introduction to Shīʿī Law: A bibliographical study. London: Ithaca Press, 1984.

Morris, H. S. *The Indians in Uganda*. London: Weidenfeld and Nicolson, 1968.

Motzki, Harald. *Die Anfänge der islamischen Jurisprudenz. Ihre Entwicklung in Mekka bis zur Mitte des 2./8. Jahrhunderts*. Stuttgart: Abhandlungen für die Kunde des Morgenlandes, 1991.

———. 'The *Muṣannaf* of ʿAbd al-Razzāq al-Ṣanʿānī as a Source of Authentic *Aḥādīth* of the First Century AH', *Journal of Near Eastern Studies* 50 (1991), 1–14.

———. *The Origins of Islamic Jurisprudence: Meccan Fiqh before the Classical Schools*. Translated from German by H. Katz. Leiden: Brill, 2002.

Mubārakpūrī, Mullā Yūnus Shakīb (trans.). *Daʿāʾim al-islām*, vol. II. Urdu Translation. Surat: Idāra-e adabiyyāt-e Fāṭimī, 1970.

———. *Daʿāʾim al-islām*, vol. II. Gujarati Translation. Surat: Idāra-e adabiyyāt-e Fāṭimī, 1972.

Murata, Sachiko (trans.). *Temporary Marriage in Islamic Law*. English translation of *Ezdivāj-e muvaqqat* (*mutʿa*) by Abu 'l-Qāsim Gurjī. Qum: Ansariyan Publications, 1986.

Musallam, Basim. *Sex and Society in Islam: Birth control before the nineteenth century*. Cambridge: Cambridge University Press, 1983.

Najafali, Abbasali. *Law of Marriage Governing Dawoodi Bohra Muslims*. Bombay: The Times of India Press, 1943.

al-Nasīmī, Maḥmūd Nāẓim. *Fi 'l-ṭibb al-islāmī*. Tripoli, Lebanon: Jarrūs Press, 1988.

Nasir, Jamil. *The Status of Women under Islamic Law*. London: Graham & Trotman, 1990.

———. *The Islamic Law of Personal status*. 3rd edn. The Hague: Kluwer Law International, 2002.

Nathwani Commission Report. Report of investigation conducted by the Commission appointed by the Citizens for Democracy into the alleged infringement of human rights of reformist members of the Dawoodi Bohras in the name of the High Priest. (Members of the Commission: N. P. Nathwani, V. M.

Tarkunde, Alam Khundmiri, Moin Shakir, and C. T. Dara.) Bombay, 1979.

al-Nu'mān al-Qāḍī. *Da'ā'im al-islām*, Vol. II, MS Collection of Mullā Qurbān Ḥusayn Godhrawala (Poonawala), transcribed in 1127/1715 (MS Q).

_______. *Kitāb al-iqtiṣār*. Edited by Muḥammad Waḥīd Mīrzā. Damascus: Institut Français de Damas, 1957.

_______. *Kitāb al-yanbū'*. MS Collection of Mullā Qurbān Ḥusayn Godhrawala (Poonawala).

_______. *Mukhtaṣar al-āthār*. MS Collection of Mullā Qurbān Ḥusayn Godhrawala (Poonawala).

_______. *Taqwīm al-aḥkām*. MS Collection of Mullā Qurbān Ḥusayn Godhrawala (Poonawala).

_______. *al-Urjūza al-muntakhaba*. MS Collection of Mullā Qurbān Ḥusayn Godhrawala (Poonawala).

Nicholson, R. A. *A Literary History of the Arabs*. Cambridge: Cambridge University Press, 1953.

Noth, Albrecht in collaboration with Lawrence Conrad. *The Early Arabic Historical Tradition: A Source-Critical Study*. 2nd edn. Translated from the German by Michael Bonner. Princeton: The Darwin Press, 1994.

Pearl, David. *A Textbook on Muslim Law*. London: Croom Helm, 1979.

Pearl, David and Werner Menski. *Muslim Family Law*. 3rd edn. London: Sweet & Maxwell, 1998.

Pedersen, Johannes. *The Arabic Book*. Translated by Geoffrey French, edited with an introduction by Robert Hillenbrand. Princeton: Princeton University Press, 1984.

Perho, Irmeli. *The Prophet's Medicine: A Creation of the Muslim Traditionalist Scholars*. Helsinki: The Finnish Oriental Society, 1995. (Studia Orientalia 74)

Peters, R., and G. De Vries. 'Apostasy in Islam', *Die Welt des Islams* 17 (1976–7), 1–25.

Poonawala, Ismail K. 'Pilgrimage to the Shrines', paper read at the second annual conference on *Sages, Shrines and Festivals: Implications for Communal Identity*, sponsored by the Institute of Diaspora Studies, San Diego State University, September 2002.

_______. 'The Beginning of the Isma'ili *Da'wa* and the Establishment of the Fatimid Dynasty as Commemorated by al-Qāḍī al-Nu'mān', in F. Daftary and J. Meri (eds.). *Culture and Memory in Medieval Islam: Essays in Honour of Wilferd Madelung*. London: I. B. Tauris, 2003, 338–63.

Powers, David. 'The Will of Sa'd b. Abī Waqqāṣ: A Reassessment', *Studia Islamica*, 58 (1983), 33–53.

_______. *Studies in Qur'an and Ḥadīth: The Formation of the Islamic Law of Inheritance*. Berkeley: University of California Press, 1986.

al-Qurṭubī, Abū 'Umar Yūsuf b. 'Abd Allāh. *al-Kāfī fī fiqh ahl al-Madīna al-Mālikī*. Beirut: Dār al-kutub al-'ilmiyya, n.d.

Rahman, Fazlur. *Islamic Methodology in History*. Karachi: Central Institute of Islamic Research, 1965.

______. *Islam*. 2nd edn. Chicago: University of Chicago Press, 1979.

______. *Islam and Modernity: Transformation of an Intellectual Tradition*. Chicago: University of Chicago Press, 1982.

______. *Health and Medicine in the Islamic Tradition*. Reprint of the 1st edn. 1987. Park Ridge Center: ABC International Group, 1998.

Rāj, Shaykh Aḥmad ʿAlī and Mullā Qurbān Ḥusayn Rājnagarwālā, trans. *Nikāḥ, Ṭalāq, aur Wirāthat ke Aḥkām*. (in Urdu). Udaipur, 1412/1991.

Rippin, A. 'Exegetical literature of abrogation: Form and content', in Hawtings et al (eds.). *Studies in Islamic and Middle Eastern Texts and Traditions in Memory of Norman Calder*. Oxford: Oxford University Press on behalf of the University of Manchester, 2000, 213–31.

Rowson, Everett. 'The Effeminates of Early Medina', *Journal of the American Oriental Society* 111 (1991), 671–93.

Rubin, Uri. '"*Al-Walad li-l-Firāsh*:" On the Islamic Campaign against "Zinā"', *Studia Islamica* 78 (1993), 5–26.

Rayner, S. E. *The Theory of Contracts in Islamic Law: A comparative analysis with particular reference to modern legislation in Kuwait*. London: Graham & Trotman, 1991.

Sachedina, A. A. *The Islamic Roots of Democractic Pluralism*. New York: Oxford University Press, 2001.

al-Ṣā'im, Muḥammad. *Bism Allāh arqīka min kulli shay'in yu'dhīka*. Cairo: Dār al-faḍīla, n.d.

Sakīna Yaʿqūb ʿAlī. *Sajda-e qalam*. Karachi, 1982.

de Santillana, David. 'Law and Society', in Arnold and Guillaume (eds.). *The Legacy of Islam*, 284–310.

Sawyer, John. *Prophecy and the Prophets of the Old Testament*. New York: Oxford University Press, 1987.

Schacht, J. 'Modernism and Traditionalism in a History of Islamic Law', [Review of N. Coulson, A *History of Islamic Law*, Edinburgh: Edinburgh University Press, 1964.] *Middle Eastern Studies* 1 (1965), 388–400.

Sezgin, Fuat. *Geschichte des Arabischen Schrifttums*. Leiden: E. J. Brill, 1967–. 12 vols. published so far.

Shabbar, ʿAbd Allāh. *Ṭibb al-a'imma ʿalayhim al-salām*. [Tehran]: Manshūrāt al-iʿtiṣām, 1415/[1995].

Shāfiʿī, Muḥammad b. Idrīs. *al-Risāla*. Edited by Aḥmad Muḥammad Shākir. 2nd edn. Cairo: Maktabat dār al-turāth, 1399/1979.

______. *Al-Shāfiʿī's Risāla: Treatise on the Foundations of Islamic Jurisprudence*. Translated with an Introduction and Notes, by Majid Khadduri. 2nd edn. London: The Islamic Texts Society, 1987.

Siddiqi, M. N. *Partnership and Profit Sharing in Islamic Law*. Leicester, 1985.

Siddiqui, Mona. 'The defective marriage in classical Ḥanafī law: Issues of form and validity', in Hawtings et al (eds.). *Studies in Islamic and Middle Eastern Texts and Traditions in Memory of Norman Calder*. Oxford: Oxford University Press on behalf of the University of Manchester, 2000, 271–86.

al-Sijistānī, Abū Ya'qūb. *Kitāb al-Iftikhār*. Edited with notes and introduction by Ismail Poonawala. Beirut: Dār al-gharb al-islāmī, 2000.

Steingass, F. *A Comprehensive Persian-English Dictionary*. New Delhi: Oriental Books Reprint Corporation, 1973.

al-Suyūṭīi, Jalāl al-Dīn. *al-Manhaj al-sawīy wa 'l-manhal al-rawīy fi 'l-ṭibb al-nabawī*. Edited by Ḥasan Muḥammad Maqbūlī. Beirut: Mu'assisat al-kutub al-thaqāfiyya, 1406/1986.

al-Ṭabarī, Abū Ja'far Muḥammad. *The History of al-Ṭabarī, Vol. VIII: The Victory of Islam*. Translated and annotated by Michael Fishbein. Albany: State University of New York Press, 1997.

______. *The History of al-Ṭabarī, Vol. XIII: The Conquests of Iraq, Southwestern Persia, and Egypt*. Translated and annotated by Gautier H. A. Juynboll. Albany: State University of New York Press, 1989.

______. *The History of al-Ṭabarī, Vol. XXVI: The Waning of the Umayyad Caliphate*. Translated and annotated by Carole Hillenbrand. Albany: State University of New York Press, 1989.

______. *The History of al-Ṭabarī, Vol. XXVIII: 'Abbāsid Authority Affirmed*. Translated and annotated by Jane McAuliffe. Albany: State University of New York Press, 1995.

______. *The History of al-Ṭabarī, Vol. XXIX: Al-Manṣūr and al-Mahdī*. Translated and annotated by Hugh Kennedy. Albany: State University of New York Press, 1990.

al-Ṭabarī, 'Alī b. Rabbān. *Kitāb al-dīn wa 'l-dawla*. Tunis, 1973.

al-Tahānawī, Muḥammad b. 'Alī. *Kashshāf iṣṭaliḥāt al-funūn*. Beirut: Dār al-kutub al-'ilmiyya, 1418/1998. 4 vols.

Taleqani, Seyyed Mahmood. *Islam and Ownership*. Translated from the Persian by Ahmad Jabbari and Farhang Rajaee. Lexington, Kentucky: Mazda Publishers, 1983.

Tewatia, D. S. and Kuldip Nayar. *Tewatia and Nayar Commission Report*. Report on violation of human rights of Dawoodi Bohras submitted to the Human Rights Commission of India and the Citizens for Democracy. Delhi, 1993.

al-Tirmidhī, Abū 'Īsā Muḥammad. *al-Jāmi' al-ṣaḥīḥ wa-huwa Sunan al-Tirmidhī*. Edited by Aḥmad Muḥammad Shākir et al. Beirut: Dār iḥyā' al-turāth al-'arabī, n.d. 5 vols.

Udovitch, A. *Partnership and Profit in Medieval Islam*. Princeton: Princeton University Press, 1970.

Ullmann, Manfred. *Die Medizin im Islam*. Leiden: E. J. Brill, 1970.

Ullmann, Manfred. *Islamic Medicine*. Edinburgh: Edinburgh University Press, 1978. (Islamic Surveys 11)

al-Wāḥidī, 'Alī b. Aḥmad al-Nīsābūrī. *Asbāb al-nuzūl*. Beirut: Dār wa-maktabat al-hilāl, 1983.

Wakin, Jeanette. *The Function of Documents in Islamic Law: The Chapters on Sale from Ṭaḥāwī's Kitāb al-Shurūṭ al-Kabīr*, edited with an Introduction and Notes. Albany: State University of New York Press, 1972.

Walbridge, Linda (ed.). *The Most Learned of the Shīʿa: The Institution of the Marjaʿ Taqlīd*. New York: Oxford University Press, 2001.

Williams, Tom. *The Complete Illustrated Guide to Chinese Medicine*. Rockport, MA, 1996.

Wilson, Sir Ronald K. *Anglo-Muhammadan Law:* A *Digest*. Revised and brought up to date by A. Yusuf Ali. Reprint. Lahore: Law Publishing Company, 1930.

Wörter buch der Klassischen Arabischen Sprache. Begun by J. Krammer and H. Gatje and continued by M. Ullmann. Wiesbaden: Harrassowitz, 1957–. 4 vols. published so far. It is a continuation of Lane's Arabic-English Lexicon, but in German beginning with the letter *kāf* until l-w-h.

Wüstenfeld-Mahler'sche. *Vergleichungs-Tabellen zur Muslimischen und Iranischen Zeitrechnung mit Tafeln zur Umrechnung Orient-Christlischer Aren*. Neu Bearbeitet von B. Spuler. Wiesbaden: Deutsche Morgenländische Gesellschaft, 1961.

Yāqūt, al-Ḥamawī. *Muʿjam al-udabāʾ*. Edited by Iḥsān ʿAbbās. Beirut: Dār al-gharb al-islāmī, 1993. 7 vols.

General Index

(It includes the translated text only, without the footnotes)

All proper names (except imam/Imams, Muslim/Muslims), pertinent Arabic words and phrases (italics), places [P], and tribes/clans [T] are included. The Arabic article 'al' and the abbreviation b. (for *ibn*, son) and bt. (for *bint*, daughter) have been ignored for purposes of alphabetization. References in square brackets are to the Qur'ānic verses.

are those who are closely related by kinship, 373
aqṭa'ahu māl[an], granted him a portion of his property, 301
Arab/s, pre-Islamic, 237; a country, 5, 460; from the country, 85
a'rābī, see Arab/s, a country
Arab/s from the country, see Arab/s, from the country
'Arafa [P], 461, see also Day of 'Arafa
'arāyā (pl. of *'arīya*), palm trees known as, 13; the term, 14; allowed the fruit of the, 15; permission granted in the, 30
'arḍ, commodity, 28,
arḍ al-ḥarb, see enemy country
'arīf, no escape from an administrative officer, 546
'āriya (pl. *'awārī*), see loan/s, commodate
'āriya maḍmūna, see loan/s, guaranteed
al-'āriya maḍmūna, see loan is guaranteed
'āriyata matā'[in], see loan, of a non-fungible object
'ārīyat al-furūj, lending women for sex, 234
arjāz, if theft occurs in the vicinity of wells, 477
arnab, see hare
'arrāf, see fortune-teller
aruzz, see rice
'asā, probability in criminal offence, 468
'aṣaba (pl. *'aṣabāt*), see agnatic heirs
aṣābi' al-rijl, blood money for a toe, 436
asad, see lion
'asal, see honey
'asal al-naḥl, see honey
'asal al-sukkar, see *'asal al-naḥl*
al-a'ṣam, a virtuous wife is as uncommon as the crow known as, 178
Aṣbagh b. Nubāta, said to 'Alī, 547
aṣḥāb al-kalām, see theologians
ashall, the right hand shall be cut, 473
ashfār (pl. of *shufr*), blood money for eyelashes, 430
'ashīra, see tribe
'aṣīr, selling of the pressed juice, 8
Asmā' bint 'Umays, beating tambourine to give pleasure to Fāṭima, 190; news of the death of Ja'far b. Abī Ṭālib, 284
aṣmayta, see *iṣmā'*
asnān (pl. of *sinn*), blood money for front teeth, 432
'aṣr, prayer, 76; late afternoon, 428
'aṭāyā (pl. of *'aṭīya*), gifts, presents, 14, 354; benefactions 313
avenger/s of blood, 342, 349, 407, 408; are infants or absent, 410; may kill him, 416; to swear and ask for retaliation, 427; forgives him, 481
āwā muḥdith[an], see *ḥadath*
al-'Awāf [P], estate inherited by Fāṭima, 333, 336
'awāhir, evidence of those who do evil acts in association with prostitutes, 519
al-awānī al-ḍārīya, vessels contaminated with traces of wine, 115
a'war, blood money for a one-eyed person, 430
al-'awārī maḍmūna, see loan, guaranteed
'awl, shares and their unjust change by, 375; the Qur'ānic shares do not deviate, 376; share was unjustly altered by, 377; who hold it permissible, 378
awlād al-a'yān, see relations by full blood
awliyā', see legal heirs
awliyā' Allāh, see Friends of God
awliyā' al-ni'ma, possessors of *walā'*, 373
awliyā' al-dam (pl. of *walīy al-dam*), see avenger/s of blood
'awra, exposed, 197
'awrāt, conceal their bodies, 198
'awratī, my shame, 139
awṣiyā' (pl. of *waṣī*), see vicegerent/s
āya muḥkama, a clear [Qur'ānic] verse, 543

Dār Furāt [P], a market place of Kūfa, 'Alī went to, 139
al-darāhim al-maḥmūl 'alayhā, alloyed dirhams, 17
al-darāhim al-mukaḥḥala, dirhams alloyed with antimony, 17
al-darāhim al-ṭazaja, new dirhams, 47
ḍarar, harm, 507; loss, 508
ḍārī, vessel contaminated with wine, 109
ḍarībatahu, the [fixed] impost of a slave, 301
David, prophet, [in 6:83–5], 363; judgments of, 403, 404, 405, 526, 527, 528
da'wa, ranks of the, 123
da'wā, see lawsuit, claim/s
dawā', see medicine
ḍawāll (pl. of *ḍālla*), no one eats the meat of lost camels, 504
Day of 'Arafa, emancipating a slave on the eve of the, 294
Day of Judgement, 3, 6, 113, 201, 442, 446, 528, 536
Day of Resurrection, 75, 76, 97, 157, 174, 181, 183, 319, 332, 343, 401, 413, 446, 447, 448, 463, 514, 540
Day of Sacrifice, 164, 165, 166, 168, 399, 489
Day of Tashrīq, the last, 166
dayn (pl. *duyūn*), see debt, loan
Days of Ignorance, see *al-jāhilīya*
debt, see loan
deposit/s, [in 4:58], restore to their owners, 497; whether he be an enemy, 498
Devil, 173,
dhabā'iḥ (pl. of *dhabīḥa*), ritually slaughtered animals, 106, 156, 159
dhabḥ, lawful slaughter of cattle and birds is by cutting the throat, 162
dhakāt, can be eaten after being slaughtered, 142; lawful slaughter, 159; knowledge of ritual slaughter, 161
dhāt maḥram, kissing a female relation not permitted for marriage, 187; women would speak only with those men who were forbidden to marry them, 198; if a man were to have intercourse with a woman forbidden to him in marriage, 458
dhawu 'l-arḥām, see cognates
dhi'b, see wolf
dhimma, responsibility, 25
dhimmī/s, should pay poll tax, 25; partnership with a, 69; not entitled to pre-empt, 71; imprecation against, 273; blood money of a, 409; inheritor for a, 411; agnatic relations of a, 415; *sufra* of a, 505; bearing witness to a Muslim's will, 520; evidence of a, 521; woman, 273
dhū bid'at[in], actions at variance with the *sunna*, 538
dhū maḥram = *dhāt maḥram*
dhū mikhlab min al-ṭayr, birds with claws are unlawful, 103
dhū nāb min al-sibā', animals with canine teeth are unlawful, 103
dhū raḥim = *dhawu 'l-arḥām*
Dhu 'l-Jaddayn [T], house of 182
dhubāb, eating of food containing dead flies, 107
dhukkiya, see *dhakāt*
ḍighth, [in 38:44], take a branch and smite therewith, 453
ḍil' (pl. *ḍulū'*, *aḍlā'*), blood money when a rib is broken, 435
ḍirār, [in 2: 231], 507
dirra, 'Alī used to walk in the markets, whip in hand, 547
discretionary punishment/s, reprimanded, 231; punished by way of correction, 461; administered a warning (verbal form *'azzara*), 464; penalty of 477; evidence of those who deserve *ta'zīr* punishments, 519
diya (pl. *diyāt*), 412; heirs inherit the blood money, 383; distribution of

blood money 391; two-thirds of blood money on paternal relations, 415; no blood money is due, 425; whole of the blood money if the chest is bent, 435; fine of one-quarter of the blood money, 523
diyās, do not pay in advance for threshing of corn, 38
drinking etiquette, 110
du'ā' (pl. *ad'iya*), 118, 187
ḍu'afā', other than the followers of the rightful imams, 83
Ḍubā'a bint al-Zubayr b. 'Abd al-Muṭṭalib, the Messenger of God contracted the marriage of Miqdād with, 183
dubayla, charity wards off tumours, 324
dubb, see bear
dubbā', see gourd
duhm, black steed is the best, 179
dukhūl, deny that they had sexual intercourse, 451,
al-dukhūl bi 'l-nisā', going into women, 188
Ḍumayra, see Ḍamīra
durrā'a, 'Alī was seen in a black woolen coat, 143

eels, eating is disapproved, 106
eggs, if oval, are lawful, 103; if round, are unlawful, 103
Egypt [P], goods of Imam al-Bāqir from, 36
Elias, prophet, [in 6:83], 363
endive, is for us, 94; the Prophet loved, 132
enemy country, a woman apostatizes and goes over to an, 484
etiquette of dress, 135
etiquette of *qāḍīs*, 534
Eve, was created from Adam's rib, 385
evil eye, 122, 124; and divination are in fact true, 125

fa-aḥṣana kathīr^an min al-nisā', Ḥasan married many women and caused them to abstain from that which is unlawful, 245
faḍl, profit, 68; [in 10: 59], bounty, 348
faḍl al-ṣadaqa, excellence of charitable gifts, 321
fahd, see lynx
faḥl (pl. *fuḥūl*), 167
fajara, see *fājir*
fājir (pl. *fawājir*), trader commits foul deeds, 5; rules regarding the marriage of immoral persons, 222; angel of death descends to take possession of the life of the wicked man, 515
fakhdh, blood money for a broken thigh, 436
fa'l, and divination are in fact true, 125
falāt, body found in an open country, 429
falcons, game captured by, 149; are of predatory birds, 151
fālūdhaj, the Messenger of God was fond of, 91; was brought and placed before 'Alī, 96: 'Alī was given, 320
faqīr, one who does not ask, 168
fāqira, blood money for a wound where the skin has broken but not the flesh, 437
farā'iḍ (pl. of *farīḍa*), see the Qur'ānic shares; compulsory religious duties, 543
faras, horse was in the throes of death, 104
farḍ, mandatory obligation, 249; a compulsory duty laid down by God, 535
Farewell Pilgrimage, the Messenger of God's sermon at, 2, 45, 241, 489; the Prophet's ritual offerings at, 68
farīḍa [in 2:236], dower, 209; prescribed share of inheritance in the Qur'ān, 375

farj, (hermaphrodite) if urine comes of the vulva, 383; blood money for the pudendum of a woman, 435
Farqad, the cupper, 65
Fārs [P], 3
fāsid, sales are defective, 10, 11; such contracts are defective, 20; the marriage is invalid, 305
fāsiq, evidence of a libertine, 518
Fātiḥat al-Kitāb, whenever you wish to seek refuge, recite the, 124
Fāṭima, 358, 363, 501, 502; carrying Ḥusayn to the Prophet, 129; on the Day of Sacrifice, 165; giving in charity at the *'aqīqa* of her sons, 170; status of, 176; on the night of her marriage, 190; she veiled, 198; her *mahr*, 206; estates inherited, 333; denial of inheritance to, 361, 362; property of, 335; testament of, 336; children of, 334, 335; daughter of Muḥammad, 336
Fāṭima bint Asad b. Hāshim, the mother of 'Alī b. Abī Ṭālib made a will, 356
fay', the Messenger of God distributed, 333; provide him from the booty, 473; distribution of war booty, 507
fayḥ, fever is from the vehemence of, 129
Feast of Sacrifice, see Day of Sacrifice,
Fenugreek, use for medicine, 133
fi'ām, group of people, 85
fī 'āmi sanat[in], commits theft in a year of famine, 477
fī ḥujūrikum, [in 4:23], who are under your protection, 219
fiqh, an expert in, 355,
firār, nothing but an evasion, 27
fiṣād, the best of medicine is bloodletting, 127
fiṣāl, weaning a baby, 282, see also *fiṭām*
fish, deep-sea fish, which have scales are lawful, 103; floating fish prohibited, 106; see also *nūn*
fiṭām, prohibited suckling after weaning, 228; mutual consent on weaning, 282
fitna, mischief, 438
followers of the rightful Imams, can a man feed poor persons other than, 83
fortune-teller, believes in what he says, is part of idolatry, 487
fosterage, 226
Friends of God, conduct of the, 101; love for the, 109; devoted to, 296
full brothers and sisters, are preferred to the consanguine kindred, 310–11
fuqqā', drinking of barley wine, 115
furqa, apostasy shall be deemed to be a divorce, 484
furūj, [in 23:5–7], 234
fusḥa, Jews may know that there is latitude in our religion, 190
fuṭis, blood money if the nose is flattened, 432

Gabriel, the angel, 2; advice concerning the neighbour, 70; descended upon him, 85; came with two *sūras* (113, 114), 121; informed the Messenger of God of the place of the charms, 122; came and said to recite the *Fātiḥa*, 129; the Holy Spirit, 317; taught how to make a testament, 340
Gammal, see *kurdī*
garlic, no one eating raw should enter a mosque, 93
ghāfilāt, [in 24:23], 459
ghalima, the best of women is the virtuous and the passionate, 181
ghalla dirhams, base quality silver coins, 26, 27, 29, 47
ghalṣama, cutting the throat below its base, 161

adhān from the, 59; forbade that the property … should escheat to the, 373; property of one who dies without leaving an heir escheats to the, 388–9; take the blood money and put it in the, 411; blood money is to be paid from the, 423; 'Alī paid the blood money from the, 429; is to add to the, 503; 'Alī provided the fodder from the, 504; remuneration of judges should come from the, 546; anyone imprisoned permanently should be given subsistence from the, 547

qabā', tailor sewed a gown but the owner of the cloth claims, 65
qabīl, guarantor, 49
qabīla, body found in a tribal habitation, 426
qābila, the hind leg of the animal sacrificed by way of *'aqīqa* should be given to the midwife, 171; a man should not marry his midwife, 224; evidence of a midwife, 521
qadar, the Divine Decree, 340
qadarī, evidence of one who believes in free will, 518
al-qadhf, slanderous accusation, 466
qādhif, evidence of a slanderer, 518
qāḍī, when the judge sells a man's goods to pay off, 43; the judge should uphold a minor's right where there is no legal guardian, 74; at Ahwāz, 158, 540; the executor refers the matter to the, 359; I am a claimant, 383–4; of Ifrīqiya, 536; I have made him a, 539; forbidden to favour one party over another, 541; not proper to pay attention to one, 542; the authority on which he decides a case, 543; forbade to pronounce judgment while he was angry, 545; office of a judge and remuneration for him, 546; does not know about the integrity of witnesses, 548
qafā', slaughtering of an animal by the nape of the neck, 163
qafīz, a dry measure, 40
qā'id, responsibility is on the leader, 419
qalansuwa, 141
qammāṭ, dealers in rope warned, 547
Qanbar, 'Alī's slave, 'Alī commanded/said, 444, 474, 486
al-qāni', [in 22:28], 168; contended, 327
qāniṣa, birds having gizzards are lawful, 103
qar' (pl. *qurū'*), [in 2:228], monthly courses, 275, 278
qar' al-ṭuhr, the state of purity between two monthly courses, 287
qarḍ, see loan/s
qarn (pl. *qurūn*), a slave can be returned if she suffers from a, 35; a woman can be rejected after marriage is she suffers from a, 217; there are four ages, and I am in the best of them, 456
Qārūn, see Croesus
qārūra, bottle [of perfume], 147
qaṣaba, blood money for one of the bones of the forearm, 434
al-qasāma, an oath pronounced fifty times in a penal procedure, 407, 426, 427; suspicious circumstances require, 428; necessary where there is suspicious in the evidence of women in cases of murder, 521
qāsim, a distributor of property, 508
qāsiṭīn, the wrongdoers, 349
qasāmat khamsīna rajul^{an}, see *al-qasāma*
al-qasma bayn al-ḍarā'ir, the right to equity between co-wives, 239
qaṣṣābīn, to perform the act of slaughter in an efficient manner, 158; do not make haste [cutting up the animals] until they are clearly dead, 547
qaṣṣār, wages of a fuller, 36

eaters, 89; women of, 179, 227; tribe of, 182; people of, 441
Qurayshī, women, 183; thieves came to a well-to-do, 499
qurū', see *qar'*
qutila fulān[un] *ṣabr*[an], confined to die while bound, 157
quṭnīya, legumes, 103

al-Rabāb, a prostitute in Mecca, 184
Rabadha [P], 'Alī sold his camel at, 21
rabā'iya, blood money for the front teeth called, 432
al-raḍā', see fosterage
radd, return or increase of shares, 366; the law of reversion, 394; the question of, 395; entitled to the, 396
rāḥat al-mawt, [restfulness which precedes] death, 339
rahbānīya, no monasticism in Islam, 177
rāhin, the giver of the pledge, 66
al-raḥīq al-makhtūm, allusion to [83:25], 85
rahn, mortgage, pledge, 38, 65
rā'igha, right of pre-emption in a byway, 71; opening a door in a by-path, 513
raj'a, witness for the resumption of married life, 247; reconciliation with a divorced wife, 286; may not have had witnesses, 287
rajul ma'mūn, regarded as trustworthy, 69
al-rajul al-sarīy, high-ranking, noble, 6
rākib, responsibility is on the rider, 419
ramad, see ophthalmia
Ramaḍān, 467, 470; fasts during, 201, 254, 296, 344, 360; month of, 467; twenty-first night of, 350
Raml 'Ālij [P], sand dunes collected together at, 376
raqīq, in the case of a slave, 35; child of the marriage is a slave, 217
raṭb, breaking fast with fresh dates, 91
ra'y, personal opinion/s, 543, 544
rayḥān, see sweet basil
relations by full blood, have precedence over relations by half blood, 370
relations by half blood, relations by full blood have precedence over, 370
retaliation for wrongs, see *al-qiṣāṣ*
ribā, fall increasingly into usury, 4; [in 2:275], is forbidden, 7; usurious interest; 22; God has cursed, 24; debt which brings a profit is, 46; double sale in one contract to evade, 48; unlawful gain, 69; expecting a return greater than the gift, that is, 321; earnings of, 322; practising, 399
rība, [in 65:4], doubt means the period, which exceeds, 280
ribā' (pl. of *rab'*), large tenement houses, 42; allowed partnership in, 68
ribḥ, profit, 53
rice, 103; good for stomach disorder, 133
ridā', should avoid taking loans, 128; out wrapping garment, 384
ridda, see apostasy
Rifā'a b. Shaddād, 'Alī's *qāḍī* at Ahwāz, 'Alī wrote to, 23, 25, 158, 246, 402, 441, 444, 462, 493, 508, 537, 540; when 'Alī appointed, 542; 'Alī said to, 546
rifq, kindness if one-half of livelihood, 241
rīḥ sawdā', plague, 456
rihān[un] *maqbūḍa*, the pledge with possession, 66
rijl, one-half of the blood money for each leg, 436
rijla, see purslane
rijrij, foul liquid, 126
riyā', hypocrisy, 139; forbade marriage for, 180; marriage feast after the second day is, 189
Riyāḥ, 'Alī's emancipated slave, 300, 334
rizq, means of livelihood, 1; bare necessities, 20

352; the shares do not vary, 376; in proportion to their shares, 395
al-saḥq fi 'l-nisā', lesbianism is like sodomy, 457
sā'id, blood money for a broken forearm, 434
sā'il, suppliant, 327
sā'iq, responsibility on the driver, 419
sa'īr, a valley in Hell called, 398
ṣakk, disapproved the practice of sale by, 12
al-salam, contract for future delivery [with prepayment], 37, 38
ṣalāt, al-awwābīn, 345,
ṣalāt al-zawāl, the prayers for the declination of the sun, 342, 344
sale, aleatory, forbidden, 9, 12; credit sale, goods delivered immediately for a deferred payment, see *al-salam*; double sale in one contract, see *bay' al-'īna*; forced sale, one who is forced to sell, see *bay' al-muḍṭarr*; resale for a fixed profit, see *bay' al-murābaḥa*
Salmān al-Fārisī, eating dates whilst he had ophthalmia, 127
salt, he who begins his meal and ends it with, 95
salūqī, greyhound hunting dog, 151
sām, death, 118, 132
sam', blood money for a man who loses his hearing, 431
samāsira (pl. *simsār*), tradesmen were called, 5
sammākīn, do not sale spoiled fish, 547
ṣammama, animals slaughtered by the knife penetrating to the neckbone be thrown away, 158
samn, clarified butter is a cure, 92; is a medicine, 132
sanā, senna pods for treatment, 133
sāq, blood money for a fractured shank, 436
ṣaqab, responsibility of the blood money on the vicinity, 428
ṣaqr (pl. *ṣuqūr*), see falcons, hawks
Sārah, a prostitute in Mecca, 184
ṣarām, no advance payment for the cutting off of the fruit, 38
saraṭān, see crabs
al-ṣarf, exchange [of money and precious metals], 24
sāriya, pillar, 404
sarīya, an expedition, 480
ṣarrāf, see money-changer/s
Satan, 99, 400; smells it, 101; arrows of, 186; snares of 197; dream was from, 329; accursed enemy, 349; to help, 485; [in 4: 60], 538; first to rely on deductive reasoning was, 544; became a rebellious, 545
sattūq, coins made of copper, 17
sawīq, parched barley, 30; dried gruel, 134; induces the growth of muscle, 134
ṣayd al-baḥr, see fish
ṣayrafī, see money-changer/s
Scroll of Inheritance, dictated by the Prophet to 'Alī, 366, 367, 368, 370, 371, 375
sectarians, the evidence of, 518
sha'ā'ir, should respect the rites of God, 164
shabaq, God has removed sexual desire from, 176
shafa, blood money for the uprooted lips, 432
shafā'a, the Messenger of God's intercession, 345; legal rights are matters on which there can be no intervention, 545
shafī', pre-emptor, 71, 72
al-shahāda 'ala 'l-khaṭṭ, providing testimony based on written evidence, 522
shāhiday 'adl, there is no marriage without a guardian and two reliable witnesses, 203
sha'īr, barley, 270

sharāb, see wine
sharī'a, 114, 427
shārib al-muskir, evidence of those who drink intoxicating liquor not admissible, 519
sharīk, co-owner legally entitled to pre-empt, 71
sharika, mercantile partnership, 68
shāt, sacrifice of sheep or ewe for *'aqīqa*, 170
shatm, intends to abuse her, 464
shaṭranj, chess is considered *laghw* [in 25:72], 192
shay', only mentioned a thing, 352
shayāṭīn (pl. of *shayṭān*), 126
Shaybānī [T], tribe of, 182
shaykh[un] *zān*[in], referred to [in 2:174], 447
sheep, lawful to eat the flesh of, 103
shellfish, disapproved, 106
shī'a, of 'Alī, 109
shī'atihi, his supporters, 342
shī'atinā, our partisans, 344, 346
shighār, prohibited in marriage, 209
shijāj, blood money for face/head wounds, 436
shimrākh, for scourging, 453
shiqṣ, a piece of land, 72; a part of the property, 74
shirb, watering right, 510
shirk, 459, 486, 515
al-shirka = *al-sharika*
shubrum, beware of spurge, 133
al-shuf'a, [right of] pre-emption, 70
shufr (pl. *ashfār*), blood money if an upper eyelid/eyelashes are injured, 430
shukkāk (pl. of *shākk*), those who entertain doubts about the Imams, 184
shūnīz, see black caraway
Shurāḥa al-Hamdānīya, stoned for adultery, 445
Shurayḥ, a *qāḍī* of Kūfa, a woman came to, 383, 384; brought them to, 403; used to decide cases in his own house, 542
shurb (pl. *ashriba*), lawful and unlawful drinks, 108
shurb al-hīm, disapproved that a man should drink like a thirsty camel, 111
al-shurūṭ fi 'l-buyū', conditions in sale, 40
al-shurūṭ fi 'l-nikāḥ, conditions in marriage, 212
si'āya, work imposed on a slave fro acquiring his freedom, 297
ṣibr, aloes spoil honey, 546
sifāḥ, this is marriage and not immorality, 189; temporary marriage is debauchery, 215
signet ring, see *khātam*
sihām, see *sahm*
siḥr, forbade the use of sorcery, 125
ṣilāt, favours, 327
silk, warp is of, 136; silk garments disapproved for men, 143
simḥāq, no retaliation for a grazing wound in the head, 420; blood money for, 437
siwāk, use of toothstick removes forgetfulness, 119; when the Prophet traveled he took with him, 147
smallpox, no *ḥadd* punishment is to be inflicted on a man who has, 453
Solomon, prophet, 124, 175; had the virility of forty men, 176; kingdom of, 487
sovereign/ sovereign authority/, if she took him before the, 268; requests him to ask the sovereign, 321; is the executor of him who has no executor, 359; should reprimand him severely, 409; if the man pardons the defamer before the case is taken to the, 465; proper authority, 470; when the thief has been brought to the, 472
sulṭān, confiscated by the ruler, 23; when the ruler sells a man's goods, 43; can be done by the state, 55; the ruling authority should divorce her, 225; the governor, 462
sum'a, show, 180, 189

Isnād Index

(For Nuʿmān's use of *isnād* see *The Pillars of Islam*, I, ix)

Index of Qur'ānic Verses

(Page numbers for this volume appear in the right column)